Travel Discount Coupon

This coupon entitles you to special discounts when you book your trip through the

TRAVEL NETWORK®
RESERVATION SERVICE

Hotels ♦ Airlines ♦ Car Rentals ♦ Cruises
All Your Travel Needs

Here's what you get: *

♦ A discount of $50 USD on a booking of $1,000** or more for two or more people!

♦ A discount of $25 USD on a booking of $500** or more for one person!

♦ Free membership for three years, and 1,000 free miles on enrollment in the unique Travel Network Miles-to-Go® frequent-traveler program. Earn one mile for every dollar spent through the program. Redeem miles for free hotel stays starting at 5,000 miles. Earn free roundtrip airline tickets starting at 25,000 miles.

♦ Personal help in planning your own, customized trip.

♦ Fast, confirmed reservations at any property recommended in this guide, subject to availability.***

♦ Special discounts on bookings in the U.S. and around the world.

♦ Low-cost visa and passport

♦ Reduced-rate cruise package programs worldwide.

D0324677

Visit our website at http://www.travelnetwork.com/Frommer or call us globally at 201-567-8500, ext. 55. In the U.S., call toll-free at 1-888-940-5000, or fax 201-567-1838. In Canada, call at 1-905-707-7222, or fax 905-707-8108. In Asia, call 60-3-7191044, or fax 60-3-7185415.

* To qualify for these travel discounts, at least a portion of your trip must include destinations covered in this guide. No more than one coupon discount may be used in any 12-month period, for destinations covered in this guide. Cannot be combined with any other discount or promotion.
**These are U.S. dollars spent on commissionable bookings.
***A $10 USD fee, plus fax and/or phone charges, will be added to the cost of bookings at each hotel not linked to the reservation service. Customers must approve these fees in advance. If only hotels of this kind are booked the traveler(s) must also purchase roundtrip air tickets from Travel Network for the trip.

Valid until December 31, 1998. Terms and conditions of the Miles-to-Go® program are available on request by calling 201-567-8500, ext 55.

NEW234

"Amazingly easy to use. Very portable, very complete."

"The only mainstream guide to list specific prices. The Walter Cronkite of guidebooks—with all that implies."

"Complete, concise, and filled with useful information."

"Hotel information is close to encyclopedic."

Frommer's® 98

New England

**by Wayne Curtis,
Herbert Bailey Livesey
& Marie Morris**

Macmillan • USA

ABOUT THE AUTHORS

Wayne Curtis (chapters 2 and 11 through 13) is the author of *Maine: Off the Beaten Path* (Globe Pequot) and numerous travel articles in newspapers and magazines, including the *New York Times, National Geographic Traveler,* and *Outside.* He lives in Portland, Maine, where he endeavors to support local microbreweries and minor-league baseball.

Herbert Bailey Livesey (chapters 8 through 10) is a native New Yorker and a former NYU administrator. After leaving his career in higher education, he worked briefly as an artist before devoting himself to writing full time. He is the author of several travel guides, nine books on education and sociology, and a novel.

Marie Morris (chapters 4 and 5) is a native New Yorker and a graduate of Harvard College, where she studied history. She has worked for the *New York Times, Boston* magazine, and the *Boston Herald,* and is also the author of *Frommer's Boston.* She lives in Boston, not far from Paul Revere.

MACMILLAN TRAVEL

A Simon & Schuster Macmillan Company
1633 Broadway
New York, NY 10019

Macmillan Publishing books may be purchased for business or sales promotional use. For information please write: Special Markets Department, Macmillan Publishing USA, 1633 Broadway, New York, NY 10019.

Find us online at **www.frommers.com**
or on America Online at Keyword: **Frommers.**

ISBN 0-02-861777-0
ISSN 1044-2286

Editor: Lisa Renaud
Contributors: Sandy MacDonald and Laura Reckford
Special thanks to Dan Glover
Production Editor: Carol Sheehan
Design by Michele Laseau
Digital Cartography by Roberta Stockwell and Ortelius Design

SPECIAL SALES

Bulk purchases (10+ copies) of Frommer's and selected Macmillan travel guides are available to corporations, organizations, mail-order catalogs, institutions, and charities at special discounts, and can be customized to suit individual needs. For more information write to: Special Sales, Macmillan General Reference, 1633 Broadway, New York, NY 10019.

Manufactured in the United States of America

Contents

List of Maps

AN INVITATION TO THE READER

In researching this book, we discovered many wonderful places—hotels, restaurants, shops, and more. We're sure you'll find others. Please tell us about them, so we can share the information with your fellow travelers in upcoming editions. If you were disappointed with a recommendation, we'd love to know that, too. Please write to:

Frommer's New England
c/o Macmillan Travel
1633 Broadway
New York, NY 10019

AN ADDITIONAL NOTE

Please be advised that travel information is subject to change at any time—and this is especially true of prices. We therefore suggest that you write or call ahead for confirmation when making your travel plans. The authors, editors, and publisher cannot be held responsible for the experiences of readers while traveling. Your safety is important to us, however, so we encourage you to stay alert and be aware of your surroundings. Keep a close eye on cameras, purses, and wallets—all favorite targets of thieves and pickpockets.

WHAT THE SYMBOLS MEAN

✪ Frommer's Favorites

Our favorite places and experiences—outstanding for quality, value, or both.

The following abbreviations are used for credit cards:

AE	American Express	JCB	Japan Credit Bank
CB	Carte Blanche	MC	MasterCard
DC	Diners Club	V	Visa

FIND FROMMER'S ONLINE

Arthur Frommer's Outspoken Encyclopedia of Travel (www.frommers.com) offers more than 6,000 pages of up-to-the-minute travel information—including the latest bargains and candid, personal articles updated daily by Arthur Frommer himself. No other Web site offers such comprehensive and timely coverage of the world of travel.

The Best of New England

One of the greatest challenges of traveling in New England is choosing from an abundance of superb restaurants, accommodations, and attractions. Where to start? Here's an entirely biased list of our favorite destinations and experiences. Over years of traveling through the region, we've discovered that these are places worth more than just a quick stop when we're in the area. They're all worth a major detour.

1 The Best of Small-Town New England

- **Marblehead** (Mass.): The "Yachting Capital of America" has major picture-postcard potential, especially in the summer, when the harbor fills with boats of all sizes. From downtown, a short distance inland, make your way toward the water down the narrow, flower-dotted streets. The first glimpse of blue sea and blue sky is breathtaking. See chapter 5.
- **Chatham** (Mass.): Located on the "elbow" of the Cape, right on Nantucket Sound, Chatham is proof that Main Street U.S.A. is alive and well on the Cape. Families throng here in the summer, to enjoy the beach and to browse through shops brimming with upscale arts, crafts, and other unique gifts. In summer, visitors and locals come together every Friday night for great outdoor concerts, while the looming Chatham Lighthouse, built in 1828, keeps a close eye on the Atlantic. See chapter 6.
- **Nantucket Town** (Mass.): This little town screams New England: cobbled streets, cozy inns, antique shops, intriguing museums, a bustling harbor and classic wharf lined with charming art galleries, and some of the best public beaches in the region. But don't be put off by the 19th-century, seafaring feel—it's subtly complemented by all the amenities and luxuries of the 20th century. See chapter 7.
- **Stockbridge** (Mass.): Norman Rockwell made a famous painting of the main street of this, his adopted hometown. Facing south, it uses the southern Berkshires as backdrop for the sprawl of the Red Lion Inn and the other late-19th-century buildings that make up the commercial district. Then as now, they service a beguiling mix of unassuming saltboxes and Gilded Age mansions that have sheltered farmers, artists, and aristocrats since the days of the French and Indian Wars. See chapter 8.

New England

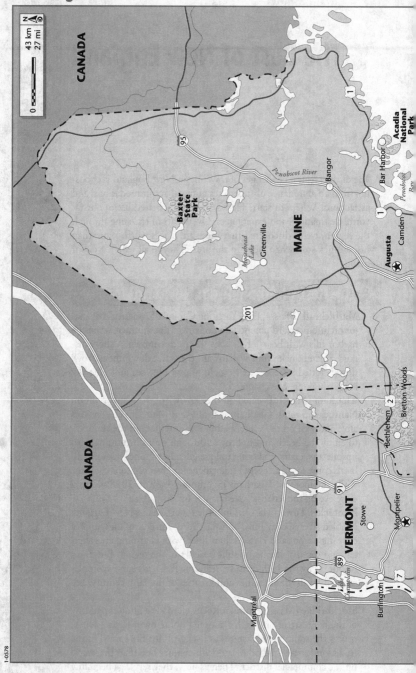

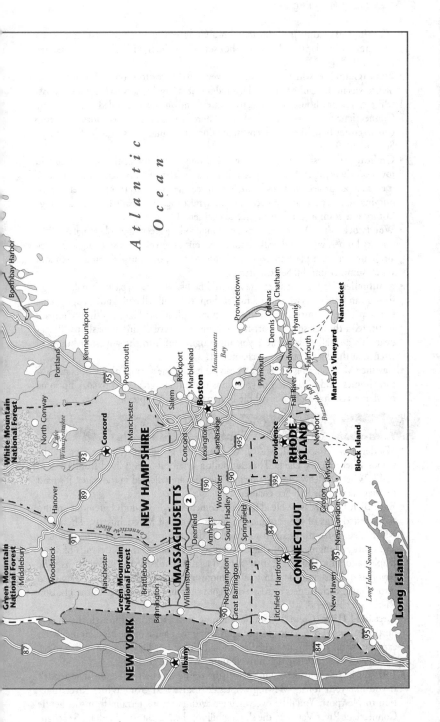

- **Washington** (Conn.): A classic, with a Congregational church facing a green surrounded by clapboard colonial houses, all of them with black shutters. See chapter 9.
- **Essex** (Conn.): A widely circulated survey voted Essex tops on its list of the 100 best towns in the United States. That judgment is largely statistical, but a walk past white clapboard houses to the active waterfront on this unspoiled stretch of the Connecticut River rings all the bells. There is not an artificial note, a blaring cookie-cutter franchise, nor a costumed docent to muddy its near-perfect image. See chapter 9.
- **Grafton** (Vt.): Just a few decades ago Grafton was a down-at-the-heels mountain town slowly being reclaimed by termites and the elements. A wealthy family took it on as a pet project and has lovingly restored the village to its former self—even burying the electric lines to reclaim the landscape. It doesn't feel like a living-history museum; it just feels right. See chapter 11.
- **Woodstock** (Vt.): Woodstock has a stunning village green, a whole range of 19th-century homes, woodland walks leading just out of town, and a settled, old-money air. This is a good place to explore by foot or bike, or to just sit on a porch and watch summer unfold. See chapter 11.
- **Montpelier** (Vt.): All state capitals should be like this: slow paced, small enough so you can walk everywhere, and full of shops that still sell nails and strapping tape to real people. Montpelier also shows a more sophisticated edge, with its Culinary Institute, a theater showing art-house films, and several fine bookshops. But at heart it's a small town, where you just might run into the governor buying a wrench at the corner store. See chapter 11.
- **Castine** (Me.): Soaring elm trees, a peaceful harborside setting, plenty of grand historic homes, and a selection of good inns make this a great spot to soak up some of Maine's coastal ambiance off the beaten path. See chapter 13.

2 The Best Places to See Fall Foliage

- **Walden Pond** (Concord, Mass.): Walden Pond is hidden from the road by the woods where Henry David Thoreau built a small cabin and lived from 1845 to 1847. When the leaves are turning and the trees are reflected in the water, it's hard to imagine why he left. See chapter 5.
- **Bash Bish Falls** (Mass.): Head from the comely village of South Egremont up into the forested hills of the extreme southwest corner of Massachusetts. The roads, which change from macadam to gravel to dirt and back, pass handmade houses and quirky Congregational chapels, and wind between crimson clouds of sugar maples and white birches feather-stroked against banks of black evergreens. The payoff is a three-state view from a promontory above a 50-foot cascade notched into a bluff, with carpets of russet and gold stretching all the way to the Hudson River. See chapter 8.
- **Litchfield Hills** (Conn.): Route 7, running south to north through the rugged northwest corner of Connecticut roughly along the course of the Housatonic River, explodes with color in the week fore and aft Columbus Day. It's something to see the fallen leaves whirling down the foaming river. See chapter 9.
- **I-91** (Vt.): An interstate? Don't scoff (the traffic can be terrible on state roads). If you like your foliage viewing wholesale, cruise I-91 from White River Junction to Newport. You'll be overwhelmed with gorgeous terrain, from the gentle Connecticut River Valley to the sloping hills of the Northeast Kingdom. See chapter 11.

- **Route 100** (Vt.): Route 100 winds the length of the Vermont from Readsboro to Newport. It's the major north-south route through the center of the Green Mountains, and it's surprisingly undeveloped along most of its length. You won't exactly have it to yourself along the southern stretches on autumn weekends, but as you head farther north you'll leave the crowds behind. One of the most spectacular stretches runs between Rochester on up to the Mad River Valley, through which the road traverses the wild, narrow Granville Gulf. See chapter 11.
- **Aboard the M/S *Mount Washington*** (N.H.): One of the more majestic views of the White Mountains is from Lake Winnipesaukee to the south. The vista is especially appealing as seen from the deck of the *Mount Washington,* an uncommonly handsome 230-foot-long vessel that offers a variety of tours through mid-October, when the lake is trimmed with a fringe of fall color along the shoreline. See chapter 12.
- **Crawford Notch** (N.H.): Route 302 passes through this scenic valley, where you can see the brilliant red maples and yellow birches high on the hillsides. Mount Washington stands guard in the background, and in fall is likely to be dusted with an early snow. See chapter 12.

3 The Best Ways to View Coastal Scenery

- **Strolling Around Rockport** (Mass.): The town centers around the small harbor and spreads out along the rugged, rocky coastline of Cape Ann. From the end of Bearskin Neck, the view is spectacular—fishing and pleasure boats in one direction, roaring surf in the other. See chapter 5.
- **Getting Back to Nature on Plum Island** (Mass.): The Parker River National Wildlife Refuge in Newburyport offers two varieties of coastal scenery—picturesque salt marshes packed with birds and other animals, and gorgeous ocean beaches where the power of the Atlantic is evident. See chapter 5.
- **Biking or Driving the Outer Cape** (Mass.): From Eastham through Wellfleet and Truro, all the way to Provincetown, Cape Cod's outermost towns offer dazzling ocean vistas and a number of exceptional bike paths, including the Province Lands, just outside Provincetown, that are bordered by spectacular swooping dunes. See chapter 6.
- **Heading "Up-Island"** (Martha's Vineyard, Mass.): Many visitors to Martha's Vineyard never venture beyond the port towns of Vineyard Haven, Oak Bluffs, and Edgartown. Though each has its charms, the scenery actually gets a lot more spectacular "up-island," in towns like Chilmark, where you'll pass moorlike meadows and family farms surrounded by stone walls. Whether biking or driving, follow State Road and the scenic Moshup Trail to the westernmost tip of the island, where you'll experience the dazzling colored cliffs of Gay Head, and beyond, the quaint fishing port of Menemsha. See chapter 7.
- **Cruising Newport's Ocean Drive** (R.I.): After a tour of the fabulously overwrought "cottages" of the hyper-rich that are strung along Bellevue Avenue, emerging onto the shoreline road that dodges the spray of the boiling Atlantic is a cleansing reminder of the power of nature over fragile monuments to the conceits of men. To extend the experience, take a 3.5-mile hike along the Cliff Walk that skirts the edge of the bluff commanded by the largest mansions. See chapter 10.
- **Biking Route 1A from Hampton Beach to Portsmouth** (N.H.): You'll get a taste of all sorts of coastal scenery pedaling along New Hampshire's minuscule coastline. You'll begin with sandy beaches, then pass rocky headlands and handsome mansions before coasting into the region's most scenic seaside city. See chapter 12.

- **Kayaking Merchant's Row** (Me.): The islands between Stonington and Isle au Haut, rimmed with pink granite and capped with the stark spires of spruce trees, are simply spectacular. Exploring by sea kayak will get you to islands inaccessible by motorboat. Outfitters offer overnight camping trips on the islands. See "Sea Kayaking & Camping Along 'Merchant's Row'" in chapter 13.
- **Hiking Monhegan Island** (Me.): The village of Monhegan is clustered around the harbor, but the rest of this 700-acre island is all picturesque wildlands, with miles of trails crossing open meadows and winding along rocky bluffs. See chapter 13.
- **Driving the Park Loop Road at Acadia National Park** (Me.): This is the region's premier ocean drive. You'll start high along a ridge with views of Frenchman Bay and the Porcupine Islands, then dip down along the rocky shores to watch the surf crash against the dark rocks. Plan to do this 20-mile loop at least twice to get the most out of it. See chapter 13.

4   The Best Places to Rediscover America's Past

- **Paul Revere House** (Boston): The history of the American Revolution is often told through stories of governments and institutions. At this little home in the North End, you'll learn about a real person. The tour is self-guided, allowing you to linger on the artifacts that hold your interest, and is particularly thought-provoking. Revere had 16 children with 2 wives, supported them with his thriving silversmith's trade—and put the whole operation in jeopardy with his role in the events that led to the Revolutionary War. See chapter 4.
- **The Old State House** (Boston): Built in 1713, the once towering Old State House is dwarfed by modern-day skyscrapers. It stands as a reminder of British rule (the exterior features a lion and a unicorn) and its overthrow—the Declaration of Independence was read from the balcony, which overlooks a traffic island where a circle of bricks represents the site of the Boston Massacre. See chapter 4.
- **Faneuil Hall** (Boston): Although Faneuil Hall is best known nowadays as a shopping destination, if you head upstairs instead of out into the marketplace, you'll find yourself transported back in time. The second-floor auditorium is in tip-top shape, and park rangers are on hand to talk about the building's role in the Revolution. Tune out the sound of sneakers squeaking across the floor, and you can almost hear Samuel Adams (his statue is out front) exhorting the Sons of Liberty. See chapter 4.
- **"Old Ironsides"** (Boston): Formally named the USS *Constitution,* the frigate was launched in 1797 and made a name for itself battling Barbary pirates and seeing action in the War of 1812. Last used in battle in 1815, it was periodically threatened with destruction until a complete renovation in the late 1920s started its career as a floating monument. The staff consists of sailors on active duty who wear 1812 dress uniforms, conduct tours, and can answer just about any question you throw at them. See chapter 4.
- **The Old North Bridge** (Concord, Mass.): British troops headed to Concord after putting down the uprising in Lexington, and the bridge (well, it's a replica) stands as a testament to the Minutemen who fought there. The Concord River and its peaceful green banks give no hint of the bloodshed here. On the path in from Monument Street, placards and audio stations provide a fascinating narrative. See chapter 5.
- **Plymouth Rock** (Mass.): Okay, so it's a fraction of its original size and looks like something you might find in your garden (especially if your garden is in rocky New

England soil), but Plymouth Rock makes a perfect starting point for exploration. Close by is the *Mayflower II*, a replica of the alarmingly small original vessel. The juxtaposition reminds you of what a dangerous undertaking the Pilgrims' voyage was, something to keep in mind as you explore the town. See chapter 5.

- **Sandwich** (Mass.): The oldest town on Cape Cod, Sandwich was founded in 1637. Glassmaking brought notoriety and prosperity to this picturesque town in the 19th century. Visit the Sandwich Glass Museum on Main Street for the whole story or one of the intriguing glassblowing studios, which are scattered throughout the town. Don't leave without visiting the 76-acre Heritage Plantation, which has a working carousel, a sparkling antique-car collection, and a wonderful collection of Americana. See chapter 6.

- **Deerfield** (Mass.): Arguably the best-preserved colonial village in New England, Deerfield has stubbornly persisted through three centuries; there are scores of houses in town dating back to the 17th and 18th centuries, and none of the clutter of modernity has intruded here. Fourteen of them on the main avenue ("The Street"), can be visited through tours conducted by the organization known as Historic Deerfield. See chapter 8.

- **Newport** (R.I.): A key port of the clipper trade long before the British surrendered their colony of "Rhode Island and Providence Plantation," Newport retains abundant recollections of its maritime past. In addition to its great harbor, clogged with cigarette boats, tugs, ferries, and majestic sloops, the City by the Sea has kept three distinctive enclaves preserved, the waterside homes of colonial seamen, the larger hillside Federalist houses of port-bound merchants, and the ostentatious mansions of America's post–Civil War industrial and financial grandees. See chapter 10.

- **Plymouth** (Vt.): Pres. Calvin Coolidge was born in this high upland valley, and the state has done a superb job preserving his hometown village. You'll get a good sense of the president's roots, but also gain a greater understanding of how a New England village works. Don't miss the cheese shop still owned by the president's son. See chapter 11.

- **Portsmouth** (N.H.): Portsmouth is a salty coastal city that just happens to boast some of the most impressive historic homes in New England. Start at Strawbery Banke, a historic 10-acre compound of 42 historic buildings. Then visit the many other grand homes in nearby neighborhoods, like the house John Paul Jones occupied while building his warship during the Revolution. See chapter 12.

- **Sabbathday Lake Shaker Community** (New Gloucester, Me.): This is the last of the active Shaker communities in the nation—the only Shaker community that voted to accept new converts rather than to die out. The 1,900-acre farm, about 45 minutes outside of Portland, has a number of exceptional buildings, including some dating back to the 18th century. Visitors come to view examples of historic Shaker craftsmanship, and buy locally grown Shaker herbs to bring home. See chapter 13.

5 The Best Literary Landmarks

- **Concord** (Mass.): Concord is home to a legion of literary ghosts. Homes of Ralph Waldo Emerson, Nathaniel Hawthorne, Henry David Thoreau, and Louisa May Alcott are popular destinations, and look much as they did during the "flowering of New England" in the mid-19th century. See chapter 5.

- **Salem** (Mass.): Native son Nathaniel Hawthorne might still feel at home here. A hotel and a boulevard bear his name, the Custom House where he found an embroidered scarlet "A" still stands, and his birthplace is open for tours. It has been moved into the same complex as the House of the Seven Gables, a cousin's home that inspired the classic novel. See chapter 5.

- **The Outer Cape** (Mass.): In the last century, the communities at the far end of the Cape—Wellfleet, Truro, and particularly Provincetown—have been a veritable HQ of bohemia. In the 19th century, Henry David Thoreau walked the 28 miles from Eastham to Provincetown and wrote about it in his classic *Cape Cod.* In the 1920s, Henry Beston spent a year living in a beach cottage and recorded his experience in *The Outermost House,* a great primer for your Cape vacation. Distinguished literati such as Edna St. Vincent Millay, Mary McCarthy, Edmund Wilson, Tennessee Williams, Norman Mailer, and many others have also taken refuge among the dunes here. See chapter 6.

- **Mark Twain & Harriet Beecher Stowe Houses** (Hartford, Conn.): Samuel Clemens's (a.k.a. Mark Twain) home is a fascinating example of the late 19th-century style sometimes known as Picturesque Gothic, and the interior shows his enthusiasm for newfangled gadgets—there is a primitive telephone in the entrance hall. About 60 yards across the lawn from the porte-cochere of the Twain residence is the smaller home of Harriet Beecher Stowe, author of *Uncle Tom's Cabin.* Come to see them during "Mark Twain Days" in mid-August, packed with such events as frog jumping and fence painting, sack races and riverboat rides, and performances of plays based on Twain's life or works. See chapter 9.

- **Robert Frost Farm** (Sugar Hill, N.H.): Two of the most famous New England poems—"The Road Not Taken" and "Stopping by Woods on a Snowy Evening"—were composed by Robert Frost at this farm just outside of Franconia. Explore the woods and read the verses posted along the pathways, and tour the farmhouse where Frost lived with his family earlier this century. See chapter 11.

- **West Branch of the Penobscot River** (Me.): Henry David Thoreau ventured down this river by canoe in the mid-19th century, and found the woods all "moosey and mossy." They're still that way along the river today. A 4-day canoe trip along part of his route includes a stop at tiny Chesuncook Village, where you can find the grave of Thoreau's host in a quiet, wooded cemetery. See chapter 13.

6 The Best Activities for Families

- **Visiting the Museum of Science** (Boston): Built around demonstrations, experiments, and interactive displays that never feel like homework, this museum is wildly popular with kids—and adults. Explore the exhibits (this can fill a couple of hours or a whole day), then take in a show at the planetarium or the Omni Theater. Before you know it, everyone will have learned something, painlessly. See chapter 4.

- **Free Friday Flicks at the Hatch Shell** (Boston): Better known for the Boston Pops' Fourth of July concert, the Esplanade is also famous for the family films (*The Wizard of Oz* or *Pocahontas,* for example) shown for free on Friday nights in summer. The lawn in front of the Hatch Shell, an amphitheater usually used for concerts, turns into a giant, carless drive-in movie as hundreds of people picnic and wait for the sky to grow dark. See chapter 4.

- **Exploring the Museum of Fine Arts** (Boston): What parents hear as "magnificent Egyptian collections" boils down to one word in kid-speak: "Mummies!" Even the most hyper youngster usually manages to take it down a notch in quiet, refined surroundings (you may have seen this phenomenon in fancy restaurants), and the collections at the MFA simultaneously tickle visitors' brains. Admission is free to those under 18. See chapter 4.

- **A Trip to Woods Hole** (Mass.): For junior oceanologists, the place to be. You can try the hands-on exhibits at the Woods Hole Oceanographic Institute, observe experiments at the Marine Biological Laboratory, explore the touch tanks at the country's oldest aquarium, and even collect crucial data with the "Ocean Quest" crew. See chapter 6.

- **Whale Watching off Provincetown** (Mass.): Boats leave Provincetown's MacMillan Wharf throughout the day for the 8-mile journey to Stellwagen Bank National Marine Sanctuary, a rich feeding ground for several types of whales. Kids will be entertained by on-board naturalists who set the stage for the showstoppers. But nothing can prepare you or the little ones for the thrill of spotting these magnificent creatures feeding, breaching, and even flipper slapping. Hands down, the best outfit in town is the **Dolphin Fleet** (☎ **800/826-9300**), which is affiliated with the Center for Coastal Studies. See chapter 6.

- **A Learn-to-Ski Vacation at Jiminy Peak** (Mass.): More than 70% of Jiminy Peak's trails are catered toward beginners and intermediates, making it one of the premier places to learn to ski in the East. The mountain is located in the heart of the Berkshires, near Mount Greylock. See chapter 8.

- **An Afternoon of Deep-Sea Fishing:** Charter fishing boats these days usually have high-tech fish-finding gear—imagine how your kids will react to reeling in one big bluefish after another. The top spots to mount such an expedition are Hyannis, on Cape Cod; Point Judith, at the southern tip of Rhode Island; and the Maine coast. See chapters 6, 10, and 13, respectively.

- **Visiting Mystic Seaport & Mystic Marinelife Aquarium** (Conn.): The double-down winner in the family-fun sweeps has to be this combination—performing dolphins and whales, full-rigged tall ships, penguins and sharks, and river rides on a perky little 1906 motor launch are the kinds of G-rated attractions that have no age barriers. See chapter 9.

- **Visiting the Montshire Museum** (Norwich, Vt.): This new children's museum, in a soaring, modern space on the Vermont–New Hampshire border, has wonderful interactive exhibits inside and nature trails winding along the Connecticut River. See chapter 12.

- **A Stay in Weirs Beach** (N.H.): This is the trip your kids would plan if you didn't get in the way. Weirs Beach on Lake Winnipesaukee offers passive amusements like train and boat rides that appeal to younger kids, and plenty of active adventures for young teens—like go-cart racing, water slides, and video arcades. Their parents can recuperate while lounging on the lakeside beach. See chapter 12.

- **A Ride on Cog Railroad** (Crawford Notch, N.H.): It's fun! It's terrifying! It's a great glimpse into history. Kids love this ratchety climb to the top of New England's highest peak aboard trains that were specially designed to scale the mountain in 1869. As a technological marvel, the railroad attracted tourists by the thousands a century ago. They still come to marvel at its sheer audacity. See chapter 12.

- **A Trip to Monhegan Island** (Me.): Kids from 8 to 12 years old especially enjoy overnight excursions to Monhegan Island. The mail boat from Port Clyde is rustic and intriguing, the hotels are an adventure, and the woods are filled with magical fairy houses. See chapter 13.

7 The Best Downhill Skiing

- **Killington** (Vt.; ☎ **802/422-3333**): Killington is your place if you like your skiing big—it boasts New England's highest vertical drop and 165 trails. You can spend days here exploring different parts of the mountain—which promises to get even bigger when it's connected to just acquired Pico. The access road sorely lacks charm, but it's got a gazillion restaurants and a raging nightlife scene that's especially appealing to singles. See chapter 11.

- **Sugarbush** (Vt.; ☎ **802/583-2381**): The resort's two big, lovely mountains (3,975-ft. Lincoln Peak and 4,135-ft. Mt. Ellen) feature the classic narrow, cascading trails that are the heart and soul of New England skiing. And the surrounding Mad River Valley retains a bucolic feel while offering most of the amenities—including good restaurants and fine inns—you'd expect at a major resort town. See chapter 11.

- **Mad River Glen** (Vt.; ☎ **802/496-3551**): This feisty ski area, just up the road from Sugarbush, hasn't given in to passing whims—like high-speed chairlifts and snowmaking—and maintains a stubborn pride in its challenging slopes and no-frills skiing. The cooperative of longtime Mad River skiers who bought the resort in 1995 seems determined to maintain its cranky charm. See chapter 11.

- **Stowe** (Vt.; ☎ **802/253-3000**): One of the oldest ski resorts in New England, Stowe deserves its reputation as one of the finest. Situated on the shoulders of Mount Mansfield, the largest and most rugged of Vermont's peaks, Stowe yields some of the most challenging old-style skiing in the East, typified by the fearsome challenge of the Front Four. See chapter 11.

- **Wildcat Mountain** (N.H.; ☎ **800/255-6439** or 603/466-3326): Wildcat is a wonderful, remote ski area deep in the White Mountain National Forest with a good range of slopes and arguably the best mountain views of any ski area in New England. See chapter 12.

- **Sugarloaf/USA** (Me.; ☎ **207/237-2000**): Stern, pyramidal Sugarloaf Mountain is an impressive sight. And this big, brooding mountain has a friendly, bustling resort at its base and some superb skiing on the upper flanks. This is the place to be after a heavy snowstorm, when the snowfields offer the only lift-served above-tree-line skiing in the East. It's popular with families. See chapter 13.

- **Sunday River** (Me.; ☎ **207/824-3000**): Sunday River came from nowhere in the last decade to blossom as one of New England's preeminent ski destinations. Sprawling across eight mountains on the Maine–New Hampshire border, it offers a wide range of terrain and a speedy assortment of lifts. See chapter 13.

8 The Best Cross-Country Ski Touring Centers

- **Woodstock Ski Touring Center** (Vt.; ☎ **802/457-2114** or 802/457-6774): Some 36 miles of groomed trails ring the base and then ascend Mount Tom and Mount Peg. The touring center also features a great backcountry run—the 6.3-mile Skyline Trail, which leads from the Suicide Six downhill area to Amity Pond. See chapter 11.

- **Trapp Family Lodge** (Vt.; ☎ **800/826-7000** or 802/253-8511): Thanks to this operation, ski touring in northern Vermont is legendary. The lodge, made famous by Maria von Trapp, whose flight from the Nazis was immortalized in *The Sound of Music,* is one of the oldest ski-touring centers in the nation. The resort features 57 miles of trails (36 of them groomed) that weave through 1,700 acres of forest and open fields on the lower flanks of Mount Mansfield. See chapter 11.

- **Craftsbury Nordic Ski Center** (Vt.; ☎ **800/729-7751** or 802/586-7767): Located in Vermont's Northeast Kingdom, Craftsbury's ski season lasts longer than the season in the rest of Vermont. The 78 miles of trails (48 groomed) rise and dip over meadows and through upland forests of maples and firs. See chapter 11.

- **Jackson Ski Touring Foundation** (N.H.; ☎ 603/383-9355): With more than 90 kilometers of trails, Jackson is one of the largest cross-country skiing networks in the Northeast. Tranquil trails lead from the peaceful village into the White Mountains, far away from the commercial clutter of North Conway. See chapter 12.

9 The Best Warm-Weather Sports

- **Nature Walks:** In every corner of New England you'll find wildlife refuges, parks, and even remote wilderness cut by trail systems that make the areas accessible to most everyone. The payoff for your exertions can be immense: thousands of nesting terns and plovers at Cape Cod's Wellfleet Bay Wildlife Sanctuary; wildflowers, rugged bluffs, and innumerable songbirds along Block Island's Greenway Trail; Newport's Cliff Walk, which both hangs above the ocean and provides views of the "cottages" of the Gilded Age industrialists who summered here; views from atop 150-foot-high cliffs at Maine's Quoddy Head State Park, at the easternmost point of the United States; a short walk through lush, mossy woods to 125-foot-high Hamilton Falls, in Vermont. You'll find suggestions throughout this book.
- **Hitting the Beach on the Cape** (Mass.): The Cape's legendary beaches live up to their billing. Yes, you'll have to fight massive crowds to get there, but once you settle on your blanket at the base of towering dunes and let the salty air waft past, it will all be worth it. The beaches of the National Seashore are among the most beautiful in the world. See chapter 6.
- **Fly-Fishing on the Housatonic River** (Conn.): Vermont's Battenkill River gets more attention—which may explain the rumors that the river is getting fished out. The stretch of the Housatonic River near Housatonic Meadows State Park is a 9-mile trout management area, with 3 miles reserved for fly-fishing. Browns and rainbows are plentiful. See chapter 9.
- **Road Biking in Central & Northern Vermont:** Arguably the best regions for cycling are the Champlain Islands, the Northeast Kingdom, and Central Vermont east of the Green Mountains. Each of these places feature plenty of elbowroom on serpentine two-lane blacktop. On the islands you'll travel through a flat, austerely beautiful landscape where a new lake vista appears at every turn; the latter two offer you verdant hills and tumbling streams—and much more challenging cycling. See chapter 11.
- **Hiking the Presidential Range** (N.H.): These rugged peaks in the White Mountains draw hikers from all over the globe, attracted by the history, the beautiful vistas, and the exceptional alpine landscapes along the craggy ridgelines. You can make day-hike forays and retreat to the comfort of an inn at night, or stay in the hills at the Appalachian Mountain Club's historic high huts. See chapter 12.
- **Backpacking the Appalachian Trail's "100-Mile Wilderness"** (Me.): It's not really wilderness—there's abundant evidence of the vast logging operations at work in the North Woods—but there is nonetheless a uniquely raw, wild feel to this 100-mile, 10-day trek on the very northern tip of the Appalachian Trail. For one thing, there's more wildlife than can be seen on any other long-distance hike in the East—black bears, moose, and loons on the many lakes. See chapter 13.
- **Mountain Biking at Acadia National Park** (Me.): Acadia's carriage roads are the perfect introduction to this sport—anyone who's reasonably fit can enjoy rides here. John D. Rockefeller, Jr., built the carriage roads of Mount Desert Island so the gentry could enjoy rambles in the woods with their horses, away from

pesky cars. Today, this extensive network makes for some of the most enjoyable, aesthetically pleasing mountain biking anywhere. See chapter 13.

- **Canoeing and Kayaking Maine's Waters:** Maine has thousands of miles of flowing rivers and streams, hundreds of glass-smooth lakes, and hundreds of miles of shorelines along remote ponds and lakes. Bring your tent, sleeping bag, and cooking gear, and come prepared to spend a night under the stars listening to the sounds of the loons. See chapter 13.

10 The Best Country Inns

- **The Hawthorne Inn** (Concord, Mass.; ☎ 508/369-5610): This inn rings all the bells. Everything—the 1870 building, the garden setting a stone's throw from the historic attractions, the antique furnishings, the eclectic decorations, the accommodating innkeepers—is top of the line. See chapter 5.
- **The Inn on Cove Hill** (Rockport, Mass.; ☎ 888/546-2701): The Inn on Cove Hill isn't in the country, but you might be fooled when you're having breakfast on the lawn at this relaxing spot near the center of this coastal town. Built in 1791 and beautifully decorated, it's a delightful place. See chapter 5.
- **The Inn at West Falmouth** (West Falmouth, Mass.; ☎ 800/397-7696 or 508/540-7696): If you're looking for a country inn worthy of *Architectural Digest,* this shingle-style 1900 manse overlooking Buzzards Bay should do the trick. New innkeepers have spruced up the exterior to equal the sumptuous interior spaces. Each individually designed room includes decorative antiques, fine linens, and a marble Jacuzzi. A deck with patio and pool overlooks the tennis court, lovely gardens, and the nearby beaches of Buzzards Bay. See chapter 6.
- **The Wequassett Inn** (Chatham, Mass.; ☎ 800/225-7125 or 508/432-5400): This Chatham institution occupies its own peninsula—22 acres—on Pleasant Bay and offers excellent sailing and tennis clinics. The oldest building on the property was built in 1740, and the inn has been operating for more than 50 years. The resort's many amenities include a health club and a first-class restaurant. Request one of the waterfront clapboard cottages, decorated in an elegant Early American style. See chapter 6.
- **The Nauset House Inn** (East Orleans, Mass.; ☎ 508/255-2195): This small, romantic 1810 farmhouse is like a sepia-toned vision of old Cape Cod. Recline in a wicker divan surrounded by fragrant flowers while the wind whistles outside. Better yet, stroll 10 minutes to Nauset Beach and take a quiet walk as the sun sets. Your genial hosts also prepare one of the finest breakfasts in town. See chapter 6.
- **Lambert's Cove Country Inn** (West Tisbury, Martha's Vineyard, Mass.; ☎ 508/693-2298): Far from the maddening crowds that can sometimes mar this popular island, Lambert's Cove offers a charming place to escape your workaday world. Down the winding dirt road is a secluded country estate with rambling gardens bordered by 150-year-old vine-covered stone walls. Amenities include a tennis court, a fine restaurant, and one of the Vineyard's best beaches. See chapter 7.
- **Mayflower Inn** (Washington, Conn.; ☎ 860/868-9466): Not a tough call at all for this part of the region: Immaculate in taste and execution, the Mayflower is as close to perfection as any such enterprise is likely to be. A genuine Joshua Reynolds hangs in the hall. See chapter 9.
- **Griswold Inn** (Essex, Conn.; ☎ 860/767-1776): "The Gris" has been accommodating sailors and travelers as long as any inn in the country, give or take a decade. For all that time, it has been the focus of life and commerce in the lower

Connecticut River Valley, always ready with a mug of suds, a haunch of beef, and a roaring fire. The walls are layered with nautical paintings and memorabilia, and there is music every night in the schoolhouse-turned-tavern. See chapter 9.

- **Windham Hill Inn** (West Townshend, Vt.; ☎ **800/944-4080** or 802/874-4080): New innkeepers made over this historic inn in recent years, adding welcome amenities like air-conditioning, a tennis court, and a swimming pool, while still preserving the antique charm of this 1823 farm house. It's at the end of a remote dirt road in a high upland valley, and guests are welcome to explore 160 private acres on a network of walking trails. The dining is superb. See chapter 11.
- **Kedron Valley Inn** (South Woodstock, Vt.; ☎ **800/836-1193** or 802/457-1473): Set at a quiet country crossroads just south of Woodstock, the Kedron Valley Inn offers genuine comfort—this is no stuffy museum-quality setting. Guests enjoy exquisite bedrooms, a private pond with two sand beaches, and a creative dining room that wins raves from discriminating diners. See chapter 11.
- **Twin Farms** (Woodstock, Vt.; ☎ **800/894-6327** or 802/234-9999): Just north of Woodstock is the most elegant inn in New England. The price will appall many of you (rooms start at $700 for two, including all meals and liquor), but you'll certainly be pampered. Novelist Sinclair Lewis once lived on this 300-acre farm, and today it's an aesthetic retreat that offers serenity and exceptional food. See chapter 11.
- **The Inn at Thorn Hill** (Jackson, N.H.; ☎ **603/383-4242**): Designed by famed architect Stanford White in 1895, this handsome inn is maintained in a style that would make the master proud. It's decorated in a Victorian motif, with comfortable guest rooms, lovely common areas, and a well-regarded dining room—all within easy walking (or skiing) distance of the town of Jackson. See chapter 12.
- **Adair** (Bethlehem, N.H.; ☎ **800/441-2606** or 603/444-2600): This is one of the newer country mansions in the White Mountains (it dates from 1927), but innkeepers Patricia and Hardy Banfield have done a stellar job of infusing this Georgian Revival with a time-honored elegance. This inn, tucked away in a little-tracked corner of the White Mountains, boasts a superb dining room on the first floor and easy access to mountain activities and golf. See chapter 12.
- **The White Barn Inn** (Kennebunkport, Me.; ☎ **207/967-2321**): Much of the White Barn staff hails from Europe, and guests are treated with a continental graciousness. The rooms are a delight, and the meals (served in the barn) are among the best in Maine. See chapter 13.
- **The Claremont** (Southwest Harbor, Me.; ☎ **800/244-5036** or 207/244-5036): The 1884 Claremont is a Maine classic. This Sound-side lodge has everything a Victorian resort should: sparsely decorated rooms, creaky floorboards in the halls, a great view of water and mountains, and perfect croquet. The dining room's only so-so, but Southwest Harbor has plenty of other dining options. See chapter 13.

11 The Best Moderately Priced Accommodations

- **Newbury Guest House** (Boston; ☎ **617/437-7666**): In the heart of the luxurious Back Bay neighborhood, you'll find this comfortable inn an oasis of affordability—rates even include breakfast. See chapter 4.
- **Harvard Square Hotel** (Cambridge, Mass.; ☎ **800/458-5886** or 617/864-5200): Smack in the middle of Cambridge's most popular destination, this hotel is a comfortable place to stay in a great location. See chapter 5.

- **John Carver Inn** (Plymouth, Mass.; ☎ **800/274-1620** or 508/746-7100): This hotel is centrally located, whether you're immersing yourself in Pilgrim lore or passing through on the way from Boston to Cape Cod. Ask about the "Passport to History" packages for a good deal. See chapter 5.

- **Summer House** (Sandwich, Mass.; ☎ **800/241-3609** or 508/888-4991): This circa 1835 Greek Revival home offers five spacious and airy rooms tastefully decorated with antiques and reproductions. All rooms have private baths and four have fireplaces, making this a good escape in winter too. New owners have made a number of improvements, but the Summer House still has its signature full breakfasts, afternoon tea, and ever-popular hammocks in the English garden. See chapter 6.

- **Isaiah Hall B&B Inn** (Dennis, Mass.; ☎ **800/736-0160** or 508/385-9928): Nestled amid oak trees in Dennis Village, not far from Cape Cod's historic Old King's Highway, this B&B has been welcoming visitors to this part of Cape Cod for more than 50 years. The inn and its gregarious owner are popular with actors starring in summer stock at the nearby Cape Cod Playhouse. Guests enjoy country-cozy rooms and a communal breakfast served on a 12-foot cherry table in the dining room. See chapter 6.

- **Even'Tide Motel** (South Wellfleet, Mass.; ☎ **800/368-0007** or 508/349-3410): That rarity, a motel with style, this popular establishment embodies the best aspects of the 1960s: handsome blond oak furniture, a rather hedonistic 60-foot heated indoor pool, and a three-quarter-mile nature trail leading to the sea. It's a low-key, low-cost family haven. See chapter 6.

- **Wesley Hotel** (Oak Bluffs, Martha's Vineyard, Mass.; ☎ **800/638-9027** or 508/693-6611): While way past its glory days as a turn-of-the-century grand hotel, the Wesley still survives as a reminder of a more refined age. Its location overlooking the busy harbor and the colorful gingerbread cottages of Oak Bluffs can't be beat, and, surprisingly, the rates remain among the most reasonable on the island. See chapter 7.

- **Tollgate Hill Inn** (Litchfield, Conn.; ☎ **800/445-3903** or 860/567-4545): No sacrifices in comfort will be made when you stay here, and you'll enjoy the marvelously atmospheric 1745 tavern that serves thoroughly up-to-date eclectic fusion cuisine. On weekends, they have live jazz, and Sunday brunch beside the fireplace in winter couldn't be more New England. See chapter 9.

- **Beech Tree** (Newport, R.I.; ☎ **401/847-9794**): Arrive on Friday afternoon at the Beech Tree in Newport and they sit you down to a complimentary bowl of chowder, fresh bread, and a glass of wine. Breakfast the next morning, huge and cooked to order, makes lunch irrelevant. All rooms have air-conditioning, TVs, and phones, unlike most B&Bs. See chapter 10.

- **Inn at the Mad River Barn** (Waitsfield, Vt.; ☎ **800/631-0466** or 802/496-3310): It takes a few minutes to adapt to the Spartan rooms and no-frills accommodations here. But you'll soon discover that the real action takes place in the living room and dining room, where skiers relax and chat after a day on the slopes, and share heaping helpings at mealtime. Rooms with breakfast are only $65 for two in summer, and $95 in winter. See chapter 11.

- **Red Hill Inn** (Center Harbor, N.H.; ☎ **800/573-3445** or 603/279-7001): Situated in the lush hills between Lake Winnipesaukee and the White Mountains, the Red Hill Inn has a faded Victorian grandeur that's been nicely updated without destroying the mood. It's hard to pry yourself away from the fireplace in the common room, but try to stir yourself, if only to explore the forest and fields around the inn. See chapter 12.

- **Philbrook Farm Inn** (Shelburne, N.H.; ☎ 603/466-3831): Go here if you're looking for a complete getaway. The inn has been taking in travelers since the 1850s, and they know how to do it right. The farmhouse sits on 1,000 acres between the Mahoosuc Mountains and the Androscoggin River, and guests can hike with vigor or relax in leisure with equal aplomb. Rooms for two are $130 and under, and that includes both breakfast and dinner. Ask about discounts for longer stays. See chapter 12.
- **Maine Stay Inn** (Camden, Me.; ☎ 207/236-9636): It's by no means a budget inn (rooms run $80 to $130 for two), but you get a lot of hospitality for the money, and the accommodations are unusually pleasant. The inn is within walking distance of both downtown Camden and the Camden Hills. See chapter 13.

12 The Best Restaurants

- **Aujourd'hui** (Boston; ☎ 617/451-1392): The exquisite setting, spectacular view, telepathic service, and, of course, marvelous food combine to transport you to a plane where you might not even notice (or care) how much it's costing. See chapter 4.
- **Durgin-Park** (Boston; ☎ 617/227-2038): A meal at this landmark restaurant might start with oysters, and it might start with a waitress slinging a handful of napkins over your shoulder, dropping a handful of cutlery in front of you, and saying, "Here, give these out." The surly service routine usually seems to be an act, but it's so much a part of the experience that some people are disappointed when the waitresses are nice (as they often are). In any case, it's worked since 1827. See chapter 4.
- **Rialto** (Cambridge, Mass.; ☎ 617/661-5050): This is a don't-miss destination if your plans include fine dining. The contemporary setting is a great match for chef Jody Adams's inventive cuisine, and the service is efficient without being too familiar—surely a draw for the visiting celebrities who flock here. See chapter 4.
- **Woodman's** (Essex, Mass.; ☎ 800/649-1773): This North Shore institution, one of the busiest restaurants anywhere, is not for the faint of heart—or the hard of artery, unless you like eating corn and steamers while everyone around you is gobbling fried clams and onion rings. The food at this glorified clam shack is fresh and tasty, and a look at the organized pandemonium behind the counter is worth the (reasonable) price. See chapter 5.
- **Martin House** (Provincetown, Mass.; ☎ 508/487-1327): Commercial Street in Provincetown is loaded with fabulous restaurants, but the Martin House definitely wins our vote. It boasts the most forward-thinking kitchen on the Cape—mostly fusion, incorporating the freshest regional delicacies—and a charming, historic ambiance. Dine inside in intimate rooms with fireplaces or in the romantic garden outside (the harbor views are breathtaking!), while you feast on highly imaginative meals. See chapter 6.
- **Chanticleer Inn** (Nantucket, Mass.; ☎ 508/257-4154): Nestled among the roses and quaint cottages of 'Sconset village on Nantucket, the Chanticleer is a jackets-required affair: classic French and continental cuisine, served in two elegant dining rooms, both with garden views. Order a bottle of wine from their extensive and stunning cellar and savor the rich desserts, but don't forget your Gold Card. See chapter 7.
- **Truc Orient Express** (West Stockbridge, Mass.; ☎ 413/232-4204): The artists and craftspeople who live in this funky Berkshires hamlet deserve something out

of the prevailing red-sauce and red-meat mode. They get it in this converted ware-house, with eye-opening Thai and Southeast Asian dishes that rarely emerge from kitchens this far west of Ho Chi Minh City. Tastes range from delicate to sinus clearing, and the service is sweetly diffident. See chapter 8.

- **Amberjacks Coastal Grill** (Norwalk, Conn.; ☎ 203/853-4332): Think Duval Street in Key West—that's where the chef/owner honed his craft before moving to this cooler shore. Such transplantations rarely work, but his uncommonly fla-vorful assemblages rouse weary palates. The menu leans to tropical fruits and aquatic denizens of the Caribbean, fired or freshened with Asian spices. See chapter 9.

- **Union League Café** (New Haven, Conn.; ☎ 203/562-4299): This august set-ting of arched windows and high ceilings is more than a century old and was long the sanctuary of an exclusive club. It still looks good, but the tone has been light-ened into an approximation of a Lyonnaise brasserie. The moderately priced menu observes the southern French tastes for curry, olive oil, pastas, lamb, and shellfish. See chapter 9.

- **Scales & Shells** (Newport, R.I.; ☎ 401/846-3474): Ye who turn aside all pre-tension get yourselves hence. There isn't a frill or affectation anywhere near this place, and since the left end of the wide-open kitchen is right at the entrance, there are no secrets, either. What we have here are marine critters mere hours from the depths, prepared and presented free of any but the slightest artifice. This might well be the purest seafood joint on the southern New England coast. See chapter 10.

- **Hemingway's** (Killington, Vt.; ☎ 802/422-3886): Killington seems an unlikely place for serious culinary adventure, yet Hemingway's will meet the loftiest expec-tations. The menu changes frequently to take full advantage of the freshest ingre-dients. If it's available, be sure to order the wild-mushroom and truffle soup. See chapter 11.

- **Daniel Webster Room** (Hanover, N.H.; ☎ 603/643-4300): Classic continen-tal fare and more is cooked to perfection and expertly served in the elegant neo-classical dining room at the Hanover Inn at the edge of the Dartmouth College campus. Try the filet mignon with foie gras. See chapter 12.

- **Chauncey Creek Lobster Pier** (Kittery Point, Me.; ☎ 207/439-1030): Perfect when you're not in the mood for anything fancy. Few places do things better than Chauncey Creek. It's a low-key affair on a tidy inlet, with bright picnic tables and a sense of adventure. See chapter 13.

- **White Barn Inn** (Kennebunkport, Me.; ☎ 207/967-2321): The setting, in an ancient, rustic barn, is magical. The tables are draped with floor-length tablecloths, and the chairs feature imported Italian upholstery. The food is to die for. Enjoy entrees such as frilled duckling breast with ginger and sun-dried-cherry sauce, or a roast rack of lamb with pecans and homemade barbecue sauce. See chapter 13.

- **Street & Co.** (Portland, Me.; ☎ 207/775-0887): Seafood is the big catch at this intimate Portland bistro, tucked down a narrow alley just a block from the water-front. Low beams, dim lighting, and drying herbs hanging from the joists overhead set the mood. Diners are seated at copper-topped tables, designed to allow the waiters to deliver steaming skillets of perfectly prepared seafood right from the stove. See chapter 13.

Planning a Trip to New England

This chapter covers most of the nuts-and-bolts travel information you'll need before setting off on a New England journey. Browse through this section before you hit the road to ensure you've touched all the bases.

1 Visitor Information

New England's leading cash crop appears to be the brochure. Shops, hotels, and restaurants often feature racks of colorful pamphlets touting local sights and accommodations. These minicenters can be helpful in turning up unexpected attractions, but for a more comprehensive overview you should head for the state information centers or the local chambers of commerce. Chamber addresses and phone numbers are provided for each region and town in the chapters that follow. If you're a highly organized traveler, you'll call in advance and ask for information to be mailed to you. If you're like the rest of us, you'll swing by when you reach town and hope the office is still open.

All six states are pleased to send out general visitor information packets and maps to travelers who call or write ahead. Here's the contact information: **Connecticut Department of Economic Development, Tourist Division,** 865 Brook St., Rocky Hill, CT 06067-3405 (☎ **800/282-6863** or 203/258-4355); **Maine Publicity Bureau,** P.O. Box 2300, Hallowell, ME 04347 (☎ **800/533-9595** or 207/623-0360); **Massachusetts Office of Travel and Tourism,** 100 Cambridge St., 13th Floor, Boston, MA 02202 (☎ **800/447-6277** or 617/727-3201); **New Hampshire Office of Travel and Tourism,** P.O. Box 1856, Concord, NH 03302 (☎ **800/258-3608** or 603/271-2343); **Rhode Island Department of Economic Development,** 7 Jackson Walkway, Providence, RI 02903 (☎ **800/556-2484** or 401/277-2601); **Vermont Travel and Tourism,** 134 State St., Montpelier, VT 05602 (☎ **800/837-6668** or 802/828-3237 for general information; 800/833-9756 for information by fax).

If you're connected to the Internet, there's a rapidly growing horde of information available on the World Wide Web. Many inns and restaurants are putting up their own sites, and entrepreneurs offer packaged tourism information. Many of these sites are simply electronic brochures, offering the same information you'd find at tourist racks. Be sure to distinguish which are paid advertising and which are the opinions of travelers or residents. (Some cagey advertisers try to make it sound as if they're offering independent advice.)

Most search engines and on-line directories—like Yahoo, AltaVista, and HotBot—will get you started if you simply type in your destination. Failing that, try official information pages maintained by each state, many of which contain links to other state-related Web sites. The Web addresses are: **Connecticut:** http://www.state.ct.us/.; **Maine:** http://www.state.me.us/.; **Massachusetts:** http://www.mass-vacation.com/.; **New Hampshire:** http://www.cit.state.vt.us/.; **Vermont:** http://www.cit.state.vt.us/.; **Rhode Island** hosts a Web site at http://www.ri.us/, but at press time it contained little useful information for travelers. You're better off starting at: http://www.ids.net/ri/.

2 When to Go

THE SEASONS

The well-worn joke about the climate in New England is that it has just two seasons: winter and August. There's a kernel of truth to that, but it's mostly a canard to keep outsiders from moving here. In fact, the ever-shifting seasons are one of those elements that make New England so distinctive.

SUMMER   The peak summer season runs from July 4 to Labor Day. Vast crowds surge into New England's tourist areas in the mountains and along the coast for the 2 months between these two holidays, and activity remains frenetic until Labor Day evening, when a calm begins to return to these regions. This should be no surprise: Summers are exquisite. Forests are verdant and lush, and in the mountains, warm (rarely hot) days are the rule, followed by cool nights. Along the coast, ocean breezes keep temperatures down; Cape Cod and the Islands, for example, are generally 10° cooler than the mainland in summer.

The weather in summer is typically determined by the winds. Southerly winds bring haze, heat, and humidity. The northwest winds bring cool weather and knife-sharp vistas. These systems tend to alternate, and the change from hot to cool will sometimes occur in a matter of minutes. Rain is never far away—some days it's an afternoon thunderstorm, other times it's a steady drizzle that brings a 4-day soaking. Regardless, travelers should come prepared for it.

For most of the region, especially the coastal areas, midsummer is the prime season for travel. Expect to pay premium prices at hotels and restaurants except at those near the empty ski resorts of northern New England, where you can often find bargains.

Also be aware that early summer brings out black flies and mosquitoes, especially in the north country. Outdoors people are best off waiting until after July 4 before setting off into the woods.

AUTUMN   Don't be surprised to smell the tang of fall approaching as early as mid-August in northern New England; a few leaves will begin to turn blaze orange in otherwise verdant trees at the edges of wetlands. Fall comes early here, puts its feet up on the couch, and stays for some time. The foliage season begins in earnest in the northern part of the region by the 3rd week in September; in the south, it reaches its peak by the middle to end of October. Figure that the change in seasons in southern Connecticut runs 3 to 4 weeks behind northern Maine. And the higher elevations of the Green and White mountains likewise start to feel wintry a month or so before coastal locations.

Fall in New England is one of the great natural spectacles of the United States, with the rolling hills blanketed with brilliant reds and stunning oranges. Autumn is garish in a way that seems determined to embarrass understated New England. Along winding country roads you'll find heaps of pumpkins for sale under fiery red sugar maples, and crisp apples available by the bushel. Take the time to scout out the farm stands, where you'll be amazed at the fertility of this otherwise flinty land.

Keep in mind that this is the most popular time of year to travel—bus tours flock here throughout October. As a result, hotels are invariably booked solid. Reservations are essential; you can also expect to pay a foliage surcharge of $10 or $20 per room at many inns.

WINTER   New England winters are like wine—some years are good, some are lousy. During a good season, plenty of light, fluffy snow covers the deep woods and ski slopes. A good New England winter offers a profound peace as the muffling qualities of fresh snow bring a thunderous silence to the region. During these winters, exploring the forest on snowshoes or cross-country skis is an experience that borders on the magical.

During the *other* winters, the lousy ones, the weather brings a nasty mélange of rain and sleet. It's bone-numbing cold, and bleak, bleak, bleak. Look into the eyes of the residents on the street during this time. They are all thinking of the Caribbean.

The higher you go in the mountains, and the farther north you head, the better your odds of finding snow and avoiding rain. Winter coastal vacations can be spectacular (nothing beats cross-country skiing at the edge of the pounding surf), but it's a high-risk venture that could definitely yield rain rather than snow.

Ski areas naturally are crowded during the winter months. They're especially so during school vacations, when most resorts tend to jack up their rates.

SPRING   New England is famous for its elusive spring, which some residents claim lasts only a weekend or so, typically around mid-May, but sometimes as late as June. One day the ground is muddy, the trees are barren, and gritty snow is still piled in shady hollows. The next day, temperatures are in the 80s, trees are blooming, and kids are swimming in the lakes. Travelers must be very crafty and alert if they want to experience spring in New England. It's also known as mud season, and many innkeepers and restaurateurs close up for a few weeks for either vacation or renovation.

And since New England is home to a slew of colleges and universities, as graduation nears (mid- to late May and early June), the region is afflicted with unusually high hotel occupancy rates, particularly around major cities like Boston. As always, it's best to book rooms in advance.

Burlington, Vermont's Average Temperatures

	Jan	Feb	Mar	Apr	May	Jun	July	Aug	Sep	Oct	Nov	Dec
Avg. High	25	27	38	53	66	76	80	78	69	57	44	30
Avg. Low	8	9	21	33	44	54	59	57	49	39	30	15

NEW ENGLAND CALENDAR OF EVENTS

January

✪ **New Year's & First Night Celebrations,** regionwide. Boston, Mass.; Portland, Me.; Providence, R.I.; Stamford, Conn.; Portsmouth, N.H.; Burlington, Vt.; and many other cities and towns, including on Cape Cod and Martha's Vineyard, celebrate the coming of the New Year with plenty of festivities. Check with local chambers of commerce for details. New Year's Eve.

February

- **Dartmouth Winter Carnival,** Hanover, N.H. Huge and elaborate ice sculptures grace the Green during this festive celebration of winter, which includes numerous sporting events and other winter-related activities. Vast quantities of beer are consumed by Dartmouth students and their guests. Call ☎ **603/646-1110.** Midmonth.
- **Mount Washington Valley Chocolate Festival,** North Conway, N.H. Earn your chocolate by cross-country skiing from inn to inn, picking up sweets at each stop. Look for other events sure to please the chocoholic in and around town. Call ☎ **800/367-3364.** Late February.
- **Stowe Derby,** Stowe, Vt. The oldest downhill/cross-country ski event in the nation pits racers who scramble from the wintry summit of Mount Mansfield into the village on the Stowe Rec path. Call ☎ **802/253-3423** for details. Late February.

March

- **St. Patrick's Day/Evacuation Day.** Parade, South Boston; Celebration, Faneuil Hall Marketplace. The 5-mile parade salutes the city's Irish heritage and the day British troops left Boston in 1776. Head to Faneuil Hall Marketplace for music, dancing, food, and plenty of Irish spirit. Call ☎ **800/888-5515.** March 17.
- **New England Spring Flower Show,** Dorchester, Mass. This annual harbinger of spring presented by the **Massachusetts Horticultural Society** (☎ **617/536-9280**) draws huge crowds starved for a glimpse of green. Second or third week of the month.
- **Super Winterfest,** Ludlow, Vt. A weeklong festival throughout the town featuring skiing, ice fishing, snow hockey, fireworks, and a parade. Call ☎ **802/ 228-1229.** Early March.

April

- ☉ **Patriot's Day,** Boston (Paul Revere House, Old North Church, Lexington Green, Concord's North Bridge). The events of April 18 and 19, 1775, which signified the start of the Revolutionary War, are commemorated and reenacted. Participants dressed as Paul Revere and William Dawes ride to Lexington and Concord to warn the Minutemen that "the regulars are out" (not that "the British are coming"— most colonists considered themselves British). Mock battles are fought at Lexington and Concord. Call the **Lexington Visitor's Center** (☎ **617/862-1450**) or the **Concord Chamber of Commerce** (☎ **508/369-3120**). Third Monday of the month, a state holiday.
- **Boston Marathon,** from Hopkinton, Mass., to Boston. International stars and local amateurs run in the world's oldest and most famous marathon. The noon start means elite runners hit Boston about 2 hours later; weekend runners stagger across the Boylston Street finish line as many as 6 hours after that. Call the **Boston Athletic Association** (☎ **617/236-1652**). Third Monday of the month.
- **Sugarbush Spring Fling,** Waitsfield, Vt. Ski-related events herald the coming of spring and the best season for skiing. Special events for kids. Call ☎ **802/ 583-2381.**
- ☉ **Daffodil Festival,** Nantucket. Spring's arrival is heralded with masses of yellow blooms adorning everything in sight, including a cavalcade of antique cars. Call ☎ **508/228-1700.** Late April.

May

- **Annual Basketry Festival,** Stowe, Vt. A weeklong event with displays and workshops by talented weavers. Call the **Stowe Area Association** at ☎ **800/ 24-STOWE.** Mid-May.

- **Lilac Sunday,** Shelburne, Vt. See the famed lilacs (more than 400 bushes) at the renowned Shelburne Museum when they're at their most beautiful. Call ☎ **802/985-3346** for details. Mid- to late May.
- **MooseMainea,** Greenville, Me. A variety of low-key events—from an antique-car show to a blackfly festival—are staged annually deep in the heart of moose territory. But the real attraction is the possibility of spotting one of the gangly beasts on a woodsy safari. Call ☎ **207/695-2702.** Mid-May to mid-June.
- **Mayfest,** Bennington, Vt. Main Street is blocked off to cars and filled with food vendors and craftsman at this late spring/early summer community event. Call ☎ **802/442-5758.** Late May.
- **Lobsterfest,** Mystic, Conn. An old-fashioned lobster bake and live music on the banks of the Mystic River. Call ☎ **860/572-5315.** Late May.
- ✪ **Brimfield Antiques Fair,** Brimfield, Mass. Up to 2,000 dealers fill several fields near this central Massachusetts town, with similar fairs in early or mid-July and mid-September. Call ☎ **508/347-2761.** Mid-May.
- **Open Studio Weekend,** throughout Vermont. Artists throughout the state open their doors to the public, offering a firsthand glimpse at how it's all done. Call ☎ **802/223-3380.** Late May.
- **Figawi Sailboat Race,** Hyannis to Nantucket. The largest race on the East Coast (☎ **508/778-1691**). Late May.

June

- **Old Port Festival,** Portland, Me. A day-long block party in the heart of Portland's historic district with live music, food vendors, and activities for kids. Call ☎ **207/772-2249.** Early June.
- **Yale-Harvard Regatta,** on the Thames River in New London, Conn. One of the oldest collegiate rivalries in the country. Early June.
- **Market Square Weekend,** Portsmouth, N.H. This lively street fair attracts hordes from throughout southern New Hampshire and Maine into downtown Portsmouth to dance, listen to music, sample food, and enjoy summer's arrival. Call ☎ **603/436-2848.** Early June.
- **Lake Champlain Balloon and Craft Festival,** Essex Junction, Vt. New England's largest balloon festival draws thousands of spectators to see these graceful craft float above the quiet landscape. Call ☎ **802/899-2993.** Early June.
- **Taste of Hartford,** Hartford, Conn. One of New England's largest outdoor festivals. Many area restaurants serve up their specialties. You'll also get a taste of local music, dance, magic, and comedy. Call ☎ **860/728-3089.** Midmonth.
- **Motorcycle Week,** Laconia and Weirs Beach, N.H. Tens of thousands of bikers descend on the Lake Winnipesaukee region early each summer to compare their machines and cruise the strip at Weirs Beach. The Gunstock Hill Climb and the Loudon Classic race are the centerpieces of the week's activities. Call ☎ **603/783-4931.** Mid-June.
- **Taste of Block Island Seafood Festival,** Block Island, R.I. Chowder cook-off, games, crafts, and live entertainment. Call ☎ **800/383-2474.** Mid-June.
- *Boston Globe* **Jazz Festival,** Boston. Big names and rising stars of the jazz world appear at lunchtime, after-work, evening, and weekend events, some of which are free. Contact the *Globe* (☎ **617/929-2000**) or pick up a copy of the paper for a schedule when you arrive in town. Some events require tickets purchased in advance. Third week of June.
- **Great Kennebec Whatever Week,** Augusta, Me. A community celebration to mark the cleaning up of the Kennebec River, culminating in a wacky race

involving all manner of watercraft, some more seaworthy than others. Call ☎ 207/623-4559 for details. Late June.

- ✪ **Jacob's Pillow Dance Festival,** Becket, Mass. The oldest dance festival in America features everything from ballet to modern dance and jazz. Tickets go on sale May 1; for a season brochure, call ☎ 413/243-0745. Late June to August.

- • **Stowe Flower Festival,** Stowe, Vt. Nearly three dozen events celebrate the joys of making the earth bloom, with offerings as diverse as garden tours and seminars by the experts. Call ☎ 800/247-8693. Late June.

- • **Williamstown Theater Festival,** Williamstown, Mass. This nationally distinguished theater festival presents everything from the classics to uproarious comedies and contemporary works. Scattered among the drama are literary readings and cabarets. Call ☎ 413/597-3399. Late June through August.

July

- • **Boston Harborfest,** along Boston Harbor and the Harbor Islands. The city puts on its Sunday best for Fourth of July, which has become a gigantic weeklong celebration of Boston's maritime history and an excuse to just get out and have fun. Events include concerts, guided tours, cruises, fireworks, the Boston Chowderfest, and the annual turnaround of the USS *Constitution.* Call ☎ 617/227-1528. First week in July.

- • **Boston Pops Concert and Fireworks Display,** Hatch Memorial Shell on the Esplanade. Independence Week culminates in the famous Boston Pops Fourth of July concert. People wait from dawn till dark for the music to start. The program includes the *1812 Overture,* complete with church bells and actual cannon fire that coincides with the fireworks. July 4.

- • **Independence Day,** regionwide. Communities throughout all six states celebrate July 4th with parades, cook-outs, road races, and fireworks. The bigger the town, the bigger the fireworks. Contact local chambers of commerce for details.

- • **Newport Music Festival,** Newport, R.I. Outdoor chamber music concerts are held among the opulent mansions. For information call ☎ 401/846-1133. Second and third weeks.

- • **Historic Homes Tour,** Litchfield, Conn. One day is your only opportunity to tour this beautiful town's historic houses and gardens. Call ☎ 860/567-9423. Midmonth.

- • **Barnstable County Fair,** East Falmouth, Mass. An old-time Cape Cod county fair complete with rides, food, and livestock contests. Call ☎ 508/563-3200. Late July.

- • **Friendship Sloop Days,** Rockland, Me. This 3-day event is a series of boat races that culminates in a parade of sloops. Call ☎ 207/596-0376. Mid-month.

- • **Wickford Art Festival,** Wickford, R.I. More than 200 artists gather in this quaint village for one of the East Coast's oldest art festivals. Call ☎ 401/295-5566. Midmonth.

- • **Vermont Quilt Festival,** Northfield, Vt. Displays are only part of the allure of New England's largest quilt festival. You can also attend classes, and have your heirlooms appraised. Call ☎ 802/485-7092. Mid-July.

- • **Revolutionary War Days,** Exeter, N.H. Learn all you need to know about the War of Independence during this historic community festival, which features a Revolutionary War encampment and dozens of reenactors. Call ☎ 603/772-2622. Mid-July.

- • **Marlboro Music Festival,** Marlboro, Vt. This is a popular 6-week series of classical concerts featuring talented student musicians performing in the peaceful hills outside of Brattleboro. Call ☎ **802/254-2394** for information. Weekends from July through mid-August.

❸ **Tanglewood,** near Lenox, Mass. The Boston Symphony Orchestra makes its summer home at this fine estate bringing symphony, chamber concerts, and solo recitals to the Berkshire Hills. For information on the season's program, call the **Tanglewood Concert Line** at ☎ **413/637-1666** (July and August only) or **Symphony Hall** at ☎ **617/266-1492.** Tickets can be charged by phone through **Symphonycharge** (☎ **800/274-0808**), and you definitely need to secure them well in advance. July through August.

August

- **SoNo Arts Festival,** South Norwalk, Conn. For 3 days artists, craftspeople, dancers, and other performers from around the country celebrate throughout South Norwalk's historic waterfront area. Call ☎ **203/866-7916.** Early August.
- **Maine Festival,** Brunswick, Me. A 3-day festival showcasing Maine-made crafts, music, foods, and performers. It's boisterous, fun, and filling. Call ☎ **207/772-9012.** Early August.
- **Maine Lobster Festival,** Rockland, Me. Fill up on the local harvest at this event dedicated to Maine's favorite crustacean. Enjoy a boiled lobster or two, and take in the ample entertainment during this informal waterfront gala. Call ☎ **800/562-2529** or 207/596-0376. Early August.
- **Southern Vermont Crafts Fair,** Manchester. More than 200 artisans show off their fine work at this popular festival, which also features creative food and good music. Early August.
- ❸ **Newport Folk Festival & JVC Jazz Festival,** Newport, R.I. Thousands of music lovers congregate at Fort Adams State Park for concerts on alternate weekends in July and August. It's one of the premier jazz concerts in the country. Performers have included big names like B. B. King, Suzanne Vega, Ray Charles, and Tony Bennett. For information on schedules and tickets call ☎ **401/847-3700** or call **Ticketmaster** (☎ **401/331-2211**). Second week.
- **Annual Star Party,** St. Johnsbury, Vt. The historic Fairbanks Museum and Planetarium hosts special events and shows, including night viewing sessions, during the lovely Perseid Meteor Shower. Call ☎ **802/748-2372.** Mid-August.
- **Martha's Vineyard Agricultural Fair,** West Tisbury, Mass. An old-fashioned country fair featuring horse pulls, livestock shows, musician and woodsman contests, and plenty of carnival action. Call ☎ **508/693-4343.** Mid-month.
- **Blueberry Festival,** Machias, Me. A festival marking the harvest of the region's wild blueberries. Eat to your heart's content. Call ☎ **207/794-3543.** Midmonth.
- **Blue Hill Fair,** Blue Hill, Me. A classic country fair just outside one of Maine's most beautiful villages. Call ☎ **207/374-9976.** Late August to Labor Day.

September

- **Vermont State Fair,** Rutland, Vt. All of Vermont seems to show up for this grand event, with a midway, live music, and plenty of agricultural exhibits. Call ☎ **802/775-5200** for details. Early September.
- **Providence Waterfront Festival,** Providence, R.I. Performances, art exhibits, games, rides, and entertainment. Don't miss the Pasta Challenge, a local restaurant competition in which the public samples and votes for the best pasta sauces. Call ☎ **401/785-9450.** Labor Day weekend.
- **Cambridge River Festival,** Cambridge, Mass. A salute to the arts, with music, dancing, children's activities, and international food in an outdoor setting. Call ☎ **617/349-4380.** Early September.

- **Norwalk Oyster Festival,** Norwalk, Conn. This waterfront festival celebrates Long Island Sound's seafaring past. Highlights include oyster-shucking and -slurping contests, harbor cruises, concerts, and fireworks. Call ☎ **203/838-9444.** Early September.
- **Windjammer Weekend,** Camden, Me. Come visit Maine's impressive fleet of old-time sailing ships, which host open houses throughout the weekend at this scenic harbor. Call ☎ **207/236-4404.** Early September.
- **Eastern States Exhibition,** West Springfield, Mass. "The Big E" is New England's largest agricultural fair, with a midway, games, rides, rodeo and lumberjack shows, country-music stars, and lots of eats. Call ☎ **413/737-2443** or 413/787-1548. Mid-September.
- **Provincetown Arts Festival,** Provincetown, Mass. One of the country's oldest art colonies celebrates its past and present with local artists holding open studios. It's an extraordinary opportunity for collecting 20th-century works. Call the **Provincetown Chamber of Commerce** (☎ **508/487-3424**). Late September.
- **Common Ground Fair,** Windsor, Me. An old-time state fair with a twist: The emphasis is on organic foods, recycling, and wholesome living. Call ☎ **207/ 623-5515.** Late September.

October

- ✪ **Northeast Kingdom Fall Foliage Festival,** northeast Vermont. A cornucopia of events staged in towns and villages throughout Vermont's northeast corner heralds the arrival of the fall foliage season. Be the first to see colors at their peak. Call ☎ **802/748-3678** for information. Early October.
- **Bourne Farm Pumpkin Festival,** West Falmouth, Mass. A fun for the whole family day of pumpkin picking, hayrides, and pony rides at a 1775 farmstead on Cape Cod. Call ☎ **508/548-0711.** Early October.
- **Fryeburg Fair,** Fryeburg, Me. Cotton candy, tractor pulls, live music, and huge vegetables and barnyard animals at Maine's largest agricultural fair. There's also harness racing in the evening. Call ☎ **207/985-3278.** A week in early October.
- **Mystic Chowderfest,** Mystic, Conn. A festival of soup served from bubbling cauldrons set on wood fires. Call ☎ **860/572-5315.** Midmonth.
- **Harvest Day,** Canterbury, N.H. A celebration of the harvest season, Shaker-style. Lots of autumnal exhibits and children's games. Call ☎ **603/783-9511.** Midmonth.
- ✪ **Cranberry Harvest Festival,** Nantucket. Bog tours, inn tours, and a cranberry cook-off, just when the foliage is at its burnished prime. The ripe cranberries blanket the landscape in incredibly intense hues. Call ☎ **508/228-1700.** Mid-October.
- **Salem Haunted Happenings,** Salem, Mass. Parades, parties, fortune-telling, cruises, and candlelight tours of historic homes. It all leads up to a ceremony on the big day. Call ☎ **508/744-0004.** Last 2 weeks of the month.
- ✪ **Head of the Charles Regatta,** Boston and Cambridge, Mass. High school, college, and postcollegiate rowing teams and individuals—some 4,000 in all—race in front of hordes of fans along the banks of the Charles River. This event always seems to fall on the crispest, most picturesque Sunday of the season. Call the **Metropolitan District Commission** Harbormaster at ☎ **617/727-0537** for information. Late October.

November

- **Thanksgiving Celebration,** Plymouth, Mass. The holiday that put Plymouth on the map is observed with a "stroll through the ages," showcasing 17th- and

19th-century Thanksgiving preparations in historic homes. Nearby Plimoth Plantation, where the colony's first years are re-created, wisely offers a Victorian Thanksgiving feast (reservations required). Call the **Plymouth Visitors Center** (☎ **800/USA-1620**) or the **Plimoth Plantation** (☎ **508/746-1622**). Thanksgiving Day.

- **Victorian Holiday,** Portland, Me. Portland dolls up its Old Port in a Victorian Christmas theme. Enjoy the window displays, take a free hayride, listen to costumed carolers sing. Call ☎ **207/772-6828** for details. Late November through Christmas.
- **Brookfield Holiday Craft Exhibition & Sale,** Brookfield, Conn. Thousands of unique, elegant, and artful gifts are displayed in gallery settings on three floors of a restored grist mill. Call ☎ **203/775-4526.** Late November to Christmas.

December

- **Christmas Prelude,** Kennebunkport, Me. This scenic coastal village greets Santa's arrival in a lobster boat, and marks the coming of Christmas with street shows, pancake breakfasts, and tours of the towns' inns. Call ☎ **207/967-3286.** Early December.
- **Christmas Tree Lighting,** Boston, Prudential Center. Carol singing precedes the lighting of a magnificent tree from Nova Scotia—an annual expression of thanks from the people of Halifax for Bostonians' help in fighting a devastating fire more than 70 years ago. Call the **Greater Boston Convention and Visitors Bureau** (☎ **617/536-4100**). First Saturday of December.
- **Boston Tea Party Reenactment,** Boston, Congress Street Bridge. Chafing under British rule, the colonists rose up on December 16, 1773, to strike a blow where it would cause real pain—in the pocketbook. Call ☎ **617/338-1773.** Mid-December.
- ✪ **Candlelight Stroll,** Portsmouth, N.H. Historic Strawbery Banke gets in a Christmas way with old-time decorations and more than 1,000 candles lighting the 10-acre grounds. Call ☎ **603/433-1100** for information. First 2 weekends of December.
- **Woodstock Wassail Celebration,** Woodstock, Vt. Enjoy classic English grog, along with parades and dances, at this annual event. Call ☎ **802/457-3555.** Early December.
- **Christmas Eve and Christmas Day.** Special festivities throughout New England. In Newport, R.I., several of the great mansions have special tours; Mystic, Conn., has a special program of Christmas festivities; Nantucket, Mass., features carolers in Victorian garb, art exhibits, and tours of historic homes. December 24 through 25.

3 The Active Vacation Planner

New England is a superb destination for those who don't consider it a vacation unless they spend more time outdoors than in. If active pursuits number among your main reasons for traveling to New England, consider adding another Frommer's publication to your library, *Outside Magazine's Adventure Guide to New England.* It covers all kinds of outings for travelers of every ability.

For pointers on where to head in northern New England, the real playground for outdoor enthusiasts, see the "Enjoying the Great Outdoors" section at the beginning of the Vermont, New Hampshire, and Maine chapters in this book. More detailed information on local services is included in each regional section.

If you're really interested in adventure, plan to stay put. I've seen too many travelers get frustrated by trying to bite off too much—some biking in the Berkshires, some canoeing in the Green Mountains, then maybe a little hiking in the White Mountains to round things off. All in 1 week. I'd advise adventurers to pick just one area, then settle in for a few days or a week, exploring locally by foot, canoe, or kayak. This way you'll have time to enjoy an extra hour lounging at a remote backcountry lake, or an extra day camping in the backcountry. You'll also learn a lot more about the region.

Guidebooks to the backcountry are plentiful and diverse. L.L. Bean in Freeport, Me., the Appalachian Mountain Club in Boston, and the Green Mountain Club in Waterbury, Vt., all have excellent selections of guidebooks, as do many local bookshops throughout the region. For a catalog of local guidebooks contact the **Appalachian Mountain Club,** 5 Joy St., Boston, MA 02108 (☎ **617/523-0636**), or **Backcountry Publications,** c/o W. W. Norton & Co., Inc., 800 Keystone Industrial Park, Scranton, PA 18512 (☎ **800/233-4830**).

Local outdoor clubs are also a good source of information, and some offer trips open to nonmembers. The most established of the bunch is the Appalachian Mountain Club (see address above). AMC regional chapters run group trips almost every weekend throughout the year, with northern New Hampshire especially well represented. Other groups include the **Green Mountain Club,** R.R. #1, Box 650, Route 100, Waterbury Center, VT 05677 (☎ **802/244-7037**), and the **Maine Outdoor Adventure Club** (☎ **207/828-0918** for a recorded hot line in Portland).

Outdoor enthusiasts with Web access will want to check out **GORP**'s resource listings for on-line information on New England–area parks and recreational activities. Head for **www.gorp.com/gorp/location/us/us.htm**, then choose from among the six New England states.

BIKING   New England's diverse terrain, rich history, and compact size have all helped to make it one of the top road-biking destinations in the country. The main attraction is the stunning scenery—steeples that dot the rolling green hills of Vermont, the sweeping mounds of sand that form Cape Cod, the rocky and rugged coast of Maine, and the towering granite of New Hampshire's White Mountains. Without much effort, you'll find thousands of miles of roads that form hundreds of loops ranging from a couple of miles on up. No matter what your stamina or ability, you'll find trips that perfectly suit you.

The hardest decision is whether you should go with an outfitter or on your own. The biggest advantage of hiring a guide is the complete and utter lack of responsibility on your part. Most outfitters will find a way to relieve all your vacation worries, from accommodations to food to equipment. The downside is the additional cost and the lack of privacy. There's no place better than a lonely backcountry road to collect your thoughts and gain a sense of serenity.

The following outfitters offer guided overnight bike trips:

Backroads, 1516 Fifth St., Berkeley, CA 94710-1740 (☎ **800/GO-ACTIVE**), features 5-day biking tours of Penobscot Bay, Me.; southern Vermont; northern Vermont; and Cape Cod and the Islands. **Bike Vermont,** P.O. Box 207, Woodstock, VT 05091 (☎ **800/257-2226**), offers weekend, 3-day, 5-day, and 6-day tours to all regions of the state. **Vermont Bicycle Touring,** P.O. Box 711, Bristol, VT 05433 (☎ **800/245-3868**), organizes six 5-day biking tours and eight weekend tours to every region of Vermont; a 5-day trip to Cape Cod and the Islands; and 3- to 5-day tours of Penobscot Bay, Boothbay Harbor, and Acadia National Park.

If mountain bikes are your thing, you'll find plenty of dirt roads and backcountry pathways to explore. Ski areas often open their lifts to bikers in the summer, and have good choices of trails in the White and Green Mountains. **Acadia National Park's carriage roads** are unique in this country, and offer a great way to spend a couple of days exploring woods and rocky hills in the saddle. **Back Country Excursions,** RFD 2, P.O. Box 365, Limerick, ME 04048 (☎ **207/625-8189**), operates a mountain-biking playground called the "Palace." The 4,000-square-foot garden has over 100 tons of stones, log-packed trailways, bridges, and stairs, all situated in a natural half-pipe. Once you grow weary of this, you can take one of the guided tours through 60 miles of connected trails in the Sebago Lake area, near the New Hampshire border.

BIRD WATCHING   Bird-watching opportunities in New England are virtually unlimited. More than 300 species have been observed in the region over the past decade, including herons, ospreys, warblers, puffins, and snowy egrets. During the spring and fall migrations, the birding is especially rich on the offshore islands.

There are so many excellent places to view birds in New England that it's a daunting task to name even a fraction of them. Some spots where you'll never go wrong include Machias Sea Island, Me. (for puffins); Wellfleet Bay Wildlife Sanctuary, Wellfleet, Mass.; Monomoy Island, Mass.; Umbagog Lake, Errol, N.H.; and Acadia National Park, Bar Harbor, Me.

Also, the **National Audubon Ecology Camp,** 613 Riversville Rd., Greenwich, CT 06831 (☎ **203/869-2017**), runs superb birding programs for both aspiring and experienced naturalists, including a study camp on 333-acre Hog Island off the Maine coast. (See the Maine chapter.)

CANOEING   New England's abundant rivers, lakes, and ponds make it a superb destination for both flat-water and white-water canoeists. Hundreds of camping sites occupy the shores and islands, tucked between tall firs and spruces.

Serious canoeists are advised to head for Maine, where the region's best long-distance canoeing is found. The 92-mile **Allagash Wilderness Waterway,** a series of remote rivers, lakes, and ponds (with a couple of portages), takes between 7 and 10 days to complete. Logging is prohibited within 500 feet of the corridor, and this linear state park has 80 authorized campsites along the route. Most of the trip is flat-water, except for two Class II and III stretches known as Chase Rapids and Twin Brook Rapids. A ranger at Churchill Dam will truck you, your equipment, and your canoe around the rapids if you're uncertain of your skills. See "Canoeing" in section 1 of the Maine chapter for more information.

If you'd prefer to travel the North Woods with a guide, you'll have no problem finding one. Among the more popular guides are Alexandra and Garrett Conover, who run **North Woods Ways,** R.R. #2 Box 159A, Guilford, ME 04443 (☎ **207/ 997-3723**). The couple offers canoe trips on several northern Maine rivers (and beyond), and are well versed in North Woods lore.

Outside of Maine, the best overnight canoeing is in Vermont, and the longest journeys are in the northern part of that state. The **Winooski, Lamoille, and Missisquoi rivers** are all tributaries of Lake Champlain. One well-regarded outfitter is **Vermont Waterways,** R.R. #1, P.O. Box 322, East Hardwick, VT 05836-9707 (☎ **800/ 492-8271**), which guides on the Winooski, Connecticut, and Lamoille Rivers on weekend or 5-day tours. Prices start at $380 per person for a 2-night tour, including accommodations and all meals. The 5-day trip is $895.

FISHING   While longtime New Englanders grouse that fishing isn't what it used to be, there are still spectacular opportunities for angling throughout the region. If you're a novice hoping for a quick return on your time, you're probably best off joining a party boat or charter for deep-sea fishing. Point Judith in Rhode Island is the best destination for this. For more information, call the **Rhode Island Party & Charterboat Association** (☎ **401/737-5812**). Many party boats also depart daily from Hyannis, Mass.

You can also surf-cast from the shores. Cape Cod and the Islands are to blues and stripers what Montana is to trout. Between late July and October, the bluefish are abundant. Striped bass are a bit more elusive, but still very catchable. Locals start hooking "keepers" in late May and continue throughout the summer.

The inland lakes and rivers will keep anglers busy throughout the season. Fishing camps are as prolific as the fish in the Maine Woods. Only serious fly fishermen need apply at **Grant's Kennebago Camps,** P.O. Box 786, Oquossoc, ME 04964 (☎ **800/633-4815** or 207/864-3608). The 18 camps, replete with dock and boat, were built on Kennebago Lake in 1905. The cost is $92 per day, including all meals. **Tim Pond Wilderness Camps,** Eustis, ME 04936 (☎ **207/243-2947**), has been in business since the 1860s and is billed as "the oldest continuously operating sporting camp in America."

If you're looking to develop your skills in fly-fishing—the most genteel form of angling—you've got your choice of two well-respected fishing schools. The **L.L. Bean Fly-Fishing School,** in Freeport, Me. (☎ **800/341-4341** ext. 6666), offers various clinics and workshops throughout the year. And **Orvis,** in Manchester, Vt. (☎ **800/235-9763**), runs one of the top fly-fishing schools in the country. The 2- or 2¹/₂-day classes are offered twice weekly from early April to mid-July, then weekends-only through August.

Information on obtaining fishing licenses may be found in the regional chapters that follow.

HORSEBACK RIDING   Kedron Valley Stables, Route 106, South Woodstock, Vt. (☎ **802/457-1480**), offers 4- to 6-day trips in the Green Mountain National Forest. You'll be guided through secluded woods and historic villages like South Woodstock, Grafton, and Proctorsville, staying at inns and eating at wonderful country restaurants.

In a state known for Morgans, the small pony-sized horses at **Vermont Icelandic Horse Farm** in Waitsfield, Vt. (☎ **802/496-7141**), are a special treat. Icelandics move at a steady gait without much rocking, much like driving with good shocks. Owner Christina Calabrese offers half-day to 3-day rides for experienced riders only.

SAILING   New England's Atlantic coast deserves its hallowed reputation as one of the world's best cruising grounds. Every day in summer, you'll see billowing sails scudding in and out of legendary bays like Narragansett in Rhode Island and Penobscot off the mid-Maine coast. With hundreds of picturesque anchorages and ample services at the dozens of harbors, New England attracts weekend luffers and celebrity yachtsmen alike. If the ocean's a bit intimidating, head to the inland lakes. Champlain, Winnipesaukee, Sebago, and Squam—along with many smaller bodies of water—are also justly popular with sailors.

There are a handful of places for bareboat charters (renting a large sailboat for day or overnight trips). Prior sailing experience is necessary for a bareboat charter, especially on the Maine coast, where fog, currents, wide tidal range, and a merciless shoreline can wreak havoc. Among the places to reserve a boat are **Hinckley Yacht Charters,** Bass Harbor Marine, Bass Harbor, Me. (☎ **800/492-7245**), on the southwestern shores of Mount Desert Island (they offer 25 boats, ranging from a 34-foot Sabre to a 49-foot Hinckley), and **Bay Island Yacht Charters** in Rockland, Me. (☎ **800/421-2492**), which has 15 boats from a 26-foot Nonsuch to a 43-foot Taswell. On New England's west coast, **Winds of Ireland,** P.O. Box 2286,

S. Burlington, VT 05407 (☎ **802/863-5090**), charters five Hunters, ranging from 30 to 40 feet.

If you lack the experience to charter a sailboat, try the next best thing—a windjammer cruise off the mid-Maine coast. For more information, see the box on windjammer tours in the Penobscot Bay section of the Maine chapter.

SKIING   Vermont is home to the region's largest ski area (**Killington**), and throughout the state you'll find the best melding of small-town life and good slopes (**Stowe, Waitsfield,** and **Okemo**). But Maine's two leading ski resorts—**Sunday River** and **Sugarloaf**—are fast putting their state on the skier's map. New Hampshire has dozens of inviting slopes in the blustery, hard-edged White Mountains, and even western Massachusetts has attractive ski areas. See the appropriate sections in each state chapter for more detailed information on alpine ski areas.

New England is also justly famed for its extensive **cross-country skiing.** A growing number of cross-country–ski centers offer professionally groomed trails through a mix of terrain. Among the best destinations in the region are the **Trapp Family Lodge Cross-Country Ski Center** (☎ **800/826-7000** or 802/253-8511) in Stowe, Vt., and the entire village of Jackson, N.H., which is laced with a network of ski trails maintained by the **Jackson Ski Touring Foundation** (☎ **603/383-9355**). Many other good choices exist; see the Maine, New Hampshire, and Vermont chapters for further guidance.

WHITE-WATER RAFTING   A couple of decades ago, adventurer Wayne Hockemeyer and some of his buddies braved the tumultuous **Kennebec River** in a 20-foot raft. Today, white-water rafting is one of the most popular attractions in Maine. Drive north on Route 201 from Bingham to West Forks and you'll soon start to think that there are as many white-water outfitters in Maine as there are doughnut shops. More than 60,000 people every summer participate. It can be risky—some are thrown off the rafts each year, and there's the infrequent fatality. But most folks just end up exhilarated and wet.

No longer is the Kennebec the only rafting river in Maine. Trips are also offered on the more technical **Penobscot and Dead rivers.** Daily water releases from dams ensure enough high water from May into October on the Kennebec and Penobscot. For contacts and more information, see the North Woods section of the Maine chapter. A directory of outfitters is available from **Raft Maine** (☎ **800/723-8633** or 207/824-3694).

4 Choosing a Small Inn or B&B

New England's inns and B&Bs offer an alternative to the homogenized, cookie-cutter hotel rooms that seem to line U.S. highways coast to coast. You can stay in inns that are 2 centuries old and sleep in quirky rooms furnished with stunning antiques and filled with intriguing geegaws that the innkeepers trust you won't walk off with.

Of course, there are reasons why some people prefer cookie-cutter rooms. Predictability isn't always a *bad* thing. In a chain hotel, you can be fairly certain water won't drip through your ceiling at night. Likewise, you can bet that beds will be firm, that the sink and bathtub will be relatively new, and that you'll have a TV and telephone.

But the only true way to develop a list of "old favorites" is to take some chances. With some luck, you'll stumble into Ralph Waldo Emerson's idea of simple contentment: "Hospitality consists in a little fire, a little food, and an immense quiet," he wrote in his journal.

Selecting an inn to start your quest can be a bit overwhelming, what with hundreds of inns and B&Bs now operating across the region, up from just a few dozen a couple of decades ago.

Indeed, the distinction between B&Bs and inns is increasingly blurred. Generally speaking, B&Bs serve just breakfast, and inns serve breakfast, dinner, and often lunch. But these differences don't always translate into the higher level of service on the part of the hosts at the inns. B&Bs can be elegant and well appointed, and can have the air of gracious inns that just happened to have overlooked serving dinner.

Because small inns reflect the personalities of their owners, you may find yourself uncomfortable even if the service is impeccable and the cleanliness unimpeachable. One place might be too "foofy," as one of my friends refers to certain inns, with ruffles everywhere, busy wallpaper, and sachets that bring to mind a tragic perfume factory explosion. Another friend of mine refuses to stay any place where he thinks the innkeepers want to be his friend. So he strikes any place with fewer than four guest rooms off his list, believing that the owners are in it mostly for the company. (Sometimes that's right, but mostly not.)

There are a few simple steps you can take to reduce the risk of wretched evenings far from home.

- **Ask your friends.** Word of mouth is the most reliable way to go, especially if you have close friends who've traveled in the region and who know your tastes and preferences.
- **Call for the brochure.** A phone call will not only bring you a brochure, which often provides clues as to the innkeeper's sense of style, but also you'll get a chance to chat briefly with the staff (or quite possibly with the owner), and gauge their friendliness and professionalism. A dog barking in the background might be a good sign, or a bad one. It all depends on your interpretation.
- **Stop by unannounced.** Don't hesitate to walk right in a place that catches your eye. Some of the best finds turn up this way. One thing I've learned after visiting hundreds of establishments in researching this book is that I still can't reliably gauge from the outside what a place will be like on the inside. An unannounced visit is also a good way to measure the hospitality of the host. Was the greeting a bit chilly? Or pleasant and warm?
- **Ask to see your room before you sign on the dotted line.** Inn rooms are almost always idiosyncratic, and often vary widely. The more lavish mansions had quarters for the servants, and no enterprising innkeeper lets these rooms go unused. Visions of upstairs grandeur can be easily deflated by downstairs reality. Innkeepers are often happy to let you look around and select from available rooms, but the nicer rooms always fetch a higher price.

5 Tips for Travelers with Special Needs

FOR TRAVELERS WITH DISABILITIES   Prodded by the Americans with Disabilities Act, a growing number of inns and hotels are retrofitting some of their rooms for people with special needs. Outdoor recreation areas, especially on state and federal lands, are also providing trails and facilities for those who've been effectively barred in the past.

Accessibility is improving regionwide, but improvements are far from universal. When in doubt, call ahead to ensure that you'll be accommodated.

Wilderness Inquiry, Fifth Street SE, Box 84, Minneapolis, MN 55414 (☎ **800/ 728-0719** or 612/379-3858), offers more than 100 adventure travel packages for travelers with disabilities nationwide, including a canoe trip on the Moose River in Maine.

FOR FAMILIES   Families rarely have trouble finding things to do with kids in New England. The natural world seems to hold tremendous wonder for the younger set—an afternoon exploring the mossy banks and rocky streambeds is an adventure. Older kids often like the challenge of climbing a high mountain peak or learning to paddle a canoe in a straight line. And there's the beach, which is always good for hours of afternoon diversion.

Be sure to ask about family discounts when visiting regional attractions. Many places offer a flat family rate that's less expensive than paying for each ticket individually. Some parks and beaches charge by the car rather than the head.

A number of New England hotels and lodges are kid-friendly, and have set aside recreation areas or established special programs to entertain the younger ones. Always ask if there are provisions for kids when you book rooms in advance, so you'll better know what to expect. And be aware that many smaller inns cater to couples, and children aren't exactly welcomed with open arms. Some inns flat out discourage kids, or strongly advise guests to bring children only if they're over a certain age. Innkeepers will typically let you know their policy regarding children when you make your reservation, but you'll reduce the likelihood of an unpleasant surprise if you ask in advance.

Recommended destinations for families include Cape Cod, with its miles of beaches and dunes, and Martha's Vineyard, with its bike paths, beaches, and kid-scaled architecture in the cottage section of Oak Bluffs. Also enjoyable are Weirs Beach and Hampton Beach in New Hampshire, and York Beach and Acadia National Park in Maine. North Conway, N.H., also makes a good base for exploring with kids. The town has lots of motels with pools, and there are nearby train rides, aquaboggans, streams suitable for splashing around, easy hikes, and the always entertaining Story Land. Excellent children's museums are located in Mystic (Conn.), Boston, Portsmouth, Portland, and Norwich (Vt.).

Several specialized guides offer more detailed information for families on the go. Try *Hikes with Children in Vermont, New Hampshire & Maine* by Cynthia and Thomas Lewis.

FOR GAY & LESBIAN TRAVELERS   Provincetown, on the tip of Cape Cod, was one of the first and is still one of the most famous gay resort communities. Gay entrepreneurs and politicians are well represented in the town's businesses and government, and much of the nightlife revolves around gay culture. By turns, the town can be wild and flamboyant, and understated and relaxed. For gay travelers somewhat anxious about being "out" in public, Provincetown is a place where they can relax and enjoy themselves with aplomb.

Outside of Provincetown, New England isn't really noted as a hotbed of gay culture. But the cities—such as Providence, Boston, Portland, and Burlington—tend to be very welcoming of alternative lifestyles. Outside of the metropolitan areas, attitudes toward homosexuality vary widely, but in general New Englanders tend to be fairly tolerant of people of all persuasions, provided they're not trying to impose a new tax on them.

A good general source of information on regional events and happenings is *In Newsweekly,* 258 Shawmut Ave., Boston, MA 02118 (☎ **617/426-8246**), a free weekly publication of news and entertainment. The 21,000-circulation publication can be found at many bookstores, restaurants, and cafes throughout New England.

In Boston, look for *One-in-Ten* (☎ **617/536-5390**), a monthly publication published by the same folks who put out the *Phoenix* newspapers in Boston, Worcester, and Providence. It often features groundbreaking articles, and has extensive listings of gay happenings around Boston and beyond. The paper also publishes events and club information on-line at **http://www.bostonphoenix.com**.

Vermont has a fine monthly newsletter covering gay, lesbian, and bisexual issues, called *Out in the Mountains* (E-mail: **oitm@aol.com**, or write P.O. Box 177, Burlington, VT 05402). Both the articles and ads will fill you in on gay happenings in the Green Mountain State. The newsletter is available free at many Vermont bookstores and other shops, or for $20 per year by mail from the address above. You can also check out the newsletter's Web site at **members.aol.com/oitm**.

Portland, Me., has a substantial gay population, attracting many refugees from Boston and New York. Portland hosts a sizable gay pride festival early each summer that includes a riotous parade and a dance on the city pier. The free newspaper, *Community Pride Reporter* (☎ **207/282-4311**), has listings of statewide events of interest to gays and lesbians.

Just south of Portland on Maine's short stretch of sandy coast is **Ogunquit,** a popular destination among gay travelers from throughout the northeast and Canada. It features a lively beach and bar scene in the summer. In the winter, it's decidedly more mellow.

For a more detailed directory of gay-oriented enterprises in New England, track down a copy of the *Pink Pages,* published by KP Media (66 Charles St., #283, Boston, MA 02114; E-mail: **kpmedia@aol.com**). The price is $8.95 plus shipping and handling. Call ☎ **800/338-6550** or visit the firm's Web site at **http://www.pinkweb.com**.

More adventurous souls should consider linking up with the **Chiltern Mountain Club,** P.O. Box 407, Boston, MA 02117 (☎ **617/859-2843**), an outdoor adventure club for gay men and lesbians that organizes trips in northern New England.

6 Getting There

BY CAR   Driving to New England by car doesn't require much in the way of special knowledge. Coming from the south, I-95 is the major interstate highway serving Connecticut, Rhode Island, Massachusetts, and Maine. The quickest route from New York to Boston is via Hartford, Conn., using I-84 and the Massachusetts Turnpike. The easiest approach to northern New England from the south is along one of the three main interstate highway corridors. I-91 heads more or less due north from Hartford along the Vermont–New Hampshire border, then angles through northern Vermont. Another major interstate is I-93, which departs from I-95 near Boston, then cuts through New Hampshire to connect with I-91 near St. Johnsbury, Vt. For Maine, continue northward on I-95, which parallels the southern Maine coast before veering inland.

The most picturesque way to enter New England is from the west. For a northern route, drive through New York's Adirondack Mountains to Port Kent, N.Y., on Lake Champlain, then catch the car ferry across the lake to Burlington. For a southern route, plan to arrive via any number of the smaller state highways that cross from New York State into Connecticut, Massachusetts, or southern Vermont. These routes, while often slow going, take you through rolling hills and farmland and are exceptionally scenic.

Be aware that the interstates leading from Boston can be extremely sluggish on Friday afternoons and evenings in the summer, especially along the routes leading to Cape Cod and Maine. A handful of choke points—particularly the Bourne Bridge to Cape Cod and the Maine tollbooths on I-95—can back up for miles. North Conway in New Hampshire is also famed for its nightmarish weekend traffic, especially during the foliage season.

BY PLANE   The central gateways to New England are Boston, New York City, and Montréal. Major commercial carriers also serve Hartford, Conn.; Burlington, Vt.; Manchester, N.H.; and Portland, Me. Several smaller airports in the region are served by feeder airlines and charter companies (see regional chapters for more information). Many of the scheduled flights from Boston to northern New England and Cape Cod and the Islands are aboard smaller prop planes; ask the airline or your travel agent if this is an issue for you.

Many people who travel to the northern reaches of New England find they pay less and have a wider choice of flight times by flying into Boston's Logan Airport, then renting a car. Boston is about 2 hours by car from Portland, less than 3 hours from the White Mountains. If you're heading to the Bennington or Manchester area of Vermont, the closest major airport is in Albany, N.Y.

Airlines serving New England include **American** (☎ 800/433-7300), **Colgan** (☎ 800/272-5488), **Continental** (☎ 800/525-0280), **Delta** (☎ 800/221-1212), **Northwest** (☎ 800/225-2525), **TWA** (☎ 800/221-2000), **United** (☎ 800/241-6522), and **USAirways** (☎ 800/247-8786).

Carriers to Cape Cod and the Islands include many of the above, plus **Cape Air** (☎ 800/352-0714 or 508/771-6944), **Island Airlines** (☎ 800/248-7779 or 508/775-6066), and **Nantucket Airlines** (☎ 800/635-8787 or 508/790-0300). Charter flights are offered by Cape Air and Nantucket Airlines, as well as by **Air New England** (☎ 508/693-8899), **Hyannis Air Service** (☎ 508/775-8171), **Island Air Charter** (☎ 508/778-8360), **King Air Charters** (☎ 800/247-2427), and **Westchester Air** (☎ 800/759-2929).

The major New England airports all host national car-rental chains. Some handy phone numbers are **Avis** (☎ 800/331-1212), **Budget** (☎ 800/527-0700), **Enterprise** (☎ 800/325-8007), **Hertz** (☎ 800/654-3131), **National** (☎ 800/227-7368), **Rent-A-Wreck** (☎ 800/535-1391), and **Thrifty** (☎ 800/367-2277).

BY BUS   Bus service is well run en route to the major cities and tourist destinations of New England, but few of the remote villages are accessible by bus.

The major bus lines serving the region are **Bonanza** (☎ 800/556-3815 or 617/720-4110), **Concord Trailways** (☎ 800/639-3317 or 617/426-8080), **Greyhound** (☎ 800/231-2222 or 617/526-1810), **Peter Pan** (☎ 800/343-9999 or 617/426-7838), **Plymouth & Brockton** (☎ 508/746-0378), and **Vermont Transit** (☎ 800/451-3292).

Plymouth & Brockton serves Massachusetts's south shore and out to Cape Cod. **Peter Pan** serves western Massachusetts and Connecticut. **Vermont Transit** is affiliated with Greyhound and serves Vermont, New Hampshire, and Maine with frequent departures from Boston. **Concord Trailways** serves New Hampshire and Maine, including some smaller towns in the Lake Winnipesaukee and White Mountains area. Concord buses are a bit more luxurious (and a few dollars more) than Vermont Transit.

BY TRAIN   Most passengers who come to New England by train take the *Northeast Direct* service offered by **Amtrak** (☎ **800/872-7245**). It runs from Washington, D.C., to Boston via Philadelphia and New York City, with New England stops in New Haven, Old Saybrook, New London, Mystic, Westerly, Kingston, and Providence. Amtrak also runs *The Cape Codder* on summer weekends from Providence to Hyannis (you can connect from New York).

Train service to Northern New England is more limited; however, Amtrak's *Vermonter* departs Washington, D.C., with stops in Baltimore, Philadelphia, and New York, before following the Connecticut River northward to Brattleboro then onward to Burlington.

The return of rail service from Boston to Portland, Me., following a hiatus of many years, has been repeatedly delayed. Service was slated to resume in 1997, but travelers should contact Amtrak for more information.

For rail service between New York and Connecticut, try the cheaper **Metro North** (☎ **800/223-6052** or 212/532-4900), which runs commuter trains connecting many towns from New Haven to New York City.

FAST FACTS: New England

AAA Members can get help with trip planning, road service in the event of a breakdown, and discount tickets to events and attractions. AAA also offers excellent free maps to members. Call ☎ **800/222-4357** for more information on membership and branch locations throughout New England.

American Express American Express offers travel services, including check cashing and trip planning, through a number of affiliated agencies spread about the region. Call ☎ **800/221-7282** to find the location nearest you.

Federal Express For the location of the nearest drop-off box, or to arrange a pickup, call ☎ **800/238-5355.**

Liquor Laws The legal age to consume alcohol is 21. In Maine, New Hampshire, and Vermont, liquor is sold at government-operated stores only; in Connecticut, Massachusetts, and Rhode Island, liquor is sold privately. Liquor is not sold on Sunday, though most restaurants and bars with liquor licenses may serve by the drink on Sundays. Restaurants that don't have liquor licenses sometime allow patrons to bring their own adult beverages. Always ask first.

Maps Maps of the region and individual states are commonly available at convenience stores and supermarkets for $2 or $3. All six states also offer free road maps at their official tourist information centers (you usually have to ask at the desk).

If you're a connoisseur of back roads and off-the-beaten-track exploring, you should consider buying one or more of Delorme's atlases, which are available for Vermont, New Hampshire, and Maine. They offer an extraordinary level of detail, right down to logging roads and public boat launches on small ponds. **DeLorme's** (☎ **888/227-1656**) headquarters and map store is located in Yarmouth (their new building was slated to open in mid-1997 at Exit 17 off I-95 near the Maine Visitors Information Center), and their products are available widely at book and convenience stores throughout the region.

Newspapers/Magazines The *Boston Globe* and the *New York Times* are distributed throughout New England, although they can sometimes be hard to come by in smaller, more remote villages. But almost every small town seems to have a daily or weekly newspaper covering local events and happenings. These are good sources of information for local events and specials at down-home restaurants—the day-to-day things that slip through the cracks at the tourist bureaus.

Speed Limits The speed limit on interstate highways in the region is generally 65 miles per hour, although this is reduced to 55 miles per hour near cities. State highways are a less formal network, and the speed limits (and the conditions of the roads) vary widely. Watch for speed limits to drop in one or two stages as you approach a town; that's where the local constabulary often lurks in search of speeders.

Taxes The current state sales taxes are: Connecticut, 6%; Maine, 6% (7% on lodging); Massachusetts, 5% (5.7% on lodging statewide; local sales taxes may also apply); New Hampshire, no general sales tax, but 8% tax on lodging and dining; Rhode Island, 7% (12% on lodging); and Vermont, 6% (7% on lodging).

For Foreign Visitors 3

Most of the information you'll need to ensure a pleasant trip will be found in the preceding chapter. Here we've outlined some aspects of U.S. laws, customs, and culture that might be perplexing to visitors from overseas.

1 Preparing for Your Trip

ENTRY REQUIREMENTS

DOCUMENTS   Canadian citizens have it easiest when visiting the United States. Canadians need only present some form of identification at the border; a passport isn't necessary unless you plan to stay more than 90 days, although it may be helpful as identification for financial transactions while you're in the States.

Two dozen nations are currently participating in the visa-waiver pilot program, which allows travelers from these countries to enter the United States for up to 90 days with just a valid passport and a visa-waiver form. Travelers under this program generally must also have a return ticket and proof of solvency. Check with your travel agency for the current rules and participating airlines and cruise lines. The countries in this program at press time were Andorra, Argentina, Australia, Austria, Belgium, Brunei, Denmark, Finland, France, Germany, Iceland, Ireland, Italy, Japan, Liechtenstein, Luxembourg, Monaco, the Netherlands, New Zealand, Norway, San Marino, Spain, Sweden, Switzerland, and the United Kingdom.

Other foreign visitors should apply for a U.S. visa at the embassy or consulate with jurisdiction over their permanent residence. You can apply for a visa in any country, but it's generally easier to get a visa in your own. Applicants must have a passport that's valid for at least 6 months beyond the dates they propose to visit, a passport-sized photo (1.5 inches square), and some indication that they have a residence outside the United States to which they plan to return. Applicants must also fill out a Form OF-156 (available free at all U.S. embassies and consulates). If you have a letter of invitation from a U.S. resident, that's sometimes helpful. Drug addicts and anarchists need not apply.

Bear in mind that the U.S. government assumes that everyone visiting the U.S. plans to immigrate here illegally. Some regard this as a little presumptuous and cynical, but that's how the system works under U.S. law. Therefore, it's up to the traveler to convince U.S. authorities otherwise. The more evidence you assemble to that effect, the easier it will be to obtain a visa. Especially helpful is an indication of how your trip will be financed.

Once in the country, foreign visitors come under the jurisdiction of the Immigration and Naturalization Service (INS). If you'd like to change the length or the status of your visa (for instance, from nonimmigrant to immigrant) contact the nearest INS office. Look in the local phone book under "U.S. Government."

Be sure to carefully check the valid dates on your visa. If you overstay 1 or 2 days it's probably no big deal. If it's more than that, you may be on the receiving end of an interrogation by customs officials on your way out of the country, and it may hinder efforts to get another visa if you apply for one in the future.

MEDICAL REQUIREMENTS   Unless you've recently been in an area suffering from an epidemic (such as yellow fever or cholera), no inoculations are needed to enter the United States.

Not all prescription drugs that are sold overseas are necessarily available in the United States. If you bring your own supplies of prescription drugs (and especially syringes), it's wise to carry a physician's prescription in case you need to convince customs officials that you're not a smuggler or drug addict.

CUSTOMS REQUIREMENTS   Jet and ship passengers will be asked to fill out a customs form declaring what goods they're bringing into the country. Visitors planning to spend at least 72 hours in the United States may bring 200 cigarettes, 3 pounds of smoking tobacco, or 100 cigars (but no Cuban cigars), and $100 worth of gifts, without paying any duties. Anything over these amounts will be taxed. No food may be brought into the country (this includes canned goods); live plants are also prohibited.

Up to U.S.$10,000 in cash may be brought in or out of the country without any formal notification. If you are carrying more than that amount, you must notify customs officials when either entering or departing the country.

MONEY

The basic unit of U.S. currency is the dollar, which is about enough to buy a large cup of coffee. The dollar consists of 100 cents. Common coins include the penny (1¢), nickel (5¢), dime (10¢), and quarter (25¢). You may come across a 50¢ or $1 coin, but these are relatively rare.

Dollar bills and coins are accepted everywhere, but some smaller shops won't accept larger bills ($50 or $100) because they lack sufficient change or are fearful of counterfeit bills. It's best to travel with a plentiful supply of $10 and $20 bills.

CURRENCY EXCHANGE   Foreign exchange bureaus, which are common in many countries, are rare in the United States, especially in New England (outside of Boston, that is). Many banks will exchange foreign currency for dollars, but it's often a time-consuming and expensive process, especially for less common currencies. It's best to plan ahead and obtain dollars or dollar-based traveler's checks in your own country before departure.

Canadian dollars are commonly accepted in Maine, New Hampshire, and Vermont (all of which border Canada), although it's generally easier to use Canadian currency very near the border. Most hotels and many restaurants will accept Canadian currency at a discount close to its current trading value. Some places will periodically accept Canadian currency at face value as a part of a promotion to attract Canadian tourists; look for signs and advertisements to this effect in your travels.

TRAVELER'S CHECKS   Traveler's checks are considered as good as cash in most U.S. shops and banks. Widely recognized brands include American Express, Barclay's, and Thomas Cook. With other types of checks, you might meet with some resistance, particularly in smaller towns. Some small shops may not cash checks of $100 or more if they have insufficient change; it's best to cash these at hotels or banks. Most banks will cash traveler's checks without charge. Only carry checks denominated in U.S. dollars; those in other currencies will be all but useless to you on the road.

CREDIT CARDS   Credit cards are becoming an increasingly common form of payment throughout the United States for everything from expensive hotel rooms to small purchases of groceries. It's not impractical to travel the country with no cash, just a credit card in your back pocket. Among the most commonly accepted credit cards are American Express, Discover, MasterCard, and Visa. Because American Express charges a higher rate for processing its transactions, a number of hotels and restaurants will claim not to accept the card, but they often will if it's the only card you have.

I highly recommended that you have at least one credit card (fully paid up) when you travel in the United States. Credit cards are commonly accepted in lieu of deposits when renting a car or a hotel room, and are often allowed as a form of identification.

Many ATMs (automatic teller machines) will debit your credit card and provide cash on the spot. (Call ahead to your credit card company before you leave and make sure your PIN number is programmed to work this way in another country.) Don't ever give your card itself to anyone as a deposit; they should record the information on it and return it to you. Also be careful with your credit-card receipts, as the information on them may be used by the unscrupulous to make purchases.

INSURANCE

Foreign visitors who are not insured are strongly urged to take out a traveler's insurance policy to cover any emergencies that may arise during their stay here. The United States does not offer national medical coverage for its residents; medical services are paid for either in cash or, more commonly, by an individual's insurance company. Be aware that hospital and doctors' fees are extremely high in the United States, and even a minor medical emergency could result in a huge extra expense for those traveling without insurance.

Comprehensive policies available in your country may also cover other disasters, including bail (in the event you are arrested), automobile accidents, theft or loss of baggage, and emergency evacuation to your country in the event of a dire medical situation. Check with your local automobile association (if there is one) or insurance company for detailed information on travelers' insurance.

Packages such as "European Worldwide Services" in Europe are sold by automobile clubs and travel agencies at attractive rates. **Travel Assistance International (TAI)** (☎ **800/821-2828** or 202/347-2025) is the agent for European Assistance Worldwide, so holders of this company's policies can contact TAI for assistance while in the United States.

Canadians should check with their provincial health offices or call **HealthCanada** (☎ **613/957-3025**) to find out the extent of their coverage and what documentation and receipts they must take home in case they are treated in the United States.

SAFETY

Most of New England—with the notable exception of parts of Boston—has a crime rate that's among the lowest in the country, and the odds of anything untoward happening during your visit here are very slight. But all travelers are advised to take the usual precautions against theft, robbery, and assault.

Travelers should avoid any unnecessary displays of wealth when in public. Don't bring out big wads of cash from your pocket, and save your best jewelry for private occasions. If you are approached by someone who demands money, jewelry, or anything else from you, do what most Americans do: Hand over what the mugger requests. Don't argue. Don't negotiate. Just comply. Afterwards, immediately contact the police (see "Emergencies," below).

The crime you're statistically most likely to encounter is theft of items from your car. Break-ins can occur any time of the day or night. Don't leave anything of value in plain view; that offers a target that's tempting for even the casual miscreant. At the least, store your valuables locked securely in your trunk. Better still, keep them with you at all times.

Late at night you should look for a well-lighted area to get gas or to step out of your car for any reason. Also, it's not advisable to sleep in your car at night at highway rest areas, which can leave you vulnerable to robbers.

Take the usual precautions against leaving cash or valuables in your hotel room when you're not present. Larger hotels have safe-deposit boxes. Smaller inns and hotels will not, although it can't hurt to ask to leave small items in the house safe. A good number of small inns don't even have locks on guest room doors. Don't be alarmed; if anything, this is a good sign, indicating that there have been no problems here in the past. If you're feeling at all nervous about this, lock your valuables in your car trunk.

2 Getting to the United States

Most international travelers come to New England via Boston's Logan Airport or the three New York City–area airports. Boston offers the easiest access to northern New England. Portland, the White Mountains, and the southern Green Mountains are 2 to 3 hours away by car. Figure on at least 5 hours of driving time to most attractions if you're coming from New York airports.

European visitors heading to Maine should inquire about flights to Bangor; while the city isn't a major European destination, a number of flights en route to the West Coast stop here to refuel and it's sometimes possible to disembark.

Dozens of airlines serve New York and Boston airports from other countries, although New York gets far more overseas traffic. Some helpful contacts include **American Airlines** (☎ 0181/572-5555), **British Airways** (☎ 0345/222-111), **Continental** (☎ 4412/9377-6464), **Delta** (☎ 0800/414-767), **United** (☎ 0181/990-9900), and **Virgin Atlantic** (☎ 0293/747-747). All of the phone numbers above are in London.

Those coming from Latin America, Asia, Australia, or New Zealand will probably arrive in the United States via gateway cities such as Miami, Los Angeles, or San Francisco, clearing customs there before connecting onward. (Most international airlines partner with one of the U.S. domestic carriers, and will be happy to book your ongoing flight for you and check for the best connection.) From any of the above-mentioned cities, it's easy to book a flight directly to Boston.

Other cities with airports that have regularly scheduled flights into the region include Portland and Bangor, Me.; Manchester, N.H.; and Burlington, Vt. Flying to Albany, N.Y., is another option, especially if your destination is southern Vermont.

Bus and train service is fairly extensive along the coast from New York to Portland, Me., but it tends to be quite spotty outside of the seaboard megalopolis.

Travelers seeking to explore the more remote regions—like the Litchfield Hills, the Berkshires, the White Mountains, or the Maine coast—will need to rent a car. You can easily do this at most airports, and there will also be many in-town locations in the larger cities. See the previous chapter for a listing of toll-free phone numbers for car-rental firms.

FAST FACTS: For the Foreign Traveler

Abbreviations   On highway signs and publications you'll often see the states of New England abbreviated. Connecticut is "Conn." or "Ct."; Massachusetts is "Mass." or "Ma."; Maine is "Me."; New Hampshire is "N.H."; Rhode Island is "R.I."; and Vermont is "Vt."

Automobile Organizations   Becoming a member of an automobile club is handy for obtaining maps and route suggestions, and can be helpful should an emergency arise with your automobile. The nation's largest automobile club is the **American Automobile Association (AAA),** which has nearly 1,000 offices nationwide. AAA offers reciprocal arrangements with many overseas automobile clubs; if you're a member of an automobile club at home, find out whether your privileges extend to the United States. For more information on AAA, call ☎ **800/222-4357.**

Business Hours   Businesses are typically open from 9am to 5pm Monday through Friday. Banks typically shut down at 3 or 4pm, although ATM machines operate 24 hours. Most restaurants and some shops stay open until 8 or 9pm. If you need something after hours, head to the nearest mall, which is typically open until 9pm or so.

Climate   See "When to Go" in chapter 2.

Currency   See "Money," in section 1 of this chapter.

Drinking Laws   You must be 21 years old to legally consume alcohol in most of the United States. No matter what your age, state laws in New England are notoriously harsh on those who drive drunk. Know your tolerance. If you plan to exceed that in an evening, allow enough time for the effects to wear off, or imbibe within walking distance of your hotel or inn.

Driving   A current overseas license is valid on U.S. roads. If your license is in a language other than English, it's recommended that you obtain an International Drivers Permit from the American Automobile Association affiliate or other automobile organization in your own country prior to departure (see "Automobile Organizations," above).

Electricity   Electrical incompatibility makes it tricky to use appliances manufactured for Europe in the United States. The current here is 110 to 120 volts, 60 cycles, compared to the 220 to 240 volts, 50 cycles used in much of Europe. If you're bringing an electric camera flash, portable computer, or other gadget that requires electricity, be sure to bring the appropriate converter and plug adapter.

Embassies/Consulates   Embassies for countries with which the United States maintains diplomatic relations are located in Washington, D.C. Call directory assistance (☎ **202/555-1212**) and request the phone number. (Directory assistance calls are free from some pay phones.)

A handful of countries maintain consulates in Boston. These include **Australia,** 20 Park Plaza, Boston, MA 02116 (☎ **617/542-8655**); **Canada,** 3 Copley Place, Suite 400, Boston, MA 02116 (☎ **617/262-3760**); **Great Britain,** Federal Reserve

Plaza, 600 Atlantic Ave. (25th Floor), Boston, MA 02210 (☎ **617/248-9555**); **Ireland,** 535 Boylston St., Boston, MA 02116 (☎ **617/267-9330**), and **Israel,** 1020 Statler Office Building, 20 Park Plaza, Boston, MA 02116 (☎ **617/542-0041**). For other countries, contact Boston directory assistance (☎ 617/555-1212).

Emergencies   In the event of any type of emergency—whether medical, fire, or if you've been the victim of a crime—simply dial ☎ **911** from any phone. You do not need a coin to make this call from a pay phone. A dispatcher will immediately send medics, police, or the fire department to assist you. If 911 doesn't work, dial "0" and report your situation to the operator. If a hospital is near when a medical emergency arises, look for the "Emergency" entrance, where you will be quickly attended to.

Gasoline   Gasoline is widely available throughout the region, with the exception of the North Woods region of Maine, where you can travel many miles without seeing a filling station. Gas prices vary throughout the region owing to varied state taxes. In general, you're better off filling up in larger cities or towns before setting off to remote or rural areas. Gas is available in several different grades at each station; the higher the octane, the more expensive it is. Cars tend to run a bit smoother and more efficiently with higher grades of gasoline, but rental cars will take any grade.

Many of the filling stations in New England have both "self-serve" and "full-serve" pumps; look for signs as you pull up. The full-service pumps are a few cents more per gallon, but an attendant will pump your gas and check your oil (you might have to ask for this). The self-serve pumps often have simple directions posted on them. If you're at all confused, ask anyone who happens to be around for instructions.

Holidays   With some important exceptions, national holidays usually fall on Mondays to allow workers to enjoy a 3-day holiday. The exceptions are New Year's Day (January 1), Independence Day (July 4), Veterans Day (November 11), Thanksgiving (last Thursday in November), and Christmas (December 25). Other holidays include Martin Luther King, Jr., Day (3rd Monday in January), Presidents' Day (3rd Monday in February), Easter (1st Sunday following a full moon occurring March 21 or later), Memorial Day (last Monday in May), Labor Day (1st Monday in September), and Columbus Day (2nd Monday in October). In Maine and Massachusetts, Patriot's Day is celebrated on the 3rd Monday in April.

On these holidays, banks, government offices, and post offices are closed. Shops are sometimes open and sometimes not on holidays, but assume that virtually all will be closed on Thanksgiving and Christmas Day.

Languages   Some of the larger hotels may have multilingual employees, but don't count on it. Outside of the cities, English is the only language spoken. The exception is along the Canadian border and in some Maine locales (including Old Orchard Beach, Biddeford, Lewiston, and Van Buren), where French is commonly spoken or at least understood.

Legal Aid   If a foreign tourist accidentally breaks a law, it's most likely to be for exceeding the posted speed limit on a road (it's the law U.S. residents frequently run afoul of). If you are pulled over by a policeman, don't attempt to pay the fine directly—that may be interpreted as a bribe, and you may find yourself in deeper trouble. You'll be issued a summons with a court date and a fine listed on it; if you pay the fine by mail, you won't have to appear in court. If you are arrested for a more serious infraction, you'll be allowed one phone call from jail—contact your embassy or consulate.

Mail Virtually every small town and village has a post office; ask anyone on the street where it is and you'll be directed there. Mail within the United States costs 32¢ for a 1-ounce letter, and 23¢ for each additional ounce; postcards are 20¢. Overseas mail to Europe, Australia, New Zealand, Asia, and South America is 60¢ for a half ounce, 40¢ for a postcard. A half-ounce letter to Mexico is 35¢; a 1-ounce letter to Canada is 40¢. If in doubt about weight or costs, ask the postal clerk.

Mail may be sent from mailboxes on the street; look for blue metal boxes with an eagle logo and the inscription U.S. MAIL or UNITED STATES POSTAL SERVICE.

If you need to receive mail during your travels, have your correspondents address it to your name, "c/o General Delivery" at the city you are visiting. Go in person to the main post office to collect it; you'll be asked for identification (a passport is ideal) before it's given to you.

Newspapers/Magazines Foreign newspapers and magazines are commonly found in Boston and Cambridge, but are harder to track down elsewhere in New England. Your best bet is to check in the phone book for one of the larger chain bookstores like Borders or Barnes & Noble. These offer a decent selection from the overseas presses.

Taxes Visitors to the United State are assessed a $10 customs tax upon entering the country, and a $6 tax on departure. The United States does not have a value-added tax (VAT). The tax you most commonly come across is a sales tax (usually 5% to 6%) added on to the price of goods and some services. New Hampshire does not have a sales tax on goods, but does levy an 8% tax on hotel rooms and meals at restaurants.

Telephone and Fax Pay phones are not hard to find except in the more remote regions. Shops that have public phones inside usually display a blue sign featuring a bell inside a circle outside the store.

Telephone numbers beginning with "800" or "888" are toll-free. Press "1" before dialing a toll-free number.

Phone directories are divided between Yellow Pages (stores and services, listed by category) and the White Pages (names, listed alphabetically). Be aware that some White Pages are further split between commercial and residential listings. The Yellow Pages section often features maps of the local area and other information of interest to travelers. Phone books are sometimes found at pay phones; failing that, ask to see one at a friendly shop or restaurant.

To find a specific local phone number, dial ☎ **411** (there's often no coin needed) and an operator will take your request.

Local calls cost 10¢ or 25¢ (depending on the state) for a limited amount of time. (You can use a quarter for a 10¢ phone call, but you won't receive change.) How far you can call on a local call varies from place to place, and the boundaries will often seem arbitrary. If you're uncertain whether a call is long distance or not, try it as a local call. If a recorded voice comes on telling you to deposit more money for the first 3 minutes, that means it's a long-distance call.

Long-distance calls at pay phones tend to be very expensive, and you'll need a lot of coins. There are other options. At some phones you can use your credit card. And prepaid phone cards are available at many convenience stores and other outlets, typically for $5 or $10. Follow the instructions on the card (you'll call a toll-free number first, then punch in a code and the number you wish to call).

Long-distance charges using the cards are usually about 30¢ per minute, and are less expensive and more convenient than feeding coins into a pay phone.

Be aware that many hotels (notably the more expensive chain hotels) tack on a surcharge for local and long-distance calls made from your room. Even toll-free calls can cost you $1 or more. Ask about these charges when you check in. If your hotel does add a high surcharge and you plan to make a lot of phone calls, you're better off using a pay phone in the lobby.

To charge the phone call to the person receiving your call, dial "0" then the area code and the number you're calling. An operator (or computer) will come on the line and ask your name, and will then call the number to ask permission to reverse the charges. If the person you're calling accepts, the call will be put through.

If you need to send or receive a fax (facsimile), ask at your hotel, or look in the Yellow Pages under "Fax Transmission Service." Many copy shops will provide this service for you.

Time   All of New England is in the Eastern Time Zone—the same as New York, and the rest of the Eastern seaboard. All states shift to Daylight Savings Time in summer, setting clocks ahead 1 hour in the spring (the 1st Sunday in April), and back again in the fall (the last Sunday in October).

Tipping   Tipping is commonly practiced in the United States to recognize good service. Be aware that in restaurants, servers are typically paid a bare minimum and depend on tips for their wage. Tipping isn't considered optional unless the service is unspeakably deplorable. For decent to good service, tip 15%; for outstanding service, 20%. Other suggestions for tipping include: bartenders, 10% to 15%; bell-hops, $1 per bag; cab drivers, 10% of fare; chambermaids, $1 per day of your stay; checkroom attendants, $1 per garment; parking attendants, $1. No tipping is expected at gas stations, or at fast-food or other self-service restaurants.

Toilets   Public toilets (commonly called "rest rooms") are increasingly scarce in the United States, and where they do exist they're often not fit for use. Restaurants have rest rooms for their customers; some will let the public use them, but many have signs indicating FOR PATRONS ONLY. This is remedied by buying a pack of gum or a cup of coffee. Fast-food restaurants (like McDonald's or Burger King) are a good bet for reasonably clean toilets when traveling on the highways; gas stations may have them, but you'd be taking your chances on cleanliness.

Boston & Cambridge 4

In a glorious waterfront setting that has attracted travelers for hundreds of years, Boston offers cosmopolitan sophistication on a comfortable scale. From the narrow, crowded streets near the harbor to the spacious boulevards along the Charles River, a sense of history permeates the city, where 18th-century landmarks sit alongside space-age office towers, and the leaders of tomorrow rush to lectures in redbrick university buildings.

Whether you want to follow in the footsteps of Paul Revere or the crew from MTV's "The Real World," you'll find that Boston balances romantic celebration of the past and forward-looking pursuit of the future. Skyscrapers bear plaques describing the deeds and misdeeds of centuries past. Museums showcase the treasures of antiquity and cutting-edge technology. And the waterfront has been reclaimed from squalor and disrepair and restored to a condition that outshines its former glory.

It's not perfect, of course. Even a brief visit will confirm that the city's drivers have earned their terrible reputation, and the local accents are as earsplitting as any in Brooklyn or Chicago. Wander into the wrong part of town and you may be ordered to "pahk yuh cah" (park your car) somewhere else—pronto. And considering that it's a great college town, there isn't much of a late-night scene outside of convenience stores and photocopy shops, although the "blue laws" restricting the sale of alcohol on Sundays have been considerably relaxed.

Cambridge is so closely associated with Boston that many people believe they're the same city—a notion both cities' residents and politicians would be happy to dispel. Cantabrigians are often considered more liberal and better educated than Bostonians, which is another idea that's sure to get you involved in a heated discussion. Harvard dominates Cambridge's history and geography, of course, but there's much more to see than just the university.

Take a few days (or weeks) to get to know the Boston area, or use it as a gateway to the rest of New England. Here's hoping your experience is memorable and delightful.

1 Orientation

ARRIVING
BY PLANE

The major domestic carriers flying into Boston are **American** (☎ 800/433-7300), **Continental** (☎ 800/523-3273), **Delta** (☎ 800/221-1212), **Northwest** (☎ 800/225-2525), **TWA** (☎ 800/221-2000), **United** (☎ 800/241-6522), and **USAirways** (☎ 800/428-4322). Most of the major international carriers also fly into Boston.

Boston's **Logan International Airport,** in East Boston at the end of the Sumner, Callahan, and Ted Williams tunnels, is one of the most accessible in the country, situated just 3 miles across the harbor from the downtown area. At the moment, it's in the throes of a massive overhaul called "Logan 2000," but you probably won't be spending much time there, and everything is clearly marked.

Access to the city is by cab, bus, and subway via underwater tunnels, or by boat. The **subway** is fast and cheap—10 minutes (to Government Center) and 85¢. Free **shuttle buses** run from each terminal to the Airport station on the MBTA Blue Line from 5:30am to 1am every day of the year. The Blue Line stops at Aquarium (for the waterfront) and at State Street and Government Center, downtown points where you can exit or transfer to the other lines.

Some hotels have their own **limos;** ask about them when you make your reservations. A **cab** from the airport to downtown costs about $18 to $24. The ride into town takes anywhere from 10 minutes to a half hour, depending on the time of day and how congested the approaches to the tunnels are. If you must travel during rush hour or on Sunday afternoon, allow extra time, or plan to take the subway.

To cruise to Rowes Wharf on Atlantic Avenue (perfect for the Boston Harbor Hotel, Marriott Long Wharf, or getting a cab elsewhere) in just 7 minutes, dock to dock, try the **Airport Water Shuttle.** Courtesy buses from all terminals connect with the weather-protected, heated boats, which sail every 15 minutes from 6am to 8pm on weekdays, and every half hour on Friday until 11pm, Saturday from 10am to 11pm, and Sundays and national holidays (except Thanksgiving Day, Christmas, New Year's Day, and the Fourth of July) from 10am to 8pm. The one-way fare is $8 for adults and children 12 and up, and $4 for senior citizens; children under 12 travel free.

The Massachusetts Port Authority coordinates **bus service** (☎ 800/23LOGAN; Web site: **http://www.Massport.com**) from the airport to South Station in Boston and suburban hubs in Braintree, Framingham, and Woburn. You can also try the **Share-A-Cab booths** at each terminal and save up to half the fare. **Limousine** and bus service north, south, and west of the city is available, usually by prearrangement. Call **Carey Limousine Boston** (☎ **800/336-4646** or 617/623-8700) or **Commonwealth Limousine Service** (☎ **800/558-LIMO** outside Mass., or 617/787-5575).

If you prefer to rent a car, the following agencies offer shuttle service from the airport to their offices: **Alamo** (☎ 800/327-9633), **Avis** (☎ 800/831-2847), **Budget** (☎ 800/527-0700), **Enterprise** (☎ 800/325-8007), **Hertz** (☎ 800/654-3131), **National** (☎ 800/227-7368), and **Thrifty** (☎ 800/367-2277).

BY CAR

Driving to Boston is not difficult. (Driving *in* Boston is another story altogether.) The major highways leading to and from Boston are I-95 (Massachusetts Route 128), which connects Boston to highways in Connecticut and New York; I-90, the Massachusetts Turnpike, an east-west toll road that links up with the New York State

Thruway; I-93/U.S. 1, extending north to Canada and leading to the Northeast Expressway, which enters downtown Boston; and I-93/Route 3, the Southeast Expressway, which connects Boston with the south, including Cape Cod.

The Massachusetts Turnpike ("Mass Pike") extends into the center of the city and connects with the Central Artery (the John F. Fitzgerald Expressway), which is linked to the Northeast Expressway. If you want to avoid Central Artery construction, exit at Prudential Center in the Back Bay. The Southeast Expressway is a busy commuter route, so try to avoid it at rush hour.

The approach to Cambridge is via either Storrow Drive or Memorial Drive, one on each side of the Charles River. Storrow Drive has a Harvard Square exit that leads you across the Anderson Bridge to John F. Kennedy Street and into the square; Memorial Drive intersects with Kennedy Street; turn away from the bridge to reach the square.

Boston is 208 miles from New York; the driving time is about 4 1/2 hours. The 992-mile drive from Chicago to Boston should take around 21 hours; from Washington, D.C., it takes about 8 hours to cover the 468 miles.

The **American Automobile Association** or AAA (☎ **800/AAA-HELP**) provides its members with maps, itineraries, and other travel information, and arranges free towing if you break down. Be aware that the Mass Pike is a privately operated road that arranges its own towing; if you break down there, wait in the car until one of the regular patrols arrives.

A word of caution about driving in the city: The Central Artery/Third Harbor Tunnel project, or "Big Dig," has begun, and while the Central Artery (the John F. Fitzgerald Expressway) is being moved underground, traffic patterns in the area change almost daily. Paradoxically, this means that streets, attractions, and businesses are well labeled, but that's because they're sometimes impossible to find in the maze of jersey barriers and construction sites. If possible, avoid the Central Artery altogether by choosing alternate routes. The Ted Williams Tunnel part of this undertaking, which will eventually connect the Pike to the airport, is complete; the connection is part of the rest of the project, and until it's finished, the tunnel is open on weekdays to commercial traffic only (at the risk of a hefty fine). Check the message boards on the major highways leading into town to see whether the tunnel is open to you when you're visiting.

It's impossible to say this often enough: When you reach your hotel, leave your car in the garage and walk or use public transportation. Use the car for trips to the suburbs, the North Shore, or Plymouth; if you must drive in town, ask at the front desk for a route around or away from the construction area.

BY TRAIN

Boston has three rail centers: **South Station** on Atlantic Avenue, **Back Bay Station** at 145 Dartmouth St., and **North Station** on Causeway Street. **Amtrak** (☎ **800/ USA-RAIL** or 617/482-3660; Web site: **http://www.amtrak.com**) has arrival and departure points at South Station and Back Bay Station. At South Station you can take the Red Line to Cambridge or to Park Street, the central hub of the **MBTA** (☎ **617/222-3200**), where you can make connections to the Green, Blue, and Orange lines. The Orange Line connects Back Bay Station with Downtown Crossing (where there's a walkway to Park Street station) and other points. The MBTA operates trains to Ipswich, Rockport, and Fitchburg from North Station, and commuter lines to points south of Boston, including Plymouth, from South Station.

Amtrak also runs to South Station from New York, with stops at Route 128 and Back Bay Station. Express trains make the trip in about 4 hours; others take 4 1/2 to

5 hours or longer. From Washington, D.C., count on $8^1/_2$ hours; traveling time from Chicago is 22 hours (sleepers are available). During slow times, excursion fares may be available. Discounts are not available Friday and Sunday afternoon. Always remember to ask for the discounted rate.

VISITOR INFORMATION

Before you travel, contact the **Greater Boston Convention & Visitors Bureau** (☎ **888/SEE-BOSTON** or 617/536-4100; fax 617/424-7664; Web site: **http://www.bostonusa.com**), which publishes a free travel-planning guide, a comprehensive guidebook, and a separate guide called *Kids Love Boston;* all three are helpful in finding accommodations that will suit your needs and can offer substantial savings. To purchase the guidebook, which comes with helpful maps, send $4.95 to the Greater Boston Convention & Visitors Bureau, P.O. Box 990468, Prudential Tower, Dept. TPO, Boston, MA 02199-0468.

Also contact the **Massachusetts Office of Travel and Tourism,** 100 Cambridge St., 13th Floor, Boston, MA 02202 (☎ **800/227-6277** or 617/727-3201; fax 617/727-6525; Web site: **http://www.mass-vacation.com**; E-mail **vacationinfo@state.ma.us**), to request the free *Getaway Guide* magazine. It's divided into six regional sections that list accommodations and attractions, and includes a map and a seasonal calendar.

Once you've arrived, the **Boston National Historic Park Visitor Center,** at 15 State St. (☎ **617/242-5642**), across the street from the Old State House and the State Street "T" station, is a good place to start exploring the city. National Park Service rangers staff the center, dispense information, and lead free tours of the Freedom Trail. The audiovisual show about the trail provides basic information on 16 historic sites. The center is accessible by stairs and ramps and has rest rooms and comfortable chairs. Open daily from 9am to 5pm except Thanksgiving Day, Christmas, and New Year's Day.

The Freedom Trail, a line of red paint or red brick on or in the sidewalk, begins at the **Boston Common Information Center,** at 146 Tremont St. on the Common. The center is open Monday to Saturday from 8:30am to 5pm and Sunday from 9am to 5pm. It's run by the Greater Boston Convention and Visitors Bureau, as is the **Prudential Information Center,** in Center Court on the main level of the Prudential Center. It's open Monday through Saturday from 9am to 8pm, and Sunday from 11am to 6pm.

At the main Harvard "T" entrance, there's an information booth run by **Cambridge Discovery, Inc.** (☎ **617/497-1630**). It's in the middle of Harvard Square at the intersection of Mass. Ave., John F. Kennedy Street, and Brattle Street. Trained volunteers dispense maps and brochures and answer questions Monday to Saturday from 9am to 5pm and Sunday from 1 to 5pm. From mid-June through Labor Day there are guided tours that include the entire old Cambridge area. Check at the booth about rates, meeting places, and times, or call ahead. If you prefer to sightsee on your own, you can purchase an old Cambridge or East Cambridge walking guide prepared by the Cambridge Historical Commission for $1.

For details on accessibility and resources, call the **Information Center for Individuals with Disabilities** (☎ 800/462-5015 in Mass. only, or 617/450-9000).

Information about the Boston area is also available on the Internet. A good place to start is **http://www.city.net/countries/united_states/massachusetts/boston**, which is packed with information and links. The city has a site (**http://www.ci.boston.ma.us**) with good links for visitors, as does the Massachusetts Port Authority (**http://www.Massport.com**). Once you're ready to start planning activities, check out Boston.com (**http://www.boston.com**), which has links to publications and other resources, including the Museum of Fine Arts, and an interactive tour of the Freedom Trail.

CITY LAYOUT

Parts of Boston still reflect the city's original layout, a seemingly haphazard plan that leaves even longtime residents tearing out their hair. Old Boston is littered with alleys, dead ends, one-way streets, streets that change names, and streets named after extinct geographical features. On the plus side, every "wrong" turn downtown, in the North End, or on Beacon Hill is a chance to see something interesting that you might otherwise have missed.

Much of the city's landscape was transformed by landfill projects of the 19th century that altered the shoreline and created the Back Bay, where the streets proceed in orderly parallel lines. After some frustrating time spent negotiating the older part of the city, this simple plan will seem ingenious.

MAIN ARTERIES & STREETS   The most "main" street downtown is **Washington Street.** As a tribute to George Washington, other streets (except Mass. Ave.) change their names when they cross Washington Street: Bromfield becomes Franklin, Winter becomes Summer, Stuart becomes Kneeland. Off Washington Street in Chinatown, several blocks inland, is Beach Street, which used to be harborfront property.

Beacon Hill is also named after a long-ago topographical feature. It seems like a big enough hill today—until you see the pillar behind the State House that rises 60 feet into the air, a reminder of its original height, before earth was taken from the top of the hill to be used as landfill. In their loftier days, Beacon, Copp's, and Fort hills gave the Shawmut peninsula the name Trimountain, today rendered as "Tremont." Copp's and Fort hills sloped down to the town dock at Dock Square, where ships could deliver their cargo directly to the first floor of Faneuil Hall. Today, Copp's Hill is smaller but still overlooks the North End; Fort Hill, which extended through downtown toward South Station, was leveled between 1869 and 1872. High Street, now flat, once lived up to its name.

When the hills were pulled down to fill in the coves that made up the shoreline, the layout of some new streets was somewhat willy-nilly. Not so in the **Back Bay,** where the streets not only line up but even go in alphabetical order, starting at the Public Garden with Arlington, then Berkeley, Clarendon, Dartmouth, Exeter, Fairfield, Gloucester, and Hereford (and then Massachusetts). In the **South End,** also mostly landfill, the grid is less pristine but still pretty logical. Streets change from West to East when they cross Washington Street, and many of the names are those of the towns with train service from South Station (for example, Concord, Worcester, and Springfield), which was new when the streets were being christened.

The most prominent feature of downtown Boston is **Boston Common.** It's bordered by **Park Street,** which is one block long (but looms large in the geography of the "T"), and four important thoroughfares. **Tremont Street** originates at Government Center and runs through the Theater District into the South End and Roxbury. **Beacon Street** branches off Tremont at School Street and curves around, passing the golden dome of the State House at the apex of Beacon Hill and the Public Garden at the foot, and slicing through the Back Bay and Kenmore Square on its way into Brookline. At the foot of the hill, Beacon crosses **Charles Street,** the fourth side of the Common and the main street of Beacon Hill. Near Massachusetts General Hospital, Charles crosses **Cambridge Street,** which loops around to Government Center and turns into Tremont Street.

On the far side of Government Center, **I-93** (the Fitzgerald Expressway) separates the North End from the rest of the city. **Hanover Street** is the main street of the North End; at the harbor it intersects with **Commercial Street,** which runs along the waterfront from the North Washington Street bridge (the route to Charlestown, a.k.a. the Charlestown bridge) until it gives way to **Atlantic Avenue** at Fleet Street. Atlantic Avenue completes the loop around the North End and runs more or less along the waterfront past South Station.

Boylston Street is the fifth side of the Common. It runs next to the Public Garden, through Copley Square and the Back Bay, and on into the Fenway. To get there it has to cross **Massachusetts Avenue, or "Mass. Ave.,"** as it's almost always called (you might as well get into the habit now). Mass. Ave. originates 9 miles away in Lexington, cutting through Arlington and Cambridge before hitting Boston at Storrow Drive, then Beacon Street, Marlborough Street, and **Commonwealth Avenue. "Comm. Ave."** starts at the Public Garden and runs through Kenmore Square, past Boston University, and into the western suburbs. Farther along Mass. Ave., Symphony Hall is at the corner of Huntington Avenue. **Huntington** begins at Copley Square and passes Symphony Hall, Northeastern University, and the Museum of Fine Arts before crossing into Brookline and becoming Mass. Route 9.

FINDING AN ADDRESS   There's no rhyme or reason to the street pattern, compass directions are virtually useless, and there aren't enough street signs. The best way to find an address is to call ahead and ask for directions, including landmarks, or leave extra time for wandering around. If the directions involve a "T" stop, be sure to ask which exit to use—most stations have more than one.

STREET MAPS   Free maps of downtown Boston and the rapid-transit lines are available at visitor information centers around the city.

The **Prudential Life Insurance Company,** 800 Boylston St. (☎ **617/236-3318**), distributes a neighborhood map of Boston at the Skywalk viewing platform; open daily from 10am to 10pm. It's helpful for walking trips of Beacon Hill, the North End, Chinatown, the South End, Charlestown, and Harvard Square.

You can also write to the **Greater Boston Convention & Visitors Bureau,** P.O. Box 990468, Prudential Tower, Suite 400, Boston, MA 02199, for the visitor information kit mentioned above under "Visitor Information"; it includes a city/subway/Freedom Trail map. Enclose a check or money order for $4.95.

The **Metropolitan District Commission (MDC)** has an excellent map of the reservations, parks, and recreation areas in Greater Boston. It tells where to find salt-and freshwater beaches and fishing, swimming and wading pools, picnic areas, foot trails and bridge paths, playgrounds, tennis and golf courses, bicycle paths, and outdoor ice-skating rinks. Contact Community Affairs at the MDC, 20 Somerset St., Boston, MA 02108 (☎ **617/727-5114,** ext. 530) for a copy.

Gousha's **Boston Fast Map** ($4.95), **Streetwise Boston** ($5.95), and **Artwise Boston** ($5.95) are sturdy, laminated maps available at most bookstores. Less detailed but more fun is MapEasy's **GuideMap to Boston** ($5.50), a hand-drawn map of the central areas and major attractions.

THE NEIGHBORHOODS IN BRIEF

The Waterfront   Boston's harbor gained its excellent reputation from the fact that it's sheltered; this neighborhood faces not the ocean but the Inner Harbor. Although for purposes of city government (notably parking regulations) it's considered part of the North End, the Waterfront neighborhood has a different feel. The narrow area along Atlantic Avenue and Commercial Street, once filled with wharves and warehouses, now boasts luxury condos, marinas, restaurants, offices, and two hotels. Also on the waterfront are the New England Aquarium and piers where you can set out on harbor cruises and whale-watching expeditions.

The North End   Crossing under I-93 from downtown on the way to the waterfront brings you to one of the city's oldest neighborhoods, the North End. Home to waves of immigrants in the course of its history, it's been predominantly Italian for 70 years or so, but the balance is shifting. It's now estimated to be about half Italian-American and half newcomers, many of them young professionals who walk to work in the Financial District. Nevertheless, you'll hear Italian spoken in the streets and find a wealth of Italian restaurants, cafes, and shops. Nearby, and technically part of the North End, is the North Station area. With the September 1995 opening of the Fleet Center to replace Boston Garden (which is slated for demolition but was still standing at press time), the restaurants and clubs in the part of the North End near Beacon Hill really started jumping. This area is, at the moment, not a place to wander around alone at night.

Faneuil Hall Marketplace/Haymarket   Employees aside, actual Boston residents tend to be in short supply at Faneuil Hall Marketplace (also called Quincy Market, the name of the central market). An irresistible draw for out-of-towners and suburbanites, the cluster of restored market buildings bounded by Government Center, State Street, the waterfront, and the North Station area is the city's most popular attraction. You'll find restaurants, bars, a food court, specialty shops, and Faneuil Hall itself. Haymarket, just off the Central Artery, is home to an open-air produce market on Fridays and Saturdays.

Government Center   Love it or hate it, Government Center introduces modern design into the redbrick facade of traditional Boston architecture. Flanked by Beacon Hill, Downtown Crossing, and Faneuil Hall Marketplace, it is home to state and federal office towers and to Boston City Hall.

The Financial District   Bounded loosely by State Street, Downtown Crossing, Summer Street, and Atlantic Avenue, the Financial District is the banking, insurance, and legal center of the city. You'll find it frantic during the day and practically empty in the evening. Several impressive office towers now loom over the Custom House, once famous for its observation deck tower and now home of corporate time-share apartments.

Beacon Hill   The tiny residential area in the shadow of the golden dome of the State House is made up of narrow, tree-lined streets and architectural showpieces, mostly in Federal style. Louisburg Square and Mount Vernon Street, two of the loveliest (and most exclusive) spots in Boston, are on Beacon Hill. Bounded by Government Center, Boston Common, and the river, it's also popular with employees of Massachusetts General Hospital, on the nominally less fashionable north side of the neighborhood. MTV fans can look for vestiges of "The Real World" at the corner of Mount Vernon and River streets, where a crew lived in a converted firehouse in 1997.

Downtown Crossing   The intersection that gives Downtown Crossing its name is at Washington Street where Winter Street becomes Summer Street, and Filene's and Macy's face off across the pedestrian mall. The name applies roughly to the shopping and business district between the Common, the Theater District, the Financial District, and Government Center. It hops during the day and slows down considerably at night, after business hours.

Chinatown   The third-largest Chinese community in the country resides in a small but growing area near the Theater District. The narrow streets jammed with Chinese and Vietnamese restaurants, groceries, and gift shops have a real neighborhood feel. As the "Combat Zone," or red-light district, shrinks under pressure from the business community, Chinatown is expanding to fill the area between Downtown Crossing and the Mass. Turnpike extension. This is the only part of the city where you can definitely find food after midnight—some restaurants are open till 3 or 4am.

Back Bay   Perpetually fashionable since its creation out of landfill a century ago, the Back Bay overflows with gorgeous architecture and chic shops. It is bounded by the Public Garden, Mass. Ave., the river, and to the south by either Huntington Avenue or St. Botolph Street, depending on who's describing it to you. Students dominate the area near Mass. Ave. and grow scarce as property values rise the closer you get to the Public Garden. Commonwealth Avenue is largely residential, Newbury Street largely commercial; both are excellent places to walk around. In the Back Bay you'll find Trinity Church, the Boston Public Library, the John Hancock Tower, Copley Place, the Prudential Center, and the Hynes Convention Center.

Huntington Avenue   Not an actual neighborhood, Huntington Avenue starts at Copley Square and separates Copley Place from the Prudential Center before heading south into the suburbs. A number of landmarks are situated along it, including the Christian Science Center, Symphony Hall (at the corner of Mass. Ave.), Northeastern University, and the Museum of Fine Arts. Parts of Huntington can sometimes be a little risky, so if you're leaving the museum at night, stick to the car or the Green Line, travel in a group, or both.

Charlestown   One of the oldest areas of Boston, this is where you'll see the Bunker Hill Monument and USS *Constitution* ("Old Ironsides"), as well as one of the city's best restaurants, Olives. Off the beaten track, Charlestown is an almost entirely white residential neighborhood with a well-deserved reputation for insularity.

The South End   Cross Stuart Street or Huntington Avenue heading south and you'll soon find yourself in a landmark district packed with Victorian row houses and little parks. Known for its ethnic, economic, and cultural diversity, galleries, and boutiques, the South End has a large gay community and some of the best restaurants in the city. With the gentrification of the 1980s, Tremont Street (particularly the end closest to downtown) gained a cachet it hadn't known for almost a century. *Note:* Don't confuse the South End with South Boston, a predominantly Irish-American residential neighborhood.

Kenmore Square   The white-and-red Citgo sign that dominates the skyline above the intersection of Commonwealth Avenue, Beacon Street, and Brookline Avenue tells you you're approaching Kenmore Square. Its shops, bars, restaurants, and clubs are a magnet for students from adjacent Boston University. The college-town atmosphere goes out the window when the Red Sox are in town and baseball fans pour into the area on the way to historic Fenway Park, three blocks away.

Cambridge   Though an independent city, Cambridge is often regarded as a Boston neighborhood, and it does often feel like one since it's so readily accessible from Boston. It's a diverse community with important historical sites, and many excellent stores, restaurants, and cultural institutions. For Ivy League atmosphere in a relaxed but expensive student environment, visit Harvard Square. For a more gritty urban feel, and budget record stores, ethnic restaurants, and vintage-clothing stores, check out Central Square.

2 Getting Around

BY PUBLIC TRANSPORTATION

The **Massachusetts Bay Transportation Authority,** or **MBTA** (☎ **617/222-3200**), is known as the "T," and its logo is the letter in a circle. It runs the subways, trolleys, and buses in Boston and many suburbs, as well as the commuter rail. The "T" Web site (**http://www.mbta.com**) gives you access to maps, schedules, and other information.

The **Boston Visitor Passport** (☎ **617/222-5218**) is one of the best deals in town. You get unlimited travel on all subway lines and local buses and Zones 1A and 1B of the commuter rail system, plus discounts on museums, restaurants, and entertainment. The cost is $5 for 1 day, $9 for 3 consecutive days, or $18 for 7 consecutive days. Passes are for sale at the Airport, Government Center, Harvard, Alewife and Riverside "T" stations, North Station, South Station, and Back Bay Station, the Boston Common and Prudential Center information centers, and Quincy Market. Your hotel might also be able to provide you with the Visitor Passport. *Tip:* Check out the discounts available before you buy your Visitor Passport, so you can coordinate trips to businesses that offer discounts with the days you're eligible.

BY SUBWAY & TROLLEY The subways and Green Line trolleys will take you around Boston faster than any other mode of transportation except walking. You might find that hard to believe when you're trapped in a tunnel during rush hour, but it's true. The oldest system in the country (it dates to 1897), recent and ongoing improvements have made it quite reliable.

The subways are color-coded and called the Red, Green, Blue, and Orange lines. The commuter rail to the suburbs shows up on system maps in purple (but it's rarely called the Purple Line). The local fare is 85¢ (you'll need a token) and can be as much as $2.25 for some surface line extensions on the Green and Red lines. Route and fare information and timetables are available at Park Street station (under the Common), which is the center of the system. Signs reading "inbound" and "outbound" refer to the location in relation to Park Street.

Note that service begins around 5:15am and shuts down between 12:30 and 1am, system-wide. The only exception is New Year's Eve, or First Night, when closing time is 2am.

Token vending machines are gaining popularity and can currently be found at Airport (Blue Line), Back Bay and Downtown Crossing (Orange Line), Government Center and Prudential (Green Line), and South Station, Downtown Crossing, and Harvard (Red Line).

The Green Line is not wheelchair accessible, but most stations on other lines are. They are indicated on system maps. To learn more, call the **Office for Transportation Access** (☎ **800/533-6282** or 617/222-5123; TDD 617/222-5415).

BY BUS The MBTA also runs buses and "trackless trolleys" (identifiable by their electric antennae but otherwise indistinguishable from buses) that provide service crosstown and to and around the suburbs. The local bus fare is 60¢; express buses are $1.50 and up. Exact change is required. Many buses are equipped with lifts for wheelchairs (☎ **800/LIFT-BUS**).

BY CAR

If you plan to confine your visit to Boston proper, there's absolutely no reason to have a car, and in fact, it's probably more trouble than it's worth. If you're driving to Boston, leave your car in your hotel garage and use it for day trips or to visit Cambridge, if you're feeling flush—you'll probably wind up paying to park there, too. If you're not motoring and you decide to take a day trip, you'll probably want to rent a car.

RENTALS The major car-rental firms have offices in Boston and at Logan Airport. (Be aware that a hefty drop-off charge is standard for most companies if you rent in one city and return in another.) If you're traveling at a busy time, reserve a car well in advance. Companies with offices at the airport include: **Alamo** (☎ 800/327-9633), **Avis** (☎ 800/831-2847), **Budget** (☎ 800/527-0700), **Enterprise** (☎ 800/325-8007), **Hertz** (☎ 800/654-3131), **National** (☎ 800/227-7368), and **Thrifty** (☎ 800/367-2277). Most companies set aside cars for nonsmokers, but you have to ask.

PARKING It's difficult to find your way around Boston and practically impossible to find parking in some areas. Most spaces on the street are metered (and patrolled until 6pm on the dot every day except Sunday), or open to nonresidents for exactly 2 hours or less between 8am and 6pm. The penalty is a $20 ticket, but should you blunder into a tow-away zone, retrieving the car will take at least $50 and a lot of running around. Read the sign or the meter carefully. In some areas parking is allowed only at certain hours. Rates vary in different sections of the city (usually $1 an hour downtown), so bring plenty of quarters and dimes. Time limits range from 15 minutes to 2 hours. *Tip:* During the day, if you're visiting the eastern part of Cambridge, near MIT, parking on Memorial Drive is free and usually not terribly hard to find.

To save yourself a lot of aggravation, leave your car in a garage or lot and walk. Most garages will charge no more than $20 for a full day, and there's often a lower flat rate if you enter and exit before certain times or if you park in the evening. Some restaurants offer reduced rates at nearby garages; ask when you call for reservations.

The two largest garages are under Boston Common and under the Prudential Center. The reasonably priced **city-run garage under the Common** (☎ 617/954-2096) at Charles Street was renovated recently, and is limited to vehicles less than 6 feet, 3 inches tall. The **garage at the Prudential Center** (☎ 617/267-1002) has entrances on Boylston Street, Huntington Avenue, and Exeter Street, and at the Sheraton Boston Hotel & Towers. Parking is discounted if you make a purchase at the Shops at Prudential Center. A similar deal is offered at the **garage at Copley Place** (☎ 617/375-4488), off Huntington Avenue.

The **All Right lot off North Street under the Expressway** (☎ 617/523-1719) offers a discount to patrons of many North End restaurants and shops—look for a sign in the window of the business.

Good-sized garages can be found at Government Center off Congress Street (☎ 617/227-0385), at the New England Aquarium (☎ 617/723-1731), at 75 State St. (☎ 617/742-7275), near the Hynes Convention Center on Dalton Street (☎ 617/247-8006), and at Zero Post Office Square (☎ 617/423-1430).

SPECIAL DRIVING RULES A right turn is allowed at a red light after stopping when traffic permits, unless a sign is posted saying otherwise (as it often is downtown). Seat belts are mandatory for adults and children, and infants and children under 5 must be strapped into car seats. You can't be stopped just for having an unbelted adult in the car, but a youngster on the loose is considered reason enough to pull you over.

Two state laws to be aware of, if only because the frequency with which they're broken will take your breath away: Pedestrians in the crosswalk have the right-of-way, and vehicles already in a rotary (traffic circle or roundabout) have the right-of-way.

Boston Transit

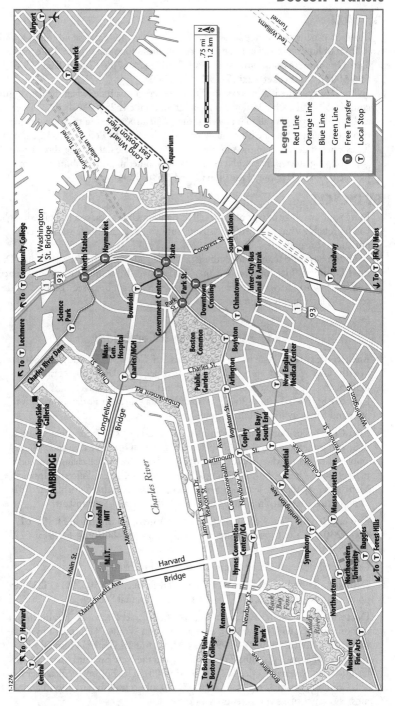

Legend

— Red Line
— Orange Line
— Blue Line
— Green Line
Ⓣ Free Transfer
Ⓣ Local Stop

N
.75 mi
1.2 km
0

Airport
Maverick
Aquarium
Long Wharf to East Boston Piers
Callahan Tunnel
Sumner Tunnel
Ted Williams Tunnel

N. Washington St. Bridge
To Community College
To Lechmere
Science Park
Charles River Dam
Charles St.
CAMBRIDGE
CambridgeSide Galleria
Longfellow Bridge
Kendall/MIT
Main St.
M.I.T.
Memorial Dr.
Massachusetts Ave.
To Harvard
Central

North Station
Haymarket
Bowdoin
Government Center
State
Congress St.
South Station
Inter-City Bus Terminal & Amtrak
Broadway
To JFK/U Mass
93
1
93

Park St.
Park St.
Downtown Crossing
Chinatown
Boylston
New England Medical Center
Boston Common
Charles St.
Public Garden
Mass. Gen. Hospital
Charles/MGH
Embankment Rd.

Charles River

Harvard Bridge
James Storrow Dr.
Beacon St.
Commonwealth Ave.
Newbury St.
Dartmouth St.
Boylston St.
Copley
Arlington
Back Bay/South End
Prudential
Columbus Ave.
Massachusetts Ave.
Tremont St.
Washington St.

Hynes Convention Center/ICA
Kenmore
To Boston Univ./Boston College
Fenway Park
Newbury St.
Back Bay Fens
Muddy River
Brookline Ave.
Museum of Fine Arts
Symphony
Huntington Ave.
Northeastern
Northeastern University
Ruggles
Forest Hills
To Arboretum

53

BY TAXI

Taxis are expensive and not always easy to find—seek out a cab stand (often found in front of hotels), or call a dispatcher. To call ahead for a cab, try the **Independent Taxi Operators Association,** or ITOA (☎ **617/426-8700**), **Town Taxi** (☎ **617/ 536-5000**), or **Checker Taxi** (☎ **617/536-7000**).

The fare structure is as follows: the first one-quarter of a mile (when the flag drops) costs $1.50, and each additional one-eighth of a mile is 25¢. "Wait time" is extra, and the passenger pays all tolls as well as the $1.50 airport fee (on trips leaving Logan only). Charging a flat rate is not allowed within the city; the Police Department publishes a list of distances to the suburbs that establishes the flat rate for those trips.

If you want to report a problem or have lost something in a cab, the Police Department runs a **Hackney Hot Line** (☎ **617/536-8294**).

BY BICYCLE

Bring your own bike or rent one—you'll fit right in. Unless you're a real pro, though, you'll probably want to stay off the streets until you're comfortable with the city layout and traffic patterns.

Boston has more than 50 miles of marked bike paths, including the 17.7-mile **Dr. Paul Dudley White loop** around the Charles River from the Museum of Science to Watertown and back. For information about renting a bike, see "Biking," under section 7, later in this chapter.

FAST FACTS: Boston & Cambridge

American Express   The main local office is at 1 Court St. (☎ **617/723-8400**), near the Government Center MBTA stop. It's open Monday through Friday from 8:30am to 5:30pm. The Cambridge office, near Harvard Square at 39 John F. Kennedy St. (☎ **617/868-2600**), is open Monday through Friday from 9am to 5pm and Saturday from 11am to 3pm.

Area Code   For Boston and the immediate suburbs, it's 617; for other suburbs, 508. You sometimes must dial "1" before a number in the same area code (for example, when calling Marblehead from Boston). Many suburbs will change area codes in May 1998. Among those switching to 978: Concord, Essex, Gloucester, Ipswich, Manchester-by-the-Sea, Newburyport, Rockport, and Salem. Switching to 781: Hull, Lexington, Lincoln, Lynn, Marblehead, Revere, and Swampscott.

Camera Repair   Try **Bromfield Camera & Video,** 10 Bromfield St. (☎ **617/ 426-5230**), or the **Camera Center,** 107 State St. (☎ **800/924-6899** or 617/ 227-7255).

Car Rentals   See "Getting Around," earlier in this chapter.

Dentists   The **Metropolitan District Dental Society** (☎ **508/651-3521**) can point you toward a member of the Massachusetts Dental Society.

Doctors   Local referral services include the Beth Israel Deaconess Health Information Line (☎ **617/667-5356**), the Brigham and Women's Hospital Physician Referral Service (☎ **800/294-9999**), the Massachusetts General Hospital Physician Referral Service (☎ **800/711-4MGH**), and the New England Medical Center Physician Referral Service (☎ **617/636-9700**). The Boston Medical Center, 388 Commonwealth Ave. (☎ **617/267-7171**), offers walk-in service and honors most insurance plans and accepts credit cards.

Embassies/Consulates   See "Fast Facts: For the Foreign Traveler," in chapter 3.

Emergencies Call ☎ **911** for fire, ambulance, or the Boston, Brookline, or Cambridge police. This is a free call from pay phones. For the state police, call ☎ **617/ 523-1212.**

Hospitals Here's hoping you won't need to evaluate Boston's reputation for excellent medical care. In case you do: **Massachusetts General Hospital,** 55 Fruit St. (☎ **617/726-2000,** or 617/726-4100 for children's emergency services), and the **New England Medical Center,** 750 Washington St. (☎ **617/636-5000,** or 617/636-5566 for emergency services), are closest to downtown Boston. At the Harvard Medical Area on the Boston-Brookline border are, among others, **Beth Israel Deaconess Medical Center,** 330 Brookline Ave. (☎ **617/667-7000**), **Brigham and Women's Hospital,** 75 Francis St. (☎ **617/732-5500**), and **Children's Hospital,** 300 Longwood Ave. (☎ **617/355-6000,** or 617/355-6611 for emergency services).

In Cambridge are **Mount Auburn Hospital,** 330 Mount Auburn St. (☎ **617/ 492-3500,** or 617/499-5025 for emergency services) and **Cambridge Hospital,** 1493 Cambridge St. (☎ **617/498-1000**).

Hot Lines In a crisis, you can call the **AIDS Hotline** (☎ 800/235-2331 or 617/ 536-7733), the **Poison Information Center** (☎ 800/682-9211 or 617/232-2120), **Rape Crisis** (☎ 617/492-7273), **Samaritans Suicide Prevention** (☎ 617/ 247-0220), **Samariteens** (☎ 800/252-8336 or 617/247-8050), or the **Travelers Aid Society** (☎ 617/542-7286).

Information See "Visitor Information," earlier in this chapter.

Liquor Laws The legal drinking age is 21. In many bars, particularly near college campuses, you may be asked for ID if you appear to be under 30 or so. At sporting events, everyone purchasing alcohol is asked to show ID. Alcohol is sold in liquor stores and a few supermarkets and convenience stores. Liquor stores (and the liquor sections of other stores) are closed on Sundays, but alcohol may be served in restaurants. Some suburban towns are "dry."

Maps See "City Layout," earlier in this chapter.

Newspapers/Magazines The "Calendar" section of the Thursday *Boston Globe* lists festivals, street fairs, concerts, films, speeches, and dance and theater performances. The Friday *Boston Herald* has a similar, smaller insert called "Scene." Both papers briefly list weekend events in their Saturday editions. The arts-oriented *Boston Phoenix,* published on Thursday, has extensive entertainment and restaurant listings.

Where, a monthly magazine available free at most hotels throughout the city, gives information about shopping, nightlife, attractions, and current shows at museums and galleries. Another freebie, *Quick Guide,* is published four times a year and offers entertainment and shopping listings, a restaurant guide, and maps.

Newspaper boxes around the city dispense free copies of the weekly *Tab,* which lists neighborhood-specific events information, the twice-monthly *Improper Bostonian,* with extensive event and restaurant listings, and the "Styles" section of the *Phoenix.* Available on newsstands, *Boston* magazine is a lifestyle-oriented monthly with cultural and restaurant listings.

Pharmacies (Late-Night) The pharmacy at the **CVS** in the Porter Square Shopping Center, off Mass. Ave. in Cambridge (☎ **617/876-5519**), is open 24 hours, 7 days a week. The pharmacy at the **CVS** at 155–157 Charles St. in Boston (☎ **617/523-1028**), next to the Charles "T" stop, is open until midnight. Some emergency rooms can fill your prescription at the hospital's pharmacy.

Police   Call ☎ **911** for emergencies. This is a free call from pay phones.

Rest Rooms   The visitor center at 15 State St. has a public rest room, as do most hotels, department stores, and public buildings. There are rest rooms at the CambridgeSide Galleria, Copley Place, Prudential Center, and Quincy Market shopping areas. One of the few public rest rooms in Harvard Square is in the Harvard Coop department store.

Safety   On the whole, Boston and Cambridge are safe cities for walking. Stay out of parks in both cities (including the Esplanade) at night unless you're in a crowd, and in general, trust your instincts—a dark, deserted street is probably deserted for a reason. Specific areas to avoid at night include Boylston Street between Tremont Street and Washington Street, and Tremont Street from Stuart Street to Boylston Street. Public transportation in the areas you're likely to be is busy and safe, but service stops between 12:30 and 1am. Always be aware of your surroundings and keep a close eye on your possessions.

Taxes   The 5% sales tax is not levied on food, prescription drugs, newspapers, or clothing worth less than $175, but there seems to be a tax on almost everything else. The lodging tax is 9.7%; the meal tax (which also applies to take-out food) is 5%; the gasoline tax (included on the price at the pump) is 10%. There is also a tax on alcohol based on alcoholic content.

Taxis   See "Getting Around," earlier in this chapter.

Transit Info   Call the **MBTA** at ☎ **617/222-3200.**

3   Accommodations

Boston regularly lands in the top 10 on lists of the most expensive destinations for business travelers, but you don't need to break the bank to have a comfortable place to stay. Rates at most area hotels are lower on weekends than on weeknights, when business and convention travelers fill rooms. Bargain hunters who don't mind cold and the possibility of snow (sometimes *lots* of snow) will want to aim for January through March, when some great deals are offered, especially on weekends. It helps to be flexible when you're selecting dates—a hotel that's full of conventioneers one week may be courting business a few days later.

It's always a good idea to make a reservation, especially during the busy spring and fall convention seasons, the vacation months of July and August, and the college graduation season of May and early June.

Boston charges a 9.7% tax on all hotel rooms (5.7% for the state, 4% for the city).

Three publications available from the **Greater Boston Convention & Visitors Bureau** (☎ **888/SEE-BOSTON** or 617/536-4100; fax 617/424-7664; Web site: **http://www.bostonusa.com**)—a free travel-planning guide, a comprehensive guidebook, and a separate guide called *Kids Love Boston*—are helpful in finding accommodations that will suit your needs and can offer substantial savings.

BED & BREAKFASTS   The following organizations can help you find a B&B:

Bed-and-Breakfast Associates Bay Colony Ltd., P.O. Box 57-166, Babson Park Branch, Boston, MA 02157 (☎ **800/347-5088** or 617/449-5302; fax 617/449-5958; Web site: **http://www.bnbboston.com**; E-mail **BnBBoston@aol.com**) lists more than 150 bed-and-breakfasts and inns in the metropolitan Boston area and throughout eastern Massachusetts, including the North Shore, South Shore, and Cape Cod.

The **Bed-and-Breakfast Agency of Boston,** 47 Commercial Wharf, Boston, MA 02110 (☎ **800/CITY-BNB** or 617/720-3540; fax 617/523-5761; from the United Kingdom, 0800/89-5128), offers accommodations in waterfront lofts and historic homes (including Federal and Victorian town houses) in Boston and Cambridge. Nightly, weekly, monthly, and special winter rates are available. Listings include 155 rooms and 60 suites as well as furnished studios and apartments, all within walking distance of downtown.

Host Homes of Boston, P.O. Box 117, Waban Branch, Boston, MA 02168-0001 (☎ **617/244-1308;** fax 617/244-5156), lists 45 homes offering personalized hospitality and clean, comfortable accommodations. Many hosts speak foreign languages, and all provide breakfast. A minimum stay of at least 2 nights is required.

Bed & Breakfast Reservations North Shore/Greater Boston/Cape Cod, P.O. Box 35, Newtonville, MA 02160-0001 (☎ **800/832-2632** outside Mass., or 617/964-1606; fax 617/332-8572; Web site: **http://www.bnbinc.com**; E-mail: **bnbinc@ix.netcom.com**) matches visitors with carefully inspected accommodations in Greater Boston and areas north of Boston, on Cape Cod, and in selected areas in Maine, New Hampshire, and Vermont. A minimum stay of at least 2 nights is required.

ON THE WATERFRONT
VERY EXPENSIVE

The newest hotel on the waterfront—technically in South Boston, next to the World Trade Center, from which it's expected to draw much of its business—is the independent **Seaport Hotel & Conference Center** (☎ **888/WTC-HOTEL**). The 427-room hotel opened in 1997 after several years of meticulous planning, and has all the features you'd expect in this price range, including shuttle service to the airport and downtown. Judging from the information available at press time, business travelers with (or without) dealings at the World Trade Center will find it a good addition to the list of hotels below.

✪ **Boston Harbor Hotel.** 70 Rowes Wharf (entrance on Atlantic Ave.), Boston, MA 02110. ☎ **800/752-7077** or 617/439-7000. Fax 617/330-9450. 230 rms, 26 suites. A/C MINIBAR TV TEL. $235–$385 double; from $350 suite. Children under 18 stay free in parents' room. Extra person $50. Weekend packages available. AE, DC, DISC, MC, V. Valet parking $26; self-parking $22 weekdays, $17 weekends. MBTA: Blue Line to Aquarium or Red Line to South Station.

The Boston Harbor Hotel is the prettiest in town, whether you approach from land or sea (the Airport Water Shuttle stops here). A dazzling six-story-high archway links the harbor and the city, and you'll forget about the Central Artery construction raging out front as soon as you glimpse the water. The hotel is within walking distance of downtown and waterfront attractions, and it prides itself on offering top-notch service. A museum-quality collection of art, prints, and nautical charts enhances the grand public spaces.

Guest rooms have a view of the harbor or the Boston skyline (rooms with city views are less expensive), and all have windows that open. Each is a luxurious bed-and living-room combination, decorated with mahogany furnishings that include an armoire, a desk, and comfortable chairs. Some suites have private terraces. Standard guest room amenities include two two-line telephones, data ports, pay-per-view movies, hair dryers, bathrobes, slippers, and umbrellas. There are three floors reserved for nonsmokers; 18 rooms are accessible for travelers with disabilities.

Dining/Entertainment: Overlooking the harbor, the noted Rowes Wharf Restaurant serves fresh seafood and American cuisine at breakfast, lunch, dinner, and Sunday

Boston Accommodations

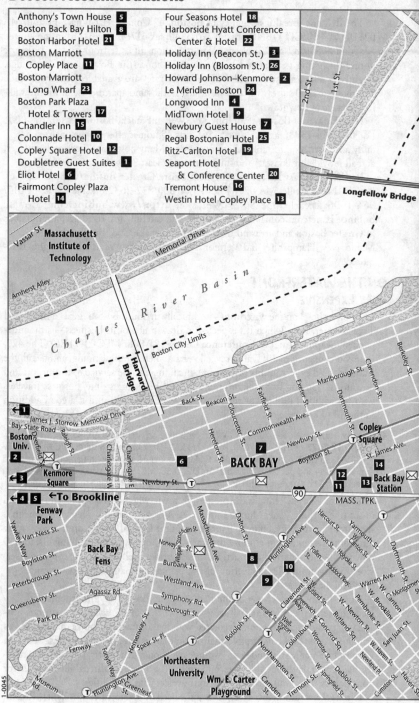

Anthony's Town House **5**
Boston Back Bay Hilton **8**
Boston Harbor Hotel **21**
Boston Marriott
   Copley Place **11**
Boston Marriott
   Long Wharf **23**
Boston Park Plaza
   Hotel & Towers **17**
Chandler Inn **15**
Colonnade Hotel **10**
Copley Square Hotel **12**
Doubletree Guest Suites **1**
Eliot Hotel **6**
Fairmont Copley Plaza
   Hotel **14**

Four Seasons Hotel **18**
Harborside Hyatt Conference
   Center & Hotel **22**
Holiday Inn (Beacon St.) **3**
Holiday Inn (Blossom St.) **26**
Howard Johnson–Kenmore **2**
Le Meridien Boston **24**
Longwood Inn **4**
MidTown Hotel **9**
Newbury Guest House **7**
Regal Bostonian Hotel **25**
Ritz-Carlton Hotel **19**
Seaport Hotel
   & Conference Center **20**
Tremont House **16**
Westin Hotel Copley Place **13**

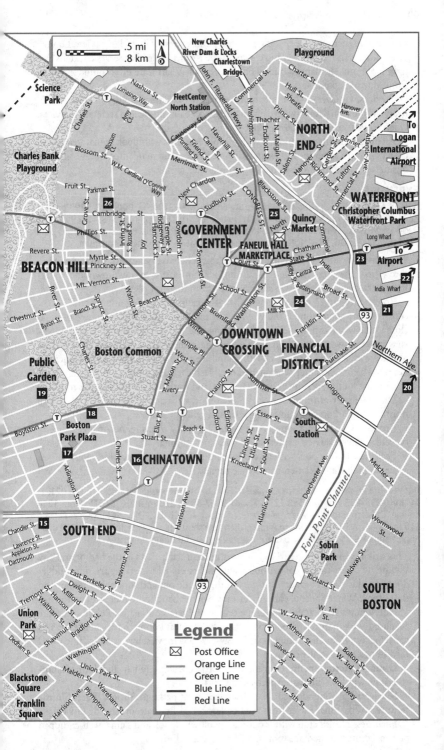

brunch (see section 4 of this chapter for a full review). The Harborview Lounge offers afternoon tea and evening cocktails; the Rowes Wharf Bar serves cocktails and light fare from 11:30am to midnight. The Rowes Wharf Café offers outdoor dining from May to September.

Services: Concierge, 24-hour room service, dry cleaning/laundry, newspaper delivery, in-room massage, twice-daily maid service, baby-sitting and secretarial services, video rentals, express checkout, valet parking.

Facilities: Health club and spa with 60-foot lap pool; whirlpool; sauna, steam, and exercise rooms; salon for facials, massage, pedicures, and manicures. State-of-the-art business center with professional staff; conference rooms.

EXPENSIVE

Boston Marriott Long Wharf. 296 State St., Boston, MA 02109. ☎ **800/228-9290** or 617/227-0800. Fax 617/227-2867. 400 rms, 12 suites. A/C TV TEL. Apr–Nov $189–$269 double; Dec–Mar $159–$229 double. Suites $450–$490. Extra person free. Weekend packages from $214 double. AE, DC, DISC, JCB, MC, V. Parking $25. MBTA: Blue Line to Aquarium.

The central location is the chief appeal of this otherwise typical Marriott. A stone's throw from the New England Aquarium, it's convenient to downtown and waterfront attractions, and just two subway stops from the airport.

Rooms face either side of Long Wharf—because of the ongoing Central Artery construction literally under the windows of the rooms near the street, ask to be as close to the water as possible. Rooms are large and decor varies, but all have pay-per-view movies, two phones, and a table and chairs in front of the window. Eighteen rooms are accessible for travelers with disabilities. The seventh floor is the Concierge Level, with complimentary continental breakfast, cocktails, and hors d'oeuvres served in a private lounge, private exercise facilities, and fresh flowers in the guest rooms.

Dining/Entertainment: Oceana Restaurant, with a 180° expanse of glass wall fronting the harbor; cafe and lounge; bar and grill.

Services: Concierge, room service until 11pm, dry cleaning, newspaper delivery, twice-daily maid service, express checkout, valet parking.

Facilities: Indoor pool with an outdoor terrace, exercise room, whirlpools, saunas, game room, business center, conference rooms.

Harborside Hyatt Conference Center & Hotel. 101 Harborside Dr., Boston, MA 02128. ☎ **800/233-1234** or 617/568-1234. Fax 617/567-8856. 270 rms. A/C TV TEL. From $214 double. Children under 12 stay free in parents' room. AE, CB, DC, DISC, JCB, MC, V. Parking $10 minimum. MBTA: Blue Line to Airport, then take shuttle bus. By car, follow signs to Logan Airport and take Harborside Dr. past the car-rental area and tunnel entrance.

This striking 14-story waterfront hotel has unobstructed views of the harbor and city skyline. It caters to the convention trade; sightseers whose transportation budget doesn't include a fair amount of time (on the shuttle bus and subway) or money (on the Airport Water Shuttle, parking, or cabs) will be better off closer to downtown.

Fiber-optic stars change color in the ceiling of the reception area. Public spaces are accented with nautical memorabilia, and the guest rooms have such extras as coffeemakers, irons and ironing boards, pay-per-view movies, luxury baths, fine wood furnishings, and excellent views.

Dining/Entertainment: The restaurant serves breakfast, lunch, and dinner. Floor-to-ceiling windows allow for spectacular views.

Services: Valet laundry, secretarial services, valet parking, Airport Water Shuttle to Rowes Wharf that leaves from the hotel dock, 24-hour airport shuttle service.

Facilities: Health club with indoor lap pool, whirlpool, and sauna; well-equipped business center; conference rooms.

FANEUIL HALL/GOVERNMENT CENTER

The **Holiday Inn Select Boston Government Center,** 5 Blossom St., Boston, MA 02114 (☎ 800/HOLIDAY or 617/742-7630), offers the features you'd expect from the international chain, including an outdoor heated pool.

The Regal Bostonian Hotel. 40 North St., Boston, MA 02109. ☎ **800/343-0922** or 617/523-3600. Fax 617/523-2454. Web site: http://www.regal-hotels.com/boston. 152 rms, 11 suites. A/C MINIBAR TV TEL. $245–$325 double; $265–$345 deluxe; $295–$375 Regal Class; $500–$775 suite. Children 18 and under stay free in parents' room. Extra person or rollaway $20. Weekend and other packages available. AE, DC, DISC, JCB, MC, V. Parking $20. MBTA: Green or Blue Line to Government Center, or Orange Line to Haymarket.

Across the street from Faneuil Hall, the relatively small Regal Bostonian is big on service and amenities. Acquired by Regal Hotels International in 1996, the four- and seven-story redbrick hotel consists of two wings—one, an old warehouse building, dates from 1824, the other from 1890. One wing is furnished in contemporary style, the other more traditionally.

All rooms have stereo VCRs, 26-inch TVs, safes, terry-cloth bathrobes, hair dryers, and two-line phones with data ports; many have French doors that open onto private balconies. Some suites have double vanities and separate dressing areas, working fireplaces, or Jacuzzis. Rooms are available for nonsmokers and travelers with disabilities.

Thanks to recently completed soundproofing, you won't be forced to choose between quiet and a nice view, but bear in mind that Faneuil Hall Marketplace is busy from early till late, the Central Artery construction is nearby, and on Friday and Saturday, the noisy Haymarket vendors are in place by 7am.

Dining/Entertainment: On the fourth-floor rooftop is the glass-enclosed Seasons restaurant. The Atrium Lounge, in the lobby, affords a great view of the marketplace.

Services: Concierge, 24-hour room service, laundry, newspaper delivery, express checkout, valet parking, complimentary morning limousine service.

Facilities: Complimentary health club privileges at the excellent Sky Club four blocks away; conference rooms.

THE FINANCIAL DISTRICT & DOWNTOWN

✪ **Le Meridien Boston.** 250 Franklin St. (at Post Office Sq.), Boston, MA 02110. ☎ **800/543-4300** or 617/451-1900. Fax 617/423-2844. 326 rms, 22 suites. A/C MINIBAR TV TEL. $285–$335 double; $450–$800 suite. Extra person $30. Weekend rates from $155 per night. AE, CB, DC, DISC, MC, V. Valet parking $26, $13 Fri–Sat; self-parking $24, $8 Fri–Sat. MBTA: Red Line to Downtown Crossing or South Station, or Blue or Orange Line to State.

Located in the old Federal Reserve Bank building, this nine-story granite-and-limestone hotel is an architectural marvel, complete with ornately carved marble fireplaces and floor-to-ceiling arched windows in the lobby. The bank's original grand marble staircase now leads to the dining areas, and there are two murals by N. C. Wyeth on the walls of the bar. Vacationers will be near the waterfront and downtown attractions, but not all that close to public transportation. "Business Traveler" rooms are available, each with a fax machine and personalized fax cover sheets, oversized desk, halogen lighting, coffeemaker, and two two-line phones. Whatever your mission, you'll find the service by the multilingual staff superb.

Guest rooms have 153 different configurations, including dramatic loft suites with first-floor living rooms, a bedroom in the loft area, and bathrooms on both levels. A glass mansard roof surrounds the top three stories, where a number of rooms have large sloped windows and extraordinary views. Each room has two telephones (one in the bathroom) and pay-per-view movies. Seven floors are reserved for nonsmokers; 15 rooms are equipped for travelers with disabilities.

Dining/Entertainment: The noted Julien restaurant serves lunch and dinner; the bar features live piano music 6 nights a week. A six-story glass atrium rises above the Café Fleuri, which serves breakfast, lunch, dinner, the Saturday "Chocolate Bar Buffet" (September through May), and Sunday jazz brunch. La Terrasse is the seasonal outdoor cafe.

Services: Concierge, 24-hour room service, dry cleaning/laundry, weekday newspaper delivery, twice-daily maid service, baby-sitting, secretarial services, express checkout, valet parking, courtesy car to Newbury Street, daily weather report.

Facilities: 40-foot indoor pool, well-equipped health club with whirlpool and sauna, full-service business center with library and full-time staff, conference rooms.

THE BACK BAY & HUNTINGTON AVENUE
VERY EXPENSIVE

The Colonnade Hotel. 120 Huntington Ave., Boston, MA 02116. ☎ **800/962-3030** or 617/424-7000. Fax 617/424-1717. 285 rms, 10 suites. A/C MINIBAR TV TEL. $240–$270 double; $450–$1,400 suite. Children under 12 stay free in parents' room. AE, CB, DC, DISC, MC, V. Parking $20. MBTA: Green Line, E train to Prudential.

The swimming pool and "rooftop resort" are probably this hotel's best-known features. Adjacent to Copley Place and the Prudential Center, the Colonnade is a slice of Europe in the all-American shopping mecca of the Back Bay. You might hear a dozen languages spoken by the guests and employees of this 10-story concrete-and-glass hotel, where the friendly, professional staff is known for its personalized VIP service.

The elegance of the quiet, high-ceilinged public spaces is reflected in the guest rooms, which have contemporary oak or mahogany furnishings, marble baths, two phones, pay-per-view movies, bathrobes, and hair dryers. The newly designed suites have dining rooms and sitting areas, and the "author's suite" features autographed copies of the work of celebrated (or at least published) literary guests.

Dining/Entertainment: In the lobby is a European-style bistro that's especially busy before and after the Symphony, and a bar with live entertainment and dancing on Friday and Saturday nights.

Services: Concierge, 24-hour room service, dry cleaning/laundry, newspaper delivery, in-room massage, baby-sitting, secretarial services, express checkout, valet parking, courtesy car, children's programs, video rentals.

Facilities: Heated outdoor pool, sundeck and fitness room, business center, conference rooms, car-rental desk.

The Fairmont Copley Plaza Hotel. 138 St. James Ave., Boston, MA 02116. ☎ **800/527-4727** or 617/267-5300. Fax 617/247-6681. 373 rms, 61 suites. A/C MINIBAR TV TEL. $289–$399 double; $395–$1,400 suite. Extra person $30. AE, CB, DC, JCB, MC, V. Valet parking $24. MBTA: Green Line to Copley or Orange Line to Back Bay.

Built in 1912, the six-story Fairmont Copley Plaza faces Copley Square, with Trinity Church on one side and the Boston Public Library on the other. The Renaissance Revival hotel overflows with opulent decorative features, including crystal chandeliers, Italian marble columns, gilded vaulted ceilings, mirrored walls, and mosaic tile floors. Guest rooms, renovated in 1996, reflect the elegance of the public spaces and are furnished with reproduction Edwardian antiques. Additional in-room features include coffeemakers, phones with data ports, hair dryers, and pay-per-view movies. Four floors are reserved for nonsmokers, and rooms for travelers with disabilities are available.

Dining/Entertainment: There are two restaurants, the Oak Room and Copley's, and two lounges, the Oak Bar and Copley's Bar.

Services: Concierge, 24-hour room service, dry cleaning/laundry, twice-daily maid service, valet parking.

Facilities: Fitness center, conference rooms, beauty salon.

✪ **Four Seasons Hotel.** 200 Boylston St., Boston, MA 02116. ☎ **800/332-3442** or 617/338-4400. Fax 617/423-0154. 288 rms, 80 suites. A/C MINIBAR TV TEL. $375–$625 double; from $1,100 1-bedroom suite; from $2,100 2-bedroom suite; from $2,150 3-bedroom suite. Weekend packages available. AE, CB, DC, DISC, JCB, MC, V. Valet parking $35. MBTA: Green Line to Arlington.

No other hotel in Boston combines every element you expect from a luxury hotel as seamlessly as the Four Seasons. Overlooking the Public Garden, the 16-story redbrick-and-glass hotel combines the traditional with the contemporary, in its architecture and in its attitude. Children receive bedtime snacks and toys. Small pets are accepted and treated as well as their traveling companions, with a special menu and amenities.

Each room is elegantly appointed and has a striking view. Beds are large and comfortable, and breakfronts conceal the 19-inch remote-control TV and refrigerated minibar. The suites range from Four Seasons Executive Suites, which have enlarged alcove areas for entertaining or business meetings, to luxurious one-, two-, and three-bedroom deluxe suites, which are the utmost in elegance, privacy, and comfort. All rooms have bay windows that open, individual climate control, pay-per-view movies, three two-line phones with computer and fax capability, hair dryers, terry-cloth bathrobes, and a safe. There are five nonsmoking floors, and rooms geared for travelers with disabilities are available.

Dining/Entertainment: The elegant restaurant Aujourd'hui, one of Boston's best, serves fine French cuisine (see section 4 of this chapter for a full review); the Bristol Lounge is open for lunch, afternoon tea, dinner, and breakfast on Sunday, and features live entertainment nightly.

Services: In general, if you want it, you'll get it. Concierge, 24-hour room service, valet service, twice-daily maid service, valet parking, complimentary limousine service to downtown Boston addresses. If you lose your luggage en route, the staff will purchase new items and provide you with a full set of toiletries and other necessities.

Facilities: Indoor heated pool and whirlpool with a view of the Public Garden; health spa with weight machines, StairMasters, treadmills, private masseuse, and sauna; excellent business center; conference rooms.

The Ritz-Carlton. 15 Arlington St., Boston, MA 02117. ☎ **800/241-3333** or 617/536-5700. Fax 617/536-1335. 278 rms, 48 suites. A/C MINIBAR TV TEL. $260–$355 double; $345–$2,000 1-bedroom suite, $710–$915 2-bedroom suite. Ritz-Carlton Club $320–$650 1-bedroom suite, $820–$1,025 2-bedroom suite. Weekend packages available. Extra person $20. AE, CB, DC, DISC, JCB, MC, V. Valet parking $24. MBTA: Green Line to Arlington.

If you have plenty of old money and are eager to part with it, this is the place for you. Overlooking the Public Garden, the Ritz-Carlton has attracted both "proper Bostonians" and celebrated guests since it opened in 1927. The 17-story hotel has the highest staff-to-guest ratio in the city, including white-gloved elevator operators.

The guest rooms have classic French provincial furnishings accented with imported floral fabrics and crystal chandeliers. Each room has two telephones (one in the bathroom), a refrigerator, a well-stocked honor bar, a safe, and an individual climate-control unit. The bathrooms are finished in Vermont marble, and terry-cloth robes are provided. All the guest rooms have closets that lock, and some have windows that open. You'll pay more for rooms with a view. Fresh flowers are provided in all suites, and many suites have wood-burning fireplaces.

Floors 15, 16, and 17 make up the Club Level, with gorgeous views and the use of the Ritz-Carlton Club, a pleasant lounge that has its own concierge and is open from 7am to 11pm, serving complimentary breakfast, afternoon tea, hors d'oeuvres, and after-dinner sweets.

Dining/Entertainment: The noted Dining Room is reviewed in section 4 of this chapter, and the Bar at the Ritz is located off the street-level lobby.

The second-floor Lounge serves afternoon tea, and from 5:30pm until midnight cigar and pipe smokers can relax over cognac, rare cordials, caviar, and desserts. On weekend evenings, there's live jazz. The Café is open from 7am to midnight. The Roof, located on the 17th floor and open seasonally, offers dinner and dancing to the Ritz-Carlton Orchestra. A famously strict dress code (the mayor of Boston was once turned away from the bar) is enforced.

Services: Concierge, 24-hour room service, dry cleaning/laundry, newspaper delivery, twice-daily maid service, baby-sitting, secretarial services, complimentary limousine service, complimentary shoeshine.

Facilities: Well-equipped fitness center with sauna and massage room, use of pool at the nearby Candela of Boston spa, conference rooms, beauty salon, gift shop.

EXPENSIVE

Boston Back Bay Hilton. 40 Dalton St., Boston, MA 02115. ☎ **800/874-0663**, 800/ HILTONS, or 617/236-1100. Web site: http://www.hilton.com/hotels/BOSBHHF. Fax 617/ 867-6104. 341 rms, 5 suites. A/C TV TEL. $210–$250 double; $400–$800 suite. Packages and AAA discount available. Extra person $20. AE, CB, DC, DISC, MC, V. Parking $15. MBTA: Green Line, B, C, or D train to Hynes/ICA or E train to Prudential.

The motto here is "We mean business," and although it's smaller than a typical Hilton, this hotel across the street from the Prudential Center complex lives up to its claim. Vacationing families will also find it convenient and comfortable, and whatever your mission, the staff is friendly and helpful. The guest rooms in the triangular 26-story hotel were renovated in 1993, the suites in 1997. Rooms are large and have modern furnishings, with windows that open, coffeemakers, hair dryers, pay-per-view movies, and irons and ironing boards. Soundproofing in the rooms helps keep the level of street noise down. Rooms for nonsmokers are available.

Dining/Entertainment: Boodles Restaurant is known for grilled steaks and seafood; Boodles Bar offers nearly 100 American microbrews; the Rendezvous Lounge serves continental breakfast, cocktails, and light meals; Club Nicole attracts a young crowd.

Services: Room service until midnight, valet laundry, currency exchange.

Facilities: Heated indoor pool, well-equipped fitness center, sundeck, business center, conference rooms.

Boston Marriott Copley Place. 110 Huntington Ave., Boston, MA 02116. ☎ **800/ 228-9290** or 617/236-5800. Fax 617/236-5885. 1,147 rms, 47 suites. A/C TV TEL. $225–$240 double; $450–$1,050 suite. Children stay free in parents' room. Weekend and other packages available. AE, DC, DISC, JCB, MC, V. Valet parking $23; self-parking $19. MBTA: Orange Line to Back Bay or Green Line to Copley.

Yes, 1,147 rooms. You won't be asserting your individuality, but you'll probably be comfortable. This 38-story tower has something for everyone—it's part of upscale Copley Place, offering complete business facilities in the heart of Boston's shopping wonderland. The giant lobby, with a four-story-long chandelier, Italian marble floors, full-size trees, and a waterfall, is almost always busy. The guest rooms, which were renovated in 1995, echo the finery of the lobby, with Queen Anne–style mahogany furniture, including a desk and table and armchairs. Rooms are equipped with full-length mirrors, hair dryers, pay-per-view movies, ironing boards, and phones with data ports. Ultrasuites feature individual whirlpool baths. Guests in Concierge Level rooms have their own concierge and access to a private lounge where complimentary continental breakfast, cocktails, and hors d'oeuvres are served. Rooms for nonsmokers and travelers with disabilities are available.

Dining/Entertainment: Champions is the city's best-known sports bar. There are two restaurants, a sushi bar, and a lounge that offers live entertainment 5 nights a week.

Services: Concierge, 24-hour room service, valet laundry, valet parking.

Facilities: Heated indoor pool; well-equipped health club with exercise room, whirlpools, and saunas; full-service business center with personal computers; conference rooms with Internet access; car-rental desk; tour desk.

Boston Park Plaza Hotel. 64 Arlington St., Boston, MA 02116. ☎ **800/225-2008** or 617/426-2000. Fax 617/426-1708. 960 rms (some with shower only), 10 suites. A/C TV TEL. $175–$265 double; $375–$2,000 suite. Extra person $20. Senior discounts and weekend and family packages available. Children under 18 stay free in parents' room. AE, CB, DC, DISC, MC, V. Valet parking $20; self-parking $14. MBTA: Green Line to Arlington.

Built as the great Statler Hilton in 1927, this hotel is proud of its history and equally proud of its renovations. The lovely old features—such as the spacious lobby with its crystal chandelier, gilt trim, and red-carpeted corridors—have been retained, and the rooms have been updated with modern comforts such as pay-per-view movies. Room size and decor vary greatly (some rooms are quite small). The location is central—just a block from Boston Common and the Public Garden, and about the same distance from the Theater District. The 15-story hotel has good facilities for business travelers and convention-goers, and child-friendly features such as special programs and a game room make it an excellent choice for families, too. Rooms for nonsmokers are available.

Dining/Entertainment: On the ground floor are four restaurants—Café Rouge, Boston's famous Legal Sea Foods and its offspring, Legal C Bar, and Red Herring—and a lounge, the cozy Captains Bar. See section 4 of this chapter for full details on Legal's.

Services: Concierge, 24-hour room service, dry cleaning/laundry, baby-sitting, express checkout, valet parking. The hotel lobby is a little commercial hub, with a travel agency, foreign currency exchange, Amtrak and airline ticket offices, and a pharmacy.

Facilities: Health club with heated pool, kids' video/game room, business center, conference rooms, beauty salon.

✪ The Eliot Hotel. 370 Commonwealth Ave. (at Mass. Ave.), Boston, MA 02215. ☎ **800/44-ELIOT** or 617/267-1607. Fax 617/536-9114. E-mail HotelEliot@aol.com. 91 suites. A/C MINIBAR TV TEL. $225–$285 1-bedroom suite; $375–$450 2-bedroom suite. Extra person $20. Children under 12 stay free in parents' room. AE, DC, MC, V. Valet parking $18. MBTA: Green Line, B, C, or D train to Hynes/ICA.

This exquisite choice combines the flavor of Yankee Boston with European-style service and amenities. Built in 1925, the nine-story hotel underwent a complete renovation from 1990 to 1994. The spacious suites are furnished with traditional English-style chintz fabrics, botanical prints, and antique furnishings. French doors separate the living- and bedrooms, and modern conveniences such as Italian marble baths, terry-cloth bathrobes, two dual-line telephones with data ports, a personal fax machine, a VCR, and two TVs are standard. Many suites also have a pantry with a microwave.

The hotel is convenient to Boston University and MIT (across the river), and the location on tree-lined Commonwealth Avenue makes for a pleasant contrast with the urban bustle of Newbury Street, a block away. Rooms for nonsmokers and travelers with disabilities are available.

Dining/Entertainment: Breakfast is served in the hotel's new restaurant, Clio, which offers contemporary French/American cuisine at dinner.

Services: Concierge, room service until midnight, dry cleaning/laundry, newspaper delivery, twice-daily maid service, baby-sitting, secretarial services, express checkout, valet parking.

Facilities: Conference rooms, safe-deposit boxes. A small but well-equipped health club is scheduled to open in late 1997.

The Westin, Copley Place. 10 Huntington Ave., Boston, MA 02116. ☎ **800/WESTIN-1** or 617/262-9600. Fax 617/424-7483. 800 rms, 45 suites. A/C MINIBAR TV TEL. $189–$305 double; $350–$1,500 suite. Extra person $25; $20 Guest Office; $30 junior suites and Executive Club Level. Weekend packages available. AE, CB, DC, DISC, JCB, MC, V. Valet parking $23. MBTA: Green Line to Copley or Orange Line to Back Bay.

Looming 36 stories in the air above Copley Square, the Westin is popular with convention-goers, sightseers, and dedicated shoppers. Determined consumers don't even have to step outside—the hotel is linked by sky bridges to Copley Place and the Prudential Center complex. Others may want to start exploring at Copley Square, across the street from the pedestrian entrance. The entrance is dominated by two-story-high twin waterfalls on either side of escalators that run to the Grand Lobby, where you'll find a multilingual staff that emphasizes quick check-in.

Upstairs, you might not notice the comfortable oak and mahogany furniture in the spacious guest rooms (at least at first), because you'll be captivated by the magnificent view. If you need to get down to business, guest rooms all have data ports, and the conference facilities are Internet accessible. Executive Club Level guests have private check-in and a private lounge where a complimentary continental breakfast and hors d'oeuvres are served. Forty guest rooms are designed for travelers with disabilities; they adjoin standard rooms to accommodate guests traveling with those with disabilities. All units have pay-per-view movies.

Dining/Entertainment: The Palm, the newest branch of the famous New York–based chain, serves lunch and dinner—steak, chops, and jumbo lobsters. Turner Fisheries features live jazz Tuesday through Saturday after 8pm. Ten Huntington is a casual bar serving light meals. The Lobby Lounge serves morning coffee and pastries.

Services: Concierge, 24-hour room service, valet service, in-room safes.

Facilities: Indoor pool, health club with Nautilus equipment, saunas, business center with computer rentals and secretarial services, conference rooms.

MODERATE

Chandler Inn. 26 Chandler St. (at Berkeley St.), Boston, MA 02116. ☎ **800/842-3450** or 617/482-3450. Fax 617/542-3428. 56 rms. A/C TV TEL. May–June $89 double; July–Oct $99 double weekdays, $109 double weekends; Nov–Apr $74 double. Children under 12 stay free in parents' room. Rates include continental breakfast. AE, CB, DC, DISC, MC, V. Parking available in nearby garages. MBTA: Orange Line to Back Bay.

This is a practical choice for bargain hunters who don't care about a tony address and a lot of extras. The Chandler Inn is technically in the South End, near the Boston Center for the Arts, but it's so convenient to the Back Bay and such a good deal that you won't mind the slightly lower-budget address. The guest rooms were recently redecorated, recarpeted, and, most importantly, air-conditioned. They're still nothing fancy, but if your needs are basic, you'll be fine. The staff is friendly and helpful.

Copley Square Hotel. 47 Huntington Ave., Boston, MA 02116. ☎ **800/225-7062** or 617/536-9000. Fax 617/236-0351. 143 rms, 12 suites. A/C TV TEL. $165–$195 double; $325 suite. Children under 18 stay free in parents' room. Packages and senior discounts available. AE, DISC, JCB, MC, V. Parking $18 (in adjacent garage). MBTA: Green Line to Copley or Orange Line to Back Bay.

Built in 1891 and located in the shadow of the megahotels near Copley Place and the Prudential Center is the seven-story Copley Square Hotel. Its relatively small size allows for attentive service, and if you're looking for a central location but don't need to run a corporate takeover out of your room, it's quite a good deal. Each attractively decorated room has a queen-sized or king-sized bed or two double beds, and a unique layout. All rooms are equipped with hair dryers, coffeemakers, safes, and phones with modem hookups and guest voice mail. Rooms for nonsmokers are available, and there is a 24-hour currency exchange in the lobby. Guests are treated to afternoon tea in the lobby and have access to the health club at the nearby Westin.

This hotel was one of the first in the country to institute an environmental policy, which includes energy and water conservation and waste reduction and recycling. Environmentally sound products are supplied in the guest rooms and are used throughout the hotel.

There are three dining options in the hotel: Speeder & Earl's serves breakfast; and Café Budapest and the Original Sports Saloon serve lunch and dinner.

The MidTown Hotel. 220 Huntington Ave., Boston, MA 02115. ☎ **800/343-1177** or 617/262-1000. Fax 617/262-8739. 159 rms. A/C TV TEL. $109–$169 double. Extra person $15. Children under 18 stay free in parents' room. 10% AARP discount; government employees' discount subject to availability. AE, DC, DISC, MC, V. Free parking. MBTA: Green Line, E train to Prudential.

Even without free parking, this two-story hotel would be a good deal. It's on a busy street within easy walking distance of Symphony Hall, the Museum of Fine Arts, and the Back Bay attractions. The good-sized rooms are bright and attractively outfitted with contemporary furnishings, and some have connecting bedrooms for families. For business travelers, the phones have data ports, and photocopying and fax services are available at the front desk. The heated outdoor pool is open from Memorial Day through Labor Day. Tables of Content, an American cafe, is open from 7am to 10pm.

✪ Newbury Guest House. 261 Newbury St. (between Fairfield and Gloucester sts.), Boston, MA 02116. ☎ **617/437-7666.** Fax 617/262-4243. 32 rms. A/C TV TEL. $105–$140 double; winter $95–$125 double. Rates may be higher during special events. Extra person $10. Rates include continental breakfast. AE, CB, DC, DISC, MC, V. Parking $10 (reservation required). Minimum 2 nights on weekends. MBTA: Green Line to Copley or B, C, or D train to Hynes/ICA.

After just a little shopping in the Back Bay, you'll appreciate what a find this cozy inn is: a bargain on Newbury Street. Two brick town houses built in the 1880s have been combined into one refined guest house with comfortable furnishings, a pleasant staff, nifty architectural details, and—*such* a deal—a buffet breakfast served in the ground-level dining room, which adjoins a brick patio. The B&B operates near capacity all year, drawing business travelers during the week and sightseers on weekends. Rooms aren't huge, but they are nicely appointed, and at these prices in this location, my only caveat is: Reserve early.

Tremont House. 275 Tremont St., Boston, MA 02116. ☎ **800/331-9998** or 617/426-1400. Fax 617/482-6730. 281 rms, 34 suites. A/C TV TEL. $139–$199 double; $170–$270 suite. Children under 16 stay free in parents' room. Extra person $10. Weekend packages and 10% AAA discount available. AE, CB, DC, DISC, MC, V. Valet parking $20. MBTA: Green Line to Boylston or Orange Line to New England Medical Center.

The Tremont House is as close to Boston's theaters as you can be without actually attending a show, and convenient to downtown and the Back Bay. The neighborhood isn't the greatest, but it is improving, and the combination of location and a recently completed $10 million renovation makes this hotel an excellent value.

The 15-story brick building captures the style that prevailed when the hotel was built in 1924. The original gold-leaf decorations and crafted ceilings in the huge lobby and ballrooms have been restored and the original marble walls and columns refurbished. The hotel is geared to travelers on a modest budget, but that's not to say there are no services—conference rooms, secretarial services, and valet laundry are available. Rooms have modern furnishings, pay-per-view movies, coffeemakers, and hair dryers. Three top-of-the-line units feature kitchenettes with a range, sink, and refrigerator (great for families who want to eat in). Four floors are reserved for nonsmokers, and there are 14 rooms equipped for travelers with disabilities.

KENMORE SQUARE & BEYOND TO BROOKLINE

EXPENSIVE

Doubletree Guest Suites. 400 Soldiers Field Rd., Boston, MA 02134. ☎ **800/222-TREE** or 617/783-0090. Fax 617/783-0897. 310 rms. A/C MINIBAR TV TEL. $169–$249 double. Extra person $20. Children 18 and under stay free in parents' room. Weekend packages from $109 per night. AAA discount available. AE, CB, DC, DISC, JCB, MC, V. Parking $14 Sun–Thurs, $7 Fri–Sat.

This hotel is one of the best deals in town—every unit is a two-room suite with a living room, bedroom, and bath. Business travelers can entertain in their rooms, and families can spread out, making this a good choice for both. Overlooking the Charles River adjacent to the Allston/Cambridge exit of the Massachusetts Turnpike, the hotel is convenient to the bike and jogging path that runs along the river, but be aware that it isn't in an actual neighborhood.

The suites, which were renovated in 1996, surround a 15-story atrium and can be reached via glass elevators. Rooms are large and attractively furnished, and most bedrooms have king-sized beds and a writing desk. Living rooms feature full-sized sofa beds, a dining table, and a good-sized refrigerator. Each suite has a coffeemaker, two TVs with pay-per-view movies, and three telephones (one in the bathroom). There are suites for travelers with disabilities on each floor.

Dining/Entertainment: Scullers Grille and Scullers Lounge serve meals from 6:30am to 11pm. Scullers Jazz Club has two nightly shows.

Services: Concierge, room service until 10pm, dry cleaning/laundry, newspaper delivery, in-room massage, twice-daily maid service, baby-sitting, secretarial services, express checkout, complimentary van service to and from Boston and Cambridge.

Facilities: Heated indoor pool, exercise room, whirlpool, sauna, game room, conference rooms, laundry room.

MODERATE

Many options in this price range and area are chain hotels, including the **Holiday Inn Boston Brookline,** 1200 Beacon St., Brookline, MA 02146 (☎ **800/ HOLIDAY** or 617/277-1200), and the **Howard Johnson Hotel—Kenmore,** 575 Commonwealth Ave., Boston, MA 02215 (☎ **800/654-2000** or 617/ 267-3100), both of which offer the reliable but unremarkable accommodations and service that each chain is known for.

INEXPENSIVE

Anthony's Town House. 1085 Beacon St., Brookline, MA 02146. ☎ **617/566-3972.** 12 rms (none with private bath). A/C TV. $45–$78 double, depending on season. Extra person $10.

Weekly rates available. No credit cards. Free on-site parking. MBTA: Green Line, C train to Hawes St. (2 stops past Kenmore).

Located 1 mile from Kenmore Square, about 10 minutes from downtown by subway, and two blocks from a busy commercial strip, this turn-of-the-century restored four-story brownstone town house is listed on the National Register of Historic Places. Each floor has three rooms and a shared bath with enclosed shower. Rooms are decorated with Queen Anne– and Victorian-style furnishings, and the large front rooms have bay windows with comfortable lounge chairs.

Longwood Inn. 123 Longwood Ave., Brookline, MA 02146. ☎ **617/566-8615.** Fax 617/738-1070. 22 rms (17 with bath). A/C TEL. Apr–Nov $69–$79 double; Dec–Mar $59–$69 double. 1-bedroom apt (sleeps 4 plus) $89 summer, $79 winter. Weekly rates available. No credit cards. Free parking. MBTA: Green Line, D train to Longwood Ave.

Located in a residential area near the Boston-Brookline border (three blocks from Boston), this three-story Victorian guest house offers comfortable accommodations at modest rates. Guests have the use of a fully equipped kitchen, coin-operated washer and dryer, common dining room, and TV lounge. Tennis courts, a running track, and a children's playground at the school next door are open to the public. Public transportation is easily accessible, and the Longwood Medical Area and busy Coolidge Corner neighborhood are close by.

CAMBRIDGE

Just about everything that's available in Boston is available in Cambridge, usually in a somewhat quieter setting. If your trip involves more than just visiting Boston, Cambridge is a good base for day trips; when you get back to the hotel, you'll still have plenty to do.

VERY EXPENSIVE

✪ **The Charles Hotel.** 1 Bennett St., Cambridge, MA 02138. ☎ **800/882-1818** outside Mass., or 617/864-1200. Fax 617/864-5715. 252 rms, 45 suites. A/C MINIBAR TV TEL. $239–$315 double; $389–$2,000 suite. Children under 18 stay free in parents' room. Weekend and spa packages available. AE, CB, DC, DISC, JCB, MC, V. Valet parking $18, self-parking $16. MBTA: Red Line to Harvard.

The Charles, a nine-story brick hotel a block from Harvard Square, is *the* place to stay in Cambridge. It became an instant classic from the day it opened in 1985. Much of its fame derives from its excellent restaurants, jazz bar, and day spa, and the service is, if anything, equally exalted.

Antique blue-and-white New England quilts, handcrafted between 1865 and 1885, hang in the lobby's oak staircase and at the entrance to each floor. In the guest rooms, the style is contemporary country, with custom-designed adaptations of Early American Shaker furniture and down quilts. Bathrooms are equipped with telephones, TVs, hair dryers, and scales. All rooms have large windows that open, incredibly comfortable beds, three phones, data ports, pay-per-view movies, and state-of-the-art Bose Wave radios. Six floors are reserved for nonsmokers; 13 rooms are accessible for travelers with disabilities.

Dining/Entertainment: Rialto, one of the best restaurants in greater Boston, serves Mediterranean cuisine by award-winning chef Jody Adams. Another excellent restaurant, Henrietta's Table, offers New England country cooking. The Regattabar features live jazz Tuesday through Saturday nights.

Services: Concierge, 24-hour room service, dry cleaning/laundry, newspaper delivery, in-room massage, twice-daily maid service, video rentals, baby-sitting, secretarial services, express checkout, valet parking. And it wouldn't be Cambridge if your

Cambridge Accommodations & Dining

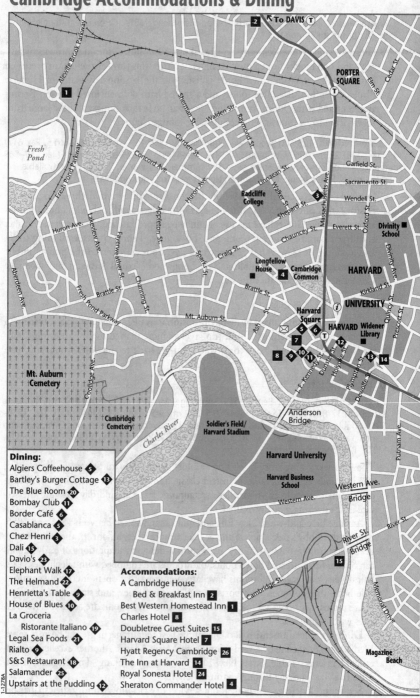

Dining:
Algiers Coffeehouse 5
Bartley's Burger Cottage 13
The Blue Room 20
Bombay Club 11
Border Café 6
Casablanca 5
Chez Henri 3
Dali 15
Davio's 23
Elephant Walk 17
The Helmand 22
Henrietta's Table 9
House of Blues 10
La Groceria
   Ristorante Italiano 19
Legal Sea Foods 21
Rialto 9
S&S Restaurant 18
Salamander 25
Upstairs at the Pudding 12

Accommodations:
A Cambridge House
   Bed & Breakfast Inn 2
Best Western Homestead Inn 1
Charles Hotel 8
Doubletree Guest Suites 15
Harvard Square Hotel 7
Hyatt Regency Cambridge 26
The Inn at Harvard 14
Royal Sonesta Hotel 24
Sheraton Commander Hotel 4

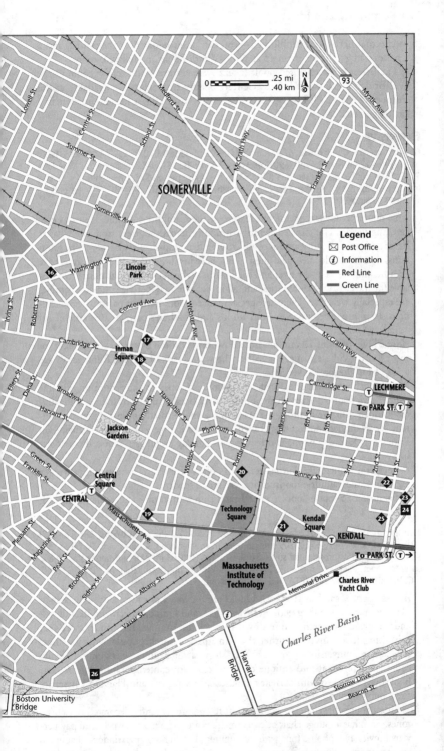

intellectual needs went unfulfilled—you can order books over the phone, and a Charles staffer will pick them up at WordsWorth Books and bill your room.

Facilities: Glass-enclosed pool, Jacuzzi, sun terrace, and exercise room at the WellBridge Health and Fitness Center. Beauty treatments are available at the European-style Le Pli Day Spa. Conference rooms; facilities for teleconferencing; car-rental desk.

EXPENSIVE

Hyatt Regency Cambridge. 575 Memorial Dr., Cambridge, MA 02139. ☎ **800/233-1234** or 617/492-1234. Fax 617/491-6906. 469 rms. A/C TV TEL. $179–$274 double on weekdays, $119–$214 double on weekends. $400–$575 suites. Extra person $25. Children under 18 stay free in parents' room. Weekend packages available. AE, DC, DISC, JCB, MC, V. Valet parking $17; self-parking $16.

This dramatic hotel, a prominent feature of the Cambridge skyline, is just as eye-catching inside. The terraced redbrick structure across the street from the Charles River encloses a 16-story atrium complete with diamond-shaped glass elevators, fountains, trees, and balconies. The guest rooms have just been renovated, and some have breathtaking views of the river and the Boston skyline. Twenty-four units are accessible for travelers with disabilities, and all rooms offer pay-per-view movies. Families are especially welcome. There are special reduced room rates for parents whose children sleep in a different room, and adult's and children's bicycles are available for rental.

The hotel is about 10 minutes from downtown Boston by car and convenient for those visiting colleges, since it's halfway between Harvard and MIT and across the bridge from Boston University.

Dining/Entertainment: Jonah's Seafood Café, open to the atrium on one side and to a view of the river on the other, serves breakfast, lunch, dinner, and Sunday brunch. On the rooftop, the revolving, glass-enclosed Spinnaker Italia restaurant serves dinner and Sunday brunch, and has a lounge where there's dancing on Friday and Saturday nights and live jazz on Sunday evenings. There's also a sports bar.

Services: Concierge, shuttle service to points of interest, baby-sitting, currency exchange, valet laundry, room service, car-rental service.

Facilities: 75-foot indoor lap pool, health club with steam room, sauna, and whirlpool.

The Inn at Harvard. 1201 Mass. Ave., Cambridge, MA 02138. ☎ **800/458-5886** or 617/491-2222. Fax 617/491-6520. 109 rms (some with shower only), 4 suites. A/C TV TEL. $165–$249 double; $450 presidential suite. Extra person $10. Children 18 and under stay free in parents' room. Packages and senior, AAA, and AARP discounts available. AE, CB, DC, DISC, MC, V. Valet parking $20. MBTA: Red Line to Harvard.

At first glance, the Inn at Harvard looks almost like a dormitory. It's adjacent to Harvard Yard at the intersection of Mass. Ave. and Quincy Street, and its redbrick and Georgian-style architecture would fit nicely on campus. But inside, there's no mistaking it for anything other than an upscale hotel, popular with business travelers and university visitors. The four-story, skylit atrium opens from the "living room," where you'll find antique tables mixed with contemporary furniture, and bookshelves stocked with current periodicals, newspapers, and Harvard University Press publications.

Guest rooms have cherry-wood furniture and are elegantly decorated in neutral tones. Each has a lounge chair or two armchairs around a table, a work area, pay-per-view movies, two phones (one with a computer modem hookup), windows that open, and an original painting from the Fogg Art Museum. Some have dormer windows and window seats. Two floors are set aside for nonsmokers; six rooms are wheelchair-accessible.

Dining/Entertainment: The small, upscale Atrium Dining Room serves seasonal New England fare at breakfast, lunch, dinner, and afternoon tea.

Services: Dry cleaning/laundry, newspaper delivery, twice-daily maid service, secretarial services, express checkout, valet parking.

Facilities: Conference rooms, safe-deposit boxes, backgammon and chess tables in the atrium library.

Royal Sonesta Hotel. 5 Cambridge Pkwy., Cambridge, MA 02142. ☎ **800/SONESTA** or 617/491-3600. Fax 617/661-5956. 400 rms, 28 suites. A/C MINIBAR TV TEL. $210–$270 double; $335–$750 suite. Children under 18 stay free in parents' room. AE, CB, DC, DISC, JCB, MC, V. Parking $15. MBTA: Green Line to Lechmere; 10-min. walk.

This hotel is in a curious location: It's close to only a few things, but it's convenient to everything. Across the street is the CambridgeSide Galleria mall, and the Boston Museum of Science is around the corner on the bridge to Boston (which is closer than Harvard Square). In the other direction, MIT is a 10-minute walk. Original contemporary artwork (including works by Andy Warhol and Frank Stella) is displayed throughout the public spaces and spacious guest rooms. Most rooms have a lovely view of the Charles River or the city. Everything is custom designed, with decorative furnishings, living-room and bedroom combinations, and luxurious bathrooms. A great new perk: cellular phone service linked to your guest-room phone. The hotel has seasonal promotions, such as free ice cream during the summer, with special rates, giveaways for children, and events for adults. Rooms for nonsmokers and travelers with disabilities are available.

Dining/Entertainment: Davio's restaurant serves breakfast, lunch, and dinner and has an outdoor patio overlooking the Charles River that's great for warm-weather dining. The casual Gallery Café also has a patio.

Services: Room service (available Sunday to Thursday from 6am to 1am, Friday and Saturday from 6am to 2am), baby-sitting, secretarial services, courtesy van service to Boston and Cambridge.

Facilities: Heated indoor/outdoor pool with retractable roof; well-equipped health club; conference rooms.

Sheraton Commander Hotel. 16 Garden St., Cambridge, MA 02138. ☎ **800/325-3535** or 617/547-4800. Fax 617/868-8322. 175 rms, 24 suites. A/C TV TEL. $165–$259 double; $330–$550 suite. Extra person $20. Children under 18 stay free in parents' room. AE, DC, DISC, JCB, MC, V. Free parking. MBTA: Red Line to Harvard.

In the heart of the historic district of Cambridge, this six-story hotel opened in 1927. It's exactly what you'd expect of a traditional hostelry within sight of the Harvard campus. The colonial-style decor begins in the elegant lobby and extends to the guest rooms, which aren't huge but are attractively furnished. Rooms have two phones with data ports, coffeemakers, hair dryers, pay-per-view movies, irons and ironing boards, and night lights. The Club Level offers additional amenities, including in-room fax machines, free local phone calls, and a private lounge where complimentary continental breakfast and afternoon hors d'oeuvres are served on weekdays. Suites have two TVs, and some have wet bars, refrigerators, and whirlpools. Four floors are reserved for nonsmokers.

Dining/Entertainment: The restaurant serves breakfast, lunch, dinner, and Sunday brunch. The cafe serves lighter fare throughout the afternoon and evening.

Services: Concierge, room service until 11pm, dry cleaning/laundry, newspaper delivery, baby-sitting, express checkout, valet parking.

Facilities: Small fitness center, sundeck, conference rooms, laundry room.

MODERATE

Best Western Homestead Inn. 220 Alewife Brook Pkwy., Cambridge, MA 02138. ☎ **800/ 528-1234** or 617/491-8000. Fax 617/491-4932. 69 rms. A/C TV TEL. Mid-Mar to Oct $109– $154 double; Nov to mid-Mar $79–$119 double. Extra person $10. Rates include continental breakfast and may be higher during special events. Children under 12 stay free in parents' room. AE, CB, DC, DISC, JCB, MC, V. Free parking. MBTA: Red Line to Alewife, then a 10-min. walk.

The gritty commercial neighborhood is nothing to write home about, but this four-story motel is comfortable and convenient if you have a car. It's about a 15-minute drive or a 30-minute ride on the "T" to Boston. Guest rooms are spacious, with contemporary or reproduction colonial furnishings, and at least one floor up from the busy street. There's an indoor pool with a Jacuzzi, and a 2^1/$_2$-mile jogging trail around Fresh Pond is across the street. Laundry service (weekdays only) and rental-car pickup and drop-off are available. There's a restaurant next door, and a shopping center with a 10-screen movie theater nearby.

A Cambridge House Bed & Breakfast Inn. 2218 Mass. Ave., Cambridge, MA 02140. ☎ **800/232-9989** or 617/491-6300; 800/96-2079 in the U.K. Fax 617/868-2848. 16 rms (13 with bath; some with shower only). A/C TV TEL. $109–$225 double. Extra person $35. Rates include breakfast. AE, DISC, MC, V. Free parking. MBTA: Red Line to Porter.

A Cambridge House is a beautifully restored 1892 Victorian home listed in the National Register of Historic Places. The three-story building is on a busy stretch of Cambridge's main drag (Mass. Ave.), set back from the sidewalk by a lawn. Rooms vary in size; all are warmly decorated with Waverly-Schumacher fabrics and period antiques. Most have fireplaces and four-poster canopy beds with down comforters. Complimentary beverages and fresh pastries are served by the fireplace in the library or parlor, and a generous buffet breakfast is offered every morning. No smoking.

Harvard Square Hotel. 110 Mt. Auburn St., Cambridge, MA 02138. ☎ **800/458-5886** or 617/864-5200. Fax 617/864-2409. 73 rms. A/C TV TEL. $125–$180 double. Children 16 and under stay free in parents' room. Corporate, AAA, and AARP rates available. AE, DC, DISC, JCB, MC, V. Parking $16. MBTA: Red Line to Harvard.

Smack in the middle of Harvard Square, this hotel is a favorite with visiting parents and budget-conscious business travelers in search of a comfortable, unpretentious atmosphere. In early 1996, the six-story brick hotel was completely refurbished and renamed (it used to be the Harvard Manor House), and the guest rooms were redecorated in contemporary style. All have data ports, hair dryers, irons, and ironing boards, and some overlook Harvard Square. Fax and copy services and complimentary newspapers (weekdays only) are available at the front desk, and there's dry cleaning and laundry service. Guests have dining privileges at the Inn at Harvard and the Harvard Faculty Club.

4 Dining

ON THE WATERFRONT
VERY EXPENSIVE

Rowes Wharf Restaurant. In the Boston Harbor Hotel, 70 Rowes Wharf (entrance on Atlantic Ave.). ☎ **617/439-3995.** Reservations recommended. Main courses $22–$32. AE, DC, DISC, MC, V. Mon–Sat 6:30–11am; Sun 7–10am; Mon–Sat 11:30am–2:30pm, Sun 10:30am–2pm; Mon–Sat 5:30–11pm, Sun 5:30–10pm. MBTA: Blue Line to Aquarium or Red Line to South Station. REGIONAL AMERICAN.

The wood-paneled Rowes Wharf Restaurant feels almost like a private club. The richly upholstered chairs encourage you to relax, and the service puts you at ease and anticipates your every desire. And that's not even mentioning the cuisine, which is among the best in the city.

The enormous picture windows afford a breathtaking harbor view, and the tables are far enough apart so that you won't hear your neighbors admiring it. You might hear them exclaiming over the food, though. Chef Daniel Bruce uses local ingredients when possible, prepared in deceptively simple ways that accent natural flavors. The signature appetizer is Maine lobster meat seasoned and formed into a sausage, then grilled, sliced, and served in a light cream sauce with lobster-claw meat and lemon pasta. Or try polenta topped with flavorful wild mushrooms. Entrees range from pan-roasted Nova Scotia salmon to pecan-smoked filet mignon grilled and served with whiskey sauce. Desserts vary with the inspiration of the chef—there's usually an excellent sorbet sampler.

EXPENSIVE

Ron's Grill & Cue. 256 Commercial St. ☎ **617/227-4454.** Reservations recommended. Main courses $8.95–$19.95. AE, CB, DC, DISC, MC, V. Sun–Wed 5–10pm (bar menu until midnight), Thurs–Sat 5–11pm (bar menu until 1am); Sun 11:30am–2am (brunch). MBTA: Blue Line to Aquarium. CONTEMPORARY AMERICAN.

From the street, this appears to be a trendy bar and upscale pool hall—but the food is much better than the pub grub you might expect. Chef Enrique Paniagua adds a Southwestern accent to many dishes, from the spices on the fries to the roasted corn and avocado salsa on the grilled salmon. Everything is good here, and there's lots of it, starting with the great bread basket and excellent soups. The extensive menu includes casual fare such as pizza, pasta, and sandwiches, as well as sturdy cuts of meat and fish—say, seared tuna with sesame seeds and mango-and-citrus relish, or grilled London broil with garlic mashed potatoes. The setting, like the food, is familiar yet daring, softly lit, with purple and black enamel accents, a tropical fish tank over the bar, and French doors that open to the street from the front dining room. The second floor is an upscale pool parlor (that's the "Cue" in the name), featuring a half-dozen imported slate tables with purple felt tops that go for as much as $18 an hour.

MODERATE

Billy Tse Restaurant. 240 Commercial St. ☎ **617/227-9990.** Reservations recommended at dinner on weekends. Main courses $5–$19.95. AE, DC, DISC, MC, V. Mon–Thurs 11:30am–11:30pm, Fri–Sat 11:30am–midnight, Sun 11:30am–11pm. MBTA: Blue Line to Aquarium, or Green or Orange Line to Haymarket. CHINESE/PAN-ASIAN.

Billy Tse's is a casual, affordable spot. Excellent renditions of the usual Chinese dishes are available, and the kitchen has its own delightful way with seafood. The "pan-Asian" selections are just as enjoyable. Start with one of the wonderful soups, sinfully good crab rangoon, or fried calamari with garlic and pepper. Move on to main dishes that range from fried rice (seven kinds) to scallops with garlic sauce to the house special fried noodles, topped with shrimp, calamari, and scallops in a scrumptious sauce. And be sure to ask about the daily specials. Lunch specials, served until 4pm, include vegetable fried rice or vegetable lo mein.

Daily Catch. 261 Northern Ave. ☎ **617/338-3093.** Reservations accepted only for parties of 8 or more. Main courses $10–$18. AE. Sun–Thurs noon–10:30pm, Fri–Sat noon–11pm. MBTA: Red Line to South Station. SOUTHERN ITALIAN/SEAFOOD.

Make sure your fellow travelers accompany you to this Fish Pier institution, because you're going to emanate garlic for at least a day and you might as well have someone to share it with. This is a basic storefront, where the staff sometimes seems overwhelmed and it can take forever to get a table, but the food is terrific. There's

Boston Dining

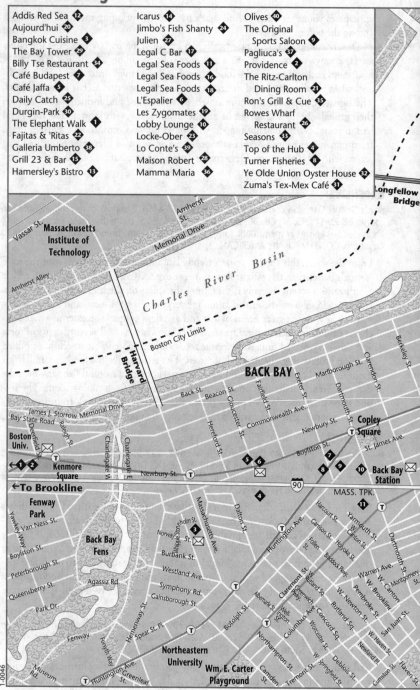

Addis Red Sea **12**
Aujourd'hui **20**
Bangkok Cuisine **3**
The Bay Tower **29**
Billy Tse Restaurant **34**
Café Budapest **7**
Café Jaffa **5**
Daily Catch **25**
Durgin-Park **30**
The Elephant Walk **1**
Fajitas & 'Ritas **22**
Galleria Umberto **38**
Grill 23 & Bar **15**
Hamersley's Bistro **13**

Icarus **14**
Jimbo's Fish Shanty **24**
Julien **27**
Legal C Bar **17**
Legal Sea Foods **11**
Legal Sea Foods **16**
Legal Sea Foods **18**
L'Espalier **6**
Les Zygomates **19**
Lobby Lounge **10**
Locke-Ober **23**
Lo Conte's **39**
Maison Robert **28**
Mamma Maria **36**

Olives **40**
The Original
   Sports Saloon **9**
Pagliuca's **37**
Providence **2**
The Ritz-Carlton
   Dining Room **21**
Ron's Grill & Cue **35**
Rowes Wharf
   Restaurant **26**
Seasons **33**
Top of the Hub **4**
Turner Fisheries **8**
Ye Olde Union Oyster House **32**
Zuma's Tex-Mex Café **31**

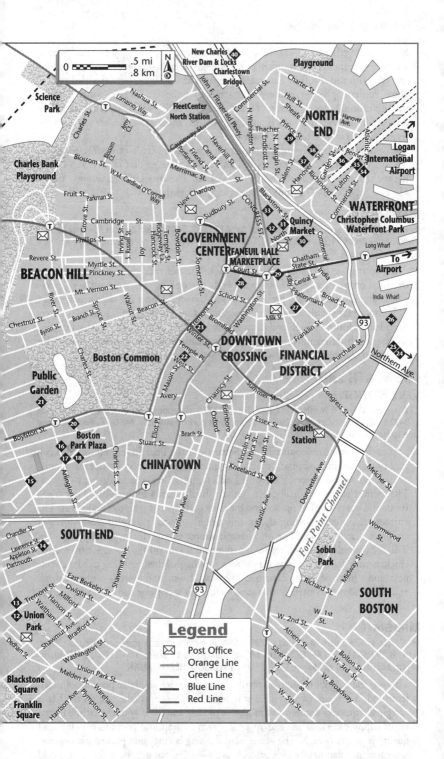

Sicilian-style calamari (squid stuffed with bread crumbs, raisins, pine nuts, parsley, and tons of garlic), freshly shucked clams, mussels in garlic-flavored sauce, and broiled and fried fish and shellfish. Calamari is prepared at least eight ways; the fried version is an excellent appetizer, and even the standard garlic-and-oil pasta sauce contains morsels of squid. And if you really want to try something different, order the squid-ink pasta puttanesca. All food is prepared to order, and some dishes are served in the frying pans in which they were cooked.

The other two branches of this minichain don't accept credit cards or reservations. The original Daily Catch, in the North End at 323 Hanover St. (☎ **617/523-8567**), keeps the same hours as the Fish Pier location. The Brookline restaurant, at 441 Harvard St. (☎ **617/734-5696**), opens at 5pm nightly.

INEXPENSIVE

Jimbo's Fish Shanty. 245 Northern Ave. ☎ **617/542-5600.** Main courses $6–$14. AE, DC, MC, V. Mon–Thurs 11:30am–9:30pm, Fri–Sat 11:30am–10pm, Sun noon–8pm. MBTA: Red Line to South Station. SEAFOOD.

Bring your sense of humor to this jam-packed restaurant, where model trains run overhead on tracks suspended from the fairly low ceiling, there are road signs everywhere, and the waitress will probably call you "honey." Under the same management as Jimmy's Harborside across the street, Jimbo's serves good, fresh seafood, skewers threaded with fish or beef, and pasta dishes (at dinner only) with varied sauces, including a lobster cream version. The truly decadent desserts generally involve ice cream and chocolate.

THE NORTH END
VERY EXPENSIVE

✪ **Mamma Maria.** 3 North Sq. ☎ **617/523-0077.** Reservations recommended. Main courses $18–$28. AE, DC, DISC, MC, V. Daily 5–10pm. Valet parking available. MBTA: Green or Orange Line to Haymarket. NORTHERN ITALIAN.

In a town house overlooking North Square and the Paul Revere House, this is a traditional-looking restaurant that offers innovative cuisine and a level of sophistication far removed from the North End's familiar "hey-whaddaya-want" service. The menu changes seasonally, but you can usually start with excellent *pasta fagioli* (bean-and-pasta soup) or risotto, and the daily pasta special is always a good bet. The entrees are unlike anything else in this neighborhood, except in size—portions are more than generous. The osso buco is almost enough for two, but you'll want it all for yourself when you realize it's so tender it falls off the bone. Or try roasted chicken with lightly steamed green beans, garlic poached to bring out its sweetness, and a hunk of potato casserole. The pasta, bread, and desserts are homemade, and the shadowy, whitewashed rooms make this a popular spot for popping the question.

MODERATE

Lo Conte's. 116 Salem St. ☎ **617/720-3550.** Reservations recommended at dinner. Main courses $9.95–$16.95. AE, DC, DISC, MC, V. Sun–Thurs 11:30am–10pm, Fri–Sat 11:30am–11pm. MBTA: Green or Orange Line to Haymarket. SOUTHERN ITALIAN.

This is a real neighborhood place, with chummy service and large portions of excellent food. There are two glorified-storefront dining rooms (the one on the left is marginally quieter) decorated with photos of Italy and filled with the satisfied chatter of happy diners. Salads and appetizers aren't cheap, but portions are large and quality is generally high. The house salad dressing is tangy and packed with cheese, and eggplant rolatini, when it's available as a special, is out of this world, but the cold antipasto is nothing to write home about (unless you don't like your relatives). The house special chicken, broccoli, and ziti is the best in town, and the daily specials actually taste as good as they sound. If seafood is involved, go for it.

Pagliuca's. 14 Parmenter St. ☎ **617/367-1504.** Reservations not accepted. Main courses $12–$22. AE, MC, V. Sun–Thurs 11am–10:30pm, Fri–Sat 11am–11pm. MBTA: Green or Orange Line to Haymarket. SOUTHERN ITALIAN.

This sparsely decorated little place doles out southern Italian cooking the way Americans like it—great pastas with lots of garlicky tomato sauce and big chunks of Italian bread to mop it up, plus such specialties as cioppino, veal chops, and chicken with peppers, onions, and potatoes. The lunch special, good until 4pm, is one of the best in town—everything on the menu is half-price.

INEXPENSIVE

Galleria Umberto. 289 Hanover St. ☎ **617/227-5709.** All items $2.50 or less. No credit cards. Mon–Sat 11am–2pm. MBTA: Green or Orange Line to Haymarket. ITALIAN.

The long, fast-moving line of businesspeople and tourists tips you off to the fact that this cafeteria-style spot is a real bargain. And the food is good, too. You can fill up on a couple of slices of pizza, but if you're feeling adventurous, try the *arancini* (a rice ball filled with gravy, ground beef, peas, and cheese). The calzones—ham and cheese, spinach, spinach and cheese, or spinach and sausage—are also tasty. Study the cases while you wait and be ready to order at once when you reach the head of the line. Have a quick lunch and get on with your sightseeing.

FANEUIL HALL/GOVERNMENT CENTER/FINANCIAL DISTRICT
VERY EXPENSIVE

The Bay Tower. 60 State St. ☎ **617/723-1666.** Reservations recommended. Jacket required for men in dining room. Main courses $18–$35. AE, CB, DC, MC, V. Mon–Thurs 5:30–10pm, Fri 5:30–11pm, Sat 5–11pm. Validated parking available. MBTA: Blue or Orange Line to State, or Green Line to Government Center. CREATIVE AMERICAN.

Let's cut to the chase: Would you pay this much at a restaurant with a view of a brick wall? No. Is it worth it? Absolutely. One of the most beautiful dining rooms in Boston, the 33rd-floor Bay Tower has glass walls facing a glorious panorama of Faneuil Hall Marketplace, the harbor, and the airport. The terraced table area is arranged so that every seat has a view, and the shiny (polished, not mirrored) surfaces lend a casinolike air to the candlelit room.

Executive chef Peter J. Patchett's menu, an intriguing variety of traditional and contemporary dishes, changes seasonally. You might start with a goat-cheese-and-artichoke napoleon or lobster bisque. Entrees include pan-seared veal served with fava-bean cassoulet, fresh pasta, and a morel mushroom sauce; for those with more traditional tastes, Dover sole meunière is filleted at the table. Special dietary preparations are available on request, and there's always at least one vegetarian entree. As you might expect at a restaurant where many people come just for dessert, drinks, and dancing, desserts are wonderful, with an emphasis on chocolate. A $12 minimum is charged in the lounge after 9:30pm on Friday and Saturday.

✪ **Maison Robert.** 45 School St. ☎ **617/227-3370.** Web site: http://www.maisonrobert.com. Reservations recommended. Main courses $16–$32. Le Café fixed-price menu $18 or $25; à la carte main courses $14–$28. AE, CB, DC, MC, V. Mon–Fri 11:45am–2:30pm; Mon–Sat 5:30–10pm. Valet parking available Wed–Sat. MBTA: Green Line to Government Center or Red Line to Park St. INNOVATIVE FRENCH.

Maison Robert is one of the finest French restaurants anywhere. It's family-owned and -operated—proprietors Lucien and Ann Robert are the parents of executive chef

Andre Robert, and Lucien's nephew Jacky Robert took over in the kitchen in 1996 after many years as a top chef in San Francisco (including 10 years at Ernie's).

A legend in Boston since it opened in Old City Hall in 1971, Maison Robert has only improved since Jacky Robert returned. The dining room was already spectacular, decorated in a formal style that complements the building's French Second Empire architecture, with majestic crystal chandeliers and tall windows. The food is every bit the equal of the setting, classic but dramatic, with unexpected but welcome Asian influences. You might start with a tender, airy Roquefort soufflé, or saffron-flavored crabmeat soup with a Chinese dumpling of shrimp. The filet mignon is a meat-lover's delight, splendid roast rack of lamb is accompanied by an equally delicious potato cake, and the savory pumpkin cheesecake is paired with a goat-cheese strudel. Desserts are truly impressive, ranging from excellent soufflés to heart-stopping chocolate concoctions to upside-down apple tart, served warm with cinnamon sabayon.

The upstairs dining room is the formal counterpart of the cozy Ben's Café on the ground floor, which has a more casual atmosphere and less expensive food, but is also thoroughly French in style. In the summer, cafe seating spills onto a lovely terrace.

EXPENSIVE

☉ Les Zygomates. 129 South St. ☎ **617/542-5108.** Reservations recommended. Main courses $12–$20; prix-fixe lunch $11, prix-fixe dinner $19. AE, MC, V. Mon–Fri 11:30am–2:30pm; Mon–Thurs 6–10:30pm, Fri–Sat 6–11:30pm. MBTA: Red Line to South Station. FRENCH/ECLECTIC.

Pick your way across the construction wasteland near South Station to this delightful bistro and wine bar. It's worth the trouble. Over the bar in the high-ceilinged, brick-walled room is a great selection of wine, available by the bottle, by the glass, and as a 2-ounce "taste." The efficient staff will recommend something or just guide you to a good accompaniment for chef and co-owner Ian Just's delicious food. Salads are excellent, lightly dressed and garden fresh, and main courses are hearty and filling but not heavy. A large piece of sautéed trout is flaky and light, and the roasted chicken leg stuffed with Vidalia onions and juniper berries is savory. The supply of baguette slices on every table is constantly replenished. For dessert, try the crème brûlée du jour, and try not to fight over the lemon mousse, a cloud of citrus and air.

Ye Olde Union Oyster House. 41 Union St. (between North and Hanover sts.) ☎ **617/227-2750.** Reservations recommended. Main courses $14.95–$27.95. AE, CB, DC, DISC, MC, V. Sun–Thurs 11am–9:30pm, Fri–Sat 11am–10pm. Lunch served until 5pm Sun–Thurs, until 6pm Fri–Sat. Union Bar 11am–3pm for lunch, 3–11pm for late-supper fare. Bar open until midnight. MBTA: Green or Blue Line to Government Center or Orange Line to Haymarket. NEW ENGLAND/SEAFOOD.

America's oldest restaurant in continuous service, the Union Oyster House opened in 1826, and the booths and oyster bar haven't moved since. The food is tasty, traditional New England fare. At the crescent-shaped bar on the lower level of the cramped, low-ceilinged building, "where Daniel Webster drank many a toddy in his day," try the sampler, a mixed appetizer of hot or cold oysters, clams, and shrimp.

Oyster stew made with fresh milk and country butter makes a good beginning. Follow that with a broiled scrod or salmon, or perhaps seafood primavera, fried seafood, or grilled pork loin. A complete shore dinner with chowder, steamers, lobster, salad, corn, and dessert is an excellent introduction to local favorites. For dessert, try gingerbread with whipped cream. Ask to be seated at John F. Kennedy's favorite booth (no. 18), which is marked with a plaque.

MODERATE

⊙ **Durgin-Park.** 340 Faneuil Hall Marketplace. ☎ **617/227-2038.** Reservations not accepted. Main courses $4.95–$17.95; specials $15.90–$24.95. AE, DC, DISC, MC, V. Mon–Thurs 11:30am–10pm, Fri–Sat 11:30am–10:30pm, Sun 11:30am–9pm. MBTA: Green or Blue Line to Government Center, or Orange Line to Haymarket. NEW ENGLAND.

People have been flocking to Durgin-Park since 1827 for huge portions of fresh, delicious food, a rowdy atmosphere where CEOs share tables with students, and famously cranky waitresses who can't seem to bear the sight of any of it. It really is everything it's cracked up to be—a tourist magnet that also attracts hordes of locals. Politicians rub shoulders with blue-haired grandmothers and everyone's disappointed when the waitresses are nice, as they often are. Approximately 2,000 people a day find their way to the end of the line that stretches down a flight of stairs to the first floor of the North Market building of Faneuil Hall Marketplace (look for the giant sign). The queue moves quickly, and you'll probably wind up seated at a long table with other people, although smaller tables are available.

The food is wonderful, and there's plenty of it—prime rib the size of a hubcap, giant lamb chops, piles of fried seafood, and roast turkey that might fill you up till Thanksgiving. Steaks and chops are broiled on an open fire over wood charcoal. Seafood, including salmon, sole, haddock, shrimp, oysters, scallops, and lobster, is received twice daily, and fish dinners are broiled to order. Vegetables are served à la carte, and if you've been waiting to try Boston baked beans, now's the time. Homemade corn bread comes with every meal. For dessert, the strawberry shortcake is justly celebrated, and molasses lovers (this is not a dish for dabblers) will want to try Indian pudding, a mixture of molasses and cornmeal slow-baked for hours and served with ice cream.

If you're going for "dinner" (otherwise known as lunch; the evening meal is called "supper"), beat the crowd by arriving when the restaurant opens. Or jump the line by starting out at the ground-floor Gaslight Pub, which has a private staircase that leads upstairs.

INEXPENSIVE

Zuma's Tex-Mex Café. 7 N. Market St., Faneuil Hall Marketplace. ☎ **617/367-9114.** Main courses $4.97–$13.99. AE, CB, DC, DISC, MC, V. Mon–Thurs 11:30am–11pm, Fri–Sat 11:30am–midnight, Sun noon–10pm. MBTA: Green or Blue Line to Government Center, or Orange Line to Haymarket. TEX-MEX.

Because of its great location on the lower level of the North Market building at Faneuil Hall Marketplace, Zuma's could probably get away with serving so-so food and still draw enormous crowds. Happily, its Southwestern cuisine is excellent, with guacamole and salsa cruda made from scratch, and tortilla chips cut and fried throughout the day right in the dining room. This casual, friendly spot is somewhat dark, spotted with neon and small lights in the ceiling. Portions are large, especially considering the low prices. An appetizer of calamari fried in a spicy batter is big enough for three, and the sizzling fajitas constantly flying out of the kitchen are substantial and delectable. Tacos are just $1.97 each; the chimichangitas are also a bargain at $1.47. The key lime pie and the margaritas (including a neon version) are justly acclaimed. And you can order lunch to go.

DOWNTOWN CROSSING

VERY EXPENSIVE

Locke-Ober. 3 and 4 Winter Place. ☎ **617/542-1340.** Reservations required. Main courses $17–$40. AE, CB, DC, DISC, MC, V. Mon–Fri 11:30am–3pm and 3–10pm; Sat 5:30–10:30pm. MBTA: Red or Green Line to Park St. or Orange Line to Downtown Crossing. AMERICAN.

"Locke's" is *the* traditional Boston restaurant, a favorite since 1875. In a tiny alley off the Winter Street pedestrian mall, it feels like a club, with carved paneling, stained-glass windows, crystal chandeliers, and silver buffet covers on the long, mirrored downstairs bar, which dates from 1880. The upstairs dining rooms are dark, elegant, and quiet. Some Boston power brokers have the same lunch every day at the same table, and probably shudder when they see "items lower in fat," if they even bother to look at a menu.

The food is magnificent, as is the service. Start with oysters (raw or Rockefeller) or the famous Jonah crab cakes, then immerse yourself in tradition—steak tartare, grilled salmon with horseradish sauce, Wiener schnitzel à la Holstein, or lobster stew. The signature dish is lobster Savannah, for which the meat of a 3-pound lobster is diced with pepper and mushrooms, bound with cheese-sherry sauce, stuffed into the shell, and baked. If your heart doesn't stop on the spot, you won't be hungry again for a long time. The dessert menu lists about two dozen items, and as you might expect, the chocolate mousse is a dish for the ages. Valet parking is available after 6pm.

INEXPENSIVE

Fajitas & 'Ritas. 25 West St. (between Washington and Tremont sts.). ☎ **617/426-1222.** Most dishes $8 and under. AE, DISC, MC, V. Mon–Wed 11:30am–9pm, Thurs 11:30am–10pm, Fri–Sat 11:30am–11pm. MBTA: Red or Green Line to Park St. MEXICAN.

This entertaining storefront restaurant may not be the most authentic place in town, but it's one of the most fun. You order by filling out a slip, checking off your choices of fillings and garnishes to go with your nachos, quesadillas, burritos, and, of course, fajitas. There's nothing exotic, just the usual beef, chicken, shrimp, beans, and so forth. A member of the somewhat harried staff relays your order to the kitchen and returns with huge portions of fresh food—this place is too busy for anything to sit around for very long. As the name indicates, 'ritas (margaritas, ordered from a list of about a dozen options using the same check-off system as the food) are a house specialty.

AT THE PUBLIC GARDEN/BEACON HILL
VERY EXPENSIVE

✪ **Aujourd'hui.** In the Four Seasons Hotel, 200 Boylston St. ☎ **617/451-1392.** Reservations recommended (imperative on holidays). Main courses $35–$45; Sun buffet brunch $44. AE, CB, DC, MC, V. Daily 6:30–10:30am; Mon–Fri 11:30am–2:30pm, Sun 11:30am–2:30pm (brunch); Mon–Sat 5:30–10:30pm, Sun 6–10:30pm. MBTA: Green Line to Arlington. CONTEMPORARY AMERICAN.

On the second floor of the city's premier luxury hotel, the most beautiful restaurant in town has floor-to-ceiling windows overlooking the Public Garden. But even if it were under a pup tent, the incredible service and food would make Aujourd'hui a hit. Executive chef David Fritchey uses regional products and the freshest ingredients available, and the wine list is one of the best in the country. Yes, the cost is astronomical, but how often can you honestly say that you get what you pay for? Here, it's true.

The menu changes often, and the selections encompass the basic offerings you'd expect in a hotel dining room as well as the flights of fancy that characterize an inventive chef. To start, you might try perfectly balanced squash-and-apple soup or a huge salad of arugula and other greens so fresh they practically crackle. Entrees might include rack of lamb served with a timbale of layered potatoes, goat cheese, mushrooms, and zucchini, or oven-roasted lobster with ginger sauce and a vegetable-filled nori roll. The "Alternative Cuisine" offerings slash calories, cholesterol, sodium, and fat, but not flavor. The dessert menu also changes, but always includes picture-perfect soufflés and homemade sorbets. A wonderful menu note (to my mind) asks that cellular phones not be used in the restaurant.

The Ritz-Carlton Dining Room. 15 Arlington St. ☎ **617/536-5700.** Reservations required. Jacket and tie required for men. Main courses $28–$43; Sun buffet brunch $47. AE, CB, DC, DISC, JCB, MC, V. Sun–Thurs 5:30–10pm, Fri–Sat 5:30–11pm; Sat noon–2:30pm, Sun 10:45am–2:30pm (brunch). Valet parking available. MBTA: Green Line to Arlington. FRENCH.

In "proper Bostonian" society, only one place will do when celebrating a special occasion: the magnificent second-floor restaurant of the elegant Ritz-Carlton, overlooking the Public Garden. Whether it's Sunday brunch or dinner under the crystal chandeliers with soft piano music playing in the background, a meal here is a memorable experience.

Less traditional dishes are available, but people come here for the French classics, such as rack of lamb with thyme, broiled sirloin in shallot sauce, and lobster "au whiskey," in a cream and bourbon sauce seasoned with tomatoes, thyme, and scallions. More than two dozen superb appetizers range from smoked north Atlantic salmon to beluga caviar with blinis. The wonderful desserts include chocolate and Grand Marnier soufflés and baked Alaska. And the service is just what you'd expect in such a splendid setting.

On Saturdays in the fall, winter, and spring, there's a series of Fashion Luncheons showcasing the work of local designers and established boutiques.

THE BACK BAY
VERY EXPENSIVE

۞ Grill 23 & Bar. 161 Berkeley St. ☎ **617/542-2255.** Reservations recommended. Main courses $19–$30. AE, CB, DC, DISC, MC, V. Mon–Thurs 5:30–10:30pm, Fri–Sat 5:30–11pm, Sun 5:30–10pm. Valet parking available. MBTA: Green Line to Arlington. AMERICAN.

Grill 23 is a wood-paneled, glass-walled room that attracts a briefcase-toting clientele—but this is more than just a steak house. Slabs of beef and chops with all the trimmings ("Grill Classics") share the menu with less aggressively carnivorous entrees ("Signature Specials") that attract equal attention from the kitchen and the diners. Steak au poivre and lamb chops are perfectly grilled—crusty and juicy, so tender that your knife glides through the meat. Sautéed salmon has an Asian accent, with bean thread noodles and baby bok choy, and the other grilled and roasted fish dishes rival those at any other Boston seafood restaurant. Side dishes, served à la carte, include huge plates of creamed spinach, home fries, and out-of-this-world garlic mashed potatoes. Desserts show as little restraint as the entrees—try the deliriously good apple crisp or pumpkin cheesecake. The service is helpful but not familiar.

Two caveats: Smoking is not only allowed but encouraged—a humidor makes the rounds of the dining room in the arms of a staff member. The ventilation is good, but you can smell smoke in your clothes and hair later. And the noise level grows louder in tiny increments as the evening progresses, but you won't realize you're shouting until you're outside yelling about what a good time you had.

۞ L'Espalier. 30 Gloucester St. ☎ **617/262-3023.** Web site: http://www.lespalier.com. Reservations required. Prix-fixe dinner (4 courses) $62; vegetable degustation menu (6 courses) $68; degustation menu (7 courses) $78. AE, DISC, MC, V. Mon–Sat 6–10pm. Valet parking available. MBTA: Green Line, B, C, or D train to Hynes/ICA. NEW ENGLAND/FRENCH.

Dinner at L'Espalier is very much like eating at the home of a dear friend who has only your pleasure in mind, and happens to have a dozen highly trained helpers in the kitchen. Owners Frank and Catherine McClelland (he's the chef) preside over three dining rooms on the second floor of an 1876 town house. Reached by a spiral mahogany staircase, the space is formal yet inviting, with fireplaces, ornately carved moldings, and bay windows. Service is beyond excellent, in that eerie realm where it seems possible that the waiter just read your mind.

The quality of the food, if anything, exceeds the trappings. The kitchen has moved beyond nouvelle cuisine into a more adventurous mode, constantly innovating with the freshest and most interesting ingredients available. The breads, sorbets, ice creams, and desserts (many adapted from the family's heirloom cookbooks) are made on the premises. The prix-fixe menu includes an *amuse geulle,* first course, main course, and dessert. There are five to seven choices in each category, always including an appetizer with caviar (for an additional charge), and all superb. A first course of shrimp, lobster, and winter squash raviolis rests in a pool of tangerine broth, and a salad of greens with warm chèvre, beets, sprouts, and bruschetta arrives dressed with a perfectly balanced pickled-ginger miso vinaigrette. Main courses usually include a game offering, perhaps grilled venison with a soufflé of celery root, apple, and cheddar. Salmon in a sesame crust over noodles in a ginger-and-sesame broth is equally impressive. Desserts are alarmingly good—even if you have one of the superb soufflés, which are ordered with dinner, ask to see the tray.

The degustation menus, both vegetarian and non-, are available to entire tables only. The vintner's tasting of wines selected from the extensive cellar to go along with each course adds $45 to the cost of the regular degustation menu. One course that's also available à la carte is the celebrated cheese tray (the Grand Fromage, which includes two local cheeses).

EXPENSIVE

✪ **Legal Sea Foods.** 800 Boylston St., in the Prudential Center. ☎ **617/266-6800.** Reservations recommended at lunch. Main courses $13.95–$23.95. AE, CB, DC, DISC, MC, V. Mon–Thurs 11am–10:30pm, Fri–Sat 11am–11:30pm, Sun noon–10pm. MBTA: Green Line, B, C, or D train to Hynes/ICA, or E train to Prudential. SEAFOOD.

The food at Legal Sea Foods ("Legal's," in Bostonian parlance) isn't the fanciest or the cheapest or the trendiest. It's the freshest, and management's commitment to that policy has produced a thriving chain. The family-owned business began as a fish market in Cambridge in 1950 and opened its first restaurant in 1968. It has an international reputation for serving only top-quality fish and shellfish—broiled, baked, stir fried, grilled, fried, steamed, and in casserole. The menu includes regular selections (haddock, bluefish, salmon, shrimp, calamari, and lobster, among others) plus whatever looked good at the market that morning, and it's all splendid. The clam chowder is a winner, or you could start with creamy, salty smoked bluefish pâté. Entrees run the gamut from plain grilled fish to seafood fra'diavolo on fresh linguine to salmon baked in parchment with vegetables and white wine. The Prudential Center branch is suggested because it takes reservations (at lunch only), a deviation from a long tradition.

In 1996, legendary New England chef Jasper White came on board as the chain's executive chef. White, who is credited with revolutionizing the concept of the hotel restaurant and the seafood restaurant, is slowly leaving his mark on the menu, which now includes such departures from tradition as red clam chowder, clam fritters, and fallen chocolate cake.

He is also expected to individualize the restaurants—the first step was the opening of **Legal C Bar** (☎ 617/426-5566) at 27 Columbus Ave., where the food and music are Caribbean. There are regular branches at the Boston Park Plaza Hotel, 35 Columbus Ave. (☎ **617/426-4444**); Copley Place, 100 Huntington Ave. (☎ **617/266-7775**); Kendall Square, 5 Cambridge Center (☎ **617/864-3400**); and eight other locations with the same blue-and-white checked decor and menu.

Top of the Hub. 800 Boylston St., Prudential Center. ☎ **617/536-1775.** Reservations recommended. Jacket advised for men. Main courses $18–$29; 6-course tasting menu $65 per person (2-person minimum); Sun brunch $29. AE, DC, DISC, MC, V. Mon–Fri 11:30am–2pm, Sat noon–3pm, Sun 11am–2:30pm (brunch); Sun–Thurs 5:30–10pm, Fri–Sat 5:30–11pm. Discounted parking available in Prudential Center garage after 4pm Mon–Fri and all day Sat–Sun. MBTA: Green Line, B, C, or D train to Hynes/ICA, or E train to Prudential. CONTEMPORARY AMERICAN.

For many years, the answer to the question "How's the food at Top of the Hub?" was, "The view is spectacular." But since a complete overhaul of the menu and the 52nd-floor space in 1995, the cuisine has improved dramatically. Even if it's still not quite a match for the panorama outside, you probably won't notice. Check the weather forecast and plan to eat here when it's clear out, taking the best advantage of the three glass-walled sides of the restaurant and lounge. Be sure to ask for a table by the window when you make your reservation, and consider coming before sunset and lingering until dark for a true spectacle.

Executive chef Dean Moore emphasizes seafood, roasting, and grilling; witness the entree of roasted monkfish flavored with 11 spices and served with orzo and seasonal vegetables. Pan-roasted medaillons of beef tenderloin is another good choice at dinner. Lunch offerings include pizzas and half a dozen tasty sandwiches. At either meal, the clam chowder is a standout, with more broth than cream. Salads are large and varied, but if you don't like your vegetables drowning in dressing, ask for it on the side.

MODERATE

Bangkok Cuisine. 177A Mass. Ave. ☎ **617/262-5377.** Reservations not accepted. Main courses $8–$15. AE, DISC, MC, V. Mon–Sat 11:30am–3pm; Mon–Thurs 5–10:30pm, Fri 5–11pm, Sat 3–11pm, Sun 4–10pm. MBTA: Green Line, B, C, or D train to Hynes/ICA. THAI.

Bangkok Cuisine, opened in 1979, was the first Thai restaurant in Boston. It has set (and maintained) high standards for the many others that followed. The dishes run the gamut from excellent chicken and basil to all sorts of curry offerings, pan-fried or deep-fried whole fish, and hot and sour salads. The green curry in coconut milk and vegetables prepared with strong green Thai chili pepper are the most incendiary. You can order nonspicy food and, of course, pad Thai, the famous noodle dish.

INEXPENSIVE

Café Jaffa. 48 Gloucester St. ☎ **617/536-0230.** Main courses $3.95–$9.25. AE, DC, DISC, MC, V. Mon–Thurs 11am–10:30pm, Fri–Sat 11am–11pm, Sun 1–10pm. MBTA: Green Line, B, C, or D train to Hynes/ICA. MIDDLE EASTERN.

A long, narrow brick room with a glass front, Café Jaffa looks more like a snazzy pizza place than the wonderful Middle Eastern restaurant it is. Young people flock here, drawn by the low prices, high quality, and large portions of food, which includes burgers and steak tips as well as traditional Middle Eastern offerings such as falafel, baba ghanoush, and hummus. Lamb, beef, and chicken kabobs come with Greek salad, rice pilaf, and pita bread. For dessert, try the baklava if it's fresh (give it a pass if not).

CHARLESTOWN

✪ **Olives.** 10 City Sq., Charlestown. ☎ **617/242-1999.** Reservations accepted only for parties of 6 or more. Main courses $15.95–$30. AE, DC, MC, V. Tues–Fri 5:30–10pm, Sat 5–10:30pm. Valet parking available. MBTA: Orange or Green Line to North Station; 10-min. walk. ECLECTIC.

This small, informal bistro near the Charlestown Navy Yard is one of the hottest spots in town. Patrons line up shortly after 5pm to get a table—you might be better off just making five friends and calling for a reservation. If you don't get there by 5:45pm, expect to wait at least 2 hours (at the bar if there's room) until a table opens. Once you're seated, you'll find many of the tables small and crowded, the service uneven, the ravenous customers festive, and the noise level high. The open kitchen in the rear of the restaurant, with a rotisserie and a huge brick oven, adds to the din.

Happily, the food is worth the aggravation. Todd English, chef and co-owner with his wife, Olivia, is a culinary genius. The menu changes regularly and always includes "Olives Classics," one of which is a meltingly delicious tart of olives, caramelized onions, and anchovies. Ginger spinach salad dressed with tahini arrives surrounded by shredded carrots with orange and cumin vinaigrette, a complex combination that works perfectly. Another Olives Classic, spit-roasted chicken flavored with herbs and garlic, oozes succulent juices into the old-fashioned mashed potatoes. Braised lamb shank with a sherry-and-olive sauce is so tender it falls off the bone. When you order your entree you'll be asked if you want falling chocolate cake with raspberry sauce and vanilla ice cream for dessert. Say yes.

THE SOUTH END
VERY EXPENSIVE

Hamersley's Bistro. 553 Tremont St. ☎ **617/423-2700.** Reservations recommended. Main courses $18.50–$27; menu degustation varies. AE, DISC, MC, V. Mon–Fri 6–10pm, Sat 5:30–10pm, Sun 5:30–9:30pm. Valet parking available. MBTA: Orange Line to Back Bay. ECLECTIC.

This is the place that put the South End on Boston's culinary map. The husband-and-wife team of Gordon and Fiona Hamersley presides over a long, narrow dining room decorated in cool yellow with lots of soft surfaces that absorb sound, so you can see but not hear what's going on at the tables around you. That means you'll have to quiz your server about the delicious-looking dish that just passed by—perhaps a marvelous appetizer of potato galette, smoked salmon, crème fraîche, and three caviars. The menu changes seasonally and offers about a dozen carefully considered entrees (always including vegetarian dishes) noted for their emphasis on taste and texture. The signature roast chicken is flavored with garlic, lemon, and parsley and served with roast potato, roast onions, and whole cloves of sweet baked garlic. Oriental salmon roulade stuffed with jasmine rice and baby bok choy is wonderful, and grilled filet of beef is served with garlic mashed potatoes and a delectable red-wine sauce. The wine list is excellent.

○ **Icarus.** 3 Appleton St. ☎ **617/426-1790.** Reservations recommended. Main courses $19.50–$29.50; "Square Meal" $38. AE, CB, DC, MC, V. Sun–Thurs 6–10pm, Fri 6–11pm, Sat 5:30–11pm; Sun 11am–3pm (brunch). Valet parking available at dinner. MBTA: Green Line to Arlington or Orange Line to Back Bay. ECLECTIC.

Every element that goes into a great dining experience is present at this subterranean restaurant, which manages to be both spacious and cozy. The upper level of the dining room overlooks the main floor, and the marble accents and dark wood trim lend an elegant air. Chef and co-owner Chris Douglass uses choice local seafoods, poultry, meats, and produce to create imaginative dishes that seem more like alchemy than cooking. The menu changes regularly—you might start with a salad of seared foie gras, apples, endive, and cider hazelnut vinaigrette, or the daily "pasta whim." Move on to cod encased in a shredded potato cake and floating in grass-green herbal broth, or garlicky grilled chicken with balsamic vinegar glaze and toasted garlic mashed potatoes so good you'll want to ask for a plate of them. But don't—save room for one of the unbelievable desserts. Chocolate coconut cake with toasted-coconut ice cream and cherry rum sauce was pronounced a favorite and instantly dethroned (even in the estimation of an unregenerate chocoholic) by a trio of fruit sorbets. The restaurant's newest offering, the prix fixe "Square Meal," consists of three courses plus dessert and derives no more than 30% of its calories from fat.

MODERATE

Addis Red Sea. 544 Tremont St. ☎ **617/426-8727.** Main courses $8.95–$12.95. AE, MC, V. Mon–Fri 5–11pm, Sat–Sun noon–11pm. MBTA: Orange Line to Back Bay. ETHIOPIAN.

If you're in the mood to experiment, Addis Red Sea is a good place to start. This dimly lit, subterranean space is decorated with colorful carpets and wall hangings, and furnished with stools and *mesobs,* traditional Ethiopian tables on which meals are served family style on a platter. They're also served without utensils—the platter is covered with a layer of *injera,* a spongy bread, and the food is spooned on top of it. Tear off a piece of injera, scoop up a mouthful of food, and dig in. Your waitress will offer advice on ordering and bring more injera if you need it to finish off the stewlike main courses. Many are vegetarian, and the vegetable combination makes a good introduction to this cuisine, with a choice of dishes that might include lentils, split peas, cracked wheat, onions, potatoes, beans, carrots, and greens. The spice level varies, but even the mildest dishes are flavorful and filling. There are also tasty meat dishes— *doro wat* is lemon-marinated chicken, and *kifto* is the Ethiopian version of steak tartare.

BROOKLINE & ENVIRONS

EXPENSIVE

✪ **Providence.** 1223 Beacon St., Brookline. ☎ **617/232-0300.** Reservations recommended. Main courses $10.95–$24.95. AE, DC, MC, V. Tues–Thurs 5:30–10pm, Fri–Sat 5:30—11pm, Sun 5–9:30pm; Sun 11am–2pm (brunch). Valet parking available Thurs–Sat. MBTA: Green Line, C train to St. Paul St. AMERICAN/ECLECTIC.

Nothing at this funky, deceptively suburban spot is quite what you'd expect. A glance around seems to reveal a typical American restaurant, until you look a little closer. There's a wood-paneled bar, but the light fixtures above it look like metal spaghetti. You're in a formal room, with columns and intricate moldings, but warm tones lend a casual air.

Chef-owner Paul O'Connell is a wizard with flavors, combining ingredients so that everything brings out the best in everything else. The menu features grilled meats and fish, but also a lot of vegetarian offerings. The courteous, helpful staff can help you navigate the list of specials, which is almost as long as the menu. It might include an appetizer of fresh fried Ipswich clams—standard stuff, until you taste the garlic-and-chipotle mayonnaise dribbled on top. The flat-bread with eggplant puree and olives could be listed on any menu with Middle Eastern influences, but here the flat-bread is made of chick peas, the eggplant exudes cardamom, and there's goat cheese on the plate. Salmon is pan-roasted and served with garlic potatoes and a ragout of artichokes, tomato, and beans. There's even pastrami, but it's veal pastrami, cured and smoked at the restaurant and served with sweet-potato dumplings. And desserts are spectacular, notably the signature warm chocolate fondant cake.

MODERATE

The Elephant Walk. 900 Beacon St., Boston. ☎ **617/247-1500.** Reservations recommended at dinner Sun–Thurs, not accepted Fri–Sat. Main courses $9.50–$18.50. AE, DISC, MC, V. Mon–Sat 11:30am–2:30pm; Mon–Thurs 5–10pm, Fri 5–11pm, Sat 4:30–11pm, Sun 4:30–10pm. MBTA: Green Line, C train to St. Mary's St. FRENCH/CAMBODIAN.

France meets Cambodia on the menu at The Elephant Walk, located four blocks from Kenmore Square on the Boston-Brookline border and decorated with lots of little pachyderms. This madly popular spot has a two-part menu (French on one side,

Cambodian on the other), but the boundary seems quite porous. Many of the Cambodian dishes have part-French names, such as poulet dhomrei (chicken with Asian basil, bamboo shoots, fresh pineapple, and kafir lime leaves) and curry de crevettes (shrimp curry with picture-perfect vegetables). The Asian influence is evident on the French side, where you'll find pan-seared duck breast and leg confit served with scallion raviolis, and pan-seared tuna served over red and green chili cream sauces. Members of the pleasant wait staff will help out if you need guidance. Ask to be seated in the plant-filled front room, which is less noisy than the main dining room and has a view of the street.

CAMBRIDGE

The MBTA Red Line runs from downtown Boston to the heart of Harvard Square. Many of the restaurants listed here can be reached on foot from there. If inexpensive ethnic food is more your speed, head for Central and Inman squares, each a virtual United Nations of budget restaurants.

See the "Cambridge Accommodations & Dining" map on pages 70–71 for the locations of the restaurants reviewed below.

VERY EXPENSIVE

✪ **Rialto.** In the Charles Hotel, One Bennett St. ☎ **617/661-5050.** Reservations recommended. Main courses $19–$29. AE, DC, MC, V. Sun–Thurs 5:30–10pm, Fri–Sat 5:30–11pm. Bar Sun–Thurs 5pm–1am, Fri–Sat 5pm–1:30am. MBTA: Red Line to Harvard. MEDITERRANEAN.

If Rialto isn't the best restaurant in the Boston area, it's close. Every element is so carefully thought out that you might find yourself pausing to admire the end product as an intellectual and culinary masterpiece. The dramatic but comfortable room has floor-to-ceiling windows overlooking Harvard Square, cushy banquettes, and standing lamps that cast a golden glow. Rialto attracts a chic crowd, but it's not a scene. The staff is solicitous without being smothering, and chef Jody Adams's food eloquently speaks for itself.

The menu changes regularly, but you might start with a blue-cheese tart in a flaky crust, or *soupe de poisson* (Provençal fisherman's soup with rouille, Gruyère, and basil oil), the very essence of seafood. Main courses are so good that you might as well close your eyes and point. Vegetarians might come up with a plate of creamy potato slices and mushrooms so thick and juicy they're almost like eating meat. Seared duck breast with foie gras, squash raviolis, and quince is wonderful, and anything involving salmon is a guaranteed winner—even those who think they don't like it will fall for the perfectly flaky, orange-pink fish, perhaps with sweet potatoes, dried cranberries, and pine nuts. For dessert, a trio of seasonal sorbets is a great choice, as is *cassata* (Sicilian sponge cake with sweet ricotta, shaved chocolate, dried cherries, and marsala).

Salamander. 1 Athenaeum St. (at First St.). ☎ **617/225-2121.** Reservations recommended. Main courses $19–$33. AE, DC, DISC, MC, V. Mon–Thurs 6–10pm, Fri–Sat 6–10:30pm. Validated parking available. MBTA: Red Line to Kendall; 10-min. walk. AMERICAN/ASIAN.

Salamander chef-owner Stan Frankenthaler is a visionary, and this is his vision. In the atrium of the Carter Ink Building, a block from the Charles River, the restaurant hums on the ground floor, a dimly lit room that centers around a wood-fired grill. Seating spills into the courtyard, where it's less warm and smoky (from the fire), but also less cozy.

The menu descriptions bubble with enthusiasm, running so long they're nearly paragraphs, and they still don't do justice to the food. Foie gras is seared and served on grilled brioche with pâté, leeks, and cherries; "fresh salad roll with noodles, many sprouts, herbs and tiny vegetables all wrapped in rice paper and served with house dipping sauces" is practically an Asian smorgasbord. And those are just the appetizers. The simplest entree (and that's a relative term here), which is almost always available, is lightly fried lobster with chilies, lemongrass, and Thai basil; you might also find black tea–flavored rotisserie-cooked chicken breast, served with regularly changing side dishes. Considering the care that's apparent in every facet of the food, service could be more attentive while the necessarily lengthy preparation process is going on.

Upstairs at the Pudding. 10 Holyoke St. ☎ **617/864-1933.** Reservations recommended. Main courses $16–$27; tasting menu $45. AE, CB, DC, MC, V. Daily 11:30am–2:30pm and 6–10pm. MBTA: Red Line to Harvard. CONTINENTAL/NORTHERN ITALIAN.

An oasis of calm above the tumult of Harvard Square, Upstairs at the Pudding is a special-occasion spot with food so good you'll want to invent a reason to go. At the top of the Hasty Pudding Club's creaky stairs, it's a high-ceilinged room with green walls and soft, indirect lighting, a perfect match for the sophistication of the food. The menu changes daily and always features hand-rolled pasta. To start, you might try fettuccine with truffle cream, or pizzetta with tomato confit, olives, garlic, chèvre, and Parmesan. You can't go wrong by ordering any main course that comes with mashed potatoes—perhaps peppered beef tenderloin with blue cheese and charred tomato coulis. Rack of lamb might be offered with braised artichokes, roasted onions, creamer potatoes, and rosemary-mustard *jus*. Portions are large, but try to save room for dessert—anything with chocolate is a good choice. There is a lovely terrace and herb garden off the dining room for seasonal alfresco dining.

EXPENSIVE

✪ **The Blue Room.** 1 Kendall Sq. ☎ **617/494-9034.** Reservations recommended. Main courses $16–$24. AE, DC, DISC, MC, V. Sun–Thurs 5:30–10pm, Fri–Sat 5:30–11pm, Sun 11am–2:30pm (brunch). MBTA: Red Line to Kendall/MIT; 10-min. walk. ECLECTIC.

The Blue Room split off from the East Coast Grill empire in 1996 and quickly carved out its own comfortable niche. The food is a rousing combination of top-notch ingredients and layers of aggressive flavors. The service is excellent, and the dining room is not as noisy as you might fear when you first spy it through the glass front wall. Part of an office-retail complex, the restaurant is a long room below plaza level (there's seating on the brick patio in warm weather) with a bar at one end and an open kitchen at the other. Upholstery, carpeting, and draperies help soften the din, but still, this is not a place for cooing lovers.

It is, however, a place for food lovers, who revel in chef and co-owner Steve Johnson's regularly changing menu. Appetizers run the gamut from salad with an assertive vinaigrette to grilled sardines to a selection of summer vegetables served with a lemony aioli. Entrees tend to be roasted, grilled, or braised, with at least two vegetarian choices. The roast chicken, served with garlic mashed potatoes, is the best in town. Grilled tuna appears often, and pork loin with cider glaze will make you think twice the next time you skip over pork on a menu to get to the steak. Be sure to check out the wine list. It's organized by characteristics (from light to rich) rather than vintage or provenance.

Casablanca. 40 Brattle St. ☎ **617/876-0999.** Reservations recommended at dinner. Main courses $10–$19. AE, MC, V. Daily 11:30am–3pm; Sun–Thurs 5:30–10pm, Fri–Sat 5:30–11pm. MBTA: Red Line to Harvard. MEDITERRANEAN.

This old-time Harvard Square favorite, perhaps better known for its hopping bar scene, moved (literally and figuratively) into the nineties when the Brattle Theater building became the Brattle Hall retail complex. But Casablanca still remains true to its reputation for serving tasty Mediterranean cuisine. The rather erratic service doesn't seem to have improved much, but luckily there's plenty to look at. The long, skylit dining room and crowded bar are decorated with murals—it's easy to imagine Humphrey Bogart leaning down to ask for a taste of the skewered lamb or the grilled chicken, served at dinner with mashed sweet potatoes or as an hors d'oeuvre in wing form, flavored with fiery North African *harissa* spice paste. Other hors d'oeuvres, from pizza with sea scallops to Provençal chick-pea fries, are so good you might want to assemble them into a meal. Just be sure to leave room for dessert—the cookies are a good choice.

Chez Henri. 1 Shepard St. ☎ **617/354-8980.** Reservations accepted only for parties of 6 or more. Main courses $14.95–$18.95; 3-course prix fixe menu $28. AE, DC, MC, V. Mon–Thurs 6–10pm, Fri–Sat 6–11pm, Sun 11am–2pm (brunch) and 6–9pm. Bar food Mon–Sat until midnight, Sun until 10pm. MBTA: Red Line to Harvard. FRENCH/CUBAN.

In a dark, elegant space off Mass. Ave. near Harvard Law School, Chez Henri is an example of how good fusion cuisine can be. Under the same ownership as Providence in Brookline, Chez Henri has a more focused menu that concentrates on French bistro-style food with Cuban accents. The menu changes regularly; it might include appetizers of spinach salad with duck tamales and mustard vinaigrette, and Swiss chard tartlette with horseradish cream. Entrees include generous portions of meat and fish—perhaps a juicy chicken breast served with black-bean sauce, avocado slaw, and two spicy *empanadas* (turnovers) filled with potato and cheese; or monkfish with mushrooms, *au gratin* potatoes, and cinnamon-scented sauce. The prix-fixe menu includes one of two appetizers and one of two entrees as well as dessert—the crème brûlée is the best in town. The food at the bar is Cuban, as are the strong specialty drinks.

✪ Dalí. 415 Washington St., Somerville. ☎ **617/661-3254.** Reservations not accepted. Tapas $2.50–$7.50; main courses $14–$19. AE, DC, MC, V. Daily 5:30–10:30pm. MBTA: Red Line to Harvard; follow Kirkland St. to intersection of Washington and Beacon sts. SPANISH.

Dali casts an irresistible spell—it's noisy and crowded, it's on a grim corner not all that close to Harvard Square (though it's a short cab ride away), it doesn't take reservations, and it still fills up with people cheerfully waiting more than an hour to get a table. The bar offers plenty to look at while you wait, including colorful paintings, dried flowers, sleeves of garlic, and a clothesline festooned with lingerie.

The crowds come for the authentic Spanish food, especially the tapas, little plates of hot or cold creations that burst with flavor, perfect for sampling and sharing. There are about a dozen entrees (including excellent paella), but most people come in a group and cut a swath through the tapas offerings, 32 on the regular menu and eight specials that change monthly. The *patatas ali-oli* (garlic potatoes) look dull but taste so good you'll want to order more immediately. But hold off while you try the crunchy-tender *gambas con gabardina* (saffron-battered fried shrimp), addictive *setas al ajillo* (sautéed mushrooms), and rich but light *queso de cabra montañes* (goat cheese baked with tomato and basil). The waiters seem a bit overwhelmed but never fail to make sure there's enough bread for sopping up juices and sangria for washing it all down.

Henrietta's Table. In the Charles Hotel, One Bennett St. ☎ **617/661-5005.** Reservations recommended. Main courses $8–$15.50. AE, CB, DC, DISC, MC, V. Mon–Fri 6:30–11am, Sat 7–11:30am, Sun 7–10:30am; Mon–Sat noon–3pm, Sun 11:30am–3pm (brunch); Sun–Thurs 5:30–10pm, Fri–Sat 5:30–11pm. Discounted parking available. MBTA: Red Line to Harvard. NEW ENGLAND.

Yes, this is Harvard Square. Don't be fooled by the country-kitchen atmosphere and homey wooden tables and chairs—Henrietta's Table looks like Grandma's house, but it's more sophisticated. The menus are built around top-quality fresh produce and change daily. Start with Maine rock crab and corn chowder or a grilled portobello mushroom, topped with Vermont Brie and served over greens dressed with walnut vinaigrette. Entrees are simple and flavorful: roast chicken is herb crusted and juicy, a grilled pork chop is smoked and served with chunky applesauce, and wood-smoked Maine salmon meshes perfectly with beach plum vinaigrette. Vegetables are served only à la carte, which can make the tab a bit higher than you might have expected. Even people who think they don't like bread pudding love the chocolate version here. The lunch menu features sandwiches, Yankee pot roast, and chicken pot pie, among other items.

The restaurant's namesake, a 1,000-pound pig who belongs to the hotel owner and lives on Martha's Vineyard, is pictured in a photograph near the front desk, but (I couldn't resist asking) is not on the menu in any way, shape, or form. The entrance is in a little farm-stand market filled with fruits, vegetables, breads, and condiments that's open weekdays from 6:30am to 10pm and Saturday and Sunday at 7am.

MODERATE

Bombay Club. 57 John F. Kennedy St., in the Galleria Mall. ☎ **617/661-8100.** Main courses $8.95–$15.95; lunch buffet $6.95 Mon–Fri, $8.95 Sat–Sun. AE, DC, MC, V. Daily 11:30am–11pm. MBTA: Red Line to Harvard. INDIAN.

Under the same ownership as the more traditional Kebab-'N'-Kurry, 30 Mass. Ave., Boston (☎ 617/536-9835), this third-floor restaurant overlooking Harvard Square doesn't look like a typical Indian restaurant and serves food that's a step up from what you'd find at one. True fame has come to this contemporary-looking spot through its lunch buffet, a generous assortment of some of the best items on the menu at a price that can't be beat. The chicken, lamb, seafood, and rice specialties are the best in town. The tandoori dishes are baked to perfection in the traditional charcoal-fired clay oven. Flavorful breads including *tandoori roti* and *tandoori nan* are also baked there. The house specials include *barra kebab,* lamb marinated in a spicy sauce for 3 days and then baked on skewers, and "royal platters" combining several items.

✪ **The Helmand.** 143 First St. ☎ **617/492-4646.** Reservations recommended. Main courses $8.95–$15.95. AE, MC, V. Sun–Thurs 5–10pm, Fri–Sat 5–11pm. MBTA: Green Line to Lechmere. AFGHAN.

Even in cosmopolitan Cambridge, Afghan food is a novelty, and if any competitors are setting their sights on the Helmand, they'll have a daunting task ahead of them. The elegant setting belies the reasonable prices at this spacious spot near the CambridgeSide Galleria mall. The courteous staff patiently answers questions about the food, which is distinctly Middle Eastern with Indian and Pakistani influences. Many vegetarian dishes are offered, and when meat appears it's often just one element of a dish rather than the centerpiece. Every meal is accompanied by delectable bread made in the wood-fired brick oven in the dining room. To start, you might try the slightly sweet baked pumpkin topped with a spicy ground-meat sauce, a good contrast of flavors and textures, or *aushak,* pasta pockets filled with leeks or potatoes and buried under a sauce of split peas and carrots. Aushak, also available as a main course, can be prepared with meat sauce as well. Other entrees include several versions of what Americans would call stew, including *deygee kabob,* an excellent mélange of lamb, yellow split peas, onions, and red peppers. For dessert, don't miss the Afghan version of baklava.

House of Blues. 96 Winthrop St. ☎ **617/491-2583,** or 617/497-2229 for tickets. Web site: http://www.hob.com. Reservations accepted only for parties of 25 or more. Main courses $5.95–$19.95; Sun brunch tickets $25. AE, DC, DISC, MC, V. Mon–Wed 11:30am–1am, Thurs–Sat 11:30am–2am, Sun 4pm–1am. Sun brunch 10am, noon, and 2pm. MBTA: Red Line to Harvard. AMERICAN.

This is the original House of Blues, a tourist magnet in a blue clapboard house near Harvard Square. Everything is blue at this noisy, crowded spot, and the walls and ceilings are dotted with folk art. On the ceiling near the bar area are plaster bas-reliefs of great blues musicians, and there's live music every night at 9 or 10pm and on Friday and Saturday afternoons.

The menu ranges far and wide (farther and wider at dinner), running from large salads to burgers to barbecue to sophisticated pasta dishes. There's also a selection of pizzas (try the one topped with feta cheese, sun-dried tomatoes, and garlic) baked in a wood-fired oven. Tickets must be purchased in advance for the Sunday Gospel buffet brunch, which usually sells out at least 2 weeks in advance.

La Groceria Ristorante Italiano. 853 Main St. ☎ **617/876-4162** or 617/547-9258. Reservations recommended at dinner. Main courses $9.95–$17.95; pizzas $6.50–$8.95; children's menu $4.95–$5.95. AE, CB, DC, DISC, MC, V. Mon–Fri 11:30am–4pm; Mon–Thurs 4–10pm, Fri–Sat 4–11pm; Sun 1–10pm. Valet parking available on weekends. MBTA: Red Line to Central Square. ITALIAN.

Just outside Central Square, this is a colorful restaurant where the Mastromauro family has dished up large portions of delicious Italian food since 1972. Foodies and bargain hunters will be equally happy here. At lunch you'll see business meetings, at dinner, family outings, and at all times, students. Cheery voices bounce off the stucco walls and tile floors, but it seldom gets terribly noisy, probably because everyone's mouth is full. Start with the house garlic bread, which overflows with chopped tomato, red onion, fennel seed, and olive oil. The antipasto platter is crowded with meats, cheeses, roasted vegetables, and whatever else the chef feels moved to include. Main dishes might include homemade pasta from the machine you see as you enter. Vegetarian lasagna is an excellent choice, as are any of the veal dishes and the savory chicken marsala. Chicken is also available roasted, and 10 varieties of brick-oven pizza are available in individual and large sizes.

✪ **S&S Restaurant.** 1334 Cambridge St., Inman Sq. ☎ **617/354-0777.** Main courses $2.95–$10.95. No credit cards. Mon–Sat 7am–midnight, Sun 8am–midnight; Sat–Sun brunch served 8am–4pm. MBTA: Red Line to Harvard, then no. 69 (Harvard–Lechmere) bus to Inman Sq. DELI.

"Es" is Yiddish for "eat," and this Cambridge classic is as straightforward as its name ("eat and eat"). Founded in 1919 by the great-grandmother of the current owners, this wildly popular weekend brunch spot is northeast of Harvard Square, west of MIT, and worth a visit during the week, too. With huge windows and lots of light wood and plants, it looks a little like a yuppie bar, but the brunch offerings run to the likes of pancakes, waffles, fruit salad, and fantastic omelets. Bagels were a tasty staple here long before they were available at every corner store, and you'll find other traditional deli items such as corned beef, pastrami, tongue, Reuben sandwiches, potato pancakes, blintzes, knockwurst, lox, and whitefish. The S&S is also a full-service restaurant with entrees of beef, chicken, and fish, plus quiche and croissants, and serves breakfast anytime during restaurant hours. Come early for brunch, or plan to spend a good chunk of your Saturday or Sunday standing around people-watching and getting hungry.

INEXPENSIVE

Algiers Coffeehouse. 40 Brattle St. ☎ **617/492-1557.** Main courses $2.50–$12. AE, CB, DC, MC, V. Daily 8am–midnight. MBTA: Red Line to Harvard. MIDDLE EASTERN.

This is an excellent place to take a break from rushing around Harvard Square and have a snack or a drink (try the special Algiers mint coffee), but you might find yourself lingering. That's the nature of coffeehouses, after all, and this is a particularly nice one. Long known as a dark, smoke-filled literary hangout, the new Algiers (which came about in the late 1980s as a result of a fire) is upstairs in Brattle Hall, and still a favorite with Cambridge intellectuals and would-be intellectuals. Smoking is allowed on the upper level. This a good spot to eavesdrop while you eat, and the soups, sandwiches, homemade sausages, falafel, and hummus are terrific. Or just order from the extensive beverage menu.

✪ **Bartley's Burger Cottage.** 1246 Mass. Ave. ☎ **617/354-6559.** Most items under $7. No credit cards. Mon–Sat 11am–10pm. MBTA: Red Line to Harvard. AMERICAN.

A cross section of Cambridge, from Harvard students to regular folks, makes this perennial favorite a regular stop for great burgers and the best onion rings anywhere. Burgers bear the names of local and national celebrities; the names change, but the ingredients stay the same. Anything you can think of to put on ground beef is available here, from American cheese to béarnaise sauce. There are also some good dishes that don't involve meat, notably veggie burgers and creamy, garlicky hummus. Bartley's is one of the only places in the area where you can still get a real raspberry-lime rickey.

5   Seeing the Sights in Boston

THE FREEDOM TRAIL

Faced with flat attendance and competition from attractions that offer more innovative exhibits, the city of Boston announced a massive overhaul of the Freedom Trail in 1996. The trail, which links 16 historical sights with a 3-mile red line on the sidewalk first painted in 1958, may be starting to change by the time you visit, but the actual plots of land aren't going anywhere.

The Freedom Trail, a line of red paint or red brick on or in the sidewalk, begins at the **Boston Common Information Center,** at 146 Tremont St. on the Common. The center is open Monday to Saturday from 8:30am to 5pm and Sunday from 9am to 5pm, and offers pamphlets to help you along your self-guided tour. You can also peel off onto the Black History Trail from here.

As you progress along the trail, you'll come across another information center further along, the **Boston National Historic Park Visitor Center,** 15 State St. (☎ 617/242-5642). Pamphlets are also available here, and from this point, you can take a free guided tour with a park ranger. If you want to start here and do the guided tour, take the "T" to the State Street station; the visitor center is across the street from the Old State House. The audiovisual show about the trail provides basic information on 16 historic sites. The center is accessible by stairs and ramps and has rest rooms and comfortable chairs. Open daily from 9am to 5pm except Thanksgiving Day, Christmas, and New Year's Day.

The hard-core history fiend can spend 4 hours or more peering at every artifact and reading every plaque along the Trail, and will wind up at Bunker Hill feeling weary but rewarded. The family with restless teenagers will probably appreciate the enforced efficiency of the 90-minute ranger-led tour, which doesn't include Charlestown.

Space doesn't permit me to detail every stop on the Trail, but one of the real highlights is the **Paul Revere House,** at 19 North Sq., in the North End (☎ 617/ 523-2338), where history is presented on a human scale. Revere set out for Lexington from here on the evening of April 18, 1775, a feat immortalized by Henry Wadsworth Longfellow ("Listen my children and you shall hear / Of the midnight

Boston Attractions

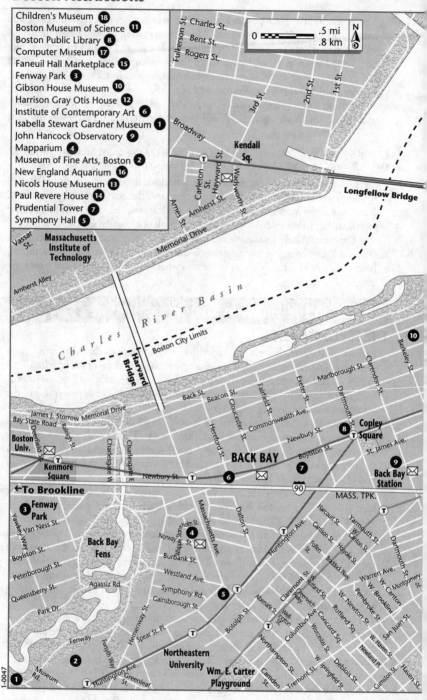

Children's Museum 18
Boston Museum of Science 11
Boston Public Library 8
Computer Museum 17
Faneuil Hall Marketplace 15
Fenway Park 3
Gibson House Museum 10
Harrison Gray Otis House 12
Institute of Contemporary Art 6
Isabella Stewart Gardner Museum 1
John Hancock Observatory 9
Mapparium 4
Museum of Fine Arts, Boston 2
New England Aquarium 16
Nicols House Museum 13
Paul Revere House 14
Prudential Tower 7
Symphony Hall 5

0   .5 mi
     .8 km

N

Charles St.
Bent St.
Rogers St.
Fullerson St.
3rd St.
2nd St.
1st St.
Broadway
Kendall Sq.
Carleton St.
Ames St.
Amherst St.
Hayward St.
Wadsworth St.
Longfellow Bridge

Vassar St.
Massachusetts Institute of Technology
Memorial Drive
Amherst Alley

C h a r l e s   R i v e r   B a s i n

Boston City Limits

Harvard Bridge

Berkeley St.
Clarendon St.
Marlborough St.
Back St.
Beacon St.
Fairfield St.
Exeter St.
Dartmouth St.
Cloucester St.
Commonwealth Ave.
Hereford St.
Newbury St.
James J. Storrow Memorial Drive
Bay State Road
Raleigh St.
Deerfield St.
Charlesgate W.
Charlesgate E.
Newbury St.

Boston Univ.
Kenmore Square
Copley Square 8
St. James Ave.
BACK BAY
7
6
9 Back Bay Station
MASS. TPK.
I-90

←**To Brookline**

3 **Fenway Park**
Yawkey Way
Van Ness St.
Boylston St.
Peterborough St.
Queensberry St.
Park Dr.
Fenway

Back Bay Fens
Agassiz Rd.

Norway St.
Westland St.
Windsor Store St.
4
Burbank St.
Westland Ave.
Symphony Rd.
Gainsborough St.
Massachusetts Ave.
Dalton St.
5
Hemenway St.
Spear St. Pl.
Forsyth Way
Huntington Ave.

Harcourt St.
Garrison St.
Follen St.
Holyoke St.
Braddock Pkwy.
Yarmouth St.
Canton St.
Claremont St.
Rutland Sq.
Greenwich Pkwy.
W. Newton St.
W. Canton St.
Warren Ave.
Pembroke St.
W. Brookline St.
W. Rutland Sq.
Montgomery St.
Dartmouth St.
Albemarle St.
Wellington St.
Concord Sq.
Columbus Ave.
Worcester St.
W. Springfield St.
Northampton St.
Camden St.
Tremont St.
W. Springfield St.
Deblois St.
Newland Pl.
San Juan St.
W. Haven St.
Haven St.
Cunston St.

Northeastern University
Wm. E. Carter Playground
2
Museum Rd.
Huntington Ave.
Greenleaf St.
1

1-0047

94

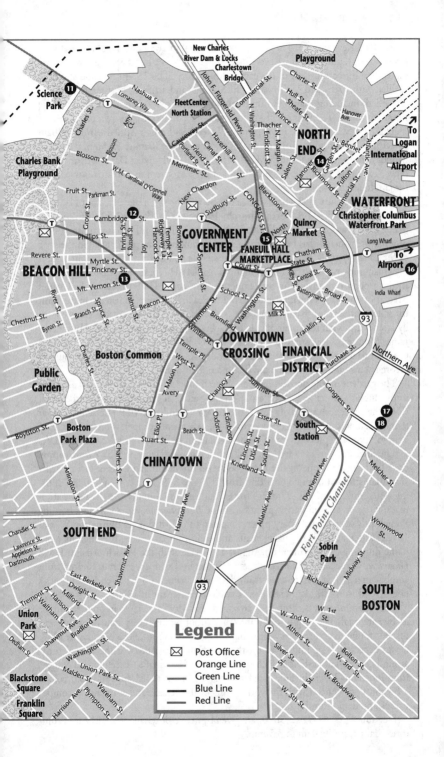

Legend

⊠ Post Office
— Orange Line
— Green Line
— Blue Line
— Red Line

ride of Paul Revere . . ."). The house was built around 1680 (it's the oldest in downtown Boston), purchased by Revere in 1770, and put to a number of uses before being turned into a museum in the early 20th century. The 2$\frac{1}{2}$-story wood structure is filled with 17th- and 18th-century furnishings and artifacts, neatly arranged and identified, including examples of the famous Revere silver, considered some of the finest anywhere. The tour is self-guided, allowing you to set your own pace.

The Paul Revere House is open from November through April 14 from 9:30am to 4:15pm, and from April 15 through October from 9:30am to 5:15pm; it's closed Mondays from January through March, as well as Thanksgiving Day, Christmas, and New Year's Day. Admission is $2.50 for adults, $2 for seniors and students, and $1 for children 5 to 17.

Paul Revere knew it was time to ride out because he saw a signal, a pair of lanterns in the steeple of the **Old North Church,** 193 Salem St. (☎ **617/523-6676**). Formally known as Christ Church, this is the oldest church in Boston standing on its original site, where it has been since 1723. The building was constructed in the style of Sir Christopher Wren, and the original steeple was the one where sexton Robert Newman hung two lanterns on the night of April 18, 1775, to indicate to Revere that British troops were setting out for Lexington and Concord in boats across the Charles River, not on foot ("One if by land, two if by sea"). The spire, long a reference point for sailors, appears on navigational charts to this day. Members of the Revere family attended this church (their plaque is on pew 54); visitors have included presidents James Monroe, Theodore Roosevelt, Franklin D. Roosevelt, and Gerald R. Ford, and Queen Elizabeth II. There are markers and plaques throughout; note the bust of George Washington, reputedly the first memorial to the first president.

The gardens on the north side of the church (dotted with more plaques) are open to the public. Church volunteers are re-creating an 18th-century garden on the south side. The church is open daily from 9am to 5pm; Sunday services (Episcopal) are at 9 and 11am and 4pm. The quirky gift shop, in a former chapel, is open daily from 9am to 5pm, and proceeds go to support the church. Donations are appreciated.

The final stops on the Freedom Trail are in Charlestown. The **USS** *Constitution,* or "Old Ironsides," one of the U.S. Navy's six original frigates, never lost a battle. It was constructed in the North End from 1794 to 1797 at a cost of $302,718, using bolts, spikes, and other fittings from Paul Revere's foundry. As the new nation made its naval and military reputation, the *Constitution* played a key role, battling French privateers and Barbary pirates, repelling the British fleet during the War of 1812, participating in 40 engagements and capturing 20 vessels. It earned its nickname during an engagement on August 19, 1812, with the French warship HMS *Guerriere,* whose shots bounced off its thick oak hull as if it were iron. Retired from combat in 1815, it was rescued from destruction when Oliver Wendell Holmes's poem "Old Ironsides" launched a preservation movement in 1830.

The *Constitution* was completely overhauled in 1995 and 1996 in preparation for its bicentennial. The ship is towed into the harbor by tugs every Fourth of July and turned around to ensure even weathering, and in honor of its 200th birthday in 1997, it was expected to be under sail for the first time since 1881 for the annual turnaround cruise. The festivities will extend into 1998, when a "Bicentennial Salute" from July 23 to 26 will include parades by visiting international ships and their sailors, a Boston Pops concert with fireworks, tours of the vessels, and seamanship competitions and demonstrations.

Free **tours** (☎ **617/242-5670**) are given by active-duty sailors in 1812 dress uniforms daily from 9:30am to 3:50pm.

The USS *Constitution* Museum (☎ 617/426-1812), just inland from the vessel, has several participatory exhibits that allow visitors to hoist a flag, fire a cannon, and learn more about the ship. The museum is open daily, June 1 to Labor Day from 9am to 6pm; March to May and the day after Labor Day through November from 10am to 5pm; December to February from 10am to 3pm; closed Thanksgiving, Christmas, and New Year's Day. Admission is $4 for adults, $3 for seniors, $2 for children 6 to 16, and free for children 5 and under. Discounted combination tickets are available if you plan to visit the Old State House during your time in Boston.

Many people, especially those traveling with fidgety children, opt to skip the final stop on the Freedom Trail. If your party's not too close to the breaking point, it's an interesting excursion. Leave the Navy Yard, cross Chelsea Street, and climb the hill, following the Freedom Trail along Tremont Street. Your guidepost is also your destination, the **Bunker Hill Monument** (☎ 617/242-5644), a 221-foot granite obelisk built in honor of the men who died in the Battle of Bunker Hill on June 17, 1775. The colonists lost the battle, but nearly half of the British troops were killed or wounded, a circumstance that contributed to the decision to abandon Boston 9 months later. The Marquis de Lafayette, the celebrated hero of the American and French revolutions, helped lay the monument's cornerstone in 1825. The top is at the end of a flight of 295 stairs—a long climb for a decent view that prominently features I-93.

In the lodge at the base of the monument are dioramas and exhibits. It's staffed by National Park Service rangers and open daily from 9am to 5pm. The monument is open daily from 9am to 4:30pm. Admission is free.

GREAT VIEWS FROM ON HIGH

Two of the city's top attractions are literally *top* attractions. From hundreds of feet in the air, you'll get an entirely different perspective on Boston. The nearest "T" stops to both are Copley on the Green Line and Back Bay on the Orange Line and the commuter rail.

The **John Hancock Observatory,** 200 Clarendon St. (☎ 617/572-6429), would be a good introduction to Boston even if it didn't have a sensational 60th-floor view. The multimedia exhibits include a light-and-sound show that chronicles the events leading to the Revolutionary War and demonstrates how Boston's land mass has changed. There's an illustrated time line, an interactive computer quiz about the city, and a display that allows you to ask for travel directions (by foot, car, and public transportation) to various points of interest. Telescopes and binoculars allow a close-up look at the faraway ground, and facsimiles of newspapers give a look at the headlines of the past. Admission is $4.25 for adults and $3.25 for seniors and children ages 5 to 15. Hours are 9am to 11pm Monday through Saturday; Sunday from 10am to 11pm from May to October, and noon to 11pm from November to April. The ticket office closes at 10pm.

The **Prudential Center Skywalk,** on the 50th floor of the Prudential Tower, 800 Boylston St. (☎ 617/236-3318), offers the only 360° view of Boston and beyond. From the enclosed observation deck you can see for miles, even (when it's clear) as far as the mountaintops of southern New Hampshire in the north or the beaches of Cape Cod to the south. Hours are 10am to 10pm daily. Admission is $4 for adults and $3 for seniors and children ages 2 to 10. On the 52nd floor the view can be enjoyed with food and drink at the Top of the Hub restaurant and lounge.

Photo Synthesis

Boston is such a magnet for shutterbugs that residents have been known to offer to snap a picture of a visiting family even before being asked. Arrange Junior and Sissy in the lap of one of the area's numerous portrait sculptures, or take a step back and capture the juxtaposition of a 19th-century steeple silhouetted against a 20th-century office tower.

Say "Cheese": At the bronze **teddy bear** in front of FAO Schwarz, 440 Boylston St. (at Berkeley). Arm-in-arm or deep in thought with Mayor **James Michael Curley,** in the park on Union Street across North Street from Faneuil Hall. Pulling the cigar away from Celtics legend **Red Auerbach,** between the South Canopy of Quincy Market and the South Market building, Faneuil Hall Marketplace. Falling at the feet of a colonial hero—pedestals support **Benjamin Franklin** (School Street, in front of Old City Hall), **Paul Revere** (Hanover Street at Clark, across from St. Stephen's Church), and **George Washington** (in the Public Garden at the foot of the Commonwealth Avenue Mall). Perched on Mrs. Mallard (or one of her babies if you fit) of *Make Way for Ducklings* fame, in the Public Garden near the corner of Beacon and Charles streets. Outdistancing the winner (or the runner-up) captured in *The Tortoise and Hare at Copley Square,* in front of Trinity Church. And at a spot so popular the grass on the area favored by photographers had to be paved over, in front of **John Harvard,** Harvard Yard, Cambridge.

Say "Ooh": Always remember to look up for a quirky perspective on the face of the city. Capture a church against a backdrop of skyscrapers on **Tremont Street** (with the Boston Common Visitor Information Center at your back, turn left toward Park Street Church) or **Boylston Street** (in front of the Four Seasons, turn left toward the Arlington Street Church; across from Trinity Church, focus on the Hancock Tower). Kill two birds with one stone: Pointing up at the Paul Revere statue on Hanover Street, you can lock in the **Old North Church** in the background, or walk around the statue for a new perspective on **St. Stephen's Church.** The Old North Church crops up all over the North End and Charlestown, as the **Hancock Tower** does throughout the Back Bay. And if your travels take you to the area around the Charles Street "T" stop, wander out onto the **Longfellow Bridge,** especially at twilight—the views of the river are splendid, and if you hit it just right, the moon appears to shine out of the Hancock Tower.

MORE BOSTON ATTRACTIONS

✪ **Faneuil Hall Marketplace.** Between North, Congress, and State sts. and I-93. ☎ **617/ 338-2323.** Marketplace Mon–Sat 10am–9pm, Sun noon–6pm; Colonnade food court opens earlier; some restaurants open early for Sun brunch and remain open until 2am daily. MBTA: Orange Line or Blue Line to State; Orange Line or Green Line to Haymarket; or Green Line to Government Center.

It's impossible to overestimate the effect of Faneuil Hall Marketplace on Boston's economy and reputation. A daring idea when it opened in 1976, the festival market concept has since been widely imitated in other cities around the country, and each new complex of shops, food stands, restaurants, bars, and public spaces tends to reflect its location. Faneuil Hall Marketplace, brimming with Boston flavor and regional goods and souvenirs, is no exception. Its success with tourists and suburbanites is so great, in fact, that you could be forgiven for thinking that the only Bostonians in the crowd are employees. The marketplace includes five buildings—the central three-building complex is listed in the National Register of Historic Places—set on brick and stone plazas that teem with crowds shopping, eating, performing, watching performers, and just people watching.

Quincy Market itself (you'll hear the whole complex called by that name as well) is a three-level Greek Revival–style building. It reopened after renovations turned it into a festival market on August 26, 1976, 150 years of hard use after Mayor Josiah Quincy opened the original market. The South Market Building opened on August 26, 1977, and the North Market Building in 1978 on, yes, August 26.

The central corridor of Quincy Market, known as the Colonnade, is the food court, where you can find anything from a bagel to a full Greek dinner, a fruit smoothie to a hunk of fudge. On either side, under the glass canopies, are pushcarts bearing the full range of crafts created by New England artisans and hokey souvenirs hawked by enterprising merchants. In the plaza between the South Canopy and the South Market Building is a **visitor information kiosk,** and throughout the complex, including the ground floor of Faneuil Hall, you'll find an enticing mix of chain stores and unique shops. On summer evenings the tables that spill outdoors from the bars fill with people unwinding, listening to or performing karaoke, or just enjoying the passing scene.

One constant since the year after the market opened—after the *original* market opened, that is—is **Durgin-Park,** a traditional New England restaurant with traditionally crabby waitresses (see section 4 of this chapter for details).

Faneuil Hall itself sometimes gets overlooked, but it's well worth a visit. Known as the "Cradle of Liberty" for its role as a center of inspirational (some might say inflammatory) speeches in the years leading to the Revolutionary War, the building opened in 1742 and was expanded using a Charles Bulfinch design in 1805. National Park Service rangers give free 20-minute talks every half-hour from 9am to 5pm in the second-floor auditorium, which, after a recent refurbishment, is now in mint condition.

New England Aquarium. Central Wharf. ☎ **617/973-5200.** Web site: http://www.neaq.org. Admission $10.50 adults, $6 children 3–11, $9.50 senior citizens; free for children under 3. $1 off all fees 4–8pm Thurs and summer Wed. No admission fee for those visiting only the outdoor exhibits, cafe, and gift shop. July 1 through Labor Day Mon–Tues and Fri 9am–6pm, Wed–Thurs 9am–8pm, Sat–Sun and holidays 9am–7pm. Early Sept through June Mon–Fri 9am–5pm, Sat–Sun and holidays 9am–6pm. Closed Thanksgiving, Christmas, and until noon New Year's Day. MBTA: Blue Line to Aquarium.

Like a crab molting its outgrown shell, the New England Aquarium has expanded into a new West Wing building that echoes the waves on adjacent Boston Harbor. The dramatic structure, scheduled to open in early 1998 (with the Aquarium operating during construction), contains an enlarged display space for temporary exhibits and a gift shop, plus a new cafe with views of the city and harbor.

The frolicking seals in outdoor enclosures have been joined by California sea otters that greet you as you approach the Aquarium—the perfect welcome to an entertaining complex that's home to more than 7,000 fish and aquatic mammals. When you head inside, buy an exhibit guide and plan your route as you commune with the penguin colony.

The focal point of the main building is the aptly named Giant Ocean Tank. You'll climb four stories on a spiral ramp that encircles the cylindrical glass tank, which contains 187,000 gallons of salt water, a replica of a Caribbean coral reef, and a conglomeration of sea creatures who seem to coexist amazingly well. Part of the reason for the prevailing calm may be that the sharks are fed five times a day by scuba divers who bring the food right to them.

Other exhibits show off freshwater specimens, denizens of the Amazon, and jellyfish. At the "Edge of the Sea" exhibit, you're encouraged to touch the starfish, sea urchins, and horseshoe crabs in the tide pool. Be sure to leave time for a show at the floating marine mammal pavilion, "Discovery," where sea lions perform every 90 minutes throughout the day.

Note: The aquarium sponsors **whale-watching expeditions** (☎ **617/973-5281**) daily from May through mid-October and on weekends in April and late October. You'll travel several miles out to sea to Stellwagen Bank, feeding ground for the whales as they migrate from Newfoundland to Provincetown. Tickets (cash only) are $24 for adults, $19 for senior citizens and college students, $17.50 for children 12 to 18, and $16.50 for children 3 to 11. Children must be 3 years old and at least 30 inches tall. Reservations are recommended and can be held with MasterCard or Visa.

Boston Public Library. 666 Boylston St. (at Copley Sq.). ☎ **617/536-5400.** Web site: http://www.bpl.org. Free Admission. Mon–Thurs 9am–9pm, Fri–Sat 9am–5pm, Sun 1–5pm. Closed Sun June–Sept and on legal holidays. MBTA: Green Line to Copley.

The central branch of the city's library system is an architectural as well as intellectual monument. The original 1895 building, a registered National Historic Landmark designed by Charles F. McKim, is an Italian Renaissance–style masterpiece that fairly drips with art. The lobby doors are the work of Daniel Chester French (who also designed the *Minute Man* statue in Concord); the murals are by John Singer Sargent and Pierre Puvis de Chavannes, among others; and you'll see notable frescoes, sculptures, and paintings. Visit the lovely courtyard or peek at it from a window on the stairs.

The adjoining addition, of the same height and material (pink granite), was designed by Philip Johnson and opened in 1972. It's a utilitarian building with a dramatic skylit atrium.

Visitors are welcome to wander throughout both buildings—the lobby of the McKim building alone could take half an hour—but you must have a library card (available to Massachusetts residents) to check out materials. The library has more than 6 million books and more than 11 million other items, such as prints, photographs, films, and sound recordings.

Free **Art & Architecture Tours** are conducted Monday at 2:30pm, Tuesday and Wednesday at 6:30pm, Thursday and Saturday at 11am, and from September through May on Sunday at 2pm. Call to arrange group tours (☎ **617/536-5400,** ext. 216).

MUSEUMS

✪ **Museum of Fine Arts, Boston.** 465 Huntington Ave. (at the Fenway). ☎ **617/267-9300.** Web site: http://www.mfa.org. Adults $10 when the entire museum is open, $8 when only the West Wing is open. Students and senior citizens $8 when the entire museum is open, $6 when only the West Wing is open. Children under 18 free. Voluntary contribution, Wed 4–9:45pm. No admission fee for those visiting only the Museum Shop, restaurants, library, or auditorium. Entire museum, Mon–Tues 10am–4:45pm, Wed 10am–9:45pm, Thurs–Fri 10am–5pm, Sat–Sun 10am–5:45pm; West Wing only, Thurs–Fri 5–9:45pm. Closed Thanksgiving Day and Christmas. MBTA: Green Line, E train, to Museum of Fine Arts or Orange Line to Ruggles. Park in the garage or in the lot off Museum Rd.

Not content with the MFA's reputation as the second-best museum in the country (after the Metropolitan Museum of Art in New York), the museum's management team works nonstop to make the collections more accessible and interesting. In recent years, the approach to raising the museum's profile even higher has run the gamut from apparently little things, such as opening the Huntington Avenue entrance, to mounting even more top-notch exhibitions, expanding educational programs, and making admission free to children under 18.

The 128-year-old museum's not-so-secret weapon in its quest is a powerful one: its magnificent collections. Your visit is guided by the best sort of curatorial attitude, the kind that makes even those who go in with a sense of obligation leave with a sense of discovery and wonder. The MFA is especially noted for its Asian and Old Kingdom Egyptian collections, classical art, Buddhist temple, and medieval sculpture and tapestries, but the works you may find more familiar are American and European paintings and sculpture, notably the Impressionist works.

Some particular favorites: John Singleton Copley's 1768 portrait of Paul Revere, Gilbert Stuart's 1796 portrait of George Washington, Winslow Homer's *Long Branch, New Jersey,* a bronze casting of Edgar Degas's sculpture *Little Dancer,* Paul Gauguin's *Where Do We Come From? What Are We? Where Are We Going?,* Fitz Hugh Lane's *Owl's Head, Penobscot Bay, Maine,* and all 43 Monets.

There are also magnificent print and photography collections, and that's not even touching on the furnishings and decorative arts, including the finest collection of Paul Revere silver in the world.

I. M. Pei designed the West Wing (1981), the latest addition to the original 1909 structure. It contains the main entrance, climate-controlled galleries, an auditorium, the excellent Museum Shop, and an atrium with a tree-lined "sidewalk" cafe. The Fine Arts Restaurant is on the second floor, and there's also a cafeteria. Pick up a floor plan at the information desk or take one of the free guided tours.

✪ **Museum of Science.** Science Park. ☎ **617/723-2500.** Web site: http://www.mos.org. Admission to the exhibit halls $8 adults, $6 seniors and children age 3–14, free for children under 3. To the Mugar Omni Theater, the Hayden Planetarium, or the laser theater, $7.50 adults, $5.50 seniors and children age 3–14, free for children under 3. Tickets to 2 or 3 parts of the complex available at discounted prices. Daily 9am–5pm (until 9pm on Fri). Closed Thanksgiving Day and Christmas. MBTA: Green Line to Science Park; the North Station commuter rail stop is a 10-min. walk from the museum.

For the ultimate pain-free educational experience, head to the Museum of Science. The demonstrations, experiments, and interactive displays introduce facts and concepts so effortlessly that everyone winds up learning something. Take a couple of hours or a whole day to explore the permanent and temporary exhibits.

Among the more than 450 exhibits, you might meet an iguana or a dinosaur, find out how much you'd weigh on the moon, or climb into a space module. There's a Discovery Center especially for preschoolers. The newest permanent exhibit is an activity center called "Investigate!" The goal is to help visitors learn to think like scientists, formulating questions, finding evidence, and drawing conclusions through activities such as strapping on a skin sensor to measure reactions to stimuli or sifting through an archaeological dig. You can also visit the theater of electricity to see lightning manufactured indoors.

The separate-admission theaters are worth planning for. If you're making a day or a half-day of it (or even if you're skipping the exhibits), try to see a show. Buy all your tickets at once, not only because it's cheaper but because they sometimes sell out. Tickets for daytime shows must be purchased in person. Evening show tickets can be ordered over the phone using a credit card, but there's a service charge for doing so.

The **Mugar Omni Theater,** one of only 31 in the country, is an intense experience. You're bombarded with images on a four-story domed screen and sounds from a 12-channel sound system with 84 speakers. Even though you know you're not moving, the engulfing sensations and steep pitch of the seating area will have you hanging on for dear life, whether you're watching a film on whales, Yellowstone, or hurricanes and tornadoes. The films change every 4 to 6 months.

The **Charles Hayden Planetarium** takes you deep into space with daily star shows and shows on special topics that change several times a year. On weekends, rock music laser shows take over the planetarium—Pink Floyd fans, this is the place for you.

The museum has a terrific gift shop where the toys and games promote learning without lecturing, and three restaurants. If you're driving, there's a garage on the premises, but entering and exiting can be a harrowing experience because the street is so busy.

✪ **Isabella Stewart Gardner Museum.** 280 The Fenway. ☎ **617/566-1401.** Admission $9 adults, $7 seniors, $5 college students with valid ID, $3 youths ages 12–17 and college students on Wed, free for children under 12. Tues–Sun 11am–5pm and some Mon holidays. Closed Mon. MBTA: Green Line, E train to Museum of Fine Arts.

Isabella Stewart Gardner (1840–1924) was an incorrigible individualist long before such behavior was acceptable for a woman in polite Boston society, and her iconoclasm has proven a great boon to art lovers. "Mrs. Jack" designed her home in the style of a 15th-century Venetian palace and filled it with European, American, and Asian painting and sculpture, much of it chosen with the help of her friend and protégé Bernard Berenson. You'll see works by Titian, Botticelli, Raphael, Rembrandt, Matisse, and Mrs. Gardner's friends James McNeill Whistler and John Singer Sargent.

The building, which was opened to the public after Mrs. Gardner's death, features furniture and architectural details imported from European churches and palaces. The *pièce de résistance* is a magnificent interior skylit courtyard filled year-round with fresh flowers (lilies at Easter, chrysanthemums in the fall, poinsettias at Christmas). Although the terms of Mrs. Gardner's will forbid changing the arrangement of the museum's content, there has been some evolution: a special exhibition gallery, which opened in September 1992, features two or three changing shows a year, and as of late 1996, the entire building was air-conditioned.

The Tapestry Room fills with music on weekends from September through April for the **concert series** (☎ 617/734-1359 for recorded information), which showcases soloists, chamber groups, and local students. The tiled floor and gorgeous wall hangings make a lovely setting for classical music. Concerts begin at 1:30pm on Saturday and Sunday. Tickets, which include museum admission, are $15 for adults, $10 for seniors and college students with valid ID, $7 for ages 12 to 17, and $5 for ages 5 to 11.

Lunch and desserts are served in the museum cafe, and unique items are available at the gift shop.

The Computer Museum. 300 Congress St. (Museum Wharf). ☎ **617/426-2800** or 617/ 423-6758 for the "Talking Computer." Web site: http://www.tcm.org. Admission $7 adults, $5 students and senior citizens; free for children under 5. Tickets half-price on Sun 3–5pm. Fall, winter, and spring Tues–Sun and Mon during Boston school holidays and vacations 10am–5pm; summer daily 10am–6pm. MBTA: Red Line to South Station. Walk north on Atlantic Ave. 1 block, past the Federal Reserve Bank, and turn right onto Congress St.

As computer technology develops, the world's premier computer museum changes and grows with it. The exhibits at the Computer Museum tell the story of computers from their origins in the 1940s to the latest in PCs and virtual reality.

The signature exhibit is the Walk-Through Computer 2000™, a networked multimedia machine 50 times larger than the real thing. When the computer's the size of a two-story house, the mouse is the size of a car, the CD-ROM drive is 8 feet long, the monitor is 12 feet high, and humans enjoying the 30 hands-on activities are the equivalent of crayon sized. The exhibit even has a 7-foot-square Pentium processor, installed in 1995 during a million-dollar upgrade.

Computers don't exist in a vacuum, of course, and a permanent exhibit called "The Networked Planet" allows visitors to explore the information superhighway and its offshoots by logging on to real and simulated networks and learning about medicine, financial markets, and air traffic control. There are also exhibits on robots, the history of the computer, and the practical and recreational uses of the PC—you might compose music, forecast the weather, or "drive" a race car.

New offerings include the "Best Software for Kids" gallery, where the selections change regularly, and kids get a chance to experience "Virtual Worlds" of race car driving and recumbent biking. In all, you'll find more than 170 hands-on exhibits, three theaters, and countless ideas to try out on your home computer.

Special activities, including Internet lessons, are offered on weekends. Call the Talking Computer for information about special programs and events. And before you leave, you can pick up some chocolate floppy disks or microchip jewelry at the Museum Store.

Boston Tea Party Ship & Museum. Congress Street Bridge. ☎ **617/338-1773.** Admission $7 adults, $5.50 students, $3.50 children 6–12, free for children under 6. Mar 1–Nov 30 daily 9am–dusk (around 6pm in summer, 5pm in winter). Closed Dec 1–Feb 28 and Thanksgiving. MBTA: Red Line to South Station. Walk north on Atlantic Ave. 1 block, past the Federal Reserve Bank, and turn right onto Congress St.

On December 16, 1773, a public meeting of independent-minded Bostonians led to the symbolic act of resistance that's commemorated here. The brig *Beaver II*, a full-size replica of one of the three merchant ships emptied by colonists poorly disguised as Indians on the night of the raid, is moored alongside a museum with exhibits on the "tea party." You can dump your own bale of tea into Boston Harbor (it will be retrieved by the museum staff), drink some complimentary tea (served iced in summer, hot in winter), and buy some tea to take home at the museum store.

☉ John F. Kennedy Presidential Library and Museum. Columbia Point, Dorchester. ☎ **617/929-4523.** Admission $6 adults, $4 seniors and students with ID, $2 children 6–16, free for children under 6. Daily 9am–5pm (last film begins at 3:50). Closed Thanksgiving, Christmas, and New Year's Day. MBTA: Red Line to JFK/UMass, then take the free shuttle bus, which runs every 20 min. By car, take the Southeast Expressway (I-93/Rte. 3) south to Exit 15 (Morrissey Blvd./JFK Library), and follow signs to parking lot.

The Kennedy era springs to life at this dramatic library, museum, and educational research complex overlooking Dorchester Bay, where the 35th president's accomplishments and legacy are illustrated with sound and video recordings and fascinating displays of memorabilia and photos.

Your visit begins with a 17-minute film narrated by John F. Kennedy himself—a detail that seems eerie for a moment, then perfectly natural. Through skillfully edited audio clips, he discusses his childhood, education, war experiences, and early political career. Then you're turned loose to spend as much time as you like on each exhibit.

Starting with the 1960 presidential campaign, you're immersed in the period. In a series of connected galleries, you'll see 3¢ newspapers and campaign souvenirs, film of Kennedy debating Richard Nixon and being sworn in, gifts from foreign dignitaries, letters, and political cartoons. There's a film about the Cuban Missile Crisis, and displays on the civil rights movement, the Peace Corps, the space program, and the Kennedy family. An expanded exhibit on First Lady Jacqueline Bouvier Kennedy opened in 1997.

There are replicas of the Oval Office and the office of Attorney General Robert F. Kennedy, the president's brother, and a darkened chamber where news reports of John Kennedy's assassination and funeral play in a continuous loop. And in a room simply called "Legacy," you'll find books, archival documents, and inter-active computers that explain the programs the president initiated and how they affect the world today.

From the final room, the soaring glass-enclosed pavilion that is the heart of the I. M. Pei–designed building, you have a glorious view of the water. Outside, JFK's boyhood sailboat, *Victura*, is on a strip of dune grass between the library and the harbor.

The Institute of Contemporary Art. 955 Boylston St. ☎ **617/266-5152.** Admission $5.25 adults, $3.25 students, $2.25 seniors and children under 16; free Thurs 5–9pm. Thurs noon–9pm, Wed and Fri–Sun noon–5pm. Closed major holidays. MBTA: Green Line, B, C, or D train to Hynes/ICA.

Across from the Hynes Convention Center, the ICA showcases rotating exhibits of 20th-century art, including painting, sculpture, photography, and video and perfor-mance art. The institute also offers films, lectures, music, video, poetry, and an edu-cational program for children and adults. The 1886 building, originally a police station, is a showpiece in its own right.

ORGANIZED TOURS

WALKING TOURS If you prefer not to explore on your own, **Boston By Foot,** 77 N. Washington St. (☎ **617/367-2345,** or 617/367-3766 for recorded informa-tion), offers excellent tours. From May through October, the nonprofit educational corporation conducts historical and architectural tours that focus on particular neigh-borhoods or themes. The rigorously trained guides are volunteers, and questions are encouraged. All tours are $8 for adults and $6 for children; reservations are not re-quired. Tickets may be purchased from the guide. The 90-minute tours take place rain or shine; call for offerings and schedules.

The **Society for the Preservation of New England Antiquities** (☎ 617/227-3956) offers a fascinating tour that describes and illustrates life in the mansions and garrets of Beacon Hill in 1800. "Magnificent and Modest," a 2-hour program, costs $10 and starts at the Harrison Gray Otis House, 141 Cambridge St., on Saturdays at 3pm May through October, and Saturdays at 10am in October. Reservations are recommended.

The **Historic Neighborhoods Foundation,** 99 Bedford St. (☎ 617/426-1885), offers 90-minute walking tours in several neighborhoods, including Beacon Hill, the North End, Chinatown, the Waterfront, and the Financial District. Schedules change with the season, and the programs highlight points of interest to visitors while cov-ering history, architecture, and topographical development. Write or call Historic Neighborhoods for current schedules, fees, and meeting places.

The **Boston Park Rangers** (☎ 617/635-7383) offer free guided walking tours of the Emerald Necklace, a loop of green spaces designed by the first landscape ar-chitect, Frederick Law Olmsted. You'll see and hear about the city's major parks and gardens, including Boston Common, the Public Garden, the Commonwealth Avenue Mall, the Muddy River in the Fenway, Olmsted Park, Jamaica Pond, the Arnold Arboretum, and Franklin Park. The full 6-hour walk includes a 1-hour tour of any of the sites. Call for schedules.

TROLLEY TOURS Take a narrated trolley tour for an overview of the sights be-fore focusing on specific attractions, or use your all-day pass as a way to hit as many places as possible in 8 hours or so. Whatever your approach, you'll have plenty of company. The business is competitive, with various companies offering different stops in an effort to distinguish themselves from the rest. All cover the major attractions and offer informative narratives and anecdotes in their 90- to 120-minute tours, as well as free reboarding if you want to visit the sites. Rates are between $17 and $20 for adults, less for children. Boarding spots are at hotels, historic sites, and tourist information centers.

Trolley companies are identified by the colors of their cars. **Old Town Trolley,** 329 W. Second St. (☎ **617/269-7010**), has orange-and-green cars; **Boston Trolley Tours** (☎ **617/269-3626**) uses blue cars; **Beantown Trolleys** (☎ **617/ 236-2148**) are red; and the **Discover Boston Multilingual Trolley Tours,** 73 Tremont St. (☎ **617/742-1440**), vehicle is white. Boston Trolley Tours has ramps to make it accessible to travelers with disabilities, and the Beantown Trolleys are the only ones that stop at the Museum of Fine Arts and the Hard Rock Cafe. Only Old Town and the Beantown Trolleys stop at the Boston Tea Party Ship & Museum. Only Old Town offers a tour of Cambridge.

SIGHTSEEING CRUISES   Take to the water for a taste of Boston's rich maritime history or a day-long break from walking and driving. You can cruise around the harbor or go all the way to Provincetown or Gloucester. If you're traveling in a large group, call ahead for information about reservations and discounted tickets.

Boston Harbor Cruises, 1 Long Wharf (☎ **617/227-4321**), offers narrated trips around the harbor. The 90-minute historic sightseeing cruises, which tour the Inner and Outer harbors, depart at 11am, 1pm, 3pm, and 7pm (the sunset cruise). Tickets are $10 for adults, $8 for seniors, $6 for children under 12. The 45-minute *Constitution* cruise takes you around the Inner Harbor and docks at Charlestown Navy Yard so you can go ashore and visit the USS *Constitution* if you like. Tours leave Long Wharf every hour on the half hour from 10:30am to 4:30pm, and on the hour from the navy yard from 11am to 5pm. The cruise is $6 for adults, $5 for seniors, and $4 for children.

The same company offers service to George's Island, where free water-taxi service to the rest of the Boston Harbor Islands is available. The 90-minute Harbor Islands cruise departs at 10am, noon, and 2pm in the spring and fall, and daily on the hour from 10am to 4pm in the summer. Tickets are $7.50 for adults, $6.50 for seniors, $5.50 for children.

Massachusetts Bay Lines (☎ **617/542-8000**) offers 55-minute harbor tours from Memorial Day through Columbus Day. Cruises leave from Rowes Wharf on the hour from 10am to 6pm; the price is $8 for adults, $5 for children and seniors. The same company offers 3-hour live-music cruises (blues, Wednesday at 7pm; rock, Thursday at 8pm) for $12. You must be at least 21 and have a photo ID.

The **Charles River Boat Company** (☎ **617/621-3001**), offers 55-minute narrated cruises around the lower Charles River basin. Boats depart from the CambridgeSide Galleria on the hour from noon to 5pm; tickets are $8 for adults, $6 for seniors, $5 for children.

For almost a full day at sea, Bay State Cruises' *MV Provincetown II* (☎ **617/ 457-1428**) sails from Commonwealth Pier daily from mid-June to Labor Day, and on weekends in May and September. Be at the pier by 8:30 (the water shuttle from Long Wharf leaves at 9am and costs $1) for the 3-hour trip to Provincetown, at the tip of Cape Cod. The return trip leaves at 3:30pm, giving you $3^{1}/_{2}$ hours for shopping and sightseeing. Same-day round-trip fares are $30 for adults, $23 for senior citizens, and $21 for children. Bringing a bike costs $5 extra each way.

Bay State also offers 3-hour cruises with live entertainment on Friday and Saturday at 8:30pm from late June through early September. Tickets are $15 to $20, depending on who's performing; you must be at least 21 and have a photo ID.

Another day trip is offered by **A.C. Cruise Line** (☎ **800/422-8419** or 617/261-6633). The *Virginia C II* sails to Gloucester from Pier 7 (290 Northern Ave.) daily from late June through Labor Day at 10am and returns at 5pm. You'll have about 2¹/₂ hours to explore Gloucester. The round-trip charge is $18 for adults, $14 for senior citizens, $12 for children under 12. A.C. Cruise Line also offers a 3-hour country-western dance cruise ($12) with live entertainment Thursdays at 8pm.

The *Spirit of Boston,* a sleek 192-foot harbor-cruise ship operated by **Bay State Cruises** (☎ **617/457-1499**), offers a New England lobster clambake luncheon cruise (daily, noon to 2:30pm) and a dinner dance cruise (nightly, 7 to 10pm). It sails from the World Trade Center. Call for reservations.

WHALE WATCHING　The New England Aquarium (see listing above) runs its own whale watches.

Boston Harbor Whale Watch (☎ **617-345-9866**) sends the 100-foot *Majestic* out to sea at speeds topping 20 knots and promises more time watching whales than trying to find them. Tours depart from Rowes Wharf beginning in mid-June and operate Friday, Saturday, and Sunday only through June. From July through early September there's daily service. Departure times are Monday through Friday at 10am, Saturday and Sunday at 9am and 2pm. Expect to spend about 4¹/₂ hours at sea. Tickets are $20 for adults, $18 for seniors and children under 13. Reservations are suggested, and discounted parking is available.

Other cruise companies offering whale watches include **A.C. Cruise Line** (☎ **800/422-8419** or 617/261-6633), with departures Tuesday through Sunday, leaving at 10:30am and returning at 5pm. The fare is $19 for adults, $15 for seniors, $12 for children under 12. **Boston Harbor Cruises** (☎ **617/227-4321**) departs daily at 10am and 11am, returning approximately 5 hours later. Tickets are $22 for adults, $16 for seniors, and $19 for children under 12. And **Massachusetts Bay Lines** (☎ **617/542-8000**) offers 5-hour cruises daily from late June through September 1. Tickets are $24 for adults, $18 for children and seniors.

DUCK, DUCK, LOOSE　The newest and perhaps best way to see Boston is with **Boston Duck Tours** (☎ **617/723-DUCK**). Sightseers board a "duck," a reconditioned World War II amphibious landing craft, on the Huntington Avenue side of the Prudential Center. The 80-minute narrated tour hits the high points, including Trinity Church, the Boston Public Library, the North End, Faneuil Hall, and the Old State House.

But the real high point comes when the duck lumbers down a ramp and splashes into the Charles River for a spin around the basin.

The tours are pricey but great fun. Tickets are $19 for adults, $16 for seniors and students, $10 for children 4 to 12, and $2.50 for children 3 and under. Tours leave every 30 minutes starting at 9am and ending 1 hour before sunset. There are no tours from December through March; call for schedules.

KID STUFF

Just about every major destination in the city either is specifically designed to appeal to youngsters or can be easily adapted to do so.

Hands-on exhibits are a big draw at several institutions: The **New England Aquarium** (☎ **617/973-5200**), the **Computer Museum** (☎ **617/426-2800** or 617/423-6758), and the **Boston Tea Party Ship & Museum** (☎ **617/338-1773**). See the listings above for full details.

You might get your hands on a baseball at a **Red Sox game,** a sure fire kid pleaser (see "Spectator Sports," below).

The **Boston Museum of Science** (☎ 617/723-2500) is not only a hands-on paradise but is also home to the **Hayden Planetarium** and the **Mugar Omni Theater.**

For those in the mood to let other people do the work, take in the shows by the street performers at **Faneuil Hall Marketplace** (☎ 617/338-2323).

Under a new policy, admission is free for those under 18 at the **Museum of Fine Arts** (☎ 617/267-9300), which has special Sunday and after-school programs.

The allure of seeing people the size of ants draws young visitors to the **John Hancock Observatory** (☎ 617/572-6429) and the **Prudential Center Skywalk** (☎ 617/236-3318).

And they can see actual ants—though they might prefer the dinosaurs—at the Museum of Comparative Zoology, part of the **Harvard University Museum of Cultural and Natural History** (☎ 617/495-3045; see section 6 for details).

Older children who have studied modern American history will enjoy a visit to the **John F. Kennedy Presidential Library and Museum** (☎ 617/929-4523).

Young visitors who have read Robert McCloskey's children's classic *Make Way for Ducklings* will relish a visit to the **Public Garden,** as will fans of E. B. White's *The Trumpet of the Swan,* who certainly will want to ride on the **swan boats** (☎ 617/ 522-1966 or 617/624-7020). Considerably less tame and much longer are **whale watches** (see "Organized Tours," above).

The walking-tour company **Boston By Foot,** 77 N. Washington St. (☎ 617/ 367-2345, or 617/367-3766 for recorded information), has a special program, **Boston By Little Feet,** geared to children 6 to 12 years old. The 60-minute walk gives a child's-eye view of the architecture along the Freedom Trail and of Boston's role in the American Revolution. Children must be accompanied by an adult, and a map is provided. Tours run from May through October and meet at the statue of Samuel Adams on the Congress Street side of Faneuil Hall, Saturday at 10am, Sunday at 2pm, and Monday at 10am, rain or shine. The cost is $6 per person.

The **Historic Neighborhoods Foundation,** 99 Bedford St. (☎ 617/426-1885), offers a 90-minute "Make Way for Ducklings" tour ($5 per person aged 5 or older). It's popular with children and adults, follows the path of the Mallard family described in Robert McCloskey's famous book, and ends at the Public Garden. Every year on Mother's Day, the HNF organizes the Ducklings Day Parade.

Children's Museum. 300 Congress St. (Museum Wharf). ☎ **617/426-8855.** Admission $7 adults, $6 children age 2–15 and seniors, $2 toddlers age 1, free for infants under age 1. Fri 5–9pm, admission is $1 for all. Sept–June Tues–Thurs and Sat–Sun 10am–5pm, Fri 10am–9pm; June–Aug Sat–Thurs 10am–5pm, Fri 10am–9pm. Closed Mon during school year, except Boston school vacations and holidays; Thanksgiving, Christmas, and New Year's Day. MBTA: Red Line to South Station. Walk north on Atlantic Ave. 1 block past the Federal Reserve Bank, and turn right onto Congress St. Call for information about discounted parking.

As you approach the Children's Museum, don't be surprised to see adults suddenly being dragged by the hand as their young companions realize how close they are and start running. You know the museum is near when you see the 40-foot-high red-and-white milk bottle out front. It makes both children and adults look small in comparison—which is probably part of the point. No matter how old, everyone behaves like a little kid at this delightful museum.

Not only is touching encouraged, it's practically a necessity if you're going to enjoy the exhibits. Children can stick with their parents or wander on their own, learning, doing, and role-playing. Some favorites: "Under the Dock," an environmental exhibit that teaches young people about the Boston waterfront and allows them to dress up in a crab suit; the "Kids' Bridge," where interactive videos allow a virtual visit to Boston's ethnic neighborhoods to learn about cultural differences and ways to combat racism; and the "Dress-Up Shop," a souped-up version of playing in Grandma's closet.

You'll also see "El Mercado," a marketplace that immerses children in Hispanic culture, surrounding them with Spanish newspapers, ethnic food products, and salsa music. The "Climbing Sculpture" is a giant maze designed especially for children (adults may get stuck). Another oversize display is a desk with a phone so big it doubles as a slide. "We're Still Here" concentrates on Northeast Native Americans and offers the chance to play in a wigwam. You can also explore a Japanese house from Kyoto (Boston's sister city) and learn about young adults in "Teen Tokyo." "Playspace" is a special room for children under 4 and their caregivers.

6 Exploring Cambridge

Harvard Square is a people-watching paradise of college and high-school students and instructors, commuters, street performers, and sightseers. There are restaurants and stores along all three streets that radiate from the center of the square and the streets that intersect them. On weekend afternoons and evenings year-round, you'll hear music and see street performers. It's a great area for just wandering. To get away from the urban bustle, stroll down to the paved paths along the Charles River.

From Boston, take the MBTA Red Line toward Alewife. In Cambridge, the subway stops at Kendall/MIT, and Central, Harvard, and Porter squares. If you're staying in or visiting the Back Bay, the longer and more colorful route is the Number 1 bus (Harvard–Dudley), which runs along Mass. Ave. It cuts through a wide variety of neighborhoods and affords a nice view of the Charles River, but can be very slow at rush hour.

If you're driving from Boston, follow Mass. Ave., or take Storrow Drive along the south bank of the river to the Harvard Square exit. Or take Memorial Drive along the north side of the river to MIT, Central Square, or Harvard. From the Massachusetts Turnpike, take the Allston/Brighton exit, then turn left onto Storrow Drive or cross the bridge to reach Memorial Drive.

Traffic in and around Harvard Square is almost as bad as in downtown Boston. Once you get to Cambridge, park the car and walk. If you prefer to ride, you can take a 75-minute narrated tour given by **Old Town Trolley** (☎ **617/269-7010**). Tours leave from the middle of Harvard Square, near **Out of Town News** (a newspaper and magazine shop right outside the Harvard "T" stop), every 45 minutes between 9am and 4pm, and you may leave the trolley and reboard anywhere along the route. Adults ride for $14, seniors $12, and children $7.

ATTRACTIONS AT HARVARD UNIVERSITY

Harvard is the oldest college in the country, and if you suggest aloud that it's not the best, you may encounter the attitude that inspired the saying "You can always tell a Harvard man, but you can't tell him much." The university encompasses the college and 10 graduate and professional schools located in more than 400 buildings around Boston and Cambridge.

Free, student-led tours of the main campus leave from the **Events & Information Center** in Holyoke Center at 1350 Mass. Ave. (☎ **617/495-1573**) during the school year, twice a day during the week and once on Saturday except during vacations, and during the summer four times a day Monday through Saturday and twice on Sunday. Call for exact times; reservations aren't necessary. You're also free to wander on

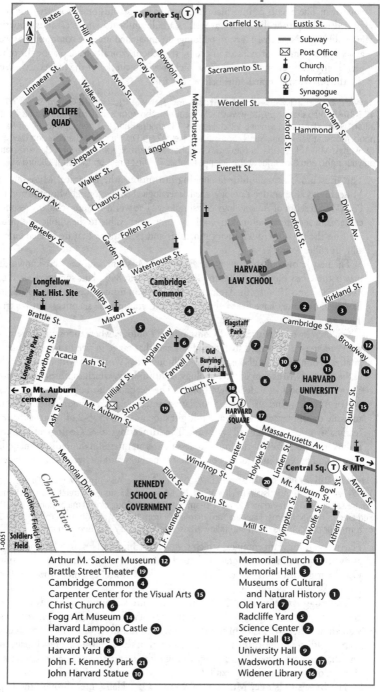

Arthur M. Sackler Museum 12
Brattle Street Theater 19
Cambridge Common 4
Carpenter Center for the Visual Arts 15
Christ Church 6
Fogg Art Museum 14
Harvard Lampoon Castle 20
Harvard Square 18
Harvard Yard 8
John F. Kennedy Park 21
John Harvard Statue 10

Memorial Church 11
Memorial Hall 3
Museums of Cultural
  and Natural History 1
Old Yard 7
Radcliffe Yard 5
Science Center 2
Sever Hall 13
University Hall 9
Wadsworth House 17
Widener Library 16

your own. The Events & Information Center has maps, illustrated booklets, and self-guided walking-tour directions, as well as a bulletin board where campus activities are publicized. Note that Harvard buildings are integrated into the community as well as set apart from it—structures in use by the school typically have plaques or other identifying features on the front. You might want to check out the university's Web site (**http://www.harvard.edu**) before your trip.

Harvard University Museum of Cultural and Natural History. 26 Oxford St. ☎ **617/495-3045.** Web site: http://fas-www.harvard.edu/~peabody/museum_cult.html. Admission $5 adults, $4 students and seniors, $3 children 3–13, children under 3 free; free to all Sat 9am–noon. Mon–Sat 9am–5pm, Sun 1–5pm; closed New Year's Day, July 4th, Thanksgiving Day, and Christmas. MBTA: Red Line to Harvard. Cross Harvard Yard, keeping the John Harvard statue on your right, and turn right at the Science Center. The first street on the left is Oxford St.

This museum is actually four fascinating institutions: the Botanical Museum, the Museum of Comparative Zoology, the Mineralogical & Geological Museum, and the Peabody Museum of Archaeology & Ethnology. The world-famous scholarly resource center is in the process of making itself even more accessible to the public and prides itself on the new interdisciplinary programs and exhibitions that tie in elements of all four collections.

The best known of the four is the **Botanical Museum,** and the best-known display is the Glass Flowers, 3,000 models of more than 840 plant species devised between 1887 and 1936 by the German father-and-son team of Leopold and Rudolph Blaschka. You may have heard about them, and you may be skeptical, but it's true: They actually look real.

Children love the **Museum of Comparative Zoology,** where dinosaurs share space with preserved and stuffed insects and animals that range in size from butterflies to giraffes. Young visitors also enjoy the dollhouselike "Worlds in Miniature" display at the **Peabody Museum of Archaeology & Ethnology,** which captures people from all over the world in scaled-down homes. The Peabody also boasts the Hall of the North American Indian, where 500 Native American artifacts representing 10 cultures are on display, and where a terrific gift shop (☎ **617/495-2248**) is packed with reasonably priced folk art and craftwork. The **Mineralogical & Geological Museum** is the most specialized of the four—unless there's an interesting interdisciplinary display or you're really into rocks, your time can be more productively spent elsewhere.

Harvard University Art Museums. 32 Quincy St. and 485 Broadway (at Quincy St.). ☎ **617/495-9400.** Admission to all 3 $5 adults, $4 seniors, $3 students, free for children under 18; free to all Sat 10am–noon. Mon–Sat 10am–5pm, Sun 1–5pm; closed major holidays. MBTA: Red Line to Harvard. Cross Harvard Yard diagonally from the "T" station and cross Quincy St., or turn your back on the Coop and follow Mass. Ave. to Quincy St., then turn left.

Harvard's art museum complex, which contains teaching and research facilities as well as exhibit spaces, houses a total of about 150,000 works of art in three collections. One-hour guided tours are available every weekday from September through June, and on Wednesdays only in July and August.

The **Fogg Art Museum,** 32 Quincy St., centers around an impressive 16th-century Italian stone courtyard, with two floors of galleries opening off it. You'll see something different in each of the 19 rooms: 17th-century Dutch and Flemish landscapes, 19th-century British and American paintings and drawings, French paintings and drawings from the 18th century through the Impressionist period, contemporary sculpture, and changing exhibits.

The **Busch-Reisinger Museum** in Werner Otto Hall (enter through the Fogg) opened in 1991 and is the only museum in North America devoted to the painting, sculpture, and decorative art of northern and central Europe—specifically Germany. Its encyclopedic collection also includes prints and illustrated books, and is particularly noted for its early-20th-century collections, including works by Klee, Feininger, Kandinsky, and artists and designers associated with the Bauhaus.

The **Arthur M. Sackler Museum,** 485 Broadway, houses the university's collections of Asian, ancient, and Islamic art. Included are an assemblage of Chinese jades and cave reliefs that's considered the best in the world, as well as Korean ceramics, Roman sculpture, Greek vases, and Persian miniature paintings and calligraphy.

A HISTORIC HOUSE

Longfellow National Historic Site. 105 Brattle St. ☎ **617/876-4491.** Guided tour $2 adults, free for seniors and children under 17. Tours June–Oct Wed–Sun and mid-Mar to May and Nov to mid-Dec Sat–Sun at 10:45am, 11:45am, 1pm, 2pm, 3pm, and 4pm. Spring and fall Wed–Fri at 12:30pm, 1:30pm, 2:30pm, and 3:30pm. Closed mid-Dec to mid-Mar. MBTA: Red Line to Harvard, then follow Brattle St. about 7 blocks; the house is on the right.

The books and furniture at this ravishing yellow mansion have remained intact since poet Henry Wadsworth Longfellow died here in 1882. It was a family residence for nearly a century afterward. Now a unit of the National Park Service, during the siege of Boston in 1775 to 1776 the house served as the headquarters of Gen. George Washington, with whom Longfellow was fascinated. The poet first lived in this house as a boarder in 1837, and when he and Fanny Appleton married in 1843, her father made it a wedding present. Rangers lead tours (the only way to see the house), which are absorbing and informative, and there are sometimes free concerts and poetry readings on the porch or lawn.

A CELEBRATED CEMETERY

Dedicated in 1831, **Mount Auburn Cemetery,** 580 Mount Auburn St. (☎ **617/ 547-7105**), was the first of America's rural, or garden, cemeteries. The establishment of burying places removed from city and town centers reflected practical and philosophical concerns. Development was encroaching on urban graveyards, and the ideas associated with the Greek Revival (the word "cemetery" derives from the Greek for "sleeping place") and Transcendentalism dictated that communing with nature take precedence over organized religion. Since the day it opened, Mount Auburn has been a popular place to retreat and reflect—in the 19th century, it was often the first place visitors from out of town were taken, and the first place they wanted to go.

A modern visitor will find history and horticulture coexisting with celebrity. The graves of Henry Wadsworth Longfellow, Oliver Wendell Holmes, Julia Ward Howe, and Mary Baker Eddy are here, as are those of Charles Bulfinch, James Russell Lowell, Transcendentalist leader Margaret Fuller, and abolitionist Charles Sumner. In season, you'll see gorgeous flowering trees and shrubs (the Massachusetts Horticultural Society had a hand in the design). Stop at the office or front gate to pick up brochures and a map or to rent the 60-minute audiotaped tour ($5; a $12 deposit is required), which you can listen to in your car or on a portable tape player. The **Friends of Mount Auburn Cemetery** (☎ **617/864-9646**) conducts workshops and coordinates walking tours. Call for topics, schedules, and fees.

The cemetery is open daily from 8am to dusk. Admission is free. Animals and recreational activities such as jogging and picnicking are not allowed. MBTA bus routes 71 and 73 start at Harvard station and stop across the street; they run frequently on weekdays, less often on weekends. From Harvard Square by car (about 10 min.) or on foot (at least 30 min.), take Mount Auburn Street or Brattle Street west; just after they intersect, the gate is on the left.

A STROLL AROUND CAMBRIDGE

To explore Harvard and the surrounding area, begin your walk in **Harvard Square.** Town and gown meet at this lively intersection, where you'll get a taste of the improbable mix of people drawn to the crossroads of Cambridge.

Start at the Harvard "T" station, with the **Harvard Coop** at your back. Walk half a block, crossing Dunster Street, and stop in front of **Holyoke Center,** an administration building designed by Josep Luis Sert with commercial space on the ground floor. Across the street at 1341 Mass. Ave. is **Wadsworth House,** a yellow wood structure that was built in 1726 as a residence for Harvard's fourth president and is now the headquarters of the alumni association. Its biggest claim to fame is a classic: George Washington slept here.

Cross the street and go left. Follow the outside of the redbrick wall past one gate until you see another "T" exit. Turn right and use Johnston Gate to enter **Harvard Yard.** "The Yard" was just a patch of grass with animals grazing on it when Harvard College was established in 1636 to train young men for the ministry. It wasn't much more when the Continental Army spent the winter here from 1775 to 1776. Some of Harvard's most interesting buildings are within this quadrangle. **Massachusetts Hall** (1720), to your right, houses the university president's office and rooms for first-year students. To your left is **Harvard Hall,** a classroom building constructed in 1765. The matching side-by-side buildings behind Harvard Hall are **Hollis** and **Stoughton halls.** Hollis dates to 1763 and has been home to many students who went on to great fame, among them Ralph Waldo Emerson, Henry David Thoreau, and Charles Bulfinch.

Across the Yard is **University Hall,** the college's main administration building, constructed between 1812 and 1813. In 1969, it was occupied by students protesting the Vietnam War, but it's best known as the backdrop of the **John Harvard Statue,** one of the most photographed objects in the Boston area. Designed by Daniel Chester French in 1884, it's known as the "Statue of Three Lies" because the inscription reads "John Harvard—Founder—1638." In fact, the college was established in 1636; Harvard (one of many people involved) wasn't the founder, but donated money and his library; and this isn't John Harvard, anyway. No portraits of him survive, so the model was, according to various accounts, either his nephew or a student. Walk over to the statue and join the throng of tourists posing for pictures with the benevolent-looking gentleman.

Walk around University Hall into the adjoining quadrangle. This is still the Yard, but it's the "New Yard," where commencement and other university-wide ceremonies are held. On your right is **Widener Library,** the centerpiece of the world's largest university library system. It was built in 1913 as a memorial to Harry Elkins Widener, a 1907 Harvard graduate who died when the *Titanic* sank in 1912 because he was unable to swim 50 yards to a lifeboat. His mother donated $2 million for the library on the condition that every undergraduate prove his ability to swim 50 yards. Today, the library holds more than 3 million volumes, including 3,500 rare volumes collected by Harry Elkins Widener.

Facing the library is **Memorial Church,** built in 1931 and topped with a tower and weathervane 197 feet tall. You're welcome to look around this Georgian Revival–style edifice unless services are going on—or to attend them if they are. Morning prayers are said daily from 8:45 to 9am, and the Sunday service is at 11am. The entrance is on the left. On the south wall, toward the Yard, the names of the Harvard graduates who died in the world wars, Korea, and Vietnam are listed, including that of Joseph P. Kennedy, Jr., the president's brother, class of 1938.

Log On, Tune In, Drop Out

Cutting-edge computer technology contributes to the local economy in many ways, most entertainingly at the area's two **Cybersmith** locations, where you can check out a selection of about 30 hot CD-ROMs, surf the World Wide Web, and take a crack at virtual reality. From businesspeople dropping in to check their E-mail to whole families "skiing," from novices to expert programmers, a wide range of people are amused and even educated at the cutting-edge business's two area locations.

Here's how it works: You're issued a "Cybercard," which works like a debit card, and the various stations deduct the appropriate amount for the activity you've chosen. Working or playing on a computer terminal (in a restaurantlike booth rather than at a desk) is $9.95 an hour, virtual reality is $2.50 per "experience," and skiing or snowboarding is $1.50 per run.

Cybersmith has a branch in the South Canopy and basement of Quincy Market (☎ **617/367-1777**) and in Harvard Square at 36 Church St. (☎ **617/492-5857**). Each has different CD-ROMs and other features. The Boston location is open Monday through Thursday from 10am to 10pm, Friday and Saturday until midnight, and Sunday from 11am to 9pm; the Cambridge location keeps the same hours except from Monday through Thursday, when it's open until 11pm.

With Memorial Church behind you, turn left toward **Sever Hall,** a classroom building designed by H. H. Richardson (the architect of Boston's Trinity Church) and built from 1878 to 1880. Notice the gorgeous brickwork that includes roll moldings around the doors, and the fluted brick chimneys. The front door is set back in the "whispering gallery." Stand on one side of the entrance arch, station a friend or willing passerby on the opposite side, and speak softly into the facade. Someone standing next to you can't hear what you say, but the person at the other side of the arch can.

Walk back across the front of Memorial Church and turn right. Follow the path out of the Yard to the **Science Center** at Zero Oxford St., a 10-story monolith said to resemble a Polaroid camera (Edwin H. Land, founder of the Cambridge-based Polaroid Corporation, was one of its main benefactors). Built from 1970 to 1972, it was designed by the Spanish architect Josep Luis Sert, the dean of the university's Graduate School of Design from 1953 to 1969, and a disciple of Le Corbusier.

On the plaza between the Science Center and the Yard is the **Tanner Rock Fountain,** a group of 159 New England field boulders artfully arranged around a small fountain. Since 1985 this has been a favorite spot for students to relax and watch unsuspecting passersby get wet; the fountain sprays a fine mist, which begins slowly and gradually intensifies. Step inside the Science Center to have a look around and perhaps a snack at the **Green House Cafe.**

To your right as you face the Science Center is **Memorial Hall,** a Victorian structure built from 1870 to 1874. The entrance on Cambridge Street puts you in the actual hall of memorials, a transept where you can read the names of the Harvard men who died fighting for the Union during the Civil War—those who died for the Confederacy are absent. Memorial Hall also houses **Sanders Theater,** prized as both a performance space and a lecture hall for its excellent acoustics and clear views, and **Annenberg Hall** (originally Alumni Hall), which underwent a massive renovation in 1995 and was turned into a dining hall. It has gorgeous stained-glass windows that you might be able to get a look at if it's not mealtime.

With the entrance to the Science Center behind you, turn right, and follow the walkway for the equivalent of a block and a half as it curves around to the right. The Harvard Law School campus is on your right. Carefully cross Mass. Ave. to **Cambridge Common.** This well-used plot of greenery and bare earth is dotted with memorials and plaques. Turn left and head back toward Harvard Square; after a block or so you'll walk near or over horseshoes embedded in the concrete. This is the path William Dawes, Paul Revere's fellow alarm sounder, took from Boston to Lexington on April 18, 1775.

Turn right onto Garden Street and continue following the Common for one block. On your right you'll see a monument marking the place where Gen. George Washington took control of the Continental Army on July 3, 1775.

Cross Garden Street and backtrack to **Christ Church** at Zero Garden St. The oldest church in Cambridge, it was designed by Peter Harrison of Newport, R.I. (who was also the architect of King's Chapel in Boston), and opened in 1761. Note the square wooden tower. Inside the vestibule you can still see bullet holes made by British muskets. At one time, the church was used as the barracks for Connecticut troops. During their stay, they melted down the organ pipes to make bullets.

Facing the church, turn right and proceed on Garden Street to the first intersection. This is Appian Way. Turn left and take the first right into **Radcliffe Yard.** Radcliffe College was founded in 1879 as the "Harvard Annex" and named for Ann Radcliffe, Lady Mowlson, Harvard's first female benefactor. Undergraduate classes were merged with Harvard's in 1943, Harvard degrees were given to Radcliffe graduates in 1963, and in 1977 responsibility for educating undergraduate women was officially turned over to Harvard. Today, Radcliffe remains an independent corporation within the university and has its own president, though its degrees, classes, and facilities are shared with Harvard. After you've strolled around, return to Appian Way and turn right. You'll emerge on Brattle Street; turn left, heading toward Harvard Square.

In about three blocks you'll find yourself in the **Brattle Square** part of Harvard Square. You may see street musicians or performers, a protest, a speech, or just more stores to explore. Cross Brattle Street at **WordsWorth Books,** turn right, and follow the curve of the building around the corner to Mount Auburn Street. Stay on the left-hand side of the street as you cross John F. Kennedy Street, Dunster Street, Holyoke Street, and Linden Street.

The corner of Mount Auburn and Linden streets is a good vantage point for viewing the **Harvard Lampoon Castle,** designed by Wheelwright & Haven in 1909. Listed on the National Register of Historic Places, this is the home of Harvard's undergraduate humor magazine, the *Lampoon.* The main tower looks like a face, with windows as the eyes, nose, and mouth, topped by what looks like a miner's hat.

Follow Mount Auburn Street back to John F. Kennedy Street and turn left. Cross the street at some point, and follow it toward the Charles River, almost to Memorial Drive. On your right is **John F. Kennedy Park.** This lovely parcel of land was an empty plot near the MBTA train yard in the 1970s (at that time the Red Line ended at Harvard), when the search was on for a site for the Kennedy Library. Traffic concerns led to the library's being built in Dorchester, but the Graduate School of Government and this adjacent park bear the president's name. Walk away from the street to enjoy the fountain, which is engraved with excerpts from the president's speeches. This is an excellent place to take a break and plan the rest of your day.

7 Spectator Sports & Active Pursuits

SPECTATOR SPORTS

Boston's well-deserved reputation as a great sports town derives in part from the days when at least one of the professional teams was one of the world's best. With all due respect to the Patriots, who play in suburban Foxboro and lost in the 1997 Super Bowl, none of them has done much lately. Passions still run deep—insult the local teams and be ready to defend yourself. This applies to some extent to college sports as well, particularly hockey, for which the Division I schools are evenly matched.

In September 1995, the **FleetCenter** opened behind 67-year-old Boston Garden and the "Gah-den" was shut down (at press time, it's still standing as various corporate entities wrangle over who will pay for the demolition). The narrow, cramped seats and obstructed views in the incredibly steep Garden were replaced by cushy chairs in a wide-open bowl-shaped arena—but the feeling of being right on top of the action was replaced by the feeling of watching at a distance. One constant is the basketball floor, a collection of wood parquet tiles that made the trip to the new building.

The FleetCenter and the **Garden History Center,** 150 Causeway St. (☎ **617/ 624-1518;** Web site: **http://www.fleetcenter.com**), are open for tours Monday through Saturday on the hour from 10am to 4pm, Sunday from 11am to 3pm, except during events. Tickets are $6 for adults, $5 for seniors and students, and $4.50 for children under 12.

BASEBALL No experience in sports matches watching the **Boston Red Sox** play at **Fenway Park,** which they do from early April to early October, and later if they make the playoffs.

In 1918, the Boston Red Sox won the World Series for the fifth time in the 15-year history of the event. And one of the most famous facts in sports history is that they have yet to win another.

Fatalistic Red Sox fans attribute the team's disastrous luck to a transaction executed after the 1919 season. Team owner Harry Frazee, a theatrical producer who needed money to mount a production of the musical *No, No, Nanette,* accepted $100,000 from the New York Yankees in exchange for a promising young pitcher and outfielder named Babe Ruth. The "Curse of the Bambino" is believed to have prevailed ever since, leading to an exorcism, a book, and an uncanny number of postseason catastrophes.

Not that the Red Sox haven't come close. They lost one-game playoffs for the pennant in 1948 and 1978. They actually went to the World Series in 1946, 1967, 1975, and 1986—and lost in the seventh and final game each time.

The curse, and the quirkiness of the oldest park in the major leagues (1912), only adds to the mystique. A hand-operated scoreboard is built into the Green Monster, or left-field wall (watch carefully during a pitching change—the left fielder from either team may suddenly disappear into the darkness to cool off), and the wall itself is such a celebrity that it's often called simply The Wall. It's 37 feet tall, a mere 298 feet from home plate, and irresistibly tempting to batters who ought to know better. On two vertical white lines on the scoreboard you'll see Morse code for the initials of legendary owners Thomas A. and Jean R. Yawkey, now dead.

The crowds can be as interesting as the architecture. Fans are jammed together in narrow, uncomfortable seats close to the field, striking up conversations with total strangers, reminiscing, and making bold predictions. A recent fan-relations campaign called "Friendly Fenway" has produced better-mannered employees, a greater variety of concession items (but not lower prices), and expanded family-seating sections, but for the most part that's window dressing. You're in an intensely green place that's older than your grandparents, inhaling a Fenway Frank and wishing for a home run—what could be better?

Practical concerns: Compared to its modern brethren, Fenway is tiny. Tickets go on sale in early December for the following season, and the earlier you order, the better chance you'll have of landing seats during your visit. Forced to choose between tickets for a low-numbered grandstand section (say, 10 or below) and less expensive bleacher seats, go for the bleachers. They can get rowdy during night games, but the view is better from there than from the deep right-field corner. If you plan to be in town around the same time as the Marathon, your chances of landing tickets for Patriots' Day are poor (the game starts at 11am so that fans can, theoretically, be in Kenmore Square to watch the leading runners pass by), but don't despair. Two or three games in April traditionally are scheduled for weekday afternoons, and they almost never sell out. Throughout the season, a limited number of standing-room-only tickets go on sale the day of the game, and there's always the possibility that tickets will be returned. It can't hurt to check, especially if the team isn't playing well. The fans are incredibly loyal, but they're not all obsessed.

The Fenway Park **ticket office** is at 24 Yawkey Way, near the corner of Brookline Avenue. Call ☎ **617/267-8661** for information, **617/267-1700** for tickets. Tickets for people with disabilities and for seating in nonalcohol sections are available. Smoking is not allowed in the park. Games usually begin at 7pm on weeknights and 1pm on weekends. Take the MBTA Green Line (B, C, or D train) to Kenmore or the D train to Fenway.

BASKETBALL   The **Boston Celtics** have fallen on hard times in recent years, but their glorious history is illustrated by the 16 National Basketball Association championship banners hanging from the ceiling of the new FleetCenter. They play from early October to April or May, and unless a top contender is visiting, you should have no trouble buying tickets. For information, call the **FleetCenter** (☎ **617/624-1000**); for tickets, call **Ticketmaster** (☎ **617/931-2000** or 617/931-ARTS). To reach the FleetCenter, take the MBTA Green or Orange Line or commuter rail to North Station.

The local college teams have yet to take their place in basketball history. Schools with teams include **Boston College,** which plays in the Conte Forum in suburban Chestnut Hill (☎ **617/552-3000**); **Boston University,** with home games in Walter Brown Arena, 285 Babcock St. (☎ **617/353-3838**); **Harvard University,** based at Lavietes Pavilion on North Harvard Street in Allston (☎ **617/495-2211**); and **Northeastern University,** at Matthews Arena on St. Botolph Street (☎ **617/ 373-4700**).

FOOTBALL   The **New England Patriots** (☎ **800/543-1776**) were playing to standing-room-only crowds even before they won the American Football Conference title in 1997 and went to the Super Bowl (they lost). They play from August through December (or January if they make the playoffs) at Foxboro Stadium on Route 1 in Foxboro, about a 45-minute drive south of the city. You can drive or catch a bus from the entrance of South Station, the Riverside "T" station, or Shopper's World in Framingham (west of the city). Tickets ($23 to $50) often sell out. Plan as far in advance as you can.

Division I-A college football is played by **Boston College,** at Alumni Stadium in Chestnut Hill (☎ **617/552-3000**). Division I-AA teams include **Boston University,** at Nickerson Field on Commonwealth Avenue (☎ **617/353-3838**); **Harvard University,** Harvard Stadium, North Harvard Street, Allston (☎ **617/495-2211**);

and **Northeastern University,** Parsons Field, Kent Street, Brookline (☎ **617/ 373-4700**).

HOCKEY   The **Boston Bruins** are in roughly the same straits as the Celtics—maybe the new FleetCenter is cursed. In 1997, for the first time in 3 decades, the Bruins failed to make the playoffs. Still, their games are exciting, especially if you happen to be in town at the same time as the archrival Montreal Canadiens.

Tickets for many games sell out early despite being among the most expensive in the league. For information, call the FleetCenter (☎ **617/624-1000**); for tickets ($43 to $70), call **Ticketmaster** (☎ **617/931-2000**). To reach the FleetCenter, take the MBTA Green or Orange Line or commuter rail to North Station.

Economical hockey fans who don't have their hearts set on seeing a pro game will be pleasantly surprised by the quality of play at the college level. Even for sold-out games, standing-room-only tickets are usually available the night of the game. Teams include **Boston College,** Conte Forum, Chestnut Hill (☎ **617/552-3000**); **Boston University,** Walter Brown Arena, 285 Babcock St. (☎ **617/353-3838**); **Harvard University,** Bright Hockey Center, North Harvard Street, Allston (☎ **617/ 495-2211**); and **Northeastern University,** Matthews Arena, St. Botolph Street (☎ **617/373-4700**). These are the Beanpot schools, who play a tradition-steeped tournament on the first two Mondays of February at the FleetCenter. The games generally sell out, but you can try to order early or wait till the day of the game and check for returned tickets.

HORSE RACING   **Suffolk Downs,** 111 Waldemar Ave., East Boston (☎ **617/ 567-3900**), reopened under new management in 1992 after being closed for several years and ghastly for years before that. Today, it's one of the best-run smaller tracks in the country, an excellent family destination (really), sparklingly clean, and the home of the Massachusetts Handicap, run in early June. Horse of the Year, Cigar, won the MassCap in 1995 and 1996, conferring instant cachet on the event and the facility.

The season runs from early October to mid-June, and there are extensive simulcasting options during and after the live racing season. The day's entries appear in the *Globe* and the *Herald.* The track is off Route 1A, about a half-mile from Logan Airport, or take the MBTA Blue Line to the Suffolk Downs station.

THE MARATHON   Every year on Patriots' Day (the 3rd Monday in April), the **Boston Marathon** is run from Hopkinton to Copley Square in Boston. Cheering fans line the entire route. An especially nice place to watch is tree-shaded Commonwealth Avenue between Kenmore Square and Mass. Ave., but you'll be in a crowd wherever you stand, particularly near the finish line in front of the Boston Public Library. For information about qualifying, contact the **Boston Athletic Association** (☎ **617/236-1652**).

ROWING   In late October, the **Head of the Charles Regatta** (☎ **617/864-8415**) attracts more rowers to Boston and Cambridge than any other crew event in the country. Some 4,000 oarsmen and oarswomen race against the clock for 4 miles from the Charles River basin to the Eliot Bridge in west Cambridge. Tens of thousands of spectators socialize and occasionally even watch the action.

Spring crew racing is far more exciting than the "head" format; the course is 2,000 meters and races last just 5 to 7 minutes. Men's and women's collegiate events take place on Saturday mornings in April and early May in the Charles River basin. You'll have a perfect view of the finish line from Memorial Drive between the MIT boathouse and the Hyatt Regency. To find out who's racing, check the Friday *Globe* sports section.

TENNIS The **U.S. Tennis Championship at Longwood** is held in August at the Longwood Cricket Club, 564 Hammond St., Brookline (☎ **617/731-4500**). Call for tickets and information about the week-long event. The finals often sell out early, but demand isn't as high for preliminary matches.

OUTDOOR ACTIVITIES

BEACHES The beaches in Boston proper are decent places to catch a cool breeze and splash around, but for real ocean surf, you'll need to head out of town.

Boston Beaches The condition of Boston Harbor has improved considerably since its pollution was an issue in the 1988 presidential campaign, and the **Metropolitan District Commission** (☎ 617/727-9547) is working to restore the run-down beaches under its purview, but the MDC sometimes still has to fly red flags when swimming is not recommended (blue flags mean the water's fine).

Be aware that these are very much neighborhood hangouts. In Dorchester, off Morrissey Boulevard, **Malibu Beach** and **Savin Hill Beach** are within walking distance of the Savin Hill stop on the MBTA Red Line. South Boston beaches are off Day Boulevard and accessible by taking the Red Line to Broadway or Green Line to Copley, then a bus marked "City Point" (routes 9, 10, and 11). Among them are **Castle Island, L Street,** and **Pleasure Bay.**

North of Boston North Shore beaches are discussed in chapter 5.

Closer to Boston are **Nahant Beach** (follow the signs from the intersection of Routes 1A and 129, near the Lynn-Swampscott border), which is large and extremely popular, and **Revere Beach.** Revere Beach is better known for its pickup scene than its narrow strip of sand, but the cruising crowds are friendly and parking on the boulevard is free. The MBTA Blue Line has a Revere Beach stop; if you're driving, head north for smaller crowds at **Point of Pines,** which has its own exit off Route 1A. Across the street from the water is **Kelly's Roast Beef,** 410 Revere Beach Blvd. (☎ 617/284-9129), a local legend for its onion rings, fried clams, and, yes, roast-beef sandwiches.

South Shore Beaches The southern suburbs are riddled with private beaches, but there are a couple of pleasant public options. In Hull (take Route 3 or 3A to Route 228), **Nantasket Beach** (☎ 617/925-4905) is right in town. It's popular with families for its fairly shallow water and the historic wooden carousel in a building across the street from the main parking lot. Nine-mile-long **Duxbury Beach** (take Route 3A to Route 139 north and go right on Canal Street) makes an enjoyable stop on the way to Plymouth, if that's in your plans. **Plymouth Beach,** off Route 3A south of Plymouth at Warren Avenue, is smaller, with mild surf.

BIKING Expert cyclists who feel comfortable with the layout of the city shouldn't have too much trouble navigating in traffic. If you don't fit that description, you're better off sticking to the many bike paths in the area and not tempting the blood-thirsty drivers.

State law requires that children under 12 wear helmets. Bicycles are forbidden on MBTA buses and the Green Line at all times and during rush hour on the other parts of the system. You must have a permit (☎ 617/222-5799) to bring your bike on the Blue, Orange, and Red lines and commuter rail during nonrush hours.

Shops that rent require you to show a driver's license or passport and leave a deposit using a major credit card. Most charge around $5 an hour, with a minimum of 2 hours, or a flat daily rate of about $20. They include **Earth Bikes,** 35 Huntington Ave., near Copley Square (☎ 617/267-4733); **Back Bay Bicycles,** 333 Newbury St., near Mass. Ave. (☎ 617/247-2336); and **Community Bicycle Supply,** 496 Tremont St., near East Berkeley Street (☎ 617/542-8623).

In case you want to see the world.

At American Express, we're here to make your journey a smooth one. So we have over 1,700 travel service locations in over 120 countries ready to help. What else would you expect from the world's largest travel agency?

do more

Travel

In case you want to be welcomed there.

We're here to see that you're always welcomed at establishments everywhere. That's why millions of people carry the American Express® Card – for peace of mind, confidence, and security, around the world or just around the corner.

do more

Cards

In case you're running low.

We're here to help with more than 118,000 Express Cash
locations around the world. In order to enroll, just call
American Express before you start your vacation.

do more

**Express
Cash**

And just in case.

We're here with American Express® Travelers Cheques and Cheques *for Two*.® They're the safest way to carry money on your vacation and the surest way to get a refund, practically anywhere, anytime.

Another way we help you...

do more®

Travelers Cheques

The **Dr. Paul Dudley White Charles River Bike Path** is a 17.7-mile circuit that begins at Science Park (near the Museum of Science) and loops along both sides of the river to Watertown and back. You can enter and exit at many points along the way. Bikers share the path with lots of pedestrians, joggers, and in-line skaters, especially in Boston near the Esplanade and in Cambridge near Harvard Square. The path is maintained by the MDC (☎ 617/727-9547), as is the 5-mile **Pierre Lallement Bike Path,** in Southwest Corridor Park. It starts behind Copley Place and runs for 5 miles through the South End and Roxbury along the route of the MBTA Orange Line to Franklin Park.

For additional information, call the **Bicycle Coalition of Massachusetts** (☎ 617/491-7433) or the **Charles River Wheelmen** (☎ 617/332-8546).

BOATING   Technically, riding a swan boat is boating. It's not exactly a transatlantic crossing, but it has been a classic Boston experience since 1877. The lagoon at the Public Garden turns into a fiberglass swan habitat every spring and summer and offers an excellent break in the midst of a busy day.

The pedal-powered **swan boats** (☎ 617/522-1966 or 617/624-7020) operate from the Saturday before Patriots' Day (the 3rd Monday in April) through September, from 10am to 6pm in summer, 10am to 4pm spring and fall. The cost is $1.75 for adults, 95¢ for children.

There are also plenty of less tame options (see "Sailing," below). The **Charles River Canoe and Kayak Center** (☎ 617/965-5110; Web site: **http://www.charlesriv.com/~infor**) has two locations, on Soldiers Field Road in Allston and at 2401 Commonwealth Ave. in Newton. Both centers rent canoes and kayaks (the Newton location also rents sculls), and lessons are available. From April through October, they open at 10am on weekdays and 9am on weekends and holidays, and close at dusk.

Noninflatable watercraft are allowed on the Charles River and in the Inner Harbor. If you plan to bring your own boat, call the Metropolitan District Commission **Harbormaster** (☎ 617/727-0537) for information about launches.

FISHING   Freshwater fishing is permitted at **Turtle Pond** in the Stony Brook Reservation in Hyde Park, at **Jamaica Pond** in Jamaica Plain, and on the banks of the **Charles River** (eating your catch is not recommended.)

For offshore saltwater fishing, the **Harbor Islands** (see below) are a good choice. You might also try fishing from the pier at **City Point** and the **John J. McCorkle Fishing Pier,** off Day Boulevard in South Boston.

For information on locations and regulations, call the **Sport Fishing Information Line** (☎ 800/ASK-FISH). Information is also available from the state **Division of Fisheries and Wildlife,** 100 Cambridge St., Room 1902, Boston, MA 02202 (☎ 617/727-3151), and in the fishing columns in the *Globe* and *Herald* on Fridays in the spring, summer, and fall.

GOLF   You won't get far in the suburbs without seeing a golf course, and with the recent explosion in the sport's popularity, you won't be the only one looking. Given a choice, opt for the lower prices and smaller crowds you'll find on weekdays.

At **Newton Commonwealth Golf Course,** 212 Kenrick St., Newton (☎ 617/630-1971), an excellent 18-hole layout is yours for greens fees of $21 on weekdays and $28 on weekends.

At 9-hole **Fresh Pond Golf Course,** 691 Huron Ave., Cambridge (☎ 617/349-6282), fees are $14, or $20 to go around twice, on weekdays, and $17 and $25 on weekends.

Within the city limits there are two 18-hole courses: **Franklin Park Golf Course,** Dorchester (☎ 617/265-4084), where greens fees are $17 on weekdays and $20 on weekends; and **George Wright Golf Course,** 420 West St., Hyde Park (☎ **617/ 361-8313**), where fees are $21 on weekdays and $24 on weekends.

The **Massachusetts Golf Association,** 175 Highland Ave., Needham, MA 02192 (☎ **617/449-3000**), represents more than 310 golf courses around the state and will send you a list of courses on request.

HARBOR ISLAND'S EXPLORATION   The **Boston Harbor Islands** (☎ **617/ 727-7676**) were right under your nose if you arrived by plane, but their accessibility isn't widely known. Newly included in the national park system and administered as a "National Park Partnership," the islands are the focus of a public-private project designed to make them more interesting and accessible. There are 30 islands in the Outer Harbor, some open for exploring, camping, or swimming. You can investigate on your own or take a ranger-led tour. Plan a day trip or even an overnight stay, but note that fresh water is not available on any of the islands.

The most popular is **George's Island,** home of Fort Warren (1834), where Confederate prisoners were kept during the Civil War. Tours are offered periodically. The island has a visitor center, refreshment area, fishing pier, picnic area, and a wonderful view of Boston's skyline. From there, free water taxis run to **Lovells, Gallops, Peddocks, Bumpkin,** and **Grape islands,** which have picnic areas and campsites. Lovells Island also has the remains of a fort (Fort Standish), as well as a sandy beach; it's the only harbor island with supervised swimming.

Boston Harbor Cruises (☎ **617/227-4321**) serves George's Island from Long Wharf. For more information, contact the **Friends of the Boston Harbor Islands** (☎ **617/740-4290**).

ICE-SKATING   The **Frog Pond** on Boston Common and the lagoon at the **Public Garden** are outdoors and open seasonally. The newly renovated Frog Pond has an ice-making system (the lagoon is dependent on the weather), and skate rentals are available. It can be great fun if the weather cooperates. For consistent conditions, you'll want to head indoors.

The **Skating Club of Boston,** 1240 Soldiers Field Rd., Brighton (☎ **617/ 782-5900**), is a training center for many competitive skaters and was 1992 Olympic silver medalist Paul Wylie's headquarters when he was a Harvard undergrad. The well-maintained surface is open to the public at least twice a week ($6 adults, $4 children), and skate sharpening and rentals are available all year.

Grooming is less consistent at the rinks maintained by the Metropolitan District Commission, which are popular with recreational hockey leagues and don't all have services and concessions. If you've brought along your own sharpened skates, try **Steriti Memorial Rink** (☎ **617/727-4708**), on Commercial Street in the North End, the only MDC rink convenient to downtown. It's open seasonally and admission is $3 for public sessions; call for days and times.

IN-LINE SKATING   As with biking, unless you're very confident of your ability with in-line skating and your knowledge of Boston traffic, staying off the streets is a good idea.

A favorite spot for in-line skaters is the **Esplanade,** between the Back Bay and the Charles River. It continues onto the bike path that runs to Watertown and back, but be aware that once you leave the Esplanade the pavement isn't totally smooth, which can lead to mishaps. Your best bet is to wait for a Sunday in the summer, when **Memorial Drive** in Cambridge is closed to traffic. It's a perfect surface.

If you didn't bring your skates, you have several options for renting. A former Olympic cyclist runs **Eric Flaim's Motion Sports,** 349 Newbury St. (☎ **617/ 247-3284**). Or try **Back Bay Bicycles,** 333 Newbury St. (☎ **617/247-2336**); the

Beacon Hill Skate Shop, 135 Charles St. S. (☎ **617/482-7400**); **Earth Bikes,** 35 Huntington Ave. (☎ **617/267-4733**); or the **Ski Market,** 860 Commonwealth Ave. (☎ **617/731-6100**).

InLine Skating in Greater Boston, a book by the **InLine Club of Boston** that's available at skate and sporting-goods shops and some bookstores, costs $8. The club has a Web site (**http://www.sk8net.com/icb**) with up-to-date event and safety information and its extremely clever logo.

JOGGING   Check with the concierge or desk staff at your hotel for a map with suggested routes.

Other sources of information include the **Metropolitan District Commission (MDC)** (☎ **617/727-1300**) and the **Bill Rodgers Running Center** in Faneuil Hall Marketplace (☎ **617/723-5612**).

The bridges across the Charles River allow for circuits of various lengths along the shore, and the path is busy and generally safe. As in any large city, you're advised to stay out of park areas (including the Esplanade) at night.

SAILING   You don't have to get wet to enjoy the glorious sight of sailboats filling up the Charles River basin or the Inner Harbor. If you want to take part, you have several options.

Community Boating, Inc., 21 Embankment Rd., on the Esplanade (☎ **617/523-1038**), offers sailing lessons and boating programs for children and adults from April to November. It runs on a co-op system; a 30-day adult membership is $65.

The **Courageous Sailing Center,** Charlestown Navy Yard (☎ **617/242-3821**), offers youth program lessons year-round. A five-lesson program (one in the classroom, four on the water) is $125.

The **Boston Sailing Center,** 54 Lewis Wharf (☎ **617/227-4198**), offers lessons for sailors of all ability levels. The center is open year-round (even for "frostbite" racing in the winter). Ten classes (five indoors, five outdoors) and a 35-day membership will run you $495.

And the **Boston Harbor Sailing Club,** 200 High St., at Rowes Wharf (☎ **617/345-9202**), offers rentals and instruction. A package of four classes, 16 hours of on-water instruction, and a 30-day membership is $414. Private lessons (3-hour minimum) are $20 an hour plus the rental of the boat (from $25 an hour) plus tax.

TENNIS   Public courts are available throughout the city at no charge. They are maintained by the **Metropolitan District Commission** (☎ **617/727-1300**). To find the one nearest you, call the MDC or ask the concierge or desk staff at your hotel.

Well-maintained courts near downtown that seldom get busy until after work are located at several spots on the Southwest Corridor Park in the South End (there's a nice one near West Newton Street) and off Commercial Street near the North Washington Street bridge in the North End. The courts in Charlesbank Park, overlooking the river next to the State Police barracks on the bridge to the Museum of Science, are more crowded during the day.

8 Shopping

The other major shopping areas in Boston have been overshadowed recently by the **Back Bay,** which seems only fitting. The Prudential Center casts a long shadow over the neighborhood, and the **Shops at Prudential Center** (☎ **800/SHOP-PRU;** Web site: **http://www.prudentialcenter.com**) are the hot new retail destination in town. You could easily spend a day browsing the stores in the Back Bay, at the "Pru," upscale Copley Place (linked by a weatherproof walkway across Huntington Avenue),

Neiman Marcus, Lord & Taylor, Saks Fifth Avenue, and the dozens of galleries, shops, and boutiques along Newbury Street.

If you're passionate or just curious about art, try to set aside a couple of hours for strolling along **Newbury Street.** You'll find an infinite variety of styles and media in the dozens of galleries at street level and on the higher floors (remember to look up). Once a year, in late June, the street is closed from the Public Garden to Mass. Ave. for a day, and more than 30 galleries are open for **Art Newbury Street.** The celebration of the area's galleries features work by regional and international artists, with special exhibits and outdoor entertainment. Contact the **Newbury Street League,** 158 Newbury St. (☎ 617/267-7961; Web site: **http://www.newbury-st.tne.com**).

Another popular destination is **Faneuil Hall Marketplace** (☎ 617/338-2323), the busiest attraction in Boston—not only because of its smorgasbord of food outlets, but also because of its shops, boutiques, and pushcarts filled with everything from rubber stamps to costume jewelry.

If the prospect of the hubbub at Faneuil Hall is too much for you, stroll over to **Charles Street,** at the foot of Beacon Hill. It's a short but commercially dense (and picturesque) street noted for its antique and gift shops.

One of Boston's oldest shopping areas is **Downtown Crossing.** Now a traffic-free pedestrian mall along Washington, Winter, and Summer streets near Boston Common, it's home to two major department stores—Filene's and Macy's—plus tons of smaller clothing and shoe stores, food and merchandise pushcarts, Woolworth's, and outlets of two major bookstore chains (Barnes & Noble and Borders). Most stores are open weeknights and Saturday until 7pm, and Sunday until 5 or 6pm.

Over in Cambridge, **Harvard Square** is packed with bookstores, boutiques, and T-shirt shops. An aggressive neighborhood association has kept the area from being consumed by chain stores, and although the bohemian days of "the Square" are long gone, you'll find a mix of national and regional outlets as well as independent retailers. A walk along Mass. Ave. in either direction to the next "T" stop (Porter to the north, Central to the southeast) will take an hour or so, time well spent for dedicated shoppers. If you just can't manage without a trip to a mall, head to East Cambridge or take the Red Line to Kendall/MIT, then the free shuttle bus to the **CambridgeSide Galleria,** 100 CambridgeSide Place (☎ 617/621-8666).

Bookworms flock to Cambridge—Harvard Square in particular caters to general and specific audiences. Check out the basement of the **Harvard Book Store,** 1256 Mass. Ave. (☎ 800/542-READ outside the 617 area code, or 617/661-1515), for great deals on remainders and used books; **WordsWorth Books,** 30 Brattle St. (☎ 800/899-2202 or 617/354-5201), for a huge selection, all (except textbooks) discounted; and **the Harvard Coop,** 1400 Mass. Ave. (☎ 617/499-2000), for textbooks, academic works, and a large general selection.

Note: Massachusetts has no sales tax on clothing priced below $175 or on food. All other items are taxed at 5%, as are restaurant meals and food prepared for takeout. With the erosion of "blue laws," Massachusetts no longer prohibits stores from opening before noon on Sunday, but many still wait till 12pm or don't open at all—call ahead before setting out.

9 Boston & Cambridge After Dark

For up-to-date entertainment listings, consult the "Calendar" section of the Thursday *Boston Globe,* the "Scene" section of the Friday *Boston Herald,* and the Sunday arts sections of both papers. The weekly *Boston Phoenix* (published on Thursday) has especially good club listings, and the twice-monthly *Improper Bostonian* (free at newspaper boxes around town) has extensive live-music listings.

The Quintessential Bargain Basement

If one store in Boston deserves to be singled out, it's **Filene's Basement,** located at 426 Washington St. (☎ **617/542-2011**). Follow the crowds to this Downtown Crossing institution, which has spoiled New England shoppers for paying retail since 1908. Far from passing off their finds as pricey indulgences, true devotees boast about their bargains.

Here's how it works: After 2 weeks on the selling floor, merchandise is automatically marked down 25% from its already discounted price. Check the boards hanging from the ceiling for the crucial dates; the original sale date is on the back of every price tag. Prices fall until, after 35 days, anything that hasn't sold (for 75% off) is donated to charity.

Filene's Basement is no longer associated with Filene's, the department store upstairs from which it leases space. The independent chain, founded in 1988, has 45 branches in the Northeast and Midwest that offer great bargains, but the automatic markdown policy is in force only at the original store, which attracts 15,000 to 20,000 shoppers a day.

The crowds swell for the special sales, which come about when a store is going out of business or a classy designer, retailer, or catalogue house (say, Neiman Marcus, Barney's, Saks Fifth Avenue, Tweeds) finds itself overstocked. You'll see the unpredictable particulars, sometimes including an early opening time, advertised in the newspapers.

Four times a year, the legendary $249 wedding dress sale sparks a truly alarming display; days are also set aside for dresses, men's and women's suits, raincoats, dress shirts, children's clothing, evening gowns, lingerie, cosmetics, leather goods, designer shoes, and anything else that looks promising to the store's eagle-eyed buyers. Two weeks later, leftovers wind up on the automatic-markdown racks, and the real hunting begins. Try to beat the lunchtime crowds, but if you can't, don't despair—just be patient.

Tip: If you're not wild about trying on clothes in the open dressing rooms, slip them on over what you're wearing, an acceptable throwback to the days before there were dressing rooms. Or make like the natives and return what doesn't suit you, in person or even by mail.

GETTING TICKETS   Ticketmaster (☎ 617/931-2000) and **Next Ticketing** (☎ **617/426-NEXT**), the major agencies that serve Boston, both levy service charges that are calculated per ticket, not per order. To avoid the service charge, visit the venue in person. If you wait until the day before or the day of a performance, you'll sometimes have access to tickets that were held back for one reason or another and have just gone on sale.

DISCOUNT TICKETS   **Yankee thrift is artistically expressed at the **BosTix booths at Faneuil Hall Marketplace and in Copley Square, where same-day tickets to musical and theatrical performances (subject to availability) are on sale for half price. A coupon book offering discounted admission to most area museums is available, too. Credit cards are not accepted, and there are no refunds or exchanges. Check the board for the day's offerings. BosTix (☎ **617/723-5181**) also offers full-price advance ticket sales (it's a Ticketmaster outlet), discounts on more than 100 theater, music, and dance events, and tickets to museums, historical sites, and attractions in and around Boston. Both locations are open Tuesday through Saturday from 10am to 6pm (half-price tickets go on sale at 11am), and on Sunday from 11am to 4pm. The Copley Square booth is also open Monday from 10am to 6pm.

THE PERFORMING ARTS

THE MAJOR COMPANIES

✪ **Boston Symphony Orchestra.** Performing at Symphony Hall, 301 Mass. Ave. (at Huntington Ave.). ☎ **617/266-1492,** 617/CON-CERT (program information), or 617/266-1200 (SymphonyCharge). Web site: http://www.bso.org. Tickets $22–$69. Rush tickets $8 (on sale 9am Fri; 5pm Tues and Thurs). Rehearsal tickets $12.50.

The Boston Symphony Orchestra, one of the world's greatest, was founded in 1881 and has performed at acoustically perfect Symphony Hall since 1900. Music director Seiji Ozawa is the latest in a line of distinguished conductors of an institution known for contemporary as well as classical music—the 1996 Pulitzer Prize in music was awarded to *Lilacs,* composed for voice and orchestra by George Walker and commissioned by the BSO.

The season runs from October through April. The orchestra performs most Tuesday, Thursday, and Saturday evenings, Friday afternoons, and some Friday evenings. Check at the box office 2 hours before show time if you weren't able to buy tickets in advance—returns from subscribers go on sale (at full price) at that time. A limited number of rush tickets (one per person) are available on the day of the performance for Tuesday and Thursday evening and Friday afternoon programs. Wednesday evening and Thursday morning rehearsals are sometimes open to the public.

✪ **The Boston Pops.** Performing at Symphony Hall, 301 Mass. Ave. (at Huntington Ave.). ☎ **617/266-1492,** 617/CON-CERT for program information, or 617/266-1200 for SymphonyCharge. Web site: http://www.bso.org. Tickets $33–$45 for tables, $12.50–$28 for balcony seats.

From early May until early July, members of the Boston Symphony Orchestra lighten up. The Pops's repertoire ranges from light classical to show tunes to popular music (hence the name), sometimes with celebrity guest stars. The floor seats at Symphony Hall are replaced with tables and chairs, and waitresses serve drinks and light refreshments. Conductor Keith Lockhart is so popular that he could almost give the orchestra its name all by himself. Performances are Tuesday through Sunday evenings. The season ends with a week of free outdoor concerts at the Hatch Shell on the Charles River Esplanade, including the traditional Fourth of July concert, which features fireworks.

Boston Ballet. 19 Clarendon St. ☎ **617/695-6955** or 617/931-ARTS (Ticketmaster). Performing at the Wang Center; tickets can be purchased at the box office at 270 Tremont St., Mon–Sat 10am–6pm. Tickets $20–$69. Student rush tickets (1 hour before curtain) $12.50, except for *The Nutcracker.*

The Boston Ballet's reputation seems to jump a notch every time someone says, "So it's not just *The Nutcracker.*" The country's fourth-largest dance company offers the holiday staple, and during the rest of the season (October through May), it presents an eclectic mix of classic story ballets and contemporary works.

CONCERT HALLS & LANDMARK VENUES

The major performance hall for the BSO is **Symphony Hall,** 301 Mass. Ave. (at Huntington Avenue), which boasts wonderful acoustics.

The **Hatch Shell** on the Esplanade (☎ 617/727-1300, ext. 555) is an amphitheater best known as the home of the Boston Pops's Fourth of July concerts. Almost every night in the summer, free music and dance performances and films take over the Hatch Shell stage to the delight of the crowds on the lawn.

FleetCenter. 150 Causeway St. ☎ **617/624-1000** (events line) or 617/931-2000 (Ticketmaster). Web site: http://www.fleetcenter.com.

The state-of-the-art FleetCenter opened in September 1995, replacing the legendary (but woefully outdated) Boston Garden. It's the home of the Bruins (hockey), the Celtics (basketball), and touring rock and pop artists of all stripes, as well as the circus (in October) and touring ice shows. Concerts are presented in the round or in the arena stage format.

✪ **Harborlights Pavilion.** Fan Pier, Northern Ave. ☎ **617/374-9000,** or 617/426-NEXT to order tickets. Web site: http://www.harborlights.com.

Soft rock, pop, folk, and jazz performers draw crowds to a giant white tent on the waterfront that holds single-level seating for evening events from June through September. The pleasant, airy setting, convenient location, and reasonable size make Harborlights a wonderful place to spend a few hours. The venue may be relocated for the 1998 season; be sure to check before setting out.

THEATER & PERFORMANCE ART

You'll find most of the shows headed to or on hiatus from Broadway in the Theater District, at the **Colonial Theatre,** 106 Boylston St. (☎ 617/426-9366); the **Shubert Theatre,** 265 Tremont St. (☎ 617/482-9393); the **Wang Center for the Performing Arts,** 270 Tremont St. (☎ 617/482-9393); and the **Wilbur Theater,** 246 Tremont St. (☎ 617/423-4008).

Harvard University's **Loeb Drama Center,** 64 Brattle St. (☎ **617/547-8300;** Web site: **http://www.amrep.org**), is the home of the **American Repertory Theatre,** which performs mainstream and experimental works year-round, except when student productions are in the spotlight for about 6 weeks in the fall and spring. Tickets are $10 to $45, depending on the show. Some ART and independent productions are at the **Hasty Pudding Theatre,** 12 Holyoke St. (☎ **617/496-8400**). It's best known for the **Hasty Pudding Theatricals** (☎ **617/495-5205;** tickets $15 to $30), all-male shows staged every March that have plenty of female characters and in-jokes. They gave the world Jack Lemmon and Fred Gwynne, among many others.

The off-Broadway sensation **Blue Man Group** branched out from New York to Boston in 1995 and immediately began selling out the Charles Playhouse. Famous (or infamous) for reducing even the most eloquent theatergoers to one-syllable stuttering, the troupe of three cobalt-colored entertainers backed by a rock band uses music, percussion, food, and audience participants in its overwhelming performance art. Props include social commentary, Twinkies, marshmallows, breakfast cereal, toilet paper, and lots of blue paint.

The **Charles Playhouse** (☎ 617/426-6912), which is also home to *Shear Madness,* is at 74 Warrenton St. in the Theater District. Performances are at 8pm Tuesday through Thursday, 7pm and 10pm Friday and Saturday, and 4pm Sunday. Tickets are $35 and $45 at the box office and through Ticketmaster (☎ **617/ 931-ARTS** or 671/931-2000).

THE CLUB & MUSIC SCENE

The club scene in Boston and Cambridge is multifaceted and constantly changing, and somewhere out there is a good time for everyone, regardless of age, clothing style, musical taste, and budget. Check the *Phoenix,* the *Improper Bostonian,* the

"Calendar" section of the Thursday *Globe,* or the "Scene" section of the Friday *Herald* while you're making plans.

At most nightspots, unless otherwise specified, the admission or cover charge varies according to the night of the week and the entertainment offered, from up to $3 for a bar to more than $20 for a well-known jazz headliner.

COMEDY

✪ Comedy Connection at Faneuil Hall. Quincy Market, Upper Rotunda. ☎ **617/ 248-9700.** Cover $8–$30.

A large room with a clear view from every seat, the oldest original comedy club in town draws top-notch talent from near and far. Big-name national acts lure crowds, and the openers are often just as funny but not as famous—yet. Shows are nightly at 8pm, with late shows on Friday and Saturday at 10:15pm. The cover charge seldom tops $12 during the week, but jumps for a big name appearing on a weekend.

FOLK

Club Passim. 47 Palmer St., Cambridge. ☎ **617/492-7679.** Cover $5–$15.

Joan Baez, Suzanne Vega, and Michelle Shocked started out here. Located in a basement on the street between buildings of the Harvard Coop, this coffeehouse is still building on a reputation for more than 30 years of nurturing new talent and showcasing established musicians. There's live music 4 to 6 nights a week and Sunday afternoons, and coffee and light meals are available all the time. Open Sunday to Thursday from 11am to 11pm, Friday and Saturday 11am to 4am.

Nameless Coffee House. 3 Church St., Cambridge. ☎ **617/864-1630.** Cover $3.

For 30 years, the Nameless has represented a foot in the door for a wide range of musicians and vocalists. The promising talent attracts a predominantly young crowd (Harvard Yard is across the street). Don't worry if half the patrons suddenly get up and leave—they're probably friends of the person who just finished performing. Open September to April, Friday and Saturday from 7:30pm to midnight.

ROCK

Middle East. 472–480 Mass. Ave., Central Sq., Cambridge. ☎ **617/864-EAST.** Cover $3–$16.

The name notwithstanding, the Middle East is a restaurant that books progressive and alternative rock in two rooms (upstairs and downstairs) 7 nights a week. Serving tasty Middle Eastern fare and showcasing top local talent as well as bands with international reputations, it's a popular hangout, especially with young people. The bakery next door, under the same management, features acoustic artists most of the time and belly dancers on Wednesdays. Many shows are for those 18 and over (you must be 21 to drink alcohol); some are all ages.

✪ The Rathskeller (The Rat). 528 Commonwealth Ave. ☎ **617/536-2750** or 617/ 536-6508 (concert line). Cover downstairs only, $5–$7.

For 24 years, the Rathskeller (known far and wide as "The Rat") has been in the heart of Kenmore Square, dispensing rock to anyone who can stand the volume and riding out the fickle whims of musical fashion. There's nothing glamorous here—come as you are for live music by up-and-coming performers Tuesday through Sunday nights and Sunday afternoons. There are tables and pool tables upstairs, and the food is pretty good. The menu features chicken, burgers, fresh seafood, vegetarian offerings, and sandwiches. The restaurant is open from 11am to 10pm, the bar until 2am, and there's patio seating in warm weather.

T.T. the Bear's Place. 10 Brookline St., Central Sq., Cambridge. ☎ **617/492-0082** or 617/492-BEAR (concert line). Cover $5–$15.

T.T.'s admits people 18 and older (you must be 21 to drink alcohol), so the crowd is on the young side, but thirty-somethings will feel comfortable too. Bookings range from cutting-edge alternative rock and roots music to ska and funk shows to up-and-coming pop acts.

JAZZ & BLUES

On summer Fridays at 6pm, the **Waterfront Jazz Series** (☎ **617/635-3911**) brings amateurs and professionals to Christopher Columbus Park, on the waterfront, for a refreshing interlude of music and cool breezes.

✪ **House of Blues.** 96 Winthrop St. ☎ **617/491-2583,** or 617/497-2229 for tickets. Web site: http://www.hob.com.

The original House of Blues packs 'em in for evening and weekend matinee shows, attracting big names—Junior Wells, Jerry Jeff Walker, and the Commitments have played recently—and hordes of fans. And there's no telling when one of the legions of out-of-towners in the audience will turn out to be someone famous who winds up on stage jamming. Advance tickets are highly recommended. Open until 1am Sunday through Wednesday, 2am Thursday through Saturday.

Regattabar. In the Charles Hotel, One Bennett St., Cambridge. ☎ **617/661-5000** or 617/876-7777 (Concertix). Tickets $5–$25.

The Regattabar's selection of local and international artists is considered the best in the area—a title Scullers (see below) is happy to dispute. Shirley Horn, Betty Carter, Tito Puente, the Count Basie Orchestra, and Karen Akers have appeared within the past 2 years. The large third-floor room holds about 200 and has a 21-foot picture window overlooking Harvard Square; unfortunately, it sometimes gets a little noisy. Buy tickets in advance from Concertix (there's a $2 per ticket service charge) or try your luck at the door 1 hour before the performance is scheduled to start. Open Tuesday through Saturday and some Sundays with one or two performances per night.

Ryles Jazz Club. 212 Hampshire St., Inman Sq., Cambridge. ☎ **617/876-9330.** Cover $5–$10.

During an evening at Ryles you can shuttle back and forth between the two levels or settle in on one floor. Music buffs turn out for dining in the downstairs room with tunes in the background, and a wide variety of first-rate jazz, world beat, and Latin performances upstairs. Both levels offer good music and a friendly atmosphere. Open Tuesday through Sunday.

Scullers Jazz Club. In the Doubletree Guest Suites hotel, 400 Soldiers Field Rd. ☎ **617/562-4111.** Web site: http://www.scullersjazz.com. Cover $6–$25.

Overlooking the Charles River, Scullers books top singers and instrumentalists—recent notables include Eartha Kitt, Branford Marsalis, and Pat Metheny—in a lovely, comfortable room. Patrons tend to be more hard-core (and quieter) than the crowds at the Regattabar, but it really depends on who's performing. Shows are usually Tuesday through Thursday at 8 and 10pm, Friday and Saturday at 8:30 and 10:30pm. The box office is open Tuesday through Saturday from 11am to 6:30pm. There's also an excellent monthly dinner/jazz show.

ECLECTIC

✪ **Johnny D's.** 17 Holland St., Davis Sq., Somerville. ☎ **617/776-2004** or 617/776-9667 (concert line). Cover $2–$16, usually $7–$10.

This family-owned and -operated restaurant and music club is one of the best in the area. You might catch acts on national and international tours, or others that haven't yet made it out of the 617 area code. The music ranges from zydeco to rock, rockabilly to jazz, blues to ska. The food's even good (try the terrific weekend brunch). Johnny D's is worth a long trip, but it's no more than 20 minutes from Harvard Square on the Red Line. Open daily from 11:30am to 1am; dinner is served Tuesday through Saturday from 4:30 to 9:30pm, with lighter fare until 11pm.

The Western Front. 343 Western Ave., Cambridge. ☎ **617/492-7772.** Cover $3–$10.

A thirtyish friend swears by the Western Front for one reason: "You're never the oldest one there." This casual spot on a nondescript street south of Central Square attracts a multicultural crowd for world-beat music, blues, and especially reggae. Sunday is dance-hall reggae night, but the infectious music makes every night dancing night. Open Tuesday through Sunday from 5pm to 1:30am; live entertainment begins at 9pm.

DANCE CLUBS

✪ **Avalon.** 15 Lansdowne St. ☎ **617/262-2424.** Cover $5–$10.

A cavernous space divided into several levels, with a full concert stage, private booths and lounges, large dance floors, and a spectacular light show, Avalon is either great fun or a sensory overload. When the stage is not in use, you'll hear international music and, particularly on Saturday (suburbanites' night out), mainstream dance hits. The dress code calls for jackets, shirts with collars, and no jeans or athletic wear; the crowd is slightly older than at Axis (see below). Open Thursday ("Euro" night) to Sunday (gay night).

Axis. 13 Lansdowne St. ☎ **617/262-2437.** Cover $7–$10.

Progressive rock and "creative dress"—break out the leather—attract a young crowd to Axis. There are special nights for alternative rock, house, techno, soul, and funk music, and for international DJs. The private room upstairs is called "DV8" (say it out loud). Open Tuesday to Sunday from 10pm to 2am.

The Roxy. 279 Tremont St., in the Tremont House. ☎ **617/338-7699.** Cover $8–$10.

A hotel ballroom turned dance club, the Roxy boasts excellent DJs and live music, a huge dance floor, a concert stage, and a balcony (perfect for checking out the action down below). In the wake of the rousing success of a performance by the Artist Formerly Known as Prince in 1996, expect the live-music offerings to be beefed up by the time you visit. Open from 10:30pm to 2am on Thursday (African-American professional night), Friday (international night), Saturday (top-40 night), and some Sundays for special events.

THE BAR SCENE

Boston Beer Works. 61 Brookline Ave. ☎ **617/536-2337.**

Across the street from Fenway Park, this cavernous, cacophonous microbrewery is chaotic at any time, and before and after Red Sox games it's a madhouse. Visit during a road trip for excellent bitters and ales, seasonal concoctions such as Bambino Ale, lager with blueberries floating in it (not as dreadful as it sounds), and especially the cask-conditioned offerings, seasoned in wood till they're as smooth as fine wine. Sweet-potato fries make a terrific snack, but don't plan to be able to hear anything your friends are saying. Open daily from 11:30am to 12:45am.

Brew Moon Restaurant & Microbrewery. 115 Stuart St. ☎ **617/523-6467.**

Handcrafted beer meets tasty edibles at this popular Theater District spot, where little plates of bar food accompany freshly made brews. The Munich Gold won a gold medal at the 1996 Great American Beer Festival; if you're looking for something lighter, try the Grasshopper IPA or the out-of-this-world house-brewed root beer. Open daily from 11:30am to 2am.

There's an equally busy branch in Harvard Square at 50 Church St. (☎ **617/ 499-2739**) that stays open till 1am (midnight on Sunday).

Bull & Finch Pub. 84 Beacon St. ☎ **617/227-9605.**

If you're out to impersonate a native, try not to be completely shocked when you walk into "the Cheers bar" and realize it looks nothing like the bar on "Cheers" (the outside does, though). The Bull & Finch really is a neighborhood bar, but today it's far better known for attracting legions of out-of-towners, who find good pub grub, drinks, and plenty of souvenirs. Food is served from 11am to 1:15am.

Custom House Lounge. In the Bay Tower, 60 State St. ☎ **617/723-1666.** $12 minimum Fri and Sat after 9:30pm.

The view from the 33rd floor of any building is bound to be amazing; sitting atop 60 State St., you'll be mesmerized by the harbor, the airport, and Faneuil Hall Marketplace directly below. There's dancing to live music Monday through Saturday (piano on weeknights, jazz quartet Friday and Saturday).

Hard Rock Cafe. 131 Clarendon St. ☎ **617/353-1400.**

This link in the 27-year-old Hard Rock chain is a fun one—just ask the other tourists on line with you. The restaurant menu leans toward salads, burgers, and sandwiches (including the legendary "pig sandwich"). The bar is shaped like a guitar; the taped music bounces off all the hard surfaces and keeps the volume at a dull roar; stained-glass windows glorify rock stars; and the room is decorated with memorabilia of John Lennon, Jimi Hendrix, Elvis Presley, the local heroes Aerosmith, and others. T-shirts and other goods are for sale. Open daily from 11am to 1am for food and until 2am at the bar.

John Harvard's Brew House. 33 Dunster St., Cambridge. ☎ **617/868-3585.**

This subterranean Harvard Square hangout pumps out English-style brews in a clublike setting (see if you can make out the sports figures in the stained-glass windows) and prides itself on its food. The selection of beers changes regularly, and aficionados will have fun sampling John Harvard's Pale Ale, Nut Brown Ale, Pilgrim's Porter, and head brewer Gwen Lloyd's other concoctions. Open Sunday from 11:30am to 11:30pm, Monday through Wednesday until 12:30am, and Thursday through Saturday until 1:30am.

Top of the Hub. Prudential Center. ☎ **617/536-1775.**

Boasting a panoramic view of greater Boston, Top of the Hub is 52 stories above the city. There is music and dancing nightly. Dress is casual but neat.

5

Side Trips from Boston: Lexington & Concord, the North Shore & Plymouth

by Marie Morris

In addition to being, as the saying goes, "the hub of the solar system," Boston is the hub of a network of wonderful day trips and longer excursions. Wherever you go, you'll find sights and attractions of great beauty and historical significance. The destinations described here—Lexington and Concord; the North Shore and Cape Ann; and Plymouth, New Bedford, and Fall River—all make fascinating, manageable day trips and also offer enough diversions to fill several days.

If you have a few days to spend exploring eastern Massachusetts and history is your main motivation, consider approaching the area in roughly chronological order. Start in Plymouth with the Pilgrims, move on to Lexington and Concord to learn about the rebellious colonists, then acquaint yourself with the North Shore and Cape Ann and the prosperity of the Federal era.

A NOTE ON AREA CODES Many of the Boston suburbs mentioned in this chapter will change area codes in May 1998. Switching to 978 are: Concord, Essex, Gloucester, Ipswich, Manchester-by-the-Sea, Newburyport, Rockport, and Salem. Switching to 781 are: Bedford, Hull, Lexington, Lincoln, Lynn, Marblehead, Revere, and Swampscott.

WEST OF BOSTON Cambridge alone can take up a day or more (see chapter 4 for details), but if time is short, a visit can be combined with a trip to Lexington and Concord for a hefty dose of American history. The route Paul Revere took out of Boston on April 18, 1775, is tough to follow (he started by crossing the harbor in a rowboat, for one thing), but his fellow rider William Dawes cut through Cambridge at Harvard Square. Both proceeded to warn the colonists that British troops were on the march, a story you'll soon know well. Before you head west, do try to stop in Cambridge, where you can explore the history-packed Harvard campus. Cambridge is about 15 minutes from Boston by subway (or longer by bus). Lexington is accessible by MBTA bus from Cambridge, and Concord can be reached by commuter rail from Boston and from Porter Square in Cambridge, north of Harvard Square.

NORTH OF BOSTON The years immediately following the Revolution brought great prosperity to eastern Massachusetts as the new nation took advantage of the lifting of British trade barriers.

The spoils of the China Trade can still be seen in the mansions and public edifices in the seaside towns and cities between Boston and the New Hampshire border. Fishing is still an important industry, but today this part of the world caters more to commuters and tourists than to those who make their living from the sea. The MBTA commuter rail and a network of bus lines run to and around the North Shore and Cape Ann. The **North of Boston Convention & Visitors Bureau,** P.O. Box 642, Beverly, MA 01915 (☎ **800/742-5306**), publishes a visitor's guide.

SOUTH OF BOSTON   The towns between Boston and Cape Cod are mostly suburban bedroom communities. The one that's famous in its own right is Plymouth. One of the oldest permanent European settlements in North America, it's a lovely town where you can walk in the footsteps of the Pilgrims—and the countless out-of-towners who make it a wildly popular destination in the summer and at Thanksgiving. Farther south, the old whaling port of New Bedford and the textile industry center of Fall River make interesting detours. All three are accessible from Boston by bus, and as of 1997, Plymouth is also served by the MBTA commuter rail.

1 Lexington

The shooting phase of the Revolutionary War started here, when British troops, marching toward Concord to destroy the colonists' stockpiles of arms, clashed with local militia members (known as Minutemen for their ability to assemble on short notice). News that eight Minutemen had died in the skirmish on Lexington's Town Green inspired their counterparts up the road to put up a fight—the Battle of Concord.

After the end of the French and Indian War, in 1763, the debt-laden British government increased taxes on the American colonies. The Crown's practical considerations ran headlong into the concerns of the notoriously independent-minded colonists, who had been exposed to the philosophical ideas of the Enlightenment, foremost among them opposition to perceived tyranny. From there it was a short jump to the cry of "no taxation without representation." Tensions rose throughout the early 1770s as British troops were quartered in colonists' homes and the "Intolerable Acts" of 1774 imposed new taxes. Mutual distrust ran high—Paul Revere wrote of helping form "a committee for the purpose of watching the movements of the British troops"—and when the British commander in Boston, General Gage, learned that the colonists were accumulating arms and ammunition, he dispatched men to destroy the stockpiles.

Troops marched from Boston to Lexington late on April 18, 1775 (no need to memorize the date; you'll hear it everywhere), preceded by Revere and William Dawes, who sounded the warning. They did their job so well that the alarm came well ahead of the advancing troops, who were forced to wade ashore in Cambridge. The Lexington Minutemen, under the command of Capt. John Parker, got the word shortly after midnight, but the redcoats had taken so long to get out of Boston that they were still several hours away. The rebels repaired to their homes and the Buckman Tavern. John Hancock and Samuel Adams, who had left Boston several days earlier upon learning that the British were after them, slept (or tried to) at the Hancock-Clarke House nearby. Five hours later, some 700 British troops under Major Pitcairn arrived.

A tense standoff ensued. Three times Pitcairn ordered them to disperse, but the patriots—fewer than 100, and some accounts say 77—refused. Parker called: "Stand your ground. Don't fire unless fired upon, but if they mean to have a war, let it begin here!" Finally, the captain, perhaps realizing as the sky grew light just how badly

Around Boston

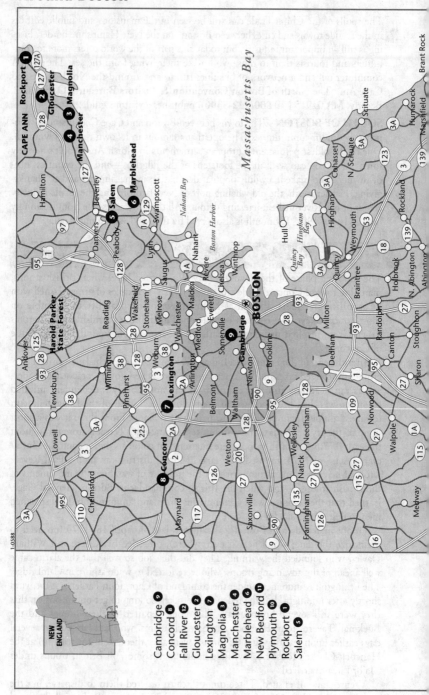

NEW ENGLAND

133

outnumbered his men were, gave the order to fall back. As the Minutemen began to scatter, a shot rang out. One British company charged into the fray, and the colonists attempted to regroup at the same time that Pitcairn tried unsuccessfully to call off his troops. Nobody knows who started the shooting, but when it was over, eight militia members were dead, including a drummer boy, and 10 wounded.

Before you set out, you might want to read "Paul Revere's Ride," Henry Wadsworth Longfellow's classic but historically questionable poem about the events of April 18 and 19, 1775.

ESSENTIALS

GETTING THERE   Modern-day Route 2A approximates Paul Revere's path, but if you attempt to follow it during rush hour, you'll wish you had a horse of your own. Instead, take Route 2 from Cambridge through Belmont. Follow signs for Route 4/225 into the center of Lexington. Or take Route 128 (I-95) to Exit 31. Mass. Ave. runs through the center of town. It's 6 miles northwest of Cambridge, 9 miles northwest of downtown Boston, and 6 miles east of Concord.

The **MBTA** (☎ **617/222-3200**) runs bus routes 62, "Bedford," and 76, "Hanscom," from Alewife Station (the last stop on the Red Line) to Lexington every hour during the day and every half hour during rush periods. There is no Sunday service. There is no public transportation between Lexington and Concord.

VISITOR INFORMATION   The **area code** is 617 through April 1998, when it will change to 781. Sketch maps and information about Lexington can be obtained at the Chamber of Commerce's **Visitor Center,** 1875 Mass. Ave. (☎ **617/862-1450**).

Some attractions are closed from November through March or mid-April, around Patriots' Day, a state holiday observed on the Monday closest to April 19. The anniversary is celebrated with a reenactment of the battle and other festivities. Make your Patriots' Day reservations well in advance: it's the day of the Boston Marathon and the start of a school vacation week.

GETTING AROUND   Downtown Lexington is easily negotiable on foot, and most of the attractions are within walking distance. If you prefer not to walk to the Munroe Tavern and the Museum of Our National Heritage, the no. 62 and 76 buses pass by on Mass. Ave.

EXPLORING THE HISTORIC SITES

Start at the **Visitor Center,** on the Battle Green. It's open daily from 9am to 5pm (9:30am to 3:30pm from October through June). The most prominent and interesting display is the diorama and accompanying narrative that illustrate the Battle of Lexington. When you step back outside, you'll have a new perspective on the events of April 19, 1775, as you explore the Green. Its best-known feature is the **Minuteman Statue** (1900) of Capt. John Parker, who commanded the militia. The **Old Revolutionary Monument** dates to 1799 and marks the grave of seven of the eight colonists who died in the conflict, which is commemorated by the **Line of Battle Boulder.** The **Memorial to the Lexington Minutemen** bears the names of the men who fell in the battle.

Across Mass. Ave., near Clarke Street, is the **Old Belfry,** a reproduction of the freestanding bell that sounded the alarm the day of the battle. **Ye Olde Burying Ground,** at the west end of the Green, dates to 1690 and contains the grave of Captain Parker.

A stop at the Visitor Center and a walk around the monuments won't take more than about half an hour, and you'll get a good sense of what went on here and why the participants are still held in such high esteem.

Lexington

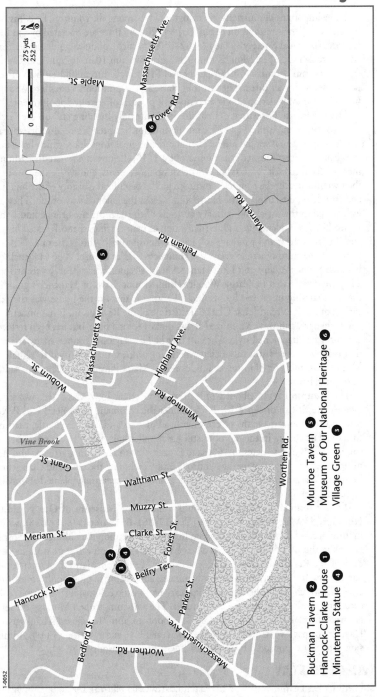

Buckman Tavern **2**
Hancock-Clarke House **1**
Minuteman Statue **4**

Munroe Tavern **5**
Museum of Our National Heritage **6**
Village Green **3**

1-0052

135

Three important destinations in Lexington were among the country's first "historic houses" when their restoration began in the 1920s. All three are operated by the **Lexington Historical Society** (☎ 617/862-1703), which conducts guided tours from April through October, Monday through Saturday from 10am to 5pm and Sunday from 1 to 5pm. Admission is $4 per house, $10 for all three; children 6 to 16, $1 per house, $2 for all three. The last tour starts at 4:30pm; tours take 30 to 45 minutes. Call for information about specialty group tours, offered by appointment.

The **Buckman Tavern,** at 1 Bedford St., is the only building still on the Green that was there on April 19, 1775, and the interior has been restored to its appearance that day. You'll see the original bar and the original front door, which has a hole in it from a British musket ball. Built around 1710, the tavern is where the Minutemen gathered to wait for word of British troop movements, and where they brought their wounded after the conflict. Costumed guides describe the history of the building and its inhabitants, explain the battle, and discuss the colonial way of life. They are well versed in the social and culinary customs of the day, the use of ingeniously designed kitchen implements, and the derivation of many sayings that originated in that era. If time is short and you have to pick one house to visit, this is the one.

About one-third of a mile away, the **Hancock-Clarke House,** at 36 Hancock St., is where Samuel Adams and John Hancock were sleeping when Paul Revere arrived. They were evacuated to nearby Woburn. Built around 1698 by Hancock's grandfather and lavishly improved by his uncle Thomas Hancock, the house was the parsonage of the Reverend Jonas Clarke at the time of the Revolution. It has undergone many changes, and was even moved across the street for a time, but has been restored and furnished in colonial style. The entrance hall display cases contain many artifacts that belong to the Historical Society, including a drum that was used to signal the Minutemen, and a set of pistols that belonged to Major Pitcairn and fell off his saddle during the battle.

The **Munroe Tavern,** about 1 mile from the Green at 1332 Mass. Ave., was taken over by the British on April 19, 1775. Under the command of General Earl Percy, some 1,000 troops made the tavern their headquarters and, after the battle, their infirmary. The ceiling in the taproom still has a bullet hole made by a careless British soldier. The building dates to 1690 and is packed with fascinating artifacts and furniture carefully preserved by the Munroe family, including the table and chair where President Washington dined in 1789. The grounds are beautifully planted and maintained.

If you continue on Mass. Ave., you'll come to the **Museum of Our National Heritage,** 33 Marrett Rd., Route 2A (☎ 617/861-6559 or 617/861-9638), which mounts accessible exhibits that explore history through popular culture. The installations in the six exhibition spaces change regularly, but you can start with another dose of the Revolution, the permanent exhibit "Lexington Alarm'd." Other topics have ranged from gravestones to jigsaw puzzles, auto racing to quilting. It's great fun, especially for children who are growing weary of nonstop colonial lore. Lectures, concerts, and family programs are also offered. The museum is open Monday through Saturday from 10am to 5pm, and Sunday noon to 5pm. It's closed Thanksgiving Day, Christmas Eve, Christmas Day, New Year's Eve, and New Year's Day. Admission is free. It's sponsored by the Scottish Rite of Freemasonry.

WHERE TO STAY

Sheraton Tara Lexington Inn. 727 Marrett Rd. (Exit 30B off I-95), Lexington, MA 02173. ☎ **800/THE-TARA** or 617/862-8700. Fax 617/863-0404. 119 rms, 2 suites. A/C TV TEL. $129–$165 double (varies seasonally); $175 suite. AE, DC, DISC, MC, V.

Overlooking the interstate, but sheltered from the noise by a stand of trees, this two-story hotel is 5 minutes from downtown by car and offers all the amenities of a chain, including room service. Rooms have colonial-style furniture and are large enough to hold a wing chair or couch. All have hair dryers, and some have balconies. An outdoor pool (open seasonally) and exercise room are available.

WHERE TO DINE

Bel Canto. 1709 Mass. Ave. ☎ **617/861-6556.** Main courses $5.50–$10.95; pizzas $5.75–$13.95. AE, DISC, MC, V. Mon–Thurs 11am–10pm, Fri–Sat 11am–11pm, Sun noon–10pm. ITALIAN/PIZZA.

One floor above the bustle of downtown Lexington, this local favorite can seem almost equally busy at peak times, but you won't feel rushed. The spacious, white-washed room fills with the chatter of diners sharing garlic bread and pizza or generous servings of pasta. The antipasto plate of meats, cheeses, tuna, and marinated vegetables makes an excellent appetizer to share. The house special pizza is served on a thick whole-wheat crust with your choice of more than two dozen toppings. Or try the light, filling chicken lasagna. There's also a children's menu ($3.50 to $4.50).

Lemon Grass. 1710 Mass. Ave. ☎ **617/862-3530.** Main courses $7–$15.50. AE, DISC, MC, V. Mon–Fri 11:30am–3pm; Mon–Thurs 5–9:30pm, Fri–Sat 5–10pm, Sun 4–9pm. THAI.

A welcome break: The only revolution going on here is in Americans' culinary habits. The space is a former coffee shop disguised with plenty of white paint, bamboo decorations, and the aromas of Asian spices. You might start with *satay* (skewers of meat served with a delectable peanut sauce), or chicken coconut soup, with a kick of pepper and plenty of chicken. Entrees range from a tasty rendition of traditional pad Thai to excellent curry dishes, and the accommodating staff will adjust the heat and spice to suit your taste.

2 Concord

Concord (say "conquered") revels in its legacy as a center of groundbreaking thought and its role in the country's political and intellectual history. After just a little time in this charming town, you may find yourself adopting the local attitude toward two of its most famous former residents: Ralph Waldo Emerson, who comes across as a well-respected uncle figure, and Henry David Thoreau, everyone's favorite eccentric cousin. Long before they wandered the countryside, the first official battle of the Revolutionary War took place at the North Bridge, now part of Minute Man National Historical Park. By the middle of the 19th century, Concord was the center of the Transcendentalist movement. Homes of Emerson, Thoreau, Nathaniel Hawthorne, and Louisa May Alcott are open to visitors, as is the authors' final resting place, Sleepy Hollow Cemetery.

ESSENTIALS

GETTING THERE   From Boston and Cambridge, take Route 2 into Lincoln. Where the road makes a sharp left, go straight onto the Cambridge Turnpike, and follow signs to "Historic Concord." From Lexington, take Route 2A west from Route 4/225 at the Museum of Our National Heritage and follow signs reading "Battle Road." Concord is 18 miles northwest of Boston, 15 miles northwest of Cambridge, and 6 miles west of Lexington.

There is no bus transportation to Concord, but **MBTA commuter trains** (☎ 617/222-3200) take about 45 minutes from North Station in Boston and stop at Porter Square in Cambridge. There is no public transportation between Lexington and Concord.

VISITOR INFORMATION   The **area code** is 508 through April 1998, then it changes to 978.

The **Chamber of Commerce,** 2 Lexington Rd., Concord, MA 01742 (☎ **508/ 369-3120**) maintains an information booth on Heywood Street, one block southeast of Monument Square. It's open weekends in April and daily May through October, from 9:30am–4:30pm. One-hour tours are available starting in May on Saturday, Sunday, and Monday holidays, or on weekdays by appointment. Group tours are available by appointment.

Concord also has a Web site (**http://www.concordma.com**), which has an area with visitor information.

GETTING AROUND   From downtown Concord, the major attractions are within easy walking distance, but if you're trying to stop everywhere in a day or are visiting Walden Pond or Great Meadows, you'll need a car.

WHAT TO SEE & DO

The town green, or **Monument Square,** at the confluence (it's not really an intersection) of Monument Street, Bedford Street, Lexington Road, Main Street, and Lowell Road, is a small green space in the middle of the sprawling town. The obelisk in the square reads "Faithful Unto Death."

At 2 Lexington Rd. is the **Wright Tavern,** which was built in 1747 and served as headquarters twice on April 19, 1775: for the Minutemen in the morning and the British in the afternoon. Today it plays the same role for the Chamber of Commerce and several businesses and is open to the public during business hours. Also overlooking the square is the **Colonial Inn,** which dates to 1716 (see "Where to Stay," below).

LITERARY LANDMARKS

The Old Manse. 269 Monument St. at North Bridge. ☎ **508/369-3909.** Guided tours $5 adults, $4 students and seniors, $3.50 ages 6–12, $12 families (3–5 people). Mid-Apr to Oct Mon–Sat 10am–5pm; Sun and holidays noon–5pm. Closed Nov to mid-Apr. From Concord Center, follow Monument St. about ³/₈ of a mile until you see signs for the North Bridge parking lot; the Old Manse is on the left.

The Reverend William Emerson built the Old Manse in 1770 and watched the Battle of Concord from the yard. He died during the Revolutionary War, and the house was occupied for almost 170 years by his widow, her second husband, their descendants—and two friends. Nathaniel Hawthorne and his bride, Sophia Peabody, moved in after their marriage in 1842 and stayed for 3 years. This is also where Ralph Waldo Emerson (William's grandson) wrote the essay "Nature." Today you'll see mementos and memorabilia of the Emerson and Ripley families and of the Hawthornes, who scratched notes on two windows with Sophia's diamond ring.

Ralph Waldo Emerson House. 28 Cambridge Tpk. ☎ **508/369-2236.** Guided tours $4.50 adults, $3 seniors and ages 7–17. Call to arrange group tours (10 people or more). Thurs–Sat 10am–4:30pm, Sun 2–4:30pm. Closed Nov to mid-Apr. Follow Cambridge Tpk. out of Concord Center; just before you reach the Concord Museum, the house is on the right.

Emerson, the philosopher, essayist, and poet, moved here in 1835, soon after his second marriage, to Lydia Jackson, and remained until his death in 1882. He called Lydia "Lydian," and she called him "Mr. Emerson," as the staff still does. You'll see original furnishings and some of Emerson's personal effects (the contents of his study at the time of his death are in the Concord Museum).

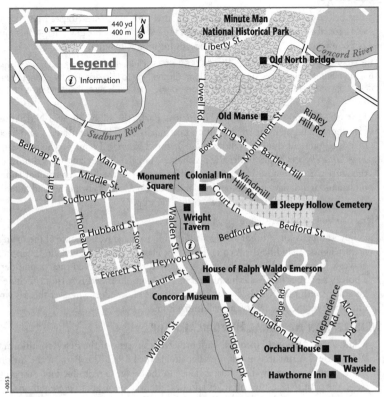

Concord

Orchard House. 399 Lexington Rd. ☎ **508/369-4118.** Guided tours $6 adults, $5 seniors and students, $4 ages 6–17, $16.50 families (up to 2 adults and 4 children). Apr–Oct Mon–Sat 10am–4:30pm, Sun 1–4:30pm; Nov–Mar Mon–Fri 11am–3pm, Sat 10am–4:30pm, Sun 1–4:30pm. Closed Jan 1–15, Easter, Thanksgiving, Christmas. Follow Lexington Rd. out of Concord Center past the Concord Museum; the house is on the left. There's overflow parking in the lot across the street.

With the theatrical and video release of the 1994 movie *Little Women* (which was filmed elsewhere), Louisa May Alcott's best-known and most popular work moved from the world of preadolescent girls back into the mainstream. The book, published in 1868, was written and set at Orchard House (though most of the actual events took place earlier—Louisa was in her mid-thirties when *Little Women* appeared), and seeing the Alcotts's home brings the family to life. Fans won't want to miss the excellent tour.

Louisa's father, Amos Bronson Alcott, was a writer, educator, philosopher, and leader of the Transcendentalist movement. He created the house by joining and restoring two early 18th-century homes already on the 12 acres of land he purchased in 1857. The family lived here from 1858 to 1877, and moved in the same circles as Emerson, Thoreau, and Hawthorne. Bronson Alcott's passion for educational reform eventually led to his being named superintendent of schools, and he ran the Concord School of Philosophy in Orchard House's backyard.

The rest of the Alcott family is known for artistic and cultural contributions, and for being the models for the characters in *Little Women.* Anna ("Meg"), the eldest, was an amateur actress, and May ("Amy") was a talented artist. Elizabeth ("Beth") died before the family moved to Orchard House. Bronson's wife, Abigail May Alcott, was a social activist and frequently assumed the role of family breadwinner—Bronson, as Louisa wrote in her journal, had "no gift for money making."

The Wayside. 455 Lexington Rd. ☎ **508/369-6975.** Guided tours $4 adults, free for ages 16 and younger. Thurs–Tues 10:30am–4:30pm. Closed Nov to mid-Apr. Follow Lexington Rd. out of Concord Center past the Concord Museum and Orchard House; the Wayside is on the left.

Part of Minute Man National Historical Park, the Wayside was Nathaniel Hawthorne's home from 1852 until his death in 1864. The Alcott family also lived here (the girls called it "the yellow house"), as did Harriett Lothrop, who wrote the *Five Little Peppers* books under the pen name Margaret Sidney and owned most of the current furnishings. The newest exhibit, housed in the barn, consists of audio presentations and figures of Louisa May and Bronson Alcott, Hawthorne, and Sidney. If you're already interested, this is a worthwhile stop.

Sleepy Hollow Cemetery. Entrance on Rte. 62 W.

Follow the signs for "Author's Ridge" up the hill to the graves of some of the town's literary lights, including the Alcotts, Emerson, Hawthorne, and Thoreau. Emerson's grave, without religious symbolism, is marked by an uncarved quartz boulder. Thoreau's grave is nearby; at his funeral in 1862, his old friend Emerson concluded his eulogy with these words: ". . . wherever there is knowledge, wherever there is virtue, wherever there is beauty, he will find a home."

MINUTE MAN NATIONAL HISTORICAL PARK

Minute Man National Historical Park preserves the scene of the first Revolutionary War battle at Concord on (all together now) April 19, 1775. Park in the lot off Monument Street and walk a short distance to the bridge (a reproduction), stopping along the path to read the narratives and hear the well-done audio presentations.

Or start your visit at the **North Bridge Visitor Center,** 174 Liberty St., off Monument Street (☎ **508/369-6993;** Web site: **http://www.nps.gov/mima**), which overlooks the Concord River and the bridge. A diorama illustrates the battle, and exhibits include surprisingly tiny uniforms, weapons, tools of colonial and British soldiers, and a film about the battle, *April Fire.* Park rangers on duty lead programs and answer questions. Outside, picnicking is allowed, and the scenery (especially the fall foliage) is lovely. The bridge isn't far; you'll still want to see the displays there, too. The Visitor Center is open daily in summer from 9am to 5:30pm and in winter from 9:30am to 4pm. Closed Christmas and New Year's.

Encouraged by their victory in Lexington, the British moved on to Concord, where the colonists were preparing to confront them. The Minutemen crossed the North Bridge, evading a group of British soldiers who were standing guard, and waited for reinforcements on a nearby hilltop. In Concord the British were searching homes for stockpiled arms (which had already been moved) and burning any guns they found along the way. The Minutemen saw the smoke and, mistakenly believing the British were burning the town, advanced against the men standing guard at the bridge. The redcoats opened fire and the colonists retaliated. At the North Bridge, the Minutemen fired what Ralph Waldo Emerson called "the shot heard round the world." (Bear in mind that he was from Concord, site of the first actual battle, but the shooting and bloodshed began in Lexington—as people there are quick to point out.)

On one side of the bridge you'll find a plaque commemorating the British soldiers who died in the Revolutionary War; on the other is Daniel Chester French's *Minute Man* statue, engraved with a stanza of the poem Emerson wrote for the dedication ceremony in 1876.

The park is open daily, year-round. At the Lexington end of the park, the **Battle Road Visitor Center,** off Route 2A, one-half mile west of I-95 (☎ **617/862-7753**) is open daily from 9am to 5pm, mid-April through October only.

The park includes the first 4 miles of the **Battle Road,** the route the defeated British troops took as they left Concord on the afternoon of April 19, 1775. They were harassed by colonial fire almost all the way back to Boston. Although this area is pretty built up, you'll still get a sense of how demoralizing the retreat must have been. At the Visitor Center, you can see displays about the Revolution, including a diorama illustrating the path of the retreat. A pamphlet is available that describes a self-guided tour of a small part of the park near the Visitor Center; on summer weekends, park rangers lead tours. Currently under construction and opening in phases is the **Battle Road Trail.** The 5.5-mile educational and interpretive path will carry pedestrian, wheelchair, and bicycle traffic. Exhibit panels and granite markers bearing information about the military, social, and natural history of the area and pointing the way along the trail are in the works.

Also on the park grounds, on Old Bedford Road, is the **Hartwell Tavern.** Costumed interpreters demonstrate daily life on a farm and tavern in colonial days. It's not Disney, but it is interesting. It's open daily from June through August and on weekends in April, May, September, and October, from 9:30am to 5pm. Admission is free.

OTHER ATTRACTIONS

✪ **Concord Museum.** Lexington Rd. and Cambridge Tpk. ☎ **508/369-9763.** Admission $6 adults, $5 seniors, $3 students and ages 15 and under, $12 families. Apr–Dec Mon–Sat 9am–5pm, Sun noon–5pm; Jan–Mar Mon–Sat 11am–4pm, Sun 1–4pm. Follow Lexington Rd. out of Concord Center and bear right at the museum onto Cambridge Tpk.; the entrance is on the left. Parking on the road is allowed.

Just when you're (understandably) suspecting that everything interesting in this area started on April 18, 1775, and ended the next day, a visit to this superb museum sets you straight. It's a great way to start your visit to the town.

The History Galleries, which opened in 1997, illustrate the town's role as a Native American settlement, Revolutionary War battleground, 19th-century intellectual center, and focal point of the 20th-century historic preservation movement. The items on display include archaeological artifacts, silver pieces from colonial churches, a fascinating collection of embroidery samplers, and rooms furnished with period furniture and textiles, all with explanatory text that places the exhibits in context. One of the lanterns that signaled Paul Revere from the steeple of the Old North Church is on display, as are the contents of Ralph Waldo Emerson's study arranged the way it was at his death in 1882, and a large collection of Henry David Thoreau's belongings. There are changing exhibits in the New Wing throughout the year. On the front lawn, what appears to be a shed is actually a replica of the cabin Thoreau lived in at Walden Pond from 1845 to 1847 (the furnishings are in the museum).

DeCordova Museum and Sculpture Park. 51 Sandy Pond Rd., Lincoln. ☎ **617/259-8355.** Web site: http://www.decordova.org. Museum $4 adults, $3 seniors, students, and ages 6–12. Tues–Sun and Mon holidays noon–5pm. Sculpture park admission free. Daily 8am–10pm. Closed July 4, Christmas, New Year's Day. From Rte. 2 E., take Route 126 to Baker Bridge Rd. (the first left after Walden Pond); when it ends, go right onto Sandy Pond Rd., and the museum is on the left. From Rte. 2 W., take I-95 to exit 28B and follow Trapelo Rd. to Sandy Pond Rd., then follow signs.

Indoors and outdoors, the DeCordova shows the work of American contemporary and modern artists, with an emphasis on living New England artists. The main building, on a leafy hilltop, overlooks a pond and the area's only outdoor public sculpture park. Extensive renovations in 1995 and 1996 made the DeCordova even more cutting edge, creating a video space for regular exhibitions and a sculpture terrace, where the work of one sculptor per year is on display. Picnicking is allowed in the sculpture park, and the **Store @ DeCordova** (☎ **617/259-8692**) has an excellent selection of prints, jewelry, clothing, and other work by local artists, including instructors at the Museum School.

Gropius House. 68 Baker Bridge Rd., Lincoln. ☎ **617/259-8843** or 617/227-3957, ext. 300. Guided tours $5. Tours on the hour June–Oct 15 Wed–Sun 11am–4pm; Oct 16–May Sat–Sun 11am–4pm. Take Rte. 2 to Rte. 126 south to left on Baker Bridge Rd.; the house is on the right. Or take I-95 to Exit 28B, follow Trapelo Rd. to Sandy Pond Rd., and go left onto Baker Bridge Rd.; the house is on the left.

The legendary German architect Walter Gropius (1883–1969), founder of the Bauhaus, accepted an appointment to teach at the Harvard Graduate School of Design in 1937 and built this home for his family on a hill in the prosperous suburb of Lincoln. The Society for the Preservation of New England Antiquities maintains the house, constructed of traditional materials such as clapboard, brick, and fieldstone, combined with materials then seldom used in domestic architecture, including glass block and welded steel. Many of the furnishings were designed by Marcel Breuer and made for the family at the Bauhaus. Decorated as it was in the last decade of Gropius's life, the house affords a revealing look at his life, career, and philosophy. Call for information on special tours and workshops.

WILDERNESS RETREATS

The titles of Henry David Thoreau's first two published works can serve as starting points: *A Week on the Concord and Merrimack Rivers* (1849) and *Walden* (1854).

To see the area from water level, there's no need to take a week; 2 hours or so should suffice. Rent a canoe at the **South Bridge Boat House,** 496 Main St. (☎ **508/369-9438**), west of the center of town, and paddle to the Old North Bridge and back. Rates are $8.50 per hour on weekends, $7.35 on weekdays; $39 per weekend day, $29 per weekday. Or opt for a small motorboat for $20 per hour, $80 per day.

At the **Walden Pond State Reservation,** Route 126 (☎ **508/369-3254**), a pile of stones marks the site of the cabin where Thoreau lived from 1845 to 1847. Today, the picturesque reservation is an extremely popular destination for hiking (a path circles the pond), swimming, and fishing. Call for the schedule of interpretive programs. Take Walden Street (Route 126) south, away from Concord Center, cross Route 2 and look for signs directing you to the parking lot. From Memorial Day through Labor Day, a daily parking fee is charged and the lot still fills early every day—call before setting out.

Another Thoreau haunt, an especially popular destination for birders, is **Great Meadows National Wildlife Refuge** (☎ **508/443-4661**). The Concord portion of the 3,400-acre refuge includes $2\frac{1}{2}$ miles of walking trails around man-made ponds that attract abundant wildlife. More than 200 species of native and migratory birds have been recorded. The refuge is open daily, sunrise to sunset, and admission is free. Don't forget your camera and sunscreen. To get there, follow Route 62 (Bedford Street) east out of Concord Center for 1.3 miles, then turn left onto Monsen Road.

WHERE TO STAY

Colonial Inn. 48 Monument Sq., Concord, MA 01742. ☎ **800/370-9200** or 508/369-9200. Fax 508/369-2170. 45 rms (some with shower only), 4 suites. A/C TV TEL. Apr–Oct $169–$175 double in main inn; $109–$169 double in Prescott wing; $230–$275 cottage. Nov–Mar

$139–$145 double in main inn; $105–$139 double in Prescott wing; $200–$235 cottage. AE, CB, DC, DISC, MC, V.

The Colonial Inn has overlooked Monument Square since 1716, when the main building was constructed. Additions since it became a hotel in 1889 have left the inn large enough to offer modern conveniences, such as conference rooms, and small enough to feel friendly. The 12 original colonial-era guest rooms (one of which supposedly is haunted) are in great demand, so reserve early if you have your heart set on staying in the main inn. Rooms in the three-story Prescott wing are a bit larger and have country-style decor. The public areas, including a sitting room and front porch, are decorated in colonial style.

Dining/Entertainment: Two lounges serve drinks and bar food, and a lovely restaurant offers salads, sandwiches, and pasta at lunch and traditional American fare at dinner. Afternoon tea is served Wednesday through Sunday; reservations (☎ **508/ 369-2373**) are required.

Services: Dry cleaning/laundry.

✪ **Hawthorne Inn.** 462 Lexington Rd., Concord, MA 01742. ☎ **508/369-5610.** Fax 508/ 287-4949. 7 rms (some with shower only). A/C TV. $95–$200 double. Extra person $15. Rates include continental breakfast. AE, DISC, MC, V. From Concord Center, take Lexington Rd. ³/₄ miles east; the inn is on the right.

Close your eyes and dream of a country inn. Open them and you may find yourself at this tree-shaded property, across the street from Hawthorne's home, the Wayside. The gorgeously decorated rooms are furnished with antiques and handmade quilts, and original art is on display throughout the two-story inn, which was built around 1870. Outside, relax in the newly landscaped garden, where there is a small pond. Gregory Burch and Marilyn Mudry have operated the inn for more than 20 years and will acquaint interested guests with the philosophical, spiritual, military, and literary aspects of Concord's history. No smoking.

North Bridge Inn. 21 Monument St., Concord, MA 01742. ☎ **508/371-0014.** Fax 508/371-6460. 6 suites (1 with shower only). A/C TV TEL. $135–$160. Extra person $15. Rates include breakfast. AE, MC, V.

A good choice for families and business travelers, the North Bridge Inn offers nicely appointed suites with kitchen facilities—all have coffeemakers, refrigerators, and microwaves, and four have stoves. The three-story inn is at the northwest corner of Monument Square, near the Colonial Inn. The rooms are spacious and have contemporary and reproduction colonial furnishings, as do the breakfast room and the lobby. Fresh-baked cookies are served every night.

A HISTORIC INN NEARBY

✪ **Longfellow's Wayside Inn.** Wayside Inn Rd., Sudbury, MA 01776. ☎ **800/339-1776** or 508/443-1776. Fax 508/443-8041. Web site: http://www.wayside.org. 10 rms (some with shower only). A/C TEL. $70–$120. Extra person $15. Rates include full breakfast. AE, CB, DC, DISC, MC, V. Closed July 4 and Christmas. From Main St. in Concord, follow Sudbury Rd. to Rte. 20 west; 11 miles after passing I-95, bear right onto Wayside Inn Rd. The inn is on the right.

Worth a visit even if you're not spending the night or dining, this local institution dates to 1716 and got its name in 1863, when Henry Wadsworth Longfellow's *Tales of a Wayside Inn* was published. Henry Ford bought the property in 1923, and it has evolved into a private, nonprofit educational and charitable trust. A Ford Foundation grant helped fund the restoration of the inn in 1956 after a devastating fire, and today it's the country's oldest operating inn. A self-guided tour of the public rooms and historical artifacts is available.

All 10 guest rooms in the two-story inn are attractively decorated and furnished with antiques, but only two (the most popular, of course) are in the original building. Make your reservations as early as possible, especially for those rooms; in addition to being a haven for travelers, the inn is a popular wedding and honeymoon destination.

It's also the centerpiece of what amounts to a tiny theme park. On the 106 acres that surround it are a restored barn, the Redstone School of "Mary Had a Little Lamb" fame (built in Sterling, Mass., in 1798 and moved to Sudbury in 1926), a wedding chapel, and a working grist mill. The mill, a reproduction built by Ford in 1929, stone-grinds the wheat flour and cornmeal that is used in the inn's baked goods and is also for sale at the gift shop. Old grindstones dot the lawn, where you're welcome to sit and sunbathe.

Dining/Entertainment: Staff members in the inn's dining rooms wear colonial costumes and dish up hearty portions of traditional New England fare that might incorporate produce grown on the inn's property. The menu changes daily, but favorite choices include prime rib, lobster casserole, and, for dessert, strawberry shortcake. You'll see lots of families and retirees. Food is served Monday through Saturday from 11:30am to 3pm and 5 to 9pm, and Sunday noon to 8pm (dinner menu only). Main courses at lunch are $7.95 to $14.50, at dinner $14.95 to $27, and portions are huge. Reservations are recommended.

WHERE TO DINE

✪ **Aïgo Bistro.** 84 Thoreau St. (Rte. 126), at Concord Depot. ☎ **508/371-1333.** Reservations recommended at dinner. Main courses $15–$25. AE, MC, V. Daily 11:30am–2:30pm and 5–10pm. MEDITERRANEAN.

"Aïgo" is Provençal patois for "garlic," which perfumes the air half a block away from this delightful spot. It's pronounced "I go," and you'll want to, for scrumptious food and top-notch service in a sophisticated setting. Settle in on a tapestry banquette, play with the brightly colored salt and pepper shakers, and prepare for hearty food, with an emphasis on garlic and grilling. You might start with the house special soup, *aïgo bouañdo,* a puree of roasted garlic, onion, and almond. Carnivores will relish the grilled fillet of beef, served with root-vegetable-and-fontina gratin, squash, and a Chianti-thyme reduction; or lamb shank with flageolet beans, sun-dried tomatoes, and baby carrots, perfumed with rosemary. At least two vegetarian entrees (one a daily special risotto) are available. The lunch menu is heavy on salads and sandwiches, served on focaccia. Desserts are few but delectable—try the fresh fruit tart.

3 Marblehead

Scenery, history, architecture, and shopping combine to make Marblehead a wonderful place to spend a few hours or a few days. The narrow streets of the historic district, known as "Old Town," lead down to the magnificent harbor that helps make this the self-proclaimed "Yachting Capital of America." The homes along the way have plaques bearing the dates of construction as well as the names of the builders and original occupants—a history lesson without any studying. Many of the houses have stood since before the Revolutionary War, when Marblehead was a center of merchant shipping. Two historic homes are open for tours, and you can shop for antiques, jewelry, clothing, and boating paraphernalia, just for starters. There is sailboat racing all summer and a Christmas celebration in early December.

None of this is secret, naturally, and in good weather visitors jam the streets and shops. If crowds aren't your cup of tea, try to visit on a weekday and definitely stay away during Marblehead Race Week at the end of July, when competitive sailors flock from all over the country.

ESSENTIALS

GETTING THERE   From Boston, drive north on Route 1A until you see signs in Lynn for Route 129; follow that along the water through Swampscott into Marblehead. Or take I-93 or Route 1 to Route 128, then Route 114 through Salem into Marblehead. It's 15 miles northeast of Boston, 4 miles southeast of Salem.

The **MBTA** (☎ **617/222-3200**) bus route 441/442 runs from Haymarket Square (Orange and Green lines) in Boston to downtown Marblehead. The trip takes about an hour. The no. 441 bus detours to Vinnin Square shopping center in Swampscott; otherwise, both routes are the same.

VISITOR INFORMATION   The **area code** is 617 through April 1998, when it will change to 781. The **Marblehead Chamber of Commerce,** 62 Pleasant St., P.O. Box 76, Marblehead, MA 01945 (☎ **617/631-2868;** Web site: **http://www.marbleheadchamber.org**), is open weekdays from 9am to 3pm and operates an information booth (daily in season, 10am to 5:30pm) on Pleasant Street near Spring Street. It also publishes a 48-page visitor's guide; individual pamphlets that list dining, shopping, and accommodations options and marine services; and a map of the historic district with two well-plotted walking tours. Marblehead also has a Web site at **http://www.marblehead.com**.

The **North of Boston Convention & Visitors Bureau,** P.O. Box 642, Beverly, MA 01915 (☎ **800/742-5306**) also publishes a visitor's guide.

GETTING AROUND   Wear your good walking shoes—the car or bus can get you to Marblehead, but it can't negotiate many of the narrow streets of Old Town. You'll also be climbing hills, especially if you do a lot of exploring.

EXPLORING THE TOWN

An aimless stroll through the winding streets of Old Town invariably leads to shopping, snacking, or gazing at something picturesque, be it the harbor or a beautiful home. If you prefer more structure, follow the Chamber of Commerce's 1- or 2-mile walking tour. Even if you don't, stop outside the **Lafayette House,** at the corner of Hooper and Union streets. Legend has it that one corner of the first floor was chopped off in 1824 to allow Lafayette's carriage to negotiate the corner. In Market Square on Washington Street, near the corner of State Street, is the **Old Town House,** in use since 1727.

Be sure to spend some time in **Crocker Park,** on the harbor off Front Street. Especially in the warmer months, when boats jam the water nearly as far as the eye can see, the view is breathtaking. There are benches and a swing, and picnicking is allowed. You may not want to leave, but snap out of it—the view from **Fort Sewall,** at the other end of Front Street, is just as mesmerizing. The ruins of the fort, built in the 17th century and rebuilt late in the 18th, are another excellent picnic spot.

By car or bicycle, the swanky residential community of **Marblehead Neck** is worth a look. Follow Ocean Avenue across the causeway and visit the **Audubon Bird Sanctuary** (look for the tiny sign at the corner of Risley Avenue) or continue on to **Castle Rock** for another eyeful of scenery. At the end of "the Neck," at Harbor and Ocean avenues, is **Chandler Hovey Park,** where there's a (closed) lighthouse and a panoramic view.

Back in town, as promised, are several destinations of historical interest.

Abbot Hall. Washington Sq. ☎ **617/631-0528.** Free admission. Year-round Mon–Tues and Thurs 8am–5pm, Wed 7:30am–7:30pm; off-season Fri 8am–1pm; May–Oct Fri 8am–5pm, Sat 11am–6pm, Sun 9am–6pm. From the historic district, follow Washington St. up the hill.

The town offices and Historical Commission share Abbot Hall with Archibald M. Willard's famous painting *The Spirit of '76,* which is on display in the Selectmen's Meeting Room. The thrill of recognizing the ubiquitous drummer, drummer boy, and fife player is the main reason to stop here. The deed that records the sale of the land by the Native Americans to the Europeans in 1684 is also on view. In the cases in the halls are objects and artifacts from the collections of the Historical Society. The building's clock tower is visible from all over Old Town.

✪ Jeremiah Lee Mansion. 161 Washington St. ☎ **617/631-1069.** Guided tours $4 adults, $3.50 students, free for children under 10. Mon–Sat 10am–4pm, Sun 1–4pm. Closed Nov to mid-May. Follow Washington St. until it curves right and heads up the hill to Abbot Hall; the house is on the right.

The prospect of seeing original hand-painted wallpaper in an 18th-century home is reason enough to visit this house, built in 1768 for a wealthy merchant and considered an outstanding example of pre-Revolutionary Georgian architecture. Original rococo carving and other details complement historically accurate room arrangements, and ongoing restoration and interpretation by the Marblehead Historical Society place the 18th- and 19th-century furnishings and artifacts in context. The friendly guides are well versed in the history of both the home and the renovations. The displays on the third floor draw on the Historical Society's collections of children's furniture, toys, and nautical and military artifacts, and work by primitivist painter J. O. J. Frost. The lawn and gardens are open to the public.

The Historical Society, which makes its headquarters in the mansion, occasionally offers walking tours of Marblehead and candlelight tours of the house. Call ahead to see if your schedules match. In 1998 the Historical Society will celebrate its centennial with special programs and exhibits, including a show of children's folk-art portraits at the mansion.

Tip: On the hill between the mansion and Abbot Hall, the private homes at no. 187, 185, and 181 Washington St. are good examples of the architecture of this period.

King Hooper Mansion. 8 Hooper St. ☎ **617/631-2608.** Donation requested for tour. Mon–Sat 10am–4pm, Sun 1–5pm. Call ahead; tours are not held during private parties. Where Washington St. curves around the foot of the hill near the Lee Mansion, look for the colorful sign.

Shipping tycoon Robert Hooper got his nickname because he treated his sailors so well, but it's easy to think he was called "King" because he lived like royalty. Located around the corner from the home of Jeremiah Lee (whose sister was the second of Hooper's four wives), the King Hooper Mansion was built in 1728 and gained a Georgian addition in 1747. The period furnishings, though not original, give a sense of the life of an 18th-century merchant prince, from the wine cellar to the third-floor ballroom. The building houses the headquarters of the Marblehead Arts Association, which stages monthly exhibits and runs a gift shop where members' work is for sale. The mansion also has a lovely garden; enter through the gate at the right of the house.

SHOPPING

Your own piece of history (contemporary or otherwise) may be waiting for you in one of Marblehead's galleries or antique, clothing, and jewelry shops. Old Town is the favored destination for shoppers, but don't forget that Atlantic Avenue and the south end of Pleasant Street are home to more mainstream businesses. This is just a selection—part of the fun of shopping, of course, is the thrill of discovery.

Along the square around the Old Town House are any number of delightful shops. Poke around in **Heeltappers Antiques,** 134 Washington St. (☎ 617/631-7722); the **Old Town Antique Co-op,** 108 Washington St. (☎ 617/631-8777), with four dealers under one roof; **Calico Country Antiques,** 92 Washington St. (☎ 617/631-3607); and **Cargo Unlimited,** 82 Washington St. (☎ 617/631-1112). **O'Rama's,** 148 Washington St. (☎ 617/631-0894), sells what it calls "miscellaneous elegancies," also known as jewelry, lingerie, accessories, and other high-end "girl stuff."

At the **Marblehead Kite Company,** 1 Pleasant St. (☎ 617/631-7166), kites are outnumbered by souvenirs, greeting cards, T-shirts, stuffed animals, and toys (including some that children of the seventies haven't seen since their youth).

Hector's Pup, 84 Washington St. (☎ 617/631-5860), an excellent toy store, is best approached from State Street, where the corner windows overflow with dollhouse furniture.

At the other end of State Street, **Brass 'n Bounty,** 68 Front St. (☎ 617/631-3864) specializes in marine antiques and antique lighting; and **Antiquewear,** 82–84 Front St. (☎ 617/639-0070; Web site: **http://www.shore.net~antiquew/**), sells 19th-century buttons ingeniously fashioned into jewelry.

Jewelry is known as "wearable art" at **Raven Gallery,** 41 State St. (☎ 617/639-3292), which also sells glass sculptures, paintings, and prints. **Arnould Gallery and Framery,** 111 Washington St. (☎ 617/631-6366), emphasizes Marblehead and New England themes. The **Art Guild Gallery,** 78 Washington St. (☎ 617/631-3791), and **Concetta's Gallery,** 11 Pleasant St. (☎ 617/639-2113), are worth a visit if you'd like to see what the local artists are up to.

WHERE TO STAY

The Chamber of Commerce accommodations listings include the town's many inns and bed-and-breakfasts. Call or write for a pamphlet (see "Visitor Information," above).

If you prefer to use an agency, try **Bed & Breakfast Reservations North Shore/ Greater Boston/Cape Cod,** P.O. Box 35, Newtonville, MA 02160 (☎ 800/832-2632 outside Mass., or 617/964-1606; fax: 617/332-8572; Web site: **http:// www.bnbinc.com**; E-mail: **bnbinc@ix.netcom.com**). A minimum stay of at least 2 nights is required.

Harbor Light Inn. 58 Washington St., Marblehead, MA 01945. ☎ **617/631-2186.** Fax 617/631-2216. 21 rms (some with shower only), 2 suites. A/C TV TEL. $95–$150 double; $160–$225 suite. Corporate rate available midweek. Rates include continental breakfast. Free parking. 2-night minimum on weekends, 3 nights on holiday weekends. AE, MC, V. Follow Washington St. 1 block north from downtown Old Town; the inn is on the right.

A stone's throw from the Old Town House, the Harbor Light Inn is two Federal-era mansions combined into one gracious lodging. From the wood floors to the original molding in the reception rooms to the 1729 beams in one of the third-floor rooms, it's both historical and relaxing, comfortably furnished in the style of the period (with some antiques). Most rooms have canopy or four-poster beds and VCRs; 11 have working fireplaces, and five of those have double Jacuzzis. There are gorgeous harbor views from some rooms and from the rooftop observation deck, which is open to all guests. All but two guest rooms are reserved for nonsmokers.

Facilities: Heated outdoor pool, sundeck, rooftop observation deck, conference room.

The Nautilus. 68 Front St., Marblehead, MA 01945. ☎ **617/631-1703.** 4 rms (none with private bath). $65–$70 double. No credit cards. Ask for parking suggestions when you call for reservations.

This guest house is as close to the harbor as you can get without being drenched. Rooms are on the second floor of a private home, plain but comfortable, and have semiprivate bathroom facilities. Make your reservations well in advance, because the combination of location and cheerful, homey service makes the Nautilus a popular destination.

Pleasant Manor Inn Bed and Breakfast. 264 Pleasant St. (Rte. 114), Marblehead, MA 01945. ☎ **800/399-5843** or 617/631-5843. 12 rms (some with shower only; one room's bath is across the hall). A/C TV. $68–$80 double. Rates include continental breakfast. 2-night minimum on weekends. No credit cards. Free parking.

Just outside the historic district, the Pleasant Manor Inn is a three-story Victorian mansion built as a private home in 1872 and operated as an inn since 1923. Innkeepers Richard and Takami Phelan took over in 1975. The spacious rooms open off a magnificent central staircase and are tastefully decorated with Victorian prints and some antiques. Aviation aficionados can request the room where Amelia Earhart stayed. Guests have the use of VCRs and a tennis court in the large backyard. Children are welcome. No smoking.

Spray Cliff on the Ocean. 25 Spray Ave., Marblehead, MA 01945. ☎ **800/626-1530** or 617/631-6789. Fax 617/639-4563. E-mail: spraycliff@aol.com. 7 rms (some with shower only). May–Oct $175–$205 double; lower rates off-season. Extra person $25. Rates include continental breakfast, evening refreshments, and use of bicycles. 2-night minimum on weekends, 3 nights on busy holiday weekends. AE, MC, V. Take Atlantic Ave. (Rte. 129) to Clifton Ave. and turn east (right driving north, left driving south); parking area is at the end of the street. Free parking. No children under 16.

Spray Cliff, a three-story Victorian Tudor built in 1910 on a cliff overlooking the ocean, is 5 minutes from town and a world away. Five of the large, sunny rooms face the water, three have fireplaces, and all are luxuriously decorated in contemporary style with brightly colored accents. Roger and Sally Plauché have run their "romantic, adult inn" on a quiet, residential street 1 minute from the beach since 1994. No smoking.

A SEASIDE INN NEARBY

Diamond District Bed and Breakfast. 142 Ocean St., Lynn, MA 01902. ☎ **800/666-3076** or 617/599-4470. Fax 617/599-5122. 9 rms (5 with bath; 1 with shower only). A/C TV TEL. Apr–Oct $90–$150 double; Nov–Mar $80–$145 double. Extra person $20. Rates include full breakfast. 2-night minimum on holiday and fall weekends and some summer weekends. AE, DC, DISC, MC, V. Take Rte. 1A north to Rte. 129 (Lynn Shore Dr.) and take it north 9/10 of a mile, past 2 traffic lights and the Christian Science Church (brick building with white pillars). Turn left onto Wolcott St., then right onto Ocean Ave.; the inn is on the right.

Travelers stopping in Lynn can take advantage of the same attribute that draws property buyers: good value. The ocean views are as breathtaking as those elsewhere on the North Shore, without the breathtaking expense of those posh communities. Marblehead is about 10 minutes away.

This comfortable B&B is in a three-story Georgian-style mansion built in 1911 as a private home, and innkeepers Jerry and Sandra Caron make it an enjoyable stop whether you're pursuing business or pleasure. The Atlantic is a block away, and the 3-mile public beach (a good place to burn off the inn's generous breakfast) is popular for jogging, skating, and biking, as well as swimming. It's visible from many of the rooms, which are good sized and tastefully decorated. All have down comforters and two-line phones with data ports, and two have alcohol-burning fireplaces. The four third-floor rooms, which share two baths and a modest living room, are smaller but no less pleasant and make a good choice for families. No smoking.

WHERE TO DINE

Iggy's Bread of the World, 5 Pleasant St. (☎ **617/639-4717**), supplies many of the Boston area's top restaurants from its headquarters on a side street in Watertown. The Marblehead branch, though hardly a sit-down dining destination, smells so good that it's tough to leave empty-handed.

The Barnacle. 141 Front St. ☎ **617/631-4236.** Reservations not accepted. Main courses $10.95–$15.95. No credit cards. Daily 11:30am–4pm and 5–10pm. SEAFOOD.

This unassuming spot doesn't look like much from the street, but at the end of the gangplanklike entrance hall is a front-row seat for the action on the water. This is an ideal place to quaff a beer and watch the boats sail by. Even if you don't land a seat on the deck or along the counter facing the windows, you'll still have a shorebird's-eye view of the mouth of the harbor and the ocean from the jam-packed dining room. The food won't provide much of a distraction, but it's tasty, plentiful, and fresh—the restaurant's own lobster boat delivers daily. The chowder and fried seafood, especially the clams, are terrific.

Driftwood Restaurant. 63 Front St. ☎ **617/631-1145.** Main courses $1.60–$9.50. No credit cards. Summer daily 5:30am–5pm; winter daily 5:30am–2pm. DINER/SEAFOOD.

At the foot of State Street next to Clark Landing (the town pier) is an honest-to-goodness local hangout. Whether you're in the mood for pancakes and hash or chowder and a seafood "roll" (a hot-dog bun filled with, say, fried clams or lobster salad), join the crowd. The house specialty, served on weekends and holidays, is fried dough, which is exactly as delicious and unhealthy as it sounds.

King's Rook. 12 State St. ☎ **617/631-9838.** Reservations not accepted. Main courses $4.50–$8. MC, V. Mon–Fri noon–2:30pm; Tues–Fri 5:30–11:30pm; Sat–Sun noon–11:30pm. CAFE/WINE BAR.

There's no better place to complete the sentence "I'm thirsty and I'd like . . ." than this cozy spot, a favorite long before coffeehouses ruled prime-time television. Coffees, teas, hot chocolates, soft drinks, and more than two dozen wines by the glass are available, and the food has a sophisticated flair. The intimate atmosphere and racks of newspapers and magazines make this a great place to linger over a pesto pizza, a salad, or a sinfully rich dessert—and, of course, a beverage.

Kitchen Witch Eatery. 78 Front St. ☎ **617/639-1475.** Most items under $6. No credit cards. Summer Sun–Thurs 11am–10pm, Fri–Sat 11am–11pm. Closed other seasons. DELI.

This storefront oasis, where you can eat in the tiny dining area or order everything you need for a picnic, is across the street from Clark Landing. Sandwiches, salads, and soups are fresh and delicious, and the muffins and other baked goods are excellent. This is also the perfect place to grab some ice cream or frozen yogurt (in dozens of flavors) and set off to explore the town.

4 Salem

Salem was settled in 1626 (4 years before Boston) and later became known around the world as a center of merchant shipping and the China Trade, but it's internationally famous today for a 7-month episode in 1692. The witchcraft trial hysteria led to 20 deaths, 3 centuries of notoriety, countless lessons on the evils of prejudice, and dozens of bad puns ("Stop by for a spell" is a favorite slogan). Unable to live down its association with witches, Salem has chosen to embrace it. The high-school sports teams are called the Witches, and the logo of the *Salem Evening News* is a silhouette of a witch.

Visitors expecting wall-to-wall witches won't be disappointed, but they will be missing another important part of the city's history. Salem flourished in the 17th and 18th centuries as its merchant vessels circled the globe, returning with treasures and artifacts that can still be seen today. Its dominance peaked between the Revolutionary War and the War of 1812 (many overseas trading partners believed that Salem was an independent country!). One reminder of that era, a replica of the 1797 East Indiaman tall ship *Friendship*, is anchored near the Salem Maritime National Historic Site.

The shipping trade was on the decline in the 1840s when Salem native Nathaniel Hawthorne worked in the Custom House, where he found an embroidered scarlet "A" that set his imagination to work.

ESSENTIALS

GETTING THERE   From Boston, take Route 1A north into downtown Salem, being careful in Lynn, where the road turns left and immediately right. Or take I-93 or Route 1 (if it's not rush hour) to Route 128, then Route 114 into downtown Salem. Keep left on 114 and ignore the signs for "Historic Salem," which lead you through downtown Peabody. In Salem, follow the signs—brown for the Visitor Center, blue for parking, and green for museums and historic sites. Salem is 16 miles northeast of Boston, and 4 miles northwest of Marblehead.

From Boston, the **MBTA** (☎ **617/222-3200**) runs bus route 450 from Haymarket Square and commuter trains from North Station. They operate often on weekdays, less frequently on weekends. The bus takes about an hour, the train 30 minutes. At the Salem station, a long staircase runs from train level to street level.

VISITOR INFORMATION   The **area code** is 508 through April 1998, when it changes to 978. An excellent place to start your visit is the **National Park Service Visitor Center** at 2 New Liberty St. (☎ **508/740-1650**; Web site: **http://www.nps.gov/sama/**), where exhibits highlight early settlement, maritime history, and the leather and textiles industries. The center (open daily 9am to 5pm) also has an auditorium where a free film on Essex County, *Where Past Is Present,* provides a good overview.

The **Salem Chamber of Commerce** in Old Town Hall, 32 Derby Sq., Salem, MA 01970 (☎ **508/744-0004**), maintains an information booth (weekdays 9am to 5pm). The chamber also collaborates with the **Salem Office of Tourism & Cultural Affairs,** 93 Washington St., Salem, MA 01970 (☎ **800/777-6848**; E-mail SalemMA@cove.com), to publish a free visitor's guide. Salem also has a Web site (**http://www.star.net/salem**).

And the **North of Boston Convention & Visitors Bureau,** P.O. Box 642, Beverly, MA 01915 (☎ **800/742-5306**) publishes a visitor's guide.

GETTING AROUND   In the immediate downtown area, walking is the way to go, but there's much more to Salem than just downtown. There's plenty of parking at meters and in lots and garages throughout the city. If you plan to spend the day and visit more than three or four places, consider buying an all-day trolley ticket (see below).

SPECIAL EVENTS   Should you find yourself in town at the end of October, you won't be able to miss **Haunted Happenings,** the city's 2-week Halloween celebration. Parades, parties, and tours lead up to a ceremony on the big day.

WHAT TO SEE & DO

Downtown Salem is spread out but flat, and the historic district extends well inland from the waterfront. Many 18th-century houses still stand, some with original furnishings. Ship captains lived near the water at the east end of downtown, in relatively small houses crowded close together. The captains' employers, the shipping company owners, built their homes away from the water (and the accompanying aromas). Many of them lived on **Chestnut Street,** which is preserved as a registered National Historic Landmark. Residents along the ravishingly beautiful thoroughfare must, by legal agreement, adhere to colonial style in their decorating and furnishings.

At the Essex Street side of the Visitor Center, you can board the **Salem Trolley** (☎ 508/744-5469; daily April through October, weekends in March and November) for a 1-hour narrated tour. Tickets ($8 adults, $7 students, $4 ages 5 to 12; family of two adults and two or more children, $20) are good all day, and you can reboard as many times as you like at any of the 15 stops. It's a great deal if you're spending the day and don't want to keep moving the car or carrying leg-weary children. In December during **Holiday Happenings,** the Salem Trolley Players' traveling presentation of *A Christmas Carol* takes place on board. Call for reservations.

To travel by sea as well as land, take a narrated 50-minute **Moby Duck Tour** (☎ 508/741-4386) from New Liberty Street in front of the Visitor Center. The amphibious tour vehicle cruises the streets of the city, then plunges into the harbor. Tickets are $12 for adults, $10 seniors, and $8 children under 12.

The **Heritage Trail** is a 1.7-mile walking route that begins at the Visitor Center, near the two-block pedestrian mall on **Essex Street.** It's marked by a red line painted on the sidewalk and connects many of the major attractions.

Pickering Wharf, at the corner of Derby and Congress streets, is a cluster of shops, boutiques, restaurants, and condos adjacent to a marina. The waterfront setting makes it a good place for strolling, snacking, and shopping. The **Pickering Wharf Antiques Gallery** (☎ 508/741-3113) collects 40 dealers of all stripes under one capacious roof. Leave at least an hour if your taste runs to antiques and collectibles. You can also take a harbor cruise or go on a whale watch organized by the **East India Cruise Company** (☎ 800/745-9594 or 508/741-0434).

Three destinations on the outskirts of the historic district are worth the trip.

By car or trolley, **Salem Willows,** a waterfront amusement park, is 5 minutes away (many signs point the way). The strip of rides and snack bars has a honky-tonk air, and the waterfront park is a good place to bring a picnic and wander along the shore. Admission and parking are free. To enjoy the great view without the arcades and rides, have lunch one peninsula over at **Winter Island Park.**

Upscale gift shops throughout New England sell the chocolate confections of **Harbor Sweets,** and you can go to the source in Salem at Palmer Cove, 85 Leavitt St. (☎ 508/745-7648). The retail store overlooks the floor of the factory—if you want to see the machinery in action, call ahead to see if it's running. Recent additions to the sinfully good product lines include sugar-free offerings and candy embossed with equestrian and golf designs. The shop is open weekdays from 8:30am to 4:30pm and Saturday from 9am to 3pm, with extended hours around candy-centered holidays.

Finally, if you can't get witchcraft off your mind, several shops specialize in the necessary accessories, including crystal balls and tarot cards. The **Broom Closet,** 3–5 Central St. (☎ 508/741-3669), and **Crow's Haven Corner,** 125 Essex St. (☎ 508/745-8763), sell everything from crystals to clothing and cast a modern-day light on age-old customs—just bear in mind that Salem is home to many practicing witches who take their beliefs very seriously.

The House of the Seven Gables. 54 Turner St. ☎ **508/744-0991.** Guided tours $7 adults, $4 ages 13–17, $3 ages 6–12. Combination discounted tickets for the House of the Seven Gables and Salem 1630 (see below) are available at both places. June 1 to Labor Day daily 9am–6pm; off-season daily 10am–4:30pm. Closed Thanksgiving, Christmas, and New Year's Day. From downtown, follow Derby St. east 3 blocks past Derby Wharf; historic site is on the right.

Built by Capt. John Turner in 1668, this building was later occupied by a cousin of Nathaniel Hawthorne's, and his 1851 novel of the same name was inspired by stories and legends of the house and its inhabitants. If you haven't read the book, don't let that keep you away—begin your visit with the audiovisual program, which tells the story. The house holds six rooms of period furniture, including pieces referred to in the book, and a narrow, twisting secret staircase. Tours include a visit to Hawthorne's birthplace (built before 1750 and moved to the grounds) and describe what life was like for the houses' 18th-century inhabitants. The costumed guides can get a little silly as they mug for young visitors, but they're well versed in the history of the buildings and artifacts, and eager to answer questions.

Also on the grounds, overlooking Salem Harbor, are period gardens, the Retire Beckett House (1655), the Hooper-Hathaway House (1682), and a counting house (1830).

✪ **Peabody Essex Museum.** East India Sq. ☎ **800/745-4054** or 508/745-9500. Web site: http://www.pem.org. Admission (good on 2 consecutive days) $7.50 adults, $6.50 seniors and students, $4 ages 6–16, $18 family (2 adults and 1 or more children). Free 1st Fri of each month 5–8pm. Mon–Sat 10am–5pm, Sun noon–5pm, Fri until 8pm. Closed Thanksgiving Day, Christmas, New Year's Day, and Mon Nov through Memorial Day. Take Hawthorne Blvd. to Essex St., following signs for Visitor Center. Enter on Essex St. or New Liberty St.

Call before dropping in on the Peabody Essex Museum in 1998, when parts will be closed for renovation and expansion, and operating hours may vary. Changes have been ongoing since the 1992 merger of the Peabody Museum and the Essex Institute, which combined fascinating collections that illustrate Salem's adventures abroad and its development at home.

The Peabody Museum, the nation's oldest in continuous operation, was founded in 1799 by the East India Marine Society, a group of sea captains and merchants whose charter included provisions for a "museum in which to house the natural and artificial curiosities" brought back from their travels. The collection of the Essex Institute (1821), the county's historical society, encompasses American art, crafts, furniture, and architecture (including nine historic houses), as well as dolls, toys, and games.

It all adds up to the impression that you're in Salem's attic, but instead of opening dusty trunks and musty closets, you find the treasures arranged in well-planned displays that help you understand the significance of each artifact. Trace the history of the port of Salem and the whaling trade, study figureheads of ships or portraits of area residents (including Charles Osgood's omnipresent rendering of Nathaniel Hawthorne), learn about the witchcraft trials, immerse yourself in East Asian art and artifacts or the practical arts and crafts of the East Asian, Pacific Island, and Native American peoples. The Asian Export Art Wing displays decorative art pieces made in Asia for Western use from the 14th to 19th centuries. Sign up for a tour of one or more houses—the Gardner-Pingree House (1804), a magnificent Federal mansion where a notorious murder was committed in 1830, has been gorgeously restored. You can also sign up for a gallery tour or select from about a dozen pamphlets for self-guided tours on various topics.

The museum has a cafe that serves lunch daily and dinner on Fridays.

Salem Maritime National Historic Site. 174 Derby St. ☎ **508/740-1660.** Free admission. Guided tours $3 adults, $2 seniors and ages 6–16, $10 family. Daily 9am–5pm. Closed

Thanksgiving, Christmas, and New Year's Day. Take Derby St. east; just past Pickering Wharf, the orientation center is on the right.

With the decline of the shipping trade in the early 19th century, Salem's wharves fell into disrepair, a state the National Park Service began to remedy in 1938 when it took over a small piece of the waterfront. Derby Wharf is now a finger of parkland extending into the harbor, part of the 9 acres, dotted with explanatory markers, that make up the historic site. An exciting addition is a full-sized replica of a 1797 East Indiaman merchant vessel, the *Friendship*. The hull was laid in Albany, N.Y., and moved (using motors) during the summer of 1997 to Salem, where construction was scheduled to be completed. The tall ship is a faithful replica with some concessions to the modern era, such as diesel engines and accessibility for people with disabilities. Fees for visitors had not been determined at press time.

On adjacent Central Wharf is a warehouse that houses the orientation center. It dates from around 1800 and was moved to the head of the wharf in the 1970s. Ranger-led tours, which vary according to seasonal schedules, expand on Salem's maritime history. Yours might include the Custom House (1819), where Nathaniel Hawthorne worked, and the Derby House (1762), a wedding gift to shipping magnate Elias Hasket Derby from his father. If you prefer to explore on your own, you can see the free film at the orientation center and wander around Derby Wharf, the West India Goods Store, the Bonded Warehouse, the Scale House, and Central Wharf.

Salem 1630: Pioneer Village. Forest River Park, off West Ave. ☎ **508/745-0525** or 508/744-0991. Admission $4.50 adults, $3.50 seniors and ages 13–17, $2.50 ages 6–12. Combination discounted tickets for Salem 1630 and the House of the Seven Gables (see above) are available at both places. Daily Memorial Day to Halloween 10am–5pm. Closed Nov 1 to last week in May. Take Lafayette St. (Routes 114 and 1A) south from downtown to West Ave., turn left and follow the signs.

A re-creation of life in Salem just 4 years after European settlement, this Puritan village is staffed by costumed interpreters who lead tours, demonstrate crafts, and tend to farm animals. They escort visitors around the various dwellings—wear sneakers, because the village isn't paved—and explain their activities. As with any undertaking of this nature, it takes a while to get used to the atmosphere, but once you do, it's great fun. When the 1996 film version of Arthur Miller's play about the witchcraft trials, *The Crucible*, was completed, the village inherited a large collection of authentic and reproduction props that have been put into use.

Salem Witch Museum. 19½ Washington Sq. ☎ **508/744-1692.** Admission $4 adults, $3.50 seniors, $2.50 ages 6–14. Sept–June daily 10am–5pm; July–Aug daily 10am–7pm. Closed Thanksgiving, Christmas, and New Year's Day. Follow Hawthorne Blvd. to the northwest corner of Salem Common.

Actually a three-dimensional audiovisual presentation with life-sized figures, the Witch Museum is a huge room lined with displays that are lighted in sequence. The 30-minute narration dramatically tells the story of the witchcraft trials and the accompanying hysteria. (One man was pressed to death by rocks piled on a board on his chest—smaller children may need a reminder that he's not real.) Translation of the narration is available in French, German, Italian, Japanese, and Spanish.

On the traffic island across from the entrance is a statue that's easily mistaken for a witch. It's really Roger Conant, who founded Salem in 1626.

WHERE TO STAY

Coach House Inn. 284 Lafayette St. (Routes 1A and 114), Salem, MA 01970. ☎ **800/688-8689** or 508/744-4092. 11 rms, 9 with bath (1 with shower only). A/C TV. $68–$75 double with shared bath; $75–$98 double with private bath; $125–$155 suite with kitchenette.

Trying Times

The Salem Witch Trials took place in 1692, a product of superstition brought to the New World from Europe, religious control of government, and plain old boredom.

The hysteria that led to the trials began in the winter of 1691 through 1692 in Salem Village (now the town of Danvers). The household of the Reverend Samuel Parris included his 9-year-old daughter, Elizabeth, her cousin Abigail, and a West Indian slave named Tituba who amused the girls and their friends during the long, harsh winter by telling them stories. Entertained by the tales of witchcraft, sorcery, and fortune-telling, the girls began acting as if they were under a spell, rolling on the ground and wailing. The superstitious settlers, aware that thousands of people in Europe had been executed for being witches in the previous 2 centuries, took the behavior seriously, and a doctor diagnosed Elizabeth, Abigail, and one of their friends as bewitched.

At first only Tituba and two other local women were accused of casting the spells, but the infighting that characterized the Puritan theocracy soon came to the fore, and an accusation of witchcraft became a handy way to settle a score. Anyone considered "different" was a potential target, from the elderly to the deaf to the poor. A special court was convened in Salem proper, and even though the girls soon recanted, the trials began. Defendants had no counsel, and pleading not guilty or objecting to the proceedings was considered the equivalent of a confession. Between March 1 and September 22, 27 of the more than 150 people accused had been convicted.

In the end, 19 people went to the gallows, and one man who refused to confess, Giles Corey, was pressed to death by stones piled on a board on his chest. Finally, cooler heads prevailed. Leading cleric Cotton Mather and his father, Harvard president Increase Mather, led the call for tolerance. With the jails overflowing, the trials were called off and the prisoners (including Tituba) freed.

The lessons of open-mindedness and tolerance that come down to us in this cautionary tale have been absorbed with varying degrees of success in the intervening years. Salem was the backdrop for the recent film version of Arthur Miller's *The Crucible*, a story of the witch trials and an allegory of the McCarthy Senate hearings of the 1950s—a time when those lessons could productively have been taught again.

Extra person $15. Rates include continental breakfast. 2- or 3-night minimum on weekends and holidays. AE, DISC, MC, V.

Built in 1879 for a ship's captain, the Coach House Inn is two blocks from the harbor. It's a good, thrifty choice if you don't mind the 20-minute walk or 5-minute drive from downtown Salem. The high-ceilinged rooms in the three-story mansion have elegant furnishings, and most have nonworking fireplaces, many of marble or carved ebony. Breakfast arrives at your door in a basket. No smoking.

Hawthorne Hotel. 18 Washington Sq. (at Salem Common), Salem, MA 01970. ☎ **800/ 729-7829** or 508/744-4080. Fax 508/745-9842. 83 rms (some with shower only), 6 suites. A/C TV TEL. $82–$162 double; $150–$275 suite. Lower rates off-season. Extra person $12. Children under 16 stay free in parents' room. Senior discount available. 2-night minimum on holiday weekends. AE, DC, DISC, MC, V.

This historic hotel, built in 1925 and nicely maintained (the lobby was remodeled in 1995, and the guest rooms are in the process of being spruced up) is as convenient as it is comfortable. The six-story building is centrally located, and some of the attractively furnished rooms overlook Salem Common. This is a busy neighborhood; ask to be as high up as possible. Guests have the use of an exercise room, and there are two restaurants on the ground floor.

Salem Inn. 7 Summer St. (Rte. 114), Salem, MA 01970. ☎ 800/446-2995 or 508/741-0680. Fax 508/744-8924. E-mail saleminn@earthlink.net. 33 rms (some with shower only), 3 suites. A/C TV TEL. Mid-Apr to mid-Oct $109–$179 double; Halloween week $140–$175 double; Nov to mid-Apr $99–$169 double. Rates include continental breakfast. 2-night minimum for special events and holidays. AE, CB, DC, DISC, MC, V.

The hubbub of downtown falls away as you enter the Salem Inn, one block from historic Chestnut Street. Both buildings, the 1834 West House and the 1854 Curwen House (around the corner on Essex Street), were homes of ship captains. Guest rooms are large and tastefully decorated. Some have fireplaces, canopy beds, and whirlpool baths, and the suites have kitchenettes. At the rear of the main building are a peaceful rose garden and brick patio.

The Courtyard Café, on the lower level, serves dinner Wednesday through Sunday from 5:30 to 9:30pm.

WHERE TO DINE

Whether you're sitting down for three courses or grabbing a muffin and running, Salem offers a good selection. In addition to the restaurants listed below, **Pickering Wharf** has a food court as well as a link in the **Victoria Station** chain (☎ 508/745-3400), where the deck has a great view of the marina. For a quick bite, try **Brothers Restaurant & Deli,** 283 Derby St. (☎ 508/741-4648), an inexpensive cafeteria-style family spot with home-cooked Greek meals that also serves breakfast all day.

The **Rockmore Restaurant** (☎ 508/740-1001 or 617/639-0600), is on a float in the middle of Salem Harbor. It's open daily from 11am to 9pm from Memorial Day weekend to Labor Day weekend, weather permitting. Main courses run $5 to $12, MasterCard and Visa are accepted, and if you're not traveling by boat, ferry service is available at Pickering Wharf or Village Street Pier in Marblehead.

In a Pig's Eye. 148 Derby St. ☎ 508/741-4436. Reservations recommended at dinner. Sandwiches and salads $3.95–$7.50, main courses $9.95–$15 at dinner Wed–Sat, $5.50–$9.95 at dinner Mon–Tues. AE, MC, V. Mon–Sat 11:30am–3pm and 6–10pm, Sun 11:30am–4pm. AMERICAN/MEXICAN.

Although it appears to be just a neighborhood bar near the House of the Seven Gables, In a Pig's Eye is more silk purse than sow's ear—the food is wonderful. The lunch menu offers bar fare that's a step up from basic, with several vegetarian options, and Mexican food, including gigantic, delicious burritos. Mexican nights are Monday and Tuesday (the Mexican pizza, mounds of vegetables and salsa served on flour tortillas, is terrific), and the rest of the week sees a change to creative pasta dishes, beef, chicken, and at least half a dozen seafood choices.

✪ Lyceum Bar & Grill. 43 Church St. (at Washington St.). ☎ 508/745-7665. Reservations recommended. Main courses $10–$19. AE, DISC, MC, V. Mon–Fri 11:30am–3pm, Sun 11am–3pm (brunch); daily 5:30–10pm. AMERICAN.

Alexander Graham Bell made the first long-distance telephone call at the Lyceum, and you may want to place one of your own, to tell the folks at home what a good meal you're having. The elegance of the high-ceilinged front rooms and glass-walled back rooms is matched by the quality of the food. Grilling is a favorite cooking technique—be sure to try the marinated, grilled portobello mushrooms, even if you have to order a plate of them as an appetizer. They're also scattered throughout the menu, say, in a delectable pasta with chicken, red peppers, and Swiss chard in wine sauce, or with beef tenderloin, red-pepper sauce, and garlic mashed potatoes. Spicy vegetable lasagna is also tasty. Try to save room for one of the traditional yet sophisticated desserts; the brownie sundae is out of this world.

Red's Sandwich Shop. 15 Central St. ☎ **508/745-3527.** Most items under $6. No credit cards. Mon–Sat 5am–3pm, Sun 6am–1pm. DINER.

This no-frills spot recently expanded, but it's still a place where locals and visitors feel equally comfortable. Hunker down at the counter or a table and be ready for your waitress to call you "dear" as she brings you pancakes and eggs at breakfast, or soup (opt for chicken over chowder) and a burger at lunch.

  Red's Winter Island Grille (☎ **508/744-0203**), under the same management, is open seasonally at Winter Island Park.

Stromberg's. 2 Bridge St. (Rte. 1A). ☎ **508/744-1863.** Reservations recommended at dinner. Main courses $9.95–$14.95; lobster priced daily. AE, DISC, MC, V. Tues–Thurs 11am–9pm, Fri–Sat until 10pm. Closed Tues after long holiday weekends. SEAFOOD.

For generous portions of well-prepared seafood and a view of the water, head to this popular spot near the bridge to Beverly. You won't care that Beverly Harbor isn't the most exciting spot, especially if it's summer and you're out on the deck enjoying the live entertainment (weekends only). The fish and clam chowders are excellent, daily specials are numerous, and there are more chicken, beef, and pasta options than you might expect. Crustacean lovers in the mood to splurge will fall for the world-class lobster roll. There's also a children's menu ($2.50 to $4.50).

5 Gloucester, Rockport & Cape Ann

Gloucester, Rockport, Essex, and Manchester-by-the-Sea make up Cape Ann, a rocky peninsula so enchantingly beautiful that when you hear the slogan "Massachusetts's *other* Cape," you may forget what the first one was. Cape Ann and Cape Cod do share some attributes—scenery, shopping, seafood, traffic—but the smaller cape's proximity to Boston and manageable scale make it a wonderful day trip as well as a good choice for a longer stay. With the decline of the fishing industry that brought great prosperity to the area in the 19th century, Cape Ann has played up its long-standing reputation as a haven for artists. In addition to galleries and crafts shops, you'll find historical attractions, beaches—and oh, that scenery!

  The public transportation to and in this area is pretty good, but if you can, try to drive—you'll be able to set your own pace and take in more sights.

  Be aware that this is anything but a four-season destination. Although plenty of people commute to Boston year-round and in recent years there's been a push to make Christmas a month-long celebration, many of the attractions that draw nonresidents are closed from fall or early winter through April or May. Rockport in particular shuts up tighter than an Essex clam.

  Cape Ann has a Web site (**http://wizard.pn.com/capeann**).

  The **Cape Ann Transportation Authority (CATA)** (☎ **508/283-7916**) runs buses from town to town on Cape Ann.

  In May 1998, the **area code** for the communities that make up Cape Ann will change from 508 to 978.

MANCHESTER-BY-THE-SEA

The scenic route from the south to Gloucester is Route 127, which runs through Manchester-by-the-Sea, a lovely village incorporated in 1645. Now a prosperous suburb of Boston, Manchester is probably best known for **Singing Beach** (see the box

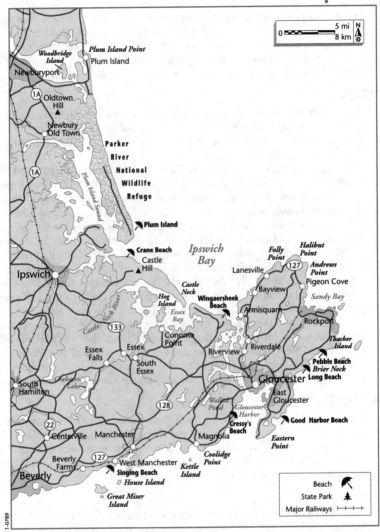

0 — 5 mi
0 — 8 km

Woodbridge Island
Plum Island Point
Plum Island
Newburyport

1A Oldtown Hill ▲

Newbury
Old Town

Parker
River
National
Wildlife
Refuge

1A

Plum Island Sound

🏖 Plum Island

🏖 Crane Beach
Castle
Hill ▲

*Ipswich
Bay*

*Folly
Point*   *Halibut
Point*

Lanesville   *Andrews
Point*
Pigeon Cove

Ipswich

*Castle
Neck*

*Hog
Island*
*Essex
Bay*

**Wingaersheek
Beach** 🏖

Bayview

Sandy Bay

Armisquam

Rockport

133

Conomo
Point

Essex

Riverview   Riverdale

*Thacher
Island*

Essex
Falls

South
Essex

Gloucester

Pebble Beach
Brier Neck
Long Beach

South
Hamilton

*Chebucco
Lake*

East
Gloucester

128

*Wallun
Pond*

*Gloucester
Harbor*

🏖 Good Harbor Beach

22

Centerville

Manchester

Magnolia

**Cressy's
Beach**

*Eastern
Point*

Beverly
Farms

127

West Manchester   *Coolidge
Point*

🏖 **Singing Beach**
House Island

*Kettle
Island*

Beverly

*Great Miser
Island*

Beach 🏖
State Park ▲
Major Railways ┼┼┼┼

1-0789

---

below on the best area beaches). The MBTA commuter rail (☎ **617/222-3200**) stops in the center of the compact downtown area, which boasts a number of shops and restaurants. Nearby **Masconomo Park** overlooks Manchester Harbor.

The home of the Manchester Historical Society is the **Trask House,** 10 Union St. (☎ **508/526-7230**), a 19th-century sea captain's home with period furnishings and costume collections. It's open in July and August, Wednesday through Saturday from 2pm to 5pm, from September through June on Thursday from 9am to 1pm, and by appointment. A donation is requested.

MAGNOLIA

Pay close attention as you head north from Manchester or south from Gloucester on Route 127—the signs for Magnolia are small and easy to miss, but the village is well worth a detour. Notable for its lack of waterfront commercial property, the village center is small and unremarkable, but the homes surrounding it, many of them one-time summer residences now occupied through the winter, are magnificent.

Less than a mile up the coast are two notable geological formations. **Rafe's Chasm** is a huge cleft in the shoreline rock, opposite the reef of **Norman's Woe,** which figures in Henry Wadsworth Longfellow's scary poem "The Wreck of the Hesperus."

ESSEX

If you approach or leave Cape Ann on Route 128, turn away from Gloucester at the Route 133 exit and head west to Essex. It's a beautiful little town known for Essex clams, salt marshes, a long tradition of shipbuilding, an incredible number of antique shops, and one celebrated restaurant.

Legend has it that ✪ **Woodman's of Essex,** on Main Street (☎ **800/649-1773** or 508/768-6451), was the birthplace of the fried clam in 1916. Today, it's a great spot to join legions of locals and out-of-towners for lobster "in the rough," steamers, corn on the cob, onion rings, and (you guessed it) fried clams. Expect the line to be long, but it moves quickly and offers a good view of the regimented commotion in the food preparation area. Eat in a booth, upstairs on the deck, or out back at a picnic table. Credit cards aren't accepted, but there's an ATM on the premises.

If this all sounds just plain uncivilized, make a reservation at **Tom Shea's,** across the street at 122 Main St. (☎ **508/768-6931**), for table service, a more sophisticated menu, and a calmer atmosphere. You'll want to be well fed before you set off to explore the numerous antique shops along Main Street.

The water views in town are of the Essex River, actually a saltwater estuary. Narrated 90-minute sightseeing tours that put you in prime birding territory are available at **Essex River Cruises,** Essex Marina, 35 Dodge St. (☎ **800/748-3706** or 508/768-6981), daily from April through October. The pontoon boat, which allows for excellent sightseeing, is screened and equipped with rest rooms. Call for reservations.

GLOUCESTER

Gloucester is the most urban of Cape Ann's communities, with a built-up downtown near the harbor and a large year-round population. Settled by Europeans in 1623 (7 years before Boston), Gloucester has made its living from the sea ever since. The depletion of the Atlantic's fishing stock in recent years has left a void now partly filled by the thriving whale-watching industry (see below).

ESSENTIALS

GETTING THERE   From Boston, the quickest route is I-93 (or Route 1, if it's not rush hour) to Route 128, which ends at Gloucester. The slower but prettier approach is to take Route 1A—all the way from East Boston, or from downtown Salem—across the bridge at Beverly and pick up Route 127. It runs through Manchester (near, not on, the water) to Gloucester. Route 128 is almost entirely inland; the exits for Manchester allow access to Route 127. Gloucester is 33 miles northeast of Boston, 16 miles northeast of Salem, and 7 miles south of Rockport.

The **MBTA** (☎ **617/222-3200**) commuter rail runs from North Station in Boston to Gloucester. The trip takes about an hour. The **Cape Ann Transportation Authority,** or CATA (☎ **508/283-7916**) runs buses from town to town on Cape Ann.

VISITOR INFORMATION   The **area code** is 508 through April 1998, when it will change to 978.

The **Gloucester Tourism Commission,** 22 Poplar St., Gloucester, MA 01930 (☎ **800/649-6839** or 508/281-8865), operates an excellent Visitors Welcoming

Where to Find Cape Ann's Best Beaches

Paradoxically, Cape Ann is almost as well known for its sandy beaches as for its rocky coastline. Two caveats: It's not Florida, so don't expect 70° water (the operative word is "refreshing"), and parking can be pricey—as much as $15 per car—and scarce, especially on weekends. If you can't set out early, wait till midafternoon and hope that the people who beat you to the beach in the morning have had enough.

During the summer, lifeguards are on duty from 9am to 5pm at larger public beaches. Surfing is generally permitted outside of those hours.

Probably the best-known North Shore beach is **Singing Beach,** off Masconomo Street in Manchester-by-the-Sea. It's named for the sound the sand makes under your feet. The legions of people walking six-tenths of a mile on Beach Street from the commuter rail station attest to both the beach's reputation and the difficulty (and expense) of parking. Save some cash and aggravation by taking the **MBTA** commuter rail (☎ **617/222-3200**) from Boston's North Station. **White Beach,** off Ocean Street, is another public beach in town.

Nearly as famous as Singing Beach and equally popular is **Crane Beach,** off Argilla Road in Ipswich, part of a 1,400-acre barrier beach reservation. Expanses of white sand and fragile dunes lead down to Ipswich Bay, with surf calmer than that at less sheltered Singing Beach, but still quite chilly. Also on Ipswich Bay is Gloucester's **Wingaersheek Beach,** on Atlantic Street off Route 133. It has its own exit (no. 13) off Route 128, about 15 minutes away. When you finally arrive you'll find beautiful white sand, a glorious view, and more dunes. Across the bay, there's a beach at **Plum Island** that's part of the **Parker River National Wildlife Refuge** (see below).

Watch out for the greenhead flies at Wingaersheek, Plum Island, and Crane beaches in late July and early August. They don't sting—they actually take little bites of flesh. Plan to bring or buy insect repellent.

Other nice beaches in Gloucester are **Good Harbor Beach,** off Route 127A at Thatcher Road in East Gloucester, **Coffin Beach,** just northwest of Wingaersheek, and **Half Moon Beach** and **Cressy's Beach,** at Stage Fort Park, off Route 127 near the intersection with Route 133. The park also contains a visitor information office (summer only), playgrounds, picnic and cookout areas, and the ruins of a Revolutionary War fort.

In Rockport, **Front Beach** and **Back Beach** are on Beach Street just a couple of blocks north of downtown, and **Old Garden Beach** is on Old Garden Road east of downtown. Heading south on Route 127A toward Gloucester, you can detour to **Pebble Beach** (which appears on some maps as "Pebbly Beach"), off Penzance Road, **Cape Hedge Beach,** off South Street, and **Long Beach,** off Thatcher Road.

If ocean beaches don't suit you, **Chebacco Lake** in Essex off Western Avenue is a freshwater option.

Center that's open daily from 9am to 5pm during the summer at Stage Fort Park, off Route 127 near the intersection with Route 133. It's well stocked with free brochures; ask for a copy of the Tourism Commission's guide to the Gloucester Maritime Trail, a pamphlet that includes descriptions of four walking tours.

The information center run by the **Cape Ann Chamber of Commerce,** 33 Commercial St., Gloucester, MA 01930 (☎ **800/321-0133** or 508/283-1601; Web site: **http://www.cape-ann.com/cacc**), is open year-round (summer, weekdays 8am to

6pm, Saturday 10am to 6pm, Sunday 10am to 4pm; winter, weekdays 8am to 5pm). Call or write for the chamber's four-color map and brochure.

The **North of Boston Convention & Visitors Bureau,** P.O. Box 642, Beverly, MA 01915 (☎ **800/742-5306**), publishes a visitor's guide. And Gloucester has a page on the Cape Ann Web site (**http://wizard.pn.com/capeann**).

GETTING AROUND   The Cape Ann Transportation Authority (see above) serves most of Gloucester on its regular routes and operates special loops during the summer, but if you can manage it, try to make this trip by car. You'll be able to make the best use of your time by making your own schedule.

SPECIAL EVENTS   The fishing fleet enjoys some divine intervention every year during **St. Peter's Fiesta,** a colorful 4-day event at the end of June. The Italian-American fishing colony's enormous festival features parades, music, food, sporting events, and, on Sunday, the blessing of the fleet.

EXPLORING THE TOWN

Start at the water, the city's lifeblood since long before the first European settlement in 1623. The French explorer Samuel de Champlain called the harbor "Le Beauport" when he came across it in 1604, some 600 years after the Vikings, and its configuration and proximity to good fishing gave it the reputation it enjoys to this day. Follow one or more of the Tourism Commission's walking tours, or explore on your own.

The fleet sets out early in the morning from the downtown part of the harbor, where processing plants—Clarence Birdseye invented the procedure for blast-freezing foods here—await the catch, which is unloaded on **State Fish Pier,** on Parker Street. Although fishing is an important industry, it doesn't carry the economic clout it once did. The depletion of New England's fishing grounds has led to the rise of another important seagoing industry: whale watching (see below).

On Stacy Boulevard west of downtown is a reminder of the sea's danger. Leonard Craske's bronze statue of the **Gloucester Fisherman,** known as *The Man at the Wheel,* bears the inscription "They That Go Down to the Sea in Ships 1623–1923." More than 10,000 fishermen lost their lives during the city's first 300 years, and a statue honoring the women and children who waited for them is currently in the works.

Driving downtown on a bad traffic day can be frustrating. But one good reason to brave the congestion on Main Street is to visit the **Cape Ann Historical Museum,** 27 Pleasant St. (☎ **508/283-0455**). The meticulously curated museum makes an excellent introduction to Cape Ann's history and artists. An entire gallery is devoted to the extraordinary work of Fitz Hugh Lane, the American Luminist painter whose light-flooded paintings show the best of his native Gloucester. The nation's single largest collection of his paintings and drawings is here, along with new galleries featuring 20th-century artists, and maritime and fisheries galleries overflowing with everything from entire vessels (including one about the size of a station wagon that actually crossed the Atlantic) to photographs and models of the Gloucester waterfront. The Capt. Elias Davis House (1804) is part of the museum and is decorated and furnished in Federal style with furniture, silver, and porcelains.

Admission is $3.50 for adults, $3 seniors, $2 students, and free for children 6 and under. The museum is open from March through January, Tuesday through Saturday from 10am to 5pm, and closed in February. Follow Main Street west through downtown and turn right onto Pleasant Street; the museum is one block up on the right. Metered parking is available on the street or in the lot across the street.

Moby Duck Tours (☎ 508/281-3825) are 50-minute sightseeing expeditions that travel on land before plunging into the water. The amphibious vehicles leave from **Harbor Loop** downtown, where tickets ($12 adults, $10 seniors, $8 children under 12) are available. Plan to take a tour if you have children along; as soon as they see the vessels, they'll want a ride.

Also at Harbor Loop, you can tour the two-masted schooner *Adventure* (☎ 508/281-8079), a 121-foot fishing vessel built in Essex in 1926. The "living museum," a National Historic Landmark under continual restoration, is open to visitors from Memorial Day to Labor Day, Thursday through Sunday from 10am to 4pm. (Suggested donation $5 adults, $4 children.)

Stage Fort Park (off Route 127 near the intersection with Route 133) offers an excellent view of the harbor and is a good spot for a picnic, swimming, or just playing on the cannons in the Revolutionary War fort.

To reach East Gloucester, follow signs as you leave downtown or go directly from Route 128, Exit 9. On East Main Street, you'll see signs for the world-famous **Rocky Neck Art Colony,** the oldest continuously operating art colony in the country. Park in the lot on the tiny causeway and walk two blocks west to Rocky Neck Avenue, which is jammed with studios, galleries, restaurants, and people. The real draw is the presence of working artists, not just shops that happen to sell art. Some of the work winds up at the **North Shore Arts Association,** 197 E. Main St. (☎ 508/283-1857), founded in 1923 to showcase local artists' work. It's open June through September, Monday to Saturday from 10am to 5pm, Sunday 1 to 5pm, and admission is free.

The high point of a trip to this part of town is a visit to **Beauport (Sleeper-McCann House),** at 75 Eastern Point Blvd. (☎ 508/283-0800). The Society for the Preservation of New England Antiquities, which operates it, describes Beauport as a "fantasy house," and that's putting it mildly. Interior designer Henry Davis Sleeper used his summer residence as a retreat and a repository for his vast collections of American and European decorative arts and antiques. From 1907 to 1934, he decorated the 40 rooms, 26 of which are open to the public, to illustrate literary and historical themes. The entertaining tour concentrates more on the house and rooms in general than on the countless objects on display. You'll see architectural details rescued from other buildings, magnificent arrangements of colored glassware, an Early American kitchen, the "Red Indian Room" (with a majestic view of the harbor), and "Strawberry Hill," the master bedroom.

If you're interested in interior design, it's worth scheduling your visit so you can see Beauport, which is closed from mid-October through mid-May and on weekends in the summer. Tours are given on the hour from mid-May through mid-October on weekdays only, from 10am to 4pm; and from mid-September through mid-October on weekdays from 10am to 4pm and weekends from 1 to 4pm. Tickets are $6 for adults, $5.50 seniors, and $2.50 ages 6 to 12. To get there, take East Main Street south to Eastern Point Boulevard (a private road), follow it one-half mile to the house and park on the left. If you're visiting from June through September, call ahead to see if afternoon tea is being offered while you're in town.

Another fantasy house is now the **Hammond Castle Museum,** 80 Hesperus Ave. (☎ 508/283-7673, or 508/283-2080 for recorded information), off Route 127 near Magnolia. Although it's equally interesting, it suffers by comparison to Beauport because the tour is self-guided and all of the artifacts aren't as carefully labeled as they might be. Still, it's worth a visit for a look inside the mind of eccentric inventor John Hays Hammond, Jr. He spent more than $6 million on his brainchild, a medieval castle constructed of Rockport granite from 1926 to 1929. There are 85-foot towers, battlements, stained-glass windows, a great hall 60 feet high, and an enclosed "outdoor" pool and courtyard lined with foliage, trees, and medieval artifacts (including the whole wooden front of a butcher shop). The pipes in the ceiling "rain" on command. Many 12th-, 13th-, and 14th-century furnishings, tapestries, paintings, and architectural fragments fill the rooms. An organ with more than 8,200 pipes is used for monthly concerts. Write for a copy of the events calendar.

The museum is open daily from May through October from 10am to 5pm, weekends only November through April, and closed Christmas and New Year's Day. Admission is $6 for adults, $5 seniors, and $4 ages 4 to 12. From Route 127, look for the tiny signs that point to Magnolia and the museum.

WHALE-WATCHING CRUISES

The waters off the coast of Massachusetts are prime whale-watching territory, and Gloucester is a center of whale-watching cruises. Stellwagen Bank, which runs from Gloucester to Provincetown about 27 miles east of Boston, is a rich feeding ground for the magnificent mammals, who dine on sand eels and other fish that gather along the ridge. The most commonly sighted species in this area are baleen whales, the finback and the humpback. The whales often perform for their audience, by jumping out of the water, and occasionally dolphins join the show.

Once the novelty of putting out to sea is behind them, children tend not to be thrilled with the amount of time it takes to reach the bank, which makes their reaction to a sighting all the more gratifying. This isn't the cheapest way to spend half a day, but it is an "only in New England" experience kids (and adults) will remember for a long time.

Dress warmly, because it's much cooler at sea than in town, and take sunglasses, sunscreen, a hat, rubber-soled shoes, and a camera with plenty of film. If you're prone to motion sickness, take appropriate precautions (ginger, whether crystallized or in ginger ale, can help alleviate nausea), as you'll be out on the open sea.

Check the local marinas for sailing times, prices ($20 to $25 for adults, less for children and seniors), and reservations, which are always a good idea. It's a competitive business—most companies guarantee sightings, offer a morning and an afternoon cruise as well as deep-sea fishing excursions, honor other firms' coupons, and offer AARP and AAA discounts. Naturalists on board narrate the trip for the companies listed here, pointing out the whales and describing the birds and fish that may cross your path.

In downtown Gloucester, **Cape Ann Whale Watch,** 415 Main St., at Rose's Wharf (☎ 800/877-5110 or 508/283-5110), is the oldest and best-known operation. Or try **Captain Bill's Whale Watch,** 33 Harbor Loop (☎ 800/33-WHALE or 508/283-6995), or **Seven Seas Whale Watch,** at Seven Seas Wharf (☎ 800/238-1776 or 508/283-1776). At the Cape Ann Marina, off Route 133, you'll find **Yankee Whale Watch** (☎ 800/WHALING or 508/283-0313).

WHERE TO STAY

Atlantis Oceanfront Motor Inn. 125 Atlantic Rd., Gloucester, MA 01930. ☎ **508/283-0014.** 40 rms (some with shower only). TV TEL. Late June through Labor Day $100–$120 double; spring and fall $65–$95 double. Extra person $8. Closed Nov to mid-Apr. 2-night minimum on spring and fall weekends, 3 nights on summer and holiday weekends. AE, MC, V. Follow Rte. 128 to the end (Exit 9, E. Gloucester), turn left onto Bass Ave. (Rte. 127A) and follow ½ mile. Turn right and follow Atlantic Rd.

The stunning views from every window of this motor inn would almost be enough to recommend it, but it also has a friendly staff and a heated outdoor pool. The redecoration of the guest rooms in comfortable, contemporary style was completed in 1995. Every room has a terrace or balcony and a small table and chairs, and the coffee shop on the premises serves breakfast until 11am. Rooms for nonsmokers are available.

Best Western Bass Rocks Ocean Inn. 107 Atlantic Rd., Gloucester, MA 01930. ☎ **800/ 528-1234** or 508/283-7600. Fax 508/281-6489. 48 rms. A/C TV TEL. Late Apr through Memorial Day $95–$125 double; Memorial Day through late June $115–$150 double; late June to late Aug $120–$160 double; Sept–Oct $115–$150 double. Extra person $8. Rollaway bed $12. Rates include continental breakfast. Children under 12 stay free in parents' room. 3-night minimum on summer weekends and some spring and fall weekends. AE, CB, DC, DISC, MC, V. Closed Nov to late Apr. Follow Rte. 128 to the end (Exit 9, E. Gloucester), turn left onto Bass Ave. (Rte. 127A) and follow ¹/₂ mile. Turn right and follow Atlantic Rd.

A family operation since 1946, the Bass Rocks Ocean Inn offers modern accommodations in a traditional setting. The guest rooms overlook the ocean from a sprawling, comfortable motel, with the office and public areas in a colonial revival–style mansion built in 1899 and known as the "wedding cake house." The rooftop sundeck, balconies, and swimming pool all offer excellent views of the surf. The large rooms have balconies or patios; each has a king-sized bed or two double beds. Each morning a cold buffet breakfast is served, and each afternoon coffee and chocolate-chip cookies are offered. A billiard room and library are available, and bicycles are at the disposal of the guests. Rooms for nonsmokers are available.

WHERE TO DINE

✪ **The Gull.** 75 Essex Ave. (Rte. 133), at Cape Ann Marina. ☎ **508/283-6565.** Reservations recommended for parties of 8 or more. Main courses $6.95–$20.95. MC, V. Daily 5am–9:30pm. Closed Nov to late Apr. Take Rte. 133 west from the intersection with Rte. 127, or approach along Rte. 133 eastbound from Rte. 128. SEAFOOD.

The Annisquam River is visible through the floor-to-ceiling windows from almost every seat at the Gull. This big, friendly restaurant specializes in seafood but is also known for its prime rib, and it draws locals, visitors, boaters, and families for large portions at reasonable prices. Ask about the daily specials. The seafood chowder is famous (with good reason), appetizers tend toward bar food, and fish is available in just about any variety and style—it seems unlikely, but the Cajun-style fish-and-chips is excellent. At lunch, there's an extensive sandwich menu. The Gull has a full bar.

The Rudder Restaurant. 73 Rocky Neck Ave., E. Gloucester. ☎ **508/283-7967.** Reservations required on weekends. Main courses $12.95–$19.95. DISC, MC, V. Memorial Day to Labor Day daily noon–10:30pm; call for open hours and days spring and fall. Closed Dec to mid-Apr. SEAFOOD/INTERNATIONAL.

A meal at the Rudder is not just a meal—it's a party. Overlooking Smith Cove, in the heart of the Rocky Neck Art Colony, the 40-year-old restaurant is packed, floor to ceiling, with gadgets, colored lights, antiques, photos, menus from around the world, and other collectibles. Ask for a seat on the deck (if it's not low tide) and be prepared for anything, because the Rudder is known for its "spontaneous entertainment." You might hear live piano music or see Susan's invisible flaming baton twirling act. The chefs are creative (try the shrimp farcis for an appetizer), and main-course offerings run the gamut from shrimp scampi over fresh linguine to chicken piccata. There's also a children's menu ($7.95).

Square on Main. 272 Main St. ☎ **508/281-3951.** Reservations recommended (off-season, weekends only). Main courses $9.50–$14.50. AE, DC, DISC, MC, V. Mon–Sat noon–3pm, Mon–Sun 5–10pm. CONTINENTAL.

A reincarnation of East Gloucester's Square Cafe (whose sign hangs outside), Square on Main is an oasis of sophistication on a congested commercial-industrial strip of downtown that draws locals and out-of-towners alike. The plain brick building belies the spacious two-level interior, which has a sunny feel even at night because of the yellow, rag-painted walls and large windows. The food is equally unexpected—for one thing, it's not all seafood, and for another, each dish has a certain flair. Fresh clam chowder is a good rendition, made even better with the addition of crunchy corn, and jalapeño-lime mayonnaise has the same effect on fried oysters. Entrees include excellent roasted chicken served with "smashed" potatoes; scallops sautéed with ginger and red, yellow, and jalapeño peppers in a hot-sweet Hong Kong–style sauce; and vegetable lasagna so rich with pesto cream sauce and cheese that the health benefits of the vegetables are almost negated. You can also dine in the small, cozy bar.

ROCKPORT

This lovely little town at the tip of Cape Ann was settled in 1690 and over the years has been an active fishing port, a center of granite excavation and cutting, and a thriving summer community whose specialty seems to be selling fudge and refrigerator magnets to out-of-towners. There's more to Rockport than gift shops—you just have to look. For every year-round resident who seems genuinely startled when legions of people with cameras around their necks descend on Rockport each June, there are dozens who are proud to show off their town.

Take a little time to explore beyond the immediate downtown area, and you'll see what Winslow Homer, Fitz Hugh Lane, Childe Hassam, and other artists were getting at when they captured Rockport in magnificent seascapes. Peer down the alleyways between the waterfront buildings or walk out to a spot with a clear view of the ocean to get your own perspective. The views from **Halibut Point State Park** (see below) are particularly dramatic. The town is still popular with painters, photographers, sculptors, and jewelry designers, and the Rockport Art Association is active all year. Many galleries show the work of local artists.

ESSENTIALS

GETTING THERE   Rockport is north of Gloucester along Route 127 or 127A. After the second Gloucester rotary at the end of Route 128, turn left at the signs for Rockport to take 127. Or continue until you see the sign for East Gloucester and turn left onto 127A, which runs along the east coast of Cape Ann. Route 127 is a loop that cuts across the peninsula inland and swings around to follow Ipswich Bay. Rockport is 40 miles northeast of Boston, 7 miles north of Gloucester.

The **MBTA** (☎ 617/222-3200) commuter rail runs from North Station in Boston to Rockport. The trip takes about an hour. The **Cape Ann Transportation Authority,** or CATA (☎ 508/283-7916) runs buses from town to town on Cape Ann.

VISITOR INFORMATION   The **area code** is 508 through April 1998, when it will become 978.

The **Rockport Chamber of Commerce and Board of Trade,** 3 Main St., P.O. Box 67, Rockport, MA 01966 (☎ 508/546-6575), is open in summer from 9am to 5pm daily, and on winter weekdays from 10am to 4pm. The chamber also operates a seasonal (mid-May to mid-October) information booth on Upper Main Street (Route 127), about a mile from downtown. At either location, ask for the pamphlet *Rockport: A Walking Guide,* which has a good map and descriptions of three short walking tours.

GETTING AROUND   Park and walk, especially downtown. The Cape Ann Transportation Authority (see above) runs within the town, but having your own car allows you to make your own itinerary.

If you can schedule only one weekday trip, make it this one. For traffic and congestion, downtown Boston has nothing on Rockport on a summer Saturday afternoon. Whenever you go, circle the square once (mind the limits on many meters), and if there's no place to park, try the back streets, even if they're some distance from the center of town. Or use the parking lot on Upper Main Street (Route 127) on weekends. Parking from 11am to 6pm will cost about $6, and a free shuttle will take you downtown and back.

SPECIAL EVENTS   Chamber-music fans might want to check out the **Rockport Chamber Music Festival** (☎ 508/546-7391), an early-summer highlight usually held on weekends in June.

WHAT TO SEE & DO

The most famous example of what to see in Rockport is surrounded by something of an Emperor's New Clothes aura—it's a wooden fish warehouse on the town wharf, or T-Wharf, in the harbor. The barn red shack (often rendered in bright red, though it's not), known as **Motif No. 1,** is the most frequently painted and photographed object in a town filled with lovely buildings and surrounded by rocky coastline. The color certainly catches the eye in the neutrals of the surrounding seascape, but you may find yourself initiating or overhearing conversations about what the big deal is. Originally constructed in 1884 and destroyed during the blizzard of 1978, Motif No. 1 was rebuilt using donations from the local community and visitors. It stands again on the same pier, duplicated in every detail, and reinforced to withstand storms. Walk to the end of T-Wharf and look to the left so you can say you saw it, then move on.

Nearby is a phenomenon whose popularity is easier to explain. **Bearskin Neck,** named after an unfortunate ursine visitor who drowned and was washed ashore in 1800, has perhaps the highest concentration of gift shops anywhere. It's a narrow peninsula with one main street (South Road) and several alleys lined—crammed, really—with galleries, snack bars, antique shops, and ancient houses. You'll find dozens of little shops carrying clothes, gifts, toys, inexpensive novelties, and expensive handmade crafts and paintings. Walk all the way to the end of the peninsula for a magnificent water view.

More than two dozen art galleries display the works of both local and nationally known artists. The **Rockport Art Association,** 12 Main St. (☎ 508/546-6604), open daily year-round, sponsors major exhibitions and special shows throughout the year.

Perhaps the mansions of Gloucester were too plush for you, or maybe you want some tips on what to do with old newspapers. Visit the **Paper House,** 52 Pigeon Hill St., Pigeon Cove (☎ 508/546-2629). It was built in 1922 entirely out of 100,000 newspapers—walls, furniture, even a piano. Every item of furniture is made from papers of a different period. It's open daily from May through October from 10am to 5pm. Admission is $1.50 for adults and $1 for children. Follow Route 127 north out of downtown until you see signs pointing to the left.

And if you'd like to indulge the inexplicable craving for fudge that overwhelms otherwise mild-mannered travelers when they get their first whiff of salt water, you can give in to temptation and then watch taffy being made at **Tuck's Candy Factory,** 7 Dock Sq. (☎ 800/569-2767 or 508/546-6352), a local landmark for nearly 70 years.

WHERE TO STAY

Reservations are essential in July and August, and they're not a bad idea in the spring and fall.

In Town

Addison Choate Inn. 49 Broadway, Rockport, MA 01966. ☎ **800/245-7543** or 508/546-7543. Fax 508/546-7638. 6 rms, 1 suite, 2 apts (some with shower only). Mid-June to mid-Sept $100 double, $130 or $730 per week suite; spring and fall $92 double, $110 suite; winter rates are lower. Extra person $15. Rates include continental breakfast. 2-night minimum on summer weekends, 3 nights 4th of July weekend. DC, MC, V. No children under 12.

Long known as Rockport's most charming place to stay, the Addison Choate Inn is a Greek Revival–style house built in 1851 and beautifully restored. Innkeepers Shirley and Knox Johnson have furnished the nicely appointed rooms with a mix of period antiques and contemporary furnishings. Some have canopy beds. The rooms range from basic to plush—the "Celebrations Suite" on the third floor has a sitting room and a view of the harbor, and the apartment units in the stable house at the back of the property have loft bedrooms and kitchenettes. Guests have the use of a TV room and the outdoor pool. The suites have cable TV, and two units are air-conditioned. No smoking.

Captain's Bounty Motor Inn. 1 Beach St., Rockport, MA 01966. ☎ **508/546-9557.** 24 rms. TV TEL. Apr to mid-May $65 oceanfront room, $68 oceanfront efficiency, $70 oceanfront efficiency suite; mid-May to mid-June and late Sept–Oct $80 oceanfront room, $85 oceanfront efficiency, $90 oceanfront efficiency suite; mid-June to late Sept $98 oceanfront room, $110 oceanfront efficiency, $120 oceanfront efficiency suite. Extra person $10; rollaway bed $5. 2-night minimum on weekends, 3 nights on holiday weekends. DISC, MC, V. Closed Nov–Mar.

To get closer to the beach than this modern, well-maintained motor inn, you'd have to sleep on a houseboat. Ocean breezes provide natural air-conditioning—each room in the two-story building overlooks the water and has its own balcony and sliding glass door. Rooms are spacious and soundproofed, and kitchenette units are available.

✪ Inn on Cove Hill. 37 Mt. Pleasant St., Rockport, MA 01966. ☎ **888/546-2701** or 508/546-2701. 11 rms (9 with bath, some with shower only). A/C TV. $67–$105 double with private bath, $50 double with shared bath. Extra person $25. Rates include continental breakfast. 2-night minimum July–Aug and weekends in June and Sept–Oct. MC, V. Closed Nov to mid-Apr. No children under 10.

This three-story inn was built in 1791 from the proceeds of pirates' gold found a short distance away. Silly pirates—they could have used the money to stay here, in an attractive Federal-style home two blocks from the head of the town wharf. Although it's close to downtown, the inn is set back from the road and has a hideaway feel. Innkeepers Marjorie and John Pratt have decorated the guest rooms in period style, with at least one antique piece in each room. Most rooms have colonial furnishings and handmade quilts, and some have canopy beds. In warm weather, a continental breakfast with home-baked breads and muffins is served on china at the garden tables; in inclement weather, breakfast in bed is served on individual trays. No smoking.

If you're coming by train from Boston, you'll be met at the station; if you drive, parking is provided.

Peg Leg Inn. 2 King St., Rockport, MA 01966. ☎ **800/346-2352** or 508/546-2352. 33 rms (some with shower only). TV. Mid-June to mid-Oct $85–$135 double, $155 2-bedroom unit. Off-season rates lower. Extra person $10. Rates include continental breakfast. 2-night minimum on weekends, 3 nights on holiday weekends. AE, MC, V. Closed Nov–Mar.

The Peg Leg Inn consists of five Early American houses with front porches, attractive living rooms, and well-kept flower-bordered lawns that run down to a gazebo at the ocean's edge. Rooms are good sized and neatly furnished in colonial style, and some have excellent ocean views. Guests at the inn may use the sandy beach across the road. No smoking.

On the Outskirts

Old Farm Inn. 291 Granite St. (Rte. 127) at Pigeon Cove, Rockport, MA 01966. ☎ **800/233-6828** or 508/546-3237. Fax 508/546-9308. 10 rms (some with shower only). A/C TEL. July–Oct $88–$130 double; Apr–June and Nov $78–$125 double. Room with kitchenette $115, 2-room suite $125. 2-bedroom housekeeping cottage $1,050 per week July–Aug. Extra person $15. Rollaway bed $20. Rates include buffet breakfast. 3-night minimum holiday and summer weekends. AE, MC, V. Closed Dec to mid-Apr. Follow Rte. 127 north from the center of town until you see signs pointing to the right for Halibut Point State Park; the inn is in front of you.

This gorgeous bed-and-breakfast is a 1799 saltwater farm with antique-furnished rooms in the Inn, the Barn Guesthouse, and the Fieldside Cottage. Each room is uniquely decorated with country-style furnishings (many have beautiful quilts on the beds), and innkeepers Susan and Bill Balzarini will make you feel at home. The excellent buffet breakfast includes fresh fruit, home-baked breads, a selection of hot and cold cereals, yogurt, and juices. Most of the rooms have a refrigerator. About $2^1/_2$ miles from the center of town, the inn is in a beautiful location a stone's throw from Halibut Point State Park.

Ralph Waldo Emerson Inn. 1 Cathedral Ave., P.O. Box 2369, Rockport, MA 01966. ☎ **508/546-6321.** Fax 508/546-7043. E-mail emerson@cove.com. 36 rms. A/C TEL. July through Labor Day $96–$137 double; spring and fall $85–$125 double. Extra person $7. Crib or cot $7. Weekly rates available. 2-night minimum on summer weekends. DISC, MC, V. Closed Dec–March; open weekends only in Apr and Nov. Follow Rte. 127 north from the center of town for 2 miles and watch for sign; turn right at Phillips St.

Somewhere in the old guest register of the Ralph Waldo Emerson Inn you might find the name of Emerson himself—the distinguished philosopher was a guest in the original (1840) inn in the 1850s. The oceanfront building was expanded in 1912 and still has an old-fashioned feel, with furnishings such as spool beds and four-posters in the nicely appointed, though not terribly large, rooms. There's no elevator—lower-priced rooms are those that require a climb and face the street or have indirect water views. A few flights of stairs seem a small inconvenience for the view from the top-floor rooms, however.

Dining/Entertainment: The dining room is open to the public when space is available. Breakfast is served from 8 to 10am, and dinner from 6 to 9pm.

Facilities: Guests have the use of a heated outdoor saltwater pool or (for a fee) the indoor whirlpool and sauna. Recreation rooms include areas for playing cards, table tennis, or watching the wide-screen TV.

Seaward Inn. 44 Marmion Way, Rockport, MA 01966. ☎ **800/648-7733** or 508/546-3471. Fax 508/546-2272. 36 rms, 9 cottages (some with shower only). TV. Mid-May to Oct $115–$175 double per night, $875–$1,600 cottage per week; mid-Apr to mid-May $100–$150 double, $130–$250 cottage per night. Extra person $20. Rates include full breakfast. AE, DC, DISC, MC, V. Closed Oct–Apr. From downtown, take Rte. 127 south about $^1/_2$ mile and turn left at the sign on Marmion Way. The inn is at the end of the street.

On 5 oceanfront acres, the Seaward Inn's three buildings and nine cottages make up a lovely complex where couples and families feel equally comfortable. The three-story main inn, two-story Carriage House, and two-story Breakers Lodge (facing the water) have comfortable rooms furnished in summer-colony style. The cottages, many of which have working fireplaces and kitchenettes, are perfect for families. The Fiumara family bought the inn from the original owners 5 years ago, and the 53-year-old property is constantly upgraded. There's a small pond for swimming, and bicycles are available if you want to explore, but you may just want to loll on the lawn and watch the ocean.

Dining/Entertainment: The SeaGarden Restaurant, on the first floor of the main inn, is open to the public for dinner. It features creative American cuisine with an emphasis on seafood.

WHERE TO DINE

Rockport is a "dry" community where the law prevents restaurants from serving alcoholic beverages—but you can bring your own bottle. There are liquor stores nearby in Gloucester and the village of Annisquam (on the west side of the peninsula off Route 127). Top prices for main dishes may be as much as $5 more if lobster is involved.

Blacksmith Shop. 23 Mt. Pleasant St. ☎ **508/546-6301.** Reservations recommended at dinner. Main courses $8.95–$16.95. AE, DC, MC, V. Mid-Apr through Memorial Day Thurs–Sun 11:30am–8pm; Memorial Day through Oct Sun–Fri 11:30am–8pm, Sat 11:30am–9pm. Closed Nov to mid-Apr. SEAFOOD.

For tasty food in a refined setting, walk one block from the town wharf to this cavernous restaurant set on stilts jutting into the harbor. The menu runs from basic seafood to more ambitious (and expensive) fare—lobster cakes or cheese tortellini with sun-dried tomatoes, for example—but everything is fresh and good. The room is as pleasing as the food, with picture windows, wooden furnishings, paintings in the gallery, and an old forge, anvil, and bellows preserved from the shop where Rockport's village smithy stood. The main dining room has been enlarged many times since its establishment in 1927; it now accommodates 200, and it still fills up. There is a children's menu ($3.95 to $4.95).

✪ **The Greenery.** 15 Dock Sq. ☎ **508/546-9593.** Reservations recommended at dinner. Main courses $9.25–$15.95. DISC, MC, V. Mid-Apr through Nov Mon–Fri 9am–10pm, Sat–Sun 8am–10pm. Closed Dec to mid-Apr. AMERICAN/SEAFOOD.

The cafelike front room of this restaurant at the head of Bearskin Neck gives no hint that at the back of the building is a dining room with a great view of the harbor. Both rooms have large windows and are decorated with plants. The terrific food ranges from crab salad quiche at lunch to grilled swordfish at dinner to steamers anytime, and there's a huge salad bar available on its own or with many entrees. Breakfast is served on weekends. All baking is done in-house, which explains the lines at the front counter for muffins and pastries. This is a good place to launch a picnic lunch on the beach, and an equally good spot for lingering over coffee and a delectable dessert and watching the action on and near the harbor.

My Place By-the-Sea. 68 South Rd., Bearskin Neck. ☎ **508/546-9667.** Reservations recommended at dinner. Main courses $12–$18. AE, CB, DC, DISC, JCB, MC, V. Apr–Nov daily 11:30–9:30pm. Closed Dec–Mar. SEAFOOD.

The lure of My Place By-the-Sea is its location at the very end of Bearskin Neck, where you'll find Rockport's only outdoor oceanfront deck. There are excellent views of Sandy Bay from the two decks and shaded patio. The menu is reliable if not exactly inspired, with many options dictated by the daily catch. The baked fish and seafood pasta entrees are good choices, and you can also have chicken or beef. The dessert menu includes excellent homemade fruit pies.

Peg Leg. 18 Beach St. ☎ **508/546-3038.** Reservations recommended. Main courses $6.95–$19. AE, MC, V. Daily 5:30–9pm. Closed off-season. AMERICAN/SEAFOOD.

For dinner in a greenhouse, complete with plants in hanging baskets, geranium trees, and flowers all around, walk through town to the end of Main Street and around the corner to the Peg Leg. The greenhouse, very romantic in the evening with its recessed spotlights and candles, is behind the cozy main restaurant. Dinner entrees include the house special chicken pie, seafood "pies" (casseroles), fresh fish, steaks, and lobster. All baking is done on the premises, and bread baskets always include tasty sweet rolls. There is also a children's menu ($6.95).

Portside Chowder House. Bearskin Neck. ☎ **508/546-7045.** Reservations not accepted. Most menu items less than $8. No credit cards. Late June through Labor Day daily 11am–8pm; Labor Day through late June daily 11am–3pm. Closed Thanksgiving and Christmas Day. SEAFOOD.

Look to the left as you set out along Bearskin Neck; the crowds in front of the small brown wooden house on the first cross street are waiting for, yes, chowder—clam and whatever else looked good that day. It comes by the cup, pint, and quart, to go or to eat in the tiny, low-ceilinged dining room with partial water views. You can also get seafood platters and surprisingly good burgers, but the real reason to come here is for tasty chowder to carry to the edge of the sea for a picnic.

A TRIP TO THE EDGE OF THE SEA

The very tip of Cape Ann is accessible to the public, and worth the trip north on Route 127 (turn right at the Old Farm Inn) to **Halibut Point State Park** (☎ 508/ **546-2997**). The surf-battered point got its name not from the fish, but because sailing ships heading for the sheltered harbors in Rockport and Gloucester must "haul about" when they reach the jutting promontory.

Walk about 10 minutes from the parking area, being careful of the wildflowers, and you'll come to a huge water-filled quarry next to a visitor center, where staffers dispense information, brochures, and bird lists. Scattered around the park are pieces of quarried granite. Swimming in the quarry is absolutely forbidden, but there are walking trails, tidal pools, a World War II observation tower that's open to visitors, and a rocky beach where you can climb around on giant boulders. Swimming is allowed there, but it isn't encouraged—the surf is rough and dangerous, and there are no lifeguards. Guided tours ($2.50 per person) are available on Saturday mornings in the summer, and there are also bird, wildflower, and tidal-pool tours; call ☎ **508/ 546-2997** or write **Friends of Halibut Point State Park,** P.O. Box 710, Rockport, MA 01966, for information and schedules. This is also a great place just to wander around and admire the scenery. On a clear day, you can see Maine.

6 Newburyport, Ipswich & Plum Island

The area between Cape Ann and the New Hampshire border is magnificent, with outdoor sights and sounds that can only be described as natural wonders, and enough impressive architecture to keep any city slicker happy. In a part of the world where the word "charming" is used almost as often as "hello," Newburyport is a singular example of a picturesque waterfront city. Downtown Newburyport is on the Merrimack River; on the town's Atlantic coast, Plum Island contains one of the country's top nature preserves, the Parker River National Wildlife Refuge. On the other side of Ipswich Bay, Ipswich itself is a lovely little town that's home to Crane Beach, on another wildlife reservation.

In May 1998, the **area code** for the communities described in this section will change from 508 to 978.

NEWBURYPORT

To get directly to Newburyport from Boston, take I-93 (or Route 1 if it's not rush hour) to I-95—not Route 128, which you'd take to most other destinations in this chapter—and follow it to Exit 57, a solid 45-minute ride. Signs lead you directly to downtown, where you can park on the street or in a lot (there's one on the waterfront at the foot of Green Street), and explore.

Perhaps because its distance from Boston makes the commute onerous (though not impossible), Newburyport has a substantial year-round population that lends it a less touristy atmosphere than its quaint appearance might suggest. Start your visit with a stop at the **Greater Newburyport Chamber of Commerce and Industry,** 29 State St., Newburyport, MA 01950 (☎ **508/462-6680**), in the heart of the redbrick downtown shopping district. You can pick up maps, brochures, shopping directories, and accommodations listings.

Market Square, the area at the foot of State Street near the waterfront, is the center of a neighborhood packed with boutiques, gift shops, plain and fancy restaurants, and many antique stores. You can also just wander over to the water, take a stroll on the boardwalk, and enjoy the action on the river. Architecture buffs will want to climb the hill to High Street, where the Charles Bulfinch–designed building that houses the Superior Court (1805) is only one of the Federal-era treasures. Ask at the Chamber of Commerce for the walking-tour map.

If you haven't gone out to sea yet, now is a good time, and here's a good place: **Newburyport Whale Watch,** Hilton's Dock, 54 Merrimack St. (☎ **800/848-1111** or 508/465-7165), offers 4¹/₂-hour cruises on a 100-foot boat with professional marine biologists on board as guides. Tickets are $24 for adults, $20 for senior citizens, and $17 for ages 4 to 16; reservations are suggested. (See "Whale-Watching Cruises," above, for more information.)

Or head to the ocean using an inland route. From downtown, take Water Street south until it becomes Plum Island Turnpike and follow it to the Parker River National Wildlife Refuge.

PARKER RIVER NATIONAL WILDLIFE REFUGE

The 4,662-acre refuge (☎ 508/465-5753) on Plum Island is a complex of barrier beaches, dunes, and salt marshes, one of the few remaining in the Northeast. There's an entrance fee for motorists, bikers, and pedestrians. The refuge is flat-out breathtaking, whether you're exploring the marshes or the seashore. More than 800 species of plants and animals (including more than 300 bird species) visit or make their home on the narrow finger of land with Broad Sound on one side and the Atlantic Ocean on the other. The seven parking lots fill up quickly on weekends when the weather is good. Plan to arrive early. South of lot 4 (Hellcat Swamp), the access road isn't paved; although it's flat and well maintained and the speed limit is low, this isn't the place for your brand-new sports car.

This is the place for some of the best ✪ **birding** anywhere, and observation of mammals and plants as well as birds. Wooden boardwalks wind through the marshes and along the shore—most don't have hand rails, so this isn't an activity for rambunctious children. You might see native and migratory species such as owls, hawks, martins, geese, warblers, ducks, snowy egrets, swallows, monarch butterflies, Canada geese, foxes, beavers, and harbor seals.

The ocean beach closes April 1 to allow piping plovers, listed by the federal government as a threatened species, to nest. The areas not being used for nesting reopen July 1, the rest in August when the birds are through. The currents are strong and can be dangerous, and there are no lifeguards—you may prefer to stick to surf fishing. Striped bass and bluefish are found in the area. A permit is required for night fishing and vehicle access to the beach. Call for information about fall and winter waterfowl hunting and the 2-day deer hunt in the fall.

IPSWICH

Across Ipswich Bay from Plum Island is the town of Ipswich. It's accessible from Route 1A (which you can pick up in Newburyport or at Route 128 in Hamilton) and from Route 133 (which intersects with Route 128 in Gloucester and I-95 in Georgetown). The **visitor center** in the Hall Haskell House on South Main Street (Route 133) is open daily in the summer, and visitor information is also available from the **Ipswich Business Association,** P.O. Box 94, Ipswich, MA 01938 (☎ **508/356-4400**).

Settled in 1630, Ipswich is dotted with 17th-century houses but is better known for two more contemporary structures. The **Clam Box,** 206 High St., Route 1A/133 (☎ **508/356-5019**), is a restaurant shaped like—you guessed it—a red-and-white-striped take-out clam box. This is a great place to try Ipswich clams to stay or to go, and not an easy place to sneak past if you have children in the car. Heading south from Newburyport, it's on the right.

South of Ipswich Center, near the intersection of Routes 1A and 133, look carefully for the Argilla Road sign (on the east side of the street). If you're traveling west on Route 133 from Gloucester and Essex, keep your eyes peeled for a sign on the right pointing to Northgate Road, which intersects with Argilla Road. Follow it east to the end, where you'll find the 1,400-acre **Crane Memorial Reservation.** The property is home to **Crane Beach** and a network of hiking trails as well as **Castle Hill.** One of the Boston area's most popular wedding locations, the exquisite Stuart-style seaside mansion known as the Great House was built by Richard Teller Crane, Jr., who made his fortune in plumbing and bathroom fixtures early in this century.

If you can't wangle an invitation to a wedding, tours of the house ($7 adults, $5 seniors and children) are given on Wednesday and Thursday in the summer and 2 Sundays a year, spring and fall. They're also offered with a themed tea on the last Thursday of the month from May through October. Call for reservations. From late May through October, you can ride in a hay wagon for a tour of the Crane Wildlife Refuge on Hog and Long islands, reached by boat across the Castle Neck River. The 90-minute **Crane Islands Tour** ($12 adults, $5 children under 12) is offered daily at 10am and 2pm. For more information, contact Castle Hill/Crane Memorial Reservation, 290 Argilla Rd., P.O. Box 563, Ipswich, MA 01938 (☎ **508/356-4351**).

Children (and adults) who can't get excited about a tour can be sent on to the beach, or they might be pacified by a stop just before Castle Hill. **Goodale Orchards Store and Winery,** 143 Argilla Rd. (☎ **508/356-5366**), is open weekends in April and daily from May through Christmas Eve. There's a picnic area, farm animals to visit, and an excellent country store where apples and baked goods are always available. Depending on the season, you might go on a hayride or participate in a fruit-wine tasting. Whatever the season, be sure to try some cider and doughnuts.

7 Plymouth

Everyone educated in the United States knows at least a little about Plymouth—about how the Pilgrims, fleeing religious persecution, left Europe on the *Mayflower* and landed at Plymouth Rock in 1620. Many also know that the Pilgrims endured disease and privation, and that just 51 people from the original group of 102 celebrated the first Thanksgiving in 1621 with Squanto, a Pawtuxet Indian associated with the Wampanoags, and his cohorts. What you won't know until you visit Plymouth is how small everything was. The *Mayflower* (a replica) seems perilously tiny, and when you contemplate how dangerous life was at the time, it's hard not to be impressed by the settlers' accomplishments.

Cape Cod was named in 1602 by Capt. Bartholomew Gosnold, and 12 years later Capt. John Smith sailed along the coast of what he named "New England." Smith called the mainland opposite Cape Cod "Plymouth." The passengers on the *Mayflower* had contracted with the London Virginia Company for a tract of land near the mouth of the Hudson River in "Northern Virginia"; in exchange for their passage to the New World, they promised to work the land for the company for 7 years. However, on November 11, 1620, rough weather and high seas forced them to make for Cape Cod Bay and anchor there, at Provincetown. Subsequently, their captain announced that they had found a safe harbor, and he refused to continue the voyage farther south to their original destination. On December 16, Provincetown having proven an unsatisfactory location, the weary travelers landed at Plymouth. They had no option but to settle in New England, and with no one to command them, their contract with the London Virginia Company became void and they were on their own to begin life in a new world.

Today, Plymouth is a manageable day-trip destination, particularly enjoyable if you're traveling with children. It also makes a good stopping point between Boston and Cape Cod.

ESSENTIALS

GETTING THERE   By car, follow the Southeast Expressway (I-93) from Boston to Route 3 south. From Cape Cod, take Route 3 north. Take Exit 6, then Route 44 east, and follow signs to the historic attractions. The 40-mile trip from Boston takes about 45 minutes if it's not rush hour. Or take Route 3 to the **Regional Information Complex** at Exit 5. To go directly to Plimoth Plantation, take Exit 4.

In September 1997, the **MBTA** (☎ **617/222-3200**) reinstituted service on the Old Colony Railroad line, which had been suspended in 1959. The new commuter rail serves Plymouth from South Station, a 58-minute trip, during the day on weekdays and all day on weekends (at peak commuting times service is to nearby Kingston). It's an especially pleasant ride when the fall foliage and cranberry bogs are at their colorful peak.

Plymouth & Brockton buses (☎ **617/773-9401** or 508/746-0378) leave from the terminal at Boston's South Station and from downtown Hyannis. You can also make connections at Logan Airport, where buses take on passengers at all airline terminals.

VISITOR INFORMATION   The **Visitor Center** (☎ **508/747-7525**) is at 130 Water St., across from the town pier. To plan ahead, contact **Plymouth Visitor Information,** P.O. Box ROCK, Plymouth, MA 02361 (☎ **800/USA-1620** or 508/747-7525; Web site: **http://media3.com/800-USA-1620**), also known as **Destination Plymouth,** or the **Plymouth Area Chamber of Commerce,** 225 Water St., Suite 500, Plymouth, MA 02360 (☎ **508/830-1620**). Off Route 3 at Exit 5 is the **Regional Information Complex,** where you can pick up maps, brochures, and information about Plymouth and the rest of eastern Massachusetts.

GETTING AROUND   The downtown attractions are accessible on foot, with a fairly shallow hill leading from the center of town to the waterfront. Note that Route 3A, which runs north to south through Plymouth, changes names as it goes, from Court to Main to Sandwich street and finally to Warren Avenue.

If you plan a lot of stops, are traveling with young children, or both, consider buying an all-day ticket for the trolley, which serves downtown and Plimoth Plantation.

Plymouth Rock Trolley, 22 Main St. (☎ **508/747-3419**), offers a narrated tour and unlimited reboarding privileges daily from Memorial Day through October and weekends through Thanksgiving. Tickets are $7 for adults and $3 for ages 3 to 12. Trolley markers indicate the stops, which are served every 20 minutes (except Plimoth Plantation, served once an hour in the summer).

A SLICE OF HISTORY

No matter how many times you suffered through elementary-school pageants wearing a big black hat and buckles on your shoes, you can still learn something about Plymouth and the Pilgrims.

The logical place to begin (good luck talking children out of it) is where the Pilgrims first set foot—at **Plymouth Rock.** The rock, accepted as the landing place of the *Mayflower* passengers, was originally 15 feet long and 3 feet wide. Time, in the form of erosion and mishandling, has left it much smaller. It was moved on the eve of the Revolution, when it broke in two, and several times thereafter. In 1867, it assumed its present permanent position at tide level, where the winter storms still break over it as they did in Pilgrim days. The McKim, Mead & White–designed portico around the rock was commissioned by the Colonial Dames of America in 1920. The rock itself is not much to look at, but the accompanying descriptions are interesting and the sense of history that surrounds it is curiously impressive.

At 6pm every Friday in August, citizens in Pilgrim costumes walk from Plymouth Rock to Burial Hill at Town Square, re-enacting a trip to church by the survivors of the settlement's first winter. Fifty-one people might sound like a lot, but you'll be struck by the small size of the group.

To put yourself in the Pilgrims' footsteps, take a **Colonial Lantern Tour** offered by New World Tours, 98 Water St. (☎ **800/698-5636** or 508/747-4161). Participants carry pierced-tin lanterns on a 90-minute walking tour of the original settlement under the direction of a knowledgeable guide. It might seem a bit hokey at first, but it's fascinating. Tours are given nightly from late March through Thanksgiving. The standard history tour leaves the New World office at 7:30pm; the "Legends and Lore" tour leaves from the lobby of the John Carver Inn, 25 Summer St., at 9pm. Tickets are $9 for adults, $7 for children. The same company offers a 90-minute tour at noon daily in July and August. The price ($15 adults, $10 children) includes a picnic lunch, and reservations are required.

A 40-minute harbor tour is another good introduction to Plymouth and a nice break from walking. You'll get a new perspective on Plymouth Rock and the *Mayflower II,* and learn about maritime history. **Capt. John Boats** (☎ **800/242-AHOY,** or 508/746-2643 for ticket information) runs tours on the hour from 11am to 7pm from June through September. They leave from State Pier, near the *Mayflower II.* Tickets are $5 for adults, $4 for seniors, $3 for children under 12. The amphibious **"duck" tours** sweeping the region arrived in Plymouth in 1997; a 1-hour ride on land and sea is $12 for adults, $8 for children under 12. The same company operates whale-watching cruises narrated by a naturalist daily from mid-May through October and on weekends in April. They leave daily at 9am and 2pm from Town Wharf, near the intersection of Water Street and Route 44. Tickets are $24 for adults, $19 for seniors, and $15 for children under 12. Reservations are recommended.

To get away from the bustle of the waterfront, you might want to relax at **Town Brook Park** at Jenney Pond, across Summer Street from the John Carver Inn. The centerpiece of the park is a beautiful tree-bordered pond that's home to many ducks and swans. Across from the pond is the **Jenney Grist Mill,** 6 Spring Lane (☎ **508/ 747-3715;** admission $2.50 adults, $2 ages 5 to 12), a working museum where you can see a reconstructed Early American water-powered mill that operates in the summer daily from 10am to 5pm. The specialty shops in the same complex, including the excellent Jenney Grist Mill Ice Cream Shoppe, are open year-round from 10am to 6pm daily. There is plenty of parking.

Also removed from the waterfront is the **National Monument to the Forefathers** (☎ 508/746-1790), a granite behemoth inscribed with the names of the *Mayflower* passengers. Heading away from the harbor on Route 44, look carefully on the right for the turn onto Allerton Street, and climb the hill. The monument is 81 feet high, elaborately decorated with figures representing various moral and political virtues, and scenes of Pilgrim history—a style of public statuary so unfashionable that it seems quite rebellious. The monument is incongruous in its little park in a residential neighborhood, but it's also quite impressive. The view from the hilltop is excellent.

Mayflower II. State Pier. ☎ **508/746-1622.** Admission $5.75 adults, $3.75 ages 6–12, children under 6 free. *Mayflower II*   and Plimoth Plantation admission $18.50 adults, $11 ages 6–12, under 6 free. Daily 9am–5pm. Closed Dec–Mar.

Berthed a few steps from Plymouth Rock, *Mayflower II* is a full-scale reproduction of the type of ship that brought the Pilgrims from England to America in 1620. Even at full scale, the vessel, constructed in England from 1955 to 1957, is remarkably small. Although little technical information is known about the original, William A. Baker, designer of *Mayflower II,* incorporated the few references in Governor Bradford's account of the voyage with other research to re-create as closely as possible the actual ship.

In 1997, 2 to 3 years of extensive reconstruction and renovation work began. The workers' explanations and interpretations of their efforts are incorporated into the exhibit, which changes regularly as the renovations proceed. (Ordinarily, costumed guides provide first-person narratives about the vessel and voyage.)

Other displays describe and illustrate the voyage and the Pilgrims' experience, including 17th-century navigation techniques, and the history of the *Mayflower II.* The vessel is owned and maintained by Plimoth Plantation, which is 3 miles south of the ship. Alongside the ship are museum shops that replicate early Pilgrim dwellings.

Pilgrim Hall Museum. 75 Court St. ☎ **508/746-1620.** Admission $5 adults, $4 seniors and AAA members, $2.50 children. Daily 9:30am–4:30pm. Closed Jan. From Plymouth Rock, walk north on Water St. and up the hill on Chilton St.

This is a great place to get a sense of the day-to-day lives of Plymouth's first white residents. Many original possessions of the early Pilgrims and their descendants are on display, including a chair that belonged to William Brewster (alongside an uncomfortable modern-day model that you can sit on), one of Myles Standish's swords, and Governor Bradford's Bible. Children 5 and up can participate in a treasure hunt. In 1998, new exhibits will include "Building a House in Plymouth Colony" and "Three Centuries of Table Settings." Among the permanent exhibits are a chunk of Plymouth Rock and the skeleton of the *Sparrow-Hawk,* a ship wrecked on Cape Cod in 1626 that lay buried in the sand and undiscovered until 1863. It's even smaller than the *Mayflower II.* Built in 1824, the Pilgrim Hall Museum is the oldest public museum in the United States and is listed on the National Register of Historic Places.

Plimoth Plantation. Rte. 3. ☎ **508/746-1622.** Admission $15 adults, $9 ages 6–12, under 6 free. Plimoth Plantation and *Mayflower II*   admission $18.50 adults, $11 ages 6–12, under 6 free. Daily 9am–5pm. Closed Dec–Mar. From Rte. 3, take Exit 4, "Plimoth Plantation Highway." From downtown, take Rte. 3A south 2¹/₂ miles.

Plimoth Plantation is a re-creation of a 1627 Pilgrim village. You enter by the hilltop fort that protects the villagers and then walk down the hill to the farm area, visiting the homes and gardens along the way, which have been constructed with careful attention to historic detail. Once you get over the feeling that the whole operation is a bit strange (I heard someone mention Pompeii), it's great fun to talk to the "Pilgrims," who, in speech, dress, and manner, assume the personalities of members of the original community. You can watch them framing a house, splitting wood, shearing sheep, preserving foodstuffs, or cooking a pot of fish stew over an open hearth, all as it was done in the 1600s. And they use only the tools and cookware available at that time. Sometimes you can join in the activities—perhaps planting, harvesting, a court trial, or a wedding party. Leave at least half a day for your visit, because once you get into the spirit, you won't want to rush. And be sure to wear comfortable walking shoes.

The community is as accurate as research can make it: Accounts of the original Pilgrim colony were combined with archaeological research, old records, and the 17th-century history written by the Pilgrims' leader, William Bradford, who often used the spelling "Plimoth" for the settlement. There are daily militia drills with matchlock muskets that are fired to demonstrate the community's defense system. In fact, little defense was needed, because the local Native Americans were friendly. Local tribes included the Wampanoags, who are represented at a homesite near the village, where members of the museum staff show off native foodstuffs, agricultural practices, and crafts. The homesite is included in admission to the plantation.

At the main entrance to the plantation you'll find two modern buildings with an interesting orientation show, exhibits, gift shop, crafts center, bookstore, and cafeteria. There's a picnic area nearby.

✪ **Plymouth National Wax Museum.** 16 Carver St. ☎ **508/746-6468.** Admission $5.50 adults, $5 seniors, $2.25 ages 5–12, children under 5 free. Mar–June and Sept–Nov daily 9am–5pm; July–Aug daily 9am–9pm. Closed Dec–Feb. From Plymouth Rock, turn around and walk up the hill or the steps.

Across New England (and probably across the United States), adults who visited this museum as children can still tell you about the history of the Pilgrims. More than 180 life-sized figures are arranged in the galleries, and dramatic sound tracks tell the story of the move to Holland to escape persecution in England, the harrowing trip across the ocean, the first Thanksgiving, and even the tale of Myles Standish, Priscilla Mullins, and John Alden. This museum is a must if children are in your party, and adults will enjoy it, too. On the hill outside is a monument at the grave site of the Pilgrims who died during the settlement's first winter.

Cranberry World. 225 Water St. ☎ **508/747-2350.** Free admission. May 1–Nov 30 daily 9:30am–5pm. Guided tours available; call for reservations. From Plymouth Rock, walk north for 10 min. right along the waterfront.

Cranberries aren't just for Thanksgiving dinner, as Ocean Spray's interesting visitor center will remind you. Displays include outdoor demonstration bogs, antique harvesting tools, a scale model of a cranberry farm, and interactive exhibits. There are daily cooking demonstrations and free cranberry refreshments. September and October are harvest time.

EXPLORING THE HISTORIC HOUSES

You can't stay in Plymouth's historic homes, but they're worth a visit to see the changing styles of architecture and furnishings since the 1600s. Costumed guides explain the homemaking details and the crafts of earlier generations. Most of the houses are open from Memorial Day through Columbus Day and during Thanksgiving celebrations; call for schedules.

Especially if you're sightseeing with children, pretend the next sentence is written in capital letters: Unless all of you have a sky-high tolerance for house tours, pick just one or two from eras that you find particularly interesting. Each has something to recommend it; the Sparrow and Howland houses are most interesting for those curious about the original settlers.

The 1640 **Sparrow House,** 42 Summer St. (☎ **508/747-1240;** admission $1), is believed to be the oldest house still standing in Plymouth. It provides a fascinating look at the home life of the early residents. Pottery made on the premises is for sale in the craft gallery. The house is near Town Brook Park, across the street from the John Carver Inn. It's open Thursday through Tuesday from 10am to 5pm.

The 1666 **Howland House,** 33 Sandwich St. (☎ **508/746-9590;** guided tour $3 adults, 75¢ ages 6 to 12), is the only house in Plymouth known to have been lived in by *Mayflower* passengers—owner Jabez Howland's parents, Elizabeth Tilley and John Howland. The tour tells about them and gives another good look at the Pilgrims' lives. The house is near the corner of Sandwich and Water streets and is open daily from 10am to 4:30pm.

The next three houses are operated by the **Plymouth Antiquarian Society** (☎ **508/746-0012**). Call ahead before you visit to make sure they're open. At each house, admission is $3 for adults, 75¢ for ages 6 to 12.

The 1677 **Harlow Old Fort House,** 119 Sandwich St., is staffed by costumed interpreters who demonstrate domestic crafts such as spinning and weaving amid period furnishings. By this time, the Pilgrims were settled, and you'll get a sense of life once mere survival stopped being a daily struggle. The house is about four blocks south of the center of town; open hours are usually from 10am to 4:30pm, Thursday through Saturday in July and August, and Friday and Saturday in June and from September through mid-October.

The 1749 **Spooner House,** 27 North St., was a family residence for more than 2 centuries and is furnished with a wealth of heirlooms that illustrate the changes in daily life over that period. The house is a few steps up the hill from Plymouth Rock and keeps the same hours as the Harlow Old Fort House, plus Sundays in July and August.

The 1809 **Hedge House,** 126 Water St., is a Federal-style mansion next door to the Visitor Center and near the Town Wharf. It has period furnishings as well as a gallery with regularly changing exhibits drawn from the Antiquarian Society's collections of textiles and decorative arts. The hours are the same as the Spooner House's.

The 1754 (with an 1898 addition) **Mayflower Society Museum,** 4 Winslow St. (☎ **508/746-2590;** admission $2.50, 75¢ ages 6 to 12), was originally the home of Edward Winslow, a great-grandson of the Pilgrim of the same name who served as governor of Massachusetts. Today, the furnishings span 3 centuries (17th, 18th, and 19th), there's a "flying" staircase that appears to defy gravity, and the formal gardens are a peaceful place to stroll. The museum is open from 10am to 5pm, daily in July and August, Friday through Sunday in June, September through mid-October, and Thanksgiving weekend. From Plymouth Rock, turn around, walk one short block up North Street, and turn right onto Winslow Street.

WHERE TO STAY

On busy summer weekends, it's not unusual for every room in town to be taken. Try to make reservations well in advance.

If you're planning a longer stay, the lodgings listed here (and a number of others) participate in Destination Plymouth's **Historic Value Vacation Package** program. Three- and four-night packages (two nights in April, May and November) include a good deal on a room and free admission to a variety of attractions. Prices start at $100 per person, double occupancy. Ask about availability when you call for reservations.

Cold Spring Motel. 188 Court St. (Rte. 3A), Plymouth, MA 02360. ☎ **508/746-2222.** 31 rms, 2 2-bedroom cottages. A/C TV TEL. $58–$78 double; $68–$88 cottage in season. Lower rates spring and fall. Extra person $5. AE, DISC, MC, V. Closed mid-Oct to Apr.

Convenient to downtown and the historic sights, this pleasant, quiet motel and the adjacent cottages surround a nicely landscaped lawn. The two-story building is two blocks inland, not far from Cranberry World, and set back from the street in a quiet part of town.

Governor Bradford Motor Inn. 98 Water St., Plymouth, MA 02360. ☎ **800/332-1620** or 508/746-6200. Fax 508/747-3032. 94 rms. A/C TV TEL. $89–$124 double in season. Extra person $10. Rates lower in off season. Children under 14 stay free in parents' room. AE, DC, DISC, MC, V.

The Governor Bradford is across the street from the waterfront, one block from Plymouth Rock, the *Mayflower II*, and the center of town. The spacious rooms, each with two double beds, have attractive, modern furnishings, refrigerators, and coffeemakers. More expensive rooms are higher up in the three-story building and have clearer views of the water. There's a small heated outdoor pool.

✪ John Carver Inn. 25 Summer St. at Town Brook, Plymouth, MA 02360. ☎ **800/274-1620** or 508/746-7100. Fax 508/746-8299. 79 rms. A/C TV TEL. Mid-Apr to mid-June $75–$95 double; mid-June to mid-Oct $85–$105 double; mid-Oct to Nov $75–$95 double; Dec to mid-Apr $65–$85 double. Children under 19 stay free in parents' room. Cribs free. Passport to History package rates change seasonally. Senior discount available. AE, CB, DC, DISC, MC, V.

A three-story colonial-style building with a landmark portico, the John Carver Inn offers comfortable, modern accommodations and a large outdoor pool. The good-sized guest rooms have been renovated recently and are decorated in colonial style. The inn is within walking distance of the main attractions, and the convenient location and easygoing staff make it an excellent choice for families. A **Hearth 'n' Kettle** restaurant is on the premises.

The hotel offers a good deal (the Passport to History Packages) that includes a 2-night, 3-day stay for two, four breakfast tickets to the restaurant, two $10 discount dinner tickets at the restaurant, two Plimoth Plantation or whale-watch tickets, and two tickets to the trolley or Wax Museum.

Pilgrim Sands Motel. 150 Warren Ave. (Rte. 3A), Plymouth, MA 02360. ☎ **800/729-SANDS** or 508/747-0900. Fax 508/746-8066. 64 rms, 2 2-bedroom suites. A/C TV TEL. Summer $90–$120 double; spring and early fall $70–$95 double; Apr and late fall $60–$80 double; Dec–Mar $50–$70 double; suites $90–$175. Higher rates for some holiday weekends. Extra person $8. AE, CB, DC, DISC, MC, V.

This attractive two-story motel is south of town, within walking distance of Plimoth Plantation. The modern units, located right on the ocean, have individually controlled heating and air-conditioning and tasteful furnishings. The more expensive rooms have ocean views. In the summer, guests have access to the private beach, terraces, whirlpool spa, and outdoor and indoor pools. Most rooms have two double or two queen-sized beds. Many rooms have refrigerators. One wing is reserved for smokers, the other for nonsmokers.

Sheraton Inn Plymouth. 180 Water St., Plymouth, MA 02360. ☎ **800/325-3535** or 508/747-4900. Fax 508/746-2609. 175 rms. A/C TV TEL. Apr–Oct $100–$160 double; Nov–Mar $85–$125 double. Children under 18 stay free in parents' room. Extra person $15. AE, CB, DC, DISC, JCB, MC, V.

Located at the Village Landing, this attractive hotel faces the harbor from a hill across the street from the waterfront. If you need the amenities of a chain and want to be near the historic sights, this is your only choice—happily, it's a good one. Rooms are tastefully furnished in contemporary style and have climate control and in-room movies, and guests have the use of a laundry room. Some rooms have small balconies that overlook the indoor swimming pool and whirlpool. The hotel also has an exercise room, a restaurant, and a pub that offers live entertainment on weekends.

WHERE TO DINE

Seafood is the specialty at almost all Plymouth restaurants, where much of the daily catch goes right from the fishing boat to the kitchen.

Lobster Hut. Town Wharf. ☎ **508/746-2270.** Fax 508/746-5655. Reservations not accepted. Lunch specials $4.50–$7.95, main courses $4.95–$12.95, sandwiches $1.75–$5.95. MC, V. Summer daily 11am–9pm; winter daily 11am–7pm. SEAFOOD.

The Lobster Hut is a self-service restaurant with a great view. Order and pick up at the counter and take your food to an indoor table or onto the large deck that overlooks the bay. For starters, have some clam chowder or lobster bisque. The seafood "rolls" (hot-dog buns with your choice of filling) are excellent. You can choose from a long list of fried seafood—including clams, scallops, shrimp, and haddock. Or you might prefer boiled and steamed items, burgers, or chicken tenders. Beer and wine are served, but only with a meal.

McGrath's Harbour Restaurant. Town Wharf. ☎ **508/746-9751.** Reservations recommended at dinner. Main courses $9.95–$14.95. AE, MC, V. Daily 11:30am–10pm. Closed Mon in winter. SEAFOOD.

McGrath's is a big, busy place, the choice of many families, local businesspeople, and tour groups. In addition to fish and seafood dinners, the extensive menu features chicken, prime rib, sandwiches, and children's offerings. Ask for a table overlooking the water—the room facing inland is on the gloomy side—and be sure you're in good company, because service can be slow.

Run of the Mill Tavern. At Jenney Grist Mill Village. ☎ **508/830-1262.** Reservations recommended at dinner. Main courses $6–$12. AE, MC, V. Mon–Sat 11:30am–10pm, Sun noon–10pm. AMERICAN.

You'll find the Run of the Mill Tavern near the water wheel at Jenney Grist Mill Village at Town Brook Park. It's an attractive setting, surrounded by trees, and the wood-paneled tavern offers good, inexpensive meals. The clam chowder is fantastic. Other appetizers include nachos, potato skins, buffalo wings, and mushrooms. Entrees are standard meat, chicken, and fish, and there are also seafood specials. The children's menu is a bargain, with burgers and fish-and-chips at $2.50 to $3.50.

8 New Bedford & Fall River

New Bedford's history is inextricably bound to the whaling industry, as Fall River's is to the textile industry. The decline of their respective lifebloods in the mid-19th and early 20th centuries led to the deterioration of the cities. Both have made great strides in recent years in a push to make themselves more attractive to the tourist trade, but it's a tough market. Almost anywhere else in the country, New Bedford and Fall River would probably be judged rousing successes. In southeastern Massachusetts, about an hour from Boston and even closer to Plymouth, Cape Cod, and Newport, they're better known for factory-outlet shopping than for historic attractions.

New Bedford and Fall River are 15 miles apart on I-195 and Route 6. From Boston, take the Southeast Expressway south to I-93 (Route 128), then Route 24 south. It runs directly to Fall River, where you can pick up I-195 or Route 6 east to New Bedford. To go straight to New Bedford, take Route 140 south off Route 24. From Plymouth, take Route 44 west to Route 24 south.

To get information before you go, phone, write or check the Internet in advance. The **Bristol County Convention & Visitors Bureau,** 70 N. 2nd St., P.O. Box 976, New Bedford, MA 02741 (☎ **800/288-6263** or 508/997-1250), distributes a factory-outlet guide. Also contact the **New Bedford Area Chamber of Commerce,** 794 Purchase St., P.O. Box 8827, New Bedford, MA 02742 (☎ **508/999-5231;** Web site: **http://www.nbchamber.com**), check **http://www.newbedford.com**, or contact the **Fall River Area Chamber of Commerce,** 200 Pocasset St., P.O. Box 1871, Fall River, MA 02722 (☎ **508/676-8226;** Web site: **http://www. frchamber.com**).

NEW BEDFORD

The downtown area near the waterfront has been nicely restored. The top attractions include the **Whaling Museum,** 18 Johnny Cake Hill (☎ **508/997-0046**), where you can board a half-scale model of a whaling bark; the **Seamen's Bethel,** 15 Johnny Cake Hill (☎ **508-992-3295**), a nondenominational chapel described in Herman Melville's classic novel *Moby Dick;* and the **New Bedford Fire Museum,** 51 Bedford St. (☎ **508/992-2162**), with historic fire-fighting equipment and uniforms children can try on.

FALL RIVER

On the waterfront, **Battleship Massachusetts,** Battleship Cove (☎ **800/533-3194** or 508/678-1100), is a five-vessel complex where you can see and board the battleship USS *Massachusetts,* a destroyer, a submarine, and two PT boats. Also at Battleship Cove is the fully restored **Fall River Carousel** (☎ **508/324-4300**), built in 1920 and moved here from a nearby park in 1992.

The **Marine Museum,** 70 Water St. (☎ **508/674-3533**), is best known for its 1-ton model of the *Titanic,* with a great number of other models and exhibits about maritime history.

Lest you think Fall River emphasizes its seafaring legacy over its ties to the textile industry, don't forget the **factory outlets.** Clustered near I-195 (start at Exit 8A) in restored mill buildings, the outlets offer just about anything that can be manufactured from thread, including clothing, outerwear, linens, and curtains. And of course you'll also need accessories, hats, housewares, books, shoes, and more. It's all here, at excellent prices. Wear comfortable shoes and bring lots of money or credit cards (many outlets also accept personal checks with proper identification).

Fall River's most famous former resident wasn't a sailor but a teacher—and an accused murderer. Although Lizzie Borden was acquitted in 1893 of killing her father and stepmother the previous year, she is remembered because of the verse: Lizzie Borden took an ax / And gave her mother forty whacks. / When she saw what she had done / She gave her father forty-one.

After many years as a public residence, the Bordens's house (where Lizzie continued to live after the murders) was painstakingly restored and opened in 1996 as a bed-and-breakfast. Tours are given during the day if you don't want to spend the night—or if you're too scared to. As you might imagine, the building is reputed to be haunted. The family bedrooms (including the one where Mrs. Borden's body was found) are on the second floor, and the third-floor rooms bear the names of the housemaid and of the lawyers who worked on the trial. And breakfast every morning (served to overnight guests only) includes some of the same dishes that were served on the fateful morning: johnnycakes, bananas, sugar cookies, and coffee.

The **Lizzie Borden Bed & Breakfast,** 92 Second St., Fall River, MA 02720 (☎ **800/700-9549** for room reservations, or 508/675-7333), is open for tours daily in the summer and on weekends the rest of the year from 11am to 3pm. The 30-minute tours leave every half-hour and cost $7.50 for adults, $3.50 for ages 6 to 12. Overnight rates are $220 per night on the second floor and $165 per night on the third floor. There is a 2-night minimum stay, and children under 12 are not permitted to stay overnight.

Cape Cod 6

Only 70 miles long, Cape Cod is a curling peninsula encompassing miles of beaches, more freshwater ponds than there are days in the year, more than a dozen lovely, richly historic New England villages, scores of classic clam shacks and custard stands—and just about everyone's idea of the perfect summer vacation.

More than 17 million visitors flock from around the world to enjoy summertime's nonstop carnival. The Cape is, if anything, perhaps a bit too popular at full swing: Connoisseurs are beginning to discover the subtler appeal of the off-season, when prices plummet along with the population. For some select travelers, the prospect of sunbathing en masse on sizzling sand can't hold a candle to a long, solitary stroll on a windswept beach, with only the gulls as company. Come Labor Day—Columbus Day, for stragglers—the crowds clear out, and the whole place hibernates till Memorial Day weekend, the official start of "the season." We've listed mostly summer rates for all the accommodations in this chapter, since that's when the vast majority of travelers plan their trips, but if you do want to explore the Cape off-season, you'll get the added benefit of lower hotel rates everywhere you go.

The **Cape Cod Chamber of Commerce,** Routes 6 and 132, Hyannis, MA 02601 (☎ **508/362-3225;** fax 508/362-3698; Web site: **www.capecod.com**), is a clearinghouse of information about vacationing here.

1 The Upper Cape

Because Sandwich and the surrounding Upper Cape towns are so close to Boston by car (a bit over an hour), they've become bedroom as well as summer communities. They may not have the let-the-good-times-roll feel of more seasonal towns farther east, but then again they're spared the fly-by-night qualities that come with a transient populace. Shops and restaurants—many catering to an older, affluent crowd—tend to stay open year-round here.

The college crowd generally gravitates to the beaches of Falmouth Heights, a bluff covered with grand, shingled Victorians built during the first wave of touristic fever in the late 1800s. The tiny enclave of Woods Hole—home at any given time to several thousand research scientists—is developing a certain neo-bohemian style, with a lively bar scene.

Cape Cod

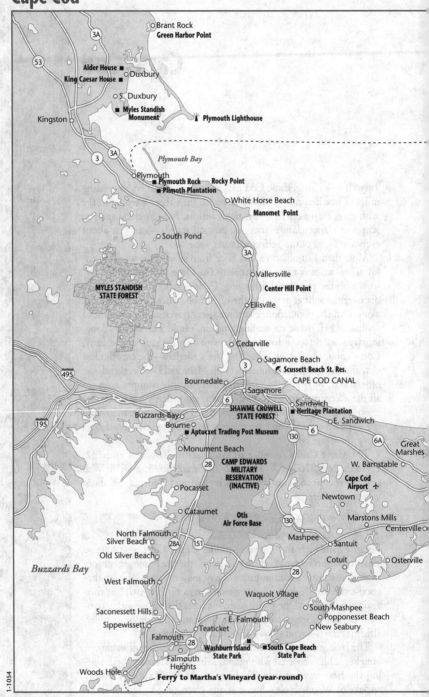

Brant Rock
Green Harbor Point

3A

53

Alder House ■
King Caesar House ■ □ Duxbury

○ S. Duxbury

■ **Myles Standish**
Monument

Kingston ○

3A   ☀ **Plymouth Lighthouse**

3

Plymouth Bay

○ Plymouth
■ **Plymouth Rock**   **Rocky Point**
■ **Plimoth Plantation**

○ White Horse Beach

Manomet Point

○ South Pond

3A

○ Vallersville

Center Hill Point

MYLES STANDISH
STATE FOREST

○ Ellisville

○ Cedarville

3

○ Sagamore Beach
↗ **Scussett Beach St. Res.**

495   Bournedale ○   CAPE COD CANAL

○ Sagamore

6   Sandwich
○   ■ **Heritage Plantation**
195   Buzzards Bay ○   **SHAWME CROWELL**   E. Sandwich
Bourne ○   **STATE FOREST**   ○

■ **Aptucxet Trading Post Museum**   130   6   6A

○ Monument Beach   Great
Marshes

28   **CAMP EDWARDS**   W. Barnstable ○
MILITARY
RESERVATION   **Cape Cod**
(INACTIVE)   **Airport** ✈

○ Pocasset   Newtown ○

Otis   Marstons Mills ○
○ Cataumet   **Air Force Base**   130   Centerville ○

Mashpee   Santuit ○
North Falmouth ○   28A   151   ○
Silver Beach ○   Cotuit   ○ Osterville
Old Silver Beach ○   ○

Buzzards Bay

West Falmouth ○   28

Waquoit Village ○   South Mashpee ○
Saconessett Hills ○   ○ Popponesset Beach
Sippewissett ○   E. Falmouth ○   New Seabury ○

○ Teaticket
Falmouth ○   ■
28   **Washburn Island**   ■ **South Cape Beach**
State Park   **State Park**
Falmouth
Heights
Woods Hole ○   **Ferry to Martha's Vineyard (year-round)**

1-1054

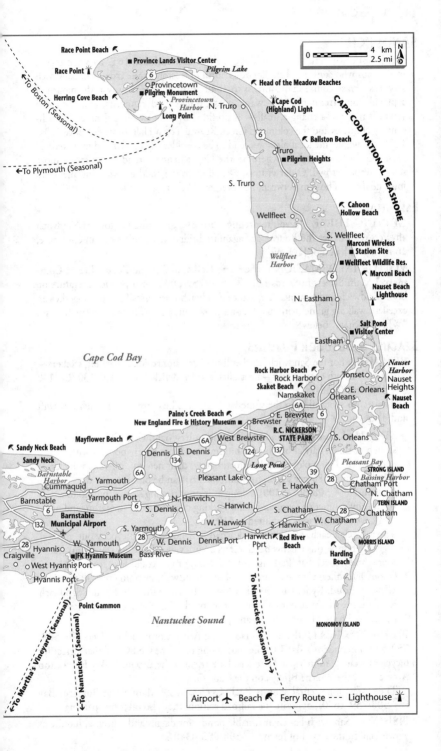

Race Point Beach

Race Point

Province Lands Visitor Center

To Boston (Seasonal)

Herring Cove Beach

6

Provincetown

Pilgrim Monument

Pilgrim Lake

Head of the Meadow Beaches

Cape Cod
(Highland) Light

Provincetown
Harbor

N. Truro

Long Point

To Plymouth (Seasonal)

6

Truro

Pilgrim Heights

Ballston Beach

S. Truro

Wellfleet

Cahoon
Hollow Beach

CAPE COD NATIONAL SEASHORE

S. Wellfleet

Marconi Wireless
Station Site

Wellfleet
Harbor

Wellfleet Wildlife Res.

6

Marconi Beach

Nauset Beach
Lighthouse

N. Eastham

Salt Pond
Visitor Center

Cape Cod Bay

Eastham

Nauset
Harbor

Rock Harbor Beach

Rock Harbor

Skaket Beach

Namskaket

Tonset

Nauset
Heights

E. Orleans

Nauset
Beach

6A

Orleans

Paine's Creek Beach

New England Fire & History Museum

E. Brewster

S. Orleans

Brewster

Mayflower Beach

6A

West Brewster

R.C. NICKERSON
STATE PARK

Sandy Neck Beach

Dennis

E. Dennis

124

137

Pleasant Bay

STRONG ISLAND

Sandy Neck

Barnstable
Harbor

134

Long Pond

39

Bassing Harbor

Chatham Port

Cummaquid

6A

Yarmouth

Pleasant Lake

28

N. Chatham

Barnstable

Yarmouth Port

N. Harwich

E. Harwich

TERN ISLAND

6

S. Dennis

Harwich

S. Chatham

28

Chatham

Barnstable
Municipal Airport

132

S. Yarmouth

W. Harwich

S. Harwich

W. Chatham

28

W. Yarmouth

28

W. Dennis

Dennis Port

Harwich
Port

Red River
Beach

MORRIS ISLAND

Hyannis

Bass River

Craigville

JFK Hyannis Museum

Harding
Beach

West Hyannis Port

Hyannis Port

Point Gammon

Nantucket Sound

MONOMOY ISLAND

To Martha's Vineyard (Seasonal)

To Nantucket (Seasonal)

To Nantucket (Seasonal)

Airport ✈   Beach ☛   Ferry Route - - -   Lighthouse ⚲

0   4 km
         2.5 mi

N

183

SANDWICH

The oldest town in this corner of the Cape (it was founded in 1637 by a contingent of Puritans who considered the environs north of Boston a mite crowded), Sandwich serves as a crash course in quaintness. A 1640 gristmill churns away at the mouth of a placid pond frequented by swans, geese, ducks, and canoeists, and the town square—more of a triangle, really—is presided over by two imposing early-19th-century churches and the columned Greek Revival Town Hall, in service since 1834.

On the whole, the local pleasures tend to be considerably quieter and more refined than the thrills offered elsewhere on the Cape; hence it tends to attract a more sedate, settled crowd. Older visitors, as well as young children, will find plenty to intrigue them. Those in between, however, are likely to get restless.

ESSENTIALS

GETTING THERE   If you're driving, turn east on Route 6A toward Sandwich after crossing either the Bourne or Sagamore bridge. It's 3 miles east of Sagamore, 16 miles northwest of Hyannis.

VISITOR INFORMATION   The **Cape Cod Canal Region Chamber of Commerce,** Main Street, Buzzards Bay (☎ **508/759-6000**), can provide literature on both Sandwich and Bourne. A group of Sandwich businesses have put together an excellent walking guide (with map). For a copy, contact the Summer House Inn (see "Where to Stay," below).

BEACHES & OUTDOOR PURSUITS

BEACHES   For the Sandwich beaches listed here, **nonresident parking stickers**— $20 for the length of your stay—are available at Sandwich Town Hall, 130 Rte. 130 (☎ **508/888-0340**).

There's no swimming in the Cape Cod Canal: The currents are much too swift and dangerous.

- **Sandy Neck Beach,** off Sandy Neck Road in East Sandwich: This 6-mile stretch of silken barrier beach with hummocky dunes is very popular with endangered piping plovers and, unfortunately, their nemesis, off-road vehicles. ORV permits ($80 per season for nonresidents) can be purchased at the gatehouse (☎ **508/362-8300**) as long as it's not nesting season, but do this fragile environment a favor and walk. Parking costs $8 a day in season, and up to 3 days of camping is permitted at $10 a night.
- **Town Neck Beach,** off Town Neck Road in Sandwich: A bit rocky but ruggedly pretty, this narrow beach offers a busy view of passing ships, plus rest rooms and a snack bar. Parking costs $5 a day, or you could hike from town (about $1^1/2$ miles) via the community-built boardwalk spanning the salt marsh.
- **Wakeby Pond,** Ryder Conservation Area, John Ewer Road (off South Sandwich Road on the Mashpee border): The beach, on the Cape's largest freshwater pond, has lifeguards, rest rooms, and parking ($4 a day).

BIKING/RECREATIONAL PATHS   The Army Corps of Engineers (☎ **508/759-5991**) maintains a **flat 14-mile loop** along the Cape Cod Canal that's great for bicyclists, skaters, runners, and strollers. Park (free) at the **Buzzards Bay Recreation Area** west of the Bourne Bridge, on the Cape side.

The closest bike rental shop is **P&B Cycles,** at 29 Main St. in Buzzards Bay (☎ **508/759-2830**), opposite the railroad station; they also offer free parking.

FISHING   Sandwich has eight fishable ponds; for details and a license, inquire at Town Hall in the center of town (☎ **508/888-0340**).

No permit is required for fishing from the banks of the Cape Cod Canal: Here your catch might include striped bass, bluefish, cod, pollock, flounder, or fluke.

Local **deep-water charters** include the *Tigger Two*, docked in the Sandwich Marina (☎ **508/888-8372**).

NATURE TRAILS   Shawme-Crowell State Forest, off Route 130 in Sandwich (☎ **508/888-0351**), offers 280 campsites and 742 acres to roam. Entrance is free; parking costs $2.

The **Sandwich Boardwalk** links the town and Town Neck Beach, by way of salt marshes that attract a great many birds, including great blue herons.

The 57-acre **Green Briar Nature Center** in East Sandwich (☎ **508/888-6870**) has a mile-long path crossing marsh and stands of white pine.

To request a map of other conservation areas in Sandwich (some 16 sites encompass nearly 1,300 acres), contact the **Sandwich Conservation Commission,** 270 Meeting House Rd. (☎ **508/888-4200**).

MUSEUMS & HISTORICAL LANDMARKS

Heritage Plantation of Sandwich. Grove and Pine sts. (about ¹/₂ mile southwest of town center), Sandwich. ☎ **508/888-3330.** Admission $8 adults, $7 seniors, $4 children 6–18. Mid-May to Oct daily 10am–5pm; no tickets sold after 4:15pm. Closed Nov to mid-May.

This is one of those rare museums equally appealing to adults and the children they drag along: The latter will leave clamoring for another visit. All ages have the run of 76 beautifully landscaped acres, crisscrossed with walking paths and riotous with color in late spring, when the towering rhododendrons are in bloom. A scattering of buildings houses a wide variety of collections, from Native American artifacts to Early American weapons. The art holdings, especially the primitive portraits, are outstanding. The high point for kids is a ride on the 1912 carousel (safely preserved indoors), where the mounts are not horses but fancifully carved animals. There's also a replica Shaker barn packed with gleaming antique automobiles. Call ahead for a schedule of outdoor summer concerts, free with admission.

Sandwich Glass Museum. 129 Main St. (in the center of town), Sandwich. ☎ **508/888-0251.** Admission $3.50 adults, $1 children 6–12. Apr–Oct daily 9:30am–4:30pm, Feb–Mar and Nov–Dec Wed–Sun 9:30am–4pm. Closed Jan.

Even if you don't consider yourself a glass fan, make an exception for this fascinating museum, which captures the history of the town and its legendary glass-making industry. A brief video introduces Deming Jarves's brilliant 19th-century endeavor: Bringing glassware, a hitherto rare commodity available only to the rich, within reach of the middle classes. Demand was such that Jarves imported hordes of immigrant workers, housing them in rather shameful shanties. All went well (for him) until Midwestern factories started using coal; unable to keep up with their level of mass production, he switched back to handblown techniques just as his workforce was ready to revolt.

None of this turmoil is evident in the dainty artifacts displayed in a series of sunny rooms. Anyone who goes in expecting not to be impressed is liable to leave dazzled. An excellent little gift shop stocks Sandwich glass replicas, as well as original glass works by area artisans.

WHERE TO STAY

The Belfry Inne. 8 Jarves St. (in the center of town), Sandwich, MA 02563. ☎ **508/888-8550.** 8 rms. Summer $95–$165 double. Rates include full breakfast. MAP plan available. AE, MC, V.

You can't miss it: It's the gaudiest "painted lady" in town, recently restored to its original flamboyant glory after skulking for decades under three layers of siding. Newly liberated, this turreted 1879 rectory has turned its fancy to romance, with queen-sized antique beds, a claw-foot tub (or Jacuzzi) for every room, and a scattering of fireplaces and private balconies.

The Dan'l Webster Inn. 149 Main St. (in the center of town), Sandwich, MA 02563. ☎ **800/444-3566** or 508/888-3623. Fax 508/888-5156. Web site: http://media3.com/dan'lwebsterinn/. 37 rms, 9 suites. A/C TV TEL. Summer $129–$169 double; $169–$325 suite. MAP plan available. AE, CB, DISC, MC, V.

On this site there once stood a colonial tavern favored by the famous orator, who came to these parts to go fishing. It unfortunately burned to the ground in 1971, but the modern replacement, operated by the Catania family, will suit modern travelers perfectly. All the rooms are ample, and nicely furnished with reproductions. The eight suites located in nearby historic houses are especially appealing; they feature fireplaces and canopy beds. The inn's common spaces are convivial, if bustling. This is a *very* popular place, among locals as well as travelers.

Dining/Entertainment: The restaurant here turns out surprisingly sophisticated fare (see "Where to Dine," below).

Facilities: A small pool; free access to nearby health club.

Pine Grove Cottages. 358 Rte. 6A (near the center of town), East Sandwich, MA 02537. ☎ **508/888-8179.** 10 cottages. TV. Summer $240–$395 double per week. Lower off-season rates. AE, DISC, MC, V. Closed Nov–Apr.

Cute as buttons, some of these one-room cottages are barely big enough to squeeze in a double bed. White walls make them seem a bit roomier, and stenciling adds a touch of romance—not that cottage fanciers would need any added inducement. With lots of families in residence, and an aboveground pool to splash in, children enjoy good odds of finding a friend.

Spring Garden Motel. 578 Rte. 6A (about 2 miles east of town center), E. Sandwich, MA 02537. ☎ **800/303-1751** or 508/888-0710. Fax 508/371-1656. 11 units. A/C TV TEL. Summer $75–$85 double. AE, DISC, MC, V. Closed mid-Nov to Mar.

Looking like an elongated rose-covered cottage, this pretty double-decker motel overlooks the Great Sandwich Salt Marsh, and every room comes with a southern-oriented patio or porch that takes in the lush green landscape. With its spacious, tree-shaded backyard, the motel is understandably popular with families. Regular summerers also appreciate the complimentary homemade continental breakfasts.

Summer House. 158 Main St. (in the center of town), Sandwich, MA 02563. ☎ **800/241-3609** or 508/888-4991. 5 rms (4 with shared bath). Summer $75–$95 double. Rates include full breakfast and afternoon tea. AE, DISC, MC, V.

The lack of private baths is the only possible explanation for the extremely reasonable rates at this elegant circa 1835 Greek Revival house. The bedrooms are all large corner rooms, brightened up with colorful home-stitched quilts and painted hardwood floors; four have working fireplaces, and a few overlook the English garden in back, which is in riotous bloom throughout the summer. It's here you'll find a hammock to hide away in, stirring only to be called in to an elaborate breakfast or a bountiful tea.

WHERE TO DINE

The Belfry Bistro. 8 Jarves St. (in the center of town). ☎ **508/888-8550.** Main courses $7–$16. AE, MC, V. Late May to mid-Oct Wed–Sun 5:30–11pm; call for off-season schedule. NEW AMERICAN.

These are not white tablecloth prices, but the damask is indeed snowy and dense, the mood luxurious, the menu most ingratiating and geared to grazers. Selections change with the seasons, but among the trio of entrees you might find a superlative spring roll served in a pool of ginger tamari, or seared scallops in their shells, cloaked in chardonnay cream sauce and served with herbed polenta.

The Dan'l Webster Inn. 149 Main St. (in the center of town). ☎ **508/888-3623.** Reservations recommended. Main courses $14–$20. AE, CB, DISC, MC, V. Daily 8am–9pm. INTERNATIONAL.

Though you have a choice of four main dining rooms—from a casual, colonial-motif tavern to a skylight-topped conservatory fronting a splendid garden—they're all served by the same kitchen, under the masterful hand of chef/co-owner Richard Catania. A devotee of fresh, local fruit and fish, he has gone so far as to build a model aquaculture farm that he can plunder at will. The results attest to his good taste. Try a classic dish like the *fruits de mer* in white wine, or entrust your palate to a seasonal highlight (the specials menu changes monthly). Desserts are also superb.

The Dunbar Tea Shop. 1 Water St. (in the center of town). ☎ **508/833-2485.** Main courses under $6. MC, V. Daily 11am–5pm. BRITISH.

Choose the cozy confines of the tearoom or, in summer, a shady grove outside. Either way, you'll get hearty, authentic English classics before moving on to sweets such as fresh-baked shortbread and seasonal pies. The Tea Shop also serves tea, of course, with all the traditional fixings and accompaniments.

FALMOUTH & WOODS HOLE

Often overlooked in the rush to catch the island ferries, Falmouth is a classic New England town, complete with white steeples encircling a town green. The area around the historic Village Green is a veritable hotbed of B&Bs, with each vying to provide the most elaborate breakfasts and solicitous advice.

Officially a village within Falmouth (one of nine), tiny Woods Hole has been a world-renowned oceanic research center since 1871, when the U.S. Commission of Fish and Fisheries set up a primitive seasonal collection station. Today, the various scientific institutes crowded around the harbor—principally, the National Marine Fisheries Service, the Marine Biological Laboratory, and the Woods Hole Oceanographic Institute—employ thousands of scientists. Woods Hole's scientific institutions offer a unique opportunity to get in-depth—and often hands-on—exposure to marine biology.

Belying stereotype, the community is far from uptight and nerdy; in fact, it's one of the hipper communities on the Cape. In the past few decades, a number of agreeable restaurants and shops have cropped up, making the small, crowded gauntlet of Water Street (don't even bother fantasizing about parking here in summer) a very pleasant place to stroll.

West Falmouth (which is really more north of town, stretched alongside Buzzards Bay) has held onto its bucolic character and makes a lovely drive, with perhaps an occasional stop for the more alluring antique stores.

Falmouth Heights, a cluster of shingled Victorian summer houses on a bluff east of Falmouth's harbor, is as popular as it is picturesque; its narrow ribbon of beach is a magnet for all, especially the younger crowd.

The Waquoit Bay area, a few miles east of town, has thus far eluded the over-commercialization that blights most of Route 28. Several thousand acres of this vital estuarine ecosystem are now under federal custody, primarily at the instigation of the region's original residents, the Mashpee Wampanoags.

ESSENTIALS

GETTING THERE   After crossing either the Bourne or Sagamore bridge, take Route 28 or 28A south. It's 18 miles south of Sagamore, 20 miles southwest of Hyannis.

The **Sea Line shuttle** (☎ 800/352-7155) connects Woods Hole, Falmouth, and Mashpee with Hyannis year-round (except Sundays and holidays); the fare ranges from 75¢ to $4, depending on distance, and children under 6 ride free.

VISITOR INFORMATION   Contact the **Falmouth Chamber of Commerce,** Academy Lane, Falmouth, MA 02541 (☎ **800/526-8532** or 508/548-8500; fax 508/540-4724).

BEACHES & OUTDOOR PURSUITS

BEACHES   Renters can obtain temporary **beach parking stickers** for Falmouth ($40 per week, $70 per month) at Falmouth Town Hall, 59 Town Hall Sq. (☎ **508/548-8623**), or at the Surf Drive Beach bathhouse in season. The town beaches all have rest rooms and concession stands; parking is usually available for a fee.

- **Old Silver Beach,** off Route 28A in West Falmouth: Western facing (great for sunsets) and relatively placid, this is a popular pick and therefore often crowded (parking costs $10 a day).
- **Nobska Beach,** by the Nobska Lighthouse in Woods Hole: Accessible by bike, via the Shining Sea Bicycle Path, this beach boasts a magnificent view.
- **Surf Drive Beach,** off Shore Street in Falmouth: About a mile from downtown and appealing to families, this is a serviceable choice with limited parking ($5 a day, $8 on weekends and holidays).
- **Falmouth Heights Beach,** off Grand Avenue in Falmouth Heights: Acknowledged college kid turf, this is where teens and 20-somethings tend to congregate. Parking is sticker only.
- **Menauhant Beach,** off Central Avenue in East Falmouth: A bit off the beaten track, Menauhant is a little less mobbed than Surf Drive Beach, and better protected from the winds. Parking is $5 a day, $8 on weekends and holidays.

BIKING/RECREATIONAL PATHS   The **Shining Sea Bicycle Path** (☎ **508/548-8500**) is a 3.6-mile beauty skirting the Sound from Falmouth to Woods Hole, by way of the scenic Nobska Lighthouse; it also connects with a 23-mile scenic road loop through pretty Sippewissett. You can park at the trailhead on Locust Street in Falmouth, or any nonmetered spot in town (parking in Woods Hole is scarce).

The closest shop—convenient to the main cluster of B&Bs, some of which offer "loaners"—is **Corner Cycle,** at Palmer Avenue and North Main Street (☎ **508/540-4195**). For a broader selection of bikes and good advice on routes, visit **Holiday Cycles,** 465 Grand Ave. in Falmouth Heights (☎ **508/540-3549**).

FISHING   Falmouth has six ponds; licenses can be obtained at Falmouth Town Hall, 59 Town Hall Sq. (☎ **508/548-7611**). Surf Drive Beach is a great spot for surf casting once the crowds have dispersed.

To go after bigger prey, book the *Thank Abba* from the Little River Boat Yard on Seconset Island in Waquoit (☎ **508/548-3511**), or head out with a group on one of the **Patriot Party Boats** based in Falmouth's Inner Harbor (☎ **800/734-0088** or 508/548-2626): the clunky *Patriot Too* is ideal for family-style "bottom fishing," and the zippy *Minuteman* is geared to pros.

Serious aficionados will want to head out with 30-year veteran Capt. John Christian on his Aquasport *Susan Jean* (☎ **508/548-6901**), moored in Woods Hole's Eel Pond, to hunt for trophy bass among the neighboring Elizabeth Islands.

NATURE TRAILS   Though hardly in its natural state, the **Ashumet Holly and Wildlife Sanctuary,** operated by the Massachusetts Aubudon Society at 186 Ashumet Rd., off Route 151 (☎ **508/563-6390**), is an intriguing 49-acre collection of more than 1,000 holly trees; native animal species flourish here, along with over 130 species of birds and a carpet of Oriental lotus blossoms that covers a kettle pond come summer. The trail fee is $3 for adults, $2 for seniors and children under 13.

The 2,250-acre **Waquoit Bay National Estuarine Research Reserve,** 149 Waquoit Hwy. in East Falmouth (☎ **508/457-0495**), charges a $2 fee in season to explore its 1-mile, self-guiding nature trail. Also inquire about WBNERR's ferry over to Washburn Island (it's about a half-hour paddle via canoe) and its 10 primitive campsites—permits cost a mere $4 a night. The reserve offers a number of interpretive programs, including the popular "Evenings on the Bluff," geared to families.

WATER SPORTS   Falmouth is something of a windsurfing mecca, prized for its unflagging southwesterly winds. Both boards and boats can be rented at **Cape Water Sports,** 145 Falmouth Heights Rd., East Falmouth (☎ **508/548-7700**), or **Cape Cod Windsurfing Academy & Watersports Rentals** (☎ **508/495-0008**), located at the Surfside Holiday motel on Maravista Beach in East Falmouth; the latter also offers classes by appointment.

Among the best sites is Old Silver Beach in North Falmouth, where tyros can take lessons—again, by appointment—at the **New England Windsurfing Academy** (☎ **508/540-8016**), located alongside the Sea Crest resort (see "Where to Stay," below), and the Trunk River area on the west end of Falmouth's Surf Drive Beach—the only public beach where windsurfers are allowed during the day.

Edward's Boat Yard, 1209 E. Falmouth Hwy., East Falmouth (☎ **508/ 548-2216**), rents out canoes for exploring Waquoit Bay (see "Nature Trails," above).

SEA SCIENCE IN WOODS HOLE

Marine Biological Laboratory. Water St. (at MBL St., in the center of town), Woods Hole. ☎ **508/289-7623.** Free admission. June–Aug Mon–Fri at 1, 2, and 3pm. Closed to the public Sept–May.

A visit to this cutting-edge think tank, housed in an 1836 candle factory, requires a little forethought—the MBL prefers that reservations be made a week in advance. After a slide presentation, a retired scientist leads a guided tour through the holding tanks, and then to the lab to observe actual research in progress.

National Marine Fisheries Service Aquarium. Albatross St. (off the western end of Water St.), Woods Hole. ☎ **508/495-2001.** Free admission. Mon–Fri 10am–4pm.

A little beat-up after a century and a quarter of service and endless streams of eager schoolchildren, this aquarium—the first such institution in the country—is no longer what you'd call state-of-the-art, but a treasure nonetheless. The displays, focusing on local waters, might make you think twice before taking a dip. Children show no hesitation, though, in getting up to their elbows in the "touch tanks"; adults are also welcome to dabble. A key exhibit that everyone should see concerns the effect of plastic trash on the marine environment. You might time your visit to coincide with the feeding of two seals who summer here: The fish fly at 11am and 3pm.

Ocean Quest

No visit to the Cape would be complete without some type of seafaring excursion on the Atlantic. If you're not a sailor or if you just don't have the time or funds for an all-day boat trip, consider a unique hands-on cruise with **Ocean Quest,** Water Street, Woods Hole (☎ **800/376-2326** or 508/457-0508). Departing from Woods Hole, these 1¹/₂-hour harbor cruises are perfect for families, as real marine research is conducted with passengers serving as bona fide data collectors.

Here's how it works. Participants divide into two teams at the outset. Up in the bow, company founder Kathy Mullin, a former grade-school teacher, or a scientist borrowed from one of the institutes, trains the new crew in the niceties of reading water temperature, assessing turbidity, and taking other key measurements; in the stern, passengers get to examine the specimens hauled up by the dredger. Midway into the trip, the teams switch stations, so that everyone gets to ponder why the water (or the sky, for that matter) looks blue or, say, the sex life of a spider crab. Little kids get a real kick out of being addressed as "Doctor," and even adults who think they know it all will probably come away much better informed.

The rides cost $14 for adults, $10 children for 3 to 12. Boats shove off daily at 10am, noon, 2pm, and 4pm from mid-June through early September.

WHERE TO STAY

Expensive

❶ Inn at West Falmouth. 66 Frazar Rd. (off Rte. 28A, in the center of town), W. Falmouth, MA 02574. ☎ **800/397-7696** or 508/540-7696. 6 rms. Summer $275–$300 double. Rates include breakfast. AE, MC, V.

This thoroughly opulent B&B occupies a turn-of-the-century shingle-style mansion, set high on a wooded hill with views to Buzzards Bay. The spacious rooms have custom linens and are accented by a few judiciously chosen, unusual antiques. The large living room is teeming with fresh flowers and heaps of best-sellers that are begging to be borrowed. After a leisurely breakfast, you might take a dip in the small heated pool or wander the beautifully landscaped grounds. On blustery days, you might take refuge in the tiny conservatory perfumed by lemon trees, sink into one of the voluminous couches by the fireplace, or retreat to your own private marble whirlpool bath.

Facilities: Small pool, one clay tennis court, and access to a nearby beach (10-min. walk).

Sea Crest. 350 Quaker Rd. (midway between N. and W. Falmouth), N. Falmouth, MA 02556. ☎ **800/225-3110** or 508/540-9400. Fax 508/548-0556. 266 rms. TV TEL. Summer $160–$240 double. AE, DC, MC, V.

Something of an anomaly in this part of the Cape, this sprawling two-story resort and conference center is a visual blight on beautiful Old Silver Beach. It might make a good choice, though, for those families who mostly want to play on the sands. The complex is undergoing renovations, so be sure to ask for an updated room. All the services and facilities one could require are right on site, too.

Dining/Entertainment: Restaurant, deli, lounge, and piano bar.

Services: A complimentary children's day camp is available.

Facilities: Indoor pool, health club, video games, four tennis courts, golf privileges, putting green, and a beach, where you can learn to windsurf (see "Water Sports," above).

Moderate

Coonamessett Inn. Jones Rd. and Gifford St. (about ¹/₂ mile north of Main St.), Falmouth, MA 02540. ☎ **508/438-2300.** 24 suites, 1 cottage. A/C TV TEL. Summer $95–$120 double. AE, CB, DISC, MC, V.

A gracious, traditional inn, the Coonamessett has been the social center of town since the century's teens. Set on 7 lushly landscaped acres overlooking a pond, it has the feel of a country club where all comers are welcome. Some of the rooms, decorated in reproduction antiques, can be a bit somber, so try to get one with good light.

Dining/Entertainment: The Coonamessett Inn Dining Room is unabashedly formal, and surprisingly good (see "Where to Dine," below). In the adjoining Eli's, a clubby tavern, a mellow jazz combo holds forth on weekends.

Inn on the Sound. 313 Grand Ave. S. (off Main St.), Falmouth Heights, MA 02540. ☎ **800/564-9668** or 508/547-9666. Fax 508/457-9631. 10 rms. Summer $95–$140 double. Rates include full breakfast. AE, DISC, MC, V.

The ambiance here is as breezy as the setting, high on a bluff beside Falmouth's premier sunning beach, with a sweeping view of Nantucket Sound. The focal point of the living room is a handsome boulder hearth (nice for those nippy nights). A couple of bedrooms have working fireplaces of their own; most have ocean views. The breakfasts, especially the banana-stuffed French toast or eggs Florentine, are reason enough to stay here.

✪ **Mostly Hall.** 27 W. Main St. (west of the Village Green), Falmouth, MA 02540. ☎ **800/682-0565** or 508/548-3786. Fax 508/457-1572. A/C. Summer $95–$110 double. Rates include full breakfast. MC, V. Closed Jan to mid-Feb.

Built by a sea captain to please his New Orleans–born bride, this plantation-style house (unique on the Cape) exudes Southern graciousness as well as style. Longtime innkeepers Caroline and Jim Lloyd have pretty much mastered the art of hospitality, providing memorable breakfasts (such as eggs Benedict soufflé), loaner bikes, and plenty of valuable advice. The six stately corner bedrooms each boasts a canopied four-poster bed, cheery floral wallpaper, and a lazily whirring ceiling fan (more for effect than function, since the inn is centrally air-conditioned). The gardens are lovely, and the gazebo makes a pleasant retreat—as does the house's cupola, a combo library/videotheque.

Nautilus Motor Inn. 533 Woods Hole Rd. (about ¹/₂ mile west of town), Woods Hole, MA 02543. ☎ **800/654-2333** or 508/548-1525. Fax 508/547-9674. 54 rms. A/C TV TEL. Summer $92–$130 double. AE, DC, DISC, MC, V. Closed mid-Oct to mid-Apr.

A crescent-shaped complex poised above Woods Hole's picturesque Little Harbor, the Nautilus doesn't have to do much to make itself attractive: Nature has already seen to that aspect. The two tiers of rooms are standard motel style, but each comes with a private balcony for taking in the view or sunning, and a very spacious wooden deck flanks the fair-sized pool. A rather curious restaurant, The Dome, is right on the premises, and the Martha's Vineyard ferry is a short stroll away.

Sands of Time Motor Inn & Harbor House. 549 Woods Hole Rd. (about ¹/₂ mile west of town), Woods Hole, MA 02543. ☎ **800/841-0114** or 508/548-6300. Fax 508/457-0160. 31 rms (2 with shared bath), 2 efficiencies. A/C TV TEL. Summer $95–$140 double. Rates include continental breakfast. AE, DC, MC, V. Closed Nov–Mar.

It's really two facilities in one. There's a two-story block of motel rooms (with crisp, above-average decor, plus private porches). Next door, there's a shingled Victorian manse, where the quarters tend to be more lavish and romantic—four-posters, working fireplaces, wicker furnishings, the works. Both types of accommodation, though, afford the same charming harbor views and share the well-kept grounds and small pool.

Woods Hole Passage. 186 Woods Hole Rd. (about 2 miles north of town center), Woods Hole, MA 02540. ☎ **508/548-9575.** Fax 508/540-9123. 5 rms. Summer $105–$115 double. Rates include full breakfast. AE, CB, DC, DISC, MC, V.

Credit the design flair to Argentinean innkeeper Christina Mozo's other occupation as graphic artist. The decorative approach is ultratasteful, yet anything but quaint. In the main building, a former carriage house, she has painted the walls a somewhat shocking pink—which actually works quite well to frame the greenery of the extensive garden out back. The two cathedral-ceiling loft rooms in the adjoining 18th-century barn are definitely tops, and seem custom-made for honeymooners.

WHERE TO DINE
Very Expensive
✪ **The Regatta at Falmouth-by-the-Sea.** 217 Clinton Ave. (off Scranton Ave., about 1 mile south of Main St.), Falmouth. ☎ **508/548-5400.** Reservations recommended. Main courses $20–$26. AE, MC, V. Daily 4:30–10pm. Closed Oct–Apr. INTERNATIONAL.

This restaurant has it all: harbor views, polished yet innovative cuisine, and superb service. You're likely to find owner Brantz Bryan affably circulating: He's the one who seems to have wandered in off a golf course. His wife and partner, Wendy Bryan, designed the decor, from the rose-petal pale walls to the custom Limoges china. Certain menu offerings are inviolable: Customers would rightfully squawk if they were to vanish. These include a celestial lobster-and-corn chowder, and the lamb *en chemise*—stuffed with chèvre, spinach, and pine nuts, baked in puff pastry, and cloaked in a cabernet sauvignon sauce. The owners have also ventured into fusion territory, with such dishes as grilled tamari-glazed shrimp and Szechuan duck served with sautéed Asian greens.

Expensive
Coonamessett Inn Dining Room. Jones Rd. and Gifford St., Falmouth. ☎ **508/548-2300.** Reservations recommended. Main courses $14–$21. AE, DC, MC, V. Daily 11am–4pm and 5–9pm. NEW AMERICAN.

If the somewhat stuffy ambiance leads you to expect bland country club fare, you're in for a pleasant surprise. Chef David Kelley cures his own salmon into superlative gravlax, and raids the inn's garden to create memorable seasonal variations on, say, lobster or lamb. Whimsical mermaid paintings, the work of local legend Ralph Cahoon, plus chandeliers shaped like hot-air balloons, accent the middle dining room.

Fishmonger's Cafe. 56 Water St. (at the Eel Pond drawbridge), Woods Hole. ☎ **508/540-5376.** Main courses $10–$19. AE, MC, V. Mid-June to mid-Oct Mon–Fri 7–11am, Sat 7–11:30am, Sun 7am–noon; Mon–Fri 11:30am–4pm, Sat noon–4:30pm, Sun 12:30–4:30pm; Mon–Thurs 5–10pm, Fri 5–10:30pm, Sat–Sun 5:30–10:30pm. Call for off-season hours. Closed Dec to mid-Mar. NATURAL.

A cherished carryover from the early 1970s, this sunny cafe attracts local grungers and execs as well as Bermuda-shorted visitors with an ever-changing menu of imaginatively prepared dishes. Regulars might grab a bite at the counter while schmoozing with staff bustling about the open kitchen. Newcomers usually go for the tables by the window, where you can watch the Eel Pond boats come and go. Lunch could be a tempeh burger, made with fermented soybeans, or ordinary beef. Longtime customers look to the blackboard for the latest innovations, which invariably include some delectable desserts, such as pumpkin-pecan pie.

Moderate

Cap'n Kidd. 77 Water St. (west of the Eel Pond drawbridge), Woods Hole. ☎ **508/548-8563.** Main courses $14–$20. AE, CB, MC, V. Daily 11am–9pm. SEAFOOD.

The semiofficial heart of town, this well-worn bistro really comes into its own once the hordes subside. It's then that the year-round scientists and fishing crews can again belly up to the hand-carved mahogany bar (thought to date from the early 1800s), or huddle around the woodstove in the glassed back porch, beside the pond, and order up reasonably priced seafood, or drink to their heart's content—mostly the latter, judging from the festive atmosphere.

Peking Palace. 452 Main St. (in the center of town), Falmouth. ☎ **508/540-8204.** Fax 508/540-8382. Main courses $8–$12. AE, DC, MC, V. June–Aug daily 11:30am–2am; Sept–May Sun–Thurs 11:30am–midnight, Fri–Sat 11:30am–1:30am. CHINESE.

This is hands down the best Chinese restaurant on the Cape. This smallish restaurant has been infused with TLC at every turn, from the fringes of bamboo gracing the parking lot to the gleaming rosewood tables. No detail has been overlooked to create a cosseting, exotic environment. There are 300-plus items on the menu, spanning three regional cuisines (Cantonese, Mandarin, and Szechuan), as well as Polynesian. Just ask your server what to order: That's how we encountered some heavenly spicy chilled squid.

Shucker's World Famous Raw Bar & Cafe. 91A Water St. ($^{1}/_{2}$ block west of the Eel Pond drawbridge), Woods Hole. ☎ **508/540-3850.** Main courses $9–$15. AE, MC, V. Daily 11am–11pm. Closed mid-Oct to mid-May. INTERNATIONAL.

A tight cluster of tables hugging the edge of Eel Pond, this outdoor cafe has a loyal following, drawn by the great prices and fresh seafood. The clam chowder is so thick with seafood (including the odd shrimp and crab) that it's truly a meal. Among the more unusual offerings are crabcaves (like a crab Welsh rarebit) and, for adventurous types, marinated grilled eel. Owner Kevin Murphy is also the force behind Falmouth's beloved local brew, Nobska Light, named for the resident lighthouse.

Inexpensive

Betsy's Diner. 457 Main St. (in the center of town), Falmouth. ☎ **508/540-0060.** Main courses $4–$8. AE, MC, V. May–Aug daily 5am–9pm; call for off-season hours. AMERICAN.

Nothing could be finer than a resurrected diner—especially one offering time-travel food. Turkey dinner, breakfast all day, homemade pies—now, these are traditions worth maintaining. The original aluminum features dazzle as they surely did back then, and the jukebox is primed with oldies.

The Clam Shack. 227 Clinton Ave. (off Scranton Ave., about 1 mile south of Main St.), Falmouth. ☎ **508/540-7758.** Main courses $5–$11. No credit cards. Daily 11:30am–7:30pm. Closed mid-Sept to late May. SEAFOOD.

"Shack" is the appropriate term. This tumble-down shanty clings to its pier like a barnacle, having weathered 3 decades of Nor'easters, not to mention the occasional hurricane. The fare has withstood the test of time, too: your basic fried clams (with belly intact, the sign of a joint that knows clams) and whatever else the nets have tossed up. Sitting at a postage-stamp table hinged to the wall, you can soak up a truly magnificent view.

FALMOUTH AFTER DARK

God knows who you'll meet in the rough-and-tumble old **Cap'n Kidd,** 77 Water St., in Woods Hole (☎ **508/548-9206**): maybe a lobsterwoman, maybe a Nobel Prize winner. Good grub, too—see "Where to Dine," above.

Casino by the Sea, at 281 Grand Ave., beneath the Wharf Restaurant (☎ **508/ 548-2772**), is essentially a dance hall catering to 20-somethings. The fun spills over from the sand; locally bred bands provide the beat. Cover $5. Closed October through April.

An alternative to rowdy bars is **The Coffee Obsession,** 110 Palmer Ave., near Route 28 (☎ **508/540-2233**), a "Friends"-style coffeehouse—something like a communal living room.

2 The Mid-Cape

If the Cape had a capital, it would have to be Hyannis. It's a sprawling monstrosity (let's be blunt), where the Kennedy mystique of the 1960s unfortunately spurred heedless development over the next several decades—a period during which, not so incidentally, the Cape's year-round population nearly doubled, to approximately 200,000. The summer crowd is about three times that, and you'd swear every single person had daily errands to run in Hyannis. And yet even this overrun town has its pockets of charm, especially the waterfront area and Main Street.

But the real beauty of the Mid-Cape is in the smaller towns: the old-money hideaways like Osterville to the west, and the historic preserve flanking the Old King's Highway (Route 6) along the bay shore. The whole architectural history of the Cape, from humble colonial saltboxes to ostentatious captains' mansions, unfurls as you meander along the winding two-lane road. Intriguing antique shops—scores of them—subtly compete for a closer look, and each village seems a throwback to a kinder, gentler era.

HYANNIS & ENVIRONS

No wonder many visitors experience "post-Camelot letdown" the first time they venture into Hyannis. The downtown area, sapped by the strip development that proliferated at the edges of town after the Cape Cod Mall was built in 1970, is only now making a valiant comeback, with attractive banners and a public park flanking the wharf where frequent ferries depart for the Islands. If you were to confine your Cape Cod visit to Hyannis alone, however, you'd get a very warped view of the Cape. Along Routes 132 and 28, you could be visiting Anywhere, U.S.A.: They're lined by the standard chain stores, restaurants, and hotels, and plagued by maddening traffic.

Hyannis has more beds (at better prices) than anywhere else on the Cape, but there's little rationale for staying right in town or along the highways—unless you happen to have missed the last ferry out. I'd recommend staying near the edge of town, in one of the moneyed villages to the west (Centerville, Osterville, Marstons Mills, and Cotuit), or, better still, head to Barnstable, due north, and just go into Hyannis to sample the restaurants and nightlife. See below for details on Barnstable.

ESSENTIALS

GETTING THERE   After crossing either the Bourne or Sagamore bridge, head east on Routes 6 or 6A. Before you reach Barnstable, pick up Route 132, which leads to Hyannis.

VISITOR INFORMATION   For information, contact the **Hyannis Area Chamber of Commerce,** 1471 Rte. 132, Hyannis, MA 02601 (☎ **800/449-6647** or 508/ 362-5230).

BEACHES & OUTDOOR PURSUITS

BEACHES   Most of the Sound beaches are fairly protected and thus not big in terms of surf. **Beach parking** costs $8 a day, usually payable at the lot; for a weeklong

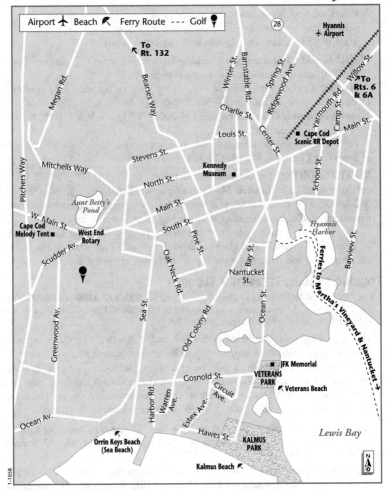

parking sticker ($35), visit the Recreation Department at 141 Basset Lane, behind the Kennedy Memorial Skating Rink (☎ **508/790-6345**).

- **Craigville Beach,** off Craigville Beach Road in Centerville: Once a magnet for Methodist "camp" meetings (conference centers still line the shore), this broad expanse of sand boasts lifeguards and rest rooms. A magnet for the bronzed and buffed, it's known as "Muscle Beach."
- **Orrin Keyes Beach** (a.k.a. Sea Beach), at the end of Sea Street in Hyannis: This little beach at the end of a residential road is popular with families.
- **Kalmus Beach,** off Gosnold Street in Hyannisport: This 800-foot spit of sand stretching toward the mouth of the harbor makes an ideal launching site for windsurfers, who sometimes seem to play chicken with the steady parade of ferries. The surf is tame, the slope shallow—the conditions are ideal for little kids, too, and lifeguards, a snack bar, and rest rooms facilitate family outings.
- **Veterans Beach,** off Ocean Street in Hyannis: A small stretch of harborside sand adjoining the John F. Kennedy Memorial (a moving tribute from the

town), this spot is not tops for swimming, unless you're very young and easily wowed. Parking is usually easy, though, and it's walkable from town. The snack bar, rest rooms, and playground will see to a family's needs.

FISHING   The **Tightlines Sport Fishing Service,** 65 Camp St., Hyannis (☎ 508/790-8600), conducts saltwater fly-fishing expeditions.

Hy-Line Cruises offers seasonal sonar-aided "bottom" or blues fishing from its Ocean Street dock in Hyannis (☎ 508/790-0696). Also departing from that dock, **Hyannis Navigator Deep-Sea Fishing** (☎ 800/771-9534 or 508/771-9500) claims the newest and fastest craft.

For a smaller, more personalized expedition, get in touch with Capt. Ron Murphy of **Stray Cat Charters** (☎ 508/428-8628).

WATER SPORTS   The **Goose Hummock Shop,** 2 Rte. 132 (☎ 508/778-0877), rents the usual craft; **Eastern Mountain Sports,** 1513 Tyanough Rd. (☎ 508/362-8690), offers rental kayaks, plus tents and sleeping bags, and sponsors occasional overnights to Washburn Island in Waquoit Bay, as well as free clinics.

For those who prefer to do their sightseeing underwater, **East Coast Divers,** 237 Rte. 28 (☎ 508/775-1185), attends to all snorkeling and scuba needs, including instruction and charters; for the super-hardy, they're open year-round.

TOURING BY RAIL, STEAMER & SLOOP

Cape Cod Scenic Railroad. 252 Main St., Hyannis. ☎ 800/872-4508 or 508/771-3788. Ticket $11.50 adult, $7.50 children 3–12. Departures Tues–Sun at 10am, 12:30pm, and 3pm June to late Oct; call for off-season hours. Closed Jan.

Here's your chance to get off the gridlocked roads and actually see the countryside. Three vintage cars make a leisurely trip to Buzzards Bay, with a stop in Sandwich; round-trip, the 42 miles take a little under 2 hours. Occasionally, special "ecology" tours are scheduled, led by a local naturalist and including a half-hour stop for a guided marsh walk in Sandwich's Talbots Point Conservation Preserve. The dinner trains are also very popular (though the food's unremarkable for the prices).

Hyannisport Harbor Cruises. Ocean St. Dock, Hyannis. ☎ 508/778-2600. Fee $8 adults, free–$3.50 children 12 and under. Late June through Aug, 16 departures daily; call for schedule. Closed Nov to early Apr.

For a fun and informative introduction to the harbor and its residents, take a leisurely (1- to 2-hour) narrated tour aboard the Hy-Line's 1911 steamer replicas *Patience* and *Prudence.* Five family trips a day in season offer free passage for children under 12, but for a real treat take them on the Sunday 3:30pm "Ice Cream Float," which includes a design-your-own Ben & Jerry's sundae, or the Thursday 9pm "Jazz Boat," accompanied by a Dixieland band.

The Hesperus. Pier 16, Ocean St. Dock, Hyannis. ☎ 508/790-0077. Fee $22 adults, $15 seniors and children 12 and under. Late May to early Sept daily departures at 12:30, 3, and 6pm; call for off-season schedule. Closed Nov–Apr.

Offering an elegant means of exploring the harbor (while sneaking a peak at the Kennedy compound), the 50-foot John Alden sloop accommodates only 22 passengers, who are welcome to help trim the sails or even steer. Most opt to luxuriate in the sparkling sun and cooling breezes. The occasional moonlight sails are especially romantic.

THE KENNEDY LEGACY

For a lovely sightseeing drive, mosey around the moneyed Sound shore to the west. Don't even bother tracking down the Kennedy Compound in Hyannisport; it's effectively screened from view, and you'll see more at the John F. Kennedy Hyannis Museum (a mostly photographic display) in town. Or if you absolutely have to satisfy your curiosity, take a harbor cruise (see above).

John F. Kennedy Hyannis Museum. 397 Main St. (in the center of town), Hyannis. ☎ **800/ 492-6647** or 508/775-2201. Admission $3 adults, children under 16 free. June–Aug Mon–Sat 10am–4pm, Sun 1–4pm; Sept–May Wed–Sat 10am–4pm.

This primarily photographic display—supplemented by a brief video program narrated by Walter Cronkite—captures the Kennedys during the glory days of 1934 to 1963. Those last 3 years were a bit chaotic (some 25,000 well-wishers thronged the roads when the senator and president-to-be returned from the 1960 Democratic Convention), but JFK continued to treasure the Cape as "the one place I can think and be alone." The candid shots included in this permanent display capture some of the quieter moments, as well as the legendary charm.

SHOPPING

Although Hyannis is undoubtedly the commercial center of the Cape, the stores you'll find there are fairly standard for the most part. Head for the wealthy enclaves west of Hyannis, and along the antiquated King's Highway (Route 6A) to the north, to find the real gems.

The Farmhouse, 1340 Main St. (about 1 mile south of Route 28), Osterville (☎ 508/420-2400), is Carolyn and Barry Crawford's 1742 farmhouse, which is set up like an adult-scale dollhouse, and the "lifelike" settings should lend decorative inspiration. Self-confident sorts will go wild in the barn; it's packed with intriguing architectural salvage.

Ex-Nantucketer Bob Marks fashions the only authentic Nantucket lightship baskets crafted off-island, and as aficionados know, they don't come cheap (a mere handbag typically runs in the thousands). Oak and Ivory is at 1112 Main St. (about 1 mile south of Route 28), Osterville (☎ 508/428-9425).

WHERE TO STAY

Expensive

Inn at Fernbrook. 481 Main St. (about ¹/₂ mile south of Rte. 28), Centerville, MA 02632. ☎ 508/775-4334. Fax 508/778-4455. 5 suites, 1 cottage. Summer $135–$290 suite, $135 cottage. Rates include full breakfast and afternoon tea. AE, DISC, MC, V.

An imposing 1881 showplace, set back from the street by a circular drive, this house has an unmistakable aura of grandeur, borne out by its pedigree and roster of former residents. Howard Marston, owner of Boston's Parker House hotel, commissioned no less a landscape architect than Frederick Law Olmsted (designer of New York's Central Park) to beautify his Queen Anne–style country retreat with a heart-shaped "sweetheart" rose garden, which remains intact and lovely. Among the subsequent owners were Dr. Herbert Kalmus, co-inventor of Technicolor (his house guests included Gloria Swanson, Cecil B. DeMille, and Walt Disney), and the Catholic Church, in the person of Cardinal Francis Spellman, who broke bread here with both Kennedy and Nixon. Current owners Brian Gallo and Sal DiFlorio restored the manse to not-too-fussy Victorian splendor, while retaining subsequent architectural quirks. The Spellman Room, which the Cardinal converted into a chapel, remains pretty much as revised—except for an elaborate and invitingly profane canopy bed where the altar once stood. The two-bedroom Olmsted Suite, occupying the entire third floor, boasts a fireplaced living room straight out of *Holiday* and steep stairs leading to a balcony and sundeck.

Moderate

Captain Gosnold Village. 230 Gosnold St. (off Ocean St., about 1 mile south of town center), Hyannis, MA 02601. ☎ **508/775-9111.** 33 rms, 8 efficiencies and suites. A/C TV TEL. Summer $75 double, $95 efficiency; $260 suite. MC, V. Closed Dec–Mar.

A cluster of grizzled cottages with pink shutters, this little compound would make a pleasant family retreat. Far enough from downtown, and a short walk from Kalmus Beach, the cottages—which can be rented by the room and day, as well as in their entirety or by the week—are remarkably cheery, with fresh, modern decor. A lifeguard watches over the small outdoor pool, and lawn games and a play area keep kids happily occupied.

East Bay Lodge. 199 East Bay Rd. (about ¹/₂ mile southeast of Main St.), Osterville, MA 02655. ☎ **800/933-2782** or 508/428-5200. Fax 508/428-5432. 18 rms. A/C MINIBAR TV TEL. Summer $135–$145 double. Rates include continental breakfast. AE, CB, DC, DISC, MC, V.

Well priced for its affluent location (in a residential section of the Cape's wealthiest town), this modern, motel-like annex to a historic restaurant isn't for those seeking a real country inn. The reproduction-appointed rooms are perfectly pretty, though, and the grounds are inviting, with a croquet course, three tennis courts, and a photogenic gazebo. Best of all is the private bay beach within a few minutes' walk.

Hyannis Harborview Resort. 213 Ocean St. (opposite the Hy-Line Ferry dock), Hyannis, MA 02601. ☎ **800/676-0000** or 508/775-4420. Fax 508/775-7995. 126 rms, 10 suites. A/C TV TEL. Summer $89–$109 double, $135–$145 suite. AE, CB, DC, DISC, MC, V. Closed Nov–Apr.

Situated right on the waterfront, this sprawling modern resort makes a convenient stopover if you're heading on to the islands. It's also a good choice for those who select Hyannis as a base for sampling the local nightlife: One of the livelier restaurant/bars, The Reach, is right on the premises, and most of the others are within an easy walk. The rooms—those higher up afford nice harbor views—are done up in pleasing color schemes with contemporary blond wood furniture. Among the other draws are outdoor and indoor pools, plus a whirlpool and exercise room.

Simmons Homestead Inn. 288 Scudder Ave. (at W. Main St. about ¹/₄ mile west of the West End Rotary), Hyannis, MA 02601. ☎ **800/637-1649** or 508/778-4999. Fax 508/790-1342. 10 rms. Summer $145–$200 double. Rates include full breakfast. AE, DC, MC, V.

A former ad exec and race car driver, innkeeper Bill Putman has a silly side and isn't afraid to show it. He started collecting animal artifacts—stuffed toys, sculptures, even needlepoint and wallpaper—to differentiate the rather traditional rooms in this rambling 1820s captain's manse and kind of got carried away. All the animals, plus his general friendliness, serve as an icebreaker, though: This is an inn where you'll find everyone milling around the hearth sipping complementary wine (served "sixish") while they compare notes and nail down dinner plans. Guests who prefer privacy may book the spiffily updated "servants' quarters," a spacious, airy cottage with its own private deck. Well-known athletes (such as O.J., in sunnier days, and Bruce Jenner) and performers from the nearby Cape Cod Melody Tent (Carly Simon) have sought refuge here over the years. Putman promises every guest a special spot that's "10 million miles from anywhere, and 2 minutes from everything."

Inexpensive

Inn at the Mills. 71 Rte. 149 (at the intersection of Rte. 28), Marstons Mills, MA 02648. ☎ **508/428-2967.** 6 rms. Summer $65–$100 double. Rates include continental breakfast. No credit cards.

This 1780 inn looks like someone's enviable private estate—an illusion maintained once you venture indoors, right into a rustic beamed kitchen. Beyond are further common rooms: a proper parlor with wingback chairs, and a sunporch harboring a white baby grand and comfy wicker couches. The view from here is of a small pool and below, beyond a sloping lawn, a good-sized pond occupied by gliding waterfowl and flanked by an inviting gazebo. The rooms are tasteful, too—except for the cathedral-ceilinged "hayloft" room, with dimensions fit for a medieval dining hall.

WHERE TO DINE

A couple of peripherals bear mention here: **Cape Cod Potato Chips,** on Breed's Hill Road at Independence Way, off Route 132 in Hyannis (☎ **508/775-7253**), really *are* the world's best. Free factory tours are offered from Monday to Friday from 10am to 4pm. And **Country Store,** 877 Main St., in the center of Osterville (☎ **508/ 428-2097**), is the essence of an old-fashioned general store.

Very Expensive

✪ **Alberto's Ristorante.** 360 Main St., Hyannis. ☎ **508/778-1770.** Reservations recommended. Main courses $13–$25. AE, CB, DC, DISC, MC, V. Daily 11am–4pm. ITALIAN.

By far the most sophisticated restaurant in town, Alberto's explores the full range of Italian cuisine, with a classicist's attention to components and composition. Chefowner Felisberto Barreiro's sole Florentine, for instance, consists of gray sole fresh from Chatham, topped with lobster, spinach, and fontina and enhanced with a beurre blanc flecked with sun-dried tomatoes. Hand-cut pasta is a specialty, including the ultrarich seafood ravioli cloaked in saffron cream sauce. Though the atmosphere is elegant, with sconces shedding a warm glow over well-spaced, linen-draped tables, the atmosphere is not one of hushed reverence: People clearly come here to have a good time, and the absolute assurance of friendly service and fabulous food ensures that they do. Locals who appreciate a bargain know to come between 4 and 6pm, when a full dinner, with soup, salad, and dessert, costs as little as $11.

The Regatta of Cotuit at the Crocker House. 4613 Falmouth Rd. (Rte. 28, near the Mashpee border), Cotuit. ☎ **508/428-5715.** Reservations recommended. Main courses $18–$26. AE, MC, V. Daily 5:30–10pm. NEW AMERICAN.

The year-round cousin of the Regatta at Falmouth-by-the-Sea (see "Where to Dine" under "Falmouth," above) serves many of the same signature dishes (such as the stellar lamb *en chemise*) in a suite of charmingly decorated Federal-era rooms. The cuisine is at once exquisite and hearty, fortified by herbs and vegetables plucked fresh from the kitchen garden, and the mood is invariably festive.

Expensive

The Black Cat. 165 Ocean St. (opposite the Ocean St. Dock), Hyannis. ☎ **508/778-1233.** Main courses $9–$24. AE, DC, MC, V. Late May to early Sept daily 11:30am–10pm; call for off-season hours. NEW AMERICAN.

Conveniently located less than a block from the Hy-Line ferries, this is a fine place to catch a quick bite or full meal while you wait for your boat to come in. The menu is pretty basic—steak, pasta, and, of course, fish—but attention is paid to the details; the onion rings, for instance, are made fresh. The dining room, with its bar of gleaming mahogany and brass, will appeal to chilled travelers on a blustery day; in fine weather, you might prefer the porch.

Ristorante Barolo. One Financial Place (297 North St., the West End Rotary), Hyannis. ☎ **508/778-2878.** Main courses $8–$20. AE, DC, MC, V. June–Sept daily 4–11pm; call for off-season hours. ITALIAN.

Part of a smart-looking brick office complex, this thoroughly up-to-date Italian restaurant does everything right, from offering extra-virgin olive oil with its crusty bread to getting those pastas perfectly al dente. A favorite dish is the filet Barolo, an Angus steak served with a reduction sauce of Barolo wine, served with sun-dried tomatoes and wild mushrooms.

Moderate

✪ Baxter's Boat House. 177 Pleasant St. (near Steamship Authority ferry), Hyannis. ☎ **508/ 755-4490.** Main courses $8–$14. AE, MC, V. Late May to early Sept Mon–Sat 11:30am–10pm, Sun 11:30am–9pm; call for off-season hours. Closed mid-Oct through Mar. SEAFOOD.

A shingled shack on a jetty jutting out into the harbor, Baxter's has catered to the boating crowd since the mid-1950s, with Cape classics such as fried clams and fish virtually any way you like it, from baked to blackened.

Tugboats. 21 Arlington St. (at the Hyannis Marina, off Willow St.), Hyannis. ☎ **508/ 775-6433.** Main courses $11–$15. AE, DISC, MC, V. July–Aug daily 11:30am–9:30pm; call for off-season hours. Closed Nov to mid-Apr. AMERICAN.

Yet another harborside perch for munching and ogling, this one's especially appealing: The two spacious outdoor decks are angled just right to catch the sunset, with cocktails/frappes to match. Forget fancy dining and chow down on blackened swordfish bites (topping a Caesar salad, perhaps) or lobster fritters, or the double-duty Steak Neptune, topped with scallops and shrimp. For dessert, try shortbread-crusted bourbon pecan pie or a key lime pie purportedly lifted straight from Papa's.

✪ Up the Creek. 36 Old Colony Blvd. (about 1 mile south of Main St.), Hyannis. ☎ **508/ 771-7866.** Reservations recommended. Main courses $9–$13. AE, CB, DC, DISC, MC, V. June– Aug daily 4:30–9:30pm; call for off-season hours. INTERNATIONAL.

Good luck finding it (tucked away in a residential area) and better luck getting in! Locals know a good deal when they see one, and dinner prices in the single digits draw an avid crowd. House specialties include a seafood strudel cloaked with hollandaise, and a broiled seafood platter comprising half a lobster, clams casino, scallops, scrod, and baked stuffed shrimp (that's the priciest entree at all of $13). Decorated like an Ivy League boathouse, the restaurant has grace and style, even when it's packed to the rafters.

Inexpensive

The Egg & I. 521 Main St. (in the center of town), Hyannis. ☎ **508/771-1596.** Most items under $10. AE, DC, DISC, MC, V. Daily 11pm–1pm. AMERICAN.

Yes, those are the correct hours. This Tudor-storefront diner *opens* at 11 at night, then serves past noon. A town with this many bars needs a place where patrons and staff alike can unwind and/or sober up after last call; a wholesome meal wouldn't hurt either. Breakfast is usually the meal of choice, especially the "create an omelet" option, but the pancakes (from chocolate chip to fruit-loaded Swedish) are strong contenders. Children go gaga over the Mickey Mouse waffle (only $2, with bacon or sausage), and those who feel silly having breakfast before bed can order sandwiches or one of a dozen or so daily specials that change with the season.

HYANNIS & ENVIRONS AFTER DARK

Try to catch any type of performance they've got on the bill at **✪ The Cape Cod Melody Tent,** West End Rotary, Hyannis (☎ 508/775-9100). Built as a summer theater in 1950, this billowy blue big-top proved even better suited to variety shows. A nonprofit venture since 1990 (proceeds fund other cultural initiatives Cape-wide), the Melody Tent hosted the major performers of the past half-century, from jazz greats to comedians, crooners to rockers. Every seat is a winner in this grand oval, only 20 banked aisles deep. There's also a children's theater program Wednesday mornings at 11am.

Another good place for mellow after-dinner entertainment is the **Roadhouse Cafe,** 488 South St., Hyannis (☎ **508/775-2386**), a dark-paneled bar resembling an English gentlemen's club. The bar stocks 48 boutique brews, in addition to all the usual hard, soft, and sweet liquors, and you won't go hoarse trying to converse over the soft jazz.

Those who have yet to give up dinner-dancing might try the **East Bay Lodge,** 199 East Bay Rd., Osterville (☎ **508/428-5200**), where a pianist playing jazz, cabaret, and oldies provides incentive to get up and sway or swing. No cover.

If you're looking for more action, you might consider **Asa Bearse House,** 415 Main St., Hyannis (☎ **508/771-4444**), a dance club that throbs to progressive rock. The "Reading Room" bar resembles a frat house in F. Scott Fitzgerald's day, complete with helter-skelter bookshelves, conversational nooks, and a moose head as mascot. Cover $3 to $5 in season.

Duval Street Station, 477 Yarmouth Road, Hyannis (☎ **508/771-7511**), is Hyannis's first (and so far, only) gay bar. The lower level of this former train station is a comfortable lounge, and upstairs there's a dance bar complete with light show and DJ mixes that spin from Latin rhythms to new wave to disco classics. Nominal cover charge Friday and Saturday in season.

Preppies convene to cut loose at **Sophie's Bar & Grill,** 334 Main St., Hyannis (☎ **508/775-1111**). The live rock leans to such freaky extremes as the Strangemen out of Martha's Vineyard, a quintet of platinum-pompadoured alien-dandies who describe their sound as "sci-fi rockabilly surf rock." Above-average pub food is another draw. Cover $3 to $5 in season.

Pufferbellies Entertainment Complex, 183R Rte. 132 at Yarmouth Road, Hyannis (☎ **800/233-4301** or 508/790-4300), is a rehabbed railroad roundhouse that's huge enough to accommodate not only 1,500 revelers but three distinct styles of revelry. The Flashbacks section is a Top 40 dance club; Little Texas goes for country-western two-stepping; and the outdoors, summers-only Caribbean Cafe brings in steel bands to accompany the barbecue. For the weekly schedule, call the 800 number listed above. Cover about $5, season pass $10.

Everyone's glowing with the day's exertions as they cram onto the deck at **Steamers Grill & Bar,** 235 Ocean St., Hyannis (☎ **508/778-0818**), to enjoy a lingering sunset over cocktails. It's a young, sporty crowd for the most part (despite the fuddy-duddy duffers' motif in the downstairs Putter's Pub), drawn by the live bands on weekends. No cover.

At **The Reach Caribbean Grill,** 213 Ocean St., Hyannis (☎ **508/778-1113**), nothing says "kick back" like the rumble of steel drums or the rhythms of reggae—except maybe a tall, cool tropical drink, perhaps prefaced by a raw cherrystone clam or oyster shooter.

BARNSTABLE & ENVIRONS

As the commercial center and transportation hub of the Cape, hyper-developed Hyannis grossly overshadows the actual seat of government in the bucolic village of Barnstable. The two locales couldn't be more dissimilar. As peaceful as Hyannis is hectic, the bay area along historic Route 6A unfolds in a blur of greenery and well-kept colonial houses. It's a perfect combination to choose your accommodation in this more peaceful setting and then venture into Hyannis for restaurants and nightlife.

Outdoor Pursuits

Barnstable's primary bay beach is **Sandy Neck,** accessed through East Sandwich; see "Beaches" under "Sandwich," above.

FISHING The township of Barnstable has 11 ponds for freshwater fishing; for **information and permits,** visit Town Hall at 367 Main St., Hyannis (☎ **508/790-6240**). Shellfishing permits are available from the Department of Natural Resources at 1189 Phinneys Lane (☎ **508/790-6272**). Surf casting, without a license, is permitted on Sandy Neck.

Among the charter boats berthed in Barnstable Harbor is the *Drifter* (☎ **508/398-2061**), a 35-foot boat offering half- and full-day trips.

KAYAKING For experienced paddlers, Barnstable's **Great Marsh,** one of the largest in New England, offers beautiful waterways out to Sandy Neck. Rent kayaks, plus tents and sleeping bags, at **Eastern Mountain Sports,** 233 Stevens St. in Hyannis (☎ **508/755-1072**).

WHALE WATCHING Provincetown is about an hour closer to the whales' preferred feeding grounds; then again, it would take you at least an hour (possibly *hours* on a summer weekend) to drive all the way down-Cape. If your time and itinerary are limited, hop aboard at **Hyannis Whale Watch Cruises,** Barnstable Harbor (about half a mile north of Route 6A on Mill Way), Barnstable (☎ **800/287-0374** or 508/362-6088; fax 508/362-9739), for a 4-hour voyage on a 100-foot high-speed cruiser. Naturalists provide the narration, and should you fail to spot a whale, your next trek is free. Tickets are $22 for adults, $19 seniors, $10 children 4 to 12 from mid-June to mid-September; call for schedule and off-season rates. Closed November to March.

Shopping

Of the hundreds of antique shops scattered through the region, perhaps a dozen qualify as destinations for real collectors. ✪ **Harden Studios,** 3264 Rte. 6A (in the center of town), Barnstable (☎ **508/362-7711**), is one such enterprise. Some items, such as the primitive portraits and mourning embroidery, are all but extinct outside of museums.

Prince Jenkins Antiques, 975 Rte. 6A (at the intersection of Route 149), West Barnstable (no phone), is one spooky shop, the piled-high kind that captivates scavengers. Make your way around the narrow path still discernible amid the heaped-up inventory, and you'll come across case upon case of vintage jewelry and watches, paintings, tapestries, urns and jade carvings, musty 18th-century garb, a Pilgrim chair or two, and all sorts of oddities. Closed mid-November to March.

Believe it or not, weathervane theft is a real threat on the Cape, so valuable are some of these copper toppers. Some of Marilyn Strauss's prize specimens, displayed in an informal museum adjoining her shop, **Salt & Chestnut Weathervanes,** 651 Rte. 6A (about one-third mile west of Route 149), West Barnstable (☎ **508/362-6085**), would fetch as much as $30,000, were she willing to part with them. Mostly she's in the business of creating replicas and custom orders. Prices range from about $200 to $2,000.

Where to Stay

The Acworth Inn. 4352 Rte. 6A (near the Yarmouth Port border), Cummaquid, MA 02637. ☎ **800/362-6363** or 508/362-3330. 6 rms. Summer $95–$115 double. Rates include full breakfast. AE, MC, V.

Cheryl Ferrell knows that it's the small touches that make a stay memorable, and anyone lucky enough to land here is sure to remember every last one, from the cranberry spritzer offered on arrival to the handmade chocolates that take the place of pillow mints. She even grinds the whole grains that go into her home-baked breakfasts, in the form of cinnamon rolls or fruit-topped waffles. She or her husband, Jack, will gladly pick you up at the Hyannis airport, if you arrange it ahead of time, and from then on their complimentary bikes may be all you need in the way of wheels.

Ashley Manor Inn. 3660 Rte. 6A (about 1 mile east of Hyannis Rd.), Barnstable, MA 02630. ☎ **508/362-8044.** 2 rms, 4 suites. A/C. Summer $120–$140 double, $165–$180 suite. Rates include full breakfast. AE, JCB, MC, V.

Nearly everyone has a vision in mind of the perfect country inn; this one could well fulfill it. The house is a much-modified 1699 colonial mansion that still retains many of its original features, including a hearth with beehive oven (the perfect place to sip port on a blustery evening), built-in corner cupboards in the wainscoted dining room, and wide-board floors. The rooms, all but one of which boast a fireplace, are spacious and inviting.

The 2-acre property itself is shielded from the road by an enormous privet hedge, and fragrant boxwood camouflages a Har-Tru tennis court. (You'll find loaner bikes beside it, ready to roll.) Romantics can seek shelter in the flower-fringed gazebo, and breakfast on the brick patio is worth waking up for: You wouldn't want to miss the homemade granola, much less the main event—quiche, perhaps, or crepes.

✪ **Charles Hinckley House.** 8 Scudder Lane (at Rte. 6A about 1¹/₂ miles east of Rte. 132), Barnstable, MA 02630. ☎ **508/362-9924.** 4 rms. Summer $119–$149 double. Rates include full breakfast. AE, MC, V.

Set atop a riotous wildflower garden, a 5-minute walk to the bay, this hip-roofed 1809 Federal manse hints at tasteful pleasures within—a promise on which it fully delivers. The period decor is almost stark, and deeply pleasing to those who prefer authenticity to misguided colonial clichés. Yet the comfort level is nonpareil: Fireplaces are a given in each room, and some have special features, such as a conservatory/sitting room with bay views. Innkeeper Miya Patrick is a caterer of local renown, and her breakfasts are eye-openers: They might begin with a fresh fruit plate and culminate in a crab-cake variation on eggs Benedict.

THE YARMOUTHS

This cross-section represents the Cape at its best—and worst. Yarmouth Port, on Cape Cod Bay, is an enchanting town, clustered with interesting shops and architectural pearls, whereas the Sound-side "villages" of West to South Yarmouth are an object lesson in unbridled development run amuck. This section of Route 28 is a nightmarish gauntlet of ticky-tacky accommodations and "attractions." Yet even here you'll find a few choice spots. You've got the north shore for culture and refinement, the south shore for kitsch. Take your pick, or ricochet back and forth, enjoying the best of both worlds.

ESSENTIALS

GETTING THERE   After crossing either the Bourne or Sagamore bridge, head east on Route 6 or 6A. Route 6A (north of Route 6's Exit 7) passes through the villages of Yarmouth Port and Yarmouth. The villages of West Yarmouth, Bass River, and South Yarmouth are located along Route 28, east of Hyannis; to reach them from Route 6, take Exit 7 south (Yarmouth Road), or Exit 8 south (Station Street).

VISITOR INFORMATION   Contact the **Yarmouth Area Chamber of Commerce,** 657 Rte. 28, West Yarmouth, MA 02673 (☎ **508/778-1008**).

BEACHES & OUTDOOR PURSUITS

BEACHES   Yarmouth boasts 11 saltwater and 2 pond beaches open to the public. The sands are packed with crowds along the Sound, but the social scene is hopping, so no one seems to mind. The beachside **parking lots** charge $7 a day; to obtain a weeklong sticker ($30), visit the Town Hall, 1146 Rte. 28, S. Yarmouth (☎ **508/398-2231**).

- **Bass River Beach,** off South Shore Drive in Bass River: Located at the mouth of the largest tidal river on the eastern seaboard, this Sound beach offers all the usual features, plus a wheelchair-accessible fishing pier.
- **Grays Beach,** off Centre Street in Yarmouth: Tame waters excellent for children; adjoins the Callery-Darling Conservation Area (see "Nature Trails," below).
- **Parker's River Beach,** off South Shore Drive in Bass River: The usual amenities, plus a 20-foot gazebo for shade.
- **Seagull Beach,** off South Sea Avenue in West Yarmouth: Rolling dunes, a boardwalk, and all the necessary facilities attract a young crowd. Bring bug spray, though: Greenhead flies get the munchies in July.

FISHING   Of the five fishing ponds in the Yarmouth area, Long Pond near South Yarmouth is known for its largemouth bass and pickerel; for details and a license (shellfishing is another option), visit the Town Hall, 1146 Rte. 28, South Yarmouth (☎ **508/398-2231**). You can cast for striped bass and bluefish off the pier at Bass River Beach (see "Beaches," above).

NATURE TRAILS   Slightly east of Yarmouth Port, follow Centre Street about a mile north and bear northeast on Homers Dock Road; from here a $2^1/2$-mile trail through the **Callery-Darling Conservation Area** leads to Grays Beach, where you can continue across the Bass Hole Boardwalk for a lovely view of the marsh.

A MUST-SEE FOR ANTIQUE LOVERS

✪ **The Winslow Crocker House.** 250 Rte. 6A (about $1/2$ mile east of town center), Yarmouth Port. ☎ **508/362-4385.** Admission $4 adults, $3.50 seniors, $2 children 5–12. June to mid-Oct Sat–Sun 11am–5pm. Closed mid-Oct to May.

The only property on the Cape currently preserved by the prestigious Society for the Preservation of New England Antiquities, this house, built around 1780, deserves every honor. Not only is it a lovely example of the shingled Georgian style, it's packed with outstanding antiques—Jacobean to Chippendale—collected in the 1930s by Mary Thacher, a descendant of the town's first land grantee.

Anthony Thacher and his family had a rougher crossing than most: Their ship foundered off Cape Ann in 1635 (near an island that now bears their name), and though their four children drowned, Thacher and his wife were able to make it to shore, clinging to the family cradle. You'll come across a 1690 replica in the parlor. Thacher's son John, a colonel, built the house next door around 1680, and—with the help of two successive wives—raised a total of 21 children.

All the museum-worthy objects in the Winslow Crocker House would seem to have similar stories to tell. For antique lovers, as well as anyone interested in local lore, this is a very worthwhile stop.

KID STUFF

ZooQuarium. 674 Rte. 28 (midway between W. Yarmouth and Bass River), W. Yarmouth. ☎ **508/775-8883.** Admission $7.50 adults, $4.50 children 2–9. July–Aug daily 9:30am–8pm; off-season daily 9:30am–5pm. Closed late Nov to mid-Feb.

This slightly scruffy wildlife museum has made great strides in recent years toward blending entertainment with education. It's a little easier to enjoy the sea lion show once you've been assured that the stars *like* performing, have been trained with posi- tive reinforcement only, and, furthermore, arrived with injuries that precluded their survival in the wild. The aquarium is arranged in realistic habitats, and the "zoo" con- sists primarily of indigenous fauna, both domesticated and wild (the pacing bobcat is liable to give you pause). Children will be entranced, and a very creditable effort is made to convey the need for ecological preservation.

SHOPPING

Route 6A through Yarmouth Port and Yarmouth remains a rich vein of antique shops. Check them all out, if you're so inclined and have the time.

Most Cape antique stores offer plenty of decorative items such as glass, china, and silver, but scant the big pieces of centuries-old furniture. There's plenty of the latter at **Nickerson Antiques,** 162 Rte. 6A (in the center of town), Yarmouth Port (☎ **508/362-6426**), mostly imported from Great Britain and much of it skillfully refinished.

The most colorful bookshop on the Cape (if not the whole East Coast) is **Parnassus Books,** 220 Rte. 6A (about a quarter mile east of the town center), Yarmouth Port (☎ **508/362-6420**). This jam-packed repository, housed in an 1858 church, is the creation of Ben Muse, who has been collecting and selling vintage tomes since the 1960s. Relevant new stock, including the Cape-related reissues pub- lished by Parnassus Imprints, is offered alongside the older treasures. Don't expect much hand-holding on the part of the gruff proprietor. You'll earn his respect by knowing what you're looking for or, better yet, being willing to browse until it finds you. The outdoor racks, maintained on an honor system, are open 24 hours a day.

WHERE TO STAY

Captain Farris House. 308 Old Main St. (about ¹/₄ mile west of the Bass River Bridge), S. Yarmouth, MA 02664. ☎ **800/350-9477** or 508/760-2818. Fax 508/398-1262. Web site: http://www.captainfarriscapecod.com. 10 rms and suites. A/C TV TEL. $85–$185 double, $185 suite. Rates include full breakfast. AE, MC, V.

Sumptuous is the only way to describe this small inn, improbably set amid a peace- ful garden a block off bustling Route 28. The central location puts the entire Cape, from Woods Hole to Provincetown, within a 45-minute drive. Lavished with a blend of fine antiques and striking contemporary touches, this 1845 manse has been carved into lovely spaces designed for relaxing. Some suites are apartment sized, with fireplaced sitting rooms and whirlpool-tubbed bathrooms bigger than the average bedroom. Innkeeper Scott Toney whips up gourmet breakfasts replete with home- baked sweet breads, and can steer you to the best restaurants around.

Ocean Mist. 97 South Shore Dr. (off Sea View Ave., east of the Bass River Bridge), S. Yarmouth, MA 02664. ☎ **800/248-MIST** or 508/398-2633. Fax 508/760-3151. 63 rms. A/C TV. Summer $169–$219 double. AE, DISC, MC, V.

If your children will settle for nothing less than a big motel on the water, this is an attractive choice. The rooms—some with duplex lofts and all with wet bars—are decorated in soothing sand tones, and the heated indoor pool, plus whirlpool, should compensate for the occasional cloudy day.

Wedgewood Inn. 83 Rte. 6A (in the center of town), Yarmouth Port, MA 02675. ☎ **508/ 362-5157**. 9 rms. A/C. Summer $115–$160 double. Rates include full breakfast. AE, DISC, MC, V.

This elegant 1812 Federal house sits atop its undulating lawn with unabashed pride: The first house in town to be designed by an architect, it still reigns supreme as the loveliest home—one that happens to welcome strangers, though you won't feel like one for long. Innkeeper Gerrie Graham provides a warm welcome, complete with tea delivered to your room. That might be one of the four formal front rooms (all with cherry-wood pencil-post beds, Oriental rugs, antique quilts, and wood-burning fireplaces; some with private porches), the two romantic hideaways under the eaves, or the three spacious rooms, with canopy beds, fireplaces, and decks, wedged into the picturesque barn in back.

WHERE TO DINE

Don't miss **Hallet's,** on Route 6A in the center of Yarmouth Port (☎ 508/362-3362): Unsuspecting passersby invariably do a double-take when they happen upon this 1889 drugstore. Mary Hallet Clark, the granddaughter of town pharmacist (and postmaster and justice of the peace) Thacher Taylor Hallet, is now the one dishing out frappes and floats from the original marble soda fountain.

✪ **abbicci.** 43 Main St. (near the Cummaquid border), Yarmouth Port. ☎ **508/362-3501.** Reservations recommended. Main courses $13–$23. AE, DC, DISC, MC, V. Tues–Sat 11:30am–2:30pm; daily 5–10pm. ITALIAN.

Don't let the glaringly modern ambiance of this upscale trattoria or the staff's city attitude fool you: This is the place to enjoy essentially rustic northern Italian cuisine. Just one taste of the veal *nocciole* (with toasted hazelnuts and a splash of balsamic vinegar), and you'll be transported straight to Tuscany. Don't miss the Sunday brunch in the fall.

Fiesta Grande. 737 Rte. 28 (midway between W. Yarmouth and Bass River), S. Yarmouth. ☎ **508/760-2924.** Main courses $5–$11. AE, DC, DISC, MC, V. June–Aug noon–10pm; call for off-season hours. MEXICAN.

Most of the Mexican food you'll encounter on the Cape is a well-intentioned approximation, but this is the real deal, whipped up by a hard-working chef from Mazatlán. Locally inspired specialties include shrimp fajitas and crabmeat enchiladas. The menu is so well priced that it's tempting to try a bit of everything.

✪ **Inaho.** 157 Main St. (in the center of town), Yarmouth Port. ☎ **508/362-5522.** Reservations recommended. Main courses $12–$20. MC, V. Early July to early Sept Tues–Sun 5–11pm; call for off-season hours. JAPANESE.

What better place than the Cape to enjoy fresh-off-the-boat sushi? You can sit at the sushi bar to watch chef-owner Yuji Watanabe perform his wizardry or enjoy the privacy afforded by a gleaming wooden booth. The minimalist decor includes traditional *shoji* screens and crisp navy-and-white banners; it's all softened by tranquil music and service. On chilly days, opt for the tempura or a steaming bowl of *shabu-shabu.*

Jack's Outback. 161 Main St. (in the center of town), Yarmouth Port. ☎ **508/362-6690.** Most items under $5. No credit cards. Daily 6:30am–2pm. AMERICAN.

This is a neighborhood cafe as Dr. Seuss might have imagined it: hyperactive and full of fun. Chef-owner Jack Braginton-Smith makes a point of dishing out good-natured insults along with the home-style grub, which you bus yourself from the open kitchen, thereby saving big bucks as well as time. This is a perfect place for impatient children, who'll find lots of familiar, approachable dishes on the hand-scrawled posters that serve as a communal menu.

Lobster Boat. 681 Rte. 28 (midway between W. Yarmouth and Bass River), W. Yarmouth. ☎ **508/775-0486.** Main courses $10–$18. AE, MC, V. May–Oct daily 4–10pm. SEAFOOD.

Just about every town seems to have one of these barnlike restaurants serving the usual array of seafood in the usual manner, from deep-fried to boiled or broiled. True to its Sound-side setting, this tourist magnet advertises itself rather flamboyantly with a facade that features the hull of a ship grafted onto a shingled shack.

THE DENNISES

In Dennis as in Yarmouth, virtually all the good stuff—pretty drives, inviting shops, restaurants with real personality—are in the north, along Route 6A. Route 28 is chockablock with more typical tourist attractions, RV parks, and family-oriented motels—some with fairly sophisticated facilities, but others undistinguished (the few exceptions are noted below). In budgeting your time, allocate the lion's share to Dennis itself, not its southern offshoots.

ESSENTIALS

GETTING THERE   After crossing either the Bourne or Sagamore bridges, head east on Route 6 or 6A. Route 6A passes through the villages of Dennis and East Dennis (which can also be reached via northbound Route 134 from Route 6's Exit 9). Route 134 south leads to the village of South Dennis; if you follow Route 134 all the way to Route 28, the village of West Dennis will be a couple of miles to your west, and Dennis Port a couple of miles east.

VISITOR INFORMATION   Contact the Dennis Chamber of Commerce, 242 Swan River Rd., W. Dennis, MA 02670 (☎ **800/243-9920** or 508/398-3568).

BEACHES & OUTDOOR PURSUITS

BEACHES   Dennis harbors more than a dozen saltwater and two freshwater beaches open to nonresidents. The bay beaches are charming, and a big hit with families, who prize the gentle surf, so soft it won't bring toddlers to their knees. The beaches on the Sound tend to attract wall-to-wall families, but the parking lots are usually not too crowded, since so many beachgoers choose accommodations within walking distance. The lots charge $8 per day; for a weeklong **parking permit** ($25), visit the Town Hall on Main Street in South Dennis (☎ **508/394-8300**).

- **Chapin Beach,** off Route 6A in Dennis: A nice, long bay beach pocked with occasional boulders and surrounded by dunes. No lifeguard, but there are rest rooms.
- **Corporation Beach,** off Route 6A in Dennis: This bay beach offers a wheelchair-accessible boardwalk, lifeguards, a snack bar, rest rooms, and a children's play area.
- **Mayflower Beach,** off Route 6A in Dennis: This 1,200-foot bay beach has the necessary amenities, plus an accessible boardwalk. The tidal pools attract lots of children.
- **Scargo Lake** in Dennis: This large kettle-hole pond (formed by a melting fragment of a glacier) actually has two pleasant beaches: Scargo Beach, accessible right off Route 6A, and Princess Beach, off Scargo Hill Road, where there are rest rooms and a picnic area.
- **West Dennis Beach,** off Route 28 in West Dennis: This long (1½-mile) but narrow beach along the Sound has lifeguards, a playground, snack bar, rest rooms, and a special kite-flying area. The eastern end is reserved for residents, but it doesn't matter: The western end tends to be less packed anyway.

BIKING/RECREATIONAL PATHS   The 25-mile **Cape Cod Rail Trail** (☎ **508/896-3491**) starts here, on Route 134, half a mile south of Exit 9 off Route 6. Once a Penn-Central track, this 8-foot-wide paved bikeway extends all the way to Wellfleet (with a few on-road lapses), passing through woods, marshes, and dunes. Sustenance is never too far off-trail, and plenty of bike shops dot the course.

The shop closest to this trailhead is **All Right Bikes,** 118 Rte. 28, West Dennis (☎ **508/394-3544**), which stocks all the relevant gear (car racks, child trailers) and in-line skates as well. It's more than a mile away, but provides a free Chamber of Commerce booklet outlining several low-traffic routes.

Another paved bike path runs along **Old Bass Road,** 3¹/₂ miles north to Route 6A.

For joggers and fitness freaks in general, the 1¹/₂-mile **Lifecourse trail,** located at Old Bass River and Access roads in South Dennis, features 20 exercise stations along its tree-shaded path.

Crow's Pasture, accessible from South Street in the northeasterly corner of East Dennis, offers 1¹/₂ miles of dirt roads leading through evergreen groves to marsh and beach.

FISHING   Fishing is allowed in **Fresh Pond** and **Scargo Lake,** where the catch includes trout and smallmouth bass; for a **license** (shellfishing is also permitted), visit the **Town Hall,** on Main Street in South Dennis (☎ **508/394-8300**). Plenty of people drop a line off the **Bass River Bridge** along Route 28 in West Dennis.

Several charter boats operate out of the Northside Marina in East Dennis's Sesuit Harbor, including the *Bluefin* (☎ **800/244-6464** or 508/697-2093).

NATURE TRAILS   Behind the Town Hall parking lot on Main Street in South Dennis, a half-mile walk along the **Indian Lands Conservation Trail** leads to the Bass River, where blue herons and kingfishers often take shelter.

Dirt roads off South Street in East Dennis, beyond the Quivet Cemetery, lead to **Crow's Pasture,** a patchwork of marshes and dunes bordering the bay; this circular trail is about a 2¹/₂-mile round-trip.

WATER SPORTS   **Cape Cod Boats,** located on the eastern side of the Bass River Bridge along Route 28 in West Dennis (☎ **508/394-9268**), rents out canoes, sailboards, Sunfish, and motorboats, by the hour, day, or week.

Located on the small and placid Swan River, **Cape Cod Waterways,** 16 Rte. 28, Dennis Port (☎ **508/398-0080**), rents canoes, kayaks, and paddleboats for exploring 200-acre Swan Pond (less than a mile north) or Nantucket Sound (2 miles south).

KID STUFF

Dennis Port boasts the best rainy-day destination for little kids on the entire Cape: the **Discovery Days Children's Museum & Toy Shop,** 444 Rte. 6A (☎ **508/398-1600**). For a nominal admission fee ($2.50 adults, $4.50 children 1 to 16 and seniors), whole families can amuse themselves in a vast educational play space equipped with a "bubble-ology" lab, a frozen-shadow wall, a transparent piano, and all sorts of other fun stuff.

On Friday mornings in season, at 9:30 and 11:30am, the **Cape Playhouse,** 36 Hope Lane, in Dennis (☎ **508/385-3911**), hosts various visiting companies that mount musicals geared to children 4 and up. At only $5, tickets go fast.

SHOPPING

You can pretty much ignore Route 28. There's a growing cluster of antique shops in Dennis Port, but the stock is flea-market level and requires more patience than most casual browsers can muster. Save your time, and money, for the better shops along Route 6A, where you'll also find fine contemporary crafts.

More than 136 dealers stock the co-op **Antiques Center of Cape Cod,** 243 Rte. 6A (about 1 mile south of the town center), Dennis (☎ **508/385-6400**); it's the largest such enterprise on the Cape. You'll find all the usual "smalls" on the first floor; the big stuff—from blanket chests to copper bathtubs—beckons above.

Eldred's, 1483 Rte. 6A (about a quarter mile west of the town center), East Dennis (☎ **508/385-3116**), where the gavel has been wielded for more than 40 years, is the Cape's most prestigious auction house. Specialties include Oriental art, marine art, and Americana. Call for a schedule.

With Eldred's so close, **Webfoot Farm Antiques,** 1475 Rte. 6A (about a quarter mile west of the town center), East Dennis (☎ **508/385-2334**)—occupying most of an 1854 captain's house—gets the cream of the crop.

WHERE TO STAY

The Beach House Inn. 61 Uncle Stephen's Rd. (about ¹/₂ mile south of town center), W. Dennis, MA 02670. ☎ **508/398-4575.** 7 rms. TV. Summer $85–$115 double. Rates include continental breakfast. No credit cards.

Families will feel right at home in this breezy B&B, set right on the beach in a residential (i.e., motel-free) community. Whereas much of Dennis's southern shore is lined with big modern resorts, this untouched area, with a smattering of weather-silvered cottages, looks and feels like a carryover from the decades before development hit. Some rooms feature private ocean-view decks, and all guests have access to a communal kitchen with two microwaves, a barbecue deck complete with grill, and a state-of-the-art climbing structure that should keep kids happily occupied should they ever tire of the beach (not likely).

Corsair & Cross Rip Resort Motels. 41 Chase Ave. (off Depot St., 1 mile southeast of Rte. 28), Dennis Port, MA 02639. ☎ **508/398-2279.** 7 rms, 40 efficiencies. A/C TV TEL. Summer $95–$200 double. Special packages available. AE, DISC, MC, V.

Of the many family-oriented motels lining this part of the Sound, these two neighbors are among the nicest, with fresh contemporary decor, two heated beach-view pools, and their own chunk of sand. As rainy-day backup, there's an indoor pool plus a game room, and even a toddler playroom equipped with toys.

The Four Chimneys Inn. 946 Rte. 6A (about ¹/₂ mile east of town center), Dennis, MA 02638. ☎ **800/874-5502** or 508/385-6317. Fax 508/385-6285. 7 rms, 1 suite. Summer $75–$115 double. Rates include continental breakfast. DISC, MC, V.

Scargo Lake is directly across the street and the village is just a brief walk away from this imposing 1881 Victorian, former home to the town doctor. Opulent tastes are evident in the high ceilings and marble fireplace of the front parlor. Rooms vary in size, but innkeeper Kathy Tomasetti has rendered them all quite appealing, with hand-painted stenciling and summery wicker furnishings. The breakfasts are knockouts, featuring such inspirations as blueberry blintz soufflé. The only elements that don't seem to fit in with all this elegance are the surprisingly reasonable rates.

✪ **Isaiah Hall B&B Inn.** 152 Whig St. (1 block northwest of the Cape Playhouse), Dennis, MA 02638. ☎ **800/736-0160** or 508/385-9928. Fax 508/385-5879. 11 rms (1 with shared bath). A/C. Summer $85–$117 double. Rates include continental breakfast. AE, MC, V. Closed mid-Oct to Mar.

So keyed-in is this Greek Revival farmhouse to the doings at the nearby Cape Playhouse that you might as well be backstage. Many stars have stayed here over the past half-century, and if you're lucky you'll find a few sharing the space. The "great room" in the carriage house annex is a virtual green room: It seems to foster late-night discussions, to be continued over home-baked breakfasts at the long plank table that dominates the 1857 country kitchen. Rooms range from retro-touristy (pine paneling, etc.) to spacious and spiffy.

○ **Lighthouse Inn.** 4 Lighthouse Rd. (off Lower County Rd., $^1/_2$ mile south of Rte. 6A), W. Dennis, MA 02670. ☎ **508/398-2244.** Fax 508/398-5658. 34 rms, 27 cottages. A/C TV TEL. Summer $174–$290 double. Rates include full breakfast and dinner. MC, V. Closed mid-Oct to mid-May.

In 1938, Everett Stone acquired a decommissioned 1885 lighthouse and built a 9-acre cottage colony around it. Today his grandsons run the show, pretty much as he envisioned it. In summer, families still gather for breakfast and dinner at group tables in the camplike dining room. With a private beach, heated outdoor pool, tennis courts, and motley amusements such as miniature golf and shuffleboard right on the premises, there's plenty to do. Most families pay a small daily surcharge to enroll their kids in "InnKids," the supervised play program, and many coordinate their vacations so that they can catch up with the same group of friends year after year. The rooms aren't what you'd call fancy, but they're adequate (some have great Sound views) and you'll probably be too busy to spend much time there anyway.

Dining/Entertainment: Serving all three meals, the loftlike dining room is open to the general public. Of course, you'll have to take pot luck in terms of whom you have at your table, but that's half the fun. The prices are quite reasonable (entrees rarely exceed $16), and the menu isn't half as stuffy as you might expect. Down the road, at the entrance to the complex, the Sand Bar serves as on-site nightspot (see "The Dennises After Dark," below).

WHERE TO DINE

Keep in mind the trendy offerings of **The Mercantile,** 766 Rte. 6A, at Mercantile Place, in the center of Dennis (☎ 508/385-3877): Picture a picnic starring shrimp salad sparked with fresh mango, perhaps, or a silky chocolate cake.

Tobey Farm, on Route 6A about half a mile west of Dennis (☎ 508/385-2930), is the place for produce. **Woolfie's Home Baking,** 279 Lower County Rd. about half a mile southwest of Dennis Port (☎ 508/394-3717), makes delicious muffins, bread, and pastries.

Expensive

The Ocean House. Depot St. (about 1 mile south of Rte. 28), Dennis Port. ☎ **508/394-0700.** Reservations recommended. Main courses $10–$20. AE, DC, MC, V. Daily 5–10pm. NEW AMERICAN.

With the Sound as a glimmering backdrop, this brick bastion could have gotten away with bridge tables and lawn chairs; instead, the decor is all-out elegant (chandeliers, wood paneling, plush window treatments—the works) to match the ambitious cuisine. Chef Alain DiTomasso is similarly forthcoming, offering broccoli mousse and potato gratin, for example, alongside perfectly grilled lamb already enrobed in a rich reduction sauce graced with asparagus and baby carrots. Pan-seared scallops come accompanied with juicy porcini mushrooms, as well as fried leeks and crisp potato curls.

○ **The Red Pheasant.** 905 Main St. (about $^1/_2$ mile east of town center), Dennis. ☎ **508/ 385-2133.** Reservations recommended. Main courses $13–$21. DISC, MC, V. Late May to early Sept daily 5–10pm; call for off-season hours. NEW AMERICAN.

An enduring Cape favorite since 1977, this handsome space—an 18th-century barn turned chandlery—has managed not only to keep pace with contemporary trends, but to remain a front-runner. Chef-owner Bill Atwood has a way with local ingredients: He transforms the ubiquitous zucchini of late summer, for instance, into homemade ravioli enfolding tasty chèvre, and his signature cherrystone-and-scallop chowder gets its zip from fresh-plucked thyme. Two massive brick fireplaces tend to be the focal point in off-season, drawing in the weary—and delighted—wanderer. In fine weather the garden room exerts its own green draw.

Moderate

Swan River Seafood. 5 Lower County Rd. (at Swan Pond River, about ²/₃ mile southeast of town center), Dennis Port. ☎ **508/394-4466.** Main courses $10–$15. AE, MC, V. Daily noon–3:30pm and 5–9:30pm. Closed Oct to late May. SEAFOOD.

Every town has its own version of the fish place with the fantastic view. Here the scenic vista is relatively low-key: a marsh punctuated by an old windmill. The fish—fresh from the adjoining market—is snapping fresh and available deep-fried, as it is everywhere, but also smartly broiled or sautéed. Go for the assertive shark steak *au poivre* (with pepper) and such specialties as scrod San Sebastian, fresh filets poached in a garlicky broth.

Inexpensive

Bob Briggs' Wee Packet. 79 Depot St. (at Lower County Rd., about ¹/₃ mile south of town center), Dennis Port. ☎ **508/398-2181.** Main courses $6–$12. MC, V. Late June to early Sept daily 8am–9pm; call for off-season hours. Closed Oct–Apr. AMERICAN.

It's been Bob Briggs's place since 1949; otherwise, the name that might leap to mind would be "Mom's." This tiny joint serves terrific diner fare, plus all the requisite seafood staples, fried and broiled.

Captain Frosty's. 219 Rte. 6A (about 1 mile south of town center), Dennis. ☎ **508/385-8548.** Main courses $2–$12. No credit cards. July–Aug daily 11am–9pm; call for off-season hours. Closed late Sept to early Apr. SEAFOOD.

We've had our share of tasteless seafood seemingly deep-fried in greasy cement, thank you very much. Here the breading is light (thanks to healthy canola oil), and the fish itself is fresh off the local day boats. You won't find a more luscious lobster roll anywhere, and the clam-cake fritters seem to fly out the door.

THE DENNISES AFTER DARK

The oldest continuously active strawhat theater in the country and still one of the best, **The Cape Playhouse,** 36 Hope Lane, on Route 6A in the center of Dennis (☎ **508/385-3911;** fax 508/385-8162), was the 1927 brainstorm of Raymond Moore, who'd spent a few summers as a playwright in Provincetown and quickly tired of the strictures of "little theater." Salvaging an 1838 meetinghouse, he plunked it amid a meadow, and got his New York buddy, designer Cleon Throckmorton, to turn it into a proper theater. Even with a roof that leaked, it was an immediate success, and a parade of stars—both established and budding—trod the boards in the coming decades, from Humphrey Bogart to Tab Hunter, from Ginger Rogers to Jane Fonda (her dad spent his salad days there, too, playing opposite Bette Davis in her stage debut). Not all of today's headliners are quite as impressive (many hail from the netherworld of TV reruns), but the theater—the only Equity enterprise on the Cape—can be counted on for a varied season of polished work. Performances late June to early September, Monday through Saturday at 8pm, and Wednesday and Thursday at 2pm. Tickets run $13 to $27.

Christine's Restaurant, 581 Rte. 28 (about a quarter mile east of West Dennis (☎ **508/394-7333**), features a 300-seat show room that draws some big acts nightly in season and weekends off-season, including local jazz-great pianist Dave McKenna and all sorts of oldies bands; also on the roster are comedy acts and a Sunday night cabaret-cum-buffet. Cover varies.

The **Sand Bar,** at the Lighthouse Inn (☎ **508/398-2244**), was built in 1949, the very year Dennis went "wet." Rock King, a combination boogie-woogie pianist and comedian, still rules the evening and wows the crowd.

Sundancers, on Route 28 in West Dennis (☎ **508/394-1600**), is one of the larger dance clubs on the Cape, attracting a young clientele with an ever-changing roster of DJs and live bands, including Sunday afternoon reggae in season. Cover varies.

The **Cape Cinema,** 36 Hope Lane, off Route 6A in the center of Dennis (☎ **508/385-2503** or 508/385-5644), part of the Cape Playhouse complex, is an art-deco surprise, with a Prometheus-themed ceiling mural and folding curtain designed by artist Rockwell Kent and Broadway set designer Jo Mielziner. Independent-film maven George Mansour, curator of the Harvard Film Archive, sees to the art-house programming. That, plus the setting and seating—black leather armchairs—may spoil you forever for what passes for cinemas today. There are shows from early April to mid-November daily at 4:30, 7, and 9pm. Closed mid-November to early April.

3 The Lower Cape

Occupying the easternmost portion of historic Route 6A, **Brewster** still enjoys much the same cachet that it boasted as a high roller in the maritime trade. But for a relatively recent incursion of condos, and of course the cars, it looks much as it might have in the late 19th century, its general store still serving as a social center point. And Brewster has lately spawned several fine restaurants and become something of a magnet for gourmets.

Their distance from Boston has helped to preserve **Harwich** and Chatham from the commercialization evident elsewhere along the Sound.

The quaint village of **Harwichport** was all set for an upscale overhaul when the recession struck; faltering funds have left it in an agreeable limbo. Here, the beach is a mere block off Main Street, so the eternal summertime pleasures of a barefoot stroll capped off by an ice-cream cone are always right at hand.

Chatham, a larger, more prosperous community, is being touted by local Realtors as "the Nantucket of the Cape." Its Main Street, a gamut of appealing shops and eateries, approaches an all-American, small-town ideal—complemented nicely by a scenic lighthouse and plentiful beaches nearby.

As the gateway to the Outer Cape, where all roads merge (annoyingly), **Orleans** is a bit too frantic to offer the peace most weary vacationers seek. Its nearby cousin, East Orleans, is on the upswing as a destination, though, offering a couple of fun restaurants and—best of all—a goodly chunk of magnificent, unspoiled Cape Cod National Seashore.

BREWSTER

Brewster somehow sets itself apart. Mostly free of the commercial encroachments that have plagued the southern shore, this thriving community goes about its business as if nothing were amiss. It has even managed to absorb an intrusively huge development within its own borders, the 380-acre condo complex known as Ocean Edge, on what was once a huge private estate. The dust settles, the trees grow back, the buildings start to blend in, and it's life as usual, if a bit more closely packed. Brewster also welcomes the tens of thousands of transient campers and day-trippers who arrive each summer to enjoy the nearly 2,000 sylvan acres of Nickerson State Park.

ESSENTIALS

GETTING THERE　After crossing either the Bourne or Sagamore bridge, head east on Route 6 or 6A. Route 6A passes through the villages of West Brewster, Brewster, and East Brewster. You can also reach Brewster by taking Route 6's Exit 10 north, along Route 124. The town lies 25 miles east of Sandwich, 31 miles south of Provincetown.

VISITOR INFORMATION   Contact the **Brewster Chamber of Commerce,** 74 Locust Lane, Brewster, MA 02631 (☎ **508/255-7045**), or the **Cape Cod Chamber of Commerce,** Routes 6 and 132, Hyannis, MA 02601 (☎ **508/362-3225;** fax: 508/362-3698; Web site: **www.capecod.com**).

BEACHES & OUTDOOR PURSUITS

BEACHES   Brewster's eight bay beaches have minimal facilities, which makes for a more natural experience. When the tide is out, the "beach" extends as much as 2 miles, leaving behind tide pools to splash in and explore, and vast stretches of rippled, reddish "garnet" sand. On a good day, you can see the whole curve of the Cape, from Sandwich to Provincetown. For a **beach parking sticker** ($8 per day, $25 per week), visit the Town Hall, 2198 Rte. 6A (☎ **508/896-3701**).

- **Breakwater Beach,** off Breakwater Road, Brewster: Only a brief walk from the center of town, this calm, shallow beach (the only one with rest rooms) is ideal for young children.
- **Flax Pond** in Nickerson State Park (see "Nature Trails," below): This large freshwater pond, surrounded by pines, has a bathhouse and offers water sports rentals. The park contains two more ponds with beaches—Cliff and Little Cliff. Access and parking are free.
- **Linnells Landing Beach,** on Linnell Road in East Brewster: This half-mile bay beach is wheelchair-accessible and an ideal family location.
- **Paines Creek Beach,** off Paines Creek Road, West Brewster: With 1 1/2 miles to stretch out in, this bay beach has something to offer sun lovers and nature lovers alike.

BIKING/RECREATIONAL PATHS   The **Cape Cod Rail Trail** intersects with the 8-mile Nickerson State Park trail system at the park entrance, where there's plenty of free parking: You could follow the Rail Trail back to Dennis (about 12 miles) or onward toward Wellfleet (13 miles).

  Idle Times (☎ **508/255-8281**) provides rentals within the park, in season. Another good place to jump in is on Underpass Road about half a mile south of Route 6A. Here you'll find **Brewster Bicycle Rental,** 442 Underpass Rd. (☎ **508/ 896-8149**). Just up the hill is the well-equipped **Rail Trail Bike & Blade,** 302 Underpass Rd. (☎ **800/896-0120** or 508/896-8200).

FISHING   Brewster offers more ponds for fishing than any other town: 14 in all. Among the most popular are Cliff and Higgins ponds within Nickerson State Park, which are regularly stocked. For a license, visit the Town Hall, 2198 Rte. 6A (☎ **508/896-3701**). Brewster lacks a deep harbor, so would-be deep-sea fishers will have to head to Barnstable or, better yet, Orleans.

NATURE TRAILS   Admission is free to the two trails maintained by the Cape Cod Museum of Natural History (see below). The **South Trail,** covering a three-quarter-mile round-trip south of Route 6A, crosses a natural cranberry bog beside Paines Creek to reach a hardwood forest of beeches and tupelos; toward the end of the loop you'll come upon a "glacial erratic," a huge boulder dropped by a receding glacier. Before heading out on the quarter-mile **North Trail,** stop in at the museum for a free guide describing the local flora, including wild roses, cattails, and sumacs.

  Also accessible from the CCMNH parking lot is the **John Wing Trail,** a 1 1/2-mile network traversing 140 acres of preservation land, including upland, salt marsh, and beach. (*Note:* This can be a soggy trip. Be sure to heed the posted warnings regarding high tides, especially in spring, or you might very well find yourself stranded.) Keep an eye out for marsh hawks and blue herons.

As it crosses Route 6A, Paines Creek Road becomes Run Hill Road. Follow it to the end to reach **Punkhorn Park Lands,** an undeveloped 800-acre tract popular with mountain bikers; it features several kettle ponds, a "quaking bog," and 45 miles of dirt paths comprising three marked trails (you'll find trail guides at the trailheads).

The small **Spruce Hill Conservation Area** behind the Brewster Historical Society Museum includes a 600-foot stretch of beach, reached by a former carriage road reportedly favored by Prohibition bootleggers.

Just east of the museum is the 1,955-acre **Nickerson State Park** at Route 6 and Crosby Lane (☎ **508/896-3491**), the legacy of a vast, self-sustaining private estate that once generated its own electricity (with a horse-powered plant) and attracted notable guests, such as Pres. Grover Cleveland, with its own golf course and game preserve. Today, it's an up-with-people, back-to-nature preserve encompassing 418 campsites (reservations pour in a year in advance, but some are held open for new arrivals willing to wait a day or two), eight kettle ponds, and 8 miles of bicycle paths. The rest is trees—some 88,000 evergreens, planted by the Civilian Conservation Corps.

WATER SPORTS   Various small sailboats, kayaks, canoes, and even aquabikes are available seasonally at **Jack's Boat Rentals** (☎ **508/896-8556**), located on Flax Pond within Nickerson State Park.

A PAIR OF MUSEUMS

✪ **Cape Cod Museum of Natural History.** 869 Rte. 6A (about 2 miles west of town center). ☎ **800/479-3867** or 508/896-3867. Admission $5 adults, $2 children 6–14. Mid-Apr to mid-Oct Mon–Sat 9:30am–4:30pm, Sun 10am–4:30pm. Closed Mon off-season.

Long before "ecology" became a buzzword, noted naturalist writer John Haye helped to found a museum that celebrates—and helps to preserve—Cape Cod's unique landscape. Open since 1954, the CCMNH was also prescient in presenting interactive exhibits. The display on whales, for instance, invites the viewer to press a button to hear eerie whale songs; the children's exhibits include an animal puppet theater. All ages are invariably intrigued by the "live hive"—like an ant farm, only with busy bees. The bulk of the museum, naturally, is outdoors, where 85 acres invite exploration (see "Nature Trails," above). There's also an ongoing, on-site archaeology lab on Wing Island, which was thought to have sheltered one of Brewster's first settlers, the Quaker John Wing, who was driven from Sandwich in the mid-17th century by religious persecution, and before him, summering native tribes dating back 10 millennia or more, when the Cape and Islands were still all of a piece. A true force in fostering environmental appreciation, the museum sponsors all sorts of activities, from lectures and concerts to marsh cruises and "eco-treks" (including a sleep-over on uninhabited Monomoy Island off Chatham).

Stony Brook Grist Mill and Museum. 830 Stony Brook Rd. (at the intersection of Satucket Rd. in town center), W. Brewster. ☎ **508/896-6745.** Free admission. July–Aug Fri 2–5pm; May–June Thurs–Sat 2–5pm. Closed Sept–Apr.

A rustic mill beside a stream. . . . It may not look it, but this was once one of the most active manufacturing communities in New England, cranking out cloth, boots, and ironwork for over a century, starting with the American Revolution. The one remaining structure was built in 1873, toward the end of West Brewster's commercial run, near the site of a 1663 water-powered mill, America's first. After decades of producing overalls and, later, ice cream (with ice dredged from the adjoining pond), the

Now that you know your way around, let's move on to something simple.

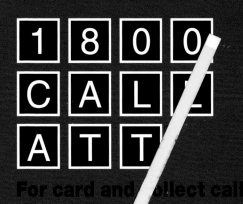

1 8 0 0
C A L L
A T T

For card and collect calls.

1 800 CALL ATT is the only number you need to know when you're away from home. Dial it from any phone, anywhere* and your calls will always go through to AT&T.

*Available in U.S. and Canada. © 1997 AT&T

AT&T

Riding the Cape Cod Rail Trail

The 25-mile Cape Cod Rail Trail is one of New England's longest and most popular bike paths. Once a bed of the Penn Central Railroad, the trail is relatively flat and straight. On weekends in summer months, you have to contend with dogs, clumsy in-line skaters, young families, and bikers who whip by you on their way to becoming the next Greg LeMond. Yet, if you want to venture away from the coast and see some of the Cape's countryside without having to drive and deal with traffic jams, this is one of the only ways to do it.

The trail starts in South Wellfleet on Lecount Hollow Road or in South Dennis on Mass. 134, depending on which way you want to ride. Beginning in South Wellfleet, the path cruises by purple wildflowers, flowering dogwoods, and small maples where red-winged blackbirds and goldfinches nest. In Orleans, you have to ride on Rock Harbor and West roads until the City Council decides to complete the trail. At least you get a good view of the boats lining Rock Harbor. Clearly marked signs lead back to the Rail Trail, on which you'll soon enter Nickerson State Park bike trails, or continue straight through Brewster to a series of swimming holes—Seymour, Long, and Hinckleys ponds. A favorite picnic spot is the Pleasant Lake General Store in Harwich. Shortly afterwards, you cross over U.S. 6 on Mass. 124 before veering right through farmland, soon ending in South Dennis.

—*by Stephen Jermanok*

factory was bought by the town and fitted out as a corn mill, with period millstones. Volunteers now demonstrate, and urge onlookers to get in on the action.

WHERE TO STAY

The Bramble Inn. 2019 Rte. 6A (about ⅓ mile east of town center), Brewster, MA 02631. ☎ **508/896-7644.** Fax 508/896-9322. 8 rms. A/C TV. Summer $95–$125 double. Rates include full breakfast. AE, DISC, MC, V. Closed mid-Jan to mid-Mar.

This is really more of a compound than an inn, per se. Cliff and Ruth Manchester oversee three lovely old buildings: two rambling mid-19th-century homes, decorated in a breezy, country-casual manner, and, across the street, a formal 1792 Federal manse done up in period style, with romantic canopied four-poster beds. Horse lovers will love the rustic-beamed suite with its vintage riding gear. Ruth is a phenomenal chef (see "Where to Dine," below), so you know you'll be in good hands come breakfast time.

✪ **Captain Freeman Inn.** 15 Breakwater Rd. (off Rte. 6, in town center), Brewster, MA 02631. ☎ **800/843-4664** or 508/896-7481. Fax 508/896-5618. 6 rms (3 with shared bath), 3 suites. A/C TV TEL. Summer $90–$205 double. Rates include full breakfast and afternoon tea. AE, MC, V.

The creation of an exemplary country inn is part business, part art, and Carol Covitz Edmondson, the ex–marketing director behind this beauty, poured plenty of both into her mint green 1866 Victorian. The "luxury suites," each complete with fireplace and a private porch with cloverleaf hot tub, incorporate all kinds of extras: a canopied, four-poster queen-sized bed; a love seat facing the cable TV/VCR (she has a store's worth of tapes available for loan); even a little fridge prestocked with cold soda, juices, and mineral water. The plainer rooms are just as pretty—one nice feature of the porch-encircled house is that the second-story windows reach almost to the floor. The three dormered third-floor rooms, though smallish, have enviable water views and are nicely priced; families often claim the whole floor. Delectable, yet healthy breakfasts are served in bed, in the elegant parlor, or on a screened porch over-looking the heated pool and a lush lawn set up for badminton and croquet. Breakwater Landing is a bucolic 10-minute walk, or just moments away if you avail yourself of a loaner bike.

Ocean Edge Resort. 2660 Main St. (about 2⅓ miles east of town center), Brewster, MA 02631. ☎ **800/343-6074** or 508/896-9000. Fax 508/896-9123. 90 rms, about 125 condos (depending on the rental pool). A/C TV TEL. Summer $250–$295 double, condo from $250. Golf, tennis, and holiday weekend packages available. AE, DC, DISC, MC, V.

If the rates strike you as high, consider the built-ins: two fitness rooms and six pools (two indoor, four outdoor) scattered around an intensively landscaped 380-acre prop-erty, part of which fronts a private 1,000-foot stretch of bay beach. If you're up for the kind of stay-put vacation where every need is met right on the premises (for a price), this might make a good choice, but you're liable to miss out on the quirks that constitute a good portion of the Cape's charms.

The entire tract, plus the nearby Nickerson State Forest, once belonged to a single family, whose prosperity appears to have been dogged by tragedy. Samuel Mayo Nickerson, a Chatham boy who made good as a Chicago banker, built the original mansion, Fieldstone Hall, in 1890 as a gift for his only son, Roland, who died 2 weeks after it burned down in 1906. His widow, Addie, built a 400-foot-long Renaissance Revival replacement—now a conference center and hotel—with an eye to meeting fire codes; it's rather homely, if grandiose, and not exactly enhanced by the addition of dense condo accommodations begun in the building boom of the early 1980s.

Dining/Entertainment: There are four restaurants on the grounds: the refined Ocean Grille and British-style Bayzo's Pub within the mansion, and Mulligan's (New American) and the Reef Cafe (casual Caribbean) overlooking the golf course.

Services: "Kidstart," a supervised program for children 4 to 12.

Facilities: The 18-hole golf course features Scottish pot bunkers. There are 11 ten-nis courts on the grounds: 5 clay and 6 Plexipave. Instruction and clinic packages are offered in both sports.

✪ Old Sea Pines Inn. 2553 Main St. (about 1 mile east of town center), Brewster, MA 02631. ☎ **800/843-4664** or 508/896-6114. Fax 508/896-2094. 19 rms (5 with shared bath), 2 suites. A/C TV. Summer $50–$105 double, $85–$135 suite. Rates include full breakfast and afternoon tea. AE, CB, DC, DISC, MC, V. Closed Jan–Mar.

In the early part of the century, this grand 1907 shingle-style mansion was the site of the Sea Pines School of Charm and Personality for Young Women. A great deal of that charm is still evident: In fact, the hosts, Michele and Steve Rowan, have done their best to re-create the gracious ambiance of days gone by. The parlor and expan-sive porch lined with rockers are just as the young ladies might have found them, as are a handful of rather minuscule boarding-school–scale rooms on the top floor. This is one of the few places on the Cape where solo travelers can find a single room and pay no surcharge. The added annex is fully wheelchair-accessible (another rarity among historic inns); its rooms are outright playful, with colorful touches, includ-ing hot pink TVs. Steve does double duty as the breakfast chef (dinner, too, in July and August) and prepares good old-fashioned food.

WHERE TO DINE
Very Expensive

✪ The Bramble Inn Restaurant. 2019 Main St. (about ⅓ mile east of Rte. 124). ☎ **508/896-7644.** Fax 508/896-9322. Reservations required. Prix fixe $38–$55. AE, DISC, MC, V. June to mid-Oct daily 6–9pm; call for off-season hours. Closed Jan–Apr. NEW AMERICAN.

There's an impromptu feel to this intimate restaurant, comprised of five small rooms, each imbued with its own personality, from sporting (the "tack room") to best Sunday behavior (the elegant parlor). One-of-a-kind antique table settings add to the charm. Such niceties fade to mere backdrop, though, beside Ruth Manchester's extraordinary cuisine. A four-course (usually six-option) menu that evolves every month gives her free rein to follow fresh enthusiasms, as well as seasonal delicacies. She has a solid grounding in Mediterranean cuisines and a gift for improvisation.

Chillingsworth. 2449 Main St. (about 1 mile east of town center). ☎ **508/896-3640.** Reservations required; jacket requested. Prix fixe $40–$56. AE, DC, MC, V. July–Aug Tues–Sun noon–2:30pm and 6–9:30pm; call for off-season hours. Closed late Nov to mid-May. FRENCH.

A longtime contender for the title of best restaurant on the Cape, Chillingsworth is certainly the fanciest, what with antique appointments reaching back several centuries and a seven-course set menu that will challenge even the most shameless of gourmands to clean their plates. There's a rote quality to the ritual, however, that can undercut what might otherwise amount to a superb culinary experience. See if you can ignore all the rigmarole and just focus on the taste sensations, which are indeed sensational. Or for a sampling, lunch or dine (sans reservations) in the à la carte Bistro.

Expensive

✪ **The Brewster Fish House.** 2208 Main St. (about ¹/₂ mile east of town center). ☎ **508/896-7867.** Reservations not accepted. Main courses $12–$22. MC, V. June–early Sept Mon–Sat 11:30am–3pm and 5–10pm; Sun noon–3pm and 5–9:30pm; call for off-season hours. Closed mid-Dec to mid-Apr. NEW AMERICAN.

Spare and handsome as a Shaker refectory, this small restaurant bills itself as "nonconforming" and delivers on the promise. The approach to seafood borders on genius: squid delectably tenderized in a marinade of soy and ginger, or silky-tender walnut-crusted ocean catfish accompanied by kale sautéed in marsala. Better get there early if you want to get in.

High Brewster. 964 Satucket Rd. (off Rte. 6A, about 2 miles southwest of town center). ☎ **508/896-3636.** Reservations required. Prix fixe $28–$46. AE, MC, V. Late May to mid-Oct daily 6–9pm; call for off-season hours. Closed Jan–Mar. NEW AMERICAN.

By candlelight, the close yet cozy keeping rooms and paneled parlors of this 1738 colonial Cape are irresistibly romantic, and Scott Anderson's sensual, sophisticated cuisine only serves to intensify the mood. His dishes tend to be bold in the modern manner—wild-mushroom ravioli, for instance, with herb aioli and candied shallots, or salmon encrusted in scallions and couscous—yet he's good at adapting local ingredients and traditional preparations. Celebrate the harvest with apple crisp topped with homemade apple rum ice cream.

Moderate

Beechcroft Bistro. At the Beechcroft Inn, 1360 Rte. 6A (about 1¹/₂ miles west of town center). ☎ **508/896-9534.** Reservations recommended. Main courses $8–$16. AE, CB, DC, DISC, MC, V. Mid-May to mid-Sept Wed–Sun 5:30–9pm; call for off-season schedule. INTERNATIONAL.

Generosity and warmth are the key ingredients of bistro fare, and you'll find plenty of both in the cozy fireplaced pub and more formal dining room. The fresh seafood "bisque du jour" is just the ticket at the end of a blustery day. Lighter options include creatively sauced pastas and Boboli pizzas such as the "Mykonos" (eggplant and feta and olives, oh my), and there's usually a choice of at least five entrees, including sole Tivoli—wrapped around a core of seafood stuffing and artichoke heart, and topped with lemon butter. You're welcome, too, to stop in just for dessert, subject to the chef's whim but usually something fiendish: Beware the Chocolate Oblivion!

The Tower House Restaurant. 2671 Rte. 6A (about 1 mile east of town center). ☎ **508/896-2671.** Reservations not accepted. Main courses $8–$18. MC, V. Late May to mid-Oct daily 8am–9pm; call for off-season hours. INTERNATIONAL.

Every beach town needs a good cafe where the hours are as you like them (so you can sun at will). This one is unusually good-looking, and the food is reliable and competently done, if not exactly radical; the "fish market specials" are apt to be your best bet.

Inexpensive

Cobie's. 3260 Rte. 6A (about 2 miles east of Brewster center). ☎ **508/896-7021.** Most items under $10. No credit cards. Daily 11am–9pm. Closed mid-Sept to late May. AMERICAN.

This picture-perfect clam shack has been dishing out exemplary fried clams, lobster rolls, foot-long hot dogs, black-and-white frappes, and all the other beloved staples of summer since 1948.

THE HARWICHES

Harwich Port is the quintessential sleepy seaside village, not too mucked up—as yet—by the creeping commercialization of Route 28. The town's main claim to fame was as the birthplace, in 1846, of commercial cranberry cultivation: The "bitter berry," as the Narragansetts called it, is now Massachusetts's leading agricultural product. The curious can find displays on this and other local distinctions at the Brooks Academy Museum in the inland town of Harwich. The incurious, or merely vacation-minded, can loll on the beach.

ESSENTIALS

GETTING THERE　From the Mid-Cape Highway, take Exit 10 south along Route 124. Harwich is located at the intersection of Route 39, where the two routes converge and head southwest to Harwich Port and West Harwich, both located on Route 28. West Harwich is also on Route 28, several miles eastward, and East Harwich (more easily reached from Route 6's Exit 11), is inland, a few miles northeast.

VISITOR INFORMATION　Contact the **Harwich Chamber of Commerce,** Route 28, Harwich Port, MA 02646 (☎ **508/432-1600;** fax 508/430-2105).

BEACHES & OUTDOOR PURSUITS

BEACHES　The Harwich coast is basically one continuous beach punctuated by the occasional harbor. Harwich Port is so close to the Sound, it's a snap to walk the block or two to the water—provided you find a **parking place** in town (try the lot near the Chamber of Commerce booth in the center of town). Parking right at the beach is pretty much limited to residents and renters, who can obtain a weekly sticker for $25 at the Town Hall, 732 Main St., Harwich (☎ **508/430-7513**).

A free trolley, the **Harwich Beach Shuttle** (☎ **800/352-7155**), heads up and down Route 28 in season, easing access for all.

- **Red River Beach,** off Uncle Venies Road, south of Route 28 in South Harwich: This is the only Sound beach in town offering parking for day-trippers (though they still have to turn up early); the fee is $5 on weekdays or $10 weekends and holidays. Marked off with stone jetties, this narrow, 2,700-foot beach has full facilities.
- **Sand Pond,** off Great Western Road near Depot Street: This area honors the weekly beach parking sticker, as do the two parking lots at Long Pond.

- **Hinckleys Pond** and **Seymour Pond,** west of Route 124 and right off the Rail Trail, and **Bucks Pond** off Depot Road at Route 39 northeast of Harwich, welcome all comers.

BIKING/RECREATIONAL PATHS   Transecting Harwich for about 5 miles, the **Cape Cod Rail Trail** skirts some pretty ponds in the western part before veering north and zigzagging toward Brewster along Route 124. For rentals and information, contact the **Harwich Port Bike Co.,** 431 Main St. (☎ **508/430-0200**), which can also provide in-line skates, kayaks, and canoes.

FISHING   There are six ponds available for fishing in the Harwich area, as well as extensive shellfishing in season; for details and a license, visit the Town Hall, 732 Main St. in Harwich (☎ **508/430-7513**).

For supplies and instruction, visit **Fishing the Cape,** at the Harwich Commons, Routes 137 and 39 (☎ **508/432-1200**); it's the official Cape headquarters for the **Orvis Saltwater Fly-Fishing School** (☎ **800/235-9763**).

Several **deep-sea fishing boats** operate out of Saquatucket Harbor (off Route 28, about half a mile east of Harwich Port), including the 33-footers *Fish Tale* (☎ **508/432-3783**) and *Arlie eX* (☎ **508/430-2454**), and the 65-foot *Yankee* (☎ **508/432-2520**). The *Golden Eagle* (☎ **508/432-5611**), offering evening bluefish trips several times a week, heads out from Wychmere Harbor.

NATURE TRAILS   The largest preserve in Harwich is the 245-acre **Bells Neck Conservation Area,** north of Route 28 near the Dennis border. It encompasses the **Herring River,** ideal for birding and canoeing (see "Water Sports," below).

WATER SPORTS   **Cape Water Sports,** 337 Rte. 28 in Harwich Port (☎ **508/432-7079**), offers lessons and rentals on several beaches: Available craft include canoes, sailboards, Sunfish, and sailboats up to 42 feet.

Meandering from a reservoir south to the Sound, West Harwich's **Herring River**—a natural herring run framed by cattail marsh—is ideal for canoeing. The **Harwich Port Bike Co.,** 431 Main St. (☎ **508/430-0200**), offers family tours, and rents out canoes and kayaks.

Cape Sail, out of Saquatucket Harbor (☎ **508/896-2730**), offers sailing lessons as well as private charters.

Cape Cod Divers, 815 Main St., Harwich Port (☎ **888/797-DIVE** or 508/432-9035), is scuba central, offering rentals and lessons, a training pool, and charter trips to shipwreck sites.

WHERE TO STAY

The Beach House Inn. 4 Braddock Lane. (off Bank St., south of Rte. 28 in the center of town), Harwich Port, MA 02646. ☎ **800/870-4405** or 508/432-4444. 10 rms. A/C TV TEL. Summer $165–$275 double. Rates include continental breakfast. DISC, MC, V.

One of the few waterside places to remain open throughout the year (a boon for solitary-minded beachcombers who don't mind the off-season chill), this intensively renovated 1920s inn is a real find. The original rooms still boast their varnished pine paneling, as well as updated whirlpool baths, and the four glorious front rooms each feature a fireplace or deck as well, plus sweeping views of Nantucket Sound.

The Commodore Inn. 30 Earle Rd. (about ¹/₂ mile south of town center, off Rte. 28), W. Harwich, MA 02671. ☎ **800/368-1180** or 508/432-1180. Fax 508/432-4634. 27 rms. A/C TV TEL. Summer $119–$175 double. Rates include full breakfast. AE, MC, V. Closed Jan–Feb.

From the outside, it looks like an especially nice motel encircling a heated pool; from the inside, the rooms resemble upscale condos, with cathedral ceilings and handsome, functional furniture. Guests are treated to a buffet breakfast, and special dinners (for example, a barbecue or clambake) are offered regularly. This is one of the few small properties on the Cape that can accommodate meetings and provide business amenities.

Sandpiper Beach Inn. 16 Bank St. (south of Rte. 28 in the center of town), Harwich Port, MA 02646. ☎ **800/432-2234** or 508/432-0485. 17 rms, 2 suites. A/C TV TEL. Summer $120–$225 double, $230 suite. Rates include continental breakfast. AE, MC, V. Closed Nov–Mar.

Plunked right on the beach, this motel looks far too tasteful to be a motel. The breezy rooms are brightened by splashy fabrics and pretty wicker furniture. For those who appreciate country-inn aesthetics but prefer a more impersonal atmosphere, this could be just the ticket.

WHERE TO DINE

The Cape SeaGrille. 31 Sea St. (south of Rte. 28 in the center of town). ☎ **508/432-4745.** Reservations recommended. Main courses $11–$20. AE, MC, V. July–Aug daily 5–9pm; call for off-season hours. Closed Jan–Mar. NEW AMERICAN.

A pair of ambitious chef-owners are the power behind the stove of this upscale enterprise occupying the pared-down, peach-toned shell of an ordinary beach house. The menu is under constant revision, the better to springboard off market finds, but among the keepers are a refreshing appetizer platter of marinated seafoods (from ceviche to salmon carpaccio), and a grilled medley starring lobster, shrimp, and bacon-wrapped swordfish. City sophisticates who insist on creativity and innovation will find this the most consistently rewarding source in town.

Goucho's Mexican Restaurant and Bar. 403 Lower County Rd. (off Rte. 28 about ¹/₂ mile west of town center). ☎ **508/432-7768.** Main courses $6–$14. MC, V. May–Sept daily 4pm–midnight. Closed mid-Oct to Mar. MEXICAN.

Something about sultry summer nights seems to call for spicy Mexican fare washed down with tart margaritas. There's nothing about this buttoned-up country house to suggest authenticity, until you reach the interior—convincingly converted with adobe-style walls and strategic serapes. All the addictive traditional dishes are available, from fajitas to flautas, along with some peculiar cross-pollinations such as the "Philly burrito" (featuring sliced steak).

L'Alouette. 787 Rte. 28 (about ¹/₂ mile east of town center). ☎ **508/430-0405.** Reservations recommended. Main courses $15–$23. AE, DC, DISC, MC, V. Tues–Sun 5–9pm; Sun noon–2:30pm. FRENCH.

Nothing can quite duplicate the seductive aromas of an authentic French restaurant. The secrets are all in the stock, and chef Louis Bastres, formerly of Biarritz, of course makes his from scratch. He's a strict classicist (none of this *nouvelle* nonsense): Specialties include such time-honored dishes as bouillabaisse and chateaubriand.

Thompson's Clam Bar. 594 Rte. 28 (in the center of town). ☎ **508/430-1239.** Reservations not accepted. Main courses $15–$22. AE, DC, DISC, MC, V. Daily noon–9pm. Closed mid-Sept to mid-June. AMERICAN.

Relocated from its perch on the harbor, where it had evolved from a fish market in 1949, this beloved local restaurant may have lost its view (and ambiance) but retains its all-American menu. Seafood—shucked, steamed, fried, baked, you name it—continues to be the main event, though carnivores are hardly ignored. Still going strong after all these years are such classic New England desserts as Indian pudding and strawberry shortcake.

CHATHAM

Sticking out like a sore elbow (and fortuitously removed from the tourist flow), Chatham was naturally one of the first spots to attract early explorers. Samuel de

Champlain stopped by in 1606 but got into a tussle with the prior occupants over some copper cooking pots and had to leave in a hurry. The first colonist to stick around was William Nickerson, from Yarmouth, who befriended a local sachem (tribal leader) and built a house beside his wigwam in 1656. To this day, listings for Nickersons still occupy a half-page in the Cape Cod phone book.

Chatham, along with Provincetown, is the only area on the Cape to support a commercial fishing fleet—against increasing odds. Overfishing has resulted in closely monitored limits, to give the stock time to bounce back. Boats must now go out as far as a hundred miles to catch their fill. Despite the difficulties, it's a way of life few locals would willingly relinquish.

As in Provincetown, there's surprisingly little animosity between the hard-working residents and the summer visitors at play, perhaps because it's clear that tourist dollars are helping to preserve this lovely town.

ESSENTIALS

GETTING THERE   After crossing either the Bourne or Sagamore bridge, head east on Route 6 and take Exit 11 south (Route 137) to Route 28. From this intersection, the village of South Chatham is about half a mile west, and West Chatham about 1¹/₂ miles east. Chatham itself is about 2 miles farther east on Route 28. The town lies 32 miles east of Sandwich, 24 miles south of Provincetown.

VISITOR INFORMATION   Contact the **Chatham Chamber of Commerce,** 533 Main St., Chatham, MA 02633 (☎ **800/715-5567** or 508/945-5199).

BEACHES & OUTDOOR PURSUITS

BEACHES   Chatham has an unusual array of beach styles, from the peaceful shores of the Nantucket Sound to the treacherous, shifting shoals along the Atlantic. For information on **beach stickers** ($7 per day, $35 per week), call Town Hall (☎ **508/945-5100**).

- **Cockle Cove Beach, Ridgevale Beach, and Hardings Beach:** Lined up along the Sound, each at the end of its namesake road south of Route 28, these family-pleasing beaches offer gentle surf suitable for all ages, as well as full facilities.
- **Forest Beach:** No longer an officially recognized town beach (there's no lifeguard), this Sound landing near the Harwich border is still popular, especially for boardsailing.
- **Oyster Pond Beach,** off Route 28: Only a block from Chatham's Main Street, this sheltered saltwater pond (with rest rooms) swarms with children.
- **Chatham Light Beach:** Located directly below the lighthouse parking lot (where stopovers are limited to 30 minutes), this narrow stretch of sand is easy to get to: just walk down the stairs. Currents here can be tricky and swift, though, so swimming is discouraged.
- **South Beach:** A former island jutting out slightly to the south of the Chatham Light, this glorified sandbar can be equally dangerous, so heed posted warnings and content yourself with strolling or, at most, wading.
- **North Beach:** Extending all the way south from Orleans, this 5-mile barrier beach is accessible from Chatham only by boat; for a fee, you can hop a **water taxi** from the Chatham Fish Pier on Shore Road (☎ **508/430-2346**). Inquire about other possible drop-off points if you'd like to beach around.

BIKING/RECREATIONAL PATHS   Though Chatham has no separate recreational path per se, a bike/blading lane makes a scenic 8-mile circuit of town, heading south onto "The Neck," east to the Chatham Light, up Shore Road all the way to North Chatham, and back to the center of town. A descriptive brochure prepared by the **Chatham Chamber of Commerce** (☎ **800/715-5567** or 508/945-0342) shows the suggested route. Rentals are available at **Bikes & Blades,** 195 Crowell Rd., Chatham (☎ 508/945-7600).

FISHING   Chatham has five ponds and lakes that permit fishing; Goose Pond off Fisherman's Landing is among the top spots. For saltwater fishing from land, try the fishing bridge on Bridge Street at the southern end of Mill Pond. First, though, get a license at the Town Hall, 549 Main St. (☎ **508/945-5101**). Shellfishing licenses are available at the Town Hall Annex on George Ryder Road in West Chatham (☎ **508/945-5180**).

If you want to go deep, sign on with the *Booby Hatch* (☎ **508/430-2312**), a 33-foot sportfisherman out of West Chatham, or the *Banshee* (☎ **508/945-0403**) in Stage Harbor.

NATURE TRAILS   Heading southeast from the Hardings Beach parking lot (see "Beaches," above), the 2-mile round-trip **Seaside Trail** offers beautiful parallel panoramas of Nantucket Sound and Oyster Pond River; keep an eye out for nesting pairs of horned lark.

Access to 40-acre **Morris Island,** southwest of the Chatham Light, is easy: You can walk or drive across and start right in on a marked three-quarter-mile trail. Heed the high tide as advised, though—it can come in surprisingly quickly, leaving you stranded.

Chatham's natural bonanza lies southward: the uninhabited ✪ **Monomoy Island,** 2,750 acres of brush-covered sand favored by some 285 species of migrating birds as the perfect pit stop along the Atlantic Flyway. Hundreds of harbor and gray seals now carpet the coastline from late November through May. Shuttle service to South Island is available aboard the *Rip Ryder* out of the Stage Harbor Marina (☎ **508/945-5450**), but you'll get a lot more out of the trip—and probably leave this unspoiled landscape in better shape—if you hire a naturalist.

Both the **Wellfleet Bay Wildlife Sanctuary,** operated by the Audubon Society (☎ **508/349-2615**), and Brewster's **Cape Cod Museum of Natural History** (☎ **508/896-3867**) offer guided trips to Monomoy Island. About a dozen times each summer, the museum even organizes sleep-overs in the island's only surviving structure, a clapboard "keeper's house" flanked by an 1849 lighthouse.

WATER SPORTS   Seaworthy vessels, from surf- and sailboards to paddle craft and Sunfish, can be rented from **Monomoy Sail and Cycle,** 275 Rte. 28, North Chatham (☎ **508/945-0811**). Pleasant Bay, the Cape's largest embayment, is the best place to play, for those with sufficient experience; if the winds don't seem to be going your way, try Forest Beach on the South Chatham shore.

SHOPPING

Chatham, with its tree-shaded Main Street lined with specialty stores, offers wonderful shopping and strolling. The goods tend to be on the conservative side, but every so often you'll happen upon some great hedonistic find.

Among the shops to check out are **Amazing Lace,** 726 Rte. 28, in the center of town (☎ **508/945-4023**), which offers one of the best collections of vintage clothing on the Cape. **Mildred Georges Antiques,** 447 Main St. (☎ **508/945-1939**), is a rewarding jumble of a shop. Nearby, **Midsummer Nights,** 471 Main St. (☎ **508/945-5562**), is a purveyor of luxurious personal-care products and boudoir accessories, and **The Spyglass,** 618 Main St. (☎ **508/945-9686**), sells ancient nautical instruments.

Other Chatham shops of note include **1736 House Antiques,** 1731 Rte. 28, about half a mile east of Route 137 (☎ **508/945-5690**); **Chatham Glass,** 17 Balfour Lane, off Route 28, about a mile west of the Chatham rotary (☎ **508/945-5547**), with outstanding handblown glassworks; and **Chatham Pottery,** 2568 Rte. 28, west of the intersection with Route 137, (☎ **508/430-2191**), where Gill Wilson (potter) and Margaret Wilson-Grey (glazer) display their striking stoneware.

WHERE TO STAY

Very Expensive

Chatham Bars Inn. Shore Rd. (off Seaview St., about ¹/₂ mile northwest of town center), Chatham, MA 02633. ☎ **800/527-4884** or 508/945-0096. Fax 508/945-5491. 132 rms, 20 suites. A/C TV TEL. Summer $190–$375 double, $405–$675 1-bedroom suite, $580–$1,000 2-bedroom suite. MAP and off-season packages available. AE, DC, MC, V.

A private hunting lodge built for a Boston family in 1914, this curved and colon-naded brick building—surrounded by 26 shingled cottages on 20 acres—has regained its glory days through renovations. It lends itself well to relaxing, with private bal-conies pitched off most of the rooms, and a large and cushy lobby that clearly invites lingering. The best spot to take in the sweeping sea views is the breezy veranda.

Dining/Entertainment: Options include the formal Main Dining Room (see "Where to Dine," below); the adjoining North Beach Tavern & Grille, which serves much the same menu, with more choices and hours; and the seasonal Beach House Grill, offering breakfast, lunch, and light dinners.

Services: Concierge, room service, baby-sitting, and "Beach Buddies," a compli-mentary children's program for ages 3¹/₂ and up.

Facilities: Fitness room, four all-weather tennis courts, putting green (Seaside Links, a town-owned 9-hole course open to the public, adjoins the resort), shuffle-board, croquet, and volleyball. There is a heated outdoor pool beside a quarter-mile private beach, where you can also catch a complimentary launch to Nauset Beach.

Pleasant Bay Village. 1191 Rte. 28 (about 3 miles north of Chatham center), Chathamport, MA 02633. ☎ **800/547-1011** or 508/945-1133. Fax 508/945-9701. 48 rms, 10 suites. A/C TV TEL. Summer $135–$245 double, $285–$415. 1- or 2-bedroom suite. AE, MC, V. Closed Nov–Apr.

Owner Howard Gamsey is a prodigious gardener: Over the past quarter-century, he has transformed what was an ordinary motel into a playful Zen paradise, where a waterfall cascades through a colorful rock garden into a stone-edged pool dotted with lily pads and flashing koi. Actually, he has poured that kind of attention into the entire 6-acre complex. The rooms and cottages, done up in restful pastels, are unusu-ally pleasant, and the breakfast room features antique tables and kilims. In summer, you can order lunch from the grill without having to bestir yourself from the heated pool.

✪ **Wequassett Inn.** 178 Rte. 28 (about 5 miles northwest of town center), Chatham, MA 02633. ☎ **800/225-7125** or 508/432-5400. Fax 508/432-1915. 104 rms. A/C MINIBAR TV TEL. Summer $230–$480 double. MAP and FAP plans available. AE, DC, DISC, MC, V. Closed Nov–May.

A virtual village occupying its own little cove, this low-key, 22-acre complex should quash any preconceived notions of what constitutes a cottage colony. Tucked amid the woods along the shore, 20 modest dwellings, built in the 1940s, harbor roomy quarters done up in an opulent country style: They cost a bit more than the 56 more modern "villa" rooms but, with their picturesque settings, are definitely worth the extra money. This is one of those places where you can escape the real world for a few days.

Dining/Entertainment: The 18th-century Eben Ryder House is home to an excellent restaurant (see "Where to Dine," below); lighter fare is served at the Pool Bar & Grille from 10am to 6pm.

Services: Concierge; instruction in tennis, sailing, and saltwater fly-fishing (inquire about clinic packages); complimentary van service to two public golf courses in Harwich and Brewster, and to Chatham and Orleans; box lunches.

Facilities: Access (for a fee) to five all-weather Plexipave tennis courts; bikes and sailboat rentals; and croquet and volleyball equipment. A fitness room (with weights and aerobics videotapes) adjoins the heated pool set at the neck of a calm beach. Nauset Beach is a 15-minute ride away via the inn's Power Skiff; bay tours and fishing charters can also be arranged. Seaplane sightseeing tours take off from the inn's own dock; charters are available to the islands or the city.

Expensive

✪ **Captain's House Inn.** 369–377 Old Harbor Rd. (about ¹/₂ mile north of the Rotary), Chatham, MA 02633. ☎ **800/315-0728** or 508/945-0127. Fax 508/945-0866. 14 rms, 2 suites. A/C. Summer $135–$325 double. Rates include full breakfast and afternoon tea. AE, MC, V.

This 1839 Greek Revival house, along with a cottage and carriage house set on 2 meticulously maintained acres, is a shining example of its era and style. The rooms, named for Capt. Hiram Harding's ships, are richly furnished, with a preponderance of canopied four-posters, beamed ceilings, and, in some cases, brick hearths.

This is one of the few B&Bs to serve the morning meal at noncommunal tables (a thoughtful touch for those of us slow to rev up, sociability-wise). The window-walled breakfast room is also the site of a traditional tea—presided over by innkeeper Jan McMasters, formerly of Bournemouth in Great Britain, who knows how to pour a proper cuppa.

Chatham Wayside Inn. 512 Main St. (in the center of town), Chatham, MA 02633. ☎ **800/391-5734** or 508/945-5550. Fax 508/945-3407. 56 rms. A/C TV TEL. Summer $145–$310 double, $285–$310 suite. Off-season packages available. AE, DISC, MC, V.

Resurrected from the brink of dereliction, this former stagecoach stop dating from 1860 has reassumed its rightful stature. Don't expect any musty antique trappings: This is a thoroughly modern renovation, with lush carpeting, a warehouse's worth of Waverly fabrics, and polished reproduction furnishings, including four-posters. The restaurant serves sophisticated New American fare, indoors and out, and the prize room boast patios or balconies overlooking the town bandstand.

✪ **Port Fortune Inn.** 201 Main St. (on the shore, near Chatham Light), Chatham, MA 02663. ☎ **800/750-0792** or phone/fax 508/945-0792. 14 rms. Summer $110–$160 double. Rates include continental breakfast. MC, V. Closed Jan–Mar.

For those never quite satisfied unless they're practically in the water, this B&B is only steps from South Beach. The flashy salmon awnings hint at high style lurking within this classic shingled cottage (formerly named Inn Among Friends), and the living room has it in spades. The bedrooms are fairly subdued by comparison, but perfectly cozy; all rooms have queen-sized beds.

Moderate

The Seafarer of Chatham. 2079 Rte. 28 (about ¹/₂ mile east of Rte. 137), W. Chatham, MA 02669. ☎ **800/786-2772** or 508/432-1739. 20 rms. A/C TV TEL. Summer $98–$145 double. AE, MC, V.

Convenient to Chatham's Sound-side beaches (Ridgevale Beach is about half a mile due south), this personable Cape-style motel is shielded from the road by stately trees. Innkeeper Cathleen Houhoulis has decorated the spotless rooms with Early American–style stenciling, and both she and her husband, John, take pains to familiarize newcomers with the area. Behind the low-slung building you'll find a sheltered garden—sans pool, the better to celebrate the peace and quiet.

WHERE TO DINE

Very Expensive

⭐ **Eben Ryder House.** Wequassett Inn on Pleasant Bay, 178 Rte. 28 (about 5 miles northwest of town center). ☎ **800/352-7169** or 508/432-5400. Fax 508/432-1915. Reservations recommended. Jacket requested. Main courses $18–$32. AE, DC, DISC, MC, V. Daily 7am–10pm. Closed Nov–May. NEW AMERICAN.

Reliably, season after season, Frank McMullen has proved himself to be a deft and often dazzling chef. Guests would surely squawk if some of his cherished dishes were ever supplanted: The saffron-suffused bisque of Nantucket scallops, for instance, is a definite keeper, as is the Lobster Sinclair—thoughtfully taken out of the shell and plumped atop a bed of saffron orzo. But it's always fun to see him kick up his heels with some world-beat concoction like duck and smoked pepper quesadilla or an incendiary Jamaican mixed grill of salmon, shrimp, and swordfish. All this, and dreamy cove views.

Expensive

Christian's. 443 Main St. (in the center of town). ☎ **508/945-3362.** Reservations recommended. Main courses $10–$20. AE, CB, DC, DISC, MC, V. Apr–Dec daily 11:30am–3pm and 5–10pm; call for off-season hours. NEW AMERICAN.

Owned by gifted, innovative chef Christian Schultz, this bilevel restaurant has a split personality: The summer-only downstairs dining rooms sport French country decor, whereas Upstairs at Christian's (open year-round) is British clubby, with leather couches, mahogany paneling, and a smattering of classic movie posters. The same cinematic-motif menu applies to both places: Famous movie titles are accorded to such specialties as escargots in marsala sauce—a.k.a. *Casablanca*.

The Main Dining Room. Chatham Bars Inn, Shore Rd. (about ¹/₃ mile northwest of town center). ☎ **800/527-4884** or 508/945-0096. Reservations and jacket required. Main courses $13–$20. AE, DC, MC, V. Mid-May to mid-Nov daily 8–11am; Sun–Fri 6–9pm, Sat 6:30–9pm; call for off-season schedule. NEW AMERICAN.

This water-view dining room is vast, of the ballroom dimensions all but lost in the modern age. In assuming the reins in the kitchen, Al Hynes has reined in the prices as well, while upping the portions. His roast rack of lamb Provençal—seasoned with three mustards, coated with herbed bread crumbs, and cloaked in a *vert pre* sauce— would set you back considerably more just about anywhere else, without presenting so interesting a twist.

Moderate

⭐ **Vining's Bistro.** 595 Main St. (in the center of town). ☎ **508/945-5033.** Reservations not accepted. Main courses $12–$17. AE, DC, MC, V. Apr to early Sept 5:30–10pm; call for off-season hours. FUSION.

If you're looking for cutting-edge cuisine in a sophisticated setting, venture upstairs at Chatham's innocuous-looking mini-mall and into this ineffably cool cafe. The film-noirish wall murals suggest a certain bohemian abandon, but the menu is up to the minute, and priced to suit Generation X. Warm lobster taco with salsa fresca and crème fraîche, a spit-roasted chicken suffused with achiote-lime marinade, served with an orange-jicama salad—these are reason enough to keep returning.

CHATHAM AFTER DARK

While most towns boast some comparable event, Chatham's free **band concerts**— 40 players strong—stand out, attracting crowds in the thousands. Held in Kate Gould Park (off Chatham Bars Avenue, in the center of town) from July through early September, they kick off at 8pm every Friday. Better come early to claim your square of lawn, and be prepared to sing—or dance—along. Call ☎ 508/945-0342 for information.

Live bands accompany the three weekly feasts held at **The Beach House Grill,** at the Chatham Bars Inn, on Shore Road (☎ **508/945-0096**): Western line-dancing to go with the Monday-night barbecue, Dixieland to accompany Wednesday's clambake, and calypso for Thursday's Caribbean blowout.

A great leveler, **The Chatham Squire,** 487 Main St. (☎ **508/945-0945**), is a local institution that attracts all the social strata in town. CEOs, seafarers, and collegiates alike convene to kibitz over the roar of a jukebox or band, and the din of their own hubbub. Cover varies.

Beloved of moneyed locals, **Upstairs at Christian's,** 443 Main St. (☎ **508/945-3362**), is a sporting piano bar with the air of a vintage frat house, with scuffed leather couches and purloined movie posters. Cinematically themed nibbles are always available to offset the generous movie-motif drinks. No cover.

ORLEANS

Orleans is where the "Narrow Land" (the early Algonquian name for the Cape) starts to get very narrow indeed: From here on up—or "down," in local parlance—it's never more than a few miles wide from coast to coast. This is where the oceanside beaches open up, into a glorious expanse some 40 miles long, framed by dramatic dunes and swept with serious surf.

All three main roads (Routes 6, 6A, and 28) converge here, so on summer weekends this spot acts as a rather frustrating funnel. Lacking the cohesiveness of smaller hamlets and somewhat chopped up by the roadways coursing through, it's not the most ideal town to hang out in, despite some appealing restaurants and shops. The village of East Orleans, however, is fast emerging as a sweet little off-beach town with both family and singles allure. About 2 miles east is seemingly endless (nearly 10-mile-long) Nauset Beach, the southernmost stretch of the Cape Cod National Seashore, and a magnet for the young and the buff.

ESSENTIALS

GETTING THERE   After crossing either the Bourne or Sagamore bridge, head east on Route 6 or 6A; both converge with Route 28 in Orleans. The town is 31 miles east of Sandwich, 25 miles south of Provincetown.

VISITOR INFORMATION   Contact the **Orleans Chamber of Commerce,** Post Office Square, Orleans, MA 02653 (☎ **800/865-1386** or 508/255-1386).

BEACHES & OUTDOOR PURSUITS

BEACHES   From here on up, on the eastern side, you're dealing with the wild and whimsical Atlantic, which can be tame one day and wild the next. Current conditions are clearly posted at the beach entrances. Weeklong **parking permits** ($25 for renters, $30 for transients) may be obtained from the Town Hall on School Road (☎ **508/240-3700**). Day-trippers who arrive early enough—say, before 9am—can pay at the gate.

- **Nauset Beach** in East Orleans (☎ **508/240-3780**): Stretching southward all the way past Chatham, this 10-mile-long barrier beach is part of the **Cape Cod National Seashore,** but is managed by the town. It's long been one of the Cape's more gonzo beach scenes—good surf, big crowds, lots of young people. Full facilities can be found within the 1,000-car parking lot; the in-season fee is $10 per car, which is also good for same-day parking at Skaket Beach (below). Substantial waves make for good surfing in the special section reserved for that purpose, and boogie boards are everywhere.
- **Skaket Beach,** off Skaket Beach Road to the west of town (☎ **508/255-0572**): This peaceful bay beach is a better choice for families with young children.

When the tide recedes (as much as a mile), little kids will enjoy splashing about in the tide pools left behind. Parking costs $8, and you'd best turn up early.

- **Pilgrim Lake,** off Monument Road about 1 mile south of Main Street: Because it's monitored by a lifeguard in season, this small freshwater beach charges an $8 parking fee.
- **Crystal Lake,** off Monument Road about three-quarter miles south of Main Street: Parking—if you can find a space—is free, but there are no facilities.

BIKING/RECREATIONAL PATHS   Orleans presents the one slight gap in the 25-mile off-road **Cape Cod Rail Trail** (☎ 508/896-3491): Just east of the Brewster border, the trail merges with town roads for about 1½ miles. The best way to avoid vehicular aggravation is to zigzag west to scenic Rock Harbor. Bike rentals are available at **Orleans Cycle,** 26 Main St. (☎ **508/255-9115**).

FISHING   Fishing is allowed in Baker Pond, Pilgrim Lake, and Crystal Lake; the latter is a likely spot to reel in trout and perch. For details and a license, visit the Town Hall at Post Office Square in the center of town (☎ **508/240-3700**). Surf casting—no license needed—is permitted on **Nauset Beach South,** off Beach Road.

Rock Harbor, a former packet landing on the bay (about 1¼ miles northwest of the town center), shelters New England's largest sportfishing fleet: some 18 boats at last count. One call (☎ **800/287-1771** or 508/255-9757) will get you information on them all. Or go look them over; the sunsets are sublime.

NATURE TRAILS   Inland there's not much, but on the Atlantic shore is a biggie, Nauset Beach. Once you get past the swarms of people near the parking lot, you'll have about 9 miles of beach mostly to yourself. You'll see tons of birds (take a field guide) and perhaps some harbor seals off-season.

WATER SPORTS   **Arey's Pond Boat Yard,** off Route 28 in South Orleans (☎ 508/255-0994), offers sailing lessons.

The **Goose Hummock Outdoor Center,** 15 Rte. 6A, south of the rotary (☎ 508/255-0455; Web site: **www.goose.com**), rents out canoes, kayaks, sailboards, and more, and the northern half of Pleasant Bay is the perfect place to use them; inquire about guided excursions.

The **Pump House Surf Co.,** 9 Rte. 6A (☎ **508/240-2226**), will meet all your scuba, sailboarding, and surfing needs, while providing up-to-date reports on where to find the best waves.

SHOPPING

Though the shops are somewhat scattered, the town is full of great finds for browsers and grazers.

Continuum Antiques, 7 S. Orleans Rd., Route 28, south of the junction of Route 6A (☎ **508/255-8513**), has some 400 vintage light fixtures here, from Victorian on down, along with a smattering of old advertising signs and venerable duck decoys. **Countryside Antiques,** 6 Lewis Rd., south of Main Street in the center of East Orleans (☎ **508/240-0525**), has a lode of stylish furnishings. **Pleasant Bay Antiques,** 540 Orleans Rd., Route 28, about half a mile south of the town center in South Orleans (☎ **508/255-0930**), is such that you'd have to head south to Sotheby's to find such a fine collection of Early American antiques.

The **Addison Holmes Gallery,** 43 Rte. 28, north of Main Street (☎ **508/255-6200**), represents such very diverse painters as Pat de Groot, whose decades' worth of Provincetown landscapes seem perennially fresh, and Susan Baker of North Truro, a deliberate primitivist with a wicked sense of humor. **New Horizons,** 35 S. Orleans Rd., Route 28, north of Main Street (☎ **508/255-8766**), shows a top-notch collection of contemporary crafts. Also look in on **Kemp Pottery,** 9 Rte. 6A, about one-eighth mile south of the rotary (☎ **508/255-5853**), and **Spindrift Pottery,** 37 Rte. 6A, about a quarter mile south of the rotary (☎ **508/255-1404**).

With Nauset Marsh and Monomoy Island so close at hand, it's great luck to have in town a place like the **Bird Watcher's General Store,** 36 Rte. 6A, south of the rotary (☎ **800/562-1512** or 508/255-6974). It stocks virtually every bird-watching accessory under the sun, from basic binoculars to costly telescopes, modest bird-houses to birdbaths fit for a tiny Roman emperor.

WHERE TO STAY

The Barley Neck Inn Lodge. 5 Beach Rd. (in the center of town), E. Orleans, MA 02643. ☎ **800/281-7505** or 508/255-8484. Fax 508/255-3626. 18 rms. A/C TV TEL. Summer $95–$115 double. Rates include continental breakfast. Off-season MAP packages available. AE, DC, MC, V.

Having radically transformed the Barley Neck Inn restaurant (see "Where to Dine," below), new owners Kathi and Joe Lewis treated the adjoining motel to an equally intensive makeover. Every room is a little different, but all boast fluffy designer com-forters and stylish appointments. There's a little pool within the complex, and Nauset Beach is less than 2 miles down the road.

The Cove. 13 S. Orleans Rd. (Rte. 28, north of Main St.), Orleans, MA 02653. ☎ **800/343-2233** or 508/255-1203. 39 rms, 7 suites, 1 efficiency. A/C TV TEL. Summer $96–$167 double, $158–$167 suite or efficiency. AE, CB, DC, DISC, MC, V.

Sensibly turning its back on busy Route 28, this well-camouflaged motel complex focuses instead on placid Town Cove, where guests are offered a free minicruise in season. The interiors are adequate, if not dazzling, and a small heated pool and a rest-ful gazebo overlook the waterfront. Meeting facilities are available for those whose business just won't wait.

Hillbourne House. 654 Orleans Rd. (Rte. 28, near the Harwich border), S. Orleans, MA 02662. ☎ **508/255-0780.** 6 rms. Summer $70–$95 double. Rates include full breakfast. No credit cards. Closed Nov to late Apr.

Overlooking a pocket of Pleasant Bay once popular with pirates, this 1798 homestead has seen a lot of history: Innkeeper Barbara Hayes can show you the trapdoor that conceals a stone pit pressed into service for the Underground Railroad. The three carriage-house rooms are beautiful examples of their era, and can be booked en masse, with their own kitchen and living room. The three more modern units carved out of the erstwhile paddocks are nearly as charming, with high ceilings countrified by wooden beams. All guests are offered a lavish breakfast and have access to the inn's little private beach and dock; in fact, some regulars arrive by sea.

Kadee's Gray Elephant. 212 Main St. (in the center of town), E. Orleans, MA 02643. ☎ **508/255-6184.** Fax 508/240-2976. 10 studio apts. A/C TV TEL. Summer $110 double. Weekly rates available. MC, V.

Available short or long term, these exuberantly decorated units (Day-Glo wicker!) are extremely cheery and ideal for families. Nauset Beach is a few miles down the road, and meanwhile everything you'll need is right in town—or right on the grounds. There's a friendly restaurant/snack bar right next door, and the little mini golf course out back is geared just right for minigolfers.

✪ **Nauset House Inn.** 143 Beach Rd. (about 1¹/₂ miles east of town center), E. Orleans, MA 02653. ☎ **508/255-2195.** 14 rms (6 with shared bath). Summer $65–$105 double. Full and continental breakfast available for a surcharge. MC, V. Closed Nov–Apr.

Heathcliff would have loved this place, or at least the surrounding moors. Modern nature lovers with a taste for creature comforts will, too. Several of the rooms located in greenery-draped outbuildings feature such romantic extras as a sunken bath or private deck. The most romantic hideaway here, though, is a 1907 conservatory appended to the 1810 farmhouse inn. It's the perfect place to lounge with a novel or lover (preferably both) as the rain pounds down and you take in the heady perfume of the profuse camellias. Breakfast would seem relatively workaday, were it not for the setting—a pared-down, rustic refectory—and innkeeper Diane Johnson's memorable muffins and pastries.

WHERE TO DINE

Very Expensive

✪ **The Barley Neck Inn.** 5 Beach Rd. (about ¹/₂ mile east of town center), E. Orleans. ☎ **800/ 281-7505** or 508/255-0212. Fax 508/255-3226. Reservations recommended. Main courses $15–$26. AE, DC, MC, V. Early July to early Sept daily 5:30pm–midnight; call for off-season hours. NEW AMERICAN.

Tastefully restored, this 1857 captain's house boasts a superb chef in Franck Champely, who came from Taillevent and Maxim's by way of New York's Four Seasons. His classical background shines in straightforward yet subtle dishes such as grilled Atlantic salmon filet with a red-pepper coulis and basil vinaigrette, or sautéed shrimp in a sauce of sweet garlic and Chablis atop lemon angel-hair pasta and shiitake mushrooms. The cuisine may be highbrow and the wine list a connoisseur's delight, but the ambiance is festive, even boisterous. It's a very good mix.

Off the Bay Cafe. 28 Main St. (at Rte. 6A, in the center of town). ☎ **508/255-5505.** Reservations recommended. Main courses $18–$26. AE, CB, DC, DISC, MC, V. July–Aug daily 11:30am–4pm and 5:30–10pm, Sat–Sun 8–11am; call for off-season hours. NEW AMERICAN.

This snappy 19th-century storefront always delivers the goods. In light of the neonautical decor (lots of varnished wood and polished brass), you might expect passable seafood; instead, it's superlative, with such brilliant accompaniments as pineapple salsa or papaya hollandaise. The rotisseried game birds are every bit as well dressed, and superb.

Moderate

✪ **Joe's Beach Road Bar & Grille.** The Barley Neck Inn, 5 Beach Rd. (about ¹/₂ mile east of town center), E. Orleans. ☎ **800/281-7505** or 508/255-0212. Reservations recommended. Main courses $7–$21. AE, DC, MC, V. Early July to early Sept daily 5:30pm–midnight; call for off-season hours. AMERICAN.

Joe Lewis's self-imposed mandate for his namesake bar is "good food, large drinks, and big fun." That's exactly what you'll find in this spacious tavern. World War II posters (found in the inn's attic) and snazzy Roaring Twenties menswear ads adorn the barn-board walls. Off-season, a fire blazes in the huge fieldstone fireplace fronted by inviting armchairs, though most everyone crowds around the 28-foot mahogany bar. Once you've secured your own table—the tablecloths are denim, the napkins bandannas—you have the run of a varied menu, which includes the exquisite dishes served in the more formal restaurant next door. If you just want to snack, consider Joe's pizza (with goat cheese, roasted peppers, and spinach) or hifalutin fish-and-chips—beer battered, with watercress aioli.

Kadee's Lobster & Clam Bar. 212 Main St. (in the center of town), E. Orleans. ☎ **508/ 255-6184.** Fax 508/240-2926. Reservations not accepted. Main courses $7–$17. MC, V. Late June to Aug daily 11:30am–9:30pm; late May to late June Sat–Sun 11:30am–9:30pm. Closed early Sept to late May. AMERICAN.

This atmospheric sea shanty has been rigged to improve on the climate. When the sun's out, the flower-print umbrellas pop up in the patio; as soon as the chilly seaborne fog moves in, a curtained awning drops down. The menu is equally adaptable: There's nothing like the classic chowders and stews or a platter of sautéed "seafood simmer" to take the chill off; fine weather, on the other hand, calls for a lobster roll, or perhaps a shore dinner splurge.

Land Ho! 38 Main St. (at Rte. 6A, in the center of town). ☎ **508/255-5165.** Reservations not accepted. Main courses $7–$15. AE, DISC, MC, V. Daily 11:30am–1am. AMERICAN.

A longtime hit with the locals (who call it, affectionately, "the Ho"), this rough-and-tumble pub attracts its share of knowledgeable visitors as well, drawn by the reasonable prices and festive atmosphere. The food may be nothing to write home about, but it's satisfying and easy on the budget. Just being there (provided you can find the door: it's around back) will make you feel like an imminent insider.

Inexpensive

Binnacle Tavern. 20 S. Orleans Rd. (Rte. 28, north of Main St.). ☎ **508/255-4847.** Most items under $12. AE, MC, V. Apr to mid-Oct daily 5–11:30pm; call for off-season hours. ITALIAN.

All sorts of strange nautical salvage adorns the barn-board walls of this popular pizzeria, where the pies—among the Cape's best—come with some very peculiar toppings, for those so inclined. More conservative combos are available, along with traditional Italian fare.

Take-Out & Picnic Fare

Pick your spot anywhere on the Cape—or within the continental United States, for that matter—and **Clambake Celebrations,** 9 West Rd., at Skaket Beach Road, about 1 mile west of the town center (☎ **800/423-4038** or 508/255-3289), will provide you with a coastal feast to go: lobsters, steamers, mussels, sausage, corn, potatoes, all packed in a steamer pot and ready to boil.

The charming little **Cottage St. Bakery,** Cottage Street off Route 28, at the junction of Route 6A (☎ **508/255-2821**), is the perfect place to grab a morning Danish (the family-sized ones resemble pizzas) or indulge in a dessert.

✪ **Fancy's Farm,** 199 Main St., in the center of East Orleans (☎ **508/255-1949**), makes vegetables look unusually appealing. The charming barnlike setting helps, as do the extras—fresh breads, pastries, juices, and exotic salads and soups to go.

ORLEANS AFTER DARK

Joe's Beach Road Bar & Grille, in the Barley Neck Inn, 5 Beach Rd., East Orleans (☎ **508/255-0212**), is a big old barn of a bar that might as well be town hall: It's where you'll find all the locals exchanging juicy gossip and jokes. On Sunday evenings in season, the weekend warriors who survived in style can enjoy live "Jazz at Joe's." There's never a cover charge.

At the **Orleans Inn,** 3 Old County Rd., on Town Cove, south of the rotary (☎ **508/255-2222**), blues, rock, and reggae, performed by popular local bands, rock the rehabbed Victorian manse throughout the summer. Call for schedule; cover varies.

4 The Outer Cape

It's only on the Outer Cape that the landscape, even the air, feels really *beachy*. You can smell the seashore just around the corner over the horizon—in fact, everywhere about you, because you're never more than a mile or two away.

And when you find it, it is a revelation. No high-rise hotels. No tacky amusement arcades. Not a whole lot of anything, other than dune grass rippling in the wind and the occasional cottage some lucky soul managed to get grandfathered before the seacoast succumbed to a federally protected slumber back in the early 1960s. Henry David Thoreau witnessed virtually the same panorama when he came roaming in the 1850s. With any luck, it will still be here, unchanged, when your great-great-grandchildren come to view this great natural wonder.

EASTHAM

One thing you won't see in Eastham is tanned socialites clutching thousand-dollar Nantucket baskets as they peruse the latest shipment of distressed continental antiques. Despite its optimal location (the distance from bay to ocean is as little as 1 mile in spots), Eastham is one of the least pretentious locales on the Cape—and yet highly popular, as the gateway to the magnificent Cape Cod National Seashore.

The downside (or upside, depending how you look at it) is that there aren't a whole lot of shops or attractions, or at least few worth checking out.

Most visitors won't bother. You can tell as soon as you pull into town: This is a place meant for kicking back—for letting the sun, surf, and sand dictate your day.

ESSENTIALS

GETTING THERE   After crossing either the Bourne or Sagamore bridge, head east on Route 6 or 6A to Orleans, and north on Route 6. Eastham is 35 miles east of Sandwich, 21 miles south of Provincetown.

VISITOR INFORMATION   Contact the **Eastham Chamber of Commerce,** Route 6 at Fort Hill Road, Eastham, MA 02642 (☎ **508/255-3444**).

BEACHES & OUTDOOR PURSUITS

BEACHES   From here on up, the Atlantic beaches are best reserved for strong swimmers: Waves are *big* (often taller than you) and the undertow can be treacherous. The flat, nearly placid bay beaches, on the other hand, are just right for families with young children.

- **Coast Guard and Nauset Light,** off Ocean View Drive: Connected to outlying parking lots by a free shuttle, these pristine National Seashore beaches have lifeguards and rest rooms. Parking is $5 per day, $15 for the season.
- **First Encounter, Thumpertown, Campground, and Sunken Meadow:** These town-operated bay beaches generally charge $5 a day; permits ($20 per week) can be obtained from the Highway Department on Old Orchard Road in North Eastham (☎ **508/255-1965**).
- **Great Pond and Wiley Park:** These two town-run freshwater beaches are also open to the public, on the same terms as the bay beaches.

BIKING/RECREATIONAL PATHS   With plenty of free parking available at the Cape Cod National Seashore's **Salt Pond Visitor Center** (☎ **508/255-3421**), Eastham makes a convenient access point for the **Cape Cod Rail Trail** (☎ **508/896-3491**). Northward, it's about 5 wildflower-lined miles to Wellfleet, where the trail currently ends (further expansion is planned); Dennis is about 20 miles southwest. A 1.6-mile spur trail, winding through locust and apple groves, links the visitors center with glorious Coast Guard Beach: It's for bikes only (no blades).

Rentals are available at the **Little Capistrano Bike Shop** (☎ **508/255-6515**), on Salt Pond Road just west of Route 6, or **Idle Times,** 4550 Rte. 6 in the center of North Eastham (☎ **800/924-8281** on the Cape, or 508/255-8281), which also carries in-line skates.

The best place for a trailside snack—fried clams, lobster, and the like—is **Arnold's** (☎ **508/255-2575**), located on Route 6 about 1 mile north of the visitors center.

FISHING   Eastham has four ponds open to fishing: **Herring Pond** is stocked. For a freshwater fishing or shellfishing license, visit the Department of Public Works on Old Orchard Road (☎ **508/255-1965**). Surf casting is permitted at **Nauset Beach North** (off Doane Road) and **Nauset Light Beach** (off Cable Road).

NATURE TRAILS   There are five "self-guiding nature trails"—for walkers only— with descriptive markers within this portion of the **Cape Cod National Seashore.** The 1¹/₂-mile **Fort Hill Trail** off Fort Hill Road (off Route 6, about 1 mile south of the town center), takes off from a free parking lot just past the Captain Edward Penniman House (open daily from 1 to 4pm in season), a fancy multicolored 1868 Second Empire manse maintained by the CCNS. Following the trail markers, you'll pass "Indian Rock" (bearing the marks of untold generations who used it to sharpen their tools) and enjoy scenic vantage points overlooking the marsh—keep an eye out for egrets and great blue herons—and out to sea. The Fort Hill Trail hooks up with the half-mile **Red Cedar Swamp Trail,** offering boardwalk views of an ecology otherwise inaccessible.

Three relatively short trails fan out from the Salt Pond Visitor Center. The most unusual is the quarter-mile **Buttonbush Trail,** specially adapted for the sight-impaired, with a guide rope and descriptive plaques in both oversized type and Braille. The **Doane Loop Trail,** a half-mile woodland circuit about 1 mile east of the visitors center, is graded to allow access to wheelchairs and strollers. The 1-mile **Nauset Marsh Trail** skirts Salt Pond to cross the marsh (via boardwalk) and open fields, before returning by way of a recovering forest.

WATER SPORTS   The best way to experience Nauset Marsh is by kayak or canoe. Rentals are available in neighboring towns: the closest source would be the **Goose Hummock Outdoor Center,** 15 Rte. 6A in Orleans (☎ **508/255-0455**). **Jack's Boat Rentals** (☎ **508/349-9808**) has a seasonal outlet on Wellfleet's Gull Pond, which connects to Higgins Pond by way of a placid, narrow channel lined with red maples and choked with yellow water lilies. In addition to watercraft to go, Jack's also offers guided paddle tours of Eastham's Herring River.

For information about other excellent naturalist-guided tours, inquire about trips sponsored by the **Cape Cod Museum of Natural History** (☎ **800/479-3867** or 508/896-3867) and the **Wellfleet Bay Wildlife Sanctuary** (☎ **508/349-2615**).

SALT POND VISITOR CENTER

Since you're undoubtedly going to spend a fair amount of time on the beach, you might as well find out how it came to be, what other creatures you'll be sharing it with, and how not to harm them or it.

Occupying more than half of the land mass north of Orleans and covering the entire 30-mile oceanfront, the 44,000-acre **Cape Cod National Seashore** was set aside as a sanctuary in 1961. Actually, it's not entirely free: If you're an American citizen, you part-own it, and contribute to its upkeep. Get your money's worth and more by taking advantage of the excellent educational exhibits and continuous film loops offered here. Particularly fascinating is a video about the accidental discovery, in 1990, of an 11,000-year-old campsite amid the storm-ravaged dunes of Coast Guard beach—which was about 5 miles inland when these early settlers spent their summers here. After absorbing some of the local history, be sure to take time to venture out—on your own or with a ranger guide—on some of the surrounding trails (see "Nature Trails," above).

The ✪ **Salt Pond Visitor Center** is on Salt Pond Road, east of Route 6 (☎ **508/ 255-0788**). Admission is free. It's open daily from June through August from 9am to 6pm; call for off-season hours.

WHERE TO STAY

Over Look Inn. 3085 Rte. 6 (about ¹/₄ mile north of town center, opposite Salt Pond Visitor Center), Eastham, MA 02642. ☎ **800/356-1121** or 508/255-1886. Fax 508/240-0345. 10 rms, 3 suites. A/C. Summer $95–$145 double, $135 suite. Rates include full breakfast and afternoon tea. AE, CB, DC, DISC, MC, V.

Henry Beston slept in this multicolored 1869 Queen Anne–style Victorian while planning his legendary sojourn at the Outermost House. You can bet it was a lot less cushy—and enchanting—before Scottish innkeepers Nan and Ian Aitchison took over in 1983. The house now reflects their many enthusiasms: The library, for instance, is dedicated to Winston Churchill, and the Ernest Hemingway Billiard Room is lined with trophies that would have done Papa proud. Their son Clive's colorful abstract canvases adorn many of the common spaces and rooms, some of which come enhanced with brass beds and claw-foot tubs. Pilgrims piking along the Rail Trail will appreciate the hearty breakfasts.

The Penny House. 4885 Rte. 6, N. Eastham, MA 02651. ☎ **800/554-1751** or 508/255-6632. Fax 508/255-4893. 11 rms. Summer $110–$175 double. Rates include full breakfast. AE, DISC, MC, V.

Whizzing past on Route 6, you'd scarcely suspect there's a peaceful inn tucked away behind a massive hedge. This neat, comfortable B&B, graced with the warmth of Australian innkeeper Margaret Keith, is clustered around a 1751 saltbox, now the setting for rich homemade breakfasts. The rooms vary widely in terms of space and price, but all are nicely appointed and meticulously maintained. A communal phone and TV in the cathedral-ceilinged "gathering room" encourage socializing.

✪ **The Whalewalk Inn.** 220 Bridge Rd. (about ³/₄ mile west of Orleans rotary), Eastham, MA 02641. ☎ **508/255-0617.** Fax 508/240-0017. 7 rms, 5 suites, 1 cottage. A/C. Summer $135–$190 double, $175 cottage, $175–$190 suite and efficiency. Rates include full breakfast. MC, V. Closed Dec–Apr.

Regularly hailed as one of the Cape's prettiest inns, this 1830s Greek Revival manse—sequestered in a quiet residential area just a few blocks off the Rail Trail—fully deserves its reputation. Innkeeper Carolyn Smith has dressed up every last space in a tasteful, mostly pastel palette more suggestive of sunny California than dour New England. Eclectic furnishings occupy the common rooms, where complimentary evening hors d'oeuvres are served. Both Carolyn and Dick, who is responsible for the indulgent gourmet breakfasts, can knowledgeably steer you to the best the area has to offer, and will lend you a bike if you like.

WHERE TO DINE

Old-timers convene at the counter of the **Hole-in-One Donut Shop,** 4295 Rte. 6A, about a quarter mile south of North Eastham (☎ **508/255-9446**), to ponder the state of the world. You can join in, or head home with your haul of hand-cut doughnuts and fresh-baked muffins and bagels.

Arnold's. 3580 Rte. 6 (about 1¹/₄ miles north of town center). ☎ **508/255-2575.** Main courses $7–$16. No credit cards. Daily 11am–10pm. Closed mid-Sept to mid-May. AMERICAN.

Offering a take-out window on the Rail Trail and a picnic grove for those who hate to waste vacation hours sitting indoors, this popular eatery dishes out all the usual seashore standards, from rich and crunchy fried clams (order whole clams, not strips) to foot-long chili dogs.

Eastham Lobster Pool. 4360 Rte. 6 (in the center of town), N. Eastham. ☎ **508/255-9706.** Reservations not accepted. Main courses $11–$25. AE, DC, DISC, MC, V. Early July to early Sept Sun–Thurs 11:30am–10pm; call for off-season hours. Closed Nov–Mar. AMERICAN.

For 3 decades, the scrape of metal chairs against the cement floor of this no-frills dining hall has been synonymous with seafood feasts. You can eye your potential entree—scrabbling among a tankful of feisty lobsters—as you wait in line to gain admittance. (The locals, along with smart visitors, know to show up in the early, early evening, or even late afternoon.) Beyond the lobsters, which come in monster proportions, there's all sorts of fish. As far back as the early 1980s, the specials were exhibiting harbingers of New American panache, and they still pack some sophisticated surprises: champagne-shallot butter, perhaps, to top a halibut steak. The bluefish, always affordable, is always fabulous. Some rather nice wines are available by the glass.

WELLFLEET

Wedged between tame Eastham and wild Truro, Wellfleet—with the well-tended look of a classic New England town—is the golden mean, the perfect destination for artists, writers, off-duty psychiatrists, and other contemplative types who hope to find more in the landscape than mere quaintness or rusticity. Distinguished literati such as Edna St. Vincent Millay and Edmund Wilson put this rural village on the map in the 1920s, in the wake of Provincetown's bohemian heyday.

Wellfleet remains remarkably unspoiled. Once you depart from Route 6, commercialism is kept to a minimum, though the town boasts plenty of appealing shops—including a score of distinguished galleries—and a couple of excellent New American restaurants. It's hard to imagine any other community on the Cape supporting so sophisticated an undertaking as the Wellfleet Harbor Actors Theatre, or hosting such a wholesome event as public square dancing on the adjacent Town Pier. And where else could you find a thriving drive-in movie theater right next door to an outstanding nature preserve?

ESSENTIALS

GETTING THERE   After crossing either the Bourne or Sagamore bridge, head east on Route 6 or 6A to Orleans, and north on Route 6. Wellfleet is 42 miles northeast of Sandwich, 14 miles south of Provincetown.

VISITOR INFORMATION   Contact the **Wellfleet Chamber of Commerce,** off Route 6, Wellfleet, MA 02663 (☎ **508/349-2510**).

BEACHES & OUTDOOR PURSUITS

BEACHES   Though these profiles are just generalizations, Wellfleet's fabulous ocean beaches tend to sort themselves demographically: **LeCount Hollow** is popular with families, **Newcomb Hollow** with high schoolers, **White Crest** with the college crowd (including surfers and off-hours hang gliders), and **Cahoon** with 30-somethings. Alas, only the latter two beaches permit parking by nonresidents. To enjoy the other two, as well as **Burton Baker Beach** on the harbor and **Duck Harbor** on the bay, plus three freshwater ponds, you'll have to walk or bike in, or see if you qualify for a **parking sticker** ($25 per week). Bring proof of residency to the seasonal Beach Sticker Booth on the Town Pier, or call the Wellfleet Recreation Department (☎ **508/349-0818**).

- **Marconi Beach,** off Marconi Beach Road in South Wellfleet: A National Seashore property, this cliff-lined beach (with rest rooms) charges an entry fee of $5 a day, or only $15 for the season. *Note:* The bluffs are so high, the beach lies in shadow by late afternoon.
- **White Crest and Cahoon Hollow beaches,** off Ocean View Drive in Wellfleet: These two town-run ocean beaches—big with surfers—are open to all. Both have snack bars and rest rooms. Parking costs $10 a day.

- **Mayo Beach,** Kendrick Avenue (near the Town Pier): Right by the harbor, facing south, this beach (with rest rooms) is hardly secluded but will please young waders and splashers. And the price is right: parking is free.

BIKING/RECREATIONAL PATHS The terminus (to date) of the 25-mile and growing **Cape Cod Rail Trail** (☎ **508/896-3491**), Wellfleet is also among its more desirable destinations: A country road off the bike path leads right to LeCount Hollow Beach. Located at the current terminus, the **Black Duck Sports Shop,** 1446 Rte. 6 (☎ **508/349-9801**), stocks everything from rental bikes to "belly boards" and inflatable boats; the deli at the adjoining **South Wellfleet General Store** (☎ **508/349-2335**) can see to your snacking needs.

FISHING For a license to fish at Long Pond, Great Pond, or Gull Pond (all stocked with trout and full of native perch, pickerel, and sunfish), visit the Town Hall, 300 Main St. (☎ **508/349-0300**). Surf casting, which doesn't require a license, is permitted at the town beaches.

Shellfishing licenses (Wellfleet's oysters are world famous) can be obtained from the Shellfish Department on the Town Pier off Kendrick Avenue. (☎ **508/349-0325**).

Also heading out from here, in season, is the 60-foot fishing boat *Nauʻiator* (☎ **508/349-6003**).

NATURE TRAILS You'll find 5 miles of very scenic trails lined with lupines and bayberries—Goose Pond, Silver Spring, and Bay View—within the **Wellfleet Bay Wildlife Sanctuary** in South Wellfleet (see below).

Right in town, the short, picturesque boardwalk known as **Uncle Tim's Bridge,** off East Commercial Street, crosses Duck Creek to access a tiny island crisscrossed by paths.

The Cape Cod National Seashore maintains two spectacular self-guided trails. The 1¼-mile **Atlantic White Cedar Swamp Trail,** off the parking area for the Marconi Wireless Station, shelters a rare stand of the lightweight species prized by Native Americans as wood for canoes; red maples are slowly crowding out the cedars, but meanwhile the tea-tinted, moss-choked swamp is a magical place, refreshingly cool even at the height of summer. A boardwalk will see you over the muck (these peat bogs are 7 feet deep in places), but the return trip does entail a calf-testing half-mile trek through deep sand. Consider it a warm-up for magnificent **Great Island,** jutting 4 miles into the bay (off the western end of Chequessett Neck Road) to cup Wellfleet Harbor. It's quite uninhabited, and a true refuge for those strong enough to go the distance. Just be sure to cover up, wear sturdy shoes, bring water, and venture to Jeremy Point—the very tip—*only* if you're sure the tide is going out.

WATER SPORTS **Jack's Boat Rentals,** located on Gull Pond off Gull Pond Road about one-half mile south of the Truro border (☎ **800/300-3787** or 508/349-9808), rents out canoes, kayaks, sailboards, Sunfish on Gull Pond, and also organizes guided paddle explorations of nearby kettle ponds and tidal rivers.

Surfing is restricted to **White Crest Beach,** and **sailboarding** to **Burton Baker Beach** at Indian Neck during certain tide conditions; ask for a copy of the regulations at the Beach Sticker Booth on the Town Pier.

The **Chequessett Yacht & Country Club,** on Chequessett Neck Road in Wellfleet (☎ **508/349-3704**), offers sailing lessons for approximately $30 an hour. For those who already know how, **Wellfleet Marine Corp.** on the Town Pier (☎ **508/349-2233**) rents 14- to 20-foot sailboats in season.

WELLFLEET BAY WILDLIFE SANCTUARY A spiffy new eco-friendly visitor's center serves as both introduction and gateway to this 1,000-acre refuge maintained by the Massachusetts Audubon Society. Passive solar heat and composting toilets are just a few of the waste-cutting elements incorporated in the seemingly simple $1.6

million building, which nestles into its wooded site. You'll see plenty of wildlife—especially lyrical red-winged blackbirds and circling osprey—as you follow 5 miles of looping trails through pine forests, salt marsh, and moors. To hone your observation skills, avail yourself of the naturalist-guided walks scheduled throughout the day: You'll see and learn so much more. Also inquire about special workshops for children, and canoeing, snorkeling, birding, and off-season seal-watching excursions. *Note:* It's worth joining the Massachusetts Audubon Society just for the chance—afforded only to members—to camp out here.

The center is located off West Road, about 1 mile north of the Eastham border, in South Wellfleet (☎ **508/349-2615;** fax 508/349-2632). Trail use is free for Massachusetts Audubon Society members; the trail fee for nonmembers is $3 adults, $2 seniors and children. Trails are open July through August from 8am to 8pm, and September through June from 8am to dusk. The visitor's center is open July and August daily from 8:30am to 5pm; during the off-season it's closed Mondays.

SHOPPING

Wellfleet has begun hailing itself as "the art-gallery town." Though it may lag behind Provincetown in terms of quantity, the quality does achieve comparable heights. Crafts make a strong showing, too, as do contemporary women's clothing and eclectic home furnishings. Just one drawback: Unlike Provincetown, which has something to offer virtually year-round, Wellfleet pretty much rolls up its sidewalks come Columbus Day.

Cherry Stone Gallery, 70 E. Commercial St., about one-eighth mile south of East Main Street (☎ **508/349-3026**), is probably more influential than all the others put together. It got a head start, opening in 1972 and showing such local luminaries as Rauschenberg, Motherwell, and, more recently, Wellfleet resident Helen Miranda Wilson.

The smallish **Cove Gallery,** 15 Commercial St., by Duck Creek (☎ **508/ 349-2530**), carries the paintings and prints of many well-known artists, including Barry Moser and Leonard Baskin. Alan Nyiri, whose dazzling color photographs are collected in the coffee-table book *Cape Cod,* shows regularly, as does Carla Golembe, whose lively Caribbean-influenced tableaux have graced several children's books.

Crafts make a stronger stand than art at **Left Bank Gallery,** 25 Commercial St., by Duck Creek (☎ **508/349-9451**). The **Left Bank Print Gallery,** 3 W. Main St. (☎ **508/439-7939**), features the spillover from the Left Bank Gallery, particularly prints.

Among the knockouts at **Swansborough Gallery,** 230 Main St. (☎ **508/ 349-1883**), are Dennis sculptor Laura Baksa's dreamy alabaster figures and fragments thereof.

WHERE TO STAY

✪ **Even'Tide.** 650 Rte. 6 (about 1 mile north of the Eastham border), S. Wellfleet, MA 02667. ☎ **800/368-0007** or 508/349-3410. Fax 508/349-7804. 28 rms, 3 apts. A/C TV TEL. Summer $75–$105 double, $105 efficiency. AE, CB, DC, DISC, MC, V.

Set back from the road in its own roomy compound complete with playground, this motel feels more like a friendly village centered around a large, heated indoor pool. The Rail Trail goes right by it, and a three-quarter-mile footpath through the woods leads to Marconi Beach.

The Holden Inn. 140 Commercial St. (about 1/8 mile north of the Town Pier), Wellfleet, MA 02663. ☎ **508/349-3450.** 26 rms (14 with shared bath), 1 suite. Summer $60–$70 double, $115 suite for 4. No credit cards. Closed mid-Oct to mid-Apr.

Run by the same family since 1924, this three-building complex—centered on an 1840 captain's house fronted by a welcoming porch and classic picket fence—projects the leisurely ease of a bygone era. Furnishings tend to be well worn but homey, and the hospitality is genuinely gracious.

WHERE TO DINE

Aesop's Tables. 316 Main St. (in the center of town). ☎ **508/349-6450.** Reservations recommended. Main courses $16–$23. AE, CB, DISC, MC, V. July–Aug Wed–Sun noon–3pm; daily 5:30–9:30pm; call for off-season hours. Closed mid-Oct to mid-May. NEW AMERICAN.

This delightful restaurant—offbeat and avant-garde enough to stay interesting year after year, since 1965—has it all: a handsome, historic setting, a relaxed and festive atmosphere, and delectable food, reliably and artistically turned out by executive chef Peter Rennert. Brian Dunne is at once owner and host; he sets the mood and provides the superb local ingredients—even growing some of the edible flowers and delicate greens that go into the "Monet's Garden" salad. The scallops (served whole) and oysters come straight from the bay to be imaginatively treated. For dessert, don't miss the "Clementine's Citrus Tart," a rich pâté sable offset by a white chocolate and fruit mousse.

☼ **Bayside Lobster Hutt.** 91 Commercial St. (about ¼ mile north of the Town Pier). ☎ **508/349-6333.** Reservations not accepted. Main courses $8–$20. No credit cards. July–Aug daily 4:30–9pm; late May to June and Sept daily 4:30–9pm. Closed Oct to late May. AMERICAN.

For your "dress down" night (or several in a row), you couldn't do better than this classic, locally owned lobster joint, housed in a grizzled 1857 oyster shack—look for the life-sized lobsterman on the roof. Streams of customers are willing to wait an hour or more to crowd into the communal mess hall at the height of summer. "Feeding frenzy" is the only way to describe the claw-cracking hordes at the long oilcloth-covered plank tables.

Finely JP's. 19 Freedjum Rd. (on Rte. 6, about 1 mile north of the Eastham border), S. Wellfleet. ☎ **508/349-7500.** Reservations not accepted. Main courses $12–$15. MC, DISC, V. July–Aug daily 5–10pm; call for off-season schedule. Closed mid-Dec to mid-Jan. NEW AMERICAN.

If you drive by and happen upon this roadside joint, you'll feel like a clever explorer indeed, even if locals have long been in on the secret. Were it not for the roadside location and nondescript, wood-paneled exterior, chef-owner John Pontius could charge a lot more for his polished cuisine. As it is, you could feast on baked oysters *Bienville* (doused with wine and cream and topped with a mushroom-onion *duxelle* and grated Parmesan) and an improvisatory "Wellfleet paella" having barely broken a twenty.

Flying Fish. 29 Briar Lane (off Main St.). ☎ **508/349-3100.** Reservations not accepted. Main courses $13–$19. MC, V. Late June to early Sept daily 7am–2pm and 6–10pm; call for off-season hours. Closed Nov–Mar. NEW AMERICAN.

Just the thing: a deli/cafe catering to esoteric cravings (such as Jamaican jerk chicken, tabouli, and Brie omelets) during the day, and loftier expectations (such as "lobster romantique" atop black-pepper fettuccine with ginger-cinnamon beurre blanc) at night. Better yet, the on-site bakery means immediate access to such devilish confections as chocolate Chambord cake. The tourists who clog Main Street haven't yet caught on.

The Lighthouse. 317 Main St. (in the center of town). ☎ **508/349-3681.** Main courses $9–$13. DISC, MC, V. Daily 6:30am–10pm. AMERICAN.

Nothing special in and of itself, this bustling year-round institution is an off-season haven for locals, and a beacon to vacationers year-round. Except on Thursday's

"Mexican Night," the menu is all-American normal, from the steak-and-eggs break-fast to the native seafood dinners. Appreciative patrons usually keep up a dull roar throughout the day, revving up to a deafening roar as the Bass and Guinness flow from the tap.

✪ **Painter's.** 50 Main St. (near Rte. 6). ☎ **508/349-3003.** Reservations recommended. Main courses $10–$18. AE, MC, V. Daily 6–10pm. Closed Nov–Apr. NEW AMERICAN.

The offspring of local literati, Kate Painter trained at some pretty fancy establish-ments: San Francisco's world-famous Stars, Boston top spot Biba, and Cape Cod's own Chillingsworth. Still, if she had her druthers—and now she does, having set up her own restaurant in a rambling 1750 tavern—she'd still prefer, in the words of her motto and mission statement, "simple food in a funky place." The modesty is mis-placed, because although the setting is pretty low-key (a wood-beamed bistro dressed up with friends' artwork), her culinary skills are top-notch. Top start, consider a warm duck-breast salad with plum-balsamic vinaigrette. The hearty entrees include such robust dishes as clams Cataplana (like a sunnily spiced Portuguese bouillabaisse), or flounder rubbed with roasted garlic. Painter's sense of humor shows up in the des-serts: "Something Chocolate" and "Something Lemon" are just that, an intriguing cross between cake and soufflé.

Picnic & Take-Out Fare

Hatch's Fish Market/Hatch's Produce, 310 Main St., behind the Town Hall (☎ 508/349-2810), is a former fishing shack and the unofficial heart of Wellfleet. You'll find the best of local bounty from fresh-picked corn and fruit-juice popsicles to steaming lobsters and home-smoked local mussels and pâté. Virtually no one passes through without picking up a little something, along with the latest talk of the town. Closed late September to late May.

WELLFLEET AFTER DARK

Arguably the best dance club on Cape Cod, **The Beachcomber,** 1220 Old Cahoon Hollow Rd., off Ocean View Drive (☎ 508/349-6055), is definitely the most sce-nic, and not just in terms of the barely legal age clientele. "The Comber" is right on Cahoon Hollow Beach—so close, in fact, that late beachgoers on summer weekends can count on a free concert: reggae, perhaps, or the homegrown "Incredible Casuals." Other nights, you might run into jazz, blues, hip-hop, or comedy, and often some very big names playing mostly for the fun of it. Cover $5 to $10.

Three restaurants become evening roosts as the hour grows later: **Duck Creeke Tavern,** 70 Main St. (☎ 508/349-7369), hosts local talent to go with its light fare; **Painter's Upstairs,** 50 Main St. (☎ 508/349-3003), features local jazz acts; and locally spawned blues and jazz usually fills the cozy attic at **Upstairs Bar at Aesop's Tables,** 316 Main St. (☎ 508/349-6450).

Wednesday nights in summer, Wellfleet's workaday fishing pier (off Kendricks Avenue) resounds to the footfalls of avid amateur **square dancers** of every age. Call ☎ 508/349-9382 for more information.

The ✪ **Wellfleet Drive-In,** 51 Rte. 6, just north of the Eastham border (☎ 800/696-3532 or 508/349-2520), clearly deserves National Landmark status: Built in 1957, it's the only drive-in left on Cape Cod, and one of a scant half-dozen surviv-ing in the state. The rituals are as endearing as ever: the playtime preceding the car-toons, the countdown plugging the allures of the snack bar, and finally, two full first-run features. Open daily from late May through mid-September; show time is at dusk. Admission is $6 adults, $3.50 seniors and children 5 to 11.

TRURO

Truro is one of those blink and you'll miss it towns. With only 1,600 year-round residents (fewer than it boasted in 1840, when Pamet Harbor was a whaling and ship-building port), the town amounts to little more than a scattering of stores and public buildings, and lots of low-profile houses hidden away in the woods and dunes. As in Wellfleet, writers, artists, and vacationing therapists are drawn to the quiet and calm. Edward Hopper lived in contented isolation in a South Truro cottage for nearly 4 decades.

If you find yourself craving excitement, however, Provincetown is only a 10-minute drive away (you'll know you're getting close when you spot the wall-to-wall tourist cabins lining the bay in North Truro). The natives manage to entertain themselves pretty well with get-togethers at the Truro Center for the Arts or, more simply, among themselves. However much money may be circulating in this rusticated community (a *lot*), inconspicuous consumption is the rule of the day. The culmination of the social season, tellingly enough, is the late-September "dump dance" held at Truro's recycling center.

ESSENTIALS

GETTING THERE   After crossing either the Bourne or Sagamore bridge, head east on Route 6 or 6A to Orleans, and north on Route 6. Truro is 46 miles east of Sandwich, 10 miles south of Provincetown.

The **North Truro Shuttle System** (☎ **508/487-6870**) connects the town with Provincetown in season, for only $2 one-way.

VISITOR INFORMATION   Contact the **Truro Chamber of Commerce,** Route 6A at Head of the Meadow Road, Truro, MA 02666 (☎ **508/487-1288**).

BEACHES & OUTDOOR PURSUITS

BEACHES   Parking at all of Truro's exquisite Atlantic beaches, except for one Cape Cod National Seashore access point, is reserved for residents and renters. To obtain a **parking sticker** ($30 for 2 weeks), inquire at the Town Hall, on Town Hall Road (☎ **508/349-3635**). On your own power—walkers and bikers are welcome—visit such natural wonders as **Ballston Beach,** where all you'll see is silky sand and grass-etched dunes.

- **Head of the Meadow,** off Head of the Meadow Road: Among the more remote National Seashore beaches, this spot (equipped with rest rooms) is known for its excellent surf. Parking costs $5 a day, or $15 a season.

- **Corn Hill Beach,** off Corn Hill Road: Offering lifeguard supervision and rest rooms, this bay beach—near the hill where the Pilgrims found the seed corn that ensured their survival—is open to nonresidents for a parking fee of $5 a day.

BIKING/RECREATIONAL PATHS   Although it has yet to be linked up to the Cape Cod Rail Trail, Truro does have a stunning 2-mile bike path of its own, the **Head of the Meadow Trail,** off the road of that name (look for a right-hand turn about half a mile north of where Routes 6 and 6A intersect). Part of the old 1850 road toward Provincetown—Thoreau traveled this route—it skirts the bluffs, passing Pilgrim Heights (where the Pilgrims found their first drinking water) and ending at High Head Road. Being fairly flat as well as short, this stretch should suit youngsters and beginners. Rentals can be arranged at **Bayside Bikes,** 102 Shore Rd., North Truro (☎ **508/487-5735**).

FISHING   Great Pond, Horseleech Pond, and Pilgrim Lake, all flanked by parabolic dunes carved by the wind, offer fishing. For a license (inquire about shellfishing, too) visit Town Hall, on Town Hall Road (☎ **508/349-3635**). Surf casting is permitted at Highland Light Beach, off Highland Road.

NATURE TRAILS   The **Cape Cod National Seashore**—comprising 70% of Truro's land—offers three informative self-guided nature trails. The half-mile **Cranberry Bog Trail** leads from the Little America youth hostel parking lot past a number of previously cultivated bogs reverting to their natural state. The **Pilgrim Spring Trail** and **Small Swamp Trail** (each a 3/4-mile loop) head out from the CCNS parking lot just east of Pilgrim Lake. Pilgrim Spring is where the parched colonists sipped their first fresh water in months—with "much delight," according to a contemporary account. Both paths overlook Salt Meadow, a freshwater marsh favored by hawks and osprey.

WATER SPORTS   The inlets of **Pamet Harbor** are great for canoeing and kayaking; when planning an excursion, study the tides so you won't be working against them. The closest rentals are in Wellfleet.

An Arts Center & a Museum

✪ **Truro Center for the Arts at Castle Hill.** 10 Meetinghouse Rd. (at Castle Rd., about 3/4 mile northwest of town center), N. Truro. ☎ **508/349-7511.** Fees vary; call for schedule. Closed Sept–June.

Send for a brochure before your visit and you could schedule some learning into your vacation. A great many celebrated writers and artists—from poet Alan Dugan to painter Edith Vonnegut—emerge from their summer hideaways to offer courses, lectures, and exhibits at this bustling little complex, an 1880s horse barn with windmill (now home to the administrative offices). The roster changes slightly from year to year, but the stellar instructors will be at the top of their form in this stimulating environment.

The center also offers lots of children's workshops, from painting to silkscreening and assemblage, for artists age 7 and up.

Truro Historical Museum. 6 Lighthouse Rd. (off S. Highland Rd., 2 miles north of town center on Rte. 6), N. Truro. ☎ **508/487-3397.** Admission $3 adults, children under 12 free. Daily 10am–5pm. Closed mid-Sept to mid-June.

Built as a hotel in 1907, the Highland House is a perfect repository for the odds and ends collected by the Truro Historical Society: ship's models, harpoons, primitive toys, a pirate's chest, and more. Be sure to visit the second floor, set up as if still occupied by 19th-century tourists.

Shopping

Susan Baker—who has personally exaggerated the rumors of her own death so as to rate her own museum without croaking—is a definite character, as original as her work. ✪ **The Susan Baker Memorial Museum,** 46 Shore Rd., Route 6A, one-quarter mile northwest of Route 6 (☎ **508/487-2557**), showcases her creative output, from fanciful/functional papier-mâché *objets* to primitivist landscapes. However, her main stock in trade—here, and at her Provincetown outlet—is humor in various media, from artist's books to very atypical T-shirts. Call ahead October through May.

Where to Stay

✪ **Kalmar Village.** 674 Shore Rd. (Rte. 6A, about 3/4 miles south of the Provincetown border), N. Truro. ☎ and fax **508/487-0585.** 9 rms, 7 efficiency suites, 60 cottages. Summer $70 double, $115 suite; cottages $895–$1,495 weekly. MC, V. Closed mid-Oct to mid-May.

A lot spiffier than many of the motels and cottages lined up along this spit of sand between Pilgrim Lake and Pilgrim Beach, this 1940s complex resembles a miniaturized Edgartown, with little white cottages shuttered in black. The clientele—largely families—can splash the day away in the 60-foot freshwater pool or on the 400-foot private beach.

Outer Reach Motel. 535 Rte. 6 (midway between N. Truro center and the Provincetown border), N. Truro, MA 02652. ☎ **800/942-5388** or 508/487-9090. Fax 508/942-5388. 59 rms. TV. Summer $79–$124 double. MC, V. Closed mid-Oct to mid-May.

This sprawling motel—the last development to sneak under the wire, pre National Seashore—offers glorious vistas of Provincetown, where guests have privileges at another big (and equally unsightly) motel, the Provincetown Inn, on a narrow bay beach at the very western end of town. On site here in North Truro, you'll find an outdoor pool and tennis court; the ocean is 1 sylvan mile east. The rooms are standard issue, but there's a terrific independent restaurant within the complex, Adrian's (see "Where to Dine," below).

✪ **South Hollow Vineyards Bed-and-Breakfast Inn.** 11 Shore Rd. (Rte. 6A off Rte. 6, ¹/₂ mile south of town center), N. Truro, MA 02652. ☎ **508/487-6200.** Fax 508/487-4248. 4 rms, 1 suite. Summer $79–$89 double, $119 suite. Rates include continental breakfast. MC, V.

You don't have to be a wine lover to appreciate this beautiful 1836 B&B set amid 5 vine-covered acres. If you are, though, you'll be in your element. Each of the five bedrooms—including the Vintage Suite, with its double Jacuzzi—comes with a four-poster bed draped in a particular wine tone, ranging from claret to burgundy. The slate-floored living room, with its exposed beams, looks more French than Federal, and is decorated with interesting oenological artifacts. For the nonconnoisseur, the draw is likely to be the bucolic setting (this is one of the last working farms on the Outer Cape) only 6 miles from the center of Provincetown.

WHERE TO DINE

Seeing as this deli/bakery/grocery is basically *it* in terms of downtown Truro, and seasonal to boot, it's a good thing **Jams,** 14 Truro Center Rd., off Route 6 in the center of town (☎ **508/349-1616**), is so delightful. It's full of tantalizing aromas: fresh creative pizzas (from pesto to pupu), rotisseried fowl sizzling on the spit, cookies straight from the oven. The pastry and deli selections deserve their own four-star restaurant, but are all the more savory as part of a picnic. Closed early September to late May.

✪ **Adrian's.** 535 Rte. 6 (midway between N. Truro center and the Provincetown border). ☎ **508/487-4360.** Fax 508/487-6510. Reservations recommended. Main courses $7–$17. AE, MC, V. Mid-June to early Sept Mon–Fri 8am–noon, Sat–Sun 8am–1pm; daily 5:30–10pm; call for off-season hours. Closed mid-Oct to mid-May. NORTHERN ITALIAN.

Sharing a bluff with the Outer Reach Motel, Adrian Salcedo Cyr's stylish restaurant is greatly prized—not just for its knockout wood-fired *pizzette* and other creative fare, but for the superb breakfasts. Try for a table on the sunny deck overlooking all of Provincetown Harbor, and sample such eye-openers as orange-cinnamon French toast or huevos rancheros. Come back for the sunset and the Tuscan bread-and-tomato soup, the grilled eggplant salad, a thin-crusted "Quattro Stagioni" pizza, some masterful pasta—oh, and don't forget the tiramisu.

Terra Luna. 104 Shore Rd. (in the center of town), N. Truro. ☎ **508/487-1019.** Main courses $8–$16. AE, MC, V. Daily 7am–1pm and 5:30–10pm. Closed Nov to late May. FUSION.

People come from miles around to sample the outstanding breakfasts at this modest restaurant: The muffins and scones emerge fresh from the oven, and entrees such as the breakfast burrito or raisin French toast stuffed with cream cheese and walnuts call for a hearty appetite. You can start in again in the evening, on well-priced Pacific Rim and/or neo-Italian fare, such as penne in a fresh tomato-and-cream sauce splashed with vodka.

5   Provincetown

You made it! To one of the most interesting, rewarding spots on the Eastern seaboard. Explorer Bartholomew Gosnold must have felt much the same thrill in 1602 when he and his crew happened upon a "great stoare of codfysshes" here (it wasn't quite the gold they were seeking, but valuable enough to warrant changing the peninsula's name).

The Pilgrims, of course, were ecstatic when they dragged into the harbor 18 years later. Never mind that they'd landed several hundred miles off-course—it was a miracle they'd made it round the treacherous Outer Cape at all.

And Charles Hawthorne, the painter who "discovered" this near-derelict fishing town in the late 1890s and introduced it to the Greenwich Village intelligentsia, was besotted by this "jumble of color in the intense sunlight accentuated by the brilliant blue of the harbor."

He'd probably be aghast at the commercial circus his enthusiasm has wrought—though proud, perhaps, to find the Provincetown Art Association & Museum, which he helped found in 1914, still going strong. This town is extraordinarily dedicated to creative expression, both visual and verbal, and right now it's on a roll. Some would ascribe the inspiration to the quality of the light (and it is particularly lovely, soft and diffuse) or the solitude afforded by long lonely winters. Still, the general atmosphere of open-mindedness certainly plays a pivotal role in allowing a varied assortment of individuals to pull together in pushing the boundaries of the avant-garde.

That same warm embrace of different lifestyles accounts in part for Provincetown's ascendancy as a gay and lesbian resort. During peak season, Provincetown's streets are a celebration of any individual's freedom to be as "out" as imagination allows. The term "family values" enjoys a very broad definition here. "Family" encompasses all the populace in its glorious diversity. Those who've settled here know they've found a very special place, and in that they have something precious in common.

ESSENTIALS

GETTING THERE   After crossing either the Bourne or Sagamore bridge, head east on Route 6 or 6A to Orleans, then north on Route 6. Provincetown is 56 miles northeast of Sandwich, 42 miles northeast of Hyannis.

Bay State Cruises (☎ **617/723-7800** or 508/487-9274) makes round-trips from Boston, daily in summer and weekends on the shoulder seasons. **Cape Cod Cruises** (☎ **508/747-2400**) connects Plymouth and Provincetown in summer.

VISITOR INFORMATION   Contact the **Provincetown Chamber of Commerce,** 307 Commercial St., Provincetown, MA 02657 (☎ **508/487-3424;** fax: 508/487-8966; Web site: **www.capcodaccess.come/provincetownchamber**). You might also try the gay-oriented **Provincetown Business Guild,** 115 Bradford St., Provincetown, MA 02657 (☎ **800/637-8696** or 508/487-2313).

BEACHES & OUTDOOR PURSUITS

BEACHES   With nine-tenths of its territory (basically, all but the "downtown" area) protected by the Cape Cod National Seashore, Provincetown has miles of beaches. The 3-mile bay beach that lines the harbor, though certainly swimmable, is not all that inviting compared to the magnificent ocean beaches overseen by the CCNS. The

Provincetown

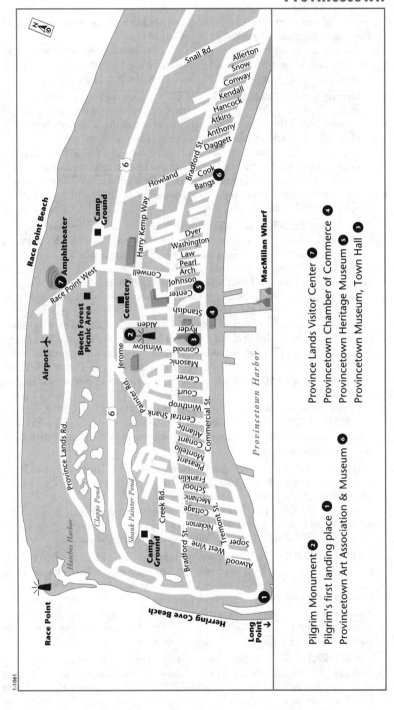

Pilgrim Monument **2**

Pilgrim's first landing place **1**

Provincetown Art Association & Museum **6**

Province Lands Visitor Center **7**

Provincetown Chamber of Commerce **4**

Provincetown Heritage Museum **5**

Provincetown Museum, Town Hall **3**

two official access areas (see below) tend to be crowded; however, you can always find a less densely populated stretch if you're willing to hike.

Note: Local beachgoers have been mobilizing for "clothing optional" beaches for years, but the rangers—fearful of voyeurs trampling the dune grass—are firmly opposed and routinely issue tickets, so stand forewarned (and fully clothed).

- **Herring Cove and Race Point:** Both CCNS beaches are known for their spectacular sunsets: Observers often applaud. Race Point, on the ocean side, is rougher, and you might actually spot whales en route to Stellwagen Bank. Accessible by shuttle, calmer Herring Cove is a haven for same-sex couples, who tend to sort themselves by gender. Parking costs $5 a day, $15 a season.

- **Long Point:** Trek out over the Breakwater and beyond, or catch a water shuttle—$7 one-way, $10 round-trip—from **Flyer's Boats** (see "Water Sports," below) to visit this very last spit of land, capped by an 1827 lighthouse. Locals call it "the end of the Earth."

BIKING/RECREATIONAL PATHS   North of town, nestled amid the Cape Cod National Seashore preserve, is one of the more spectacular bike paths in New England, the 7-mile **Province Lands Trail,** a heady swirl of steep dunes (watch out for sand drifts on the path) anchored by wind-stunted scrub pines. With its free parking, the **Province Lands Visitor Center** (☎ 508/487-1256) is a good place to start: You can survey the landscape from the observation tower to try to get your bearings before setting off amid the dizzying maze. With any luck, you'll find a spur path leading to one of the beaches—Race Point or Herring Cove—lining the shore.

Bike rentals are offered seasonally, practically on-site, by **Nelson's Bike Shop,** 43 Race Point Rd. (☎ 508/487-0034). It's also an easy jaunt from town, where you'll find plenty of good bike shops. Try the centrally located **Ptown Bikes,** 306 Commercial St. (☎ 508/487-TREK), though it's smart to reserve several days in advance.

In-line skates can be rented at **Oceana Sportswear,** 210A Commercial St. (☎ 508/487-7276), but remember, they're banned on the CCNS paths, and unless you're a pro, you'll have a tough time wending through the pedestrian crush along Commercial Street.

FISHING   Surf casting is permitted at **New Beach** (off Route 6) and **Race Point Beach** (near the Race Point Coast Guard Station); also, many people drop a hand line or light tackle right off the West End breakwater.

For low-cost **deep-sea fishing** via party boat, board the *Cee Jay* (☎ 508/487-4330) or *Captain Bill* (☎ 800/675-6723). For serious fishing, sign on for the *Shady Lady* (☎ 508/487-1700). All three depart from MacMillan Wharf.

NATURE TRAILS   Within the Province Lands (off Race Point Road, half a mile north of Route 6), the CCNS maintains the 1-mile self-guided **Beech Forest Trail,** a shaded path which circles a shallow freshwater pond blanketed with water lilies before heading into the woods. (Watch for sunning turtles.) You can see the shifting dunes (much of this terrain is soft sand) gradually encroaching on the forest. Another wonderful walk (though only half "natural") is along the **West End breakwater** out to the end of Long Point, about 3 miles round-trip.

WATER SPORTS   In addition to operating a Long Point shuttle from its own dock and MacMillan Wharf (see "Beaches," above), **Flyer's Boat Rental** at 131 Commercial St. in the West End (☎ 508/487-0898) offers all sorts of craft, from canoes and dinghies to sailboats of varying sizes; they also give sailing lessons and organize fishing trips and outings with aquaculturists.

WHALE WATCHING   The Stellwagen Bank feeding area, 8 miles off Provincetown, is a rich feeding ground for whales, and **Dolphin Fleet,** on MacMillan Wharf (☎ **800/826-9300** or 508/349-1900), was the first, and by most accounts still the best, outfit running whale watches at Stellwagen. Most cruises carry a naturalist (a very vague term) to provide running commentary; the difference on the Dolphin is that scientists from the Center for Coastal Studies are out there doing research crucial to the whales' survival, and part of the proceeds goes to further their worthwhile efforts. Serious whale aficionados will want to try one of the day-long trips to the Great South Channel, where humpbacks and finbacks are likely to be found by the dozen.

Some tips for first-timers: Dress very warmly, in layers (it's cold out on the water), and definitely take along a windbreaker—waterproof, if you've got one, or maybe your innkeeper can offer a spare. Tickets are $16.50 to $17.50 adults, $14.50 to $15.50 seniors and children 7 to 12, and free to children under 7. From April through October, there are three 3¹/₂-hour trips daily; in July and August there's also one 8-hour trip each week. Call for schedule and reservations (required). Closed November through March.

ORGANIZED TOURS & CRUISES

Art's Dune Tours. At the corner of Commercial and Standish sts. (in the center of town), Provincetown. ☎ **800/894-1951** or 508/487-1950. Fee $9 adults, $7 children under 12. Call for schedule and reservations.

In 1946, Art Costa started driving sightseers out to ogle the decrepit "dune shacks" where transient genii such as Eugene O'Neill, Jack Kerouac, and Jackson Pollock found their respective muses; in one such hovel, Tennessee Williams cooked up the steamy *Streetcar Named Desire.* The Park Service wanted to raze these eyesores, but luckily saner heads prevailed: They're now National Historic Landmarks. Art's tours, via Chevy Suburban, typically take about 1¹/₄ hours, and though he "narrates" straight through, his stories never seem scripted; you'll suspect (rightly) that he has scores more up his sleeve.

Bay Lady II. MacMillan Wharf (in the center of town), Provincetown. ☎ **508/487-9308.** Fee $10–$13 adults, $5 children under 12. Mid-May to mid-Oct four 2-hour sails daily; call for schedule and reservations. Closed mid-Oct to mid-May.

In sightseeing aboard this 73-foot reproduction gaff-rigged Grand Banks schooner, you'll actually be adding to the scenery for those onlookers onshore. The sunset trip is especially spectacular.

MUSEUMS

✪ **The Expedition** *Whydah* **Sea Lab & Learning Center.** MacMillan Wharf (in the center of town), Provincetown. ☎ **508/487-3688.** Fax 508/487-7955. Admission $5 adults, $3.50 children 3–12. July–Aug daily 9am–7pm; call for off-season hours. Closed Jan–Mar.

Cape Cod native Barry Clifford made headlines in 1984 when he tracked down the wreck of the 17th-century pirate ship *Whydah* (pronounced "*Wid*-dah," like Yankee for "widow") 1,500 feet off the coast of Wellfleet, where it had lain undisturbed since 1717. Only 10% excavated to date, it has already yielded over 100,000 artifacts, including 10,000 gold and silver coins, plus its namesake bell, proving its authenticity. In this museum/lab, visitors can observe the reclamation work—involving electrolytic reduction—as it's done, and discuss the ship, its discovery, and its significance with the scientists and scholars on hand, while studying the many interpretive exhibits. You may never approach the beach in quite the same way again: Thousands more wrecks are out there, awaiting the patient and clever.

Province Lands Visitor Center. Race Point Rd. (about 1 1/2 miles northwest of town center), Provincetown. ☎ **508/487-1256.** Free admission. July–Aug daily 9am–6pm; call for off-season hours. Closed Dec–Mar.

Though much smaller than the Salt Pond Visitor Center, this satellite also does a good job of explicating this special environment, where plant life must fight a fierce battle to maintain its toehold amid shifting sands buffeted by salty winds. After perusing the exhibits, be sure to circle the observation deck, for great views of the "parabolic" dunes. Also inquire about any special events scheduled, such as guided walks and family campfires.

Pilgrim Monument & Provincetown Museum. High Pole Hill Rd. (off Winslow St. north of Bradford St.). ☎ **800/247-1620** or 508/487-1310. Admission $5 adults, $3 children 4–12 (includes 2 hours free parking). July–early Sept daily 9am–7pm; off-season daily 9am–5pm; last admission 45 minutes before closing. Closed Dec–Mar.

You can't miss it: Anywhere you go in town, this granite tower looms, ever ready to restore your bearings. Climb up the 60 gradual ramps interspersed with 116 steps—a surprisingly easy lope—and you'll get a gargoyle's-eye view of the spiraling coast and, in the distance, Boston against a backdrop of New Hampshire mountains. Definitely devote some time to the curious exhibits in the museum at the monument's foot, chronicling Provincetown's checkered past as both fishing port and arts nexus. Among the memorabilia, you'll find polar bears brought back from MacMillan's expeditions, and early programs for the Provincetown Players.

✪ **Provincetown Art Association & Museum.** 460 Commercial St. (in the East End). ☎ **508/487-1750.** Suggested donation $3 adults, $1 seniors and children under 12. Late May to early Sept daily noon–5pm and 8–10pm; call for off-season hours.

This extraordinary cache of 20th-century American art began with five paintings donated by local artists, including Charles Hawthorne, the charismatic teacher who first "discovered" this picturesque outpost. Founded in 1914, only a year after New York's revolutionary Armory Show, the museum was the site of innumerable "space wars" as classicists and modernists vied for square footage; an uneasy truce was finally struck in 1927 when each camp was accorded its own show. In today's more ecumenical atmosphere, it's not unusual to see a tame still life hanging alongside a statement of Gen-X angst, or an acknowledged master sharing space with a less skilled upstart. Nor is there a hard and firm wall between creators and onlookers. Juried members' shows usually accompany the in-depth retrospectives, so there are always new discoveries to be made. The museum sponsors a full schedule of concerts, lectures, readings, and classes.

SHOPPING

Of the several dozen art galleries in town, only a handful (noted below) are reliably worthwhile. (For in-depth coverage of the local arts scene, look to *Provincetown Arts,* a glossy annual sold at the Provincetown Art Association & Museum shop.) In season, most of the galleries and even some of the shops take a suppertime siesta so as to reopen later and greet visitors as late as 10 or 11pm. Shows usually open Friday evening, prompting a "stroll" tradition spanning the many receptions.

ANTIQUES/COLLECTIBLES The second-story **Clifford-Williams Antiques,** 225 Commercial St. (☎ **508/487-4174**), is packed to the gills with substantial English furniture.

You'd have to go to Boston—or abroad—to view estate jewelry as fine as that at **Small Pleasures,** 359 Commercial St. (☎ **508/487-3712**). Virginia McKenna's hand-selected stock ranges from romantic Victorian settings to sleek silver for the 1920s-era male.

Two others: **Remembrances of Things Past,** 376 Commercial St. (☎ 508/487-9443), is a fun kitsch fest; **West End Antiques,** 146 Commercial St. (☎ 508/487-6723), is more of a nostalgia fest.

ART/CRAFTS   Berta Walker is a force to be reckoned with, having nurtured artists such as Charles Hawthorne, Milton Avery, and Robert Motherwell. Whoever has her current attention—such as figurative sculptor Romolo Del Deo—warrants watching at the **Berta Walker Gallery,** 208 Bradford St., in the East End (☎ 508/487-6411). Closed late October to late May.

Not content to have cornered some of the best fine art around, Berta has now opened a small storefront satellite gallery, **Walker's Wonders,** 153 Commercial St., in the West End (☎ 508/487-8794), to showcase folk and functional art, including furniture, jewelry, and sundry "imaginative objects and special delights."

Founded in 1994 by artist and publishing scion Nick Lawrence, ✪ **dna gallery,** 286 Bradford St., in the East End (☎ 508/487-7700), has attracted such talents as photographer Joel Meyerowitz (Provincetown's favorite portraitist, known for such tomes as *Cape Light*) and sculptor Conrad Malicoat, whose free-form brick chimneys and hearths can be seen and admired about town. Another contributor is local conceptualist/provocateur Jay Critchley, whose latest enterprise involves condoms adorned with an image of the Virgin Mary. It's a very lively bunch, appropriately grouped under the rubric "definitive new art," and readings by cutting-edge authors add to the buzz. Closed mid-October to late May.

Bunny Pearlman, the gallery director at **East End Gallery,** 349 Commercial St. (☎ 508/487-4745), and an artist herself, has an eye for iconic art. Closed late November to mid-April.

Julie Heller, owner of, you guessed it, the **Julie Heller Gallery,** 2 Gosnold St., off Commercial Street (☎ 508/487-2169), started collecting early Provincetown paintings as a child. She chose so incredibly well, her roster (shown in a rustic fishing shack) now reads like a who's who of local art. Hawthorne, Avery, Hofmann, Lazzell, Hensche—all the big names are here, as well as some contemporary artists.

Artists invited to show with the venerable **Long Point Gallery,** 492 Commercial St., in the East End (☎ 508/487-1795), are among the elect. Paul Resika's Provincetown landscapes, for example, perfectly capture the intensity of color, the sense of suspension in time. Closed mid-September to mid-June.

The art shown at **Rice/Polak Gallery,** 430 Commercial St., in the East End (☎ 508/487-1052), has a decorative bent and a certain stylish snap. Several gallery artists have fun with dimensions—such as painter Tom Seghi with his mammoth pears, and sculptor Larry Culkins with his assemblages of undersized, antique-look dresses. Closed December through April.

Splashy both in selection and in presentation, **UFO Gallery,** 424 Commercial St., in the East End (☎ 508/487-4424)—short for Universal Fine Objects—is not afraid to delve into the decorative and functional. Boston *fauve* Todd McKie, for instance, contributes colorful platters painted like tribal masks. The art can be quite distinguished, with such respected figures as Michael Mazur (*Dante's Inferno*) and Helen Miranda Wilson delivering their latest musings. Closed early September to late May.

The **William-Scott Gallery,** 439 Commercial St., in the East End (☎ 508/487-4040), is so tiny that it may look, on the surface, like one of those roadside galleries geared to impulsive tourists. But take a closer look. John Dowd's straightforward house portraits are not as simple as they might seem: Still quite young, he's shaping up as Hopper's heir apparent. Closed November to late May.

DISCOUNT SHOPPING   Adams' Pharmacy, 254 Commercial St. (☎ **508/ 487-0069**), is Provincetown's oldest business (established in 1868), and still has an old-fashioned soda fountain. We—and apparently, a great many drag queens—like it for the cheapo makeup (two-for-$1 lipsticks) in outrageous colors.

Veteran scavengers won't be put off by the musty backstage aroma at the **Provincetown Second Hand Store,** 389 Commercial St. (☎ **508/487-9153**). There are prime pickings to be had here, including some extremely glam outfits and shoes in petite to he-man sizes, and an assortment of firsthand vintage lingerie culled from the owner's family business. Closed January and February.

WHERE TO STAY
EXPENSIVE

✪ **The Brass Key Guesthouse.** 9 Court St. (in the center of town), Provincetown, MA 02657. ☎ **800/842-9858** or 508/487-9005. Fax 508/487-9020. 10 rms, 2 cottages. A/C TV TEL. Summer $155–$220 double, $190 cottage. Rates include continental breakfast. AE, DISC, MC, V.

Michael MacIntyre and Bob Anderson could give lessons in how to set up and operate the ideal inn. They've inaugurated three so far: the original Brass Key in Key West, this beauty, and a new satellite on Bradford Street. What was their secret? Take one lovely old captain's house on a quiet street, enhance its privacy with a decorative wooden fence, its beauty with intensive landscaping, and install a 17-foot cerulean whirlpool for soaking under the stars. The superattentive service and top-notch amenities (every room has its own minifridge and VCR) reflect Michael's Ritz-Carlton background, and the tasteful country-style decor, Bob's Greenwich, Connecticut, upbringing. Together, they're a powerful social force in town, sponsoring a series of wine-maker dinners and importing the occasional cultural event. Staying here is like visiting rich relatives in Bar Harbor, except that they probably wouldn't provide a rooftop deck for nude sunbathing.

✪ **The Tides.** 837 Commercial St. (near the Truro border), Provincetown, MA 02657. ☎ **800/ 528-1234** or 508/487-1045. 62 rms, 2 suites. Summer $129–$179 double, $249 suite. AE, DC, DISC, MC, V. Closed Nov–Apr.

Located on a peaceful 6-acre parcel well removed both from Provincetown's bustle and North Truro's congestion, this surprise oasis—part of the Best Western chain, which takes pride in individualized excellence—boasts every feature you might require of a beachfront retreat, including a nice wide beach you can literally flop onto from the ground-level units. Most of the rooms overlook Provincetown's quirky skyline, as does the generously proportioned outdoor pool. Every inch of this complex has been groomed, including the green grounds, the Wedgwood blue breakfast room, which seems to have been lifted whole from an elegant country inn, and the spotless rooms decorated in a soothing palette of ivory and pale pastels. And the only sound you'll hear at night is the mournful refrain of a foghorn.

✪ **Watermark Inn.** 603 Commercial St. (in the East End), Provincetown, MA 02657. ☎ **800/ 734-0165** or 508/487-0165. Fax 508/487-2383. 10 suites. TV, TEL. Summer $130–$275 double. AE, MC, V.

If you'd like to experience Provincetown without being stuck in the thick of it (the carnival atmosphere can get tiring at times), this contemporary inn at the peaceful edge of town is the perfect choice. Resident innkeeper/architect Kevin Shea carved this beachfront manor into 10 dazzling suites: The prize ones, on the top floor, have peaked picture windows and sweeping views from their own 80-foot deck. Innkeeper/

designer Judy Richland, his wife, saw to the interior decoration—bold Marimekko quilts and plenty of primary colors.

MODERATE

The Boatslip Beach Club. 161 Commercial St. (in the West End), Provincetown, MA 02657. ☎ **800/451-7547** or 508/487-1669. Fax 508/487-6021. 45 rms. TV TEL. Summer $125–$160 double. MC, V. Closed Nov to early Apr.

Pack your party clothes. As the site of Provincetown's incomparable "tea dances," this modernized waterside motel is Party Central—mostly for gay men, but women, too, and anyone else who wants to hang around. There are some rather snazzy human specimens draped around the pool, the SRO sundeck, and one another. Just as you can expect to be scoped out, you can pretty much count on making interesting new friends.

Hargood House at Bayshore. 493 Commercial St. (in the East End), Provincetown, MA 02657. ☎ and fax **508/487-9113.** 2 studios, 17 efficiencies. TV TEL. Summer $99–$103 studio, $132–$194 efficiency. AE, MC, V.

This cherished beachfront complex is enjoying a new lease on life. While retaining some of their original charm, such as a few select antiques and salvaged architectural details, the rooms have been lightened up, the better to reflect the waterside setting. The prize rooms surround a flower-lined lawn, with pride of place going to a cathedral-ceiling loft right over the water; several more apartments, including a freestanding little house, can be found across the street. The decor is not quite designer level, but the big plus is the opportunity to live among artworks on loan from the Walker Gallery, many of which would rightly hang on a museum wall.

Land's End Inn. 22 Commercial St. (in the West End), Provincetown, MA 02657. ☎ **800/276-7088** or 508/487-0706. 17 rms (1 with separate bath), 2 apts, 1 suite. Summer $85–$190 double, $140–$150 apt, $285 suite. Rates include continental breakfast. No credit cards.

Enjoying a prime 2-acre perch atop Gull Hill, this 1907 bungalow is stuffed to bursting with rare and often outlandish antiques. Some rooms would suit a 19th-century sheik, others your everyday hedonist. In the dark-paneled living room, it's always Christmas: The ornate decorations never come down. The place is guaranteed to delight some guests and overwhelm others. There's no denying that the octagonal loft suite, a virtual goldfish bowl poised to take in views in every direction, is a spectacular setting for romance (shy types need not apply). Though the inn is predominantly gay, cosmopolitan visitors will be made to feel welcome, regardless of gender or orientation.

INEXPENSIVE

✪ **The Black Pearl Bed & Breakfast.** 11 Pearl St. (off Commercial St., near the center of town), Provincetown, MA 02657. ☎ **508/487-6405.** Fax 508/487-7412. 6 rms, 1 cottage. Summer $70–$85 double, $150 cottage. Rates include continental breakfast. MC, V. Closed Jan–Feb.

Every room in this cheerily updated captain's house has a look all its own, from bold Southwestern to fanciful Micronesian, and several boast skylights and private decks. The Connemara Cottage takes the cake, with an antique bedstead, wood-burning fireplace, and double Jacuzzi, plus such niceties as air-conditioning and a cable TV with VCR.

The Fairbanks Inn. 90 Bradford St. (near the center of town), Provincetown, MA 02657. ☎ **800/324-7265** or 508/487-0386. 13 rms (4 with shared bath), 1 efficiency, 1 apt. Summer $75–$95 double, $85 efficiency, $175 apt. Rates include continental breakfast. AE, DC, MC, V.

Bargain-priced because of its Bradford Street location, this colonial mansion (built in 1776) looks its era without looking its age. Beautifully maintained, it boasts gleaming wooden floors softened by rich Orientals, and romantic bedding—sleigh beds and four-posters. A patio, porch, and rooftop sundeck lend themselves to pleasant socializing.

Holiday Inn. 6 Snail Rd. (at Rte. 6A, in the East End), Provincetown, MA 02657. ☎ **800/465-4329** or 508/487-1711. Fax 508/487-3929. 78 rms. A/C TV TEL. Summer $129–$139 double. AE, CB, DC, DISC, MC, V. Closed Nov–Apr.

A good choice for first-timers not quite sure what they're getting into, this no-surprises motel-with-pool at the eastern edge of town is a bit far from the action but congenial enough. Guests get a nice view of town, along with free movies in the restaurant/lounge.

✪ **The Inn at Cook St.** 7 Cook St. (at Bradford St., in the East End), Provincetown, MA 02657. ☎ **888/COOK-655** or 508/487-3894. 3 rms, 2 suites, 1 cottage. TV. Summer $90 double, $125 suite, $100 cottage. Rates include continental breakfast. MC, V.

A welcome addition to the B&B scene, this 1836 Greek Revival beauty, tucked away in a quiet neighborhood, exudes tasteful warmth, from its pale yellow exterior trimmed with black shutters to its hidden garden, complete with goldfish pool. All the handsomely appointed rooms are oriented to this oasis, with an assortment of private and shared decks, and the tiny rose-trellised cottage, with sleeping loft, is an integral part of its charm.

The Rose & Crown. 158 Commercial St. (in the West End), Provincetown, MA 02657. ☎ **508/487-3332.** Web site: ptown.com/ptown/rosecrown/. 6 rms (3 with shared bath), 1 apt, 1 cottage. Summer $65–$95 double, $110 apt or cottage. Rates include continental breakfast. DC, MC, V.

Follow the yellow brick road, over a tiny footbridge spanning a minilagoon full of disporting Barbies and Kens, to enter a world where, as the brochure brags, "Anything worth doing is worth overdoing!" That maxim is borne out at every turn, in the lace-draped lamps and movie-star dolls; even the resident cat, a magnificent Persian, seems to have gotten the message and shamelessly vogues. The kitschy front yard of this 1780s Georgian "square rigger" has secured the inn's title as Provincetown's most photographed, and any pennies you care to toss in Barbie's Dream Pool go toward the fight against AIDS.

✪ **White Horse Inn.** 500 Commercial St. (in the East End), Provincetown, MA 02657. ☎ **508/487-1790.** 12 rms (9 with shared bath), 6 efficiencies. Summer $70 double, $100–$125 efficiency. No credit cards.

The rates are a literal steal, especially given the fact that this inn is the very embodiment of Provincetown's bohemian mystique. Frank Schaefer has been tinkering with this late-18th-century house since 1963. The rooms may be a bit austere, but each is enlivened by some of the artwork he has collected over the decades. A number of his fellow artists helped him out in cobbling together the studio apartments out of salvage: There's an aura of beatnik improv about them still.

WHERE TO DINE
VERY EXPENSIVE

✪ **Front Street.** 230 Commercial St. (in the center of town). ☎ **508/487-9715.** Reservations recommended. Main courses $17–$24. AE, MC, V. June–Oct daily 6–10:30pm; call for off-season hours. Closed Jan–Apr. NEW AMERICAN.

A longtime fave, this bustling little bistro—housed in the brick basement of a Victorian manse—continues to surprise and delight year after year. Chef Donna Aliperti revises her menu weekly, so aficionados know to check the latest posting, even if they've already reserved prime seating—the high-backed wooden booths—weeks in advance. Among the signature dishes that regularly surface in season are the grilled salmon splashed with raspberry balsamic vinegar, tea-smoked duck, and an unforgettable nectarine croustade.

✪ **Martin House.** 157 Commercial St. ☎ **508/487-1327.** Fax 508/487-4514. Reservations recommended. Main courses $14–$26. AE, CB, DC, DISC, MC, V. July–Oct Mon–Sat 6–11pm, Sun 3:30–11pm; call for off-season hours. Closed early Dec. FUSION.

Easily one of the most charming restaurants on the Cape, this snuggery of rustic rooms also just happens to contain one of the Cape's most forward-thinking kitchens. Co-owner Gary Martin is the conceptualizer behind the inspired regional menu, and chef Alex Mazzocca the gifted creator. Both favor regional delicacies, such as the unusual *mizuma* (a Japanese bitter herb) that jazzes up a gingered dipping sauce for the Asian steamed buns, or the local littlenecks that appear in a kafir lime–tamarind broth with green chili paste. The dinners, pleasantly delivered, exceed every expectation: They're like nothing you've ever had before, and the peaceful, softly lit rooms make an optimal setting for exploring new tastes. On Sunday afternoons, the rose-choked garden terrace lends itself beautifully to a traditional Sunday afternoon tea, featuring faithful renditions of the customary savories and sweets.

EXPENSIVE

✪ **Cafe Edwige.** 333 Commercial St. ☎ **508/487-2008.** Reservations recommended. Main courses $15–$18. AE, DC, MC, V. July–Aug daily 8am–1pm and 6–11pm; call for off-season hours. Closed late Oct to Mar. NEW AMERICAN/FUSION.

The tourist throngs generally walk right on by this second-story eatery, little suspecting what they're passing up. To start: superlative breakfasts in a healthful mode, featuring everything from tofu frittatas to broiled flounder with stir-fried vegetables. The cathedral-ceilinged space, with hippie-era wooden booths and deco accents, is a great place to greet the day. At night it's commensurately romantic, with subdued lighting and the masterful cuisine of chef Steve Frappolli, a veteran of New York's New American landmark, An American Place. He's in his element here, dishing up the likes of planked codfish with ginger-carrot broth and wild-berry shortcake.

✪ **The Mews Restaurant & Cafe Mews.** 429 Commercial St. ☎ **508/487-1500.** Reservations recommended. Main courses $8–$29. AE, CB, DC, DISC, MC, V. Mid-June to mid-Sept daily 11am–3pm and 5:30–10pm; call for off-season hours. Closed late Dec (except New Year's Eve) to mid-Feb. NEW AMERICAN.

An enduring favorite, the Mews boasts a century-old carved mahogany bar. You can always bank on fine food and suave service. The formal dining room, downstairs, is right on the beach—practically *of* the beach, with its sand-toned walls warmed by toffee-colored Tiffany table lamps. Standouts include the marsala-marinated portobello mushrooms and a mixed seafood carpaccio. Among the showier entrees is "captured scallops": prime Wellfleet specimens enclosed with a shrimp-and-crab mousse in a crisp wonton pouch and served atop a petite filet mignon with chipotle aioli. Desserts and coffees—you might take them upstairs in the cafe, to the accompaniment of improvisatory soft jazz piano—are delectable.

Scruples World Bistro. 149 Commercial St. (in the West End). ☎ **508/487-1076.** Main courses $14–$22. AE, DISC, MC, V. Late June to early Sept 11am–1am; call for off-season hours. Closed Nov to mid-May. INTERNATIONAL.

HOSTESS WILL EAT YOU reads the altered sign in the window, the site of many an alternative tourist photo. Actually, the hostess—often a drag performance artist—is more likely to entertain you, as will the wild mix of cuisines. Thai predominates, from classic coconut soup and chicken satay through lemongrass shrimp; other influences include Caribbean and Tex-Mex. All that spice makes an excellent foil for the bar's "beach cocktails": Blue Hawaii, Bahama Mama, and more.

MODERATE

Bubala's by the Bay. 183 Commercial St. (in the West End). ☎ **508/487-0773.** Main courses $9–$19. AE, DISC, MC, V. Daily 8am–10:30pm. Closed Nov–Mar. ECLECTIC.

Once a nothing special seaside restaurant, this trendy bistro—miraculously transformed with a gaudy yellow paint job and Picassoesque wall murals—promises "serious food at sensible prices." That it delivers, all day long—from buttermilk waffles with real maple syrup through lobster tarragon salad and creative focaccia sandwiches to fajitas, Cajun calamari, and pad Thai.

✪ The Commons Bistro & Bar. 386 Commercial St. ☎ **508/487-7800.** Reservations recommended. Main courses $9–$19. AE, MC, V. Late June to early Sept daily 8:30am–1pm; call for off-season hours. ECLECTIC.

It's a toss-up: The sidewalk cafe provides a great view of Provincetown's inimitable street life, whereas the plum-colored dining room inside affords a refuge adorned with the owners' extraordinary collection of original Toulouse-Lautrec prints. Either way, you'll get to partake of tasty and creative fare. At lunchtime, the overstuffed "lobster club" sandwich on lemon bread is outstanding, and the grilled duck medaillons served atop soba, Asian greens, and shredded jicama is the ultimate summertime refresher. The Commons boasts the only wood-fired pizza oven in town to date, and the soft-crusted pizzette with various toppings—consider the crisped duck, scallions, chèvre, and wild mushrooms—makes a great snack whatever the hour. Another long overdue first for this seafaring town is a seasonal sushi bar.

✪ The Dancing Lobster Cafe/Trattoria. 9 Ryder St. Extension (on Fisherman's Wharf, off Commercial St.). ☎ **508/487-0900.** Reservations not accepted. Main courses $10–$14. No credit cards. Daily 5:30–11pm. Closed Nov–Apr. MEDITERRANEAN.

One way or another, your jaw is bound to drop—whether at the scenic location of this glass-sided restaurant, or the easy-on-the-pocket prices that prevail. It's worth lining up for 90 minutes or more for one of the 20 hotly contested tables to feast on the sunny output of this open kitchen. Where to begin? With the grilled-squid *bruscetta,* the saffrony Venetian *zuppa di pesce,* or perhaps the asparagus ravioli or steamed mussels with a basil aioli? You'll appreciate the Italian tradition of *primi* and *secondi,* even if it curbs your craving for tiramisu—but you could always take it with you, or better yet, use it as an excuse to come back.

Iguana Grill. 135 Bradford St. (in the center of town). ☎ **508/487-8800.** Fax 508/487-8267. Main courses $8–$14. AE, DISC, MC, V. July–Aug Daily 5–10pm; call for off-season hours. Closed Nov–Feb. LATIN AMERICAN.

Healthful Mexican? It might seem an oxymoron, except that co-owner Eric Ovalle insists on substituting low-fat updates for the rich fare he grew up on. You won't find a single fried food on the menu, and in fact not so much as a morsel of beef. Lean ground turkey fills in nicely for the usual *carne* in such traditional dishes as tacos, burritos, fajitas, and enchiladas. Be sure to try something cloaked in *mole,* a chocolate-based sauce that's spicy rather than sweet. And then, since you've been good, blow all your resolve on a *postre* like go, a Santo Domingan corn pudding.

The Lobster Pot. 321 Commercial St. (in the center of town). ☎ **508/487-0842.** Reservations not accepted. Main courses $14–$19. AE, DISC, DC, MC, V. Mid-June to mid-Sept daily 11:30am–10:30pm; call for off-season hours. Closed Jan. SEAFOOD.

Snobbish foodies might turn their noses up at a venue so flagrantly Olde Cape Coddish, but for Provincetown regulars, no season seems complete without at least one pilgrimage. Pilgrimage is the right word, because you have to suffer somewhat to get in: The line, which starts near the aromatic, albeit frantic kitchen, often snakes into the street. A lucky few will make it all the way to the outdoor deck; however, most tables, indoor and out, afford nice views of MacMillan Wharf.

INEXPENSIVE

Cafe Heaven. 199 Commercial St. (in the center of town). ☎ **508/487-9639.** Reservations not accepted. Most items under $10. No credit cards. Late May to early Sept daily 8am–3pm and 6:30–10pm; call for off-season hours. Closed Nov–Apr. AMERICAN.

Prized for its leisurely country breakfasts (served till midafternoon, for you reluctant risers), this modernist storefront—adorned with big, bold paintings, locally produced—also turns out substantive sandwiches, such as avocado and goat cheese on a French baguette. The salads are appealing as well—especially the "special shrimp," lightly doused with dilled sour cream and tossed with tomatoes and grapes. Innumerable "pasta possibilities," plus "heavenly" burgers with a choice of internationally inspired toppings, are the main event come evening.

BAKED GOODS & LATE-NIGHT DINING

You absolutely have to peruse the cases of *pasteis* (meat pies) and pastries at the **Provincetown Portuguese Bakery,** 299 Commercial St., in the center of town (☎ 508/487-1803). Point to a few and take your surprise package out on the pier for snacking. Though perhaps not the wisest course for the whale watch bound, it's the best way to sample the scrumptious international output of this beloved institution. Closed November through March.

A local landmark, **Spiritus,** 190 Commercial St. (☎ 508/487-2808), is an outré pizza parlor known for post–last-call cruising: It's open till 2am. The pizza's good, as are the fruit drinks, specialty coffees, and premium ice cream. For a peaceful morning repast—and perhaps a relaxed round of bocce—check out the little garden in back. Closed November through March.

PROVINCETOWN AFTER DARK

There's so much going on in season on any given night, you might want to simplify your search by calling or stopping in at the **Provincetown Reservations System** office at 293 Commercial St. in the center of town (☎ 508/487-6400).

THE CLUB SCENE

The Atlantic House. 6 Masonic Place (off Commercial St., 2 blocks west of Town Hall). ☎ **508/487-3821.** Cover for the Big Room $5.

Open year-round, the "A-house"—the nation's premier gay bar—also welcomes straights of both sexes, except in the leather-oriented Macho Bar upstairs. Late in the evening, there's usually plenty going on in the Big Room dance bar. Check out the Tennessee Williams memorabilia, including a portrait *au naturel;* there's more across the street, in a new restaurant called Grand Central.

The Boatslip Beach Club. 161 Commercial St. ☎ **508/487-2660.** Cover varies.

Come late afternoon, if you wonder where all the beachgoers went it's a safe guess that a goodly number are attending at the gay-lesbian tea dance held daily in season from 3:30 to 6:30pm on the hotel's pool deck. Later in the evening, after a post tea dance at Pied Piper (see below), they'll probably be back for some disco or two-stepping.

Crown & Anchor. 247 Commercial St. (in the center of town). ☎ **508/487-1430.** Cover varies; call for schedule.

There's something for everyone at this warren of specialty bars, spanning leather (in "The Vault"), disco, comedy, drag shows (including headliner "Musty Chiffon" singing 1960s camp classics), and cabaret (such as the irresistible trio known simply as Betty). Facilities include a pool bar and game room.

Pied Piper. 293A Commercial St. (in the center of town). ☎ **508/487-1527.** Cover varies; call for schedule. Closed Nov to mid-Apr.

In season, a "parade" of gay revelers descends in early evening from the Boatslip to "the Pied," for its After Tea T-Dance. The late-night wave consists of a fair number of women, or fairly convincing simulations thereof (Monday and Wednesday nights feature the "female illusionists" of the Drag Factory). For a glimpse of stars in the making, check out "Putting on the Hits," a sampling of local talent held Tuesday nights at 10pm.

Vixen. Pilgrim House, 336 Commercial St. (in the center of town). ☎ **508/487-6424.** Cover varies; call for schedule.

Provincetown's oldest hotel was overhauled in 1995, yielding this chic new women's bar. On the roster are jazz, blues, and comedy acts—including the unabashedly butch (even in a prom dress) and very funny Lea Delaria, who resembles a punk Bud Costello.

THE BAR SCENE

Governor Bradford. 312 Commercial St. (in the center of town). ☎ **508/487-9618.** Cover varies; call for schedule.

It's a good old bar, featuring a summer-long lineup of blues acts, plus the inimitable home-grown, gender-bending rock group known as Space Pussy.

Larry's Bar. At Sebastian's Waterside Restaurant. ☎ **508/487-3286.** No cover. Closed late Oct to mid-Apr.

Mrs. Wald did not raise a retiring child. The irrepressible Larry—perennial chair and chief cheerleader for Provincetown's campy Carnival Week—is a drink-dispensing one-man entertainment committee. Once he gets going on one of his riffs (usually centered on an assortment of mutant Barbie dolls), you can just sit back and enjoy the show. This tiny bar is the place to go when you need a good laugh.

Martha's Vineyard & Nantucket

7

For those who seek refuge here, from megastars and CEOs to middle-class families and penniless students, Martha's Vineyard and Nantucket are the ultimate escape. Time has a way of dropping away once you set off for these naturally isolated ports. Not that you'll be leaving the 20th century far behind: Laptops and cell phones, FedEx and satellite dishes can be found in abundance here. The difference is, you'll find yourself more inclined to ignore them.

Though geologically similar, each island has a distinct personality. Martha's Vineyard, large enough to support a year-round population spanning a broader socioeconomic spectrum, is not quite so rarefied as is Nantucket. Islanders pride themselves on their Democratic liberalism. True, a prime ocean-side estate might fetch millions here, but the lucky local denizens still dicker over the price of zucchini at the local farmers' market.

Whereas Nantucket is pretty much a unified whole centered on one small town, the Vineyard, with its colorful villages, is multifaceted. Edgartown comes closest to Nantucket in formality and architecture. Oak Bluffs, with its gaudily painted gingerbread cottages, is a religious community turned nightlife carnival. Bucolic Chilmark looks like a chunk of northern New England, complete with stone fences and farmhouses, while commercial Vineyard Haven could easily be plunked back on the Cape.

Nantucket, flash-frozen in the mid-19th century through zealous zoning, has long been considered a Republican haven. It's rich and traditional, as the stereotype goes, and if your great-grandparents didn't summer here, you might as well not bother: You'll just be roundly ignored. The younger generations, however, many of whom did indeed grow up summering here among the old guard, tend to be more welcoming. In fact, there's a small creative buzz that's making itself heard on Nantucket in the form of brave new enterprises, especially shops and restaurants.

In other words, there's something for everyone on both islands, and it's fun to keep exploring and comparing until you happen upon a niche that feels just right.

1 Martha's Vineyard

For a place with such a chichi reputation—especially since the Clintons and Princess Diana recently put in well-publicized appearances—this 100-square-mile island can seem surprisingly dowdy at first glance. It presents its showiest side in the trim port of Edgartown, where impressive captain's mansions bespeak the riches that prior generations wrested from the sea. Inland, the rolling meadows and dense forests might make you forget you're on an island at all.

Most visitors cling to the shore, usually making a circuit of Vineyard Haven (the only truly year-round town); Oak Bluffs, with its colorful cluster of carpenter's Gothic cottages; buttoned-down Edgartown, still the seat of money and power; and Gay Head, where the remarkable multicolored clay cliffs remain under the stewardship of their original caretakers, the Wampanoag Indians. Visitors with a bit more time and latitude will also want to take in the rough-hewn fishing port of Menemsha and wander the rural back roads of Chilmark, where a loose-knit federation of artists, writers, actors, and musicians—some rather well known—seek and sometimes even find inspiration.

GETTING THERE

BY FERRY   Most visitors take ferries from the mainland to the Vineyard. If you're traveling via car or bus, you will most likely catch a boat from Woods Hole on Cape Cod; however, boats also run from Falmouth, Hyannis, New Bedford, and Nantucket.

From Woods Hole, the state-run **Steamship Authority** (☎ **508/477-8600**) operates daily, year-round, weather permitting. It also maintains the only car ferries, which make the 45-minute trip to Vineyard Haven throughout the year, and to Oak Bluffs from late May to early September (call for seasonal schedules). A one-way car passage from mid-May to mid-October is $38; in the off-season, it's $18 to $24. During the summer, you'll need a reservation to bring your car over and you must book months in advance. If you arrive without a reservation, come early and be pre-pared to wait in the standby line for hours.

Many people prefer to leave their cars on the mainland, take the ferry (often with their bikes), and then rent a car, jeep, moped, or bicycle on the island. You can park your car at Woods Hole or at one of the many lots in Falmouth; parking is $7.50 per day. Free shuttle buses (equipped for bikes) run regularly from the outlying lots to the ferry terminal.

A one-way passenger ticket from mid-May to mid-October is $4.75 for adults, $2.40 for children 5 to 12 (kids under 5 ride free); in the off-season, $4.25 for adults, $2.15 for children. If you're bringing your bike, it's an extra $3 each way, year-round. You do not need a reservation on the ferry if you're traveling without your car.

From Falmouth, you can board the *Island Queen* at Falmouth Harbor (☎ **508/548-4800**) for a 40-minute cruise to Oak Bluffs (passengers only; no cars). The boat runs from mid-May through mid-October and a one-way fare costs $6 for adults, $3 for children under 13, and an extra $3 for bikes. Parking near the harbor is $8 to $10 per day.

From Hyannis, you can take the **Hy-Line** from the Ocean Street Dock (☎ **508/778-2600**) to Oak Bluffs, May through October. Trip time is about 1 hour and 45 minutes and a one-way trip costs $11 for adults, $5.50 for children 5 to 12 ($4.50 extra for bikes). In July and August, it's a good idea to reserve a parking spot in Hyannis by calling the number above; the all-day fee is $9.

From New Bedford, Massachusetts, the *Schamonchi* at Billy Woods Wharf (☎ **508/997-1688**) takes island-goers to Vineyard Haven from mid-May through mid-October. Trip time is about 1½ hours and a 1-day/round-trip ticket is $16 ($9 for children under 13, and $2.50 for bikes).

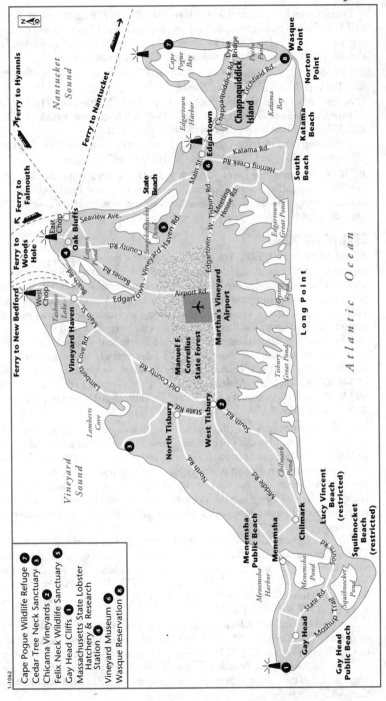

Cape Pogue Wildlife Refuge **7**
Cedar Tree Neck Sanctuary **3**
Chicama Vineyards **2**
Felix Neck Wildlife Sanctuary **5**
Gay Head Cliffs **1**
Massachusetts State Lobster Hatchery & Research Station **4**
Vineyard Museum **6**
Wasque Reservation **8**

1-1062

From Nantucket, you can take the **Hy-Line** (☎ 508/778-2600) to Oak Bluffs, mid-May through mid-September. Trip time is 2 hours and 15 minutes and the one-way fare is $11 for adults, $5.50 for children 5 to 12, and $4.50 extra for bikes. It's the only passenger service between the islands (no cars allowed, though).

BY PLANE   You can also fly into the **Martha's Vineyard Airport** (☎ 508/693-7022) in West Tisbury, about 5 miles outside Edgartown.

Airlines serving the Vineyard include: **Cape Air** (☎ 800/352-0714 or 508/771-6944); **Continental Express** (☎ 800/525-0280); **Northwest Airlink** (☎ 800/225-2525); and **USAirways Express** (☎ 800/428-4322).

Two companies offering year-round charter service are: **Air New England** (☎ 508/693-8899) and **Direct Flight** (☎ 508/693-6688).

BY BUS   **Bonanza Bus Lines** (☎ 800/556-3815) serves the Woods Hole ferry port from Boston (new South Station), New York City, and Providence, Rhode Island. The trip from Boston takes about an hour and 35 minutes and costs $12.50 one-way; from New York, it's about an 8-hour trip.

GETTING AROUND

BY BICYCLE & MOPED   You shouldn't leave the Vineyard without exploring on two wheels, if only for a couple of hours. There's a little of everything, from paved paths to hilly country roads (see "Beaches & Outdoor Pursuits" below for details on where to ride). Mopeds are also a popular way to navigate Vineyard roads, but some roads tend to be narrow and rough—the number of accidents involving mopeds seems to rise every year. You'll need a driver's license to rent a moped.

Bike- and moped-rental shops are clustered throughout all three down-island towns. Bike rentals will cost about $8 to $18 a day, mopeds $25 to $50. In Vineyard Haven, try **Martha's Vineyard Scooter & Bikes,** on Union Street (☎ 508/693-0782); in Oak Bluffs, **Anderson's,** on the Circuit Avenue Extension (☎ 508/693-9346), or **DeBettencourt's Bike Shop** (☎ 508/693-0011); and in Edgartown, **R. W. Cutler Bike,** 1 Main St. (☎ 508/627-4052).

BY CAR   If you're coming to the Vineyard for a few days and you're going to stick to the down-island towns, it's best to leave your car on the mainland. Traffic and parking on the island can be brutal in summer, and it's easy to take the shuttle buses (see below) from town to town or simply bike your way around. But, if you're staying longer or want to do some exploring up-island, bring your car or rent one on the island—my favorite way to tour the Vineyard is by jeep. Keep in mind, however, that car-rental rates can soar during peak season, and gas is also much more expensive on the island.

There are representatives of the national car-rental chains at the airport and in Vineyard Haven and Oak Bluffs. Local agencies also operate out of all three port towns and many of them also rent jeeps, mopeds, and bikes. The national chains include: **Alamo** (☎ 800/327-9633); **Avis** (☎ 800/331-1212); **Budget** (☎ 800/527-0700); **Hertz** (☎ 800/654-3131); **National** (☎ 800/227-7368); and **Thrifty Rent-a-Car** (☎ 800/FOR-CARS).

Local agencies include: **Adventure Rentals,** on Beach Road (☎ 508/693-1959), or **Atlantic** (☎ 508/693-0480), both in Vineyard Haven; **Vineyard Classic Cars** of Oak Bluffs (☎ 508/693-5551), which rents classic Corvettes, plus standard vehicles; and **AAA Island Rentals** (☎ 508/627-6800) in Edgartown. Another recommendable island company that operates out of the airport is **All Island Rent-a-Car** (☎ 508/693-6868).

BY SHUTTLE BUS & TROLLEY   Low-cost ($1 to $3, depending on distance) shuttle buses make the circuit around the down-island towns in season (late June to early September) from 7am to midnight; for information and a schedule call the **Martha's Vineyard Transit Authority** (☎ 508/627-7448). Buses also go out to Gay Head (via the airport, West Tisbury, and Chilmark) every few hours from 9am to 5pm in July and August.

Edgartown operates its own trolleys in season, which circle throughout town or out to South Beach. They also stop at the free parking lots just north of the town center—this is a great way to avoid circling the streets in search of a vacant spot on busy weekends. A one-way trip in town is just 50¢; a trip to South Beach is $1.50. For more information, call ☎ **508/627-9663.**

BY TAXI   Upon arrival, you'll find taxis at all ferry terminals and at the airport, and there are permanent taxi stands in Oak Bluffs (at the Flying Horses Carousel) and Edgartown (next to the Town Wharf). Rates from town to town in summer are generally flat fees based on where you're headed and the number of passengers. A trip from Vineyard Haven to Edgartown would probably cost around $10 for two people. Rates double after midnight. Two reliable companies are **Adam Cab** (☎ **800/281-4462** or 508/693-3332) and **All Island Taxi** (☎ **800/693-TAXI** or 508/693-2929).

THE CHAPPAQUIDDICK FERRY   The *On Time* ferry (☎ **508/627-9427**) runs the 5-minute trip from Dock Street in Edgartown to Chappaquiddick Island from June to mid-October, 7:30am to midnight. Passengers, bikes, mopeds, dogs, and cars (three at a time) are all welcome. The one-way cost is $1 per person, $4 for one car/one driver, $2.50 for one bike/one person, and $3.50 for one moped or motorcycle/one person.

ESSENTIALS

VISITOR INFORMATION   Contact the **Martha's Vineyard Chamber of Commerce** at Beach Road, Vineyard Haven, MA 02568 (☎ **508/693-0085;** fax: 508/693-7589) or visit their Web site: at **http://www.mvy.com**. The office is just two blocks up from the ferry terminal in Vineyard Haven. There are also **information booths** at the ferry terminal in Vineyard Haven; across from the Carousel in Oak Bluffs, and on Church Street in Edgartown.

Always check the two local newspapers, *The Vineyard Gazette* and *The Martha's Vineyard Times,* for information on current events.

EMERGENCIES   In case of an emergency, call ☎ **911** and/or head for the **Martha's Vineyard Hospital,** Linton Lane, Oak Bluffs (☎ **508/693-0410**), which has a 24-hour emergency room.

BEACHES & OUTDOOR PURSUITS

BEACHES   Most of the Vineyard's magnificent shoreline, alas, is privately owned or restricted to residents, and thus off-limits to visitors. Renters, however, can obtain a **beach sticker** by applying with a lease at the relevant town hall (Vineyard Haven, ☎ 508/696-4200; Oak Bluffs, ☎ 508/693-5511; Edgartown, ☎ 508/627-6180; West Tisbury, ☎ 508/693-9659; Chilmark, ☎ 508/645-2651; or Gay Head, ☎ 508/645-9915). Also, many up-island inns offer temporary passes to such restricted hot spots as Chilmark's **Squibnocket** and **Lucy Vincent** beaches (the latter features high bluffs and, to the left, bathers in the buff).

In addition to the public beaches listed below, you might also track down a few hidden coves by requesting a map of conservation properties from the **Martha's Vineyard Land Bank** (☎ **508/627-7141**). Below is a list of public beaches:

• **East Beach,** Wasque Reservation, Chappaquiddick: Relatively few people go to the bother of getting to Chappaquiddick and then biking and hiking (or four-wheel driving) this far, so you'll have the sands almost to yourself. It's one of the Vineyard's best-kept secrets and an ideal spot for bird watching. Sorry, no facilities.

- **Gay Head Beach (Moshup Beach),** off Moshup Trail: Parking costs $15 a day (in season) at this peaceful half-mile beach just east of the colorful cliffs. Remember that climbing the cliffs or stealing clay for a souvenir here is against the law for environmental reasons—the cliffs are suffering from rapid erosion. Rest rooms are near the parking lot and lifeguards patrol the beach.
- **Joseph A. Sylvia State Beach,** midway between Oak Bluffs and Edgartown: Stretching a mile and flanked by a paved bike path, this placid beach has views of Cape Cod and Nantucket Sound and is prized for its gentle and warm waves, which make it perfect for swimming. The wooden drawbridge is a local landmark, and visitors and islanders alike have been jumping off of it for years. Be aware that State Beach is one of the Vineyard's most popular and come midsummer it's packed. The shuttle bus stops here, and roadside parking is available, but it fills up fast, so stake your claim early. There are no rest rooms, and only the Edgartown end of the beach, known as Bend in the Road Beach, has lifeguards.
- **Lake Tashmoo Town Beach,** off Herring Creek Road, Vineyard Haven: The only spot on the island where the lake meets the ocean, this tiny strip of sand is good for swimming and surf casting, but is somewhat marred by limited parking and often brackish waters.
- **Lobsterville Beach,** at the end of Lobsterville Road in Gay Head: This 2-mile beauty on Menemsha Pond boasts calm, shallow waters, ideal for children. It's also a prime spot for birding—just past the dunes are nesting areas for terns and gulls. The only drawback is that parking is for residents only.
- **Menemsha Beach,** next to Dutchers Dock in Menemsha Harbor: Despite its rough surface, this small but well-trafficked strand—with lifeguards and rest rooms—is popular with families. Nearby food vendors in Menemsha, who sell everything from ice cream and hot dogs to steamers and shrimp cocktail, are also a plus here.
- **Oak Bluffs Town Beach,** Seaview Avenue: This sandy strip extends from both sides of the ferry wharf, which makes it a convenient place to linger while waiting for the next boat. The surf is consistently calm and the sand smooth, so it's also ideal for families with small children. Public rest rooms are available at the ferry dock. No lifeguards.
- **Owen Park Beach,** off Main Street in Vineyard Haven: A tiny strip of harborside beach adjoining a town green with swings and a bandstand will suffice for young children, who, by the way, get lifeguard supervision. No rest rooms.
- **South Beach (Katama Beach),** about 4 miles south of Edgartown on Katama Road: If you only have time for one trip to the beach and you can't get up-island, I'd go with this popular, 3-mile barrier strand that boasts heavy wave action (check with lifeguards for swimming conditions), sweeping dunes, and most importantly, relatively ample parking space. It's also accessible by bike path or shuttle. Lifeguards patrol some sections of the beach, and there are sparsely scattered toilet facilities. *Tip:* Families tend to head to the left, college kids to the right.
- **Wasque Beach,** Wasque Reservation, Chappaquiddick: Surprisingly easy to get to (via the *On-Time* ferry), this half-mile-long beach has all the amenities—lifeguards, parking, rest rooms—without the crowds; in season, a $3 entrance fee is charged per car and per adult over 15.

Exploring the Vineyard on Two Wheels

What makes biking on the Vineyard so memorable is that you'll not only find the smooth, well-maintained paths indigenous to the Cape, but also long stretches of virtually untrafficked roads. They may be rough in spots, but they reveal breath-taking country landscapes and sweeping ocean views.

A triangle of paved bike paths, roughly 8 miles to a side, links the down-island towns of Oak Bluffs, Edgartown, and West Tisbury (the Sound portion along Beach Road, flanked by water on both sides, is especially enjoyable). From Edgartown, you can also follow the bike path to South Beach. For a more woodsy ride, there are paved paths in the **Correllus State Forest** (☎ 508/693-2540), a vast spread of scrub oak and pine smack dab in the middle of the island.

The up-island roads leading to Chilmark, Menemsha, and Gay Head are a cyclist's dream, with sprawling, unspoiled pastureland, old farmhouses, and brilliant views of the sea. But keep in mind that the terrain is often hilly and the roads are narrow and a little rough around the edges. Try **South Road** from the town of West Tisbury to Chilmark Center (about 5 miles), or **Middle Road,** another lovely ride that will also get you from West Tisbury to Chilmark (it's usually less trafficked, too).

My favorite up-island route, though, is the 6-mile stretch from Chilmark Center out to Gay Head via State Road and ✪ **Moshup Trail.** The ocean views along this route are nothing less than spectacular. About 2 miles down State Road don't miss the **Quitsa Pond Lookout,** an amazing place to watch the sunset on a clear day. A bit farther, just over the Gay Head town line, is the **Gay Head spring,** a roadside iron pipe where you can refill your water bottle with the freshest and coldest water on the island. At the fork after the spring, turn left on Moshup Trail and follow the coast, with gorgeous views of the water and the sweeping sand dunes. You'll soon wind up in Gay Head, where you can explore the red-clay cliffs and pristine beaches.

Bike-rental operations are ubiquitous near the ferry landings in Vineyard Haven and Oak Bluffs, and there are also a few outfits in Edgartown. For information on bike-rental shops, see "Getting Around," at the beginning of this section.

FISHING   For shellfishing, you'll need to get information and a permit from the appropriate town hall (for the telephone numbers, see "Beaches," above). Popular spots for surf casting include Wasque Point on Chappaquiddick (see "Nature Trails," below), South Beach, and the jetty at Menemsha Pond.

The party boat *Skipper* (☎ 508/693-1238), usually used for narrated celebrity sightings, offers half-day trips out of Oak Bluffs harbor in season. Deep-sea excursions can be arranged aboard the *Slapshot II* (☎ 508/627-8087) or **Big Eye Charters** (☎ 508/627-3659), both out of Edgartown, or **North Shore** (☎ 508/645-2993) in Menemsha, locus of the island's commercial fishing fleet.

Cooper Gilkes III, proprietor of **Coop's Bait & Tackle,** 147 W. Tisbury Rd., Edgartown (☎ 508/627-3909), which offers rentals as well as supplies, is another acknowledged authority. He's available as an instructor or charter guide.

GOLF   President Clinton helped to publicize the 9-hole **Mink Meadows Golf Course** off Franklin Street in Vineyard Haven (☎ 508/693-0600). It's open to the public, as is the semiprivate, championship-level 18-hole **Farm Neck Golf Club,** off Farm Neck Road in Oak Bluffs (☎ 508/693-3057).

IN-LINE SKATING   The perfect activity on the island's paved paths. You'll find rentals at **Jamaikan Jam,** 154 Circuit Ave. (☎ 508/693-5003) or **M. V. Blade Runners,** Circuit Avenue Extension (☎ 508/693-8852), both in Oak Bluffs; the latter offers renters complimentary introductory clinics twice daily in season.

NATURE TRAILS   About a fifth of the Vineyard's land mass has been set aside for conservation. The **West Chop Woods,** off Franklin Street in Vineyard Haven, comprise 85 acres with marked walking trails. Midway between Vineyard Haven and Edgartown, off Edgartown–Vineyard Haven Road, the **Felix Neck Wildlife Sanctuary** (☎ 508/627-4850) includes a 6-mile network of trails over varying terrain, from woodland to beach.

Accessible by ferry from Edgartown, quiet Chappaquiddick is home to two sizable preserves: the **Cape Pogue Wildlife Refuge** and **Wasque Reservation** (☎ 508/627-7260), covering much of the island's eastern barrier beach, comprise 709 variegated acres that draw flocks of nesting or resting shorebirds. The 4,000-acre **Correllus State Forest** occupies a sizable, if not especially scenic, chunk mid-island; it's riddled with mountain-bike paths and riding trails.

The ✪ **Cedar Tree Neck Sanctuary,** off Indian Hill Road southwest of Vineyard Haven (☎ 508/693-5207), offers some 300 forested acres that end in a stony beach, where, alas, swimming and sunbathing are prohibited.

WATER SPORTS   **Wind's Up,** 95 Beach Rd. in Vineyard Haven (☎ 508/693-4252), rents out canoes, kayaks, and various sailing craft, including Windsurfers, and offers instruction on-site, on a placid pond; they also rent out surfboards and boogie boards.

John Moore (☎ 508/693-1385) is considered the Vineyard's top kayaking instructor. Contact him for lessons or tours, or just general guidance.

For scuba equipment, visit **Vineyard Scuba** on South Circuit Avenue in Oak Bluffs (☎ 508/693-0288).

Rank beginners may enjoy towing privileges at **M. V. Parasail** and **M. V. Ski** off Owen Park Pier in Vineyard Haven Harbor (☎ 508/693-2838): For the former you're airborne by parachute, for the latter you straddle water skis, a knee board, or an inner tube.

A STROLL AROUND EDGARTOWN

A good way to get yourself acclimated to the pace and flavor of the Vineyard is to walk the streets of Edgartown. This walk starts at the Dr. Daniel Fisher House and meanders along for about a mile. Depending on how long you linger at each stop, it should take about 2 to 3 hours.

If you're driving, park at the free lots at the edge of town (you'll see signs on the roads from Vineyard Haven and West Tisbury) and bike or take the trolley (it only costs 50¢) to the **Edgartown Visitors Center** on Church Street. Around the corner (you just passed them) are three local landmarks: the Dr. Daniel Fisher House, Vincent House Museum, and Old Whaling Church.

The **Dr. Daniel Fisher House,** 99 Main St. (☎ 508/627-8017), is a prime example of Edgartown's trademark Greek Revival opulence. A key player in the 19th-century whaling trade, Dr. Fisher amassed a sufficient fortune to found the Martha's Vineyard National Bank. Built in 1840, his mansion boasts classical elements like colonnaded porticos and a delicate roof walk. The only way to view the interior (now headquarters for the Martha's Vineyard Preservation Trust) is with a guided **Edgartown Historic Walking Tour** (☎ 508/627-8619), originating next door at the Vincent House Museum, off Main Street between Planting Field Way and Church Street; tours run from June through October, daily from 11am to 3pm, and

Charlotte Inn ❺
Dr. Daniel Fischer
House ❷
Edgartown
Lighthouse ❼
Old Whaling Church ❸
Town Wharf ❻
Vincent House
Museum ❶
Vineyard Museum ❹

↖To Oak Bluffs

↖To
Vineyard
Haven

Eel Pond

SHERIFFS MEADOW

Starbuck Neck

Plaintingfield Way

Pierce Ln.

Pease's Point Way

Fuller St.

Cottage St.

Morse St.

N. Water St.

Pine St.

Upper Main St.

Church St.

Winter St.

Cooke St.

Pent Ln.

Main St.

Davis Ln.

Daggett St.

Lighthouse
Beach ↖

Edgartown Harbor

Robinson Rd.

Pease's Point Way

Kelly St.

Norton St.

High St.

School St.

S. Summer St.

S. Water St.

CHAPPAQUIDDICK
ISLAND

Mullins Way

Katama Rd.

Atwood
Circle

Dunham Rd.

Katama Bay

↘To South Beach
& Katama Beach

Beach ↖ Ferry Route - - -

J-1063

cost $5 for adults; free for children 12 and under. The Vincent House is a transplanted 1672 full Cape that's considered to be the oldest surviving dwelling on the island.

The tour also takes in the neighboring **Old Whaling Church,** 89 Main St. (☎ **508/627-4442**), a magnificent 1843 Greek Revival edifice built out of massive pine beams. With its 27-foot windows and 92-foot tower (a landmark easily spotted from the sea), this is a building that knows its place in the community: central. Maintained by the Preservation Trust and still supporting a Methodist parish, the building is now primarily used as a performance hall (see "Martha's Vineyard After Dark," below).

Continuing down Main Street and turning right onto School Street, you'll pass the 1839 **Baptist Church,** which, having lost its spire, was converted into a private home with a rather grand, column-fronted facade. Two blocks farther, on your left, is **The Vineyard Museum,** 59 School St. (☎ **508/627-4441**), a fascinating complex assembled by the Dukes County Historical Society. This cluster of buildings contains exhibits of early Native American crafts; an entire 1765 house with period furnishings; an extraordinary collection of maritime art; and the Gay Head Light Tower's decommissioned Fresnel lens (see "Museums & Historic Landmarks," below).

Give yourself enough time to explore the museum's curiosities before heading south one block on Cooke Street. Catercorner across South Summer Street, you'll spot the 1828 **Federated Church.** One block left are the offices of the *Vineyard Gazette,* 34 S. Summer St. (☎ **508/627-4311**). Operating out of a 1760 house, this exemplary small-town newspaper has been going strong since 1846, and its 14,000 subscribers span the globe.

Heading toward Main Street, you'll happen upon the **Charlotte Inn,** 27 S. Summer St. (☎ 508/627-4751), among the most charming on the entire East Coast (see "Where to Stay" below). You don't have to be a guest here to appreciate the English gardens, and in fact, the in-house **Edgartown Art Gallery** provides a good excuse to explore the common rooms.

Head down Main Street toward the water, stopping in at any inviting shops along the way. Veer left on Dock Street to reach the **Old Sculpin Gallery,** 58 Dock St. (☎ 508/627-4881). The output of the Martha's Vineyard Art Association displayed here tends to be amateurish, but you might happen upon a find. The real draw is the stark old building itself, which started out as a granary (part of Dr. Fisher's vast holdings) and spent the better part of the 20th century as a boat-building shop.

Keep an eye out for vintage boats when you cross the street to survey the harbor from the deck at **Town Wharf.** It's from here that the tiny *On-Time* ferry makes its 3-minute crossing to **Chappaquiddick Island.** Just so you don't waste time tracking it down, the infamous **Dyke Bridge,** scene of the Kennedy/Kopechne debacle, has been dismantled and, at long last, replaced.

Mere strollers might want to remain in town to admire the many formidable captain's homes lining North Water Street, many of which have been converted into inns. Each has a tale to tell. The 1750 **Daggett House** (no. 59), for instance, expanded upon a 1660 tavern, and the original beehive oven is flanked by a "secret" passageway. Nathaniel Hawthorne holed up at the **Edgartown Inn** (no. 56) for nearly a year in 1789. Head back toward Main Street and the center of town.

MUSEUMS & HISTORIC LANDMARKS

Cottage Museum. 1 Trinity Park (within the Camp Meeting Grounds), Oak Bluffs. ☎ **508/ 693-0525.** Admission $1 (donation). Mon–Sat 10am–4pm. Closed mid-Sept to mid-June.

Oak Bluffs' famous "Camp Ground"—a 34-acre circle encompassing more than 300 multicolored, elaborately trimmed carpenter's Gothic cottages—looks very much the way it might have more than a hundred years ago. These adorable little houses, loosely modeled on the revivalists' canvas tents that inspired them, have been handed down through the generations. Unless you happen to know a lucky camper, your best chance of getting inside one is to visit this homey little museum.

The compact architecture is at once practical and symbolic. The Gothic-arched French doors off the peak-roofed second-story bedroom, for instance, lead to a tiny balcony used for keeping tabs on community doings. The daily schedule was, in fact, rather hectic. In 1867, when this cottage was built, campers typically attended three lengthy prayer services daily. Today's residents tend to blend in with the visitors, though the opportunities for worship remain manifold: at the 1878 Trinity Methodist Church within the park, or just outside, on Samoset Avenue, at the nonsectarian 1870 Union Chapel.

At the very center of the Camp Grounds is the striking **Trinity Park Tabernacle.** Built in 1879, the open-sided chapel is the largest wrought-iron structure in the country. Thousands can be accommodated on its long wooden benches, which are usually filled to capacity for the Sunday-morning services in summer, as well as for weekly community sings and occasional concerts.

✪ **Flying Horses Carousel.** 33 Circuit Ave. (at Lake Ave.), Oak Bluffs. ☎ **508/693-9481.** Tickets $1 per ride, or $8 for 10 rides. Late May to early Sept daily 9:30am–10pm; call for off-season hours. Closed mid-Oct to mid-Apr.

You don't have to be a kid—although it helps—to enjoy the colorful mounts adorning what might be the oldest working carousel in the country. Built in 1876 at Coney Island, this National Historic Landmark maintained by the Martha's Vineyard Preservation Trust predates the era of horses that "gallop." Lacking the necessary gears, these merely glide smoothly in place to the joyful strains of a calliope. The challenge lies in going for the gold ring—brass, actually—that entitles the lucky winner to a free ride. Some regulars, adults included, have grown rather adept—you'll see them scoop up several in a single pass. In between rides, take a moment to admire the intricate hand carving and real horsehair manes.

✪ **The Vineyard Museum.** 59 School St. (2 blocks southwest of Main St.), Edgartown. ☎ **508/627-4441.** Fax 508/627-4436. Admission in season $5 adults, $3 seniors and children 12–17. Early July to early Sept Tues–Sat 10am–4:30pm, Sun noon–4:30pm; call for off-season hours and rates.

All of Martha's Vineyard's history is captured here, in a compound of historic buildings. To proceed chronologically, start with the precolonial artifacts—from arrowheads to vibrant Gay Head clay pottery—displayed in the 1845 Captain Francis Pease House; there's also a small gift shop here, and a Children's Gallery to showcase the output of visiting youngsters.

The Gale Huntington Reference Library houses rare documentation of the island's history, from genealogical records to whaling ship logs. There's also some extraordinary memorabilia, including scrimshaw and portraiture, on view in the adjoining Francis Foster Museum. To get a sense of daily life during the era when the waters of the East Coast were the equivalent of a modern highway, visit the Thomas Cooke House, a shipwright-built full Cape, built in 1765, where the customs collector lived and worked. Further curiosities are stored in the nearby Carriage Shed.

The latest—and flashiest—addition to the museum's holdings is the Fresnel lens, lifted from the Gay Head Lighthouse in 1952 after nearly a century of service. Though it no longer serves to warn ships of dangerous shoals (that light is automated now), it still lights up the night every evening in summer, just for show.

CRUISES

Hugh Taylor (James's equally musical brother) alternates with a couple of other captains in taking the helm of ✪ *Arabella,* at North Road, Menemsha Harbor (☎ **508/645-3511**). This swift 50-foot catamaran makes daily trips to Cuttyhunk and sunset cruises around Naushon Island; private charters can also be arranged. This is a great way to see lovely, hidden coves and vistas. Evening sails are $30; day sails, $50 adults, $27.50 children. Departures are mid-June to mid-September, daily at 11am and 6pm. Reservations are required.

Gosnold Cruises, at Pier 44, Vineyard Haven Harbor (☎ **800/693-8001** or 508/693-8900), offers a range of excursions on its 65-foot cruiser, the *Andy Rosse.* Trips include a brief "Learn about Lobsters" jaunt featuring narration researched by the Dukes County Historical Society. Other options involve food and/or music. Rates are $15 to $40 for adults, $10 to $25 for children 3 to 12; call for schedule and reservations. Closed October through May.

John and Mary Clarke, innkeepers at the Lothrop Merry House (see "Where to Stay," below), offer half-day and day-long sails aboard their 54-foot 1962 Alden ketch, *Laissez Faire,* at Vineyard Haven Harbor (☎ **508/693-1646**). Refreshments—including wine and hors d'oeuvres—are included. Rates are $60 to $100 per person; call for details and reservations. Closed October through May.

Black Dog owner Robert Douglas's prized 110-foot topsail schooner, *The Shenandoah,* Beach Street Extension, Vineyard Haven (☎ **508/693-1699**), is modeled after an 1849 revenue cutter and fitted out with period furnishings. It spends most of the summer doing windjammer duty, transporting some 26 lucky souls wherever the wind happens to take them in the course of a week. Occasional day sails ($50) are offered in July and August—a great way to preview the weeklong $750 cruise. Reservations are required. Closed mid-September through mid-June.

SHOPPING

ANTIQUES/COLLECTIBLES   You don't have to be a bona fide collector to marvel over the nautical haul at **C. W. Morgan Marine Antiques,** Beach Road, just east of town center, Vineyard Haven (☎ **508/693-3622**). Frank Rapoza's collection encompasses paintings and prints, intricate ship models, sailors' chests and scrimshaw, and anything remotely boating related.

ARTS & CRAFTS   Stop by **C. B. Stark Jewelers,** 126 Main St., Vineyard Haven (☎ **508/693-2284**), where proprietor Cheryl Stark started fashioning island-motif charms back in 1966. The latest iconic accessory is jewelry fashioned from "wampum" (purple-shaded quahog shells) by Kate Taylor, James's sister and a fantastic singer/songwriter in her own right.

   Chilmark Pottery, off State Road (about 4 miles southwest of Vineyard Haven), West Tisbury (☎ **508/693-6476**), features tableware fashioned to suit its setting. Geoffrey Borr borrows his palette from the sea and sky and produces highly serviceable stoneware with clean lines and a long life span. There's also a branch at 170 Circuit Ave., Oak Bluffs (☎ **508/693-5910**).

   One of my favorites is ♦ **The Field Gallery,** State Road (in the center of town), West Tisbury (☎ **508/693-5595**). Marc Chagall meets Henry Moore in this rural pasture, where Tom Maley's playful figures have been enchanting locals and passersby for decades. The Sunday evening openings are high points of the summer social season.

   If you've only time to make one art stop, visit **The Granary Gallery,** at the Red Barn Emporium, Old County Road (off Edgartown–West Tisbury Road, about a quarter mile north of the intersection), West Tisbury (☎ **800/472-6279** or 508/693-0455), which displays astounding prints by the late Alfred Eisenstaedt, dazzling color photos by local luminary Alison Shaw, and a changing roster of fine artists.

   World-renowned master glassblowers sometimes lend a hand at ♦ **Martha's Vineyard Glass Works,** State Road (in the village center), North Tisbury (☎ **508/693-6026**), just for the fun of it. The three resident artists—Andrew Magdanz, Susan Shapiro, and Mark Weiner—are no slouches themselves, having shown nationwide to considerable acclaim. It's fascinating to witness a work in progress here.

   Another notable stop is **Peter Simon Photography Gallery,** at the Feast of Chilmark, State Road (in the center of town), Chilmark (☎ **508/645-9575**). Singer Carly Simon's brother, Peter, has the family ear for music—he has produced two albums of local talent, called *Vineyard Sound*—but has also made his own name behind a camera, chronicling island life since its great hippie heyday in the 1970s. The Feast's cafe/bar serves as a permanent gallery for his work, some of it hand-tinted by his wife, Ronni. Usually, one of them is on hand weekday mornings to greet curiosity seekers and collectors.

   In the words of owner Doug Parker, the **Vineyard Studio/Gallery,** on State Road in Vineyard Haven (☎ **508/693-1338**), offers "a glimpse of indigenous creativity few tourists get to see." Parker has transformed the barn of his summertime home into an artists' co-op, more or less as "a philanthropic gesture." Artists here pay only a nominal fee to cover overhead. The shows are ambitious, sophisticated (no lighthouses or jetties here), and worth a deliberate detour. Be sure to wander out back to admire the impressive perennial gardens.

BOOKS A year-round institution and heaven for browsers, ✪ **Bunch of Grapes,** 68 Main St. (in the center of town), Vineyard Haven (☎ **800/693-0221** or 508/ 693-2291), offers the island's broadest selection of books.

FASHION It may date back to 1969, but ✪ **The Great Put On,** Mayhew Lane (in the center of town), Edgartown (☎ **508/627-5495**), always manages to keep up with the latest styles, including lines by Norma Kamali, Vivienne Tam, and BCBG.

Jamaikan Jam, 154 Circuit Ave. (in the center of town), Oak Bluffs (☎ **508/ 693-5003**), is one of the best ethnic shops along Circuit Avenue, carrying colorful and comfortable clothes and Jamaican tchotchkes. You can also buy or rent in-line skates here.

LeRoux, 89 Main St. (in the center of town), Vineyard Haven (☎ **508/ 693-6463**), stocks functional and fashionable labels (for men and women), including some nationally known names, like Patagonia and even some low-key Betsey Johnson pieces. They also carry Woodland Waders, an island-made line of sturdy woolen outerwear. There's also a branch at Nevin Square in Edgartown (☎ **508/627-7766**).

GIFTS/HOME DECOR The owners of **Bramhall & Dunn,** 61 Main St., Vineyard Haven (☎ **508/693-6437**), have a great eye for the extras that lend character to country homes. Expect to find rag rugs, rustic pottery, rugged antiques, and sensuous linens. They're also located at The Red Barn, Old County Road, West Tisbury (☎ **508/693-5221**).

WHERE TO STAY
IN EDGARTOWN
Very Expensive
✪ **Charlotte Inn.** 27 S. Summer St. (in the center of town), Edgartown, MA 02539. ☎ **508/ 627-4751.** Fax 508/627-4652. 22 rms, 2 suites. A/C TV TEL. Summer $295–$575 double, $495–$675 suite. Rates include continental breakfast and afternoon tea. Lower rates off-season. AE, MC, V. Open year-round.

Ask anyone to recommend the best inn on the island, and this is the name you're most likely to hear—not just because it's the most expensive, but because it's easily the most refined. Owners Gery and Paul Conover have been tirelessly fine-tuning this cluster of 18th- and 19th-century houses (five all together, counting the Carriage House, a Gery-built replica) since 1971. Surrounded by formal gardens, each house has a distinctive look and feel—though the predominant mode is English country house, with hunting prints and quirky decorative accents. In the elegant 1860 Main House, the common rooms double as the Edgartown Art Gallery. Though the Carriage House was built much later, it blends right in and contains some of the more desirable quarters.

Dining/Entertainment: However sterling the accommodations at the Charlotte Inn, the restaurant may actually gather more laurels: l'étoile is one of Edgartown's finest. See "Where to Dine," below, for more information.

✪ **Harbor View Hotel.** 131 N. Water St. (about ½ mile northwest of Main St.), Edgartown, MA 02539. ☎ **800/255-6005** or 508/627-7000. Fax 508/627-7566. 124 units. A/C TV TEL. Summer $260 double; $435–$525 suite. Lower rates off-season. AE, DC, MC, V. Open year-round.

Grander than grand, this shingle-style complex started out as two Gilded Age hotels, ultimately joined by a 300-foot veranda. Treated to a massive centennial makeover in 1991, it now boasts every modern amenity, while retaining its retro charm—and a lobby that's right out of an Adirondack lodge. Front rooms overlook little Lighthouse Beach; in back, there's a large pool surrounded by newer annexes. The hotel is located just far enough from "downtown" to avoid the traffic hassles, but close enough for a pleasant walk past impressive captain's houses.

Dining/Entertainment: The casual Breezes restaurant is open daily for breakfast, lunch, and dinner; you can ask to be served on the veranda or by the pool, if you like. Starbuck's (see "Where to Dine," below) serves more formal meals in an elegant setting.

Service: Concierge, room service, overnight laundry, baby-sitting.

Facilities: Small beach, pool, tennis courts; guests enjoy privileges at the Farm Neck Golf Club (see "Beaches & Outdoor Pursuits," above).

Kelly House. 23 Kelley St. (in the center of town), Edgartown, MA 02539. ☎ **800/225-6005** or 508/627-4394. Fax 508/627-4394. 51 rms, 8 suites. A/C TV TEL. $225 double, $330–$525 suite. Rates include continental breakfast and afternoon tea. AE, CB, DC, MC, V. Closed Nov–Apr.

The setting couldn't be more central—plunk in the middle of prime shopping/strolling territory—and the rooms, many with harbor views, are large and airy, with handsome pine furnishings and low-key country accents. There's scarcely any vestige of the inn's origins as a 1742 tavern, except in its reconstituted cellar pub. If fresh decor and luxurious amenities are important to you, this place might win out over a more intimate B&B—and they do provide some nice personal touches, such as milk and cookies at bedtime.

Service: Overnight laundry and baby-sitting can be arranged.

Facilities: There's a small heated outdoor pool on the property, and guests are welcome to use the tennis courts at the Harbor View Hotel, under the same management.

✪ **Tuscany Inn.** 22 N. Water St. (in the center of town), Edgartown, MA 02539. ☎ **508/627-5999.** Fax 508/627-6605. 8 rms. A/C. Summer $185–$295 double. Rates include full breakfast. Lower rates off-season. AE, DC, MC, V. Closed Feb.

Innkeepers Rusty Scheuer and Laura Sbrana-Scheuer have transformed a derelict captain's house into a winning little inn. The interior decor is straight from sunny Italy, with warm colors and an abundance of fine old paintings—anything but the usual Yankee austerity. Past a little library lined with leather-backed books is Laura's open kitchen, where she gives cooking classes off-season (she's from Florence, and a formidable chef). Lavish breakfasts (say, blueberry buttermilk pancakes or frittata with focaccia) are served here when the weather precludes a patio feast. Each of the eight rooms is a gem, with hand-painted antique armoires and fanciful beds—and, in some cases, skylights, marble whirlpools, and harbor views.

Expensive

✪ **Point Way Inn.** 104 Main St. (at Pease's Point Way, in the center of town), Edgartown, MA 02539. ☎ **800/942-9569** or 508/627-8633. Fax 508/627-8579. 15 rms. A/C. Summer $150–$185 double. Rates include continental breakfast and afternoon tea. Lower rates off-season. AE, MC, V. Open year-round.

Run by avid sailors and croquet players—the inn's little green serves as headquarters for the Edgartown Mallet Club—this homey inn really gives you a sense of what island life is all about. Ben and Linda Smith are real hands-on hosts. Ben likes to take guests clamming in his special spot, or give them croquet pointers—visitors will feel like house guests who happen to be paying. You can even arrange to reserve the inn's loaner car. Days begin with the scent of Linda's delectable breakfast breads wafting from the cozy farmhouse-style kitchen; you'll also get an afternoon boost of lemonade and cookies in the gazebo. The living room, featuring but one of the rambling inn's 11 fireplaces, is especially welcoming in the pre- and postdinner hours. Rooms are not too fancy, but rather effortlessly romantic.

Moderate

✪ The Arbor. 222 Upper Main St. (on the western edge of town, about 3/4 miles from the harbor), Edgartown, MA 02539. ☎ **508/627-8137.** 10 rms (2 with shared bath). A/C. Summer $100–$150 double. Rates include continental breakfast. MC, V. Closed Nov–Apr.

This unassuming house hugging the bike path at the edge of town packs surprising style: Innkeeper Peggy Hall tacked a lovely cathedral-ceilinged living room onto her 1880 farmhouse to add the light and liveliness you'll find as you compare notes with other travelers or peruse a fine collection of coffee-table books from the comfort of an overstuffed chintz couch. The guest rooms themselves range from tiny to spacious, but all are nicely appointed, largely with antiques, and the rates are a good deal, especially considering the fresh-baked breakfast served on fine china.

Edgartown Inn. 56 N. Water St., Edgartown, MA 02539. ☎ **508/627-4794.** 20 rms (5 with shared bath). A/C TV. Summer $85–$185 double. No credit cards. Closed Nov–Mar.

Nathaniel Hawthorne holed up here for nearly a year—secretly courting a Wampanoag maiden, it is rumored, who inspired *The Scarlet Letter.* This is also where a young and feckless Ted Kennedy sweated out that shameful, post-Chappaquiddick night. Questionable karma aside, it's a lovely 1798 Federal manse, a showplace even here on captain's row. Rooms are traditional but not overdone. Modernists might prefer the two cathedral-ceilinged quarters in the annex out back, which offer lovely light and a sense of seclusion.

IN OAK BLUFFS

Expensive

Island Inn. Beach Rd. (about 1 mile south of the town center), Oak Bluffs, MA 02557. ☎ **800/ 462-0269** or 508/693-2002. Fax 508/693-7911. 51 units. A/C TV TEL. Summer $130–$300 double. Lower rates off-season. AE, DC, MC, V. Closed Dec–Mar.

Ideally located between Oak Bluffs and Edgartown on a verdant, 7-acre triangle of land (shared with the popular Farm Neck Golf Club), this modern complex is ideal for families. It's the kind of place where you'll feel comfortable letting your older kids wander about on their own (they'll head straight for the heated pool), while you hone your golf swing or tennis serve. All the units, from studios to a two-bedroom, two-fireplace cottage that sleeps six, are perfect for an extended stay and include fully equipped kitchens.

Facilities: Heated pool; access to tennis courts and golf course at the adjacent Farm Neck Golf Club.

✪ The Oak House. Seaview Ave. (on the Sound), Oak Bluffs, MA 02557. ☎ **508/693-4187.** Fax 508/696-7385. 8 rms, 2 suites. A/C TV TEL. Summer $140–$180 double, $250 suite. Rates include continental breakfast and afternoon tea. AE, DISC, MC, V. Closed mid-Oct to mid-May.

An 1872 Queen Anne bayfront beauty, this one time home of former Massachusetts governor William Claflin has preserved all the luxury and leisure of the Victorian age. The rooms toward the back are quieter; then again, the front ones have water views. The common rooms, like the 10 bedrooms (two are suites), are furnished in an opulent Victorian mode. Innkeeper Betsi Convery-Luce serves fabulous pastries at breakfast and teatime.

Moderate

✪ **Wesley Hotel.** 1 Lake Ave. (on the harbor), Oak Bluffs, MA 02557. ☎ **800/638-9027** or 508/693-6611. Fax 508/693-5389. 82 rms (20 with shared bath). A/C TV. Summer $135–$175 double. AE, CB, DC, DISC, MC, V. Closed mid-Oct to mid-May.

This 1879 grand hotel, right on the harbor, is the last of its kind and hardly shows its age—unless you count the rockers that line the spacious wraparound porch. The Wesley has retained its historic charm with old photographs on the walls, dark-stained oak trim, an old-fashioned registration desk, and plenty of antiques. Rooms are spacious and are furnished with Victorian reproductions. *Note:* Reserve early and you might get a harbor view without the surcharge.

Inexpensive

Attleboro House. 11 Lake Ave. (on the harbor), Oak Bluffs, MA 02557. ☎ **508/693-4346.** 11 rms (all with shared bath). Summer $60–$85 double. Rates include continental breakfast. MC, V. Closed Oct–May.

As old-fashioned as the afghans that proprietor Estelle Reagan crochets for every bed, this harborside guest house—serving Camp Meeting visitors since 1874—epitomizes the simple, timeless joys of summer. None of the 11 rooms has a private bath, but the rates are so retro, you may not mind.

IN VINEYARD HAVEN & THE TISBURYS

✪ **Lambert's Cove Country Inn.** Lambert's Cove Rd. (off State Rd., about 3 miles west of Vineyard Haven), W. Tisbury, MA 02568. ☎ **508/693-2298.** Fax 508/693-7890. 15 rms. A/C. Summer $135–$175 double. Rates include full breakfast. Lower rates off-season. AE, MC, V. Open year-round.

A dedicated horticulturist created this haven in the 1920s, expanding on a 1790 farmstead. You can see the old adzed beams in some of the upstairs bedrooms. Among his more prized additions is the Greenhouse Room, a bedroom with its own conservatory. You'll find an all-weather tennis court on the grounds, and the namesake beach nearby. Brunch on the patio is a beloved island tradition, as are the skillfully prepared New American dinners (see "Where to Dine," below). Set far off the main road and surrounded by apple trees and lilacs, this secluded estate is the perfect place to relax.

The Lothrop Merry House. Owen Park (off Main St.), Vineyard Haven, MA 02568. ☎ **508/693-1646.** 7 rms (3 with shared bath). Summer $129–$195 double. Rates include continental breakfast. Lower rates off-season. MC, V. Open year-round.

You'll get more than the superficial Vineyard experience if you stay at this nicely weathered 1790 B&B overlooking the harbor, with its own little stretch of beach and a canoe and Sunfish to take out at your leisure. Innkeepers Mary and John Clarke also charter cruises aboard their ketch, the *Laissez Faire.* A few of the simply furnished rooms have fireplaces (the island is especially lovely and exceedingly private in winter), and the two without water views compensate with air-conditioning.

UP-ISLAND: CHILMARK, MENEMSHA & GAY HEAD

The Captain R. Flanders House. North Rd. (about a mile northeast of Menemsha), Chilmark, MA 02535. ☎ **508/645-3123.** 5 rms, 2 cottages. Summer $150 double; $205 cottage. Rates include continental breakfast. Lower rates off-season. AE, MC, V. Closed mid-Nov to Apr.

Set amid 60 acres of rolling meadows crisscrossed by stone walls, this late-18th-century farmhouse, built by a whaling captain, has remained much the same over 2 centuries. The living room, with its broad plank floors, is full of astonishing antiques, but there's no self-conscious showiness. This is a working farm, so there's no time for posing (even if it *was* featured in Martha Stewart's *Wedding Book*). After fortifying themselves with homemade muffins, honey, and jam at breakfast, guests are free to fritter the day away however they like. Passes are provided to nearby Lucy Vincent Beach, or you might just take a long country walk.

✪ **The Inn at Blueberry Hill.** North Rd. (about 4 miles northeast of Menemsha), Chilmark, MA 02535. ☎ **800/356-3322** or 508/645-3322. Fax 508/645-3799. 25 rms. TV TEL on request. Summer $190–$350 double; $275–$700 suite/cottage. Rates include continental breakfast. Lower rates off-season. AE, MC, V. Closed Jan–Mar.

Energetic young owners Bob and Carolyn Burgess bought this one time white elephant while on their honeymoon, which may partly explain its runaway romanticism. Their goal was to create a spalike retreat of the utmost luxury without in any way compromising the lovely natural setting—56 acres of former farmland, surrounded by vast tracts of conservation forest. They've succeeded splendidly. The 1792 farmhouse has been spruced up to suit a more modern aesthetic—still simple, but full of light. The same is true of the scattered cottages (some tucked under towering spruces), where the decor has been kept intentionally minimal, so as to play up the natural beauty all around. Tasteful, handcrafted furnishings are complemented by such gentle touches as fluffy comforters.

Dining/Entertainment: Local ingredients are showcased on the menu at Theo's (see "Where to Dine," below, for details).

Facilities: The renovated barn contains a full-scale Cybex fitness center overlooking a solar-heated outdoor lap pool and hot tub. Equipment is provided for croquet, boule, horseshoes, and volleyball. Beyond the tennis court, miles of walking paths branch out through the woods. A personal trainer can fashion a custom fitness program on request and oversee workouts, or arrange for massages and facials. Complimentary passes and shuttles to Lucy Vincent and Squibnocket beaches.

Menemsha Inn and Cottages. Off North Rd. (about 1/2 mile northeast of the harbor), Menemsha, MA 02552. ☎ **508/645-2521.** 9 rms, 6 suites, 12 cottages. TV. Summer $115–$170 double; $170 suites. Room rates include continental breakfast. Cottages $1,075–$1,475 per week. Lower rates off-season. No credit cards. Closed Dec–Apr.

There's an almost Quaker-like plainness to this weathered waterside compound, though many of the rooms are quite inviting. Mostly it's a place to revel in the outdoors (11 seaside acres), without needless distractions. The late *Life* photographer Alfred Eisenstaedt summered here for 4 decades, and the interior aesthetics would please any artist. There's no restaurant—just a restful breakfast room with a piano. The most luxurious suites are located in the Carriage House, which has a spacious common room with a fieldstone fireplace and inviting rattan-and-chintz couches. These rooms have private decks: If you just want to sit and gaze out to sea, you're all set.

Outermost Inn. Lighthouse Rd. (about 1/4 mile northeast of the lighthouse), Gay Head, MA 02535. ☎ **508/645-3511.** Fax 508/645-3514. 6 rms, 1 suite. TV on request. Summer $250–$285 double or suite. Rates include full breakfast. Lower rates off-season. AE, DC, MC, V. Closed Nov to mid-Apr.

Location, location, location—you'd have to camp out at Gay Head lighthouse to get a better view. Commanding a grassy bluff overlooking the Vineyard Sound, with the Elizabeth Islands off in the distance, this comfortable, shingled house was built by Jean and Hugh Taylor (JT's sibling) in 1971. Each bedroom features floors of a distinctive wood, from cherry to ash, and all the furnishings—wool rugs, down comforters—are low-key and natural, though upscale. The sitting room contains all sorts of musical instruments, ready for improvisation ("We encourage guests to play if they know how—and not to, if they don't," says Jean with a laugh).

Dining/Entertainment: Specializing in straightforward seafood, the dining room enjoys a splendid ocean view.

WHERE TO DINE

Outside Oak Bluffs and Edgartown, all of Martha's Vineyard is "dry," including Vineyard Haven, so bring your own bottle; some restaurants charge a fee for uncorking.

Locals love the two dozen enticing flavors of homemade ice cream at **Mad Martha's,** 117 Circuit Ave., in the center of Oak Bluffs (☎ 508/693-9151). Bill Clinton opted for a relatively restrained mango sorbet, which isn't to say you shouldn't go for a good old-fashioned hot-fudge sundae.

IN EDGARTOWN
Very Expensive

✪ **l'étoile.** In the Charlotte Inn, 27 S. Summer St. (off Main St.). ☎ 508/627-5187. Reservations required. Jacket recommended. Prix fixe $62 and up. AE, MC, V. May to early Sept daily 6:30–9:45pm; call for off-season hours. Closed late Dec to Apr. FRENCH.

Every signal (starting with the price!) tells you that this is going to be one very special meal. Having passed through a pair of sitting rooms that double as the Edgartown Art Gallery, you'll come upon a conservatory sparkling to the light of antique brass sconces and fresh with the scent of potted citrus trees. Everything is exquisite, from the table settings (gold-rimmed Villeroy & Boch) to a nouvelle cuisine menu that varies with the seasons.

Chef Michael Brisson is determined to dazzle, and he does, with an ever-evolving menu of delicacies flown in from the four corners of the earth. *Sevruga* usually makes an appearance—perhaps as a garnish for chilled leek soup. An *étouffée* of lobster with champagne sauce might come with flying-fish roe ravioli, or warm Mission figs might offset seared pheasant breast in an Armagnac-sage sauce.

Expensive

✪ **Savoir Fare.** 14 Church St. (Old Post Office Sq., off Main St. in the center of town). ☎ 508/627-9864. Reservations recommended. Main courses $27–$32. AE, MC, V. Late May to mid-Oct Mon–Sat 11:30am–2:30pm; daily 6–10pm; call for off-season hours. Closed Nov to mid-Apr. NEW AMERICAN.

Scott Caskey initially opened this stylish cathedral-ceiling space as a gourmet deli/catering concern. Spurred by a rumor of impending competition (which never did materialize), he switched over to haute restaurateuring and has no regrets. Some of the prettiest seating is outside, under the graceful pergola (you'd never guess you were surrounded by parking lot), where champagne and shellfish are always on ice. The mostly Mediterranean fare is both substantial and lyrical, and Scott has a winning way with unusual desserts.

Starbuck's. At the Harbor View Hotel, 131 N. Water St. ☎ 508/627-7000. Reservations recommended. Main courses $18–$29. AE, MC, V. Mon–Sat 7–11am and noon–2pm; Sun 8am–2pm; daily 6–10pm. NEW AMERICAN.

Starbuck's is resolutely grand, lushly draped and formally decorated with lute-back chairs and tasseled curtains. The menu is far less stuffy, encompassing such rustic dishes as mussel soup Provençale, or risotto with wild mushrooms and artichokes. Most diners favor substantial slabs of fish and beef, and that's what they'll get, prepared however they like it. The elaborate breakfast menu is also a highlight, featuring Yankee red flannel hash and choose-your-own-combo griddle cakes.

Moderate

The Newes from America. The Kelley House, 23 Kelley St. ☎ **800/225-6005** or 508/627-7900. Fax 508/627-8142. Main courses $7–$22. AE, DC, MC, V. Daily 11am–11pm. PUB GRUB.

The pub grub is better than average at this subterranean tavern, built in 1742 and only recently resurrected. The decor may be more Edwardian than colonial, but those who come to quaff don't seem to care. Try a rack of five esoteric brews, or choose the perfect suds to accompany your dinner, which could be anything from a wood-smoked oyster "Island Poor Boy" sandwich with linguica relish to an 18-ounce porterhouse steak. Other sandwich choices include Brazilian chicken salad and grilled eggplant—reliable and filling.

Inexpensive

The **Main Street Diner,** Old Post Office Square, off Main Street in the center of town (☎ **508/627-9337**), is open daily from 7am year-round, and is a solid choice for a cheap breakfast or lunch, with no-nonsense selections that seem straight out of the 1950s.

Among the Flowers. Mayhew Lane. ☎ **508/627-3233.** Main courses $9–$11. DC, MC, V. July–Aug 8am–11pm; call for off-season hours. Closed mid-Oct to Apr. INTERNATIONAL.

Everything's fresh and appealing at this outdoor cafe near the dock. Sit under the awning and you'll just catch a glimpse of the harbor. The breakfasts are the best around, and crepes, waffles, and eggs remain available at lunch. The comfort food dinners (lemon chicken, lobster Newburg crepe, and others) are some of the best buys in this pricey town. There's almost always a wait, not just because it's so picturesque and appealing, but because the food is homey, hearty, and kind on the wallet.

IN OAK BLUFFS

Expensive

⭘ **Jimmy Seas Pan Pasta Restaurant.** 32 Kennebec Ave. ☎ **508/696-8550.** Reservations not accepted. Main courses $13–$23. No credit cards. May to mid-Oct daily 5–10pm; call for off-season hours. Closed Jan–Mar. MEDITERRANEAN.

If you're wondering why the luncheonette-level decor at this restaurant doesn't quite mesh with the menu prices, it's because chef Jimmy Cipolla gives his all to his one-pot pasta dishes, served right in the pan. Pasta comes in such intriguing guises as pumpkin tortellini in a creamy sage sauce, and everything's fair game for toppings, from chicken and shrimp with fresh pesto to swordfish in a balsamic vinaigrette.

Moderate

Zapotec. 10 Kennebec Ave. (in the center of town). ☎ **508/693-6800.** Reservations not accepted. Main courses $10–$17. AE, MC, V. Daily noon–2:30pm and 5–10pm. Closed mid-Oct to mid-May. MEXICAN.

Look for the chili-pepper lights entwining the porch of this clapboard cottage: They're a beacon leading to tasty regional Mexican cuisine, from mussels Oaxaca (with chipotle peppers, cilantro, lime, and cream) to crab cakes Tulum (mixed with codfish and grilled peppers, and served with dual salsas), plus the standard chicken and beef burritos. A good *mole* is hard to find; here you can accompany it with Mexico's unbeatable beers (including several rarely spotted north of the border).

Inexpensive

Dee's Harbor Cafe. 1 Lake Ave., on the harbor (☎ **508/693-6506**), gives you gourmet breakfasts on the cheap, plus well-priced sandwiches, quesadillas, and salads at lunchtime. Open daily in season for breakfast and lunch.

Papa's Pizza. 158 Circuit Ave. ☎ **508/693-1400.** Most items under $8. MC, V. June–Aug 11am–11pm; call for off-season hours. PIZZA.

The pizza at this vintage-look parlor tends to be on the tame side (you won't have to pick off the arugula). For families with kids, it's ideal. Stop in if only to see the vintage photographs of the local "campers."

In Vineyard Haven & the Tisburys

Just around the corner from the Black Dog Tavern, on Water Street near the ferry terminal, is the **Black Dog Bakery** (☎ **508/693-4786**). The doors to this fabled bakery open at 5:30am, and from midmorning on, it's elbowroom only as customers line up for fresh-baked muffins, cookies, and breads.

You might also want to check out **Alley's General Store,** on State Road, in the center of West Tisbury (☎ **508/693-0088**), which has been in business since 1858, for picnic fixings and a bulletin board that offers a local view of noteworthy activities and events.

Very Expensive

Lambert's Cove Country Inn. Lambert's Cove Rd. (off State Rd., about 3 miles west of Vineyard Haven), W. Tisbury. ☎ **508/693-2298.** Reservations recommended. Main courses $18–$23. AE, MC, V. June–Sept daily 6–8pm; call for off-season hours. NEW AMERICAN.

Whether you choose to dine outdoors, canopied by wisteria, or indoors over candlelit lace tablecloths, the setting is sheer romance, and the country-house cuisine shows just enough quirks to tickle the tired palate. The domestic rack of lamb, for instance, is dressed with raspberry-blackberry mint vinegar, and the cheese-and-walnut ravioli in Gorgonzola cream are bejeweled with asparagus and roasted red peppers.

✪ **Le Grenier.** 96 Main St. (in the center of town), Vineyard Haven. ☎ **508/693-4906.** Reservations recommended. Main courses $18–$30. AE, DC, MC, V. July–Aug daily 6–10pm; call for off-season hours. Closed mid-Oct to mid-Mar. FRENCH.

If Paris is the heart of France, Lyons is the belly, and that's where chef-owner Jean Dupon grew up on his Maman's hearty cuisine (she now helps out here, cooking lunch). Dupon has the moves down, as evidenced in such classics as steak *au poivre* (with black pepper), calf's brains Grenobloise with beurre noir and capers, or lobster Normande flambéed with calvados, apples, and cream. For an "attic" (the literal translation, and the actual location), Le Grenier is rather romantic, especially when aglow with hurricane lamps.

Red Cat Restaurant. 688 State Rd. (in the village center), N. Tisbury. ☎ **508/693-9599.** Reservations recommended. Main courses $19–$29. DISC, MC, V. Mon 6–10pm, Tues–Sun 5:30–9:30pm. Closed late Nov to spring. NEW AMERICAN.

Native son and chef Benjamin DeForest may have honed his skills at Boston's formidable Four Seasons, but the laid-back island style comes naturally. At this straightforward roadside cafe, all the artistry is concentrated on the plate: in a tasty "fresca" of tomatoes, corn, and basil, for instance, or a showy dish involving a hefty 14-ounce pork chop sauced with calvados, pears, and blond raisins and topped with crispy sweet-potato curls. Try the home-comfort chocolate bread pudding for dessert, and come early (and midweek) if you can.

Moderate to Expensive

✪ **Black Dog Tavern.** Beach St. Extension (on the harbor), Vineyard Haven. ☎ **508/693-9223.** Reservations not accepted. Main courses $10–$25. AE, MC, V. June to early Sept Mon–Sat 7–11am and 11:30am–2:30pm; Sun 7am–1pm; daily 5–10pm; call for off-season hours. NEW AMERICAN.

How does a humble harbor shack come to be a national icon? Location helps. Soon after *Shenandoah* captain Robert Douglas decided, in 1971, that this hardworking

The Quintessential Lobster Dinner

When only a huge lobster and a sunset will do, visitors and locals alike head to ✪ **The Home Port** on North Road in Menemsha (☎ **508/645-2679**). At first glance, prices for the lobster dinners may seem a bit high, but they include an appetizer of your choice (go with the stuffed quahog), salad, amazing fresh-baked breads, a nonalcoholic beverage (remember, it's BYOB in these parts), and dessert. The decor is on the simple side, but who really cares? It's the scintillating harbor views that have drawn the faithful hordes to this family-friendly place for more than 60 years. Locals not keen on summer crowds prefer to order their lobster dinners for pickup (half-price) at the restaurant door, then head down to Menemsha Beach for a private sunset supper. Reservations are highly recommended and the prix-fixe platters range from $19 to $30 (MasterCard, Visa, and American Express accepted). The Home Port is open June through September, daily from 6 to 10pm; call for off-season hours. Closed mid-October through mid-April.

port could use a good restaurant, influential vacationers, stuck waiting for the ferry, would wander in to tide themselves over with a bit of "blackout cake" or peanut-butter pie. The rest is history, as smart marketing moves followed on word of mouth. The smartest of these was the invention of the signature "Martha's Vineyard Whitefoot," a black Lab whose profile now adorns everything from baby's overalls to doggy bandannas.

Still, visitors love this rough-hewn tavern, and it's not just the hype that keeps them happy. The food is home-cooking good—heavy on the seafood, of course (including grilled swordfish with banana, basil, and lime, and bluefish with mustard soufflé sauce). Though the lines grow ever longer (there can be a wait to get on the wait list!), nothing much has changed at this beloved spot. Eggs Galveston for breakfast at the Black Dog Tavern is still one of the ultimate Vineyard experiences.

UP-ISLAND: CHILMARK, MENEMSHA & GAY HEAD

Expensive

✪ **The Feast of Chilmark.** State Rd. (in the center of town), Chilmark. ☎ **508/645-3553.** Reservations recommended. Main courses $15–$29. AE, MC, V. July–Aug daily 6–10pm; call for off-season hours. Closed Nov–Apr. NEW AMERICAN.

Capturing the essence of "up-island," this clapboard house conceals a sophisticated bilevel restaurant with lots of exposed wood and a menu to make even jaded New Yorkers sit up and take notice. Chef Tony Saccocia's specialties include quahog chowder, lobster turnovers with shrimp and lemon cream, and rack of local lamb with a spinach-cognac glaze. On premises is the Peter Simon Photography Gallery (see "Shopping," above).

✪ **Theo's.** At the Inn at Blueberry Hill, North Rd. (about 4 miles northeast of Menemsha), Chilmark. ☎ **800/356-3322** or 508/645-3322. Reservations required. Prix fixe $38–$50. AE, MC, V. Daily 7:30–9:30am, noon–1:30pm, and 6–9pm. Closed Jan–Mar. NEW AMERICAN.

Theo's is quite a combination: Formal yet soothing and relaxed, satisfying to all the senses yet subtly health-conscious. Renowned local chef Robin Ledoux Forte plucks up each tender vegetable herself from the inn garden; her husband often hauls in the catch of the day. And while her preparations may be minimalist, she's awfully good at finding delicious combinations—surrounding noisettes of Menemsha swordfish, for instance, with sesame aioli and a spicy Asian slaw. The lighting, cast by candles in blue goblets across rag-painted walls, creates an aura of unhurried comfort and a pervasive sense that all is as it should be, here in the unspoiled countryside.

Inexpensive

The Menemsha Bite. Basin Rd. (off North Rd., about ¼ mile northeast of the harbor), Menemsha. ☎ **508/645-9239.** Most items under $9. No credit cards. Daily 11am–9pm. Closed mid-Sept to June. SEAFOOD.

It's usually places like "The Bite" that folks crave when they think of New England: a classic "chowdah" and clam shack, flanked by picnic tables. Run by two sisters employing their grandmother's recipes, this place makes superlative chowder, potato salad, fried fish, and so forth.

MARTHA'S VINEYARD AFTER DARK
BARS & CLUBS

The Vineyard isn't exactly known for its nightlife scene, partly because of the island's low-key personality and partly because of its strict liquor laws—all towns except for Oak Bluffs and Edgartown are dry and last call at bars and nightclubs is at midnight. Still, if you're craving a little action, Oak Bluffs is probably your best bet. Here are a few options:

The **Atlantic Connection,** 124 Circuit Ave., Oak Bluffs (☎ **508/693-7129**), is a popular nightclub where disco lives on, along with—uh-oh—karaoke. Celebrity regulars such as Spike Lee and Ted Danson seem to love the hodgepodge of entertainment, and the unofficial house band, Entrain, has begun to attract a wide following (both on the island and on the mainland) with their funky, reggae-laced rock. Cover varies here; call for nightly schedules. It's closed mid-September through April.

The Lamppost and **The Rare Duck,** 111 Circuit Ave., in the center of Oak Bluffs (☎ **508/696-9352**), are a pair of clubs that teem with rambunctious college kids all summer long. The latter, smaller one (in the basement) is more bearable and usually features acoustic acts. Its bilevel counterpart (upstairs) is more rowdy with live rock bands and a dance floor. Covers vary; call for nightly schedules. Closed November through March.

Locals and visitors alike flock to **The Ritz Cafe,** 1 Circuit Ave., in the center of Oak Bluffs (☎ **508/693-9851**), a down-and-dirty blues club that features live music on the weekends.

Outside of Oak Bluffs, ✪ **The Hot Tin Roof,** Airport Road at Katama Airport (☎ **508/693-1137**), is a worthy stop if you're out on the town. It's actually a nightclub in a hangar, and somewhat of a Vineyard institution. Carly's back (as in Simon), and the joint is jumping. The singer/songwriter first opened this place in the early 1970s and eventually lost interest (while it lost cachet). Now with backing from a handful of high-rollers, it's on a roll again. Notoriously stage shy, Carly will sometimes take the mike herself, but is mostly content to attract an eclectic roster including such notables as Jimmy Cliff, Peter Wolf, Hall & Oates, and the Bacon Brothers (including Kevin). Comedians command the stage on Tuesday. Cover varies; call for nightly schedules. It's closed mid-September through April.

LOW-KEY EVENINGS

Try one of these unique places for a more mellow, island evening:

At **David's Island House,** 120 Circuit Ave., Oak Bluffs (☎ **508/693-4516**), pianist/proprietor David Crohan draws steady crowds—and occasional star collaborators—to his restaurant/lounge with his classical/pop music and winning personality.

The cocktail lounge, where David and his guests perform, is open nightly May through September. No cover.

Try to attend a concert, play, or lecture at the **Old Whaling Church,** 89 Main St., Edgartown (☎ **508/627-4442**). This magnificent 1843 Greek Revival church functions primarily as a 500-seat performing arts center. Such island luminaries as actress Patricia Neal and the late *Life* photographer Alfred Eisenstaedt have spoken from the pulpit here and plenty of locally loved musicians like James Taylor, Carly Simon, and Livingston Taylor have been known to give performances. The acoustics here are fantastic. Ticket prices vary; call for schedule. Closed October through April.

The ✪ **Wintertide Coffeehouse,** Beach Street Extension, Vineyard Haven (☎ **508/693-8830**), is another great hang-out. It's a community-run, alcohol-free folkie haven that not only keeps the natives entertained through the long, lonely winters, but also has been hailed by *Billboard* as one of the country's top 10 coffeehouses. The Black Dog Bakery provides the nibbles; some big names on the folk, blues, and jazz circuits provide the live soundtrack. You'll also catch an occasional comic, including the homegrown troupe W.I.M.P. (as in Wintertide Improv). Cover varies; call for schedule.

✪ **The Vineyard Playhouse,** 10 Church St., Vineyard Haven (☎ **508/696-6300**), is an intimate (112-seat) black-box theater where equity professionals put on a rich season of chestnuts and challenging new work—followed, on summer weekends, by musical or comedic cabaret in the gallery/lounge. Townspeople often get involved in the outdoor Shakespeare production, a 3-week run starting in mid-July at the Tashmoo Overlook Amphitheatre about a mile west of town. The playhouse is open late June to early September, Tuesday through Sunday; call for off-season hours.

2 Nantucket

Nantucket is a world unto itself, light years removed from the frenetic pace of any big city. This island of only 50 square miles reigned as the world capital of the whaling industry for more than 100 years and it retains the same aura of prim prosperity today. Cottages weathered gray by the salt air line cobblestone streets that amble up to a picturesque harbor with a working fishing fleet. Bicycle trails and roads lead past estates and mansions to open moors and dunes and then on to uncrowded beaches. Elegant shops and restaurants crowd the town's narrow streets. To the east, the pretty village of Siasconset (pronounced *scon*-set) has merely a clutch of facilities to accompany its sun-splashed beaches. (And dog owners, rejoice: Nantucket is a very dog-friendly place where Fido can romp on the beach. The chamber of commerce, listed below under "Essentials," can supply the names of several lodgings that accept pets.)

GETTING THERE

BY FERRY   Ferry service to Nantucket is frequent, but often crowded, especially for visitors bringing their cars. But remember, the island is so compact that a car really isn't a neccessity.

From Hyannis (South Street Dock), the **Steamship Authority** (☎ 508/477-8600; on Nantucket, 508/228-3274) operates year-round ferry service (including cars, passengers, and bicycles) to Steamship Wharf in Nantucket, which lies about 30 miles south. If you bring your car in summer, reserve months in advance—only six boats make the trip daily and they fill up fast. If you come without a reservation and plan to go standby, there's no guarantee you'll get to the island that day. Arrive at least 30 minutes before departure to avoid your space being released to standbys. The penalty for canceling an auto reservation can be as high as 50% of the fare, depending upon when you cancel; check the policy when you make reservations. No advance reservations are required for passengers.

Total trip time is 2 hours and 15 minutes. A one-way fare with car costs $90, mid-May to mid-October; $70, mid-March to mid-May and mid-October through November; and $50, December to mid-March. For passengers, a one-way ticket is $10 for adults, $5 for children 5 to 12, and $5 extra for bikes. Parking at the ferry dock costs $7.50 per day.

Passenger ferries from the Ocean Street Dock in Hyannis to Nantucket's Straight Wharf are also operated by **Hy-Line Cruises** (☎ **508/778-2600**). In December of 1995, Hy-Line began year-round service with its new high-speed passenger ferry, *The Grey Lady*, which cuts trip time from 2 hours to 1. The cost of a one-way fare is $29 adults ($52 round-trip), $23 for children 4 to 12 ($39 round-trip), and $4.50 extra for bicycles. The boat seats 40 and makes five round-trips daily to Nantucket; reserve in advance. From mid-May through October, Hy-Line's standard, 2-hour ferry service is also offered. A one-way ticket is $11 adults, $5.50 for children 4 to 12, and $4.50 extra for bikes. On busy holiday weekends, you may want to order tickets in advance; otherwise, be sure to buy your tickets at least half an hour before departure. For all Hy-Line ferry service, it's a good idea to reserve a parking spot in Hyannis in July and August; the all-day fee is $9.

Hy-Line's *MV Great Point* (2-hour trip) has a first-class section with a private lounge, bathrooms, bar, and snack bar; the one-way fare is $21 for adults and children. Their **"Around the Sound"** cruise is a 1-day, round-trip excursion from Hyannis with stops in Nantucket and Martha's Vineyard that runs from June through mid-September. The price is $33 for adults, $16.50 for children 4 to 12, and $13.50 extra for bikes.

From Martha's Vineyard, Hy-Line runs passenger-only ferries to Nantucket from June through mid-September (there is no car-ferry service between the islands). Trip time from Oak Bluffs is 2 hours and 15 minutes. The one-way fare is $11 for adults, $5.50 for children 4 to 12, and $4.50 extra for bikes.

From Harwich Port, you can avoid the summer crowds in Hyannis and board one of **Freedom Cruise Line's** (☎ **508/432-8999**) passenger-only ferries to Nantucket. From mid-May through September, boats leave from Saquatucket Harbor in Harwich Port, making the trip in just under 2 hours. A one-way ticket is $13.50 adults, $7.50 for children 5 to 12, and $4.75 extra for bikes. Parking is free for the first 24 hours; $8 for each day thereafter. Reserve in advance.

BY PLANE   You can fly into **Nantucket Memorial Airport** (☎ **508/325-5300**), about 3 miles south of Nantucket Road on Old South Road. Flight time from Boston to Nantucket is about 30 minutes.

Airlines serving Nantucket include: **Business Express/Delta Connection** (☎ 800/ 345-3400), with flights from Boston (year-round) and New York (seasonally); **Cape Air** (☎ 800/352-0714), which flies year-round from Boston, Martha's Vineyard, and New Bedford; **Colgan Air** (☎ 800/272-5488), which flies year-round from Newark and Hyannis; **Continental Express** (☎ 800/525-0280), which flies from Newark (seasonally); **Island Airlines** (☎ 508/228-7575) and **Nantucket Airlines** (☎ 800/ 635-8787), with service year-round from Hyannis; **Northwest Airlink** (☎ 800/

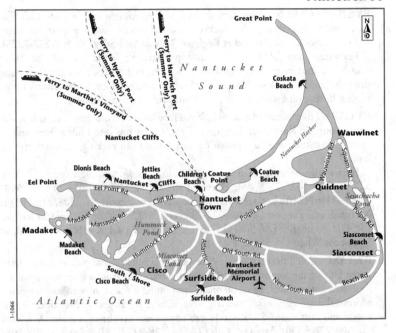

225-2525), with flights from Boston (year-round) and Newark (seasonally); and **USAirways Express** (☎ 800/428-4322), which flies year-round from Boston.

Island Airlines and Nantucket Airlines (see above) both offer year-round charter service to the island.

GETTING AROUND

Small and compact, Nantucket is easily navigated on bike, moped, or foot, and also by shuttle buses or taxis. The chamber of commerce strongly suggests that visitors opt not to bring cars to minimize congestion and environmental impact. If you're staying outside of Nantucket Town, however, or if you simply prefer driving, you might want to bring your car or rent one here. If you do opt to drive, in-town traffic can reach gridlock in the peak season, and parking can be a nightmare.

BY BIKE & MOPED   When I head to Nantucket for a few days, I prefer to get around by bike. The island itself is relatively flat (and only 14 by 3 ½ miles) and paved bike paths abound. There are also many unpaved back roads to explore, which make mountain bikes a wise choice. Mopeds are also prevalent here, but be aware that local rules and regulations do exist and are strictly enforced. (For example, mopeds are not allowed on sidewalks or bike paths.) You'll need a driver's license to rent a moped, and state law requires that you wear a helmet. Here are some shops that rent bikes and mopeds (all are within walking distance of the ferries): **Cook's Cycle Shop Inc.,** 6 S. Beach St. (☎ 508/228-0800); **Holiday Cycle,** 4 Chester St. (☎ 508/228-3644); **Nantucket Bike Shops,** at Steamboat Wharf and Straight Wharf (☎ 508/228-1999); and **Young's Bicycle Shop,** at Steamboat Wharf (☎ 508/228-1151), which also does repairs. You can also bring your own bike over on all the ferries for a small additional charge.

BY SHUTTLE BUS   From June through September, free shuttle buses, with bike racks, make a loop through Nantucket Town and to a few outlying spots; for routes and stops, contact the **Nantucket Regional Transit Authority** (☎ **508/228-7025**).

For a reasonable fee ($2 to $5 round-trip), **Barrett's Tours** (☎ **508/228-0174**) runs beach shuttles to Jetties, Madaket, 'Sconset, and Surfside beaches from June through Labor Day; buses leave every 15 minutes across from the Nantucket Information Bureau on Federal Street (see "Visitor Information," below).

BY CAR   I'd recommend a car only if you'll be here for more than a week, if you're staying outside Nantucket Town, or if you're just not into biking. Remember, though, that there are no in-town parking lots and so parking, although free, is limited.

Here's a list of rental agencies on the island: **Budget,** at the airport (☎ 800/527-0700 or 508/228-5666); **Hertz,** at the airport (☎ 800/654-3131 or 508/228-9421); **Nantucket Jeep Rental,** across from airport (☎ 508/228-1618); **National,** at the airport (☎ 800/222-7368 or 508/228-0300); **Thrifty Car Rental,** 150 Old South Rd. (☎ 508/325-4616); and **Young's 4 X 4 & Car Rental,** at Steamboat Wharf (☎ 508/228-1151).

BY TAXI   You'll find taxis (many are vans) waiting at the airport and at all ferry ports. During the summer, reserve a taxi in advance to avoid a long wait upon arrival. Rates are flat fees, based on one person riding before 1am with surcharges for additional passengers, bikes, and dogs. A taxi from the airport to Nantucket Town hotels will cost about $8. Reliable cab companies on the island are: **A-1 Taxi** (☎ **508/228-3330**), **Aardvark Cab** (☎ **508/228-9227**), **All Point Taxi** (☎ 508/228-5779), and **Peterson's Taxi** (☎ **508/228-9227**).

ESSENTIALS

VISITOR INFORMATION   Contact the **Nantucket Island Chamber of Commerce,** 48 Main St., Nantucket, MA 02554 (☎ **508/228-1700**). When you arrive, you should also stop by the **Nantucket Visitors Service and Information Bureau** in Nantucket Town at 25 Federal St. (☎ **508/228-0925**), open daily July through Labor Day, weekdays Labor Day through June. There are also **information booths** at Steamboat Wharf and Straight Wharf.

The island's two newspapers, *The Inquirer & Mirror* and *The Nantucket Beacon,* have information on current events and activities around town.

EMERGENCIES   In case of a medical emergency, the **Nantucket Cottage Hospital,** 57 Prospect St. (☎ **508/228-1200**), is open 24 hours.

BEACHES & OUTDOOR PURSUITS

BEACHES   In distinct contrast to Martha's Vineyard, virtually all of Nantucket's 110-mile coastline is open to the public—on purpose. The following areas each tend to attract a different crowd:

- **Children's Beach:** This small beach is a protected cove just west of busy Steamship Wharf. Appealing to families, it has a park, playground, rest rooms, lifeguards, a snack bar (the beloved Downy Flake, famous for their homemade doughnuts), and even a bandstand for free weekend concerts.
- **Cisco Beach:** About 4 miles from town, in the southwestern quadrant of the island (from Main Street, turn onto Milk Street, which becomes Hummock Pond Road), Cisco enjoys vigorous surf—great for the surfers who flock here, not so great for the waterfront homeowners. Lifeguards patrol here and rest rooms are available.

- **Coatue Beach:** This fishhook-shaped barrier beach, on the northeastern side of the island at Wauwinet, is Nantucket's outback, accessible only by four-wheel drive vehicles, watercraft, or the very strong-legged. Swimming is strongly discouraged because of fierce tides.
- **Dionis Beach:** About 3 miles out of town (take the Madaket bike path to Eel Point Road), is Dionis, which enjoys the gentle Sound surf and steep, picturesque bluffs. It's a great spot for swimming, picnicking, and shelling, and you'll find fewer children than at Jetties or Children's beaches. Stick to the established paths to prevent further erosion. Lifeguards patrol here and rest rooms are available.
- **Jetties Beach:** Located about a half-mile west of Children's Beach on North Beach Street, Jetties is about a 20-minute walk, or an even shorter bike ride, bus ride, or drive from town (there's a large parking lot, but it fills up early on summer weekends). It's a family favorite, with mild waves, lifeguards, a bathhouse and rest rooms, and an affordable restaurant, The Jetties Cafe & Grille. Facilities include the town tennis courts, volleyball nets, a skate park, and a playground; water-sports equipment and chairs are also available to rent. Every August Jetties hosts an intense sand castle competition, and the Fourth of July fireworks are held here.
- **Madaket Beach:** Accessible by Madaket Road, the 6-mile bike path that runs parallel to it, and by shuttle bus, this westerly beach—with lifeguards, rest rooms, and a food van—is narrow and subject to pounding surf and sometimes serious cross-currents. Unless it's a fairly tame day, you might content yourself with wading. This is the best spot on the island for a sunset.
- **Siasconset Beach:** The easterly coast of 'Sconset is as pretty as the town itself and rarely, if ever, crowded, perhaps because of the water's strong sideways tow. You can reach it by car, shuttle bus, or by a less scenic and somewhat hilly (at least for Nantucket) 7-mile bike path. There are usually lifeguards on duty, but the closest facilities (rest rooms, grocery store, cafe) are back in the village.
- **Surfside Beach:** Three miles south of town via a popular bike/skate path, broad Surfside—equipped with lifeguards, rest rooms, and a surprisingly accomplished little snack bar—is appropriately named and commensurately popular. It draws thousands of visitors in high season, from college students to families, but the free parking lot can only fit about 60 cars—you do the math, or better yet, ride your bike or take the shuttle bus.

BIKING   Several lovely, paved bike paths radiate out from the center of town to outlying beaches. The main paths run about 6.2 miles west to Madaket, 3.5 miles south to Surfside, and 8.2 miles east to Siasconset. To avoid backtracking from Siasconset, continue north through the charming village, and return on Polpis Road. Polpis does not yet have a bike path (it's getting one soon), but traffic is relatively light.

Strong riders could do a whole circuit of the island in a day but most will be content to combine a single route with a few hours at a beach. You'll find picnic benches and water fountains at strategic points along all the paths.

For a great free map of the island's bike paths (it also lists Nantucket's bicycle rules), stop by **Young's Bicycle Shop,** near Steamship Wharf (☎ **508/228-1151**). It's definitely the best place for rentals. See "Getting Around," above, for more bike-rental shops.

FISHING   For shellfishing you'll need a permit from the **harbormaster's office** at 38 Washington St. (☎ **508/228-7260**). You'll see surf casters all over the island (no permit is required); for a guided trip, try Mike Mont of **Surf & Fly-Fishing Trips** (☎ **508/228-0529**).

Deep-sea charters heading out of Straight Wharf include *The Albacore* (☎ **508/ 228-1439**) and *Monomoy* (☎ **508/228-6867**).

IN-LINE SKATING   Cyclists share the island's paved paths with in-line skaters, who can gear up at **Nantucket Sports Locker on Wheels,** 14 Cambridge St. (☎ **508/228-6610**).

NATURE TRAILS   Through preservationist foresight, about one-third of Nantucket's 42 square miles are protected from development. Contact the **Nantucket Conservation Foundation,** 118 Cliff Rd. (☎ **508/228-2884**), for a map of their holdings ($3), which include the 205-acre **Windswept Cranberry Bog** (off Polpis Road), where bogs are interspersed amid hardwood forests, and a portion of the 1,100-acre **Coatue-Coskata Wildlife Refuge,** comprising the barrier beaches beyond Wauwinet. The **Trustees of the Reservations** (☎ **508/228-6799**), who oversee the bulk of this tract, offer 3-hour naturalist-guided tours out past the Great Point Lighthouse. **The Maria Mitchell Association** (see "Museums & Historic Landmarks," below) also sponsors guided birding and wildflower walks in season.

WATER SPORTS   **Force 5,** with its office at 37 Main St. (☎ **508/228-0700**), and a seasonal satellite at Jetties Beach (☎ **508/228-5358**), offers lessons and rents out kayaks, sailboards, sailboats, and more. **Sea Nantucket,** on tiny Francis Street Beach off Washington Street (☎ **508/228-7499**) also rents kayaks; it's a quick sprint across the harbor to beautiful Coatue.

Nantucket Island Community Sailing (☎ **508/228-6600**) gives relatively low-cost lessons for adults (16 and up) and families; a seasonal adult membership covering open-sail privileges costs $150.

Scuba gear and lessons are available at the **Sunken Ship,** on South Water and Broad streets near the Steamship Wharf (☎ **508/228-9226**).

MUSEUMS & HISTORIC LANDMARKS

Jethro Coffin House. Sunset Hill Rd. (off W. Chester Rd., about ¹/₂ mile northwest of town center). ☎ **508/228-1894.** Admission $3 adults, $2 children 5–14; also included in Nantucket Historical Association pass ($8 adults, $5 children). July–Aug daily 10am–5pm; call for off-season hours. Closed mid-Oct to Apr.

Built around 1696, this saltbox is the oldest building left on the island. A National Historical Landmark, it is also known as the Horseshoe House for the brick design on its central chimney. It was struck by lightning and severely damaged (in fact, nearly cut in two) in 1987, prompting a long-overdue restoration. Dimly lit by lead glass diamond-pane windows, it's filled with period furniture such as lathed ladder-back chairs and a clever trundle bed on wooden wheels. Nantucket Historical Association docents will fill you in on all the related lore.

The Maria Mitchell Science Center. 2 Vestal St. (at Milk St., about ¹/₂ mile southwest of town center). ☎ **508/228-9198.** Admission $5 adults, $3 children under 12, $2 seniors. Early June to late Aug Tues–Sat 10am–4pm; call for off-season hours.

This is a group of buildings organized and maintained in honor of distinguished astronomer and Nantucket native Maria Mitchell (1818–89). The **science center** consists of astronomical observatories, with a lecture series, children's science seminars, and stellar observation opportunities (when the sky is clear). The Hinchman House, at 7 Milk St., is home to the **Museum of Natural Science,** and offers evening lectures, bird watching, wildflower and nature walks, and children's nature classes. The **Mitchell House,** 1 Vestal St., the astronomer's birthplace, features a children's history series and adult-artisans seminars, and has wildflower and herb gardens. The **Science Library** is at 2 Vestal St. and the tiny, child-oriented **aquarium** is at 28 Washington St.

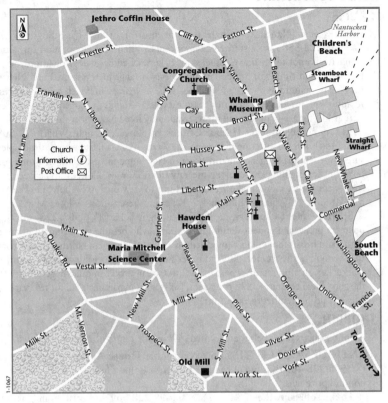

Map labels: Jethro Coffin House, Cliff Rd., Easton St., Nantucket Harbor, Children's Beach, W. Chester St., Steamboat Wharf, N. Water St., S. Beach St., Franklin St., Congregational Church, Whaling Museum, N. Liberty St., Lily St., Gay, Quince, Broad St., Easy St., Straight Wharf, New Lane, Church, Information, Post Office, Hussey St., India St., Center St., S. Water St., New Whale St., Liberty St., Gardner St., Main St., Fair St., Commercial St., Hawden House, Main St., Quaker Rd., Pleasant St., Maria Mitchell Science Center, Vestal St., Washington St., South Beach, New Mill St., Mill St., Pine St., Orange St., Union St., Francis St., Milk St., Mt. Vernon St., Prospect St., S. Mill St., Silver St., Dover St., To Airport, Old Mill, W. York St., York St.

1-1067

Old Mill. S. Mill and Prospect sts. (about ½ mile south of town center). ☎ **508/228-1894.** Admission $2 adults, $1 children 5–14; also included in the Nantucket Historical Association pass ($8 adults, $5 children). July–Aug daily 10am–5pm; call for off-season hours. Closed mid-Oct to Apr.

Four windmills once stood on the hills west of town; this 1746 structure is the only one remaining. A 50-foot Douglas fir pole (the original was a mast) turns the 30-by-6-foot sailcloth-covered arms into the wind, setting in motion a wooden gear train that grinds corn between millstones weighing more than a ton apiece. You can buy some fresh meal after watching it being made (wind permitting).

✪ **Whaling Museum.** 13 Broad St. (in the center of town). ☎ **508/228-1736.** Admission $5 adults, $3 children 5–14; also included in the Nantucket Historical Association pass ($8 adults, $5 children). Late May to mid-Oct daily 10am–5pm; call for off-season hours. Closed early Dec to mid-Apr.

Housed in a former spermaceti candle (candles made from a waxy fluid that's extracted from sperm whales) factory, this museum is a must-visit—if not for the awe-inspiring skeleton of a 43-foot finback whale (stranded in the 1960s), then for the exceptional collections of scrimshaw and nautical art. Check out the action painting, *Ship Spermo of Nantucket in a Heavy Thunder-Squall on the Coast of California 1876*, executed by a captain who survived the storm. The price of admission includes daily lectures on the brief and colorful history of the industry, like the beachside "whalebecue" feasts that natives and settlers once enjoyed. There's quite a nice gift shop, too.

CRUISES

The Endeavor (Nantucket Whaleboat Adventures), at Slip 15, Straight Wharf (☎ 508/228-5585), is a spirited 31-foot replica Friendship sloop, ideal for jaunts across the harbor to pristine Coatue; skipper James Genther will gladly drop you off for a bit of sunbathing or beachcombing, or even arrange for a treasure hunt. New to his fleet is a faithfully re-created whaleboat, the *Wanderer,* in which crews of six can recapture the arduous experience of chasing a whale—minus the target, of course. Fees start at $15 for a 1-hour sail; call for reservations. Closed November through April.

In summer, **Nantucket Harbor Cruises,** at Slip 12, Straight Wharf (☎ 508/228-1444), offers lobstering demos on the *Anna W. II,* a lobster boat turned pleasure barge, and passengers sometimes get to take home the proceeds. In winter, the boat runs seal-sighting cruises along the jetty (no stowaways allowed). In between seasons, Capt. Bruce Cowan takes groups out just to view the lovely shoreline. Fees are $22.50 adults, $17.50 for children 4 to 12; call for reservations. Closed May.

Sparrow Yacht Charters, at Slip 19, Straight Wharf (☎ 508/228-6029), is operated by naval architect Randolph Watkins, who became so enamored of cruising aboard his 40-foot sailboat (modeled on a 1900s Norwegian North Sea pilot boat) that he took to the seas in 1983 and never stopped, except for his annual sojourn in Nantucket. In a brief cruise, perhaps out to Coatue, you can quickly get a taste for the good life. Fees start at $25 per person (six-person maximum); call for reservations. Closed mid-September to early June.

SHOPPING

All of the shops listed below are located right in the center of Nantucket Town.

ANTIQUES/COLLECTIBLES   Nantucket House Antiques, 1 Beach St. (☎ 508/228-4604), is full of genuine treasures—some affordable, some with astronomical price tags.

Tonkin of Nantucket, 33 Main St. (☎ 508/228-9697), specializes in brass and silver knickknacks and antique Nantucket lightship baskets—those peculiar woven purses you see dangling from tanned, moneyed arms.

ARTS & CRAFTS   Widely copied, the miniaturized jewelry versions of Nantucket's trademark lightship baskets were introduced at ✪ **The Golden Basket,** 44 Main St. (☎ 800/582-8205 or 508/228-4344), with another branch at Straight Wharf (☎ 508/228-1019). The baskets, complete with gold penny, represent a small portion of the inventory, all of which is exquisite.

Like many seaside resort communities, Nantucket tends to foster pretty imagery more than serious art; however, **Main Street Gallery,** 2 S. Water St. (☎ 508/228-2252), offers more challenging and substantial work.

Appealing vintage prints are available from **Paul LaPaglia Antique Prints,** 38 Centre St. (☎ 508/228-8760).

In 1966, two Rhode Island School of Design grads opened **The Spectrum,** 26 Main St. (☎ 800/221-2472 or 508/228-4606), in a country schoolhouse, and quickly developed it into a premier showcase for crafts. The stock is accessible and appealing, from Josh Simpson's glass marble "planets" to Thomas Mann's old-fashioned charms.

FASHION   **Force 5 Water Sports,** 37 Main St. (☎ 508/228-0700), is the place for wet suits, Windsurfers, boogie boards, surfboards, and more. But it also stocks the best bathing suit selection in town.

Martha's Vineyard may have spawned the Black Dog, but this island boasts the inimitable "Nantucket reds"—cotton clothing that starts out tomato red and washes out to salmon pink. The fashion originated at **Murray's Toggery Shop,** 62 Main St.

(☎ **800/368-2134** or 508/228-0437). Roland Hussey Macy, founder of Macy's, got his start here in the 1830s.

GIFTS/HOME DECOR   Claire Murray, 11 S. Water St. (☎ **800/252-4733** or 508/228-1913), designs and creates extraordinary latch-hook rugs. If you want to try your own hand at it, the store also sells kits, plus ready-made quilts, sweaters, hand-painted furniture, and more.

Warm and welcoming ✪ **Erica Wilson Needle Works,** 25–27 Main St. (☎ **508/228-9881**), spills over with needlepoint kits, richly textured sweaters, baby clothes, and home accessories.

TOYS   Long a local fixture, **Pinwheel Toys,** 38 Centre St. (☎ **508/228-1991**), offers a great selection of playthings, both mass market and customized, such as "Cisco the Steamer," a little wooden car ferry.

✪ **The Toy Boat,** Straight Wharf (☎ **508/228-4552**) is keen on creative toys that are also educational (delighted beneficiaries will never suspect). In addition to the top commercial lines, owner Loren Brock stocks lots of locally crafted playthings, such as "mermaid purses" and little working sailboats.

WHERE TO STAY
VERY EXPENSIVE

✪ **Summer House.** 17 Ocean Ave. (a 5-min. walk south of the village center), Siasconset, MA 02564. ☎ **508/257-4577.** Fax 508/257-4590. 10 rms. TEL. Summer $300–$425 double. Rates include continental breakfast. Lower rates off-season. AE, MC, V. Closed Nov–Apr.

Romance incarnate, these former fishing shacks, entwined with roses, fragrant honeysuckle, and ivy, hug a bluff overlooking the sea. Adirondack chairs are scattered casually across the lush, shady lawn encircled by the cottages. At the bottom of the bluff is a small sparkling pool, where lunch is served, and beyond it, miles of scarcely populated beach. The cottages are outfitted with charming English country antiques and luxurious linens, and baths in all but one of the 10 rooms have a marble Jacuzzi.

Dining/Entertainment: On the premises is a celebrated restaurant of the same name serving cutting-edge cuisine.

The Wauwinet. 120 Wauwinet Rd. (about 8 miles east of Nantucket center), Wauwinet, MA 02554. ☎ **800/426-8718** or 508/228-0145. Fax 508/228-6712. 25 rms, 5 cottages. A/C TV TEL. Summer $270–$760 double; $610–$1,290 cottage. Rates include full breakfast and afternoon port. Lower rates off-season. AE, DC, MC, V. Closed Nov to mid-Apr.

Stephen and Jill Karp renovated this deluxe retreat in 1988 for roughly $3 million, and it has since earned several nicknames, including "The Ultimate," or, as the staff has been known to joke, the "We Want It." With 25 rooms in the main building (which started out as a restaurant in 1850) and 10 more in five modest-looking shingled cottages, the complex can only hold about 80 spoiled guests, tended to by 100 staffers. The lovely rooms—all with a cozy nook from which to gaze out across the water—each have a unique decorating scheme, with pine armoires, plenty of wicker, exquisite Audubon prints, handsome fabrics, and antique accessories.

Dining/Entertainment: Guests can dine in the highly acclaimed Topper's restaurant (see "Where to Dine," below).

Services: The staff will go to great lengths to please, jitneying you into town, for instance, in a 1936 "Woody," or dispatching you on a 21-foot launch across the bay to your own private strip of beach.

Facilities: The inn is the last stop on an 8-mile road to nowhere (actually, a wildlife sanctuary), and boasts several clay tennis courts with a pro shop and teaching pro, a croquet lawn, a platform for nearly life-size "beach chess," and plenty of boats and bikes to borrow.

White Elephant Hotel. Easton and Willard sts., Nantucket, MA 02554. ☎ **800/475-2637** or 508/228-2500. Fax 508/325-1195. 72 rms, 8 cottages. A/C TV TEL. Summer $295–$495 double, $145–$675 cottage. Lower rates off-season. AE, CB, DC, DISC, MC, V. Closed Nov–Apr.

Belying its name, this luxury property, right on the harbor, is the ultimate in-town lodging. Rooms (distributed among 2 buildings and 18 cottages) are big and airy, with picturesque views and country-chic decor. Every space is fresh and breezy, and none more so than the outdoor heated pool and hot tub surrounded by tasteful gray arbors. The hotel's location welcomes "sail in" guests.

EXPENSIVE

Beachside at Nantucket. 30 N. Beach St. (about ³/₄ miles west of the town center), Nantucket, MA 02554. ☎ **800/322-4433** or 508/228-2241. Fax 508/228-8901. 90 rms. A/C TV TEL. Summer $185–$225 double. Lower rates off-season. AE, DC, DISC, MC, V. Closed mid-Oct to mid-Apr.

This is not your ordinary motel. The Beachside's 90 air-conditioned bedrooms and lobby have been lavished with Provençal prints and handsome rattan and wicker furniture; the patios and decks overlooking the central courtyard with its heated pool have been prettified with French doors and latticework. If you prefer the laissez-faire lifestyle of a motel to the sometimes constricting rituals of a B&B, you might find this the ideal base.

Fair Winds. 29 Cliff Rd. (about ¹/₂ mile west of the town center), Nantucket, MA 02554. ☎ **508/228-1998.** 8 rms. Summer $165–$195 double. Rates include continental breakfast. MC, V. Closed mid-Oct to mid-May.

A short walk from town, this B&B offers the peace many visitors are seeking. In fact, a lot of first-time guests spot the house while out cycling and, after coming in for a look, decide to stay here on their return visit to the island. The bright common rooms lead to a 50-foot deck with a panoramic view of the Sound; it's here that guests tend to bring their breakfast of fresh-baked breads and muffins. Four of the prettily decorated bedrooms enjoy that same priceless view.

✪ **Four Chimneys.** 38 Orange St. (about ¹/₄ mile east of Main St.), Nantucket, MA 02554. ☎ **508/228-1912.** Fax 508/325-4864. 10 rms. A/C. Summer $165–$275 double. Rates include continental breakfast. Lower rates off-season. AE, DC, MC, V. Closed Nov to mid-May.

The Four Chimneys is a bed-and-breakfast of rare charm, stylishly outfitted with a grand piano in the front parlor and a crystal chandelier dining room. For privacy seekers, there's a beautiful little Japanese garden in back. Down comforters and authentic antiques, including some stunning colonial chests, adorn the bedrooms; some rooms have fireplaces and/or terraces.

Jared Coffin House. 29 Broad St. (at Centre St.), Nantucket, MA 02554. ☎ **800/248-2405** or 508/228-2405. Fax 508/228-8549. 60 rms. A/C TV TEL. Summer $165–$275 double. Rates include full breakfast. AE, DC, DISC, MC, V.

Built to the specs of the social-climbing Mrs. Coffin in 1845, this grand brick manse was renovated to its original splendor by the Nantucket Historical Trust. It is the social center of town, as well as a mecca for visitors. Accommodations range from well-priced singles (rare in these parts) to roomy suites. Rooms in the neighboring annex houses are equally grand. (The front rooms can be quite noisy.) The staff is extremely helpful and gracious. Twenty-minute waits for breakfast are not unusual—though the cranberry pancakes are worth the wait. Pets are accepted.

Westmoor Inn. Westmoor Lane (off Cliff Rd., about a mile west of the town center), Nantucket, MA 02554. ☎ **508/228-0877.** 14 rms. Summer $135–$255 double. Rates include continental breakfast. Lower rates off-season. AE, MC, V. Closed early Dec to Mar.

This yellow 1917 Federal-style mansion has all its original detailing—from the grand portico to the widow's walk—plus a new interior design that makes the most of the mansion's sunny hilltop setting. The spacious living room is full of thoughtful touches, perhaps a vase of magnificent gladiolas on the baby grand, and a 1,000-piece puzzle of Nantucket arrayed as a work in progress. There's even a cozy little TV room (anathema at most B&Bs) with sporting wicker couches and framed architectural blueprints. The 14 bedrooms, including a ground-floor suite with a full-size Jacuzzi and French doors leading to the lawn, are as romantic as one would expect. After breakfasting to classical music in the conservatory, you can head off down a sandy lane to a quiet stretch of bay beach or hop on a bike and explore the island.

The Woodbox Inn. 29 Fair St. (about a 5-min. walk east of the town center), Nantucket, MA 02554. ☎ **508/228-0587.** 7 rms, 2 suites. Summer $125 double, $160–$210 suite. Rates include full breakfast. No credit cards. Closed Jan to late May.

The oldest inn on the island, this shingled 1709 house is easily the most evocative. The sleeping quarters include seven queen-bedded rooms and two suites with fireplaces. Breakfasts in the keeping room feature delicious egg dishes and popovers.

MODERATE

India House. 37 India St. (about a 5-min. walk west of Centre St.), Nantucket 02554. ☎ **508/228-9043.** 9 rms. Summer $85–$135 double. Rates include continental breakfast. MC, V.

This wonderfully simple and spare B&B has wide plank floors and plenty of canopied four-posters. Guests are treated to one of the best breakfasts around, featuring such treats as blueberry-stuffed French toast and soft-shell crabs filled with scallop mousse, in addition to fresh juice and homemade breads and muffins. The private garden out back is a lovely spot in which to sip a cocktail.

✪ **Martin House Inn.** 61 Centre St. (between Broad and Chester sts.), Nantucket, MA 02554. ☎ **508/228-0678.** 13 rms (4 with shared bath). Summer $90–$160 double. Rates include continental breakfast. AE, MC, V.

This is one of the most affordable B&Bs in town, but also one of the most stylish, with a formal parlor and dining rooms and a spacious side porch, complete with hammock. The garret rooms with a shared bath are a real deal. Other higher-priced rooms have four-posters and fireplaces.

The Quaker House. 20 Chestnut St. (in the center of town), Nantucket, MA 02554. ☎ **508/228-0400.** 8 rms. A/C. Summer $120–$170 double. Rates include full breakfast. AE, MC, V. Closed mid-Oct to late May.

This pretty B&B, built in 1847, is right in the center of town—a plus for those who like to be centrally located, maybe a minus for those who prefer to retire early. It's not that the street life is rowdy, but people do tend to stroll and socialize till all hours, and the houses are closely packed. All of the comfortable rooms have queen-sized beds, and are simply but tastefully decorated.

WHERE TO DINE
VERY EXPENSIVE

✪ **Chanticleer Inn.** 9 New St., Siasconset. ☎ **508/257-4154.** Reservations recommended. Jacket required. Main courses $28–$35; prix fixe $65 and up. AE, MC, V. Tues–Sun noon–2:30pm and 6:30–9:30pm. Closed mid-Oct to mid-May. FRENCH.

Definitely the priciest restaurant throughout the Cape and Islands, this rose-covered cottage turned French *auberge* has fans who don't begrudge a penny and who insist they'd have to cross an ocean to savor the likes of this classic cuisine. I've highlighted just a few glamorous options on the prix-fixe menu: *gateau de grenouilles aux pommes de terre* (a frogs' legs "cake" in a potato crust); *tournedos de lotte marinee au gingembre, sauce au rhum, croquettes d'ail* (a gingered monkfish scallopini with a lemon-rum sauce and sweet garlic fritters); and *pain perdu, glace au chocolat blanc, coulis d'abricots secs* (a very classy bread pudding with white-chocolate ice cream and apricot sauce). The restaurant also has a stellar wine cellar with 38,000 bottles.

DeMarco. 9 India St. (between Federal and Centre sts.). ☎ **508/228-1836.** Reservations recommended. Main courses $18–$30. AE, MC, V. June to mid-Sept daily 6–10pm; call for off-season hours. Closed Dec–Mar. NORTHERN ITALIAN.

This frame house carved into a cafe/bar and loft pioneered haute northern Italian cuisine on the island. A forward-thinking menu and attentive service ensure a superior meal, which might include fettuccine with grilled duck breast, porcini mushrooms, sun-dried tomatoes, and arugula.

✪ Topper's. In The Wauwinet, 120 Wauwinet Rd. (off Squam Rd.), Wauwinet. ☎ **508/ 228-8768.** Reservations recommended. Jacket required. Main courses $26–$36. AE, DC, MC, V. Mon–Sat noon–2pm, Sun 11am–2pm; daily 6–9:30pm. Closed Nov–Apr. NEW AMERICAN.

This 1850 restaurant—part of a secluded resort—is a tastefully subdued knockout, with wicker armchairs, splashes of chintz, and a two-tailed mermaid to oversee a chill-chasing fire. Peter Wallace's cuisine is regionalism at its best: Lobster, in his hands, becomes a major event (it's often sautéed with champagne beurre blanc), and he also has a knack for unusual delicacies such as arctic char. Desserts are fanciful and fabulous: Consider the "chocolate boat."

EXPENSIVE

The Hearth. At the Harbor House, 7 S. Beach St. ☎ **800/475-2637** or 508/228-1500. Reservations recommended. Main courses $12–$18. AE, DC, DISC, MC, V. Mid-June to mid-Sept daily 7:30–10:30am, 11:30am–5pm, and 6–10pm; call for off-season hours. Closed Jan–Mar. NEW ENGLAND.

This is one of the larger, more formal dining rooms in town, and a traditional spot for lavish Sunday brunches (followed, at night, with an all-you-can-eat prime-rib buffet). While taking a firm meat-and-potatoes stance, the restaurant is not oblivious of culinary trends: The pan-roasted crab cakes come on a bed of corn salsa, with an apricot demiglaze dipping sauce, and the house-specialty steak is enrobed in cracked peppercorns and drizzled with a Jack Daniel's reduction. The Hearth is one of the few island restaurants to offer an early-bird discount (call them "sunset dinner specials" here), and the prix-fixe menu is also a good deal.

Local musicians often perform in the adjoining Hearth Lounge, a barnlike space with a carved whale hanging over the fireplace and a huge chandelier sporting brass weather vanes.

✪ India House Restaurant. 37 India St. (about ⅛ mile west of Centre St.). ☎ **508/ 228-9043.** Reservations recommended. Prix fixe $44. MC, V. July–Aug Tues–Sun seatings at 7pm and 9pm; call for off-season hours. Closed mid-Oct to late May. NEW AMERICAN.

Three small dining rooms, with listing floors and low-slung ceilings, make a lovely, intimate setting for superb candlelit dinners. A longtime favorite dish is Lamb India House, cloaked in rosemary-studded breading and béarnaise sauce. However, new influences have recently surfaced: for example, Asian (as demonstrated in the 12-spice salmon sashimi with garlic and mint soy oil) and Southwestern (Texas wild-boar ribs with grilled pineapple barbecue sauce). The menu changes weekly, so you can be sure that this wonderful restaurant won't be resting on its well-deserved laurels.

RopeWalk. At Straight Wharf. ☎ **508/228-8886.** Reservations not accepted. Main courses $17–$22. MC, V. Mid-May to mid-Oct daily 11:30am–1am. Closed mid-Oct to mid-May. NEW AMERICAN.

Making the most of its harborside setting, this open, airy cafe offers stellar seafood with interesting asides, such as polenta or risotto. The raw bar—which sometimes serves sushi—can't be beat.

'Sconset Cafe. Post Office Sq. (in the village center), Siasconset. ☎ **508/257-4008.** Reservations recommended. Main dinner courses $17–$22. No credit cards. Daily 8:30am–9:30pm. Closed mid-Sept to mid-May. NEW AMERICAN.

Chummy as a friend's kitchen, this small bistro turns out three great meals a day, starting with hearty waffles and ending, perhaps, with fork-tender veal or duck confit. Seafood is also a forte.

✪ **Ship's Inn.** 13 Fair St. (2 blocks southeast of Main St.). ☎ **508/228-0040.** Reservations recommended. Main courses $15–$24. AE, DISC, MC, V. Mid-June to mid-Oct Wed–Mon 5:30–9:30pm; call for off-season hours. Closed mid-Oct to mid-May. CALIFORNIAN/FRENCH.

Within the peach walls of this windowed bistro, the chef finesses a hybrid of French and Californian cuisines. The island's homegrown produce is put to good use in the intensely flavored chilled soup of pureed vegetables.

MODERATE

Arno's. 41 Main St. ☎ **508/228-7001.** Reservations recommended. Main courses $9–$18. AE, DISC, MC, V. Apr–Dec 8am–9pm; call for off-season hours. Closed Jan. ECLECTIC.

A storefront facing the passing parade of Main Street, this institution packs surprising style within its bare brick walls (Molly Dee's mostly monochrome paintings, like vintage photographs, are especially nice). The internationally influenced menu yields tasty, bountiful platters.

✪ **The Brotherhood of Thieves.** 23 Broad St. (at Federal St.). No phone. Reservations not accepted. Main courses $8–$15. No credit cards. June–Sept daily 11:30am–12:30pm; often closes early off-season. Closed Feb. AMERICAN.

An authentic 1840s whaling bar, this candlelit boîte is loaded with ambiance. But what keeps would-be patrons lining up to enter is the well-priced, down-home food. The curly fries alone are certifiably addictive, and the warm soups, mulled ciders, and camaraderie help locals get through the off-season.

Obadiah's. 21 India St. (between Federal and Centre sts.). ☎ **508/228-4430.** Main courses $10–$20. AE, MC, V. Mon–Sat noon–3pm; daily 5:30–10pm. Closed late Sept to mid-June. REGIONAL AMERICAN.

Finding a reasonably priced restaurant in Nantucket is no mean feat. This one is a gem. You can eat outdoors, on a lantern-lit patio, or in the atmospheric brick-walled basement of the 1840s house. The cuisine is not all that daring, but reliably and substantially good. Portions are generous; service is swift and friendly.

✪ **Sushi by Yoshi.** 2 E. Chestnut St. ☎ **508/228-1801.** Most sushi combinations under $25. No credit cards. Daily 11:30am–9:30pm. Closed mid-Dec to Mar. JAPANESE.

This place is Nantucket's best source for great sushi. The super-fresh local fish is artfully presented by chef Yoshihisa Mabuchi, who also dishes up such healthy, affordable staples as miso or *udon* (noodle) soup. It's tempting to order a raft of Rhoda rolls (with tuna, avocado, and caviar), especially when a portion of the proceeds goes toward AIDS support.

INEXPENSIVE

✪ **Espresso Cafe.** 40 Main St. ☎ **508/228-6930.** Most items under $7. No credit cards. Late May to Nov daily 7:30am–11pm; call for off-season hours. INTERNATIONAL.

This reliable self-service cafe is in the heart of town. Pastries, sandwiches, and international dishes are affordably priced and delicious, and the cafe has some of the best coffee in town (the "Nantucket" and "Harvard" blends are perennial favorites). In good weather, enjoy a leisurely snack on the sunny patio out back.

TAKE-OUT & PICNIC FARE

You can get fresh-picked produce right in town from Bartlett's traveling market (there's a truck parked on Main Street in season), or head out to **Bartlett's Ocean View Farm,** 33 Bartlett Farm Rd. (☎ **508/228-9403**), where, in June, you might get to pick your own strawberries.

Home-baked goodies spruce up the breakfasts and lunches prepared at **Claudette's,** Post Office Square (in the village center), Siasconset (☎ **508/257-6622**), which can be enjoyed on the small terrace or carted straight to the beach. Closed mid-Oct to mid-May.

✪ **The Juice Bar,** 12 Broad St. (☎ **508/228-5799**), is a humble hole-in-the-wall that scoops up some of the best ice cream around, complemented by superb home-made hot fudge. The pastries are also excellent, and yes, you can also get juice, from refreshing lime rickeys to healthful carrot cocktails. Closed mid-October to March.

NANTUCKET AFTER DARK

Nantucket has a handful of bars and nightclubs, many of which have live music in summer.

Acoustic performers from all over the country hold fort in **The Brotherhood of Thieves,** 23 Broad St. (in the center of Nantucket Town; no phone), an atmospheric restaurant/nightclub where you'll find live folk music just about every night in season, when lines tend to form out the door. It's closed in February; no cover.

The Hearth Lounge, in Harbor House, 23 S. Water St. (☎ **508/228-1500**), is a handsome, beamed hall with elegant appointments where a duo by the name of Phil & Elizabeth crank out stirring R&B on weekend evenings in summer. No cover.

Midway to Surfside Beach, **The Muse,** 44 Atlantic Ave., about 1½ miles south of the town center (☎ **508/228-6873**), attracts hard-rocking bands and the island's younger crowd with salvage yard decor and late-night pizza. Cover varies; call for schedule. Closed October through April.

The Nantucket Arts Alliance (☎ **800/228-8118** or 508/228-8118) operates Box Office Nantucket, offering tickets for all sorts of cultural events around town. They operate out of the Macy Warehouse on Straight Wharf in season, Monday through Saturday from 9am to 1pm, Sundays from 11am to 3pm.

Theater buffs will want to spend an evening at the **Actors' Theatre of Nantucket,** Methodist Church, 2 Centre St. (☎ **508/228-6325**). Drawing on some considerable local talent of all ages, this shoe-box theater stages thought-provoking plays as readily as summery farces. Tickets are $15, and the theater is open from late May to mid-September, Tuesday through Sunday at 8:30pm; call for off-season hours. You can catch the children's productions (tickets $10) from mid-July to mid-August, Tuesday through Saturday at 5pm.

Central & Western Massachusetts

by Herbert Bailey Livesey

While Boston and its maritime appendages of Cape Ann and Cape Cod face the sea and gingerly embrace it, inland Massachusetts turns in upon itself. Countless ponds and lakes pool in its folds and hollows, often hidden by deep forests and granite outcroppings, but the region grew linearly, along the north-south valleys of the Connecticut and Housatonic rivers.

The heartland Pioneer Valley, embracing the Connecticut River, was just that in the early 18th century, when trappers and farmers first began to push west from the colonies clinging to the edges of Massachusetts Bay. They were followed by visionary capitalists who erected redbrick mills along the river for the manufacture of textiles and paper. Most of those enterprises failed or faded in the post–World War II movement to the milder climate and cheaper labor of the South, leaving a miasma of economic hardship that has yet to be dispelled. But those industrialists also helped fund several distinguished colleges for which the valley is now known, and those educated populations provide for much energy and a rich cultural life.

Roughly the same pattern applied in the Berkshires, the twin ranges of rumpled hills that define the western band of the state. There is only one college of note, however, and the development of the region in the 19th century owed more to the fact that it became accessible by railroad from New York and Boston. Artistic and literary types made a favored summer retreat of it, followed by wealthy folks attracted by the region's new reputation for creativity and bohemianism (many of their extravagant mansions, dubbed the "Berkshire Cottages," still survive). And to this day, the region still attracts the Town & Country crowd, who support a vibrant summer schedule of the arts, then steal away as the crimson leaves fall and the Berkshires fall quiet beneath 6 months of snow.

1 Enjoying the Great Outdoors

Both the mildly sedentary and the cut-and-toned hyper-fit visitor will find outdoor pursuits aplenty in inland Massachusetts. A state park or forest is never more than minutes away—there are dozens in the region, and the entire width of the state from Worcester to the Berkshires can be traversed in an hour. Even the smallest and most undeveloped of these parks have picnic areas and walking trails; most offer camping, fishing, boating, hiking, and cross-country skiing as well. **October Mountain,** near Lee, and **Pittsfield State Forest,** both in the Berkshires, have an especially wide variety of possible pursuits.

The Pioneer Valley, with its generally low hills and underused back roads near the Connecticut River, is ideal for **biking;** most of the larger towns have rental shops. The 8½-mile trail that follows an old railroad bed connecting Amherst and Northampton is especially convenient.

Birders and those who enjoy viewing native wildlife are served by local chapters of the Audubon Society and other organizations that set up preserves and sanctuaries with **observation trails,** as on the outskirts of Worcester, in Easthampton, and near Sheffield and Lenox, in the Berkshires. The Massachusetts branch of the **Audubon Society** (☎ 617/259-9500) produces a *Guide to Wildlife Sanctuaries, Nature Centers, and Policy Offices* that lists every sanctuary throughout the state, with descriptions of each, plus hours, facilities, directions, and fees.

While the state's **ski resorts** can't match the vertical drops and variety of trails found in Vermont and New Hampshire, they are nearer for New Yorkers and Bostonians, and often more family-friendly. Even the relatively flat Pioneer Valley has illuminated trails and a 3,600-foot run at Mount Tom, and the Berkshires check in (from south to north) with Catamount (Egremont), Butternut Basin (Great Barrington), Bousquet (Pittsfield), Jiminy Peak (Hancock), and Bodie Mountain (New Ashford). All are covered in more detail later in this chapter.

Most **golf courses** are private, but there are exceptions. Waubeeka Golf Links in South Williamstown, Pontoosuc Lake Country Club in Pittsfield, and the Egremont Country Club at the edge of Great Barrington are open to the public and greens fees are reasonable. You'll find phone numbers for each one later in this chapter.

Those who enjoy mildly strenuous organized outings might want to contact **Greylock Discovery Tours,** based in Lenox (☎ 800/877-9656 or 413/637-4442), which organizes **hikes** and **canoe trips** from May to October. On their own, hikers are rewarded with 360° views at the summits of several peaks. Perhaps the most unexpected site of a scenic elevation is Joseph Skinner State Park, near South Hadley, which has been popular for leisure outings since the early 19th century. In the far southwestern corner, so near the border that it can be entered from New York State, is Bash Bish Falls. Its waters tumble between two peaks, affording a vista that stretches all the way across the Hudson River to the Catskill Mountains. The highest peak in the state, however, is Mount Greylock, near Williamstown, a state reservation with a rustic overnight lodge near its top and a three-state panorama.

2 Worcester

There is a dispirited air clinging to Massachusetts's second-largest city, especially around the dilapidated edges. That observation applies to many of the region's cities, most of which reached their apogees in the late 19th century. Worcester has undergone bootstrapping efforts with varying degrees of success, especially downtown around the Romanesque City Hall. And its citizens haven't given up. Those with the wherewithal have invested in a surprising number of museums, historic buildings, and theatrical venues. Worcester (pronounced *Wuss*-ter, or *Woos*-tah locally) was the site of the first National Women's Rights Convention, held here in 1850, and the city's annual music festival claims to be the oldest in the country.

While it can't be regarded as a must stop, the city offers a few worthwhile diversions.

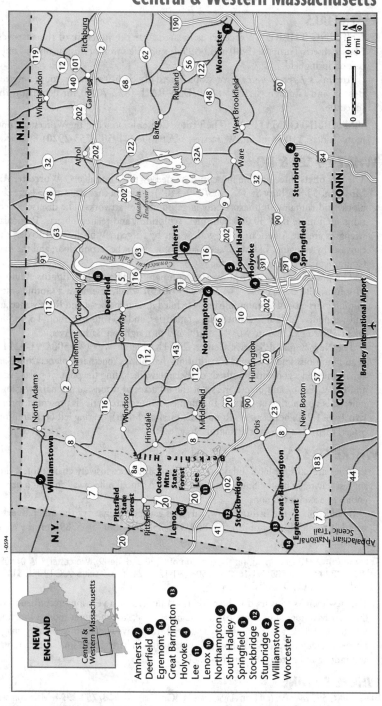

N.H.

VT.

CONN.

N.Y.

CONN.

Bradley International Airport

Fitchburg
Winchendon
Gardner
Rutland
Barre
Athol
Ware
West Brookfield
Worcester 1
Sturbridge 2
Quabbin Reservoir
Amherst 7
South Hadley
Holyoke 5
Springfield 3
Deerfield 8
Greenfield
Conway
Connecticut Fall River
Northampton 6
Huntington
North Adams
Charlemont
Windsor
Hinsdale
Middlefield
Otis
New Boston
Williamstown 9
Berkshire Hills
October Mtn. State Forest
Lee 11
Stockbridge 12
Great Barrington 13
Egremont 14
Pittsfield State Forest
Pittsfield
Lenox 10
Appalachian National Scenic Trail

190
119
12
101
140
2
62
56
122
68
202
148
32
202
78
122
32A
32
63
202
63
9
116
202
116
5
391
291
90
84
90
90
112
112
9
143
66
10
202
112
20
2
16
112
20
90
20
23
57
8
8
8a
9
20
102
41
7
183
44
7
20

1-0594

N
10 km
6 mi
0

ESSENTIALS

GETTING THERE Worcester is located near the juncture of the east-west Massachusetts Turnpike (I-90) and I-395. It's 43 miles west of Boston, and 51 miles east of Springfield.

Amtrak's *Lake Shore Limited* stops here daily each way on its route between Boston and Chicago. Call ☎ **800/USA-RAIL** (872-7245) for details on the schedule.

VISITOR INFORMATION The **Visitor Center** is located at the Worcester Common Outlets, 110 Front St., Worcester, MA 01608 (☎ **508/753-2920**).

WHAT TO SEE & DO

The city offers three notable museums, headed by the admirable ✪ **Worcester Art Museum,** 55 Salisbury St. (☎ **508/799-4406**), which occupies most of a large city block, and contains an unexpectedly large number of artworks. The diverse collections total more than 30,000 paintings, sculptures, and related objects. Particular strengths are the American wing, with works by Sargent, Whistler, and Ryder; the canvases by Gauguin, El Greco, and Gainsborough on the second floor; and the pre-Columbian artifacts on the fourth.

The president of a steel-processing company endowed the **Higgins Armory Museum,** 100 Barber Ave. (☎ **508/853-6015**), which resembles a Gothic castle shining in its coat of aluminum paint. He filled it with medieval and Renaissance art and weaponry, including stained glass, tapestries, and 60 suits of armor. To find it, take I-190 to Exit 1, onto MA 12 north, and turn right on Barber Avenue.

The **New England Science Center,** 222 Harrington Way (☎ **508/791-9211**), is an ambitious family-oriented institution that brings together a planetarium, an aquarium, and a zoo with hundreds of specimens, including the popular polar bears and eagles. Ponds and picnic areas dot the 60 acres of woods, and a narrow-gauge railroad is yet another attraction. In summer, a sunset jazz series is presented. From Exit 14 of I-290, head east on Route 122 (Grafton Street), bearing left on Hamilton Street, then left again on Harrington Way.

WHERE TO STAY

Pickings are slim for local lodgings, which are almost exclusively chain motels. I'd suggest staying in nearby Sturbridge, which is less than 20 miles away and has a better choice of accommodations.

In addition to the listing below, business travelers might try the quiet **Beechwood Inn,** 363 Plantation St. (☎ **800/344-2589** or 508/754-5789), on the edge of town.

Crowne Plaza. 10 Lincoln Sq. (at the junction of I-290 and Rte. 9), Worcester, MA 01608. ☎ **800/227-6963** or 508/791-1600. Fax 508/791-1796. 243 rms, 7 suites. A/C TV TEL. $119–$139 double. AE, CB, DC, DISC, MC, V.

The new owners (this used to be a Marriott) undertook a year-long reconstruction that involved upgrading every part of the hotel, especially the guest rooms. In addition to the usual gadgets (radios, hair dryers), they have added coffeemakers, magnifying makeup mirrors, and phones with data ports. There's also a small fitness room and indoor and outdoor swimming pools.

WHERE TO DINE

Bergamo's. 592 Main St. (off Franklin Sq., west of City Hall). ☎ **508/753-2994.** Main courses $5.95–$11.95. AE, DC, DISC, MC, V. Mon–Wed 11:30am–9pm, Thurs 11:30am–10pm, Fri 11:30am–midnight, Sat 4pm–midnight. ITALIAN/AMERICAN.

Head here for the kind of pub grub that gets little attention from restaurant reviewers, but is nearly always satisfying. Bubbly, gooey, laden pizzas fit that description, as do the pasta variations and thick sandwiches. The atmosphere is fern bar sans greenery, with a handsome mahogany bar in front.

3 Sturbridge & Old Sturbridge Village

First things first. Sturbridge and Old Sturbridge Village aren't a single entity. The former is an organic community, populated by working people with real lives. But why so many motels and restaurants in a town of fewer than 8,000 residents? That's due to the latter, a fabricated early-19th-century village composed of authentic buildings moved here from other locations and peopled by docents pretending to pursuits of 170 years past. It is one of the two most prominent tourist destinations in central Massachusetts.

ESSENTIALS

GETTING THERE   Leave the east-west Massachusetts Turnpike (I-90) at Exit 9, or the north-south I-84 at Exit 3B. Sturbridge is 18 miles southwest of Worcester, and 32 miles east of Springfield.

VISITOR INFORMATION   The **Sturbridge Area Visitors Center,** 380 Main St., Sturbridge, MA 01566 (☎ **508/347-2761**), is open weekdays during regular business hours.

SPECIAL EVENTS   Highly popular annual occasions are the **Brimfield Antique and Collectible Shows,** when at least 3,000 dealers gather for up to 6 days in mid-May, mid-July, and mid-September. Call ☎ **508/347-2761** for details. Brimfield is an otherwise sleepy village adjoining Sturbridge on the west. Since it has so few hotels, most of the dealers and seekers stay in Sturbridge, so you'll need to reserve your own rooms far in advance.

   Thanksgiving and Christmas weeks at Old Sturbridge Village are particularly special. Traditional New England dinners, concerts, and candlelit nights are only a few of the events brightening the calendar. Call ☎ **800/733-1830** or 508/347-3362 for details.

EXPLORING A 19TH-CENTURY VILLAGE

There is only one sight of significance in this otherwise pleasantly unremarkable town. Expect crowds on long holiday weekends in summer and during the October foliage season.

✪ **Old Sturbridge Village.** 1 Old Sturbridge Rd. ☎ **800/733-1830** or 508/347-3362. Fax 508/347-0375. Admission (2-day pass) $15 adults, $13.50 seniors, $7.50 for ages 6–15, free for children under 6. Apr to late Oct daily 9am–5pm; late Oct to Dec Tues–Sun 10am–4pm; Jan and 1st 2 weeks in Feb, weekends only 10am–4pm; mid-Feb to Mar Tues–Sun 10am–4pm. Take Exit 3B off I-84 or Exit 9 off I-90 and drive west on Rte. 20 to the entrance to the village, on the left.

Only one of the more than 40 restored structures in the complex stands on its original site—the Oliver Wight House, now part of the OSV Lodges, beside the entrance road. The rest were transported here from as far away as Maine, starting 50 years ago. All are authentic buildings, not re-creations, and they represent the living quarters and places of trade and commerce of a settlement of the 1830s. Among these are a Quaker meeting house, a sawmill, a bank, and a school.

   Costumed docents perform carefully researched demonstrations of blacksmithing, hearth cooking, glassmaking, printing, potting, and carpentry. Visitors are welcome to question them as they go about their daily tasks. These change with the seasons, and special events and activities mark such dates as Washington's Birthday, Mother's Day, and the Fourth of July. Town meetings, weddings, militia drills, and a harvest fair are staged. A new boat ride has proved popular.

Meals are available in Bullard Tavern, and a gift shop and bookstore are open during museum hours.

WHERE TO STAY

When the choices below are full, try the **EconoLodge,** 262 Main St. (☎ **508/ 347-2324**), or the **Colonial Quality Inn,** on Route 20 (☎ **508/347-3306**). Both are located near Exit 9 of I-84.

Old Sturbridge Village Lodges. Rte. 20 west, Sturbridge, MA 01566. ☎ **508/347-3327.** Fax 508/347-3018. 59 rms. A/C TV TEL. May–Oct $85–$130 double; Nov–Apr $65–$85 double. Extra person $5. AE, DISC, MC, V.

Apart from the centerpiece Oliver Wight House, which is more than 200 years old, these six barnlike structures arranged around a common and a swimming pool are of post–World War II origin. Rooms are fresh, spacious, and straightforward, with colonial reproductions. Free morning coffee is available in the office.

Publick House. Rte. 131 (Box 187), Sturbridge, MA 01566. ☎ **508/347-3313.** Fax 508/ 347-5073. 17 rms. A/C TEL. $85–$155 double (historic rms); $55–$90 double (motel rms). AE, CB, DC, MC, V. From Exit 3B of I-84, drive 1.5 miles south of Rte. 20 on 131.

This four-building complex is the high-profile lodging in the Sturbridge area. Apart from the main structure, a tavern built in 1771, additional accommodations are in the Colonel Ebenezer Crafts Inn, a 1786 Federalist farmhouse; the Chamberlain House, adjacent to the Publick House; and the Country Motor Lodge, which is what it sounds like. Go for the peaceful, freestanding Ebenezer Crafts Inn, a bed-and-breakfast a mile from the Publick House with its own swimming pool. There are no room TVs throughout, though the management will wheel one into your room on request and there's a TV in the common room.

Dining/Entertainment: There are three restaurants associated with the Publick House, serving traditional New England dishes.

Sturbridge Coach Motor Lodge. 408 Main St., Sturbridge, MA 01566. ☎ **508/347-7327.** Fax 508/347-2954. 54 rms. A/C TV TEL. May–Oct $60–$95 double; Nov–Apr $45–$60 double. Higher rates on long weekends and during special events. AE, MC, V.

You've seen it all before, from the avocado bathroom fixtures to the wrapped plastic cups. But the rates are among the lowest in the area and the location is 200 yards from the entrance to Old Sturbridge Village. There's a pool next to the parking lot.

WHERE TO DINE

Rom's. Rte. 131 (2 miles south of Rte. 20). ☎ **508/347-3349.** Main courses $5.95–$12.95. AE, DISC, MC, V. Sun–Thurs 11am–9pm, Fri–Sat 11am–10pm. ITALIAN/AMERICAN.

This was once a hot-dog and fried-clam roadside stand that grew over 40 years like a multigenerational New England farmhouse. Today, it can seat 700 diners at a time on two levels, but remains a near-ideal family restaurant, with something to please everyone. Liquor is available, but only from a service bar, discouraging the hard-drinking crowd. The Wednesday night (5 to 9pm) and Thursday lunch (11:30am to 2pm) buffets are crowd pleasers, as are the always low prices. A take-out window spoons out "buckets of rigatoni," fish-and-chips, and shrimp in a basket, among other favorites.

The Whistling Swan/Ugly Duckling. 502 Main St. (Rte. 20). ☎ **508/347-2321.** Main courses $12.95–$23.95. AE, CB, DC, MC, V. Whistling Swan, Mon–Sat 11:30am–2:30pm; Mon–Fri 5:30–9:30pm, Sat 5:30–10pm; Sun noon–8pm. Ugly Duckling, Tues–Thurs 11:30am–11pm, Fri–Sat 11:30am–11:30pm. CONTINENTAL/AMERICAN.

This 1855 Greek Revival mansion houses two restaurants that share a kitchen. On the main floor are the rooms of the Whistling Swan, with widely spaced tables, wall sconces, and Sheraton-style chairs. The menu lists "continental" dishes—frogs' legs Provençal, sole with orange-lime sauce, even surf-and-turf. The execution is safe and careful, and the service is efficient if not terribly sophisticated.

Upstairs, the Ugly Duckling packs tables together under the rough-cut board roof and a big brass chandelier. Patrons strive to be heard over the live piano—it's loud, even boisterous. The food is simple and hearty.

Which venue to choose? I'd mount the stairs, in a New York minute.

4 Springfield

Times have been tough in this once prosperous manufacturing city on the east bank of the Connecticut River. But its loyal citizens haven't given in to the consequences of job flight and high unemployment, and there is evidence of redevelopment throughout the downtown district, with recycled loft and factory buildings standing beside modern glass towers. Springfield remains the most important city in western Massachusetts, and has succeeded in attracting new enterprises, notably in plastics, toolmaking, and electronic equipment.

ESSENTIALS

GETTING THERE   Springfield is located near the juncture of the east-west Massachusetts Turnpike (I-90), a toll highway, and north-south I-91, and is readily accessible from every city in the Northeast. It's 89 miles west of Boston, and 32 miles north of Hartford.

Bradley International (☎ 203/627-3000) in Windsor Locks, Conn., is the nearest major airport, about 20 miles to the south of Springfield. Here you can rent a car from any of the major companies, or catch a bus, cab, or limo into Springfield. Major airlines serving Bradley include **American** (☎ 800/433-7300), **Continental** (☎ 800/525-0280), **Delta** (☎ 800/221-1212), **Northwest** (☎ 800/225-2525), **United** (☎ 800/241-6522), and **USAirways** (☎ 800/247-8786).

Amtrak's *Lake Shore Limited* stops both ways in Springfield on its daily run between Boston and Chicago, as does the daily *Vermonter* between Washington, D.C., and Burlington, Vt., with connecting buses from Montréal, Québec, and intermediate stops at New York and Hartford, among others. Schedules change often, however, so call ☎ **800/USA-RAIL** (872-7245) for up-to-date information and reservations.

VISITOR INFORMATION   The **Greater Springfield Convention and Visitors Bureau** (☎ 413/787-1548) is at 34 Boland Way, Springfield, MA 01103.

SPECIAL EVENTS   A highlight of the annual calendar is the **Eastern States Exposition,** a huge old-fashioned agricultural fair with games, rides, a midway, and entertainment. It's held on a fairground on the opposite side of the Connecticut River in West Springfield in mid-September. Call ☎ **413/737-2443** for details. Also on the grounds is the **Old Storrowtown Village,** a collection of restored colonial buildings, accessible by guided tour, Monday to Saturday, from June to Labor Day.

MUSEUMS & HISTORIC SITES

Springfield has enjoyed its share of wealthy benefactors, and enough of them gave back to their community to produce a number of museums of varying levels of interest. The more conventional are the four clustered around the grassy quadrangle behind the Springfield Library. In addition, there are three specialized museums that do their duty well but can easily be skipped by those who don't share those interests, including the Basketball Hall of Fame, described below. Bikers devout and fantasizing will want to check out the **Indian Motorcycle Museum,** 33 Hendee St. (☎ 413/737-2624), while weaponry enthusiasts are sure to be intrigued by the 1840s **Springfield Armory,** 1 Armory Sq. (☎ 413/734-8551), now a museum tracing the evolution of weapons once made here.

Basketball Hall of Fame. W. Columbus Ave. (at Union St.). ☎ **413/781-6500.** Fax 413/781-1939. Admission $8 adults 16 and over, $5 seniors and children 7–15, free for children 6 and under. Daily Sun–Tues and Thurs 9am–6pm, Wed and Fri–Sat 9am–8pm.

Dr. James Naismith invented basketball in Springfield in 1891, providing the logic for this memorial and entertainment center. A definite must for fans, it is painless even for those who regard the game as a blur of 7-foot armpits.

Take the elevator to the third floor and work your way down. Up there are the inductees and displays recalling the history of the game. Descriptions of the early years are surprising. Remember the Waterloo Hawks? The Pittsburgh Ironmen? The Indianapolis Kautskys? Or the Philadelphia Hebrews? The Hall covers every aspect of the game, from high school to the NBA to the Olympics, as well as such offshoots as wheelchair leagues and the Harlem Globetrotters. An updated map of the United States announces the latest boys' and girls' champs in every state. No aspect of the sport is too small, attested to by the collections of Topps cards and sneakers.

On the ground floor is a shooting court with baskets at various heights, and next to it a virtual-reality display, in which visitors can insert themselves on a large viewing screen and play against the pros.

Museums at the Quadrangle. 220 State St. (corner of Chestnut St.). ☎ **413/263-6800.** Admission $4 adults, $1 ages 6–18; free for children under 6. $1 more for the planetarium. Wed–Sun noon–4pm.

Four museums and a library surrounding a single inner quadrangle constitute this unusually rich resource, much of it built from the generosity of prosperous local industrialists who flourished in Springfield during the 19th and early 20th centuries.

A good way to begin a tour is by entering the library from State Street and walking through to the back. Out there, on the right, is the first museum; the others can be visited around the quad in a counterclockwise circuit. A ticket bought in any of the museums is good for all the others. Before setting out, note the limited hours above.

The **George Walter Vincent Smith Art Museum**'s eponymous donor, a wealthy carriage manufacturer, assembled an extensive, eclectic collection he installed in this 1896 Italian Renaissance–style mansion. Proceeding upstairs, you'll find a gallery of largely sentimental pastoral scenes, with a few small landscapes by George Inness, Thomas Cole, and Alfred Bierstadt. Subsequent rooms house substantial numbers of Apulian red-figured vases and Chinese cloisonné, a form of pottery that employs metal, glass, and enamel. They are followed by rooms of Oriental carpets and prettily inconsequential Italian landscapes, many of Venice. On the main floor are cases of Japanese samurai armor and weaponry surrounding an arresting, heavily carved Shinto shrine dating from 1805.

And to Think That I Saw It on Mulberry Street

The grandparents of Theodor Seuss Geisel lived on Springfield's Mulberry Street, and in 1937 the writer and illustrator later known as Dr. Seuss named the first of his dozens of children's books for the neighborhood. He followed up with such classics as *How the Grinch Stole Christmas* (1957), *Horton Hatches the Egg* (1940), and *The Cat in the Hat* (1957). Every last title is still in print, and more than 100 million copies have been sold.

Though Geisel spent most of his adult life in California, the result of a nearly 2-decade career in documentary films during which he won two Academy Awards, much of his inspiration for his children's books can be traced to Springfield.

Mulberry Street is no longer the august avenue it once must have been, its Victorian manses now crowded by undistinguished apartment blocks and commercial strips. And the former Central High School from which Geisel graduated is now a condominium. But Seuss's drawing of Bartholomew Cubbins's castle bears a strong resemblance to the Howard Street Armory, now a community center, and certain of his landscapes look as if they were recalled from his playtimes in Forest Park, near his boyhood home at 74 Fairfield St.

Likely to be the biggest winner with children, the **Science Museum** contains a planetarium (show time at 2:45pm), dioramas of large African animals, and downstairs, the Monsato Eco-Center. This new section strives for elusive cohesion with some interactive devices, aquariums with native and tropical fish, a boa and poisonous frogs, and scattered other exhibits.

Enter the **Connecticut River Valley Historical Museum** through a gateway that is a representation of the headgear worn by Dr. Seuss's famous Cat in the Hat. (The children's author grew up in Springfield.) Inside are examples of weapons made by the city's firearms manufacturers, including a blunderbuss and an unusual 1838 rifle with a revolving cartridge chamber. Exhibits pertaining to local history and a genealogy library are of limited interest, but some may find the temporary exhibits upstairs appealing.

The strongest and most professionally organized repository of the lot is the ✪ **Museum of Fine Arts,** which has 20 galleries with canvases by European and American artists. The latter are the most interesting, with examples of colonial paintings on through Gilbert Stuart and John Copley to early 20th-century realists George Bellows and Reginald Marsh and culminating with both magic realists and abstract expressionists of recent decades, sampling Frank Stella, Helen Frankenthaler, Don Eddy, and George Sugarman. Make a particular effort to view the remarkable serigraph of lower Manhattan by Richard Estes.

Matoon Street Historic District. Between Chestnut and Elliot sts.

Built between 1870 and the 1890s, this largely unsullied block of Queen Anne–style Victorian and Romanesque Revival row houses is worth a short detour after visiting the Quadrangle Museums. One of the semifamous residents was Lawrence O'Brien, postmaster general in the Kennedy administration and former Commissioner of the National Basketball Association. He lived at numbers 29 and 43. The street is dominated at the eastern end by a looming church designed by H. H. Richardson, the architect of Boston's Trinity Church. Turn south at the church onto Elliot Street, where there are a couple of impressively proportioned wooden Victorians.

WHERE TO STAY

Directly across the street from the Marriott is the entirely comparable **Sheraton Monarch Place,** 1 Monarch Place, Springfield, MA 01104 (☎ **413/781-1010;** fax 413/734-3249), with similar prices and amenities.

Marriott Springfield. Boland and Columbus aves., Springfield, MA 01115. ☎ **413/ 781-7111.** Fax 413/731-8932. 265 rms. A/C TV TEL. $98–$115 double. AE, DC, DISC, MC, V.

Easy to find, just off the Springfield Center exit of I-91, this can be a real treat after a few nights in quirky New England inns. Predictable, yes, but tuck into a room with all these goodies (cable TV with hit movies on order, hair dryer, coffeemaker, and phone with data port) and lack of charm can suddenly seem unimportant—especially when it's combined with room service, a parking garage, indoor pool, exercise room, a friendly bar, a capable grill restaurant, and an executive floor with a private breakfast lounge.

WHERE TO DINE

Pioneer Valley Brew Pub. 51–59 Taylor St. (near Dwight St.). ☎ **413/732-2739.** Main courses $7.95–$18.95. Mon–Wed 11:30am–9pm, Thurs–Sat 11:30am–10pm, Sun 1–9pm. AE, MC, V. ECLECTIC AMERICAN.

Only open since March 1995, this self-described "Deco Diner" is a welcome addition to the forlorn local dining scene. The main room is spacious, and a second one in the back overlooks a dining terrace. In addition to a regular slate of ales and lagers on tap (try Armory Amber), there are seasonal special brews to wash down such tasty dishes as Flemish stew in a sourdough bowl and beer-battered chicken with a cashew dipping sauce.

Student Prince and The Fort. 8 Fort St. (west of Main St.). ☎ **413/734-7475.** Main courses $7.95–$21.75. Mon–Sat 11am–11pm, Sun noon–10pm. AE, CB, DC, DISC, MC, V. GERMAN/ AMERICAN.

In 1935, German immigrants opened a cafe they called the Student Prince and began serving beer in steins with schnitzels, sauerbraten, and hasenpfeffer. That might not have seemed the precise historical moment to ensure the success of such an enterprise, but it thrived. In 1946, they were able to add a large dining room next door, which they chose to call The Fort. The resulting complex is the most popular place in town. Waitresses rush about in sensible shoes, slapping plates down and tolerating no lip from playful patrons. Monster portions are the rule, with veal shanks as thick as a linebacker's forearm and plates of wurst heaped high with sausages, boiled potatoes, and sauerkraut. Check out the enormous stein collection at the bar.

Tavern Inn. 91 W. Gardner St. (on the corner of W. Columbus Ave.). ☎ **413/736-0456.** Main courses $5.95–$13.95. Mon–Fri 11:30am–2:30pm; Mon–Wed 4:30–9pm, Thurs–Fri 4:30– 10pm, Sat 11:30am–midnight, Sun noon–9pm. AE, MC, V. ITALIAN/AMERICAN.

Guileless as they come, this place is exactly what it seems to be. Two blocks south of the Basketball Hall of Fame, the Tavern has a sports bar–style atmosphere, with big TVs in both rooms, silently tuned to whatever game is on, but the mood is affable rather than raucous. Meal options include manicotti and veal Florentine, and just about everything comes with salad and a choice of pasta or potatoes.

SPRINGFIELD AFTER DARK

The **Springfield Symphony Orchestra** offers performances at **Symphony Hall,** 127 Main St. (☎ 413/787-6610), from October to May.

Stagewest produces a September-to-May theatrical series that concentrates on late 20th-century plays by such luminaries as A. R. Gurney and Edward Albee. The shows are mounted at **One Columbus Center** (☎ 413/781-2340) between Worthington and Bridge streets. The nearby **Paramount Performing Arts Center,** 1700 Main St. (☎ 413/734-5706), is a restored 1920s movie palace that hosts concerts by traveling pop, rock, comedy, and country performers.

5 The Pioneer Valley

In the Pioneer Valley, low billowing hills and quilted fields embrace the Connecticut River as it runs south to the Atlantic. The earliest European settlers came here for what proved to be uncommonly fertile soil, and were followed in the 19th century by men who harnessed the power of the river and became wealthy textile and paper manufacturers.

These industrialists took the lead in funding the institutions of higher learning that are now the pride of the region. Prestigious Smith, Mount Holyoke, and Amherst are here, as are innovative Hampshire College and the sprawling main campus of the University of Massachusetts, with its enrollment of more than 25,000 students. All five contribute mightily to the cultural life of the valley, and Northampton, Amherst, and South Hadley are invigorated by the vitality of thousands of college-age young people.

In the north, near Vermont, the living village of Deerfield preserves the architecture and atmosphere of colonial New England, but without the whiff of sterility that afflicts artificial gatherings of old buildings with costumed docents.

Interstate 91 and Route 5 both traverse the valley from south to north. The trip from edge to edge on the Interstate takes less than an hour, while Route 5 tenders more of the flavor of pastoral vistas and colorful mill towns.

There are ample numbers of motels along the way, but if you're looking for lodgings more representative of the character of the region, you might contact the **Folkstone Bed & Breakfast Reservation Service** (☎ 800/762-2751 or 508/480-0380). They have listings throughout Central Massachusetts with rates of $50 to $150 a night; all accept MasterCard and Visa.

ESSENTIALS

GETTING THERE   From Boston and upstate New York, take the Massachusetts Turnpike (I-90), a toll highway, to Springfield, then follow I-91 or Route 5 north. While there are local buses, you'll want a car.

The nearest major airport is **Bradley International** (☎ 203/627-3000), just south of Springfield, in Connecticut. (See section 4 of this chapter for a list of airlines that serve Bradley.) A private service called **Valley Transporter** (☎ 800/872-8752 or 413/549-1350) offers van shuttles between the airport and Amherst, Northampton, Hadley, Holyoke, and Deerfield.

Amtrak's *Vermonter* stops in Amherst and Northampton on its daily trips between Burlington, Vt., and Washington, D.C., but schedules change at least twice yearly, so call ☎ 800/USA-RAIL (872-7245) for up-to-date information and reservations.

VISITOR INFORMATION   The **Pioneer Valley Tourist Information Center** (☎ 413/665-7333) is at the intersection of Routes 5 and 10 in South Deerfield, at Exit 24 of I-91.

HOLYOKE

Once an important paper manufacturing center, Holyoke, which lies 8 miles north of Springfield and 88 miles west of Boston, has suffered a long economic slide since World War II. Abandoned factories and the dissolute air of the commercial center don't bolster first impressions. Still, there are a couple of modestly worthwhile sights and a pleasant inn for a meal or an overnight stay.

WHAT TO SEE & DO

Canals dug during the city's heyday as a paper manufacturing center still cut through the downtown area (they were intended to allow access to the mills and bypass a dam in the Connecticut River). Linear **Heritage State Park,** entrance at 221 Appleton St. (☎ 413/534-1723), runs beside one of the canals, and has an interpretive center that offers walking tours and exhibits limning the history of the industrial glory days. On most Sundays from mid-June to late August, the ancient locomotive of the **Heritage Park Railroad** pulls three cars of train buffs on a 2-hour, 5-mile trip downriver from the park to Holyoke Mall at Ingleside. Times and fares vary, since demand and funds fluctuate. Call Heritage State Park for more information.

For skiing, hit **Mount Tom,** 2 miles north of the city center off Route 5 (☎ 800/545-7163). At 1,150 feet, it won't remind anyone of the Jungfrau, but still, there are 17 mostly intermediate trails, and a long run of 3,600 feet. They are illuminated at night and snowmaking equipment is at hand. Rentals are available. All-day lift tickets are $30 for adults, $26 for seniors and children ages 9 to 12. Summer recreational facilities include an artificial wave pool, water slide, and water tube ride, as well as hiking trails.

Volleyball Hall of Fame. 44 Dwight St. (next to Heritage Park). ☎ **413/536-0926.** Free admission. Tues–Sat 9:30am–4:30pm, Sun noon–5pm.

The valley abounds with specialized museums that needn't detain any traveler who doesn't harbor the specific interests they address, and this is one of them. Volleyball was invented in Holyoke by one William Morgan in 1895, an event commemorated by this one room in a converted mill shared with a **children's museum.** If you're a passionate volleyball fan, you'll find this place at least intriguing; if you barely know the difference between volleyball and basketball, you'll be underwhelmed. Your call.

Wistariahurst Museum. 238 Cabot St. ☎ **413/534-2216.** Fax 413/534-2344. Free admission for tours; special musical events $5–$10. Apr–Oct Wed and Sat–Sun 1–5pm; Nov–Mar Wed and Sat–Sun noon–4pm. Closed last 2 weeks of Aug.

Skinner is a name that pops up with some regularity in these parts. This was once the home of William Skinner, a silk manufacturer, and though it looks a little the worse for wear of late, it retains a fine marble vestibule, coffered ceilings, and Tiffany windows. This is essentially a house museum, with paintings, objects, and furnishings of the late 19th century. The museum's great hall is a venue for frequent musical events.

WHERE TO STAY & DINE

Yankee Pedlar Inn. 1866 Northampton St. (Rte. 5), Holyoke, MA 01040. ☎ **413/532-9494.** Fax 413/536-8877. 32 rms. A/C TV TEL. $65–$125 double. Rates include breakfast. AE, CB, DC, DISC, MC, V. Take Exit 16 off I-91 and head east for 5 blocks.

A vigorous young manager has big plans for this Victorian inn, and renovations and new construction continue at a brisk pace. Of the five buildings in the complex, the 1850 house has the most modern rooms. Some rooms have canopied beds, and 4 of the 15 suites have kitchenettes.

Dining/Entertainment: The main dining room, with its breezy menu and lively bar, is popular with locals as well as travelers. Live musical entertainment is presented on weekends.

SOUTH HADLEY

Pioneer educator Mary Lyon founded Mount Holyoke Female Seminary in 1836 and presided over it for 12 years. One of the Seven Sisters group of prestigious women's colleges, it emphasizes liberal arts and preparation for the service professions such as law, medicine, teaching, and social work.

Strung along the eastern side of Route 116 (College Street), the college is the essential reason for the existence of this small town (population 13,600), although it was settled in the late 17th century. It lies 15 miles north of Springfield, and 7 miles south of Amherst.

On the campus is an admirable **Art Museum** (☎ **413/538-2245**), which focuses on art of the Orient, Egypt, and the Mediterranean, but also mounts temporary exhibits on a considerable range of topics. Admission is free. Hours are Tuesday to Friday from 11am to 5pm, Saturday and Sunday from 1 to 5pm. It's closed during school holidays, but not in summer. To find it, take Park Street from the east side of the Y intersection in the center of town and follow the signs.

Joseph Skinner State Park (☎ **413/586-0350**) straddles the border between South Hadley and Hadley. On its 390 acres are miles of walking trails, picnic grounds, and the historic Summit House. The building (open weekends only from May to October) was erected in a single day in 1821 by a group of energetic male friends who wanted a place to party with copious quantities of gin, rum, cigars, and panoramic views of the valley.

A tastefully designed mall called **The Village Commons** (☎ **413/532-3600**) stands alongside Route 116 opposite the Mount Holyoke campus. More than 30 shops, including a movie theater, three restaurants, and the admirable **Odyssey Bookshop,** are clustered in white clapboard buildings suggesting a classic New England village.

NORTHAMPTON

Smith College, with its campus sprawling along Main Street slightly west of the commercial center, is Northampton's dominating physical and spiritual presence. One of the original Seven Sisters (before that informal league of women's colleges was broken up by coeducation), Smith is the largest female liberal-arts college in the United States.

Lying 21 miles north of Springfield and 16 miles south of Deerfield, Northampton was long the home of Calvin Coolidge, who pursued his law practice here before and after his monosyllabic occupancy of the Oval Office. (At a White House dinner, the laconic Silent Cal was seated next to a woman who said she had made a bet she could get three words out of him. "You lose," he said.) He lived in houses at 21 Massasoit St. and on Hampton Terrace, but the homes are privately owned and not open to the public. A room containing many of his papers is maintained by the **Forbes Library,** 20 West St. (☎ **413/584-6037**).

SEEING THE SIGHTS

Historic Northampton. 46 Bridge St. (east of the railroad bridge). ☎ **413/584-6011.** Admission $3 adults, $1 children 7–12. Tours Mar–Dec Wed–Sun noon–4pm.

Among Northampton's most popular attractions are the Museum Houses, three expertly restored and maintained historic homes still standing on their original sites. They are the 1730 Parsons House, the 1796 Shepherd House, and the 1812 Isaac Damon House, which contains a furnished parlor true to 1820.

Smith College

To a considerable extent, the campus buildings that line Elm Street are a testament to the excesses of late-19th-century architecture. Their often egregious admixtures of Gothic, Greco-Roman, Renaissance, and medieval esthetic notions lend a Teutonic sobriety to the west end of town.

That aside, one of those ponderous brown monoliths houses a worthwhile **Museum of Art,** 76 Elm St. at Bedford Terrace (☎ 413/584-2700). Included in its permanent holdings of more than 24,000 works of the late-19th and 20th centuries are paintings by Degas, Monet, Picasso, and Winslow Homer. Admission is free. It's open September to June Tuesdays, Fridays, and Saturdays from 9:30am to 4pm, Wednesdays and Sundays noon to 4pm, and Thursdays noon to 8pm; in July and August hours are Tuesday to Sunday from noon to 4pm.

Words & Pictures Museum. 140 Main St. ☎ **413/586-8545.** Admission $3 adults, $1 children under 18. Tues–Wed and Sat–Sun noon–5pm, Thurs noon–8pm.

Don't let the fact that funding is provided in part by a creator of the Teenage Mutant Ninja Turtles lead to the conclusion that this repository of comic-book illustrations is just the place to take the kiddies. Most of the work on display, while expertly rendered, is of the decidedly adult variety, with action characters demonstrating a predilection for violence as well as for costumes of an S&M persuasion (and displaying more than a few bared breasts and buttocks). Parents with children should escort their charges through the mock "cave" entrance onto the elevator directly to the second floor, where there are interactive computer games and a replica of a Ninja Turtles movie set. An addition is being built to display a Batmobile.

Outdoor Pursuits

Three miles southwest of town on Route 10 in Easthampton is the **Arcadia Nature Center and Wildlife Sanctuary** (☎ 413/584-3009), a 700-acre preserve operated by the Massachusetts Audubon Society. It contains a mixed ecology of marshes and woods bordering the Connecticut River. Over 5 miles of well-tended trails provide access to a variety of flora and fauna. The Sanctuary is open dawn to dusk, Tuesday to Sunday. Admission is $3 for nonmember adults, $2 for seniors and ages 3 to 15.

Cyclists make good use of the **Norwottuck Trail Bike Path,** an 8¹/₂-mile trail that follows a former railroad bed running between Northampton and Amherst, reached by an old bridge across the river. Access is via Damon Road and at Mount Farms Mall. Bikes can be rented at **Valley Bicycles,** 319 Main St. (☎ 413/256-0880), across the river in Amherst.

Look Memorial Park, 300 N. Main St. (☎ 413/584-5457), is northwest of town off Route 9, with 157 acres of woods, a 5-acre lake, picnic grounds, and a small zoo of native animals. Boats are available for rent. There are musical and theatrical events, including puppet shows, in summer.

Shopping

One of the pleasures of college towns for bibliophiles and browsers is the larger than usual number of bookstores, often dealing in exotica not found in the big national chains. Northampton has those, in abundance, but also enjoys the most diverse shopping in the valley. All of the following stores are open 7 days a week.

The **Antique Center of Northampton,** 9¹/₂ Market St. (☎ 413/584-3600), contains the stalls of more than 60 independent dealers on three floors. **Pinch Pottery and the Ferrin Gallery,** 179 Main St. (☎ 413/586-4509), offers superb contemporary jewelry, glassware, and ceramics, and represents elite craftspeople whose works are found in the distinguished White House Collection. There are no bargains, but there are affordable pieces. CDs, greeting cards, and stationery supplement the extensive stock of the two-level **Beyond Words Bookshop,** 189 Main St. (☎ 413/586-6304), which has a second-floor cafe. The store motto is "Book lovers never go to bed alone." A former department store has been reconfigured into **Thorne's Marketplace,** 150 Main St. (☎ 413/584-5582), which now contains more than 30 specialty boutiques on five floors.

WHERE TO STAY

This being a college town, with frequent influxes of parents and alumnae during graduations, homecomings, and other events, anticipate higher rates and limited vacancies at those times, in addition to the usual holiday weekends.

Autumn Inn. 259 Elm St., Northampton, MA 01060. ☎ **413/584-7660.** Fax 413/586-4808. 28 rms, 2 suites. A/C TV TEL. $82–$98 double. AE, CB, DC, MC, V.

A genteel motel with a vaguely Georgian style, the Autumn is conveniently situated opposite the quieter northern end of the Smith campus. There is a restaurant with a huge wood-burning fireplace serving breakfast and lunch (not dinner). In summer, an unheated pool beckons. Smoking isn't permitted on the second floor, in the lobby, or in the dining room.

Hotel Northampton. 36 King St., Northampton, MA 01060. ☎ **413/584-3100.** Fax 413/584-9455. 77 rms. A/C TV TEL. $83–$180 double. AE, CB, DC, DISC, MC, V.

Built in 1927, this five-story brick building at the center of town looks older. An admirable restoration and modernization has brought it up to date, with rooms containing lots of wicker and colonial reproductions, feather duvets, and assorted Victoriana. Many front rooms have balconies overlooking King Street, some have canopied beds, a few have Jacuzzis. No smoking.

Dining/Entertainment: Service in the hotel's Coolidge Park Cafe is pleasant enough, but glacial in execution. Downstairs, Wiggins Tavern is an authentic colonial watering hole that predates the hotel by a couple of centuries, with dark beams and stone fireplaces. If you value your limited time, eat elsewhere.

Inn at Northampton. Rte. 5 and I-91 (just west of Exit 18), Northampton, MA 01060. ☎ **413/586-1211.** Fax 413/586-0630. 124 rms. A/C TV TEL. $69–$129 double. Rates include breakfast. AE, CB, DC, DISC, MC, V.

Easily accessible, this inn is hidden behind a Mobil gas station, and the entrance isn't clearly marked. Renovations have elevated it from a standard motel to something less readily categorized, closer to a modest resort, with its lighted tennis court and two swimming pools, one of them indoors. Though the recreational amenities are impressive, the management needs to work on the breakfasts, which primarily consist of canned juice and boxed cereals. The restaurant on the premises also serves dinner, though it's not particularly noteworthy.

WHERE TO DINE

Eastside Grill. 19 Strong Ave. (1 block south of Main St.). ☎ **413/586-3347.** Main courses $8.95–$14.95. AE, MC, V. Mon–Sat 11:30am–2:30pm; Mon–Thurs 5–10pm, Fri–Sat 5–11pm, Sun 4–9pm. REGIONAL AMERICAN.

The consensus choice for tops in town, this white clapboard building with a nautical look is small for the amount of business it does. The far-reaching menu has bayou riffs, such as chicken etouffée and shrimp and andouille jambalaya. But while the Cajun/Creole dishes obviously absorb much of the kitchen's attention, there are ample alternatives. The seafood is impressive, and you'd do well to end your meal with New Orleans pudding—pecans, coconut, and raisins in a bread custard doused with a bourbon sauce.

Fitzwilly's. 21 Main St. (near Pleasant St.). ☎ **413/584-8666.** Main courses $9.95–$13.95. AE, DC, DISC, MC, V. Daily 11:30am–midnight. AMERICAN.

Occupying a building constructed in 1898, this ingratiating pub makes the most of its high stamped-tin ceilings and ample space. Big copper brewing kettles constitute much of the decor, signaling the intriguing selection of beers on tap, some from regional microbreweries. Beyond the two long bars are curtained booths where patrons dive into grilled pizzas, burgers, and ribs. There are also low-cal "spa" dishes.

La Cazuela. 7 Old South St. (down the hill from Main St.). ☎ **413/586-0400.** Main courses $8–$12.95. AE, DISC, MC, V. Mon–Thurs 5–9pm, Fri 5–10pm, Sat 3–10pm, Sun 3–9pm. SOUTHWESTERN/MEXICAN.

The menu at this restaurant mixes recipes of the American Southwest with those of Mexico, and the kitchen takes its job quite seriously. In addition to the predictable flautas, enchiladas, and chimichangas, frequently changing dinner specials explore lesser-known regional cuisines with such dishes as *pollo asado de Yucatán,* chicken roasted in a banana leaf. La Cazuela is in a rustic 1850 building, with earth tones and Mexican artifacts that give the interior a Santa Fe look. No smoking.

La Veracruzana. 31 Main St. (near Pleasant St.). ☎ **413/586-7181.** Main courses $5.45–$7.95. No credit cards. Sun–Wed 11am–10pm, Thurs 11am–11pm, Fri–Sat 11am–midnight. SOUTHWESTERN/MEXICAN.

Choose from the big handwritten menu over the counter next to the kitchen in back—lunch or snack items like burritos, tacos, and fajitas, plus more serious plates like *pechuga de pollo en mole poblano:* chicken breast in the famous Mexican chocolate-based (but spicy, not sweet) sauce. Go with a friend and share the six-taco package deal (in any style or combination) for only $7.95. There's a free salsa bar, and beer and wine are available.

Vermont Country Deli & Cafe. 48 Main St. (near Pleasant St.). ☎ **413/586-7114.** Main courses $5.50–$7.95. MC, V. Daily 7am–7pm (until 9pm Fri–Sat in summer). ECLECTIC.

The eye-catching sign out front only says "French Bakery," but the appetizing sights glimpsed through the window drag people inside. On the right is a long case crowded with platters of tantalizing salads and main courses, like Hunan orange chicken, sesame noodles, grilled vegetables, Vietnamese pasta salad, and spinach knishes. Fat focaccia sandwiches are made to order, including one with "Cajun" turkey and co-riander horseradish dressing. On the opposite side of the room are plump sticky buns, lemon muffins, sourdough baguettes, and several urns of various coffees. Eat at one of the tables in back, or keep it in mind for a take-out picnic.

NORTHAMPTON AFTER DARK

The presence of Smith College only partially accounts for the large number of music bars and clubs in town, making Northampton the nightlife magnet of the valley. In April, the **Loud Music Festival** rattles walls with more than 250 alternative rock bands from around the country.

For a rundown of what's happening, pick up a copy of the *Optimist,* a weekly handout.

Still thriving after 104 years, the **Academy of Music,** 74 Main St. (☎ **413/584-8453**), serves several functions, and has done so since the acting Barrymores came through town. It shows big-screen films as well as providing a venue for op-era, ballet, and pop performers on tour. The hall operates irregularly, and the acts and prices vary, so call ahead for details.

Another old favorite, the **Iron Horse Music Hall,** 20 Center St. (☎ **413/584-0610**), has played host to an enormous variety of artists, from Bonnie Raitt and Richie Havens, to jazzmen Dave Brubeck and Pat Metheny, to obscure but no less gratifying Celtic fiddlers, blues belters, and grunge rockers. It's open nightly from 5:30pm to 1am, but covers vary, so call ahead.

Live alternative bands alternate with DJ dance parties at the two-floor **Pearl Street Nightclub,** 10 Pearl St. (☎ **413/584-7771**). There are often dance-party nights targeted at teenagers, or gay nights (usually Wednesdays). Call ahead for details on specific events. Closed on Mondays.

You might also stop in for a pint of microbrewed suds at **Fitzwilly's,** 21 Main St., near Pleasant Street (☎ **413/584-8666**).

AMHERST

Winter naturally suppresses the street activity of this otherwise lively college town, but any hint of a break in the weather has students, faculty members, and townspeople jogging, bounding, strolling, and greeting each other as they gravitate toward the shops and cafes clustered around the downtown intersection of Pleasant, Amity, and Main streets. Yet another Pioneer Valley town (situated 7 miles east of Northampton, 16 miles southeast of Deerfield) defined by its educational institutions, this one has an even bigger student population than most, with distinguished Amherst College occupying much of its center, the large University of Massachusetts campus to its immediate northwest, and Hampshire College off South Pleasant Street.

Near the town green is a seasonal **information booth.** Its hours vary, and when it is closed, visitors can consult the **Chamber of Commerce** office (☎ **413/253-0700**) in the Lord Jefferey Inn (entrance at 11 Spring St.).

HISTORIC HOMES & COLLEGES

Most of the historic homes are within a few blocks of the Amity/Main/Pleasant street crossing. **Amherst College,** which has two museums of interest, lies mostly along the east side of the town common. At the northeast corner of the green is the **Town Hall,** another fortresslike Romanesque Revival creation of Boston's H. H. Richardson.

Amherst College. S. Pleasant and College sts. ☎ **413/542-2000.**

Named for Baron Jefferey Amherst, a British general during the last of the French and Indian Wars, the illustrious liberal-arts college for men maintains a cooperative relationship with Smith, Mount Holyoke, the University of Massachusetts, and the experimental Hampshire College. It was founded in 1821, with Noah Webster on its first board of trustees. Robert Frost was a member of the faculty for more than a decade.

Its large campus cuts through the heart of the town, and contains two museums open to the public. The **Pratt Museum of Natural History** (☎ 413/542-2165), at the southeast corner of the main quadrangle, boasts a large number of dinosaur tracks collected from sedimentary rocks of the Connecticut Valley, as well as fossils, a mastodon skeleton, and rocks and minerals indigenous to the valley. The **Mead Art Museum** (☎ 413/542-2335), at the intersection of Routes 116 and 9, displays varied collections of sculptures, paintings, photographs, and antiquities. Its strengths lie in the works of 19th- and 20th-century American artists and French Impressionists. Admission to both museums is free.

Amherst History Museum at the Strong House. 67 Amity St. (1 block west of the main intersection). ☎ **413/256-0678.** Admission $2. Mid-May to mid-Oct Wed and Sat 12:30–3:30pm; mid-Oct to mid-May Thurs only 12:30–3:30pm.

Built around 1744, this is one of the oldest houses in town. That's its principal appeal, for the collection of furniture, clothing, and accessories it contains are in need of a firm curatorial hand and the funds to pull it all together in an organized fashion. Volunteers gamely lead the guided tours.

Dickinson Homestead. 280 Main St. (2 blocks east of the Town Hall). ☎ **413/542-8161.** Admission $4 adults, $3 students, $2 children 6–11; free for children under 6 and students from the 5 area colleges. Admission by guided tour only. Tours: Mar Wed and Sat 1:30, 2:15, 3, and 3:45pm; Apr–May and Sept–Oct Wed–Sat 1:30, 2:15, 3, and 3:45pm; June–Aug Wed–Sun

1:30–4pm (Sat also 10:30 and 11:30am); Nov to mid-Dec Wed and Sat 1:30, 2:15, 3, and 3:45pm. Reservations recommended.

Designated a National Historic Monument, this is the house where Emily Dickinson was born in 1830 and where she lived until her family moved in 1840. They returned in 1855, and the famous poet stayed here from then until her death 31 years later. The "Belle of Amherst" was the granddaughter and daughter of local movers and shakers, the source of her support while she produced the poetry that was to be increasingly celebrated even as she withdrew into near-total seclusion.

University of Massachusetts. Visitors Center (MA 116). ☎ **413/545-2511.** Free admission. Campus tours, intended primarily for prospective students and their parents, are available by appointment.

Though the university was founded in 1863, this 1,200-acre campus north of the town center dates only from the 1960s. Its 25,000 students study for degrees in 90 academic fields. The university's recent success in intercollegiate basketball (the team made it to the Final Four in 1996) has provoked the enthusiasm of sports fans all over the state.

Art is given a high priority by the administration, with six galleries scattered around the campus. Foremost among these is the University Gallery in the **Fine Arts Center,** beside the pond in the quadrangle. Its permanent collection and frequent temporary exhibitions focus on works of 20th-century artists. The Center also mounts productions in dance, music, and theater. Call the box office (☎ **413/545-2511**) for information about current and upcoming performances.

BIKING

An 8¹/₂-mile bicycle trail following a former railroad bed between Amherst and Northampton is well used by residents of both towns. Bicycles can be rented at **Valley Bicycles,** 319 Main St. (☎ **800/831-5437** or 413/256-0880), in Amherst.

SHOPPING

Atticus/Albion Bookstore, at 8 Main St. (☎ **413/256-1547**), has a rumpled aspect that is catnip for readers who like to poke among the piles of books and take a seat on the window sofa to skim their finds. The nearby **Jefferey Amherst Bookshop,** at 55 S. Pleasant St. (☎ **413/253-3381**), is tidier, emphasizing paperbacks and specializing in Emily Dickinson and academic texts.

WHERE TO STAY

Allen House. 599 Main St. (5 blocks east of the Town Hall), Amherst, MA 01430. ☎ **413/ 253-5000.** 7 rms. A/C. $45–$135 double. Rates include breakfast. AE, DISC, MC, V. No children under 10.

The colorful exterior paint job makes this Queen Anne–style Victorian, built in 1886, easy to spot. The interior is fitted out in the manner of the eye-blink moment of the Aesthetic artistic movement, which had Oscar Wilde as one of its boosters but barely lasted 10 years. In any event, the parlor and bedrooms are lovingly decorated and highly visual, embellished with tracery and curlicues that are somehow Arabic in feel. The Eastlake Room is the prize. Free pickup service from the Amtrak station is provided. No smoking.

Lord Jefferey Inn. 30 Boltwood Ave. (next to the Town Hall), Amherst, MA 01002. ☎ **800/ 742-0358** or 413/253-2576. Fax 413/256-6152. 50 rms. A/C TV TEL. $68–$118 double. AE, DC, MC, V.

Perhaps it is inevitable that the principal lodging in a college town is going to look a little battered and threadbare. The Lord Jeff does, and not just because it's been around since 1926 (which isn't *that* old anyway). But despite the wear and tear of more than 70 years of graduations, homecomings, and conferences, the inn offers an environment that is as warm as its several working fireplaces. Robert Frost stayed here for two of his last years as an English professor at the college.

Dining/Entertainment: The main dining room is open for all meals, including Sunday brunch, and the less formal Boltwood's Tavern, recently expanded, serves plain food from 11:30am to 10pm.

WHERE TO DINE

Judie's. 51 N. Pleasant St. (north of Amity and Main sts.). ☎ **413/253-3491.** Main courses $4.99–$14.95. AE, DISC, MC, V. Sun–Thurs 11:30am–10pm, Fri–Sat 11:30am–11pm. ECLECTIC AMERICAN.

As popular as any place in town, Judie's does its best to suit every taste. Just to keep things ticking, for example, there's a "Munchie Madness" period from 3 to 6pm, with a half-price snacks menu. Throughout the day, folks drop by for just a cup of soup and one of the trademark popovers. A glass-enclosed porch fronts the converted house, which has several interior rooms. Typical of the posted lunch specials is sautéed chicken with broccoli, mushrooms, and onions with a bordelaise sauce, all in a baked stuffed potato—for just $4.99.

Rasa Sayang. 13 N. Pleasant St. (near intersection of Amity and Main sts.). ☎ **413/ 253-7888.** Main courses $4.25–$13.95. AE, CB, DC, DISC, MC, V. Sun–Thurs 11:30am–10pm, Fri–Sat 11:30am–10:30pm. MALAYSIAN.

Opened in 1995 at a site that has seen several failed ventures, this operation seems to have what it takes to survive. Prices are reasonable, service is warm and efficient, and the food is just different enough to pique jaded taste buds. Malaysia is at that Asian cultural crossroads that brings together the curries of India and the variegated cooking styles of China, and the food attests to it. There is a lengthy menu to sample, with 21 varieties of "noodles in soup," incorporating pork, seafood, chicken and duck, not to mention the daily specials. Beer, wine, and a limited selection of liquors are available.

AMHERST AFTER DARK

Students and young adults tend to gravitate toward the livelier music scene in Northampton, but Amherst itself does offer some nighttime entertainment. Close at hand is the **Black Sheep Cafe,** 79 Main St. (☎ **413/253-3442**), which is active nightly, with folk and blues singers, poetry readings, chamber music . . . a broad, unpredictable selection. Entrance is usually free.

Throughout the school year, Amherst College's **Buckley Recital Hall** (☎ **413/ 542-2195**) and **The Millins Center** (☎ **413/545-0505**) at UMass mount a variety of pop, classical, dance, and theatrical performances that might include, for example, the Cincinnati Symphony, Mummenschantz, or Elton John.

DEERFIELD

Meadows cleared and plowed more than 300 years ago still surround this historic town between the Connecticut and Deerfield rivers. Every morning tobacco and dairy farmers leave houses fronting the main street to work their land nearby. Students attend the distinguished prep school, Deerfield Academy, founded in 1797. Lawyers maintain offices here, while other residents commute to and from jobs elsewhere. Deerfield is an invaluable fragment of American history, and it isn't one of those New England village exhibits with costumed performers who go home to their condos at night.

A town still exists here, 16 miles north of Northampton and 16 miles northwest of Amherst, because the earliest English settlers were determined to thrive despite their status as a frontier pressure point in the wars that tormented colonial America. Massacres of Deerfield's settlers by the French and Indian enemies of the British nearly wiped out the town in 1675 and again in 1704. In the latter raid, 49 people were killed and more than 100 were taken prisoner and marched to French Québec.

The main avenue, simply called The Street, is lined with more than 80 houses built in the 17th, 18th, and 19th centuries. Most are private, but 14 of them can be visited through tours conducted by Historic Deerfield, a local tourism organization (see below). And all along The Street there is not a single tube of neon nor a commercially franchised intrusion.

MUSEUMS & HISTORIC HOMES

"The Street" is a mile long, with most of the museum houses concentrated along the long block north of the central town common. There are two buildings operated by organizations other than Historic Deerfield. One is Memorial Hall Museum, east of the town common on Memorial Street, for which a separate admission is charged. (For the slightly larger fee of $12 adults, $5 children 6 to 21, tours of the 14 museum houses can be combined with a visit to Memorial Hall through Historic Deerfield.) The other is the Indian House Memorial, north of the Deerfield Inn, also maintained by a separate organization. A teepee is pitched in the front yard, rather chummily, considering the depth of hostility between the colonists and Native Americans in this region. Since it is only a 1929 reproduction of an earlier house, it is of less interest than the other structures.

Special celebrations in the town are held on Patriots Day (the 3rd Monday in April), Washington's Birthday, Thanksgiving, and over the Christmas holidays. In summer, there is an antique and classic car show; call the information center at **Historic Deerfield** (☎ 413/774-5581) for details.

Memorial Hall Museum. Memorial St. (between The Street and Routes 5 and 10). ☎ **413/774-3768.** Admission $5 adults, $3 children 6–21. May 1–Nov 2 daily 10am–4:30pm.

Deerfield Academy's original 1798 classroom building was converted into this museum of village history in 1880. A popular, if suggestively grisly, exhibit is the preserved door of a 1698 home that shows the gashes made by weapons of the French and Indian raiders in 1704. Should the point be too muted, a hatchet is imbedded in the door.

Five period rooms are also on view, and 14 other exhibition rooms contain substantial collections of colonial furniture, vintage clothing, quilts, paintings, pottery, and pewter, as well as examples of Native American weapons and tools.

✪ **Historic Deerfield.** Information Center, Hall Tavern, The Street. ☎ **413/774-5581.** Admission (good for 1 week) $10 adults, $5 children 6–21. Daily 9:30am–4:30pm.

Begin with a visit to the Hall Tavern, opposite the post office, where tickets are sold and maps and brochures are available. This is also the departure point for guided tours, which customarily leave on the half hour during busier seasons (April through October), and according to demand during the slower months.

While there are no charges for simply strolling The Street, the only way to get inside the museum houses is by tour. One attraction that is also free is the new **Channing Blake Meadow Walk.** Open from 8am to 6pm in good weather, the trail begins beside the Rev. John Farwell Moors House, a relatively recent Historic Deerfield acquisition on the west side of The Street. The walk is marked by interpretive tablets, and goes through a working farm, past the playing fields of Deerfield

Academy, and through pastures beside the Deerfield River. Along the trail you can see sheep and cattle up close (which will delight the kids), but for that reason, dogs aren't allowed on the trail. Wheelchairs should be able to negotiate the trail in most seasons.

The 14 houses on the tour were constructed between 1720 and 1850. They contain more than 20,000 furnishings, silver and pewter pieces, textiles, ceramics, and implements used from the early 17th century to 1900. Included are imports from China and Europe as well as items made in the Connecticut River Valley during its prominence as an industrial center. The objects are all tidily arranged and displayed to good effect, and the tour guides provide interesting descriptions and background.

Historic Deerfield's **Museum Store** (☎ **413/774-5581**) is in a weathered shack between the post office and the Deerfield Inn. While it does stock a few T-shirts, the general run of its merchandise is a cut above most similar enterprises. Judicious selections include weather vanes, hand-dipped candles, relevant books, fruit preserves, and reproductions of light fixtures found in the village houses. It's open during museum hours.

WHERE TO STAY & DINE

✪ **Deerfield Inn.** 81 Old Main St., Deerfield, MA 01342. ☎ **800/926-3865** or 413/774-5587. Fax 413/773-8712. 23 rms. A/C TV TEL. $122–$156 double. Rates include breakfast and afternoon high tea. AE, DC, MC, V.

Even if it had any significant local competition, this inn would attract more than its share of guests. Built in 1884, the Deerfield is conveniently located in the middle of The Street, with all the historic houses within easy walking distance, and is one of the stellar stopping places in the valley. The innkeepers restlessly scour their establishment, recently replacing all the bathroom fixtures, refinishing the older furniture, and installing new carpeting. Six of the bedrooms, named after people who lived in the village, have four-posters, while others have various combinations of beds and foldout sofas to accommodate different family configurations. No smoking.

Dining/Entertainment: On premises are both a full-service dining room and an informal cafeteria. Afternoon high tea is included.

6 The Berkshires

They are more than hills, but less than mountains, so the Taconic and Hoosac ranges that define this region at the western end of the state go by the collective name of "The Berkshires." The hamlets, villages, and two small cities that have long drawn energy and sustenance from the region's kindly Housatonic River and its tranquil tributaries are as New England as New England can be.

Mohawks and Mohegans lived and hunted here, and while white missionaries established settlements at Stockbridge and elsewhere in an attempt to Christianize the native tribes, the Indians eventually moved on west. Farmers, drawn to the narrow but fertile floodplains of the Housatonic, were supplanted in the 19th century by manufacturers, who erected the brick mills that drew their power from the river. Many of these factories survive, largely abandoned or converted to other functions.

At the same time, artists and writers came here for the mild summers and seclusion that these hills and many lakes offered. Nathaniel Hawthorne, Herman Melville, and Edith Wharton were among many who put down temporary roots. By the last decades of the 19th century and the arrival of the railroad, wealthy New Yorkers and Bostonians had discovered the region and began to erect extravagant summer "cottages" with dozens of bedrooms on scores of tailored wooded acres. With their support, culture and the performing arts found a hospitable reception. By the 1930s, theater, dance, and concerts had established themselves as regular summer fixtures. Tanglewood, Jacob's Pillow, and the Berkshire and Williamstown Theatre Festivals are events that draw tens of thousands of visitors every July and August.

When making reservations, note that the many inns in the region routinely stipulate minimum 2- or 3-night stays in summer and over holiday weekends and often require advance deposits.

BERKSHIRE ESSENTIALS

GETTING THERE   The Massachusetts Turnpike (I-90) runs east-west from Boston to the Berkshires, with an exit near Lee and Stockbridge. From New York City, the scenic Taconic State Parkway connects with I-90 not far from Pittsfield.

Amtrak's *Lake Shore Limited* runs daily between Boston and Chicago, stopping in Pittsfield each way. Call ☎ **800/USA-RAIL** (872-7245) for details on schedules and fares.

VISITOR INFORMATION   Pittsfield's **Berkshire Visitors Bureau,** Berkshire Common (off South Street, near the entrance to the Hilton), Pittsfield, MA 01201 (☎ **800/237-5747** or 413/443-9186), provides brochures and answers questions for the entire region. In addition, local chambers of commerce and other civic groups maintain information booths at central locations in Great Barrington, Lee, Lenox, Pittsfield, Stockbridge, and Williamstown (details are found in the sections that follow below). Internet surfers can find on-line information on what's happening in Berkshire County at: **http://berkcon.com**.

SHEFFIELD: ANTIQUES CAPITAL OF THE BERKSHIRES

The first settlement of any size encountered when approaching from Connecticut on Route 7, Sheffield, 11 miles south of Great Barrington, occupies a floodplain beside the Housatonic River, with the Berkshires rising to the west.

Agriculture has been the principal occupation of its residents, and still is to a large degree. Everyone else sells antiques, or so it might seem as you drive along Route 7 (a.k.a. Main Street or Sheffield Plain). The wide road and generously spaced, well-maintained houses cultivate an impression of prosperous tranquillity.

A PIONEER'S HOME

May through October, you can make a short excursion to see the **Colonel Ashley House,** Cooper Hill Road (☎ **413/229-8600**), in Ashley Falls. Built in 1735, this small, gray, modified saltbox is believed to be the oldest house in Berkshire County. Its builder, Colonel Ashley, was a person of considerable repute in colonial western Massachusetts, a pioneer in the area, an officer in one of the French and Indian Wars, and later a lawyer and a judge. Furnishings and farm tools appropriate to the period inform the interior. To find it, drive south on Route 7, watching for Route 7A on the left toward Ashley Falls. After a short distance on 7A, bear right on Rannappo Road. At the Y intersection, turn right on Copper Hill Road and drive for about 200 yards. Visiting times are sharply restricted. The house is open from 1 to 5pm on Saturday, Sunday, and holiday Mondays in June, September, and October; Wednesday to Sunday July through Labor Day.

OUTDOOR PURSUITS AT BARTHOLOMEW'S COBBLE

The 278-acre nature reservation called **Bartholomew's Cobble,** on Route 7A (☎ **413/229-8600**), lies beside an oxbow bend in the Housatonic. It is latticed with 6 miles of trails for hiking or cross-country skiing. They cross pastures, penetrate forests, and provide vistas of the river valley from the area's high point, Hurlburt's

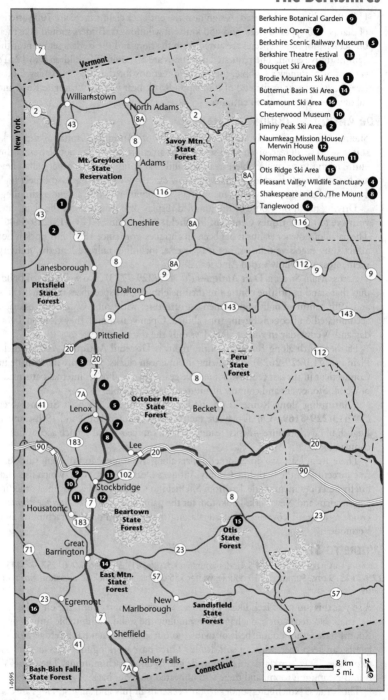

The Berkshires

Berkshire Botanical Garden **9**
Berkshire Opera **7**
Berkshire Scenic Railway Museum **5**
Berkshire Theatre Festival **13**
Bousquet Ski Area **3**
Brodie Mountain Ski Area **1**
Butternut Basin Ski Area **14**
Catamount Ski Area **16**
Chesterwood Museum **10**
Jiminy Peak Ski Area **2**
Naumkeag Mission House/
   Merwin House **12**
Norman Rockwell Museum **11**
Otis Ridge Ski Area **15**
Pleasant Valley Wildlife Sanctuary **4**
Shakespeare and Co./The Mount **8**
Tanglewood **6**

Vermont

New York

Williamstown

North Adams

Savoy Mtn.
State
Forest

Mt. Greylock
State
Reservation

Adams

Cheshire

Lanesborough

Dalton

Pittsfield
State
Forest

Pittsfield

Peru
State
Forest

Lenox

October Mtn.
State
Forest

Becket

Lee

Stockbridge

Housatonic

Beartown
State
Forest

Otis
State
Forest

Great
Barrington

East Mtn.
State
Forest

Egremont

New
Marlborough

Sandisfield
State
Forest

Sheffield

Bash-Bish Falls
State Forest

Ashley Falls

Connecticut

0   8 km
0   5 mi.

N

313

Hill. Picnicking is permitted. A sign near the entrance claims there are 700 varieties of plants, 125 types of trees, and 450 kinds of wildflowers. Birders should take their binoculars, for many species are attracted to the flora and the feeders set up near the administrative cabin. The requested donations arc $3 adults, $1 children 6 to 12. To get to Bartholomew's Cobble, follow the directions for the Colonel Ashley House (see above), except at the end of Rannappo Road, bear left on Weatogue Road and follow it to the reservation entrance.

FOR ANTIQUES HOUNDS

Sheffield can legitimately lay claim to the title of "Antiques Capital of the Berkshires"—no small feat, given what seems to be an effort by half the population of this entire region to sell collectibles, treasures, and near antiques to the other half. These are canny, knowledgeable dealers who know exactly what they have, so expect high quality and no bargains. Of the many, many possibilities, here is a slender sampling.

Driving north on Route 7, the jumbled display of birdhouses on the right drag your eye to the **Antiques Center of Sheffield,** 33 S. Main St. (☎ **413/229-3400**). The garrulous owner claims it has been an antiques store since 1860. His stock is not afflicted by excessive tidiness, but it is diverse, including railroad lanterns, military mementos, and wildly varied Americana.

Across Main Street is **Darr Antiques** (☎ **413/229-7773**), two well-ordered buildings that stand in pristine contrast to their neighbor. Darr specializes in formal 18th- and 19th-century English and American furniture, with some Chinese accessories, accumulated on frequent buying trips abroad. Open year-round, they close on Tuesday and Wednesday in winter, Tuesdays only the rest of the year.

Farther north along Route 7, on the right, is **Dovetail Antiques,** 440 Sheffield Plain (☎ **413/229-2628**), specializing in American clocks, primarily those made in Connecticut in the last century. Some have gears, cogs, and other internal parts made of wood. Stoneware and country furniture are also available.

Continuing along Route 7, on the left at the edge of town, is **Susan Silver** (☎ **413/229-8169**). On display are meticulously restored 18th- and 19th-century English library furniture—desks, reading stands, cabinets—and French accessories of comparable age.

There are at least two dozen other dealers along this route. Most of them stock the **free directory** of the Berkshire County Antiques Dealers Association, which lists and briefly describes member dealers from Sheffield to Cheshire and across the border in Connecticut and New York. Look, too, for the pamphlet called *The Antique Hunter's Guide to Route 7,* covering 81 dealers along that road in both Massachusetts and Vermont.

WHERE TO STAY

Ivanhoe Country House. 254 S. Undermountain Rd. (Rte. 41), Sheffield, MA 01257. ☎ **413/229-2143.** 9 rms. Summer $110 double; winter $55 double. Rates include breakfast. No credit cards.

A stay at this inn most feels like a visit to a gregarious country aunt, the one who has her rules. No decorator had a hand in assembling the stolid, comfortable furnishings. Rooms have either double beds or twins (no queens) and each has a refrigerator so guests can keep beer, wine, or soft drinks. Three have working fireplaces and access to porches. Tray breakfasts are left outside guests' doors each morning. The only TV is in the common room, and there's an unheated pool out back.

Those rules? No children under 15 on weekends in July and August. Dogs are accepted, for an extra $10 a day, but must be leashed at all times and cannot be left alone in guests' rooms.

SOUTH EGREMONT

As the larger, busier half of the town of Egremont, this diverting village 5 miles south-west of Great Barrington borders Route 23, the most used gateway to the southern Berkshires from Route 22 and the Taconic Parkway in New York State. It was once a stop on the stagecoach route between Hartford and Albany, and retains many structures from that era, including mills that utilized the stream that still rushes by. Those circumstances make it a magnet for antique dealers, restaurateurs, and refugee urban professionals who have made the precarious leap into innkeeping and retailing.

OUTDOOR PURSUITS

HIKING   In warmer months, scenic ✪ **Bash Bish Falls State Park,** on Route 23 (☎ **413/528-0330**), makes a rewarding day outing for hiking, birding, and fishing. (No camping or picnicking, though.)

Getting there from South Egremont isn't too complicated. Drive west on Route 23 from the town center, turning south on Route 41, and immediately right on Mount Washington Road. Keep alert for signs directing the way to Mount Washington State Forest and Bash Bish Falls. After 8 miles, past fallow fields, summer houses, and groves of white birch bright against the deep green of dense pine, a sign indicates a right turn toward the falls. Look for it opposite a board-and-batten church with an unusual steeple. The road begins to follow the course of a mountain stream, going downhill. In about 3 miles, on the left, is a large parking place next to a craggy promontory and a sign prohibiting alcohol, camping, and fires.

The sign also points off to a trail down to the falls, which should only be negotiated by reasonably fit adults. First, mount the promontory for a splendid view across the plains of the Hudson Valley to the pale blue ridgeline of the Catskill Mountains, between two rounded peaks off to the west. The falls can be heard, but not yet seen, down to the left. If the trail seems too steep, continue down the road to another parking area, on the left. From here, a gentler trail a little over a mile long leads in to the falls. The falls themselves are quite impressive, crashing down from over 50 feet into a deep pool. The park is open from dawn to dusk. Admission is free.

SKIING   At the western edge of the township, touching the New York border, is the **Catamount Ski Area,** on Route 23 (☎ **413/528-1262**). About 2 hours from Manhattan, it is understandably popular with New Yorkers, who must drive twice as long to get to Vermont's higher peaks. It has 24 trails, including the daunting "Catapult," the steepest run in the Berkshires (to be attempted by experts only), and four double chairlifts. There is also night skiing on 13 of the area's trails.

SHOPPING

Fans of 19th-century weather vanes and museum-quality folk arts, or of painted country furniture of America, Québec, and Bavaria, are delighted by the offerings of **The Splendid Peasant,** on Route 23 (☎ **413/528-5755**). Evidently, they have much company, for the owners have recently expanded their galleries into a second building.

WHERE TO STAY

Egremont Inn. Old Sheffield Rd. (P.O. Box 418), S. Egremont, MA 01258. ☎ **413/528-2111.** Fax 413/528-3284. 18 rms. A/C TEL. July–Aug $90–$165 double. Lower rates off-season. Rates include breakfast. AE, DISC, MC, V.

You can slip into this friendly former stagecoach stop as easily as into a pair of beloved old slippers. Tens of thousands of travelers have preceded you, for the Egremont has been a tavern and inn since 1780. That longevity shows, in tilting floors and lintels and a grand brick fireplace constructed over an ancient blacksmith hearth. The present owners have been on the scene for a little over 3 years, and their renovations have included the merging of smaller bedrooms to create five suites. The only TV is the satellite-fed set in one of the common rooms. Children are welcome.

Dining/Entertainment: Dinner is served Wednesday to Sunday year-round, and there's Sunday brunch from July to mid-October. Main courses of "Country American" food go for $15 to $22 in the dining room, $9 to $13.50 in the informal tavern. A guitar player performs on Thursdays and a jazz ensemble on Saturdays and at Sunday brunch.

Facilities: There are two tennis courts and a pool out back.

Weathervane Inn. Rte. 23, S. Egremont, MA 01258. ☎ **800/528-9580** or 413/528-9580. Fax 413/528-1713. 12 rms. A/C. Sun–Thurs $95–$135 double, including breakfast and afternoon tea; Fri–Sat $175–$205 double, including breakfast, tea, and dinner. MAP (breakfast and lunch or dinner included in rate) and 2-night minimum required weekends (3-night minimum July–Aug); no dinner Mar–Apr. No children under 7. AE, DISC, MC, V.

"Screw the Golden Years," reads a sampler pillow in the sitting room, a reflection of the owners' nose-thumbing views on life. An affectionate cat is more welcoming, as are the bedrooms, many of which have four-poster beds with quilts. The core of the building was a 1735 farmhouse, but the Greek Revival appearance of the property dates to an 1835 renovation. An unheated pool is available. No smoking.

WHERE TO DINE

✪ **John Andrew's.** Rte. 23. ☎ **413/528-3469.** Reservations recommended on weekends. Main courses $13–$22. MC, V. June–Aug Mon–Sat 5:30–10pm, Sun 11am–3pm; Sept–May Thurs–Tues 5:30–10pm. ECLECTIC AMERICAN.

Appetizing aromas drift on the air of this made-over farmhouse, alerting arrivals that this is no barbecue or fish joint. A fertile imagination is at work behind the kitchen doors, one that conjures such refreshing culinary departures as seared sea scallops with couscous and sweet pea mint coulis. A variety of breads arrives with the generous cocktails—rosemary focaccia, pita, and sourdough. Rows of windows in the rear dining room let in the fading summer light, which falls on Parsons chairs, wood floors, and sponged walls of dusky rose. All is very near countrified faultlessness; my quibbles are few.

Mom's Cafe. Main St. ☎ **413/528-2414.** Main courses $4.95–$12.95. MC, V. Daily 6:30am–9:30pm. ECLECTIC.

"Mom" is a guy, who keeps his informal drop-in place perking from early breakfast to late cappuccino. His menu runs from omelets and pancakes to pizzas with toppings as diverse as avocado and pineapple. He has added Spanish tapas in the evening, including such standards as *mejillones a la vinegreta* (mussels in vinaigrette) and *gambas en salsa verde* (shrimp in green sauce). They go well with sangria. In good weather, eat on the deck over the stream that runs behind the building. The restaurant also serves beer and wine.

GREAT BARRINGTON

Even with a population well under 8,000, this pleasant commercial and retail center, 7 miles south of Stockbridge, is the largest town in the southernmost part of the county. Rapids in the Housatonic provided power for a number of mills in centuries past, most of which are now gone, and in 1886, it was one of the first communities in the world to have electricity on its streets and in its homes. More recently, it was spared by the killer tornado of Memorial Day 1995 that hopped over Great Barrington only to touch down again a few miles east around Monterey, tearing off hundreds of trees halfway up their trunks. That devastation will be seen along Route 23 for decades to come.

Great Barrington has no sights or monuments of significant interest, leaving ample time to browse its many antique galleries and growing number of specialty shops. Convenient as a home base for excursions to such nearby attractions as Monument Mountain, Bash Bish Falls, Butternut Basin, Tanglewood concerts, and the museums and historic houses of Stockbridge, it has a number of unremarkable but entirely adequate motels along Route 7 north of the town center that tend to fill up slower on weekends than the better-known inns in the area. It is something of a dining center, too, compared to other Berkshire towns.

The **Southern Berkshire Chamber of Commerce** maintains an information booth at 362 Main St. (☎ 413/528-1510), near the town hall. It's open Monday to Thursday 9:30am to 4:30pm, Friday 9:30am to 5pm, and Saturday 9:30 to 3:30pm.

OUTDOOR PURSUITS

The **Egremont Country Club,** on Route 23 (☎ 413/528-4222), is open to the public. Its facilities include an 18-hole golf course, tennis courts, and an Olympic-sized pool.

Butternut Basin, also on Route 23, 2 miles east of town (☎ 413/528-2000), is known for its strong family ski programs. A children's center provides day care for kids ages $2^1/2$ to 6 daily from December 23rd to the end of the season, and the SKIwee program offers full- and half-day programs for children 4 to 12 that include lunch, ski instruction, and a lift ticket. Six double and quad chairlifts provide access to 22 trails, the longest of which is a $1^1/2$-mile run. There are also 5 miles of cross-country trails.

A little over 4 miles north of town, west of Route 7, is **Monument Mountain,** with two hiking trails to the summit. The easier one is called the Indian Monument Trail, about an hour's hike to the top; the more difficult route, the Hickey Trail, isn't much longer, but takes the steep way up, and should probably be avoided by novice hikers. The summit, called Squaw Peak for an Indian maiden who allegedly leapt to her death from the spot, offers splendid panoramic views. Nathaniel Hawthorne and Herman Melville, two members of the remarkable mid-19th-century literary set that summered in the Berkshires, first met here on a hiking trip.

Camping, climbing, and hiking equipment, as well as canoe rentals and free advice on area trails, are available at **Appalachian Mountain Gear,** 777 S. Main St. (☎ 413/528-8881). The owner guides free hikes on Sundays.

SHOPPING

Shoppers will want to turn off Main Street onto **Railroad Street,** the town's best shopping strip.

Start on the corner, at **T. P. Saddle Blanket & Trading Co.,** 304 Main St. (☎ 413/528-6500), an unlikely but fascinating emporium that looks as if it had been lifted whole from the Colorado Rockies. Packed to the walls with country furniture and Western gear—boots, hats, plates, Indian jewelry, pitchers, jars of salsas, rugs, blankets—it's open every day.

Down the left side of Railroad Street is **Mistral's,** Route 7 (☎ 413/528-1618), whose French Canadian owner parades her good taste with a stock of Gallic tableware, bed linens, fancy foods, furniture, and night wear. Open daily.

Several antique and art galleries and other enterprises mingle kitsch and class at **Jennifer House Commons,** Route 7 (☎ 413/528-2690), on the right, north of town on Route 7.

In town, just before Route 7 turns right across a short bridge, Route 41 goes straight, toward the village of Housatonic. In about 4 miles is a long, low shed that houses the kiln and workrooms of **The Great Barrington Pottery** (☎ **413/274-6259**). Owner/master Richard Bennett has been throwing pots according to ancient Japanese techniques for over 30 years. His separate showroom is open year-round.

WHERE TO STAY

North of town on U.S. 7 are a number of motels, including economical **Monument Mountain,** 249 Stockbridge Rd. (☎ **413/528-3272**), which has a pool, tennis courts, and a riverside location.

✪ **The Old Inn on the Green & Gedney Farm.** Rte. 57, New Marlborough, MA 01230. ☎ **800/286-3139** or 413/229-3131. Fax 413/229-2053. 8 rms, 5 suites. TEL. $120–$285 double. Rates include breakfast. AE, MC, V. Take Rte. 23 east from Great Barrington, picking up Rte. 57 after 3.4 miles. After 5.7 miles, you'll see The Old Inn on the left. Continue another 1/4 mile to the barns on the left. Registration is on the ground floor of the gray barn.

This two-part establishment is comprised of a former 1760 tavern/general store/post office on the village green and a pair of converted dairy barns down the road. While the baths in the Old Inn have recently been redone, the most desirable rooms are in the barn, combining contemporary furnishings and accessories with Oriental rugs. Given the steep prices, guests might reasonably expect television and air-conditioning. They don't get them.

Dining/Entertainment: The restaurant, which has built a reputation based on the creativity of its admirable kitchen, is in the Old Inn, and is open only for dinner (Thursday to Sunday November through June, Wednesday to Monday July through October).

Windflower Inn. 684 S. Egremont Rd. (P.O. Box 25), Great Barrington, MA 01230. ☎ **800/992-1993** or 413/528-2720. Fax 413/528-5147. 13 rms. A/C TV. $170–$220 double with breakfast and dinner; $100–$160 double with breakfast and afternoon tea. AE.

A roadside lodging for decades—veteran Berkshire lovers might remember it as the Fairfield Inn—the Windflower has attained its highest order of quality under the current owners, who have operated it since 1980. Built in the middle of the last century in Federal style, it commands a large plot of land opposite the Egremont Country Club on Route 23 between Great Barrington and South Egremont. All rooms have small black-and-white televisions, six have fireplaces, and four have canopied beds. Dinner is served Thursday to Sunday in summer. Out back is an unheated pool. Smoking is allowed only in the living room. Children are welcome.

WHERE TO DINE

Barrington Brewery. Rte. 7 (in the Jennifer House complex, north of town). ☎ **413/528-8282.** Main courses $8.95–$14.95. AE, MC, V. Daily 11:30am–10 or 11pm (depending on business). ECLECTIC AMERICAN.

This converted barn hasn't been "done" to death, and retains its rough siding and beams. All beers and ales are made in the brewery upstairs, and they are good enough to distract even devoted oenophiles (although wines are also available). A fun gimmick is the selection of 3-ounce shot glasses of currently available brews. Grub is of the bratwurst, burger, and nacho variety, but good pot pies and grilled strip steaks are also on the card. The restaurant bakes its own breads and desserts. The ground floor is all nonsmoking, even at the bar. In summer, a tented dining area is erected outside.

Boiler Room Cafe. 405 Stockbridge Rd. (Rte. 7). ☎ **413/528-4280.** Main courses $9–$21. MC, V. Tues–Sat 5–10pm. Closed Tues in winter. ECLECTIC.

They need a new sign out front, for you can sail past on the way to Stockbridge without spotting the current one (on the left). What's more, the menu describes the fare as "cuisine locale," but it's hard to say where that "locale" might be, since the menu is replete with such items as raclette, tuna marinated in soy sauce with sesame noodles, and Mexican braised lamb shanks with avocado salsa. Whatever.

The only real problem here is deciding what to order, since everything sounds good. One recent possibility (the menu is changed once or twice a month) was a "Mediterranean Platter," which included homemade sausage of lamb, pork, and fennel, white beans, shrimp, asparagus, goat cheese, olives, smoked mussels, and grilled bread. The decor is as offbeat and amusing as the food.

✪ **Castle Street Cafe.** 10 Castle St. (near the Town Hall). ☎ **413/528-5244.** Main courses $9–$21. AE, DISC, MC, V. Wed–Thurs and Sun–Mon 5–9pm, Fri–Sat 5–10pm. NEW AMERICAN.

This storefront bistro has ruled the Great Barrington roost for some time now, with such Francophilic fare as grilled veal chop with roast garlic sauce and roast duck with black-currant sauce. Pastas are so big that half portions are available. There's a short bar at the back of the room to have a drink while checking out the night's menu. An award-winning wine list is another reason to stop in.

GREAT BARRINGTON AFTER DARK

Baroque and classical music performed on period instruments constitutes the **Aston Magna Festival,** held at 6pm on five Sundays in July and August at the St. James Church, Main Street and Taconic Avenue (☎ **413/528-3595**). Also in July and August, the **Berkshire Opera Company** (☎ **413/528-4420**) offers several performances each of two operas. Sung in English, they are presented in the theater of the Monument Mountain Regional High School on U.S. 7.

STOCKBRIDGE

Stockbridge's ready accessibility to Boston and New York, each about 2¹⁄₂ hours away by today's highways and reachable by rail since the second half of the 19th century, transformed the original frontier settlement into a Gilded Age summer retreat for the superrich and the merely wealthy. The town has long been popular with artists and writers as well, including Norman Rockwell, who lived here for 25 years and who rendered the Main Street of his adopted town in a famous painting. Along and near Main Street are a number of historic homes and other attractions, enough to fill the hours of a long weekend, even without the Tanglewood concert season in nearby Lenox.

Stockbridge lies 7 miles north of Great Barrington, and 6 miles south of Lenox. The chamber of commerce maintains a self-service seasonal **information booth** opposite the row of stores Rockwell depicted. It is open 24 hours a day from May through October, with stocks of pamphlets and notices about area attractions and lodgings.

SEEING THE SIGHTS

✪ **Norman Rockwell Museum.** Rte. 183. ☎ **413/298-4100.** Admission $9 adults, $2 children 6–18, $20 family. May 1–Oct 31 daily 10am–5pm; Nov 1–Apr 30 Mon–Fri 11am–4pm, Sat–Sun 10am–5pm. Take Main St. (Rte. 102) west to the junction with Rte. 183, with its traffic signal. Turn left (south) at the traffic signal. In about ¹⁄₂ mile, the entrance to the museum is on the left.

This striking building of generous proportions was erected in 1993, at a cost of $4.4 million, to house the works of Stockbridge's favorite son.

The beloved illustrator used both his neighbors and the town where he lived for the last third of his life to tell stories about an America rapidly fading from memory. Most of Rockwell's paintings adorned covers of the weekly *Saturday Evening Post;* warm and often humorous depictions of homecomings, first proms, and visits to the doctor and the marriage license bureau. He displayed serious concerns, too, notably with his series on the "Four Freedoms" and his poignant portrait of a little African-American girl in a white dress being escorted by U.S. marshals into a previously segregated school. Art critics and intellectuals routinely denounced his work as saccharine and sentimental, but the self-effacing artist didn't fire back, instead expressing his admiration for the work of the abstract expressionists.

Selections of his illustrations are rotated into view from the large permanent collection, the pity being that none of his ingenious *April Fool's* covers are included. A couple of galleries show the works of other illustrators of the past hundred years, including Howard Pyle, Charles Dana Gibson, and N. C. Wyeth.

The lovely 36-acre grounds also contain Rockwell's last studio, moved here to a point overlooking a bend in the Housatonic. Picnic tables are provided.

Chesterwood. 4 Williamsville Rd. ☎ **413/298-3579.** Admission $7 adults, $3.50 youths 13–18, $1.50 children 6–12. May 1–Oct 31 daily 10am–5pm. Drive west on Main St., south on Rte. 183 about 1 mile to the Chesterwood sign.

Sculptor Daniel Chester French used this estate as his summer home and studio for over 30 years. His famous statue of the Minute Man at the Old North Bridge in Concord, completed in 1875 at the age of 25, launched his highly successful career. Subsequent commissions included a bust of Ralph Waldo Emerson at Harvard, the statue of *Alma Mater* at Columbia University, and one of the most moving monuments in America, the Abraham Lincoln Memorial in Washington, D.C. His house and studio here were designed by his friend and collaborator on the Lincoln Memorial, Henry Bacon. A visit can easily be combined with one to the Rockwell Museum, which is less than a mile away.

Naumkeag. Prospect Hill. ☎ **413/298-3239.** Admission $7 adults, $2.50 children. Daily Memorial Day to Columbus Day 10am–5pm. From the Cat & Dog Fountain in the intersection next to the Red Lion Inn, drive north on Prospect Hill Rd. about 2 miles.

Architect Stanford White of the celebrated New York firm of McKim, Mead & White designed this 26-room house, a classic Berkshire cottage of the Gilded Age, for Joseph Hodge Choate and his family in 1886. His client dubbed it "Naumkeag," an Amerindian name for Salem, Mass., which was his childhood hometown. Choate was a lawyer and served as U.S. ambassador to the Court of St. James's. His many-gabled and -chimneyed house is largely of the New England Shingle style, surrounded by impressive gardens. Admission is by guided tour only, but worth it for the glimpses of the rich interior, fully furnished and decorated in the manner of the period, including many paintings and an extensive collection of Chinese export porcelain.

Berkshire Botanical Garden. Routes 102 and 183. ☎ **413/298-3926.** Admission $5 adults, $4 seniors; free for children under 12. May–Oct daily 10am–5pm. Drive west from downtown Stockbridge on Main St., picking up Church St. (Rte. 102) northwest and driving about 2 miles.

These 15 acres of flower beds, shrubs, ponds, and raised vegetable and herb gardens are an inviting destination for strollers and picnickers. The 1st weekend in October is devoted to a harvest festival, which features jugs of cider, displays of pumpkins, and hayrides.

Children's Chime Bell Tower. Main St. No phone. Free admission.

West of the town center, the Greek Revival Town Hall and a mid-19th-century redbrick Congregational church face the old village green. The campanile out front is the Children's Chime Bell Tower. Dating from 1878, its bells are tolled every evening from spring to first frost.

Merwin House. 14 Main St. ☎ **413/298-4703.** Admission $4 adults, $3.50 seniors, $2 children 6–12. Tours June to Oct 15, Tues, Thurs, Sat, and Sun on the hour, noon–4pm.

A small brick Federalist house with a later wood-frame extension, this 1825 residence contains furnishings true to the period. The lawn runs down to the Housatonic.

Mission House. Main and Sergeant sts. (Rte. 102). ☎ **413/298-3239.** Admission $5 adults, $2.50 children. Daily Memorial Day to Columbus Day 10am–5pm.

The Rev. John Sergeant had the most benevolent, if paternalistic, of intentions: He sought to build a house among the Stockbridge Indians of the Housatonic tribe, hoping to convert them to civilized (i.e., English) ways through proximity to his godly self and his small band of settlers. The Mission House, built in 1739, was the site of this Christianizing process, and it was moved here, understandably weathered, in 1928. A few of the furnishings were owned by Sergeant. Visits are by guided tour, and include a stroll around the herb garden.

THE BERKSHIRE THEATRE FESTIVAL

In summer, the **Berkshire Theatre Festival,** P.O. Box 797, Main St. (☎ **413/298-5536**), holds its annual June to late-August season of classic and new plays, often with marquee names starring or directing, Dianne Wiest and Joanne Woodward among them. Its venue is a "casino" built in 1887 to plans by Stanford White. A second stage, the Unicorn Theatre, was opened in 1996. Each summer's program is announced in February or March. Tickets are usually pretty affordable and easy to get, unless you're trying for a weekend night or a performance with a name star.

WHERE TO STAY

Inn at Stockbridge. 30 East St. (Rte. 7; Box 618), Stockbridge, MA 01262. ☎ **413/298-3337.** Fax 413/298-3406. 12 rms. A/C TEL. June–Oct $100–$260 double; Nov–May $98–$190 double. Rates include breakfast. AE, DISC, MC, V. No children under 12.

A mile north of Stockbridge center, this 1906 neoclassical building, with its grandly columned porch, is set well back from the road on 12 landscaped acres. The former New Yorkers who own and run the inn are almost painfully anxious to please, serving full breakfasts by candlelight and afternoon spreads of cheese and wine (hot cider in cold weather). Carafes of brandy are in each room. They have added another four rooms, but the best of the older accommodations is the "Terrace Room," with a deck, a private entrance, Jacuzzi, and the only bedroom TV. There is also a pool. No smoking.

The Red Lion. Main St., Stockbridge, MA 01262. ☎ **413/298-5545.** Fax 413/298-5130. 111 rms. A/C TEL. Late Apr to late Oct $94–$159 double; Late Oct to late Apr $87–$123 double. AE, CB, DC, DISC, MC, V.

So well known it serves as an all-inclusive symbol of the Berkshires, this eternally busy inn had its origins as a stagecoach tavern in 1773. That original building is long gone, and the summer hotel that grew up on the site burned to the ground in 1896. It was quickly rebuilt into what is essentially the structure extant today. Many of the antiques arranged in both public and private rooms survived the fire, including a collection of colonial table china. Most rooms have TVs. Make reservations even further in advance than is recommended for other Berkshire inns.

Dining/Entertainment: Guests can dine in the moderately formal dining room (main courses $16.50 to $26.50), in the casual Widow Bingham Tavern (main courses $9.95 to $15.95), in the basement Lion's Den (main courses $6.95 to $12.95), and, in good weather, in the courtyard out back. Many of the guests pass a daily hour or two in rocking chairs on the long porch, chatting and people watching in a New England version of a sidewalk cafe.

Facilities: Outdoor pool.

The Taggart House. Main St., Stockbridge, MA 01262. ☎ and fax **413/298-4303.** 4 rms. A/C. July–Oct $275–$355 double; Nov–June $175–$275 double. Rates include breakfast. 2- and 3-day minimum stays apply on summer and fall weekends. AE, CB, DC, DISC, MC, V.

Ordinarily, an inn with only four guest rooms wouldn't merit space here. But what rooms! The decor and furnishings of this outwardly sedate 1850 Victorian/colonial mansion, a block west of the Red Lion, are breathtaking. Start with the theatrical main floor—the dining room, perhaps. The inlaid mahogany table was once a centerpiece in an Argentine palace and is now the site of candlelight breakfasts that more nearly resemble brunch. Wallpapers and fabrics throughout the house are mostly of the complex arts-and-crafts variety. A birch-bark canoe hangs above the billiards table, only the largest item of a collection of Amerindian arts and artifacts. There is a paneled library, a ballroom that is often the scene of weddings, a handsome harpsichord, and nine beguiling fireplaces. And upstairs, beds with fur throws or East Indian silk coverlets or velvet canopies and chests painted with turtle-shell and bois effects . . . it would take many more pages than I have available to adequately describe this immersion in the Gilded Age.

WHERE TO DINE

The Red Lion (see "Where to Stay," above) offers three venues for dining. Its **Lion's Den** also has nightly live entertainment, usually of the folk-music variety.

Michael's. Elm St. (off Main St.). ☎ **413/298-3530.** Main courses $8.95–$16.95. AE, CB, DC, MC, V. Mon–Sat 11:30am–midnight, Sun noon–10pm (bar until 1am). ITALIAN/AMERICAN.

This tavern, with a decided sports tilt and its adjoining dining room, is one of the few nearby alternatives to the Red Lion Inn. Bar snacks served around the 60-inch TV are nachos and fried mozzarella sticks, as expected in such environs. The food is pretty good, the greeting offhanded but friendly, and the place stays open throughout the day. Upstairs are pool tables and video games.

WEST STOCKBRIDGE

The hills around this Stockbridge satellite (it's just 5 miles northwest) are alive with the sounds of creativity. Potters, painters, writers, sculptors, weavers, and glassblowers pursue their compulsions summers or year-round, selling the results from their studios and several galleries. A pamphlet called *The Art of West Stockbridge* is available in display racks throughout the area and describes the work of some of the most important artisans and where it can be found.

One of the most ambitious new creative enterprises is the **Berkshire Center for Contemporary Glass,** 6 Harris St. (☎ 413/232-4666). The spanking new building has ample space for a showroom and a large work area. Kids find the process fascinating and are even allowed to participate. Classes and workshops are scheduled, and artisans can rent studio time. The Center, located in the heart of the village, is open daily 10am to 10pm May through October, 10am to 6pm November through April.

WHERE TO STAY & DINE

Williamsville Inn. Rte. 41 (about 5 miles south of West Stockbridge Center), W. Stockbridge, MA 01266. ☎ **413/274-6118.** Fax 413/274-3539. 16 rms. A/C. July–Oct $120–$185 double; Nov–June $105–$160 double. AE, MC, V.

Rooms are in the 1797 main house, the converted barn, or in the no-frills cottages. Some have woodstoves or fireplaces, full baths or shower stalls, and some are more expensive than they should be.

Dining/Entertainment: The kitchen has received good notices for its "eclectic country cuisine," and the two dining rooms are open for dinner from 6 to 9pm— Wednesday to Monday from June to October, Thursday to Sunday from November to May. A popular storytelling series is held Sunday nights November through April, with a fixed-price $15.95 dinner.

Facilities: On the grounds are a clay tennis court, a pool, and a summer sculpture garden.

WHERE TO DINE

La Bruschetta. 1 Harris St. ☎ **413/232-7141.** Reservations advised. Main courses $8.95–$16.95. AE, MC, V. May–Oct Thurs–Tues 5–9pm; Nov–Apr Fri–Sun 5–9pm. NEW ITALIAN.

Forgive them their too brief hours, for the chef-owners create splendidly aromatic dishes that require care and advanced technique. Pre-appetizers are the eponymous *bruschettas,* grilled slices of bread piled with a variety of fragrant toppings. A basket of warm bread and a saucer of olive oil follow, so you might want to skip the appetizers. Rich, long-simmered sauces characterize the entrees, whether pastas, meats, or fowl, demanding to be sopped up to the last drop. Wines are as carefully selected as the ingredients. Just make sure the place is open before making the trip.

✪ **Truc Orient Express.** 2 Harris St. ☎ **413/232-4204.** Main courses $7.50–$11. AE, MC, V. Daily 11:30am–3pm and 5–10pm. Closed Tues in winter. VIETNAMESE.

If La Bruschetta is closed, as is often the case, just walk across the yard to Truc, in a rambling onetime warehouse. The menu is full of revelatory taste sensations. *Mai Tuyet Nhi* is a soup adrift with snow mushrooms and lobster meat, a suitable lead-in to the extravaganza called *Lauthap Cam-Chap Pin Loo,* a hot pot crowded with meatballs, shrimp, squid, scallops, and assorted veggies simmered tableside in a shiny brass pot and ladled over rice noodles. I can't wait to get back to try *Bo Luc Lac* ("Shaking Beef").

LEE

While Stockbridge and Lenox were developing into luxurious recreational centers for the upper crust of Boston and New York, Lee, which lies just 5 miles southeast of Lenox, was a thriving paper-mill town. That inevitably meant it was shunned by the wealthy summer people and thus remained essentially a town of workers and merchants. It has a somewhat raffish, although not unappealing, aspect, its center bunched with shops and offices, and few of the stately homes and broad lawns that characterize its neighboring communities.

The town's contribution to the Berkshire cultural calendar is the Jacob's Pillow Dance Festival, which first thrived on a fabled alliance between founder Ted Shawn and Martha Graham.

The Lee Chamber of Commerce operates an **information center** during summer and early fall on the Town Common, Route 20 (☎ **413/243-0852**).

THE JACOB'S PILLOW DANCE FESTIVAL

Jacob's Pillow, George Carter Road, Becket (☎ **413/243-0745**), is to dance what Tanglewood is to classical music, each showcasing talent of stature in its respective field. Known as a regular summer venue for famed dancer and choreographer Martha Graham, who died in 1991 after a 70-year career, the theater has long welcomed troupes of international reputation, of late including the Mark Morris Dance Group, the Paul Taylor Company, and Feld Ballet/NY, as well as repertory companies whose work is based on jazz, flamenco, and Indian and Asian music. The season is from late June to late August, and tickets go on sale May 1 (the summer's program is announced in January or February; call the number above to have a schedule mailed to you). The more prominent companies are seen in the main Ted Shawn Theatre, where tickets are in the $27-to-$43 range; other troupes are assigned to the Studio/Theatre, where tickets are $12 to $15. Tickets are usually readily available, unless the performance in question is a big-name event, or you've decided to go at the last minute.

A BERKSHIRE ART GALLERY

With no immediate obligatory historic homes or museums to see, visitors in search of attractions routinely make the short excursion to the hamlet of Tyringham. To get there, take Route 20 south to Route 102, near the no. 2 interchange of the Massachusetts Turnpike. Following the signs through the complicated intersection, pick up Tyringham Road and drive south about 4 miles.

You'll know when you get where you're going. It's on the left, an odd fairy-tale structure often called the "Gingerbread House." At the front wall are jagged limestone outcroppings, in back are conical turrets topping towers, and the shingled roof rolls like waves on the ocean. Erected at the turn of the century as a studio for sculptor Henry Hudson Kitson, it now houses the **Tyringham Art Galleries** (☎ 413/243-0654), showcasing the works of competent, if not breathtaking, Berkshire artists. Open daily 10am to 5pm, Memorial Day to Columbus Day. Admission is $1 adults; free for children.

CAMPING

October Mountain State Forest offers 50 campsites (with showers) and more than 16,000 acres for hiking and walking, canoeing and other nonmotorized boating, cross-country skiing, and snowmobiling. To get there, drive northwest on Route 20 into town, turn right on Center Street, and follow the signs.

WHERE TO STAY

The **Lee Chamber of Commerce,** which operates an information center during summer and early fall on the Town Common, Route 20 (☎ 413/243-0852), can help you find lodging in the area, often in modest guest houses and B&Bs—rarely as grand as those in Lenox, but nearly always significantly cheaper. That's something to remember when every other place near Tanglewood seems to be fully booked or quoting prices of $200 a night or more.

A lakeside motel on the road to Lenox, the **Black Swan,** 435 Laurel St., MA 20 (☎ 413/243-2700), has a pool and sauna.

✪ **Applegate.** 279 W. Park St., Lee, MA 01238. ☎ **800/691-9012** or 413/243-4451. 6 rms. A/C. $85–$225 double. MC, V. From Stockbridge, drive north on Rte. 7. In about ¹/₂ mile, take a right on Lee Rd. The inn is 2¹/₄ miles ahead, on the right. No children under 12.

This paragon of the B&B trade utilizes a gracious 1920s Georgian colonial manse to full advantage. The most desirable lodging has a huge canopied bed with a puffy comforter, Queen Anne reproductions, sunlight filtering through gauzy curtains, a walk-around steam shower, and a fireplace with real wood instead of pressed logs. Two robes hang ready for guests' use, and a complimentary carafe of brandy is also waiting. Wing chairs have good reading lights. Other rooms are similar, albeit somewhat smaller. The two-bedroom carriage house suite has a Jacuzzi and a kitchenette. No room TVs, but there's a large set with VCR on the sunporch.

Breakfast is by candlelight, and the innkeepers set out wine and cheese in the afternoon. There's a swimming pool, and across the street is a 9-hole golf course. The inn doesn't allow pets, although five cats call Applegate home.

Chambéry Inn. 199 Main St., Lee, MA 01238. ☎ **413/243-2221.** Fax 413/243-3600. 9 rms. A/C TV TEL. July–Aug and Oct $99–$195 double; Sept and Nov–June $65–$155 double. Rates include breakfast. AE, DISC, MC, V. No children under 18.

This was the Berkshires' first parochial school (1885), and it is named for the French hometown of the nuns who ran it. That accounts for the extra-large bedrooms, which used to be classrooms. Seven of these "suites," with 13-foot ceilings and the original woodwork and blackboards still in place, have been equipped with whirlpool baths and gas fireplaces. Room-service dinners are provided by the restaurant in back, itself a converted train station. No smoking.

Federal House. Main St. (Rte. 102), S. Lee, MA 01260. ☎ **800/243-1824** or 413/243-1824. 7 rms. A/C. Memorial Day to Oct $85–$165 double; Nov–May $75–$125 double. Rates include breakfast. AE, MC, V.

Built in 1824 in the gracious Federalist style, including a portico with fluted columns, this distinguished little inn still sports antiques belonging to the original family in its upstairs bedrooms, which are perfectly nice if a bit pricey. Dining is the reason to go.

Dining/Entertainment: The Federal House made a name for itself with sumptuous "event" and holiday meals. The understated elegance fashioned by the owners is made warm by the presence of fireplaces in both dining rooms, the one in the front parlor carved from black marble. Food is essentially contemporary French, but with many excursions farther afield. It is complemented by an impressive wine cellar. Dinner is served 5:30 to 9:30pm Thursday to Sunday from November through April, nightly from May through October. Reservations are recommended. Dinner for two, before wine and tip, should be under $70.

WHERE TO DINE

The Federal House (see "Where to Stay," above) offers the best dining in town. Here's a more casual alternative.

Cactus Café. 54 Main St. ☎ **413/243-4300.** Main courses $8.50–$16.50. AE, DC, DISC, MC, V. Daily 11:30am–2pm; Sun–Thurs 5–9pm, Fri–Sat 5–10pm. TEX-MEX.

What must have been a 1930s luncheonette has had a few coats of pastel paint slapped on the walls and stamped-tin ceiling, with serapes and sombreros hung from nails. The food is as artlessly homemade, heaped on thick white china. It's filling and tastes good, although the seasoning cries for a little more zing.

An adjoining room, **Y Mas!,** serves espresso and pastries and has live music from time to time.

LENOX & TANGLEWOOD

Stately homes and fabulous mansions mushroomed in this former agricultural settlement from the 1890s until around 1910. By 1913, the 16th Amendment, authorizing income taxes, put a severe crimp in that impulse. But Lenox remains a repository of extravagant domestic architecture surpassed only in such fabled resorts of the wealthy as Newport and Palm Beach. And since many of the cottages have been converted into inns and hotels, it is possible to get inside some of these beautiful buildings, if only for a cocktail or a meal.

The reason for so many lodgings in a town with a permanent population of barely 5,000 (more than two dozen buildings post signs and others take in guests through B&B networks) is Tanglewood, a nearby estate where a series of concerts by the Boston Symphony Orchestra is held every summer. While the weekend performances of the BSO are the big draw, there are also solo recitals, chamber concerts, and appearances by the privileged young musicians who study at the prestigious Tanglewood Music Center.

Lenox lies 7 miles south of Pittsfield and 23 miles south of Williamstown. The **Lenox Chamber of Commerce** operates an information center in the Lenox Academy Building, 75 Main St. (☎ **413/637-3646**). It has public rest rooms, and attendants can assist in obtaining lodgings.

TANGLEWOOD & THE PERFORMING ARTS SCENE

Lenox is filled with music every July and August, and the undisputed headliners are Seiji Ozawa and the Boston Symphony Orchestra, of which he is music director. Their concerts are given at the famous **Tanglewood** estate, usually beginning the last weekend in June and ending the weekend before Labor Day. The estate is on West Street (actually in Stockbridge township, although it's always associated with Lenox); drive 1 1/2 miles southwest of Lenox on Route 183.

While the BSO is Tanglewood's 800-pound cultural gorilla, the program features a menagerie of other performers and musical idioms. These run the gamut from popular artists (past performers have included James Taylor and Peter, Paul & Mary) and jazz vocalists and combos (including Dave Brubeck, Betty Carter, Joe Williams, and George Shearing), to choral groups like the Robert Shaw choral troupe and guest soloists and conductors such as André Previn, Itzak Perlman, and Jessye Norman. Large visiting ensembles like the Kirov Orchestra and Chorus and the Boston Pops are also featured.

Such prominent groups and individual artists usually appear in "The Shed," an open-ended auditorium that seats 5,000, supplemented by a surrounding lawn where an outdoor audience lounges on folding chairs and blankets. Less known performers and chamber groups appear in Ozawa Hall and the separate theater. Seats in The Shed range from $14 to $76, while lawn tickets are usually $12 to $17.50. (Higher prices apply for some special appearances.)

For **information on programs,** call ☎ **617/266-1492** (Boston) or 413/637-5165 (Lenox). For weekly updates on the performance schedule, call ☎ **413/637-1666.** To order tickets by mail before June, write the Tanglewood Ticket Office at Symphony Hall, Boston, MA 02115. After the 1st week in June, write the Tanglewood Ticket Office, Lenox, MA 01240. Tickets can be charged by phone through **Symphonycharge** (☎ **800/274-0808** outside Boston, or 617/266-1200 in Boston). Tentative programs are available before Christmas; the summer's schedule is locked in by February. It's not too hard to get tickets in advance (before June), but it's trickier after that. If you decide to go at the last minute, take a blanket or lawn chairs and get tickets for the lawn, which are almost always available. You can also attend rehearsals during the week.

The estate itself (☎ **413/637-5165** June through August), with more than 500 gorgeous acres of manicured lawns, gardens, and groves of ancient trees, much of it overlooking Stockbridge Bowl lake, was put together starting in 1849 by William Aspinwall Tappan. Admission to the grounds is free.

At the outset, the only structure on the property was a modest something referred to as the Little Red Shanty. In 1851, it was rented to Nathaniel Hawthorne and his wife Sophia. The author of *The Scarlet Letter* and *The House of the Seven Gables* stayed there long enough to write a children's book, *Tanglewood Tales,* and meet Herman Melville, who lived nearby in Dalton and became a close friend. The existing Hawthorne Cottage is a replica, now serving as practice studios. (It isn't open to the public.) On the grounds is the original Tappan mansion, with fine views. Two smaller structures of more recent vintage provide space for recitals, lectures, and chamber concerts.

As consuming as the events at Tanglewood are, there's even more. **Shakespeare & Company** uses buildings and outdoor amphitheaters on the grounds of The Mount to stage its late-May to Labor Day season of plays by the Bard, works by Edith Wharton, and new American playwrights. (See the listing for the Edith Wharton Restoration below.) Performances by dance troupes, student actors, and even puppets flesh out the schedule. The venues are the outdoor amphitheaters, Mainstage and Oxford Court, and two indoor stages, Stables and Wharton. Staggered performances take place Tuesday through Sunday, usually at 3, 5, or 8pm. Tickets range from $12.50 to $27.50, and are generally easy to get, since the theater rarely draws name actors. Call the box office at ☎ **413/637-3353;** the summer's schedule is announced by February or March. Lunch and dinner picnic baskets can be purchased on site.

In addition, from June to September, the **National Music Center,** 70 Kemble St. (☎ **413/637-4718** for tickets and information), presents a July to August season of music—jazz, pop, folk, and blues—in its 1,200-seat hall. And, on selected Saturdays between October and May, chamber music recitals are presented at the Lenox Town Hall by **Armstrong Chamber Concerts,** P.O. Box 367, Washington Depot, CT 06794 (☎ **860/868-0522**).

A LITERARY LANDMARK & A STOP FOR TRAIN BUFFS

Edith Wharton Restoration, The Mount. Plunkett St. (at the intersection of Routes 7, 20, and 7A). ☎ **413/637-1899.** Guided tours given Memorial Day through Oct daily 9am–2pm. Admission $6 adults, $4.50 children 13–18; free for children under 13.

Wharton, who won a Pulitzer Prize for her novel *The Age of Innocence,* was singularly equipped to write that subtle and deftly detailed examination of the upper classes of the Gilded Age and the first decades of this century. She was born into that stratum of society in 1862 and traveled in those circles that made the Berkshires a regular stop on their restless movements between New York, Florida, Newport, and the Continent. She had her own "cottage" built on this 130-acre lakeside property in 1902 and lived there 10 years before leaving for France, never to return.

Wharton took an active hand in the overall design of her home and the execution of its details. She was, after all, the author of an upscale 1897 how-to guide called *The Decoration of Houses.* Grand by today's standards, the house wasn't especially large for that time in Lenox history. Called "The Mount," it is often used by the actors of the Shakespeare & Co. troupe (see "Tanglewood & the Performing Arts Scene," above) to stage on-site productions based on the author's works. Restoration is ongoing, but tours continue as scheduled.

Berkshire Scenic Railway Museum. Housatonic St. and Willow Creek Rd. ☎ **413/637-2210.** Guided tours given Memorial Day weekend through Oct on Sat, Sun, and holidays 10am–4pm.

Housed in a deactivated and restored train station, the Berkshire Scenic Railway Museum has displays of model railroads, a gift shop, and a real caboose. Fifteen-minute train rides are also offered. This is one of the few attractions in Lenox likely to appeal to children.

OUTDOOR PURSUITS

Pleasant Valley Wildlife Sanctuary, West Mountain Road (☎ **413/637-0320**), has a small museum and 7 miles of hiking and snowshoeing trails crossing its 1,500 acres. Beaver lodges and dams can be glimpsed from a distance and waterfowl and other birds are found in abundance, rewarding targets for those who come equipped with binoculars. Open Tuesday to Sunday, dawn to sunset. Admission is $3 adults, $2 children 3 to 15. To get there, drive north 6.6 miles on Routes 7 and 20 and turn left on West Dugway Road.

In town, **Main Street Sports & Leisure,** 48 Main St. (☎ **413/637-4407**), rents bicycles, canoes, in-line skates, snowshoes, cross-country skis, tennis rackets, and related equipment. They can also advise on routes and trails, and provide guided outdoor trips.

Kennedy Park, right down the street from the store, is a lovely spot for cross-country skiing in winter, or for a ramble in any season. Dogs are allowed off-leash.

WHERE TO STAY

While it may seem that every other house in town puts up guests—the long list below is only partial—most can accommodate only small numbers. The Tanglewood concert season is a powerful draw, so prices are highest in summer and the brief fall foliage season, usually around Columbus Day. Rate schedules are marked by Byzantine complexity, with tariffs set according to wildly varying combinations of seasons and days of the week, as well as specific facilities, including private or shared baths, fireplaces, views, air-conditioning, and size of quarters. Minimum 2- or 3-night stays are usually required during the Tanglewood weeks, October foliage, and long holiday weekends. None of this forewarning will matter if you don't make your reservations well in advance.

Not all the bed-and-breakfasts hang signs out front. Some aren't permitted to, due to zoning restrictions, while others prefer to operate through a referral service. One of these is **Berkshire B&B Homes,** Main Street, Box 211, Williamsburg, MA 01096 (☎ **413/268-7244;** fax 413/268-7243).

Given the substantial numbers of lodging places and the limited space to describe them, admittedly arbitrary judgments have been made to winnow the list. Some inns, for example, are so rule ridden and facility free they come off as crabby—no smoking, no children, no pets, no phones, no TV, no credit cards, no breakfast before 9am, shared bathrooms, checkout at 11am, check-in after 3pm—and cost twice as much as nearby motels that have all those conveniences. Let them seek clients elsewhere.

Others are open only 6 or 7 months a year, and charge the world for a bed or a meal. In this latter category, though, one place demands at least a mention. **Blantyre,** 16 Blantyre Rd. (☎ **413/637-3556** in summer, or 413/298-3806 in winter), in its 1902 Tudor-Norman mansion, bestows its guests with a soak in undeniable luxury, both in dining room and bedchamber.

When all the area's inns are fully booked or if you want to be assured the full quota of 20th-century comforts and gadgets, Routes 7 and 20 north and south of town harbor a number of conventional motels. Among the possibilities are the **Mayflower Motor Inn** (☎ **413/443-4468**), the **Susse Chalet** (☎ **413/637-3560**), and the **Lenox Motel** (☎ **413/499-0324**).

Very Expensive

Canyon Ranch in the Berkshires. 165 Kemble St., Lenox, MA 01240. ☎ **800/326-7080** or 413/637-4100. Fax 413/637-0057. 120 rms. A/C TV TEL. 3-night packages from $1,620–$2,740 double. Rates include all meals. Taxes and 18% service charge extra. AE, DC, MC, V.

Welding turn-of-the-century opulence to the contemporary impulses for dietary deprivation and masochistic physicality isn't the way most people choose to spend their leisure time—at least not at these prices. But for the too rich and too thin set or for those who'd like to splurge just once, this is the place.

A polite but firm security guard turns away the unconfirmed at the gate, so there's no popping in for a look around. The core facility is the 1897 extravaganza of a mansion, Bellefontaine, said to be modeled after Le Petit Trianon at Versailles. While it has been painstakingly restored, it is difficult to say what was lost in the disastrous fire of 1949, which left only the magnificent library untouched.

Dining/Entertainment: After being steamed, exhausted, massaged, and showered, the real events of each day are mealtimes; "nutritionally balanced gourmet," natch.

Facilities: Sweat away the pounds in the huge spa complex, with 40 exercise classes a day, weights, an indoor running track, racquetball, squash, indoor and outdoor pools, tennis, and canoeing and hiking outings. But first have a consultation with a staff member who "can help you enhance your wellness opportunities."

Cranwell Resort & Golf Club. 55 Lee Rd., Lenox, MA 01240. ☎ **800/272-6935** or 413/637-1364. Fax 413/637-4364. 65 rms. A/C TV TEL. Jan–May $99–$239 double; June through Labor Day $199–$389 double; Sept–Dec $99–$329 double. Rates include breakfast. 3-night minimum stay July–Aug. AE, DC, DISC, MC, V. From Lenox Center, go north to Rte. 20 east. The resort is on the left.

Yet another century-old mansion, this one in modified Tudor style, stands at the center of this 380-acre resort. That's where the most expensive rooms are; the rest are in a number of surrounding smaller buildings. Some of the latter have wet bars or kitchenettes. Rooms are unremarkable but very comfortable, like those in a good chain hotel.

Dining/Entertainment: Three dining rooms range from formal to pubby, and there is live musical entertainment on weekend nights.

Facilities: The lovely grounds and the 18-hole, par 71 golf course are the best features, but there are two tennis courts and a large heated pool, too. In winter, the gentle slopes serve as cross-country ski trails.

✪ Wheatleigh. W. Hawthorne Rd., Lenox, MA 01240. ☎ **413/637-0610.** Fax 413/637-4507. 17 rms. A/C TV TEL. $175–$565 double. AE, DC, MC, V.

On my first stay at Wheatleigh, years ago, a bevy of glamorous young New Yorkers, all dressed in white, draped themselves in Gatsbyesque poses around the lavishly appointed Great Hall. They all contrived to look elaborately bored, no easy feat in this persuasive 1893 replica of a 16th-century Italian *palazzo*, which matches the highest standards of the moneyed Berkshires. Wheatleigh was very expensive then, and still is. But other places are catching up, and the new French manager is striving to give requisite value. In addition to refurbishing some of the recreational facilities, he has added TV sets, for example, with stands that don't clash with the superb decor. (Innkeepers are fond of saying that people don't visit them to watch *Seinfeld,* but at these prices, guests should be able to at least catch the evening news if they wish.) It may sound paradoxical, but the cheapest units are too expensive (they average only 11 by 13 feet), while the priciest rooms are almost reasonable.

Dining/Entertainment: The dining room admirably rounds out the experience, with immaculate floral arrangements on white napery, original contemporary art on the walls, muted chamber music playing just below recognition level. The year-round prix-fixe menu is $68; reservations recommended on weekends.

Facilities: Exercise room, pool, tennis court.

Expensive

Brook Farm Inn. 15 Hawthorne St., Lenox, MA 01240. ☎ **800/285-7638** or 413/637-3013. Fax 413/637-4751. 12 rms. July through Labor Day $105–$190 double; Sept–Oct $70–$145 double; Nov–June $85–$125 double. Rates include breakfast buffet and afternoon tea. DISC, MC, V. No children under 12. From the town center, go south 1 block on Old Stockbridge Rd. Turn right.

"There is poetry here," insist the owners of this picture-pretty 1870 farmhouse, and an afternoon idle in the hammock overlooking the pool or a curled-up read by the fireplace will have you agreeing. Breakfast is an ample buffet. Five of the rooms have air-conditioning, a huge plus if it's a hot summer, as the last few have been. None of them have phones. No smoking.

Facilities: Outdoor pool.

Cliffwood Inn. 25 Cliffwood St., Lenox, MA 01240. ☎ **413/637-3330.** 7 rms. A/C. July through Labor Day and foliage season $109–$200 double; May 15–June and Sept after Labor Day $82–$145 double; Nov–May 14 $73–$132. Rates include breakfast (except during midweek in low season). No credit cards.

One of the relatively compact manses of the Vanderbilt era, this has a long veranda in back overlooking the outdoor pool. Antiques of many styles and periods fill the common and private spaces. Six of the seven bedrooms have working fireplaces (including one in a bathroom!). Only one unit has a TV. The owners will loan beach chairs to use on the lawn at Tanglewood.

Facilities: Outdoor pool and an year-round countercurrent workout pool.

Gables Inn. 103 Walker St., Lenox, MA 01240. ☎ **800/382-9401** or 413/637-3416. 15 rms, 3 suites. A/C TV. $80–$210 double. Rates include breakfast. DISC, MC, V. No children under 12.

Edith Wharton, who spent more than 2 decades in Lenox, made this Queen Anne mansion her home for 2 years while her house, The Mount, was being built. That may be enough to interest fans of the novelist, but there is much more to appeal to potential guests, including the canopied four-poster and working fireplace in Edith's bedroom, which was recently redone. Meticulously maintained Victoriana and related antiques are found in every corner, most notably in the eight-sided library. No rooms have phones, but suites have VCRs and refrigerators.

Facilities: A heated outdoor pool and tennis court are available.

Gateways Inn. 51 Walker St., Lenox, MA 01240. ☎ **413/637-2532.** Fax 413/637-1432. 12 rms. A/C TV TEL. $95–$325 double. Rates include breakfast. AE, DC, DISC, MC, V. No children 12 or under.

Harley Procter, who hitched up with a man called Gamble and made a bundle, had this house, christened "Orleton," built as his summer home in 1912. Its most impressive feature is the eye-catching staircase that winds down into the lobby. You'll probably hear the oft-repeated myth that it was designed by Stanford White, but that would have been quite a trick—White died in 1906. Still, whoever did it, it's a stunner, just the thing for a grand entrance. Equally impressive is the suite named for conductor Arthur Fiedler, with not one but two fireplaces, a big four-poster on the sunporch, and a Jacuzzi in the new bathroom. No smoking.

Dining/Entertainment: While the kitchen has long been regarded as very capable, the tone in the dining room went beyond formal to stuffy. It's loosened up of late, and dining here is one of Lenox's greater pleasures. (Dinner entrees run $15.50 to $21.50; reservations recommended on weekends.)

Whistler's Inn. 5 Greenwood St., Lenox, MA 01240. ☎ **413/637-0975.** Fax 413/637-2190. 14 rms. A/C TEL. July–Oct $90–$200 double or suite. Rates 20%–35% lower rest of the year. Rates include breakfast. AE, DISC, MC, V.

Both innkeepers are compulsive travelers, hitting every continent, but with particular fondness for India and Africa. They bring things back from every trip, filling the cavernous rooms of their Tudor mansion with clusters of cut glass, painted screens, assorted Victoriana, grandfather clocks, Persian rugs, landscape paintings, ormolu candelabras, a grand piano, shelf after shelf of books (both of them are writers), and lavish furniture. The result is rooms that are not so much decorated as gathered, without a single boring corner. A white rag mop of a dog called Pushkin races around demanding attention. Breakfast is suitably proportioned (to the surroundings, not the dog) and a bottle of sherry or port is kept in the library for guests to pour themselves a drink to sip with tea and cookies. Ten of the guest rooms are air-conditioned; TV is available on request.

Moderate

Amadeus House. 15 Cliffwood St. (near corner of Main St.), Lenox, MA 01240. ☎ **800/ 205-4770** or 413/637-4770. Fax 413/637-4484. 8 rms (7 with private bath). July through Labor Day $60–$175 double; mid-May to June and Sept–Oct $60–$150 double; Nov to mid-May $60–$125 double. Rates include breakfast. AE, DISC, MC, V. No children under 10.

As can be assumed from the name, the owners are lovers of classical music. That theme carries through with the names given the guest rooms—Bach, Bernstein, and Brahms—and the fact that the usual common-room TV is replaced by a stereo and stacks of CDs. "Beethoven" is a two-bedroom suite with a sitting area and fully stocked kitchen. Only one room has air-conditioning; most of the rest have ceiling fans. The central part of the house dates from 1820. Breakfast incorporates a hot entree and afternoon tea is served. No pets are allowed, though there is a resident Labrador retriever named Bravo.

Candlelight Inn. 53 Walker St., Lenox, MA 01240. ☎ **413/637-1555.** 8 rms. A/C. $70–$155 double. Rates include breakfast. AE, MC, V. No children under 10.

A folksy gathering place for locals as well as guests, the bar at the end of the center hall in this 1885 Victorian sees a friendly, not raucous, nightly trade, and the four dining rooms are often full. In winter, clink glasses beside a crackling fire; in summer, reserve a table in the courtyard beneath Campari umbrellas. (Main courses are $13.95 to $22.95.) Dinner is served year-round, lunch from Memorial Day to late October. While the Candlelight does most of its business on the restaurant side, the upstairs rooms are routine but comfortable. No smoking.

Village Inn. 16 Church St., Lenox, MA 01240. ☎ **800/253-0917** or 413/637-0020. Fax 413/ 637-9756. 32 rms. A/C TEL. Summer–fall $80–$210 double; winter–spring $60–$140 double. AE, DC, DISC, MC, V. No children under 6.

An inn since 1775, with occasional periods when it was put to other uses, this place hasn't a whiff of pretense. Its unusually large number of rooms come in considerable variety, and are categorized as "Superior," "Standard," or "Economy." That means four-posters in the high-end rooms, some of which have fireplaces and/or whirlpool baths, and constricted quarters with double beds at the lower prices. Claw-foot tubs are common in rooms in all categories.

Afternoon tea and dinner are served June to October in the restaurant, light meals in the tavern (the only room where smoking is allowed). Small combos play on some weekends, and there have been poetry readings.

WHERE TO DINE

See also "Where to Stay," above, since many of the local inns have fine dining rooms.

✪ **Church Street Cafe.** 65 Church St. ☎ **413/637-2745.** Reservations recommended on weekends. Main courses $14.95–$17.95. MC, V. Daily 11:30am–2pm and 5:30–9pm. Closed Sun–Mon in winter. ECLECTIC AMERICAN.

The most popular place in town got that way by delivering fanciful combinations that please the eyes and pique the taste buds without scaring off timid diners. Such innovative cuisine includes the lunchtime "cafe sandwich," a layered production of grilled disks of eggplant, roasted sweet red peppers, goat cheese, watercress, red onion slices, and tomato on nubby whole-grain bread. So many powerful flavors seep and mingle here that even carnivores hardly notice the absence of meat. Similar creativity informs the dinner plate of pan-seared cod with a bouillabaisse of shrimp, potatoes, fennel, and tomatoes. Surroundings are unembellished, plain wood chairs and tables and crocks of flowers. The large dining deck fills up whenever the weather allows.

Lenox 218. 28 Main St. (Rte. 7A). ☎ **413/637-4218.** Main courses $12.95–$21.95. AE, CB, DC, DISC, MC, V. Mon–Sat 11:30am–2:30pm and 5–10pm, Sun 10:30am–10pm. ITALIAN/ AMERICAN.

Largely black and white, with hanging pots of ivy, the decor at this restaurant falls short of the urban sophistication it evidently seeks. So does the food, which mainly consists of simple, familiar fare like veal piccata, chicken cacciatore, and meat loaf with peas, carrots, and mashed potatoes. But that's okay. It's cooked and assembled well enough, and the service is pleasant. Lunch might be the better time, when the bar in front is quiet.

PITTSFIELD

Berkshire County's largest city (in 1990, the population was over 48,000) gets little attention in most tourist literature, and there's good reason. A commercial and in-dustrial center—Martin Marietta is the largest employer—it presents little of the charm that marks such popular destinations as Stockbridge and Lenox. Still, it is a convenient base for day excursions to attractions elsewhere in the region, including several ski centers, the summer concert season at Tanglewood, and Hancock Shaker Village, a few miles to the west. Pittsfield is also home to the house where Herman Melville wrote *Moby Dick,* and an eccentric little museum with a theater showing art films much of the year.

The **Berkshire Visitors Bureau** (☎ **800/237-5747** or 413/443-9186) is located in the same block of buildings as the Hilton, on Berkshire Common. Pittsfield lies 137 miles west of Boston, and 7 miles north of Lenox.

A LITERARY LANDMARK & A LOCAL MUSEUM

Arrowhead. 780 Holmes Rd. ☎ **413/442-1793.** Admission $5 adults, $4.50 seniors, $3.50 children 6–16, $15 for families. Late May to Labor Day 10am–5pm; Labor Day to end of Oct Fri–Mon 10am–5pm; rest of year by appointment only. Drive east from Park Square on East St., turn right on Elm St. and right again on Holmes Rd.

Herman Melville, just one prominent member of the literary and artistic community that kept summer homes in the Berkshires, bought this house in 1850 and lived here until 1863. It was during this time that he wrote his masterpiece, *Moby Dick,* and a number of lesser works. One of his best friends was Nathaniel Hawthorne, and they conversed regularly in the upstairs study and at a table beside the large fireplace in the kitchen. In truth, however, the house is only likely to be interesting to literature students and avid readers. Visits are by guided tour only.

Berkshire Museum. 39 South St. (Rte. 7, 1 block south of Park Sq.). ☎ **413/443-7171.** Ad-mission $3 adults, $2 seniors and students, $1 children 12–18. Tues–Sat 10am–5pm, Sun 1–5pm. Also open Mon in July–Aug.

It began in 1903 as the "Museum of Natural History and Art," the words chiseled in stone above the entrance. The holdings bounce from Babylonian cuneiform tab-lets to stuffed birds to mineral displays to tanks of live fish in the basement aquarium. An auditorium seating 300 serves as the "Little Cinema," which has a season of art and foreign films during the warmer months.

Apart from the aquarium, the greatest interest may be generated by the art and archaeological artifacts assembled on the second floor. A sculpture gallery has full-size casts of important 16th-century Italian sculptures and a 19th-century *Diana* by

American Augustus Saint-Gaudens. While those looking for name artists will generally be disappointed, there are a number of canvases and sculptures by contemporary artists that deserve attention, and here and there are minor Alexander Calders, a Reginald Marsh, and a couple of landscapes by Alfred Bierstedt. Among cases of 2nd-century Mediterranean glassware and Roman funerary busts are pieces of pre-Christian Egyptian jewelry and pottery and a delicate necklace from Thebes dating to at least 1500 B.C. Kids will love the mummy, of course, and the tropical and native fish and amphibians in the basement.

OUTDOOR PURSUITS

A useful Pittsfield store to know is **Plaine's Bike Golf Ski,** 55 W. Housatonic St. (☎ 413/499-0294), which rents bikes by the day and week and carries equipment for all the sports its name suggests. Open daily, it's on Route 20, west of downtown, at the corner of Center Street.

A prime recreational preserve is **Pittsfield State Forest,** entered on Cascade Street (☎ 413/442-8992), a little over 3 miles west of the center of town on West Street. Its 10,000 acres have 31 campsites, boat ramps, streams for canoeing and fishing, and trails for hiking, horseback riding, and cross-country skiing. Open daily 8am to 8pm. Admission is $2 per car.

BOATING   **Onota Boat Livery,** 463 Peck Rd. (☎ 413/442-1724), rents canoes and motorboats for use on Onota Lake, conveniently located at the western edge of the city.

GOLF   Nonmember golfers are welcome on the 18-hole course at **Pontoosuc Lake Country Club,** Kirkwood Drive (☎ 413/445-4217), for reasonable greens fees.

SKIING   South of the city center, off Route 7 near the Pittsfield city limits, is **Bousquet Ski Area,** Dan Fox Drive (☎ 413/442-8316). It has 21 trails, the longest over 1 mile long with a vertical drop of 750 feet, with two double chairlifts and two rope tows. Night skiing is on Monday to Saturday, when trails are open until 10pm; equipment can be rented for moderate rates.

About 9 miles in the other direction, off Route 7 in the town of New Ashford, is **Brodie Mountain Ski Area** (☎ 413/443-4752), with a vertical drop of 1,250 feet and a long run of 2^1/$_2$ miles. Midweek ski-school packages are attractive, and in summer they offer racquetball, tennis, and campsites.

Alternatively, turn west a mile short of Brodie Mountain on Brodie Mountain Road and continue about 3 miles to **Jiminy Peak,** Hancock, MA 01237 (☎ 413/738-5500, or 413/738-7325 for 24-hour ski reports). This expanding resort aspires to four-season activity, so skiing on 28 trails (18 are open at night) with seven lifts is supplemented the rest of the year with horseback riding, trapshooting, fishing in a stocked pond, six tennis courts, mountain biking, pools, and golf at the nearby Waubeeka Springs course. Ample lodging is available (see "Where to Stay," below.)

WHERE TO STAY

The Country Inn at Jiminy Peak. Brodie Mountain Rd. (near Rte. 43), Hancock, MA 01237. ☎ **800/882-8859** or 413/738-5500. Fax 413/738-5513. 105 suites. A/C TV TEL. $95–$209 suite. Rates include breakfast. AE, CB, DC, DISC, MC, V.

The "Jiminy Peak" moniker might suggest a mock-Alpine enclave with rapacious singles and indefatigable social directors in Tyrolean pants. On the contrary, this is one of the better lodging deals in the Berkshires, especially if your idea of luxury is space. All units are one-bedroom suites with full kitchens and pullout sofas, suitable for families or two couples traveling together. A buffet breakfast is served in the Founders' Grill in season, meaning late June to mid-October and mid-December to

April. Some signs of the robust use to which ski resorts are subject can be seen in nicks on furniture legs and around elevators, though maintenance is otherwise relatively good. And guests could live without the constant reminders that they, too, "could be part of the Jiminy Peak family" by buying a condo. But these shortcomings pale beside the two pools and abundant recreational facilities (mentioned above in the description under "Outdoor Pursuits"), and Tanglewood is less than 30 minutes away.

Hilton Inn Berkshire. West St., Pittsfield, MA 01201. ☎ **800/445-8667** or 413/499-2000. Fax 413/442-0449. 175 rms. A/C TV TEL MINIBAR. $79–$189 double. Children stay free in parent's room. AE, CB, DC, DISC, MC, V.

The tallest building in town at 14 stories, this Hilton isn't hard to find, although it takes a little round-the-block maneuvering to get to the front door. (Look for signs to Berkshire Common, west of South Street, the main drag.) It has most of the bells and whistles expected of a first-class chain hotel, and is more family-friendly than many lodgings in the region. (And most rooms have two double or queen-sized beds, with sleep sofas, perfect for families.) With all the rooms, you've got a pretty good chance of copping a bed on Tanglewood weekends. Some rooms have hair dryers and fully stocked minibars. Cable TV and in-room movies are standard. Seven floors are nonsmoking.

Facilities: There is a newly outfitted fitness room and a heated indoor pool to keep the kids occupied.

WHERE TO DINE

Giovanni's. 1331 North St. (Rte. 7N, north of the center). ☎ **413/443-2441.** Main courses $7–$18. AE, DC, DISC, MC, V. Mon–Sat noon–3pm, Sun 10am–2pm; Mon–Thurs 5–10pm, Fri–Sat 4–11pm, Sun 4–10pm. ITALIAN/AMERICAN.

Four rows of hanging fake Tiffany lamps date the room to the disco decade. The menu is as retro as the decor. Large portions are opportunities for enough carbo-loading to propel a marathon runner 5 miles past the finish line. One of the house specialties, for example, heaps chicken, shrimp, broccoli, mushrooms, onions, and strips of bell peppers on a half-pound of linguine. Meant for one, it'll serve two. Seniors are fond of the early-bird specials, priced at under $10, including a glass of wine.

ON THE SHAKER TRAIL

Mother Ann arrived in near-revolutionary New York State in 1774 with eight disciples. The former Ann Lee, previously imprisoned for her excess of religious zeal, had proclaimed a vision that anointed her the leader of the United Society of Believers in Christ's Second Coming. That austere Protestant sect was popularly known as "The Shakers" for their spastic movements when in the throes of religious ecstasy.

Mother Lee established their first communal settlement in Watervliet, near Albany, N.Y. By the time of her death in 1784, she had made many converts, who then fanned out across the country to form colonies from Maine to Indiana. Two of the most important communities straddled the Massachusetts–New York border, within miles of each other near Pittsfield and New Lebanon, N.Y. Farther west, a Shaker Museum has been established at Old Chatham.

Shaker society produced highly disciplined farmers and craftspeople, whose products were much in demand in the outside world. They sold seeds, invented early agricultural machinery and hand tools, and erected large buildings of several stories and exquisite simplicity. Their spare, clean-lined furniture and accessories anticipated the so-called Danish Modern style by a century, and in recent years have drawn astonishingly high prices at auction.

All of these accomplishments required a verve owed at least in part to sublimation of sexual energy—a fundamental Shaker tenet was total celibacy. They kept going with converts and adoptions, but by the 1970s the inevitable result of that short-sighted policy left the movement with a bare handful of adherents. The string of Shaker settlements and museums that remain is testament to their dictum, "Hands to work, hearts to God."

To tour the region's Shaker attractions, start out in Pittsfield, heading west on Route 20. In about 5 miles, on the left, is Hancock Shaker Village.

✪ Hancock Shaker Village. Routes 20 and 41, Pittsfield, MA 01202. ☎ **800/817-1137** or 413/443-0188. Admission Memorial Day to late Oct $12.50 adults, $5 children 6–17, $30 families (2 adults and children under 18); Apr to Memorial Day and late Oct to Nov $10 adults, $5 children 6–17, $25 families. Apr to Memorial Day and late Oct to late Nov daily 10am–3pm (guided tours), Memorial Day through the 3rd week in Oct daily 9:30am–5pm. Also open 1st weekend in Dec, Christmas weekend, and 3rd week in Feb (call ahead for times and events).

Of the 20 restored buildings that make up the village, the signature structure is clearly the 1826 round stone barn. The Shaker preoccupation with functionalism and purity of line and material is no more clear than here—the shape of the building expedited the chores of feeding and milking livestock by arranging cows in a circle. The precise joinery of the roof beams and support pillars is a joy to examine.

The second "must-see" on the grounds is the brick dwelling that contained the communal dining room, kitchens, and upstairs sleeping quarters. Sexes were separated at meals, work, and religious services, and equality was served by such features as the opposing staircases leading to male and female "retiring rooms."

Other buildings of note include the Meeting House, where religious services were held, and the 1792 laundry and machine shop, where a reproduction of a 19th-century water turbine has been installed.

While present-day artisans and docents labor in herb and vegetable gardens and in shops demonstrating Shaker crafts and techniques, they are not in costume, nor do they pretend to be Shaker inhabitants. They are knowledgeable about their subject in varying degrees, however, and dispense such nuggets as explanations of the Shaker discipline that required members to dress the right side first, to button from right to left, and to step with the right foot first.

The museum shop is excellent, with books and replicas of Shaker baskets, boxes, and small furniture.

A cafe serves lunches during the main Memorial Day to October season, with some dishes based on Shaker recipes. On Saturday nights in July, August, September, and October, the Village presents tours and Shaker four-course dinners by candlelight at a cost of $38 per person. Reservations for these are essential (☎ **413/443-0188**).

Mount Lebanon Shaker Village. Rte. 20, New Lebanon, NY 12125. ☎ **518/794-9500.** Admission $6 adults, $3 children 7–18. Memorial Day to Labor Day weekends (and some Mon holidays) 10am–4pm. Continue to the far end of the village, taking the rutted gravel road down to the red barn on the left.

From Hancock Shaker Village, turn left (west) on Route 20. In about 5 miles, on the left, is the private Darrow School, which has taken over most of the buildings that were once part of one of the Shaker movement's most important communities. They're easy to spot after a visit to Hancock Shaker Village, with their sober, simple dimensions and utter lack of ornamental detailing. Some of the buildings have been set aside as the Mount Lebanon Shaker Village.

This was the first self-contained Shaker community in America, established in 1787. In the red barn is a gift shop and a small museum of tools, furniture, farm implements, and related items. Guided tours are available (on a sporadic basis) of buildings not in use by the school, the most interesting of which are the meetinghouse and a stone dairy barn.

Past fund-raising auctions held on the school grounds helped send prices for antique Shaker furniture and artifacts into the stratosphere, especially after enthusiasts Oprah Winfrey and Bill Cosby showed up and added their figurative two cents to the bidding.

Shaker Museum and Library. 88 Shaker Museum Rd., Old Chatham, NY 12136. ☎ **518/ 794-9100.** Admission $6 adults, $5 seniors, $3 children 8–17. Late Apr to early Nov Wed–Mon 10am–5pm. Leaving the Mt. Lebanon Shaker Village, turn left (west) again on Route 20. After Brainard (about 8 miles), watch for the turn south on Rte. 66. Continue to the hamlet of Old Chatham, picking up County Road 13. This is tricky, so watch closely for the sign next to the general store pointing to the Shaker Museum and Library.

Obviously better funded and pampered than the Mount Lebanon Shaker Village, this concentration of barns and outbuildings contains a substantial collection of about 8,000 Shaker tools, pieces of furniture, machinery, and smaller items, such as the famous oval boxes that held everything from seeds to sewing materials. They fill 24 galleries, most of which offer illuminating essays, reproductions of Shaker writings, and helpful descriptive labels. Many of the galleries are arranged as period rooms, including living quarters, kitchen areas, weaving shops, a classroom, and a blacksmith's shop. All is displayed with curatorial taste and painstaking care, and, except when school groups are about, can be contemplated at leisure and in rural calm. Periodic special events are mounted, which have included, in the recent past, antique fairs, apple harvest breakfasts, herb and plant sales, concerts, and kite-flying demonstrations.

After a visit, the perfect overnight retreat is directly at hand . . . right across the road.

WHERE TO STAY & DINE

✪ **Old Chatham Sheepherding Company Inn.** 99 Shaker Museum Rd., Old Chatham, NY 12136. ☎ **518/794-9774.** Fax 518/794-9779. 10 rms. A/C TEL. $150–$350 double. Rates include breakfast. AE, MC, V. "Special arrangements" must be made for children under 12.

This 1995 newcomer demanded instant recognition as one of the most accomplished inns in the Northeast. The 1790 Georgian manor may seem too grand and sumptuously appointed for association with the stringently ascetic Shakers, but there are connections. A previous owner gave his collection of Shaker artifacts to the museum across the street. And the new owners, who have put together 500 acres of gorgeous rolling farmland, built vast barns in the spare Shaker style. In no time, they have assembled and nurtured a flock approaching 1,000 sheep. Guests are welcome to witness the operation of the 48-station milking parlor, and in the adjoining barn, adorable newborn lambs cavort and gambol around their mothers.

Rooms in the main house and in adjoining cottages are faultlessly decorated. Four-poster beds have mattresses covered with fleece-filled pads, the baths have etched glasses and more thick, wraparound towels than any two people are likely to need. Most rooms have views of the flocks whirling across the meadows; four have working fireplaces. At night, a sheepskin is laid beside the bed to cuddle the feet upon arising. No smoking.

Dining/Entertainment: Those cute animals on the grounds might make it hard for sensitive folk to dine at night on leg of lamb and spicy lamb sausage in the 45-seat dining room, but there are always options on a menu that is changed daily. Chef Melissa Kelly makes maximum use of the farm's products and of produce from the upper Hudson Valley.

WILLIAMSTOWN

Entering the town on Route 7 or intersecting Route 2, 23 miles north of Lenox, you'll arrive at a central green shaded by tall trees. In the middle is a weathered building that looks authentic, but turns out to be a replica of a 1753 dwelling. It was made with period tools in celebration of the town's bicentennial. Both the community and its prestigious liberal-arts college were named for Col. Ephraim Williams, who was killed in 1755 in one of the French and Indian Wars. He bequeathed the land for creation of a school and a town. His college grew, spreading east from the central common along both sides of Main Street (Route 2). Since it has been around for more than 200 years, every new building was erected in one of the styles popular at the time of construction. That makes Main Street a virtual museum of institutional architecture, with representatives of the Georgian, Federalist, Gothic Revival, Romanesque, and Victorian modes and a few that are yet to be labeled. They stand at dignified distances from each other, so what might have been a tumultuous visual hodgepodge is a stately lesson in historical design.

A free weekly newspaper, *The Advocate,* produces useful guides to both the northern and southern Berkshires. For a copy, send a check for $3.50 to *The Advocate,* P.O. Box 95, 38 Spring St., Williamstown, MA 01267. An unattended **information booth** at the corner of North Street (Route 7) and Main Street (Route 2) has an abundance of pamphlets and brochures free for the taking.

THE WILLIAMSTOWN THEATRE FESTIVAL

Williamstown's premier attraction each summer is the **Williamstown Theatre Festival,** Adams Memorial Theatre, Main Street, P.O. Box 517, MA 01267 (☎ **413/ 597-3400**). Staging classic and new plays during its performance season (late June through August), the festival attracts many top actors and directors. There are two venues: The Main Stage presents works by major playwrights, while the Other Stage sometimes features more experimental plays. Ticket prices range from $14 to $32, depending upon venue and performance date. The summer's schedule is usually announced by March. It's not too difficult to get tickets, except at the last minute.

ART MUSEUMS

✪ **Sterling and Francine Clark Art Institute.** 225 South St. ☎ **413/458-9545.** Admission free. Sept–June Tues–Sun 10am–5pm; July–Aug daily 10am–5pm.

The eponymous Mr. Clark was an art lover. He was also an heir to the Singer fortune, which allowed him to pursue his avocation and bestow this remarkable repository upon his community. Clark's endowment funded the modern wing to the original white marble neoclassical building and covered all acquisitions, upkeep, and recent renovations; in addition, he specified in his bequest that no admission fees be charged.

It is a remarkable gift, for this is not the collection of an undisciplined, self-absorbed millionaire. Within these walls are canvases by Renoir (34), Degas, Gauguin, Toulouse-Lautrec, Pissarro, and their predecessor, Corot. While they are the stars, there are also 15th- and 16th-century Dutch portraitists, English and European genre and landscape painters, and Americans Sargent and Homer, as well as fine porcelain, silverware, and antique furnishings. This qualifies as one of the great cultural resources of the Berkshires and the state.

Williams College Museum of Art. Main St. ☎ **413/597-2429.** Admission free. Tues–Sat (and some Mon holidays) 10am–5pm, Sun 1–5pm.

The second, lesser leg of Williamstown's two prominent art repositories exists in large part due to the college's collection of almost 400 paintings by the American modernists Maurice and Charles Prendergast. Some of their works are always rotated into view, and while they are of moderate interest, visitors are more likely to be drawn to such names as Juan Gris, Fernand Léger, Giorgio De Chirico, James Whistler, and Pablo Picasso. These are salted with more contemporary pieces by Andy Warhol and Edward Hopper and supplemented by frequently changed temporary exhibitions. The striking three-story entrance atrium was designed by prominent architect Charles Moore.

Outdoor Pursuits

Waubeeka Golf Links, Routes 7 and 43, South Williamstown, MA 01267 (☎ 413/458-5869), is open to the public, with highest weekend greens fees of $30. The clubhouse can seat 150 people in three dining rooms.

Mount Greylock State Reservation contains the highest peak (3,487 ft.) in Massachusetts and a section of the Appalachian Trail. A road allows cars to be driven almost to the summit, where the War Memorial Tower is located—even the sedentary visitor can enjoy 360° vistas of the Taconic and Hoosac ranges, far into Vermont and New York.

More active people will find hiking trails radiating from the parking lot near **Bascom Lodge,** P.O. Box 1800, Lanesboro, MA 01237 (☎ 413/743-1591 or 413/443-0011), a grandly rustic creation of the Civilian Conservation Corps in the New Deal thirties. Simple dormitory beds and four private rooms are available by the night from mid-May to late October. Rates on Fridays and Saturdays and all of August are $20–$25 for adults in bunk rooms, $62 for private rooms. Members of the Appalachian Mountain Club receive discounts. Dinners are available by reservation. Look for North Main Street off Route 7 in Lanesboro.

Shopping

In South Williamstown, the white frame building on the right (going north on Route 7) looks like a recycled general store, and it is. Once a basic small town emporium, **The Store at Five Corners,** Routes 7 and 43 (☎ 413/458-3176), now stocks gifts and upscale food for takeout, picnics, and eating on premises: pàtés, baguettes, French cheeses, wines, deli meats, and salads.

Saddleback Antiques, 1395 Cold Spring Rd. (☎ 413/458-5852), features country, wicker, and Victorian furniture and a variety of collectibles, while **Collectors Warehouse,** 105 North St. (☎ 413/458-9686), has a little bit of everything—jewelry, books, dolls, furniture, glassware. Both are on Route 7, the first to the south of the town center, the second slightly to the north.

Where to Stay

This is a college town, so in addition to the usual peak periods of July, August, and the October foliage season, lodgings fill up during graduation (late May to early June) and on football weekends.

Field Farm Guesthouse. 554 Sloan Rd., Williamstown, MA 01262. ☎ and fax **413/458-3135.** 5 rms. TEL. $100 double. DISC, MC, V. Follow Rte. 7 to its intersection with Rte. 43. Turn west, then make an immediate right turn on Sloan Rd. Continue 1 mile to the Field Farm entrance, on the right.

After an extended vacation of B&B hopping, there may come a time when one more tilted floor or wobbly Windsor chair will send even a devout inn lover over the edge. Here's one antidote. In 1948, this pristine example of postwar modern architecture rose in the middle of a spectacularly scenic 294-acre estate. Most of the rooms look over meadows to Mount Greylock. The living room is equipped with a telescope to view the beavers and waterfowl on the lake a hundred yards away. The setting is so lovely, actor Christopher Reeve used it as a backdrop for his wedding. Most of the furniture, of the Scandinavian Modern school, was made to order for the house. Rooms are spare, in muted colors. Three have decks; two have fireplaces. A pool and tennis court are available to guests. Breakfasts are hearty meals of waffles and five-cheese omelets utilizing fruits, herbs, and vegetables grown on the property. Well-behaved children are welcome. No smoking.

Orchards Inn. 222 Adams Rd., Williamstown, MA 01267. ☎ **800/225-1517** (outside MA) or 413/458-9611. Fax 413/458-3273. 49 rms. $125–$225 double. AE, CB, DC, MC, V.

Most guests seem satisfied with this small hotel at the eastern edge of town, although little about it will quicken your heartbeat. The management tries hard, though. Rooms have reproductions of English furniture, with fewer antiques than claimed in the brochures. Room fridges are stocked with soft drinks, the TVs have VCRs, and many rooms have working fireplaces. Terry-cloth robes are provided.

Dining/Entertainment: The restaurant kitchen seeks no new frontiers, with offerings like veal marsala and broiled salmon with broccoli and wild rice (main courses $16.50 to $23).

Services: The nightly turndown service includes a plate of cookies.

Facilities: There's an exercise room with Jacuzzi and sauna, an outdoor pool, and access to nearby tennis and golf.

Williams Inn. 1090 Main St. (Routes 7 and 2), Williamstown, MA 01267. ☎ **800/828-0133** or 413/458-9371. Fax 413/458-2767. 100 rms. A/C TV TEL. $100–$150 double. Children under 14 stay free in parent's room. AE, CB, DC, DISC, MC, V.

Despite the name, this is a standard motel, built in 1974 and containing most of the gadgets and conveniences today's traveler has come to expect. Even the smallest rooms are ample in dimension. The management accepts many bus tours, and this place is well suited to them. Pets are permitted on the first floor.

Dining/Entertainment: The main dining room serves such familiar fare as veal scallopini and chicken amandine (main courses $13.95 to $19.95) and there is also a tavern menu with burgers and such ($4.95 to $9.95). Weekend nights, live bands play forties music.

Facilities: Guests have access to an indoor pool, a Jacuzzi, and saunas.

WILLIAMSTOWN AFTER DARK

In addition to the Williamstown Theatre Festival (see above), the Williams College Department of Music sponsors diverse concerts and recitals, from choral groups to jazz ensembles. Call their 24-hour recorded **Concertline** at **413/597-3146** to learn of upcoming events. In addition, the Clark Art Institute (see "Art Museums," above) hosts frequent classical music events.

9

Connecticut

by Herbert Bailey Livesey

Connecticut resists generalization and confounds spinners of superlatives. It doesn't rank at the top or bottom of any major chart of virtues or liabilities, which makes it impossible to stuff into pigeonholes. Certainly compact—only 90 miles from west to east and 55 miles south to north—it is still three times the size of the smallest state, which happens to lie right next door. While parts of it are clogged with humanity, there are three other states even more congested—and much of the state is as empty and undeveloped as inland Maine.

By some measures, Connecticut's citizens are as wealthy as any in the country, but dozens of its cities and large towns are hollow shells of their prosperous 19th-century selves, beset by crime and poverty as bleak and intractable as they get. It can boast no dramatic geographical feature—no Smuggler's Notch, no Cape Cod—and its highest elevation is only 2,380 feet, a hill so far north it almost tips into the next state. Established in 1635 by disgruntled English settlers who didn't like the way things were going at the Plymouth Colony, it has long seemed spiritually divorced from the rest of New England, an appendage of New York, or a place to be traversed on the way from there to Boston.

All that might seem to constitute an identity crisis, and hardly makes Connecticut seem an appealing vacation destination. But a closer look reveals an abundance of reasons to slow down, to linger.

To a great extent, the state owes its existence to the presence of water. In addition to having Long Island Sound off of its southern coast, several significant rivers and their tributaries slice through the hills and coastal plain—the Housatonic, Naugatuck, Quinnipiac, Connecticut, and Thames. They provided power for the mills along their courses and the towns and cities that grew around them. Industry still drives most of the economy, despite the bucolic image that mention of the state often conjures, but the pollution of the water that it helped cause is being cleaned up, both in the rivers and the Sound.

Development, too, has slowed, helping to preserve for a little longer the scores of classic colonial villages from the Litchfield Hills to the Mystic coast. They are as placid and timeless as they have been for more than 3 centuries or as polished and sophisticated as transplanted urbanites can make them.

Connecticut

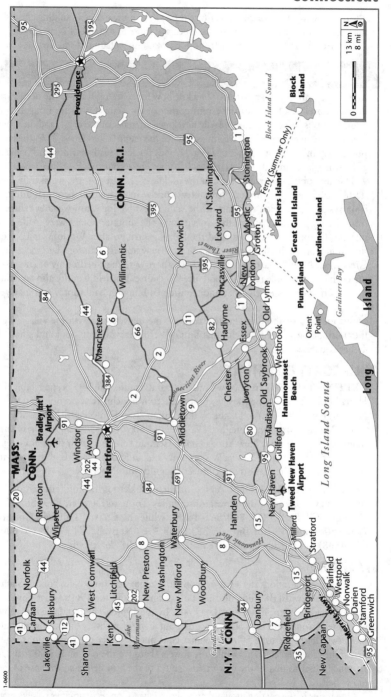

And the state's salty maritime heritage is palpable in the old boatbuilding and fishing villages at the mouths of its rivers, especially those to the east of New Haven.

Connecticut is New England's front porch. Pull up a chair and stay awhile.

1 The Gold Coast

Mansions, marinas, and apartment blocks elbow for space right up to the deeply indented shoreline of this southwestern corner of the state bordering Long Island Sound. This is one of the most heavily developed stretches of the coast, and, in terms of family incomes, one of the wealthiest (hence the name "Gold Coast"). As the land rises slowly inland from the water's edge, woods thicken, roads narrow, and pockets of New England unfold. Yacht country becomes horse country.

The first suburbs started to form in the middle of the last century, when train rails started radiating north and east from New York's Grand Central Terminal into the countryside. That made this part of the state accessible for warm-weather refugees from the big city, and eventually—inevitably—the summer homes were made permanent. Corporate executives liked the life of gentry, so after World War II, they started moving their companies closer to their new homes. Stamford became a city; Greenwich, New Canaan, Darien, and Westport were their bedrooms of choice—pricey, haughty, redolent of the good life. (Of course, Fairfield County also contains Bridgeport, a depressed city that once considered filing for bankruptcy and may yet do so.)

But for visitors, the fashionable exurbs are the draw, along with the villages farther north, especially Ridgefield, that hint of Vermont within an hour and a half of Times Square.

GOLD COAST ESSENTIALS

GETTING THERE   From New York and points south, take I-95 or, preferably the Hutchinson and Merritt parkways. From eastern Massachusetts and northern Connecticut, take I-84 south to Danbury, then Route 7 south into Fairfield County.

The **Metro North** commuter line (☎ **800/223-6052** or 212/532-4900) has many trains daily to and from New York's Grand Central Terminal, with stops at Greenwich, Stamford, Darien, Norwalk, Westport, and additional stations all the way to New Haven. Less frequent trains connect Danbury with Norwalk.

VISITOR INFORMATION   An information booklet for the northern part of the county is available from the **Housatonic Valley Tourism District,** P.O. Box 406, Danbury, CT 06813 (☎ **800/841-4488**), while the **Coastal Fairfield County Convention and Visitor Bureau,** 383 Main Ave., Norwalk, CT 06851 (☎**800/ 473-4868**) can provide informative materials about the Coast itself.

STAMFORD

A trickle of corporations started moving their headquarters from New York to Stamford (which lies just 38 miles northeast of Manhattan) in the 1960s. That flow became a steady stream, if not exactly a flood, by the 1980s. The trend was cut short by the recession at the end of that decade, but signs of recovery are strong, and almost two dozen Fortune 500 companies continue to direct their operations from here. They have erected shiny mid-rise towers that give the city of 108,000 an appearance closer to that of the new urban centers of the Sun Belt than to those of the Snow Belt.

One result is a lively downtown that other, weaker, Connecticut cities sorely envy. Roughly contained by Greylock Place, Tresser Boulevard, and Atlantic and Main streets, it has two theaters offering live entertainment, tree-lined streets with many viable shops and a large mall, pocket parks and plazas, and a number of stylish restaurants, sidewalk cafes, and nightclubs.

For further information, contact the **Greater Stamford Convention & Visitors Bureau,** One Landmark Sq., Stamford, CT 06902 (☎ **203/359-4761**).

AN ART MUSEUM

Whitney Museum of American Art at Champion. One Champion Plaza (Atlantic St. and Tresser Blvd.). ☎ **203/358-7630** or 203/358-7652. Free admission. Tues–Sat 11am–5pm.

This outpost of the generous parent institution in New York is housed on the ground floor of one of Stamford's shiny new downtown office towers. It displays the kinds of cutting-edge contemporary art that routinely infuriates and amuses critics and art-lovers at the mother museum. With no permanent collection, the artworks on view are traveling exhibitions, changed every 5 or 6 weeks.

OUTDOOR PURSUITS

A fine family-oriented resource is the **Stamford Museum & Nature Center,** 39 Scofieldtown Rd. (☎ **203/322-1646**), a mile north of Exit 35 of the Merritt Parkway (Route 15) and about 5 miles north of the city center. The Center has a large lake with mallards and Canada geese who brazenly waddle out of the water to beg tidbits from the picnickers at the nearby tables. Farther along is an open pen with a pair of river otters, and beyond that, the edge of the Hecksher Farm, a real, not re-created, complex of weathered barns and zigzag rail fences housing goats, sheep, chickens, dairy cattle, and—an exotic surprise!—peacocks. May and June are good months to go, when the animal population expands with the arrival of newborn chicks, kids, calves, and lambs. Feeding time is 9am. The farm has a country store stocked with souvenirs and snacks, and on the grounds are nature trails, an imaginative playground, a small planetarium, and an oddball Tudor-Gothic main house that has an art gallery. Open Monday to Saturday and holidays from 9am to 5pm. Admission $4 adults, $3 seniors and children under 14.

The **Bartlett Arboretum,** 151 Brookdale Rd. (☎ **203/322-6971**), is less compelling, perhaps, but quieter and as soothing as only a garden in the woods can be. Operated by the University of Connecticut, which has an adjoining campus, the horticultural preserve has several walking trails, none of them strenuous, and gardeners working with their blossoming charges are happy to chat with visitors about techniques and choices. The grounds are open daily from 8am to sunset year-round. Admission is free.

Recreational sailors might want to consider the bareboat fishing charters at **Yacht Haven,** Washington Boulevard (☎ **203/359-4500**), while less experienced or venturesome folk may prefer joining the professional crew of the *SoundWaters* (☎ **203/323-1978**), an 80-foot three-masted schooner. The 3-hour sailing trips are intended to be educational lessons on the ecology of the Sound. There are, however, sunset dinner cruises and singles sails, a total of 10 or so each summer. Fees are $10 to $25, depending on the event.

SHOPPING

Dedicated antique hounds and the simply curious will want to make time for **United House Wrecking,** 535 Hope St. (☎ **203/348-5371**). The name may not sound promising, but the company got its start selling architectural remnants salvaged from demolitions. When these pillars and mantelpieces were increasingly augmented with decorative garden fixtures and used antique furniture and accessories, they had to move here to contain the exploding inventory. Hankering for a stone pig? A 2-foot *David?* A pagoda? A 1930s gas pump? An amusement park bumper car? Or perhaps a chandelier with monkeys in frock coats holding candlesticks? They're here. Open Monday to Saturday from 9:30am to 5:30pm, Sunday noon to 5pm. (It's tough to find. From exit 9 of I-95, pick up Route 1, then Route 106 north, make a left on Glenbrook Road, which becomes Church Street, then turn right on Hope Street. Be sure you have a map, or detailed directions.)

WHERE TO DINE

Hacienda Don Emilio. 222 Summer St. (north of Main St.). ☎ **203/324-0577.** Main courses $10.95–$17.95. AE, CB, DC, DISC, MC, V. Mon–Fri 11:30am–2:30pm; Mon–Thurs 5–10pm, Fri 5–11pm, Sat noon–11pm, Sun 1–9pm. MEXICAN/SEAFOOD.

Expect no surprises on the menu, but aficionados of mainstream Mexican cookery aren't necessarily looking for invention. More important here is the quality of ingredients and their preparation (a noted cookbook author and the executive chef conduct regular on-site training of the kitchen staff). Specialties are the *pollo en mole poblano* and *puerco en salsa bruja*—chicken in chocolate-based sauce and pork simmered with tomatoes, onions, and hot peppers. A tasty bar menu has carefully executed smaller dishes, just the thing for a light lunch. Skip the ordinary combination plates.

Kathleen's. 25 Bank St. (between Park and Atlantic sts.). ☎ **203/323-7785.** Reservations recommended. Main courses $15.50–$22. AE, CB, DC, DISC, MC, V. Mon–Thurs 11:30am–3pm and 5–10pm; Fri–Sat 5–11pm. NEW AMERICAN.

This popular restaurant was named after the owner's mother and has the relaxed and informal ambiance that suggests it. In warm weather, tables with umbrellas take up the sidewalk outside, facing a leafy triangular plaza across the street. When the snow flies, the interior has a clubby atmosphere, with a paneled ceiling above the bar and baskets of flowers. Shirt-sleeved regulars occupy the bar, while garden club ladies mingle with executives in suits in the back. The menu ranges around the hemisphere, Jamaican jerk pork chop with black-bean salsa sharing menu space with a Tabasco-fired seafood gumbo, crowded with whole clams and plump shrimp. With the Palace Theatre, Rich Forum, and a new cineplex nearby, Kathleen's does brisk business at night, too.

STAMFORD AFTER DARK

Community and corporate leaders have long supported the cultural and popular performing arts in the city, which also gives rise to commercial performance spaces and nightclubs. The **Rich Forum** of the **Stamford Center for the Arts,** Atlantic Street and Tresser Boulevard (☎ 203/325-4466), presents professional productions with name actors of such successful Broadway and off-Broadway plays as *After-Play* and Edward Albee's *Three Tall Women,* while the **Palace Theatre,** 61 Atlantic St. (☎ 203/325-4466), offers musicals, rotating appearances by the Stamford Symphony Orchestra, Connecticut Grand Opera and Orchestra, and the Connecticut Ballet, and one-night stands by solo acts and traveling troupes like George Carlin, Judy Collins, and the Alvin Ailey Dance Theater.

Among the handful of downtown clubs is the **Art Bar,** 84 W. Park Place (☎ 203/973-0300), which has DJ rock for dancing, and jazz in a smaller room Thursday to Saturday, usually for a small cover charge. The **Terrace Club,** 1938 W. Main St. (☎ 203/961-9770), alternately features live acts and DJ dance nights.

NORWALK

Given the despair that grips many crime-ridden New England cities, the improvement of this city's once notorious South Norwalk neighborhood gladdens the heart. The rehabilitation of several blocks of 19th-century row houses is effectively transforming the T-shaped waterfront district into an increasingly prosperous and trendy area that has come to be called, inevitably, "SoNo." The transformation is far from complete, and decay still festers around the edges, but new shops, restaurants, and nightspots open weekly, a process that looks to be self-generating. The opening of the Maritime Aquarium was a prime motivation, and the district—bounded by Washington, Water, and North and South Main streets—is readily accessible from the South Norwalk railroad station.

SEEING THE SIGHTS

✪ Maritime Aquarium. 10 N. Water St. ☎ **203/852-0700.** Admission $7.75 adults, $7 seniors, $6.50 children 2–12; IMAX $6.50 adults, $5.50 seniors, $4.75 children; combination packages $12 adults, $10.50 seniors, $9.50 children. July through Labor Day daily 10am–6pm; Labor Day through June 10am–5pm.

Formerly the Maritime Center at Norwalk, this facility may have changed its name, but it remains the centerpiece of revitalized SoNo. In fact, the earlier name seems more inclusive, since part of the complex includes exhibits of dive suits, model ships, and full-sized vessels, including the *Tango,* which was *pedaled* across the Atlantic Ocean.

The main attractions, though, are the marine creatures and mammals on view. On the ground floor is an indoor-outdoor tank of harbor seals, which are found in nearby Long Island Sound. They are fed at 11:45am, and 1:45 and 3:45pm, when they wriggle up on the rocks and all but rest their heads in their handler's lap. Another exhibit features a pair of river otters, and the tanks beyond focus on fish and sea creatures found in Sound waters, from monster lobsters, flounder, and pollack to the more exotic sea robin, skate, and bristling sea ravens. And to make sure no one's expectations are unmet, there is a large tank of tiger sand sharks, swimming silently and eerily in unending circles, their fearsome mouths inches away from onlookers.

There are frequent, but palatable, ecological messages. The giant IMAX screen shows nature films that aren't necessarily confined to the seven seas. One recent show, for example, was *Africa: The Serengeti.*

Lockwood-Mathews Mansion Museum. 295 West Ave. ☎ **203/838-1434.** Admission $5 adults, $3 seniors and children 12 and under. Tues–Fri 11am–3pm, Sun 1–4pm. Closed mid-Dec to Jan. From I-95 southbound, take Exit 15; from I-95 northbound, take Exit 14.

Erected in 1864 for a financier by the unlikely name of LeGrand Lockwood, this four-story granite mansion covered with peaked and mansard slate roofs has 50 rooms arranged around a stunning skylit octagonal rotunda. Marble, gilt, intricately carved wood, marquetry, etched glass, and frescoes were commissioned and incorporated with abandon. It cost $1.2 million (real money back then). Visits are by 1-hour guided tour only.

CRUISES

Excursions to **Sheffield Island** and its historic lighthouse are offered by the **M/V Island Girl** (☎ 203/838-9444), a 60-passenger vessel that departs from Hope Dock, near the Maritime Aquarium at Washington and North Water streets. Weather permitting, the boat sets out two to four times daily, weekends from late May to late September and weekdays from late June to Labor Day. The round-trip takes about 1¹/₂ hours, with a 15-minute layover on the island. Fares are $9 for adults, $8 seniors, $7 children under 12. Special outings at extra cost include Thursday evening clambakes and occasional Sunday picnics. Call ahead.

Similarly, the oyster sloop *Hope* has "creature cruises" in winter to spot seals and bird life, and marine study cruises at other times, a service of the Marine Aquarium. Fares are $15 per person. Inquire and reserve ahead at ☎ 203/852-0700, ext. 206.

SHOPPING

Don't make a special trip, but **Stew Leonard's,** 100 Westport Ave. at Route 1 (☎ **203/847-7213**), isn't your average grocery store and is worth a quick look in passing. They say so themselves, with humongous signs reading WORLD'S LARGEST DAIRY STORE AS FEATURED IN *RIPLEY'S BELIEVE IT OR NOT.* The store's general jokey tone is established by a sign at the door, RULE #1: THE CUSTOMER IS ALWAYS RIGHT. RULE #2: IF THE CUSTOMER IS EVER WRONG, RE-READ RULE #1. Inside, you'll find a wall of signed photos of celebrity visitors and model trains running around the walls. Otherwise, those expecting a Disneyland of dairy and produce will be disappointed (talking, singing barnyard figures notwithstanding). Bulk quantities rather than wide selection is the name of the game, and most shoppers will find less variety than they expect of their neighborhood supermarket, despite the hoopla.

Serious shoppers have several choices. Mainstream goods are on sale at the renovated **Factory Outlets,** East Avenue (☎ **203/838-1349**), with discounted items from prominent manufacturers. Open daily, it's half a mile from Exit 16 of I-95, opposite the South Norwalk railroad station.

And poking among the boutiques and galleries along Washington and Main streets may produce a bargain or at least a surprise.

WHERE TO DINE

✪ **Amberjacks Coastal Grill.** 99 Washington St. (between Broad and Main sts.). ☎ **203/ 853-4332.** Main courses $16.95–$19.95. AE, MC, V. Daily noon–3pm; Sun–Thurs 5:30–10pm, Fri–Sat 5:30–11pm. CONTEMPORARY AMERICAN.

The Grill's owner/chef used to run a restaurant in Key West and this room looks as if he brought it with him intact from Duval Street. There's the bar, shaped like the prow of a boat, the colorful paintings with watery motifs, and the spidery Italianate lights. And there's the food—bold, distinctive flavors, with liberal use of tropical fruits and Asian spices. A simple example is the yellowfin tuna burger with ginger and mango-papaya "ketchup" on a Portuguese onion roll, accompanied by an Oriental vegetable salad with a pile of taro chips. The chef also offers "small plates"— essentially large appetizers costing $5.95 to $8.95—perfect for a light lunch or as side orders to be shared at dinner. There is a jazz combo Thursday night, blues on Fridays, local bands on some Saturdays, and outdoor tables on pleasant days. The lively Friday happy hour draws attractive 30-ish singles.

Barcelona. 63 N. Main St. (east of Washington St.). ☎ **203/899-0088** or 203/854-9088. Main courses $16–$18. MC, V. Sun–Thurs 5pm–midnight, Fri–Sat 5pm–2am. TAPAS/ MEDITERRANEAN.

This used to be a two-part operation, but the cosmopolitan tapas bar drew the lion's share of attention, so it now occupies the entire space. Dressed up to look like a designer bar from Barcelona's tony Eixample district, it features tapas, the Spanish bar snacks, along with larger appetizers and entrees. The kitchen isn't doctrinaire about recipes, which range all over the Mediterranean for inspiration, from *antipasti* to *meze*. The back bar is lined with cracked ice, the bed for platters of the night's delectables. They might include grilled chorizos with green lentils, leg of lamb with white-bean salad, or the potato called *tortilla*. Barcelona is fully licensed, with 8 beers on draft and 12 red and white wines sold by the glass.

WESTPORT

After World War II, the housing crunch had young couples scouring the metropolitan area for affordable housing lying along the three main routes of what is now known as the Metro North transit system. Some of them wound up in this pretty village beside the Saugatuck River, several miles inland from Long Island Sound (47 miles northeast of New York City, 29 miles southwest of New Haven). Most of the new commuter class thought it too far away from Manhattan—3 hours a day on the train plus additional transport at either end—and it was deemed the archetype of the far-out bedroom communities that were dubbed the "exurbs"—beyond suburban. Notable for its large contingent of people in the creative crafts, primarily commercial artists, advertising copywriters, art directors, and their fellows, the town was also appealing to CEOs and higher-level executives, many of whom solved their commuting problem by moving their offices to nearby Stamford. The result is a bustling community with surviving elements of its rural New England past wrapped in a sheen of Big Apple panache.

For further information contact the **Westport Chamber of Commerce,** 180 Post Rd. E., Westport, CT 06881 (☎ **203/227-9234**).

A NEARBY TRIBUTE TO A CHARLATAN

The Barnum Museum. 820 Main St. (at Frontage St.), Bridgeport, CT 06604. ☎ **203/ 331-9881.** Admission $5 adults, $4 seniors and students, $3 children 4–18. Tues–Sat 10am–4:30pm, Sun noon–4:30pm; in July–Aug also Mon 10am–4:30pm.

Phineas T. Barnum was Bridgeport's most colorful citizen, even though his career as huckster extraordinaire took him around the world. While this museum doesn't contain all his collections of circus art and memorabilia, there's enough here to justify an in-and-out trip to seedy downtown Bridgeport. See the famous Fiji "mermaid"! A two-headed calf! A detailed scale model of the Barnum & Bailey Three-Ring Circus! A thorough renovation was completed in 1989, and a new wing by architect Richard Meier contains temporary exhibits.

OUTDOOR PURSUITS

One of several state parks making the most of their Sound-side locations, **Sherwood Island State Park,** P.O. Box 188, Green Farms, CT 06436 (☎ **203/226-6983**), has two long swimming beaches separated by a grove of trees sheltering dozens of picnic tables with grills. Surf fishing is a possibility from designated areas, and the park has concession stands and rest rooms. Don't make a special effort to check out the amateurish "nature center." Open from 8am to sunset. Pets aren't allowed April 15 to September 30. Get there from Exit 18 of I-95 or U.S. 1, following the road called the Sherwood Island Connector. Admission is $8 for out-of-state cars.

West of the town center is **The Nature Center for Environmental Activities,** 10 Woodside Lane (☎ **203/227-7253**). Its 62 acres have several walking trails, a wildlife rehab center, and a building with live animals and an aquarium. Admission is $1 adults, 50¢ children 3 to 14. Open Monday to Saturday 9am to 5pm, Sunday 1 to 4pm.

Sailboats can be rented and lessons arranged at the **Longshore Sailing School,** Longshore Club Park, 260 S. Compo Rd. (☎ **203/226-4646**), about 2 miles south of the Boston Post Road (U.S. 1).

SHOPPING

Window-shopping along Main Street is diverting, although most of the shops are outlets of the chains often seen in malls, including **Brooks Brothers, Talbots, The Gap, Eddie Bauer, Banana Republic, Williams-Sonoma, Crabtree & Evelyn,** and **Ann Taylor.** Less conventional is **Lillian August,** 17 Main St. (☎ **203/ 629-1539**), with a large collection of paintings, rugs, overstuffed chairs and sofas, and related accessories. Owing allegiance to no specific style, it looks as if it might have been put together by Laura Ashley on speed.

The Greatest Flack on Earth

Bombast, hyperbole, and boggling fabrication were the tools of his trade, and Phineas Taylor Barnum wielded them with whatever surgical or blunderbuss skill the situation required. His name is forever linked to the Barnum & Bailey Circus—"The Greatest Show on Earth"—but he didn't get into that relatively respectable business until he was past 60. He was one of the most flamboyant figures of the last tumultuous century, and his life spanned most of it.

Born in Bethel, Conn., in 1810, he is most often associated with New York, where he fashioned a career based largely upon his ability to grab the spotlight and bang the drums until everyone wanted to believe his latest outrageous tale.

There was his trumpeted exhibit of the "Fiji Mermaid," a monkey's upper body sewn to the stuffed tail end of a fish. And his copy of the 10-foot stone creature called the "Cardiff Giant," the original of which proved to be a sculpture, not a fossil, making P.T.'s version a hoax of a fraud.

Tom Thumb was real, though, if not his name (which was Charles Stratton) or the title of "General" that Barnum bestowed upon him. Thumb was 33 inches tall, and Barnum took him around the world, making them both rich. Chang and Eng, Siamese twins, were genuine, too, but are said to have hated P.T. for adding them to his horde of bearded ladies and other "freaks." Barnum's greatest coup may have been arranging the wildly successful tour of the Swedish singer Jenny Lind, whom he dubbed "The Swedish Nightingale," even though he had never seen or heard her.

Retiring from show biz in 1855, Barnum served terms as a Republican representative from Fairfield in the Connecticut legislature and a 1-year term as mayor of Bridgeport. He also spent some time in the Danbury jail, for libel.

It wasn't until he lost his fortune through bad investments that he created his circus, in 1871. After becoming partners with James A. Bailey, he procured the services of one of his greatest attractions, Jumbo, a $6^1/_2$-ton elephant. Jumbo was hit by a freight train in 1885. His corpse was stuffed and presented to the Barnum Museum at Tufts University in Medford, Mass.

Barnum outlived his prized pachyderm, but only by a few years; he died in 1891, one of the greatest showmen and hucksters the world had ever seen.

WHERE TO STAY & DINE

✪ **Inn at National Hall.** 2 Post Rd. (at the west end of the Saugatuck Bridge), Westport, CT 06880. ☎ **800/628-4255** or 203/221-1351. Fax 203/221-0276. 15 rms, 7 suites. A/C TV TEL. $195–$395 double. Rates include continental breakfast. AE, DC, MC, V.

It's nearly impossible to go wrong choosing a member of Relais & Chateaux for a night's stay, assuming money is no object. This riverside hotel was offered virtually instant membership into that association, and, if anything, stands above the already high standards. You know something special is going on as soon as you enter the elevator, which turns out to be a trompe l'oeil representation of an estate library, complete with a skulker betwixt the volumes. There is, in fact, a playful elegance on display throughout.

Space doesn't allow me to detail the voluptuous furnishings, baroque canopied beds, and the rarely seen antiques that fill the public rooms and bilevel suites. (Bathrobes and slippers conveniently placed at hand, plus VCRs in the rooms, are only the latest examples of the management's constant fine-tuning.) But it's improbable that you've seen anything like this elsewhere. The Inn's 1873 brick building was a furniture store, bank, town hall, and office building before it finally realized its destiny as an exquisitely decorated and furnished hotel. No smoking.

Dining/Entertainment: The in-house restaurant, Zanghi, is superior to anything within miles. Its cuisine is updated French/Italian, with unrepentantly lavish use of foie gras and similar ingredients. Main courses are $16.50 to $28.50.

Services: Concierge, 24-hour room service, dry cleaning/laundry, newspaper, nightly turndown, in-room massages, twice-daily maid service, secretarial services, valet parking.

WESTPORT AFTER DARK

One of the oldest theaters on the strawhat circuit, the **Westport Playhouse,** 25 Powers St. (☎ **203/227-4177**), is nearing its 70th year. Outdoor musical performances are offered at **Levitt Pavilion,** off Jesup Green (☎ **203/226-7600**). Both are near the center of town.

RIDGEFIELD

No town in Connecticut has a more imposing main street—Ridgefield's is almost 100 feet wide, lined with ancient towering elm, maple, and oak trees, and bordered by massive 19th-century houses set well back on plush carpets of lawn. Impressive at any time of the year, it is in its glory during the brief blaze of foliage season. Only a little over an hour from New York City (58 miles northeast, to be exact), the town is nonetheless a true evocation of the New England character, a popular weekend getaway for stressed Manhattanites.

There was a settlement here as early as 1709—and at least one building, the Keeler Tavern, survives from those years. In 1777, Benedict Arnold, who was to cause mischief all over this state and nearby New York, was still on the side of the rebels. That April he commanded American troops against a British force retreating from Danbury to the north. After a fierce skirmish, the Redcoats smashed through Arnold's barricades and escaped to the coast. It remains known as the Battle of Ridgefield.

AN ART MUSEUM & HISTORIC TAVERN

Aldrich Museum of Contemporary Art. 258 Main St. (near the intersection of Routes 35 and 33 at the south end of Main St.). ☎ **203/438-4519.** Admission $3 adults, $2 seniors and students. Tues–Sun 1–5pm.

The eponymous patron of the museum is past 90, but his superb collection of paintings and sculptures from the second half of the 20th century continues to grow. The original white clapboard structure has been more than doubled in size with a harmonious addition, and a professional curator now oversees the permanent holdings and organizes frequent temporary exhibitions, concerts, films, lectures, and other events. The outdoor sculptures set up in the side and backyards can be viewed anytime, even when the museum itself is closed (which may happen, as hours fluctuate with the season and current exhibitions).

Keeler Tavern. 132 Main St. ☎ **203/431-0815.** Admission $4 adults, $2 seniors, $1 children. Wed and Sat–Sun 1–4pm.

This 1715 tavern was providing sustenance to travelers between Boston and New York long before the Revolutionary War, but that conflict provided it with its object of greatest note. A British cannonball is imbedded in one of its walls, presumably fired during the Battle of Ridgefield in 1777. Period furnishings have been installed to set the tone, and costumed guides tell the story.

And the tavern has another claim to fame: It was long the summer home of architect Cass Gilbert (1849 to 1934), who designed the Supreme Court Building in

Washington and was a key figure in the construction of the George Washington Bridge.

Shopping

Apart from the usual antique shops and the funk of strip malls and franchise enterprises north of the town center on Route 35, one of the most interesting stops for devoted foodies is the **Hay Day Market,** 21 Governor St. (☎ **203/431-4400**), in a shopping center behind the shops that line Main Street. Open daily, it is about as upscale a food market as exists outside of Beverly Hills or Manhattan, with sections devoted to excellent produce, prepared foods, baked goods, charcuterie, cheeses, and fresh flowers. Check out items like Camembert en brioche and platters of pasta primavera.

Where to Stay & Dine

The Elms. 500 Main St. (Rte. 35, at the north end of town), Ridgefield, CT 06877. ☎ **203/ 438-2541.** 20 rms. A/C TV TEL. $99–$130 double. Rates include breakfast. AE, CB, DC, MC, V.

A pair of buildings constitute Ridgefield's oldest (1799) operating inn. Facing them from the street, the one on the right has the reception desk and most of the rooms. Inside, it has the ambiance of a contemporary small hotel with the conveniences many travelers desire as well as rooms with canopied four-poster beds.

Dining/Entertainment: The Elms Restaurant & Tavern (☎ **203/438-9206**), now in the hands of a celebrated chef, is in the other building, where a 1996 renovation has freshened the dining room and informal tavern (where the prices are lower) without masking its 18th-century origins. Food served is of the Creative American variety, utilizing regional ingredients. Reservations are essential on weekends. A dining porch is inviting in good weather.

West Lane Inn. 22 West Lane (off Rte. 35), Ridgefield, CT 06877. ☎ **203/438-7323.** Fax 860/438-7325. 20 rms. A/C TV TEL. $115–$165 double. Rates include breakfast. AE, DC, MC, V. Driving north from Wilton on Rte. 7, turn west on Rte. 35 at the edge of town.

An inn to fit most images of a romantic country getaway, this place also works for businesspeople, since it offers modem jacks and voice mail in every room. Several rooms have fireplaces and all have queen-sized four-poster beds. The 1849 house sports a fine oak staircase and stands on a property blessed with giant shade trees.

While there is no formal dining room, the **Inn at Ridgefield** (☎ **203/438-8282**) next door serves lunch and dinner daily. (Reservations are required on weekends, and men are expected to wear jackets at dinner.)

2 The Litchfield Hills

When the Hamptons got too pricey, too visible, and too chichi back in the 1980s, a lot of stockbrokers, CEOs, and celebs started discovering the Litchfield Hills, arguably the most fetchingly rustic yet sophisticated part of Connecticut.

The topography and, to an extent, the microculture of the region are defined by the river that runs through it, the Housatonic. Broad but not deep enough for vessels larger than canoes, it waters farms and villages and forests along its course, provides opportunities for recreational angling and float trips, and, over the millennia, has helped to shape these foothills, which merge with the Massachusetts Berkshires.

Men in overalls and CAT caps still stand on the porches of general stores, their breath steaming in the bracing autumn air. Others wade into the river, working the riffs and rills with long looping casts of trout flies hand-tied over the winter. Churches

The Litchfield Hills

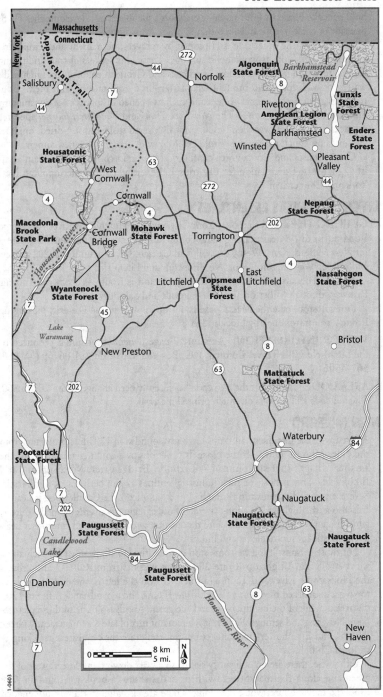

hold pancake breakfast fund-raisers; neighbors squabble about development. That's one side of these bucolic hills, less than 2 hours from Times Square.

Increasingly, the other side is fashioned by refugees, permanent and temporary, from New York and its workaholic suburbs. These chic seekers of tranquillity and real estate fled to pre-Revolutionary saltboxes and Georgian colonials on Litchfield's warren of back roads and brought Manhattan-bred expectations with them. Boutiques fragrant with designer coffees and cachets opened in spaces once occupied by luncheonettes and feed stores. The *New York Times* and *Wall Street Journal* appeared on racks next to local weeklies. Restaurants discovered sushi and sun-dried tomatoes and just how much money they could get away with charging the newcomers.

Compromises and city-country conflicts aside, the Litchfield Hills remain a satisfying all-season destination for day trips and overnights from metropolitan New York and Connecticut.

LITCHFIELD HILLS ESSENTIALS

GETTING THERE   From New York City, take the Hutchinson River Parkway to I-684 north to I-84 east, taking Exit 7 onto Route 7 north. Continue on Route 7 for New Milford, Kent, West Cornwall, and Canaan. Or, pick up Route 202 at New Milford for Washington Depot, New Preston, and Litchfield.

An especially attractive entrance into the region is Route 44 from the Taconic Parkway, through Millerton and into Lakeville and Salisbury.

From Boston, take the Massachusetts Turnpike west to the Lee exit, picking up Route 7 south from nearby Stockbridge.

VISITOR INFORMATION   A useful 40-page *Unwind* brochure is produced by the **Litchfield Hills Travel Council,** P.O. Box 968, Litchfield, CT 06759 (☎ **860/ 567-4506**).

AREA CODE   Note that the area code has recently been changed from 203 to 860. The old code still appears on much printed material.

NEW MILFORD

A gateway to the Litchfield Hills, this town was founded in 1703 by immigrants from the older Milford, down on the coast. It functions as a commercial center for the smaller villages that surround it—Roxbury, Bridgewater, Washington, and Brookfield—and as host for such industrial entities as Kimberly-Clark and Nestlé. Several rivers and streams run through it, and dammed Lake Candlewood is nearby. It is also at the high end of a long stretch of the egregiously overdeveloped Route 7, which is clogged with minimalls, auto dealerships, and ill-conceived enterprises dealing in plastic lawn ornaments and hubcaps.

For those reasons, it is a welcome stop on the drive north, if only for lunch and a short stroll. Turn right on Route 202 where it splits from Route 7 and crosses the Housatonic River and a railroad track. Up on the left is one end of the long town green, marked by an early–World War II tank and a bandstand. A fire in 1902 destroyed many of the buildings around the green, so this isn't one of those picture-book New England settings. Rather, it is a pleasant mix of late Victoriana, early Greek Revival, and Eisenhower-era architecture, not to ignore the requisite First Congregational Church.

Otherwise, there are no obligatory sights, so a walk down Bank Street, west of the green and along Railroad Street, with its crafts shops, a bookstore, and an Arte Moderne movie house, won't take long. There are also almost a dozen unheralded restaurants of various levels of accomplishment (from pizza-and-brew to ambitious storefront fusion), and at least half of them family-friendly.

CANDLEWOOD LAKE

Candlewood Lake (☎ 860/354-6928) is the third-largest man-made lake in the eastern United States. It has a finger that pokes into New Milford, but the area with the most recreational facilities is a few miles to the east. From New Milford, drive north on Route 7 about 2¹/₂ miles, turn west on Route 37 toward and through Sherman, then south on Route 39 to the unfortunately named **Squantz Pond State Park** (☎ 860/424-3200). With over 170 acres along the lakeshore, it offers swimming, ice-skating, fishing, hiking and cycling trails, picnic grounds, rental canoes, and a boat launch.

SHOPPING

When conductor Skitch Henderson and his wife Ruth decided to put together **The Silo,** 44 Upland Rd. (☎ 860/355-0300), they didn't allow themselves to be hemmed in by conventional categories. Housed in their old farm buildings are an arts-and-crafts gallery, a store selling kitchen implements and packaged food products, and a cooking school where noted chefs and food critics give classes most weekends. Open daily from 10am to 5pm. Find it off Route 202, 4 miles north of New Milford center; watch closely for the unobtrusive sign on the right.

WHERE TO STAY

There are good reasons for families to consider making New Milford their base for exploring the Litchfield Hills. Inns in the towns farther north typically exclude children under 12 (not to mention pets). Smokers are restricted, too, and room rates fluctuate wildly according to the day of the week and season. But the following inn welcomes children and smokers and is relatively inexpensive. Because it does good business during the week as well as on weekends, its rates are stable.

Heritage Inn. 34 Bridge St. (opposite Railroad Station), New Milford, CT 06776. ☎ **860/ 354-8883.** Fax 860/350-5543. 20 rms. A/C TV TEL. $79–$94 double. Rates include breakfast. Children under 5 stay free in parent's room; older kids sharing their parents' room are charged $15. AE, DISC, MC, V.

This sky blue building started life as a tobacco warehouse in 1870, but after the conversion to an inn over a century later, it looks more like a railroad hotel in the Old West, with its high ceilings and long central hall that runs all the way from front to back. The heavy old beams were left exposed, a nice touch, for the decor is otherwise uninspired, though perfectly comfortable and hardly claustrophobic. The somewhat more spacious upstairs rooms pull together better visually, and several have sitting areas. Breakfast goes well beyond the continental standard, with French toast, pancakes, and eggs any way, including made-to-order omelets with a variety of fillings. The *New York Times* is available. While the inn stands next to the railroad tracks, only an occasional freight train rumbles past, since commuter service was ended years ago. In deference to the inn's many business guests, smoking is permitted. Pets are accepted.

WHERE TO DINE

There are many dining choices along Bank and Railroad streets and out along nearby Route 7.

The Bistro Café. 31 Bank St. (west of the town green). ☎ **860/355-3266.** Main courses $13.95–$17.95. AE, MC, V. Mon–Sat 11am–3pm and 4:30–10pm, Sun noon–4pm and 4:30–10pm. NEW AMERICAN & THAI.

Consensus points to this redundantly named eatery as the pick of the local litter. The late-19th-century structure has served many functions, including funeral parlor. Now, its walls are stripped to the brick and the tables are dark polished wood, each set with a blue flask of olive oil. The lunch menu runs to soups, salads, and sandwiches, most of it given interesting twists, as with the chicken club with spicy andouille sausage. At night, there are a few Southern flourishes—oven-roasted catfish and Cajun fries, for example—but no fervid culinary allegiances. In fact, one member of the squad of chefs specializes in Thai dishes, making it necessary to add a special page of his creations to the already eclectic menu.

Upstairs is the **Tap Room,** with a convivial bar at its center, open only in the evenings and offering a menu of light dishes. It's closed Sunday and Monday.

WOODBURY

The chief distinction of this attractive town strung along several miles of Route 6, west of Waterbury, is its number of antique stores—at least 40, by rough count. That means that on weekends in good weather the main road is clogged with cars trolling for treasures and progress can be slow.

ANTIQUES

Shoppers are drawn here for antiques of every sort, from funky to obscure to elegant, with a few contemporary crafts thrown in. Pick up a copy of the directory of shops produced by the **Woodbury Antiques Dealers Association** at one of the member stores to winnow down the list.

Two to check are at the intersection of Routes 6 and 317. **Rosebush Farm,** 289 Main St. (☎ **860/266-9114**), traffics in the kinds of outsized "statement" pieces that are catnip for interior designers, while **Nancy Fierberg Antiques,** 289 Main St. (☎ **860/263-4957**), carries American country furniture and folk art such as weather vanes and barbershop poles.

A variation on the prevailing menu of aged or collectible goods is **A Merry-Go-Round of Fine Crafts,** 319 Main St. (☎ **203/263-2920**). Crowding its six rooms are traditional crafts of every sort, all by Connecticut artisans. Among the items on display are wheat weavings, handmade picture and mirror frames, dolls, samplers, stenciled floorcloths, and, for reasons known only to the artist, pictures painted on saw blades—something for every taste. Open Wednesday to Monday from January to Easter.

MORE TO SEE & DO

About the only scrap of surviving history worth mentioning is the 1750 **Glebe House,** on Hollow Road (☎ **203/263-2855**), a quarter mile west of Route 6 on a street of fine 18th-century houses. A *glebe* was a property given to a preacher, in this case an Episcopal bishop, as partial compensation for his services. Inside are furnishings true to the period; outside is the **Gertrude Jekyll Garden,** named for a prominent landscape gardener of this century. Open April through November, Wednesday to Sunday from 1 to 4pm. Admission is $4 for adults, $1 children under 12.

North of Woodbury on Route 6, watch for Flanders Road forking to the left. Three miles along, on the right, is the office building for **Flanders Nature Center** (☎ **203/263-3711**). The organization that runs it is also a land trust, keeping its 1,300 acres in four different towns out of the hands of developers. Trail maps of the various properties are available in the office, which is open Monday to Friday from 9am to 5pm; the trails, dawn to dusk.

WHERE TO STAY

Merryvale. 1204 Main St. (Rte. 6), Woodbury, CT 06798. ☎ **860/266-0800.** 4 rms. $105–$130 double. Rates include breakfast. MC, V.

South of the town center, this 2-century-old house was converted into a B&B back in 1951, but the present owners took over only a few years ago. A striking focal point is a wall painting of an American eagle, original to the house, revealed during the renovation process. One of the owners is an architect and the other worked in fashion, accounting for the remarkably good taste displayed throughout. The 4-acre property slopes down to the Pomperaug River. Breakfasts are described as "historic," featuring dishes from the colonial and Federal periods.

WHERE TO DINE

Good News Café. 694 Main St. (Rte. 6). ☎ **203/266-4663.** Reservations recommended on weekends. Main courses $12–$20. AE, MC, V. Mon and Wed–Sat 11:30am–2:30pm and 5–10pm, Sun noon–3pm and 5–10pm (continuous service in cafe bar). NEW AMERICAN.

Owner Carole Peck used to have a restaurant in New Milford, where she packed a scrapbook with glowing reviews. She's doing the same at this location. Part of the secret is that she doesn't see her work as nuclear fission. It's a fun place, with a cheery young staff, a constantly changing menu, and rooms painted in blazing primary colors. The informal cafe-bar has old 45 records hanging from the ceiling, and the paintings on the walls—many of them quite good—are all for sale. There is a dining terrace and jazz combos perform Saturday night.

And the food? Make it Europe meets Asia, touching down in various parts of America along the way, with the resulting concoctions often deployed on the same plate. Examples: curried linguine in apple-carrot sauce with Asian vegetables or roasted monkfish with tomato-fennel essence and caramelized red-onion ravioli. If that sounds too clever, be assured that it works—usually—and with the bonus that nearly all the entrees qualify as heart-healthy. Desserts, however, tend to the rich, gooey, and caloric.

WASHINGTON & WASHINGTON DEPOT

Settled in 1734, its name changed in 1779 to honor the first American president, Washington occupies the crown of a hill beside Route 47. Its village green, with the impressive 1802 Congregational Meeting House surrounded by uniformly white buildings with black shutters and sheltered by towering shade trees, is an example of a municipal arrangement found all over New England but rarely to such near-perfection. The village is home to the exclusive Gunnery School and the renowned Mayflower Inn.

Adjacent Washington Depot, down the hill beside the Shepaug River, serves as the commercial center, with a small cluster of mostly upscale shops.

WHAT TO SEE & DO

Nearby **Steep Rock Reservation** is a lovely spot for hiking, fly-fishing, or cross-country skiing. (Dogs are allowed here off-leash.)

The traveling series of musical events known as the **Armstrong Chamber Concerts** usually alights in Washington on four Sunday afternoons in spring and fall (other appearances are in Greenwich and Lenox, Mass.). Performances are in the Congregational Church.

A worthwhile detour takes drivers down Curtis Road, past the private Gunnery School to **The Institute for American Indian Studies,** on Route 199 (☎ **860/868-0518**). The small repository of Native American crafts and artifacts is presented with sensitivity and, for the most part, without polemics. A sound track of birdsong and running water plays in the galleries of permanent and temporary exhibits. These baskets, pots, tools, and artworks are fascinating in themselves, but they are used to tell the story of Amerindians past and present, mostly of those who lived and still live in this region. Displays are supplemented by workshops, performances, films, and storytelling sessions. Down a nearby path is a re-creation of an Algonquian Village. Open Monday to Saturday from 10am to 5pm, Sunday noon to 5pm (closed Monday and Tuesday from January through March). Admission is $4 adults, $2 children 6 to 16.

In Washington Depot, consider putting together a picnic from the delectable array of quiches, pizzas, and salads at **The Pantry,** 5 Titus Rd. (☎ 860/868-0258). Also available are an abundance of cookware and other kitchen gizmos and necessities. Nearby is the beguiling **Hickory Stick Bookshop,** 2 Greenhill Rd. (☎ 860/868-0525).

WHERE TO STAY & DINE

✪ **Mayflower Inn.** 118 Woodbury Rd. (Rte. 47), Washington, CT 06793. ☎ **860/868-9466.** Fax 860/868-1497. 25 rms. A/C TV TEL. $230–$375 double. AE, MC, V. Take Rte. 202 north 2 miles past New Preston, turning south on Rte. 47 through Washington Depot and up the hill past Washington Common. The entrance is on the left. No children under 12.

These words can do little to burnish the reputation of Connecticut's courtliest (and most expensive) manor inn. Galaxies of stars, diamonds, and flags have already been showered upon it by the usual arbiters of taste.

While the main building is almost entirely new, some elements survive from the original 1894 structure. The most delightful of these is the richly paneled library, nearly intact from the days before the present owners took over in 1990. Porches look out across manicured lawns to flower beds and deep woods, from which deer routinely emerge. Furnishings throughout reflect a sensibility honed by knowledge of sumptuous English country houses and French provincial *auberges*—a genuine Joshua Reynolds portrait hangs in the parlor, and Tabriz carpets lie on gleaming wood floors.

Unlike lesser inns that cut corners on modern conveniences, the Mayflower makes available everything that a superior urban hotel might offer. That includes minibars in all rooms and gas fireplaces in most; baths are done with tapestry rugs, Limoges fittings, and mahogany wainscoting.

In sum, this is as close to perfection as any such enterprise is likely to be, almost justifying the breathtaking prices. The fact that the clientele is largely drawn from the martini-and-manhattan generation may not endear it to affluent younger people who aren't on honeymoons. No smoking in the bedrooms.

Dining/Entertainment: Three dining rooms of differing styles present dishes created by the Culinary Institute of America–trained chef. He transforms humble tapioca into something rivaling crème brûlée. Service is intelligent and alert.

Facilities: Heated outdoor pool, tennis court, and a fully equipped fitness center (with saunas, weights, StairMasters, treadmills, and classes). Massages can be booked at the fitness center.

NEW PRESTON & LAKE WARAMAUG

Never more than a few houses and retailers at the juncture of two country roads, this hamlet long served primarily as a supplier for local residents and, starting in the middle of the 19th century, the large families who summered each year on nearby Lake Waramaug (which is named, by the way, for a Chief Waramaug, whose daughter Lillinoah was one of the countless Indian maidens alleged to have leapt off ledges across North America). More recently, New Preston's small grocery and hardware stores have been converted to antiques emporia of high order, and they and a couple of casual cafes find themselves surrounded on weekends by BMWs and Volvos.

WHAT TO SEE & DO

At the northwest tip of the L-shaped lake, **Lake Waramaug State Park,** Lake Waramaug Road (☎ **860/868-0220**), gives the public access to a beautiful body of water that is otherwise monopolized by the private homes and inns that border it. Canoes and paddleboats are for rent, there is a swimming beach, picnic tables, food concessions, and a total of almost 80 camping and RV sites.

In no time, the intersecting streets that form the center of the village have gone from sleepy to spiffy, catering to nouveau Nutmeggers from Manhattan and weekend tourists from all over the Northeast. Especially notable among the antique shops is **J. Seitz & Co.,** Main Street (☎ **860/868-0119**), featuring painted furniture from New Mexico displayed in 3,800 square feet of showroom.

A former dairy farm on a wide promontory above Lake Waramaug was converted into the **Hopkins Vineyard,** Hopkins Road (☎ **860/868-7954**), in 1979. Headquartered in a 19th-century barn across the street from the Hopkins Inn (see below), its tasting and sales rooms are open in January and February, Friday to Saturday from 10am to 5pm, Sunday from 11am to 5pm; March and April, Wednesday to Saturday from 10am to 5pm, Sunday from 11am to 5pm; and May through December, Monday to Saturday from 10am to 5pm, Sunday 11am to 5pm.

The 10 or so bottlings range from a sparkling white to a surprising hard cider, with chardonnays and a pinot noir in between. They won't make anyone forget the Napa Valley, but prices are fair and the wines make worthy mementos of a good weekend. A new wine bar overlooks the lake and serves pâté and cheese.

WHERE TO STAY & DINE

The Boulders. East Shore Rd. (Rte. 45), New Preston, CT 06777. ☎ **860/868-0541.** Fax 860/868-1925. 17 rms. A/C TEL. $200–$250 double. Rates are $50 lower in midweek Nov–Apr, $50 higher on Fri–Sat Memorial Day through Oct. Rates include full breakfast. MAP (which includes dinner) $50 more than B&B rate. AE, MC, V. Drive north from New Preston about 2 miles on Rte. 45.

This once rustic lakeside inn has been nudged upward in both price and quality. Part of the improvement lies with the outlying "guest houses," four new buildings with two spacious units each. All enjoy private decks, fireplaces, whirlpool tubs, and refrigerators. These have contemporary furnishings, while the tone of the rooms in the 1895 main house is set by antiques and reproductions of country styles. Plates of cookies await arriving guests, and the *New York Times* is provided daily.

Dining/Entertainment: Great views are bonuses of the sitting and dining rooms. A serious wine cellar complements the acclaimed cuisine (entrees run $18.50 to $22). Guests are encouraged to take the MAP rates, and they're a bargain of sorts.

Facilities: Down by the shore is the private boathouse with canoes, rowboats, and paddleboats available free to guests.

Hopkins Inn. 22 Hopkins Rd., New Preston, CT 06777. ☎ **860/868-7295.** Fax 860/868-1768. 12 rms (10 with private bath). $63–$140 double. No credit cards. Closed Jan to early Mar. From New Preston, take Rte. 45 north about 2¹/₂ miles, and look for the sign on the left.

A family named Hopkins started farming this land in 1787, and its descendants were still around in 1979, when they turned the farm into a vineyard and winery. The yellow frame farmhouse with black shutters that is now the inn sits atop a hill with the best views of Lake Waramaug. Food is the main event at the inn, since the guest rooms are on the Spartan side, with no phones, air-conditioning, or TV.

Dining/Entertainment: A dining terrace takes maximum advantage of the lake view. The continental menu features dishes of the Swiss and Austrian Alps, like backhendl with lingonberries, supplemented with such dishes as trout bleu or meunière, the central ingredient of which is netted live on order from a tank. Entrees run $16.25 to $19.25. Breakfast, lunch, and dinner are served Tuesday to Sunday May through October, but only breakfast and lunch are offered in April, November, and December. Reservations are required for meals.

Inn at Lake Waramaug. 107 N. Shore Rd., New Preston, CT 06777. ☎ **800/525-3466** or 860/868-0563. Fax 860/868-9173. 23 rms, 1 suite. A/C TV TEL. $155–$275 double, MAP. Rates include breakfast and dinner. AE, MC, V. Drive north on Rte. 45 from New Preston about 2¹/₂ miles to the sign on the left, then 1 mile to the inn.

In recent years, guests could never be sure what they might find here, due to many ownership changes. For the moment, its operation has settled into a reassuring steady hum, with most facets running smoothly. The many public and private rooms ramble through several buildings, some old, some fairly new, from the high end of a slope down to the waterside cafe called The Boathouse. The dining room and some guest rooms are nonsmoking.

Dining/Entertainment: The reputation of the kitchen has jumped, too, so the mandatory MAP (breakfast and dinner) isn't the straitjacket it might have been.

Facilities: Canoes and a Sunfish are available at the inn's beach. An indoor pool and sauna in the main house have been upgraded, and there is a tennis court.

LITCHFIELD

Possessed of a long common with stately trees reconfigured around the turn of the century by the Frederic Law Olmsted landscaping firm (designers of New York's Central Park), Litchfield is testimony to the taste and prosperity of the Yankee entrepreneurs who built it in the late 18th and early 19th centuries from a colonial farm community to an industrial center. The factories and mills were dismantled toward the end of the 19th century, and the men who built them settled back to enjoy their riches.

Their uncommonly large homes, either authentic Federalists and Greek Revivals or later remodeled to look that way, are set well back from the streets. The commercial district is a block of late-19th-century houses facing the common, with gaudier enterprises kept to the outskirts.

Litchfield has produced its share of notables, including Harriet Beecher Stowe, author of *Uncle Tom's Cabin,* and her abolitionist preacher brother, Henry Ward Beecher.

In recent decades, the town has been discovered by fashionable New Yorkers, who find it less frenetic than the Hamptons of Long Island. Their influence is seen both in the quality of store merchandise and restaurant fare and the lofty prices they command.

A WALK THROUGH HISTORY

Litchfield's houses and broad tree-lined streets reward leisurely strolls, whether kicking through piles of fallen leaves in autumn or passing through shafts of sunlight piercing the canopy of arching trees.

From the stores and restaurants along West Street, walk east (that's to the right when you're facing the common), then turn right on South Street. On the opposite corner is the **Litchfield Historical Society,** at South and East streets (☎ **860/ 567-4501**), containing exhibits outlining life in the area during the late-colonial and post-Revolution periods, with paintings, furniture, and household utensils. Inquire here about tours of private homes conducted every July. It's open mid-April to October, Tuesday to Saturday from 11am to 5pm, Sunday 1 to 5pm. Admission is $3.

Walking down South Street, on the right behind a white picket fence, is one of the few historic houses regularly open to the public, the 1773 **Tapping Reeve House**

& Law School (☎ 860/567-4501). It was the earliest American law school, established before this was a country, and counted among its students Aaron Burr, Noah Webster, and three Supreme Court justices. The house was Mr. Reeve's, who taught his classes in the small building to the left. Hours are the same as those of the Litchfield Historical Society, which maintains it.

When the street starts to peter out into more modern houses, cross over and walk back toward the common and cross to the north side. Over there on the right is the magisterial **First Congregational Church,** built in 1828. Turn left, then right on North Street, where the domestic architecture matches the quiet splendor of South Street.

OUTDOOR PURSUITS

The **White Memorial Foundation,** Route 202 (☎ 860/567-0857), is a 4,000-acre wildlife sanctuary and nature conservancy about 4 miles southwest of Litchfield. It has campsites and 35 miles of trails for hiking, cross-country skiing, and horseback riding. On the grounds is a small museum of natural history with nature exhibits, stuffed native animals, and a gift shop.

This is horse country, so consider a canter across the meadows and along the wooded trails of **Topsmead State Park** (☎ 860/567-5694). The park has a wildlife preserve and a Tudor-style mansion that can be toured in the summer. Follow Route 118 1 mile east of town. Horses can be hired nearby at **Lee's Riding Stables** (☎ 860/868-7954).

SHOPPING

Most of the interesting shops are in the row of late-19th-century brick buildings on the south side of the town green. In the front of **Barnidge & McEnroe,** 7 West St. (☎ 860/567-4670), is a coffee bar for espressos and lattes, which will keep you going as you browse through its entertaining selection of books, gifts, and ceramics at the rear of the store. Open daily.

Black Swan Antiques, Litchfield Commons, south of the center on Route 202 (☎ 860/567-4429), has relocated from New Preston, but continues to specialize in English and European provincial furniture and accessories.

It isn't often that a commercial nursery becomes a tourist attraction, but **White Flower Farm,** Route 63 (☎ 860/567-8789), is special. For avid gardeners across the country, this is the L.L. Bean of the mail-order plant and seedling trade. The four main sections strung out along Route 63 (3 miles south of Litchfield center) display perennials, flats of seedlings, bulbs, herbs, florals, potted plants, and shrubs. A featured attraction is the greenhouse full of rare tuberous begonias. A new visitors' center has informative attendants and rest rooms. The farm is usually closed from December through March, but days and hours vary, so call ahead.

Chardonnays and merlots don't spring to mind as likely Connecticut products, but the **Haight Vineyard,** 29 Chestnut Hill Rd. (☎ 860/567-4045), corrects that impression. Established in 1978, it has grown and prospered, presently offering 11 drinkable bottlings, including a respectable Riesling, a couple of sturdy picnic-style reds, and a traditional apple wine. They range in price from $7 to $11 per bottle. The tasting room is open year-round Monday to Saturday from 10:30am to 5pm, Sunday noon to 5pm. There is a second winery in Mystic.

WHERE TO STAY

✪ **Tollgate Hill Inn.** Rte. 202 (Tollgate Rd., 2¹/₂ miles northeast of Litchfield), Litchfield, CT 06759. ☎ **800/445-3903,** 860/567-4545, or 860/567-3821. Fax 860/567-8397. 21 rms. A/C TV TEL. $90–$175 double. Rates include breakfast. AE, DC, DISC, V.

Three barn red buildings on 10 wooded acres, including the 1745 tavern that is the main house, constitute the liveliest, most atmospheric lodging in Litchfield. The bedrooms are comfortable, with all the electronic conveniences you could need. Morning coffee is free for the pouring at the registration desk, next to the parrot.

Dining/Entertainment: The busy restaurant may have wavy wide-board floors and high-backed wooden booths in its oldest room, but the food is thoroughly contemporary, of the New American variety (main courses $18 to $24). Shellfish pie—puff pastry encasing lobster chunks, crabmeat, scallops, and shrimp—is one delectable possibility. A Bloody Mary at the table in front of the fireplace in the bar is a treat on a frosty Sunday. Weekends from mid-June through October, jazz combos perform on Saturday nights in the cellar or for Sunday brunch.

WHERE TO DINE

The County Seat. 3 West St. (on the green). ☎ **860/567-8069.** Main courses $6.95–$8.50. AE, MC, V. Sun–Thurs 7am–11pm, Fri–Sat 7am–midnight. ECLECTIC.

Not easy to describe, but a pleasure to experience, The County Seat has a store in front selling kitchenware, coffee beans, baskets, and espresso machines. In back is a soda fountain, and in between is a coffee bar/lunch counter/dining room offering soups, sandwiches, salads, and light meals. One featured sandwich is a smoked mozzarella quesadilla with mixed greens and olive mayonnaise. There is table service now, and upholstered chairs and sofas are available for lounging and chatting. Live music of many kinds is on tap Friday and Saturday nights, with a modest cover charge.

Spinell's Litchfield Food Company. West St. (on the green). ☎ **860/567-3113.** Main courses $3.95–$8.95. MC, V. Daily 8am–6pm. ECLECTIC.

Ensconced in one of a row of late-19th-century buildings facing the town green, this is essentially a take-out shop with a cafe attached, but its proprietor has infused it with a sensibility honed in some of New York's most celebrated restaurants. The cold case has the makings of a marvelous picnic, displaying such appetizing platters as seasonal fiddlehead salad, wild rice with dried cranberries, and black-bean and corn salad. Supplement those with some exotic French and Spanish cheeses, Thai chicken sausage, salmon cakes, and soups of squash and onion or fennel with ham. There are house-made pies and breads and just about anything can be ordered for an eat-in lunch. Breakfast possibilities include buttermilk pancakes and three-egg omelets and big or bigger cups of espresso or cappuccino.

The Stone House Café & Gallery. 637 Bantam Rd. (Rte. 202, 5 miles south of town). ☎ **860/567-3326.** Main courses $10.95–$18.95. AE, MC, V. Tues–Sat 11:30am–2:30pm, Sun 10am–4pm; Tues–Thurs 5:30–9pm, Fri–Sat 5:30–10pm, Sun 6–9pm. NEW AMERICAN.

It stands on 9 acres beside a swift-running stream, a handsome 1849 house that is part art gallery and all restaurant. A graduate of the Culinary Institute of America ("the other CIA") and Boston's Ritz-Carlton shakes the skillets, cranking out such wintry delectables as leg of lamb stuffed with herbed feta and spinach propped beside a white-bean ragout, and summery fare like pan-seared sea bass with a tumble of Mediterranean veggies. A cheerful young staff brings it all upstairs, downstairs, and out on the deck. Mostly Californian and French wines are available by the glass. The photos and paintings on the wall are for sale.

West Street Grill. 43 West St. (on the green). ☎ **860/567-3885.** Reservations required on weekends. Main courses $14.95–$25.95. AE, MC, V. Mon–Thurs 11:30am–3pm and 5:30–9pm; Fri–Sun 11:30am–4pm and 5:30–10pm. NEW AMERICAN.

Known as an incubator for some of Connecticut's best chefs, several of whom have gone off to open their own places, this sprightly contemporary bistro hasn't lost a step, despite the frequent changes. Entrees tend towards Asian-tinged Cal-Ital renditions of meats, fowl, and grilled fish dressed with innovative sauces and garnishes. The trendiest spot for miles, it attracts the weekend celebrity set, with vaguely familiar faces exchanging confidences at every other table. Some patrons complain that people not known to the staff get short shrift, but that seems more likely due to excess sensitivity than reality.

LITCHFIELD AFTER DARK

No one goes to Litchfield for its pounding nightlife, but movie-lovers might consider the **Bantam Cinema** (☎ 860/567-0006) in the otherwise unremarkable village of Bantam, about 3 miles southeast on Route 209. Don't expect the latest Schwarzenegger action flick, since the managers concentrate on art and foreign films that don't get wide distribution. Otherwise, consider dropping by **The County Seat** (above) for one of its weekend musicales.

KENT

A prominent prep school of the same name, a history as an iron-smelting center, and a continuing reputation as a gathering place of artists and writers define this town of fewer than 2,000. Noted 19th-century landscape painter George Inness helped establish that assessment, and several galleries represent the works of his creative descendants. They are joined by a multiplicity of antiques shops and bookstores, most of them strung along Route 7. South of town on the same road is the hamlet of Bull's Bridge, named for one of the two remaining covered bridges in the state that can be crossed by cars.

North of Kent center, near Kent Falls, is the double-duty **Sloane-Stanley Museum & Kent Furnace,** on Route 7 (☎ 860/927-3849). Fans of the books of illustrator-author Eric Sloane, who celebrated the work and crafts of rural America, will enjoy this replica of his studio, exhibits of tools he depicted, and the drawings and paintings that adorn the walls. On the grounds are the ruins of an iron furnace that was in operation for much of the 19th century, one of many once active ironworks in the Kent area. Open mid-May through October, Wednesday to Sunday from 10am to 4pm. Admission is $3 adults, $1.50 seniors and children.

Four miles north of Kent is the handily accessible **Kent Falls State Park,** on Route 7 (☎ 860/927-3238). Its centerpiece, a 250-foot cascade, is clearly visible from the road, and picnic tables are set about the grounds. A path mounts the hill beside the falls, and there are a total of 295 wooded acres to explore. Rest rooms are available. A parking fee of $8 per car is charged on weekends and holidays, June through October. Serious hikers have a greater challenge nearby, should they choose to undertake it: On the opposite side of Route 7, the Appalachian Trail follows a stretch of the Housatonic River north toward Cornwall Bridge and West Cornwall and all the way into Massachusetts.

WEST CORNWALL

Not to be confused with Cornwall, about 4 miles to the southeast, nor Cornwall Bridge, about 7 miles to the south, this tiny hamlet is best known for its picturesque covered bridge, one of only two in the state that still permit the passage of cars. The bridge connects Routes 7 and 128, crossing the Housatonic. With a state forest to the north and a state park to its immediate south, Cornwall, a cluster of houses and a handful of commercial enterprises, enjoys a piney seclusion that remains welcoming to passersby.

EXPLORING THE AREA

Housatonic Meadows State Park, on Route 7 (☎ 860/672-6772 in summer, 860/927-3238 the rest of the year), is comprised of 452 acres bordering both sides of the Housatonic River immediately south of West Cornwall, and provides access to fishing, canoeing, and picnicking.

A couple of local organizations offer equipment and guidance. One is **Housatonic Anglers** (☎ 860/672-4457), whose owners offer float trips, weekend fly-fishing schools, lodging in two streamside cottages, and guided fishing trips (lunch is included). The other is **Clarke Outdoors,** 163 Rte. 7, Cornwall (☎ 860/672-6365), which provides rentals of river craft, including kayaks and rafts, as well as instruction and guided white-water trips.

Just outside Cornwall proper, off Route 4, is **Mohawk Mountain Ski Area,** 46 Great Hollow Rd. (☎ 800/895-5222 or 860/672-6100). "Mountain" is an overstatement, but this is the state's oldest ski resort, with 5 chairlifts, 23 trails, and snowmakers. The main base lodge has a fireplace and outdoor deck. Rentals and instruction are provided.

Apart from a couple of antiques shops, shoppers are drawn to **The Cornwall Bridge Pottery Store,** Route 128 (☎ 860/672-6545), catercorner from the Brookside Bistro. In addition to handmade and manufactured ceramics, the store has counters and shelves of lamps, copper pots, wind chimes, kitchen gadgets, and even knitwear.

WHERE TO DINE

Brookside Bistro. Rte. 128 (near the covered bridge). ☎ 860/672-6601. Reservations recommended on weekends. Main courses $10.75–$19.95. MC, V. Daily noon–2:30pm and 6–9:30pm. Closed Mar and Mon–Wed in winter. COUNTRY FRENCH.

More truly a bistro than most places that so describe themselves, this nicely situated restaurant traffics in such classic Gallic recipes as *coq au vin* (chicken cooked in wine), lamb shank, and eggplant tart. None of that tricky nouvelle gimmickry, just carefully rendered, very tasty food. Portions are sizable—so large, in fact, that many of the patrons leave with their leftovers in plastic containers. Usually this would lead me to suggest that appetizers and/or desserts be avoided, but who can resist the herbed chicken sausage in brioche with mustard-cream sauce? Or the airy cheesecake or earthy tarte tartin? The screened dining deck hangs over a tumbling brook, the seating area of choice in good weather. Closings aren't always predictable, so call ahead.

SHARON

Early on, this attractive hamlet near the New York border established a reputation for its manufactures, which included mousetraps and cannon shells. Those industries no longer exist, and Sharon is now primarily residential, a picturesque village with many houses made of brick or fieldstone in an area where wood-frame houses prevail.

The **Sharon Audubon Center,** Route 4 (☎ 860/364-0520), is a 758-acre nature preserve with herb and flower gardens, a shop and interpretive center, and 11 miles of hiking and nature trails. Injured birds are brought to the center for rehabilitation, and there are usually several raptors (birds of prey) on display. The grounds are open dusk to dawn, the main building Monday to Saturday from 9am to 5pm and Sunday from 1 to 5pm. Admission to trails is $3 adults, $1.50 seniors and children.

WHERE TO DINE

West Main Cafe. 13 W. Main St. ☎ **860/364-9888.** Main courses $12.95–$17.95. AE, MC, V. Mon and Thurs–Sat 11:30am–2:30pm, Sun 10am–3pm; Thurs and Sun–Mon 5:30–9pm, Fri–Sat 5:30–10pm. NEW AMERICAN.

One of the most celebrated of the chefs who have passed through the West Street Grill in Litchfield, Matthew Fahrner has taken a flier on this once scorned eatery in his hometown. There are only a few tables in the frame house, steps from the village green, and decor is minimal—a few unremarkable paintings. That leaves the spotlight on Fahrner's fancies of the moment, which bound around the culinary map, but seem most often to play on Southwestern, Asian, and Caribbean themes. There are no guarantees of what will next capture his imagination, and the menu changes monthly.

LAKEVILLE & SALISBURY

These two attractive villages share a common history and a main street lined with 19th-century houses stretching along Route 44. The "lake" in question is Lake Wononscopomuc, slightly south of the town center, its shoreline dotted with summer homes.

The discovery in the area of a particularly pure iron ore led to the development of mines and forges as early as the mid-1700s. One of the ironworkers was the eccentric Ethan Allen, later to become the leader of the Green Mountain Boys and a hero for his capture of Fort Ticonderoga from the British in 1775. The forges of the area supplied Washington's army with many cannons in the critical early years of the Revolution.

WHAT TO SEE & DO

One wealthy forge owner and manufacturer, John Milton Holley, bought a 1768 mansion and doubled its size in 1808. The result is the **Holley House,** 15 Millerton Rd., Route 44 (☎ **860/435-2878**), a Federalist and Greek Revival architectural mix. One of the few historic houses in the area open to the public, it contains furnishings and collections of china, silverware, and glass collected by Holley and his descendants over the continuous 173 years the family lived there. Open mid-June to mid-September, Saturday and Sunday from noon to 5pm. Admission is free.

Not far from Lakeville center (south on Route 41, then east on Route 112) is **Lime Rock Park** (☎ **860/435-2571**), one of the premier auto racing courses in the Northeast. It has garnered even greater attention since Paul Newman, a Connecticut resident, started piloting his own car around the turns. While sports cars are the central attraction, there are special races with vintage vehicles and NASCAR stock cars, and the famous Skip Barber driving school is located here. Races are held late April through mid-October, Saturdays and Monday holidays.

In Salisbury, the **Salisbury Antiques Center,** 46 Library St. (☎ **860/435-0424**), deals in exalted forms of English and American furniture and accessories.

WHERE TO STAY & DINE

White Hart. The Village Green (P.O. Box 385), Salisbury, CT 06068. ☎ **860/435-0030.** Fax 860/435-0040. 26 rms. A/C TV TEL. $85–$195 double. AE, CB, DC, MC, V.

Fortunes have fluctuated in the White Hart's 180-plus years, but lately this white clapboard inn at the end of Salisbury's main street is on the rise. The front porch, with its voluptuously curved wicker furniture, is the prime summertime site. A front parlor with fireplace long ago replaced a cheesy gift shop. Apart from the three suites and the large Ford Room (which go for around $190), most of the rooms are on the small side.

Dining/Entertainment: The ambitious main restaurant, June's New American Sea Grill, has gathered kudos for its creative way with seafood. Informal meals and snacks are served in the Tap Room.

NORFOLK

Founded in 1758, Norfolk was long popular as a summer vacation destination for industrialists who owned mills and factories along Connecticut's rivers. At the least, drive into the center for a look at the village green. It is highlighted by a monument that involved the participation of two of the late 19th century's most celebrated creative people—sculptor Augustus Saint-Gaudens and architect Stanford White.

At the opposite corner is the 90-year-old "Music Shed," a closed auditorium on the Ellen Battell Stoeckel Estate that is the venue for an eagerly awaited series of summer events, the **Norfolk Chamber Music Festival,** P.O. Box 545, Routes 44 and 272, Norfolk, CT 06058-0545 (☎ **860/542-3000**). Held from late June to mid-August, it hosts evening performances by such luminaries as the Tokyo String Quartet and the Vermeer Quartet. These are augmented by morning recitals by young musicians in training.

Two prime recreational areas are near each other on Route 272, north of town. One mile from the village green is **Haystack Mountain State Park** (☎ **860/482-1817**). Its chief feature is a short trail leading up from the parking lot to a stone tower at the 1,715-foot crest. On clear days, the splendid views from the top take in a panorama stretching from the Catskill Mountains in New York to Long Island Sound. Picnicking is allowed.

Another 5 miles further north, on the Massachusetts border, is **Campbell Falls** (☎ **860/482-1817**), which enjoys an abundance of streams, rapids, and cascades. Fishing is a possibility, as are hiking and picnicking.

3 New Haven

The approach to New Haven via Interstate 95 isn't a paean to positive urban planning. What you'll first see, at the waterfront, are acres of railroad switchyards, oil storage tanks, warehouses, and grimy factories. Inland are a few half-hearted efforts at mid-rise office buildings that look less like a skyline than a jaw of broken teeth. The streets approaching the downtown district are dissolute, untended, radiating a sense of hopes unfulfilled. It is easy to just continue on to Mystic.

But that would be shortchanging both the city and yourself. For while New Haven suffers the routine roster of afflictions of most of Connecticut's cities—nearly a quarter of its citizens live at or below the poverty line and street crime is high—it also has a great deal to offer the leisure traveler. Ready and waiting to fill out a rewarding weekend are four active performing-arts centers and theaters with September-to-June seasons of first-rate professional caliber, three outstanding small museums, autumn renewals of college football rivalries that date back 120 years, and a variety of ethnic restaurants that will drive foodies mad with choices.

Much of what is worthwhile about New Haven can be credited to the presence of one of the world's most prestigious universities. It both enriches its community and exacerbates the usual town-gown conflicts—a paradox with which the institution and civic authorities have struggled since the colonial period. But there can be no denying that the city would be reduced to a lump of queasy urban malaise were the university to evaporate.

Relatively little serious history has happened here. But there are a number of amusing "firsts" that boosters love to trumpet. Yale awarded the first Doctor of Medicine degree in 1729 to a man who never practiced medicine. The first hamburger was allegedly made and sold here, as was, even less certainly, the first pizza. Noah Webster compiled his first dictionary here, and Eli Whitney perfected his cotton gin. A resident invented the corkscrew in 1860, and a candy company came up with the name "lollipop" for one of its products. The first telephone switchboard was made here, necessitated by a Reverend John E. Todd, who was the first person in the world to request telephone service. Charles Goodyear of New Haven came up with a way to vulcanize rubber, and a local man named Colt invented a revolver in 1836.

ESSENTIALS

GETTING THERE Interstate 95 between New York and Providence skirts the shoreline of New Haven, and I-91 from Boston and Hartford ends there. Connections can also be made from the south along the Merritt and Wilbur Cross parkways.

Tweed–New Haven Airport receives feeder flights connecting with several major airlines, including **Continental** (☎ **800/525-0280**), **USAirways** (☎ **800/428-4322**), and **United** (☎ **800/241-6522**). It's located southeast of the city, near Exits 50 and 51 of I-95.

Amtrak (☎ **800/523-8760** for Metroliners, 800/872-7245 for all other trains) has several trains daily that run between Boston and New York and stop in New Haven.

Metro-North (☎ **800/METRO-INFO**) commuter trains make many daily trips between New Haven and New York. The trip to or from New York takes 1 1/2 hours; to or from Boston, about 3 hours. Metro-North tickets are much cheaper than Amtrak's.

PARKING Downtown traffic isn't too congested, except at the usual rush hours, and there are ample parking lots and garages near the green and Yale University, where most visitors spend their time. Even on-street spots aren't difficult to find most of the day.

VISITOR INFORMATION The **Greater New Haven Convention & Visitors Bureau** maintains an attended office at One Long Wharf Drive, New Haven, CT 06511 (☎ **203/777-8550**), visible and easily reached from Exit 46 of I-95. It's open from Memorial Day to Labor Day. An especially useful detailed map of New Haven that even points out restaurants and store locations is *Professor Pathfinder's Yale University & New Haven,* available in bookstores.

SPECIAL EVENTS Important seasonal events are the new **International Festival of Arts & Ideas,** held at many sites around the city in late June, and a free **jazz festival** on the green in late July through early August. Call the visitors bureau at ☎ **203/777-8550** for additional details.

EXPLORING YALE & NEW HAVEN

The major attractions are all associated with Yale University, and except for the Peabody Museum, are within walking distance of each other near the **New Haven Green,** which is bounded by Elm, Church, Chapel, and College streets.

The flat green, about one-third the size of Boston Common, is divided into two unequal parts by north-south Temple Street. It was set aside by town elders in the earliest colonial days as a place for citizens to graze their livestock, bury their dead, and spend leisure hours strolling its footpaths. Government and bank buildings border it on the east, a retail district on the south, and some older sections of the vast Yale campus to the north and west.

Facing Temple Street are three historic churches, all dating from the early 19th century. Next to Chapel Street is **Trinity Episcopal,** a brownstone Gothic Revival structure, the Georgian **First Church of Christ/Center Congregational,** and the essentially Federalist **United Congregational.** The First Church of Christ is of the greatest interest, built atop a crypt with tombstones inscribed as early as 1687. Tours are conducted Tuesday to Friday 10:30am to 2:30pm.

The oldest house in New Haven is now the **Yale University Information Center,** a white colonial facing the north side of the green at 149 Elm St., near College Street (☎ 203/432-2300). While its primary mission is to familiarize prospective students and their parents with the hour **guided walking tour** (Monday to Friday 10:30am and 2pm, Saturday and Sunday at 1:30pm). The center has an introductory video and maps for self-guided tours; it's open Monday to Friday from 9am to 4:45pm, Saturday and Sunday from 10am to 4pm.

It is impossible to imagine New Haven (or, for that matter, the United States) without Yale, so pervasive is its physical and cultural presence. After all, it helped educate our last two presidents, as well as Gerald Ford, William Howard Taft, Noah Webster, Nathan Hale, and Eli Whitney. Established in 1702 in the shoreline town now known as Clinton, the young college was eventually moved here in 1718 and named for Elihu Yale, who made a major financial contribution. It has many prestigious schools and divisions, including those devoted to medicine, law, theology, architecture, and engineering.

The most evocative quadrangle of the sprawling institution is the **Old Campus,** which can be entered from College, High, or Chapel streets. Inside, the mottled green is enclosed by Victorian Gothic and Federalist buildings and dominated by **Harkness Tower,** a 1920 Gothic Revival campanile that looks much older. Sculptures of notable Yale alumni constitute much of the exterior ornamentation.

Yale Center for British Art. 1080 Chapel St. (at High St.). ☎ **203/432-2800** or 203/432-2850. Free admission. Tues–Sat 10am–5pm, Sun noon–5pm.

What looks like a parking garage from outside is a great deal more impressive once you step inside. The museum claims to be the most important collection of British art outside the United Kingdom, and I can't see any reason to dispute it.

Take the elevator to the fourth floor, where the bulk of the permanent collection is exhibited. It is arranged chronologically, from the 16th century to the early 19th, so turn right from the elevator to enter the Elizabethan Age and proceed clockwise. The paintings—portraits, in the main—are carefully hung and illuminated by many translucent skylights. It's a dazzling progression, some 250 canvases in all, by such luminaries as Hogarth, the landscapist Antonio Canal, Gainsborough, Joshua Reynolds, Benjamin West, and the glorious Turner, from his early realistic seascapes to the lyrical visions that anticipated Impressionism toward the end of his life (1851).

On the third floor are temporary exhibits, and on the second floor the visual narrative is picked up with works from the second half of the 19th century and the 20th, culminating with such familiar contemporary artists as Barbara Hepworth and Henry Moore. On the ground floor is the museum shop and a lecture hall.

Yale University Art Gallery. 1111 Chapel St. (at York St.). ☎ **203/432-0600.** Admission $3 (suggested donation). Tues–Sat 10am–5pm, Sun 2–5pm.

This museum displays the artworks of many epochs and regions, but is most noted for its collections of French Impressionists and American realists of the late 19th and early 20th centuries. It's a satisfying collection for connoisseurs, but won't test the patience of most teenagers and those adults who aren't regular museum-goers.

Architect Louis I. Kahn, responsible for the nearby Center for British Art, also designed the larger of these two buildings.

Following my standard recommendation, take the elevator to the fourth floor and work your way down. Asian arts and crafts command the top floor, a permanent core of them surrounded by temporary displays. The tiny Netsuke ivories at the center bear close examination, as do the bronze, porcelain, and ceramic vessels in nearby cases. On the third floor, to the right, are 14th- to 18th-century Gothic ecclesiastical panels, mainly tempera on wood with prodigious amounts of gilt. To the left are 16th-century Italian and Dutch portraits and allegorical scenes, among them paintings by Rubens and Frans Hals.

In sharp contrast are adjoining galleries of avant-garde 20th-century Americans of the abstract expressionist school—Rothko, Rauschenberg, Stella, Ellsworth Kelly, and Kenneth Noland—as well as Europeans Braque, Brancusi, Klee, Picasso, Mondrian, Duchamp, and Miró.

Peabody Museum of Natural History. 170 Whitney Ave. (at Sachem St.). ☎ **203/ 432-5050** (recording). Admission $5 adults, $3 seniors and children 3–15. Mon–Sat 10am– 5pm, Sun noon–5pm.

Start on the third floor and work your way down, especially if a school group has just entered—the assault on adult eardrums can be fearsome, for this is probably the most popular field trip destination in town.

Up on the third floor there are dioramas with stuffed animals in various environments, abetted by quite effective backdrop paintings. There are bighorn sheep, wading marsh birds, a leopard, Alaskan brown bears, Southwestern javelina, mule deer, bison, musk oxen, and the assorted birds, snakes, and rodents with which they share their natural settings of desert, jungle, or tundra. An adjoining gallery has mounted birds representing every species found in Connecticut. On the same floor is a small but illuminating collection of ancient Egyptian artifacts, including pottery, funerary objects, and fragments of reliefs and hieroglyphics.

The second floor doesn't hold a great deal of general interest, but down on the first is a "bestiary" of large stuffed animals, from a single-wattled cassowary to a type of needle-nosed Indian crocodile called a gavial. This display leads logically into the Great Hall of Dinosaurs, its assembled fossils ranging from a pea-brained stegosaurus and mastodons to the fearsome brontosaurus.

Remaining galleries deal with animal and human evolution, including displays of the weapons, headdresses, clothing, and body ornaments of Polynesian, Plains Indian, and pre-Columbian cultures.

SHOPPING

A retail time machine, **Group W Bench,** 1171 Chapel St. (☎ **203/624-0683**), celebrates an eye-blink epoch that lasted about 3 years in real time but has continued to reverberate through the terms of five presidents. Started in 1968, the store is packed with beads, chimes, peace emblems, peacock feathers, Mexican yo-yos, rubber chickens, and bumper stickers reading THANK YOU, JERRY (as in "Garcia"). You can get a 1960s nostalgia contact high just walking in the door. The bearded founder also owns the **Gallery Raffael,** 1177 Chapel St. (☎ **203/772-2258**) next door, which showcases mostly American arts and crafts, including his own.

Farther east on the same street is **WAVE,** 1046 Chapel St. (☎ **203/782-6212**), a more upscale operation with a wealth of handblown glassware, brightly colored ceramics, candles, fragrances, toiletries, and mirrors with hand-painted frames.

Atticus Bookstore & Café, 1082 Chapel St. (☎ **203/776-4040**), might as easily be listed under "Where to Dine," for one end of this bookstore consists of an always occupied lunch counter and take-out section. Famous for its scones, the cafe also sells delectable pastries, crusty loaves of bread, soups like black bean and gazpacho, and hero sandwiches stuffed with meats, cheeses, and vegetables. The New Orleans–style muffeletta is especially good. The rest of the space is devoted to what many call the best bookstore in town. It's open daily from 8am to midnight.

WHERE TO STAY

New Haven lodgings are both limited and, with one notable exception, devoid of either charm or distinctiveness. Still, its motels and hotels fill up far in advance for football weekends, alumni reunions, and graduation. One hotel reports reservations for graduation weeks into the next century.

Among the national chains represented in town are the **Holiday Inn,** 30 Whalley Rd. (☎ **203/777-6221**); **Howard Johnson,** 400 Sargent Dr. (☎ **203/562-1111**); and the **Marriott Residence Inn,** 3 Long Wharf Dr. (☎ **203/777-5337**).

The visitors bureau has a **hotel reservation service** (☎ **800/332-7829**).

The Colony. 1157 Chapel St. (between Park and York sts.), New Haven, CT 06511. ☎ **800/ 458-8810** or 203/776-1234. Fax 203/772-3929. 86 rms. A/C TV TEL. $98–$108 double. AE, CB, DC, MC, V.

It may be a conventional hotel that looks a little dated and worn, but The Colony offers a great location on a decent stretch of one of the city's better streets. It's within easy walking distance of the green, the Yale campus, theaters, most of my recommended restaurants, and two of the Yale museums.

Dining/Entertainment: Charlie B's Steakhouse serves decent food (including seafood from a raw bar) and features jazz combos on weekend nights.

Services: Concierge, room service.

✪ **Three Chimneys Inn.** 1201 Chapel St. (between Park and Howe sts.), New Haven, CT 06511. ☎ **203/789-1201.** Fax 203/776-7363. 10 rms. A/C TV TEL. $155 double. Rates include breakfast. AE, DISC, MC, V. No children under 6 accepted.

This 1870 mansion, with its arresting paint job and formal front garden, long did business as the Inn at Chapel West. Then, unexpectedly, it plunged into bankruptcy, and it was stripped of many of its furnishings and fixtures to placate creditors. A new management has resurrected this favorite inn of Yalies and their parents. The parking lot was repaved, a new roof was added, and all rooms were retrofitted with custom-made medicine cabinets, armoires to hide the TVs, and four-poster kings and queens, some with canopies. Many rooms have stuffed chaises, and all have at least two reading chairs. Two-line phones with data ports have been installed.

In the morning, a selection of newspapers waits outside the dining room. The "enhanced" continental breakfast typically includes cereal, fresh fruit, yogurt, and a hot dish. Afternoon tea is served, and in the parlor across the hall, a tray of cordials is set out for guests to pour themselves.

WHERE TO DINE

The Brü Rm at BAR. 254 Crown St. (between High and College sts.). ☎ **203/495-1111.** Pizzas $5–$11. MC, V. Mon 5pm–1am, Tues–Wed 11:30am–2:30pm and 5pm–1am, Thurs 11:30am–1am, Fri 11:30am–2am, Sat 5pm–2am, Sun 2pm–1am. PIZZA.

Yes, those spellings and capitalizations are correct. This place is a 1996 brew pub tacked onto a slightly older nightclub ("BAR").

It's also a naked challenge in the eternal New Haven pizza wars. If Frank Pepe's is the champ, as local consensus insists, this whippersnapper takes over as the new leading contender. This, of course, assumes that you share the local conviction that the thinner the crust the better. The pizzas here easily meet that requirement—if they were any thinner you could read this page through them.

Basic categories are red, red with cheese, and white (cheese only), with 20 additional toppings to choose from. The smallest size can feed two people, especially if they start with the house salad, a concoction of pears and pecans atop mixed greens with crumbled blue cheese scattered over all. The shiny chrome and copper vats on the ground floor and open mezzanine produce five beers and ales, from the BAR Blonde to the Damn Good Stout. They are drawn as half-pints, pints, and pitchers.

Caffé Adulis. 228 College St. (near Crown St.). ☎ **203/777-5081.** Main courses $8.95–$12.95. AE, MC, V. Thurs–Fri noon–3pm; Sun–Thurs 5–10pm, Fri–Sat 5–11:30pm. ERITREAN.

Talk about specialization. Eritrea recently won its independence from Ethiopia after a 30-year civil war, and the Eritrean owners insist there are differences between their cuisines, too.

This successful ethnic eatery rewards the slightly venturesome diner with novel taste experiences at soothingly low prices. There is, for example, *injera,* a spongy, sour flat-bread made of millet that figures in most of these dishes, including *tsebhe Derho* (chicken simmered with hot peppers) and shrimp *barka,* jumbo crustaceans pan-seared and tumbled together with tomato-basil sauce, coconut, and dates ladled over fragrant basmati rice. About half the dishes are vegetarian, and most are spicy-hot, but the chef will adjust the seasonings if you ask. A familiar touchstone is the authentic presence of pasta, introduced by the Italians during their long colonial rule of the region. Beer goes better with this peppery food than wine. Local Elm City Ale is a good choice, one of several regional microbreweries represented.

Claire's Corner Copia. 100 Chapel St. (at College St.). ☎ **203/562-3888.** Main courses $4.50–$6.75. No credit cards. Sun–Thurs 8am–10pm, Fri–Sat 8am–11pm. VEGETARIAN.

Few college towns are without at least one cheap vegetarian restaurant. This one has ruled in New Haven since 1975, long enough for the founder to produce her own cookbook, copies of which she happily sells to satisfied customers. Dining options include curried couscous, eggplant rollatini, and a number of Mexican entrees, but the stars might well be the veggie burgers and the four different pizzettes. Breakfast brings a bounty of plump scones and massive muffins. A big blackboard lists many choices for all three meals and in-between snacks. On occasion the restaurant has live entertainment. All this, and the kitchen keeps kosher, too. A quibble: The Mexican and Indian dishes could use a little more zip.

Frank Pepe's. 157 Wooster St. (between Olive and Brown sts.). ☎ **203/865-5762.** Pizzas $4.95–$10. No credit cards. Mon and Wed–Thurs 4–10:30pm, Fri–Sat 11:30am–midnight, Sun 2:30–10:30pm. PIZZA.

On the scene for most of this century, Pepe's has long claimed the local pizza crown while fighting off perpetual challenges. In exchange for truly super, almost unimaginably thin-crusted pies, pilgrims put up with long lines, minimal decor, and a sullen staff that brooks no hesitancy or questioning from the paying supplicants.

If the wait looks to be especially long, you can do about as well, quality- and personnel-wise, at **Sally's,** 237 Wooster St. (☎ **203/624-5271**), just down the street.

Louis' Lunch. 261–263 Crown St. (between High and College sts.). ☎ **203/562-5507.** Burgers $3.90–$4.25. No credit cards. Mon–Thurs 11am–4pm, Fri–Sat 11am–1am. AMERICAN.

Here's history on a bun. The claim, unprovable but gaining strength as the decades roll on, is that America's very first hamburger was sold in 1900 at this boxy little brick luncheonette with the shuttered windows.

Louis' Lunch wasn't always at this location—it was moved a few years ago to escape demolition—but not much else has changed. The tiny wooden counter and tables are carved with the initials of a century of patrons. The beef is freshly ground each day, formed into crude patties, squeezed into vertical grills, thrust into gas-fired ovens almost as old as the building, and then served (medium rare, usually) on two slices of white toast on paper plates. The only allowable garnishes are slices of tomato and onion—add cheese and you'll have a Louis burger with "the works." There's no mustard and no ketchup, so don't even ask. And no fries, either, just potato chips. They usually have three or four kinds of pie, though, and if they have time, they might make a tuna or steak sandwich. Just don't expect history to make compromises.

Pika Tapas Café. 39 High St. (south of Chapel St.). ☎ **203/865-1933.** Main courses $9–$14, tapas $2–$7. MC, V. Mon–Thurs 11:30am–10:30pm, Fri–Sat 11:30am–11:30pm. SPANISH.

Tapas, for those still uninitiated, are the tasty snacks served in Spanish taverns as accompaniments to wine or beer. Comparable to hors d'oeuvres or antipasti, they come in an infinite variety of tastes and combinations. Among the most common are *tortilla,* a firm potato-and-egg omelet; *pan Catalan,* thick slices of bread moistened with tomato pulp and topped with cured ham; and *gambas al ajillo,* shrimp sautéed with garlic. All these and at least 20 more are offered at the big semicircular bar in front of the Miró-like mural at this sprightly new enterprise. Keep it in mind for light meals before or after curtain at the nearby theaters. There are also larger portions of such classics as paella and clams with chorizo sausage and white beans.

✪ **Union League Café.** 1032 Chapel St. (between High and College sts.). ☎ **203/562-4299.** Main courses $15–$19. AE, MC, V. Mon–Fri 11:30am–2:30pm; Mon–Thurs 5:30–9:30pm, Fri–Sat 5:30–10pm, Sun 4–8:30pm. CREATIVE FRENCH.

These grand salons with high arched windows opening onto Chapel Street retain an air of their aristocratic origins, which date back to 1854. Even the name fairly shrieks—with genteel Yankee reticence, of course—of its former status as a bastion of WASP privilege, the Union League Club. Now, however, it has loosened up considerably, and jeans-clad Yalies, their doting parents, philosophizing profs, and deal-making execs are all equally comfortable. The atmosphere is now closer to that of an updated Provençal brasserie than to that of a gentlemen's sanctuary, with waiters in aprons and butcher paper on the tables. Dinner entrees routinely tinker with tradition; witness the *medaillons de lotte en croute de pomme terre* (monkfish in potato crust) or *poulet grillé aux éspices* (grilled marinated chicken with curry, ginger, and cumin over a basmati risotto). The welcoming bar in back has a menu of light snacks. Lunch is mostly salads and sandwiches, but with twists, as in the leaves of roast lamb dressed with pesto and tomatoes on toasted slabs of great bread.

NEW HAVEN AFTER DARK

The presence of Yale and a highly educated faction of the general population ensures a cultural life equal to that in many larger cities. A reliable source of information about cultural events and nightlife is the free weekly newspaper, the *New Haven Advocate,* widely available at hotels, bookstores, and restaurants.

Within a couple of blocks of the green are the **Shubert Performing Arts Center,** 247 College St. (☎ **800/955-5566** or 203/562-5666), which presents such touring troupes as the Bolshoi Ballet and the Alvin Ailey Dance Theater, musical plays, opera, cabaret, and miscellaneous musical organizations; and the **Palace Performing Arts Center,** 248 College St. (☎ **203/789-2120**), with a more erratic schedule of pop singers and bands.

A deconsecrated church is the home of the **Yale Repertory Theatre,** Chapel and York streets (☎ **203/432-1234**), west of the green, which mounts an October-through-May season of lesser-known plays by known playwrights as diverse as David Mamet and George S. Kaufman. Away from downtown, but worth the taxi fare, is the **Long Wharf Theatre,** 222 Sargent Dr. (☎ **203/787-4282**), known for its success in producing new plays (October through June) that often make the jump to off Broadway and even Broadway.

Sprague Memorial Hall, 470 College St. (☎ **203/432-4157**), and **Woolsey Hall,** College and Grove streets (☎ **203/432-2310**), are two important additional venues on the Yale campus that host the performances of many resident organizations, including the New Haven Symphony Orchestra, the New Haven Civic Orchestra, the Yale Concert Band, the Yale Glee Club, Yale Philharmonia, and Yale Symphony Orchestra.

Bars and clubs also thrive, in considerable variety. The biggest and best venue for live rock and pop is **Toad's Place,** 300 York St. (☎ **203/562-5694**), which has welcomed the likes of the Rolling Stones, U2, Phoebe Snow, Bob Dylan, and Johnny Winter. Admission charges can get up to $15 or more for the top acts, but are much lower most of the time. The club usually features live music Wednesday to Sunday, with dancing (to a band or DJ) on most Saturday nights.

A less frenetic evening of music and conversation can be spent at **Xando,** 338 Elm St. (☎ **203/495-7166**). A bilevel postmodernist environment with brick walls and track lighting, it has an espresso bar and a segregated smoking section downstairs and less crowded tables on the upper level, where folk singers often perform.

For something in between, there's **BAR,** 254 Crown St. (☎ **203/495-1111**), which has a lounge in front—open to the street on warm nights—and a pool table, a terrace, and a dance floor with another bar in back. Connected to BAR is the Brü Rm, described above in "Where to Dine."

4 Hartford

The second-largest city of the Constitution State shares with its urban siblings a visible malaise it can't seem to shake, even with its status as state capital and the political clout to prop it up. It is not, after all, a Worcester sharing territory with a Boston, nor an Albany with a New York. Yet even while straining to focus on its grand edifices—the divinely overwrought gold-domed Capitol, the Mark Twain House, the august Wadsworth Athenaeum—it is impossible to ignore the miles of distressed housing, hollow-eyed office and industrial structures, and weed-strewn lots that radiate out from the center. Unattended grime, street crime, youth gangs, and visible poverty are persistent thorns in the civic hide. On top of all that, the bedrock insurance business has been in the doldrums and companies have been dispersing to the suburbs and farther away, taking jobs and taxes with them. It didn't help that the Hartford Whalers NHL team left town at the end of the 1996–97 season.

None of this grief is unique to Hartford, certainly, but this is not a place likely to attract vacationers who don't have business here (at least not for long).

It isn't as if they don't try. A civic center was completed in 1975 in an attempt to attract business downtown, and an above-street walkway connects it with the newer, 39-story CityPlace. Both venues offer special concerts and art exhibits, and the 489-seat Hartford Stage Company has a 10-month theatrical season in its own 1977 building catercorner from the center. A block away, the gracious Old State House recently reopened after 4 years of careful renovation, and across Main Street a shed has been provided for a daily farmers' market and a local paper sponsors noontime rock concerts during the summer. All these efforts have encouraged the establishment of a few cosmopolitan restaurants and a couple of good hotels, so most of a day trip or overnight visit will be contained within only a few square blocks.

Hartford was founded in 1636 by dissidents fleeing the rigid religious dictates of the Massachusetts Bay Colony. Three years later, they drafted what were called the "Fundamental Orders," the basis of a subsequent claim that Connecticut was the first political entity on earth to have a written constitution. From 1701 until 1875, Hartford shared the status of capital with New Haven, undergirding the municipal rivalry that continues today.

ESSENTIALS

GETTING THERE   I-84 and I-91 intersect in central Hartford. It's just about at the halfway point between New York City and Boston (115 miles northeast of New York, 103 miles southwest of Boston).

Several major U.S. airlines provide direct or feeder-line service to **Bradley International Airport** in Windsor Locks, about 12 miles north of the city. Buses, cabs, and limousines shuttle passengers into the city and to other points in the state. Major airlines serving Hartford include **American** (☎ 800/433-7300), **Continental** (☎ 800/525-0280), **Delta** (☎ 800/221-1212), **Northwest** (☎ 800/225-2525), **United** (☎ 800/241-6522), and **USAirways** (☎ 800/247-8786).

Amtrak (☎ **800/872-7245**) has several trains daily following the inland route between New York City and Boston, stopping at Hartford and Windsor Locks. The trip to either New York or Boston takes about $2^1/2$ hours.

VISITOR INFORMATION   A counter on the main floor of the Civic Center, at Trumbull, Asylum, and Church streets, has informational materials, and is manned by members of the **Hartford Guides.** Highly knowledgeable about their city, they not only provide information about sightseeing, shopping, restaurants, and hotels, they conduct walking tours and can provide escort service for women and seniors from lodgings or eating places to their cars or buses. To obtain their assistance or suggestions, call ☎ **860/293-8105.**

SPECIAL EVENTS   Hartford makes the most of its association with one of America's most beloved authors, Mark Twain. His image is seen everywhere, and the city puts on three "Mark Twain Days" in mid-August, packed with such events as frog jumping, fence painting, riverboat rides, and performances of plays based on Twain's life or works. Most activities are free.

In late July, there is a **Festival of Jazz** with free performances at the pavilion in Bushnell Park.

SEEING THE SIGHTS

The Old State House. 800 Main St. (at Asylum Ave.). ☎ **860/522-6766.** Free admission. Jan–Oct Mon–Fri 10am–4pm, Sat 10am–3pm; Nov–Dec Mon–Sat 10am–5pm, Sun noon–5pm.

After closing for a 4-year $12-million renovation, the 1796 State House opened in time to celebrate its bicentennial. Costumed "interpreters" stand ready, even eager, to answer questions. Upstairs, on the right, is the restored Senate chamber, with an original full-length painting of the first president by that indefatigable Washington portraitist, Gilbert Stuart. Across the hall is the room that housed the city council after the state government moved to a larger facility. These days, the plan is to use the building for temporary art exhibitions, changed two or three times yearly. If subsequent shows live up to the standard of the opening exhibit—contemporary paintings by Latino artists—this will become a must stop on the local cultural circuit. There is a museum shop in the basement.

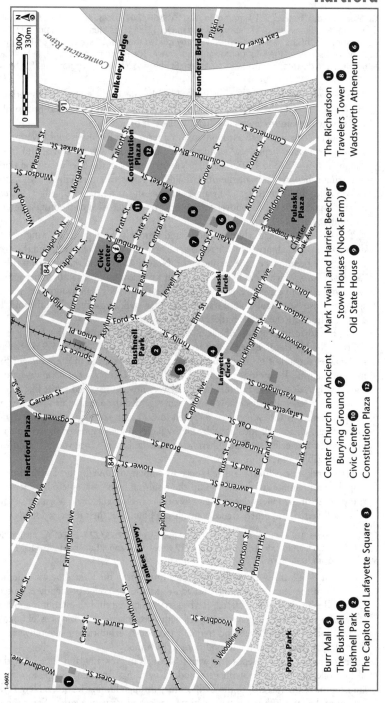

Hartford

Connecticut River

Bulkeley Bridge

Founders Bridge

Burr Mall 5
The Bushnell 4
Bushnell Park 2
The Capitol and Lafayette Square 3

Center Church and Ancient Burying Ground 7
Civic Center 10
Constitution Plaza 12

Mark Twain and Harriet Beecher Stowe Houses (Nook Farm) 1
Old State House 9

The Richardson 11
Travelers Tower 8
Wadsworth Atheneum 6

1-0602

⊗ **Mark Twain House.** 351 Farmington Ave. ☎ **860/247-0998.** Admission $7.50 adults, $7 seniors, $3.50 children 6–12. Memorial Day to Oct 15 and Dec Mon–Sat 9:30am–5pm, Sun noon–5pm; rest of the year closed Tues. Visits by guided tour only. Take Exit 46 off I-84, turn right onto Sisson Ave., then right onto Farmington Ave. The house is on the right, in less than a 1/2 mile. From downtown, drive west on Asylum St., bearing left on Farmington Ave. The house is on the left.

This 19-room house is a fascinating example of the late-19th-century style sometimes known as "Picturesque Gothic," with several steeply peaked gables and brick walls whose varying patterns are highlighted by black or orange paint.

Samuel Clemens, whose pseudonym was a term used by Mississippi River pilots to indicate a water depth of 2 fathoms, lived here with his wife, Olivia, and three daughters from 1873 to 1897. The high-Victorian decor of the interior was the work of distinguished designers of the time, including Louis Comfort Tiffany, who provided advice and stained glass. Twain's enthusiasm for newfangled gadgets— *Tom Sawyer* is said to be the first novel written on a typewriter—led to the installation of a primitive telephone in the entrance hall.

The guided tour takes about an hour, and proceeds through the drawing room, dining room, and library (which has a magnificent carved mantelpiece), and then up through the bedrooms on the second floor. Note the picture in the playroom titled *Life And Death,* which looks like two people in a window up close but becomes a skull when viewed from a distance. On the top floor is the writer's main workroom, a large space that also has a pool table. Twain would often walk across the hall in the middle of the night and wake up his butler to play a few games.

On the adjacent property, about 60 yards across the lawn from the Twain residence, is the **Harriet Beecher Stowe House,** 73 Forest St. (☎ 860/525-9317). This is a smaller version of its neighbor, built in 1871. Stowe lived in the "cottage" for most of the time Twain resided in his. The author of *Uncle Tom's Cabin* was hardly a great writer, despite the fact that her antislavery novel is regarded as the first international best-seller. Perhaps that is why Twain regarded the older woman with neighborly equanimity. (He was not so disposed toward many of his contemporary and earlier rivals. Of an acclaimed novel by Henry James, Twain expressed the sentiments of countless university students when he commented that "Once you put it down, it isn't possible to pick it up again.")

Prices and policies for the Stowe House are similar to those for the Twain House. Couples and families may want to skip the resulting high cost, especially since the competence of the guides depends greatly on the luck of the draw. Most are admirably well versed, but others are lost outside the bounds of their rehearsed spiels.

⊗ **Wadsworth Atheneum.** 600 Main St. (at Gold St.). ☎ **203/278-2670.** Admission $6 adults, $4 seniors and students, $3 children 6–17 (free Thurs and 11am–noon on Sat). Tues–Sun 11am–5pm (until 8pm 1st Thurs of month).

Opened in 1842, this was the first public art museum in the United States. It looks its age from the outside, its wings and additions a hodgepodge of ineptly executed Gothic, Renaissance, and Victorian Revival styles. The refurbished interior is another story, with its soaring atrium courts ringed with open galleries and balconies, although a confusion of varying levels and frequent temporary exhibitions make movement difficult from one part of the second floor to the other.

Persevere, for this is a repository with few equals in New England. The strengths of the collection lie primarily in its American paintings, spanning the period from landscapists of the first half of the 19th century through luminaries of the New York School of the mid-20th to the provocative work of today's young artists. Some space is also devoted to 17th- and 18th-century European artworks of lesser magnitude.

For an overview, proceed by elevator to the top floor. In a far corner is a room devoted to Thomas Cole, accorded a leadership role among artists of the Hudson River School. Adapting the then prevailing romanticism of European artists to lush depictions of American landscapes, he was one of the most restrained in his use of color but didn't neglect the drama of the Catskill Mountains and the Hudson Highlands.

In the next gallery are works by Frederick Church, a Hartford native, and the flamboyant Albert Bierstadt, who fashioned huge, sumptuous portrayals of the Rocky Mountains and the West. On the balcony outside that section are more Americans—Frederic Remington, Andrew Wyeth, Ben Shahn, Reginald Marsh, Milton Avery, even Norman Rockwell. Watch for the shadow box by Joseph Cornell. These lead naturally to a gallery of the so-called American Impressionists, whose work bore resemblances to their European colleagues but never achieved their acclaim.

The highlights of the second floor are rooms of early Connecticut furniture, most of it elaborately carved in a form of utilitarian folk art. On the first floor is the MATRIX Gallery, full of rule-bending multimedia works. It makes the adjacent rooms of large canvases by abstract expressionists and Pop and Op artists of the 1950s and 1960s look familiar and accessible, hardly the reactions they provoked at their first exposures. Here, find stellar examples by de Kooning, Rauschenburg, Frankenthaler, Albers, and Kline, as well as sculptures by Donald Judd and David Smith. Looking right at home is a splendid desk by Frank Lloyd Wright.

On the same floor is the **Museum Café,** which has surprisingly good light items that alone are reason enough for a visit. There are tables out on the terrace in good weather. Lunch is served Tuesday to Saturday, brunch on Sunday, and dinner on the first Thursday of each month, when the museum is open until 8pm.

WHERE TO STAY

The Goodwin Hotel. 1 Haynes St. (at Asylum St.), Hartford, CT 06103. ☎ **800/922-5006** or 860/246-7500. Fax 860/247-4576. 124 rms. A/C TV TEL. $89–$233 double. AE, CB, DC, DISC, MC, V. Valet parking $13.

In a state with few luxury hotels, this quiet hostelry opposite the Civic Center stands out. It is housed in a Queen Anne–style Victorian built in 1881 as a residence for J. P. Morgan, the 19th-century industrialist, financier, and railway tycoon. While its understated public areas are lovely, the bedrooms are not as plush or spacious as one might hope. VCRs are available on request. Valet parking, though it can be painfully slow at checkout time, is a blessing along this crowded block.

Dining/Entertainment: Pierpont's is the capable in-house restaurant, serving New American cuisine that is creative and satisfying without being too startling.

Services: Concierge, room service (6am to midnight), secretarial services.

Facilities: Modest health club.

Sheraton. 315 Trumbull St. (Civic Center Plaza), Hartford, CT 06103. ☎ **860/728-5151.** Fax 860/522-3356. 388 rms. A/C TV TEL. $120 double. AE, CB, DC, DISC, MC, V. Parking $10.

You can spot it from just about anywhere, highways or downtown. The 22-story slab is everything expected of a Sheraton, with conveniences such as coffee in the rooms and VCRs supplied on request. Its rates are no bargain, but aren't a rip-off, either.

Services: Room service, dry cleaning/laundry, secretarial services.

Facilities: Indoor pool, health club with whirlpool and sauna.

WHERE TO DINE

Bombay's. 89A Arch St. (at the corner of Columbus Blvd.). ☎ **860/724-4282.** Main courses $8.95–$17.95. MC, V. Daily 11:30am–2:30pm and 4:30–9:30pm. INDIAN.

Hartford's burgeoning population of immigrants from the Indian subcontinent is responsible for several exotic restaurants, including this one, the best of the lot. A gaudy interior doesn't raise high hopes, with its pictures of camels and caravans and an acoustical tile ceiling. But wait! Even if Indian menus seem to you only a blur of *tikka* this and *tandoori* that, there's no mistaking the tantalizing aromas issuing from the curtained kitchen.

It would be no deprivation to lunch only on one or two of the appetizers and a big basket of *nan,* the puffy flat-bread warm from the oven, its bigger bubbles nicely singed. But that would mean missing such flavor-packed entrees as chicken *tikka sang* or lamb *dhansak* (cubes of lamb cooked with lentils in a stew seasoned with ginger and curries). Dishes are spicy enough to pop a few beads of sweat, but won't take the top of your head off. Prices are about 40% less at lunch than in the evening.

Civic Café. 150 Trumbull St. (near Asylum St.). ☎ **860/493-7412.** Main courses $15.95–$23.95. AE, DC, DISC, MC, V. Mon–Sat 11am–2:30pm; Mon–Wed 5–11pm, Thurs–Sat 5pm–midnight, Sun 4–10pm. ECLECTIC.

The prosperous, self-satisfied bunch who frequent this restaurant would be at ease in Boston or New York, and they have found a place that looks like it belongs in a hipper city. Up above, it's postindustrial ducts, pipes, and whirring fans. Air-conditioning is glacial, and so, sometimes, is the service. No one seems to mind, so busy are they watching the collisions of egos. Suits dominate at lunch, when the raw bar near the front is a big draw, and at happy hour, when patrons down fruit-colored martinis around the rectangular bar. The food itself gets your attention, not least for the gobs of salsas and dustings of herbs cast over each plate. "Lemon herb-rubbed rotisserie chicken with buttermilk mashed potatoes and roast garlic" is as simple as things get, and of course tuna is served rare. T-shirts and shorts are no-nos.

A similar formula and clientele is evident at the even newer **Max Downtown,** a block away on Asylum Street, opposite the Civic Center.

Hot Tomato's. 1 Union Place (at the corner of Asylum St.). ☎ **860/249-5100.** Main courses $13.95–$19.95. AE, CB, DC, MC, V. Sun–Mon 5:30–9:30pm, Tues–Thurs 5:30–10pm, Fri–Sat 5:30–11pm. ITALIAN.

The admirable renovation of Union Station spawned this popular trattoria in one wing. Walk from the host's podium past the ordered frenzy of the open kitchen and down into a large glass-sided dining room or out onto the dining terrace. A knowing crowd, most of it casually dressed, tucks into black bowls of pasta, which they are usually unable to finish.

Many of the recipes are infrequently available this side of Bologna. Especially spicy dishes are marked with a star, and one such is ziti tossed with grilled chicken strips, olive oil, roasted garlic cloves, and bitter broccoli rabe (admittedly an acquired taste). Main courses come with a house salad, which may be replaced with a "petite" Caesar salad for $1.95 extra. The waitress produces a pepper grinder from a pouch on her belt or a wedge of Parmesan for fresh gratings to order.

HARTFORD AFTER DARK

A widely available free weekly paper, the *Hartford Advocate,* provides useful information on cultural, sports, and musical events.

Several downtown clubs and bars put on live bands, usually Thursday to Saturday. Assuming they're still in operation (never something to be assumed), check out the **bar with no name,** 115 Asylum St. (☎ 860/522-4646), **The Russian Lady,** 191 Ann St. (☎ 860/525-3003), and **Arch Street Tavern,** 85 Arch St. (☎ 860/246-7610).

For beer by the pint or pitcher and Monday Night Football with the guys (and the women who are game), where better than **Coach's,** 187 Allyn St. (☎ **860/ 522-6224**)? It has 32 TVs and serves such dainties as chili in scooped-out loaves of bread. A similar sports bar is **Huskies,** 356 Asylum St. (☎ **860/278-4747**), which has various drink and food promotions as well as a patio overlooking Bushnell Park.

The Bushnell Performing Arts Center, 166 Capitol Ave. (☎ **860/246-6807**), is the venue for the **Hartford Ballet,** a classical and contemporary troupe that doesn't neglect to stage the obligatory Christmas season *Nutcracker.* It is also home to the **Hartford Symphony** and the **Hartford Pops,** when it isn't hosting visiting orchestras or road companies of Broadway plays like *Miss Saigon.*

Hartford Stage, 50 Church St. (☎ **860/527-5151**), mounts a variety of traditional and mainstream plays, occasionally interspersed with introductions of new productions, while **Theatreworks,** 233 Pearl St. (☎ **860/527-7838**), explores new frontiers.

5 The Way East: Guilford to Old Saybrook

Usually ignored by vacationers anxious to get on to Mystic and Essex and the new casinos, the stretch of coast between New Haven and the Connecticut River, known simply as the Shoreline, has its gentle pleasures, enough to justify a short detour for lunch, a walk on a beach, a spell of shopping, or even a proper British high tea (in Madison). When lodgings are difficult to find at the better-known destinations, Shoreline's inns and resorts are logical alternatives within easy driving distance.

THE SHORELINE ESSENTIALS

GETTING THERE   The Shoreline can be reached from Exit 57 of I-95. Pick up Route 1 (a.k.a. Boston Post Road), which serves as the main street of several Shoreline towns.

Several daily **Amtrak** trains stop at Old Saybrook, and the **Shoreline East** (☎ **800/255-7433**) commuter line uses the same tracks to service towns between there and New Haven, but only Monday through Friday.

VISITOR INFORMATION   Informational materials can be obtained in advance from the **Connecticut River Valley and Shoreline Visitors Council,** 393 Main St., Middletown, CT 06457 (☎ **800/486-3346** or 860/347-0028).

GUILFORD

One of the state's oldest colonial settlements (1639), this village, 13 miles east of New Haven, is embraced by the West and East rivers and has an uncommonly large green bordered by churches, shops, and public buildings.

SEEING THE SIGHTS

There are dozens of historic houses to see in town, most of them privately owned and a few others open to the public on a limited seasonal basis, typically Memorial Day weekend to Labor Day or Columbus Day. **Hyland House,** 84 Boston St. (☎ **203/ 453-9477**), built around 1660, and the **Thomas Griswold House,** 171 Boston St. (☎ **203/453-3176**), from 1774, are two of these. The Whitfield House (below) is open year-round.

Henry Whitfield State Museum. 248 Whitfield St. (east of the green). ☎ **203/453-2457.** Admission $3 adults, $1.50 seniors and children 6–17. Feb–Dec 14 Wed–Sun 10am–4:30pm; Dec 15–Jan 30 by appointment only.

The Whitfield Museum's billing as the "oldest house in Connecticut and the oldest stone house in New England" is misleading. In addition to undergoing frequent alterations over the years, the house was devastated by a major fire in 1860 that left little more than the granite walls. After reconstruction, it was inhabited until the turn of the century, and by the 1930s it had deteriorated from neglect, and had to be rebuilt once again.

Most of what you can see now, including the leaded windows, dates from that time, not from the mid-1600s, when the original structure went up. It is instructive, nonetheless, and is presented as a museum, not a historic home. The furnishings inside are authentic to the period, and there are displays of powder horns, flintlock rifles, spinning wheels, and a loom.

The Puritan settlers of Guilford were fearful of hostile action from nearby English and Dutch colonies. This building was one of four that served as part of a fortification system. Look for the unusual corner window on the second floor, which was used as a lookout over Long Island Sound, though the water is no longer visible due to tree growth.

WHERE TO DINE

An American Bistro. 25 Whitfield St. ☎ **203/458-9059.** Main courses $9.95–$18.95. AE, MC, V. Daily 11:30am–3:30pm; Tues–Sun 5–9pm. FRENCH/ECLECTIC.

Formerly known as The Bistro on the Green, this locally popular spot touches on the conventions in decor and menu that both names suggest. Butcher paper is laid over white tablecloths under vases of fresh flowers, and escargot and cassoulet are among the regular offerings. But the new chef is pushing the edges, so there is a *bruschetta du jour,* as well as various pastas and loosely "New American" dishes like pistachio-crusted salmon.

They are also open mornings from 10am for late breakfasts, and serve "light bites" between lunch and dinner.

MADISON

Madison, 19 miles east of New Haven, is home to a historic architectural district that stretches west of the business district along the Boston Post Road, from the main green to the town line, and boasts many examples of 18th- and 19th-century domestic styles and few commercial intrusions.

EXPLORING THE TOWN

Prosperous Madison has completed the transition from colony to seaside resort to year-round community, a process begun when the first house was built in 1651. Today there are two dwellings from the early years that can be visited on limited summer schedules. **Deacon John Grave House,** 581 Boston Post Rd. (☎ **203/245-4798**), dates from 1685, and the **Allis-Bushnell House,** 853 Boston Post Rd. (☎ **203/245-4567**), from 1785.

Off the Boston Post Road east of the town center, also reached from Exit 62 off I-95, is **Hammonasset Beach State Park** (☎ **203/245-1817**), a more than 900 acre peninsula jutting into Long Island Sound that has the only public swimming beach in the area. The park also has a nature center, picnic areas, and campgrounds, and offers boating, too. Cars with Connecticut license plates get in for $5 Monday to Friday and $7 weekends; out-of-state plates mean you'll be charged $8 and $12, respectively.

Madison's central commercial district may look ordinary at first glance, but several specialty shops along Boston Post Road and intersecting Wall Street provide entertaining browsing. These are the remaining holdouts against the magnetic pull of the monster outlet malls recently opened in neighboring Clinton and Westbrook.

One of the most active stores in the community is **R. J. Julia Booksellers,** 768 Boston Post Rd. (☎ **203/245-3959**), which holds frequent author readings and poetry slams. Many books on the store's two levels have annotation cards offering the specific observations of obviously well-read staff members. There is a large, separate children's section.

A few steps east is **Walker-Loden,** 788 Boston Post Rd. (☎ **203/245-8663**), which inadequately describes its wares as "gifts, antiques, and artwork." On hand are diverse souvenir and household items, such as straw hats, cookbooks, nonmechanical toys, greeting cards, pillboxes, prayer rugs, silk ties and scarves, and much more.

Cross the street, head north, and you'll come across several other shops. One of them, in a 1690 plum-colored saltbox, is **The British Shoppe,** 45 Wall St. (☎ **203/ 245-4521**), which stocks such English favorites as kippers, bangers, pork pies, boxes of various teas, and several sublime cheeses, all imported from Blighty. (The breads are from Old Saybrook, down the road.) Gifts and housewares of British origin are on sale, and lunches and afternoon teas are served in the "Front Parlor." Classic Ploughman's Lunches of cheese, bread, tomato, lettuce, and pickled onions recall those in English pubs (unfortunately, without pints of English beer, licensing requirements being too tough to meet). Lunch is served 11:30am to 1:30pm Monday to Saturday, and afternoon teas are Monday to Saturday 2 to 4pm and Sunday 12:30 to 4pm, offering properly brewed loose teas with finger sandwiches and cakes.

WHERE TO STAY

Tidewater Inn. 949 Boston Post Rd. (east of the business district), Madison, CT 06443. ☎ **203/245-8457.** 9 rms. A/C TV TEL. $80–$160 double. Rates include breakfast. AE, MC, V.

The bland exterior isn't promising, but impressions change once you step inside. The new owners have lowered rates and upgraded facilities, and the inn is now as useful to business travelers as it is comforting to vacationers. Decor hasn't changed much, with floral wallpapers and four-poster beds alongside collections of Chinese porcelains, Japanese prints, and related Orientalia. It is as if the New England wife of a long-absent merchant captain had embellished the house's standard trimmings with all of the gifts and souvenirs he carried back from his trade in Asia. (The abundance of fake wreaths, lacy padded hearts, and silk flowers won't suit every taste, however.) Most of the rooms have two reading chairs and desks with utilitarian brass office lamps. Breakfasts are substantial, with fresh fruit followed by waffles, pancakes, or other hot items. A fridge with soft drinks and an iron and ironing board are available to guests.

WESTBROOK

In Westbrook, a roadside sprawl more plebeian in character than Guilford and Madison, intermittent houses share space with strip malls, fish shanties, cookie-cutter franchises, marinas, and enterprises dedicated to boating services. Only the town center, 28 miles east of New Haven, preserves a touch of its New England character.

Giving a boost to the local economy is the new outlet mall, **Westbrook Factory Stores,** 314 Flat Rock Place (☎ **860/399-8656**), north of town at Exit 65 of I-95. Expected to eventually house 80 or more outlets, the complex observes an architectural style that might be described as Rural Railroad Revival, actually a pleasant change from the cell-block design common to many malls. Name dealers include Reebok, Timberland, Dockers, Bugle Boy, Olga/Warner's, Haggar, Corning/Revere, American Tourister, Nordic Track, Springmaid/Wamsutta, J. Crew, Jockey, and Oshkosh B'Gosh. Open daily.

WHERE TO STAY

Water's Edge. 1525 Boston Post Rd. (Rte. 1), Westbrook, CT 06498. ☎ **800/222-5901** or 860/399-5901. Fax 203/399-6172. 32 rms. A/C TV TEL. $110–$300 double. AE, DC, DISC, MC, V.

Water's Edge started out as Bill Hahn's Resort, a shambling family getaway spot that had the feel of a Catskills resort transplanted to the Connecticut coast. It grew and grew into what is now a full-service hotel which also has time-share condo units. Used for corporate conferences as well as by families and couples, it has sacrificed a reputed former coziness in favor of efficiency and a measure of gloss. Families may want to inquire about renting one of the unoccupied villas instead of the standard hotel rooms.

Dining/Entertainment: The hotel restaurant is a tony pink-and-buff affair with terraces overlooking the lawn and the wide sandy beach. While the kitchen is capable, the best deal is the generous Sunday brunch. There's live music and dancing on weekends.

Services: Supervised summer play program for kids.

Facilities: All manner of recreational facilities are available, including two pools (one indoor), paddleboats and sailboats, a fitness center, and tennis courts.

WHERE TO DINE

Lenny & Joe's Fish Tale. 86 Boston Post Rd. (Rte. 1). ☎ **203/669-0767.** Main courses $6.75–$13.95. No credit cards. Sun–Thurs 11am–9pm, Fri–Sat 11am–10pm. SEAFOOD.

This is a rough-and-ready fish shack with low ceilings, few pretenses to decor, and waitresses in shorts, aprons, and sneakers. On each bare table is a ketchup bottle and a canister of sea salt. Fish is the thing, of course, most of it fried. And while it is sure to elevate triglyceride counts, the nutty, crunchy coating on superfresh whole clams, oysters, shrimp, or calamari is hard to resist, especially on a summer evening when the air carries the scent of oceans and distant islands. The menu is printed daily to reflect market prices and availability.

There is another Fish Tale in Madison, at 1301 Boston Post Rd. (☎ **860/245-7289**).

OLD SAYBROOK

Its location at the mouth of the Connecticut River (35 miles east of New Haven, 26 miles west of Mystic) is this otherwise nondescript town's principal lure.

You'll have to get off Route 1 to see it at its best. Pick up Route 153 south at the western edge, following its nearly circular route as it touches the shore and passes through the hamlets of Knollwood and Fenwick and across the causeway to Saybrook Point before ending up back in the main business district.

Movie buffs will get a kick out of cruises on *The African Queen*, moored at the River Landing Marina, Ferry Road (☎ **860/388-2007**), the actual steam-powered launch from the 1951 film starring Humphrey Bogart and Katherine Hepburn. It makes voyages May to October, Wednesday through Sunday, from 11am to 6:30pm. The fare for the half-hour trip is $15.

WHERE TO DINE

Cuckoo's Nest. 1712 Boston Post Rd. (Rte. 1). ☎ **860/399-9060.** Main courses $10.95–$15.95. AE, DC, DISC, MC, V. Mon–Wed 11:30am–10pm, Thurs–Sat 11:30am–11pm, Sun 11am–10pm. TEX-MEX/CAJUN.

"Mexican Food Plus Cajun & Creole," crows the ecumenical menu, so sanctimonious sticklers for gastronomic authenticity had better look elsewhere. The rest of us can have a good time at moderate cost at this unabashedly raffish roadhouse, which comes complete with wooden chairs, tables, and floors that haven't seen fresh coats of shellac since the 1976 opening. On the walls are old advertising signs and English street markers; pierced-tin lamps hang over some of the tables, and fans rotate lazily overhead. A jazz duo performs Thursday nights, a pianist on Sundays.

As for the food, corn-crusted codfish with yellow rice and roasted garlic salsa may or may not be truly Mexican, but it tastes mighty good. So do the pork-loin fajitas, topped with shredded cheese and pico de gallo. As for the "Cajun & Creole" offerings, check out the New Orleans popcorn shrimp or the catfish Creole. A little jambalaya couldn't hurt, either. Sunday brunch is all you can eat for only $9.95. Begin your visit with a mango margarita, out on the terrace if it's a warm night.

6   The Connecticut River Valley

New England's longest river originates in the far north near the Canadian border, 407 miles from Long Island Sound. It separates Vermont from New Hampshire, splits Massachusetts in half, then takes a 45° turn at Middletown, south of Hartford, to make its final run to the sea.

Native Americans of the region called the river *Quinnehtukqut,* which, to the linguistically tin ears of the English settlers, sounded like "Connecticut." The colonists encroached upon Indian territory as far north as present-day Windsor, which ignited a brief war with the Pequot, who occupied the land.

Since the river was navigable by relatively large ships as far as Hartford, the sheltered lower Connecticut became important for boatbuilding and to industries associated with the international clipper trade. The Connecticut River retains that nautical flavor, and the valley has miraculously avoided the industrialization, development, and decay that afflicts most of the state's other rivers.

CONNECTICUT RIVER VALLEY ESSENTIALS

GETTING THERE   Limited-access state highway 9 runs parallel to the river, along the west side of the valley, connecting I-91 south of Hartford with I-95 near Old Saybrook. The lower valley is therefore readily accessible from all points in New England and from the New York metropolitan area and points south.

Amtrak (☎ **800/872-7245**) trains stop at Old Saybrook, at the mouth of the river, several times daily on their runs between New York and Boston. In addition, **Shoreline East** (☎ **800/255-7433**) commuter trains operate Monday to Friday between New Haven and Old Saybrook.

VISITOR INFORMATION   The **Connecticut River Valley and Shoreline Visitors Council,** 393 Main St., Middletown, CT 06457 (☎ **800/486-3346** or 860/347-0028), is a source of pamphlets, maps, and related materials.

A NOTE ON LODGINGS   There aren't a great many motels between Haddam and Old Lyme, the southernmost segment of the valley that is of greatest interest to tourists, but there are several excellent full-service inns and many bed-and-breakfasts, some independent and some that can only be found through referral agencies. Two such B&B referral companies are **Bed & Breakfast, Ltd.,** P.O. Box 216, New Haven, CT 06513 (☎ **203/469-3260**), and **Nutmeg Bed & Breakfast Agency,** P.O. Box 1117, West Hartford, CT 06127 (☎ **800/727-7592** or 860/236-6698).

OLD LYME

As quiet a town as the coast can claim, with tree-lined streets largely free of traffic, Old Lyme (40 miles east of New Haven, 21 miles west of Mystic) was the favored residence of generations of seafarers and ship captains. Many of their 18th- and 19th-century homes have survived, some as summer residences of the artists who established a colony here around the turn of the century, a few as inns and museums.

A MANSION OF ART

Florence Griswold Museum. 96 Lyme St. (Rte. 1). ☎ **860/434-5542.** Admission $4 adults, $3 seniors and students, children under 12 free. June–Nov Tues–Sat 10am–5pm, Sun 1–5pm; Dec–May Wed–Sun 1–5pm.

Once the shipbuilding and merchant trade had all but flickered out at the end of the last century, artists who came to be known as the "American Impressionists" took a fancy to this area. Encouragement, patronage, and even food and shelter were offered them by Ms. Griswold, the wealthy daughter of a sea captain. Her 1817 Federalist mansion was the temporary home for a number of painters, most of whom left samples of their work in gratitude, including pictures painted directly on the walls of the dining room. Visitors can walk across the mansion's 6 acres to the Lieutenant River, a brief course that flows slightly to the west of the Connecticut.

Rotating temporary exhibits are held on the first and second floors. The restored studio of Impressionist William Chadwick is also on view.

OUTDOOR PURSUITS

One of several state parks located at the edge of Long Island Sound, **Rocky Neck State Park,** Route 156 (☎ **860/739-5471**), east of Old Lyme, has a half-mile, scimitar-shaped beach and over 560 acres for camping, picnicking, fishing, and hiking. Reach it from Exit 72 of I-95, picking up Route 156 south.

Although headquartered in New York's Hudson Valley, **Atlantic Kayak Tours,** 320 W. Saugerties Rd., Saugerties, NY 12477 (☎ **914/246-2187**), conducts many tours along Connecticut's rivers and shoreline, as well as crossings to Long Island. Most excursions are in the 6- to 14-mile range, with levels of difficulty ranging from beginner to highly advanced. With some exceptions, tours are $45 per person, plus $30 for kayak rental.

WHERE TO STAY & DINE

Bee and Thistle Inn. 100 Lyme St. (Rte. 1), Old Lyme, CT 06371. ☎ **800/622-4946** or 860/434-1667. Fax 860/434-3402. 11 rms (9 with private bath), 1 cottage. A/C TEL. $75–$155 double. Approaching from the south, take Exit 70 from I-95; turn left, then right on Rte. 1 north. No children under 12 accepted.

The core structure of the inn dates from 1756, with the usual wings and additions. Every corner of the place is an enjoyable clutter of antiques and collectibles. A small detached cottage is the best lodging, with the only room TV and a fireplace.

Dining/Entertainment: A skilled professional kitchen staff prepares three meals a day, served on dining-room tables near fireplaces by an eager-to-please wait staff. Musicians are on hand weekend evenings. Diners are asked to wear jackets (or the female equivalent) to dinner.

Old Lyme Inn. 85 Lyme St. (Rte. 1), Old Lyme, CT 06371. ☎ **800/434-5352** or 860/434-2600. Fax 860/434-5352. 13 rms. A/C TV TEL. $99–$158 double. Rates include breakfast. AE, CB, DC, DISC, MC, V. To get there, follow the directions for the Bee and Thistle, above.

Most of the bedrooms in this 1850s farmhouse are spacious, and furnished with pieces such as Victorian chairs, love seats, and four-poster or "cannonball" beds.

Dining/Entertainment: The dining rooms are even more impressive, especially the Grill, which features an entire antique bar and marble-manteled fireplace—

admirers of Victorian taverns might not want to leave. The Grill offers a light dinner menu, with live music on weekends. The other dining rooms are more formal (but not stuffy) and serve more substantial creative American meals prepared by a highly competent chef. Entrees in the Grill are $15.65 to $16.75, in the main rooms $19.95 to $27.95.

ESSEX

It is hard to imagine what improvements might be made to bring this dream of a New England town closer to perfection. In fact, a recently published survey book, *The 100 Best Small Towns in America,* ranked Essex, a waterside village just 35 miles east of New Haven, number one. (Among the criteria were low crime rates, per-capita income, proportions of college-educated residents, and numbers of physicians. Essex ranked with the leaders in every category.) Residents insist they can still leave their doors unlocked.

Tree-bordered streets are lined with shops and homes that retain an early-18th-century flavor without the unreal frozen-in-amber, precious quality that often afflicts other towns as postcard-pretty as this. People live and work and play here, and bustle busily along a Main Street that runs down to Steamboat Dock and its flotilla of working vessels and pleasure craft.

SEEING THE SIGHTS

Clustered along the harbor end of Main Street are three historic houses that can be visited on limited schedules. No. 40 is the **Richard Hayden House,** an 1814 brick Federalist that was home to the namesake merchant and shipbuilder. During the War of 1812, British raiders burned Hayden's entire fleet. He was ruined, and died soon after, still a young man. Next door, at no. 42, is a mid-1700 center-hall colonial that was also the home of a boatbuilder, the **Noah Tooker House.** And at no. 51 is the **Robert Lay House,** completed around 1730 and thought to be the oldest original structure in town.

Connecticut River Museum. Steamboat Dock (at the foot of Main St.). ☎ **860/767-8269.** $4 adults, $3 seniors, $2 children 6–12. Tues–Sun 10am–5pm.

Anglers wet their lines from the dock; gulls and ducks hang around hoping for a discarded tidbit. Steamboat service was fully operational here from 1823, and the existing dock dates from 1879. Designated a National Historic Site, the museum proper is a converted warehouse, which has two floors of intricately detailed model ships, marine paintings, and various artifacts. They relate the story of shipbuilding in the valley, which began in 1733 and helped make this a center of world trade far into the 19th century. Essex had as many as nine boatyards, and the first American warship constructed for the War of Independence, the *Oliver Cromwell,* was finished here in 1775. Also in the museum is a replica of the first submersible vessel deployed in wartime, the *Turtle.*

The museum usually has walking-tour maps ($1) of Essex, making this a good first stop on a visit.

Essex Steam Train. Railroad Ave. (Rte. 154). ☎ **860/767-0103.** Fares, train and boat $15 adults, $7.50 children 3–11; train only $10 adults, $5 children 3–11. Daily trips June through Labor Day, less frequently Sept–Apr.

Steam locomotives from the 1920s chug along a route from this station on the road between Essex center and Ivoryton to a boat landing in the hamlet of Deep River, a mildly engrossing excursion of about an hour. It can be combined with an optional additional cruise on the river, for a total of $2^1/_2$ to 3 hours. Special events include a Halloween "ghost" train, a Christmas express with Santa Claus, a jazz festival in June, and dinner trains.

WHERE TO STAY & DINE

✪ **Griswold Inn.** 36 Main St. (center of town), Essex, CT 06426. ☎ **860/767-1776.** 30 rms. A/C TEL. $90–$185 double. Rates include breakfast. AE, MC, V.

Gloss over the assertion that "The Gris" is the oldest inn in America (there are other claimants). What's more important to locals and regular guests from out of town is that the inn has been rescued from a rumored takeover by outsiders harboring dark plans for its transformation. Three brothers who grew up in town with the inn as a focal part of their lives (as it is for every Essex native) have bought it. Managing partner Doug Paul vows that there will be no dramatic changes, and that maintenance and modest alterations will proceed at a measured pace. That's a relief, for it is difficult to imagine this corner of New England without The Gris. Rumpled, cluttered, folksy, and forever besieged by drop-in yachtspeople, anglers, locals, guests, and tourists, the main building dates to 1776. The Brothers Paul are now directing their efforts at upgrading the too often plain and unadorned bedrooms scattered through six buildings. Several new suites are now available. Viva Gris!

Dining/Entertainment: The taproom, one of the most atmospheric taverns north of Key West, started life as a schoolhouse and was moved here in 1800. Its vaulted ceiling is said to be made of crushed shells and horsehair, seemingly held up there by the centuries of wafting tar and nicotine that turned it a deep tobacco brown. The walls are layered with nautical memorabilia, as are most of the public rooms. There is live entertainment every night, be it a Dixieland band or only a man with a banjo. The several dining rooms are nearly as colorful, named for their displays of books, antique weapons, or marine paintings. The food is hearty, no-foolin' victuals—turkey with stuffing, roast loin of pork, mixed grill with sauerkraut. Creative risks are restricted to the menu's descriptive prose, which employs titles like "The Awful Awful NY Sirloin—awful big and awful good." Forgive them their excesses, for servings are large, the cooking is straightforward, and prices are fair.

IVORYTON

Once a center for the ivory trade, where factories fabricated piano keys and hair combs—hence the name—Ivoryton has since subsided into a residential quietude. A virtual suburb of the only slightly larger Essex, a few miles east, the town perks up a bit in the summer, when the **Ivoryton Playhouse** (☎ **860/767-3075**) opens its June-to-August theatrical season. The Playhouse's repertoire runs to revivals of Broadway and off-Broadway comedies and mysteries.

WHERE TO STAY & DINE

✪ **Copper Beech Inn.** 46 Main St., Ivoryton, CT 06442. ☎ **860/767-0330.** Fax 860/767-7840. 13 rms. A/C TV TEL. $105–$175 double. Rates include breakfast. AE, CB, DC, MC, V. Take Exit 3 from Rte. 9 and head west on Main St.

Comparisons with the Griswold Inn in nearby Essex are inevitable, but these are two very different animals. Where The Gris is decidedly populist, perennially busy, and well into its 3rd century, the Copper Beech has much less traffic, and is stately in its pace, without a single figurative hair out of place. The previous owners rescued this 19th-century home of an ivory importer hours before it was to be burned to the ground in a fire department training exercise. It was gutted and rebuilt from the studs out, and the present innkeepers have expanded on the earlier effort. The nine rooms in the converted barn they call the "Carriage House" have ample elbow room, cushy chairs, expensive reproductions of 19th-century furniture styles, and not much character. They compensate with whirlpool tubs, phones, and TVs. The four rooms in the main room tuck right into country inn stereotypes, with original turn-of-the-century bath fixtures and plenty of antiques. They have phones but no TVs, and staying there can be as nostalgic as a visit to Aunt Edna's. Obviously, which sort of room to book is a matter of taste. No smoking anywhere on the property.

Dining/Entertainment: The Copper Beech is home to one of the most honored kitchens in the region. "New Traditionalist" might describe the chef's take on French recipes and techniques as applied to his high-quality ingredients. Service is seamless in the three formal dining areas, with rolled napkins in the water glasses standing as alert as rabbit ears in a meadow. The restaurant is closed Mondays from April to December, and Mondays and Tuesdays January to March.

CHESTER

Hardly more than a three-block business center with a few side streets that straggle off past stone fences into the countryside, Chester can be dismissed easily enough. After all, it's small enough to barely require downshifting. But pause a moment, for this is a riverside hamlet that deserves savoring. Along Main Street are antique shops and art galleries, the post office, a library, and several eating places that range from sandal informal to dressy casual. The two small streams that once provided power for early grist- and sawmills are canalized and all but hidden.

Downtown Chester doesn't have much room for shops, but it squeezes in at least a couple that deserve a closer look. At **Naturally, Books and Coffee,** 16 Main St. (☎ 860/526-3212), a small selection of books occupies the front of the store, and there's an espresso bar in the back. They have outdoor tables on warm days and live acoustic jazz, folk, and pop performers on weekends. **Ceramica,** 36–38 Main St. (☎ 860/526-9978), an outlet of a small chain with branches in SoHo (Manhattan), West Hartford, and Scarsdale, N.Y., carries a line of mostly Italian and uniformly gorgeous hand-painted platters, bowls, pitchers, vases, cups, tureens, and teapots. Open daily.

WHERE TO DINE

Fiddlers. 4 Water St. (behind Main St.). ☎ **860/526-3210.** Main courses $12.50–$18.95. MC, V. Tues–Sat 11:30am–2pm; Tues–Thurs 5:30–9pm, Fri 5:30–9:30pm, Sat 5:30–10pm, Sun 4–9pm. SEAFOOD.

Have your fish any way you want—poached, sautéed, broiled, baked, or grilled over mesquite—or leave it up to the skillful kitchen, for they can come up with some eye-openers. Topping that list is the "lobster au pêché" (fat chunks of lobster meat married to peach nubbins, shallots, mushrooms, cream, and peach brandy). Not for lobster purists, certainly, but a downright revelatory example of what an imaginative chef can do. All entrees come with a starch, vegetable, and garlic bread with an aioli dip. The rooms are cheerfully unremarkable, with bentwood chairs, marine prints, and ruffled curtains.

The Wheatmarket. 4 Water St. ☎ **860/526-9347.** Soups, salads, and sandwiches $3.20–$5. MC, V. Mon–Sat 9am–6pm. DELI.

Eat out or eat in at this upwardly mobile country delicatessen, next door to Fiddlers. The staff is eager to please, and will even make up full picnic baskets for $9.50 to $16 per person. "The Gourmet" version includes smoked salmon with capers, cream cheese, and red onion; mousse truffée with toast points, chicken-and-grape salad, Caesar salad, cheesecake, and sparkling cider. Or put together your own from the appetizing array of breads, cheeses, pâtés, cold cuts, soups, salads, and sandwiches.

Shelves are stocked as well with bottled jams, olive oils, a variety of coffee beans, mustards, and vinegars.

EAST HADDAM

Hardly more than a wide spot in a country road surrounded by woods and meadows, Hadlyme (a jurisdiction of the town of East Haddam) wouldn't attract much attention at all if a wealthy thespian hadn't decided to build his hilltop redoubt here.

To get there, take the **Chester-Hadlyme Ferry,** at the end of Route 148, slightly less than 2 miles from Chester. A ferry has operated here since 1769, and the current version takes both cars and pedestrians ($2.25 for vehicles plus $1.50 for trailers, 75¢ for walk-on passengers). It operates (when it feels like it) from 7am to 6:45pm in the warmer months. If it's closed down, there will be a sign posted out at the intersection of Routes 148 and 154, in which case you have to drive north on 154 to Haddam and take the bridge.

AN ECCENTRIC'S CASTLE

Gillette Castle State Park. River Rd. ☎ **860/526-2336.** Admission $4 adults, $2 children 6–11. Grounds open daily 8am–sunset; castle Memorial Day to Columbus Day daily 10am–5pm, Columbus Day to the end of Nov weekends 10am–4pm.

William Gillette was a successful actor and playwright known primarily for his theatrical portrayals of Sherlock Holmes. He took the money and ran to this hill rearing above the Connecticut River, where he had his castle built.

It's difficult to believe that he really thought the result resembled the Norman fortresses that allegedly were his inspiration. Rock gardens by roadside eccentrics in South Dakota or Death Valley are closer relations. Gillette felt it necessary, for one example, to design a dining-room table that slid into the wall, an inexplicable space-saving effort by a bachelor rattling around in 24 oddly shaped rooms.

But whatever Gillette's deficiencies as an architect and designer, no one can argue with his choice of location. The castle sits atop a hill above the east bank, with superlative vistas upriver and down. Nowhere else is the blessed underdevelopment of the estuary more apparent.

Since the terrace of the "castle" can be entered for free, many visitors just come to take in those views and avoid the fees for entering the interior. The 184-acre grounds have picnic areas, nature trails, and fishing sites. There is a snack bar at the edge of the parking lot.

RIVER CRUISES

A voyage on the river is a near-irresistible outing. Cruises of a variety of lengths, times, and themes are offered by **Camelot Cruises,** 1 Marine Park (☎ **860/ 345-8591**). The pride of their fleet is the M/V *Camelot,* a 160-foot vessel carrying as many as 500 passengers. In addition to dinner and mystery cruises (in which the passengers solve a staged "murder"), there are summer and fall excursions to Sag Harbor, Long Island.

EAST HADDAM AFTER DARK

From Gillette State Park, turn north on Route 82 and make the short drive to East Haddam proper. The dominant building is a restored six-story Victorian of splendid proportions that opened in 1877 and is now the **Goodspeed Opera House,** Goodspeed Landing (☎ **860/873-8668**). A century ago, it presented such productions as *All is Not Gold that Glitters* and *Factory Girl.* Now it mostly stages revivals of Broadway musicals on the order of *Sweeney Todd* and *Annie,* but has made room for more experimental shows that have eventually made it all the way to the Big Apple. The Goodspeed's season is usually from April to December.

7 Mystic & the Southeastern Coast

If a whirlwind driving tour of New England leaves only 2 or 3 days for all of Connecticut, I'd say you should spend them in this section of the coast that segues into the mainland beach resorts of Rhode Island. And go soon, because it's impossible to predict the eventual effects that the gushers of money produced by two new and immensely successful gambling casinos will have on the character of this region.

The town of Mystic and its singular attraction, the living, working museum that is Mystic Seaport, are the prime reasons for a stay—the Seaport alone can easily occupy most of a day and the two-part town itself sustains a delightful nautical air, with fun shops and restaurants to suit most tastes and every budget.

But that's not a complete list of the region's charms. The tranquil neighboring village of Stonington is home to an active commercial fishing fleet, the last in the state; nearby Groton, on the Thames River, offers tours of the world's first nuclear submarine; there are several enchanting inns in the area; many companies and individuals offer their vessels for whale watching, dinner cruises, and deep-sea fishing excursions. And yes, for those with a taste for the adrenaline rush of a winning streak, there are those two casinos.

If at all possible, avoid July and August, when the crowds are oppressive, restaurants are packed, and rooms are booked months in advance.

SOUTHEASTERN COAST ESSENTIALS

GETTING THERE   From New York City, take I-95 to Exit 84 (New London), 86 (Groton), 90 (Mystic), or 91 (Stonington). Or, to avoid the heavy truck and commercial traffic of the western segment of I-95, use the Hutchinson River Parkway, which becomes the Merritt Parkway (Route 15) and merges with the Wilbur Cross Parkway. Continue to Exit 54, connecting with I-95 for the rest of the trip. From Boston, take the Massachusetts Turnpike to I-395 south to Exit 75, then south on Route 32 to New London and I-95 west.

Amtrak (☎ **800/872-7245**) has six trains daily (three each way) on its Northeast Direct route between New York, Providence, and Boston, with intermediate stops at New Haven, Old Saybrook, New London, and Mystic.

The regional bus company, **SEAT** (☎ **860/886-2631**), connects the more important towns and villages of the district, except for North Stonington.

VISITOR INFORMATION   The **Southeastern Connecticut Tourism District,** P.O. Box 89, 470 Bank St., New London, CT 06320 (☎ **800/863-6569** or 860/444-2206), can provide free vacation kits.

AREA CODE   Note that the local area code changed from 203 to 860 in 1995, although some printed tourist materials still carry the old code.

A NOTE ON LODGINGS   Motels do abound, especially in clusters around the several exits off I-95, and can handle the load most of the year (though it's tight in July and August). But travelers who seek lodgings of a more intimate and sometimes less expensive sort can contact the Southeastern Connecticut Tourism District (see above) to request a folder describing the loosely affiliated **Bed & Breakfasts of Mystic Coast,** which lists 23 establishments in the area, including four just across the Rhode Island state line. Most are in the $50-to-$110 range and accept credit cards.

NEW LONDON

Founded in 1646 and first known by the Pequot name *Nameaug,* New London's protected deep-draft harbor at the mouth of the Thames River was responsible for its long and influential history as a whaling port. That heritage lingers, but its years of great prosperity are behind it.

Possessed of an architecturally interesting but somnolent downtown district, New London, which lies 46 miles east of New Haven and 45 miles southeast of Hartford, is of note to travelers primarily because it's a transit point for three ferry lines connecting Block Island, R.I., and Long Island, N.Y., with the mainland. **Connecticut College** has a large campus at the northern edge of the city, along Route 32 and Williams Street. The **U.S. Coast Guard Academy** is also here, but while it welcomes visitors, it is of interest primarily to alumni and prospective students and their parents.

An attended **visitor information booth** is located in downtown New London at the corner of Eugene O'Neill Drive and Golden Street (no phone). It's open June through August daily from 10am to 4pm; May, September, and October, Friday to Sunday from 10am to 4pm.

SEEING THE SIGHTS

Coast Guard Academy. 15 Mohegan Ave. (off Williams St., north of Exit 84 of I-95). ☎ **860/444-8611.** Free admission. Grounds, Mon–Fri 10am–5pm; Visitors Pavilion, May 1–Oct 31 daily 10am–5pm, Apr Sat–Sun 10am–5pm. Pavilion closed in Nov–Mar.

A guard takes names at the gate, and directs cars to the Visitors Pavilion on the other side of the base, overlooking the Thames. The Pavilion doesn't offer much except views of the river and shores; the short film run on request is a public-relations exercise designed to recruit students, not enlighten the public.

A full-rigged sailing vessel, the *Eagle,* is the academy's principal attraction, available to visitors only on a limited basis. The latest in a line of Coast Guard cutters that goes back to 1792, it was built as a training ship for German Naval cadets in 1936 and taken as a war prize after World War II. Renamed the *Eagle,* the barque continues that instructional function at the academy. When in port, usually only in April and May, it can be boarded Monday to Friday from 4pm to sunset, Saturday and Sunday from noon to sunset. Its dock can be seen from the Visitors Pavilion.

If you're here on a Friday in spring or early fall, there might be a dress parade by the corps of cadets.

Lyman Allyn Art Museum. 625 Williams St. ☎ **860/443-2545.** Admission $3 adults, $2 seniors and students, children under 12 free. July through Labor Day Tues–Sat 10am–5pm, Sun 1–5pm; Labor Day through June Tues–Sun 1–5pm. From Exit 84 of I-95, proceed north on Rte. 32 to the first exit, following brown signs to the museum.

This neoclassical granite pile stands on a hill looking across Route 32 toward the Coast Guard Academy. Its holdings are the results of the enthusiasms of private collectors, and therefore hold to no particular curatorial or scholarly vision. The various parts are interesting, however, even if they don't belong to a harmonious whole.

The basement contains detailed room settings of Victorian dollhouse furniture, right down to tiny ladles on the kitchen counter and buttonhooks on the bureau. On the main floor are American paintings and furnishings dating to the colonial period, including landscapes by Hudson River School artists Frederic Edwin Church, George Inness, and Albert Bierstadt. Upstairs are galleries with exhibits as diverse as Asian temple castings, African carvings, Japanese lacquerware, and paintings related to New London's past.

OUTDOOR PURSUITS

Not far from downtown is **Ocean Beach Park,** at the south end of Ocean Avenue (☎ **800/510-7263** or 860/447-3031), a 40-acre recreational facility with a broad sand beach, a boardwalk, a 50-meter-long freshwater pool, a miniature golf course, and a triple water slide. Also available are a bathhouse with lockers and showers, concession stands, and a lounge. Live entertainment is scheduled throughout the summer. Open Saturday before Memorial Day through Labor Day, daily from 9am to 10pm. The parking fee also covers admission for all occupants of the car.

From June to September, waterborne excursions run by **Thames River Cruises** (☎ **860/444-7827**) carry passengers up past the *Nautilus* submarine base (see "Groton," below). Daily departures are made hourly from 9am to 5pm; home dock is the City Pier at the foot of State Street, behind the railroad station. The fare is $10 for adults, $6 for children 6 to 13.

The ferries that ply Long Island Sound from New London have a recreational aspect, as well as simply serving as transport between Block Island and Long Island. Year-round service to Orient Point on Long Island is provided by **Cross Sound Ferry** (☎ **860/443-5281**). Departures are every hour or two during the day, and the one-way voyage takes about an hour and 20 minutes. Call ahead both to confirm departure times and make reservations, especially when taking a car. The **Fishers Island Ferry** (☎ **860/443-6851**) also has daily departures for Long Island. **Nelseco Navigation Co.** (☎ **860/442-7891** or 860/442-9553) operates its ferry once a day (with an extra trip Friday evenings) from mid-June to early September between New London and the Old Harbor on Block Island. The one-way trip takes about 2 hours. An advance reservation for cars is essential, but a call ahead is also important to determine fares and current sailing times.

WHERE TO STAY

Queen Anne Inn. 265 Williams St. (east of Rte. 32), New London, CT 06320. ☎ **800/ 347-8818** or 860/447-2600. 10 rms (8 with private bath). A/C. $89–$175 double. Rates include breakfast. AE, CB, DISC, DC, MC, V.

Parents visiting their kids at the area colleges are frequent guests at the Queen Anne, as are businesspeople who prefer to avoid the anonymity of highway motels. This relatively steady occupancy flow is why rates don't fluctuate as much here as at many inns.

The inn's name refers to the building's late Victorian architectural style. An oak staircase reaches up three floors (there's no elevator) to the Tower Room, probably the best of the lot. It is equipped with a TV and phone as well as a kitchen with stove, fridge, and coffeemaker. These extras are not features of all the rooms, however—two rooms share a bath, and only some have phones and TVs, so make your needs known when reserving. A couple of rooms have fireplaces, and most have four-posters or canopy beds.

Breakfast is an extravaganza of Mexican quiches, chocolate waffles, and citrus French toast with strawberry cream sauce. That treat is complemented with high teas (3 to 9pm) of coffee cakes, scones, and delicate sandwiches. You may not care to eat a single meal out during your stay.

GROTON

The future is uncertain for this naval-industrial town on the opposite side of the Thames from New London, for it has long been dependent on the presence of the Electric Boat division of General Dynamics and the Navy's Submarine Base, and cutbacks in military budgets show no signs of reversal. Whatever happens, the principal tourist attraction will probably remain the famous USS *Nautilus,* the world's first nuclear-powered vessel.

SEEING THE SIGHTS

After a visit to the submarine museum, history buffs may wish to stop for a stroll around **Fort Griswold Battlefield State Park,** Monument Street and Park Avenue

(☎ **860/445-1729** or 860/449-6877). It was here, in 1781, that the traitor Benedict Arnold led a British force against American defenders, ruthlessly ordering the massacre of his 88 prisoners after they had surrendered. Museum open Memorial Day to Labor Day daily from 10am to 5pm and Labor Day to Columbus Day, Saturday and Sunday 10am to 5pm. Free admission.

Submarine Force Museum. Submarine Base. ☎ **800/343-0079** or 860/449-3174. Free admission. May 15–Oct 31 Wed–Mon 9am–5pm, Tues 1–5pm; Nov 1–May 14 Wed–Mon 9am–4pm. Take Exit 86 from I-95, driving north on Rte. 12 and following signs to the museum.

Outside the museum are battered minisubs used by the Axis powers in World War II. The entry hall and adjoining galleries display models of submarines, torpedoes, missiles, deck guns, hands-on periscopes, and a full-scale cross-section of Bushnell's *Turtle,* the "first submersible ever used in a military conflict" in 1776—unsuccessfully, as it happens.

Continuing out the back and across a set of railroad tracks, the USS *Nautilus* itself stands at its mooring, ready for inspection. Before descending into the sub, keep in mind that large people or those with arthritis or similar afflictions might find it difficult to negotiate some of the hatchways and steep staircases. The somewhat claustrophobic walk through the control rooms, attack center, galley, and sleeping quarters is aided by listening devices handed out to each visitor that click on with audio descriptions at appropriate points along the tour. The self-guided tour only takes about 10 minutes.

FISHING TRIPS

A number of companies offer full- and half-day fishing trips. Typical of the party boats is the 114-foot *Hel-Cat II,* 181 Thames St. (☎ **860/535-2066** or 860/535-3200), operating from its own pier about 2 miles south of Exit 85N or 86S of I-95.

Both charter and party boats are available from the **Sunbeam Fleet** based at **Captain John's Sport Fishing Center,** 15 First St., Waterford (☎ **860/443-7259**). Fishing party boats sail twice daily Friday to Sunday in June, Thursday to Tuesday July through Labor Day. The same firm has day-long whale-watching voyages Sunday, Tuesday, and Thursday in July and August. Nature cruises are available in February and March (an eagle watch) and March to May (harbor seals). A substantial variety of fishing trips are offered. The whale-watch boat has a galley and bar. Waterford is the town immediately south of New London; the dock is next to the Niantic River Bridge.

UNCASVILLE & THE MONHEGAN SUN CASINO

About halfway between New London and Norwich, this blue-collar town once hardly provided sufficient reason even to downshift your car. That's changed, for good.

In October 1996, the Mohegan tribe opened its gambling casino, **Mohegan Sun,** Mohegan Sun Blvd. (☎ **888/226-7711**). It directly competes with Foxwoods (see below), the hugely successful hotel/casino complex of the Mashantucket Pequots, only 10 miles away. While it is early to predict its fiscal success, the signs are good, given the tribe's outlay of well over $300 million for land and construction. They sit in the middle of a potential $1 billion annual market, and were drawing thousands of gamblers a day within a few weeks of opening.

The central building has a circular arrangement, with four entrances named for the seasons. The core of 150,000 square feet is devoted to the games, everything from blackjack and baccarat to craps and Pai Gow poker, supplemented by 3,000 slot machines. In the center is a nightclub featuring stars of secondary magnitude, and overhead are simulated peeled log constructions meant to suggest ancient lodge houses. It is an esthetically pleasing space (as casinos go), although few of the avid players seem to notice. A hotel and additional recreational facilities are planned.

The casino is right off Exit 79A of I-395, which makes for easy on/off access for players who don't want to deal with that onerous 20-minute drive to Foxwoods before emptying their bank accounts.

NORWICH

There is tourist potential here, where the Yantic and Shetucket rivers converge to form the Thames. Blocks of Broadway and Union Street are lined with substantial mansions in styles ranging from the Federalist and classical revival of the first half of the 19th century to the Italianate, French Second Empire, and eclectic Victorian conceits of the second. They survive from the city's golden era, when the abolitionist preacher Henry Ward Beecher was inspired to compare the hills of Norwich to the petals of a rose, prompting the oft-repeated reference to the city as the "Rose of New England."

There is no pretending, however, that this historic old mill town isn't in the doldrums. Until efforts to reverse that decline take hold, the principal reason for a visit is the wonderful lodging described below.

WHERE TO STAY & DINE

✪ **Norwich Inn & Spa.** 607 W. Thames St. (Rte. 32), Norwich, CT 06360. ☎ **800/267-4772** or 860/886-2401. Fax 860/886-9483. 65 rms and suites. A/C TV TEL. $115–$245 double. AE, DC, MC, V. From New Haven and New York, take Exit 76 off I-95 onto I-395 north, Exit 79A onto Rte. 2A east, then exit onto Rte. 32 north and drive 1.5 miles to the inn entrance.

You could spend a long weekend here without experiencing a whiff of deprivation, for the Norwich Inn & Spa has none of that tone of rigidly enforced self-denial that exists at many other places that call themselves "spas." The property is now owned by the Pequot tribal organization, but that association isn't noticeable. Foxwoods Casino is about 15 minutes away, making this a soothing and convenient respite from the glitz.

The complex is set among woods on a 40-acre property, the main building augmented by outlying clapboard "villas" with 160 condo units, about half of which are available for overnight guests. (These are in addition to the 65 inn rooms mentioned above.) A typical villa has a fully equipped kitchen, a large sitting area with logs and paper laid in the fireplace, two double beds in the separate bedroom, and a deck overlooking the woods and a pond. Inn rooms aren't as expansive and don't have fireplaces, but they are hardly Spartan.

Dining/Entertainment: The dining room is called the Prince of Wales, blessed with a versatile kitchen staff capable of producing meals either conventional or fitness minded, both uncommonly satisfying.

Facilities: Everyone has access to two outdoor pools, an indoor pool, a golf course, and a gym with stationary bikes, treadmills, StairMasters, and weight machines, as well as steam rooms and saunas. Massages are available, too, at $69 for a 50-minute session. Make reservations for fitness classes when arranging for lodging.

MYSTIC

The spirit and texture of the maritime life and history of New England are captured in many ports along its indented coast, but nowhere more cogently than along the Mystic River estuary, its harbor nearly enclosed by Mason Island. This was a highly active whaling and shipbuilding center during the colonial period and into the last century, but the discontinuation of the first industry and the decline of the second haven't adversely affected the community. No derelict barges nor rotting piers degrade the views and waterways (or at least not many).

Mystic and West Mystic are stitched together by a drawbridge, the raising of which, mostly for sailboats, causes traffic stoppages at a quarter past every hour but rarely shortens tempers, except for visitors who don't leave their urban impatience behind. There are complaints by some that the two-part town has been commercialized, but the incidence of T-shirt shops and related tackiness is limited, and the more garish motels and attractions have been restricted to the periphery, especially up near Exit 90 of Interstate 95. The congestion at that busy cloverleaf is sure to increase if plans for a new all-weather theme park, Fun-Plex, come to fruition.

The town is home to one of New England's most singular attractions, the Mystic Seaport museum village. Far more than the single building the name might suggest, it is a re-created seaport of the mid-1800s, with dozens of buildings and watercraft of that romantic era of clipper ships and the China trade. The spidery webs of full-rigged sailing ships beckon visitors almost as soon as they leave the highway, and the briny tang of the ocean air draws them on.

A **visitor information center** is located in the Olde Mistick Village shopping center, at Route 27 and Coogan Boulevard, near the Interstate (☎ **860/536-1641**). Mystic is 55 miles east of New Haven.

SEEING THE SIGHTS

✪ **Mystic Seaport.** 75 Greenmanville Ave. (Rte. 27). ☎ **860/572-0711** or 860/572-5315. Admission $16 adults, $8 children 6–15 (2nd day included with validation). AE, MC, V. Jan–Mar and Oct–Dec daily 10am–4pm; Apr–June and Sept–Oct daily 9am–5pm; July–Aug daily 9am–8pm. Take Exit 90 from I-95, driving about 1 mile south on Rte. 27 toward Mystic. Parking lots are on the left, the entrance on the right.

Few visitors fail to be enthralled by this evocative museum village. It encompasses an entire waterfront settlement, more than 60 buildings on and near a 17-acre peninsula poking into the Mystic River. With all there is to see and do, and considering the hefty admission charges, plan to set aside at least 2 or 3 hours for a visit. In fact, you could easily fill an entire day here, especially if you're one of those folks who thrill at the sight of full-rigged tall ships standing at their wharves as if readying for voyages to Cathay and the Spice Islands.

Deciding where to start and what to see is something of a challenge. A useful guide map is available at the ticket counter in the Visitor Center in the building opposite the Museum Stores (which can be saved for later, since they stay open later than the village most of the year).

A recommended route, exiting the Center, is to bear right along the path leading between the Galley Restaurant and the village green. It bends to the left, intersecting with a street of shops, public buildings, and houses. At that corner, for example, is an 1870s hardware and dry goods store.

Turning right there, pass a one-room schoolhouse, a chapel, a furnished 1830s home, and a **children's museum.** The museum, which invites youngsters to play games characteristic of the seafaring era, faces a small square that is the starting point for horse-drawn wagon tours of the village.

From there, one of the proudest possessions of the seaport fleet of over 400 craft is only a few steps away—the three-masted barque *Charles W. Morgan.* It was built in 1841, a whaler that called New Bedford home.

Facing the *Morgan* is a row of shops and services that did business with the whalers and clipper ships that put in at ports such as this. Bearing left along the waterfront, they include a tavern (nonfunctional), an 1833 bank with an upstairs shipping

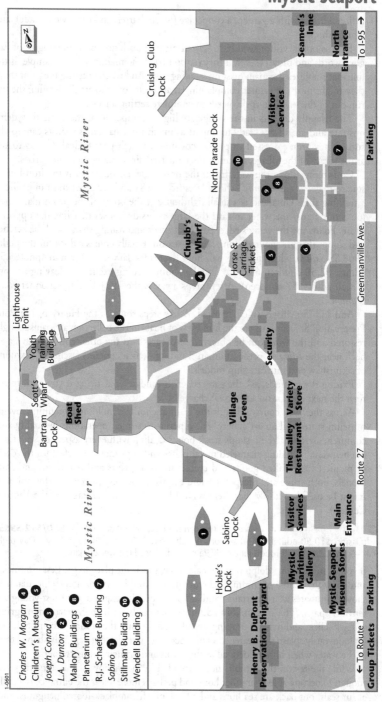

Mystic Seaport

Charles W. Morgan **4**
Children's Museum **5**
Joseph Conrad **3**
L.A. Dunton **2**
Mallory Buildings **8**
Planetarium **6**
R.J. Schaefer Building **7**
Sabino **1**
Stillman Building **10**
Wendell Building **9**

Mystic River

Lighthouse
Point

Youth
Training
Building

Scott's Wharf

Bartram
Dock

Boat
Shed

Cruising Club
Dock

Mystic River

North Parade Dock

Chubb's Wharf

Horse &
Carriage
Tickets

Seamen's
Inne

Visitor
Services

North
Entrance

To I-95 →

Parking

Security

Village
Green

Variety
Store

The Galley
Restaurant

Greenmanville Ave.

Sabino Dock

Hobie's Dock

Visitor
Services

Main
Entrance

Mystic
Maritime
Gallery

Mystic Seaport
Museum Stores

Henry B. DuPont
Preservation Shipyard

← To Route 1

Group Tickets

Parking

Route 27

I-0601

office, a house with a garden, a cooperage (where barrels and casks were made), and a print shop.

By this point, visitors will have started picking up hints about the origins of English words and phrases, even if they haven't tried. A "mainstay," for example, is the line that stabilizes the main mast on a sailing ship. And when entering the print shop, they might hear the printer complaining that she is "out of sorts," meaning she has run out of the lead letters she needs to complete setting a page.

The friendly docents in the village are highly competent at the crafts they demonstrate and are always ready to impart as much information as visitors care to absorb. They aren't dressed in period costumes, which paradoxically lends to the authenticity of the village, avoiding the contrived air of many such enterprises.

Continuing along the waterfront, the next vessel encountered is the iron-hulled square-rigger *Joseph Conrad,* which dates from 1881 and has spent most of its life as a training ship. Up ahead is a small lighthouse at the point of the peninsula, which looks out across the water toward the large riverside houses that line the opposite shore. Following the water's edge, pass boat sheds and fishing shacks and the ketches and sloops that are moored along here in season. Finally comes a dock for the perky 1908 SS *Sabino,* which provides half-hour river rides daily from 11am to 4pm ($3.50 adults, $2.50 children 6 to 15) and $1^1/_2$-hour evening excursions leaving at 5pm ($8.50 adults, $7 children). A few steps away is the 1921 fishing schooner, *L.A. Dunton.*

And still the village isn't exhausted. A few steps south is the Henry B. Du Pont Preservation Shipyard, where the hundreds of boats in the collection are painstakingly restored and the work can be observed in progress. At the other end of the village, back near the *Morgan,* is the Stillman Building, which contains fascinating exhibits of scrimshaw and intricate ship models.

Exiting the grounds, ask the gatekeeper to validate your ticket if you wish to return the next day for no additional charge.

Across the brick courtyard with the giant anchor is a building containing several museum stores and an art gallery. Far superior to similar operations in quality and comprehensiveness, these shops stock books dealing with every aspect of seafaring; kitchenware, including enameled metal plates and cups that are perfect for the deck or picnics; fresh-baked goods and coffee; nautical prints and paintings; and ship models, both crude and inexpensive and exquisite and very pricey. (At this point, it might be useful to know that there is an ATM next to the entrance of the Visitors Center.)

✪ **Mystic Marinelife Aquarium.** 55 Coogan Blvd. (at Exit 90 of I-95). ☎ **860/572-5955.** Admission $10.50 adults, $9.50 seniors, $7 children 3–12. July through Labor Day daily 9am–6pm; Labor Day through June daily 9am–5pm. Closed last week in Jan.

If you've never seen a dolphin and whale show, this is the place to go. Less gimmicky and glitzy than those of commercial enterprises found in Florida and California, this show illuminates as it entertains, and at 15 minutes in length doesn't test young attention spans. The undeniably adorable mammals with their permanent grins squawk, click, and make thumping sounds, roll up onto the apron of their pool, tail walk, joyously splash the nearer rows of spectators, and pick out variously shaped toys in the water when blindfolded, all at the command of their young trainers.

While the rest of the exhibits necessarily fall in the shadow of the stars, they are enough to occupy at least another hour and perhaps more. Near the entrance is a tank of fur seals, out back are sea lions and a flock of African black-footed penguins, and in between are some of the most remarkable marine creatures you'll ever see eye to eye. Among them are scorpion fish, spider crabs, and sea horses propelled on gossamer fins; billowing, translucent moon jellyfish; sea ravens; and the pugnacious yellow-head jaw fish, which spends its hours digging fortifications in the sand. The shrieks of excited children rend the air, not too great a price for observing their delighted discoveries.

OUTDOOR PURSUITS

For a change from salt air and ship riggings, drive inland to the **Denison Pequotsepos Nature Center,** 109 Pequotsepos Rd. (☎ **860/536-1216**), a 125-acre property with more than 7 miles of trails. The center building has a thrown-together quality, with stuffed birds next to plaster snakes and dog-eared books next to the live boa constrictor and worm farm. Younger children are nonetheless fascinated, and outside are picnic tables and cages of raptors—two horned owls, last time we looked. There are five marked nature trails. Admission is $3 adults, $1 children. Open Monday to Saturday 9am to 5pm, Sunday 1 to 5pm (closed Sundays January through April and Mondays September through April).

Across the road is the **Denison Homestead** (☎ **860/536-9248**), a 1717 farmhouse that sheltered 11 generations of Denisons and is filled with that family's antique furnishings. Admission is $4 adults, $1 children under 16. Open Thursday to Sunday from 1 to 5pm.

To get to the Nature Center and Homestead, take Route 27 north from Mystic, make a right on Mistuxet Avenue, then turn left on Pequotsepos Road.

Several operators offer **sailing and fishing cruises.** One of the most convenient is the *Argia* (☎ **860/536-0416**), which docks only 100 feet south of the drawbridge in downtown Mystic. Morning sails on this 81-foot replica of a 19th-century schooner are from 10am to 1pm, afternoon sails are from 2 to 5pm, and evening cruises are from 6 to 8pm. Refreshments are served. Fares are $30 to $32 adults, $20 children under 18. Longer sailing possibilities are the outings of the windjammer *Mystic Whaler* (☎ **800/697-8420** or 860/536-4218), which offers 3-hour lobster dinner sails, day trips, and extended cruises that can last 2, 3, or 5 days. Corresponding rates go from as little as $50 per passenger to $695. Voyages set out from a pier at 7 Holmes St., off Route 27, 1 mile south of Mystic Seaport.

SHOPPING

Olde Mistick Village, Route 27 and Coogan Boulevard (☎ **860/536-4941**), is essentially a conventional mall, but it's housed in new buildings that attempt to simulate a colonial village. More than 60 shops and restaurants are on site, including two bank branches, cinemas, and a winery. The Village is open daily, year-round.

Downtown Mystic has limited shopping. One of the most engaging choices is **Bank Square Books,** 53 W. Main St. (☎ **860/536-3795**). Maybe they don't actually have any volume you want in their jumble of shelves and racks, as they might appear to, but it's fun looking anyway.

WHERE TO STAY

There are plenty of ho-hum but adequate motels in the area that can soak up the traffic at all but peak periods, meaning weekends from late spring to early fall and high season weekdays in July and August, when it is necessary to have reservations. Within a block north and south of Exit 90 are the **Best Western Sovereign** (☎ **800/ 528-1234**), **Comfort Inn** (☎ **800/228-5150**), **Howard Johnson Motor Lodge** (☎ **800/654-4656**), **Days Inn** (☎ **800/325-2525**), and **Residence Inn** (☎ **800/ 331-3131**). For more distinctive accommodations, try one of the inns listed below.

The Inn at Mystic. Routes 1 and 27, Mystic, CT 06355. ☎ **800/237-2415** or 860/536-9604. 67 rms. A/C TV TEL. $55–$250 double. AE, DC, DISC, MC, V.

A splendid variety of lodgings and prices are offered at this inn occupying 13 hillside acres overlooking Long Island Sound, and the complex also incorporates one of the area's better restaurants.

At the crest of the hill is the impressive inn, a 1904 classical revival mansion with rooms as grand as the exterior, enhanced by whirlpool baths, fireplaces, and canopied beds. Bogart and Bacall spent part of their honeymoon here. Down the hill a way is the intimate Gatehouse, similarly accoutred, and furnished with a scattering of antiques. Some of the rooms in the new motel sections are equally well appointed, including a few with balconies; others are modest and conventional. All rooms have hair dryers and clock radios.

Dining/Entertainment: See "Where to Dine," below, for a complete review of Flood Tide, the inn's restaurant. Don't miss the bounteous and relatively inexpensive breakfasts, which feature stuffed crepes, three-egg omelets, Belgian waffles, and eggs Benedict . . . with lobster! A complimentary afternoon tea is served as well.

Facilities: A tennis court and an outdoor pool are on the premises, and guests have access to a nearby health club and to paddleboats and canoes down on the water.

Mystic Hilton. 20 Coogan Blvd., Mystic, CT 06355. ☎ **800/445-8667** or 860/572-0731. Fax 860/572-0328. 184 rms. A/C TV TEL. $125–$205 double. AE, CB, DC, DISC, MC, V. Take Exit 90 of I-95 and drive south 1 block to Coogan Blvd.

This is your basic Hilton. That means generally crisp efficiency, if not much personality, plus all the useful room amenities such as in-room movies and hair dryers . . . you get the picture. The front desk was reluctant to quote room rates, which I suspect indicates a willingness to negotiate on prices according to season and demand (give it a try). The hotel is now owned by the Pequot tribe.

Dining/Entertainment: There's a theme restaurant called The Moorings, and a piano player entertains in the evenings.

Services: Room service until 1am.

Facilities: Indoor pool, fitness room.

✪ **Steamboat Inn.** 73 Steamboat Wharf, Mystic, CT 06355. ☎ **860/536-8300.** Fax 860/536-9258. 10 rms. A/C TV TEL. $95–$275 double. Rates include breakfast. AE, DISC, MC, V. Look for the inn sign pointing down an alley on the west bank of the Mystic River, just before the drawbridge. No children under 9.

Mystic's most appealing lodging is easily overlooked from land, but readily apparent from the river. Perched on the riverbank, the yellow clapboard structure first served as a warehouse in the early part of this century and was converted to a luxury bed-and-breakfast only a few years ago. Its four downstairs rooms are larger, with double whirlpool baths, wet bars, and some kitchen facilities, while the upstairs six have smaller whirlpools and wood-burning fireplaces. While every room is decorated differently, they are uniformly attractive, and all but one have water views. Antique armoires hide the TVs.

Breakfast in the fetching common room is "hearty continental," with ample quantities of plump homemade muffins, fresh bagels, granola, and fruit compote. Sherry is left out all day for guests to pour themselves. The sailing ship *Argia* is moored outside, enhancing the nautical aspect of the inn. No smoking.

Taber Inne. 66 Williams Ave. (Rte. 1; 2 blocks east of the intersection with Rte. 27), Mystic, CT 06355. ☎ **860/536-4904.** Fax 860/572-9140. 25 rms. A/C TV TEL. $85–$310 double. AE, MC, V.

The Taber Inne has something to suit almost all tastes and budgets, with seven buildings containing both simple motel units and hedonistic two-bedroom duplex suites with whirlpool baths, decks, and fireplaces. For larger family groups, the homey "Little House" has two bedrooms, a sitting room, and a kitchen with microwave oven and dishwasher. It will sleep up to six in relative comfort for only $195 in high season. Some accommodations have porches, some have gas- or wood-burning fireplaces, and some have canopied beds. While breakfast isn't served, there's a coffeepot waiting in the reception area, and the manager hands out discount coupons for village restaurants.

Facilities: Guests have access to a community center with indoor pool, tennis, racquetball, and a fitness room.

Whaler's Inn. 20 E. Main St., Mystic, CT 06355. ☎ **800/243-2588** or 860/536-1506. Fax 860/572-1250. 41 rms. A/C TV TEL. $82–$210 double. Children under 16 stay free in parents' room. AE, MC, V.

The most commendable aspects of this downtown inn are its restaurant and its relatively low rates. (The high price above is for a suite. Doubles run only to $135 in summer.) Decor slips from bleakly old-fashioned to gaudy faux Victorian, and the reception staff could apply a touch more warmth. The rooms are deployed in four adjacent buildings, one of which is a house constructed in 1865, another a three-story building dating from 1917 that was once the "U.S. Hotel." The rooms are comfortable enough, if not particularly pleasing to the eye, and can be useful to businesspeople on a tight budget as well as leisure travelers. Phones have data ports, beds are queens or doubles, and half the bathrooms only have showers. Most rooms are nonsmoking.

Dining/Entertainment: See "Where to Dine," below, for a full review of the hotel's restaurant, Bravo Bravo.

WHERE TO DINE

Abbott's Lobster in the Rough. 117 Pearl St., Noank. ☎ **860/572-9128.** Main courses $15–$23 (but subject to market fluctuations). MC, V. 1st weekend in May through Labor Day daily noon–9pm; Labor Day to Columbus Day Fri–Sun noon–7pm. Drive south from downtown Mystic on Rte. 215, alert for signs to Noank, and cross a railroad bridge. At Main St. in Noank, turn left, then take an immediate right on Pearl St. Be prepared to ask for directions anyway. SEAFOOD.

It's as if a wedge of the Maine coast had been transplanted to the Connecticut shore. This is a nitty-gritty lobster shack at the edge of the Sound, with plenty of indoor and outdoor picnic tables and not a frill to be found. While there are many options and combinations, including hot dogs and chickens for the crustaceaphobic, the classic shore dinner rules. That means clam chowder, a mess of boiled shrimp in the shell, a bowl of steamed clams and mussels, and a small but tasty lobster. That'll be $21.95 (or thereabouts), with coleslaw, potato chips, and drawn butter thrown in. Smaller appetites might settle for selections from the raw bar, clams and oysters shucked to order. Dessert can be cheese- or carrot cake. Bring your own beer or wine.

Bravo Bravo. In the Whaler's Inn, 14 E. Main St. ☎ **860/536-3228.** Main courses $13.95–$24.95. AE, MC, V. Sun and Tues–Thurs 5–9pm, Fri–Sat 5–10pm. NEW ITALIAN/AMERICAN.

Ask locals about the best restaurant in town and as often as not they'll enthusiastically send you to this trattoria. In warm weather, Bravo Bravo has an adjoining tented deck, and the resulting combination is a money machine for the owners, even on a nondescript Tuesday evening. Inside and out, it is filled with families, couples, and men in suits or polo shirts and khakis. As the night wears on, it can get as noisy as a disco, and the wait staff is asked to cover too many tables, so getting refills of wine or water is nigh impossible.

A basket of marvelous bread arrives with the drinks, along with a ramekin of a spread comprised of emulsified white beans, sun-dried tomatoes, and roasted garlic. That will have to keep you happy until someone shows up for your order. When the time finally comes, keep it simple. Some of the dishes sound appealing—the tomato fettuccine with lobster nubbins, scallops, mussels, tomato, and asparagus, for example—but are overloaded with ingredients. The daily specials are apt to be better choices. And, note that prices out on the deck are lower for less complicated dishes.

Flood Tide. In The Inn at Mystic, Routes 1 and 27. ☎ **860/536-8140.** Main courses $16.95–$26.95. AE, DC, DISC, MC, V. Mon–Sat 7–10:30am; Mon–Sat 11:30am–2:30pm, Sun 11am–2:30pm; Sun–Thurs 5:30–9:30pm, Fri–Sat 5:30–10pm. CONTINENTAL.

Peel back about 3 decades and this place looks more familiar. In the 1960s, elaborate table-side preparations were big, and they're still doing them here, especially the Caesar salad and fettuccine Alfredo, but also with beef Wellington, chateaubriand, and rack of lamb, carved showily before your eyes. The performance is unabashedly retro, but reminds us why we used to relish this celebratory stuff in the years before Nouvelle-Pan-Asian-Italo-Southwestern-Fusion firecracker pseudo food was invented. Flood Tide even has a pianist plinking at the baby grand nightly and at Sunday brunch. The two dining rooms look out over the Sound, and smoking is confined to the handsome bar. Lunch is cheaper and less fussy, and breakfast is a particular treat.

PizzaWorks. 12 Water St. (Rte. 215, south of Main St.) ☎ **860/572-5775.** Pizzas $5–$11.95. MC, V. Daily 4–9 or 10pm. PIZZA.

Mystic Pizza is still on Main Street, much gussied up since Julia Roberts made her debut there in the movie of the same name. But if a good pizza is more important to you than dimly reflected Hollywood glory, get here fast. In appearance, PizzaWorks is your basic pizza parlor, with checked oilcloth on the tables, brick walls, and neon signs on the walls. Pizzas are "red"— with tomato sauce—or "white"— without. Toppings are inventive but well short of gimmicky (none of that pineapple foolishness), but while extras can be piled on, the regular recipes stand alone. The "white" clams casino and the barbecued chicken with onion and bacon are super, and the "red" sausage cacciatore matches them. But then almost any of the 25 possible toppings make eyeballs roll in pleasure. The long beer list includes Nantucket Amber, Lightship, and Elm City Ale. This is brew-and-pie nirvana. There is another PizzaWorks branch in Old Saybrook.

Quiambaug House. 29 Old Stonington Rd. (off Half Moon Rd., Rte. 1). ☎ **860/572-8543.** Main courses $14.95–$19.95. AE, DC, DISC, MC, V. Dining room Mon–Sat 11:30am–3pm, Sun 11am–3pm; daily 5–10pm. Club Room daily 11:30am–midnight. SEAFOOD.

The owners of this sprawling roadside establishment used to operate the Harbor View in Stonington, before it went into bankruptcy under subsequent management. Retirement was boring, so here they are again, with a proven formula that brought big-time business from the day they opened.

The food doesn't strike off in daring directions, which can be a relief. Many dishes have Mediterranean touches, as with the fragrant bouillabaisse and the grilled swordfish Niçoise with roasted peppers and black olives. The catches of the day veer toward traditional New England preparations (think steamed lobster with mussels) and other dishes are similarly classic, such as the duck breast with plums and port. All this arrives in several commodious rooms that resulted from the expansion of a humble 1924 clam shack.

The chummy bar at one end has a less ambitious but satisfying menu at lower prices ($7.95 to $9.95). An amusing sidelight: The fish-and-chips are "served in the *London Times* when available."

STONINGTON & NORTH STONINGTON

Not much seems to happen in these slumbering villages, only lightly brushed by the 20th century despite all the thrashing about over in heavily touristed Mystic. That suits most of the residents just fine, explaining why most of them are not thrilled by the strong possibility that a giant Six Flags theme park will soon be erected in their midst. It is difficult to imagine what that will do to inland North Stonington, as peaceful a New England retreat as can be found, with hardly any commercialization beyond a couple of inns. Sound-side Stonington has a pronounced maritime flavor, sustained by the presence of the state's only remaining fishing fleet. Its two length-wise streets are lined with well-preserved Federalist and Greek Revival homes.

WHAT TO SEE & DO

For an introduction, drive south to **Cannon Square** along Stonington's **Water Street,** which has most of the town's shops and restaurants. Standing in the raised grassy main square are two 18-pound cannons that were used to fight off an attack by British warships during the War of 1812. Opposite is a lovely old granite house, and on the corner, a neoclassical bank.

Continue south to the end of Water Street, where there is a parking lot and the small **town beach** (admission $2 to $3 per person, $5 to $6 per family). The misty blue headland directly south across the Sound is Montauk Point, the eastern extremity of New York's Long Island. Return along Main Street, which is almost exclusively residential except for a few government buildings.

You might also check out the **Old Lighthouse Museum,** 7 Water St. (☎ 860/535-1440). Built of stone in 1823, this two-story lighthouse with its short tower was moved here from a hundred yards away and deactivated. Most of the exhibits inside relate to the maritime past of the area, with scrimshaw tusks, a whalebone wool-winding wheel, a tortoiseshell serving dish, and export porcelain that constituted much of the 19th-century China Trade. There are also weapons and relics of the Revolutionary period and the War of 1812, but the most interesting item might be the carved ivory pagoda. Upstairs are kitchen tools and Shaker boxes and trays. Climb the tower for a view of coast and sea. Admission is $3 for adults, $1 for children 6 to 12. Open May through October, Tuesday to Sunday from 11am to 5pm.

Duffers who feel overwhelmed by all the nautical talk and activity of the area can retreat to the fairway familiarity of their favorite game at the **Pequot Golf Club,** on Wheeler Road in Stonington (☎ 860/535-1898). It has a par 70, 18-hole course and is fully open to the public, including the restaurant. Cart and club rentals are available. Call ahead to make reservations for weekend tee times. Take Exit 91 from I-95 north to Taugwonk Road, turn west on Summers Lane, and south on Wheeler Road.

One of the Nutmeg State's handful of earnest wineries, **Stonington Vineyards,** 523 Taugwonk Rd., Stonington (☎ 860/535-1222), has a tasting room in a barn beside its vineyard. There are usually six or seven pressings to be sampled, from a blush to a Riesling, with a chardonnay leading the pack, at least according to most taste buds. Bottles cost from $8 to $16. Open daily from 11am to 5pm, with a cellar tour at 2pm. To get there, take Exit 91 from I-95 and drive north 2½ miles.

WHERE TO STAY

Antiques & Accommodations. 32 Main St., N. Stonington, CT 06359. ☎ **800/554-7829** or 860/535-1736. Fax 860/535-2613. 7 units. A/C. $99–$229 double. Rates include breakfast.

A Casino in the Woods

What has been wrought in the woodlands north of the Mystic coast is nothing less than astonishing.

There was very little there when the Mashantucket Pequot tribe received clearance to open a gambling casino on their ancestral lands in rural Ledyard. Virtually overnight, the tribal bingo parlor was expanded into a full-fledged casino and a hotel was built.

That was in 1992. Within 3 years, it had become the single most profitable gambling operation in the world. Money cascaded over the Pequot (pronounced "*Pee-kwat*") in a seemingly endless torrent. Expansion was immediate—another hotel, then a third, more casinos, plans for a $13 million museum of Native American arts and culture, golf courses, a monorail, perhaps even a new theme park. The tribe bought up adjacent lands, at least two nearby inns and another hotel, and contemplated opening casinos in other cities.

All this prosperity came to a tribe of only 350 acknowledged members, many of them of mixed ethnicity. Residents of surrounding communities—indeed, of the whole state—were ambivalent, to put the best face on it. When it was learned that one of the tribe's corporate entities was to be called Two Trees Limited Partnership, a predictable query was, "Is that all you're going to leave us? Two trees?"

But while there is a continuing danger of damage to the fragile character of this most authentically picturesque corner of Connecticut, it is also a fact that due to the recent development, thousands of non-Pequots have found employment at a time of economic stagnation and corporate and military downsizing throughout the region.

The complex is reached through forested countryside and quiet hamlets that give little hint of the behemoth rising above the trees in Ledyard township. There are no signs screaming "Foxwoods." Instead, watch for plaques with the symbols of tree, wolf, and fire above the word "Reservation." The widening of Route 2 is one of the first indications that something is up. As you enter the property, platoons of

MC, V. Take Exit 92 of I-95, drive west on Rte. 2 for 2¹/₂ miles, then turn right onto Main St. at the sign.

Gardens, porches, and patios invite lounging and ambling at this converted 1820 farmhouse and 1861 Victorian. Rooms and suites vary substantially in dimension and fixtures. The largest has three bedrooms with a dining room and kitchen; another has two bedrooms sharing a kitchen and sitting room; the "bridal suite" has a canopied queen-sized bed. Four rooms have cable TV, and three have working fireplaces, but none have phones. Obviously, it is necessary to make your wishes known at the outset. Everyone, though, shares the four-course candlelit breakfast, with such surprises as cantaloupe soup and walnut-and-banana waffles. Guests who take a liking to any of the antique silver or crystal pieces or furnishings will be pleased to know that just about everything is for sale.

Randall's Ordinary. Rte. 2, N. Stonington, CT 06320. ☎ **860/599-4540.** Fax 860/599-3308. A/C. $75–$195 double. Rates include breakfast. AE, MC, V. Take Exit 92 from I-95, head north on Rte. 2.

The oldest structure on this 27-acre estate dates from 1685. The three rooms upstairs in the old building have fireplaces and are charmingly furnished with four-poster and canopied beds, but have no phones or TVs. Those amenities are found in most of attendants point the way to parking and hotels. Ongoing construction surrounds the dark glassy tower of the hotel and sprawling casino. Though busy and bustling, it doesn't look like Vegas from the outside—happily, there are no Sphinxes, no pyramids, no 20-story neon palm trees.

Inside, the glitz gap narrows, but it is still relatively restrained as such temples to chance go. The gambling rooms have windows, for example, when the prevailing wisdom among casino designers is that they should not give customers any idea what time of day or night it is.

And no one is allowed to forget that this whole eye-popping affair is owned and operated by Native Americans. Prominently positioned around the main buildings are larger-than-life sculptures by Alan Houser and Bruce LaFountain, of Chiricahua and Chippewa descent, respectively, depicting Amerindians in a variety of poses and artistic styles. One other Indian-oriented display is *The Rainmaker,* a glass statue of an archer shooting an arrow into the air. Every hour on the hour, he is the focus of artificial thunder, wind-whipped rain, and lasers pretending to be lightning bolts, and the action is described in murky prose by a booming voice-of-Manitou narrator. That's as close as the chest thumping gets to going over the top, although some visitors might reflect upon the political correctness of the non-Indian cocktail waitresses outfitted in skimpy Pocahontas minidresses with feathers in their hair.

The pace of all this might be slowing, at least temporarily, for another tribe has built the **Mohegan Sun Resort** in Uncasville, barely 6 miles away as the crow flies. The Pequots are watching closely to see what the new competition will do to their business, and are ready to make adjustments.

Two dozen bus companies provide daily service to Foxwoods from Boston, Hartford, Providence, New York, Philadelphia, and Albany, among many other cities—too many to list here. For information about transit from particular destinations, call ☎ **860/885-3000.**

the rooms of the nearby barn, moved here from upstate New York and converted for this purpose. While the barn interior is dramatic, with heavy hand-cut beams and banisters made of stripped logs, the furnishings are, well, ordinary, albeit comfortable enough, if you don't mind bare floors. Coffee is set out in the lobby, near the parrot. Randall's Ordinary is now owned by a Pequot tribal organization, but that affiliation isn't noticeable.

Dining/Entertainment: The central gimmick of the inn: Meals are cooked at an open hearth and served by a staff in period costumes. Considering the primitive circumstances under which the food is prepared, it turns out to be hearty and tasty, if a tad too simple for refined tastes. Reserve ahead for dinner, which is a set price of $30. This nightly event takes place on the ground floor of the John Randall House, the farmhouse that has been occupied continuously by members of the Randall family for over 200 years.

FOXWOODS RESORT CASINO

The casino-hotel complex (☎ **860/885-3000**) is a moving target, forever changing, adding, renovating, and expanding. There are, in fact, several cavernous gambling rooms, one of the most popular being the hall containing the 4,500 slot machines. A high-tech horse parlor, with tote boards and live feeds from tracks around the country, is an impressive newcomer. All the usual methods of depleting wallets are at hand—blackjack, bingo, chuck-a-luck, keno, craps, baccarat, roulette, acey-deucy, money wheel, and several variations of poker. To keep players at tables, there is food service in the poker parlor and complimentary drinks are served at craps and black-jack tables.

WHERE TO STAY

The resort has three hotels, the newest one still unnamed at this writing, but sure to be operational by the time these words are printed. With more than 900 rooms, it more than doubles the resort's housing capacity. Unlike Las Vegas and other gambling centers, room rates aren't kept artificially low as an inducement to visit, although that policy may change in the future depending upon competitive pressures from the rival Mohegan Sun Resort.

Foxwoods Resort Hotel. Rte. 2, Ledyard, CT 06339. ☎ **800/369-9663** or 860/885-3000. Fax 860/885-4040. 312 rms. $190–$300 double. AE, DISC, MC, V. From Boston, take I-95 south to exit 92 onto Rte. 2 west. From New Haven and New York, take I-95 to I-395 north to Exit 79A onto Rte. 2A east, picking up Rte. 2 east.

Don't even bother trying to park your car in the huge garage. It takes forever, and the valet parking at the front door is free.

Well maintained despite the heavy foot traffic, this hotel has eight floors adjoining the casinos. Rooms are colorful, but not too gaudy (except for the suites for high rollers on the top floor), and are provided with the usual amenities. There are no premium channels or in-room movies on the TV, though; the management doesn't want you lolling around your room watching the tube when you could be downstairs losing money.

Facilities: There's a spa and indoor pool to relax those neck muscles knotted from hours spent hunched over a card table.

Two Trees Inn. 240 Lantern Hill Rd. (off Rte. 2), Ledyard, CT 06339. ☎ **800/369-9663** or 860/885-3000. Fax 860/885-4050. 280 rms. $140–$200 double. Rates include breakfast. AE, DISC, MC, V. Follow directions for Foxwoods Resort Hotel above, continuing past the entrance to the casino on Rte. 2 to Lantern Hill Rd.

This was the first Foxwoods hotel, built in less than 3 months, now a short shuttle-bus ride or 10-minute walk from the casino complex. Essentially a conventional motor hotel, it attracts large numbers of bus tours. A skimpy continental breakfast is set out each morning in the small woody lobby, an occasion to contemplate your fellow guests' taste in white pants and hot pastel tops . . . in January. A nonsmoking floor is available.

Dining/Entertainment: There is a busy middling restaurant, Branches.
Facilities: Heated indoor pool, fitness room.

WHERE TO DINE

Nine sit-down restaurants and five fast-food operations situated throughout the casino complex cover the most popular options. Only a couple aspire to even moderately serious culinary achievement.

Cedars Steak House (☎ **860/885-3000,** ext. 4252) grills beef and seafoods that are supplemented by a raw bar, while **Al Dente** (ext. 4090) does designer pizzas and pastas. Both expect their guests to be dressed at least a notch better than tank tops and shorts. They are the only ones that accept reservations.

The most popular dining room is the **Festival Buffet** (ext. 3172), which charges $10 for an all-you-can-eat spread that usually includes five or six main courses plus soups, salads, sides of vegetables and starches, and desserts.

Other self-explanatory possibilities are **Han Garden** (ext. 4093), **Pequot Grill** (ext. 2690), and **The Deli** (ext. 5481).

FOXWOODS AFTER DARK

Just as in Vegas and Atlantic City, big showbiz names are whisked onto the premises, usually on weekends. Expect no surprises. Even Wayne Newton makes the scene, as do the likes of Tony Bennett, Paul Anka, Loretta Lynn, Jackie Mason, Luther Vandross, Willie Nelson, Tom Jones, and the usual testaments to nostalgia—The Monkees, Frankie Avalon, and Fabian. For information about current headliners, call ☎ **800/200-2882.**

For a break from the whirring of the slots and the insistent chatter of the croupiers, and to occupy underage kids, Foxwoods has created **Cinetropolis,** an entertainment center that looks like a cleaned-up futuristic Gotham. This is the electronic age at its most playfully frantic. *Turbo Ride* lets you pretend you are experiencing the rumbling takeoffs and powerful G-forces of jets taking off, this by way of giant films and machinery that makes your seat rock and roll as if in a cockpit. *Fox Giant Screen Theatre* is an IMAX-like production that features front-row rock concerts and exploding volcanoes, and *Virtual Adventures* lets you take control of an undersea vessel slipping past the dangers of the ocean depths. Once all that is exhausted, the *Fox Arcade* has pinball and video games that might seem a little pallid after the rest of these diversions.

10 Rhode Island

by Herbert Bailey Livesey

Water defines "Little Rhody" as much as mountain peaks character-ize Colorado. The Atlantic thrusts all the way to the Massachusetts border, cleaving the state into unequal halves and filling the geological basin that is Narragansett Bay. That leaves 400 miles of coastline and several large islands.

A string of coastal towns runs in a northeasterly arc from the Connecticut border up to Providence, the governmental and business capital, which lies at the point of the bay, 30 miles from the open ocean. It was here that Roger Williams, banned from the Massachusetts Bay Colony in 1635 for his outspoken views on religious freedom, established his colony. Little survives from that first century, but a large section of the city's East Side is composed almost entirely of 18th- and 19th-century dwellings and public buildings.

Another group of Puritan exiles established their settlement a couple of years after Providence, on an island known to the Narragansett as "Aquidneck." Settlers thought their new home resembled the Isle of Rhodes in the Aegean, so the official name became "Rhode Island and Providence Plantations," a moniker that was subsequently applied to the entire state.

The most important town on Aquidneck is Newport, and it's the best reason for an extended visit to the state. Its first era of prosperity was during the colonial period, when its ships not only plied the new mercantile routes to China but engaged in the reprehensible "Triangular Trade" of West Indies molasses for New England rum for African slaves. Their additional skill at smuggling and evading taxes brought them into conflict with their British rulers, whose occupying army all but destroyed Newport during the Revolution. After the Civil War, the town began its transformation from commercial outpost to resort with the arrival of the millionaires of what Mark Twain sneeringly described as the "Gilded Age." They built astonishingly extravagant mansions, their contribution to Newport's bountiful architectural heritage. With their winning of the America's Cup and subsequent defenses of yachting's most famous trophy, the town became a recreational sailing center with a packed summer cultural calendar. So travelers who want nothing more than a deep tan by Monday can coexist with history buffs and music lovers, who come to attend concerts held against a backdrop of waves hissing across packed sand.

Finally, there is Block Island, which lies a 1-hour ferry ride from Point Judith. A classic summer resort, it has avoided the imposition of Martha's Vineyard chic and Provincetown clutter. It has also sidestepped history (even though it was first settled in 1661), so there are few mandatory sights. That leaves visitors free simply to explore its lighthouses, hike its cliff-side trails, and hit the beach.

1 Providence

Roger Williams knew what he was doing. Admired for his fervent advocacy of religious and political freedom in the early colonial period, he obviously had good instincts for town building as well. He planted the seeds of his settlement on a steep rise overlooking a swift-flowing river at the point where it widened into a large protected harbor. That part of the city, called the East Side and dominated by the ridge now known as College Hill, remains the most attractive district of a New England city second only to Boston in the breadth of its cultural life and rich architectural heritage.

College Hill is so named because it is the site of Rhode Island College, which started life in 1764 and was later renamed Brown University, a member of the elite Ivy League. The Hill is further enhanced by the presence of the highly regarded Rhode Island School of Design, whose buildings are wrapped around the perimeter of the Brown campus. In and around these institutions are several square miles of 18th- and 19th-century houses, colonial to Victorian, lining often gaslit streets. At the back of the Brown campus is the funky shopping district along Thayer Street, while at the foot of the Hill is the largely commercial Main Street.

While most points of interest are found on the East Side, the far larger collection of neighborhoods west of the river has its own attractions. The level downtown area is the center for business, government, and entertainment, with City Hall, a new convention center, the two best large hotels, some small parks and historic buildings, and several theaters for music, dance, and theatrical productions. To its north, across the Woonasquatucket River, is the imposing State House and the Amtrak railroad station. And to its west, on the other side of Interstate 95, is Federal Hill, a residential area bearing a strong ethnic identity, primarily Italian, but increasingly leavened by numbers of more recent immigrant groups.

This is a city of manageable size—the population is about 170,000—that can easily occupy 2 or 3 days of a Rhode Island vacation. Locals are proud of the burgeoning reputation of the city's dining scene, pointing to ambitious new restaurants that are nearly always less expensive than their counterparts in Boston and New York. College Hill is only one of 26 National Historic Districts, the calendar is full of concerts and special events, and the presence of so many young people promotes a lively nightlife. Thanks, Rog.

ESSENTIALS

GETTING THERE I-95, the logical route from either Boston or New York, runs right through the city, which lies 45 miles south of Boston, 55 miles northeast of New London. From Cape Cod, pick up I-195 west.

T. F. Green/Providence Airport (☎ 401/737-8222) in Warwick, south of Providence (Exit 13, I-95), handles all national flights. Major airlines serving this airport include: **American** (☎ 800/433-7300), **Continental** (☎ 800/525-0280), **Delta** (☎ 800/221-1212), **Northwest** (☎ 800/225-2525), **United** (☎ 800/241-6522), and **USAirways** (☎ 800/247-8786). The Rhode Island Public Transit Authority (RIPTA) provides transportation between the airport and the city center. Taxis are also available, costing about $20 for the 20-minute trip.

Providence

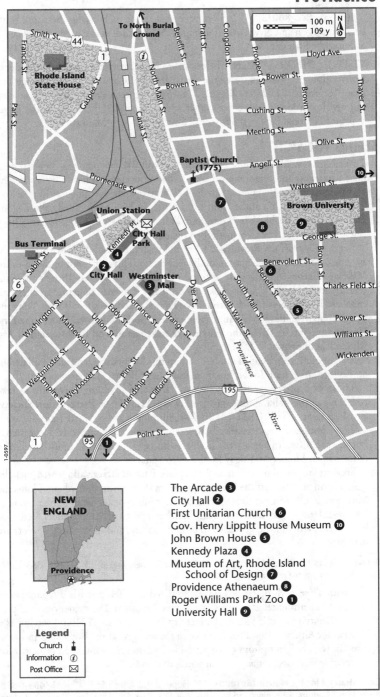

The Arcade ③
City Hall ②
First Unitarian Church ⑥
Gov. Henry Lippitt House Museum ⑩
John Brown House ⑤
Kennedy Plaza ④
Museum of Art, Rhode Island
   School of Design ⑦
Providence Athenaeum ⑧
Roger Williams Park Zoo ①
University Hall ⑨

Legend
Church ⌖
Information ⓘ
Post Office ✉

Amtrak (☎ 800/872-7245) runs several trains daily along the shore route between Boston and New York, stopping at the attractive new station at 100 Gaspee St., near the State House.

VISITOR INFORMATION   Before your visit, contact the **Greater Providence Convention and Visitors Bureau** of the Chamber of Commerce, 30 Exchange Terrace, Providence, RI 02903 (☎ **401/274-1636**). Once in Providence, you can consult a visitor information center at that address, or check the center at the Roger Williams National Park at the corner of Smith and North Main streets.

SEEING THE SIGHTS

Two leisurely walks, one short, another longer, will take you past most of the prominent attractions and offer up a palpable sense of the city's evolution from a colony of dissidents to a contemporary center of commerce and government.

Downtown, chart a route from the 1878 City Hall on Kennedy Plaza along Dorrance Street one block to Westminster, turning left past The Arcade (see "Quick Bites & Lowbrow Treats," below), then right on Weybosset.

Better still, cross the Providence River and walk down South Water Street as far as James, turn left, then left again on Benefit Street. This is the start of the so-called **Mile of History.** Lined with restored or carefully preserved 18th- and 19th-century houses, it is a feast for aficionados of Early American domestic architecture, enhanced by sections of brick herringbone sidewalks and gas street lamps. Along the way are opportunities to visit, in sequence, the 1786 **John Brown House,** the **First Unitarian Church** (1816), the **Providence Athenaeum,** and the **Museum of Art, Rhode Island School of Design.**

Two of our recommended inns are also on this lovely street, and an uphill detour on College Street leads to the handsome campus of Brown University.

Those who prefer expert direction to haphazard rambling may want to take advantage of the walking tours provided by the **Providence Preservation Society,** 21 Meeting St. (☎ **401/831-7440**). Two 90-minute audiocassette tours are available, in addition to booklets describing several historic neighborhoods. The cassettes can be rented (with your driver's license as hostage), the booklets purchased. The office is open Monday to Friday from 9am to 5pm.

Boosters are proud of their new **Waterplace Park & Riverwalk,** which encircles a tidal basin and borders the Woonasquatucket River down past where it joins the Moshassuck to become the Providence River. It incorporates an amphitheater, boat landings, landscaped walkways with benches and trees, and vaguely Venetian bridges that cross to the East Side. Summer concerts and other special events are held here.

Brown University. Office of Admissions, 45 Prospect St. (near Angell St.). ☎ **401/863-2378.** Free admission. Mon–Fri 9am–5pm.

The nation's seventh-oldest college was founded in 1764, and has a reputation as the most experimental among its Ivy League brethren. The evidence of its pre-Revolutionary origins is seen in **University Hall,** built in 1771 and serving as a barracks for American and French troops in the war against the British. Tours of the campus, with buildings from every period in its history, are intended primarily for prospective students, but anyone can join (call ahead).

Gov. Henry Lippitt House Museum. 199 Hope St. (at Angell St.). ☎ **401/453-0688.** Admission $4 adults, $2 seniors and students. Apr–Dec Tues–Fri 11am–3pm, Sat–Sun 1–3pm; Jan–Mar by appointment only.

Visits to the museum are by guided tour only, and these leave on the hour, so plan your trip accordingly, for this house is as magnificently true to its grandiose Victorian era as any residence on the Continent.

Its style is technically Renaissance Revival—which really meant that the architect brought to bear any motif or notion that took his fancy. Meticulously detailed stenciling, expanses of stained glass, ornately framed mirrors, inlaid floors, and wood intricately carved or made to look like marble combine to make this mansion one of the treasures of College Hill. The fact that the governor and his descendants lived in the house until 1981 helped enormously in its preservation.

John Brown House. 52 Power St. (at the corner of Benefit St.). ☎ **401/331-8575.** Admission $5 adults, $3.50 seniors and students, $2 children 7–17. Tues–Sat 10am–4:30pm, Sun noon–4pm; Mon–Fri in Jan–Feb by appointment only.

A three-story mansion made of brick (in contrast to the mostly wood-frame houses of the same late-18th-century era), this was the home of a man who made his fortune as a master of the China Trade. He is said to have been responsible for the burning of a British warship, the *Gaspee,* 4 years before the start of the Revolution. John was also a slave trader, in contrast to his industrialist brother, Moses, who was an abolitionist.

The style of the house is Georgian, although no doubt the owner preferred to think of it as Federalist after the war was won. His widow, children, and grandchildren lived here until 1846. Subsequent owners made additions and redecorated in the Victorian fashion. Their efforts were reversed after the house was bequeathed to the Rhode Island Historical Society in 1941, which restored it to its original condition. Brown University was named in honor of the family, members of which were generous contributors. The mansion faces Power Street, laid out in 1638 for Roger Williams's town.

Museum of Art, Rhode Island School of Design. 224 Benefit St. (between Waterman and College sts.). ☎ **401/454-6100.** Admission $2 adults, $1 seniors, 50¢ students and children 5–18. Summer Wed–Sat noon–5pm; winter Tues–Wed and Fri–Sat 10:30am–5pm, Thurs noon–8pm, Sun and holidays 1–5pm.

Prestigious RISD (pronounced "*Riz*-dee") supports this ingratiating center that houses the 65,000 artworks of the permanent collection and frequent temporary exhibitions. Demonstrating its considerable breadth, on display are Chinese terra-cotta sculptures, Greek statuary, French Impressionist paintings, and Early American decorative arts, with frequent illuminating stops in between.

Probably of greatest general interest are the rooms of works by such masters as Monet, Cézanne, Rodin, Picasso, and Matisse. But allow time for the American wing, which contains not only fine antique furnishings and accessories but paintings by Gilbert Stuart, John Singleton Copley, and John Singer Sargent.

The Providence Athenaeum. 251 Benefit St. (at College St.). ☎ **401/421-6970.** Free admission. Mon–Fri 8:30am–5:30pm, Sat 9:30am–5:30pm, Sun 1–5pm. In summer, open until 8:30pm on Wed; closed Sat.

The Providence Athenaeum, a learned society that was founded in 1753, commissioned this granite 1838 Greek Revival building to house its lending library, the fourth oldest in the United States and an innovative concept at the time.

Edgar Allan Poe courted Sarah Whitman, his "Annabel Lee," between these shelves. Random glances through the old card catalog reveal handwritten cards dating well back into the 1800s. It has a large and active children's section and is a marvelous place in which bibliophiles can lose themselves.

Roger Williams Park Zoo. 950 Elmwood Ave. (at Exit 17 off I-95). ☎ **401/785-3510.** Admission $5 adults, $2.50 seniors and children 3–12. Apr–Oct daily 9am–5pm; Nov–Mar daily 9am–4pm.

In a 430-acre park that also contains a museum of natural history and a planetarium, the zoo is divided into habitats: Tropical America, the Farmyard, and the Plains of Africa. Of the more than 150 species on view, the most popular are the polar bears, giraffes, penguins, the birds of the walk-through rain forest, and the cuddly critters of the petting zoo. Ongoing renovations have removed the prisonlike structures of the Victorian era in which the zoo was created, replacing them with concealed moats and hidden fences so that the animals can be viewed with less obvious barriers.

Children can also be treated to rides on the carousel, a little train, on real ponies, and in paddleboats on the lake. Families might want to take a picnic and make a day of it.

Rhode Island State House. 82 Smith St. (between Francis and Hayes sts.). ☎ **401/277-2357.** Free admission. Mon–Fri 8:30am–4:30pm.

Constructed of Georgian marble that blazes in the sun, the 1900 Capitol building dominates the city center by virtue of its hilltop location and superior aesthetic. This near-flawless example of neoclassical governmental architecture is given room to flaunt, with open spaces all around. Its self-supported dome is one of the largest in the world, reminding many viewers of that on St. Peter's Cathedral in Rome. The gilded figure on top represents *Independent Man,* the state symbol. Inside, a full-length portrait of George Washington is given pride of place, one of many depictions of the Father of His Country by Gilbert Stuart, one of Rhode Island's own. Guided tours by appointment.

SHOPPING

Thayer Street, which is the main commercial district for the university, has the official **Brown Bookstore** at no. 244 (at the corner of Olive Street), open daily, but not in the evenings, and the **College Hill Bookstore** at no. 252, funkier and wider ranging in its selections and open daily until midnight. Also in the vicinity are **Urban Cargo** (at no. 224), with casual clothes and jewelry for college-age women, and **Hillhouse** (no. 135), long in the business of providing male Brownies with Ivy dress-up clothes for interview weeks and parent days.

WHERE TO STAY

Assuming charm and character aren't paramount criteria in lodging, the clusters of motels around most of the exits from I-95 and I-195 are routinely comfortable and offer decent value, especially since you're not likely to stay more than 1 or 2 nights. Among these possibilities are the **Ramada Inn,** 940 Fall River Ave., Seekonk, MA 02771 (☎ **508/336-7300**), and the **Marriott,** 1 Orms St., Providence, RI 02904 (☎ **401/272-2400**).

Alternatives are provided by B&B referral agencies, such as **Bed & Breakfast of Rhode Island,** P.O. Box 3291, Newport, RI 02840 (☎ **800/828-0000** or 401/849-1298). These are rooms in private homes, so sometimes quirky rules and limitations apply, to be ascertained at the time of booking. Remember, too, that they are rarely as inexpensive as local branches of motel chains.

Lodgings in the historic districts are required to provide off-street parking—and it's free in the case of the three inns recommended below (the C. C. Ledbetter, the Old Court, and the State House Inn).

C. C. Ledbetter. 326 Benefit St., Providence, RI 02903. ☎/fax **401/351-4699.** 5 rms (3 with private bath). A/C TV. $70–$125 double. AE, DISC, MC, V. Rates include continental breakfast. No credit cards.

There's no sign out front, because the eponymous owner doesn't want to attract a boozy football weekend crowd or bother her neighbors. Look for the 1780 clapboard building with the olive green exterior. Things are a lot more colorful inside, with a substantial collection of contemporary artworks, much of it museum quality. Two rooms share a bath; another might be the only one in the state to contain a rowing machine. A hearty continental breakfast is served around a common table downstairs, where you'll usually find the two resident dogs.

While the owner isn't enthusiastic about accepting children and pets, she'll consider both or either. And she makes no bones about the fact that she ups her rates on parents' and alumni weekends and at graduation (which is already booked through the end of the century).

Days Hotel. 220 India St., Providence, RI 02903. ☎ **800/325-2525** or 401/272-5577. 140 rms. A/C TV TEL. $80–$125 double. AE, CB, DC, DISC, MC, V.

Don't demand a room with a view. This vertical motel has an expressway on one side and an unsightly section of waterfront on the other. Nevertheless, this place represents an attempt by Days Inn to upgrade its image (slightly). The usual conveniences are in place. Keep asking for cheaper rooms, for even on a weeknight in summer they can be had for $60 or less, depending on the occupancy rate. Most of Providence's attractions are within a 10-minute drive.

Dining/Entertainment: Serviceable dining room.

Services: 24-hour shuttle service to and from the airport and bus and train stations (make arrangements when you reserve).

Facilities: Modest exercise room with whirlpool.

The Old Court. 144 Benefit St., Providence, RI 02903. ☎ **401/751-2002** or 401/351-0747. 10 rms. A/C TEL. $75–$135 double. Rates include breakfast. DISC, MC, V.

This was once a rectory, built in 1863, and the furnishings reflect that period in surprising diversity. There are examples of rococo-revival and Eastlake styles, as well as secretaries embellished with marquetry and Oriental rugs on bare floors, standouts amid more familiar Victoriana. Most traces of the building's tenure as a boarding-house for college students have been expunged. Breakfast is a production, always with a hot entree, and served in a room with eight tables. Only three rooms have TVs so far, but the management expects to add more.

Families or longer-term visitors may be interested in the apartment across the street. It has one bedroom, a living room, and a full kitchen with dining nook. Admittedly a little dowdy, it does offer a good deal of space and the opportunity to save money on meals.

Providence Biltmore. Kennedy Plaza, Providence, RI 02903. ☎ **800/294-7709** or 401/421-0700. Fax 401/455-3050. 217 rms. A/C TV TEL. $114–$199 double. AE, CB, DC, MC, V.

The centrally located Biltmore is the equal of the newer Westin (nearby), and these two choices share honors as the capital's prime business hotels. (Given its relatively moderate rates, vacationing couples and families might be inclined to splurge.)

A grand staircase beneath the deco-ish bronze ceiling dates the building to the 1920s, and a plaque on a column in the lobby shows the nearly 7-foot-high water level of the villainous 1938 hurricane. A dramatic new feature is the glass elevator that starts in the lobby and exits outdoors to scoot up the side of the building. In the rooms you'll find pay-per-view movies and phone service that includes voice mail and modem ports; some suites have kitchenettes.

Dining/Entertainment: There's a new restaurant called D'Avios (though no room service, oddly).

Services: Concierge, dry cleaning/laundry, newspaper delivery, nightly turndown, twice-daily maid service, baby-sitting, express checkout, valet parking, free coffee in lobby.

Facilities: Exercise room, business center, conference rooms.

State House Inn. 43 Jewett St., Providence, RI 02908. ☎ **401/785-1235.** 10 rms. A/C TV TEL. $99–$109 double. Rates include breakfast. Lower weekday corporate rates. AE, MC, V. From the easily identified State House, drive west on Smith St., over I-95, then left on Holden and right on Jewett.

The neighborhood isn't the best (though downtown restaurants are only minutes away), but the owners compensate with lower rates and hotel conveniences, including hair dryers and clock radios; guests also have access to a fax and copier. Some rooms have canopy beds or fireplaces. Breakfast is substantial, with at least one hot dish. Children are welcome. No smoking. Reserve well in advance for special events at local colleges.

Westin Providence. 1 W. Exchange St., Providence, RI 02903. ☎ **800/228-3000** or 401/598-8000. Fax 401/598-8200. 363 rms. A/C MINIBAR TV TEL. $140–$195 double. AE, DC, MC, V.

With its luxurious interior and downtown location next to the convention center, this is a business hotel of high order (with rates considerably lower than siblings in Boston and New York). Bedrooms have pay-per-view movies and phones with data ports and voice mail. Executive floors are available. The chilly grandeur of the architectural spaces hasn't seemed to afflict the sunny personalities of most of the staff.

Dining/Entertainment: Its rotunda lobby is filled with oversized chairs set around a white piano. To one side is a lounge with the buffed glow of an exclusive men's club, and upstairs are adjoining bars featuring sports and live jazz. There are two restaurants.

Services: Concierge, room service (limited hours), dry cleaning/laundry, newspaper delivery, baby-sitting, express checkout, valet parking, courtesy limo.

Facilities: Health club and heated indoor pool on the roof, plus Jacuzzi, sauna, business center, conference rooms.

WHERE TO DINE

Providence has a sturdy Italian heritage, resulting in a profusion of tomato sauce and pizza joints, especially on Federal Hill, the district west of downtown and I-95. Since they are so many and so obvious, the suggestions below focus—a bit perversely, perhaps—on restaurants that have broken away from the red-sauce imperative.

One fruitful strip to explore for dining options is that part of **Thayer Street** that borders the Brown University campus, which counts Thai, Tex-Mex, barbecue, Indian, and even Egyptian restaurants among its possibilities.

Adesso. 161 Cushing St. (off Thayer St.). ☎ **401/521-0770.** Main courses $9.95–$23.95. AE, MC, V. Mon–Thurs 11:45am–10:30pm, Fri–Sat 11:45am–11:30pm, Sun 4:30–10pm. FUSION.

They call it a "California Café," and follow through with Wolfgang Puck–ish designer pizzas from the wood-burning grill in the obligatory open kitchen. Go for the pizzas (but not the view, which is of the parking lot). One typical production combines strips of smoked chicken breast, curls of bacon, sun-dried tomatoes, mozzarella, and blanched garlic and scallions in a mustard-dill sauce. A nonpizza possibility is the grilled sea bass with a port wine cream sauce and portobello mushrooms. No one goes hungry, not with portions large enough to quell the raging metabolism of a Brown defensive end. In back is a liquor and espresso bar. Adesso is all but hidden down unmarked Cushing Street, off Thayer.

Cafe Nuovo. 1 Citizens Plaza. ☎ **401/421-2525.** Main courses $14.50–$23.95. AE, DC, DISC, MC, V. Daily 11:30am–2:30pm; Sun–Thurs 5–10pm, Fri–Sat 5–11pm. MEDITERRANEAN FUSION.

This sleek relative newcomer occupies part of the ground floor of a postmodernist office tower that looks out at the confluence of the Moshassuck and Woonasquatucket rivers. Its reputation as a see-and-be-seen hotbed shortchanges the skill of its capable chefs. While grounded in the Italian repertoire, they skip lightly among other inspirations—Thai, Greek, and Portuguese among them. That restlessness brings them to dishes like lamb shank baked in a clay pot with orzo and rosemary and a cioppino of lobster chunks, shrimp, littlenecks, calamari, and whitefish. If that isn't enough, start with an appetizer-sized pizza while casting an eye around the room of glass and marble and burnished wood. There are tables outside in warm weather. Access is from the Steeple Street bridge.

✪ The Gatehouse. 4 Richmond Sq. (east end of Pitman St.) ☎ **401/521-9229.** Reservations recommended on weekends. Main courses $16.95–$22.95. AE, DC, MC, V. Mon–Fri noon–2:30pm, Sun 10am–2pm; daily 5:30–10pm. NEW AMERICAN.

This is where I'd send you if you can only have one meal in Providence. Step inside a refined taproom with a green marble bar on the left, a working fireplace and elegantly set tables over to the right. Downstairs is a candlelit lounge and an outdoor deck perched above the Seekonk River. Jazz pianists or duos perform down there Wednesday to Saturday, and a pub menu offers burgers and pastas.

Service and edibles are more polished on the main floor. Try to imagine the signature appetizer: A fig wrapped in a crispy phyllo husk combines with tastes of Stilton cheese, toasted pine nuts, prosciutto, cream, and port with a balsamic glaze. It's a perfect marriage, unlikely as it may sound. Most of the entrees are grilled, at least in part, as with roasted tomato polenta, portobello mushrooms, and julienned vegetables cooked over hickory and rolled in a warm burrito. Presentation is careful but unfussy. The clever wine list sweeps from Australia's Hunter Valley to the Rhone and on to the Napa, with pauses at Rhode Island's own Sakonnet Vineyard.

Pot au Feu. 44 Custom St. (off Weybosset St.) ☎ **401/273-8953.** Main courses, salon $19.50–$26.50; bistro $13.95–$19.95. AE, CB, DC, MC, V. Salon, Tues–Fri noon–1:30pm and 6–9pm, Sat 6–9:30pm; bistro, Mon–Fri 11:30am–2pm; Mon–Thurs 5:30–9pm, Fri–Sat 5:30–10pm. TRADITIONAL FRENCH.

Named for the classic boiled dinner of chicken, beef, and root vegetables, this is, remarkably, one of only two French restaurants in town. They do it up right, and if English weren't being spoken all around, you'd think the restaurant was on a village square in Provence. Dishes like steak au poivre, *suprême de volaille Colbert,* and *lotte à la niçoise* are all exactly as they should be, remembrances of what made Gallic cooking memorable long before the excesses of the food revolution set in sometime around the first Reagan administration.

Unless someone else is paying or you absolutely must have a tablecloth, there's no good reason not to head straight downstairs, especially at dinner, when the price gap widens between the salon and the basement bistro. The stone walls and bare floors do nothing to muffle the din down there, but that deliciously earthy food comes from the same kitchen. Smoking is confined to the bar.

QUICK BITES & LOWBROW TREATS

A bona fide National Historic Landmark is an unlikely venue for snaffling up cookies, salads, souvlaki, doughnuts, and egg rolls. But **The Arcade,** 65 Weybosset St. (☎ 401/456-5403), is a 19th-century progenitor of 20th-century shopping malls, an 1828 Greek Revival structure that runs between Weybosset and Westminster streets. Its main floor is given over largely to fast-food stands and snack counters of the usual kinds—yes, the Golden Arches, too—while the upper floor is primarily clothing and jewelry boutiques and toy and souvenir shops. Open daily.

Another local culinary institution arrives in Kennedy Plaza on wheels every afternoon around 4:30. The grungy aluminum-sided, trailer-sized **Haven Bros.** (☎ 401/861-7777) food truck deals in decent burgers and better fries from its usual parking space next to City Hall. No new frontiers here, except that it hangs around until way past midnight to dampen the hunger pangs of club goers, overworked lawyers, assorted night people, and workaholic pols (the mayor is a regular).

PROVIDENCE AFTER DARK

The southern end of Water Street has four bar/restaurants functioning essentially as nightspots. **The Hot Club,** 575 S. Water St. (☎ 401/861-9007), opens at noon and keeps its door open past midnight, with live jazz two or more nights a week. Other nearby possibilities, last I looked, are **Steam Alley, Fish Co.** and **Grappa** (both on South Water Street). Around the corner on South Main Street, **Clef No. 580** has live jazz most nights.

Concerts by star acts like Joe Cocker and B. B. King, as well as mainstream and alternative bands, are held at **The Strand,** 79 Washington St. (☎ 617/423-6398).

For art-house films and midnight cult movies, there is the **Avon Repertory Cinema,** on Thayer Street, near Meeting Street.

The **Ocean State Light Opera** (☎ 401/331-6060) often performs at the Wheeler School Theater, and the **Rhode Island Philharmonic** (☎ 401/831-3123) usually appears at the Providence Performing Arts Center.

2   Between Providence & Newport: A Bucolic Detour to Sakonnet Point & Little Compton

As a break from the rushed urbanity of Providence or the concentration of sights and activities that is Newport, a side trip down the length of the oddly isolated southeastern corner of the state is a soothing excursion.

No one has thought to throw a bridge or run a ferry across the water between Newport and Sakonnet Point, prospects the reclusive residents would no doubt resist to the last lawsuit. They have been known to steal away with road signs to discourage summer visitors, and there are almost no enterprises geared to attract tourists. Things are quiet in these parts, and they intend to keep it that way.

To get there from Providence or Boston, pick up I-195 east, then I-24 south, toward Newport. Take Exit 3 for Route 77 south, just before the Sakonnet River Bridge. From Newport, take Route 138 toward Fall River, and exit on Route 77 south immediately after crossing the bridge.

After a welter of small businesses, most of them involved in some way with the ocean, Route 77 smooths out into a pastoral Brigadoon, not quite rural, but more rustic than suburban. Colonial farmhouses, real or replicated, bear sidings and roofs of weathered shakes the color of wood smoke. They are centered in tidy lawns, with fruit trees and firs as sentinels, bordered by miles and miles of low stone walls assembled with a sculptural sense of balanced shapes and textures. No plastic deer, no faded flamingoes, no tomato plants in the front yard, none of those cute little banners hung from porches to herald seasons and holidays. It is as if a requirement of residence were attendance at a school of good taste.

There are a few antique shops and roadside farm stands, of both the permanent and card-table variety, as well as a snack shop or two and a garden store, but nothing even remotely intrusive to sour the serenity.

One of the few good reasons to pull off the road is **Sakonnet Vineyards,** 162 W. Main Rd. (☎ **401/635-8486**), with an entrance road on the left, about 3 miles south of the traffic light in Tiverton Four Corners. In operation over 20 years, it is one of New England's oldest wineries, and produces 50,000 cases of creditable wines annually. Types range from a popular pinot noir to a dry gewürztraminer, abetted by such whimsical bottlings as their Eye of the Storm blush, commemorating the 1985 arrival of Hurricane Gloria. If you've had the foresight to bring along a picnic lunch, you can buy a bottle or two and retire to one of the tables beside the pond near the tasting room. The "hospitality center" is open daily, from 10am to 6pm in summer, 11am to 5pm in winter.

Continuing south on Route 77, the road skirts Little Compton and heads on to **Sakonnet Point,** where the inland terrain gives way to stony beaches and coastal marshes. There's a wetlands wildlife refuge (where you might glimpse snowy egrets and herons), a small harbor with working boats, and not much else.

Now head back north on Route 77; watch for the sign pointing toward Adamsville (if the natives haven't made off with it). Take the second right turn from the Stone House Club (described below), onto a road that doesn't appear to have a name. Shortly, it arrives at a T intersection surrounded by a Congregational church, a few small shops, a post office, law and real-estate offices, and the Commons restaurant. That's downtown **Little Compton.** Turn left (north) and you're back in the country before you shift into third gear. In about 4 miles, the road ends at Peckham Road. Turn right, in the faith that you are heading toward **Adamsville;** you'll arrive there in about 8 miles. It's here that you'll come across Abraham Manchester's (see below).

From Adamsville, return to Route 77 via Route 179 to Tiverton Four Corners to get back to Newport, or take Route 81 to Route 24 if returning to Providence or Boston.

WHERE TO STAY ALONG THE WAY

Stone House Club. 122 Sakonnet Point Rd., Little Compton, RI 02837. ☎ **401/635-2222.** 13 rms (4 with shared bath). $58–$125 double, depending on season and type of accommodation. Rates include breakfast. Additional membership fee as noted below. MC, V.

From our last stop in Sakonnet Point, return along Route 77, where you'll shortly note the entrance to this restaurant/tavern/inn. It's open to the public, but it must observe the wink-wink subterfuge of being a private club because it serves spirits and there is a church next door. That means a $20 membership fee for individuals and $36 for couples, in addition to room rates. Furnishings are worn and unstylish, but look oddly right for their location. No TVs or phones in the rooms (though there is an intercom). Two private swimming beaches are available to guests.

Dining/Entertainment: The cellar Tap Room and more formal dining room upstairs traipse all over the gastronomic map—traditional, nouvelle, Italian, Asian—with a predisposition to seafood. They are open Tuesday to Sunday in summer, Friday to Sunday November through April.

WHERE TO DINE ALONG THE WAY

Abraham Manchester's. Main Rd. ☎ 401/635-2700. Main courses $6.85–$21.95. AE, MC, V. Daily 11:30am–10pm. ECLECTIC.

Adamsville, the claimed birthplace of the Rhode Island Red chicken, is a less pristine hamlet than its neighbor Little Compton, with a disheveled aspect and more pickup trucks than sports utility vehicles. At its center is Abraham Manchester's, which serves as much as the town's social center as a restaurant. The gregarious owner and her staff greet almost everyone by name, bantering as old friends do. The building is a former general store, but not much attention is paid the niceties of historic preservation. There are splintery beams of indeterminate age, and the mounted stag head and wagon wheel are typical of the decor.

The menu is unexpectedly imaginative, with, for example, a smoked chicken Alfredo over spinach fettuccine, and a production called the "Manchester Medley Platter." That's a jumble of shrimp marinated in red wine, blackened swordfish, pieces of barbecued chicken, and a slab of sautéed tenderloin, an assemblage fragrant with garlic, herbs, and balsamic vinegar. Portions are daunting.

If you've come before 11:30am, note that the owner's daughter runs **The Barn** on the other side of the parking lot, offering freshly baked breads and pastries with her elaborate breakfasts.

3 Newport

The "City by the Sea" is the singularly unimaginative nickname an early resident unloaded on Newport. At least it was accurate, since for a time during the colonial period it rivaled Boston and even New York as a center of New World trade and prosperity. Newport occupies the southern tip of Aquidneck Island in Narragansett Bay, and is connected to the mainland by three bridges and a ferry.

Wealthy industrialists, railroad tycoons, coal magnates, financiers, and robber barons made respectable by political connections and vast fortunes were drawn to the area in the 19th century, especially between the Civil War and World War I. They bought up property at the ocean's rim, building summer mansions, patterned after European palaces, that they used as summer "cottages."

Their toys were equally extravagant yachts meant for pleasure, not commerce, and competitions between them established Newport's reputation as a sailing center. In 1851, the sporting schooner *America* defeated a British ship in a race around the Isle of Wight. The prize trophy became known as the America's Cup, which remained in the possession of the New York Yacht Club (with an outpost in Newport) until 1983. In that shocking summer, *Australia II* snatched the Cup away from *Liberty* in the last race of a four-out-of-seven series. Though the cup was regained by an American team in 1987, it was won by New Zealand in 1995 and remains down under. The strong U.S. yachting tradition has endured despite the loss of the Cup, and Newport continues as a bastion of world sailing and a destination for long-distance races.

The perimeter of the city resembles a heeled boot, its toe pointing west. About where the "laces" of the "boot" would be is the downtown business and residential district. Several wharves push into the bay, providing support and mooring for flotillas of pleasure craft, from stubby little inboards and character boats to graceful sloops and visiting tall ships. Much of the strolling, shopping, eating, quaffing, and gawking is done along this waterfront and its parallel streets, America's Cup Boulevard and Thames Street. (The latter used to be pronounced "Tems," in the British manner, but was Americanized to "Thaymz" after the Revolution.)

Newport

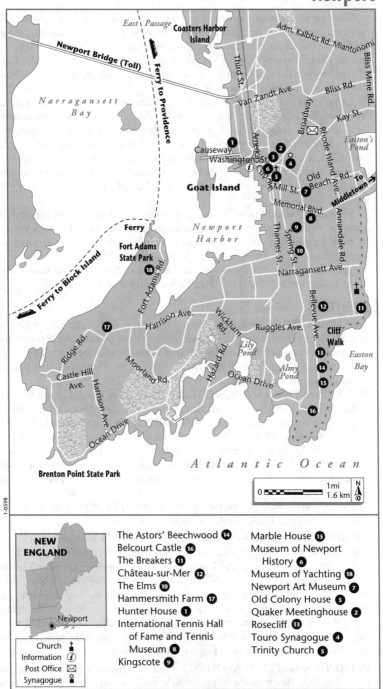

The Astors' Beechwood ⑭
Belcourt Castle ⑯
The Breakers ⑪
Château-sur-Mer ⑫
The Elms ⑩
Hammersmith Farm ⑰
Hunter House ①
International Tennis Hall
of Fame and Tennis
Museum ⑧
Kingscote ⑨

Marble House ⑮
Museum of Newport
History ⑥
Museum of Yachting ⑱
Newport Art Museum ⑦
Old Colony House ③
Quaker Meetinghouse ②
Rosecliff ⑬
Touro Synagogue ④
Trinity Church ⑤

Church ✝
Information ⓘ
Post Office ✉
Synagogue ✡

NEW
ENGLAND

Newport

0 ▬▬▬ 1mi
1.6 km

N

The navy has pulled out its battleships, causing a decline in the local economy, but it's hardly proven to be the disaster predicted by some. And this area has thus far been spared the coarser intrusions that afflict so many coastal resorts. Monster RVs and motorcycle bands rarely arrive to complicate the heavy traffic of July and August, and T-shirt emporia have kept within reasonable limits. Considering it has over 3.7 million visitors a year, that's remarkable.

Immediately east and north of the business district are blocks of colonial, Federal, and Victorian houses of the 18th and 19th centuries, many of them restored and bearing plaques designating them as National Historic Sites. Happily, they are not frozen in amber, but are very much in use as residences, restaurants, offices, and shops. Taken together, they are as visually appealing in their own way as the 40-room cottages of the superrich. Steven Spielberg found them sufficiently authentic to spend several weeks there in the spring of 1997 filming *Amistad,* an epic set in the early 19th century.

So despite Newport's prevailing image as a collection of stupefyingly ornate mansions and regattas of sailing ships inaccessible to all but the rich and famous, the city is, for the most part, middle class and moderately priced. Summer evenings are often cool enough for a cotton sweater. Scores of inns and bed-and-breakfasts assure lodging even during festival weeks, at rates and fixtures from budget to luxury level. In nearly every regard, this is the "First Resort" of the New England coast.

ESSENTIALS

GETTING THERE From New York City, take I-95 to the third exit, picking up Route 138 east (which joins briefly with Route 4) and crossing the Newport toll bridge slightly north of the downtown district. From Boston, take Route 24 through Fall River, picking up Route 114 into town. Newport lies 75 miles south of Boston, 115 miles northeast of New Haven.

T. F. Green/Providence Airport (☎ 401/737-8222) in Warwick, south of Providence (Exit 13, I-95), handles national flights into the state. Major airlines serving this airport include: **American** (☎ 800/433-7300), **Continental** (☎ 800/525-0280), **Delta** (☎ 800/221-1212), **Northwest** (☎ 800/225-2525), **United** (☎ 800/241-6522), and **USAirways** (☎ 800/247-8786). A few of the larger Newport hotels provide shuttle service, as does **Cozy Cab** (☎ 401/846-2500). **Pineapple Beantown Express** (☎ 401/841-8989) has shuttle service between Newport and Boston's Logan Airport.

The **Interstate Navigation Company** (☎ **401/783-4613**) provides ferries between Providence, Block Island, and Newport's Fort Adams.

VISITOR INFORMATION Before you visit, call the 24-hour **visitor information line** (☎ **800/263-4636** outside Rhode Island, or 401/848-2000 in Rhode Island). After you've arrived, check in at the excellent **Newport Gateway Visitors Center,** 23 America's Cup Ave. (☎ **800/326-6030** or 401/849-8040). Open daily from 9am to 5pm (until 6pm Friday and Saturday), it has several attendants on duty to answer questions, brochures for attractions and accommodations, a lodging-availability service, rest rooms, and panoramic photos showing the locations of mansions, parks, and other landmarks. They even validate parking in the adjacent lot for up to the first half-hour. The building is shared with the bus station.

PARKING & GETTING AROUND Most of Newport's attractions can be reached on foot, except for the mansions, so leaving your car at your hotel or inn is wise. Parking lots and garages aren't cheap, especially at the waterfront, and many streets are too narrow. The metered parking slots along Thames Street are closely monitored by police and fines are steep (although in the off-season, the meters are hooded and parking is free for up to 3 hours). Renting or bringing a bicycle is an attractive option.

The **Rhode Island Public Transit Authority** (RIPTA; ☎ 401/781-9400) has a free shuttle bus that follows a roughly circular route through town, making stops at major sights.

SPECIAL EVENTS   Arrive any day between Memorial Day and Labor Day and expect to find at least a half-dozen festivals, competitions, or other events in progress. Following is only a partial list of some of the more prominent. (Specific dates often change from year to year, so it is necessary to call ahead to confirm; ☎ **800/ 263-4636** outside Rhode Island, or 401/848-2000 in Rhode Island).

While there are a few substantive events in the off-season months, notably the **February Winter Festival** (call ☎ 401/849-8048 for details), which focuses on food and winter sports, the pace ratchets up in June, starting with the annual **Great Chowder Cook-Off** at the Newport Yachting Center (☎ **401/845-1600** for details). In the 3rd week of June is the 3-day **Secret Garden Tour** (☎ **401/847-0514**), when the gardens of the Point section of town are open to visitors.

In July, the principal music events are the **Newport Music Festival** (☎ 401/ 86-1133), which offers three classical music concerts daily at various venues during the middle 2 weeks of the month, and the **Rhythm and Blues Festival** (☎ 401/ 847-3700), held outdoors in Fort Adams Park for 2 days at the end of the month. The 2nd week of July sees the **Hall of Fame Tennis Tournament** (☎ 401/ 849-6053), the only U.S. men's ATP tournament held on grass, overlapping the days of the pro women's **Hall of Fame Invitational.** In the 3rd week of the month is the **Black Ships Festival** (☎ 401/847-3700), a celebration of all aspects of Japanese culture.

August brings the 2-day **Ben & Jerry's Folk Festival** and the 3-day **JVC Jazz Festival** (☎ 401/847-3700 for both), both held at Fort Adams Park. Things wind down after Labor Day, though there's still the 2-day **Irish Music Festival** (☎ 401/ 849-2028) toward the end of the month and the annual **Bowen's Wharf Waterfront Seafood Festival** (☎ 401/849-2243) in the 3rd week of October.

Rosters of scheduled performers for the blues, folk, and jazz festivals are usually released by May. While tickets are often available near concert time, it's wise to purchase them at least a month in advance for the best-known groups and soloists. Newport somehow contrives to absorb the throngs that descend upon it for these events, but lodgings for weekends from Memorial Day to Labor Day should be secured at least 2 months in advance, and sooner is better.

THE COTTAGES

That's what wealthy summer people called the almost unimaginably sumptuous mansions they had built in Newport in the last decades before the 16th Amendment to the Constitution (the one that allowed the imposition of an income tax).

Say this for the wealthy of the Gilded Age, many of whom obtained their fortunes by less than honorable means: They knew a good place to put down roots when they saw it. These are the same ones, after all, who developed Palm Beach in winter, the Hudson Valley in spring, the Berkshires in autumn, and Newport in summer, sweeping from house to luxurious house with the insouciance of a bejeweled matron dragging her sable down a grand staircase. They were Vanderbilts and Astors and their blue-blooded friends and rivals, and they rarely stayed in any one of their mansions for more than a few weeks a year.

When driving or biking through the cottage district (walking is impractical for most people), consider the fact that most of these astonishing residences are still privately owned—that's almost as remarkable as the grounds and interiors of the nine that are open to the public.

When you set out, ask if Rough Point, the fabled 1887 Tudor mansion of the late Doris Duke (still protected by high walls topped with barbed wire at this writing), has begun to welcome visitors, too; it is slated to open sometime in the near future. To find it, continue south on Bellevue from Belcourt Castle. It's on the left, just before a sharp turn west along what becomes Ocean Drive.

Also, resolve to visit only one or two homes per day. The sheer opulence of the mansions can soon become numbing, an effect not unlike touching down in five European countries in a week and touring the most lavish palaces in each.

Each residence requires 45 minutes to an hour for its guided tour. The aptitude and personality of individual docents is generally good, apart from their understandable tendency to take on a robotic tone. If at all possible, go during the week. Weekend foot and vehicular traffic can resemble Times Square at curtain time.

Six of the mansions are maintained by the **Preservation Society of Newport County,** 118 Mill St. (☎ 401/847-6543), which also operates the 1748 Hunter House and the Green Animals Topiary Gardens in Portsmouth. They sell a **combination ticket,** good for a year, to eight properties; it's $35.50 for adults, $10 for children 6 to 11. Tickets for individual mansions are $6.50 to $10 for adults, $3 to $3.50 for children. Strip tickets for two to six mansions are also available. They can be purchased at any of the properties.

The cottages are **open** daily from 10am to 5pm from late May to Labor Day; November to April they're open Saturday and Sunday from 10am to 4pm. The mansions that aren't operated by the Preservation Society but are open to the public are Belcourt Castle, Beechwood, and Hammersmith Farm.

Following are descriptions of the nine in the order they are encountered when driving south from Memorial Boulevard along Bellevue Avenue, then west on Ocean Avenue.

Kingscote. Bowery St. (west of Bellevue Ave.) See above for admission details.

Built in 1839, this mansion (on the right-hand side of the avenue) is a reminder that well-to-do Southern families often had second homes north of the Mason-Dixon line to avoid the sultry summer of the deep South. Richard Upjohn was the architect, and Kingscote reflects the Gothic Revival style he used for Trinity Church in New York.

Although considered one of the Newport "cottages," the mansion's existence precedes the Gilded Age to which the others belong (a period usually delineated as starting around 1875 and ending with the outbreak of World War I), and its inclusion in the group is largely due to its acquisition in 1864 by the sea merchant William Henry King. His family's furnishings are those now on view, many of them porcelains and textiles accumulated in the China Trade. Shortly after the purchase, he went mad and spent the rest of his life in an asylum. The New York architectural firm of McKim, Mead & White was commissioned to design the 1881 dining room, notable for its Tiffany glass panels.

The Elms. Bellevue Ave. See above for admission details.

Architect Horace Trumbauer is said to have been inspired by the Chateau d'Asnieres outside Paris, and a first look at the ornate dining room of The Elms, suitable for at least a marquis, buttresses that claim. So, too, do the sunken gardens, laid out and maintained in the formal French manner.

The owner was a first-generation millionaire, a coal tycoon named Edward J. Berwind. His cottage was completed in 1901, and he filled it with genuine Louis XIV and XV furniture and paintings and accessories true to the late 18th century.

Château-sur-mer. Bellevue Ave. See above for admission details.

William S. Wetmore was yet another Rhode Island merchant who made his fortune in the lucrative China Trade. The entrance to this "Castle by the Sea" is on the left-hand side of Bellevue, driving south.

High Victorian in style, which means it drew from many inspirations (including Italian Renaissance and French Second Empire), the Château features a central atrium four stories high with a glass skylight and balconies at every level.

✪ **The Breakers.** Ochre Point Ave. (east of Bellevue Ave.) ☎ **401/847-6543.** See above for admission details. After Château-sur-mer, turn left on Ruggles Ave., then left again on Ochre Point Ave. The Breakers is on the right, a parking lot on the left.

If you only have time to see one of the "cottages," make it this one.

Architect Richard Morris Hunt was commissioned to create this replica of a generic Florentine Renaissance palazzo, and was apparently unrestrained by cost considerations. The high iron entrance gates alone weigh over 7 tons. Such mind-numbing extravagance shouldn't really be surprising—Hunt's patron was, after all, Cornelius Vanderbilt II, grandson of railroad tycoon Commodore Vanderbilt and a superstar spender of the Gilded Age.

Had Vanderbilt been European royalty, The Breakers would have provided motive for a peasant revolt. Vanderbilt's small family, their guests, and their staff of 40 servants had 70 rooms in which to roam. Nearly 3 years in construction, completed in 1892, the mansion's foundation is approximately the size of a football field. Platoons of artisans were imported from Europe to apply gold leaf and carve wood and marble and provide mural-sized baroque paintings. The furnishings you'll see are original.

Rosecliff. Bellevue Ave. See above for admission details. From The Breakers, return to Bellevue Ave. and turn left (south). Rosecliff is on the left.

Stanford White, of McKim, Mead & White, thought the Grand Trianon of Louis XVI at Versailles a suitable model for this 1902 commission for Mr. Hermann Oelrichs.

With a middling 40 rooms, it doesn't overwhelm, at least not on the scale of The Breakers. But it has the largest ballroom of all the cottages—the crossbar in the H layout of the house—not to mention a storied heart-shaped grand staircase.

All this was made possible by one James Fair, an immigrant who made his fortune after he unearthed the thickest gold and silver vein of Nevada's Comstock Lode and bought this property for his daughters, Theresa and Virginia (a.k.a. Tessie and Birdie). Theresa was the sister who married Hermann Oelrichs, a highly successful New York businessman.

In 1941, the mansion and its contents were sold for $21,000. It was used as a setting for some scenes in the Robert Redford movie of Fitzgerald's *The Great Gatsby* and for a ballroom scene in Arnold Schwarzenegger's *True Lies.*

Beechwood. 580 Bellevue Ave. ☎ **401/846-3772.** Admission $8.50 adults, $6.50 seniors and children 5–12. Mid-May to Oct 31 daily 10am–5pm, Nov–May Fri–Sun 10am–4pm (tours on the half-hour, except at 12:30pm).

Mrs. William Backhouse Astor—*the* Mrs. Astor, as every brochure and guide feels compelled to observe—was, during her active life, the arbiter of exactly who constituted New York and Newport society. "The 400" list of socially acceptable folk was influenced or perhaps even drawn up by her, and that roster bore meaning, in some quarters, well into the second half of the 20th century. Being invited to Beechwood was absolutely critical to a social pretender's sense of self-worth, and elaborate machinations were set in motion to achieve that goal. (It may be of some comfort to the descendants of the failed supplicants that Mrs. Astor spent her last few years at the cottage greeting imaginary guests.)

Built in 1852, the mansion isn't as large or impressive as some of its neighbors. But unlike those managed by the Preservation Society, it provides a little theatrical pizzazz with a corps of actors who pretend to be friends, children, and servants of Mrs. Astor.

✪ **Marble House.** Bellevue Ave. See above for admission details.

Architect Richard Morris Hunt, another favorite of the cottage builders, outdid himself for his clients William and Alva Vanderbilt. Several types of marble were used both outside and inside with a lavish hand that rivals the palaces of the Sun King, reaching its apogee in the ballroom, which is encrusted with three kinds of gold.

It cost William $2 million to build Marble House and another $7 million to decorate it, but Alva divorced him 4 years after the project was finished. She got the house, which she soon closed after marrying William's friend and neighbor. When her second husband died, Alva discovered the cause of female suffrage, and reopened Marble House in 1913 to hold a benefit for the campaign for women's right to vote.

Belcourt Castle. Bellevue Ave.(at Lakeview Ave.) ☎ **401/846-0669.** Admission $7.50 adults, $6 seniors and college students, $5 children 13–18, $3 children 6–12. Feb–May Sat–Sun and holidays 10am–3pm; Memorial Day to mid-Oct daily 9am–5pm; mid-Oct to Nov daily 10am–4pm; Dec (special tours) 10am–3pm. Closed Jan.

This was the (only slightly) less grand mansion to which Alva Vanderbilt repaired after her second marriage. While the Vanderbilts were avid yachtsmen, her new husband, Oliver Hazard Perry Belmont, was a fanatical horseman. His 62-room house, also a design by Richard Morris Hunt, actually contained stables on the ground floor, where his beloved steeds slept under monogrammed blankets (the Belmonts were instrumental in building New York's Belmont Racetrack).

Alva and Oliver entertained frequently, and counted among their guests Kaiser Wilhelm and the Duke of Windsor. The castle, meant to resemble a royal hunting lodge, contains a collection of European stained glass, scores of Oriental carpets, and French Renaissance furniture and artifacts. Thomas Edison designed the lighting.

Hammersmith Farm. Ocean Dr. (past Castle Hill Ave.). ☎ **401/846-7346.** Admission $8.50 adults, $3 children 6–12. Memorial Day–Labor Day daily 10am–7pm; Apr–May and Sept to mid-Nov daily 10am–5pm. Closed mid-Nov to Mar.

Built for John W. Auchincloss in 1887 on a farm established in the 17th century, this house was used for the wedding reception of one of his descendants, Jacqueline Bouvier, in 1953. Set on a rise with an unimpeded view across 50 acres of manicured lawns and gardens to Narragansett Bay, it subsequently became the unofficial summer White House of the short Kennedy presidency. John-John and Caroline played here in a small outbuilding near the gardens that is now the gift shop. Out in the meadows beyond are the miniature horses and equally diminutive donkey that are descendants of animals raised by the Auchinclosses.

Despite an impressive porte cochere, its substantial size, and its superb setting, the cottage is hardly pretentious, managing to seem as homey inside as the Hudson Valley residence of another millionaire and inspiration to Jack Kennedy, Franklin D. Roosevelt. There is a certain irony in the location of the Kennedy summer White House, for on the adjoining property, Fort Adams State Park, was the Dwight D.

Summers in Camelot

There comes a moment in every tour of the mansion when the group lets loose an involuntary sound that is part starstruck gasp, part sad sigh. It is when the guide at **Hammersmith Farm** pauses at the foot of the main staircase.

Up there at the top, on September 12, 1953, she says, Jaqueline Bouvier Kennedy stood in her ivory silk wedding gown and tossed her bouquet to the single women at her reception. She was in the first day of her 10 years as the wife of America's youngest elected president.

Jack Kennedy had wasted no time after his service in the navy in World War II, either in ascending the political ladder or in sowing wild oats. At the arranged dinner where he first met Jackie, an erstwhile Deb Queen and Inquiring Photographer, Washington's most eligible bachelor "reached across the asparagus and asked her for a date." It was time for a man of high ambition to take a politically acceptable wife, and, soon after, he did.

Jack lost a bid for the vice presidency 3 years after his marriage to Jackie, but won the nomination and the presidency in 1960. The shingled Victorian "cottage" on a hill overlooking Narragansett Bay became his summer White House. Despite its 28 rooms and the extensive gardens designed by Frederic Law Olmsted, the designer of New York's Central Park, it seems a relatively modest residence. (At least it does after visits to a few of Newport's other fabled mansions, such as the 70-room neo-Renaissance palazzo, The Breakers, built for Cornelius Vanderbilt.) Hammersmith has antiques, but not all that many, and its other furnishings are rather ordinary, in rooms of no great size.

But here is a history we know. The president's desk is on display, as are photos of Jacqueline and their children. They lived and worked and played here. The presidential yacht, *Honey Fitz,* used to be moored down at the dock. Also seen are images of members of her side of the family, the aristocratic Auchinclosses. One of them, John, built the cottage in 1887. His son Hugh married Janet Lee Bouvier, Jackie's mother, and yet another Auchincloss—Louis—is the lawyer and novelist who has chronicled the lives and times of the well-bred and well-heeled of New York and New England. It is the whispers of the minglings of those lives that lend the cottage at Hammersmith an air of profound purpose and loss.

Eisenhower summer White House. It makes concrete the symbolism mentioned by Kennedy in his inaugural address, the passing of power from men born in the last century to those born in this one.

Admission fees are not by the carload, the way most people arrive, but by individual, which means that a car with five adults will be charged more than $40. That will separate true Kennedy lovers from the merely curious. Even though it is open to the public, Hammersmith is privately owned, and is up for sale at an asking price of $9.5 million. There is no way to tell whether it will remain open or in what ways it will be changed after that future change in ownership.

ANOTHER HISTORIC HOME

Hunter House. 54 Washington St. (at Elm St.). ☎ **401/847-6543.** Admission $6 adults, $3 children 6–11. May–Sept daily 10am–5pm; Apr and Oct Sat–Sun 10am–5pm. Closed Nov–Mar.

Another property of the Preservation Society, this 1754 colonial with its gambrel roof and widow's walk is one of the most impressive dwellings in the lightly touristed neighborhood known as The Point, north of downtown.

Above the doorway, within the broken pediment, is a carved wooden pineapple. This symbol of welcome derived from the practice of placing a real pineapple at the door to announce that the sea captain owner had returned from his long voyage and was ready to receive guests. The interior displays furniture crafted by Newport's famed 18th-century cabinetmakers, Townsend and Goddard.

OTHER ATTRACTIONS

In addition to checking out the attractions described below, you might want to stroll along **Spring Street** between Memorial Boulevard and Touro Street. **Historic Hill** is the large district of colonial Newport that rises from America's Cup Boulevard, along the waterfront, to Bellevue Avenue, the beginning of Victorian Newport. Spring Street serves as the Hill's main drag, and it's a treasure trove of colonial, Georgian, and Federal structures serving as residences, inns, and antique and other shops. There are no 20th-century architectural intrusions. Chief among its visual delights is the 1725 **Trinity Church,** at the corner of Church Street. Said to be fashioned in the manner of the legendary British architect Christopher Wren, it certainly reflects that inspiration in its belfry and distinctive spire, seen from all over downtown Newport and dominating Queen Anne Square, a greensward that runs down to the waterfront. The church is sheathed in beige clapboard and has two stained-glass windows by Tiffany.

International Tennis Hall of Fame. 194 Bellevue Ave. (at the corner of Memorial Blvd.). ☎ **401/849-3990.** Admission $8 adults, $6 seniors, $4 children under 13; $12 family. Daily 9:30am–5pm (except during tournaments).

On Bellevue Avenue, there was (and is) an exclusive men's club called the Newport Reading Room. One member was James Gordon Bennett, Jr., the wealthy publisher of the *New York Herald.* He persuaded a friend to ride a horse into the club. The outraged members reprimanded Bennett, who had an instant snit that they hadn't enjoyed his little jest. He went right out and bought a property on the other side of Memorial Boulevard, and ordered a structure built for his own social and sports club.

The New York architectural firm of McKim, Mead & White produced a shingle-style edifice of lavish proportions with turrets and verandas and an interior piazza for lawn games, equestrian shows, concerts, and a new game called tennis. As Bennett hoped, his Newport Casino swiftly became the premier gathering place of his privileged compatriots.

Now those grass courts not only host important professional tournaments, but are open to the public for play (phone ahead to make reservations, May to October). The building itself houses the Hall of Fame, recently renovated at a cost of $6 million, containing trophies, memorabilia, and computerized interactive exhibits. The Hall is of interest primarily to fans of the game, but has photographic highlights recognizable to casual observers.

Museum of Newport History. Washington Sq. (at Thames and Touro sts.). ☎ **401/ 841-8770.** Admission $5 adults, $4 seniors, $3 children 6–12. Mid-May to Oct Mon and Wed–Sat 10am–5pm, Sun 1–5pm; Nov to mid-May Fri–Sat 10am–4pm.

One of five properties maintained by the Newport Historical Society, this museum is in the refurbished 1772 Brick Market (not to be confused with the nearby shopping mall, Brick Marketplace). The architect was Peter Harrison, also responsible for the Touro Synagogue (below), and the market has been refurbished and reconfigured to contain this professionally installed illumination of the city's history. The museum houses boat models, paintings, antique silverware, old photos, a ship figurehead, and features videos and occasional audio commentaries on Newport history. A printing press used by Benjamin Franklin's brother James is also on display.

Newport Art Museum. 76 Bellevue Ave. (at the corner of Beach Rd.) ☎ **401/848-8200.** Admission $4 adults, $3 seniors, free for children under 18. Memorial Day–Labor Day daily 10am–5pm; Labor Day–Memorial Day Tues–Sat 10am–4pm, Sun 1–4pm.

Standing across the avenue from Touro Park, this was the first Newport commission of Richard Morris Hunt, who went on to design many of the Cottages along Bellevue Avenue. Unlike most of his later Newport houses, this 1862 structure is in the Victorian Stick style, a wood construction that had origins in earlier Carpenter Gothic. This, the former Griswold Mansion, is often cited as a supreme example of the style.

Now a museum and headquarters of the local art association, it mounts exhibitions of the works of Newport artists, offers classes and lectures, and serves as a venue for concerts of the city's frequent music festivals.

Touro Park. Bellevue Ave. (between Pelham and Mill sts.)

Opposite the Newport Art Museum, this small park provides a shaded respite from shopping. Its center is the Old Stone Mill. Dreamers like to believe that the eight columns of the roughly circular structure were erected by Vikings. Realists say it was built by Benedict Arnold, a governor of the colony long before his great-great-grandson committed his infamous act of treason during the War for American Independence.

Touro Synagogue. 72 Touro St. (Spring St.) ☎ **401/847-4794.** Free admission. Labor Day–Oct 15 and Memorial Day–July 4 Mon–Fri 1–3pm, Sun 11am–3pm; Oct 16–Memorial Day Mon–Fri at 2pm, Sun 1–3. Guided tours only.

This is the oldest existing synagogue in the United States, dating from 1763. A Sephardic Jewish community existed in Newport from the mid-17th century, largely refugees from Portugal, but it was over a hundred years before this building was erected. It was designed by Peter Harrison, who was also responsible for the Brick Market, which now houses the Museum of Newport History. The synagogue was closed at the end of its first century for lack of a congregation of sufficient size. It had come back into use in yet another hundred years and was designated a National Historic Site in 1946. On display inside is a 500-year-old Torah.

Next door is the **Newport Historical Society,** 82 Touro St. (☎ **401/846-0813**). In addition to its displays of colonial Newport furnishings and decorative arts, the Society sponsors walking tours (details in "Tours & Cruises," below).

OUTDOOR PURSUITS: THE BEACH & BEYOND

Fort Adams State Park, Harrison Ave. (☎ **401/847-2400**), is on the thumb of land that partially encloses Newport Harbor. It can be seen from the downtown docks and reached by driving or biking south on Thames Street, west on Wellington Avenue (a section of Ocean Drive, which becomes Harrison Avenue). The fort for which the park is named is being restored. Boating, ocean swimming, fishing, and sailing are all available on its 105 acres. Open Memorial Day to Labor Day; admission is $2 per car (state residents, seniors), $4 for nonresidents.

Also on the grounds is the **Museum of Yachting** (☎ **401/847-1018**), housed in a stone barracks of the early 19th century. Photographs, videos, paintings, and models chart the history of competitive sailing. Open mid-May to October 31 daily from 10am to 5pm, by appointment the rest of the year. Admission is $3 for adults, $2.50 for seniors, free for children under 12.

Farther along Ocean Drive, past Hammersmith Farm, is **Brenton Point State Park,** a dramatically scenic preserve that borders the Atlantic, with nothing to impede the waves rolling in and collapsing on the rock-strewn beach. These aren't the towering breakers of the West Coast, but are usually high enough for rather sedate surfing. Scuba divers are seen surfacing offshore and anglers enjoy casting from the long breakwater.

There are other beaches more appropriate for swimming. The longest (over a mile long) and most popular is **Easton's Beach,** which lies along Route 138A, the extension of Memorial Boulevard, east of town. It's the best choice for families, since the breakers are usually very gentle, and there are plenty of facilities, including a very large bathhouse, eating places, picnic areas, lifeguards, a carousel, and the **Newport Aquarium** (☎ 401/849-8430).

On Ocean Drive, less than 2 miles from the south end of Bellevue Avenue, is **Gooseberry Beach,** which is privately owned but open to the public.

Cliff Walk skirts the edge of the southern section of town where most of the Cottages were built, and provides better views of many of them than can be seen from the street. Traversing its length, high above the crashing surf, is more than a stroll, but less than an arduous hike. Think of it as a highly scenic fitness walk. For the full 3.5-mile length, start at the access point near the intersection of Memorial Boulevard and Eustis Avenue. (For a shorter walk, start at the Forty Steps, at the end of Narragansett Avenue, off Bellevue. Leave the walk at Ledge Road and return via Bellevue Road.) Figure 2 to 3 hours for the round-trip, and be warned that there are some rugged sections to negotiate.

Biking is one of the best ways to get around town, especially out to the mansions and along Ocean Drive, about 18 miles in a circular route from downtown and back. Among several rental shops are **Firehouse Bicycle,** 25 Mill St. (☎ **401/847-5700**); **Ten Speed Spokes,** 18 Elm St. (☎ **401/847-5609**); and **Fun Rentals,** 1 Commercial Wharf (☎ **401/846-3474**). The last firm also rents mopeds.

Adventure Sports Rentals, at the Inn on Long Wharf, 142 Long Wharf (☎ **401/849-4820**), not only rents bikes and mopeds, but outboard boats, kayaks, and sailboats, and arranges parasailing outings.

Guided fly-fishing trips and fly-casting instruction are offered by **The Saltwater Edge,** 561 Lower Thames St. (☎ **401/842-0062**). Captain Weatherby takes anglers out in his Boston Whaler on half- and full-day quests for yellowfin tuna, blue shark, white marlin, and dorado. He also sells topflight gear in his pro shop, which is open daily.

TOURS & CRUISES

Several organizations conduct tours of the mansions and the downtown historic district. In summer, the **Newport Historical Society,** 82 Touro St. (☎ **401/846-0813**), has two itineraries. Tours of Historic Hill leave at 10am and 3pm Thursday and Friday and 10am Saturday, and tours of Cliff Walk at 10am and 3pm on Saturdays. Prices are $5 and $7, respectively.

Newport on Foot leaves the Gateway Visitors Center twice daily on 90-minute tours.

If your car has a cassette deck or you have a portable player, a company called **CCInc Auto Tape Tours** produces a 90-minute recorded tour of the mansions for $12.95. It is well done, with an intelligent narration backed by music and sound effects, although it takes a little while to get the hang of when to turn it on and off. The tapes are available at a booth in the Gateway Visitors Center (see "Visitor Information," above) for $12.95 each or directly from the company at P.O. Box 227, 2 Elbrook Dr., Allendale, NJ 07401 (☎ **201/236-1666**).

Viking Tours, based at the Gateway Visitors Center (☎ **401/847-6921**) has narrated bus tours of the mansions and 1- and 2 1/2-hour harbor cruises.

Yankee Boat Peddlers, Bannister's Wharf (☎ 401/847-0298), schedules several daily departures of its 72-foot schooner *Madeleine* and its classic powerboat *RumRunner II.*

One-and-a-half-hour cruises of the bay and harbor are given by **Newport Navigation** on its *Spirit of Newport,* Newport Harbor Hotel & Marina (☎ 401/849-3575), twice daily Monday to Friday, three times on weekends.

And the **Old Newport Scenic Railway,** 19 America's Cup Ave. (☎ 401/624-6951), has 3-hour excursions in vintage trains along the edge of the bay to the Green Animals Topiary Gardens in Portsmouth, at the northerly end of the island.

SHOPPING

At the heart of the downtown waterfront, **Bannister's Wharf, Bowen's Wharf,** and **Brick Marketplace** have about 60 stores between them, none of them especially compelling.

More interesting, if only for their quirky individuality, are the shops along **Lower Thames Street.** For example, **Aardvark Antiques** (no. 475) specializes in salvaged architectural components and larger items rescued from old houses. Books, nautical charts, and sailing videos are offered at **Armchair Sailor** (no. 543), and for vintage clothing, visit **Cabbage Rose** (no. 493).

Spring Street is noted for its antique shops, but purveyors of crafts, jewelry, and folk art are also scattered among them. One of these is **MacDowell Pottery** (no. 140), a studio and retail shop selling ceramics and gifts by Rhode Island artisans; another, the nearby **J. H. Breakell & Co.** (no. 135), is a good source for handcrafted sterling and gold jewelry. Antique boat models, including mounted half-hulls and miniatures in bottles, are displayed along with charts and navigational instruments at **The Nautical Nook** (no. 86). For a pricey memento of Newport's middle history, check out **The Drawing Room/The Zsolnay Store** (no. 152–154), which stocks 19th-century estate furnishings and specializes in Hungarian Zsolnay ceramics. Folk art and furniture are primary goods at **Liberty Tree** (no. 104).

Spring intersects with **Franklin Street,** which harbors even more antique shops in its short length, alongside the post office. **Newport China Trade Co.** (no. 8) deals in export porcelain and objects associated with 19th-century China. Take a fat wallet to **The John Gidley House** (no. 22) for European antiques of high order. **Patina** (no. 32) is another dealer in Americana and folk art.

Note that most of these dealers have their own notions about what are appropriate operating hours and may not be open when other stores are.

WHERE TO STAY

The **visitor information office** (☎ 401/849-8040) provides a useful service to those who arrive in town without reservations. Motels, hotels, and inns that have vacancies that night are listed on a frequently updated board. Most have a number next to their names, to be called from the free direct-line phones located nearby. With dozens of possibilities, there is nearly always something available, even in summer, but less impulsive travelers will want to make reservations in advance to be certain of getting what they want, especially for weekends from June through Labor Day.

Newport Reservations (☎ 800/842-0102 or 401/842-0102, fax 401/842-0104) is one free service representing a number of hotels, motels, inns, and B&Bs. **Anna's Victorian Connection** (☎ 401/849-2489) is similar, but charges a fee and doesn't represent hotels or motels. They accept credit cards.

The better motels are located in Middletown, about 3 miles north of downtown Newport. Possibilities include the **Courtyard by Marriott,** 9 Commerce Dr. (☎ **401/849-8000**), the **Quality Inn Suites,** 936 W. Main Rd. (☎ **401/846-7600**), and the **Howard Johnson Lodge,** 351 W. Main Rd. (☎ **401/849-2000**).

The rates given below generally have very large ranges. Newport hotel rates shift dramatically to meet seasonal demand—so don't assume that a room with a $200 price tag on weekends in July won't be half that price in the spring. It always pays to call around.

VERY EXPENSIVE

✪ **Cliffside Inn.** 2 Seaview Ave. (near Cliff Ave.), Newport, RI 02840. ☎ **800/845-1811** or 401/847-1811. Fax 401/848-5850. 15 rms and suites. A/C TV TEL. $175–$325 double. Rates include breakfast. AE, DC, DISC, MC, V.

Assuming that money is no object, there are really only two places to stay in Newport—this and the Francis Malbone House (see below).

It is difficult to imagine what further improvements might be made in these accommodations. Taking it from the top, 11 of the 15 units have whirlpool baths and working fireplaces; all have nightly turndown service and terry-cloth robes. Antiques and admirable reproductions are generously deployed, including Eastlake originals and Victorian fancies that include an amusing "birdcage" shower from 1890. Favorite units are the "Garden Suite," a duplex with private garden and a big double bath with radiant heat beneath the Peruvian tile floors, and the "Tower Suite," with a green marble bath, a fireplace, and a cedar-lined steeple above the bed. A conscientious staff anticipates your needs, as with coffee and juice delivered to rooms in anticipation of the full breakfast. Afternoon tea is a bonus.

✪ **Francis Malbone House.** 392 Thames St. (east of Memorial Blvd.), Newport, RI 02840. ☎ **800/846-0392** or 401/846-0392. Fax 401/848-5956. 18 rms. A/C TV TEL. $135–$325 double. Rates include breakfast. AE, MC, V. No children under 12.

Nine new rooms have been added in a wing of the original 1760 Colonial house. Very nice, they are, with king-sized beds, working fireplaces, and excellent reproductions of period furniture. Four of them share two sunken gardens and three have whirlpool baths built for two. But given a choice, take a room in the old section. There, antiques outnumber repros, glowing Oriental rugs lie upon buffed wide-board floors, and silks and linens are deployed unsparingly. (There are no TVs in the main building, though. They'd destroy the effect.) In the front hall is a print of a painting by Gilbert Stuart of shipping merchant Francis Malbone and his brother. A full breakfast is served in the morning and afternoon refreshments are set out. The most interesting parts of the waterfront are right outside the door. No smoking.

EXPENSIVE

Doubletree Islander. Goat Island, Newport, RI 02840. ☎ **800/222-8733** or 401/849-2600. Fax 401/846-7210. 253 rms. A/C TV TEL. $99–$189 double. AE, CB, DC, DISC, MC, V.

More than 25 years old (and previously a Hilton and then a Sheraton), the Doubletree is notable primarily for its full hotel services and its location on an island at the northern end of Newport Harbor. You might expect such a place to be impersonal, but most of the staff endeavors to be pleasant. There are delightful views from most of the guest rooms.

Dining/Entertainment: Both formal and casual restaurants are on the premises, along with a lounge.

Facilities: Fitness center, indoor and outdoor pools, two tennis courts.

Elm Tree Cottage. 336 Gibbs Ave., Newport, RI 02840. ☎ **888/356-8733** or 401/849-1610. Fax 401/849-2084. 5 rms, 1 suite. A/C. $135–$225 double. Rates include breakfast. AE, MC, V. No children under 14.

Only a couple of blocks from the beach, this B&B gets enough good reviews to place it among Newport's best-known inns. The flamboyant Victorian manse is a pleasure to behold, inside and out. In an agreeable deviation from local convention, many of the furnishings are French, though they do reflect the Victorian time period. Louis XV is a central inspiration, but much of the decor was obtained at estate auctions. All but one of the rooms have fireplaces (Duraflame logs only). One of the owners creates stained-glass panels and plays musical instruments in the spare time that only busy innkeepers seem to be able to find. Look for the bar with silver dollars imbedded in its surface in the sitting room, where she has two pianos and puts out refreshments in the afternoon. Breakfasts are ample. No smoking.

MODERATE

Admiral Fitzroy. 398 Thames St. (south of Memorial Blvd.), Newport, RI 02840. ☎ **800/ 343-2863** or 401/848-8000. Fax 401/848-8006. 19 rms. A/C TV TEL. $85–$225 double. Rates include breakfast. AE, DISC, MC, V.

The largest of a group of four local inns, the Admiral Fitzroy attracts many Europeans and Australians drawn to the international yachting events that begin or end in Newport. Despite the current name, the antique barometers, and the ship model at the end of the reception desk, this used to be a nunnery—but that doesn't mean Spartan gloom. Rehabilitating old buildings is a central interest of the owners, whose attention to detail is seen in the hand-painted floral renderings found in every room. Many rooms have "peek" harbor views, but better still, take a glass of wine up to the roof deck, which offers a 360° panorama. In addition to the breakfast buffet, the kitchen serves a choice of hot dishes each morning. The staff is unfailingly pleasant. Since they accept children, as many inns do not, lots of families make this home base.

If the 1854 Fitzroy is full, reservations can be made through the same telephone numbers for the similar **Admiral Benbow,** at 93 Pelham St., and the **Admiral Farragut,** at 31 Clarke St. These places rotate 2- to 4-week closings each winter.

✪ **Beech Tree.** 34 Rhode Island Ave., Newport, RI 02840. ☎ **401/847-9794.** 8 rms, 1 suite. A/C TV TEL. $79–$215 double. Rates include breakfast. AE, DISC, MC, V. Drive north on Broadway from downtown and turn right on Rhode Island Ave. It's the 8th house on the left.

Arrive here on a Friday evening and the avuncular owner will sit you down to a bowl of Newport chowder, bread, and a glass of wine. After that, a lot of guests skip dinner and go straight upstairs to soak in a whirlpool bath. On the dining-room wall are photos of the owner with Sandy Dennis and Soupy Sales, and one of their sons with George Bush. They are brief distractions from the other big event of the day— perhaps the most elaborate and filling breakfast served by any B&B in Newport. There are bagels, muffins, pastries, fruit bowls, and five juices to pave the way for plates heaped with eggs, waffles, pancakes, sausages, and/or bacon. Lunch becomes irrelevant. The owners even leave out brandy and cordials and invite guests to help themselves.

The rooms have king- or queen-sized beds and good reading chairs. The flowery decor isn't to everyone's taste, but this place offers such good value that you can easily ignore it (the $215 rate quoted above is for the inn's single suite in summer). A chatty family atmosphere prevails.

Castle Hill. Ocean Dr., Newport, RI 02840. ☎ **401/849-3800.** Fax 401/849-3838. 40 units. TEL. $65–$300 double. Weekly cottage rentals $750–$850. Rates include breakfast. AE, MC, V.

The setting, with 40 beautiful oceanfront acres on a near island, is the overwhelming attraction of this venerable resort. But now that a sorely needed renovation of the 1874 Victorian mansion and its outbuildings is bearing fruit, even a visit in foul weather is a treat. The former summer camp dowdiness of the bedrooms is fast approaching mere memory, and new marble bathrooms, televisions, and air conditioners in most units now help to justify the high summer rates (the $300 rate quoted above is the summer rate for the bridal suites). The best values are the "Harbor Houses," which have been gutted and completely overhauled, with new furniture, TVs, whirlpools, and porches overlooking the bay. Still, primitive lodgings are deemed desirable by many guests, who choose the separate "Beach Cottages" down by the entrance road. With rudimentary furnishings and no central heating, they are available only in summer. Renovations are underway, however, and children and smoking are acceptable, although not in the main house.

Dining/Entertainment: Meals in the newly revived dining room keep guests on the premises to sample the earnest young chef's inventive cuisine, which is inadequately described as "Northeastern Regional." Use of native produce is paramount. The handsome taproom is sheathed in wood, with a riveting view of sailing ships on Narragansett Bay that is shared with the dining room, deck, and many of the bedrooms. Breakfast buffets are expansive, with daily hot entrees; main courses at dinner cost $18 to $27.

Clarkeston. 28 Clarke St., Newport, RI 02840. ☎ **800/524-1386,** 401/846-8242, or 401/849-7397. 9 rms. A/C TEL. $95–$245 double. Rates include breakfast. MC, V.

The charcoal gray exterior enhances the house, built around 1705, one of the oldest in town. Rooms tend to be small, but not oppressively so. They are named for famous Newport residents—Doris Duke, Mrs. Astor, Harry Belmont—none of whom stayed here, as far as is known. The owners have dressed it up with his-and-her walk-around shower stalls and feather-padded mattress covers. Whirlpools and Jacuzzis have also been installed, and there are a few working fireplaces. Hot water comes up almost instantly, which seems not all that important unless you have waited 10 minutes in other inns for that to happen. Guests are welcome to store food in the fridge in the lobby, and a full breakfast is served in the front parlor.

If the inn is full, the same owners have the less elegant **Cleveland House,** directly across the street. Built in 1885, this former rooming house has been perked up with marble baths and four-poster beds, but is well short of memorable. The best rooms are in back. Breakfast is skimpier than across the street. Prices are as low as $55 for a double. Both inns are a short block off Mary Street, west of Spring Street.

Inntowne. Thames and Mary sts., Newport, RI 02840. ☎ **800/457-7803** or 401/846-9200. Fax 401/846-1534. 26 rms. A/C TEL. $95–$179 double. Rates include breakfast and afternoon tea. AE, MC, V.

While Inntowne may not be among the elite Newport lodgings, it outdoes many equally visible operations along the waterfront, and has more available rooms than most. Location is paramount here: Inntowne is at the edge of one of the most active strips of Thames Street and within walking distance of everything appealing along the waterfront. Parking is a bummer—$12.25 a night across the street in a municipal lot. The reception can be either cordial or unresponsive. Either way, the rooms are comfortable, most with four-poster or canopied beds. Breakfast is a little skimpy, but afternoon tea is an agreeable extra. TV is available only in the common room.

Mill Street. 75 Mill St., Newport, RI 02840 (2 blocks east of Thames). ☎ **800/392-1316** or 401/849-9500. Fax 401/848-5131. 23 suites. A/C TV TEL. $65–$295 suite. Rates include breakfast. Children under 16 stay free in parent's room. AE, CB, DC, MC, V.

Something different from most Newport inns, this turn-of-the-century sawmill was scooped out and rebuilt from the walls in. Apart from exposed expanses of brick and an occasional wood beam, all of it is new. The designers chose to create an all-suite facility, each with a queen-sized bed in the bedroom and a convertible sofa in the sitting room. It's a good deal for families. The more expensive duplexes have private balconies, but everyone can use the rooftop deck, where breakfast is served on warm days. While the staff doesn't prohibit smoking on premises, they don't put out ashtrays, either.

The Victorian Ladies. 63 Memorial Blvd. (east of Bellevue Ave.), Newport, RI 02840. ☎ **401/849-9960.** 11 rms. A/C TV. $85–$165 double. Rates include breakfast. MC, V. Closed Jan. No children under 10.

The owners of this little compound of four small buildings tirelessly add new rooms, fixtures, and comforts. They have chosen a version of Victorian decor in keeping with the age of the main house, but updated to suit contemporary tastes. Every guest room is different from the others, but most have queen-sized beds, often four-postered. Six rooms have phones. Full breakfasts include homemade breads and hot entrees. Newport's main shopping district is nearby. No smoking.

INEXPENSIVE

Jailhouse. 13 Marlborough St. (east of Thames St.), Newport, RI 02840. ☎ **401/847-4638.** Fax 401/849-3023. 21 rms. A/C TV TEL. $45–$215 double. Rates include breakfast and afternoon tea. AE, MC, V.

They claim that this was once a colonial jail, although it doesn't look as if it's that old or served that purpose. In any case, the management hams up the incarceration theme, with references to its "prison staff," the "cell block" rooms, legal notices, and speed limit signs. Someone thinks this is cute and clever. It isn't, but there are compensations—the price, primarily. Even during a festival week in July, a room can be had here for as little as $55 (the high rate noted above is for a two-bedroom "maximum security" suite.) And that includes motel conveniences like cable TV with HBO, as well as breakfasts, afternoon tea, and a minifridge in every room. Listless efforts at decor have pegboards instead of closets, but also new baths and carpeting. It's on the same block as the White Horse Tavern. Maybe they'll think better of the caged reception desk before you get there.

Pilgrim House. 123 Spring St. (between Mary and Church sts.), Newport, RI 02840. ☎ **800/525-8373** or 401/846-0040. Fax 401/848-0357. 11 rms (2 sharing a bath). A/C TEL. $60–$175 double. Rates include breakfast. MC, V. Often closed in Jan. No children under 12.

This narrow, four-story, elevatorless mid-Victorian has a rooftop deck with unobstructed harbor views. On good days, the "enhanced" continental breakfast can be taken out there. Afternoon refreshments might be sherry and shortbread. While rooms are without phones or TV, they do have clock radios, and the cozy common room has a fireplace, TV, and VCR. The two cheapest rooms share a bath, logical for a family of three or four. No smoking.

WHERE TO DINE
EXPENSIVE

Canfield House. 5 Memorial Blvd. (behind the Tennis Hall of Fame). ☎ **401/847-0416.** Reservations recommended on summer weekends. Main courses $14.95–$24.95. AE, DC, DISC, MC, V. Daily 5–10pm. NEW AMERICAN.

Named for the gambler who ran a casino in this house from 1897 to 1907, this restaurant still possesses a grandeur suitable for the society swells who were his customers. The main room has a high-vaulted mahogany ceiling, and the lounge, a fireplace and leaded glass panels above the bar. Male patrons are often sockless, in Guccis, with green trousers and blue blazers carrying about 30 gold buttons each. They are with bronzed and shiny women who look as if they spend 10 months of the year in San Diego. Sprinkled among them are officers attending the Navy War College and yachtsmen just in from Bermuda.

The restaurant closed briefly for retooling in 1996, and word of its improvement led to hefty business within a few weeks. The food isn't haute, by any means, despite some of the fevered hoorahs it has received. But it is prepared to order and attractively presented—things like grilled tuna with mango salsa ringed with garlic mashed potatoes, baby carrots, asparagus, roasted tomatoes, dressed greens, and yellow squash (all on one plate!).

Patrick's Pub in the basement serves tavern snacks and pizzas. There are three spacious bedrooms upstairs renting for $85 to $125 a night.

Le Bistro. Bannister's Wharf (near America's Cup Ave.). ☎ **401/849-7778.** Reservations recommended on summer weekends. Main courses $14.95–$26.95. AE, DC, DISC, MC, V. Mon–Sat 11:30am–3pm, Sun 11am–3pm; daily 5–11pm. FRENCH.

Some of the prices slip over the edge of reason, given the fairly routine surroundings. Still, the kitchen is among the most capable in town, assembling lightened versions of French country standards. A rough country pâté is worth the wait, which can be spent nibbling at the crusty bread while checking out fellow guests. They are a prosperous and congenial lot, Rolexes peeking out from the cuffs of Ralph Lauren sweats when they lean over to strike up conversations with their neighbors. (It helps if you have a 50-footer moored in the harbor.) Once they get caught up in seeing and being seen, they barely notice the excellent bouillabaisse, the Burgundian sausage with hot potato salad, the spicy fettuccine with fresh fat clams and big chunks of tomato. The second-floor dining room is somewhat more formal than the third floor, which contains the bar and a few tables.

◆ White Horse Tavern. Marlborough and Farewell sts. ☎ **401/849-3600.** Reservations recommended. Jackets required for men at dinner. Main courses $18–$33. AE, DC, DISC, MC, V. Wed–Mon noon–3pm; daily 6–10pm. NEW AMERICAN.

It may not be the oldest operating tavern in America, as is claimed, but since it's still going strong after 324 years, there can't be too many other healthy contenders. It was once the two-story residence of Francis Brinley, a pirate turned tavern keeper, and while it has obviously undergone many alterations and renovations, it retains its authenticity. On the ground floor are a bar and two dining rooms, with a big fireplace once used for cooking. The upstairs has a similar arrangement.

Given the setting, the kitchen could have chosen to coast on boiled dinners and baked apples. But the food is quite good, from the daily soup-and-sandwich lunch specials to the thick, mesquite-grilled veal chop with an ancho rub and applejack reduction sauce. About a third of the dishes involve seafood. They wouldn't be so gauche as to call it "surf 'n' turf," but the grilled lobster and veal paillard braised in a roasted-garlic and lemon broth scented with rosemary is a highly refined version of the same. Prices are significantly lower at lunch and at Sunday brunch.

MODERATE TO EXPENSIVE

Black Pearl. Bannister's Wharf. ☎ **401/846-5264.** Reservations required for dinner in Commodore's Room. Jackets required for men for dinner in Commodore's Room. Main courses $12.75–$22 in the Tavern, $17.50–$28.50 in the Commodore's Room. AE, MC, V. Tavern daily 11am–11pm; Commodore daily 11:30am–2:30pm and 6–11pm. SEAFOOD/AMERICAN.

This long building near the end of the wharf is divided into two sections. The Tavern has an atmospheric bar and a room painted mostly in black with framed marine charts on the walls. The Commodore's Room isn't all that different, except it's green, more formal, and a 2-pound lobster goes for $35, with trimmings. The simpler preparations of fish, duck, and beef are the ones to order. In the Tavern, don't miss the definitive Newport chowder, followed by a Pearlburger or one of the other overstuffed sandwiches. And in summer, the menu is similar at the dining patio and an open-air bar out on the wharf.

Cooke House. Bannister's Wharf. ☎ **401/849-2900.** Reservations recommended on summer weekends. Main courses $11.95–$21.95 in the Candy Store and Grill, $21–$30 in the Dining Room. AE, DC, DISC, MC, V. Candy Store and Grill daily 11:30am–10:30pm; Dining Room daily 6–10pm. ECLECTIC.

For many, this is the quintessential Newport restaurant. Most of its several levels are open to the air in summer and glassed-in in winter, with overhead fans dispersing the sea breezes. Several bars lubricate conversation. The one on the main floor has a 5-foot model of a schooner on the back wall and the real thing straining at hawsers right outside. The 19th-century structure was moved to the wharf from America's Cup Boulevard in the 1970s.

Up on the formal third floor, they sauté your lobster out of the shell while you put away appetizers of wild mushrooms with leeks and morels bound with mushroom butter ($9.50) or duck foie gras terrine with black mission fig compote ($17.50). If that seems too rich for wallet or liver, spare the walk upstairs and opt for swordfish with red-pepper coulis or the Thai-style whole-wheat spaghetti with jalapeño, shrimp, cilantro, and peanuts. At one side is an espresso bar, and people stop in throughout the day for a latte, a beer, or a sandwich.

✪ **Scales & Shells.** 527 Lower Thames St. ☎ **401/846-3474.** Reservations not accepted. Main courses $9.95–$18.95. No credit cards. Sun–Thurs 5–10pm, Fri–Sat 5–11pm. SEAFOOD.

That graceless name is an accurate reflection of the uncompromising character of this clangorous fish house. Diners who insist upon a modicum of elegance should cross this off their list, or at least head for the upstairs room, called "Upscales," which is less boisterous, if hardly sedate. Fans of Boston's Legal Sea Foods will recognize the drill, if not the more rugged surroundings. A waiting list lengthens at the door as the evening wears on.

Lots of different fish and shellfish at midrange prices are listed on the big black-board in back. An open kitchen with a low counter starts almost at the door—no secrets there. They put together ingredients in guileless preparations that allow the natural tastes to prevail. Salmon with a puddle of crab dill butter and bluefish with black olives and grilled yellow peppers are typical. Also in front is a three-sided bar, where the stressed bartender not only pours every drink, but opens every clam and oyster served. Ask him for the tasty New England brew by the unfortunate name of Smuttynose, and give the man a good tip.

Yesterday's & The Place. 28 Washington Sq. ☎ **401/847-0116.** Reservations recommended for The Place. Main courses $11.95–$27.95. AE, MC, V. Yesterday's daily 11:30am–10pm; The Place daily 5:30–10pm. ECLECTIC.

Turn left into a sprawling space filled with wooden booths around a squared bar. That's Yesterday's, an amiable saloon that goes in for sandwiches, pastas, and simple one-plate meals like herbed roast chicken. The seafood ravioli, with salad, is only $7.95 at lunch. They have 36 microbrews on draft.

Turn right into The Place, a tablecloth and candlelight room that indulges in the sorts of cross-border and transoceanic gastronomic explorations that fit, very loosely, under the "New American" rubric. Expect to see Thai, Mexican, French, and

Italian influences at play. Wait staffs of the dual operations are at least efficient and usually pleasant.

INEXPENSIVE TO MODERATE

Anthony's Seafood. Waites Wharf (off Thames St.). ☎ **401/848-5058.** Reservations not accepted. Main courses $5.95–$14.95. AE, MC, V. Daily 11am–9pm. Closed Dec to mid-Apr. AMERICAN/SEAFOOD.

It couldn't be less casual, with paper plates of food set down on wooden picnic tables. The star meal combo is a New England shore dinner, encompassing chowder, steamed clams, Portuguese sausage, corn on the cob, and lobster. Or choose from an extensive list of sandwiches (such as lobster or clam rolls), salads, pastas, and fried dinners of shrimp, scallops, oysters, and combo plates. A free cup of chowder comes with every entree. The restaurant is fully licensed.

Brick Alley Pub. 140 Thames St. ☎ **401/849-6334.** Reservations recommended for dinner. Main courses $8.95–$17.95. AE, DC, DISC, MC, V. Mon–Fri 11:30am–midnight, Sat–Sun 11am–midnight. ECLECTIC.

Just so you know what you're getting into, the cab of a red Chevy pickup truck is next to the soup and salad bar. Walls are covered with old advertising posters and a room in back has a pool table, pinball machine, and video games. Families, tourists, working stiffs, and yachtsmen squeeze through the doors into the thronged front dining rooms, the bar in the middle, and out onto the tree-shaded terrace in back. They're big on frozen daiquiris. The voluminous menu doesn't leave out much: baked stuffed clams, six Caesar salads, hot cherry peppers stuffed with prosciutto and provolone, Cajun catfish, nachos, 20 kinds of burgers, seven pizzas, chicken teriyaki, and "triple hot buffalo shrimp pasta" (whatever that might be)—with the admonition, "No crybabies!" It's loud and good-natured and prices are palatable if you avoid lobster. The bars stay open later than the kitchen.

Music Hall Café. 250 Thames St. ☎ **401/848-2330.** Main courses $9.50–$17.50. AE, DISC, MC, V. Daily noon–2:30pm and 5:30–10pm. TEX/MEX.

Named for the 1894 building in which it is located, this restaurant looks straight out of Santa Fe. Windows and arches painted on one wall suggest haciendas, and there are carvings of howling coyotes, a kiva ladder, bleached skulls, and hand-painted Mexican tiles on the bar. Under the tricolored awning out front is a row of green tables, ideal for evaluating the Thames Street scene. Barbecued meats are prominent, along with the usual enchiladas, tamales, soft tacos, and a number of grilled items. Vegetarian fare with a kick is also on the card. Even when every chair is occupied, the place isn't crowded.

NEWPORT AFTER DARK

The most likely places to spend an evening of elbow bending, conversation, or listening to music lie along **Thames Street.** Bars are unthreatening and casual. The **Candy Store** of Cooke House, at Bannister's Wharf, has a classic waterside bar. Nearby, two of the most obvious possibilities are **The Red Parrot,** at Memorial Boulevard and Thames Street, which has the look of an Irish saloon and jazz combos Thursday to Sunday year-round, and **One Pelham East,** at Thames and Pelham streets, with a cafe to one side, a small dance floor, and a stage for rockers at the front.

A full schedule of live music is on the plate at the **Newport Blues Café,** at Thames and Green streets, with bands and shouters Monday to Saturday evenings in season (Thursday to Saturday off-season) and a Sunday gospel brunch. Meals are available from 5 to 10pm.

David's, 28 Prospect Hill St., north of Thames, is Newport's only gay and lesbian bar, with an old-fashioned taproom and an adjoining disco right out of the 1970s.

While the Basque sport of jai alai is proclaimed the fastest in the world, the real reason for the existence of **Newport Jai Alai,** 150 Admiral Kalbfus Rd. (☎ **401/ 849-5000**), is gambling. In addition to the game itself, and its highly complicated scoring and odds systems, there are 432 video slot machines and simulcasts of horse and dog races from around the country. Slots are open daily from 10am until 1am, and jai alai games, from May to October, start at 7pm Wednesday to Friday, at noon Monday and Saturday, and at 1pm on Sunday.

4 South County: From Wickford to Watch Hill

Travelers rushing along the Boston–New York corridor inevitably choose I-95 to get from Providence to the Connecticut border. They either do not have the time for a detour or don't know that the nearby shore has some of the best beaches and most congenial fishing and resort villages of New England.

This is called "South County," a designation that has no official status, but refers to the coast that is the southerly edge of Bristol County. Definitions are fuzzy, but for our purposes, South County runs from Wickford, near Providence, to Westerly, nudging Connecticut.

SOUTH COUNTY ESSENTIALS

GETTING THERE   To get to South County from Providence or Boston, take I-95 south, leaving it at Exit 9 to pick up Route 4, also a limited-access highway. In about 7 miles, exit onto Route 102 east, and you'll soon arrive in Wickford. From Newport, cross the Newport and Jamestown bridges on Route 138 to Route 1A north, and take it to Wickford.

Narragansett, at the center of South County's beach country, is 32 miles southwest of Providence, and 14 miles west of Newport.

CROWDS   Try to avoid weekends in July and August, when the crush of daytrippers can turn these two-lane roads into parking lots. Worst of all is arriving on a Friday afternoon and departing on a Sunday evening. If those are your only options, however, lock in lodging reservations well in advance.

WICKFORD

Apart from those crowded summer weekends, a day or two in South County is as stress free and laid back as an outing can be. There is nothing that can be regarded as a must-see sight, hardly any museums to speak of, and only a couple of historic houses to divert from serious cafe sitting, sunbathing, and shopping—and these are the chief pursuits in Wickford, a tidy village that crowds the cusp of a compact harbor.

Sailors and fishermen, artists and craftspeople are among the residents, all of them evident within a block on either side of the **Brown Street** bridge that crosses the narrow neck of the waterway connecting Academy Cove with the harbor. Most of the shopping of interest is there, slipping over to adjoining **Main Street.** Buildings in the area are largely survivors from the 18th and 19th centuries. Parking is usually easy to find, for this is the quiet end of South County.

One place that catches the eye is **The Shaker Shop,** 16 W. Main St. (☎ **401/ 294-7779**), which features handcrafted replicas of the clean-limbed furniture of the eponymous religious sect. Quilts, baskets, and boxes are also displayed. Next to the shop, at the same street address, is **Seaport Tavern** (☎ **401/294-5771**), a re-do of the former occupant, a tearoom called Peaches. Its deck is just the spot for a snack, a light meal, or a glass of iced tea.

Proceed south on Route 1A, known through here as Boston Neck Road. About a mile south of Hamilton, watch for the side street on the right marked for the **Gilbert Stuart Birthplace,** 815 Gilbert Stuart Rd. (☎ 401/294-3001). This may be the one historic homestead in South County that is worth a detour, and not because the painter famous for his portraits of George Washington was born here. (After all, he left for good in young adulthood, and none of his original art is on display.) Rather, it is the setting and the two preserved buildings that reward a visit. First is a weathered gristmill dating from the late 1600s; second, the Stuart birthplace itself, built over his father's snuff mill. The undershot waterwheel and millstones still work, powered by controlled discharges from the adjacent pond. Admission is $3 for adults, $1 for children 6 to 12, and you have to go on the guided tour. Open from April through October, Thursday to Monday from 11am to 4:30pm.

Still on Route 1A, on the right, south of Saunderstown, is the **Casey Farm** (☎ 401/295-1030). Owned by the Society for the Preservation of New England Antiquities, the working 300-acre farmstead is a handsome 18th-century complex of barns and houses. Free-range chickens hop along the carefully laid stone walls that section the fields. Unfortunately, the farm is only open to visitors June 1 to October 15, Tuesday, Thursday, and Saturday from 1 to 5pm. Adults $3, children $1.50.

NARRAGANSETT & THE BEST LOCAL BEACHES

Continuing south on 1A from the Casey Farm, the pace quickens, at least from late spring to foliage season. After crossing the Narrow River Inlet, the road bends toward the series of consecutive beaches around **Narragansett Pier,** the name of which derives from a 19th-century amusement wharf that no longer exists.

Since ocean waves break upon the sand at an angle, there is enough action to permit decent surfing at **East Matunuck State Beach.** In the middle of it all is **The Towers,** a massive stone structure that spans the road between cylindrical towers with conical roofs. It is all that remains of the Gilded Age Narragansett Casino, which was designed by the New York firm of McKim, Mead & White. In the seaward tower is the **Narragansett Tourist Information Office** (☎ 401/783-7121), run by the local chamber of commerce, which can help you find lodging.

Nearby, on the left, the 1888 **Coast Guard House,** 40 Ocean Rd. (☎ 401/789-0700), is now a highly regarded restaurant. It has recovered from a devastating 1991 hurricane, and enjoys unobstructed views of the beach and ocean from its wraparound picture windows.

There are several inns and hotels in the vicinity, many of them looking out over the water across wide lawns. McKim, Mead & White had yet another commission in what is now a B&B, **Stone Lea,** 40 Newton Ave. (☎ 401/783-9546). Situated near the crest of a cliff that falls into the ocean, it is an antiques-filled delight to wander through, if a bit formal in tone. Fresh paint and new wallpaper have been applied recently. Eight rooms rent for $100 to $150 double, including breakfast. MasterCard and Visa are accepted.

A few blocks before The Towers, Route 1A makes a sharp right turn (west), but stick to the shore, proceeding south on Ocean Road. Soon you'll come to **Scarborough State Beach,** a favorite destination of veteran beachgoers, although often jammed with frolicking young people.

POINT JUDITH & GALILEE

Following that road to the end, you'll reach the **Point Judith Lighthouse,** 1460 Ocean Rd. (☎ 401/789-0444). Built in 1816, the brick beacon is a photo op that can be approached but not entered.

Backtrack along Ocean Road, turning left on Route 108, then left again on Sand Hill Cove Road, past the dock of the only year-round ferries to Block Island, and into the Port of Galilee.

The impulse to drive as far as you can without winding up in the drink may account for the popularity of **George's of Galilee,** 250 Sand Hill Cove Rd. (☎ 401/783-2306). It can't be the food, which is ordinary, nor the service, which is slap-dash. Anyway, prices aren't exorbitant, and while it can be brassy on weekends, its decks give good vantage to watch the heavy boat and ferry traffic on the adjacent channel. As for food, any of the nearby eating places are likely to do as well.

Beyond George's parking lot is the redundantly named **Salty Brine State Beach.** Though small, it is protected by a long breakwater that blunts the waves produced by the passing vessels and is a good choice for families with younger children.

To get a better sense of the area from the water, consider the 1$^{3}/_{4}$-hour tour on the *Southland,* which departs from State Pier, in Galilee (☎ **401/783-2954**); it's a renovated Mississippi riverboat that hugs the coast as it moves past fishing villages and beaches. Prices are $6 for adults, $4 for children 4 to 12. Reservations aren't necessary and there's a bar and snack counter on board.

Another possible excursion is a **whale-watching cruise** on one of the three boats of the *Frances Fleet,* 2 State St., Point Judith (☎ **800/662-2824** or 401/783-4988). Cruises are made July 1 through Labor Day, Monday to Saturday from 1pm to about 6pm, depending on the location of the whales. It isn't cheap, at $30 for adults, $27 for seniors, and $20 for children under 12; but the sight of a monster humpback leaping from the water is unforgettable. Numerous **party and charter boats** leave for fishing expeditions from Point Judith.

WESTERLY & WATCH HILL

Leaving Galilee, drive north on 108 to Route 1, turning west on Route 1, toward Connecticut. Before long, it joins Route 1A and enters the township of Westerly, although the immediate area remains semirural.

If it is time to stop for the night, or for dinner, watch for the entrance on the left to the **Shelter Harbor Inn,** 10 Wagner Rd. (☎ 401/322-8883). Parts of the main building date to 1810, and a genteel tone prevails. Several of the 23 rooms in three buildings have fireplaces, decks, or both. A rooftop whirlpool, two paddle-tennis courts, and a croquet green are available and a shuttle takes guests to the private beach a mile away. A creative restaurant and honored wine cellar round out the picture. Rates are $72 to $136 double. American Express, MasterCard, and Visa are accepted.

Follow Route 1A west toward **Watch Hill,** a beautiful land's end village that achieved its desirable resort status during the post–Civil War period and has retained it ever since. Many grand shingled summer mansions and Queen Anne gingerbread houses remain from that time.

The north side of the point is the harbor, packed with pleasure boats, and along the south shore is **Misquamicut State Beach,** a long but often crowded strand.

South of town on Watch Hill Road is the picturesque **Watch Hill Lighthouse** (viewable only from outside). Back in town at the small **Watch Hill Beach,** kids are sure to get a kick out of the nearby carousel, which dates to 1867 and recently was the beneficiary of a 3-year restoration. Shoppers have more than 50 boutiques to explore.

And for a rare East Coast treat, find a seat to watch the sun drop into the ocean. A good place to do that would be the **Watch Hill Inn,** 38 Bay St. (☎ 401/348-8912). All meals are served, largely in the unsurprising New England tradition, but with superb sunset views.

From Watch Hill, take Route 1A toward the Westerly Airport and pick up the Route 78 bypass around Westerly to Route 2 in Connecticut, following signs onto Interstate 95.

5 Block Island

Viewed from above or on a map, the island resembles a pork chop or a lumpy pear with a big bite out of the middle. Only 7 miles long and 3 miles wide, it is edged with long stretches of beach lifting at points into dramatic bluffs. The interior is dimpled with undulating hills, only rarely reaching above 150 feet in elevation. Its hollows and clefts cradle an alleged 365 sweet-water ponds, some no larger than a backyard swimming pool. That "bite" out of the western edge of the chop/pear is **Great Salt Pond,** which almost succeeds in cutting the island in two, but, as it is, serves as a fine protected harbor for fleets of pleasure boats.

The only notable concentration of houses, businesses, hotels, and people is at **Old Harbor,** on the lower eastern shore, where the ferries from the mainland arrive and most of the remaining commercial fishing boats moor.

For the record, the island was named for Adrian Block, a Dutch explorer who briefly stepped ashore in 1641. The earliest European settlement was in 1661, and the island has since attracted the kinds of people who nurture fierce convictions of independence fueled in part by the streaks of paranoia that leads them to live on a speck of land with no physical connection to the mainland. That has meant farmers, pirates, fishermen, smugglers, scavengers, and entrepreneurs, all of them willing to deal with the realities of isolation, lonely winters, and occasional killer hurricanes. Today, that means about 800 permanent residents who tough it out 9 months a year waiting for the sun to stay a while.

The challenges of island living aren't readily apparent to the tens of thousands of visitors who arrive every summer for a day or a season. They are wont to describe this as paradise, a commendation that seems to be assigned only to islands. And they are correct, at least if sun and sea and zephyrs are paramount considerations. Those elements transformed the island from an offshore afterthought into an accessible summer retreat for the urban middle class after the Civil War, in America's first taste of mass tourism.

Unlike other such regions throughout the country that have lost their sprawling Victorian hotels to fire or demolition, Block Island has preserved many of its buildings from that time. They crowd around Old Harbor, providing most of the lodging base. Smaller inns and bed-and-breakfasts add more tourist rooms, most in converted houses built at the same time as the great hotels. There are only a bare handful of establishments that even look like motels, and building stock is marked, with few exceptions, by tasteful Yankee understatement. Angular structures covered in weathered gray shingles prevail.

Away from the sand and surf, it is an island of peaceful pleasures and gentle observations. Police officers wear Bermuda shorts. Children tend semipermanent lemonade stands in front of picket fences and low hedges. Old-timers work their morning route along Water Street, barely making it to the other end in time for lunch, so many are the opportunities to exchange views and news.

ESSENTIALS

GETTING THERE   The Interstate Navigation Company, P.O. Box 482, New London, CT 06320 (☎ **401/783-4613**), provides most of the surface service, including passengers-only ferries on daily triangular routes between Providence, Newport, and Block Island from June 22 to September 2. Bicycles may be taken on board for

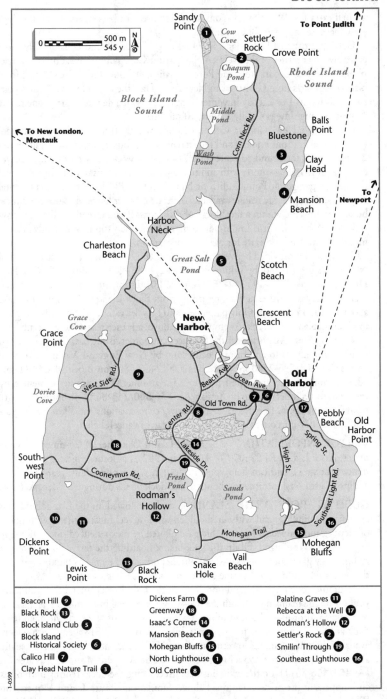

Block Island

Block Island Sound

To Point Judith

Sandy Point 1

Cow Cove

Settler's Rock 2

Grove Point

Rhode Island Sound

Chaqum Pond

Middle Pond

Corn Neck Rd.

Balls Point

Bluestone

Clay Head

Wash Pond

3

To New London, Montauk

4

Mansion Beach

To Newport

Harbor Neck

Charleston Beach

Great Salt Pond

5

Scotch Beach

Grace Cove

Grace Point

New Harbor

Crescent Beach

Dories Cove

West Side Rd.

9

Beach Ave.

Ocean Ave.

Old Harbor

Southwest Point

Center Rd.

7 6

Old Town Rd.

17

Pebbly Beach

Old Harbor Point

8

18

14

High St.

Spring St.

Cooneymus Rd.

19

Lakeside Dr.

Fresh Pond

Sands Pond

Southeast Light Rd.

Rodman's Hollow

12

10

11

Mohegan Trail

15

16

Dickens Point

13

Black Rock

Snake Hole

Vail Beach

Mohegan Bluffs

Lewis Point

0   500 m
     545 y

N

1-0599

a small extra fee. While reservations aren't required for passengers, get to the dock early, because the boats fill up quickly.

Getting a car to Block Island is something of a hassle and considerably more expensive. Car ferries of the **Nelseco Navigation Company** (same address and telephone as above) depart from the Port of Galilee at Point Judith, R.I. Apart from blacked-out days from Christmas to New Year's Day, there are daily departures year-round, as few as 1 or 2 a day in winter to as many as 10 a day from early June to late August. Sailing time is usually 1 hour, 10 minutes.

Ferries leave New London, Conn., daily from early June to Labor Day at 9am (extra trips at 7:15pm Fridays) and return daily at 4:30pm. Sailing time is a little over 2 hours. Since the round-trip fare for a 2- or 3-day weekend for a car and a driver can total nearly $80—more, with additional passengers—consider parking in one of the nearby garages at Point Judith or New London. Block Island is small, rental bicycles and mopeds are readily available, there are cabs for longer distances, and most hotels and inns are within a few blocks of the docks. If you intend to take a car anyway, understand that it is important to make ferry reservations well in advance—a month or two isn't too early for weekend departures.

Service is also provided between Block Island and Montauk, at the eastern end of New York's Long Island, by **Viking Ferry Lines,** R.D. #1 (P.O. Box 159), West Lake Drive, Montauk, NY 11954 (☎ **516/668-5700**). From late May to mid-October, there are daily departures at 9am, returning from Block Island at 4:30pm. Trips take about 1 hour 45 minutes. Only passengers and bicycles can be accommodated; parking is available in Montauk. As emphasized above, advance reservations are advised.

Westerly State Airport, near the Connecticut border, is the base for over a dozen regular daily flights to and from Block Island by **New England Airlines** (☎ **800/ 243-2460,** 401/596-2460 in Westerly, or 401/466-5881 on Block Island). Flights take 12 minutes, and are more frequent in the summer. They are supplemented by the June-to-October service of **Action Air** (☎ **800/243-8623** or 860/448-1646) from Groton, Conn. In either case, make advance reservations and allow for the possibility that not-infrequent coastal fogs will delay or cancel flights.

VISITOR INFORMATION   The **Block Island Chamber of Commerce,** Water Street, Block Island, RI 02807 (☎ **401/466-2982**), has knowledgeable attendants, many brochures, and can help you find lodging. It is open daily year-round. In addition, a seasonal information booth at the dock opens during ferry debarkations.

GETTING AROUND THE ISLAND   Cars are allowed on the island, but roads are narrow, winding, and without shoulders, and drivers must contend with flocks of bicycles and mopeds, many of which are piloted by inexperienced riders. If you're taking a car to the island, fill up the tank before boarding the ferry. There is only a rudimentary gas station—no signs, just a trailer office and nameless pumps—next to the post office. (On the other side of the post office is a bank with an ATM.)

Assuming your physical condition is up to the task, I recommend that you leave your car on the mainland and join the two-wheelers. Several in-town shops and stands rent bikes and/or mopeds, most of them within a couple of blocks of the main ferry dock at Old Harbor. Rates for mountain bikes are typically $18 a day, with widely available discount coupons lowering that to $15. Moped rates vary, but are usually about $75 a day. One convenient source is **The Moped Man,** 435 Water St. (☎ **401/466-5011**), on the main business street facing the dock, renting both bikes and mopeds at the prices mentioned above. Similar outlets are **Island Moped and Bike,** behind the Harborside Inn on Water Street (☎ **401/466-2700**), and **Esta's Bike Rentals,** Water Street (☎ **401/466-2651**).

Several inns also rent bicycles, so a possible plan is to take a taxi from the ferry or airport to one of them, drop off luggage, and get around by bike after that. Two such inns are the **Seacrest,** 207 High St. (☎ **401/466-2882**), and **Rose Farm,** on Roslyn Road (☎ **401/466-2034**), but inquire about rentals when making room reservations—most hotels and inns have ready sources.

EXPLORING THE ISLAND

Little on the island distracts from the central missions of most visitors—sunning, cycling, lolling, and ingesting copious quantities of lobster, clams, chowders, and alcohol. There is only one museum, and it takes only about 20 minutes to cover, even for those enamored of local history. Add a couple of antique lighthouses, a wildlife refuge, and three topographical features of note, and that's about it, enough to provide destinations for a few leisurely bike trips. A driving tour of every site on that list takes no more than 2 hours.

A couple of miles south of Old Harbor on what starts out as Spring Street is the **Southeast Lighthouse.** By the road is a tablet that claims that in 1590 a war party of 40 Mohegans was driven over the bluffs by the Manisseans, the Indians of Block Island. An undeniably appealing Victorian structure, the lighthouse's claim for attention lies primarily in the fact that it had to be moved 100 feet back from the eroding precipice a couple of years ago to save it. There is a free small exhibit on the ground floor, but the admission fee to the top is as steep as the stairs ($5).

Continuing a hundred feet or so along the same road to the **Edward S. Payne Overlook,** paths from the small parking lot lead out to a promontory with views of the 160-foot-high **Mohegan Bluffs,** cliffs plunging down to the ocean. Pretty, yes; stunning, no.

Continuing in the same direction along the same road, which goes through other names and soon makes a sharp right turn inland, watch for the left (west) turn onto Cooneymus Road. In a few hundred yards, pull over near the sign for **Rodman's Hollow,** a geological dent formed by a passing glacier. Claims of its magnificence pale before the reality of undeveloped acres of low trees laced with walking trails.

Back in Old Harbor, proceed north on Corn Neck Road, skirting Crescent Beach, on the right. The paved road ends at **Settler's Rock,** with a plaque naming the English pioneers who landed here in 1661. This is one of the loveliest spots on the island, with mirrored **Chaqum Pond** (suitable for swimming) behind the Rock and a scimitar beach curving out to **North Lighthouse,** erected in 1867. In between is a **National Wildlife Refuge** that will be of interest primarily to bird-watchers. The lighthouse, best reached by foot along the rocky beach, is now an interpretive center of local ecology and history, open late June to Labor Day daily from 10am to 5pm.

Back in Old Harbor, the **Block Island Historical Society Museum,** Old Town Road and Ocean Avenue (☎ **401/466-2481**), was an 1871 inn converted to this use in 1945. The ground floor contains a miscellany of photos, ship models, a World War I uniform, a wicker baby carriage, tools, and an old cash register. Upstairs is a room set up to reflect the Victorian period. The rest of the floor is given to temporary exhibits.

Apart from sunbathing, the island's most popular pursuit is biking. The ferries allow visitors to bring their own bicycles, but several local agencies rent 21-speed mountain bikes (see "Getting Around the Island," above).

Use your bike to get to the many beaches. The longest (about 3 miles long) and most popular strand is **Crescent Beach,** which runs over 2 miles along the shore north of Old Harbor and has a pavilion halfway along the beach. (It changes names, to Scotch Beach and then Mansion Beach as you head farther north from Old

Harbor.) Mostly sand, if a little rocky in places, it is lifeguarded and family oriented, with a bathhouse. The sections nearest Old Harbor are the most crowded, but the more northerly stretches are more secluded, even on July weekends.

Parasailing has become popular here, and striped chutes can be seen daily, lifting riders up to 600 feet above the ocean. Athletic ability isn't necessary, and participants take off and land on the deck of the tractor boat. Contact **Block Island Parasail,** Old Harbor (☎ **401/466-2474**).

Other beaches on the island, such as the aptly named **Pebbly Beach** (which is also very crowded because it is just south of the main harbor), are shorter and rockier.

Fishing, kayaking, and canoeing are hugely popular, and the name to know is **Oceans & Ponds,** at Ocean and Connecticut avenues (☎ **800/678-4701** or 401/466-5131). Loquacious owner Bruce Johnson possesses an encyclopedic knowledge of his island and doesn't stint on sharing it. His high-quality stock features Orvis clothing, duffels, and fishing gear. Kayaks and canoes are available for rent, and he can arrange charter trips on three sportfishing boats. Twice a summer, he hosts 1-day fly-fishing schools with Orvis instructors.

WHERE TO STAY

When you get off the ferry at Old Harbor, you'll be facing Water Street and its row of looming Victorian hotels. Reading from right to left, they are the Surf, the National, the Water Street Inn, the New Shoreham House, and the Harborside Inn. Their accommodations range from barely adequate to satisfactory, and they are a logical option for people who arrive without reservations (not a good idea on weekends).

High cost can't be equated with luxury on the island, the proclamations of hoteliers notwithstanding. Just because your room costs $225 for a Saturday night in July, don't expect 24-hour room service, a fitness center, or even a TV. That doesn't happen. Even in a low-end B&B, a midweek night in high season is likely to cost at least $90. Keep in mind that very few island lodgings have air-conditioning, but sea breezes make it unnecessary on all but a few days each summer. Two- or 3-day minimum stays apply on weekends.

For help in finding lodging, try the chamber of commerce on Water Street, to the left and around the corner from the dock. They stay in touch with the island's inns and B&Bs and can offer suggestions.

Anchor House Inn. 253 Spring St., Block Island, RI 02807. ☎ **800/730-0181** or 401/466-5021. Fax 401/466-8887. 4 rms (all with showers only). TV TEL. $99–$150 double. Rates include breakfast. AE, MC, V. No children under 12.

A huge anchor out front marks this former eyesore, transformed into a virtually new B&B in 1996. Two more rooms may have been added by the time you call. Room decor is spare and restful, avoiding froufrou—quilts on the beds and a few pictures by island artists are about it. All rooms have ceiling fans. Breakfasts are of the hearty continental variety, typically including fruits, juices, bagels, fresh muffins, and quiche. No smoking. Parking is limited.

Atlantic Inn. High St., Box 188, Block Island, RI 02807. ☎ **800/224-7422** or 401/466-5883. Fax 401/466-5678. 21 rms. TEL. $99–$210 double. Rates include breakfast. AE, MC, V. Closed Nov to mid-Apr.

Perched upon 6 rolling acres south of downtown, the 1879 Atlantic has a beguiling veranda. Drawn by the promise of spectacular sunsets and a special menu of nibbles and drinks, including the most diverse beer-and-wine selection on the island, guests and others start assembling from 3:30pm on. The flowers that brighten the many public and private rooms are grown on the property. Bedrooms are decorated almost entirely with antiques, a departure from the common practice at other inns of sprinkling a token few among the many reproductions. Note, for example, the magnificent grandfather clock in the lobby. Children are welcome. No smoking.

Dining/Entertainment: The Atlantic shines most in its dining room, where six-course fixed-price dinners ($45) are offered, and changed weekly. Ingredients are the freshest available and presentations are as eye pleasing as the food is gratifying. The well-versed chef might decide on sea scallops marinated in citrus juices, swiftly seared, tossed in an orange-lime butter and with baby asparagus on one night, then move on to herb-encrusted game hen served with red-onion jam and grilled polenta the next. Reservations are recommended on summer weekends.

Facilities: Two all-weather tennis courts.

✪ **Champlin's.** Great Salt Pond, P.O. Box J, Block Island, RI 02807. ☎ **800/762-4551** or 401/466-2641. 30 rms. A/C TV. $125–$225 double. AE, MC, V. From Old Harbor, drive west on Ocean Ave. and turn left on West Side Rd. The entrance road to Champlin's is on the right. The ferry from Long Island docks nearby.

Families with kids are welcome at this all-inclusive resort, and there are 220 transient slips in the marina for visiting yachtspeople (for reservations, call ☎ **800/762-4541**). Those who can live without the tilted floors and idiosyncratic adornments of the Victorian inns will be pleased by the clean lines and muted fabrics of the bedrooms and the standard microwave ovens and compact fridges. Once you've unpacked, there isn't much to compel you to leave.

Dining/Entertainment: Restaurant, pool bar, snack shop, and even a theater showing first-run movies. There's live music on weekends.

Services: A shuttle van is provided for trips to other parts of the island.

Facilities: On the premises are a large freshwater pool, two tennis courts, a minimart, and a Laundromat. Cars, mopeds, bicycles, kayaks, and paddleboats are all available for rent.

Rose Farm. Roslyn Rd., Box E, Block Island, RI 02807. ☎ **401/466-2034.** 19 rms. TV TEL. $75–$179 double. Rates include breakfast. AE, DISC, MC, V. Closed at least 2 months in winter. From Old Harbor, drive south on Spring St. and turn left at the entrance to the Spring House Hotel. Follow the road around the back of the hotel to Rose Farm. No children under 12.

The remodeled 1897 farmhouse that was the original inn has now been joined by an additional house across the driveway. Four of the rooms in the new building have large whirlpool baths and decks. One room is fully accessible for guests with disabilities. Some have canopied beds, most have ocean views, and all have Victorian reproduction furnishings with a few antiques, including a handsome Eastlake bedstead. The inn rents 21-speed mountain bikes. Afternoon refreshments are served, usually iced tea and pastries. Smoking is limited to the decks.

The 1661 Inn & Hotel Manisses. 1 Spring St., Block Island, RI 02807. ☎ **800/626-4773** or 401/466-2063. Fax 401/466-3162. 25 rms (some with shared bath) in main inn, plus 23 in satellite buildings. TEL. $80–$265 double. Rates include breakfast. AE, MC, V. No children under 12.

Pulling into the parking space up the hill from Old Harbor, many guests are delighted to see llamas grazing in the meadow down to the left. There are emus, goats, geese, and a Scottish Highland ox down there, too. They belong to the Manisses, which itself is only the most visible of a small hospitality empire. Other properties include the 1661 Inn, farther up the hill, and the Dodge, Sherman, and Nicholas Ball cottages. Reception personnel are gracious and helpful, and are kept aware of vacancies at the other houses.

The upstairs guest rooms use oak antiques and lots of wicker. Their size varies widely; the corner rooms are largest, and have whirlpool tubs. Each room has a tray of soft drinks, cordials, and snacks next to a carafe of sherry. No smoking.

Dining/Entertainment: All meals are served, often extracting such superlatives as "impressive" and "sophisticated" from restaurant reviewers. Next to the front desk are two inviting rooms, one with a bar. In the evening, it serves as a dessert parlor, where you can order up flaming coffees.

Spring House. 902 Spring St., P.O. Box 902, Block Island, RI 02807. ☎ **800/234-9263** or 401/466-5844. 49 rms. TEL. $99–$275 double. Rates include breakfast. AE, MC, V.

Marked by its red mansard roof and wraparound porch, the island's oldest hotel (1852) has hosted the Kennedy clan, Mark Twain, Ulysses S. Grant . . . and Billy Joel. The young staff is congenial, if occasionally a bit scattered. Swimming is allowed in the freshwater pond on the property.

There are three styles of bedrooms, most of good size, with dusky rose carpeting, queen-sized beds, and pullout sofas. They don't have TVs or air-conditioning, but wet bars are standard. Kids are accepted.

Dining/Entertainment: A considerable attraction is the all-you-can-eat barbecue lunch next to the bar on the veranda. Alert to trends, the management boasts of its portable humidor with expensive cigars that it trots out in the spacious lounge, Victoria's Parlor. On the other side of the lobby is a sitting area with a fireplace, not common at island hostelries, and from there stretches the bright white dining room, with a conventional menu that's executed very competently.

Water Street. Water St., Block Island, RI 02807. ☎ **800/825-6254** or 401/466-2605. 10 rms. TV TEL. $35–$220 double. Rates include breakfast. AE, MC, V. Closed a few months in winter.

Less conspicuous than the larger Victorians lining Water Street, but of the same era, this inn is known more for its ground-floor restaurant, Mohegan Café, than for the comfortable rooms and suites upstairs. Even the cheapest (and noisiest) room at the top of the stairs is large enough for a pullout sofa. Baths are a little primitive, with dim lighting and toilets that tend to tilt on the sloping floor, but all rooms have clock radios and ceiling fans, and some have air-conditioning and harbor views. A coupon provided at check-in entitles bearers to breakfast at the Portfolio Coffeehouse around the corner. Children are welcome.

Show up an hour or so after the last ferry and they might lower the rate if they still have rooms left. The reception is on the right side of the building, in a converted closet.

WHERE TO DINE

Apart from a couple of kitchens that aspire to more rarefied levels of achievement, expect boiled or broiled lobsters, lots of fried and grilled fish and chicken, and the routine varieties of burgers and beef cuts. Chowders are usually surefire, especially but not exclusively the creamy New England version. Clam cakes are ubiquitous. (Actually, deep-fried fritters containing more dough than clams, they are still fun eating, especially when dipped in tartar sauce.)

Several inns and hotels on the island have dining rooms worth noting, especially the Atlantic.

Ballard's. Old Harbor. ☎ **401/466-2231.** Main courses $9.50–$21.95. MC, V. Daily 11:30am–11pm. Closed mid-Oct to Apr. AMERICAN.

Sooner rather than later, everyone winds up at Ballard's, so I might as well mention it. Behind the long porch is a warehouselike interior hung with nautical flags that was once a cavernous clambake hall. Beyond that is a cement terrace with resin tables and chairs beside a long, crowded beach. Several bars fuel the late-evening crowd that piles in for frequent live entertainment, much of which was in style 50 years ago.

The menu ranges all over the map, with something for everyone, though the execution is pretty ordinary. One surprising appetizer is "Ballard's Clam Cake Special," comprised of a bowl of chowder, six clam cakes, and a wedge of watermelon. At only $5.50, it makes an ample and inexpensive lunch.

Dead Eye Dick's. Payne's Dock, New Harbor. ☎ **401/466-2654.** Main courses $13.95–$19.95. AE, MC, V. Daily noon–3pm and 5pm–midnight. Closed mid-Sept to Memorial Day. SEAFOOD/AMERICAN.

Its name and chosen logo—a shark with an eye patch—suggest the kind of joint that sponsors wet T-shirt contests. But Dead Eye Dick's doesn't. Feel free to take either kids or grandparents. Neither picky appetites nor touchy stomachs will have trouble finding something suitable on the menu. Appetizers include conventional clams casino and Maryland crab cakes, but also designer pizzas and bruschettas. Follow with grilled or blackened fish steaks, often accompanied by jalapeño jelly. Salads are ordinary, but come with good crusty bread and a garlicky dipping sauce. While seafood is the kitchen's focus, they also do well by beef and pork cuts, grilled to juicy near perfection. The bar has some offbeat brews on tap or in bottles, including a microbrew from Vermont called Otter Creek.

Ernie's/Finn's. Water St. ☎ **401/466-2473.** Breakfasts $2.95–$5.50; main courses $3–$20.45. Daily Ernie's 6:30am–noon; Finn's 11:30am–10pm. Closed Columbus Day–Memorial Day. AMERICAN.

Breakfast, and nothing but, is what they've been doing at street-level Ernie's for more than 35 years. That means an early crowd of serious anglers and insomniacs and, later, stumble-in visitors so relaxed they can barely move. They have choices of low-fat plates of scrambled egg substitutes and turkey sausages or thick dipped-in-batter French toast drenched with maple syrup and heaped with hash browns and rashers of bacon. (Guess which breakfast most people pick.)

Downstairs, Finn's specializes in ultrafresh seafood at decent prices—the top price listed above is for the twin lobster dinner. Burgers and steaks are also available.

The Oar. West Side Rd. ☎ **401/466-8820.** Sandwiches and salads $2.75–$11.75. AE, MC, V. Daily 6:30–midnight. Closed mid-Oct to late Apr. AMERICAN.

The Oar is more good-time bar than eating place. The best reason to seek it out (at the B.I. Marina) is the view of the Great Salt Pond and the myriad pleasure boats that cover its surface all summer. Take it in from either the deck or the cool bar, with its wide picture window. The restaurant's name should be plural, since the ceiling and walls are hung with scores of oars—all of them painted with cartoons, graffiti, names, and assorted messages of obscure or ribald intent. Commemorating races, anniversaries, important events, or simply some really good parties, they provide such idle diversions as "find the oldest" (1965).

The menu is largely old reliables, from Buffalo wings and fried calamari to burgers and lobster rolls. The only things resembling an actual dinner are plates and buckets of fried chicken, which come with fries or rice and beans. The 20-piece bucket costs $32. Drinks are served until 1am.

BLOCK ISLAND AFTER DARK

Nightlife isn't of the guzzling, rollicking south Florida variety, but neither do they close the bars at sunset. Prime candidates for a potential rockin' good time are

Captain Nick's, on Ocean Avenue (☎ 401/466-5670), with pool tables and live bands supplemented by disco, and the year-round **Yellow Kittens,** on Corn Neck Road (☎ 401/466-5855), also presenting live bands in high season.

Ballard's (see "Where to Dine," above) has music nightly, often of the accordion or "big band" variety. Pitchers of beer, pool tables, pinball, and foozeball are the attractions at **Club Soda,** on Connecticut Avenue (☎ 401/466-5912), but there is live music once or twice a week. Find it under the Highview Inn, off Ocean Avenue. Another live music venue is the lounge of the **National Hotel,** on Water Street (☎ 401/466-2901).

Two cinemas show current films: **Oceanwest,** Champlin's Marina, New Harbor (☎ 401/466-2971), and the **Empire,** Water Street, Old Harbor (☎ 401/466-2555), which also has a video game room.

Vermont

by Wayne Curtis

A pair of East Coast academics raised a ruckus recently with a proposal to turn much of the Great Plains into a national park and let the buffalo roam free again.

With all due respect, if there's any state that should be turned wholesale into a national park, it's Vermont. This would preserve a classic American landscape of rolling hills punctuated with slender white church spires and covered bridges (Vermont has more than 100). It would preserve the perfectly scaled main streets in towns like Woodstock and Bennington and Middlebury and Montpelier. It would save the dairy farms that fan across the shoulders of verdant ridges. But most of all, it would preserve a way of life that, one day, America will wish it had done more to save.

Without feeling in the least like a theme park, Vermont captures a sense of America as it once was. Vermonters still share a strong sense of community, and they still respect the ideals of thrift and parsimony. They prize their small villages and towns, and they understand what makes them special. In a recent speech, Gov. Howard Dean said that one of Vermont's special traits was in knowing "where our towns begin and end." It seems simple, but that speaks volumes when you consider the erosion of identity that has afflicted many small towns that have been swallowed up by some creeping megalopolis.

Of course, it's not likely that Vermont residents would greet a national park proposal with much enthusiasm. Meddlesome outsiders and federal bureaucrats don't rank high on their list of folks to invite to Sunday supper. At any rate, such a preservation effort would ultimately be doomed to failure. Vermont's impeccable sense of place is tied to its autonomy and independence, and any effort to control it from above would certainly cause it to perish.

Happily for travelers exploring the state, it's not hard to get a taste of Vermont's way of life. You'll find it in almost all of the small towns and villages. And they are *small.* Let the numbers tell the story: Burlington, Vermont's largest city, has just 39,127 residents; Montpelier, the state capital, 8,247; Brattleboro, 8,612; Bennington, 9,532; Woodstock, 1,037; Newfane, 164. (All these figures are from the 1990 census.) The state's entire population is just 560,000—making it one of a handful of states with more senators than representatives in Congress.

Of course, numbers don't tell the whole story. You have to let the people do that. One of Vermont's better-known residents, Nobel Prize–winning author Sinclair Lewis, wrote 70 years ago: "I like Vermont because it is quiet, because you have a population that is solid and not driven mad by the American mania—that mania which considers a town of four thousand twice as good as a town of two thousand. . . . Following that reasoning, one would get the charming paradox that Chicago would be ten times better than the entire state of Vermont, but I have been in Chicago and not found it so."

With all due respect to our readers from Chicago, that still holds true today.

1 Enjoying the Great Outdoors

BACKPACKING   The **Long Trail,** running 270 miles from Massachusetts to the Canadian border, was the nation's first long-distance hiking path and remains one of the best. This high-elevation trail follows Vermont's gusty ridges and dips into shady cols, crossing federal, state, and private lands. Open-sided shelters are located about 1 day's hike apart, making this a convenient way to traverse the backcountry. The trail can be quite demanding in parts, and hiking the entire length requires stamina and experience. Shorter excursions of 2 or 3 days are, of course, entirely possible.

The best source of information about the Long Trail and other backcountry opportunities in Vermont is the **Green Mountain Club,** R.R. #1, Box 650, Route 100, Waterbury Center, VT 05677 (☎ **802/244-7037;** E-mail: **gmc@sover.net**), which publishes the *Long Trail Guide.* Club headquarters is located on Route 100 between Waterbury and Stowe, and its newly expanded hikers information center is open weekdays until about 4:30pm. Annual membership dues, which will get you a newsletter and discounts on guides, are $27 for an individual, or $35 for a family.

BIKING   Vermont's back roads offer some of the most superb biking in the Northeast. Even **Route 100**—the state's main north-south artery—is inviting along many stretches; especially appealing is Route 100 north of Killington to Sugarbush. While sheer hills on some back roads can be excruciating for those who've spent too much time behind a desk, close scrutiny of a map should reveal routes that follow rivers and offer less grueling pedaling.

Vermont also lends itself to superb mountain biking. Numerous county and town roads have been abandoned and offer superior backcountry cruising. Most **Green Mountain National Forest trails** are also open to mountain bikers (but not the Appalachian or Long trails). Mountain bikes are prohibited from state park and state forest hiking trails, but are allowed on the gravel roads through these lands. There's also a 10-mile pilot trail for mountain bikers in the Little River area of **Mount Mansfield State Forest** that's worth checking out. **Mount Snow and Jay Peak ski areas,** among others, will bring you and your bike to blustery ridges via lift or gondola, allowing you to work with, rather than against, gravity on your way down. **Craftsbury Center** is your best bet if you're looking for back-road cruising through farmland rather than forest.

Organized **inn-to-inn bike tours** were invented in Vermont, and they remain a great way to see the countryside by day while relaxing in luxury at night. Tours are typically self-guided, with luggage transferred for you each day by vehicle. Try **Vermont Bicycle Touring** (☎ 802/453-4811), **Country Inns Along the Trail** (☎ 802/247-3300), **Bike Vermont** (☎ 800/257-2226), and **Cycle-Inn-Vermont** (☎ 802/228-8799).

Vermont

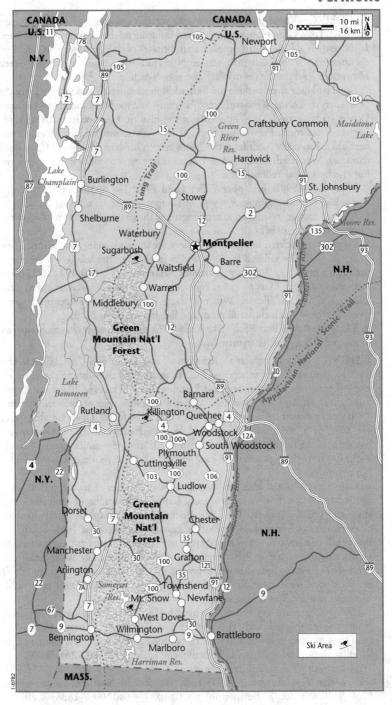

CANOEING　Vermont offers exceptionally pleasant canoeing on a number of rivers and lakes. **Lake Champlain** offers protected canoeing on the east side of North Hero Island and Grand Isle; outside these waters, be wary of sudden winds that can come up unexpectedly with disastrous results. Numerous small ponds within the **Green Mountains** lend themselves to a lazy afternoon's paddle.

Good paddling rivers include the **Battenkill** in southwest Vermont, the **Lamoille** near Jeffersonville, the **Winooski** near Waterbury, and the **Missisquoi** from Highgate Center to Swanton Dam. The whole of the historic **Connecticut River,** while frequently interrupted by dams, offers uncommonly scenic paddling through rural farmlands. Especially beautiful is the 7-mile stretch between Moore and Comerford dams near Waterford. Rentals are easy to come by near Vermont's major waterways; just check the local Yellow Pages.

In the early 1990s, the **Upper Valley Land Trust** (☎ 603/643-6626) set up a network of primitive campsites along the Connecticut River, allowing canoeists to paddle and portage its length and camping along the riverbanks at night. Two of the campsites are accessible by car. Call for a brochure.

Vermont also offers a novel way to explore the state: **canoeing inn to inn**. These trips can usually be tailored for most ability levels and offer leisurely touring at a pace that's perfect for Vermont. **Vermont Waterways** (☎ 800/492-8271) offers weekend and 5-day tours by canoe and sea kayak on the Connecticut River, Lake Champlain, the Lamoille, and Winooski rivers. Prices start at $380 per person for a weekend trip, which includes all meals and lodging at inns or B&Bs.

A helpful guide is Roioli Schweiker's *Canoe Camping Vermont & New Hampshire Rivers,* published by Countryman Press.

FISHING　Vermont attracts anglers from all over the eastern United States, who flock to its banks with spinners and flies. Both lake and river fishing can be excellent—if you know what you're doing. Vermont has 288 lakes of 20 acres or larger, hundreds of smaller bodies of water, and nearly countless miles of rivers and streams.

Novice fly fishermen would do well to stop by the famed **Orvis Catalog Store** (☎ 802/362-3750) in Manchester to ask for some friendly advice, then perhaps try out some of the tackle on the store's small ponds. If time permits, sign up for one of the Orvis fly-fishing classes and have an expert critique your technique and offer some pointers.

Vermont's rivers and lakes are home to 14 major species of sport fish, including landlocked salmon, four varieties of trout (rainbow, brown, brook, and lake), and large- and smallmouth bass. The 100-mile-long **Lake Champlain** attracts its share of enthusiasts angling for bass, landlocked salmon, and lake trout. In the south, the **Battenkill** is perhaps the most famed trout river (thanks in part to the proximity of Orvis), although veteran anglers contend that it's lost its luster. The **Walloomsac** and **West rivers** have also been rumored to give up a decent-sized trout or two. And don't overlook the **Connecticut River,** which the Fish and Wildlife Department calls "probably the best-kept fishing secret in the Northeast."

Fishing licenses are required and are available by mail from the state or in person at many sporting goods and general stores. License requirements and fees change from time to time, so it's best to write or call for a complete list: **Vermont Fish & Wildlife Dept.,** 103 S. Main St., Waterbury, VT 05671 (☎ 802/241-3700).

Two invaluable guides are *The Atlas of Vermont Trout Ponds* ($14.95), and *Vermont Trout Streams* ($24.95), both published by **Northern Cartographic,** 4050 Williston Rd., S. Burlington, VT 05403 (☎ 802/860-2886; Web site: **www.together.net/~ncarto.html**).

HIKING   Vermont offers a spectacular range of hiking trails, from gentle woodland strolls to lengthy treks along rugged, windswept ridges.

The two premier long-distance pathways in Vermont are the **Appalachian** and **Long trails,** which traverse some of the most dramatic terrain the state has to offer. Day hikes are easily carved out of these longer treks; see "Backpacking," above, for information on the **Green Mountain Club,** which is the best source of advice on Vermont's trails.

The **Green Mountain National Forest** offers a total of 500 miles of hiking trails, from the Long Trail to pathways through lowland valleys. There is no single best area for hiking; just head to any of those big green areas on the state map and search out local information on trails. Any of the four Green Mountain offices will make a good stop for picking up maps and requesting hiking advice from rangers. The main office is in Rutland (☎ **802/747-6700**). District ranger offices are in Middlebury (☎ **802/388-6688**), Rochester (☎ **802/767-4261**), and Manchester (☎ **802/362-2307**).

In addition to the national forest, Vermont has around 80 state forests and parks, many of which set the stage for superior hiking. Guides to hiking trails are essential to getting the most out of a hiking vacation in Vermont. Recommended guides include the Green Mountain Club's *Day Hiker's Guide to Vermont,* and *50 Hikes in Vermont,* published by Countryman Press. Both are widely available in bookstores throughout the state.

SKIING   Vermont has been eclipsed by upscale Western and Canadian ski resorts in the past few decades, but in many minds Vermont is *still* the capital of downhill skiing in the United States. The nation's first ski lift—a rope tow—was rigged up off a Buick engine in 1933 near Woodstock. The first lodge to accommodate skiers was built in Vermont at Sherburne Pass.

Downhill ski areas in Vermont vary widely, but each has its appeal. For those looking for the allure of big mountains, steep faces, and a lively ski scene, there's Killington, Sugarbush, Stratton, and Stowe. Families and intermediates find their way to Mount Snow, Pico, Okemo, Bolton Valley, and Smuggler's Notch. For old-fashioned New England ski mountain charm, there's Mad River Glen, Ascutney, Burke, and Jay Peak. Finally, those who prefer a small mountain with a smaller price tag make tracks for Middlebury Snow Bowl, Bromley, Maple Valley, and Suicide Six.

Recorded information on **current ski conditions** is available by calling ☎ **800/837-6668.**

Vermont is also blessed with about 50 **cross-country ski areas** throughout the state. These range from modest mom-and-pop operations to elaborate destination resorts with snowmaking that extends the season and tides skiers over during snow droughts. Many of these are connected by the 200-mile **Catamount Trail,** which runs the length of the state parallel to but lower than the Long Trail. For more information, contact the Catamount Trail Association, P.O. Box 1235, Burlington, VT 05402 (☎ **802/864-5794.**)

The best general advice for cross-country skiers is to head north, and head to higher elevations, where the most persistent snow is usually found. Among the snowiest, best-run destinations are the Trapp Family Lodge in Stowe, the Craftsbury Nordic Center in the Northeast Kingdom, and Mountain Top near Killington. For a free brochure listing all the cross-country facilities, contact the **Vermont Dept. of Travel and Tourism** (☎ **800/837-6668**).

The state also updates a **recorded cross-country ski report** every Thursday (☎ **802/828-3239**). A fax of the report is available by calling ☎ **800/833-9756.**

Inn-to-inn ski touring is growing in popularity. **Country Inns Along the Trail** (☎ 802/247-3300) offers a 4-night trip along the Catamount Trail that connects three inns in central Vermont. The cost is approximately $500 per person, double occupancy, and includes lodging and all meals. Customized trips can also be arranged.

SNOWMOBILING   Vermont boasts a lengthy, well-developed network of snowmobile trails throughout the state. That's the good news. The bad news is that out-of-staters must pay a pound of flesh for the privilege of riding in Vermont. Nonresidents pay $22 to register their sled, and an additional $25 to join the Vermont Association of Snow Travelers (VAST). Snowmobilers must also join a local snowmobile club, with fees of $7 to $10. The fine for ignoring these rules is $117.50.

The best source of information on snowmobiling in Vermont is **VAST,** P.O. Box 839, Montpelier, VT 05601 (☎ 802/229-0005), which produces a great newsletter and can help point you and your machine in the right direction.

Snowmobile rentals are hard to come by in Vermont, although guided tours are common. In southern Vermont, **High Country Snowmobile Tours,** located 8.5 miles west of Wilmington (☎ 800/627-7533 or 802/464-2108), offers tours between 1 hour and overnight. If you've never been on a snowmobile before but want to give it a whirl, rides around a 1.5-mile track are offered just south of Stowe at **Nichols Snowmobile Rentals** (☎ 802/253-7239).

2 Bennington, Manchester & Southwestern Vermont

Southwestern Vermont is the turf of Ethan Allen, Robert Frost, Grandma Moses, and Norman Rockwell. It may very well feel familiar to you even if you've never been here before. Over the decades, it has subtly managed to work itself into America's cultural psyche.

The region is sandwiched between the Green Mountains to the east and the rolling hills along the Vermont–New York border to the west. If you're coming from the southwest, the first town you're likely to hit is Bennington—a commercial center that offers up a selection of goods for residents and tourists alike. Northward toward Rutland the terrain is more intimate than intimidating, with towns clustered in broad and gentle valleys along rivers and streams. Former 19th-century summer colonies and erstwhile lumber and marble towns exist side by side, with both offering pleasant accommodations, delightful food, and, in the case of Manchester Center, world-class shopping.

These outposts of sophisticated culture are within easy striking distance of the Green Mountains, allowing you to enjoy the outdoors by day and goose-down duvets by night. The region also attracts its share of weekend celebrities, as well as shoppers, gourmands, and those simply looking for a brief fantasy detour in the elegant inns and B&Bs.

Keep in mind when exploring the area that two Route 7s exist. Running high along the foothills is the new Route 7, which offers limited access and higher speeds, resulting in a speedy trip up the valley toward Rutland. Meandering along the valley floor is Historic Route 7A, a more languorous route with plenty of diversions (antique shops, historic views). If you've got the time, take the slow road from Bennington to Manchester.

BENNINGTON

Bennington owes its fame (such as it is) to a handful of eponymous moments, places, and things—like the Battle of Bennington, fought in 1777 during the American War of Independence. There's Bennington College, a small but prestigious liberal-arts school that's produced a bumper crop of well-regarded novelists in recent years. And then there's Bennington pottery, which traces its ancestry back to the first factory built here in 1793, and is today prized by collectors for its superb quality.

Bennington is a pleasant, no-frills town with a handful of restaurants and stores still selling things that people actually need. The surrounding countryside, while defined by rolling hills, is afflicted with fewer abrupt inclines and slopes than many of Vermont's towns. The downtown is compact, low, and handsome, and boasts a fair number of architecturally striking buildings. In particular, don't miss the stern marble Federal building (formerly the post office) with its six fluted columns at 118 South St.

ESSENTIALS

GETTING THERE   Bennington is located at the intersection of Routes 9 and 7. The nearest interstate access from the south is via the New York Thruway at Albany, N.Y., about 35 miles away. From the east, I-91 is about 40 miles away at Brattleboro.

VISITOR INFORMATION   The **Bennington Area Chamber of Commerce,** Veterans Memorial Drive, Bennington, VT 05201 (☎ **802/447-3311**), maintains an information office on Route 7 north near the veterans' complex. The office is open during business hours; after hours, you can pick up a map of Bennington and a list of attractions from the box outside the front door. Information is also available on the Internet at **www.bennington.com**, or by E-mail from **benncham@sover.net**.

EXPLORING THE TOWN

Bennington's claim to history is the fabled Battle of Bennington, which took place on August 16, 1777. Though it was a relatively minor skirmish, it had major implications for the outcome of the American Revolution.

The British had devised a grand strategy to defeat the impudent colonies: Divide the colonies from the Hudson River through Lake Champlain, then concentrate forces to defeat one half followed by the other. As part of the strategy, British General John Burgoyne was ordered to attack the settlement of Bennington and capture the military supplies that had been squirreled away there by the Continental militias in anticipation of hostilities. There, he came upon the colonial forces led by Gen. John Stark, a veteran of Bunker Hill. After a couple of days playing cat and mouse, Stark ordered the attack on the afternoon of August 16, proclaiming, "There are the redcoats, and they are ours, or this night Molly Stark sleeps a widow!" (Or so the story goes.)

The battle was over in less than 2 hours—the British and their Hessian mercenaries were defeated, with more than 200 enemy troops killed; the colonials lost but 30 men. This cleared the way for another vital colonial victory at the Battle of Saratoga, ended the British strategy of divide and conquer, and set the stage for a colonial victory in the War of Independence.

That battle is commemorated by northern New England's most imposing monument. You can't miss the **Bennington Battle Monument** if you're passing through the surrounding countryside. This 306-foot obelisk of blue limestone atop a low rise was dedicated in 1891. It resembles a shorter, paunchier Washington Monument. Note also that it's actually about 6 miles from the site of the actual battle; the monument marks the spot where the munitions were stored.

The monument's viewing platform, which is reached by elevator, is open from 9am to 5pm daily from April through October. A fee of $1 is charged.

Along the highway between Old Bennington and the current town center is the **Bennington Museum** (☎ **802/447-1571**). This intriguing collection traces its roots back to 1875; the museum has occupied the current stone-and-column building overlooking the valley since 1928. Nine galleries feature a wide range of exhibits,

Southern Vermont

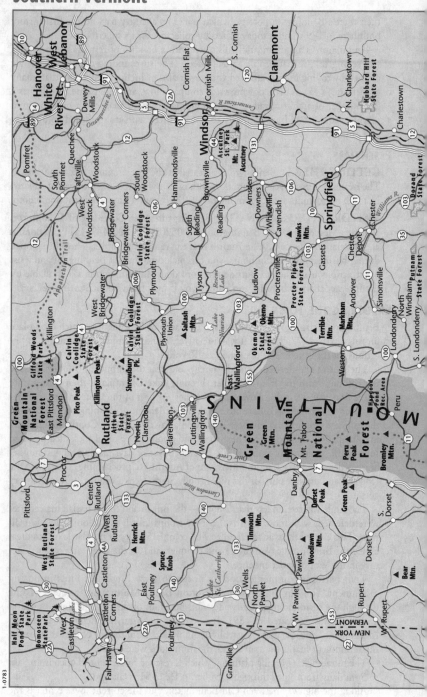

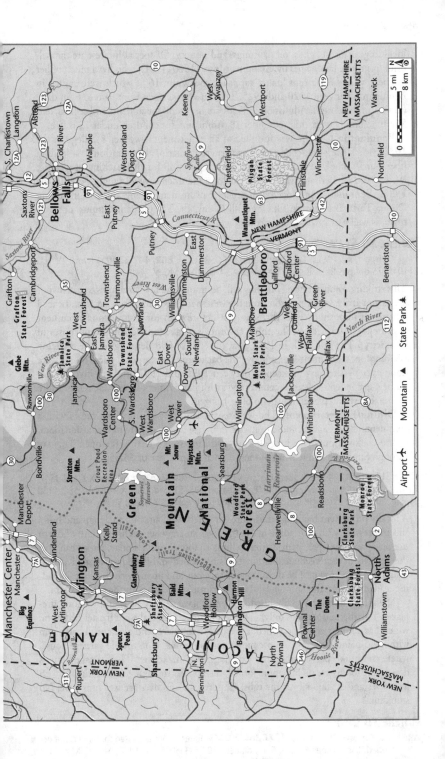

Airport ✈   Mountain ▲   State Park ▲

455

including furniture, glass, oil paintings, and pottery. Of special interest are the colorful, primitive landscapes by Grandma Moses (1860–1961), who lived much of her life nearby, and a glorious luxury car called the Wasp, 16 of which were crafted in Bennington between 1920 and 1925. The museum is open from 9am to 6pm daily (until 5pm in winter). Admission is $5 for adults, $4.50 for students and seniors, and $12 for a family with children under 18. Admission for children under 12 is free.

Bennington College was founded as an experimental women's college in the 1930s. It's since gone coed, and has garnered a national reputation as a leading liberal-arts school. Bennington has a great reputation for the teaching of writing; W. H. Auden, Bernard Malamud, and John Gardner have all taught here. In the 1980s, Bennington produced a number of prominent young authors, including Donna Tartt, Bret Easton Ellis, and Jill Eisenstadt. The pleasant campus, north of town, is well worth wandering about.

WHERE TO STAY

Four Chimneys. 21 West Rd., Bennington, VT 05201. ☎ **802/447-3500.** 11 rms. TV TEL. $110–$175 double. Rates include breakfast. AE, DC, DISC, MC, V.

This striking colonial revival building will be among the first structures to catch your eye as you arrive in Bennington from the west. Set off Route 7 on a large, landscaped lot, it's an imposing white, three-story structure with (of course) four prominent chimneys. (*Local secret:* The third chimney's a fake, added for the purposes of symmetry.) The inn, built in 1912, is at the edge of Old Bennington; the towering Bennington Monument looms above the backyard. The carpeted guest rooms were done over by the new innkeepers between 1996 and 1997, and are inviting and homey, decorated in a casual country style with Early American reproductions. More than half have fireplaces; most also offer Jacuzzis.

Dining/Entertainment: The well-regarded dining room offers meals with a continental flair. Guests choose from two dining areas—the more formal inside room, or the enclosed porch with brick floor and cane-seated chairs. It's open Tuesday through Sunday for lunch and dinner; dinner is a prix fixe of $32.50.

South Shire Inn. 124 Elm St., Bennington, VT 05201. ☎ **802/447-3839.** Fax 802/442-3547. 9 rms (1 with shower only). A/C TEL. Peak season $95–$145 double; off-season $80–$130 double. Surcharge in foliage season. Rates include full breakfast. AE, MC, V.

A locally prominent banking family hired architect William Bull to design and build this impressive Victorian home in 1880. It was an era when architects knew how to use big space, and their patrons were willing to foot the bill. Today, guests can reap the benefits of that vision at Bennington's finest bed-and-breakfast, located a short walk from downtown. The downstairs is spacious and open, with detailing including leaded glass on the bookshelves, and intricate plasterwork in the dining room.

The guest rooms are richly hued, and most have canopy beds and working fireplaces (Duraflame-style logs only). The best of the bunch is the old master bedroom, which has a king-sized canopy bed, a tile hearth fireplace, and a beautiful bathroom with hand-painted tile. Four more modern guest rooms are in the old carriage house, where the innkeepers spared little expense in the makeover. The carriage house's downstairs rooms are slightly more formal; the upstairs rooms are more intimate, with low eaves and skylights over the tubs. Children 12 and over are welcome here. No smoking.

WHERE TO DINE

Alldays & Onion. 519 Main St. ☎ **802/447-0043.** Reservations accepted for dinner, but not often needed. Sandwiches $2.25–$6.95; dinner $10.95–$19.95. AE, DISC, MC, V. Mon–Tues 8am–6pm, Wed–Sat 8am–8pm. ECLECTIC.

First off, the name. For reasons that are not entirely clear, this eminently casual place is named after a turn-of-the-century British automobile manufacturer.

Locals flock here to enjoy the wholesome, tasty sandwiches, the filling deli salads (like Cajun chicken and pasta salads), and tasty quiches and soups. More ambitious dinners are served later in the week, with entrees ranging from Southwest cowboy steak with skillet corn sauce to soba and stir-fried vegetables. The atmosphere is that of a small-town restaurant gussied up for a big night out—the fluorescent lights are bright, but the dark hues of the walls knock down the intensity a notch, and folk-rock background music mellows it further still. In summer, enjoy the airy screened-in patio.

✪ Blue Benn Diner. North St. (Rte. 7). ☎ **802/442-5140.** Breakfast $1.25–$5.95; sandwiches and main courses $1.95–$5.75; dinner $7.95. No credit cards. Mon–Tues 6am–5pm, Wed–Fri 6am–8pm, Sat 6am–4pm, Sun 7am–4pm. DINER.

Diner aficionados make pilgrimages here to enjoy the ambiance of this 1945 Silk City classic, with barrel ceiling and copious amounts of stainless steel. Blue stools line the laminate counter, on which you see plain evidence that more people are right-handed than left-handed by the wear marks. But even folks who don't give a fig for diners flock here for the tremendous value on food. The printed menu is vast, but don't overlook the specials scrawled on paper and taped all over the walls. Blue plate dinner specials are $7.95, and include vegetables, rice, soup or salad, rolls, and Indian pudding for dessert. There's also a great selection of pies, like blackberry, pumpkin, and chocolate cream, that sell for $2.50 a slice (add 25¢ if you want it à la mode).

ARLINGTON, MANCHESTER & DORSET

Vermont's rolling Green Mountains are rarely out of view from this cluster of hamlets. And in midsummer the lush green hereabouts gives Ireland a good run for its money—verdant hues are found in the forests blanketing the hills, the valley meadows, and the mosses along the tumbling streams, making it obvious how these mountains earned their name.

These quintessential Vermont villages make ideal destinations for romantic getaways, aggressive antiquing, and serious outlet shopping. Each of the towns is worth visiting, and each has its own peculiar charm. Arlington has a quaint town center that borders on the microscopic. To the north, Manchester and Manchester Center share a blurred town line, but maintain distinct characters. The more southerly Manchester has an old-world, old-money elegance, with a campuslike town center centered around the columned Equinox Hotel. Just to the north, Manchester Center is a major mercantile center with dozens of outlets offering discounts on brand-name clothing, accessories, and housewares. A worthy detour off the beaten track is Dorset, an exquisitely preserved town of white clapboard architecture and marble sidewalks.

ESSENTIALS

GETTING THERE   Arlington, Manchester, and Manchester Center are located north of Bennington on Historic Route 7A, which runs parallel to and west of the more modern, less interesting Route 7. Dorset is north of Manchester Center on Route 30, which intersects with Route 7A in Manchester Center.

VISITOR INFORMATION   The **Manchester and the Mountains Chamber of Commerce,** R.R. #2, Box 3451, Manchester Center, VT 05255 (☎ **802/362-2100**), maintains a year-round information center in Manchester Center four blocks north of the blinking light. Look for the white house on Adam Park Green. Hours are 9am to 5pm Monday through Saturday (from Memorial Day weekend through October it's also open Sunday from 9am to 2pm).

For information about outdoor recreation, the Green Mountain National Forest maintains a district **ranger office** (☎ 802/362-2307) in Manchester on Routes 11 and 30 east of Route 7. It's open from 8am to 4:30pm Monday through Friday.

EXPLORING THE AREA

Arlington has long been associated with painter and illustrator Norman Rockwell, who resided here from 1939 to 1953. Arlington residents were regularly featured in Rockwell covers for the *Saturday Evening Post.* ("Moving to Arlington had given my work a terrific boost. I'd met one or two hundred people I wanted to paint . . . the sincere, honest, homespun types that I love to paint," Rockwell wrote in his autobiography.)

Visitors can catch a glimpse of this long relationship in a 19th-century Carpenter Gothic–style church in the middle of town, **The Norman Rockwell Exhibition** (☎ 802/375-6423). This small museum features a variety of displays, including many of those famous covers, along with photographs of the original models. Sometimes you'll find the models working as volunteers. Reproductions are available at the gift shop. Open from 9am to 5pm daily in summer; open in the off-season (closed January) from 10am to 4pm weekdays and 10am to 5pm weekends. Admission is $1.

Between Arlington and Manchester you'll pass the entrance to **Skyline Drive** (☎ 802/362-1113), a looping toll road that takes you to the summit of 3,835-foot **Mount Equinox**—which, incidentally, is the highest peak in Vermont not traversed by the Long Trail. The toll is $6 per car and driver, plus $2 per passenger for the 5-mile trip to the top, which affords open views of the Green Mountains to the east. Don't expect wilderness; there's even an inn up top that's open May through October. The mountaintop is also accessible by hiking trail from the village of Manchester. The trail departs from behind the Burr and Burton Seminary on Seminary Road.

Manchester has long been one of Vermont's more moneyed resorts, attracting prominent summer residents like Mary Todd Lincoln and Julia Boggs Dent, the wife of U. S. Grant. This town is well worth visiting just to wander its quiet streets, bordered with distinguished homes dating from the early Federal period. It feels a bit like you've entered a time warp here, and the cars driving past the green seem strangely out of place. Be sure to note the sidewalks made of irregular marble slabs. The town is said to have 17 miles of such sidewalks, made from the castoffs of Vermont's marble quarries.

Seven miles north of Manchester on Route 30 is the village of **Dorset.** Fans of American architecture owe themselves a visit. While not as grand as Manchester, this quiet town of white clapboard and black and green shutters has a quiet and appealing grace. The elliptical green is fronted by early homes that are modest by Manchester standards, but nonetheless are imbued with a subtle elegance. In fact, Dorset feels more like a Norman Rockwell painting than many Norman Rockwell paintings. The main action here is at **Peletier's Store,** which has been provisioning villagers for more than 175 years, although the shelf stock is decidedly more upscale these days.

Museums & Historic Homes

✪ **Hildene.** Rte. 7A, Manchester. ☎ **802/362-1788.** $7 adults, $3 children 6–14. Tours daily mid-May to Oct 9:30am–4pm; grounds close at 5:30pm. Special holiday tours Dec 27–29.

Robert Todd Lincoln was the only son of Abraham and Mary Todd Lincoln to survive to maturity. But he's also noted for his own achievements. He earned millions as a prominent corporate attorney and served as secretary of war and ambassador to Britain under three presidents. He also was president of the Pullman Company (makers of deluxe train cars) from 1897 to 1911, stepping in after the death of company founder George Pullman.

What did one do with millions of dollars in an era when that was still something more than pocket change? Build lavish summer homes, for the most part. And Lincoln was no exception. He summered in this stately, 24-room Georgian Revival mansion between 1905 and 1926, and delighted in showing off its remarkable features, including a spectacular sweeping staircase and a 1908 Aeolian organ with its 1,000 pipes (you'll hear it played on the tour). And what summer home would be complete without formal gardens? Lincoln had gardens designed after the patterns in a stained-glass window and planted on a gentle promontory with outstanding views of the flanking mountains.

A tour of the estate will give you a good sense of life here—descendants of Lincoln occupied the home until 1975, when they donated the property to the Church of Christ, Scientist, which later sold the property to the Friends of Hildene. Many of the furnishings are original, and a number of family mementos are on display.

Special Christmas candlelight tours are held at the end of December, and in winter 9 miles of cross-country skiing trails are maintained on the property, with the carriage house serving as a warming hut. Visitors pay a $10 skiing fee.

American Museum of Fly-Fishing. Rte. 7A (a block north of the Equinox Hotel), Manchester. ☎ **802/362-3300.** Adults $3, children and students free. May–Oct daily 10am–4pm; Nov–Apr Mon–Fri 10am–4pm.

This is probably not the place to take diffident teenagers who complain that adults do boring things on vacation. It is, however, the place for serious anglers interested in the rich history and delicate art of fly-fishing. The museum includes exhibits on the evolution of the fly-fishing reel, paintings and sculptures of fish and anglers, displays of creels, and dioramas depicting fishing at its best. You can see the fly-fishing tackle of some of the nation's more notable anglers, including Herbert Hoover, Andrew Carnegie, and Ernest Hemingway. And, naturally, there are extensive exhibits of beautifully tied flies, displayed in oak-and-glass cases.

MANCHESTER CENTER SHOPPING

Manchester Center is one of several upscale factory outlet meccas in northern New England. Retailers include (take a deep breath) Pendleton, Bass Shoes, Timberland, Burberry's, Polly Flinders, Christian Dior, J. Crew, Seiko, Donna Karan, Coach, Van Heusen, Giorgio Armani, and Dansk. The shops conveniently cluster along a T intersection in the heart of Manchester Center. Most are readily accessible on foot, while others are a bit further afield, requiring scuttling from one to the next by car.

A couple of local shops are worth seeking out amid the high fashion names. Orvis, which has crafted a worldwide reputation for manufacturing topflight fly-fishing equipment, is based in Manchester. The **Orvis Catalog Store** (☎ 802/362-3750) is located between Manchester and Manchester Center, and offers rustic housewares, sturdy outdoor clothing, and, naturally, fly-fishing equipment. Two small ponds just outside the shop allow prospective customers to try before they buy.

Near the middle of Manchester Center at the intersection of Routes 7A and 30 is the **Northshire Bookstore** (☎ 802/362-2200), one of the best bookshops in a state where reading is a popular pastime. In addition to great browsing, the store sponsors frequent readings by prominent authors, both local and otherwise.

OUTDOOR PURSUITS

HIKING & BIKING   Superb hiking trails ranging from challenging to relaxing can be found in the hills a short drive from these towns. Get acquainted with what's where at the **Green Mountain District Ranger Station** (see "Visitor Information," above). Ask for the free brochure *Day Hikes on the Manchester Ranger District*.

The **Long Trail** and **Appalachian Trail** (they overlap in southern Vermont) run just east of Manchester; one of the more popular day treks runs along these trails to **Spruce Peak**. Five miles east of Manchester Center on Routes 11 and 30, look for parking where the Long Trail/Appalachian Trail crosses the road. Strike out southward on foot over rocky terrain for 2.2 miles to the peak, looking for the blue-blazed side trail to the open summit with its breathtaking views of the Manchester Valley.

A scenic drive northwest of Manchester Center you'll come to the **Delaware and Hudson Rail-Trail,** of which 20 miles have been built in two sections in Vermont. (Another 14 miles will eventually be developed across the state line in New York.) The southern section of the trail runs about 10 miles from West Pawlet to the state line at West Rupert, over trestles and past vestiges of former industry, such as the old Vermont Milk and Cream Co. Like most rail trails, this is perfect for exploring by mountain bike. To reach the trailhead, drive north on Route 30 from Manchester Center to Route 315, then continue north on Route 153. In West Pawlet, park across from Duchie's General Store (a good place for refreshments), then set off on the trail southward from the old D&H freight depot across the street.

ON THE WATER   For a duck's-eye view of the rolling hills, stop by **Battenkill Canoe Ltd.** (☎ **800/421-5268** from out of state, or 802/362-2800; E-mail: **info@battenkill.com**) in Arlington. This friendly outfit offers daily canoe rentals on the scenic Battenkill and surrounding areas. Trips range from 2 hours to a whole day, and multiday inn-to-inn canoe packages are also available. The shop is open daily in season (May to October) from 9am to 5:30pm.

Aspiring anglers can sign up for fly-fishing classes taught by skilled instructors affiliated with **Orvis** (☎ **800/548-9548**), the noted fly-fishing supplier and manufacturer. The 2¹/₂-day classes include instruction in knot tying and casting; students practice catch-and-release fishing on the company pond and the Battenkill River. Classes are held from mid-April through Labor Day.

SKIING

Bromley. P.O. Box 1130, Manchester Center, VT 05255. ☎ **802/824-5522,** or 800/865-4786 for lodging. Web site: www.bromley.com. Vertical drop: 1,334 ft. 6 chairlifts, 3 surface lifts. Skiable acreage: 175. Lift tickets $39 weekends, $19 weekdays.

Bromley is a great place to learn to ski. Gentle and forgiving, the mountain also features long, looping intermediate runs that are tremendously popular with families. The slopes are mostly south facing, which means some protection from the winter winds and the warmth of the sun. (Of course, it also means that the snow melts here first.) The base lodge scene is more mellow than at many resorts, and your experience here is certain to be quite relaxing.

Stratton. Stratton Mountain, VT 05155. ☎ **802/297-2200,** or 800/843-6867 for lodging. Web site: www.stratton.com. Vertical drop: 2,003 ft. 1 gondola, 9 chairlifts (including 1 6-person high-speed), 2 surface lifts. Skiable acreage: 500. Lift tickets $49 weekends and holidays, $44 weekdays.

Stratton is striving to reinvent itself. Founded in the 1960s, it labored in its early days under the belief that Vermont ski areas had to be Tyrolean to be successful (hence a Gothic clock tower, Swiss Chalet Nightmare architecture, and the overall feel of being Vail's younger, less affluent sibling). Stratton is working to leave that image of Alpine quaintness behind in a bid to attract a younger, edgier set. The jury is still out, but the resort appears to be heading in the right direction. The slopes are especially popular with snowboarders, a sport that was invented here when bartender Jake

Burton slapped a big plank on his feet and aimed down the mountain. Expert skiers should seek out Upper Middlebrook, a fine, twisting run off the summit.

WHERE TO STAY & DINE

✪ **Arlington Inn.** Rte. 7A (P.O. Box 369), Arlington, VT 05250. ☎ **800/443-9442** or 802/375-6532. 19 rms (some with showers only, 1 with detached bath). A/C. Summer, Christmas, Thanksgiving, and Presidents' and Memorial Day weekends $80–$160 double; foliage season $90–$195 double; late fall to spring $70–$150 double. Rates include breakfast. AE, CB, DC, DISC, MC, V.

This stout, cream-colored Greek Revival home, built in 1848 for a railroad baron, seems better suited to the Virginia countryside. But it anchors the village well here, set back from the road on a lawn bordered with sturdy maples. Inside, the inn boasts a similarly courtly feel, with unique wooden ceilings adorning the first floor rooms, and a tavern that borrows its atmosphere from an English hunt club.

Innkeepers Deborah and Mark Gagnon have taken great strides to improve the inn's regal decor. In 1996, they purchased the 1830 parsonage next door and added six guest rooms there, each with telephone and television. Room rates vary widely, but even the least expensive rooms are well appointed with period reproductions. The quietest rooms are in the detached carriage house, which many guests specifically request. The inn is nonsmoking.

Dining/Entertainment: Dinners, served in the main dining room, include native produce and meats when available. Dinner choices change frequently, but might include the popular dim sum with shrimp; steamed mussels with linguica, saffron, and cilantro; and scallopini of veal cadori, prepared with wild mushrooms, rosemary, and a cognac cream sauce. Entrees are priced from $18 to $24.

Services/Facilities: Tennis court, conference room, baby-sitting. There's a municipal golf course nearby.

Barrows House. Rte. 30, Dorset, VT 05251. ☎ **800/639-1620** or 802/867-4455. Fax 802/867-0132. Web site: www.barrowshouse.com. 28 rms (1 with shower only). A/C. $190–$245 double, including breakfast and dinner. B&B rates also available. Discounts available in the off-season and midweek. 2-day minimum on weekends, 3-day minimum on some holiday weekends. AE, DISC, MC, V.

Within easy strolling distance of the village of Dorset stands this compound of eight Early American buildings set on nicely landscaped grounds studded with birches, firs, and maples. The main house was built in 1784, and it's been an inn since 1900. Some of the guest rooms have gas- or wood-burning fireplaces, and all share a small, country-style common area in the main inn. The inn offers limited rooms for smokers, and only some rooms have telephones.

Dining/Entertainment: Enjoy a before-dinner drink in the casual and cozy tavern with the trompe l'oeil bookshelves. The main dining area is a happy marriage of classical and contemporary. Sit in either the traditional country inn room, or the more modern greenhouse addition. The cuisine is contemporary New England, with entrees like Atlantic salmon with a sun-dried tomato pesto cream, or pan-roasted chicken breast with roasted peppers, shiitake mushrooms, and artichoke hearts. Entrees range from $9.95 to $18.75.

Services/Facilities: Outdoor heated pool, bicycle rental, game room, sauna, two tennis courts.

✪ **1811 House.** Rte. 7A, Manchester Village, VT 05254. ☎ **800/432-1811** or 802/362-1811. 14 rms, including 3 cottage rms. A/C. $160–$200 double. Rates include full breakfast. AE, DISC, MC, V.

This historic Manchester Village home, the first part of which was built in the mid-1770s, started taking in guests in 1811 (hence the name). And it often seems that not much has changed here in the intervening centuries. The warrenlike downstairs common rooms are rich with history—the pine floors are uneven, the doors out of true, and everything is painted in earthy, colonial tones. The antique furniture recreates the feel of the house during the Federal period, and a delightful English-style pub lies off the entryway, complete with tankards hanging from the beams. For aficionados of Early American culture, this is without question the place to be. No evening meals are served.

The Equinox. Rte. 7A (P.O. Box 46), Manchester Village, VT 05245. ☎ **800/362-4747** or 802/362-4700. Fax 802/362-1595. 180 rms and suites (8 with shower only). A/C TV TEL. $169–$299 double; $369–$659 suite. AE, DC, DISC, MC, V.

A blue-blood favorite, the Equinox dominates Manchester Village with its gleaming white clapboard and trim rows of columns. And make no mistake, its historic lineage notwithstanding (it was established in 1769), this is a full-blown resort with sports facilities, two dining rooms, and all the in-room amenities. As is fitting for its faux-Anglo charm, there's a even a British school of falconry affiliated with the inn that offers introductory classes at princely fees ($65 per person for a 45-min. introductory lesson). New in 1997 was the Land Rover Off-Road Driving School, the only permanent Land Rover course in the United States.

Guest rooms are by and large decorated similarly in a country pine motif. The suites are a bit richer hued. Room prices vary based on size, but in truth there's really not all that much difference between the largest and smallest rooms.

Next door to the inn is the grand Charles Orvis Inn, an 1812 home renovated by The Equinox in 1995. It offers nine elegantly appointed suites for $659 to $899 per night, including breakfast. You might think this is a bit high-priced for an overnight. You might be right.

Dining/Entertainment: Choose the dining room to fit your mood: There's the continental elegance of The Colonnade, where men are requested to wear jackets at dinner, or the more relaxed, clubby comfort of Marsh's Tavern.

Services: Concierge, limited room service, dry cleaning and laundry, nightly turndown, baby-sitting, express checkout, valet parking, safe-deposit boxes.

Facilities: Golf course, indoor and outdoor pools, nature trails, health club, sauna, sundeck, beauty salon, boutiques, and a falconry school.

Inn at Ormsby Hill. Rte. 7A (near Hildene, south of Manchester Village), Manchester Center, VT 05255. ☎ **800/670-2841** or 802/362-1163. Fax 802/362-5176. 10 rms. A/C. $115–$225 double. Rates include full breakfast. Discounts midweek and off-season. AE, MC, V. Closed briefly in Apr.

The oldest part of the handsome Inn at Ormsby Hill dates to 1764 (the revolutionary Ethan Allen was said to have hidden out here). Today, it's a harmonious medley of eras and styles, with inspiring views out toward the Green Mountains, and wonderful hospitality offered by innkeepers Chris and Ted Sprague. The common rooms are comfortable and spacious.

Guest rooms vary in size and style. Among the best are the Taft Room, with its vaulted wood ceiling, and the first-floor library, with many of Isham's books still lining the shelves. The newer rooms, in what used to be a dormitory (when the inn served as a home for underprivileged boys), are somewhat smaller, but still tastefully done. Nine of the ten rooms feature two-person Jacuzzis and fireplaces.

Dining/Entertainment: Chris offers guests a light supper upon arrival on Friday nights (at $20 per couple), and an optional four-course dinner Saturday night ($60 for two). (Go with the dinner. You won't be disappointed.) The intriguing dining room was built by prominent 19th-century attorney Edward Isham to resemble the interior of a sumptuous steamship. Here guests also enjoy Chris's otherworldly breakfasts as they admire the views.

The Reluctant Panther. West Rd. (P.O. Box 678), Manchester Village, VT 05254. ☎ **800/ 822-2331** or 802/362-2568. Fax 802/362-2586. 16 rms (some with showers only). A/C TV TEL. $175–$355 double. Rates include breakfast and dinner. AE, MC, V. No children under 14.

The Reluctant Panther, located a short walk from the Equinox, is easy to spot: It's painted a pale eggplant color and has faded yellow shutters, making it stand out in this staid village of white clapboard. It's run with couples in mind. This 1850s home is elegantly furnished throughout (as are guest rooms in an adjacent building, built in 1910), and features nice touches, including goose-down duvets in every room. Ten of the rooms have fireplaces, and one, the Mark Skinner suite, even features a wood-burning fireplace and a double Jacuzzi in the bathroom. Smoking is permitted in the lounge only.

Dining/Entertainment: As nice as the inn is, the Reluctant Panther is perhaps better known locally for its dining. The first-floor dining room, decorated with floral prints, is intimate without feeling crowded. (There's also a greenhouse with slate floor, which is very pleasant in summer.) The cuisine is European, prepared by Swiss-German chef Robert Bachofen, a former director at the Plaza Hotel in New York. The menu changes frequently, but expect entrees like broiled salmon with a tomato crust served on a kidney-bean salad or a shank of veal served with a pepper Parmesan polenta. Entree prices range from $21 to $27.

West Mountain Inn. River Rd., Arlington, VT 05250. ☎ **802/375-6516.** Fax 802/375-6553. E-mail: info@westmountaininn.com. Web site: www.westmountaininn.com. 18 rms (2 with shower only). A/C. Spring weekends, summer, and winter $169–$209 double; foliage season $199–$219 double; spring midweek $145 double. Rates include breakfast and dinner. AE, DISC, MC, V.

The West Mountain Inn is a handsome, rambling, white clapboard building dating back a century and a half. Sitting atop a grassy bluff at the end of a dirt road one-half mile from the center of Arlington, it's a perfect place for travelers seeking sanctuary from the hectic modern age. The guest rooms, named after famous Vermonters, are nicely furnished with country antiques and Victorian reproductions. The rooms vary widely in size and shape, but even the smallest has plenty of charm and character. Some of the rooms in outlying cottages feature kitchenettes. No smoking.

Dining/Entertainment: The inviting dining room is furnished in a hearty rather than cloying country style, with maple floors, pine walls, and green-and-white plaid tablecloths. Dinners include regional fare prepared and served with flair. Guests are served hors d'oeuvres before dinner; typical entrees are roasted quail with an orange-kiwi glaze, and steak au poivre in a mushroom merlot demi. Dinner for nonguests is by reservation only, and is $30 fixed price.

Service/Facilities: Conference rooms, nature trails, nearby health club; in-room massage and baby-sitting by prior arrangement.

WHERE TO DINE

✪ **Chantecleer.** Rte. 7A, 3¹/₂ miles north of Manchester Center. ☎ **802/362-1616.** Reservations recommended. Main courses $18.75–$27.50. AE, DC, MC, V. Wed–Mon 6–9:30pm. Closed Mon–Tues in winter and for 2–3 weeks in both Nov and Apr. CONTINENTAL.

If you like superbly prepared continental fare but are put off by the stuffiness of high-brow Euro wanna-be restaurants, this is the place for you. Rustic elegance is the best description for the dining experience in this century-old dairy barn. The oddly slick exterior, which looks as if it could house a Ponderosa-style chain restaurant, doesn't offer a clue to just how pleasantly romantic the interior is. Heavy beams define the soaring space overhead, the walls are appropriately of barn board, and the small bar is crafted of a slab of pine. A rooster motif predominates (predictably enough, since *chantecleer* is French for rooster), fresh flowers decorate the tables, and, when the weather's right, a fire blazes in the arched fieldstone fireplace. Swiss-born chef Michel Baumann, who's owned and operated the inn since 1981, changes his menu every 3 weeks, but his selections might feature entrees such as veal sweetbreads in a Madeira morel sauce, grilled prime veal chop, or frog legs Provençal. Arrive expecting an excellent meal; you won't go away disappointed.

3 Brattleboro & the Southern Green Mountains

The southern Green Mountains are New England writ large. If you've developed a preconception of what New England looks like but haven't ever visited, this is probably what you've been picturing.

The hills and valleys around the bustling town of Brattleboro, in Vermont's southeast corner, contain some of the state's best-hidden treasures. Travel along the main valley floors—on roads along the West or Connecticut rivers, or on Route 100—tends to be quick. To really soak up the region's flavor, turn off the main roads and wander up and over rolling ridges, and into narrow folds in the mountains that hide peaceful villages. If it seems to you that the landscape hasn't changed all that much in the past 2 centuries—well, you're right. It hasn't.

This region is well known for its pristine and historic villages. You'll stumble across them as you explore—you can't help but find them. And no matter how many other people have found them before you, there's almost always a sense that these are your own private discoveries.

A good strategy is to stop for a spell in Brattleboro to stock up on supplies or sample some local food or music. Then set off for the southern Green Mountains, settle in to a remote inn, and continue your explorations by foot, bike, or canoe. In winter, you can plumb the snowy white hills by cross-country ski or snowshoe.

The single best source of travel information on the region is the **state visitor's center** (☎ 802/254-4593) on I-91 in Guilford, south of Brattleboro.

BRATTLEBORO

Deeply set in a scenic river valley, Brattleboro is not only a good spot for last-minute provisioning, but it also has a funky, slightly dated charm that's part 1940s, part 1960s. The rough brick texture of this compact, hilly city has aged nicely, its flavor only enhanced with its adoption by "feral hippies" (as a friend of mine calls them), who live in and around town and operate many of the best local enterprises.

While Brattleboro is very much part of the 20th century, its heritage runs much deeper. In fact, Brattleboro was Vermont's first permanent settlement. (The first actual settlement, which was short-lived, was at Isle La Motte on Lake Champlain in 1666.) Soldiers protecting the Massachusetts town of Northfield built an outpost here in 1724 at Fort Dummer, about 1¹/₂ miles south of the current downtown. The site of the fort is now a small state park with a campground. In later years, Brattleboro became a center of trade and manufacturing, and was the home of the Estey Organ Co., which once supplied countless home organs, carved in an ornate Victorian style, to families across the nation.

Brattleboro remains the commercial hub of southeast Vermont, located at the junction of I-89, Routes 5 and 9, and the Connecticut River. It's also the most convenient jumping-off point for those arriving from the south via the interstate.

ESSENTIALS

GETTING THERE   From the north or south, Brattleboro is easily accessible via Exit 1 or 2 on I-91. From the east or west, Brattleboro is best reached via Route 9.

VISITOR INFORMATION   The **Brattleboro Chamber of Commerce,** 180 Main St., Brattleboro, VT 05301 (☎ **802/254-4565**), next to the Dunkin' Donuts, dispenses travel information year-round between 8:30am and 5pm weekdays. Or request information via E-mail at **bratchmb@sover.net**; the Web address is **www.sover.net/~bratchmb**.

EXPLORING THE TOWN

Here's a simple, straightforward strategy for exploring Brattleboro: Park. Walk.

The commercially vibrant downtown is blessedly compact, and strolling around on foot is the best way to appreciate its very human scale and handsome commercial architecture. Even if you're en route to a destination to the north, it's well worth a stop for a bite to eat and some light shopping.

Enjoyable for kids and curious adults is the **Brattleboro Museum & Art Center** (☎ **802/257-0124**) at the Union Railroad Station, with wonderful exhibits highlighting the history of the town and the Connecticut River Valley, along with paintings and sculpture by artists of local and international repute. The museum is open Tuesday through Sunday from noon to 6pm from mid-May through October. It's located downtown near the bridge to New Hampshire. Admission is $3 for adults, $2 for seniors and college students, free for children under 18.

North of town on Route 5, where the highway crosses the West River (a Connecticut River tributary), you can sign up for a guided river tour on the *Belle of Brattleboro* (☎ **802/254-1263**). This sturdy, wood-decked riverboat, which may recall the *African Queen* among incurable romantics or those with poor vision, seats about 50 at picnic table–style seating under a yellow canopy. A variety of cruises is offered, but all offer a glimpse of Brattleboro's wildlife and small-town allure from the languid West and Connecticut rivers. Tours run frequently in summer, and cost $7 for adults and $4 for children; there's an additional fee for cruises featuring meals or on-board entertainment.

OUTDOOR PURSUITS

A soaring aerial view of Brattleboro can be found atop **Wantastiquet Mountain,** which is just across the Connecticut River in New Hampshire. You can drive to the trailhead, but somehow it's more adventurous to walk from downtown (figure on a round-trip of about 3 hours). To reach the base of the "mountain" (a term that's just slightly grandiose), cross the river on the two green steel bridges, then turn left on the first dirt road; go two-tenths of a mile to a parking area on your right. The trail begins here; trekkers ascend via a carriage road (stick to the main trail and avoid the side trails) that winds about 2 miles through forest and past open ledges to the summit, which is marked by a monument dating from 1908. From here, you'll be rewarded with sweeping views of the river, the town, and the landscape beyond. Retrace your steps back to town or your car.

Serious canoeists and dabbling paddlers alike will find contentment at **Connecticut River Safari** (☎ **802/257-5008** or 802/254-3908), headquartered where Route 5 spans the West River north of town. Located in a shady riverside glen, this is a fine spot to rent a canoe or kayak to poke around for a couple of hours ($10 for two people), a half day ($15), or a full day ($20). Explore locally, or arrange for a shuttle upriver or down. The owners are exceedingly helpful about providing information and maps to keep you on track. Among the best areas for snooping, especially for bird-watchers, are the marshy areas along the lower West River and a detour off the Connecticut River locally called "The Everglades." Pack a lunch and make a day of it.

WHERE TO STAY

Latchis Hotel. 50 Main St., Brattleboro, VT 05301. ☎ **802/254-6300.** Fax 802/254-6304. 30 rms. A/C TV TEL. $52–$125 double. AE, MC, V.

This wonderful downtown hotel fairly leaps out in Victorian-brick Brattleboro. Built in 1938 in an understated art deco style, the Latchis was once the cornerstone for a small chain of hotels and theaters. It no longer has its own orchestra or commanding dining room (although the theater remains), but it's still owned by the Latchis family and has an authentic if slightly dated flair.

Guests enter through a narrow lobby decorated with subtle art-deco detailing, then walk or ride the elevator to guest rooms on the three upstairs floors. The mysterious angled hallways are reminiscent of a film-noir piece—you can't help but wonder what's going on behind all the doors. For the most part, the guest rooms are comfortable, but not luxurious, with simple maple furniture and old-time radiators that keep the place toasty in winter. From the hotel, it's easy to explore town on foot, or you can wander the first-floor hallways to take in a first-run movie at the Latchis Theatre or quaff a fresh pint at the Windham Brewery. The deluxe rooms feature refrigerators and coffeemakers, and come with continental breakfast and free movie passes.

Dining/Entertainment: The Latchis Grille is located beneath the hotel and offers well-prepared lunches (summer only) and dinners, with both New England and global fare including grilled pork chops, seafood tagliatelle, and a Vermont roast dinner. Entrees range in price from $6 to $17.

40 Putney Rd. 40 Putney Rd., Brattleboro, VT 05301. ☎ **800/941-2413** or 802/254-6268. Fax 802/258-2673. E-mail: frtyptny@sover.net. Web site: www.putney.net/40putneyrd/. 4 rms. A/C TV TEL. $82–$145 double. Rates include breakfast. 2-night minimum on major holidays. AE, DISC, MC, V.

This stately home of white brick and gray slate sits off Route 5 at the northern edge of downtown Brattleboro. Built in the early 1930s, this small French chateau–style mansion was converted to a B&B in 1991 and now offers Brattleboro's most elegant accommodations. The common rooms have hardwood floors and dark wood detailing, which nicely offsets the pale muted colors of the walls. Wingback chairs and a bow-back sofa face the fireplace; there's always a decanter of port set out for guests. Innkeepers Joan and Pete Broderick are gracious hosts, offering complimentary juices in an upstairs refrigerator, and the *New York Times* and *Boston Globe* on Sundays.

Guest rooms are well appointed with country modern furnishings, including hooked and chenille rugs. Two rooms feature gas fireplaces. The best of the four rooms is the two-room suite, which features built-in bureaus and a large tiled bathroom. Guests are welcome to enjoy the landscaped backyard and restored gardens along the West River, or stroll into town on a riverside path. Breakfasts are at the gourmet end of the scale, and are served on the pleasant backyard patio in summer. Children 12 or older are welcome. No smoking.

WHERE TO DINE

Common Ground. 25 Eliot St. ☎ **802/257-0855.** Reservations not accepted. Lunch $2.50–$7.50; dinner $3–$7. No credit cards. Mon and Wed–Thurs 11:30am–8pm, Fri–Sat 11:30am–9pm, Sun 10:30am–2pm and 5:30–9pm. WHOLE FOODS.

Common Ground opened 2 years after the Woodstock Music Festival, which establishes it both chronologically and spiritually. This culinary landmark occupies a funky, hectic space on the second floor of a downtown building—the tone is set walking up the stairway, where business cards tout trauma touch therapy and meditation and movement services. At the top of the stairs, diners choose from a well-worn dining room with flea-market tables, or a pleasant greenhouse addition. The Common Ground is operated as a worker-owned cooperative, and service is cordial if not always brisk.

There's little variation between the lunch and dinner menus; both draw heavily from local and organic ingredients. A meal might include grilled tofu with tahini, brown rice with tamari ginger sauce, or a marinated sea vegetable salad. Or stick with the basics: a bowl of brown rice, beans, and a tortilla costs just $2.50. Sandwiches include tempeh Reuben, Vermont cheddar, and the classic peanut butter and jelly (made with organic Valencia peanut butter and cider jelly and served on whole-wheat bread). There's often live folk music on the weekends.

Curtis Bar-B-Q. Rte. 5, Putney. ☎ **802/387-5474.** Main courses $4–$20. No credit cards. Wed–Sun 10am–dark. Closed Nov–spring. BARBECUE.

Just uphill from Exit 4 off I-91 (about 9 miles north of Brattleboro), you suddenly smell the delicious aroma of barbecue sizzling over open pits. Do not pass this place by, because you *will* change your mind later and waste a lot of time and gasoline backtracking. After all, this is the best barbecue in Vermont, and possibly in New England.

This classic roadside food joint, situated on a scruffy lot next to a Mobil station, has a heap of charm despite itself. (The five signs commanding ALL DOGS MUST BE LEASHED set a strangely appropriate mood for dining here.) This self-serve restaurant consists of two blue school buses and a tin-roofed cooking shed; guests take their booty to a smattering of picnic tables scattered about the lot. Place your order, grab a seat, dig in, and enjoy.

Peter Havens. 32 Eliot St. ☎ **802/257-3333.** Reservations strongly recommended. Main courses $15–$21. MC, V. Tues–Sat 6–9pm. REGIONAL/AMERICAN.

Peter Havens has been serving up the most consistently reliable fine dining in Brattleboro since it opened in 1989. Situated downtown in an upscale, contemporary building, Peter Havens doesn't offer a creative menu. You won't find towering appetizers that defy architectural principles, or wheelbarrow-loads of this year's trendy herb in your meal, but you will get choice ingredients served with panache and flair. The restaurant has but a handful of tables, so make a reservation if you have your heart set on dining here.

All appetizers are priced at $6.50 (except for soup at $4), and range from pâté to gravlax to a smoked filet of lemon-peppered trout. Fewer than 10 entrees are on the menu, but among these you'll find a grilled filet mignon served with a green peppercorn bourbon sauce, and duck breast roasted with a black-currant and port sauce. For seafood, there's scallops with roasted peppers and crabmeat in a light cream sauce, and salmon with a delicately sweet zinfandel and shallot sauce. Wines are limited, but the selection is decent.

THE WILMINGTON REGION

Set high in the hills on the winding mountain highway midway between Bennington and Brattleboro, Wilmington has managed to retain its charm as an attractive crossroads village despite its location on two busy roads. The town draws its share of tourists (especially from New York and New Jersey) but still has the feel of a gracious mountain village.

From Wilmington, the ski resort of Mount Snow/Haystack is easily accessible to the north via Route 100, which is brisk, busy, and close to impassable on sunny weekends in early October. Heading north, you'll first pass through West Dover, an attractive, classically New England town with a prominent steeple and acres of white clapboard.

Between West Dover and Mount Snow, it becomes increasingly evident that developers and entrepreneurs discovered the area in the years following the founding of Mount Snow in 1954. Some regard this stretch of highway as a monument to lack of planning. While development isn't dense (this is no North Conway, N.H.), the buildings represent a not entirely savory mélange of architectural styles, the most prominent of which is Tyrolean Chicken Coop. Many of these buildings began their lives as ski lodges and have since been reincarnated as boutiques, inns, and restaurants. The silver lining is this: The unsightly development prompted Vermont to later pass a progressive and restrictive environmental law called Act 250, which has preserved many other areas from degradation.

Happily, much of the development along Route 100 ceases just north of Mount Snow. Also, remember that you're not restricted to Route 100, no matter what the locals tell you. The area is packed with smaller roads, both paved and dirt, that make for excellent exploring.

ESSENTIALS

GETTING THERE   Wilmington is located at the juncture of Routes 9 and 100. Route 9 offers the most direct access from both Bennington and Brattleboro. The Mount Snow area is located north of Wilmington on Route 100.

VISITOR INFORMATION   The **Mount Snow/Haystack Region Chamber of Commerce,** Main Street, P.O. Box 3, Wilmington, VT 05363 (☎ **802/464-8092**), maintains an information booth May through September at the intersection of Routes 9 and 100. Information may be requested via E-mail at **info@visitvermont.com**. The **Mount Snow Lodging Bureau and Vacation Service** (☎ **800/245-7669**) can assist with booking rooms in the area.

THE MARLBORO MUSIC FESTIVAL

The renowned Marlboro Music Festival offers classical concerts performed by highly talented younger musicians as well as accomplished masters on weekends from mid-July through mid-August in the agreeable town of Marlboro, east of Wilmington on Route 9. The retreat was founded in 1951, and has hosted countless noted musicians, including Pablo Casals, who participated between 1960 and 1973. Concerts take place in the 700-seat auditorium at Marlboro College, and advance ticket purchases are strongly recommended. Call or write for a schedule and ticket forms. Ticket prices range from $5 to $25. Between September and June contact the festival's winter office at **Marlboro Music,** 135 S. 18th St., Philadelphia, PA 19103 (☎ **215/569-4690**). In summer, write Marlboro Music, Marlboro, VT 05344, or call the box office (☎ **802/254-2394**).

OUTDOOR PURSUITS

Mountain Biking

Mount Snow was one of the first resorts to foresee the growing appeal of mountain biking, and the region remains one of the leading destinations for those whose vehicle of choice has knobby tires. Mount Snow established the first mountain-bike school in the country, and it remains one of the best places to be formally introduced to the sport. The **Mountain Bike Center** (☎ 800/245-7669) at the base of the mountain offers equipment rentals, maps, and advice. Independent mountain bikers can also explore some 140 miles of trails and abandoned roads that lace the region. For a small fee, you can take your bike to the mountaintop by chairlift and coast your way down along marked trails, or earn the ride by pumping out the vertical rise to the top. Fanning out from the mountain are numerous abandoned town roads that make for less challenging but no less pleasant excursions.

Skiing

The Mount Snow area offers several excellent **cross-country ski centers.** The 10 miles of groomed trails at **Timber Creek Cross-Country Touring Center** (☎ 802/464-0999), in West Dover near the Mount Snow access road, is popular with beginners and holds snow nicely, thanks to its high elevation. A weekend ticket price is $13. The **Hermitage Ski Touring Center** (☎ 802/464-3511) attracts more advanced skiers to its varied terrain and 33 miles of trails. The weekend cost is $12. The **White House Ski Touring Center** (☎ 802/464-0999), at the inn by the same name on Route 100, offers the easiest access to the Vermont woods, a good range of terrain, and 25 miles of trail ($10). And the **Sitzmark** ski center (☎ 802/464-3384) maintains 24 miles of cross-country trail that covers terrain with 550 feet of elevation gain ($10).

Mount Snow/Haystack. Mt. Snow, VT 05356. ☎ **802/464-3333,** or 800/245-7669 for lodging. E-mail: mtsnow@mtsnow.com. Web site: www.mountsnow.com. Vertical drop: 1,700 ft. 20 lifts (2 high-speed), 4 surface lifts. Skiable acreage: 767. Lift tickets $47 weekends, $45 midweek. Haystack only $39 holiday, $37 weekend, $25 midweek.

These two former ski resorts, once competitors, are now both owned by American Skiing Company, which also owns Killington and numerous other New England resorts. The main mountain is noted for its widely cut runs on the front face (disparaged by some as "vertical golf courses"), and is an excellent destination for intermediates and advanced intermediates. More advanced skiers migrate to the North Face, which is its own little world of bumps and glades. New in the 1996–97 season were 16 additional acres of glade skiing, and a new snowboard half-pipe. Plans for the next season include a new high-speed quad and night lighting for the half-pipe.

Because it's the most southerly of the Vermont ski areas and the closest to the Boston–New York megalopolis (it's just over 4 hours from New York), the mountain can get crowded, especially on weekends. Haystack, which is 10 miles' distance by car (it's much closer as the crow flies), is a classic older New England ski mountain, with challenging, narrow runs. Lift lines are typically much shorter at Haystack.

Mount Snow's village is attractively arrayed along the base of the mountain. The most imposing structure is the balconied hotel overlooking a small pond, but the overall character is shaped more by the unobtrusive smaller lodges and homes. Once famed for its groovy singles scene, Mount Snow's postskiing activities have mellowed somewhat, although twenty-somethings will find no shortage of après-ski activities.

WHERE TO STAY

The Mount Snow area has a surfeit of lodging options, ranging from basic motels to luxury inns to slope-side condos. Rates drop quite a bit in the summer when the region slips into a pleasant lethargy. In the winter, the higher prices reflect relatively easy access to skiers from New York and Boston.

The best phone call to make first is to **Mount Snow's lodging line** (☎ 800/245-7669) to ask about vacation packages and condo accommodations.

A good budget option is the **Snow Creek Inn** (☎ 802/464-5632) in West Dover, which has a range of rooms with weekend rates starting at $80 per night double during ski season.

Skiers enjoy the **Inn at Mount Snow,** a contemporary lodge featuring nice views of the mountain from suites and motel-style rooms. Winter weekend rates are $116 to $141 per night double, including breakfast.

Willing to pay for luxury? Try the deluxe **Inn at Saw Mill Farm** (☎ 802/464-8131), on 28 acres in West Dover; a 2-night winter weekend package including gourmet meals is about $720 double.

Trail's End. 5 Trail's End Lane (^{1}/$_2$ mile off Rte. 100 between Haystack and Mt. Snow), Wilmington, VT 05363. ☎ **800/859-2585** or 802/464-2727. 15 rms (2 with shower only). Summer $95–$145 double; fall $105–$165 double; winter $115–$185 double. Rates include full breakfast. 2-night minimum on weekends, 3 nights on holidays. AE, MC, V. Closed mid-Apr to mid-May.

When the current innkeepers bought Trail's End in 1985, it was a rough ski lodge 30 years old, with bunk beds nailed into the walls. Since acquiring it, Bill and Mary Kilburn have carved out an inviting, friendly spot that attracts repeat visitors who come for the instant camaraderie with other guests and their gregarious hosts.

Trail's End, located a short drive off Route 100 on 28 forested acres, features carpeted guest rooms that are spotlessly clean, styled in a light country fashion with pine and wicker furniture. Six feature fireplaces and two have Jacuzzis. But few guests seem to spend much time in their rooms. They congregate around the 22-foot stone fireplace in the main common room, in the stone-floored library and game room, or in the informal second-floor loft—or they hang out in the kitchen with Bill as he obsessively polishes his gleaming stove. At breakfast, the congregating continues around three massive round tables. The incurably shy, it should go without saying, will not be happy here. Others will.

Facilities: Heated outdoor pool (summer only), clay tennis court, game rooms, sundeck.

White House of Wilmington. Rte. 9, Wilmington, VT 05363. ☎ **800/541-2135** or 802/464-2135. E-mail: whitehse@sover.net. 23 rms. $128–$178 double. Rates include full breakfast. Fireplace rms $30 less in summer. 2-night minimum reservation on weekends. AE, MC, V.

The White House of Wilmington, a fanciful Greek Revival–style home with two prominent porticos (built in 1915 by a wealthy lumber baron), sits impressively on the crest of an open hill just east of Wilmington. The interior is spacious and open, with hardwood floors, arched doorways, and superb detailing throughout. The guest rooms are comfortably furnished; nine have wood-burning fireplaces, and four feature whirlpools. Formal without being stuffy, the inn has an especially appealing bar on its enclosed porch, which can't be beat as a spot to sip something soothing while watching the sun sink over the Vermont hills.

Dining/Entertainment: The inn's restaurant is well regarded for its continental cuisine, served in an attractive dining room with hardwood floors, dark wood trim, pink tablecloths, and an intricate fireplace mantel. Entrees include duck stuffed with walnuts, apples, and grapes (the chef's specialty); veal piccata; and filet mignon au poivre.

Facilities: Outdoor heated swimming pool, tennis courts, Jacuzzi, nature trails, conference rooms, sauna, 22 miles of groomed cross-country ski trails. The inn also accommodates snowmobilers.

WHERE TO DINE

✪ **Inn at Sawmill Farm.** Rte. 100, West Dover. ☎ **802/464-8131.** Reservations recommended. Main courses $27–$32. AE, MC, V. Daily 6–9:30pm. Closed last week of Apr through the 1st week of May. CONTINENTAL.

Let's talk wine. About 36,000 bottles of wine. That's what's lurking in the inn's custom-made wine cellar, and what garnered it a coveted "Grand Award" from *Wine Spectator* magazine. The inn offers a decent selection by the glass, and if you feel like splurging on a $400 bottle of wine, this is the place.

But the wine is only one of the reasons the inn has long been popular with upscale diners. The food is deftly prepared by innkeeper/chef Brill Williams (son of innkeepers Ione and Rodney Williams), with entrees ranging from pan-seared salmon in saffron sauce to breast of pheasant with a *forestiere* sauce. Feeling a bit more adventurous? Opt for the sautéed breast of chicken, served with a surprisingly delicate Indonesian curry sauce and caramelized banana.

The atmosphere is near perfect. While the garden dining room is less posh than the formal dining room (housed in a portion of an old barn), the soft tones, wide pine planks in the floors, and live piano music filling the air lend the whole dining room a soft and romantic feel. Well-selected silverware and glassware lend a classical elegance. The service is superb, although the slavish attention of the servers and their overall formality (one waiter lavished grated cheese on my salad while another simultaneously proffered pepper) puts some folks on edge. In an effort to attract a broader clientele, the inn recently dropped its long-standing jackets-on-men policy and now allows neat but casual evening attire.

Le Petit Chef. Rte. 100, Wilmington. ☎ **802/464-8437.** Reservations recommended. Main courses $15–$25 (mostly $19–$22). AE, MC, V. Wed–Thurs and Sun–Mon 6–9pm, Fri–Sat 6–10pm. FRENCH.

Situated in an old Cape Cod–style farmhouse, Le Petit Chef has attracted legions of satisfied customers who flock here to sample Betty Hillman's superb and creative fare. The interior has been updated and modernized at the expense of some historic character, but the quality of the food usually makes diners overlook the made for ski crowds ambiance. By all means, start with the signature "Bird's Nest," an innovative mélange of shiitake mushrooms and onions cooked in a cream sauce and served in a basket of deep-fried potato. The main courses are equally succulent, with selections like a filet of salmon baked in a horseradish crust, loin of venison sautéed and served with a red currant sauce, and chicken breast rolled with blue cheese and pear and served on bulgur with a pear chutney.

NEWFANE & TOWNSHEND

For many travelers, these two villages about 5 miles apart on Route 30 are the epitome of Vermont. Both are set deeply within the serpentine West River Valley, and both are built around open town greens. Both towns consist of impressive white clapboard homes and public buildings that share the grace and scale of the surrounding homes. Both towns boast striking examples of Early American architecture, notably Greek Revival.

Don't bother looking for strip malls, McDonald's, or garish video outlets hereabouts. Newfane and Townshend feel as if they've been idled on a sidetrack for decades while the rest of American society steamed blithely ahead. That's not to say these villages have the somber feel of a mausoleum. On a past visit during a breezy autumn afternoon, a swarm of teenagers skateboarded off the steps of the courthouse in Newfane, and a lively basketball game was underway at the edge of the green in Townshend. There's life here.

For visitors, inactivity is often the activity of choice. Guests find an inn or lodge that suits their temperament, then spend the days strolling the towns, undertaking aimless back-road driving tours, soaking in a mountain stream, hunting up antiques at the many shops, or striking off on foot for one of the rounded, wooded peaks that overlook villages and valleys.

ESSENTIALS

GETTING THERE   Newfane and Townshend are located on Route 30 northwest of Brattleboro. The nearest interstate access is off Exit 3 from I-91.

VISITOR INFORMATION   There's no formal information center serving these towns. Brochures are available at the **state visitor's center** (☎ 802/254-4593) on I-91 in Guilford, south of Brattleboro. Visitors might also try the Townshend Country Store for local advice.

EXPLORING THE AREA

Newfane was originally founded on a hill a few miles away in 1774; in 1825 it was moved down to the valley floor. Some of the original buildings were dismantled and rebuilt, but most date from the early- to mid-19th century. The **National Historic District** is comprised of some 60 buildings around the green and on nearby side streets. You'll find styles ranging from Federal through colonial revival, although Greek Revival appears to carry the day. A strikingly handsome courthouse—where cases are still heard, as they have been for 170 years—dominates the shady green. This structure was originally built in 1825; the imposing portico was added in 1853. For more detailed information on area buildings, obtain a copy of the free walking tour brochure at the Moore Free Library on West Street.

About a dozen **antique shops** line Route 30 through the West River Valley, as well as on Route 35 north of Townshend. They provide good grazing on lazy afternoons, and are a fine resource for serious collectors. The **Newfane Antiques Center** (☎ 802/365-4482) houses 20 dealers on three floors and offers a broad selection ranging from bric-a-brac to quality furniture. **Schommer Antiques** (☎ 802/365-7777) on Route 30 in Newfane Village carries a good selection of 19th-century furniture and accessories in a shop that's listed on the National Register.

Hard-core treasure hunters should time their visit to hit the **Newfane Flea Market** (☎ 802/365-4000), which features 100-plus tables of assorted stuff. The flea market is held Sundays from May through October on Route 30 just north of Newfane Village.

OUTDOOR PURSUITS

Three miles outside of Townshend are **Townshend State Park** (☎ 802/365-7500) and **Townshend State Forest.** Located at the foot of Bald Mountain, the park consists mostly of a solidly built campground constructed by the Civilian Conservation Corps in the 1930s. But you can park here to hike **Bald Mountain,** one of the better short hikes in the region. A 3.1-mile loop trail begins behind the ranger station, following a bridle path along a brook. The ascent soon steepens, and at 1.7 miles you'll arrive at the 1,680-foot summit, which turns out not to be bald at all. Open ledges offer views toward Mount Monadnock to the east, and Bromley and Stratton mountains to the west. The descent is via a steeper 1.4-mile trail that ends behind the campground. The park is open early May through Columbus Day; the day use fee is $1.50 for adults, $1 for children. Ask for trail maps at the park office. The park is reached by crossing the Townshend Dam (off Route 30), then turning left and continuing to the park sign.

Continuing northwest on Route 30, you'll come to the photogenic town of Jamaica. **Jamaica State Park** (☎ **802/874-4600**) offers campsites and picnicking along the West River (there's good swimming and splashing in the river), and a trail to Ball Mountain Reservoir, where there's lake swimming and boating. Some of New England's premier white-water canoeing and kayak racing takes place on the river below the dam in the spring and fall; races are scheduled around controlled releases.

WHERE TO STAY

Four Columns Inn. West St. (P.O. Box 278), Newfane, VT 05345. ☎ **800/787-6633** or 802/365-7713. Fax 802/365-0022. E-mail: frcolinn@sover.net. Web site: www.fourcolumnsinn.com. 15 rms (1 with shower only). A/C TEL. Most of the year $110–$195 double, including continental breakfast; foliage season $200–$295 double, including breakfast and dinner. 2-day minimum on major holiday weekends. AE, CB, DC, DISC, MC, V. Pets accepted.

You can't help but notice The Four Columns Inn in Newfane: It's the regal, white clapboard building with four Ionic columns just off the green. This perfect village setting hides a near-perfect inn within. Pam and Gorton Baldwin, who bought the inn in 1996, have done a wonderful job retaining the best parts of the inn (the chef, for instance, has been here for more than 2 decades), while improving those areas where quality had slipped over the years. Dogs are welcome here.

The guest rooms, which are decorated in a light country Victorian style, are all inviting. Be aware that rooms in the Main House and Garden Wing are somewhat larger than those above the restaurant (and there's no chance you'll overlook the kitchen vents). Among the best rooms are no. 18, with its handsome cherry sleigh bed and two-person Jacuzzi, and no. 3, with its grand four-poster bed and huge Jacuzzi enclosed in the sort of dark wooden framework you might see in a Gothic cathedral. My favorite, sheerly for its funky character, is no. 1 on the top floor of the main house. The low angled ceilings lend it an intimate feeling, and the skylights and terra-cotta bathroom floor are nice touches. But the best part is the semiprivate sitting area across the hall that's tucked under the eaves next to the eponymous four columns.

Dining/Entertainment: The inn's dining room is extremely well regarded, and folks come from miles around to sample the fine fare here. There's a pleasing atmosphere with low beams and white damask tablecloths, but the place isn't quite as historic or romantic as other dining rooms in the region (Windham Hill and the Old Tavern both come to mind). Main courses feature delectable New American cuisine, with entrees like pheasant with wild rice, chestnuts, and clementine and red-currant sauce; and sauté of shrimp and scallops with tomato, mushrooms, and chipotle peppers. The innkeepers are just as proud of their pastry chef, so be sure sample the delicious desserts.

Services/Facilities: Outdoor pool, hiking trails on 150 private acres, sundeck, baby-sitting, limited room service.

✪ **Windham Hill Inn.** Windham Hill Rd., W. Townshend, VT 05359. ☎ **800/944-4080** or 802/874-4080. E-mail: windham@sover.net. Web site: windhamhill.com. 21 rms (2 with shower only). A/C TEL. $195–$245 double. Rates include breakfast and dinner. 2-night minimum on weekends; 3-night minimum on Columbus Day weekend. AE, DC, DISC, MC, V. Closed Apr and week prior to Dec 27. No children under 12. Turn uphill across from the country store in W. Townshend and climb 1¹/₄ miles up a demanding hill to a marked dirt road; turn right and continue to end.

The Windham Hill Inn is about as perfect as an inn gets, especially if you're looking for a romantic getaway. Situated on 160 acres at the end of a dirt road in a high upland valley, the inn was originally built in 1823 as a farmhouse, and remained in the same family until the 1950s, when it was converted to an inn. Under the ownership of innkeepers Pat and Grigs Markham, the Windham Hill has ratcheted up several notches in quality as extensive renovations have managed to meld the best of the old and the new.

The guest rooms are wonderfully appointed in an elegant country style; a half-dozen have Jacuzzis or soaking tubs, nine have balconies or decks, 13 have gas fireplaces, and all feature views. Especially nice is Jesse's Room on the third floor, with soaking tub, gas woodstove, a large bathroom, and lustrous pine floors; and Forget-Me-Not, with soaking tub and four-poster bed. Even the smallest room—Susie L. Keach—is welcoming and comfortable.

The common areas, like the guest rooms, are appointed in a restrained country fashion that's more refined than rustic. Several rooms on the first floor invite guests to sit and thumb through a book or enjoy a drink from the bar; one of the common rooms even has a Steinway baby grand and game alcove with dozens of CDs.

Windham Hill is at the pricey end of the scale, but a stay here offers tremendous value. It's a guaranteed treat if you have limited leisure time and can't afford to take a chance with your vacation. No smoking.

Dining/Entertainment: The dining room, which is open to the public, is the picture of elegant simplicity, with ash flooring, subtle lighting, and simple table settings. The views of the small pond and stately maples on the hillside behind the inn are lovely, but not enough to distract from the delicious meals, which feature exceptionally creative cooking with a strong emphasis on local and seasonal ingredients. Recent entrees have included pecan-brioche-encrusted salmon and pheasant breast. The prix-fixe five-course dinner is $35 and well worth it.

Facilities: Hiking trails, outdoor heated pool, clay tennis court, game alcove, conference rooms, 6 miles of groomed cross-country ski trails.

WHERE TO DINE

For fine dining, make tracks to either the Windham Hill Inn or Four Columns (see above). For a quick lunch or breakfast, see below.

Townshend Corner Store. Corner of Routes 30 and 35, Townshend. ☎ **802/365-4624.** Breakfast $1.55–$4.25; lunch and dinner items $1.60–$4.05. No credit cards. Daily 6:30am–10pm (closes at 7pm in winter). LUNCHEONETTE.

SIT LONG—TALK MUCH reads the sign behind the counter. It's posted over the day's ice-cream selections, which, quite frankly, don't vary much from yesterday's selections. Or tomorrow's. But the sign offers good advice for getting the most out this classic country store, located on the green in Townshend. The small dining area is likely to be occupied by a mix of locals and tourists, each eyeing the other warily. Just sidle up to the worn, red laminate counter with the red toadstool-shaped stools, and enjoy the simple, filling luncheonette fare. Particularly good are the old-fashioned milkshakes and muffins, and the thick slabs of bacon that come with breakfast.

GRAFTON & CHESTER

When I first visited Grafton, I was fully prepared to dislike it. I'd heard that it was pristine and quaint, the result of an ambitious preservation plan by wealthy benefactors. I figured it would be too precious, too fussy, too much an overwrought picture-book re-creation of New England as envisioned by the D.A.R.

But it only took me about a half-hour of aimless wandering to come away a serious booster of the place. It's not a museum like Sturbridge Village or Colonial Williamsburg, but an active town with some 600 residents. It just happens to have dozens of museum-quality homes and buildings.

More commercial Chester, in contrast, is less pristine and feels more lived in. The downtown area has a pleasant neighborly feel to it, along with a handful of intriguing boutiques and shops along the main road. Chester is a great destination for antiquing, with several good dealers in the area. When heading north of town on Route 103, go slow enough to enjoy the Stone Village, where a neighborhood of well-spaced, austere stone homes line the roadway. Many of these homes were said to be major stopping points on the Underground Railroad.

ESSENTIALS

GETTING THERE   The most direct route to Bellows Falls is via I-91; get off at either Exit 5 or 6 and follow signs to town via Route 5. Grafton is 12 miles west of Bellows Falls on Route 121, at the intersection of Route 35. *Tip:* The trip north on Route 35 from Townshend to Grafton is exceedingly scenic and pastoral.

VISITOR INFORMATION   The **Grafton Information Center,** Grafton, VT 05146 (☎ **802/843-2255**), is located on Route 35 just south of the village. For information about Chester, contact the **Chester Chamber of Commerce,** P.O. Box 623, Chester, VT 05143 (☎ **802/875-2939**).

EXPLORING GRAFTON

Grafton is best seen at a languorous pace, on foot, when the weather is welcoming. Don't expect to be overwhelmed with grandeur. Instead, keep a keen eye out for telling historical details.

Start at the **Grafton Information Center** (see above), which offers parking and access to the rest of the village. Exhibits in the main center provide some background on the village's history. Barns nearby house other informative exhibits.

From here, follow a footpath past the barns and through a small covered bridge to the **Grafton Cheese Co.** (☎ **800/472-3866**), a small, modern building where you can buy a snack of award-winning cheese and peer through plate-glass windows to observe the cheese-making process. (One caveat: Outwardly, cheese making is neither very complicated nor interesting.)

Cross back over the covered bridge and bear right on the footpath along the cow pasture to the **Kidder Covered Bridge,** then head into town via Water Street, continuing on to Main Street. Toward the village center, white clapboard homes and shade trees abound. This is about as New England as New England gets.

On Main Street, stop by the **Grafton Historical Society Museum** (☎ **802/843-2344;** open weekends only) to peruse photographs, artifacts, and memorabilia of Grafton. The nearby **Grafton Museum of Natural History** (☎ **802/843-2347;** open weekends only) offers intriguing displays on Vermont wildlife.

Afterwards, stop by the **Old Tavern at Grafton,** the impressive building that anchors the town and has served as a social center since 1801, and partake of a beverage at the rustic Phelps Barn Lounge, or a meal in one of the dining rooms. (See below.) From here, you can make your way back to the information center by wandering on pleasant side streets. If you'd like to expand your range and cruise the outlying areas by bike, ask about rentals at the tavern. Horse and buggy rides are also available here.

If you're visiting in winter, Grafton offers superb cross-country skiing at the **Grafton Ponds Cross-Country Ski Center** (☎ **802/843-2400**), located just south of the cheese factory on Route 35. Managed by the Old Tavern, Grafton Ponds has 18 miles of groomed trails and a warming hut near the ponds where you can sit by a woodstove and enjoy a steaming bowl of soup. The Big Bear loop runs high up the flanks of a hill and is especially appealing; travel counterclockwise such that you walk up the steep hill and enjoy the rolling descent. Ski and snowshoe rentals are available; a trail pass costs $12 for adults, $8 for seniors, and $6 for children 12 and under. Half-day passes are also available.

WHERE TO STAY & DINE

Chester Inn at Long Last. Rte. 11 (P.O. Box 589), Chester, VT 05143. ☎ **802/875-2444.** 26 rms (some with shower only). $160 double, including breakfast and dinner; $110 double on Mon, including breakfast only. MC, V. Closed Apr and mid-Nov.

The Chester Inn at Long Last (formerly the Inn at Long Last) was in transition when I last visited in early 1997. Longtime owner Jack Coleman was stepping aside, a new name had just been unveiled, and changes in decor were under discussion. But the overall atmosphere is likely to remain small-town rustic and quaint. It's more of a hotel than an country inn, located in a tall building smack in the middle of Chester's one-street downtown. The eclectically furnished guest rooms are set off long upstairs hallways and feature themes—like the Frederick Law Olmsted Room, which has prints of Olmsted-designed parks and books about the landscape architect on the bedside table.

Downstairs the lobby has the feel of an informal old roadhouse (you half expect to see Willy Loman trudging through with his weary bags), but with polished floors, braided and Oriental rugs, and a handsome stone fireplace it's a welcoming spot. There's a small taproom off the main lobby, as well as a quiet sitting room.

Dining/Entertainment: The dining room has a quasi-formal, old-world setting (except for the clunky ship captains' chairs) that masks an informal character. And that character comes through in the creative menu by chef Russ Jones. Appetizers include crab cakes and blue-corn tortellini, with entrees along the lines of broiled salmon with citrus crust and rosemary aioli, and a duck breast with bourbon-molasses glaze. The restaurant, which is open to the public, is closed on Mondays. Main courses run between $12 and $20.

The Old Tavern at Grafton. Routes 35 and 121, Grafton, VT 05146. ☎ **800/843-1801** or 802/843-2231. E-mail: tavern@sover.net. 66 rms (7 with shower only). $120–$230 double. Rates include continental breakfast. Discounts available May–June and midweek in summer. 2- or 3-day minimum on winter weekends, some holidays, and during foliage season. MC, V. Closed Apr. No children under 8.

Countless New England inns seek to replicate the service and gracious style of a far larger resort, but fall short because of understaffing and a woeful lack of capital. But the Old Tavern at Grafton succeeds, and wildly so. It should be noted that this is called Old Tavern, not "Ye Olde Taverne," a good reflection of the understated quality and professional service that has pervaded this place since a management change a few years ago. Note also that the Old Tavern advertises only lightly, yet still draws capacity crowds through word of mouth.

The inn seems more intimate than its 66 guest rooms would suggest, since the rooms are spread throughout the town. Fourteen are in the exceptionally handsome colonnaded main building, 22 are across the street in the Homestead Cottage, and the remaining rooms are scattered among seven historic guest houses in and around the village. All rooms are decorated with antiques and an upscale country elegance, but the rooms in the Homestead Cottage (which is actually two historic homes joined together) have a more modern, hotel-like character. Children over 8 years old are welcome.

The common areas in the inn are formal in a Federal-style sort of way, but those determined to relax can still do so. And, of course, there's the village of Grafton to reconnoiter, which requires but a few steps from the front door.

Dining/Entertainment: "Appropriate dinner attire" is requested, but there's still a fairly loose, relaxed air to the three dining rooms in the evening. The menu features classic New England fare, updated for more adventurous palates. Dinner features entrees like roasted rack of lamb, salmon Wellington, and maple roast duckling. Lower-key entrees include cheddar-and-ale soup and a selection of pastas. Lunch prices range from $5.75 to $9.75; dinner prices from $14 to $22.

Facilities: Sand-bottomed pool, bicycle rentals, game room, nature trails, conference rooms, laundry facility, Jacuzzi, two tennis courts.

LUDLOW & OKEMO

Ludlow is home to Okemo Mountain, a once sleepy ski resort that's been nicely upgraded and updated in the past decade. Ludlow is also notable as one of the few Vermont ski towns that didn't go through one of those unfortunate Tyrolean identity crises.

Centered around a former mill that produced fabrics and, later, aircraft parts, Ludlow has an unpretentious made in mill town Vermont character that seems quite distant from the prim grace of white clapboard Grafton. Low-key and unassuming, it draws skiers by the busload in winter (it's especially popular with travelers from the New York City metropolitan area); in summer, it's a good place to put your feet up on the porch rail and watch the clouds float over the mountaintops.

ESSENTIALS

GETTING THERE   Ludlow is situated at the intersection of Routes 193 and 100. The most direct route from an interstate is Exit 6 off I-91; follow Route 103 westward to Ludlow.

VISITOR INFORMATION   The **Ludlow Area Chamber of Commerce,** P.O. Box 333, Ludlow, VT 05149 (☎ **802/228-5830**), staffs a helpful information booth at the Okemo Marketplace, at the foot of Mountain Road.

SKIING

Okemo. Ludlow, VT 05149. ☎ **802/228-4041,** or 800/786-5366 for lodging. Vertical drop: 2,150 ft. 10 chairlifts (2 high-speed), 2 surface lifts. Skiable acreage: 470. Lift tickets $48 weekend, $44 weekday.

Okemo fans like to point out a couple of things. First, this is one of the few family-owned mountains remaining in Vermont (it's been owned by Tim and Diane Mueller since 1982). Second, it now has more varied terrain, including challenging advanced trails on the south face, ridding it of the charges that it's only a mountain for intermediates. (Especially enticing for expert skiers are the two bumped-out glade trails.) Fans also point out that Okemo doesn't attract yahoos, who gravitate to way-gnarlier Killington to the north.

It's still first and foremost a mountain for families, who not only like the varied terrain but the friendly base area that's of a scale not too intimidating for kids. Families should note also that the mountain offers three levels of ticket prices, with $8 off the above prices for young adults (ages 13 to 18) and $18 off for juniors (7 to 12). Children 6 and under ski free.

WHERE TO STAY

During ski season, contact the **Okemo Mountain Lodging Service** (☎ **800/ 786-5366** or 802/228-5571) for reservations at a variety of area accommodations, including slope-side condos. Those looking for an extended stay might also check with **Strictly Rentals** (☎ **802/228-3000**), which can arrange for stays of a weekend or longer.

The Castle. Rte. 103 (at Rte. 131; P.O. Box 207), Proctorsville, VT 05153. ☎ **800/697-7222** or 802/226-7222. Fax 802/226-7853. 10 rms (2 with shower only). $135–$185 double, including breakfast; $190–$240 double, including breakfast and dinner. Off-season discounts available. AE, MC, V. Closed 2 weeks in Apr.

The original owner of this stone mansion, situated on a rise overlooking Route 103, had an obvious thing for wood. The 1901 home is opulent with a dark, chocolaty woodworking. Somewhat paradoxically, this makes the house a little gloomy during the day, but it glows with a golden luster at night, warmly lit by burning logs in the fireplaces. The mansion has come a long way since Boston corporate refugees Erica and Richard Hart bought the place in early 1995. But there's still a ways to go—some of the old details are nice, like the spherical glass doorknobs; others aren't, like cracked and discolored tiles in some of the bathrooms, and outdated electrical fixtures. And be forewarned that some of those bathrooms are quite small. On the other hand, six of the guest rooms feature wood-burning fireplaces, which are wonderful in the winter. The innkeepers have embarked on a 6-year plan to restore the place; look for improvements with each passing season.

Dining/Entertainment: The Castle's dining area occupies two rooms with exquisite woodworking on the first floor. The kitchen produces tasty meals with a classical French touch. You might start with crab-stuffed prawns or a baked Roquefort and pear tart, then graduate to veal with artichoke and capers, or a delicious brook trout stuffed with prawns and served with a citrus beurre-blanc sauce. Leave some room for desserts, which might include a lemon tartlet, apple-cranberry cobbler, or maple crème brûlée. Entrees range in price from $14.25 to $24.

Facilities: Outdoor swimming pool, tennis court.

The Governor's Inn. 86 Main St., Ludlow, VT 05149. ☎ **800/468-3766** or 802/228-8830. 8 rms (some with shower only). $180–$230 double; $300–$325 suite. Rates include full breakfast and dinner. MC, V.

This attractive village home was built in 1890 by Vermont governor William W. Stickney (hence the name), and is the very picture of Victorian elegance. The downstairs lobby and common room (both with gas fireplaces) are richly hued with time-worn hardwood, and the walls are filled with photos and mementos of the innkeeper's ancestors. The rooms vary in size (some are quite small), but each is comfortably appointed with antiques. Nice touches abound, like a turndown service with chocolates and a shot of Benedictine & Brandy delivered before bedtime.

Dining/Entertainment: Chef-innkeeper Deedy Marble is proud of her culinary accomplishments, and rightly so. The noted six-course dinners are served in a handsome Victorian dining room, with tables set with antique knife holders and bone china. The fare might be described as New England Deluxe, with entrees like polenta-crusted native game birds, or scallops in a brandied cream sauce. Just one entree is offered each night, so ask when you make reservations to ensure it's a good match with your appetite. Dinner is included in the room rates; for outside diners, the fixed-price meal varies from $45 to $50.

WHERE TO DINE

Fine dining is available at the two local inns mentioned above. For less demanding palates and thinner wallets, see below.

Harry's Cafe. Rte. 103 (5 miles north of Ludlow), Mount Holly. ☎ **802/259-2996.** Reservations recommended on weekends. Main courses $10.95–$16.95. AE, MC, V. Wed–Sun 5–10pm. ECLECTIC.

Along a dark stretch of road north of Ludlow you'll pass a brightly lit roadside cafe with a red neon HARRY'S over the door. This isn't a hamburger joint, as you might assume, but a great family restaurant with a menu that spans the globe. Entrees are a veritable culinary U.N., with New York sirloin, jerk pork, flautas, spicy Thai curry, fish-and-chips, Portuguese seafood stew, and chicken breast stuffed with ricotta cheese, basil, and sun-dried tomatoes. You'll likely be most content with the Thai fare, which seems to be the house specialty. On the downside, the interior is more blandly efficient than cozy, and the service can bog down on busy nights.

4 Woodstock

In 1847, Woodstock native and noted sculptor Hiram Powers unveiled his statue of a nude, entitled *Greek Slave.* It caused a huge uproar nationwide, not only because of Powers's depiction of nudity, but because of his depiction of slavery at a time when slavery was emerging as the nation's most divisive issue.

Woodstock seems an odd spawning ground for someone who would foment a national scandal. Because today Woodstock is dedicated to preserving the mannered past, not to challenging the unsettled future. Travelers simply can't drive to Woodstock on a route that *isn't* pastoral and scenic, putting one in mind of an earlier, more peaceful era. The superb village green is surrounded by handsome homes, creating what amounts to a comprehensive review of architectural styles of the 19th and early 20th centuries.

Much of the town is on the National Register of Historic Places, and 500 acres surrounding Mount Tom (see below) has been deeded to the National Park Service by the Rockefeller family and is in the process of becoming a National Historic Park (it's expected to open by the year 2000).

In fact, some joke that downtown Woodstock might as well be named Rockefeller National Park, given the attention and cash the Rockefeller family has lavished upon the town in the interest of preservation. (For starters, Rockefeller money built the faux-historic Woodstock Inn and paid to bury the unsightly utility lines around town.)

Woodstock, which sits on the banks of the gentle Ottauquechee River, was first settled in 1765, rose to some prominence as a publishing center in the mid-19th century (no fewer than five newspapers were published here in 1830), and began to attract wealthy families who summered here in the late 19th century. To this day, Woodstock feels as if it should have a prestigious prep school just off the green, and it comes as some surprise that it doesn't.

Wealthy summer rusticators were instrumental in establishing and preserving the character of the village, and today the very wealthy have turned their attention to the handsome farms outside of town. Few of these former dairy farms still produce milk; barns that haven't been converted to architectural showcase homes more than likely house valuable collections of cars or antiques.

Woodstock is also notable as a historic center of winter outdoor recreation. The nation's first ski tow (a rope tow powered by an old Buick motor) was built in 1933 at the Woodstock Ski Hill near today's Suicide Six ski area. While no longer the skiing center of Vermont, Woodstock remains a worthy destination during the winter months for skating, cross-country skiing, and snowshoeing.

One caveat: Woodstock's excellent state of preservation hasn't gone unnoticed, and it draws hordes of travelers. During the peak foliage season, it can even be hard to view the town green because of all the tour buses driving around it.

ESSENTIALS

GETTING THERE   Woodstock is 13 miles west of White River Junction on Route 4 (take Exit 1 off I-89). From the west, Woodstock is 20 miles east of Killington on Route 4.

VISITOR INFORMATION   The **Woodstock Area Chamber of Commerce,** 18 Central St., Woodstock, VT 05091 (☎ **802/457-3555**), staffs an information booth on the green between June and October. Ask about the guided village walking tours.

EXPLORING THE REGION

IN TOWN   Few other New England villages can top Woodstock for sheer grace and elegance. The heart of the town is the shady, elliptical Woodstock Green. Admiral George Dewey spent his later years in Woodstock, which may help explain the canard promulgated by some that the green was laid out in the shape of Dewey's flagship. In fact, the town's basic design was more or less laid out by 1830, 7 years before Dewey was born.

At the east end of the green is Woodstock's compact commercial area, with a small but good selection of boutiques and restaurants. To the south is the regal Woodstock Inn (see below). To the north is **Middle Covered Bridge,** one of three in town and I'd argue one of the most photographed covered bridges in existence. Although many photographers believe it's a historical artifact, it was actually built in 1969 by one of the few master craftsmen still living. Around the rest of the green and along the leafy side streets are architecturally outstanding buildings where you can neatly trace the evolution of American architecture.

To put local history in perspective, stop by the **Woodstock Historical Society,** 26 Elm St. (☎ **802/457-1822**). Housed in the 1807 Charles Dana House, this beautiful home has rooms furnished in Federal, Empire, and Victorian styles, and offers displays of dolls, costumes, and examples of early silver and glass. The Dana House is open from May through October. Hours are 10am to 5pm Monday through Saturday, and Sunday from noon to 5pm. Admission is $1.

OUTSIDE WOODSTOCK   Less than a half-mile north of town on Route 12 (Elm Street) is the **Billings Farm and Museum** (☎ **802/457-2355**), a working farm well worth visiting for a glimpse of life in a grander era. The farm was built by Frederick Billings, the man who is credited with completing the Northern Pacific Railroad. (The town of Billings, Mont., is named after him.) This dairy farm was renown late in the last century for its scientific breeding of Jersey cows and its fine architecture, especially the gabled 1890 Victorian farmhouse. Now owned by Billings's granddaughter and her husband, Laurence Rockefeller, the farm includes hands-on demonstrations of farm activities, exhibits of farm life, an heirloom kitchen garden, and active milking barns.

The museum is open daily May through October from 10am to 5pm, and on weekends in November and December. The farm is also open for special events in winter, including sleigh rides. Admission is $7 adults, $6 seniors, $5 children 13 to 17, $3 children 5 to 12, and $1 children 3 to 4.

Bird-watchers will enjoy a trip to the **Vermont Institute of Natural Science** (☎ **802/457-2779**), which also houses the Vermont Raptor Center. The center is home to 25 species of birds of prey that have been injured and can no longer survive in the wild. The winged residents change from time to time, but typically range from majestic bald eagles to the diminutive saw-whet owl. Serious birders might also choose to spend some time in the institute's Pettingill Ornithological Library. Other attractions include an herbarium, nature trails, and exhibits of live animals, including snakes, bees, and tarantulas. The institute is located 1¹/₂ miles south of the village on Church Hill Road. It's open daily 10am to 4pm, but is closed Sundays from November through April. Admission is $5 for adults, $2 for children.

About 5 miles east of Woodstock is the riverside village of **Quechee.** Formerly a town of prosperous woolen mills, Quechee is emerging as a huge if low-key resort community. Some 6,000 acres of the surrounding countryside is owned by the Quechee Lakes Corporation, which has developed second homes and other amenities, including a golf course and polo field.

The small village, with a handful of boutiques and restaurants, still revolves spiritually and economically around the restored brick mill building along the falls. **Simon Pearce Glass** (☎ **802/295-2711**), which makes exceptionally fine (and exceptionally expensive) glassware and pottery, occupies the former Downer's Mill, where it houses its glassmaking operation, a retail store, and a well-respected restaurant (see below). Visitors can watch glassblowing take place weekdays and on summer weekends from a downstairs viewing gallery. Open daily from 9am to 9pm.

WARM-WEATHER OUTDOOR PURSUITS

Outdoor activities in the Woodstock area aren't as rugged as those you'll find in the Green Mountains to the west, but they'll easily occupy you for an afternoon or two.

Don't leave the village without climbing **Mount Tom,** the prominent hill that overlooks Woodstock. Start your ascent from Faulkner Park, named after Mrs. Edward Faulkner, who created the park and had the mountain trail built to encourage healthful exercise. (To reach the trailhead from the Woodstock Green, cross Middle Covered Bridge and continue straight on Mountain Avenue. The road bends left and soon arrives at a grassy park at the base of Mt. Tom.)

The trail winds up the hill, employing one of the most lugubrious sets of switchbacks I've ever experienced. Designed after the once popular "cardiac walks" in Europe, the trail sometimes seems to require hikers to walk for miles only to gain a few feet in elevation. But persevere. This gentle trail eventually arrives at a clearing overlooking the town. A steeper, rockier, and more demanding trail continues 100 yards or so from here to the summit. At the top, a carriage path encircles the summit like a friar's fringe of hair, offering fine views of the town and the Green Mountains to the west. You can follow the carriage path down to Billings Farm, or retrace your steps back to the park.

Experienced and aspiring equestrians should head to the **Kedron Valley Stables** (☎ **802/457-1480**), about 4^1/$_2$ miles south of Woodstock on Route 106. A full menu of riding options is available, ranging from a 1-hour beginner ride ($30) to a 5-night inn-to-inn excursion ($1,375 per person including all meals and lodging, double occupancy). The stables rent horses to experienced riders for local trail rides, offers sleigh and carriage rides, and has an indoor riding ring for inclement weather. It's open every day except Thanksgiving and Christmas.

Five miles east of town, Route 4 crosses **Quechee Gorge,** a popular if overrated tourist attraction. The sheer power of the glacial runoff that carved the gorge some 13,000 years ago must have been dramatic, but the 165-foot gorge itself isn't all that impressive today. More impressive is the engineering history. This chasm was first spanned in 1875 by a wooden rail trestle, when 3,000 people gathered along the gorge to celebrate the achievement. The current steel bridge was constructed in 1911 for the railroad, but the tracks were torn up in 1933 and replaced by Route 4.

The best view of the bridge is from the bottom of the gorge, which is accessible by a well-graded gravel path that descends south from the parking area on the gorge's east rim. The round-trip requires no more than a half-hour. If the day is warm enough, you might also follow the path northward, then descend to the river to splash around in an inviting rocky swimming hole near the spillway.

SKIING

The area's best cross-country skiing is at the **Woodstock Ski Touring Center** (☎ **802/457-2114** or 802/457-6774) at the Woodstock Country Club, just south of town on Route 106. The center maintains 36 miles of trails, including 12 miles of trails groomed for skate-skiing. And it's not all flat; the high and low points along the trail system vary by 750 feet in elevation. There's a lounge and restaurant at the ski center, and a large health and fitness center accessible via ski trail. Lessons and picnic tours are available. The full-day trail fee is $11 for adults and $8 for children under 14.

Suicide Six ski area (☎ **802/457-6661**) may have an intimidating name, but at just 650 vertical feet it doesn't pose much of a threat to either life or limb. Owned and operated by the Woodstock Inn, this venerable family ski resort (it first opened in 1934) has two double chairlifts, a complimentary J-bar for beginners, and modern base lodge. Beginners, intermediates, and young families will be content here. Weekend lift tickets are $34 for adults, $21 for seniors and children under 14; midweek it's $19 and $15, respectively. The ski area is located 2 miles north of Woodstock on Pomfret Road.

WHERE TO STAY

Jackson House Inn. 37 Old Rte. 4 west, Woodstock, VT 05091. ☎ **800/448-1890** or 802/457-2065. Web site: www.govermont.com/jacksonhouse. 12 rms, all with shower only. A/C. $150–$250 double. 2-day minimum during weekends, holidays, and foliage season. Rates include full breakfast. MC, V.

Antique buffs will be at home in the Jackson House Inn, located just west of Woodstock en route to Killington. The furnishings in this yellow 1890 Victorian are immaculate and perfectly chosen, from the Oriental rugs to the antique chests. The home was built by a lumber baron who hoarded the best wood for himself; cherry-and-maple floors are so beautiful you'll feel guilty for not taking off your shoes. (Not to worry: There's shoe storage and slippers for guests in the front hallway.) Even the wainscoting is lustrous. The guest rooms, which are each decorated in different period styles (Empire, Federal, etc.), are equally well appointed, although some are rather small.

The inn features the elegant touches you'd expect for the high price, like robes, decanters of brandy, and Bose speakers in the rooms. But there are others you wouldn't expect, like the small fitness room in the basement with a steam room and the 3-acre backyard with formal English gardens and a pond stocked with rainbow trout.

New innkeepers took over in early 1997, and the prognosis is very good. At press time, two historically sympathetic additions were underway. One will house four luxury guest suites with fireplaces and Jacuzzis. Another will be home to a new restaurant, where guests can enjoy elegant French fare while overlooking the gardens.

The Jackson House is a wonderful retreat, although guests should be aware that its location, a stone's throw off a busy stretch of Route 4, detracts somewhat from the graceful tranquillity the innkeepers have succeeded in achieving in the rest of the property. Children over the age of 13 are welcome. No smoking.

✪ **Kedron Valley Inn.** Rte. 106, S. Woodstock, VT 05071. ☎ **800/836-1193** or 802/457-1473. Fax 802/457-4469. E-mail: kedroninn@aol.com. 27 rms (2 with shower only). TV. $120–$195 double; foliage season and Christmas week $140–$215 double. Rates include full breakfast. Discounts available spring and midweek. Inquire about packages. AE, DISC, MC, V. Closed Apr and briefly prior to Thanksgiving.

This is a standout inn. Located in a complex of Greek Revival buildings at a country crossroads about 5 miles south of Woodstock, the inn is run by Max and Merrily Comins, a cordial couple who offer guests a bit of history, a bit of country style, and a whole lot of good food and wine. The attractive guest rooms in all three buildings are furnished with a mix of antiques and reproductions, and all have heirloom quilts from Merrily's collection; 14 feature wood-burning fireplaces. Don't be alarmed if you're put in the newer, motel-like log building by the river. The rooms are equally well appointed, with canopy beds, custom oak woodwork, and fireplaces. Room 37 even has a private streamside terrace. *Editor's note:* My dog, Lucy, loves this place!

Dining/Entertainment: The country-elegant dining room has two fireplaces, a nice view of the grounds, and an inviting wine list. The menu is contemporary American cooking built on a classical French foundation. You might start with a rich pheasant ragout, then move on to salmon stuffed with a scallop, shrimp, and salmon mousse and wrapped in a puff pastry. There are also vegetarian courses and a lighter tavern menu. The main entrees are priced from $16 to $21. Breakfasts are terrific and gargantuan.

Services/Facilities: Baby-sitting (extra charge), safe, private swimming pond with two beaches, conference rooms, health club nearby ($10 extra).

✪ **Twin Farms.** Barnard, VT 05031. ☎ **800/894-6327** or 802/234-9999. Fax 802/234-9990. 14 rms and cottages. A/C TEL TV. $800–$950 double; $1,150–$1,500 cottage. Rates include all meals, liquor, and many amenities. AE, MC, V. Closed Apr. Not suitable for children under 18.

Twin Farms offers uncommon luxury—at an uncommon price. Housed on a 300-acre farm that was once home to Nobel Prize–winning novelist Sinclair Lewis and his wife, journalist Dorothy Thompson, Twin Farms has carved out an international reputation as a low-key, exceptionally tasteful small resort. The clientele includes royalty and corporate chieftains looking for simplicity and willing to pay dearly for it. Rates include open bar, use of all recreational equipment, and more.

The compound consists of the main inn with four guest rooms, and 10 outlying cottages. The rooms are impeccable, designed by talented interior decorators who commissioned craftsmen and artisans to create much of the furniture and adornment. The inn is owned by the Twigg-Smith family, who are noted art collectors in Hawaii. Some of the work on display at the inn and in guest rooms includes originals by David Hockney, Roy Lichtenstein, Milton Avery, and William Wegman.

Dining/Entertainment: Meals are understatedly sumptuous affairs served at locations of your choosing—at your cottage, along a stream, or in one of the dining areas around the estate. Don't bother looking for a menu; the gourmet chefs serve what's fresh, and your meal is likely to include ingredients from the organic vegetable and herb gardens on the property. If you have any special requests, don't hesitate to make them.

Services: Concierge, limited room service, newspaper delivery, in-room massage, twice-daily maid service, valet parking, safe-deposit boxes.

Facilities: Lake swimming, bicycle rental, game rooms, Jacuzzi, nature trails, conference rooms, two tennis courts, fitness center, canoes, fishing pond, croquet.

Woodstock Inn & Resort. 14 The Green, Woodstock, VT 05091. ☎ **800/448-7900** or 802/457-1100. Fax 802/457-6699. 141 rms, 3 town houses. A/C TV TEL. $155–$295 double. AE, MC, V.

The Woodstock Inn, an imposing white-brick structure set behind a garden off the Woodstock Green, appears a venerable and long-established institution at first glance.

But it's not—at least not *this* building. Constructed between 1968 and 1969, the inn happily shunned the more unfortunate trends in sixties architecture for a dignified look suitable for Woodstock. Everyone's the better for it. Inside, guests are greeted by a broad stone fireplace, and sitting areas are tucked throughout the lobby in the manner of a 1940s-era resort. Guest rooms are tastefully decorated in either country pine or a Shaker-inspired style. The best rooms are in the new wing (built in 1991), and feature lush carpeting, refrigerators, fireplaces, and built-in bookshelves.

Dining/Entertainment: The dining room is classy and semiformal, with continental and American dishes served on elegant green-bordered custom china. Entrees are in the $20-to-$25 price range.

Facilities: Robert Trent Jones, Jr.–designed golf course (at the inn-owned Woodstock Country Club), two swimming pools (indoor and outdoor), nature trails, putting greens, fitness center with tennis, squash, racquetball, and steam rooms. In winter, 36 miles of groomed cross-country ski trails.

WHERE TO DINE

The Kedron Valley Inn and the Woodstock Inn also have fine dining rooms that are open to the public; see above.

✪ **The Prince and the Pauper.** 24 Elm St. ☎ **802/457-1818.** Reservations recommended. Fixed-price dinner $34. DISC, MC, V. Sun–Thurs 6–9pm, Fri–Sat 6–9:30pm. Lounge opens at 5pm. NEW AMERICAN/CONTINENTAL.

It takes a bit of sleuthing to find The Prince and the Pauper, located down Dana Alley (next to the Woodstock Historical Society's Dana House). But it's worth the effort. This is Woodstock's finest restaurant, with an intimate but informal setting. Ease into the evening with a libation in the tap room (it's open an hour before the restaurant), then move over to the rustic but elegant dining room. Start with an appetizer of lobster ravioli or smoked coho salmon, then enjoy the grilled boneless rack of lamb baked in a puff pastry with spinach and mushroom duxelles, or a grilled Delmonico steak with shallots and shiitakes. The $34 fixed-price dinner offers good value, but if that's out of your budget, head to the lounge and order off the bistro menu ($10.95 to $15.95), with selections like barbecue pork, Maryland crab cakes, and Indonesian curried lamb. There's also a selection of pizzas at $9.95.

Simon Pearce Restaurant. The Mill, Quechee. ☎ **802/295-1470.** Reservations recommended for dinner. Lunch items $6.75–$11.50; dinner main courses $16–$24. AE, DC, DISC, MC, V. Daily 11:30am–2:45pm and 6–9pm. REGIONAL/AMERICAN.

The setting can't be beat. Housed in a restored 19th-century woolen mill with wonderful views of a waterfall (it's spotlit at night), Simon Pearce's is a collage of exposed brick, buttery yellow pine floorboards, and handsome wooden tables and chairs. Meals are served on Simon Pearce pottery and glassware (if you like your setting, you can buy it afterwards at the sprawling retail shop in the mill). The restaurant atmosphere is a wonderful concoction of formal and informal, ensuring that everybody feels comfortable here whether in white shirt and tie or (neatly pressed) jeans.

You might start off your evening with Maine crab cakes with *roille,* or cheese croquettes with tomato chutney. Then move on to the chili-cured roast tenderloin of pork with grilled corn salsa, or perhaps the seared tuna with sesame, noodle cakes, wasabi, and pickled ginger. Simon Pearce is also open for lunch, when the menu lightens to include entrees like warm goat-cheese salad, grilled chicken sandwich with roasted peppers and parmigiana aioli, and tarragon chicken salad with scallions and toasted almonds.

Wild Grass. Rte. 4 (east of the village), Woodstock. ☎ **802/457-1917.** Reservations advised during peak season. Main courses $10.50–$16.50. DISC, MC, V. Sun–Thurs 6–9pm, Fri–Sat 6–9:30pm. ECLECTIC.

Wild Grass is a welcome addition to the Woodstock dining scene, offering well-prepared fare at reasonable prices. It's located in one of the few charmless parts of town, along the main drag in a sort of contemporary minimall. The interior has an unfortunate chain-bistro kind of feel to it, with painted grapevines and plate-glass windows. But the food rises above the prosaic surroundings, and the menu typically has some genuinely creative offerings. Especially appealing are two appetizers: the unique crispy sage leaves with tangy dipping sauces, and the roll-it-yourself spring rolls. The fresh fish is grilled to perfection, and sauces are pleasantly zesty and piquant.

5 Killington

In 1937, a travel writer described the town near Killington Peak as "a small village of a church and a few undistinguished houses built on a highway three corners." The area was rugged and remote, isolated from the commercial centers to the west by imposing mountains, and accessible only through daunting Sherburne Pass.

That was before Vermont's second highest mountain was developed as the Northeast's largest ski area. And before a wide, 5-mile-long access road was slashed through the forest to the mountain's base. And before Route 4 was widened and improved, easing access to Rutland. In fact, that early travel writer would be hard-pressed to recognize the region today.

Since the mountain was first developed for skiing in 1957, dozens of restaurants, hotels, and convenience stores have sprouted along Killington Road to accommodate the legions of skiers who descend upon the area during the long skiing season, which typically runs from October into May.

Killington Road is a brightly lit, highly developed modern ski-resort access road. There's not much to remind visitors of classic Vermont between the highway and the base lodge. Suburban-style theme restaurants dot the route (The Grist Mill has a waterwheel; Casey's Caboose has a red caboose), along with dozens of hotels and condos ranging from high-end fancy to low-end dowdy.

It's also become a choice destination for those who ski for the nightlife as much as for the moguls. With some 60 bars within striking distance, Killington cultivates a hard-partying personality. The area has a frenetic, where-it's-happening feel in winter. (That's not the case in summer, when the empty parking lots can trigger mild melancholia.) Those most content here are skiers who like their skiing *big,* singles in search of aggressive mingling, and travelers who want a wide selection of amenities and are willing to sacrifice charm for choice.

ESSENTIALS

GETTING THERE   Killington Road extends southward from Routes 4 and 100, just east of the intersection with Route 100 North. It's about 12 miles east of Rutland on Route 4. Many of the inns offer shuttles to the Rutland airport. In 1996, Amtrak began offering service from New York to Rutland, with connecting shuttles to the resorts. Call ☎ **800/872-7245** for more information.

VISITOR INFORMATION   The **Killington and Pico Areas Association,** P.O. Box 114, Killington, VT 05751 (☎ **802/773-4181**), supplies lodging and travel-package information. For ski resort information, contact the **Killington Travel Service** (☎ **800/372-2007**) or the **Killington Lodging Bureau** (☎ **800/621-6867**).

ALPINE SKIING

✪ **Killington.** Killington, VT 05751. ☎ **802/422-3261,** or 800/621-6867 for lodging. Vertical drop: 3,150 ft. 2 gondolas, 16 chairlifts (2 high-speed), 2 surface lifts. Skiable acreage: 1,200. Lift tickets $48.

Killington is by far New England's largest ski area, and some critics say it's the skier's equivalent of the Mall of America: improbably huge, run with brisk efficiency but no personal touch. True, in part. But like the megamall, Killington has an unrivaled selection, with trails ranging from long, old-fashioned narrow runs with almost no discernible downhill slope, to killer bumps high on its flanks. Thanks to this diversity, Killington has long been the destination of choice for serious skiers.

In 1996, Killington's new owner—the megalithic American Skiing Company—acquired struggling Pico, a middling but well-respected ski area just over the ridge. Plans call for connecting the two areas with ski trails and lifts, making Killington even more gargantuan. When this will occur is uncertain, but the odds favor either the 1997–98 season or the following year. Until then, Pico is being marketed as "Pico at Killington." Killington lift tickets are valid at Pico, and a cheaper Pico-only ticket is also available.

Even before the new acquisition, first-time skiers at Killington were in a bit of a quandary. The two-sided trail map is virtually worthless since it's impossible to make sense of. But make one wrong turn and you'll end up on a no-slope green trail practically walking back to the bottom.

My advice: At the outset, focus on one lift and follow the lift signs—don't even try to figure out the trail signs. After a couple of runs, the layout will start to make sense. Then move on to another lift. Killington is a superb mountain for both experts and beginners. Intermediates might be more content heading over to Pico, which has six chairlifts (including two high-speed).

CROSS-COUNTRY SKIING

The intricate network of trails at the **Mountain Top Inn** (☎ 800/445-2100 or 802/483-2311) has had a loyal local following for years, but it's now attracting considerable attention from far-flung skiers as well. The 66-mile trail network runs through mixed terrain with fabulous pastoral views, and is nicely groomed for both traditional and skate-skiing. The area is often deep with snow owing to its high ridge-top location in the hills east of Rutland, and snowmaking along key portions of the trail ensure that you won't have to walk across bare spots during snow droughts. The resort maintains three warming huts along the way, and lessons and ski rentals are available. The trails have a combined elevation gain of 670 feet. Trail passes are $13 for adults, $10 for children.

SUMMER FUN

MOUNTAIN BIKING Mountain bikers challenge themselves on Killington's five mountains as they explore 50 miles of trails. The main lift is equipped to haul bikes and riders to the summit, delivering spectacular views. Riders then give their forearms a workout applying breaks with some vigor and frequency while bumping down the slopes. Explore on your own, or sign up for a full- or half-day tour.

The **Mountain Bike Shop** (☎ 802/422-6232) is located at the Killington Base Lodge and is open from June through mid-October from 9am to 6pm daily. A trail pass is $5; trail pass with a onetime chairlift ride is $15; unlimited chairlift rides are $25 per day. Bike rentals are also available, starting at $20 for 2 hours, or $32 for a day. Helmets are required ($3 per day).

HIKING Those who'd like to explore the rocky highlands but are a bit unsure of themselves in the wilds should head for the **Merrell Hiking Center** (☎ 802/422-6708) at the Killington Base Lodge. The center's staff can offer helpful recommendations on area trails based on your experience and inclinations. Five dollars gets you a trail pass for hiking on Killington Peak, a map, and a pocket field guide. Another $5 will allow you to cut to the chase by taking the chairlift to the 4,195-foot summit to explore the ridgeline before hiking down. (This also offers a way for hikers with bad knees to stay active: Hike to the summit, then avoid the knee-jarring descent by riding the chairlift down.) Guided nature hikes and other specialized tours are available on request, as are rentals of boots and backpacks.

Hikers on their own might set their sights on **Deer Leap Mountain** and its popular 3-hour loop to the summit and back. The trail departs from the Inn at Long Trail off Route 4 at Sherburne Pass. Park across from the inn, then head north through the inn's parking lot onto the Long Trail/Appalachian Trail and into the forest. Follow the white blazes (you'll return on the blue-blazed trail you'll see entering on the left). In half a mile, you'll arrive at a juncture. The Appalachian Trail veers right to New Hampshire's White Mountains and Mount Katahdin in Maine; Vermont's Long Trail runs to the left. Follow the Long Trail, and after some hiking through forest and rock slab over the next half-mile or so, turn left at the signs for Deer Leap Height. Great views of Pico and the Killington area await you in four-tenths of a mile. After a snack break here, continue down the steep, blue-blazed descent back to Route 4 and your car. The entire loop is about 2.5 miles.

AN ADVENTURE IN HISTORY

President Calvin Coolidge State Historic Site. Rte. 100A, Plymouth. ☎ **802/672-3773.** Admission $5 adults, children under 14 free. Daily 9:30am–5:30pm. Closed late Oct to mid-May.

When told that Calvin Coolidge had died, literary wit Dorothy Parker is said to have responded, "How can they tell?" Even in his death, the nation's most taciturn president had to fight for respect. A trip to the Coolidge Historic District should at the least raise Silent Cal's reputation among visitors, who'll get a strong sense of the president raised in this mountain village, a man shaped by harsh weather, unrelieved isolation, and a strong sense of community and family.

Situated in a high upland valley, the historic district consists of a group of about a dozen unspoiled buildings open to the public, and a number of other private residences that may be observed from the outside only. It was at the Coolidge Homestead (open for tours) that in August 1923 Vice President Coolidge, on a vacation from Washington, was awakened in the middle of the night and informed that President Warren Harding had died unexpectedly. His father, a notary public, administered the oath of office.

With sloping, open meadows surrounding the village, visitors can plainly see the distinct patterns of life in an early Vermont town, where commerce and residential life clustered tightly and barn animals roamed the rest. A new mile-long walking trail offers access to the area's meadows and woods.

Be sure to stop by the **Plymouth Cheese Factory** (☎ 802/672-3650) in a trim white shop just uphill from the Coolidge Homestead. Founded in the late 1800s as a farmer's cooperative by President Coolidge's father, the factory is still owned by the president's son, who in his nineties still stops by daily in summer. Excellent cheeses are available here, including a spicy pepper cheddar. "It's got some authority," an elderly clerk warned me, and she was right. It's open daily in summer from 8am to 5:30pm.

WHERE TO STAY

Killington offers hundreds of guest rooms along the access road between Route 4 and the mountain. Prospective visitors can request lodging information from the **Killington and Pico Areas Association** (☎ 802/773-4181). Or they can line up a vacation with a single phone call to the **Killington Lodging Bureau** (☎ 800/ 621-6867). The accommodating staff will take care of all your travel needs, including air or train reservations.

Other options include the **Vermont Inn** (☎ 800/541-7795 or 802/775-0708), on Route 4 on the west side of Sherburne Pass. This 1840 farmhouse was reborn as a ski dorm a few decades back, then again as an inn. Guest rooms tend to be on the cozy side, but many have touches like gas fireplaces and country stenciling. The inn also has a well-regarded dining room. Rates are $70 to $110 in summer, $80 to $120 in winter. **Butternut on the Mountain Motor Inn** (☎ 800/524-7654 or 802/ 422-2000) is on the Killington access road and features 18 motel-like guest rooms along with extras like a tiny indoor pool and small whirlpool. There's also a restaurant on the premises. Rates run from $70 to $110 in midwinter; ask about discounts in the off-season.

Cortina Inn. Rte. 4 (1.5 miles west of Pico), Killington, VT 05751. ☎ **800/451-6108** or 802/ 773-3333. Fax 802/775-6948. E-mail: cortina1@aol.com. Web site: www.cortinainn.com. 97 rms. A/C TV TEL. Winter and foliage season $129–$179 double. Rates include breakfast. Rates higher during holidays. AE, CB, DC, DISC, MC, V.

Travelers seeking modern amenities within striking distance of Vermont's wilds and ski mountains will be content at the Cortina Inn. The original lodge, situated on Route 4 between Pico and Rutland, was built in 1966, with additions in 1975 and 1987. The interior still feels a bit like a private ski chalet dating from the 1970s— albeit one with *really* long hallways. There's even a sunken conversation pit with a two-sided fireplace, and a spiral staircase twisting up to a second level.

Guest rooms vary slightly in their modern country style, but all are comfortably furnished. Especially nice is Room 201 (the priciest of the bunch) with a loft, fan window, refrigerator, and Adirondack-style log furniture. Innkeepers Bob and Breda Harnish do a good job making this inn, with nearly 100 rooms, feel like a smaller and more intimate place. Especially appealing is the attention paid to detail—the hotel staff even brushes off the windows of guests' cars each morning after a snowstorm.

Dining/Entertainment: Evening meals are available on premises at Zola's Grill. There's also a tavern for lighter appetites, and afternoon tea is served in the fireplaced lobby in winter.

Services: Free shuttles to both Killington and Pico during ski season, concierge, limited room service, dry cleaning, laundry service, newspaper delivery, baby-sitting, currency exchange, express checkout, safe-deposit box.

Facilities: Indoor pool, fitness room, Jacuzzi, sauna, sundeck, mountain-biking center, eight tennis courts, two game rooms (one for adults only), small canoeing pond, children's center, conference rooms.

Inn at Long Trail. Rte. 4, Killington, VT 05751. ☎ **800/325-2540** or 802/775-718. E-mail: ilt@vermontel.com. 22 rms, 5 with showers only. Midweek $78–$98 double, including full breakfast. 2 nights on weekends and during foliage season, $300–$398 double, including 2 dinners and 2 breakfasts. 2-night minimum on weekends and during foliage season, 3-night minimum on holiday weekends. AE, MC, V. Closed late Apr to late June.

The Inn at Long Trail, situated in an architecturally undistinguished building at the intersection of busy Route 4 and the Long and Appalachian trails, is not a drive-by. The interior of this rustic inn is far more charming than the exterior. "Rustic" can be a travel guide code word for "shabby," but that's not the case here. Tree trunks support the beams in the lobby, which sports log furniture and banisters of yellow birch along the stairway. The older rooms in this three-floor hotel (built in 1938 as an annex to a long-gone lodge), are furnished simply in ski-lodge style. Comfortable, more modern suites with wood-burning fireplaces, telephones, and TVs are offered in a motel-like addition.

Just off the lobby is a relaxing, woody pub—an ideal place to knock back a pint of Guinness after a day on the trails. The back dining room maintains the Keebler elf theme, with a stone ledge that juts through the wall from the mountain behind. Innkeepers Murray and Patty McGrath (along with their children Connor and Brogan) emphasize the Gaelic in both atmosphere and cuisine. The menu features a selection of hearty meals popular with hungry hikers and skiers, including the inn's famed Guinness stew, corned beef and cabbage, and Irish poached salmon. Delicious homemade bread accompanies the meals. And there's live Irish music in the pub on weekends during the busy seasons.

Inn of the Six Mountains. Killington Rd. (P.O. Box 2900), Killington, VT 05751. ☎ **800/ 228-4676** or 802/422-4302. Fax 802/422-4321. 103 rms. TV TEL. Winter $139–$179 double midweek; $179–$249 double weekends; $249–$289 double holidays. Off-season discounts available. Rates include full breakfast. AE, CB, DC, DISC, MC, V.

With its profusion of gables and dormers, the Inn of the Six Mountains stands as the most architecturally dramatic of the numerous hotels along Killington Road. The lobby is welcoming in a modern, Scandinavian sort of way, with lots of blond wood and stone, and the location is convenient to Killington's base lodge, just a mile up the road. But for a luxury hotel that offers only deluxe rooms and suites, and charges accordingly, the attention to detail often comes up short. While the guest rooms are tastefully decorated in a Shaker-inspired sort of way, many feature scuffed walls, weary carpeting, and bruised furniture.

Dining/Entertainment: The inn features dining on the premises.

Facilities: Indoor pool, health club, Jacuzzi, sauna, sundeck, tennis court, game rooms, conference rooms.

Mountain Top Inn. Mountain Top Rd., Chittenden, VT 05737. ☎ **800/445-2100** or 802/ 483-2311. Fax 802/483-6373. 35 rms plus 20 units with 1–4 bedrooms. A/C TEL. Summer and fall $176–$226 double; winter $176–$226 double midweek, $196–$246 double weekends and holidays; off-season $98–$168 double. AE, MC, V.

The Mountain Top Inn was carved out of a former turnip farm in the 1940s, but has long since left its root vegetable heritage behind. Situated on 1,300 ridge-top acres with expansive views of the rolling Vermont countryside, the inn has the feel of a classic, small Pocono resort hotel, where the hosts make sure you've got something to do every waking minute. Overall, the Mountain Top doesn't offer good value to those only looking for simple room and board. But those who like to be active outdoors and who prefer to stay put during their vacation will be kept nicely busy for their money.

Dining/Entertainment: The pleasant dining room, with heavy beams and rustic, rawhide-laced chairs, features regional American cuisine with a continental flair. Entrees, which range from $12.95 to $20.95, might include pork tenderloin served with apples and an applejack brandy sauce, or New England seafood pie.

Facilities: Sixty-six miles of cross-country ski trails, horseback riding.

WHERE TO DINE

Charity's. Killington Rd. ☎ **802/422-3800.** Reservations not accepted. Lunch items $5.95– $6.75; main dinner courses $12.95–$16.95. AE, DC, MC, V. Daily 11:30am–11pm. PUB FARE.

Rustic, crowded, bustling, and boisterous, Charity's is the place to head after a day on the slopes—especially if you like your food big and your company young.

(Lunchtime in summers is a decidedly more mellow affair.) The centerpiece of this barnlike restaurant, adorned with stained-glass lamps and turn-of-the-century prints, is a handsome old bar crafted in Italy, then shipped to West Virginia, where it completed a run of nearly a century before being dismantled and coming to Vermont in 1971. The menu offers a good selection of burgers, plus a half-dozen vegetarian entrees, like veggie stir-fry and red-pepper ravioli. A Sunday brunch is offered until 2:30pm.

Choices. Killington Rd. (at Glazebook Center). ☎ **802/422-4030.** Main courses $11.95–$21. AE, DC, MC, V. Sun–Thurs 5–10pm, Fri–Sat 5–11pm; Sun brunch 11am–2pm. BISTRO.

One of the locally favored spots for consistently good fare at a reasonable price is Choices, located on the access road. Full dinners come complete with salad or soup and bread, and will amply restore calories lost on the trail. Fresh pastas are a specialty (try the Cajun green peppercorn fettuccine), and other inviting entrees include jambalaya, lamb cutlets, or salmon in phyllo. Somewhat more upscale entrees are available next door at Claude's, owned by the same chef.

✪ Hemingway's. Rtes 100 and 4. ☎ **802/422-3886.** Reservations strongly recommended. Fixed-price menu $42–$50; vegetarian menu $36–$40; tasting menu $60–$68 (with wines). AE, MC, V. High season Tues–Sun 6–10pm; off-season Wed–Sun 6–9pm. Closed in mid-Apr and early Nov. AMERICAN/ECLECTIC.

Hemingway's is an extraordinarily elegant spot. Opened by Linda and Ted Fondulas in 1982, the restaurant is recognized nationally and was named one of the nation's 25 top restaurants by *Food & Wine* magazine in 1992, and one of the 50 most distinguished U.S. restaurants by *Condé Nast Traveler* in 1993. By all accounts, it's continued to improve since then.

Located in the 1860 Asa Briggs House, a former stagecoach stop now fronting a busy stretch of highway between Killington and Woodstock, Hemingway's offers dining in three formal areas. The wine cellar has an old-world intimacy and is suited for groups out for a celebration; the two upstairs rooms are elegant with damask linen, silver flatware, crystal goblets, fresh flowers, and contemporary art on the walls. Diners tend to be dressed casually but neatly (no shorts or T-shirts). The food is top-notch, and a four-course dinner (plus extras like bread, canapés, and coffee) is offered at a price that turns out to be rather reasonable given the quality of the kitchen and the superb service. (The cost of dining here is much less than at any other of the *Food & Wine* 25.) *One warning:* The flavors are subtle and may be lost on those more accustomed to the fireworks of Thai curries or Sour Patch Kids.

The menu changes frequently to reflect available stock. A typical meal might start with a wild-mushroom ravioli with basil and lemon, followed with a Napoleon of sea bass and lobster with champagne sauce. Then it's on to the main course: perhaps a grilled venison chop, or potato-crusted Atlantic salmon. Desserts are typically the highlight of the meal and are stunningly presented. The chocolate chocolate charlotte with raspberries is wonderful; for sheer architectural bravado, try one of the caged desserts, like the caged pumpkin crème brûlée with apple cider sauce.

Mother Shapiro's. Killington Rd. ☎ **802/422-9933.** Reservations not accepted. Breakfast $2.50–$8.95; sandwiches $5.25–$7.95; main dinner courses $11.95–$18.95. AE, DISC, MC, V. Daily breakfast 7am–1pm, lunch and munchies 11:30am–2am, dinner 4:30–10pm. PUB FARE.

Mother Shapiro's motto is "Such a nice place." That tongue-in-cheek approach sets the tone for this funky spot that typically has a higher percentage of Vermont license plates in the parking lot than other restaurants around Killington. "Mother" is actually Jay Shapiro, a mustachioed entrepreneur who founded the restaurant in

1980. He's made this a relaxed place, done up in a sort of Victorian vaudeville/brothel look. The menu nags ("No whining," "Don't make a mess," "No substitutions concerning this menu unless it's not too busy, then we'll talk") while offering a decent selection of dishes that favors dressed-up pub fare (for example, veggie fajitas, smoked barbecue ribs). Individual breakfasts are nearly large enough for two. Mother Shapiro's also offers a decent bar menu after hours for those whose hunger catches up with them long after the sun has set.

Panache. Killington Access Rd., Killington. ☎ **802/422-8622.** Reservations recommended. Main courses $21–$59 (mostly $21–$26). AE, CB, DC, DISC, MC, V. Sun–Thurs 6–9pm, Fri–Sat 6–10pm. EXOTIC GAME.

Panache isn't for everyone. For starters, there's giraffe and lion and other fare that I'll bet won't show up anytime soon on the McDonald's menu. The exotic dinner offerings—which also include musk ox, wildebeest, and African ornyx—attracts adventurous gourmands in search of new flavors, but there's also a good selection of more traditional fare, like bison, elk, filet mignon, and duck. And once you get beyond the eye-popping menu (zebra!?), you'll discover a superior restaurant with a deft touch and creative flair. It's located in a modern building that also houses the spa at The Woods condo complex, and the sleek, contemporary interior could easily be on Manhattan's Upper East Side. The service is good, and the presentation world-class. The more exotic entrees are naturally more pricey (the African sampler costs $59), but more familiar fare is around $20 to $25.

As an added bonus, parents who make reservations can drop off their kids (no infants or toddlers) at a wonderful adjacent game room with air hockey and video games; the staff will keep an eye on them and feed them free pizza.

6 Middlebury

Middlebury is a gracious college town set amid bucolic countryside. The town center is idyllic in a New England as envisioned by Hollywood sort of way. It's centered around a slightly awkward, sloping green; above the green is the commanding Middlebury Inn. Shops line the downhill sides. In the midst of the green is a handsome chapel, and the whole scene is lorded over by a fine, white steepled Congregational church built between 1806 and 1809. Otter Creek tumbles dramatically through the middle of town, and is flanked by a historic district where you can see the intriguing vestiges of former industry. In fact, Middlebury has 300 buildings listed on the National Register of Historic Places. About the only disruption is the frequent growl of trucks downshifting as they drive along the main routes through town.

Historic Middlebury College, which is within walking distance of downtown, doesn't so much dominate the village as coexist nicely alongside it. The college has a sterling reputation for its liberal-arts educations, but may be best known for its intensive summer language programs. Don't be surprised if you hear folks gabbing in exotic tongues while walking through town. Students commit to total immersion, which means no lapsing by speaking in English while they're enrolled in the program.

ESSENTIALS

GETTING THERE Middlebury is located on Route 7 about midway between Rutland and Burlington.

VISITOR INFORMATION The **Addison County Chamber of Commerce,** 2 Court St., Middlebury, VT 05753 (☎ **800/733-8376** or 802/388-7951; Web site: **middlebury-info.com**), is located in a handsome, historic white building just off the green, facing the Middlebury Inn. Brochures and assistance are available weekdays during business hours. Ask also for the map and guide to downtown Middlebury, published by the Downtown Middlebury Business Bureau, which lists shops and restaurants around town. Downstairs is the **Vermont Folklife Center,** offering exhibits on the crafts, arts, and culture of Vermont.

SEEING THE SIGHTS

The best place to begin a tour of Middlebury is the Addison County Chamber of Commerce (see above), where you can request the chamber's self-guided walking tour brochure.

The historic **Otter Creek** district, set along a steep hillside by the rocky creek, is well worth exploring. While here, you can peruse top-flight Vermont crafts at the **Vermont State Crafts Center at Frog Hollow,** 1 Mill St. (☎ **802/388-3177**). The center, picturesquely situated overlooking tumbling Otter Creek, is open daily and features the work of some 300 Vermont craftspeople, with exhibits ranging from extraordinary carved wood desks to metalwork to glass and pottery. The Middlebury center also features a pottery studio and a resident potter who's often busy at work. The Crafts Center also maintains shops in Manchester Village and at the Church Street Marketplace in Burlington. Visit the center's Web site for a listing of monthly exhibits: **www.sover.net/~vsccfrog/**.

Beer hounds should schedule a stop at the **Otter Creek Brewing Co.,** 85 Exchange St. (☎ **800/473-0727**), for a tour and free samples of their well-regarded beverages, including the flagship Copper Ale and a robust Stovepipe Porter. The brewery opened in 1989; by 1995 it had outgrown its old space and moved into the new 40-barrel brew house on 10 acres. The facility and gift shop are open for tours daily 10am to 6pm.

Located atop a flat ridge with beautiful views of both the Green Mountains and farmlands rolling toward Lake Champlain, prestigious **Middlebury College** has a handsome, well-spaced campus of gray limestone and white marble buildings that's best explored by foot. The architecture of the college, founded in 1800, is primarily colonial revival, which lends it a rather stern and Calvinist demeanor. Especially appealing is the prospect from the marble Mead Memorial Chapel, built in 1917 and overlooking the campus green.

At the edge of campus is the **Middlebury College Center for the Arts,** which opened in 1992. This architecturally engaging center houses the **Middlebury College Museum of Art** (☎ **802/443-5000,** ext. 5007), a small museum with a selective sampling of European and American art, both ancient and new. Classicists will savor the displays of Greek painted urns and vases; modern art aficionados should head for the powerful *Imagem da Minha Revolta,* a 1988 installation by Brazilian artist Franz Krajcberg that deftly depicts the tragedy of the destruction of the rain forest. The museum is located on Route 30, and is open Tuesday to Friday 10am to 5pm, and weekends noon to 5pm. Admission is free.

Horse fans should head 2.5 miles outside of Middlebury to the **Morgan Horse Farm** (☎ **802/388-2011**), which is owned and administered by the University of Vermont. The farm has roots dating back to the late 1800s, and was for a time owned by the federal government, which in turn gave the farm to the university in 1951. Col. Joseph Battell, owner of the farm from the 1870s to 1906, is credited with preserving the Morgan breed, a horse of considerable beauty and stamina that has served admirably in war and exploration. The breed is now prized as show horses and family pleasure horses alike. The farm with its 70 registered stallions, mares, and foals is open for guided tours daily May through October from 9am to 4pm. There's also a picnic area and gift shop with loads of horse-related items. Admission is $3.50 for adults, $2 for teens, and free for children under 12. To reach the farm, head past the college on Route 125 to Weybridge Street (Route 23); turn right and follow signs for approximately 2.5 miles.

OUTDOOR PURSUITS

HIKING The Green Mountains roll down to Middlebury's western borders, making for easy access to the mountains. Stop by the **U.S. Forest Service's Middlebury Ranger District office,** south of town on Route 7 (☎ 802/388-4362), for guidance and information on area trails and destinations. Ask for the brochure *Day Hikes on the Middlebury & Rochester Ranger Districts,* which lists 14 hikes.

One recommended stroll for people of all abilities—and especially those of poetic sensibilities—is the **Robert Frost Interpretive Trail,** dedicated to the memory of New England's poet laureate. Frost lived in a cabin on a farm across the road for 23 summers. (The cabin is now a National Historic Landmark.) Located on Route 125 about 6 miles east of Middlebury, this relaxing loop trail is just a mile long, and excerpts of Frost's poems are placed on signs along the trail. Also posted is information about the trail's natural history. The trail, which is managed by the Green Mountain National Forest, offers pleasant access to the gentle woods of these lovely intermountain lowlands.

SKIING Downhill skiers looking for a low-key, low-pressure mountain invariably head to **Middlebury College Snow Bowl** (☎ 802/388-4356), near Middlebury Gap on Route 125 east of town. This historic ski area, founded in 1939, has a vertical drop of just over 1,000 feet served by three chairlifts. The college ski team uses the ski area for practice, but it's also open to the public at rates of about half what you'd pay at Killington. The ski area recently spruced up its compact base area. Adult tickets are $26 weekend, $20 midweek; juniors are $20 and $15.

There's also cross-country skiing nearby at the **Rikert Ski Touring Center** (☎ 802/388-2759), at Middlebury's Bread Loaf Campus on Route 125. The center offers 25 miles of machine-groomed trails through a lovely winter landscape.

WHERE TO STAY

Middlebury offers a handful of motels in addition to several inns. Two well-kept, inexpensive motels are located south of town on Route 7: The **Blue Spruce Motel** (☎ 802/388-4091) and the **Greystone Motel** (☎ 802/388-4935).

Middlebury Inn and Motel. 14 Courthouse Sq., Middlebury, VT 05753. ☎ **800/842-4666** or 802/388-4961. E-mail: midinnvt@sover.net. Web site: www.middleburyinn.com. 80 guest rms (3 with shower only). A/C TV TEL. Double $70–$155 midweek, $88–$165 weekends; suite $124–$146 weekdays, $146–$260 weekends. Rates include continental breakfast. MC, V.

The historic Middlebury Inn traces its roots back to 1827, when Nathan Wood built a brick public house he called the Vermont Hotel. It's come a long way since then, and now contains 80 modern guest rooms equipped with most conveniences. The rooms are good sized and most come furnished with a sofa or upholstered chairs in addition to the bed; rooms are decorated in rich, dark hues and colonial reproduction furniture. The eight guest rooms in the Porterhouse Mansion next door also have a pleasant, historic aspect. An adjacent motel is decorated in an Early American motif, but it feels like veneer—underneath it's still a motel.

The inn's spacious lobby is decorated in an aggressive colonial American style, but has a nice feel with a creaky floor, leather chairs, and bow-back sofas. Late in the day, the lobby is filled with the rich golden glow of the setting sun, making the wonderful colors come even more alive.

Dining/Entertainment: Three dining rooms offer breakfast, lunch, and dinner. Meals tend toward basic American fare (like broiled lamb chops with mint jelly, or seafood gratinée), with some dinners that are moderately more exotic (veggie stir-fry and sole paupiettes). Guests can enjoy both breakfast and dinner for $34.50 per person; outside diners should expect to pay $9.95 to $19.95 for entrees.

Swift House Inn. 25 Stewart Lane, Middlebury, VT 05753. ☎ **802/388-9925.** Fax 802/388-9927. 21 rms (1 with shower only). A/C TV TEL. $70–$175 double. Rates include continental breakfast. AE, CB, DC, DISC, MC, V.

The Swift House Inn is a compound of three graceful old homes set in a residential area just a few minutes' walk from the town green. The main Federal-style inn dates back to 1814; inside, it's splendidly decorated in a simple, historical style that still bespeaks a modern crispness.

Guests rooms are uncommonly well designed with antique and reproduction furnishings. Especially appealing is the Swift Room, with its oversized bathroom, whirlpool, and private terrace. About half of the 21 rooms have fireplaces or whirlpools or both; most also have coffeemakers and hair dryers. Light sleepers may prefer the main inn or the Carriage House rather than the Gatehouse down the hill; the latter is on Route 7 and the truck noise can be a minor irritant at night. The Swift House offers lodging at reasonable prices considering what guests receive, and the less expensive rooms are among the better deals in the state.

Dining/Entertainment: There's a dining room and tiny pub, and common rooms that are comfortable if not terribly cozy. See "Where to Dine," below.

Facilities/Services: Jacuzzi, steam room, sauna, safe, conference rooms.

WHERE TO DINE

Swift House Inn. 25 Stewart Lane. ☎ **802/388-9925.** Reservations recommended during peak seasons, weekends, and college events. Main courses $8.95–$22 (mostly $15–$17). AE, CB, DC, DISC, MC, V. Thurs–Mon 6–9:30pm. REGIONAL.

Guests here might feel as if they're having an exceedingly pleasant dinner in the house of an elderly, wealthy relative who appreciates traditional New England cooking. The dining room on the first floor of this wonderful inn is divided among three rooms, some of which are detailed with lustrous cherry woodwork and 12-over-12 windows. In the cooler seasons, request a seat near the fireplace with its gorgeous mantle of polished cherry and marble. If time permits, arrive early for a single-malt scotch at the cozy pub. Then, to food.

For starters, you might opt for the jumbo shrimp or the stuffed portobello mushrooms. Next it's the venison with burgundy and lentil sauce, the steamed lobster, or the Black Angus New York strip steak. Desserts are excellent; the crème brûlée is among the tastiest in the state.

Woody's. 5 Bakery Lane (on Otter Creek just upstream from the bridge in the middle of town). ☎ **802/388-4182.** Reservations recommended on weekends and during college events. Lunch items $3.95–$6.95; main dinner courses $9.95–$16.95. AE, MC, V. Mon–Sat 11:30am–10pm, Sun 10:30am–9pm. Light menu only 3–5pm. Closed Tues in winter. PUB FARE/PASTA.

Woody's is not Olde New Englande. Set down a small alley in the middle of town, it features dining on three levels overlooking the creek in an exuberantly retro interior with a huge neon clock, lots of brushed steel, soaring windows, and red-and-black checkered linoleum floors. It's the kind of fun, hip place destined to put you in a good mood the moment you walk in. Lunches include burgers, sandwiches, and salads, along with burritos and pita melts. Dinner is heavy on the pasta selections (the bourbon shrimp with linguine is good), but also features appetizing selections from the grill, like Cajun-grilled salmon and a leg of lamb with roasted eggplant salad.

7 Montpelier & Barre

Montpelier is easily the most down-home, low-key state capital in the United States. There's a hint of that in every photo of the glistening gold dome of the state capitol. Rising up behind it isn't a bank of mirror-sided skyscrapers, but a thickly forested hill. Montpelier, it turns out, isn't a self-important center of politics, but a small town that just incidentally happens to be home to the state government.

The state capitol is worth a visit, as is the local art museum and historical society. But more than that, it's worth visiting just to experience a small, clean, New England town that's more than a little friendly. Montpelier centers around two main boulevards: State Street, which is lined with state government buildings, and Main Street, where many of the town's shops are located. It's all very compact, manageable, and cordial. If you so much as think about crossing the street, the driver of the next car will probably stop and wave you across.

Lots of people I know have visited Montpelier and come away thinking, "Hey, I could live here!" The downtown has two hardware stores next door to one another (one had this sign posted on its front door when I visited: WE JUST OILED OUR FLOOR AND IT MAY BE SLIPPERY WHEN WET UNTIL IT GETS WORE IN), and two movie theaters, including the **Savoy** (☎ **802/229-0509**), one of the best art-movie houses in northern New England. At the Savoy, a large cup of cider and a popcorn slathered with real, unclarified butter cost me less than a small popcorn with oil would at a mall cinema.

Nearby Barre (pronounced "Barry") is more commercial, but shares an equally vibrant past. (Between Montpelier and Barre is an unlovely 6-mile stretch of road with motels, fast-food restaurants, and many of the other conveniences sought by travelers.) Barre has a more commercial, blue-collar demeanor than Montpelier. The historic connection to the thriving granite industry is seen here and there, from the granite curbstones lining its long Main Street, to the signs for commercial establishments carved out of locally hewn rock. Barre attracted talented stone workers from Italy and Scotland (there's even a statue of Robert Burns), which gave turn-of-the-century Barre a lively, cosmopolitan flavor.

ESSENTIALS

GETTING THERE   Montpelier is accessible via Exit 7 off I-89. For Barre, take Exit 8.

VISITOR INFORMATION   The **Central Vermont Chamber of Commerce,** P.O. Box 336, Barre, VT 05641 (☎ **802/229-5711**), is located on Stewart Road off Exit 7 of I-89. Turn left at the first light; it's one-half mile on the left. Information is available on the Web at **www.central-vt.com**.

EXPLORING THE TOWNS

Start your exploration of Montpelier with a visit to the gold-domed **State House** (☎ **802/828-2228**). If you're in a hurry, you can take a self-guided tour, admiring the statue of Ethan Allen guarding the doors, and the long, stately halls with marble floors. If time allows and you're here in the right season, take one of the free guided tours, which are offered July through mid-October. The tours leave on the half-hour Monday to Friday 10am to 3:30pm, and on Saturdays from 11am to 2pm.

Central Vermont & the Champlain Valley

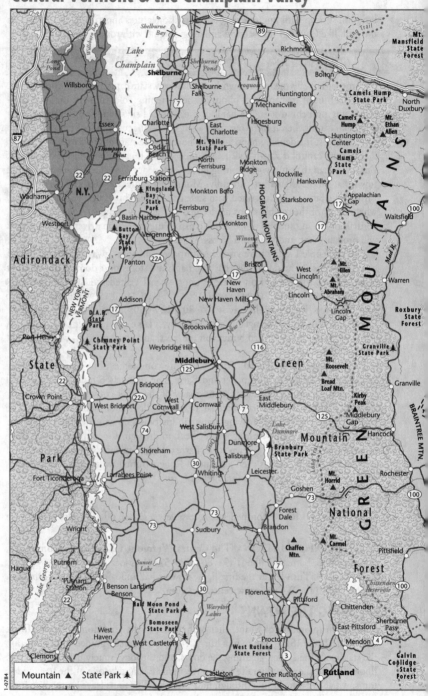

Mountain ▲   State Park ⚕

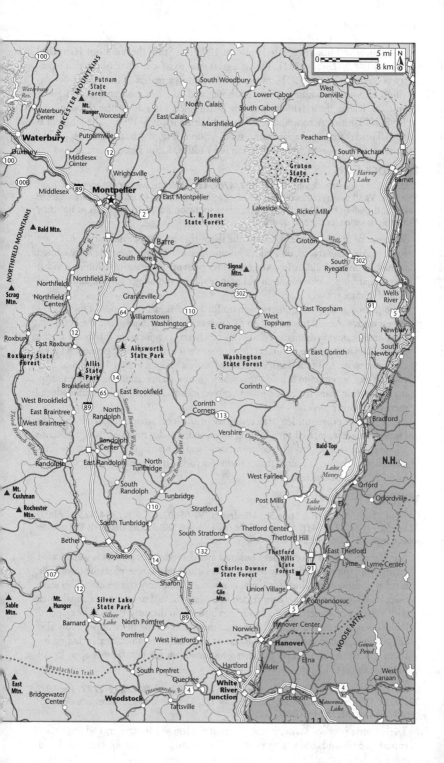

497

A short stroll from the State House, at 109 State St., is the **Vermont Historical Society** (☎ 802/828-2291). This is a great spot to admire some of the rich tapestry of Vermont's history. The museum is housed in a replica of the elegant old Pavilion House, a prominent Victorian hotel, and contains a number of intriguing artifacts, such as the gun once owned by Ethan Allen. On exhibit here through June 1998, is "Tourists Accommodated: Visiting Vermont 1895–1995." The museum is open Tuesday through Friday from 9am to 4:30pm, Saturday from 9am to 4pm, and Sundays from noon to 4pm. Admission is $3 adults, $2 for students and seniors.

FOR ROCK FANS

Rock of Ages Quarry. Graniteville. ☎ 802/476-3119. Web site: www.rockofages.com. Tours $4 adults, $3.50 seniors (62 and over), $1.50 children 6–12. Mon–Fri 9:15am–3:30pm. Closed July 4 and mid-Oct to May. From Barre, drive south on Route 14, turn left at lights by McDonald's; watch for signs to quarry.

When in or around Barre, listen for the deep, throaty hum of industry. That's the Rock of Ages Quarry, set on a rocky hillside high above town near the aptly named hamlet of Graniteville. A free visitors center presents informative exhibits, a video about quarrying, a glimpse at an old granite quarry (no longer active), and a selection of granite gifts.

For a look at the active quarry, sign up for a guided half-hour tour of the world's largest quarry. An old bus groans up to a viewer's platform high above the 500-foot, man-made canyon (dramatic enough to be chosen as a location for scenes of the movie *Batman IV*), where workers cleave huge slabs of fine-grained granite and hoist them out using 150-foot derricks anchored with a spider's web of 15 miles of steel cable. It's an operation to behold. Afterwards, visitors are invited to stop by the nearby manufacturing plant to see the granite carved into memorials, architectural adornments, and other pieces.

For a more poignant, less staged display of the local stonecutters craft, head to **Hope Cemetery,** located on a hillside in a wooded valley north of Barre on Route 14. The cemetery is filled with columns, urns, and human figures carved of the fine-grained gray granite. It's more than a memorial park—it's a remarkable display of the talent of area stonecutters.

WHERE TO STAY

Capitol Plaza Hotel. 100 State St., Montpelier, VT 05602. ☎ **800/274-5252** or 802/223-5252. Fax 802/229-5427. 46 rms. A/C TV TEL. Midweek $82 double; weekends $92 double; foliage season $102 double. AE, DISC, MC, V.

The Capitol Plaza is Montpelier's business and conference hotel, but is well located (across from the state capitol) to serve travelers whose goal is to explore the town. The hotel is nothing fancy, but it is clean, comfortable, and very convenient. This solid brick building was originally constructed in the late 1950s, but underwent a makeover with a change of ownership to a family-run business in the early 1990s. The carpeted lobby is small and has a colonial cast to it; the rooms on the three upper floors also adopt a light, faux-colonial tone, and feature the usual hotel amenities, including in-room coffeemakers. A simply decorated restaurant on the first floor is open for all three meals.

Inn at Montpelier. 147 Main St., Montpelier, VT 05602. ☎ **802/223-2727.** Fax 802/223-0722. 19 rms (4 with showers only). A/C TV TEL. $99–$155 double. Rates include continental breakfast. AE, DC, DISC, MC, V.

Two historic in-town homes house guests at the Inn at Montpelier, and both offer superb accommodations with most major amenities. The main cream-colored

Federal-style inn, built in 1827, features a mix of historical and up-to-date furnishings, along with a sunny sitting room and deck off the rear of the second floor. The larger front rooms are nicely appointed, but so too are the much smaller rooms in the former servants' wing. If you'd prefer not to catch the wafting scents of dinner cooking, ask for a room at the adjacent house, built in 1807, and decorated with comparable flair. Room 27 is especially pleasant, and features a large private deck. The inn tends to be a shade more antiseptic and Spartanly furnished than other historic inns, but it's more intriguing and comfortable than any chain hotel.

Dining/Entertainment: The inn's restaurant, open Tuesday through Sunday, is very well regarded, with appealingly prepared entrees such as pheasant breast, salmon filets, and hand-rolled fettuccine. Entrees are priced from $13 to $21.

WHERE TO DINE

A creation of the New England Culinary Institute, **La Brioche Bakery & Cafe** (☎ **802/229-0443**) occupies the corner of Montpelier's State and Main streets. It's a little bit of Europe in one of New England's more continental cities (Montpelier could slip into the Black Forest or the Vienna Woods without causing much of a stir). A deli counter offers baked goods like croissants and baguettes. Get them to go, or settle into a table in the afternoon sun outdoors.

✪ **Horn of the Moon.** 8 Langdon St., Montpelier. ☎ **802/223-2895.** Reservations not accepted. Breakfast $2.50–$6; lunch $4–$6; dinner $6–$10. No credit cards (out-of-state checks accepted). Tues–Sat 7am–9pm, Sun 9am–7pm. VEGETARIAN.

This relaxed, informal restaurant overlooking a tributary of the Winooski River was the first vegetarian restaurant in Vermont, and it remains one of the best. In fact, it's appealing enough to attract plenty of carnivores, drawn by the robust pastas, tasty sandwiches made on whole-wheat flat-bread, and the Mexican-style dishes like burritos and tostadas. If you're looking for a full three-course meal with dinner rolls and linens, you're better off around the corner at the Main Street Grill. But if you want wholesome, inexpensive food, get here early and get here often. A terrific value.

Main Street Grill & Bar. 118 Main St., Montpelier. ☎ **802/223-3188.** Reservations usually not needed. Lunch items $3.75–$6.50; main dinner courses $5.95–$12.75. AE, DC, DISC, MC, V. Mon–Fri 7–10am, Sat 8–10am; Mon–Sat 11:30am–2pm, Sun 10am–2pm; daily 5:30–10pm. AMERICAN/ECLECTIC.

This airy, modern grill serves as classroom and ongoing exam for students of the New England Culinary Institute, which is located just down the block. It's not unusual to see knots of students, toques at a rakish angle, walking between the restaurant and class. Diners can eat on the first-level dining room, watching street life through the broad windows (in summer, there's seating on a narrow porch outside the windows), or burrow in the homey bar downstairs. Dishes change with the semester, but might include a vegetarian chili, vegetable stir-fry, portobello mushroom sandwich, or a robust penne with chicken, artichokes, and sun-dried tomatoes in a fennel cream sauce. The breakfast burrito is served with a tangy corn salsa, and is nearly large enough for two.

For fancier, more formal dining, head to the second-floor Chef's Table, which is also part of the Culinary Institute. Entrees here range from $15.25 to $18.75.

8 Mad River Valley

The Mad River Valley is one of Vermont's best-kept secrets, and has something of a Shangri-la quality to it. In places it appears to have changed little since it was first settled in 1789 by Gen. Benjamin Wait and a handful of Revolutionary War veterans, including half a dozen said to have served as Minutemen at the battles of Concord Bridge and Lexington.

Since 1948, ski-related development has competed with the early farms that were the backbone of the region for 2 centuries. But the newcomers haven't been too pushy or overly obnoxious. Save for a couple of telltale signs, you could drive Route 100 through the sleepy villages of Warren and Waitsfield and not realize that you've passed close to some of the choicest skiing in the state. The region hasn't fallen prey to condo or strip-mall developers, as have some other ski areas in Vermont, and the valley seems to have learned the lessons of haphazard development that afflicted Mount Snow and Killington to the south. Longtime Vermont skiers say the valley is like Stowe was 25 years ago.

The region's character becomes less pastoral along the Sugarbush Access Road, but even then, development isn't heavily concentrated, not even at the base of Sugarbush, the valley's preeminent ski area. The better lodges and restaurants tend to be tucked back in the forest or set along streams, and it behooves travelers to make sure they have good directions before setting out in search of accommodations or food. Hidden up a winding valley road, Mad River Glen, the area's older and grumpier ski area, has a pleasantly dated quality that eschews glamour in favor of the rustic. Its slogan: "Ski It If You Can." As yet, the whole valley still maintains a friendly and informal attitude, even during the peak of ski season. And valley residents hope to keep it that way, even in the face of certain growth.

ESSENTIALS

GETTING THERE   Warren and Waitsfield straddle Route 100 between Killington and Waterbury. The nearest interstate access is from Exit 10 (Waterbury) on I-89; drive south on Route 100 for 14 miles to Waitsfield.

VISITOR INFORMATION   The **Sugarbush Chamber of Commerce,** P.O. Box 173, Waitsfield, VT 05673 (☎ **800/828-4748** or 802/469-3409), on Route 100, is open Monday through Saturday 9am to 5pm.

SKIING

✪ **Sugarbush.** Warren, VT 05674. ☎ **802/583-2381,** or 800/537-8427 for lodging. Web site: www.sugarbush.com. Vertical drop: 2,600 ft. 14 chairlifts (4 high-speed), 4 surface lifts. Skiable acreage: 432. Lift tickets $47.

After absorbing nearby Glen Ellen Ski Area in 1979, Sugarbush struggled with solvency under several owners. Once noted for its icy and rocky runs, the mountain tended to attract young kids and older skiers who prized the classic New England ski trails. The neon ski-suit and grunge snowboard crowd stuck with Killington, 1 hour south.

With the purchase of Sugarbush by Les Otten in 1995—and $28 million in improvements—Sugarbush has added some flash and zip to broaden its appeal. The "new" Sugarbush announced its intentions by first linking the two main ski mountains—Lincoln Peak and Mount Ellen—with a 2-mile, 10-minute high-speed chairlift that crosses three ridges (no more irksome shuttle buses), and installing additional high-speed, detachable quad chairlifts at both mountains. Snowmaking has been significantly upgraded (Otten is a master of snowmaking, if nothing else), and the improved slopes are generating some buzz among ski bums far and wide.

Happily, Sugarbush is still a low-key area with great intermediate cruising runs on the north slopes and some challenging expert slopes to the south, but expect a glossier edge as the resort races to make up for lost time. The most notable change will be the new Grand Summit Hotel and Crown Club at the base of Lincoln Peak, which at press time was slated to open in late 1997.

✪ **Mad River Glen.** Waitsfield, VT 05763. ☎ **802/496-3551.** Vertical drop: 2,000 ft. 4 chairlifts. Skiable acreage: 115. Lift tickets $28 midweek, $32 weekends, $34 holidays.

Mad River Glen is the curmudgeon of the Vermont ski world (motto: "Ski It If You Can"). High-speed detachable quads? Forget it. The main lift is a 1948 *single*-chair lift that creaks its way 1 mile to the summit. Snowmaking? Don't count on it. Only 15% of the terrain benefits from the fake stuff; the rest is dependent on Mother Nature. Snowboarding? Nope. It's forbidden at Mad River.

Mad River's slopes are twisting and narrow, and hide some of the steepest drops you'll find in New England (nearly half of the slopes are classified as expert). Mad River Glen long ago attained the status of a cult mountain among serious skiers, and its fans seem bound and determined to keep it that way. In recent *Snow Country* rankings, Mad River came in number one in the East for terrain, bumps, steeps, and value.

Longtime owner Betsy Pratt sold the ski area to a cooperative of about 1,000 Mad River skiers in 1995, making it the only cooperative-owned ski area in the country. The new owners seem especially proud of the mountain's funky traditions (how *about* that single chair?), and say they're determined to maintain the spirit. Watch for a festive 50th anniversary bash celebrating that spirit in 1998.

HIKING & BIKING

A rewarding **14-mile bike trip** along paved roads begins at the village of Waitsfield. Park your car near the covered bridge, and follow East Warren Road past the Inn at Round Barn Farm and up into the hilly, farm-filled countryside. Near the village of Warren, turn right at Brook Road to connect back to Route 100. Return north on bustling but generally safe and often scenic Route 100 to Waitsfield.

Bike rentals, repairs, and advice are available in Waitsfield at **Mad River Bike Shop** (☎ **802/496-9500**). The shop is located on Route 100 just south of the junction with Route 17, and is open daily from 9am to 6pm (until 5pm on Sunday).

Hikers in search of good exercise and a spectacular view should strike for **Mount Abraham,** west of Warren. Drive west up Lincoln Gap Road (it leaves Route 100 just south of Warren Village), and continue until the crest, where you'll cross the intersection with the Long Trail. Park here and head north on the trail; about 2 miles along you'll hit the Battell Shelter, which can sleep eight hikers. (There's also a spring nearby.) Push on another eight-tenths of a mile up a steep ascent to reach the panoramic views atop 4,006-foot Mount Abraham. Enjoy. Retrace your steps back to your car. Allow 4 or 5 hours for the round-trip hike.

For a less demanding adventure that still yields great views, head *south* from Lincoln Gap Road on the **Long Trail.** In about six-tenths of a mile, look for a marked spur trail to Sunset Rock with open vistas of the Champlain Valley. A round-trip hike requires about 1 hour.

EXPLORING THE VALLEY

Without a doubt the most unique way to explore the region is atop an Icelandic horse. The **Vermont Icelandic Horse Farm** (☎ **802/496-7141**) specializes in tours on these small, sturdy, strong horses. Day and half-day rides are available, but to really appreciate both the countryside and the horses, you should sign up for one of the multiday treks. These range from 2 to 5 nights, and include lodging at area inns, all your meals (lunches are either picnics or enjoyed at a local restaurant), your mount, and a guide to lead through the lush hills around Waitsfield and Warren. In winter, there's also skijoring, which can best be described as waterskiing behind a horse. The overnight trips range from $385 (based on double occupancy) for the 2-day trip, to $1,245 for the 6-day fall foliage trip. Call for information and reservations for day and half-day trips.

The classic **Warren General Store** (☎ 802/496-3864) anchors the former bustling timber town of Warren. Set along a tumbling stream, the store has uneven wooden floorboards, a potbellied stove, and shelf stock fully updated for the 1990s with a good selection of gourmet foods and wines. Get a coffee or a sandwich at the back deli counter, and enjoy it on the deck overlooking the water. Afterwards, browse upstairs, where you'll find an assortment of leather goods, clothing, and jewelry. The store is located in Warren Village just off Route 100 south of the Sugarbush Access Road.

Visitors can explore local rivers or lakes with the help of **Clearwater Sports** (☎ 802/496-2708) on Route 100 in Waitsfield, just north of the covered bridge. These outgoing guides rent canoes and kayaks, and offer shuttle services for intrepid paddlers looking for adventures ranging from white water (best in the spring) to a placid summer afternoon paddle on the Waterbury Reservoir. Rates are $35 per day for canoe rental; guided tours run from 9am to 3pm and cost $45 per person, including transportation, equipment, and instruction (bring your own picnic lunch). In a romantic mood? Ask about Clearwater's moonlight cruises. In winter, Clearwater offers snowshoe, ice skate, and telemark ski rentals, and hosts 2- and 4-hour snowshoe tours.

Also in Waitsfield is the **Mad River Canoe Factory Showroom** (☎ 802/496-3127). Experienced canoeists will recognize the name of this respected canoe manufacturer, which makes fiberglass and other canoes of complex laminates suitable for running raging rivers and poking around placid ponds. The showroom, located on Mad River Green, is open weekdays from 10am to 4pm. Paddling accessories (and some good advice) are also available here.

South of Warren, Route 100 pinches through **Granville Gulf,** a wild and scenic area of tumultuous streams and sheer hillsides. The highway twists and winds through this troll-like defile, which stands in contrast to the more open vistas along most of Route 100. Look for the roadside pull-off at **Moss Glen Falls,** one of the state's loveliest cascades.

WHERE TO STAY

Sugarbush isn't overrun with condos and lodges like some other ski areas, but still offers a suitably wide range of choices. Some 200 of the condos nearest the mountain are managed by the **Sugarbush Resort** (☎ 800/537-8427 or 802/583-3333), with facilities ranging from one to four bedrooms. Guests have access to a range of amenities, including a modern health club and five pools. The resort also manages the attractive **Sugarbush Inn,** right on the access road, with 46 hotel rooms and two restaurants. Shuttle buses deliver guests around the mountain, keeping driving to a minimum. During major winter holidays, there's a minimum stay of 5 days. Rates vary widely and most rooms are sold as packages that include lift tickets in winter; call for information. Also on the drawing board is the new **Grand Summit Hotel,** to be built at the base of Lincoln Peak with a scheduled opening date of Christmas 1997. The condominium-hotel will feature a restaurant, health club, and an outdoor heated pool, among other amenities.

◐ Inn at Round Barn Farm. E. Warren Rd., Waitsfield, VT 05673. ☎ 802/496-2276. Fax 802/496-8832. E-mail: roundbarn@madriver.com. 11 rms (1 with shower only). $115–$220 double. Rates include full breakfast. AE, MC, V.

"We're basically for romantics," says a staffer at this extraordinary inn. And that's the all-encompassing definition of "romantic." Those seeking the romance of Vermont will find it here in spades. You arrive at the inn after passing through a covered bridge off Route 100; a mile later you come upon this wonderful barn and farmhouse, set along a sloping hill with views of fields all around. The centerpiece of the inn is the eponymous Round Barn, a strikingly beautiful 1910 structure that's used variously for weddings, arts exhibits, and Sunday church services. The Simko family has improved the grounds bit by bit since opening in 1987, and they're now beautifully landscaped with stone walls, gardens, and a duck pond. A new sculpture garden invites contemplation of 25 pieces along a mile-long wood-chip path.

Elegant, pine-floored guest rooms will appeal to couples looking to kindle their own romance. Each room is furnished with an impeccable country elegance so deft that it doesn't overstay its welcome. Especially deluxe is the new Joslin Room, which features a whirlpool, steam shower, and a Queen Anne vanity. Common rooms downstairs are furnished with comparable flair (although the breakfast room with its views across the fields was sacrificed in 1996 to add a guest room), and are simple and elegant at the same time. No smoking.

Facilities/services: Indoor lap pool, 18-mile cross-country ski center, games rooms, health club nearby, safe-deposit boxes, free refreshments.

Inn at the Mad River Barn. Rte. 17 (R.R. #1; P.O. Box 88), Waitsfield, VT 05673. ☎ 800/631-0466 or 802/496-3310. 15 rms (3 with shower only). TV. Summer $65 double; winter $95 double. Rates include breakfast. AE, DISC, MC, V.

The Inn at the Mad River Barn, run by former Mad River Glen Ski area owner Betsy Pratt, is a classic, 1940s-style ski lodge that attracts a clientele nearly fanatical in its devotion to the place. It's best not to come here expecting anything fancy. Do come expecting to have some fun once you're settled in. It's all knotty pine, with Spartanly furnished guest rooms, and rustic common rooms where visitors feel at home putting their feet up. Most guests stay in a two-story barn behind the white clapboard main house; some stay at the annex up the lawn. In winter, guests can elect to get their dinners on the premises, served in boisterous family style. In summer, the mood is slightly more sedate (only breakfast is offered), but enhanced by a beautiful pool a short walk away in a grove of birches. The Mad River Barn isn't so much an institution or accommodation as a big family, and guests who approach it in that spirit won't go away disappointed. A great value.

West Hill Inn. W. Hill Rd. (R.R. #1, Box 292), Warren, VT 05674. ☎ 802/496-7162. 7 rms (4 with shower only). Summer, foliage, and ski seasons $95–$135 double; spring $85–$115 double. Rates include full breakfast. AE, MC, V.

Nestled on a forested hillside along a lightly traveled country road, the West Hill Inn offers the quintessential New England experience with an easy commute to the slopes at Sugarbush. Built in the 1850s, this farmhouse was expanded in the summer of 1995 with a modern common room, which offers a handsome fireplace for warmth in winter and an outdoor patio for summer lounging. The guest rooms vary, but all are well appointed in an updated country style. A room with a fireplace sits atop a spiral staircase; two Hobbit-like rooms are tucked under the eaves above a narrow staircase in the old part of the home. Two recently upgraded guest rooms include a steam shower and double Jacuzzi.

Guests often linger amid the rich, colorful tones of the library, with its woodstove and walls of books, or borrow a VCR and one of the 120 movies before retreating to their rooms. Country breakfasts are served around a large dining-room table, and the day's first meal tends to be an event as much as it is nourishment. It often takes some effort to pry yourself away from the good company to get outdoors before lunchtime rolls around.

WHERE TO DINE

The Common Man. German Flats Rd., Warren. ☎ **802/583-2800.** Reservations highly recommended in season. Main courses $10–$19.95. AE, DISC, MC, V. Daily 6:30–9pm. Open at 6pm on Sat and till 10pm on busier nights. Closed Mon from mid-Apr to mid-Dec. CONTINENTAL.

Dapper proprietor Mike Ware greets guests arriving at The Common Man, and it's clear by the warm response from returning patrons that he and chef Patrick Matecat are doing something quite right. It's spectacularly located in a century-old barn moved here in 1987, and the interior is soaring and dramatic, but manages to be intimate as well. Chandeliers, floral carpeting on the walls (weird, but it works), and candles on the tables meld successfully and coax all but coldhearted guests into a relaxed frame of mind. You'll be halfway through the meal before you notice there are no windows.

The menu strives to be as ambitious and appealing as the decor. It often hits the mark, although it sometimes misses with a bland offering or two. Guests might start with an appetizer of duck salad or rabbit sausage. The feast continues with dishes ranging from a traditional cassoulet to Vermont veal sautéed with apple slices, calvados, and fresh cream. Try the sinful *Schneeballe* (vanilla ice cream with coconut and hot fudge) for dessert.

The Den. Junction of Routes 100 and 17, Waitsfield. ☎ **802/496-8880.** Reservations not accepted. Lunch items $3.50–$6.95; main dinner courses $8.50–$13.95. AE, MC, V. Daily 11:30am–11pm. AMERICAN.

Jonesing for a juicy burger without frills or fancy service? Then head to The Den. A local favorite with a comfortable, neighborly feel, it's the kind of spot where you can plop yourself down in a pine booth, help yourself to the salad bar while waiting for your main course, and cheer on the Red Sox (or Patriots or Celtics) on the tube over the bar. The menu offers the usual pub fare, with all manner of burgers, plus Reubens, roast-beef sandwiches, chicken in a basket, and even pork chops with apple sauce and french fries.

John Eagan's Big World Pub. At Madbush Falls Country Motel, Rte. 100, Warren. ☎ **802/ 496-3033.** Reservations not accepted. Main courses $9.75–$16.25; burgers and sandwiches $6.25. AE, MC, V. Daily 5:30–9:30pm. GRILL/INTERNATIONAL.

Extreme skier John Eagan starred in 10 Warren Miller skiing films over the years, but *really* took a risk when he opened his own restaurant in December 1994. It offers terrific value. Located in a 1970s-style motel dining room that's sorely lacking in charm or élan (save for the bar made of ski sections signed by skiing luminaries), the Big World Pub compensates with a small but above-average pub menu that the chef pulls off with unexpected flair. Dishes include wood-grilled chicken breast glazed with Vermont cider, ginger, and lime; pan-roasted pork loin brushed with Dijon; and a tangy Hungarian goulash. Try the unique "dog bones" appetizer—Polish sausage wrapped in puff pastry and served with sauerkraut and mustard. Wash your meal down with a pint of custom Eagan's Extreme Ale, brewed by Vermont's Catamount Brewery.

9 Stowe

There's no getting around it: Stowe is a tourist town. That's even evident in summer, when the telltale ski racks disappear. How else could you explain a shop called "Everything Cows" that sells bovine-themed giftware?

But Stowe, which bills itself as the "Ski Capital of New England," has managed the juggernaut of steady growth reasonably well and with good humor. There are condo developments and strip-mall-style restaurants, to be sure. In fact, this small town with a year-round population of just 3,400 boasts some 62 lodgings and more than 50 restaurants. But there are still spectacular views of the gentle mountains, and wonderful vistas across the fertile farmlands of the valley floor. The village of Stowe has managed to retain much of its charm and small-town feel. And the place never really feels overrun—except when the ski slopes empty out in the late afternoon and traffic clogs Mountain Road.

Stowe is quaint, compact, and contains what may be Vermont's most gracefully tapered church spire, located atop the Stowe Community Church. Most of the recent development has taken place along Mountain Road (Route 108), which runs northwest of the village to the base of Mount Mansfield and the Stowe ski area. Here you'll find an array of motels, restaurants, shops, bars, and even a three-screen cinema. A free trolley connects the village with the mountain during ski season, so you can let your car get snowed in, avoid the valley traffic, and still not miss out on anything.

ESSENTIALS

GETTING THERE　Stowe is located on Route 100 north of Waterbury and south of Morrisville. In summer, Stowe may also be reached via Smugglers Notch on Route 108. This pass, which squeezes narrowly between the rocks and is not recommended for RVs or trailers, is closed in winter.

VISITOR INFORMATION　The **Stowe Area Association,** P.O. Box 1320, Stowe, VT 05672 (☎ **800/247-8693** or 802/253-7321), maintains a handy office in the village center. Ask for advice, pick up brochures, or make lodging reservations at area inns and hotels. This is a good first stop if you show up in town without a place to stay. Stowe's home-page on the Internet may be found at **http:// www.stoweinfo.com/saa.**

The **Green Mountain Club** (☎ **802/244-7037**), a venerable statewide association devoted to building and maintaining backcountry trails, has a visitor's center on Route 100 between Waterbury and Stowe. This is a good place to buy detailed hiking guides, and to ask the staff for hiking and camping suggestions.

WARM-WEATHER OUTDOOR PURSUITS

Stowe's forte is winter (see the sections on skiing, below), but it's also an outstanding fair-weather destination, surrounded by lush, rolling green hills and open farmlands, and towered over by craggy **Mount Mansfield,** Vermont's highest peak at 4,393 feet.

Deciding how to get atop Mount Mansfield is half the challenge. The **toll road** (☎ **802/253-7311**) traces its lineage back to the 19th century, when it served horses bringing passengers to the old hotel sited near the mountain's crown. (The hotel was demolished in the 1960s.) Drivers now twist their way up this road and park below the summit of Mansfield; a 2-hour hike along well-marked trails will bring you to the top with its unforgettable views. The toll road is open from late May through mid-October. The fare is $12 per car with up to six passengers, $2 per additional person; $7 per motorcycle (two people). Ascending by foot or bicycle is free.

Another option is the **Stowe gondola** (☎ **802/253-7311**), which whisks skiless travelers to within 1¹/₂ miles of the summit at the Cliff House Restaurant. Hikers can explore the rugged, open ridgeline, then descend just before twilight. The gondola runs from mid-June through mid-October and costs $9 round-trip for adults, $4 for children 6 to 12.

The budget route up Mount Mansfield, and to my mind the most rewarding, is by foot, and you have at least nine options for an ascent. The easiest but least pleasing route is up the toll road. Other options require local guidance and a good map. Ask for information from knowledgeable locals (your inn might be of help), or stop by the Green Mountain Club headquarters, open weekdays, on Route 100 about 4 miles south of Stowe. GMC can also assist with advice on other area trails.

One of the most understated, most beloved local attractions is the **Stowe Recreation Path,** which winds 5.3 miles from behind the Stowe Community Church up the valley toward the mountain, ending behind the Topnotch Tennis Center. This exceptionally appealing pathway is heavily used by locals for transportation and exercise in the summers; in the winter, it serves as a cross-country ski trail. Connect to the pathway at either end, or at points where it crosses side roads that lead to Mountain Road. No motorized vehicles or skateboards are allowed.

All manner of recreational accoutrement is available for rent at **The Mountain Bike Shop** (☎ **802/253-7919**), located in the Big Red Building along the Rec Path. This includes full suspension demo bikes, baby joggers, and bike trailers. Basic bike rentals are $16 for 4 hours; the shop is open from 9am to 6pm daily in summer. (This is also a good spot for cross-country ski and snowshoe rentals in winter.)

Anglers should allow ample time to peruse **The Fly Rod Shop** (☎ **800/535-9703** or 802/253-7346), located on Route 100, 2 miles south of the village. This well-stocked shop offers fly and spin tackle, along with camping gear, antique fly rods, and rentals of canoes and fishing videos.

A short drive from Waterbury is **Camel's Hump,** the state's fourth highest peak at 4,083 feet. (It's also the highest Vermont mountain without a ski area.) Once the site of a popular Victorian-era summit resort, the mountain still attracts hundreds of hikers who ascend the demanding, highly popular trail to the barren, windswept peak. It's not the place to get away from crowds on sunny summer weekends, but it's well worth the effort for the spectacular vistas and to observe the unique alpine terrain along the high ridge.

One popular round-trip loop hike is about 7.5 miles (plan on 6 hours or more of hiking time), and departs from the Couching Lion Farm 8 miles southwest of Waterbury on Camel's Hump Road. (You're best off asking locally for exact directions.) At the summit, seasonal rangers are on hand to answer questions and to admonish hikers to stay on the rocks to avoid trampling the rare and delicate alpine grasses, found in Vermont only here and on Mount Mansfield to the north.

ALPINE SKIING

✪ **Stowe Mountain Resort.** Stowe, VT 05672. ☎ **802/253-3000,** or 800/253-4754 for lodging. Web site: www.stowe.com/smr. Vertical drop: 2,360 ft. 1 gondola, 8 chairlifts (1 high-speed), 2 surface lifts. Skiable acreage: 487. Lift tickets $50 holiday, $48 nonholiday.

Stowe has been knocked from its perch as the shining ski capital of New England in recent years (Killington, Sunday River, and Sugarloaf have all poached on its territory). But this historic resort, first developed in the 1930s, still has lots of charm and plenty of great runs. Especially notable are its legendary "Front Four" trails (National,

The Story of Ben & Jerry

The doleful cows standing amid a bright green meadow on Ben & Jerry's ice-cream pints have become almost a symbol for Vermont. But Ben & Jerry's cows—actually, they're Vermont artist Woody Jackson's cows—have also become a symbol for friendly capitalism ("hippie capitalism," as some prefer).

The founding of the company has become a legend in business circles. Two friends from Long Island, N.Y., Ben Cohen and Jerry Greenfield, started up their company in Burlington in 1978 with $12,000 and a few mail-order lessons in ice-cream making. The pair experimented with the flavor samples they obtained free from salesmen, and sold their products out of an old gas station in town. Embracing the outlook that if it's no fun, why do it, they gave away ice cream at community events, staged free outdoor films in summer, and plowed profits back into the community. This approach, along with the exceptional quality of their product, built a successful corporation with sales topping $150 million.

While competition from other gourmet ice-cream makers and a widespread consumer desire to cut back fat consumption has made it tougher to have fun and turn a profit at the same time, Ben and Jerry are still at it, expanding their manufacturing plants outside New England and concocting new products like fruit sorbet. While their products are sold almost worldwide, the company's heart is still in New England. Look for their shops in and around many towns and villages, and watch for their trucks with the cows on the side.

The main factory in Waterbury, about 10 miles south of Stowe, is among the most popular tourist attractions in Vermont. The plant is located about a mile north of I-89 on Route 100, and the grounds have a festival marketplace feel to them, despite the fact that there's no festival and no marketplace. During peak summer season crowds mill about waiting for the 30-minute, $1 tours (the afternoon tours fill up quickly, so get there early if you want to avoid a long wait). Once you've got your ticket, browse the small ice-cream museum (learn the long, strange history of Cherry Garcia), buy a cone of your favorite flavor at the scoop shop, or lounge along the promenade, which is scattered with Adirondack chairs and picnic tables.

For kids, there's the "Stairway to Heaven," which leads to a playground, and a "Cow-Viewing Area," which is pretty much self-explanatory. The tours are informative and fun, and conclude with a sample of the day's featured product. For more information on the tours, call ☎ 802/244-8687.

Starr, Lift Line, and Goat), which have humbled more than a handful of skiers attempting to claw their way from intermediate to expert. The majority of the slopes are located on Mount Mansfield; other trails are on adjacent Spruce Peak, which has a vertical drop of 1,550 feet. Other facilities include eight restaurants and limited night skiing.

CROSS-COUNTRY SKIING

Stowe is an outstanding destination for cross-country skiers, offering no fewer than four groomed ski areas with a combined total of 93 miles of trails traversing everything from gentle valley floors to challenging mountain peaks.

The **Trapp Family Lodge Cross-Country Ski Center,** on Luce Hill Road, 2 miles from Mountain Road (☎ **800/826-7000** or 802/253-8511; Web site: **www.trappfamily.com**), was the nation's first cross-country ski center. It remains one of the most gloriously situated in the Northeast, set atop a ridge with views across the broad valley and into the folds of the mountains flanking Mount Mansfield. The center features 36 miles of groomed trails on its 2,200 acres of rolling forestland. Rates are $12 for a trail pass, $13 for equipment rental, and $15 for a group lesson. A package of all three is $30.

The **Edson Hill Manor Ski Touring Center** (☎ **800/621-0284** or 802/253-8954) has 33 miles of wooded trails just off Mountain Road. Also offering appealing ski touring are the **Stowe Mountain Resort Cross-Country Touring Center** (☎ **800/253-4754** or 802/253-7311), with 48 miles at the base of Mount Mansfield, and **Topnotch Resort** (☎ **800/451-8686** or 802/253-8585), with 15 miles of groomed trails in the forest flanking Mountain Road.

WHERE TO STAY

✪ Green Mountain Inn. Main St. (P.O. Box 60), Stowe, VT 05672. ☎ **800/253-7302** or 802/253-7301. Fax 802/253-5096. 65 rms. A/C TV TEL. Winter and summer $113–$250 double. Higher rates on holidays, lower during off-season. Ask about packages. 3-night minimum Christmas week. AE, DISC, MC, V.

This tasteful, historic structure is the only inn right in the village. It's a big place, with 65 rooms spread through three buildings, but it feels far smaller, with personal service, cozy rooms, and narrow hallways. Guest rooms are decorated with an early-19th-century motif that befits the 1833 vintage of the main inn. Primitive art, braided rugs, and stenciling on the wall in the guest rooms all blend nicely to create a mood that's pleasantly historic but not overzealously so. About half the rooms are carpeted, so if you want the buttery golden wood floors, be sure to ask when you book. Even the motel-style annex rooms, built some 25 years ago, have a pleasantly antiquarian flair. About a dozen rooms feature Jacuzzis and/or gas fireplaces. But the older rooms are heated with sometimes balky radiators, and a few of the guest rooms overlook noisy kitchen ventilators and a gas station; ask when you book.

Dining/Entertainment: The inn has two restaurants, the seasonal Main Street Dining Room and The Whip Bar and Grill. The Whip is a small, classy grill with loads of pubby charm and a menu featuring a good selection of salads, sandwiches, and burgers.

Services/Facilities: Heated outdoor pool (summer), fitness club, Jacuzzi, sauna, library, games (chess, badminton, volleyball, croquet), conference rooms, limited room service, in-room massage, afternoon tea and cookies, safe-deposit boxes.

Stowehof. 434 Edson Hill Rd. (P.O. Box 1139), Stowe, VT 05672. ☎ **800/932-7136** or 802/253-9722. Fax 802/253-7513. 50 rms plus 2 guest houses. A/C TV TEL. $70–$190 double. Rates include full breakfast. 4-night minimum during holidays; 2-night minimum on some weekends. AE, DC, DISC, MC, V.

Stowehof is well situated on a hillside and feels far removed from the hubbub of the valley floor. Its exterior architecture is mildly alarming in that aggressive neo-Tyrolean ski chalet kind of way. But inside, the place comes close to magic—it's pleasantly woodsy, folksy, and rustic, with heavy beams and pine floors, ticking clocks, and massive maple-tree trunks carved into architectural elements. Guests may feel a bit like characters in *The Hobbit*. The guest rooms are furnished simply, each decorated individually: some are bold and festive with sunflower patterns, others subdued and quiet. Four have wood-burning fireplaces, and all have good views.

Dining/Entertainment: Diners are served in a cozy, multilevel dining room, with entrees like Vermont venison stew, smoked pork chop, and the house specialty, Wiener schnitzel. Entrees range from $14.95 to $21.95.

Services/Facilities: All-weather tennis courts, outdoor pool, game room, nearby jogging track, nature trails, business center, conference rooms, nearby health club, sauna, sundeck, dry cleaning, laundry service, in-room massage, valet parking, safe. Winter brings sleigh rides and naturalist-led snowshoe hikes.

☀ **Topnotch.** 4000 Mountain Rd. (P.O. Box 1458), Stowe, VT 05672. ☎ **800/451-8686** or 802/253-8585. Fax 802/253-9263. 90 rms. A/C TV TEL. Ski season $188–$570 double; off-season $130–$496 double; summer $198–$600 double. Town-home accommodations $185–$695 depending on season and size. 6-night minimum during Christmas week. AE, DC, DISC, MC, V.

A boxy, uninteresting exterior hides a creatively designed interior at this upscale resort and spa. The main lobby is imaginatively conceived and furnished, with lots of stone and wood and an absolutely huge moose head hanging on the wall. There's even a telescope to watch skiers schuss down the slopes across the valley. The guest rooms, linked by long, motel-like hallways, are nicely appointed if basic; ask for one of the top-floor rooms with cathedral ceilings.

Dining/Entertainment: Well-prepared, healthy dishes are offered in the inn's stone-walled dining room. Entrees are priced $18 to $26.

Facilities: The spa facilities are the real draw here. Guests spend much of their time around the exceptionally appealing 60-foot indoor pool with bubbling fountain and 12-foot whirlpool. There's an outdoor pool for summer use as well. Fitness classes are offered throughout the day. Other activities include horseback riding, tennis (indoor courts provide for tennis year-round), and cross-country skiing on the inn's property.

☀ **Trapp Family Lodge.** Luce Hill Rd., Stowe, VT 05672. ☎ **800/826-7000** or 802/ 253-8511. Fax 802/253-5740. E-mail: info@trappfamily.com. Web site: www.trappfamily.com. 93 rms. TV TEL. Winter $138–$198 double (higher during school vacation); summer $118–$168 double. Breakfast $10 extra per person. Discounts available in spring and late fall. 3-night minimum stay during Christmas week, Presidents' Day week, and foliage season. AE, DC, DISC, MC, V. Depart Stowe village westward on Rte. 108; in 2 miles bear left at fork near the white church; continue up the hill following signs for the lodge.

The Trapp family, of *Sound of Music* fame, bought this sprawling farm high up in Stowe in 1942, just 4 years after fleeing the Nazi takeover of Austria. Maria and Baron von Trapp's family continue to run this Tyrolean-flavored lodge to great acclaim. The original lodge burned in 1980, and some longtime guests still grouse that its replacement lacks the character of the old place. But it's still a comfortable resort hotel, if designed more for efficiency than elegance. The guest rooms are a shade or two better than your standard hotel room, and most come with fine valley views and private balconies. Common areas with blond wood and comfortably upholstered chairs abound, and make for comfortable idling. Especially nice is the second-floor library with fireplace.

Dining/Entertainment: The restaurant offers wonderful views for the lucky few with tables along the window, and well-prepared continental fare for all. A good selection of vegetarian entrees is available. The informal Austrian Tea Room across the road from the main inn offers three kinds of wurst.

Services: Newspaper delivery, in-room massage, baby-sitting, children's program, currency exchange (Canadian), courtesy shuttle to mountain for skiing, guest safe.

Facilities: Fitness center, heated indoor pool, two outdoor pools (one adults only), sauna, extensive cross-country ski network (see above), game rooms, four clay tennis counts, gift shops.

WHERE TO DINE

The **Harvest Market,** 1031 Mountain Rd. (☎ **802/253-3800**), is the place for gourmet-to-go. The market offers basics like fruit and dairy products, but this isn't the place for the mundane. Browse the Vermont products and exotic imports (they've got eight different kinds of olives), then pick up some of the fresh-baked goods, like the pleasantly tart raspberry squares, to bring back to the ski lodge or take for a picnic along the bike path. If you're renting a condo, there's a great selection of gourmet meals to go—just reheat them in your room. The market also features a great selection of wine and beer.

Blue Moon Cafe. 35 School St. ☎ 802/253-7006. Reservations recommended, especially during ski season. Main courses $12.95–$16.95. AE, DISC, MC, V. Daily 6–9:30pm. NEW AMERICAN.

The delectable crusty bread on the table and Frank Sinatra crooning in the background offer up clues that this isn't your typical ski-shack restaurant. Located a short walk off Stowe's main drag in an old village home accented with wood barn beams and salmon-colored walls, the Blue Moon serves up the village's most reliably fine meals. The menu is always in play, changing every Friday. But count on at least one lamb, beef, and veggie dish, plus a couple of seafood offerings. Chef Jack Pickett has superb instincts for spicing, and creates inventive dishes like chicken with black beans and mango, or venison with a green tomato and chipotle sauce. This place gets my vote if you're looking for a low-key and rewarding meal by candlelight after a long day exploring the great outdoors.

Cliff House. Atop Mt. Mansfield (gondola access). ☎ 802/253-3665. Reservations required. Fixed-price dinner $39. AE, DC, DISC, MC, V. Open in winter for lunch Wed–Sun, and nights when night skiing is offered 5:30–9pm. Open irregularly evenings in summer, typically Thurs–Sun; call first. REGIONAL/AMERICAN.

The setting is a somewhat stark, modern ski lodge. But talk about views! Those are reason to hop the gondola to this high-altitude restaurant on the shoulders of Mount Mansfield. Plan to arrive early enough to stroll around on the deck outside the restaurant; in summer, you can even come up in the late afternoon for sunset atop Mansfield, then hike down to the Cliff House for diner. The restaurant offers a fixed-price dinner, with the price including appetizer, salad, entree, dessert, *and* the round-trip gondola ride. Entrees draw on regional products, and might include cedar-planked salmon with an herb crust, or a filet mignon with a red-wine sauce and caramelized shallots.

Miguel's Stowe-Away. Mountain Rd. ☎ 802/253-7574. Reservations recommended weekends and peak ski season. Main courses $9.50–$13.95. AE, DC, DISC, MC, V. Summer daily 5:30–10pm; other seasons daily 5–10pm. MEXICAN.

Located in an old dark red farmhouse midway between the village and the mountain, Miguel's packs in the locals who come for the tangiest Mexican and Tex-Mex food in the valley. Start off with a margarita or Vermont beer, then try out appetizers like the empanadas, or the exceptionally flavorful chili verde. Follow up with fajitas or one of the filling combo plates. (The snow crab enchiladas are tasty and unique.) Miguel's offers superb quality for the money, and the kitchen pays attention to the little things, like using only Hass avocados for its guacamole. Like the big national chains, Miguel's has grown popular enough to offer its own brand of chips, salsa, and other products, which turn up in specialty food shops throughout the Northeast. If you're heading south, Miguel's also operates a branch on the Sugarbush Access Road in Warren.

The Shed. Mountain Rd. ☎ 802/253-4364. Reservations recommended weekends and holidays. Lunch items $4.50–$7.95; main dinner courses $8.25–$15.95. AE, DC, DISC, MC, V. Daily 11:30am–midnight (only light fare served 10pm–midnight); Sun brunch 10am–2pm. PUB FARE.

When The Shed burned down in early 1994, the gnashing of teeth and the tearing of sackcloth could be heard throughout the valley. Since it first opened 3 decades ago, this friendly, informal place won converts by the sleigh-load with its solid pub food and feisty camaraderie. The good news is that the replacement structure has recaptured much of the original charm—especially the bar, with a barnlike interior that's already been worn to a nice patina. (The main dining room, alas, has the somewhat more sterile atmosphere of a chain restaurant.) The best news is that a new brewery was built along with the restaurant, and The Shed is cranking out some fine brews. Especially excellent is the dark Mountain Ale. The bar also serves up some fairly toxic West Indian rum drinks.

10 Burlington

Burlington is a vibrant college town that's continually, valiantly resisting the onset of middle age. It's the birthplace of hippies turned mega-corporation Ben & Jerry's. It elected a socialist mayor in 1981, Bernie Sanders, who's now Vermont's representative to the U.S. Congress. Burlington is also home to the eclectic rock band Phish, which has been anointed by some as the heirs to the Grateful Dead hippie music tradition. And just look at the signs for offices as you wander downtown—an uncommonly high number seem to have the word "polarity" in them.

It's no wonder that Burlington has become a magnet for those seeking alternatives to big-city life with its big-city problems. The city has a superb location overlooking Lake Champlain and beyond to the Adirondacks of northern New York. To the east, visible on your way out of town, the Green Mountains rise dramatically, with two of the highest points (Mt. Mansfield and Camel's Hump) soaring above the undulating ridge.

In this century, Burlington turned its back for a time on its spectacular waterfront. Urban redevelopment focused on parking garages and high-rises; the waterfront lay fallow, open to development by light industry. In recent years the city has sought to regain a toehold along the lake, acquiring and redeveloping parts for commercial and recreational use. It's been successful in some sections, less so in others.

In contrast, the downtown is thriving. The pedestrian mall (Church Street) works here as it has failed in so many other towns. As a result, the scale is skewed toward pedestrians in the heart of downtown. It's best to get out of your car as soon as feasible.

ESSENTIALS

GETTING THERE   Burlington is at the junction of I-89, Route 7, and Route 2.

Burlington International Airport, about 3 miles east of downtown, is served by **Continental Express** (☎ 800/732-6887), **United Airlines** (☎ 800/241-6522), **USAirways** (☎ 800/428-4322), and **Delta Connection** (☎ 800/345-3400).

Amtrak's *Vermonter* offers daily departures for Burlington from Washington, Baltimore, Philadelphia, New York, New Haven, and Springfield, Mass. Call ☎ **800/ 872-7245** for more information.

Vermont Transit Lines (☎ 802/864-6811), with a depot at 135 St. Paul St. facing City Hall Park, offers bus connections from Albany, Boston, Hartford, New York's JFK Airport, and other points in Vermont, Massachusetts, and New Hampshire.

VISITOR INFORMATION   The **Lake Champlain Regional Chamber of Commerce,** 60 Main St., Burlington, VT 05401 (☎ **802/863-3489**), maintains an information center in a handsome brick building on Main Street just up from the waterfront and a short walk from Church Street Market. The center is open weekdays from 8:30am to 5:30pm.

A seasonal **information booth** is also staffed summers on the Church Street Marketplace at the corner of Church and Bank streets. There's no phone. Information can also be requested via E-mail (**vermont@vermont.org**) or the Web (**www.vermont.org/chamber**).

Burlington has three free weeklies that keep residents and visitors up to date on local events and happenings. (To confuse matters somewhat, the *Free Press* is the one paper that costs money.) *Seven Days* carries topical and lifestyle articles along with listings. The *Vermont Times* emphasizes local politics. And *Vox,* a *Vermont Times* product, has an extensive cultural and nightlife calendar. All three are widely available at downtown stores and restaurants.

ORIENTATION Burlington is comprised of three distinct areas: the UVM campus atop the hill, the downtown area flanking the popular Church Street Marketplace, and the waterfront along Lake Champlain.

University of Vermont The University of Vermont was founded in 1791, funded by a state donation of 29,000 acres of forestland spread across 120 townships. In the 2 centuries since, the university has grown to accommodate 7,700 undergraduates and 1,200 graduate students, plus 300 medical students. The school is set on 400 acres atop a hill overlooking downtown and Lake Champlain to the west, and offers a glorious prospect of the Green Mountains to the east. The campus has more than 400 buildings, many of which were designed by the most noted architects of the day, including H. H. Richardson and McKim, Mead & White. (By the way, UVM stands for "Universitas Virdis Montis," which translates as University of the Green Mountains.)

UVM doesn't have a college neighborhood with bars and bookstores immediately adjacent to the campus, as is common at many universities. Downtown serves that function. The downtown and the campus are five blocks from one another, connected via aptly named College Street. A shuttle, which looks like an old-fashioned trolley, runs daily on College Street between the Community Boathouse on the waterfront and the campus. It's in operation year-round between 11am and 9pm, and it's free.

Church Street Marketplace The downtown centers around the Church Street Marketplace, a pedestrian mall that's alive with activity throughout the year. (See "Shopping," below.) Fanning from Church Street are a number of side streets containing an appealing amalgam of restaurants, shops, offices, and malls. This is the place to wander without purpose and watch the crowds; you can always find a cafe or ice-cream shop to rest your feet. While the shopping and grazing is good here, don't overlook the superb historic commercial architecture that graces much of downtown.

Waterfront The waterfront has benefited recently from a $6-million renovation centered around Union Station at the foot of Main Street. This includes some new buildings, including The Wing Building, an appealingly quirky structure of brushed steel and other offbeat materials, which blends in nicely with the more rustic parts of the waterfront. (A little too nicely, some of the tenants complain, noting a lack of foot traffic.) Next door is the new Cornerstone Building, with a restaurant and offices, which offers better views of the lake from its higher vantage. Nearby is the city's Community Boathouse, which is an exceptionally pleasant destination on a summer's day (see below).

Burlington

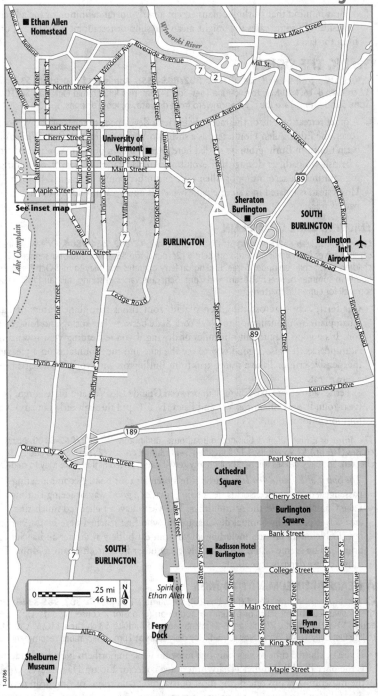

Ethan Allen
Homestead

Route 127 Beltline

Winooski River

East Allen Street

North Avenue

Park Street

N. Champlain St

North Street

Riverside Avenue

N. Winooski Ave.

N. Prospect Street

Mansfield Ave.

Mill St.

N. Union Street

Colchester Avenue

Grove Street

Pearl Street

Cherry Street

S. Winooski Avenue

University of
Vermont

University Pl.

College Street

Main Street

East Avenue

Battery Street

Church Street

Maple Street

See inset map

Lake Champlain

St. Paul St.

S. Union Street

S. Willard Street

S. Prospect Street

BURLINGTON

Howard Street

Sheraton
Burlington

SOUTH
BURLINGTON

Burlington
Int'l
Airport

Williston Road

Patchen Road

Hinesburg Road

Ledge Road

Pine Street

Shelburne Street

Spear Street

Dorset Street

Flynn Avenue

Kennedy Drive

Queen City Park Rd.

Swift Street

Lake Street

Cathedral
Square

Pearl Street

Cherry Street

Burlington
Square

Bank Street

Battery Street

Radisson Hotel
Burlington

College Street

SOUTH
BURLINGTON

Spirit of
Ethan Allen II

Ferry
Dock

S. Champlain Street

Pine Street

Main Street

Saint Paul Street

King Street

Maple Street

Flynn
Theatre

Church Street Market Place

Center St.

S. Winooski Avenue

0   .25 mi
    .46 km

N

Allen Road

Shelburne
Museum

1-0786

513

Bear in mind that Burlingtonians accept a fairly liberal definition of the adjective "lakeside." In some cases this might mean the shop or restaurant is 100 yards or so from the lake.

SEEING THE SIGHTS

Ethan Allen Homestead. Rte. 127. ☎ **802/865-4556.** Admission $3.50 adults, $3 seniors, $2 children 6–16. Mid-May to mid-June Tues–Sun 1–5pm; mid-June to mid-Oct Mon–Sat 10am–5pm, Sun 1–5pm. Take Rte. 127 northward from downtown; look for signs.

A quiet retreat on one of the most idyllic, least developed stretches of the Winooski River, the Ethan Allen Homestead is a shrine to Vermont's favorite son. While Allen wasn't born in Burlington, he settled here later in life on property confiscated from a British sympathizer during the Revolution. An orientation center offers an intriguing multimedia accounting of Allen's life and other points of regional history. The Homestead is located in a sizable park, which is open year-round. Admission to the park is free.

ENJOYING LAKE CHAMPLAIN

Lake Champlain Ferries. King St. Dock, Burlington. ☎ **802/864-9804.** One-way fare for car and driver from Burlington to Port Kent $12; round-trip $5.50 for adult passengers; $1.50 children 6–12; children under 6 free. Burlington ferry operates mid-May to mid-Oct. Departures hourly in summer between 7:45am and 7pm. Schedule varies in spring, fall, and foliage season; call for current departures.

Car ferries chug across the often placid, sometimes turbulent waters of Lake Champlain from Burlington to New York State between late spring and foliage season. It's a good way to cut out miles of driving if you're heading west toward the Adirondacks. It's also a good way to see the lake and the mountains on a pleasant, inexpensive cruise. Take a round-trip from Burlington with your binoculars; bring a bite to eat.

Ferries also cross Lake Champlain between Grande Isle, Vt., and Plattsburgh, N.Y. (year-round), and Charlotte, Vt., and Essex, N.Y. (April through early January). Call for more information.

The Spirit of Ethan Allen II. Burlington Boathouse, Burlington. ☎ **802/862-8300.** Narrated cruises (1¹/₂ hr.) $7.95 adults, $3.95 children 3–11. Sunset cruises (2¹/₂ hr.) $8.95 adults, $4.95 children. Specialty cruises (dinner, brunch, mystery theater) priced higher. Late May to mid-Oct.

The Spirit of Ethan Allen II is Burlington's premier tour boat. Accommodating 500 passengers on three decks, this sleek ship provides a good way of seeing Burlington, Lake Champlain, and the Adirondacks. The views haven't changed much since the area was explored by Samuel de Champlain, who first reached here in 1609. Food is available on all cruises, including all-you-can-eat buffets at dinner and at Sunday brunch. The scenic cruise departs daily every other hour from 10am to 4pm. The sunset cruise departs at 6:30pm.

A NEARBY MUSEUM NOT TO MISS

✪ **Shelburne Museum.** Rte. 7 (P.O. Box 10), Shelburne, VT 05482. ☎ **802/985-3346.** Web site: www.shelburnemuseum.org. Summer admission (good for 2 consecutive days), $17.50 adults, $10.50 students, $7 children 6–14; winter tours, $7 adults, $3 children. MC, V. Late May to late Oct daily 10am–5pm; Nov to mid-May daily tours at 1pm (reservations recommended).

If you've allotted time to visit only one museum while in northern New England, this is the one. Established in 1947 by Americana collector Electra Havermeyer Webb, the museum contains one of the most outstanding collections of American decorative, folk, and fine art. The museum is spread over 45 beautiful acres 7 miles south of Burlington; the collections occupy some 37 buildings. The more mundane exhibits include quilts, early tools, decoys, and weather vanes. But the museum also collects and displays *whole buildings* from around New England and New York State. These include an 1890 railroad station, a lighthouse, a stagecoach inn, an Adirondack lodge, and a round barn from Vermont. There's even a 220-foot steamship, eerily land-locked on the museum's grounds. Spend a few hours here and you're bound to come away with a richer understanding of regional culture. The grounds also contain a museum shop, cafeteria, and picnic area.

In the winter, much of the museum is closed but tours of selected collections are offered daily at 1pm. Dress warmly.

SHOPPING

The **Church Street Marketplace** is one of the more notable success stories of down-town development. Situated along four blocks between Main Street and Pearl Street, extending southward from the austerely elegant 1816 Congregational Church, the marketplace buzzes with the sort of downtown energy that makes urban planners everywhere envious. While decidedly trendy (there are Banana Republic and The Nature Company stores), the marketplace still makes room for a used-book store and a $10 astrological reading joint. In summer, leave time to be entertained by buskers, sidewalk vendors, and knots of young folks just hanging out. In winter, there's the warm comfort of the **Burlington Square Mall,** an adjacent enclosed mall that's doing an admirable job of beating the suburbs at their own game.

North of Burlington in the riverside town of Winooski is the **Champlain Mill** (☎ 802/655-9477), an attractive 1910 woolen mill that was converted to shops, restaurants, and offices in 1981. The mill hosts some three dozen retailers selling national brands like **Kenneth Cole** and **Patagonia,** along with vendors of uniquely Vermont products, like **Dakin Farms** with its selection of locally smoked meats and cheeses.

OUTDOOR PURSUITS

On the downtown waterfront, look for the **Burlington Community Boathouse** (☎ 802/865-3377), a modern structure built with Victorian flair. A lot of summer action takes place at this city-owned structure and along the 900-foot boardwalk. You can rent a sailboat or rowboat, sign up for kayak or sculling lessons, or just wander around and enjoy the sunset.

Burlington's commitment to taking back its lake is best seen in the 9-mile **Burlington Bike Path,** which runs picturesquely along the shores of Lake Champlain to the mouth of the Winooski River. A superb way to spend a sunny afternoon, the paved bike route over a former rail bed passes through shady parklands and Burlington's backyards. Along the banks of the Winooski, you can admire the re-mains of an old bridge and scout around for marble chips.

Bike rentals are available downtown at the **Skirack,** 85 Main St. (☎ 802/658-3313), at $14 for 4 hours (enough time to do the whole trail), and up to $22 for a whole day. Skirack also rents in-line skates ($8 for 4 hours), which are also com-monly used on the bike path. **Earl's Cyclery,** 135 Main St. (☎ 802/863-3832), and **North Star Cyclery,** 100 Main St. (☎ 802/863-3832), also rent bicycles.

WHERE TO STAY

Burlington's motels are located along the two major access roads to the south and east. On Route 7 south of town, try the **Super 8 Motel** (☎ 800/800-8000 or 802/862-6421), the **Bel-Aire Motel** (☎ 802/863-3116), or the **Town & Country Motel** (☎ 802/862-5786). Clustered along Route 2 near I-89 and the airport are the **Holiday Inn** (☎ 802/863-6363), **EconoLodge** (☎ 800/371-1125 or 802/863-1125), and the clean, budget-priced **Swiss Host Motel and Village** (☎ 800/326-5734 or 802/862-5734).

✪ **The Inn at Shelburne Farms.** Harbor Rd., Shelburne, VT 05482. ☎ **802/985-8498.** 24 rms (17 with private bath). TEL. Spring $90–$225 double; summer $95–$235 double; fall $100–$265 double. Closed mid-Oct to mid-May. AE, DC, MC, V.

The numbers behind this exceptional turn-of-the-century mansion on the shores of Lake Champlain tell the story: 60 rooms, 10 chimneys, 1,000 acres of land. Built in 1899 by William Seward and Lila Vanderbilt Webb, this sprawling Edwardian "farmhouse" is the place to fantasize about the lifestyles of the *truly* rich and famous. From the first glimpse of the mansion as you come up the winding drive, you'll realize you've left the grim world behind. That's by design. Noted landscape architect Frederick Law Olmsted had a hand in shaping the grounds, and noted forester Gifford Pinchot helped with the planting.

The 24 guest rooms are splendidly appointed. Meals aren't included in the rates, but a restaurant on the property offers outstanding breakfasts and dinners. If you're traveling on a tight budget, do this: Camp for a few nights, stay in a cheap motel—whatever it takes to free up a few dollars. Then pool your savings and book the least expensive room with the shared bath just to gain access to the mansion and the grounds. You'll feel like royalty for a day.

Radisson Hotel Burlington. 60 Battery St., Burlington, VT 05401.☎ **800/333-3333** or 802/658-6500. Fax 802/658-4659. 255 rms. A/C TV TEL. Winter $105–$129 double; summer $144–$174 double. AE, DISC, MC, V.

The nine-story Radisson offers the most extraordinary views and the best location in the city. As might be expected, it also offers all the amenities of an upscale national hotel chain, including an indoor pool, fitness room, covered parking, and two dining areas. Though the hotel was built in 1976, renovations of the public areas in 1993 and the guest rooms in 1995 have kept the weariness at bay.

The hotel charges about $10 more for a lakeside room, and it's worth it. The views of the lake and the Adirondacks are spectacular; request a room ending with a "43"— these southwest corner rooms are bright and offer superb panoramas. Families with kids should angle for one of the five cabana rooms, which open up to the pool area.

Dining/Entertainment: If you end up with a city-view room, at least stop by the tiered bar and dining room, Seasons on the Lake, to savor the lake and mountain vistas.

Services/Facilities: Concierge, dry cleaning, laundry service, newspaper delivery, express checkout, courtesy car to airport, safe-deposit boxes, indoor pool, fitness room, Jacuzzi, conference rooms, gift shop.

Willard Street Inn. 349 S. Willard St. (2 blocks south of Main St.), Burlington, VT 05401. ☎ **800/577-8712** or 802/651-8710. Fax 802/651-8714. 15 rms (8 share 3 baths; 1 with private hall bath). TV TEL. $75–$200 double. Rates include continental breakfast. AE, DISC, MC, V.

This impressive inn, which opened in the fall of 1996, is a welcome addition to the Burlington lodging pool, which until now had few alternatives to big, modern hotels and strip-mall motels. Located in a fine Queen Anne–style brick mansion near the university, the Willard Street Inn has soaring first-floor ceilings, cherry woodwork, and a beautiful window-filled breakfast room with a bold black-and-white tile floor. The home was originally built in 1881 by a bank president, and served a stint as a retirement home before its conversion to an inn.

As is common in many older inns, the rooms are eclectic and about half share hall baths, so make inquiries when you book. Rooms in the former servants wing are more cozy than those in the core of the house, and the third-floor rooms are slightly less elegant. (Note also that the top-floor rooms are equipped with ceiling fans, but no rooms have air-conditioning.) Among the best rooms are no. 12, which boasts a small sitting area and the best views of the lake, and no. 4, which is spacious, has a sizable private bath, and also features lake views. Don't leave without asking about the curious history of "Martha," the resident ghost.

WHERE TO DINE

Al's. 1251 Williston Rd. (Rte. 2, just east of I-89), S. Burlington. ☎ **802/862-9203.** Sandwiches 75¢–$3.55. No credit cards. Mon–Wed 10:30am–11pm, Thurs–Sat 10:30am–midnight, Sun 11am–10pm. BURGER JOINT.

Two words: french fries.

Daily Planet. 15 Center St. ☎ **802/862-9647.** Reservations recommended for parties of 4 or more. Lunch items $4.95–$6.50; main dinner courses $5.95–$18.50 (mostly $12–$14). AE, DC, DISC, MC, V. Mon–Fri 11:30am–3pm; Sun–Thurs 5–9:30pm, Fri–Sat 5–11pm. Sept–May Sat–Sun brunch 11am–3pm. ECLECTIC.

This popular spot is usually brimming with college students and downtown workers on evenings and weekends. But it's worth putting up with the mild mayhem for some of the more uncommonly creative food in town. The restaurant consists of three informal, comfortable dining rooms, including a solarium (pleasant during a winter brunch) and an adjacent bar, which has a loud, smoky saloon atmosphere with a stamped-tin ceiling and a judicious use of neon.

The menu is eclectic, and the dishes better than the usual pub fare you might expect at a spot like this. For lighter appetites, the selection ranges from burgers to muffaletta. Heartier eaters should consider the grilled flank steak, Moroccan vegetable sauté, and Yucatán ravioli made with ancho chili pasta and filled with spicy black beans.

✪ **Five Spice.** 175 Church St. ☎ **802/864-4045.** Reservations recommended on weekends and in summer. Lunch items $5.25–$7.95; main dinner courses $7.75–$14.95. AE, CB, DC, MC, V. Sun–Thurs 11:30am–10pm, Fri–Sat 11:30am–11pm. PAN-ASIAN.

Five Spice is the best of Burlington's bumper crop of Asian restaurants. Located upstairs and down in an intimate setting with rough wood floors and aquamarine wainscoting, Five Spice is a popular draw among college students and professors. But customers pour in for the exquisite food, not for the scene. The cuisine is multi-Asian, drawing on the best of Thailand, Vietnam, China, and beyond. Try the excellent hot and sour soup. Then gear up for Indonesian beef or the superior kung pao chicken. The dish with the best name on the menu—Evil Jungle Prince with Chicken—is made with a light sauce featuring a winning combination of coconut milk, garlic, and lemongrass. If you're looking to save money, come for lunch rather than dinner. The menu's the same but the prices are about half the dinner menu.

At press time, the restaurant was weighing a move to larger quarters nearby; call first to confirm its location.

Mona's. 3 Main St. (in the Cornerstone Building). ☎ **802/658-6662.** Reservations recommended. Lunch items $5.25–$7.95; main dinner courses $12.95–$17.95 (mostly $10–$14). AE, CB, DC, MC, V. Mon–Thurs 11:30am–10pm, Fri–Sat 11:30am–11pm, Sun 10am–9pm. Valet parking on weekends. CASUAL AMERICAN.

This elegant but relaxed restaurant overlooking the waterfront is sleeker and more modern than the average Burlington bistro, and serves up meals to match. Located next to the old train station at the foot of Main Street, Mona's is an up-tempo place rich with copper tones throughout. The first-floor ceiling in the first-floor jazz bar (you can order from a less pricey bistro menu here) is made of copper, and seems to emit a lurid, unearthly glow at sunset. For the best views of Lake Champlain and the Adirondacks, head to the upstairs dining room. In good weather, angle for a table on the 65-seat deck.

Since opening in 1995, Mona's has revised its menu and curbed some of its inventiveness, but the bustling open kitchen still produces some surprises with its bold use of big spices. The sea meets the Southwest with both the grilled shrimp (basted with a hot lime habenero paste) and chipotle shrimp; meat lovers will enjoy the sirloin or prime rib. Sundays (until 3pm) there's a lavish buffet brunch ($12.95), with selections ranging from the usual suspects (waffles and bagels) to vegetable tarts and marinated flank steak.

BURLINGTON AFTER DARK

There's always something going on in the evening, although it might take a little snooping to find it. Burlington—home to the hippie rock group Phish—has a thriving local music scene. The city government, recognizing a potential economic boon when it sees one, has worked to incubate this scene. Check the free local weeklies for information on festivals and concerts during your visit, and to find out who's playing at the clubs.

The most popular clubs are located near the juncture of Main and College streets. At 188 Main St., **Nectar's** (☎ 802/658-4771), half of which is a funky cafeteria-style restaurant, features live bands 7 days a week and no cover charge. On weekends it's packed with UVM students and abuzz with a fairly high level of hormonal energy. Look for the revolving neon sign.

One flight above Nectar's is **Club Metronome** (☎ 802/865-4563), a loud and loose nightspot that features a wide array of acts with a heavy dose of world beat. This is a no-frills place with tomato-red walls and disco mirror ball where you can dance or shoot a game of pool (or do both at once, as seems popular). The cover is generally around $5, although national touring acts might run $15 or so. This is a good spot to hear some of the local talent pool, which runs quite deep.

Around the corner at 165 Church St. is **Club Toast** (☎ 802/660-2088), which benefited from a full makeover in 1996, making it a bit more open and cheery than it had been. National, regional, and local bands all pass through, with performers like Marshall Crenshaw and Groove Collective alternating with up and coming Burlington garage bands. Cover charges range from $3 to $15. For an upcoming schedule, call or visit their Web site at **members.aol.com/clubtoast**.

Other nighttime options include the **Comedy Zone** (☎ 802/658-6500) at the Radisson Hotel, and **CB's Dance Club** (☎ 802/878-5522) in Essex, which features country dancing most nights. Call for the evening lineup and directions.

For gay nightlife, head to **135 Pearl** (☎ 802/863-2343), Burlington's leading gay club, located naturally enough at 135 Pearl St. Get a bite to eat, dance, or listen to live music Wednesday through Saturday. Open from noon until 2am, it's a friendly place that attracts a diverse clientele.

11 The Northeast Kingdom

Vermont's Northeast Kingdom is one of northern New England's more spectacularly remote regions. Consisting of Orleans, Essex, and Caledonia counties, the region was given its memorable name in 1949 by Sen. George Aiken, who understood the area's allure at a time when few others paid it much heed.

Contrasts with southern Vermont aren't hard to find. Rather than pinched, narrow valleys, the Kingdom's landscape is far more open and spacious, with rolling meadows ending abruptly at the hard edge of dense boreal forests. The leafy woodlands of the south give way to spiky forests of spruce and fir. And rather than Saabs and Volvos, you'll see pickup trucks dominating the roads, and plenty of them. Accommodations and services for tourists aren't as plentiful or easy to find here as in the southern reaches of the state, but some superb inns are tucked among the hills and in the forests.

This section includes a loose, slightly convoluted driving tour of the Northeast Kingdom, along with some suggestions for outdoor recreation. If your time is limited, make sure you at least stop in St. Johnsbury, which has two of my favorite attractions in the state—the Fairbanks Museum and St. Johnsbury Athenaeum.

Visitor information is available from the **Northeast Kingdom Chamber of Commerce** in St. Johnsbury (☎ **800/639-6379** or 802/748-3678). Other helpful **chambers of commerce** in the region include Barton (☎ **802/525-3242**), Lake Willoughby (☎ **802/525-4496**), Hardwick (☎ **802/472-5906**), Island Pond (☎ **802/723-4316**), Lyndon (☎ **802/626-9696**), and Newport (☎ **802/ 334-7782**).

TOURING THE NORTHEAST KINGDOM

Your first stop should be **Hardwick,** a small town with rough edges set along the Lamoille River. It has an attractive, compact commercial main street, some quirky shops, and a couple of informal restaurants.

From here, head north on Route 14 a little over 7 miles to the turnoff toward Craftsbury and **Craftsbury Common.** An uncommonly graceful village, Craftsbury Common is home to a small academy and a large number of historic homes and buildings spread along a sizable green and the village's broad main street. The town occupies a wide upland ridge and offers sweeping views to the east and west. Be sure to stop by the old cemetery on the south end of town, where you can wander among the historic tombstones of pioneers, which date back to the 1700s. Craftsbury is an excellent destination for mountain biking and cross-country skiing, and is home to the region's finest inn (see below).

From Craftsbury, continue north and reconnect to Route 14. You'll wind through the towns of Albany and Irasburg as you head north. At the village of Coventry, veer north on Route 5 to the lakeside town of **Newport.** This commercial outpost (pop. 4,400) is set on the southern shores of **Lake Memphremagog,** a stunning 27-mile-long lake that's just 2 miles wide at its broadest point, and the bulk of which is located in Canada.

Newport, improbably enough, has a small outlet zone on Main Street. Look for discounted outdoor gear from **Bogner** (☎ 802/334-0135), **Louis Garneau** (☎ 802/ 334-5885), and **Great Outdoors** (☎ 802/334-2831).

Newport's only lakeside restaurant is **The East Side,** located at 25 Lake Rd. (☎ 802/ 334-2340). It's a good spot for lunch or a refreshing beverage while admiring the hill-flanked azure waters of Lake Memphremagog.

From Newport, continue north on Route 5, crossing under I-91, for about 7 miles to the town of **Derby Line** (pop. 2,000). This border outpost has a handful of restaurants and antique shops; you can park and walk across the bridge to poke around the Canadian town of Rock Island without much hassle. (The weaker Canadian dollar will likely yield a cheap lunch if you've held out this long.)

Maple Syrup & How It Gets That Way

Maple syrup is at once simple and extravagant: simple because it's made from the purest ingredients available, extravagant because it's an expensive luxury.

Two elemental ingredients combine to create maple syrup: sugar maple sap and fire. Sugaring season slips in between northern New England's long winter and short spring; it usually lasts around 4 or 5 weeks, typically beginning in early to mid-March. When warm and sunny days alternate with freezing nights, the sap in the maple trees begins to run from roots to the branches overhead. Sugarers drill shallow holes into the trees and insert small taps. Buckets (or plastic tubing) are hung from the taps to collect the sap that drips out bit by bit.

The collected sap is then boiled off. The equipment for this ranges from a simple backyard fire pit cobbled together of concrete blocks, to elaborate sugarhouses with oil or propane burners. It requires between 32 and 40 gallons of sap to make 1 gallon of syrup, and that means a fair amount of boiling. The real cost of syrup isn't the sap; it's in the fuel to boil it down.

Vermont is the nation's capital of maple-syrup production, producing some 550,000 gallons a year, with a value of about $12 million. The fancier inns and restaurants all serve native maple syrup with breakfast. Other breakfast places will charge $1 or so for real syrup rather than the flavored corn syrup that's so prevalent elsewhere. (Sometimes you have to ask if the real stuff is available.)

You can pick up the real thing in almost any grocery store in the state, but I swear it tastes better if you buy it right from the farm. Look for handmade signs touting syrup, posted at the end of driveways around the region throughout the year. Drive on up and knock on the door.

A number of sugarers invite visitors to inspect the process and sample some of the fresh syrup in the early spring. Ask for the brochure *Maple Sugarhouses Open to Visitors,* available at information centers, from the **Vermont Travel Division,** 134 State St., Montpelier, VT 05602, or from the agriculture department at ☎ **802/ 828-2416.**

Back in Derby Line, look for the **Haskell Free Library and Opera House,** at the corner of Caswell Avenue and Church Street (☎ **802/873-3022**). This handsome neoclassical building contains a public library on the first floor, and an elegant opera house on the second that's modeled after the old Boston Opera House. The theater opened in 1904 with advertisements promoting a minstrel show featuring "new songs, new jokes, and beautiful electric effects." It's a beautiful theater, with a scene of Venice painted on the drop curtain and carved cherubim adorning the balcony.

What's most curious about the structure, however, is that it lies half in Canada and half in the United States. (The Haskell family donated the building jointly to the towns of Derby Line and Rock Island.) A thick black line runs beneath the seats of the opera house, indicating who's in the United States and who's in Canada. Because the stage is set entirely in Canada, apocryphal stories abound from the early days of frustrated U.S. officers watching fugitives perform on stage. More recently, the theater has been used for the occasional extradition hearing.

From Derby Line, retrace your path south on Route 5 to Derby Center and the juncture of Route 5A. Continue south on Route 5A to the town of Westmore on the shores of **Lake Willoughby.** This glacier-carved lake is best viewed from the north,

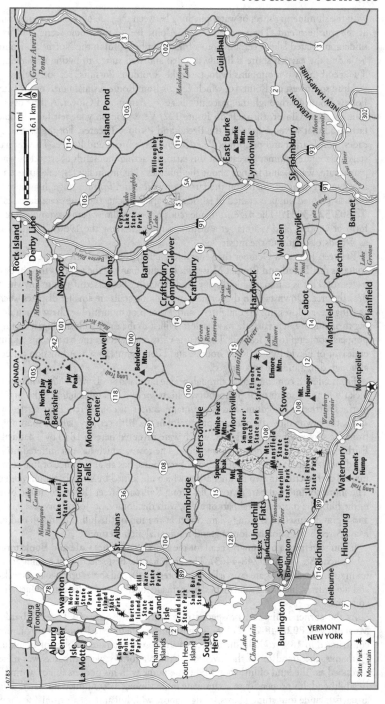

with the shimmering sheet of water pinching between the base of two low mountains at the southern end. There's a distinctive Alpine feel to the whole scene, and this underappreciated lake is certainly one of the most beautiful in the Northeast. Route 5A along the eastern shore is lightly traveled and well suited to biking or walking. To ascend the two mountains by foot, see the "Outdoor Pursuits" section, below.

Head southwest on Route 16, which departs from Route 5A just north of the lake. Follow Route 16 through the peaceful villages of Barton and Glover. A little over a mile south of Glover, turn left on Route 122. Very soon on your left look for the farmstead that serves as home to the **Bread and Puppet Theater.** For the past 3 decades, Polish artist and performer Peter Schumann's Bread and Puppet Theater has staged elaborate summer pageants at this farm, attracting thousands of attendees who participate, watch, and lounge about the hillsides. The multiday fest takes place in a grown-over former quarry on the farm's property, and features huge, lugubrious, brightly painted puppets crafted of fabric and papier-mâché. (For the exact dates, call ☎ 802/525-3031.) The pageant theme tends to be rebellion-against-tyranny of one form or another, and visitors get a distinct sense of reliving the 1960s. Think of it as Woodstock without the music.

Between June and October the venerable, slightly tottering barn on the property contains the **Bread and Puppet Museum,** housing many of the puppets used in past pageants. This is a remarkable display, and shouldn't be missed if you're anywhere near the area. Downstairs in the former cow-milking stalls are smaller displays, such as King Lear addressing his daughters, and a group of mournful washerwomen doing their laundry. Upstairs, the vast hayloft is filled to the eaves with soaring, haunting puppets, some up to 20 feet tall. The style is witty and eclectic; the barn seems a joint endeavor of David Lynch, Red Grooms, and Hieronymus Bosch. Admission is free, although donations are encouraged.

From Glover, continue south through serene farmlands to Lyndonville, where you pick up Route 5 south to **St. Johnsbury.** This town of 7,600 inhabitants is the largest in the Northeast Kingdom, and is the major center of commerce. First settled in 1786, the town enjoyed a buoyant prosperity in the 19th century, largely stemming from the success of platform scales, which were invented here in 1830 by Thaddeus Fairbanks. They're still manufactured here. The town, which has not suffered from the depredations of tourist boutiques and brew pubs, has an abundance of fine commercial architecture in two distinct areas, which are joined by steep Eastern Avenue. The more commercial part of town lies along Railroad Street (Route 5) at the base of the hill. The more ethereal part of town, with the library, St. Johnsbury Academy, and a grand museum, is along Main Street at the top of the hill. The north end of Main Street is also notable for its grand residential architecture.

If you're getting a bit hungry, head for the **Northern Lights Café and Bookstore,** 79 Railroad St. (☎ 802/748-4463). This shop has the best selection of reading matter in town (local works are especially well represented), and serves up delicious snacks and light meals, including sandwiches, homemade muffins, and a delectable blueberry coffee cake.

At the corner Main and Prospect streets in St. Johnsbury, ✪ **The Fairbanks Museum** (☎ 802/748-2372) is an imposing Romanesque red sandstone structure constructed in 1889 to hold the collections of obsessive amateur collector Franklin Fairbanks, the grandson of the inventor of the platform scale. Fairbanks was once described as "the kind of little boy who came home with his pockets full of worms." In adulthood, his propensity to accumulate indiscriminately continued unabated. His artifacts include four stuffed bears, a huge moose with full antlers, art from Asia, and 4,500 stuffed native and exotic birds. And that's just the tip of it.

The soaring, barrel-vaulted main hall, reminiscent of an old-fashioned railway depot, embodies Victorian grandeur. Among the assorted clutter, look for the unique mosaics by John Hampson. Hampson crafted scenes of American history—such as Washington bidding his troops farewell—entirely of mounted insects. In the Washington scene, for instance, iridescent green beetles form the epaulets, and the regal great coat is comprised of hundreds of purple moth wings. Words fail me here; you must see these works of art, which alone are worth the price of admission.

There's also a planetarium and weather station. The museum is open Monday to Saturday from 10am to 4pm, and Sunday from 1 to 5pm (open daily until 6pm in July and August). Admission is $4 for adults, $3 for seniors, $2.50 for children 5 to 17, and $10 per family (maximum of three adults, unlimited children).

Also in town, at 30 Main St., **The St. Johnsbury Athenaeum** (☎ 802/748-8291) is in an Edward Hopper–esque brick building with a truncated mansard tower and prominent keystones over the windows. This is the town's public library, but it also houses an extraordinary art gallery dating to 1873. It claims to be the oldest, unadulterated art gallery in the nation, and I see no reason to dispute that claim. Your first view of the gallery is spectacular: After winding through the cozy library stacks with its ticking regulator clock, you round a corner and find yourself gazing across Yosemite National Park. This luminous 10-by-15-foot oil was created by noted Hudson River School painter Albert Bierstadt, and the gallery was built specifically to accommodate this work. (Not everyone was happy about the work moving here. "Now 'The Domes' is doomed to the seclusion of a Vermont town, where it will astonish the natives," groused the *Boston Globe* at the time.) The natural light flooding in from the skylight above nicely enhances the painting. Some 100 other works fill the walls. Most are painted reproductions of other paintings (a common teaching tool in the 19th century), but look for originals by other Hudson River School painters including Asher B. Durand, Thomas Moran, and Jasper Cropsey.

The Athenaeum is open Monday and Wednesday from 10am to 8pm, Tuesday through Friday from 10am to 5:30pm, and Saturday from 9:30am to 4pm. Admission is free, but donations are encouraged.

OUTDOOR PURSUITS IN THE NORTHEAST KINGDOM
HIKING

At the southern tip of Lake Willoughby, two rounded peaks rise above the lake's waters. These are the biblically named Mount Hor and Mount Pisgah, both of which lie within **Willoughby State Forest.** Both summits are accessible via footpaths that are somewhat strenuous but yield excellent views.

For **Mount Pisgah** (elev. 2,751 ft.), look for parking on the west side of Route 5A about 5.7 miles south of the junction with Route 16. The trail departs from across the road and runs 1.7 miles to the summit.

To hike **Mount Hor** (elev. 2,648 ft.), drive 1.8 miles down the gravel road on the right side of the above-mentioned parking lot, veering right at the fork. Park at the small parking lot, and continue on foot past the parking lot a short distance until you spot the start of the trail. Follow the trail signs to the summit, a round-trip of about 3.5 miles.

MOUNTAIN BIKING

The Craftsbury ridge offers several excellent variations for bikers in search of easy terrain. Most of the biking is on hard-packed dirt roads through sparsely populated countryside. The views are sensational, and the sense of being well out in the country very strong. The **Craftsbury Center at Craftsbury Common** (☎ 800/729-7751 or 802/586-7767) rents mountain bikes and is an excellent source for maps and local information about area roads. Bike rentals are $12 per day.

At **Jay Peak** (☎ 802/988-2611), mountain bikers can take their bikes via tram to the summit of the 3,968-foot mountain, then explore some 20 miles of trail while gravity does most of the heavy lifting.

CROSS-COUNTRY SKIING

The same folks who offer mountain biking at the Craftsbury Center also maintain 61 miles of groomed cross-country trails through the gentle hills surrounding Craftsbury. The trails, maintained by ✪ **Craftsbury Nordic** (☎ 800/729-7751 or 802/586-7767), are pleasant, old-fashioned trails that emphasize pleasing landscapes rather than fast action. Trail passes are $11 for adults, $5 for juniors 6 to 12, and $7 for seniors (discounts available midweek.) **Highland Lodge** (☎ 802/533-2647) on Caspian Lake offers 36 miles of trails (about 10 miles groomed) through rolling woodlands and fields. You might also give snowshoeing a try. Craftsbury Nordic rents snowshoes for $8 per day, and a snowshoe trail pass costs $5.

ALPINE SKIING

Jay Peak. Rte. 242, Jay, VT 05859. ☎ **802/988-2611** or 800/451-4449 for lodging. E-mail: skijayvt@aol.com. Vertical drop: 2,153 ft. 1 tram, 4 chairlifts, 2 surface lifts. Skiable acreage: 300-plus. Lift tickets $39.

Located just south of the Canadian border, Jay Peak is Vermont's best ski mountain for those who get away just to ski and prefer to avoid all the modern-day glitter and trappings that seem to clutter ski resorts elsewhere. While some new condo development has been taking place at the base of the mountain, the mountain still has the feeling of a remote, isolated destination, accessible by a winding road through unbroken woodlands.

More than half of Jay's 62 trails are for intermediate skiers. But experts haven't been left behind. Jay has developed extensive glade skiing since 1994, taking excellent advantage of its sizable natural snowfall, which averages more than 300 inches annually (more than any other New England ski area). Jay has also reopened its extreme chutes, which appeal to advanced skiers in search of a challenge. Jay Peak's ski school emphasizes glade skiing, making it a fitting place to learn how to navigate these exciting, challenging trails that have cropped up at most New England ski areas in recent years.

WHERE TO STAY

Highland Lodge. Caspian Lake, Greensboro, VT 05841. ☎ **802/533-2647.** 11 rms plus 11 cottages (2 rms with tub only). $190–$230 double. Rates include breakfast and dinner. DISC, MC, V. Closed mid-Mar to May and mid-Oct to Christmas. From Hardwick, drive on Rte. 15 east 2 miles to Rte. 16; drive north 2 more miles to E. Hardwick. Head west and follow signs to the inn.

The Highland Lodge was built in the mid-19th century, and has been accommodating guests since 1926. It's a great destination for a relaxing, old-fashioned holiday. Located just across the road from lovely Caspian Lake, this lodge has 11 rooms furnished in a comfortable country style. A wide porch runs the length of the inn, and white Adirondack chairs are well placed for shady reading or dozing. The main activities here tend to be relaxing rather than hectic: There's swimming and boating in the lake in summer, along with tennis on clay courts; in winter, the lodge maintains its own cross-country ski area with 30 miles of groomed trail. Behind the lodge is a nature preserve, which makes for quiet exploration. Bored? There's also badminton, croquet, and horseshoes.

✪ **Inn on the Common.** Craftsbury Common, VT 05827. ☎ **800/521-2233** or 802/586-9619. Fax 802/586-2249. 16 rms (3 with shower only). $220–$270 double; foliage season $250–$270 double. Rates include breakfast and dinner ($30 less for breakfast only). AE, MC, V.

This exceedingly handsome complex of three Federal-style buildings anchors the charming ridge-top village of Craftsbury Common. Innkeepers Penny and Michael Schmitt have run this place with panache since 1973, and have created a beautiful, comfortable inn that offers just the right measures of history and luxury. Guests can unwind in the nicely appointed common rooms, or stroll the 15 acres of beautifully landscaped grounds.

Dining/Entertainment: Dinner starts with cocktails at 6pm, then guests are seated amid elegant Federal-era surroundings at 7:30pm. The menu changes nightly, but includes well-prepared dishes like venison ravioli and jumbo shrimp stuffed with scallops and served with a sherry sauce.

Facilities: Outdoor pool, clay tennis court, croquet, 250-video library. In winter, there's cross-country skiing and snowshoeing.

12

New Hampshire

by Wayne Curtis

There are two ways to get old-time New Hampshirites riled up and spitting vinegar. First, tell them you think that Vermont is a truly great state. Then tell them you think it's weird that they don't have a state income tax or sales tax.

At its most basic, New Hampshire defines itself by what it isn't—and that, more often than not, is Vermont, a state regarded by local old-timers as one of the few communist republics still remaining. No, New Hampshire is not Vermont, and they'll thank you not to confuse the two.

Keep in mind that New Hampshire's state symbol is the Old Man of the Mountains, which is an actual site you can visit in the White Mountains. You'll see this icon just about everywhere you look—on state highway signs, on brochures, on state police cars. And it's an apt symbol for a state that relishes its cranky old man demeanor. New Hampshire has long been a magnet for folks who talk of government with tones normally reserved for scabies. That "Live Free or Die" license plate? It's for real. New Hampshire stands behind its words. It hasn't quite accepted state planning as a legitimate task. Nor does New Hampshire have a bottle-deposit law, or a law banning billboards. (Godless Vermont has both, as does its other heathen neighbor, Maine.)

New Hampshire savors its reputation as an embattled outpost of plucky, heroic conservatives fighting the good fight against intrusive laws and irksome bureaucrats. Without a state sales tax or state income tax, it's had to be creative. Many government services are funded through the "tourist tax" (an 8% levy on meals and rooms at restaurants and hotels) along with a hefty local property tax (the mere mention of which is another way to get folks riled up). In fact, candidates for virtually every office with the possible exception of dogcatcher must take "The Pledge," which means they'll vow to fight any effort to impose sales or income tax. To shirk The Pledge is tantamount to political suicide.

The state's cranky spirit is perhaps best captured by its leading newspaper, the *Manchester Union Leader*. This conservative powerhouse has made and broken candidates in their quest for the White House during New Hampshire's influential first-in-the-nation primary. The paper's attitude has mellowed somewhat since the demise of cantankerous editor William Loeb, and it's dropped the vitriolic

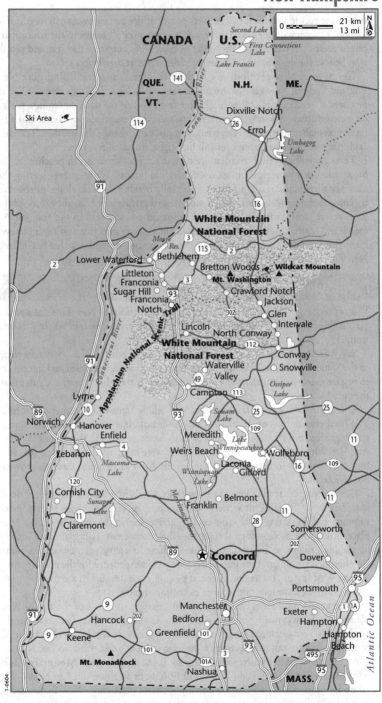

New Hampshire

front-page editorials. But it still delivers plenty of fire and brimstone in its editorial section. (The newspaper also has the policy of printing all letters to the editor it receives. As such, it has become the outlet of choice for conspiracy theorists and people who believe the government is beaming radio waves at their brain.)

Get beyond New Hampshire's affable crankiness, and you'll find pure New England. Indeed, New Hampshire may represent the New England ethic distilled to its essence. At its core is a mistrust of those from outside the state, a premium placed on independence, a belief that government should be frugal above all else, and a laconic acceptance that, no matter what, you just can't change the weather. Travelers exploring the state with open eyes will find these attitudes in spades.

Travelers will also find wonderfully diverse terrain—from ocean beaches, to the broad lakes, to the region's most impressive mountains. Without ever leaving the state's borders you can toss a Frisbee on a sandy beach, ride bikes along quiet country lanes dotted with covered bridges, hike rugged granite hills blasted by some of the most severe weather in the world, and canoe on a placid lake in the company of moose and loons. You'll also find good food and country inns you won't want to ever leave. But most of all, you'll find vestiges of that feisty independence that has defined New England since the first settlers ran up their flag 3 1/2 centuries ago.

1 Enjoying the Great Outdoors

Visitors coming from the West scoff at the low elevations of New England's peaks. ("Four thousand feet? *Four thousand feet?* That's not even a foothill where we come from!")

Savvy Eastern hikers indulge their guests with good humor. Then they take them to the White Mountains' brutally rugged, steep trails to snap their will and force them to beg for mercy—never mind the plentiful oxygen at these low elevations. After that, they tend to stay quiet.

The White Mountains' famed network of hiking trails will test anyone's mettle. The hard granite hills of the ancient mountains of New England resist the sort of gently graded trail through the crumbly earth found so often in the American West. And the White Mountains' early trailblazers were evidently a humorless lot, who found amusement in building trails straight up sheer pitches and through tortuous boulder fields.

Despite (or perhaps because of) these trails, the White Mountains are *the* destination in New England for serious outdoors people. There's superb hiking in the summer, and fine skiing (both cross-country and alpine) in the winter. It's also a good place to test your meteorological acumen—the weather can change almost instantly on the high ridges, so backcountry explorers have to keep a keen eye out. A pleasant afternoon picnic can turn into a harrowing, cold experience for the unwary. Atop Mount Washington, the region's highest peak, it's not unusual to see snow anytime of the year—midsummer flurries aren't that uncommon.

More gentle outdoor recreation is found throughout much of the rest of New Hampshire, from canoeing on the meandering Connecticut River (which forms the border with Vermont), to sailing on vast Lake Winnipesaukee. If you're so inclined, come prepared for outdoor recreation, because it doesn't take much to find it.

An excellent general source of information is the **Appalachian Mountain Club,** 5 Joy St., Boston, MA 02108 (☎ **617/523-0636,** or 603/466-2727 in N.H.). The group sponsors outings and instructional workshops throughout New England, but especially in the White Mountains. Signing up for a trip is an excellent way to get to know the area under the leadership of someone who knows the area well.

BACKPACKING   The White Mountains of northern New Hampshire offer the most extensive, most challenging, most beautiful backpacking in the Northeast. The bulk of the best trails are located within 773,000-acre **White Mountain National Forest,** which encompasses several 5,000-plus-foot peaks and more than 100,000 acres of designated wilderness. Trails range from easy lowland walks along bubbling streams to demanding ridgeline paths buffeted by fierce winds. AMC huts offer shelter in eight dramatically situated cabins that offer Spartan comfort. (Reservations are essential; call ☎ **603/466-2727**).

In addition, a number of three-sided Adirondack-style shelters are located throughout the backcountry on a first come, first served basis. Some are free; at others a small fee is collected. Pitching a tent in the backcountry is free subject to certain restrictions (for example, no camping within a certain distance of a trail or river), and no permits are required. It's best to check with the **forest headquarters** (☎ **603/ 528-8721**) or a district ranger station for current rules and regulations.

The ridges around Mount Washington attract the densest crowds. Backpackers in search of a more remote experience should head for trails in the Mount Moosilauke/ Kinsman Notch area west of I-93, and the northern unit of the forest just west of Berlin.

The **Appalachian Trail** passes through New Hampshire, entering the state at Hanover, running along the highest peaks of the White Mountains, and exiting into Maine along the Mahoosuc Range northeast of Gorham. The trail is well maintained, although it tends to attract teeming crowds along the highest elevations in summer.

Rental equipment—including sleeping bags and pads, tents, and packs—is available at **Eastern Mountain Sports** (☎ **603/356-5433**) in North Conway at reasonable rates.

BIKING   There's superb road biking throughout the state. The best advice is to sacrifice the direct-line convenience of the major roads for the winding, twisting back roads. Southwest New Hampshire near Mount Monadnock offers a multitude of shady back roads for exploring, especially around Hancock and Greenfield.

In the White Mountains, my favorite 1-day loop (bring lunch) is on the east side of the mountains outside of North Conway. Start in Conway and follow the Kancamagus Highway (Route 112) to Bear Notch Road. Turn right, then climb Bear Notch before descending to the town of Bartlett; turn right and follow busy Route 302 (the worst part of the trip) to River Road, which connects to West Side Road and continues back to Conway.

The White Mountains also offer plenty of opportunities for mountain bikers; trails are open to bikers unless otherwise noted. Bikes are not allowed in wilderness areas. The upland roads outside of Jackson offer some superb country biking, as does the steep terrain around Franconia and Sugar Hill. **Great Glen Trails** (☎ **603/ 466-2333**), near Mount Washington, and **Waterville Valley Base Camp** (☎ **800/ 468-2553**), at the southwest edge of the park, both offer bike rentals and maintained mountain-bike trails for a fee.

Mountain Road Tours (☎ **603/532-8708**) in southern New Hampshire can arrange inn-to-inn biking tours in the state.

CAMPING   Campers shouldn't have any problem finding a place to pitch a tent or park an RV in New Hampshire, especially in the northern half of the state.

The **White Mountain National Forest** maintains 20 campgrounds with a total of 819 sites (no hookups), some very small and personal, others quite large and noisy. Sites tend to be fairly easy to come by midweek, but on summer weekends (along with foliage weekends) you're taking your chances if you arrive without reservations. Reservations are accepted by the **Forest Service** (☎ **800/280-2267**) at 11 of the campgrounds from 14 to 180 days before arrival. There's an additional reservation fee of $7.85 added to the campground fee.

Fifteen of New Hampshire's **state parks** allow camping (two of these offer camping for RVs only). About half of these parks are located in and around the White Mountains. The New Hampshire state park system accepts advance reservations for many of its campgrounds. Between January and May call ☎ **603/271-3628;** during summer, call the campground directly to reserve. Not all campgrounds participate; some remain first come, first served. A list of parks and phone numbers is published in the *New Hampshire Visitor's Guide,* which is distributed widely through information centers, or by contacting the **Office of Travel and Tourism Development,** P.O. Box 1856, Concord, NH 03302 (☎ **603/271-2343**).

New Hampshire also has more than 150 private campgrounds. For a free directory, get in touch with the **New Hampshire Campground Owners' Association,** P.O. Box 320, Twin Mountain, NH 03595 (☎ **800/822-6764** or 603/846-5511; Web site: **www.ucampnh.com**).

CANOEING New Hampshire has a profusion of rivers and lakes suitable for paddling, and canoe rentals are available widely around the state. Good flat-water paddling may be found along the **Merrimack and Connecticut rivers** in the southern parts of the state. Virtually any lake is good for dabbling about with canoe and paddle, although beware of stiff northerly winds when crossing large lakes like vast **Winnipesaukee.** In the far north, 8,000-acre **Lake Umbagog** is home to bald eagles and loons, and is especially appealing to explore by canoe. In general, the farther north you venture, the wilder and more remote the terrain.

In the north, the **Androscoggin River** offers superb Class I–II white water and swift flat water upstream of Berlin; below, the river is fetid with paper-mill pollution and is best avoided.

Serious white-water enthusiasts head to the upper reaches of the **Saco River** during spring runoff, where the Class III–IV rapids are intense if relatively short-lived along a 6.5-mile stretch paralleling Route 302.

FISHING New Hampshire ponds, streams, and rivers offer good fishing throughout the state. A vigorous stocking program keeps the waters active with fish. Brook trout account for about half of all trout stocked in the state's waters; lake and rainbow trout are also stocked. Other sport fish include small- and largemouth bass, landlocked salmon, and walleye.

Fishing licenses are required for freshwater fishing throughout the state, but not for saltwater fishing. For detailed information on regulations, request the free *Freshwater Fishing Digest* from the **New Hampshire Fish and Game Department,** 2 Hazen Dr., Concord, NH 03301 (☎ **603/271-3211**). Fishing licenses for nonresidents range from $18.50 for 3 days to $35.50 for the season. Another helpful booklet, also available free from the Fish and Game Department, is *Fishing Waters of New Hampshire.* For on-line information, set your Web browser to www.wildlife.state.nh.us.

HIKING New Hampshire has hiking trails in abundance. The White Mountains alone offer 1,200 miles of trails; state parks and forests add considerably to the mileage.

Serious hikers will want to make a beeline for the Whites. The essential guide to hiking trails is the Appalachian Mountain Club's *White Mountain Guide,* which contains up-to-date detailed descriptions of every trail in the area. The guide is available at most book and outdoor shops in the state. See the section on the White Mountains later in this chapter for further suggestions on hikes.

In southwest New Hampshire, the premier hike is **Mount Monadnock,** said to be one of the world's two most popular hikes (second only to Mt. Fuji in Japan). This lone massif, rising regally above the surrounding hills, is a straightforward day hike accessible via one of several trails.

For other hiking opportunities outside the Whites, two recommended guidebooks are *50 Hikes in New Hampshire,* and *50 More Hikes in New Hampshire,* both written by Daniel Doan and published by **Backcountry Publications,** c/o W. W. Norton & Co., Inc., 800 Keystone Industrial Park, Scranton, PA 18512 (☎ **800/ 233-4830**).

SKIING   New Hampshire offers a good selection of slopes, with everything from challenging steeps to gentle runs at 22 downhill ski areas.

New Hampshire's forte may be the small ski area that caters to families. These include Gunstock, Temple Mountain, Mount Sunapee, King Pine, and Pats Peak, all with vertical drops of 1,500 feet or less. The more challenging skiing is in the White Mountains region; the best areas are Cannon Mountain, Loon Mountain, Waterville Valley, Wildcat, and Attitash. These all have vertical drops around 2,000 feet, and feature services one would expect at a professional ski resort.

Ski NH (☎ **800/343-2250** or 603/745-9396) distributes a ski map and other information helpful in ski-trip planning. To check on **current downhill ski conditions,** call ☎ **800/258-3608.**

The most impressive ski run in New Hampshire isn't served by a lift. **Tuckerman Ravine** drops 3,400 feet from a lip on the shoulder of Mount Washington down to the valley floor. Skiers arrive from throughout the nation to venture here in the early spring (it's dangerously avalanche prone during the depths of winter), first hiking to the top then flying to the bottom of this dramatic glacial cirque. The slope is sheer and unforgiving; only very advanced skiers should attempt it. Careless or cocky skiers are hauled out every year on stretchers, and few years seem to go by without at least one skier's death. Contact the AMC's **Pinkham Notch camp** (☎ **603/ 466-2725**) for information on current conditions.

Ample **cross-country skiing** opportunities also exist. The state boasts some 26 cross-country ski centers, which groom a combined total of more than 500 miles of trails. The state's premier cross-country destination is the town of **Jackson** (☎ **603/ 383-9355**), with 55 miles of groomed trails in and around an exceptionally scenic village in a valley near the base of Mount Washington. Other favorites include **Bretton Woods** (☎ **800/232-2972** or 603/278-5181), at the western entrance to Crawford Notch, also with more than 50 miles of groomed trails, and the spectacularly remote **Balsams/Wilderness cross-country ski center** (☎ **800/255-0600** or 603/255-3951) in the farthest reaches of the state.

My favorite inn with its own cross-country ski center is the **Franconia Inn** (☎ **800/473-5299** or 603/823-5542), which has nearly 40 miles of groomed trails on the scenic western edge of Franconia Notch.

SNOWMOBILING   Sledders will find nearly 6,000 miles of groomed, scenic snowmobile trails lacing the state. These are interconnected via an intricate trail network that is maintained by local snowmobile clubs. All sleds must be registered with the state; this costs $29 and can be done through any of the 200 off-highway recreational-vehicle agents in the state. More information about snowmobiling in the state may be obtained from the **New Hampshire Snowmobile Association,** 722 Rte. 3A, Bow, NH 03304 (☎ **603/224-8906**).

The state's most remote and spectacular destination for snowmobilers is that nubby finger that thrusts up into Canada. It also happens to be the snowiest part of the state.

The **Connecticut Lakes Tourist Association** (☎ **603/538-7405**) can provide information on services and lodging in the area. Your best bet for rentals or snow-mobile tours of the area is **Pathfinder Sno-Tours,** based at Timberland Lodge in Pittsburg (☎ **603/538-6613**).

2 Portsmouth

Portsmouth is a civilized seaside city of bridges and brick and seagulls, and is far and away one of the most attractive small cities on the whole of the eastern seaboard. Filled with elegant architecture that's more intimate than intimidating, this bonsai-sized city projects a strong and proud sense of its heritage without being overly precious about it.

Part of the city's appeal is its variety. Upscale coffee shops and fancy art galleries exist alongside old-fashioned barbershops and tattoo parlors. There's been a steady gentrification in recent years, which has brought a surfeit of twee shops, but the town still has a fundamental earthiness that serves as a tangy vinegar for the overly saccharine spots. Portsmouth's humble waterfront must actually be sought out, and when found it's rather understated.

Portsmouth's history runs deep, a fact that's instantly evident when you walk through town. For the past 3 centuries, the city has served as a hub for the region's maritime trade. In the 1600s, Strawbery Banke (it wasn't renamed Portsmouth until 1653) was a center for the export of wood and dried fish to Europe. In the 19th century, it prospered as a center of regional trade. Across the river in Maine, the Portsmouth Naval Shipyard was founded in 1800, and evolved into a prominent base for the building, outfitting, and repair of U.S. Navy submarines.

Today, Portsmouth's maritime tradition continues with a lively trade in bulk goods (look for scrap metal and minerals stockpiled along the shores of the Piscataqua River on Market Street); the city's de facto symbol is the tugboat, one or two of which are almost always tied up near the waterfront's picturesque "tugboat alley."

Visitors to Portsmouth will find there's a whole lot to see in a little space. There's good shopping in the boutiques that now occupy much of the historic district, good eating at the many small restaurants, and plenty of history to explore among the historic homes and museums that crop up on almost every block.

ESSENTIALS

GETTING THERE   Portsmouth is served by Exits 3 through 7 on I-95. The most direct access to downtown is via Market Street (Exit 7), which is the last New Hampshire exit before crossing the river to Maine. By bus, Portsmouth is served by Concord Trailways and Vermont Transit.

VISITOR INFORMATION   The **Greater Portsmouth Chamber of Commerce,** 500 Market St., Portsmouth, NH 03802 (☎ **603/436-1118**), operates a very helpful tourist information center year-round between Exit 7 and downtown. The office is open daily in summer, weekdays only the remainder of the year. In summer, the chamber staffs a second information booth at Market Square in the middle of the historic district.

ORIENTATION   Portsmouth consists of two main areas of interest to travelers. First, there's the historic commercial district, located around Market Square and extending to the shores of the Piscataqua River. Second, there's Strawbery Banke, the city's premier historic neighborhood, now an outdoor museum (admission charged), which is near the public gardens and a waterfront park.

Portsmouth

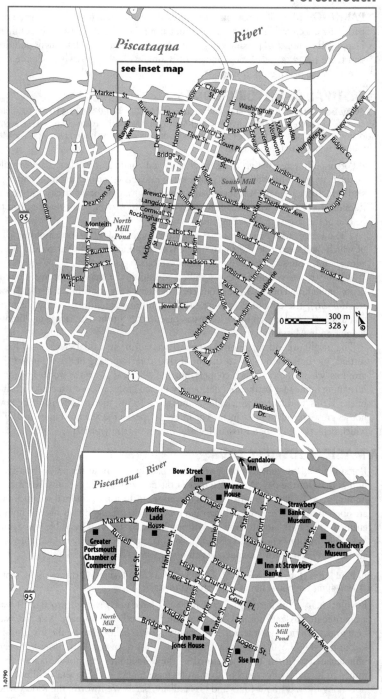

Piscataqua River

see inset map

Market St.
Russell St.
Raynes Ave.
High St.
Bow St.
Chapel St.
Court St.
Washington St.
Marcy St.
Franklin
Melcher
Wentworth
Edward
Humphreys Ct.
New Castle Ave.
Ridges Ct.

Deer St.
Hanover St.
Fleet St.
Church St.
Court Pl.
Pleasant St.
Livermore
Junkins Ave.
Bridge St.
Rogers St.
South Mill Pond
Kent St.
Clough Dr.

Brewster St.
Summer St.
Langdon St.
Richards Ave.
Rowland
Sherburne Ave.
Cornwall St.
Rockingham St.
Dearborn St.
Monteith St.
North Mill Pond
Cabot St.
McDonough St.
Union St.
Austin
Miller Ave.
Broad St.
Burkitt St.
Stark St.
Madison St.
Wibird St.
Union St.
Lincoln Ave.
Hawthorne St.
Broad St.
Whipple St.
Albany St.
Park St.
Middle St.
Jewell Ct.
Aldrich Rd.
Thaxter Rd.
Mendum
Central
Fells Rd.
Monroe St.
Summit Ave.
Spinney Rd.
Hillside Dr.

0   300 m
    328 y

Piscataqua River

Gundalow Inn
Bow Street Inn
Warner House
Strawbery Banke Museum
Moffet-Ladd House
Market St.
Russell
Greater Portsmouth Chamber of Commerce
Bow St.
Chapel St.
Daniel St.
State St.
Marcy St.
Court St.
Washington St.
Gates St.
The Children's Museum
Deer St.
Hanover St.
High St.
Church St.
Fleet St.
Congress St.
Pleasant St.
Court Pl.
Inn at Strawbery Banke
North Mill Pond
Bridge St.
Middle St.
Porter St.
State St.
John Paul Jones House
Slse Inn
Rogers St.
South Mill Pond
Junkins Ave.
95

1-0790

533

PARKING   Most of Portsmouth can be easily reconnoitered on foot, so you need park only once. Parking can be tight in and around the historic district in summer. Happily, the municipal parking garage costs just 25¢ per hour; look for signs pointing you there just west of Market Square off Congress Street. Strawbery Banke also offers limited parking for visitors.

A FESTIVAL OF HISTORIC HOMES

✪ **Strawbery Banke.** P.O. Box 300, Portsmouth, NH 03802. ☎ **603/433-1100.** $10 adults, $9 seniors, $7 children 7–17, $25 families. Mid-Apr to early Nov daily 10am–5pm. Special events held around Thanksgiving and the first 2 weekends of Dec; otherwise closed Nov–Apr. Look for directional signs posted around town.

If Portsmouth were a festival of historic homes and buildings, Strawbery Banke would be the main stage. In 1958, the city planned to raze this venerable neighborhood, first settled in 1653, to make way for urban renewal. A group of local citizens resisted the tides of progress and won, establishing an outdoor history museum that's grown to be one of the largest in New England.

The museum today consists of 10 downtown acres and 42 historic buildings, 10 of which have been restored to 10 different eras and are open to the public. (One admission fee buys access to all homes and exhibits.)

While Strawbery Banke employs staffers to assume the character of historic residents (including Thomas Bailey Aldrich, a frequent early contributor to the *Atlantic Monthly*), the emphasis is more on the buildings, architecture, and historic accoutrement, and less on living history as practiced at Sturbridge Village or Plimoth Plantation in Massachusetts.

The neighborhood surrounds an open lawn (formerly a tidal creek), and has a settled, picturesque quality to it. You'll find three working crafts shops on the grounds, where you can watch coopers, boatbuilders, and potters at work. The most intriguing home may be the split personality Drisco House, half of which depicts life in the 1790s, and half of which shows life in the 1950s, nicely demonstrating how houses grow and adapt to each era. The museum opened the Shapiro House in 1997, which depicts the life of a Russian Jewish immigrant family in 1919.

A MAGICAL HISTORY TOUR

Portsmouth's 18th-century prosperity can be plainly seen in the regal Georgian-style homes that dot the city. A walking tour of the city will take in the most significant homes, many of which are maintained by various historical or colonial societies and are open to the public. A helpful map and brochure describing the key historic homes entitled "The Portsmouth Trail: A Historic Walking Tour" is available free at the city's information centers (see above). If you plan to tour more than one home, ask about the **Portsmouth Passport,** which offers a small discount.

John Paul Jones House. 43 Middle St. ☎ **603/436-8420.** $4 adults, $2 children 6–14. Mon–Sat 10am–4pm, Sun noon–4pm. Closed late Oct to May.

Revolutionary War hero John Paul Jones ("I have not yet begun to fight") was a boarder in this handsome 1758 home during the Revolutionary War. He was here to oversee the construction of his sloop, *Ranger,* believed to be the first ship to sail under the U.S. flag (there's a model of it on display). The home has been immaculately restored and maintained by the Portsmouth Historical Society; costumed tour guides offer tours of 45 minutes to an hour, providing a raft of information along the way about Jones and his landlady, Sarah Wentworth, the widow who took in guests at her large, Georgian-style home to support her sizable family. The house, which was built by six carpenters working 6 days a week for 2 years, contains a handsome collection of period furniture; there are also collections of china and period clothing, including elaborate wedding gowns.

Moffatt-Ladd House. 154 Market St. ☎ **603/436-8221.** $4 adults, $1 children under 12. Mon–Sat 10am–4pm, Sun 2–5pm. Closed Oct 16–June 14.

The Moffatt-Ladd House, built for a family of prosperous merchants and traders, is as notable for its elegant garden as for the 1763 home, with its Great Hall and elaborate carvings throughout. Remarkably, the home remained in one family between 1763 and 1913, when it became a museum. Many of the furnishings have never left the house. The home will especially appeal to aficionados of Early American furniture and painting; it's hung with portraits of some 15 family members. Don't overlook the 1815 Dufour wallpaper in the Great Hall. The terraced garden's design dates to the mid-19th century, but some of the roses can be traced back to plantings in 1768 and 1776.

Warner House. 150 Daniel St. ☎ **603/436-5909.** $4 adults, $2 children 7–12. Tues–Sat 10am–4pm, Sun 1–4pm. Closed Nov to early June.

The Warner House, built in 1716, was the governor's mansion in the mid-18th century when Portsmouth served as state capital. This stately brick home with graceful Georgian architectural elements (note the alternating arched and triangular pediments above the dormer windows) is a favorite among architectural historians for its circa 1716 wall murals (said to be the oldest murals still in place in the U.S.), the early wall marbleizing, and the original white pine paneling. Benjamin Franklin visited the house in 1763 to personally supervise the installation of a lightning rod on the west wall.

Wentworth-Gardner House. 50 Mechanic St. ☎ **603/436-4406.** $4 adults, $2 children 6–14. Tues–Sun 1–4pm. Closed late Oct–early June.

The Wentworth-Gardner is arguably the most handsome mansion in the entire Seacoast region, and is widely considered to be one of the best examples of Georgian architecture in the nation. Built in 1760, the home features many of the classic period elements, including very pronounced quoins (the blocks on the building's corners), pedimented window caps, plank sheathing (this was meant to make it appear as if made of masonry), and an elaborate doorway featuring Corinthian pilasters, a broken scroll, and a paneled door topped with a pineapple, the symbol of hospitality. The inside is no less impressive, with hand-painted Chinese wallpaper and a vast fireplace in the kitchen featuring a windmill spit. This waterfront house was once owned by Wallace Nutting, the noted chronicler of old New England ways, and at one point was owned by the Metropolitan Museum of Art in New York, which considered moving the house to Central Park.

BOAT TOURS

Portsmouth is especially attractive when seen from the water. A small fleet of tour boats ties up at Portsmouth, offering scenic tours of the Piscataqua River and the historic Isle of Shoals throughout the summer and fall.

The **Isle of Shoals Steamship Co.** (☎ **800/441-4620** or 603/431-5500) sails from Baker Wharf on Market Street and is the most established of the tour companies. The firm offers a variety of tours on the 90-foot, three-deck *Thomas Laighton* (it's a modern replica of a turn-of-the-century steamship) and the 70-foot *Oceanic,* which was especially designed for whale watching. Among the most popular excursions are to the Isle of Shoals, allowing passengers to disembark and wander about **Star Island,** a dramatic, rocky island that's part of an island cluster far out in the offshore swells. Star Island has a rich history and today serves as the base for a summer religious institute. Reservations are strongly encouraged for this trip. Other popular trips include 6-hour whale-watching voyages and a sunset lighthouse cruise. Fares range from $9 to $25 for adults, $5 to $16 for children.

Portsmouth Harbor Cruises (☎ 800/776-0915 or 603/436-8084) specializes in tours of the historic Piscataqua River aboard the *Heritage,* a 49-passenger cruise ship with plenty of open deck space. Cruise by five old forts during the harbor cruise, or enjoy the picturesque tidal estuary of inland Great Bay, a scenic trip upriver from Portsmouth. Trips run daily, and reservations are suggested. Fares are $7.50 to $15 for adults, $5 to $8 for children.

SHOPPING

Portsmouth's compact historic district has dozens of unique boutiques selling items you're not likely to find at the mall, including many handcrafted products. The selection ranges from urban funky to country casual, so few leave disappointed. If you're serious about browsing, allow at least a couple of hours to wander through town. The following are just a sampling of the more intriguing places.

The most creative shoe store in the city, **Choozy Shooz,** 19 Market St. (☎ 603/433-4455), offers a wide selection of hip as well as eminently practical footwear, including an array of English funky styles. **Slackers,** 51 Ceres St. (☎ 603/427-1425), an appealing shop tucked away near Tugboat Alley, features a selection of casual, contemporary clothing and footwear, including plenty from Patagonia. It's a draw for college students and skateboarders.

Teens tend to like **Macro Polo,** 89 Market St. (☎ 603/436-8338), which specializes in retro-chic. This pleasantly cluttered shop stocks pink flamingos, refrigerator magnets, movie kitsch, candies, coffee mugs, and T-shirts, most of which are embellished with off-beat humor. Packed to the eaves with small stuff, **Paradise Garage,** 63 Penhallow St. (☎ 603/431-0180), offers up an array of clever postcards, jewelry, imported soaps, greeting cards, a good selection of car models (the kind you put together with glue), and vintage automobile bric-a-brac.

City & Country, 50 Daniel St. (☎ 603/433-5353), is a contemporary housewares store—a sort of Pottery Barn Lite—and offers a small but intriguing selection of glasses, table settings, flatware, and cooking implements, along with a mix of furniture and wrought-iron accessories.

Harbour Treats, 4 Market Sq. (☎ 603/431-3228), is a chocoholic's paradise, with a good selection of homemade fudges, chocolates, and truffles. Don't leave without trying the chocolate turtles.

A contemporary gallery featuring the work of area craftspeople, the elegant **N. W. Barrett Gallery,** 53 Market St. (☎ 603/431-4262), offers up a classy selection of creative, exuberant crafts, including ceramic sculptures, glassware, lustrous woodworking, and a wide array of handmade jewelry.

WHERE TO STAY

Portsmouth has a good selection of places to stay within walking distance of the downtown historic area. Less expensive, less stylish options include several chain hotels at the edge of town near I-95. Among them are the **Anchorage Inn,** 417 Woodbury Ave. (☎ 603/431-8111); **Susse Chalet,** 650 Borthwick Ave. (☎ 603/436-6363); and the **Holiday Inn of Portsmouth** (☎ 603/431-8000), also on Woodbury Avenue.

Bow Street Inn. 121 Bow St., Portsmouth, NH 03801. ☎ **603/431-7760.** Fax 603/433-1680. 9 rms. A/C TV TEL. Aug to mid-Sept $105–$139 double; mid-May to July $99–$130 double; off-season $89–$119 double. Rates include continental breakfast. 2-night minimum on holidays. AE, DISC, MC, V.

This is a fine spot for travelers willing to give up charm to gain convenience. This former downtown brewery was made over in the 1980s in a bit of inspired adaptive reuse—condos occupy the top floor, and the respected **Seacoast Repertory Theatre** (☎ 603/433-4472) occupies the first.

The second floor is the Bow Street Inn, a modern nine-room hotel that offers superb access to historic Portsmouth. The guest rooms, set off a somewhat sterile hallway, are clean, comfortable, and for the most part unexceptional, although rooms 6 and 7 both feature fine views of the harbor. Parking is on the street or at a nearby paid lot. If you're looking for entertainment, the theater's right downstairs, and all of historic Portsmouth lies a few steps outside your door. That's where the Bow Street's value lies.

Inn at Strawbery Banke. 314 Court St., Portsmouth, NH 03801. ☎ **800/428-3933** or 603/436-7242. 7 rms (5 with shower only). Peak season $95–$100 double; off-season $75 double. Rates include full breakfast. AE, DISC, MC, V.

The Inn at Strawbery Banke, located in a home built in the early 1800s on historic Court Street, is ideally located for exploring Portsmouth. Strawbery Banke is but a block away, and Market Square is just two blocks away. Innkeeper Sarah O'Donnell is a young and friendly host, and has done a nice job taking this antique home and making it comfortable for her guests. Rooms are small but bright, and feature stenciling, wooden interior shutters, and beautiful pine floors; one has a bathroom down the hall. There are two sitting rooms with televisions, and a dining room where a full breakfast is served between 8 and 9am.

✪ **Sise Inn.** 40 Court St., Portsmouth, NH 03801. ☎ **603/433-1200.** Fax 603/433-1200. 34 rms. A/C TV TEL. Late May to Oct $89–$175 double; Nov to early May $79–$150 double. Rates include continental breakfast. AE, DC, MC, V.

The Sise Inn is basically a modern, elegant, small hotel in the guise of a country inn. This solid gray Queen Anne–style home with jade and cream trim overlooks the busy intersection of Court and Middle streets, but inside it's peaceful and a world removed from the bustle of town. The original home was built for a prominent merchant in 1881; the hotel addition was constructed about a decade ago. The effect is surprisingly harmonious, with the antique stained glass and copious oak trim meshing well with the more contemporary elements. An elevator serves the three floors and there's modern carpeting throughout, but many of the rooms and suites feature antique armoires and updated Victorian styling. Among the most appealing rooms is no. 302, a two-level room with an upstairs bedroom and a private downstairs living room. (The sofa folds out and there are two bathrooms, making this a good choice for families.)

An elaborate continental breakfast is served in the huge old kitchen and adjoining sunroom, and there's usually something to snack on in the afternoon. Be sure to admire the lustrous butternut trim surrounding the fireplace in the parlor.

WHERE TO DINE

The **Ceres Bakery,** 51 Penhallow St. (☎ **603/436-6518**), is Portsmouth's original funky bakery, set off on a quiet side street. It's less trendy than Café Brioche on Market Square, and is a better place for local flavor and good home baking. It's a tiny space with just a handful of tables, so you might be better off getting a cookie or slice of cake to go and then walk the couple of blocks to the waterfront rose gardens.

Blue Mermaid World Grill. The Hill (between Hanover and Deer sts. near the municipal parking garage). ☎ **603/427-2583.** Reservations recommended for parties of 6 or more. Lunch items $5.25–$8.75; main dinner courses $9.95–$15.95. AE, DC, DISC, MC, V. Sun–Thurs 11:30am–9pm, Fri–Sat 11:30am–10pm. Open 1 hour later in summer. ECLECTIC.

This place ranks among my favorites in Portsmouth for its good food, good value, and good attitude. The Blue Mermaid is a short walk from Portsmouth's mainstream tourist destinations in a historic area called The Hill, whose main feature today is a large parking lot and old homes converted to offices. Sited in an antique house with lots of exterior charm, inside there's a certain Zen-like grace to the spare bar downstairs and dining room upstairs. It's not a pretentious place—Tom Waits drones on in the background, and the service is casual but professional. More locals than tourists congregate here.

The simple surroundings contrast nicely with the adventurous menu, which creatively builds on cuisines from around the world. You might try the spicy grilled Thai-spiced shrimp and scallop skewers with grilled pineapple, pan-seared haddock in a coconut cream, or the creative pizzas with toppings like roasted corn and black beans. More mainstream entrees include barbecued ribs, lamb with couscous, and salmon fillet.

Muddy River Smokehouse. 21 Congress St. ☎ **603/430-9582.** Reservations not accepted Fri–Sat. Sandwiches $4.95–$6.95; main courses $7.95–$17.95 (mostly $9–$12). AE, MC, V. Sun–Thurs 11am–10pm, Fri–Sat 11am–11pm. BARBECUE.

"So authentic you'll get a notion to marry your sister," claims the Muddy River T-shirt. As you might expect from that, this is a lively restaurant that doesn't take itself too seriously. You enter through an unremarkable, narrow storefront just down the block from historic Market Square, then pass through a long, open, brick-walled bar area decorated with neon and garbage can lampshades. Suddenly, you arrive in a surprisingly cavernous, cacophonous dining room that has a cafeterialike feel to it. Done up in a festive, faux-bayou atmosphere (there's an impressive wall mural), the dining room offers an appealingly wide-ranging menu. There's a superb assortment of barbecued beef ribs, pork ribs, chicken, and sausage (they're slow-smoked over hickory or apple wood), and there are also sandwiches, burgers, and chili. The barbecue is OK, not great, and you can find better in New England. But this is definitely the place for the carnivore in your life in Portsmouth. A limited menu is offered through midnight weekends downstairs in the lounge.

Portsmouth Brewery. 56 Market St. ☎ **603/431-1115.** Reservations accepted only for parties of 10 or more. Lunch items $4.50–$8.95; main dinner courses $8.95–$12.95. AE, CB, DC, DISC, MC, V. Mon–Sat 11:30am–12:30am, Sun 10am–12:30am (Sun brunch served until 2pm). PUB FARE.

Located in the heart of the historic district (look for the tipping tankard suspended over the sidewalk), the Portsmouth Brewery opened in 1991 and quickly attracted a young clientele drawn by the superb beers. The tin-ceilinged, brick-walled dining room is open, airy, echoey, and redolent of hops. (Alberta Hunter may be playing in the background.) The brews are made in 200-gallon batches, and include specialties like Old Brown Ale, Murphy's Law Red Ale, and the delightfully creamy Black Cat Stout. The eclectic menu complements the robust beverages, with selections including burgers (try the "murder burger" with Cajun spices), stir fry, burritos, white or red pizza, and beer-marinated beef kabobs. The food's OK; the beer is well above average.

Press Room. 77 Daniel St. ☎ **603/431-5186.** Reservations not accepted. Sandwiches $3.25–$5.25; main courses $5.25–$8.25. AE, DC, DISC, MC, V. Tues–Sat 11:30am–1am, Sun–Mon 5pm–1am. PUB FARE.

Diners flock here more for the convivial "Cheers"-like atmosphere and the easy-on-the-budget prices than for creative cuisine. Opened in 1976, the Press Room likes to boast that it was the first in the area to serve Guinness Stout, so it's appropriate that the atmosphere reflects a certain Gaelic charm. It's the sort of place where locals like to gather to discuss the issues of the day ("BMWs? I *hate* BMWs!") and feel at home. As for character, it's got plenty. During winter and cool coastal days, a fire burns in the woodstove and quaffers flex their elbows at darts amid brick walls, pine floors, and heavy wooden beams overhead. Choose your meal from a basic bar menu, with inexpensive selections including a variety of burgers, nachos, fish-and-chips, stir-frys, and a selection of salads. A great value.

PORTSMOUTH AFTER DARK

Portsmouth's nightlife typically takes place in downtown bars over a pint or two of locally brewed beers. If you're geared up for something more active, check out the following options.

Live jazz, classical guitar, and low-key folk rock is offered most Tuesday through Sunday evenings at the **Dolphin Striker,** 15 Bow St. (☎ **603/431-5222**). Blues are the thing in the downstairs lounge of the **Muddy River Smokehouse,** 21 Congress St. (☎ **603/430-9582**), which is open evenings Wednesday through Saturday. Wednesday nights draw the region's aspiring blues artists to open mike night; weekends offer wrenching blues with well-known performers from Boston, Maine, and beyond.

A popular local bar and restaurant (see "Where to Dine," above), the **Press Room,** 77 Daniel St. (☎ **603/431-5186**), offers casual entertainment most evenings, either upstairs or down. Tuesday nights are the popular Hoot nights, with an open mike hosted by local musicians. Friday nights are typically set aside for contemporary folk, starring name performers from around the region. But the Press Room might be best known for its live jazz on Sunday night, when the club brings in quality performers from Boston and beyond. The cover charge is usually under $10.

The **Elvis Room,** 142 Congress St. (☎ **603/436-9189**), has fought battles against The King's lawyers (they didn't like the name) and unruly local teens who adopted the place as their own. The owners prevailed in both instances, and today this smoky, relaxed coffeehouse is a fine place to read a book, play some chess, or listen to eclectic live music. It's open later than anyplace else in the city.

Portsmouth also boasts a historic theater, the **Music Hall,** 28 Chestnut St. (☎ **603/433-2400**), which dates back to 1878, and was recently brought back to its former glory by a nonprofit arts group. A variety of shows are staged here, from magic festivals to comedy revues to concerts by the visiting symphonies and pop artists. Call for the current lineup.

3 Hanover & Environs

If your idea of New England involves a sweeping green edged with stately brick buildings, be sure to visit Hanover, a thriving university town agreeably situated in the Connecticut River Valley. First settled in 1765, the town was home to the early pioneers who were granted a charter by King George III to establish a college. The school was named after the 2nd Earl of Dartmouth, the school's first trustee. Since its founding, Dartmouth College, the most northerly of the Ivy League schools, has had a large hand in shaping the community. One alumnus has aptly said of the school, "Dartmouth is the sort of place you're nostalgic for even if you've never been there."

Dartmouth has produced more than its share of illustrious alumni, including Robert Frost, Nelson Rockefeller, Supreme Court Justice Salmon P. Chase, Louise

Erdrich, Robert Reich, C. Everett Koop, and Dr. Seuss. Perhaps the most famous son of Dartmouth was renowned 19th-century politician and orator Daniel Webster. In arguing for the survival of Dartmouth College in a landmark case before the U.S. Supreme Court in 1816 (when two factions vied for control of the school), Webster offered his famous closing line: "It is a small college, gentlemen, but there are those who love it." This has served as an informal motto for the school alumni ever since.

Today, a handsome, oversized village green marks the permeable border between college and town. In the summer, the green is an ideal destination for strolling and lounging. In the winter, look for the massive, intricate ice sculptures from the winter carnival. The best way to explore Hanover is by foot, so your first endeavor is to park your car, which can be trying during peak seasons. Try the municipal lots west of Main Street.

The town boasts a compact and prosperous commercial area, offering some good browsing and shopping. While the area clearly caters to the affluent with its shops like Simon Pearce, The Gap, and several excellent bookshops, there's a good selection of small stores that are light on frills and fluff.

Just south of Hanover is the working-class town of **Lebanon,** another commercial center, which in many ways has a less artificial New England air to it. This colorful community has a village green to be proud of, a variety of shops, some appealing restaurants, and a quirky mall carved out of an old brick powerhouse. If you're looking for the *New York Times,* head to Hanover; if you need a wrench, head for Lebanon.

ESSENTIALS

GETTING THERE   Lebanon and its sibling, West Lebanon, are located on I-89 (Exits 17 to 20), and just across the river from I-91 (Exit 10). Hanover is north of Lebanon via Route 10 or Route 120. **Amtrak** serves White River Junction, Vt., just across the river.

VISITOR INFORMATION   Dartmouth College alumni and other volunteers maintain an **information center** (☎ 603/643-3512) on the green in the summer and fall. Good sources of local information in the off-season are the **Hanover Chamber of Commerce,** P.O. Box 5105, Hanover, NH 03755 (☎ 603/643-3115), located on Main Street across from the post office, and the **Lebanon Chamber of Commerce,** 2 Whipple Place, Lebanon, NH 03766 (☎ 603/448-1203).

SPECIAL EVENTS   The **Dartmouth Winter Carnival,** held annually in mid-February, is the best way to make the most of the region's notorious cold weather. The festival features winter sporting competitions such as ski jumping, but it may be best known for the ice sculpture contest, in which elaborate if ephemeral artworks and cartoon characters grace the green. The festival is not necessarily family oriented—it's largely for college kids to break the winter doldrums with the copious consumption of alcohol. Contact Dartmouth College (☎ 603/646-1110) for more information.

EXPLORING HANOVER

Hanover is a superb town to explore by foot or on bike. Start by picking up a map of the campus, available at the Dartmouth information center on the green or at the Hanover Inn. (Free guided tours are also offered in the summer.) The expansive, leafy campus is a delight to walk through; be sure to stop by the **Baker Memorial Library** to view the murals by Latin American painter José Orozco. He painted *The Epic of*

American Civilization while teaching here between 1932 and 1934. The huge murals wrap around a basement study room, and are as colorful as they are densely metaphorical. There's a helpful printed interpretation of the murals in a free brochure available at the front desk in the room.

South of the green next to the Hanover Inn is the modern **Hopkins Center for the Arts** (☎ **603/646-2422**). The center attracts national acts to its 900-seat concert hall, and stages top-notch performances at the Moore Theater. Call for information on current shows. If the building looks vaguely familiar, that may be because it was designed by Wallace Harrison, the architect who later went on to design New York's Lincoln Center. It seems this could have been a trial run for his later work.

Adjacent to the Hopkins Center is the **Hood Museum of Art** (☎ **603/646-2808**). Although it houses one of the oldest college museums in the nation, it's in a decidedly contemporary, open building, constructed in 1986. The austere, three-story structure displays selections from the permanent collection, including a superb selection of 19th-century American landscapes and a fine grouping of Assyrian reliefs dating from 883 to 859 B.C. The museum is open Tuesday through Saturday from 10am until 5pm (open until 9pm on Wednesdays), and Sunday from noon to 5pm. Admission is free.

THE NEARBY MONTSHIRE MUSEUM: A GRADE A FAMILY OUTING

The **Montshire Museum of Science,** Montshire Road, Norwich, Vt. (☎ **802/649-2200**), is not your average New England science museum of dusty stuffed animals housed in a creaky building. Located on the border between New Hampshire and Vermont (hence the name), the Montshire is a new, architecturally engaging, hands-on museum that draws kids back time and again. The Montshire took root in 1976, when area residents gathered up the leavings of Dartmouth's defunct natural-history museum and put them on display in a former bowling alley in Hanover. The museum grew and prospered, largely owing to the dedication of hundreds of volunteers. In 1989, the museum moved to this beautiful 100-acre property sandwiched between I-91 and the Connecticut River.

Exhibits are housed in an open, soaring structure inspired by the region's barns. The museum contains some live animals (don't miss the leaf-cutter ant exhibit on the second floor), but it's mostly fun, interactive exhibits that involve kids deeply, teaching them the principles of math and science on the sly. Even preschoolers are entertained here at "Andy's Place," a play area with aquariums, bubble-making exhibits, and other magical things. Outside, there's a science park masquerading as a playground, and four nature trails that wend through this riverside property of tall trees and chirpy birds. The high pedestrian bridge from the tower to the hillside is especially popular with kids, and features exhibits on New England weather. Admission is $5 for adults, $4 for children 3 to 17 (free for kids under 3). Hours are daily from 10am to 5pm. To get there, use Exit 13 off I-91 and head east; look for museum signs almost immediately.

WHERE TO STAY

Several hotels and motels are located off the interstate in Lebanon and West Lebanon, about 5 miles south of Hanover. Try the **Airport Economy Inn** (☎ **800/433-3466** or 603/298-8888), **Holiday Inn Express** (☎ **603/448-5070**), the **Radisson Inn North Country** (☎ **603/298-5906**), or **The Sunset** (☎ **603/298-8721**).

"An Aristocracy of Brains": Cornish's 19th-Century Arts Colony

Artists flocked to the quiet Cornish area in the late 19th century, and the subtle beauty of the region, still prevalent today, makes it abundantly clear why. The first artistic immigrants to arrive were the painters and sculptors, who showed up in the late 1880s and early 1890s, building modest homes in the hills. They were followed by politicians and the affluent, who eventually established a thriving summer colony. Among those who populated the rolling hills that looked across the river toward Ascutney were sculptor Daniel Chester French, painter Maxfield Parrish, and *New Republic* editor Herbert Crowley. Prominent visitors included Ethel Barrymore and presidents Woodrow Wilson and Theodore Roosevelt. A 1907 article in the *New York Daily Tribune* noted that artists made their homes in Cornish not "with the idea of converting it into a 'fashionable' summer resort, but rather to form there an aristocracy of brains and keep out that element which displays its lack of grey matter by an expenditure of money in undesirable ways."

The social scene eventually peaked, and the area has lapsed into a peaceful slumber. Those who come here now do so for the beauty and seclusion, not for the gatherings and parties. Indeed, the country's most famous recluse, J. D. Salinger, lives in Cornish today.

The region lacks obvious tourist draws—there are no fancy hotels, no five-star restaurants—but it's well worth visiting and exploring. At twilight, you can see where Maxfield Parrish found his inspiration for the rich, pellucid azure skies for which his prints and paintings are so noted.

The region's premier monument to its former arts colony is the **Saint-Gaudens National Historic Site** (☎ **603/675-2175**), located off Route 12A. Noted sculptor Augustus Saint-Gaudens first arrived in this valley in 1885, shortly after receiving an important commission to create a statue of Abraham Lincoln. His friend

Alden Country Inn. On the Common, Lyme, NH 03768. ☎ **800/794-2296** or 603/795-2222. Fax 603/795-9436. 15 rms (some with shower only). A/C TEL. Summer and fall $125–$160 double; off-season $105–$145 double. Rates include breakfast or Sun brunch. 2-night minimum on weekends Apr to mid-Oct. AE, DC, DISC, MC, V.

Ten miles north of Hanover is the quiet crossroads village of Lyme, with its tidy common and handsome church. Overlooking the common is the 1809 Alden Country Inn, a regal four-story building with a high triangular gable. Over the years it served as a stagecoach stop and Grange Hall. The guest rooms are varied but decorated with light historic styling; some are simply furnished with white walls and stenciling, others are more floral in character. Most feature painted floors that show off the wide boards. My favorite: Room no. 9 with its mustard yellow floors and somewhat larger bathroom. (As is common in many old inns, the bathrooms are usually on the small side, often tucked into closets.) Beware that stairs get narrower and steeper the higher your room is in the building.

Dining/Entertainment: The Alden Tavern and Grille on the first floor (open to the public) has a nice burnished glow, with maple and pine floors, a fireplace, and a collection of colonial era tools on the walls. Meals are traditional New England, with entrees like Shaker cranberry pot roast and crisp-roasted maple duck. Entrees are $14.95 to $17.95.

Hanover Inn. Wheelock St. (P.O. Box 151), Hanover, NH 03755. ☎ **800/443-7024** or 603/643-4300. Fax 603/646-3744. E-mail: hanover.inn@dartmouth.edu. 92 rms. A/C TV TEL. $207–$277 double. Valet parking. AE, DC, DISC, MC, V.

Charles Beaman, a lawyer who owned several houses and much land in the Cornish area, assured him he would find a surfeit of "Lincoln-shaped men" in the area. Saint-Gaudens came, and pretty much stayed the rest of his life.

His home and studio, which he called "Aspet" after the village in Ireland where he was raised, is a superb place to learn more about this extraordinary artist. A brief tour of the house, which is maintained much as it was when Saint-Gaudens lived here, provides a brief introduction to the man. Visitors learn about the artist at several outbuildings and while exploring the grounds, where many replicas of Saint-Gauden's most famous statues are on display. The 150-acre grounds also feature short nature trails, where visitors can wander the hilly woodlands, descending down a rocky vale to a placid millpond.

The historic site is open daily 9am to 4:30pm from late May through October. Admission is $2 for adults 17 and over; free for children under 17.

Covered-bridge aficionados should seek out the **Cornish-Windsor Covered Bridge,** which is the nation's longest covered bridge. Spanning the Connecticut River between Vermont and New Hampshire, this bridge has an ancient and intriguing lineage. A toll bridge was first built here in 1796 to replace a ferry; the current bridge was built in 1866 and extensively restored in 1989. When the late afternoon light hits it right, this just may win the title of most handsome covered bridge in New England.

For a view of the bridge and the scenic shores of the Connecticut River, rent a canoe a few miles downstream from the bridge at **Northstar Canoe Livery,** R.R. #2, Box 894, Cornish, NH 03745 (☎ **603/542-5802**). For $17 per person, Northstar will shuttle you 12 miles upstream, allowing a leisurely paddle back to your car over the next few hours. Or rent by the day ($30) and dabble in the currents.

The Hanover Inn, New Hampshire's oldest continuing business, was born in 1780. But Gen. Ebenezer Brewster, who founded it, would be hard-pressed to recognize it today. This large, modern hotel is thoroughly up-to-date; guests with laptops even have on-line access to Dartmouth's mainframe. (The inn is owned and operated by Dartmouth College.) An expansion of the lobby in 1996 included a much-needed common area, making this exceptionally well run and well maintained hotel all the more inviting. Yet it has an old-world graciousness, and it's perfectly situated for exploring the town. The hotel connects via tunnels and enclosed walkways to the Hopkins Center and the Hood Museum, so it's easy to get around, even in the dead of winter.

Rooms are priced according to size and view, and each is nicely furnished in a contemporary colonial style. Most have canopy or four-poster beds and down comforters along with welcome amenities like hair dryers, multiple phones, and bathrobes.

Dining/Entertainment: The inn has two excellent dining rooms; see below.

Services/Facilities: Valet parking, laundry service, dry cleaning, safe-deposit boxes, turndown service, conference rooms, newspaper delivery. Guests have access to the university's gym, which is a short walk away; ask at the front desk.

Mary Keane House. Lower Shaker Village, Enfield, NH 03748. ☎ **603/632-4241.** 7 rms (1 with shower only). TV. $89–$129 double. Higher rates in foliage season. Rates include breakfast. AE, MC, V.

Situated at Lower Shaker Village, about 25 minutes from Dartmouth, the Mary Keane House is an ideal spot for the gentle recuperation of a harried soul. Built in

1929 (2 years after the Shakers had abandoned the village), this two-story yellow Georgian Revival doesn't share much with the Shaker village in architecture or spirit—in fact, it's filled with lovely Victorian antiques, which seem anathema to the Shaker sensibility. But it's kept immaculately clean (something the Shakers would appreciate), and it's right in the Shaker village, so guests can explore the buildings and museum by day (the grounds are especially peaceful at twilight), paddle one of the inn's canoes on Lake Mascoma, or swim at the small private beach. Room no. 3 is a particular gem, with Corinthian columns, a formal sitting room, plenty of space to unwind, and a refined country-Victorian elegance. No smoking.

WHERE TO DINE

Café Buon Gustaio. 72 S. Main St. ☎ **603/643-5711.** Reservations recommended. Main courses $8–$19. AE, CB, DC, DISC, MC, V. Tues–Thurs 5:30–9pm, Fri–Sat 5:30–9:30pm. NORTHERN ITALIAN.

Four words sum up Café Buon Gustaio: simple setting, elegant fare. Located on Hanover's Main Street in a 19th-century home, the cafe is a trattoria-style restaurant with a menu that changes frequently and a kitchen staff with the proven ability to pull off a good meal night after night. A handsome bar occupies part of one parlor; diners adjourn to the second, more intimate parlor. Begin your meal with a grilled portobello mushroom with artichoke salad, or a lobster ravioli with roasted red-pepper cream. Then feast on spaghettini served with tuna, capers, olives, and beans; or canneloni of smoked chicken, peppers, scallions and ricotta in a d'Abruzzi sauce. If you don't pine for pasta, there's usually a selection of pizzettas and grilled dishes, such as Black Angus steak with a five-peppercorn butter, and swordfish with a spicy shrimp salsa.

✪ Daniel Webster Room. In the Hanover Inn, Wheelock St. ☎ **603/643-4300.** Reservations recommended. Breakfast items $4.25–$9.50; lunch items $6.95–$13.50; main dinner courses $15–$23. AE, DC, DISC, MC, V. Daily 7:30–10:30am and 11:30am–1pm; Tues–Sat 6–9pm. CONTINENTAL.

The neoclassical Daniel Webster Room of the Hanover Inn will appeal to those looking for exceptionally fine dining amid a formal New England atmosphere. The inn's proper dining room is reminiscent of a 19th-century resort hotel, with fluted columns, floral carpeting, and regal upholstered chairs. The only concession to frivolity are the Tavern on the Green–style white lights adorning the potted plants. The dinner menu isn't extensive, but that doesn't make it any less appealing. Entrees range from oatmeal-crusted trout amandine with chanterelles and leeks, to sautéed rabbit au jus. The restaurant has a commendable wine list, and is one of only two restaurants in New Hampshire to receive AAA's four-star rating.

Also off the lobby of the inn is the more informal **Ivy Grill,** set in contemporary, vaguely retro surroundings that come as a bit of a surprise at this staid inn. It's open daily from 11:30am to 10pm, and serves up lunches for under $10 and dinners like crispy half duck with glazed acorn squash and cider, and lobster and crab ravioli. Most dinner entrees are $13 to $15.

Lou's. 30 S. Main St. ☎ **603/643-3321.** Breakfast items $2.10–$6.50; lunch items $3.85–$6.25. AE, MC, V. Mon–Fri 6am–3pm, Sat–Sun 7am–3pm. Bakery open for snacks until 5pm. BAKERY/DINER.

Lou's is a Hanover institution, attracting large crowds for breakfast on weekends and a steady clientele for lunch throughout the week. The mood is no-frills New Hampshire, with a black-and-white linoleum checkerboard floor and maple-and-vinyl booths updated with a modern country look. Breakfast is served all day here (real maple syrup on your pancakes is $1 extra), and the sandwiches are huge and delicious, served on fresh-baked bread. If you're inclined to blow your calorie budget, the baked goods are a fine temptation. The macaroons are especially good. A great value.

4 The Lake Winnipesaukee Region

New Hampshire's largest lake rarely seems all that huge. That's because Winnipesaukee's 180-mile shoreline is convoluted and twisting, wrapped around dozens of inlets, coves, and bays, and further fragmented with some 274 islands. As a result, intermittent lake views from the shore give the illusion you're viewing a chain of smaller lakes and ponds rather than one massive body of water that measures 12 miles by 20 miles at its broadest points.

How to best enjoy the lake? If you've got kids, settle in at Weirs Beach for a few days and take in the gaudy attractions. If you're looking for isolation, consider renting a lakeside cabin for a week or so on the eastern shore, find a canoe or sailboat, then explore much the same way travelers did a century ago. If your time is limited, a driving tour around the lake with a few well-chosen stops will give you a nice taste of the region's woodsy flavor.

See the map entitled "The White Mountains & the Lake Country" in the next section of this chapter.

WESTERN SHORE

Lake Winnipesaukee's western shore has a more frenetic atmosphere than its sibling shore across the lake. That's partly for historic reasons (the main stage and rail routes passed along the west shore), and partly for modern reasons—I-93 runs west of the lake, serving as a sluice for hurried visitors streaming in from the megalopolis to the south. The western shore offers more diversions for short attention spans, plus more hotels, restaurants, and shops, especially in Laconia and Meredith.

ESSENTIALS

GETTING THERE   Interstate access to the west shore is from I-93 at Exit 20 or Exit 23. From Exit 20, follow Route 3 north through Laconia to Weirs Beach. (It's less confusing and more scenic to stay on Business Route 3.) From Exit 23, drive 9 miles east on Route 104 to Meredith, then head either south on Route 3 to Route 11, or strike northwest on Route 25.

VISITOR INFORMATION   The **Greater Laconia/Weirs Beach Chamber of Commerce,** 11 Veterans Sq., Laconia, NH 03246 (☎ **800/531-2347**), maintains a seasonal information booth on Business Route 3 about halfway between Laconia and Weirs Beach. It's open daily in summer from 9am to 6pm. Information is also available year-round at the chamber's office at the old railway station in Laconia. It's open Monday through Friday from 9am to 5pm and on Saturdays from 10am to 2pm.

The **Lakes Region Association,** P.O. Box 1545, Center Harbor, NH 03226 (☎ **800/605-2537** or 603/253-8555), doesn't maintain an information booth but is happy to send out a handy vacation kit with maps and extensive information about local attractions.

KID STUFF IN WEIRS BEACH

Weirs Beach is a compact resort town that reflects its Victorian heritage. Unlike beach towns that sprawl for miles, Weirs Beach clusters in that classic turn-of-the-century fashion along a boardwalk, which happens to be near a sandy beach. At the heart of the town is a working railroad that still connects to the steamship line—a nice throwback to an era when summer vacationers weren't dependent on cars. The town

Hog Heaven!

Laconia and Weirs Beach get *very loud* in mid-June, when some 150,000 motorcyclists descend on the towns to fraternize, party, and race during what's become the legendary **Motorcycle Week.**

This bawdy event dates back to 1939, when motorcycle races were first staged at the newly built Belknap Gunstock Recreation Area. The annual gathering gained some unwelcome notoriety in 1965, when riots broke out involving bikers and locals. The then mayor of Laconia attributed problems to the Hell's Angels, claiming he had evidence that they had trained in Mexico before coming here to foment chaos. This strange episode was documented in Hunter S. Thompson's classic 1966 work, *The Hells Angels.*

Laconia and Weirs Beach eventually recovered from that unwanted publicity, and today bike races take place at the Loudon Speedway just north of Concord, and at the Gunstock Recreation Area, which hosts the Hill Climb. But the whole Weirs Beach area takes on a leather-and-beer carnival atmosphere throughout the week, with bikers cruising the main drag and enjoying one another's company until late at night. Many travelers would pay good money to avoid Weirs Beach at this time, but they'd be missing out on one of New England's more enduring annual phenomena.

attracts a broad mix of visitors, from history and transportation buffs to beach nuts and young video-game warriors.

But most of all, it attracts families. Lots of families. In fact, Weirs Beach is an ideal destination for parents with kids possessed by an insatiable thirst for novelty and flashing lights. Families might start the morning at **Endicott Beach** (named after the Royal Governor of Massachusetts Bay Colony, who sent surveyors here in 1652), swimming in the clear waters of Winnipesaukee. Arrive early if you want to find public parking, which costs 50¢ an hour with a 5-hour maximum.

Afterwards stroll along **the boardwalk** into town, which offers a modest selection of penny arcades, bumper cars, jewelry outlets, leather shops, and tasty if unnutritious fare like crispy caramel corn.

Along the access roads to Weirs Beach are a number of activities that delight young kids and parents desperate to take some of the energy out of them. **The Surfcoaster** (☎ 603/366-4991) has a huge assortment of wave pools, water slides, and other moist diversions. It's on Route 11B just outside of Weirs Beach. Also on Route 11B is **Daytona Fun Park** (☎ 603/366-5461), which has go-carts, minigolf, and batting cages. The **Weirs Beach Waterslide,** on Route 3 (☎ 603/366-5161), has four slides that produce varying levels of adrenaline. And the **Funspot** (☎ 603/366-4377) will keep kids (and uninhibited adults) occupied with video games, candlepin bowling, and a driving range.

EXPLORING BY LAND & BY LAKE

Scenic train rides leave from town on the **Winnipesaukee Scenic Railroad** (☎ 603/279-5253 or 603/745-2135), which offers 1- and 2-hour excursions from Weirs Beach throughout the day during the summer. It's a unique way to enjoy views of lake and forest; kids are provided a hobo lunch packed in a bundle on a stick. Fares for adults are $8.50 for the 2-hour ride and $6.50 for the 1-hour ride. Children ages 4 to 11 are charged $5.50 and $4.50.

After riding the rails, head out onto the waters on the stately **M/S *Mount Washington,*** an exceptionally handsome 230-foot-long vessel with three decks and a capacity for 1,250 passengers (☎ **603/366-2628**). This ship, by far the largest of the lake tour boats, is the best way to get to know Winnipesaukee, with excellent views of the winding shoreline and the knobby peaks of the White Mountains rising over the lake's north end. As many as four cruises a day are offered in summer, ranging from a 2¹/₂-hour excursion ($15 adults, $7 children 4 to 12) to a 3- hour dinner cruise ($29 to $35) that includes dinner and live entertainment on two decks. The dinner cruises offer different themes, but don't look for alternative rock; most are along the lines of classic rock, oldies nights, and country/western. The ship operates from the end of May through mid-October, departing from the train station in Weirs Beach. (You can't miss it when it's at the dock.)

Gunstock, on Route 11A between West Alton and Gilford (☎ **800/486-7862**), is a fine destination for families and intermediate skiers who like good views and great grooming as part of their ski experience. This venerable state-run ski area, with a vertical drop of 1,420 feet, has the comfortably burnished patina of a rustic resort dating from a much earlier era—no garish condos, no ski theme lounges, no forced frivolity. But the mountain managers pride themselves on maintaining excellent ski conditions throughout the day on its 45 trails and even closes several hours during lunch for midday grooming. Gunstock skiers have a choice of two double chairlifts, two triples, and a quad (plus two surface lifts); from the slopes, the views of iced-over Winnipesaukee and the White Mountains to the north are superb. Gunstock also offers night skiing on 15 trails served by five lifts. Adult lift tickets in the winter of 1996–97 were $28 midweek and $39 weekends and holidays. For juniors (ages 6 to 12) and seniors (65 and over), rates are $20 midweek and $24 weekends and holidays.

WHERE TO STAY

Creeping condomania has reduced the number of guest rooms in the lake area, but Business Route 3 (which runs picturesquely along Paugus Bay) still offers a good selection of motels, cottages, and motor courts, including many that will delight aficionados of 1950s-style architecture and neon. Try the **Naswa Lakeside Resort** (☎ 603/366-4341), which offers simple cottages and motel-style rooms on a sandy beach and features a popular restaurant and bar. The resort has been in the same family for more than 6 decades, but it hasn't been sitting still. In 1996, the resort purchased the motel across the street, bringing the number of rooms to 80.

The **Hi-Spot Motor Court** (☎ 603/524-3281) has its own beach and rowboats for guests, who choose from housekeeping cottages and motel rooms. If you'd prefer to be within walking distance of Weirs Beach attractions, the **Half Moon Motel and Cottages** (☎ 603/366-4494) is perfectly situated on a hillside overlooking the town and the lake beyond. Summer rates are $67 to $79.

Inn at Mill Falls. Routes 3 and 25, Meredith, NH 03253. ☎ **800/622-6455** or 603/ 279-7006. Fax 603/279-6797. 78 rms in 2 buildings. A/C TV TEL. Summer and fall $79–$249 double; winter and spring $69–$235 double. AE, DISC, MC, V.

Located in the middle of Meredith, the Inn at Mill Falls is part of a complex of two dozen shops and restaurants in a renovated and expanded mill built around a small waterfall. The inn, which opened in 1985, has loads of architectural integrity, but it's best suited for those who prefer the amenities of a modern hotel to the charm of a country inn. It's a thoroughly up-to-date hotel with nicely decorated guest rooms (the maple and pine furniture is by New Hampshire craftsmen), and views across the highway to the Meredith Bay. Fifty-four of the guest rooms are at the old mill site;

another 24 are across the way at Bay Point, a four-story building with superior lake views and turn-of-the-century boathouse styling.

Dining/Entertainment: Several dining options are available at the adjacent mill complex, including the Millworks Restaurant, Giuseppe's Pizzeria and Cafe, and Mame's.

Services/Facilities: Indoor pool, lake beach swimming, Jacuzzi, conference rooms, nearby health club, limited room service, safe.

✪ **Red Hill Inn.** Rte. 25B, Box 99M, Center Harbor, NH 03226. ☎ **800/573-3445** or 603/279-7001. Fax 603/279-7003. E-mail: info@redhillinn.com. Web site: www.redhillinn.com. 21 rms (4 with shower or tub only). TEL. $95–$175 double at inn and farmhouse; $150–$200 cottage. Rates include full breakfast. 2-day minimum on weekends. Good-value midweek packages available. AE, CB, DC, DISC, MC, V. From Center Harbor, drive northwest 2.9 miles on Rte. 25B.

The Red Hill Inn is tucked in the rolling hills between Winnipesaukee and Squam Lake (where *On Golden Pond* was filmed), but borrows more of its flavor from the mountains than the lakeshore. Housed in an architecturally austere, three-story brick home dating from the turn of the century, the inn looks down a long meadow toward a small complex of elegant green-and-red shingled farm buildings at the foot of a hill. (Two of these have been converted to well-appointed guest quarters.)

The rooms and common areas in the main inn are handsomely furnished in low Victorian style with floral wallpaper and maple floors. Room prices are based on views and size, but my favorite room (the Kearsarge) is one of the least expensive, with a very private brick and chocolatey brown paneled sitting room, off which lies a small bathroom with a claw-foot tub.

Dining/Entertainment: The inn's dining room serves lunch, Sunday brunch, and dinner, with classic entrees such as medaillons of venison au poivre, or rack of lamb with a feta-cheese and Dijon-mustard topping. Prices range from $9.95 to $26.95 (most are $15 to $18).

WHERE TO DINE

Kellerhaus (☎ **603/366-4466**) is *the* classic house of sweets. Located in a storybook-like stone and half-timber structure on Route 3, a third of a mile north of Endicott Beach, this old-fashioned place with bull's-eye windows on a hillside overlooking the lake features a diet-busting ice-cream buffet, where fanatics can select from a battery of toppings including macaroon crunch, butterscotch, chocolate, and whipped cream. The smorgasbord is $3.25 to $5.95, depending on the number of scoops you begin with. There's also a sizable gift shop with homemade candies, providing snacks for the road.

Hart's Turkey Farm Restaurant. Rte. 3, Meredith. ☎ **603/279-6212.** Reservations recommended during peak season. Main courses $7.95–$17.50. AE, CB, DC, DISC, MC, V. Summer daily 11:15am–9pm; fall–spring daily 11:15am–8pm. POULTRY/AMERICAN.

Hart's Turkey Farm Restaurant is not good news if you're a turkey. On a typically busy day, this popular spot dishes up more than a ton of America's favorite bird, along with 4,000 dinner rolls and 1,000 pounds of potatoes. Let's not even talk about Thanksgiving.

Judging by name alone, Hart's Farm sounds more rural than it is. In fact, there are no turkeys to be seen nearby. It's in a nondescript roadside building on a busy, nondescript part of Route 3. Inside, it's comfortable in a faux–Olde New Englande sort of way, and the service has that brisk efficiency found only in places where waitresses have been hoisting heavy trays for years, and are nonplused even when bus tours show up unexpectedly for a meal. But diners don't flock to Harts for the charm. They come for filling meals that range from fried fish to filet mignon. And most off all, they come for turkey that's cooked right every time.

Hickory Stick Farm. 60 Bean Hill Rd., Belmont. ☎ **603/524-3333.** Web site: www.hickorystickfarm.com. Reservations recommended. Main courses $10.95–$18.95. AE, DISC, MC, V. Memorial Day to Columbus Day Tues–Sun 5–8pm; limited schedule remainder of the year. AMERICAN.

The Hickory Stick Farm is well off the beaten path in the countryside outside of Laconia (ask for directions when you make reservations), but has managed to attract and keep happy diners since it first opened its doors in 1950 (it's still operated by the same family). Ask for a seat in the screened-in gazebo room during the balmy weather. When it turns chilly, angle for a table near the fireplace in the brick-floored dining room.

The restaurant is famous for its distinctive duck dishes, served with an orange-sherry sauce. The duck is slow-roasted for 4 to 5 hours, and the fatty layer is removed from beneath the skin. This method yields delicate and crispy skin, but moist meat. The duck attracts gourmands from Boston and beyond, but tasty country fare like sirloin and roast rack of lamb keeps the locals coming in night after night.

Las Piñatas. 9 Veteran's Sq., Laconia. ☎ **603/528-1405.** Reservations suggested for parties of 5 or more. Lunch items $4–$8; main dinner courses $10–$13. AE, MC, V. Mon–Sat 11am–2pm; Mon–Thurs 5–9pm, Fri–Sat 5–9:30pm, Sun 5–8pm. MEXICAN.

Armando Lezama first came to Laconia from Mexico City in 1979 as a high-school exchange student. He liked it. So he moved here with his family, opening what's most certainly the most authentic Mexican restaurant in New Hampshire. Housed in the handsome stone railroad station on the edge of Laconia's downtown, Las Piñatas has a good menu of genuine Mexican dishes and frozen margaritas that seem especially tasty after a long day at the lake. While diners might gripe about the lackadaisical service or the overabundance of iceberg lettuce, the entrees boast authentic spicing—the beans are earthy and the salsa tangy. Everything is uniformly well prepared, and offered at excellent prices. The menu includes Mexican regulars like as empanadas, tacos al carbón, and fajitas. Among the specialties are the delicious enchiladas de mole, made with the Lezama's homemade mole sauce. For dessert, try the coconut flan, or a bunuelo with maple syrup. There's often local live entertainment on weekends.

EASTERN SHORE

Winnipesaukee's eastern shore sometimes recalls Gertrude Stein's comment about Oakland: "There's no there there." Other than the low-key town of **Wolfeboro,** the eastern shore is mostly islands and coves, mixed forests and rolling hills, rocky farms and the occasional apple orchard. While it's a large lake, its waters are also largely inaccessible from this side. Old summer homes and new gated condominium communities occupy some of the best coves and points. But narrow roads do touch on the lake here and there, and most roads are nicely engineered for leisurely cruising. The secret to getting the most out of the eastern shore is to take it slow and enjoy the small villages and quiet forests as if they were delicately crafted miniatures, not vast panoramas.

ESSENTIALS

GETTING THERE   Lake Winnipesaukee's eastern shore is best explored on Route 28 (from Alton Bay to Wolfeboro) and Route 109 (from Wolfeboro to Moultonborough). From the south, Alton Bay can be reached via Route 11 from Rochester, or from Route 28, which intersects Routes 4 and 202 about 12 miles east of Concord.

VISITOR INFORMATION The **Wolfeboro Chamber of Commerce,** P.O. Box 547, Wolfeboro, NH 03894 (☎ **800/516-5324** or 603/569-2200), offers regional travel information and advice from its offices in a converted railroad station at Depot Square, one block off Main Street in Wolfeboro (turn on Railroad Avenue).

EXPLORING WOLFEBORO

The town of Wolfeboro (pop. 2,800) claims to be the first summer resort in the United States, and the documentation makes a pretty good case for it. In 1763, John Wentworth, the nephew of a former governor, built a summer estate on what's now called Lake Wentworth, along with a road to it from Portsmouth. Wentworth didn't get to enjoy his holdings for long—his Tory sympathies forced him to flee when the political situation heated up in 1775. The house burned in 1820, but the site now attracts archaeologists.

Tourists are lured to **Wentworth State Beach** (☎ 603/569-3699) not so much because of history but because of the attractive beach, refreshing lake waters, and shady picnic area. The park is located 5 miles east of Wolfeboro on Route 109.

Wolfeboro has a vibrant, homey downtown that's easily explored on foot. Park near Depot Square and the gingerbread Victorian train station, and stock up on brochures and maps at the Chamber of Commerce office inside. Behind the train station, running along the former tracks of the rail line, is the **Russell C. Chase Bridge-Falls Path,** a rail trail that (so far) runs pleasantly about half a mile along Back Bay to a set of small waterfalls. (Plans call for extending the pathway farther in coming years.)

A QUIRKY CASTLE

Castle in the Clouds. Rte. 171 (4 miles south of Rte. 25), Moultonborough. ☎ **800/ 729-2468** or 603/476-2352. $10 adults, $9 seniors, $7 students. (Grounds only, $4.) Mid-May to mid-June Sat–Sun 9am–5pm; mid-June to Labor Day daily 9am–5pm; Labor Day to 3rd week of Oct daily 9am–4pm. Closed Nov–Apr.

Cranky millionaire Thomas Gustav Plant built this eccentric stone edifice high atop a mountain overlooking Lake Winnipesaukee early in this century. Completed in 1913 at a cost of $7 million, the home is a sort of rustic San Simeon East, with orange roof tiles, cliff-hugging rooms, stained-glass windows, and unrivaled views of the surrounding hills and lakes. Visitors drive as far as the carriage house (nicely converted to a snack bar and restaurant), where they park and are taken in groups through the house by knowledgeable guides.

Even if the castle holds no interest, the 5,200-acre grounds themselves are worth the admission price (there's a discount for those visiting the grounds only). The long access road is harrowingly narrow and winding (kids, don't try this in your mobile home), with wonderful vistas and turnouts for stopping and exploring along the way. I'd advise taking your time on the way up; the exit road is fast, straight, and uninteresting.

Equestrians can rent horses to explore the hills at $25 for a 1-hour ride (reservations required).

On your way out, you're invited to visit the modern bottling plant and brewery, where Castle Springs Water is packaged for shipment to shops throughout the Northeast, and a new brewery produces tasty microbrews for local consumption. There's no additional charge for the tour.

WHERE TO STAY & DINE

Wolfeboro Inn. 90 N. Main St., Wolfeboro, NH 03894. ☎ **800/451-2389** or 603/569-3016. Fax 603/569-5375. 44 rms. A/C TV TEL. $79–$229 double. Rates include continental breakfast. Add $20 on weekends. 2-night minimum in peak season. AE, MC, V.

This small, elegant hotel strives to mix modern and traditional, and succeeds admirably in doing so. Located a short stroll from downtown Wolfeboro, the inn dates back to 1812 but was extensively expanded and updated between 1985 and 1986. The modern lobby features a small atrium with wood beams, slate floor, and a brick fireplace, and has managed to retain an old-world elegance and grace. Comfortable guest rooms vary in size, and most are furnished with Early American reproductions. Some have fireplaces; others have views of Wolfeboro Bay. The inn also has some nice extras, including its own 75-passenger excursion boat (a free trip is included in room rates). On the downside, for an inn of this elegance and price it has only a disappointing sliver of lakeshore and a miniature beach for guests.

Dining/Entertainment: The main dining room has two areas to suit your mood: Sit near the fireplace in a low-ceilinged room decorated in a traditional Early American style, or choose the upper, gazebolike room, which is airy and summery. The dining room is open daily in summer; Thursday through Saturday in winter. The atmospheric Wolfe's Tavern is open daily year-round. With pewter tankards hanging from the low beams, 60 brands of beer, and a selection of basic pub fare, this is a good destination for salads, burgers, and a variety of pasta dishes.

Services/Facilities: Beach swimming, conference rooms, nearby health club, concierge, limited room service, dry cleaning, laundry service, baby-sitting.

5 The White Mountains

The White Mountains are northern New England's undisputed outdoor recreation capital. This cluster of ancient mountains is a sprawling, rugged playground that attracts kayakers, mountaineers, rock climbers, skiers, mountain bikers, bird-watchers, and hikers.

Especially hikers. The **White Mountain National Forest** encompasses some 773,000 acres of rocky, forested terrain, more than 100 waterfalls, dozens of remote backcountry lakes, and miles of clear brooks and cascading streams. An elaborate network of 1,200 miles of hiking trails dates back to the 19th century, when the urban gentry took to the mountains in droves to build character, build trails, and experience the raw sublimity of nature. Trails ranging from easy to extraordinarily demanding lace the hillside forests, run along remote valley rivers, and traverse barren, windswept ridgelines where the weather can change dramatically in less time than it takes to eat your lunch.

The spiritual center of the White Mountains is its highest point: 6,288-foot **Mount Washington,** an ominous, brooding peak that's often cloud capped, and often mantled with snow early and late in the season. This blustery peak is accessible by train, car, and foot, making it one of the most popular spots in the region. You won't find wilderness here, but you will find a surfeit of natural drama.

Flanking this colossal peak are the brawny **Presidential Mountains,** a series of wind-blasted granite peaks named after U.S. presidents and offering spectacular views. Surrounding these are numerous other rocky ridges that lure hikers looking for challenges and a place to experience raw and elemental nature.

As for **camping,** simple but comfortable huts (managed by the Appalachian Mountain Club) and three-sided lean-tos are scattered throughout the White Mountains, providing overnight shelter for backcountry campers. Meals are included at the huts, but the whole package is surprisingly pricey. Shelters are sometimes free; sometimes a backcountry manager will collect a small fee. Backcountry tent camping is free throughout the White Mountains, and no permit is needed, although you'll need to purchase a parking permit to leave your car at the trailhead. Check with one of the ranger stations for current restrictions on where you can camp in the backcountry.

The White Mountains & Lake Country

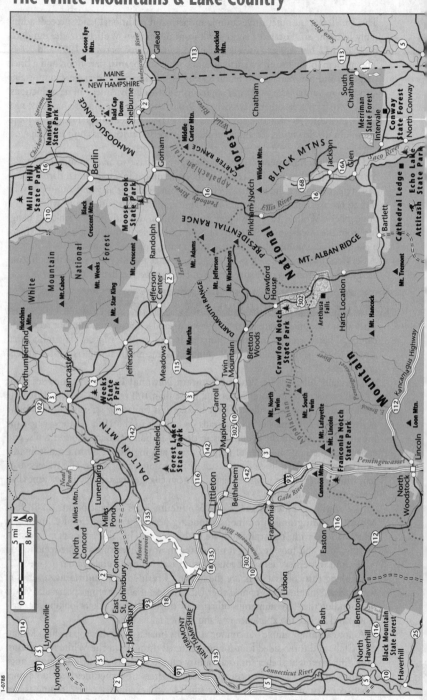

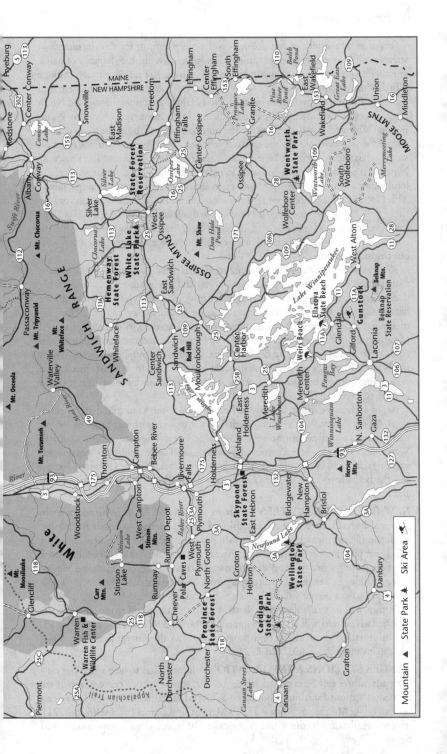

Mountain ▲   State Park ≛   Ski Area ⛷

Travelers whose idea of fun doesn't involve steep cliffs or icy dips in mountain streams still have plenty of opportunities for milder adventure. A handful of major arteries provide easy access to mountain scenery. **Route 302** carries travelers through North Conway and Crawford Notch to the pleasant towns of Bethlehem and Littleton. **Route 16** travels from southern New Hampshire through congested North Conway before twisting up dramatic Pinkham Notch at the base of Mount Washington. Wide and fast **Route 2** skirts the northern edge of the mountains, offering wonderful views en route to the town of Jefferson. **I-93** gets my vote for the most scenic interstate in northern New England, passing through spectacular Franconia Notch as it narrows to a two-lane road in deference to its natural surroundings (and local political will). And finally, there's the **Kancamagus Highway,** linking Conway with Lincoln, and providing some of the most spectacular White Mountain vistas in the region. Along the way, frequent roadside pull-offs and interpretive exhibits allow casual explorers to admire cascades, picnic along rivers, and enjoy sweeping mountain views. Several less demanding nature hikes are also easily accessible from various roadside turnouts.

Keep in mind that the White Mountains are a national *forest,* not a national *park,* a distinction that's sometimes lost on urbanites and foreign travelers. There's a big difference. National forests are managed for multiple uses, which includes timber harvesting, wildlife management, recreational development, and the like. This may disappoint those offended by clear-cutting and logging roads. Fortunately, the level of cutting is not as excessive as at many Western forests, and the regrowth here also tends to be more rapid than in the arid West. Also bear in mind that about 15% of the White Mountains is formally designated as wilderness, from which mechanical devices (including mountain bikes) are prohibited. Strike out for these areas if you're looking to step deep into the wilds.

As for accommodations, it's easy to find an area to suit your mood and inclinations. North Conway is the motel capital of the region, with hundreds of rooms, many quite charmless but at very reasonable rates. The Loon Mountain and Waterville Valley area have a sort of planned condo village graciousness that delights some travelers and creeps out others. Jackson, Franconia Notch, Crawford Notch, and the Bethlehem-Littleton area are the best destinations for old-fashioned hotels and inns.

NEW BACKCOUNTRY FEES   Starting in May 1997, the White Mountain National Forest will require anyone using the backcountry—whether for hiking, mountain biking, picnicking, or skiing—to pay a recreation fee. This new fee is part of a 3-year pilot project mandated by Congress, which decided that backcountry users had been getting a free ride and should now pony up. The new program will require anyone parking at a trailhead to display a permit on the dashboard of their car. Those who don't have a permit will likely get a ticket and face a fine.

Permits will be available widely, both at ranger stations and many stores in the region. Two permits will be sold: an annual permit for $20, and a 7-day pass for $5. For information about the permit program, contact the **Forest Service**'s White Mountains office at ☎ **603/528-8721.**

RANGER STATIONS & INFORMATION   Information to help with your outdoor adventures can be obtained at the national forest visitor's centers, which are located in various locations around the White Mountains. The **Forest Service**'s central White Mountains office is at 719 Main St. in Laconia (☎ **603/528-8721**), which actually isn't in the White Mountains but near Lake Winnipesaukee. (Go figure.)

Your best source of information in the mountains is at the **Saco Ranger Station** (☎ 603/447-5448) in Conway; the office is on the Kancamagus Highway just 100 yards west of Route 16. Other district offices are the **Androscoggin Ranger Station** (☎ 603/466-2713), which is at 80 Glen Rd. in Gorham. The **Ammonoosuc Ranger Station** (☎ 603/869-2626) is on Trudeau Road in Bethlehem. The **Pemigewasset Ranger Station** (☎ 603/536-1310) is on Route 175 in Plymouth. And the **Evans Notch Ranger Station** (☎ 207/824-2134), which covers the Maine portion of the White Mountains (about 50,000 acres), is located in Bethel at 18 Mayville Rd., off Route 2 just north of town.

Additional information and advice about recreation in the White Mountains is also available at the **AMC's Pinkham Notch Camp** (☎ 603/466-2721) on Route 16 between Jackson and Gorham. The center is open daily from 6am to 10pm.

SPECIALIZED GUIDEBOOKS If you're serious about exploring the wind-scoured crags and mossy ravines of the White Mountains, you'll need supplemental guides and maps to keep you on track in the great outdoors. Here's a short list of recommended guides, most of which are available at area bookstores:

- *AMC White Mountain Guide* (Appalachian Mountain Club, 1992, $16.95). This compact, 638-page book (no, that's not an oxymoron) is chock-full of detailed information on *all* the hiking trails in the White Mountains. It's printed in small type in a size suitable to throwing in your pack, and comes with a handy set of maps. This is the hiker's bible for the region.
- *Mount Washington: A Guide and Short History* (Countryman Press, 1992, $9.95). Peter Randall originally wrote this handy and informative guide in 1983, updating it in 1992. The guide will appeal to those interested in the history and hiking of the Northeast's tallest peak.
- *Fifty Hikes in the White Mountains* (Backcountry Publications, 1994, $14). The fourth edition of this popular guide, written by John Doan, offers a good selection of mountain rambles ranging from easy strolls to overnight backpack trips.
- *Ponds & Lakes of the White Mountains* (Backcountry Publications, 1993, $16). The White Mountain high country is studded with dramatic tarns (many left by retreating glaciers). This 350-page guide by Steven D. Smith offers 68 trips to help get you there.
- *Waterfalls of the White Mountains* (Backcountry Publications, 1990, $17). Waterfall lovers will get their money's worth from Bruce and Doreen Bolnick's guide to 100 mountain waterfalls, including roadside cascades and backcountry cataracts.

NORTH CONWAY & ENVIRONS

North Conway is the commercial heart of the White Mountains. Shoppers adore it because of the profusion of outlets, boutiques, and restaurants along Routes 302 and 16. (The two state highways overlap through town.) Outdoor purists abhor it, considering it a garish interloper to be avoided at all costs, except when looking for pizza.

No doubt North Conway itself won't strike anyone as nature's wonderland. The shopping strip south of the village is basically a long turning lane flanked with outlet malls of every architectural stripe, motels, and chain restaurants. On rainy weekends and during the foliage season, the road can resemble a linear parking lot.

Regardless, North Conway is beautifully situated along the eastern edge of the broad and fertile Saco River Valley (often called the Mt. Washington Valley by local tourism boosters). Gentle, forest-covered mountains, some with sheer cliffs that suggest the distant, stunted cousins of Yosemite's rocky faces, border the bottomlands.

Northward up the valley, the hills rise in a triumphant crescendo to the blustery, tempestuous heights of Mount Washington.

The village itself is trim and attractive (if often congested), with an open green, quaint shops, Victorian frontier town commercial architecture, and a distinctive train station. It's a good place to park, stretch your legs, and find a cup of coffee or a snack.

Visitors who'd prefer a more scenic, less commercial route bypassing North Conway's strip malls should detour to **West Side Road.** Arriving from the south, turn north at the light in Conway Village on to Washington Street. One-half mile farther, bear left on West Side Road. The road passes near two covered bridges in the first half-mile, then dips and winds through the broad farmlands of the Saco River Valley. You'll pass working farms and farm stands, and some architecturally distinctive early homes. You'll also come upon dramatic views of the granite cliffs that form the western wall of the valley. Stop for a swim at **Echo Lake State Park** (it's well marked, on your left). At the first stop sign, turn right for North Conway Village, or turn left to connect to Route 302 in Bartlett, passing more ledges and cliffs.

ESSENTIALS

GETTING THERE   North Conway and the Mount Washington Valley are on Routes 16 and 302. Route 16 connects to the Spaulding Turnpike outside of Portsmouth, N.H. Route 302 begins in Portland, Maine.

VISITOR INFORMATION   The **Mount Washington Valley Chamber of Commerce,** P.O. Box 2300, North Conway, NH 03860 (☎ **800/367-3364** or 603/ 356-3171), operates a seasonal information booth opposite the village green with brochures about attractions and inns. The staff can arrange for local accommodations. It's open daily in summer, Monday to Friday from 9am to 6pm and weekends from 9am to 8pm. In winter, it's open weekends only.

The state of New Hampshire also operates an **information booth** with rest rooms and telephones at a vista with fine views of Mount Washington on routes 16 and 302 north of North Conway.

RIDING THE RAILS

A unique way to view the mountainous landscape around North Conway is via train. The **Conway Scenic Railroad** (☎ **800/232-5251** or 603/356-5251; Web site: **www.conwayscenic.com**) offers regularly scheduled trips in comfortable cars pulled by either steam or sleek early diesel engines. Trips depart from an 1874 train station just off the village green, recalling an era when tourists arrived from Boston and New York to enjoy the country air for a month or two each summer. The 1-hour excursion heads south to Conway; the more scenic 1$\frac{3}{4}$-hour trip heads north to the village of Bartlett. For a real show, sign up for the 5$\frac{1}{2}$-hour excursion through dramatic Crawford Notch (I think of this as equivalent to the old "A" ticket at Disneyland), with stupendous views of the mountains from high along this beautiful glacial valley. You even get a great view of the remarkable Mount Washington Hotel. Ask also about the railway's dining excursions.

The train runs April through mid-December, with more frequent trips scheduled daily in midsummer. Tickets are $8.50 to $16.50 for adults ($31.95 to $39.95 for Crawford Notch), $5.50 to $11.50 for children 4 to 12 ($16.95 to $21.95 for Crawford Notch). Kids under 4 ride free on the Conway trip only. Reservations are suggested for the dining car and the Notch train.

SHOPPING, SHOPPING & MORE SHOPPING

Consumers who find themselves suffering from mall withdrawal after being amid all those trees and mountains can indulge themselves in North Conway. You could easily fill a day or two combing through bargain racks of name-brand clothing and other merchandise. You won't have to search hard to find these 200-plus shops. They're easily found along "the strip," which extends about 3 miles from the junction of Route 302 and Route 16 north of Conway into to the village of North Conway itself. It's a town planner's nightmare, but a shopper's paradise.

Among the more notable outlet clusters are **Outlet Village Plus at Settler's Green,** with better than 30 name-brand shops; the **Tanger Factory Outlet,** which hosts the popular L.L. Bean shop; and **Willow Place,** with 11 shops like Dress Barn, Bed & Bath, and Lingerie Factory. Other outlets scattered along the strip include Anne Klein, American Tourister, Izod, Dansk, Donna Karan, Levi's, Polo/Ralph Lauren, Reebock/Rockport, J. Crew, and Eddie Bauer.

For those setting out on a White Mountain expedition, outdoor equipment suppliers in town include **International Mountain Equipment** (☎ 603/356-7013) and **Eastern Mountain Sports** (☎ 603/356-5433), both on Main Street just north of the green. There's also **Ragged Mountain Equipment** (☎ 603/356-3042), 3 miles north of town in Intervale on Routes 16 and 302. All three shops are excellent sources of advice on local destinations and weather conditions; Ragged Mountain offers its own free brochures outlining suggested day hikes and mountain bike rides in the area.

A final testimonial: A favorite shop of mine is **Chuck Roast Mountainwear** (☎ 603/356-5589), a North Conway–based manufacturer of outerwear, backpacks, and soft luggage. The day pack I purchased from them 5 years ago has held up superbly despite constant battering. All their goods come with a lifetime guarantee. Their outlet is at the Mount Washington Outlet Center, the plaza next door to the L.L. Bean outlet.

ROCK CLIMBING

The impressive granite faces on the valley's west side are for more than admiring from afar. They're also for climbing. Cathedral Ledge and Whitehorse Ledge attract rock climbers from all over the Eastern seaboard, who consider these cliffs (along with the Shawangunks in New York State and Seneca Rocks in West Virginia) as sort of an Eastern troika where they can put their grace and technical acumen to the test.

Experienced climbers will have their own sources of information on the best access and routes. (Guidebooks are also available at the outdoor outfitters mentioned above.) Inexperienced climbers should sign up for a class taught by one of the local outfitters, whose workshops run from 1 day to 1 week. Try the **Eastern Mountain Sports Climbing School** (☎ 603/356-5433), the **International Mountain Climbing School** (☎ 603/356-7064), or the **Mountain Guides Alliance** (☎ 603/356-5310).

To tone up or keep in shape on rainy days, the **Cranmore Sports Center** (☎ 603/356-6301) near the Mount Cranmore base lodge has an indoor climbing wall open weekdays from 5 to 9pm and weekends from 2 to 8pm. The fee is $10 Monday to Friday, and $12 on weekends. Newcomers must pass a belay test (free) before climbing; if their skills aren't up to snuff, they'll be asked to take a lesson. Private, semiprivate, and group lessons are available.

SKIING

Mount Cranmore. North Conway Village, NH 03860. ☎ 603/356-5544. Vertical drop: 1,200 ft. 6 chairlifts (1 high-speed quad), 4 surface lifts. Skiable acreage: 190. Lift tickets $39 weekends for adults, $22 children under 12; midweek $31 adults, $17 children under 12.

Mount Cranmore is within walking distance of downtown North Conway (although I wouldn't try it in ski boots). The oldest operating ski area in New England, Mount Cranmore is unrepentantly old-fashioned, and doesn't display an iota of pretense. It's not likely to challenge advanced skiers, but it will delight beginners and intermediates, as well as those who like the old-style New England cut of the ski trails.

WHERE TO STAY

Route 16 through North Conway is packed with basic motels that are reasonably priced in the off-season, but may be pricey during peak travel times such as fall foliage season. Fronting the commercial strip, these motels don't offer much in the way of a pastoral environment, but most are comfortable and conveniently located. Try the **School House Motel** (☎ 603/356-6829), with a heated outdoor pool; **the Yankee Clipper Motor Lodge** (☎ 800/343-5900 or 603/356-5736), with a pool and minigolf; or the slightly more pricey **Green Granite Motel** (☎ 800/468-3666 or 603/356-6901), with whirlpool suites, 88 rooms, and a free continental breakfast.

Albert B. Lester Memorial Hostel. 36 Washington St., Conway, NH 03818. ☎ 603/447-1001. Fax 603/447-1011. E-mail: hiconway@nxi.com. Web site: www.angel.net/~hostel. 45 beds. $16 per person. $45 for private rooms. Rates include continental breakfast. JCB, MC, V. Closed Nov. Turn north at the light in Conway on Washington St.; it's the second house on the left.

Conveniently situated near the center of Conway Village, the Lester Hostel is the best choice for those traveling on a shoestring but not enamored of camping. Rooms in this gracious black-and-white farmhouse are set up hostel-style and accommodate 45 people (some family rooms are available), but guests, many of whom are young Europeans, generally spend their time in the yard knocking around a volleyball or availing themselves of the barbecue. A new bike room and repair shop make this the premier destination (or base) for bike travelers. In the summer, weekly lobster bakes will fill you with lobster, clams, mussels, and corn for just $10. Not only will you save money here, but the congenial atmosphere is a great way to swap tips on area trails and bike rides with newfound friends. The hostel is open for check-in or checkout daily from 7:30am to 9:30am, and 5 to 10pm. Ask about shuttle service to the Portland, Me., hostel.

Cranmore Inn. 80 Kearsarge St., N. Conway, NH 03860. ☎ 800/526-5502 or 603/356-5502. 18 rms (4 share hall baths; 7 rms with showers only). Summer $59–$78 double; foliage season and ski weekends $79–$98 double; off-season $49–$68 double. Rates include full breakfast. AE, MC, V.

The Cranmore Inn has the feel of a 19th-century boardinghouse—and that's what it is. Open since 1863, this three-story Victorian home is hidden on a side street a short walk from North Conway's main attractions. Its distinguished heritage (it's the oldest continuously operating hotel in North Conway) adds considerable charm and quirkiness, but comes with some minor drawbacks, like uneven water pressure in the showers and some sinks with cracked or stained enamel. During my last visit, I had a window that wouldn't stay up and a window shade that wouldn't stay down. Ask to see your room before you hand over your credit card.

That said, I'd return here in a second because of its charm, its graciousness, and the good humor of the innkeepers. The inn also has nice details like guests' names on placards at breakfast in the dining room. The old-fashioned downstairs parlors are great for cribbage or mingling with other guests; the front porch allows you to monitor the rather sedate comings and goings of Kearsarge Street. There's also an outdoor pool in summer to cool off after a day of hiking.

Red Jacket Mountain View. Rte. 16 (P.O. Box 2000), N. Conway, NH 03860. ☎ 800/752-2538 or 603/356-5411. Fax 603/356-3842. E-mail: rjacket@nxi.com. 164 rms. A/C TV TEL. $89–$245 double, depending on season, time of week, and view. AE, CB, DC, DISC, MC, V.

Set high on a grassy ridge overlooking the Saco Valley, this Best Western facility is a 1970s-era resort that's managed to avoid a dated disco-era look through constant renovations. A modern, two-story building with two wings flanking a reception area, dining room, and indoor pool, the Red Jacket presents a quiet oasis on 30 hillside acres overlooking the hubbub of the highway. The spacious guest rooms are nicely furnished with colonial reproductions, and many offer private patios or balconies. If the weather's nice, splurge on a mountain-view room and enjoy the vistas of the Moat Mountains across the valley.

Dining/Entertainment: As for food, you're better off exploring locally. The resort's Champey's Restaurant is a rather dim and gloomy hotel dining room that's overdue for renovation. Not even wonderful views and a decent menu can enliven the atmosphere.

Services: Concierge, limited room service, dry cleaning, laundry, baby-sitting, valet parking, safe-deposit boxes.

Facilities: Heated indoor and outdoor swimming pools, two tennis courts (lit for night play), game rooms, jogging track, nature trails, conference rooms, laundry room, sauna, sundeck.

Stonehurst Manor. Rte. 16 (1.2 miles north of North Conway Village; P.O. Box 1937), N. Conway, NH 03860. ☎ **800/525-9100** or 603/356-3271. Web site: www.stonehurstmanor.com. 24 rms (2 with shared bath, some with showers only). A/C TV. $80–$140 double; $106–$166 double with breakfast and dinner included. $20–$30 surcharge during foliage season. MC, V.

The Stonehurst Manor seems determined to confound expectations. This imposing, eclectic Victorian stone-and-shingle mansion, set amid white pines on a rocky knoll above Route 16, wouldn't seem at all out of place in the south of France or on the moors of Scotland. The immediate assumption is that it caters to the stuffy and affluent. But don't assume. The main focus here is on outdoor adventure vacations, and it attracts a youngish crowd. And the rates aren't nearly as prohibitive as you might expect.

My advice is to request one of the 14 rooms in the regal 1876 mansion itself (another 10 are in a comfortable but less elegant wing built in 1952). These mansion rooms are all unique and furnished appropriately to the building's era. Room no. 21A, for instance, one of the nicest in the inn, has stained-glass windows and a wicker-furnished private porch with sunset views toward Humphrey's Ledge. It's easy to slip into a fantasy that you're the guest of the Bigelow carpet tycoons—the wealthy Victorians who originally built this endearing edifice. Relax and enjoy it.

Dining/Entertainment: The restaurant makes the best wood-fired pizza in the area (see "Where to Dine," below).

✪ **White Mountain Hotel and Resort.** W. Side Rd. (5.4 miles west of N. Conway; P.O. Box 1828), N. Conway, NH 03860. ☎ **800/533-6301** or 603/356-7100. 80 rms. A/C TV TEL. Summer $89–$179 double; foliage season $109–$189 double; winter $69–$139 double; off-season $59–$119 double. AE, DISC, MC, V.

This modern, upscale resort has the best location of any lodge in the North Conway area. Sited at the base of dramatic White Horse Ledge near Echo Lake State Park and amid a golf course community, the White Mountain Hotel was built in 1990 but borrows from the rich legacy of classic White Mountain resorts. Its designers have managed to take some of the more successful elements of a friendly country inn—a nice deck with a view, comfortable seating in the lobby, a clubby tavern area—and incorporate them into a thoroughly modern resort. The tones throughout are muted and rich, and overall sensibility seems more influenced by a European elegance than Early American rusticity.

Guest rooms are comfortably appointed with dark wood and an earthy maroon carpeting, and are a solid notch or two above standard hotel furnishings. All feature hair dryers and coffeemakers. Minisuites offer a bit more elbowroom and small refrigerators.

Services/Facilities: 9-hole golf course, two tennis courts, game rooms, outdoor heated pool, Jacuzzi, sauna, fitness center, nature trails, conference rooms, self-service Laundromat, limited room service, dry cleaning, laundry service, baby-sitting.

WHERE TO DINE

Bellini's. 33 Seavey St., N. Conway. ☎ **603/356-7000.** Reservations not accepted. Main courses $10–$19. AE, CB, DC, DISC, MC, V. Sun–Mon and Wed–Thurs 5–10pm, Fri–Sat 5–11pm. Closed 2 weeks in Nov and 2 weeks during mud season. ITALIAN.

Bellini's has a fun, quirky interior that's more informal than its Victorian exterior might suggest. Inside it features Cinzano umbrellas and striped awnings, black-and-white checkerboard floors, and huge potted plants—it's the kind of place to put you in a good mood right off. And the food, which runs the Italian gamut from fettuccine chicken pesto to braciola, can only but further improve your spirits. The pleasantly garlicky marinara sauce is only a notch above average, but much of the rest of the fare shines brighter. Particularly good are the toasted raviolis. This is a great place to sup with a gaggle of friends or your extended family, but a moon-eyed couple might also find a quiet niche to make a romantic evening of it.

Stonehurst Manor. Rte. 16 (1.2 miles north of the village), N. Conway. ☎ **603/356-3113.** Reservations recommended. Main courses $12.75–$21; pizza $8.95–$10.95. MC, V. Daily 6–10pm. AMERICAN/PIZZA.

It's likely these are the most elegant surroundings in which you'll ever eat a pizza. Wood-fired pizza was added to the menu about a decade ago, just ahead of the national trend, when the restaurant noticed that inn guests arriving late from Boston didn't feel up to a full meal. So they added pizza in a number of elegant variations (chicken sausage and wild mushrooms; grilled vegetables), and the word spread. The pizza became a local institution, complementing the other superb dishes served here.

Diners have a choice of four dining areas on the first floor of this sumptuous 1876 mansion, and each area is decorated informally and comfortably. (The deep, low rattan chairs, however, may have outlived their charm.) In the summer, head for the screened patio overlooking the garden. In addition to pizza, the chef serves up a raft of other creative dishes, including wood-fired roast duck with blackberry sauce, and baked haddock in parchment with vegetables.

JACKSON & ENVIRONS

Jackson is an eddy swirling gently on its own, just out of the flow of the tourist mainstream. Situated in a picturesque valley just off Route 16 about a 15-minute drive north of North Conway, Jackson still attracts plenty of travelers, but history is strong enough here to absorb much of the tourist impact.

You enter Jackson, somewhat tentatively, on a single-lane covered bridge. The village center is tiny, but touches of old-world elegance remain here and there—vestiges of a time when Jackson was a premier destination for the East Coast affluent, who fled the summer heat in the cities to board at rambling wooden hotels or retire to shingled country estates.

With the depression and the subsequent rise of the motel trade in the 1940s and 1950s, Jackson and its old-fashioned hostelries slipped into a decades-long slumber. Then along came the 1980s, which brought developers winging in and out of the valley in private helicopters, condo projects sprouting in fields where cows once roamed, and the resuscitation of the couple of vintage wooden hotels that didn't burn or collapse during the dark ages.

Thanks to a rebuilt golf course and one of the most elaborate and well-maintained cross-country ski networks in the country, Jackson is today again a thriving resort, both in summer and winter. It's still out of the mainstream, and a peaceful spot quite distant in character from commercial North Conway. Settle in to one of the old summer homes converted to an inn, park yourself on a rocker on a porch, and you'll find that not all that much has changed in the intervening century.

ESSENTIALS

GETTING THERE   Jackson is just off Route 16 about 11 miles north of North Conway. Look for the covered bridge on the right when heading north.

VISITOR INFORMATION   The **Jackson Chamber of Commerce,** P.O. Box 304, Jackson, NH 03846 (☎ **800/866-3334** or 603/383-9356), can answer your questions about lodging and attractions.

EXPLORING MOUNT WASHINGTON

Mount Washington is home to numerous superlatives. At 6,288 feet, it's the highest mountain in the Northeast. (Mt. Mitchell in North Carolina is slightly higher, robbing Mt. Washington of the "highest in the East" title.) It's said to have the worst weather in the world outside of the polar regions. And it holds the world's record for the highest surface wind speed—231 miles per hour, set in 1934. Consider also that winds over 150 miles per hour are routinely recorded every month except June, July, and August, the result of the mountain's location at the confluence of three major storm tracks.

Mount Washington may also be the mountain with the most alternatives for getting to the summit. Visitors can ascend by cog railroad (see the "Crawford Notch" section, below), by car, by guide-driven van, or by foot. There's an annual bike race and foot race to the summit, and each year winter mountaineers test their mettle by inching their way to the top equipped with crampons and ice axes.

The summit of Mount Washington is a highly developed place, and not the best destination for those seeking brutish wilderness. There's a train platform, a parking lot, a snack bar, a gift shop, a museum, and a handful of outbuildings, some of which house the weather observatory, which is staffed year-round. And there are the crowds, which can be thick on a clear day. Then again, on a clear day the views can't be beat, with vistas extending into four states and to the Atlantic Ocean.

The best place to learn about Mount Washington and its approaches is the rustic **Pinkham Notch Camp** (☎ **603/466-2721**), operated by the Boston-based Appalachian Mountain Club. Located at the crest of Route 16 between Jackson and Gorham, Pinkham Notch offers overnight accommodations and meals (see below), maps, a limited selection of outdoor supplies, and plenty of advice from a helpful staff. A number of hiking trails depart from Pinkham Notch, allowing for several loops and side trips.

About a dozen trails lead to the mountain's summit, ranging in length from 3.8 to 15 miles. (See Peter Randall's *Mount Washington: A Guide and Short History,* mentioned above, for details.) The most direct and, in many ways, most dramatic trail is the **Tuckerman Ravine Trail,** which departs from Pinkham Notch. Healthy hikers should allow 4 to 5 hours for the ascent, an hour or two less for the return trip. Be sure to schedule in time to enjoy the dramatic glacial cirque of **Tuckerman Ravine,** which attracts extreme skiers to its snowy chutes and sheer drops as late as June, and often holds patches of snow well into summer.

The **Mount Washington Auto Road** (☎ 603/466-3988) opened in 1861 as a carriage road, and has since remained one of the most popular White Mountain attractions. The steep, winding 8-mile road (it has an average grade of 12%) is partially paved and incredibly dramatic; your breath will be taken away at one turn after another. The ascent will test your iron will; the descent will test your car's brakes. If you're nervous at all, consider that there have been only two fatalities in more than a century, making it one of the safest stretches of road anywhere.

If you'd prefer to leave the driving to someone else, custom vans ascend regularly allowing you to relax, enjoy the views, learn about the mountain from informed guides, and leave the fretting about overheating brakes to someone else.

The **Auto Road,** which is on Route 16 north of Pinkham Notch, is open mid-May to late-October from 7:30am to 6pm (shorter hours early and late in the season). The cost for cars is $15 for vehicle and driver, and $6 for each additional passenger ($4 for children 5 to 12). The fee includes an audiocassette featuring a narrator pointing out sights along the way. Van rates are $20 for adults, $10 for children 5 to 12. More information is available on the Internet at **www.mt-washington.com**.

One additional note: The *average* temperature atop the mountain is 30°. (The record low was -43°, and the warmest temperature *ever* recorded atop the mountain, in August, was 72°.) Even in summer visitors should come prepared for blustery, cold conditions.

If you'd prefer to observe Mount Washington from a safe and respectful distance, head up **Wildcat Mountain** (☎ 800/255-6439 or 603/466-3326) on the enclosed gondola for a superb view of Tuckerman Ravine and Mount Washington's summit. The lift operates weekends from Memorial Day to mid-June, then daily through October. The base lodge is located just north of Pinkham Notch on Route 16.

CROSS-COUNTRY SKIING

Jackson regularly makes the experts' short list of the top five cross-country ski resorts in the nation, and there's one reason for that: the nonprofit ☉ **Jackson Ski Touring Foundation** (☎ 603/383-9355), which created and now maintains the extensive trail network. The terrain around Jackson is wonderfully varied, with 93 miles of trails maintained by the foundation (56 miles are regularly groomed).

Start at the foundation headquarters in the middle of Jackson, then head right out the back door and ski through the village. Gentle trails traverse the valley floor, with more advanced trails heading up the flanking mountains. One-way ski trips with shuttles back to Jackson are also available; ask if you're interested. Trail fees are $10 for adults, $5 for children 10 to 15, and free for children under 10. Ski rentals are available at the Jack Frost ski shop in the ski center.

ALPINE SKIING

Black Mountain. Jackson, NH 03846. ☎ 800/475-4669 or 603/383-4490. Web site: www.blackmt.com. Vertical drop: 1,100 ft. 4 lifts. Skiable acreage: 101. Lift tickets $32 weekends for adults, $20 juniors; weekdays $19 adults, $15 juniors.

Dating back to the 1930s, Black Mount is of the White Mountains' pioneer ski areas. It remains the quintessential family mountain—modest in size, entirely non-threatening, and perfect for beginners. And the mountain offers some great views from the top to boot. It feels a bit like you're skiing in a farmer's unused hayfield, which just adds to the charm. The original lift was a tow where skiers held on to shovel handles to get to the top.

☉ **Wildcat.** Rte. 16, Pinkham Notch, NH 03846. ☎ 800/255-6439 or 603/466-3326. Internet: http://www.skiwildcat.com. Vertical drop: 2,100 ft. 1 gondola, 5 chairlifts.

Skiable acreage: 120. Lift tickets $39 weekends and holidays for adults, $23 juniors 6–12; mid-week $27 adults, $20 juniors 6–12.

Wildcat Mountain has a rich heritage as a venerable New England ski mountain. It also happens to offer the best mountain views of any ski area in the Whites. Situated on national forestland just across the valley from Mount Washington and Tuckerman Ravine, Wildcat has strong intermediate trails and some challenging expert slopes, including a newly cut double diamond with 60% steeps. This is skiing as it used to be—there's no base-area clutter, just a simple ski lodge. While that also means there's no on-slope accommodations, you've got an abundance of choices within a 15-minute drive. Spend the night bunkhouse-style just up the road at AMC's Pinkham Notch Camp, or enjoy the luxury comforts of Jackson's inns. A short trip to the north is the unassuming town of Gorham, which offers several good motels at accommodating rates along with a handful of basic-fare restaurants.

KID STUFF

Parents with young children who find majestic mountains even less interesting than watching C-Span can buy peace of mind at two area attractions. **StoryLand,** at the northern junction of Routes 16 and 302 (☎ **603/383-4293**), is filled with 30 acres of improbably leaning buildings, magical rides, fairy-tale creatures, and other enchanted beings. Kids can take a ride in a Pumpkin Coach, float in a swan boat, ride the watery Bamboo Chute, wander through a Dutch village, or spin on an antique carousel. A "sprayground" features a 40-foot happy octopus—if they're so inclined, kids can get a good summer soaking. Live shows and snacks easily fill out an afternoon; plan on spending 5 or 6 hours here to take it all in. StoryLand is open daily mid-June through Labor Day from 9am to 6pm, and Labor Day to Columbus Day on weekends from 10am to 5pm. Admission, which includes all rides and entertainment, is $16 for visitors over 4 years old. American Express, MasterCard, and Visa are accepted.

Next door is **Heritage New Hampshire** (☎ **603/383-9776**), which endeavors to make state history easily digestible for both adults and kids. It's an indoor theme park in a Georgian-style building with a theme of old-time New Hampshire. Visitors learn about the famous Concord Coach and hear prominent politician Daniel Webster discourse about his life and times. You'll come away with some context for the rest of your stay in the state. The attraction is open daily mid-May to mid-October from 9am until 5pm (until 6pm mid-June to Labor Day). Admission is $10 for adults, $4.50 for children 6 to 12, and free for kids under 6.

WHERE TO STAY & DINE

Eagle Mountain House. Carter Notch Rd., Jackson, NH 03846. ☎ **800/966-5779** or 603/383-9111. Fax 603/383-0854. 93 rms. TV TEL. $79–$149 double; $109–$169 suite. AE, DC, DISC, MC, V.

The Eagle Mountain House is a fine and handsome relic that happily survived the ravages of time, fire, and the capricious tastes of tourists. Built in 1916 and fully renovated in 1986, this five-story wooden classic is set in an idyllic valley above the village of Jackson. The lobby is rich with earth tones, polished brass, and oak accenting. The guest rooms, set off wonderfully wide and creaky hallways, are furnished with a country pine look and feature stenciled blanket chests, pine armoires, and feather comforters. There's a premium for rooms with mountain views, but it's not really worth the extra cash. Just plan to spend your free time lounging on the wide porch with the views across the golf course toward the mountains beyond.

Dining/Entertainment: There's a handsome oak tavern off the lodge for light snacks. The spacious, formal dining room seats about 150 guests, and provokes a distinct "well, here we are!" sense of glee when you first settle in for dinner under the high ceilings. The menu features creative New England classics, with offerings like Maine lobster pie and roasted cranberry duck.

Services/Facilities: 9-hole golf course, two tennis courts (one lit for night play), heated outdoor pool (summer), small health club, game room, conference rooms, dry cleaning, safe-deposit boxes.

✪ **Inn at Thorn Hill.** Thorn Hill Rd. (P.O. Box A), Jackson, NH 03846. ☎ **603/383-4242.** E-mail: thornhill@ncia.net. 19 rms (9 with shower only). A/C TEL. $150–$200 double; peak season (foliage and Christmas) $186–$232 double; cottages $230–$275. All rates include breakfast and dinner. 2-day minimum on holidays and weekends. AE, DC, DISC, MC, V.

This is a truly elegant inn. Housed in a classic shingle-style home designed by scandalplagued architect Stanford White in 1895 (although now swathed in yellow siding), the Inn at Thorn Hill is just outside of town, surrounded by wooded hills that seem to greet it in a warm embrace. Inside, there's a comfortable Victorian feel, mercifully sparing on the frilly stuff. The two sitting parlors are well designed for lounging—one boasts a woodstove, piano, and views toward the mountains (cookies and tea are served here in the afternoon). There's also a TV room with jigsaw puzzles and a decent selection of books on the shelves. Classical music is piped throughout. Three of the guest rooms have gas fireplaces.

Dining/Entertainment: The dining room is decorated in what might be called Victorian great-aunt style, with rich green carpeting, press-back oak chairs, and pink tablecloths. The inn serves some of the best meals in the valley.

Facilities: Outdoor pool, nature trails, conference rooms.

The Lodge at Pinkham Notch. Rte. 16, Pinkham Notch, NH (Mailing address: AMC, 5 Joy St., Boston, MA 02108). ☎ **603/466-2727.** 108 beds in bunk rooms of 2, 3, and 4 beds. All have shared bath. Sun–Fri (except Aug) $42 per adult, $24 per child (discount for AMC members); Sat and Aug, $47 adults, $29 children. All rates include breakfast and dinner. MC, V.

Guests flock to the Pinkham Notch Camp for the camaraderie as much as for the accommodations. Situated spectacularly at the base of Mount Washington and with easy access to numerous hiking trails, the lodge is operated like a Scandinavian youth hostel, with guests sharing bunk rooms with new friends, and enjoying boisterous, filling meals at long family-style tables in the main lodge. A zealous warden even walks the hallways near dawn beating a pot with a wooden spoon to ensure no slackers try to shirk their obligation to *Get Up and Hike!*

The accommodations are Spartan and basic, but that's overcome by the often festive atmosphere. Think of it as a field trip with a bunch of excitable teens—although the teens in this case often happen to be hardy mountain veterans in their sixties or seventies. In the winter, I've been awoken in the predawn darkness by eager mountaineers preparing their ascents in the parking lot to blaring Grateful Dead tapes. In the summer, I've spent hours swapping late-night tips on hiking destinations with grizzled hikers twice my age. It's not a place to be an introvert, but it *is* a place to feel part of the rich heritage of local mountain recreation.

Wentworth Resort Hotel. Jackson, NH 03846. ☎ **800/637-0013** or 603/383-9700. Fax 603/383-4265. 58 rms. A/C TV TEL. $149–$159 double, including breakfast and dinner; $89–$99 room only. Higher rates during foliage season and Christmas week; discounts available Mar to mid-June. AE, MC, V.

The venerable Wentworth sits in the middle of Jackson Village, all turrets and eaves and awnings. Built in 1869, this Victorian shingled inn edged to the brink of deterioration in the mid-1980s, but was pulled back by a plucky entrepreneur, who added a number of condominiums clustered around the golf course. The large guest rooms are a good value for the money, decorated with a Victorian grace and elegance. Some rooms feature fireplaces, whirlpools, or claw-foot tubs. Or for those of stouter constitutions, you can stroll just up the road and plunge into the cold waters of Jackson Falls.

Dining/Entertainment: The regal first-floor dining room serves up regional favorites like garlic-and-herb chicken and char-grilled salmon.

Facilities: Outdoor heated pool, 18-hole PGA golf course, clay tennis courts, billiards, close proximity to hiking.

Wildcat Inn & Tavern. Rte. 16A, Jackson, NH 03846. ☎ **800/228-4245** or 603/383-4245. 15 rms (some with shower only, 2 with hall bathrooms). Summer $69–$96 double. Surcharge during foliage season. Rates include breakfast. AE, DC, MC, V.

The Wildcat Inn occupies a three-story farmhouse-style building in the middle of Jackson, directly across from the cross-country ski center. It's a comfortable, informal kind of place, better known for its restaurant and tavern than for its accommodations. Most guest rooms are cozy, two-room suites, carpeted and furnished eclectically. Sitting rooms typically contain contemporary sofas, chairs, and pine furniture, and offer cozy sanctuary after a day hiking or skiing.

Dining/Entertainment: The downstairs dining room resembles a traditional country farmhouse, with old wood floors and pine furniture. Country-style meals are prepared with considerable flair, and include a tenderloin of beef topped with lobster, asparagus, and hollandaise sauce (main courses are $13.95 to $21.95). In the winter, the smart money stakes out a toasty spot in front of the tavern fireplace—one of the most popular gathering spots in the valley—to sip soothing libations and order from the bar menu, which has lighter fare like chicken quesadillas and spanakopita ($6.95 to $8.95).

CRAWFORD NOTCH

Crawford Notch is a wild, rugged mountain valley that runs through the heart of the White Mountains. Within the Notch itself lies a lot of legend and history. For years after its discovery by European settlers (Timothy Nash stumbled upon it in 1771), it was an impenetrable wilderness, creating a barrier to commerce by blocking trade between the upper Connecticut River Valley and commercial harbors in Portland and Portsmouth. That was eventually surmounted by a plucky crew who hauled the first freight through.

As the traffic picked up, the Crawford family, who were among the region's pioneers, began offering lodging to the first teamsters, and later to the tourists who flocked here to experience the sublime feelings triggered by contact with raw nature. The Crawfords also led tours to the summit of Mount Washington, and built the first horseback trail.

Nathaniel Hawthorne immortalized the Notch with a short story about a real-life 1826 tragedy. One dark and stormy night (of course), the Willey family fled its home when they heard an avalanche roaring toward the valley floor. As fate would have it, the avalanche divided above the inn and spared the structure; the seven who fled were killed in tumbling debris. The only survivors were the family dog and two oxen. (You can still visit the site of the Willey home today.)

The Notch is accessible via Route 302, which is wide and speedy on the lower sections, and becomes challenging only in its steepness as it approaches the narrow defile of the Notch itself. (Modern engineering has taken most of the kinks out of the road.) The views up the cliffs from the road can be spectacular on a clear day; on an overcast or drizzly day, the effect is slightly foreboding and medieval.

ESSENTIALS

GETTING THERE   Route 302 runs through Crawford Notch for about 25 miles between the towns of Bartlett and Twin Mountain.

VISITOR INFORMATION   Twin Mountain Chamber of Commerce, P.O. Box 194, Twin Mountain, NH 03595 (☎ **800/245-8946** or 603/846-5407), offers general information and lodging referrals at their information booth near the intersection of Routes 302 and 3. Open year-round, but hours are shorter in the off-season.

WATERFALLS & SWIMMING HOLES

Much of the mountainous land flanking Route 302 falls under the jurisdiction of **Crawford Notch State Park,** which was established in 1911 to preserve land that elsewhere had been decimated by overly aggressive logging. The headwaters of the Saco River form in the Notch, and what's generally regarded as the first permanent trail up Mount Washington also departs from here. Several turnouts and trailheads invite a more leisurely exploration of the area. The trail network on both sides of Crawford Notch is extensive; consult the *AMC White Mountain Guide* for detailed information (see "Specialized Guidebooks," earlier in this chapter).

Engorged by snowmelt in the spring, the Saco River courses through the Notch's granite ravines and winds past sizable boulders that have been left by retreating glaciers and crashed down from the mountainsides above. It's a popular destination among serious white-water boaters, and makes for a good spectator sport if you're here early in the season. During the lazy days of summer, the Saco offers several good swimming holes just off the highway. They're unmarked, but where you see local cars parked off the side of the road for no apparent reason, you should be able to find your way to a good spot for soaking and splashing.

Up the mountain slopes that form the valley, hikers will spot a number of superb waterfalls, some more easily accessible than others. A day spent exploring the falls is a day well spent. A few to start with:

Arethusa Falls has the highest single drop of any waterfall in the state, and the trail to the falls passes several attractive smaller cascades en route. These are especially beautiful in the spring or after a heavy rain, when the falls are at their fullest. The trip can be done as a 2.6-mile round-trip to the falls and back on Arethusa Falls Trail, or as a 4.5-mile loop hike that includes views from stunning Frankenstein Cliffs. (These are named not after the creator of the famous monster, but after a noted landscape painter.)

If you're arriving from the south, look for signs to the trail parking area shortly after passing the Crawford Notch State Park entrance sign. From the north, the trailhead is half a mile south of the Dry River Campground. At the parking lot, look for the sign and map to get your bearings, then cross the railroad tracks to start up the falls trail.

Another hike begins a short drive north on Route 302. Reaching tumultuous **Ripley Falls** requires an easy hike of a little more than 1 mile round-trip. Look for the sign to the falls on Route 302 just north of the trailhead for Webster Cliff Trail. (If you pass the Willey House site, you've gone too far.) Drive in a piece and park at the site of the Willey Station. Follow trail signs for the Ripley Falls Trail, and allow about a half-hour to reach the cascades. The most appealing swimming holes are at the top of the falls.

Two attractive falls may be seen from the roadway at the head of the Notch, just east of the crest. **Flume Cascades** and **Silver Cascades** tumble down the hills in white braids that are especially appealing during a misty summer rain. These falls were among the most popular sites in the region when tourists alighted at the train station about 1 mile away. They aren't as spectacular as the two mentioned above, but they're accessible if you're in a hurry. Travelers can park in the lots along the road's edge for a slower-paced view.

A Historic Railway

Mount Washington Cog Railway. Rte. 302, Bretton Woods. ☎ 800/922-8825 or 603/846-5404. Fare $39 adults, $26 children 6–12, kids under 5 free. MC, V. Runs daily Memorial Day to late Oct, plus weekends in May. Frequent departures; call for schedule. Reservations recommended.

The cog railway was a marvel of engineering when it opened in 1869, and it remains so today. Part moving museum, part slow-motion roller-coaster ride, the cog railway steams to the summit with a determined "I think I can" pace of about 4 miles per hour. But there's still a frisson of excitement on the way up and back, especially when the train crosses Jacob's Ladder, a rickety-seeming trestle 25 feet high that angles upward at a grade of more than 37%. Passengers enjoy the expanding view on this 3-hour round-trip (there are stops to add water to the steam engine, to check the track switches, and to allow other trains to ascend or descend). There's also a 20-minute stop at the summit to browse around. Be aware that the ride is noisy and sulfurous, and you should dress expecting to acquire a patina of cinder and soot.

But it's hard to imagine anyone (other than those fearful of heights) not enjoying this trip—from kids marveling at the ratchety-ratchety noises and the thick plume of black smoke, to curious adults trying to figure out how the cog system works, to naturalists who get superb views of the boney, brawny uplands leading to Mount Washington's summit.

Skiing

Attitash Bear Peak. Rte. 302, Bartlett, NH 03812. ☎ 800/223-7669 or 603/374-2368. E-mail: info@attitash.com. Web site: www.attitash.com. Vertical drop: 1,750 ft. 10 chairlifts (including 1 high-speed quad), 1 surface lift. Skiable acreage: 214. Lift ticket $44 weekends and holidays, $37 weekdays.

Attitash Bear Peak is a good intermediate-to-advanced skier mountain with a selection of great cruising runs and a handful of more challenging drops. The mountain includes two peaks—the 1,750-foot Attitash and the adjacent 1,450-foot Bear Peak. The main attraction here is the skiing and the great views of the White Mountains from the peaks; not much happens locally at night, so those looking for action typically head 15 minutes away to North Conway. With the scheduled opening of the Grand Summit Hotel at the base in 1997 (right at press time), there's more reason to stick around in the evening, but there's still not the lively scene found at many ski areas.

Attitash Bear Peak also offers the Smart Ticket program, which allows skiers to buy as many "points" as they'd like on a ticket. Points are deducted for each run (more points on weekends and on longer lifts). The advantage? If conditions deteriorate or if you're seized by the urge to shop in North Conway, you can do so and then use up the rest of your points the next day. Points can also be transferred to others and are good for 2 years from the date of purchase. Attitash Bear Peak is owned by the American Skiing Co., and discount books of tickets are available that can be used here as well as at Sunday River, Sugarloaf, Killington, Mount Snow, and elsewhere.

Bretton Woods. Rte. 302, Bretton Woods, NH 03575. ☎ 800/232-2972 or 603/278-5000. Vertical drop: 1,500 ft. 4 chairlifts (including 1 high-speed quad), 1 surface lift. Skiable acreage: 150. Lift tickets $38 weekends and holidays for adults, $25 children 6–15; weekdays $31 adults, $15 children 6–15.

Bretton Woods is solid beginner-to-intermediate mountain with a pleasant family atmosphere and great views of Mount Washington. The resort does a good job with kids, and offers some nice intermediate cruising runs and limited night skiing. There's even a speedy detachable quad chair, which skiers don't often find at resorts of this size. Accommodations are available on the mountain and nearby, but evening entertainment tends to revolve around hot tubs, TVs, and going to bed early. There's also an excellent cross-country ski center nearby.

WHERE TO STAY & DINE

✪ **Mount Washington Hotel.** Rte. 302, Bretton Woods, NH 03575. ☎ **800/258-0330** or 603/278-1000. 195 rms (6 with shower only). TEL. Midweek $185–$315 double, up to $585 suites; weekends and holidays $225–$315 double, up to $620 suites. All rates include breakfast and dinner. AE, DISC, MC, V. Closed mid-Oct to mid-May.

Your first response to the Mount Washington Hotel will likely be one of disbelief. It seems as if some bizarre Edwardian glacier had flowed down from the mountains and settled resolutely in the valley. This five-story wooden resort, with its gleaming white clapboards and cherry red roof, seems something out of a fable. Built in 1902 by railroad and coal magnate Joseph Stickney ("Look at me gentlemen . . . for I am the poor fool who built all this," he said at the grand opening), the resort attracted luminaries like Babe Ruth, Thomas Edison, Woodrow Wilson, and silent-screen star Mary Pickford. In 1944, it hosted the famed Bretton Woods International Monetary Conference, which secured the dollar's role as the world's currency.

After large resorts fell out of fashion, the Mount Washington went through a succession of owners and fell on hard times. Threatened with demolition and put on the auction block in 1991, it was purchased for just over $3 million by a group of dedicated local business folks who launched the long process of bringing it back from the brink. Being frugal Yankees, they're renovating with operating profit, not with borrowed money. The improvements are moving along nicely, but the hotel still can seem a bit shabby and threadbare in parts and it will be a while before it displays a consistent gloss.

The guest rooms are furnished simply but comfortably (the less expensive rooms still have the old reproduction French Empire furniture, which is a bit cheesy), but as at most other grand resorts, The Mount Washington was designed around public areas. Wide hallways and elegant common areas on the first floor invite strolling and indolence. A broad 900-foot wraparound veranda makes for relaxing afternoons.

The main hotel is open only seasonally, but three other properties—including a smaller 1896 inn, a motor inn, and contemporary town homes—are open year-round.

Dining/Entertainment: Meals are enjoyed in the impressive octagonal dining room, designed such that no guest would be slighted by being seated in a corner. (Jackets are requested for men at dinner.) A house orchestra provides entertainment during the dinner, and guests often dance between courses. The meals tend to be delicious, with a continental bent but global influences. The sunset, reflected off the mountains through the oversized windows, is often spectacular. The fixed-price meal is $40 per person for outside visitors or non-MAP guests.

Facilities: 27-hole golf course, 12 red-clay tennis courts, indoor and outdoor pools, stables, game room, gift shop.

✪ **Notchland Inn.** Rte. 302, Hart's Location, NH 03812. ☎ **800/866-6131** or 603/374-6131. Fax 603/374-6168. E-mail: notchland@aol.com. 12 rms, 6 with shower only. Midweek $175–$220 double; foliage season and holidays $205–$260 double. Rates include breakfast and dinner; B&B rates available for $40. 2-night minimum on weekends; 3-night minimum some holidays. AE, DISC, MC, V.

The Notchland Inn appears just off Route 302 in a wild, remote section of the valley, looking every bit like a redoubt in a Sir Walter Scott novel. Built of hand-cut granite between 1840 and 1862 by a prosperous Boston dentist, Notchland is a classy yet informal inn and perfectly situated for exploring the wilds of the White Mountains. All 12 guest rooms are tastefully appointed with antiques and traditional furniture, and feature wood-burning fireplaces, high ceilings, and individual thermostats. The new suite has a Jacuzzi and private deck, with more of a modern, condolike air about it that sets it apart in spirit from the other rooms. The two suites in the old schoolhouse next door are comfortable and spacious, decorated in a modern country style.

A stay typically begins with a brief tour of the home, including the common rooms, one of which, according to local lore, was remodeled at the turn of the century by Gustav Stickley himself, the father of the mission style. There are other treasures to be found, like an original oil painting by George L. Frankenstein, the prominent 19th-century artist whose name graces nearby cliffs, and a wood-fired hot tub in a gazebo overlooking a small pond. If the weather's not conducive to skiing or hiking, there's backgammon, Scrabble, and jigsaw puzzles in the common rooms (although no TV). Ed Butler and Les Schoof, the two New York refugees who own the place, are exceptionally friendly and accommodating. The Notchland is appropriate for children over 12. No smoking.

Dining/Entertainment: Dinners in the bright, often noisy dining room tend to be eclectic and nicely presented. Five-course dinners are served at 7pm, with a choice of three creative entrees or so each evening. These might include a Thai curry, five-pepper-crusted roast beef, or scallops with walnuts and a lime-ginger sauce. Dinners are available to the public (space permitting) at a prix fixe of $32 not including tax, tip, or beverage.

Services: In-room massage and baby-sitting by advance appointment.

Facilities: River swimming (just across the road), outdoor hot tub, nature trails, game room, safe.

WATERVILLE VALLEY & LINCOLN

On the southwestern edge of the White Mountains are two ski resorts hidden away in mountain valleys. Both have blossomed in recent years, not always with favorable results. Waterville Valley, which lies at the end of a 12-mile dead-end road, was the first to be developed. Incorporated as a town in 1829, Waterville Valley became a popular destination for summer travelers during the heyday of mountain travel late in the 19th century. Skiers first started descending the slopes in the 1930s after a few ski trails were hacked out of the forest by the Civilian Conservation Corps and local ski clubs. But it wasn't until 1965, when a skier named Tom Corcoran bought 425 acres in the valley, that Waterville began to assume its current modern air.

While the village has a decidedly manufactured character (it easily has as many parking lots as the average regional mall), Corcoran's vision has kept the growth within bounds. There's not much in the way of sprawl here; the village is reasonably compact, with modern lodges, condos, and restaurants clustered around the "Town Square," itself a sort of mall complex. The architecture is inspired by New England vernacular; there's not a Swiss chalet to be found. The village is also quite pleasant in summer, when the place abounds with outdoor activities like mountain biking, hiking, and swimming.

Some 25 miles to the north is Loon Mountain, which is located just outside the former paper-mill town of Lincoln. (That's the distance by major roads in winter; it's shorter in summer by crossing Thornton Gap on Tripoli Road.) The resort was first conceived in the early 1960s by Sherman Adams, a former New Hampshire governor and Eisenhower administration official. The mountain opened in 1966 and was quickly criticized for its mediocre skiing, but continual upgrading and expanding since then has brought the mountain greater respect.

Loon has since evolved from a friendly intermediate mountain served by a few motels to a friendly intermediate mountain served by dozens of condos and vast, modern hotels. Lincoln seems to embrace sprawl with the same zeal that Waterville Valley shuns it. At times it seems that Lincoln underwent not so much a development boom in the 1980s as a development spasm. Clusters of chicken-coop-style homes and condos now blanket the lower hillsides of this narrow valley, and fast-food restaurants and strip mall–style shops line Route 112 from I-93 to the mountain.

The Loon area includes the adjacent towns of Lincoln and North Woodstock on either side of I-93. North Woodstock has more of the feel of a town that's lived in year-round. The Lincoln and Loon Mountain base village are both lively with skiers in the winter, but in the summer the area can have a post–nuclear fallout feel to it, with lots of homes but few people in evidence despite efforts to stage special events like lumberjack shows. The ambience is also compromised by that peculiar style of resort architecture that's simultaneously aggressive and bland.

ESSENTIALS

GETTING THERE   Waterville Valley is located 12 miles northwest of Exit 29 on I-93 via Route 49. Lincoln is accessible off I-93 on Exits 32 and 33.

VISITOR INFORMATION   The **Waterville Valley Chamber of Commerce,** RFD #1, Box 1067, Campton, NH 03223 (☎ **800/237-2307** or 603/726-3804), staffs an information booth on Route 49 in Campton, just off I-93. The **Lincoln-Woodstock Chamber of Commerce,** P.O. Box 358, Lincoln, NH 03251 (☎ **800/ 227-4191** or 603/745-6621), has an information office open daily at Depot Plaza on Route 112 in Lincoln.

The most comprehensive place for information about the region from Lincoln northward is the **White Mountains Visitor Center,** P.O. Box 10, North Woodstock, NH 03262 (☎ **800/346-3687** or 603/745-8720), located just east of Exit 32 on I-93. They'll send you a visitor's kit, and they offer brochures and answer questions from their center, which is open from 8:30am to 5pm daily. On the Internet, head to **www.whitemtn.org,** or E-mail **pmack@whitemtn.org.**

HIKING & MOUNTAIN BIKING

Impressive mountain peaks tower over both Lincoln and Waterville Valley, making both areas great for hiking and mountain biking. As always, your single best source of information is the Appalachian Mountain Club's *White Mountain Guide* (see "Specialized Guidebooks," earlier in this chapter), which offers a comprehensive directory of area trails. Also check with Forest Service staff at the White Mountains Visitor Center for information on local outdoor destinations.

From Waterville Valley, a popular 4-hour hike runs to the summit of **Mount Tecumseh,** the shoulders of which host skiers in winter. The hiking trail starts about 100 yards north of the ski lodge and offers wonderful views as you climb. From the 4,003-foot summit, you can return via the **Sosman Trail,** which winds its way down beneath the ski lifts and along ski runs closed for summer.

Outdoor novices who prefer their adventures neatly packaged will enjoy the **Waterville Valley Base Camp** (☎ **800/468-2553**). The "camp," located at the Waterville Valley Town Square, offers mountain-bike rentals, in-line skates, guided tours, lift access for bikers and hikers, and information on area trails. Rates start at

$5 for a single ride on the lift, to $55 for a private 4-hour guided hike. (The Base Camp also offers cross-country skiing and snowshoeing in winter.)

In the Lincoln area, a level trail that's excellent for hikers in any physical shape is the **Wilderness Trail** along the east branch of the Pemigewasset River. Head eastward on Route 112 (the Kancamagus Highway) from I-93 for 5 miles then watch for the parking lot on the left just past the bridge. Both sides of the river may be navigated; the Wilderness Trail on the west side runs just over 3 miles to beautiful, remote Black Pond; on the east side, an abandoned railroad bed makes for smooth mountain biking. The two trails may be linked by fording the river where the rail bed is crossed by a gate.

The **Loon Mountain Bike Center** (☎ **603/745-8111,** ext. 5566) offers more than 70 mountain bikes for rent at its facility at the mountain's base. There's also in-line skating at Loon's **skating center** (☎ **603/745-8111,** ext. 5568), which features a skate arena and half-pipe.

Additionally, hikers will find easy access to various trailheads along the Kancamagus Highway (see below).

THE KANCAMAGUS HIGHWAY

The Kancamagus Highway—locally called "The Kanc"—is the White Mountain's most spectacular road. Officially designated a national scenic byway by the U.S. Forest Service, the 34-mile roadway joins Lincoln with Conway through 2,860-foot Kancamagus Pass. When the highway was built between 1960 and 1961, it opened up 100 square miles of wilderness—a move that irked preservationists but has proven very popular with folks who prefer their sightseeing by car.

The route begins and ends along wide, tumbling rivers on relatively flat plateaus. The two-lane road, which the U.S. Forest Service has declared a national scenic byway, rises steadily to the pass. Several rest areas with sweeping vistas allow visitors to pause and enjoy the mountain views. The highway also makes a good destination for hikers; any number of day and overnight trips may be launched from the roadside. One simple, short hike along a gravel pathway (it's less than one-third of a mile each way) leads to **Sabbaday Falls,** a cascade that's especially impressive after a downpour. Six national forest campgrounds are also located along the highway.

Be sure to take your time and stop frequently. Think of it as a scavenger hunt as you look for a covered bridge, cascades with good swimming holes, a historic home with a fascinating story behind it, and spectacular mountain panoramas. All these things and more are along the route.

The highway is popular with serious bikers in training, but it's also a strong draw for casual peddlers in reasonable physical shape. The shoulders are wide enough to accommodate both bikes and RVs, and the grade is reasonably forgiving, especially on the eastern slope. Make sure your brakes are in good working order before setting off down the long descent.

SKIING

Loon Mountain. Lincoln, NH 03251. ☎ **603/745-8111,** or 800/227-4191 for lodging. Web site: http://www.loonmtn.com. Vertical drop: 2,100 ft. 8 chairlifts (1 high-speed), 1 high-speed gondola, 1 surface lift. Skiable acreage: 250. Lift tickets $45 weekends, $38 weekdays.

Located on U.S. Forest Service land, Loon has been stymied in past expansion efforts by environmental concerns regarding land use and water withdrawals from the river. Loon finally got the go-ahead for expansion in 1994, and is now in the midst of a $12-million, 6-year effort to expand and reshape the ski mountain, add uphill capacity, and improve snowmaking. (The summer of 1997 added two lifts and three trails.)

The expansion plans should reduce some of the congestion of this popular area and open up more room to roam. Today, most of the trails still cluster toward the bottom, and most are solid intermediate runs. Experts head to the north peak, which has a challenging selection of advanced trails served by a triple chairlift.

Waterville Valley. Waterville Valley, NH 03215. ☎ **800/468-2553** or 603/236-8311. E-mail: info@waterville.com. Web site: www.waterville.com. Vertical drop: 2,020 ft. 8 chairlifts (1 high-speed), 4 surface lifts. Skiable acreage: 255. Lift tickets $43 weekends, $37 weekdays.

While Waterville Valley has some good, steep drops, it's known mostly as a superb intermediate's mountain, albeit one with fairly limited terrain compared to the bigger ski areas in the region. There's been a recent effort to upgrade the mountain and offer more challenging trails, and the resort has also taken strides to accommodate snowboarders—management built a snowboard playground called The Boneyard on Mount Tecumseh (it features a bus buried up to its roof in snow and some hairy jumps), and it decreed that Snow Mountain (the beginners mountain) is open *only* to snowboarders on weekends. (Snowboarders are welcome anywhere else on the mountain as well, of course.) There's also a good snowboard shop in the base complex.

WHERE TO STAY
In Waterville Valley

Golden Eagle Lodge. Snowsbrook Rd., Waterville Valley, NH 03215. ☎ **800/910-4499** or 603/236-4600. Fax 603/236-4947. 118 rms. TV TEL. Winter $89–$239 per unit; summer $98–$188 per unit; spring $78–$158 per unit. Premium charged on holidays. All rates subject to a "resort fee" of 10% in winter, 15% in spring and summer. Children stay free in parents' room. Some minimum stay requirements on certain holidays. AE, DC, DISC, MC, V.

This sprawling, contemporary condo project is centrally located in the village and is the most regal of the bunch. The lodge can accommodate two to six people in one and two-bedroom units, all of which have kitchens and basic cookware. The five-story resort strives for a modern-meets-rustic lodge appearance, generally to good effect. But guests don't travel great distances for the decor here; they come for the resort's amenities and location (an easy shuttle bus ride to the slopes).

Facilities: Indoor and outdoor pools, whirlpool, bike rental, nearby 9-hole golf course, game rooms, nearby indoor jogging track, nature trails, conference rooms, nearby health club, self-service Laundromat, sauna, 12 outdoor and four indoor tennis courts nearby.

Snowy Owl Inn. Village Rd., Waterville Valley, NH 03215. ☎ **800/766-9969** or 603/236-8383. Fax 603/236-4890. 80 rms. TV TEL. Winter $119–$249 double. Discounts in off-season and summer. Rates include continental breakfast. AE, DISC, MC, V.

The Snowy Owl will appeal to those who like the amiable character of a country inn but demand all the modern conveniences. Another modern resort project near Town Square, it offers a number of pleasant extras like a towering fieldstone fireplace in the lobby and a rooftop observatory that offers a fine panorama of the surrounding hills. The rooms are basic motel style, decently furnished and featuring pine accenting; about half have whirlpools and wet bars, and a few feature air-conditioning.

Facilities: Indoor and outdoor pools, game room, nearby health club (access included in room rates).

In Lincoln & North Woodstock

In addition to the places listed below, Lincoln offers a range of motels that will appeal to budget travelers. Among those worth seeking out are the **Kancamagus Motor Lodge** (☎ 800/346-4205 or 603/745-3365), the **Mountaineer Motel**

(☎ **800/356-0046** or 603/745-2235), and **Woodward's Motor Inn** (☎ **800/ 635-8968** or 603/745-8141).

Mountain Club at Loon. Rte. 112 (R.R. #1; Box 40), Lincoln, NH 03251. ☎ **800/229-7829** or 603/745-2244. Fax 603/745-2317. 234 rms. A/C TV TEL. Winter $149–$219 double mid-week, $199–$299 double weekend; summer and off-season from $109 double. AE, DC, DISC, MC, V.

Set at the edge of Loon Mountain's slopes, the Mountain Club is a huge, contemporary resort built during the real-estate boom of the 1980s. It was managed for several years as a Marriott, and the decor tends to reflect its chain hotel heritage. The lobby is done up in dark green tones with leatherlike couches arrayed before a polished granite fireplace, and the rooms are adorned with copious oak veneer. Guest rooms are designed to be rented either individually or as two-room suites; each pair features one traditional hotel-style bedroom with king-sized bed, and one studio with a kitchen, sitting area, and a fold-down queen-sized bed. (The studio option is perfect for couples who'd rather have extra space and cooking facilities than a king-sized bed.) The high room rates reflect the proximity to the slopes and the excellent health-club facilities connected to the hotel via covered walkway. The free covered parking will be appreciated during heavy snowstorms, as will the resort's in-house restaurant and lounge.

Facilities: Ski-out access, indoor and outdoor pools, year-round outdoor whirl-pool, health club and fitness facility (including basketball, volleyball, and aerobics rooms), and two outdoor tennis courts.

Wilderness Inn. Rte. 3 (just south of Rte. 112), N. Woodstock, NH 03262. ☎ **800/200-9453** or 603/745-3890. 6 rms, plus a cottage (2 rms share 1 hall bath). $40–$115 double. Rates include full breakfast. MC, V.

The Wilderness Inn is located at the southern edge of North Woodstock village–it's not the wilderness that the name or the brochure might suggest. But it's a friendly, handsome bed-and-breakfast, with six guest rooms in a large bungalow-style home that dates to 1912. The interior features heavy timbers in classic Craftsman style, creaky maple floors, a somewhat spare mix of antiques and reproductions, and games to occupy an evening. The breakfasts are very filling and very good.

Woodstock Inn. Main St. (P.O. Box 118), N. Woodstock, NH 03262. ☎ **800/321-3985** or 603/745-3951. Fax 603/745-3701. 19 rms (11 with private bath). A/C TV TEL. Summer and winter $54–$140 double; foliage season $75–$140 double; off-season $49–$95 double. Rates include breakfast. AE, DC, DISC, MC, V.

The Woodstock Inn shares some qualities with Dr. Jekyll and Mr. Hyde. In the front, it's a fusty white Victorian with black shutters amid Woodstock's commercial downtown area. In the back, it's a modern, boisterous brew pub that serves up tasty fare along with its robust ales (see below). The inn features 19 guest rooms spread among 3 houses. If you're on a tight budget, go for the shared bathrooms in the main house and the nearby Deachman house; the slightly less personable Riverside building across the street offers rooms with private baths, but at a premium. Rooms are individually decorated in a country Victorian style, furnished with both reproductions and antiques. There's a pervasive aroma of sachet and cedar in the main building that adds to the period mood. (Sort of.) The Woodstock Inn is a fun place to hang your hat, and is a reasonable alternative to modern, oversized hotels.

WHERE TO DINE

The Lincoln–North Woodstock area isn't known for its haute cuisine, but you can get decent burgers and other filling fare.

If you're in a condo or suite with an oven or microwave, your best option for a delicious, reasonably priced meal is at **Half Baked,** 27 S. Main St., North Woodstock (☎ **603/745-3811**). For the past dozen years, the shop has offered dinners to go from an old farmhouse just south of North Woodstock village—just reheat when you get back to your room. A half-dozen Greek triangles are $3.95; homemade pasta is 75¢ a serving with sauces extra; a family-sized lasagna is $29.50.

Woodstock Station. In the Woodstock Inn, Main St. ☎ **603/745-3951.** Reservations accepted for Clement Room only. Breakfast items $3.95–$9.50; lunch and dinner items $5.50–$16 (dinner in Clement Room $11.95–$22.95). AE, DC, DISC, MC, V. Clement Room 7–11:30am and 5:30–9:30pm; Woodstock Station 11:30am–10pm. PUB FARE/AMERICAN.

You've got a choice here: Dine amid the Victorian frippery of the Clement Room on the enclosed porch of the Woodstock Inn, or head to the relaxed brew pub in the back, housed in a heavily doctored old train station. In the Clement Room, the offerings tend toward classic American fare like chicken breast with wild mushrooms, shrimp stuffed with clams, or beef Wellington. (But good luck getting seated: Last time I stopped through for Sunday brunch, the hostess rather ungraciously decided that it was so crowded she wouldn't even put me on the waiting list.)

The pub is far more informal, with high ceilings, knotty pine, and decorations consisting of vintage winter recreational gear. There's a large-screen TV, a group computer trivia game, and live local music on some nights. The menu rounds up the usual pub suspects, like nachos, chicken wings, burgers, and pasta, all of which are prepared decently if without much creative flair. A new craft brewery opened on the premises in 1995, and serves up well-brewed porters, stouts, and brown and red ales.

FRANCONIA NOTCH

Franconia Notch is rugged New Hampshire writ large. As travelers head north on I-93, the Kinsman Range to the west and the Franconia Range to the east begin to converge, and the road angles upward. Soon, the flanking mountain ranges press in on either side, forming tight and dramatic Franconia Notch, which offers little in the way of civilization but a whole lot in the way of natural drama. Most of the Notch is included in a well-run state park that to most travelers will be indistinguishable from the national forest. Travelers seeking the sublime should plan on a leisurely trip through the Notch, allowing enough time to get out of the car and explore forests and craggy peaks.

ESSENTIALS

GETTING THERE   I-93 runs through Franconia Notch, gearing down from four lanes to two (where it becomes the Franconia Notch Parkway) in the most scenic and sensitive areas of the park. Several roadside pullouts and scenic attractions dot the route.

VISITOR INFORMATION   Information on the park and surrounding area is available at the state-run **Flume Information Center** (☎ 603/823-5563) at Exit 1 off the parkway. The center is open during the summer Monday through Saturday from 9am to 4:30pm. North of the Notch, head to the **Franconia/Eaton/Sugar Hill Chamber of Commerce,** P.O. Box 780, Franconia, NH 03580 (☎ 603/823-5661) on Main Street next to the town hall. It's open Monday through Saturday from 9am to 3pm; you can also call ☎ 800/866-3334 for a lodging brochure nightly until 9pm, until 6pm on Friday and Saturday.

FRANCONIA NOTCH STATE PARK

Franconia Notch State Park's 8,000 acres, nestled within the surrounding White Mountain National Forest, hosts an array of scenic attractions easily accessible from

I-93 and the Franconia Notch Parkway. For information on any of the follow attractions, contact the park offices (☎ **603/823-5563**).

Without a doubt, the most famous park landmark is the **Old Man of the Mountains,** located near Cannon Mountain. From the right spot on the valley floor, this 48-foot-high rock formation bears an uncanny resemblance to the profile of a craggy old man—early settlers said it was Thomas Jefferson. If it looks familiar, it's because this is the logo you see on all the New Hampshire state highway signs. The profile, which often surprises visitors by just how tiny it is when viewed from far below (bring binoculars), is best seen from the well-marked roadside viewing area at Profile Lake. In years past, harried tourists craning their necks to glimpse the Old Man while speeding onward resulted in some spectacular head-on collisions. Take your time and pull over. It's free.

The Flume is a rugged, 800-foot gorge through which the Flume Brook tumbles. The gorge, a hugely popular attraction in the mid-19th century, is 800 feet long, 90 feet deep, and as narrow as 20 feet at the bottom; visitors explore by means of a network of boardwalks and bridges. If you're looking for simple and quick access to natural grandeur, it's worth the money. Otherwise, set off into the mountains and seek your own drama with fewer crowds. Admission is $6 adults and $3 for children 6 to 12.

Echo Lake is a picturesquely situated recreation area, with a 28-acre lake, a handsome swimming beach, and picnic tables scattered about all within view of Cannon Mountain on one side and Mount Lafayette on the other. This is the best spot for a relaxing afternoon when the weather's in an agreeable mood. A bike path runs along the lake and continues onward both north and south. Admission to the park is $2.50 for visitors over 12 years old.

For a high-altitude view of the region, set off for the alpine ridges on the **Cannon Mountain Tramway.** The old-fashioned cable car serves skiers in winter; in summer, it whisks up to 80 travelers at a time to the summit of the 4,180-foot mountain. Once at the top, you can strike out by foot along the Rim Trail for superb views. Be prepared for cool, gusty winds. The tramway costs $8 for adults, $4 for children 6 to 12. It's located at Exit 2 of the parkway.

Also near the base of Cannon Mountain is the **New England Ski Museum** (☎ **603/823-7177**), with its compact but interesting collection of ski memorabilia like early clothing, posters, and historic equipment. The old ski films shown in the theater are especially entertaining. It's open daily from the end of May to mid-October, and Thursday through Tuesday during ski season. Admission is free.

HIKING

Hiking opportunities abound in the Franconia Notch area, ranging from demanding multiday hikes high on exposed ridgelines to gentle valley walks. Consult AMC's *White Mountain Guide* (see "Specialized Guidebooks," earlier in this chapter) for a comprehensive directory of area hiking trails.

A pleasant woodland detour of 2 hours or so can be found at the **Basin-Cascades Trail** (look for well-marked signs for the basin off I-93 about 1 ½ miles north of the Flume). A popular roadside waterfall and natural pothole, the Basin attracts teeming crowds, but few visitors slip away from the masses by continuing on the trail to a series of other cascades beyond. Look for signs for the trail, then head off into the woods. After about half a mile of easy hiking you'll reach **Kinsman Falls,** a beautiful 20-foot cascade. Continue on about six-tenths of a mile beyond that to **Rocky Glen,** where the stream plummets through a craggy gorge. Retrace your steps back to your car.

For a more demanding hike, set off for rugged **Mount Lafayette,** with its spectacular views of the western White Mountains. Hikers should be well experienced, well equipped, and in good physical condition. Allow 6 to 7 hours to complete the hike. A popular and fairly straightforward ascent begins up the **Old Bridle Trail,** which departs from the Lafayette Place parking area off the parkway. This trail climbs steadily with expanding views to the AMC's **Greenleaf Hut** (2.9 miles). From here, continue to the summit of Lafayette on the **Greenleaf Trail.** It's only 1.1 miles farther, but it covers rocky terrain and can be demanding and difficult, especially if the weather turns on you. If in doubt about conditions, ask advice of other hikers or the AMC staff at Greenleaf Hut.

SKIING

Cannon Mountain. Franconia Notch Pkwy., Franconia. ☎ **603/823-5563.** Vertical drop: 2,146 ft. 1 80-person tram, 6 chairlifts. Skiable acreage: about 200. Lift tickets $37 weekends, $28 weekdays.

Cannon Mountain, a state-run ski area, was once *the* place to ski in the East. One of New England's first ski resorts, Cannon remains famed for its challenging runs and exposed faces, and the mountain still attracts skiers serious about getting down the hill in style. Many of the old-fashioned New England–style trails are narrow and fun (if sometimes icy, scoured by the notch's winds), and the enclosed tramway is an elegant way to get to the summit. There's no base scene to speak of; skiers tend to retire to inns around Franconia or retreat southward to the condo villages around Lincoln.

WHERE TO STAY & DINE

Franconia Inn. 1300 Easton Rd., Franconia, NH 03580. ☎ **800/473-5299** or 603/823-5542. Fax 603/823-8078. E-mail: info@franconiainn.com. Web site: www.franconiainn.com. 30 rms (2 with shower only), 2 suites. Midweek $79–$98 double; weekends $93–$113 double. Rates include breakfast. MAP rates also available. AE, MC, V. Closed Apr to mid-May.

This is a pleasant inn that offers good value. Owned by Alec and Richard Morris, two brothers who bought the inn in 1981, the Franconia Inn is set along a quiet road in a bucolic valley 2 miles from the village of Franconia. A grass airstrip lies across the road; it's used by glider pilots (you can sign up for an hour-long soaring excursion over dramatic Franconia Notch).

The inn itself, built in 1934 after a fire destroyed the original 1886 inn, has a welcoming, informal feel to it, with wingback chairs around the fireplace in one common room, and jigsaw puzzles half completed in the paneled library. Families are always welcome; kids tend to gravitate to the basement game room for pinball, video games, and Ping-Pong. Guest rooms are nicely appointed in a relaxed country fashion, and three feature gas fireplaces.

Dining/Entertainment: The handsome first-floor dining room serves a delicious breakfast and dinner daily (entrees priced between $14.95 and $18.95).

Facilities: Heated pool, outdoor hot tub, four clay tennis courts, bikes (free), game rooms, sauna, golf course nearby, tour desk, bridle trails, and horse rentals. The inn maintains some 38 miles of groomed trails that start right outside the front door.

BETHLEHEM & LITTLETON

A century ago, Bethlehem was about the same size as North Conway to the south, boasting an impressive number of sprawling resort hotels, summer homes, and even its own semiprofessional baseball team. (Joseph Kennedy, patriarch of the Kennedy clan, played for the team.) Bethlehem subsequently lost the race for the riches (or won, depending on your view of outlet shopping), and today is again a sleepy town high on a hillside.

Famous for its lack of ragweed and pollen, Bethlehem was once teeming with vacationers seeking respite from the ravages of hay fever. When antihistamines and air-conditioning appeared on the scene, the sufferers stayed home. Empty resorts burned down one by one. Around the 1920s, Bethlehem was discovered by Hasidic Jews from the New York City area, who soon arrived in numbers to spend the summers in the remaining boardinghouses. In fact, that tradition has endured, and it's not uncommon today to see bearded men wearing black walking the village streets or rocking on the porches of Victorian-era homes.

Nearby Littleton, set in a broad valley along the Ammonoosuc River, is the area's commercial hub, but it boasts a surfeit of small-town charm. The town's long main street is still vibrant in an era when many main streets have been abandoned by retailers scrambling for the mall. (That hasn't been a problem here because there *is* no mall.) The street has an eclectic selection of shops—you can buy a wrench, a foreign magazine or literary novel, locally brewed beer, pizza, whole foods, or camping supplies.

These two towns don't offer much in the way of must-see attractions, but both have good lodging, decent restaurants, and pleasant environs. Either town makes a peaceful alternative for travelers avoiding the tourist bustle to the south.

ESSENTIALS

GETTING THERE   Littleton is best reached via I-93; get off at either Exit 41 or 42. Bethlehem is about 3 miles east of Littleton on Route 302. Get off I-93 at Exit 40 and head east. From the east, follow Route 302 past Twin Mountain to Bethlehem.

VISITOR INFORMATION   The **Bethlehem Chamber of Commerce,** P.O. Box 748, Bethlehem, NH 03574 (☎ **603/869-2151**), maintains an information booth in summer on Bethlehem's Main Street near the golf course. The **Littleton Area Chamber of Commerce,** P.O. Box 105, Littleton, NH 03561 (☎ **603/ 444-6561**), offers information from its office at 120 Main St. Or request information by E-mail from **chamber@moose.ncia.net.**

EXPLORING BETHLEHEM

Bethlehem once was home to 38 resort hotels, but little evidence of that remains today. For a better understanding of the town's rich history, track down a copy of *An Illustrated Tour of Bethlehem, Past and Present,* available at many shops around town. This unusually informative guide offers a glimpse into the town's past, bringing to life many of the most graceful homes and buildings.

Bethlehem consists of a Main Street, and a handful of side streets. Several antique stores clustered in what passes for downtown are well worth browsing.

Harking back to its more genteel era, Bethlehem still offers two well-maintained 18-hole golf courses amid beautiful North Country scenery. Call for hours and greens fees. Both the municipal **Bethlehem Golf Course** (☎ **603/869-5754**) and private **Maplewood Casino and Country Club** (☎ **603/869-3335**) are on Route 302 (Main Street) in Bethlehem.

Just west of Bethlehem on Route 302 is **The Rocks** (☎ **603/444-6228**), a classic, Victorian gentleman's farm that today is the northern headquarters for the Society for the Protection of New Hampshire Forests. Set on 1,200 acres, this gracious estate was built in 1883 by John J. Glessner, an executive with the International Harvester Company. A well-preserved shingled house and an uncommonly handsome barn grace the grounds. Several hiking trails meander through meadows and woodlands on a gentle hillside, where visitors can enjoy open vistas of the wooded mountains across the rolling terrain. The Society operates a Christmas tree farm here, as well as regular nature programs. Admission is free.

WHERE TO STAY

✪ **Adair.** 80 Guider Lane (just off Exit 40 on Rte. 93), Bethlehem, NH 03574. ☎ **800/441-2606** or 603/444-2600. Fax 603/444-4823. E-mail: adair@connriver.net. Web site: www.adairinn.com. 9 rms. $135–$220 double. Rates include breakfast. 2-night minimum on weekends, 3-night minimum on holidays. AE, MC, V.

Adair opened in 1992 and rapidly became one of New England's most esteemed inns. Guests arrive via a long, winding drive flanked by birches and stone walls to arrive at a peaceful, Georgian Revival home that seems far more regal than its years. Built by Washington attorney Frank Hogan (of Hogan & Hartson fame) as a wedding gift for his daughter in 1927, the inn is set on beautifully landscaped grounds. Inside, the common rooms are open, elegant, and spacious. Downstairs is the memorable Granite Tap Room, a huge, wonderfully informal, granite-lined, stone-floored rumpus room with a VCR, antique pool table, fireplace, and self-service bar.

The guest rooms are impeccably well furnished with a mix of antiques and reproductions in a light country fashion. (Six feature fireplaces.) The best of the lot is the Kinsman suite, with a Jacuzzi the size of a small swimming pool and a tiny balcony looking out toward the Dalton range. Another favorite room is Dalton, with its views of the Presidential Range and unique desk made of an old piano.

Innkeepers Patricia, Hardy, and Nancy Banfield have carved a wonderful retreat out of an extraordinary estate, and are helpful hosts who have mastered the art of being both welcoming and unobtrusive. It's the sort of place guests will return to time and again. Not appropriate for younger children. No smoking.

Dining/Entertainment: See Tim-Bir Alley, below.

Facilities: All-weather tennis court, nature trails, game room with billiards.

Hearthside Village. Rte. 302 (midway between Bethlehem Village and I-93), Bethlehem, NH 03574. ☎ **603/444-1000.** 16 cottages (all with showers only). TV. $49.95–$59.95 ($10 less in off-season). 2- or 3-day minimum during foliage season. MC, V. Closed mid-Oct to mid-May.

Hearthside Village is a quirky motel court that seems partly conceived by Alfred Hitchcock, partly by Red Grooms. A little bit weird and a little bit charming at the same time, Hearthside says it was the first motel court built in New Hampshire. The village—a colony of steeply gabled miniature homes—was built by a father and son in two constructive bursts, the first in the 1930s, the second in the late 1940s. The six forties-era cottages are of somewhat better quality, with warm knotty pine interiors. But all cottages are nicely if simply furnished, and all but three have fireplaces (Duraflame-style logs only) and handy kitchenettes. Since acquiring the motel in 1990, Rhonda and Steve Huggins have done an outstanding job making it a friendly, fun place that appeals especially to families. There's a pool, an indoor playroom for tots filled with toys, and another recreation room with video games and Ping-Pong for older kids. A great value.

Rabbit Hill Inn. Rte. 18, Lower Waterford, VT 05848. ☎ **800/762-8669** or 802/748-5168. Fax 802/748-8342. Web site: rabbithillinn.com. 20 rms. A/C. $189–$289 double. Rates include breakfast and dinner. Honeymoon packages available. AE, MC, V. Closed early Apr and early Nov. From I-93, take Rte. 18 northwest from Exit 44 for approximately 2 miles.

A short hop across the Connecticut River from Littleton is the lost-in-time Vermont village of Lower Waterford, with its perfect 1859 church and small library. Amid this cluster of buildings is the stately Rabbit Hill Inn, constructed in 1795. With its prominent gabled roof and imposing columns, the inn easily ranks among the most refined in the Connecticut River Valley. From the porch and many of the guest rooms, the views of the northern White Mountains are unrivaled. The inn's interior is richly furnished with Federal-era antiques. More than half of the rooms have gas fireplaces, most have air-conditioning, and the innkeepers go the extra mile to make this an appealing destination for couples in search of quiet romance. Children over the age of 12 are welcome. No smoking.

Dining/Entertainment: Dinner is included in the rates, and features regional classics along with more creative fare like fresh tomato fettuccine tossed in a jalapeño sunflower seed pesto, and braised Vermont pheasant breast with bacon, grapes, and baby artichokes. Jacket and tie aren't required, but proper attire is expected in the dining room.

Thayers Inn. Main St., Littleton, NH 03561. ☎ **800/634-8179** or 603/444-6469. 40 rms (3 with shared bath, some with shower only). TV TEL. $39.95–$59.95 double. AE, DC, DISC, MC, V.

Last century President Ulysses S. Grant addressed a street-side crowd from one of the balconies under the grand eaves of Thayers Inn. You might try that, too, although it's not likely you'll be as successful at scaring up a crowd. My advice: Just grab a book, have a seat on the balcony, and watch life pass by on Littleton's Main Street. Offering good value for your money, Thayers is a clean, well-run hostelry in an impressive historic building. That's an all too rare sight in small towns these days. This solid 1850 inn has a variety of rooms furnished comfortably and eclectically on four floors. Notable guests who have stayed here include Bette Davis, Horace Greeley, Nelson Rockefeller, and Richard Nixon. Each room on the floors is different, and guests are encouraged to poke around and see what's available before deciding on their evening quarters.

WHERE TO DINE

✪ **Tim-Bir Alley.** At Adair, Old Littleton Rd., Bethlehem. ☎ **603/444-6142.** Reservations recommended. Main courses $13.95–$18.50. No credit cards. Wed–Sun 5:30–9pm. Closed Apr, Nov, and Sun in off-season. REGIONAL/CONTEMPORARY.

Hands down, the best dining in the White Mountains is at Tim-Bir Alley, housed in the area's most gracious country inn. Owned by Tim and Biruta Carr, Tim-Bir Alley began a few years ago in a miniature storefront off a small alley in Littleton. Its reputation for gourmet cuisine outgrew its tiny size, and the pair eventually moved up the hill to Adair, occupying the beautiful dining room. The setting is elegant and romantic, the meals always memorable, the service . . . well, the service can be a bit poky, so come expecting to enjoy a leisurely meal.

The ingredients are wholesome and basic, but the real art is in the preparation and presentation. Even the simple side dishes flirt with the remarkable—the squash and brussel sprouts (the latter prepared with a liberal dose of ginger) were among the best I've ever tasted. Diners might start with chicken and water chestnut wontons with a spicy peanut sauce, then follow with quail with a wild-mushroom, smoked-bacon, and merlot sauce; or tournedos of beef with mozzarella and roasted tomato and basil sauce. Save room for the superb deserts, which range from cranberry-almond cake with a warm honey sauce, to a chocolate-hazelnut pâté.

6 The North Country

I've been traveling to New Hampshire's North Country for more than 25 years, and it's come to serve as a touchstone for me. Errol is a town that seems to never change, and that held true even during the boom times of the 1980s. The clean Errol Motel is always there. The Errol Restaurant still serves the best homemade donuts north of Boston. And the land surrounding the town remains an outpost of rugged, raw grandeur that hasn't been at all compromised, as have many of the former wildlands to the south.

Of course, there's a problem with these lost-in-time areas. It's the nothing to see, nothing to do syndrome that seems to especially afflict families with young children. You drive for miles and see lots of spruce and pine, an infrequent bog, a glimpse of a shimmering lake, and—if you're lucky—a roadside moose chomping on sedges.

But there *is* plenty to do. White-water kayaking on the Androscoggin River. Canoeing on Lake Umbagog. Bicycling along the wide valley floors. And visiting one of the Northeast's grandest, most improbable turn-of-the-century resorts, which is thriving despite considerable odds against it.

Some recent developments are encouraging for those who'd like to see the area remain unchanged. In what may be one of the last bursts of federal largess for a long time to come, the piney shoreline around spectacular Lake Umbagog was protected as a National Wildlife Refuge a few years ago. Part was acquired outright by the federal and state governments (Umbagog straddles the Maine–New Hampshire border), and part was protected through the purchase of development rights from timber companies. The upshot? Umbagog should remain in its more or less pristine state for all time.

As for Errol, some shops have closed, some have opened. But the Androscoggin River still flows through. And the police still set up radar at the bend near the river to catch Canadian speeders heading south toward Old Orchard Beach on Friday, then turn around to catch them heading north on Sundays.

ESSENTIALS

GETTING THERE   Errol is at the junction of Route 26 (accessible from Bethel, Me.) and Route 16 (accessible from Gorham, N.H.).

VISITOR INFORMATION   The **Northern White Mountains Chamber of Commerce,** 164 Main St., Berlin, NH 03570 (☎ **603/752-6060**), offers travel information from its offices weekdays between 8:30am and 4:30pm.

OUTDOOR RECREATION

Dixville Notch State Park (☎ **603/788-2155**) offers limited hiking, including a delightful 2-mile round-trip hike to Table Rock. Look for the small parking area just east of The Balsams resort (from Colebrook, head east on Route 26) on the edge of Lake Gloriette. The loop hike (it connects with a half-mile return along Route 25) ascends a scrabbly trail to an open rock with fine views of the resort and the flanking wild hills.

If you're heading to the North Country, be sure to bring your canoe or kayak, since this is a superb area for both white-water and flat-water paddling.

A great place to learn the fundamentals of white-water paddling is at **Saco Bound's Northern Waters** white-water school (☎ **603/482-3848**), located where the Errol bridge crosses the Androscoggin River. The school offers 3- and 5-day workshops in the art of getting downstream safely, if not dryly. Many of the students camp along the river at the school's campground, although some bivouac a short walk away at the Errol Motel. Classes involve videos, dry-land training, and frequent forays onto the river—both at the Class I–III rapids at the bridge, and more forgiving rips downstream. The base camp is also a good place for last-minute boat supplies and advice for paddlers exploring the river on their own.

Excellent lake canoeing may be found at **Lake Umbagog,** which sits between Maine and New Hampshire. The lake, which is home to the **Lake Umbagog Wildlife Refuge** (☎ **603/482-3415**), has some 40 miles of shoreline, most of which is wild and remote. Look for osprey and eagles, otter and mink. Some 30 primitive campsites are scattered around the shoreline and on the lake's islands. These are managed by **Umbagog Lake Campground** (☎ **603/482-7795**), and are extremely pricey for backcountry sites ($18 for two). On the other hand, they're well maintained and you get a lot of wildlands for your money. The campground, which is located on Route 26 at the lake's southern tip, also rents canoes.

The area around Errol offers excellent roads for **bicycling**—virtually all routes out of town make for good exploring (although it's mighty hilly heading east). An especially nice trip is south on Route 16 from Errol. The occasional logging truck can be unnerving, but mostly it's an easy and peaceful riverside trip. Consider pedaling as far as what's locally called the Brown Co. Bridge—a simple, wooden logging road bridge that crosses the Androscoggin River. It's a good spot to leap in the river and float through a series of gentle rips before swimming to shore. Some small ledges on the far side of the bridge provide a good location for sunning and relaxing.

Biking information and rentals ($24 per day) are available in Gorham at **Moriah Sports,** 101 Main St. (☎ **603/466-5050**).

WHERE TO STAY & DINE

✪ **Balsams Grand Resort Hotel.** Dixville Notch, NH 03576. ☎ **800/255-0600** (800/255-0800 in N.H.) or 603/255-3400. Fax 603/255-4221. E-mail: thebalsams@aol.com. Web site: www.thebalsams.com. 200 rms (1 with shower only). TEL. Winter $288–$308 double, including breakfast, dinner, and lift tickets; summer $338–$390 double, including all meals and entertainment; year-round $508–$575 suite. 4-night minimum on weekends in July–Aug. AE, DISC, MC, V. Closed early Apr to late May and mid-Oct to Christmas.

Located on 15,000 private acres in a notch surrounded by 800-foot cliffs, the Balsams is a rare surprise hidden deep in the northern forest. The inn is but one of a handful of great resorts dating back to the 19th century still in operation, and its survival is all the more extraordinary given its remote location. What makes this Victorian grande dame even more exceptional has been its refusal to compromise or bend to the trend of the moment. Bathing suits and jeans are prohibited from the public areas, you'll be ejected from the tennis courts or golf course if you're not neatly attired, and men are required (not requested) to wear jackets at dinner. The resort has also maintained strict adherence to the spirit of the "American plan"—everything but booze is included in the room rate, from greens fees to tennis to boats on Lake Gloriette to entertainment in the three lounges in evening. Even the lift tickets at the resort's downhill ski area are covered.

The Balsams's rigorous old-world decorum only enriches the mood at this sprawling resort. The rooms are spacious and attractive; the public areas tastefully appointed with resort-style furnishings representing almost every decade between 1866, when the place first opened, and today. Navigating your way through the winding halls is not for the directionally challenged.

Dining/Entertainment: Meals are superb. Especially famous is the sumptuous luncheon buffet served in summer, featuring delightful salads, filling entrees like linguine with clam sauce and fried shrimp, and time-honored desserts (when did you last gorge yourself on chocolate éclairs?). There are also three lounges.

Services: Concierge, limited room service, dry cleaning, laundry service, newspaper delivery, turndown service, baby-sitting, currency exchange, and valet parking.

Facilities: Two golf courses (one 18-hole, one 9-hole), six tennis courts, heated outdoor pool, 45 miles of groomed cross-country ski trails, bicycle rentals, game rooms, nature trails, children's programs, business center, conference rooms, sundeck, water sports equipment, beauty salon, boutiques, shopping arcade.

✪ **Philbrook Farm Inn.** North Rd. (off Rte. 2 between Gorham, N.H., and Bethel, Me.), Shelburne, NH 03581. ☎ **603/466-3831.** Web site: www.innbook.com. 18 rms, plus 5 summer cottages (6 rooms have shared baths; of the private baths, 1 is tub only, 2 are shower only). $110–$140 double, including full breakfast and dinner; cottages $575 weekly. No credit cards. Closed Apr and Nov–Dec 25.

The Philbrook Farm Inn is a true New England classic. Set on 1,000 acres between the Mahoosuc Range and the Androscoggin River, this country inn has been owned and operated by the Philbrook family continuously since 1853. The inn has grown haphazardly since the Philbrooks acquired the early farmhouse, with additions in 1861, 1904, and 1934. As a result, the cozy guest rooms on three floors are eclectic—some have a country farmhouse feel, others a more Victorian flavor. Rooms are named after favored guests. I stayed in the room named after Albert Payson Briggs, who was a frequent visitor between 1872 and 1954.

The common areas are spacious and comfortable, with jigsaw puzzles and a century and a half's worth of books lining the shelves. Guests spend their days swimming in the pool, playing croquet, or exploring trails in the nearby hills. Philbrook Farm is a wonderful retreat, well out of the tourist mainstream, and worthy of protection as a local cultural landmark.

Dining/Entertainment: The dining room has a farmhouse-formal feel to it; guests are assigned one table for their stay, and are served by waitresses in crisp, white uniforms. Meals tend toward basic New England fare, with specialties like cod cakes and baked beans with brown bread. Potatoes are served with almost every meal.

Maine 13

by Wayne Curtis

Humorist Dave Barry once wryly suggested that Maine's state motto should be "Cold, but damp."

Cute, but true.

There's spring, which tends to last a few blustery, rain-soaked days. There's November, in which Arctic winds alternate with gray sheets of rain. And then winter brings a character-building mix of blizzards and ice storms to the fabled coast. (The inland mountains are more or less blessed with uninterrupted snow.)

Ah, but then there's summer. Summer in Maine brings ospreys diving for fish off wooded points; gleaming cumulus clouds building over the steely blue rounded peaks of the western mountains; and the haunting whoop of loons echoing off the dense forest walls bordering the lakes. It brings languorous days when the sun rises before most visitors and it seems like noontime at 8am. (There's a tiny but vocal movement afoot to shift Maine to Canada's Atlantic time zone, which would move some of the precious daylight from 4 or 5am to the evening, where it might be put to better use.) Maine summers bring a measure of gracious tranquillity, and a placid stay in the right spot can rejuvenate even the most jangled nerves.

The trick comes in finding that right spot. Those who arrive here without a clear plan may find themselves cursing their travel decision. Maine's Route 1 along the coast has its moments, but for the most part it's rather charmless—an amalgam of convenience stores, tourist boutiques, and restaurants catering to bus tours. Acadia National Park can be congested, Mount Katahdin's summit crowded, and some of the more popular lakes become obstacle courses for jet skis.

But Maine's size works to the traveler's advantage. Maine is nearly as large as the other five New England states combined. It has 3,500 miles of coastline, some 3,000 coastal islands, and millions of acres of undeveloped woodland. In fact, more than half of the state exists as "unorganized territories," where no town government exists, and the few inhabitants look to the state for basic services. With all this space, and a little planning, you'll be able to find your piece of Maine.

Wherever your travels take you, be sure to look for the varied layers of history, both natural and human. You'll find the mark of the great glaciers on the scoured mountaintops. You'll find the hand of man in 2-century-old mansions on remote coves that bespeak a former affluence when Maine ruled the waves (or at least much of the early trade on those waves). You'll find the 18th and 19th centuries overlapping in coastal villages, where handsome Georgian and Victorian homes sit side by side. Picking these layers apart is much of the fun in exploring Maine.

1 Enjoying the Great Outdoors

Bring your mountain bike, hiking boots, sea kayak, canoe, fishing rod, and snowmobile—there'll be plenty for you to do here.

If your outdoor skills are a bit rusty or nonexistent, consider brushing up at the **L.L. Bean Outdoor Discovery Schools** (☎ **800/341-4341**, ext. 6666). The "schools" are actually a series of lectures and workshops that run anywhere from 2 hours to 3 days. Classes are offered at various locations around the state covering a whole range of subjects, including map and compass, fly tying, bike maintenance, canoeing, kayaking, and cross-country and telemark skiing. L.L. Bean also hosts popular canoeing, sea kayaking, and cross-country skiing "festivals" that bring together instructors, lecturers, and equipment vendors for 2 or 3 days of learning and outdoor diversion. Call for a brochure.

BACKPACKING   Compared to camping by canoe or sea kayak, backpacking opportunities are relatively limited in Maine. A couple of notable exceptions exist. The 2,000-mile **Appalachian Trail,** which ends (or begins, depending on your direction) at Maine's highest peak, is nothing short of spectacular as it passes through Maine. En route to Mount Katahdin, it winds through the "100-Mile Wilderness," a remote, bosky, and boggy stretch where the trail crosses few roads and passes no settlements. It's the quiet habitat of loons and moose, and hikers are transients. Trail guides are available from the **Appalachian Trail Conference,** P.O. Box 807, Harpers Ferry, WV 25425 (☎ **304/535-6331**), or the **Maine Appalachian Trail Club,** P.O. Box 283, Augusta, ME 04330.

Another excellent destination for backcountry exploration is 200,000-acre **Baxter State Park,** with administrative offices at 64 Balsam Dr., Millinocket, ME 04462 (☎ **207/723-5140**), in the north-central part of the state. The park maintains about 180 miles of backcountry hiking trails, and more than 25 backcountry sites, some of which are accessible only by canoe. The vast majority of travelers coming to the park are intent on ascending 5,267-foot Mount Katahdin. But dozens of other peaks are well worth scaling, and just traveling through the deep woods hereabouts is a sublime experience. Reservations are required for backcountry camping, and many of the best spots fill up shortly after the first of the year. Reservations can be made by mail or in person, but not by phone.

Note that backcountry camping is not permitted at Acadia National Park.

BEACHGOING   Swimming at Maine's ocean beaches is for the hearty. The Gulf Stream, which prods warm waters toward the Cape Cod shores to the south, veers toward Iceland south of Maine and leaves the state's 3,500-mile coastline washed by the brisk Nova Scotia current, an offshoot of the arctic Labrador current. During summer, water temperatures along the south coast can top 60° during an especially warm spell where the water is shallow, but it's usually cooler than that. The average ocean temperature at Bar Harbor in summer is 54°.

Maine's beaches are found mostly between Portland and the New Hampshire border. Northeast of Portland a handful of fine beaches await—including popular **Reid State Park** and **Popham Beach State Park**—but rocky coast defines this territory for the most part. The southern beaches are beautiful, but rarely isolated. Summer

Maine

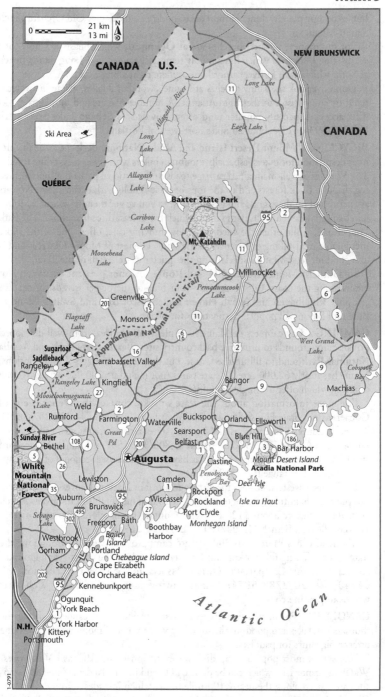

homes occupy the low dunes in most areas; mid-rise condos give Old Orchard Beach a mini-Miami air.

For my money, the best beaches are at **Ogunquit,** which boasts a 3-mile-long sandy strand, some of which has a mildly remote character, and **Long Sands Beach** at York, which has a festive, carnival atmosphere right along Route 1A.

Don't overlook the sandy beaches at Maine's wonderful lakes, where the water is tepid by comparison to the frigid Atlantic. A number of state and municipal parks offer access. Especially popular (and often crowded) is **Sebago Lake State Park** (☎ 207/693-6613), about 20 miles northwest of Portland.

BICYCLING   Mount Desert Island and **Acadia National Park** comprise the premier destination for bikers, especially mountain bikers who prefer easy-riding terrain. The 57 miles of well-maintained carriage roads in the national park offer superb cruising through thick forests and to the tops of rocky knolls with ocean views. No cars are permitted on these grass and gravel roads, so you've got them to yourself. Mountain bikes may be rented in Bar Harbor, which has at least three bike shops. The Park Loop Road, while often crowded with slow-moving cars, offers one of the more memorable road-biking experiences in the state. The rest of Mount Desert Island is also good for road biking, especially on the quieter western half of the island.

In southern Maine, **Route 103** and **Route 1A** offer pleasant excursions for bikers along the coast. Offshore, bring your bike to the bigger islands for car-free cruising. **Vinalhaven** and **North Haven** in Penobscot Bay, and **Swan's Island** in Blue Hill Bay are all popular destinations for bikers.

CAMPING   Car campers in Maine have plenty of choices, from well-developed private campgrounds to primitive backcountry sites. **Baxter State Park** and **Acadia National Park** tend to fill up the fastest, but there's no shortage of other options. Maine has nearly 62,000 acres in state parks (not including 200,000-acre Baxter), a dozen of which offer overnight camping.

For more information about the state's parks, contact the **Department of Conservation,** State House Station #22, Augusta, ME 04333 (☎ 207/287-3821). To make camping reservations at 12 of the state park campgrounds, call between January and August (☎ 207/287-3824, or 800/332-1501 in Maine). MasterCard and Visa are accepted. For reservations at Baxter State Park, see section 8 of this chapter. Campsite fees range from $10 to $16.

On Maine's western border, the **White Mountain National Forest** offers superb camping at a handful of campgrounds in the rolling mountains of the Evans Notch area. Rates average about $12 per night. Contact Evans Notch Ranger District, 18 Mayville Rd., Bethel, ME 04217 (☎ 207/824-2134).

Maine also has more than 200 private campgrounds spread throughout the state, many offering full hookups for RVs. For a guide to the private campgrounds, contact the **Maine Campground Owners Association,** 655 Main St., Lewiston, ME 04240 (☎ 207/782-5874; E-mail: **info@campmaine.com**; Web site: **www.campmaine.com**).

CANOEING   For many outdoors enthusiasts, Maine means canoeing. From the thousands of lakes and ponds to the tumbling white water of mountain rivers, Maine offers a big allure for paddlers.

The state's most popular long-distance excursion is the **Allagash Wilderness Waterway** canoe trip, which can be done end to end in 7 to 10 days. Some 80 campsites are spaced along the nearly 100-mile route, which includes a 9-mile stretch of Class I–II white water. For a map and brochure, contact the Bureau of Parks and Recreation, Maine Department of Conservation, State House Station 22, Augusta,

ME 04333 (☎ **207/287-3821**). The Allagash is also served by a number of outfitters, who can provide everything from a complete guide service to a simple car shuttle. (See section 8 of this chapter.)

You can't travel very far in Maine without stumbling upon a great canoe trip. Two excellent sources of information are the *AMC River Guide: Maine* and *Quiet Water Canoe Guide: Maine,* both published by the Appalachian Mountain Club, 5 Joy St., Boston, MA 02108.

FISHING   Maine draws anglers from throughout the Northeast who indulge their grand obsession on Maine's 6,000 lakes and ponds and its countless miles of rivers and streams. Among the most appealing areas for serious freshwater anglers is the **Grand Lake Stream** region deep in the woods of Washington County, not far from the New Brunswick border and Canada. This area has a strong heritage as a fisherman's settlement, and a number of camps and outfitters cater to the serious angler.

Nearby **Dennys River** and the **St. Croix River** are good destinations for Atlantic salmon; troll the numerous lakes for trout and smallmouth bass. Among the classic fishing lodges in this area are **Weatherby's** (☎ **207/796-5558**) and **Indian Rock Camps** (☎ **800/498-2821** or 207/796-2822).

For other options on rustic fishing camps statewide, request one of the attractive brochures that lists more than 50 sporting camps between the Rangelely Lakes and Eagle Lake near Fort Kent: **Maine Sporting Camp Association,** P.O. Box 89, Jay, ME 04239.

Nonresident **licenses** are $50 for the season, or $21 for 3 days. Seven- and 15-day licenses are also available. You can purchase licenses at many outdoor shops or general stores. For a booklet of fishing regulations, contact the **Department of Inland Fisheries and Wildlife,** State House Station #41, Augusta, ME 04333 (☎ **207/287-3371**).

HIKING   Maine has surprisingly limited hiking opportunities, given that it's home to 10 peaks that are over 4,000 feet high. But the reason is simple. Outside of Baxter State and Acadia National parks, Maine has very limited public lands. Recreation has historically occurred on the millions of acres of privately owned timber company land, and the emphasis there has been on canoeing, fishing, and hunting, not on recreational hiking.

That's not to say that Maine lacks great places to hike. Trails abound, if you know where to look. **Acadia National Park** offers superb and surprisingly tranquil hiking, given the huge popularity of the park. Happily for hikers, few visitors venture far from their cars, leaving the trail system relatively unpopulated. In western Maine, 50,000 acres of the **White Mountains** spill over the border from New Hampshire and boast an excellent network of trails. There are a number of pathways in and around Evans Notch that offer opportunities for hikers of all levels. Finally, there's the excellent and generally unheralded **Bigelow Range** near the Sugarloaf/USA ski resort, which offers challenging trails and stunning vistas from high, blustery ridges. The Appalachian Trail traverses the range; a good source of trail information is in the AT guide (see "Backpacking," above).

Two guides to the state's trails are highly recommended. *50 Hikes in Southern and Coastal Maine* by John Gibson is a reliable directory to trails at Evans Notch, Acadia, and the Camden Hills area. *50 Hikes in the Maine Mountains* by Chloe Chunn is the best guide for the Bigelow Range and Baxter State Park. Both are available from **Backcountry Publications,** c/o W. W. Norton & Co. Inc., 800 Keystone Industrial Park, Scranton, PA 18512.

SEA KAYAKING   Sea kayakers nationwide migrate to Maine in the summer for world-class sea kayaking. The 3,500 miles of rocky coastline and the thousands of offshore islands have created a wondrous playground. Paddlers can explore protected estuaries far from the surf, or test their skills and determination with excursions across the choppy, open sea to islands far offshore. It's a sport that can be extremely dangerous (the seas can turn on you in a matter of minutes), but can yield plenty of returns for those with the proper equipment and skills.

The nation's first long-distance "water trail" was created here in 1987 when the **Maine Island Trail** was established. This 325-mile waterway winds along the coast from Portland to Machias, and incorporates some 70 state and privately owned islands along the route. Members of the Maine Island Trail Association, a private nonprofit organization, help maintain and monitor the islands and in turn are granted permission to visit and camp on them as long as they follow certain restrictions (for example, don't visit designated islands during seabird nesting season). The association seeks to encourage low-impact, responsible use of these natural treasures. A guidebook, published annually, provides descriptions of all the islands in the network and is free with association membership (note that it's available *only* to members). Membership is $40 per year; contact the **Maine Island Trail Association,** P.O. Box C, Rockland, ME 04841 (☎ **207/596-6456** or 207/761-8225).

For novices, Maine has a number of kayak outfitters offering guided excursions ranging from an afternoon to a week. Outfitters include the **H2Outfitters**, P.O. Box 72, Orr's Island, ME 04066 (☎ **800/205-2925**), and **Maine Sports Outfitters,** P.O. Box 956, Rockport, ME 04856 (☎ **800/244-8799** or 207/236-8797). Write or call and request information on upcoming trips.

SKIING   Maine has 2 major downhill ski resorts along with 10 smaller areas. The two big resorts, **Sugarloaf** and **Sunday River,** came under the same ownership in 1996, but both maintain distinct characters. Sugarloaf is compact and manageable, and offers the highest vertical drop in New England after Vermont's Killington. The resort's base area is self-contained like a campus and is a big hit with families. Sunday River is a younger resort and its base area is still a bit rough around the edges—think of it as more of a brash community college. But it offers diverse skiing terrain and state-of-the-art snowmaking and grooming. I'd go to Sugarloaf if I were expecting heavy natural snowfall; I'd choose Sunday River if the natural snow conditions were marginal or poor.

The medium and small mountains cater primarily to the local market but offer good alternatives for travelers who'd just as soon avoid the flash and crowds of a larger area. Of the midsized areas, **Shawnee Peak** and **Saddleback** have small resort complexes at or near their bases, and offer better bargains and fewer crowds; Shawnee Peak is open for night skiing until 10pm 6 nights each week. **Mount Abram,** which is near Sunday River, has developed a solid reputation among telemark skiers.

For a pamphlet listing basic information about all of Maine's ski areas, contact the **Ski Maine Association,** P.O. Box 7566, Portland, ME 04112 (Web site: **www.skimaine.com**). The association maintains a recorded announcement of current downhill ski conditions statewide in season, call ☎ **800/533-9595,** or 207/773-7669 in Maine.

Cross-country skiers have a glorious mix of terrain to choose from, although groomed cross-country ski areas aren't as extensive in Maine as in neighboring New Hampshire or Vermont. Sunday River, Saddleback, and Sugarloaf all feature cross-country ski areas at or near their downhill complexes. A more remote destination is **The Birches** (☎ **800/825-9453**) on Moosehead Lake, with 24 miles of groomed trails. The best place to combine remote backcountry lodging and skiing is **Little Lyford Pond Camps** (☎ **207/695-2821,** via radio phone) outside of Greenville—it's accessible in winter only by ski-plane or snowmobile.

For further information about cross-country ski areas in Maine, contact the **Maine Nordic Council** (☎ **800/754-9263**).

SNOWMOBILING   Snowmobiling is in the midst of a boom in Maine. Restaurants and lodges that were until recently shuttered through winter are now doing more business in the snowy months than the rest of the year. Communities throughout northern Maine, in particular, are spending tens of thousands of dollars grooming trails nightly for snowmobilers in a bid to attract their attention. Maine's **Interconnected Trail System (ITS)** serves as a superhighway for the North Woods; the woods are also laced with an elaborate network of local trails maintained by local snowmobile clubs. Overall, Maine has 11,000 miles of groomed trails maintained by 260 snowmobile clubs. If you plan your trip right, stops for gas, food, and warming up will be no more than 30 miles apart.

The farther north you go, the better the conditions are likely to be. Of particular note is the sled trail that follows the perimeter of **Moosehead Lake,** with stops possible at Mount Kineo and Seboomook, Northeast Carry, and Kokadjo, all of which offer food and lodging. For more information on the trail or rentals, contact the **Moosehead Region Chamber of Commerce,** P.O. Box 581, Greenville, ME 04441 (☎ **207/695-2702**).

WHITE-WATER RAFTING   Maine has three northern rivers that get the adrenaline pumping: the Dead, the Kennebec, and the Penobscot. All three are dam-controlled, which means that good rafting is available throughout the season. The **Dead River** has a limited release schedule; during the average season, it's opened only a half-dozen times for rafting in early summer and fall; smaller releases allow paddling in inflatable kayaks during the summer. The **Kennebec River** offers monstrous waves just below the dam (some say they're comparable to the big water you'll find out West), then tapers off into a gentle afternoon paddle as you float out of a scenic gorge. The West Branch of the **Penobscot River** has a challenging, technical section called the Cribworks at the outset, several serious drops and falls after that, and dramatic views of Mount Katahdin along the route.

For a list of outfitters, contact **Raft Maine,** P.O. Box 3, Bethel, ME 04217 (☎ **800/723-8633** or 207/824-3694).

WINDJAMMING   An ideal way to combine time in the outdoors with relative luxury and an easy to digest education in maritime history is aboard a windjammer cruise on the coast. Maine boasts a sizable fleet of vintage sailing ships that offer private cabins, meals, entertainment, and adventure. The ships range in size from 53 to 132 feet, and most are berthed in the region between Bath and Belfast. You choose your adventure: An array of excursions are available, from simple overnights to week-long expeditions among Maine's thousands of scenic islands and coves.

2 The South Coast

There are two good reasons to visit Maine's south coast: the long, sandy beaches and the almost tactile sense of history you'll find in the coastal villages.

Thanks to quirks of geography, almost all of Maine's sandy beaches are located in the 60-mile stretch of coastline between Portland and Kittery. And you're likely to find a sandy spot that appeals to you, whether you prefer dunes and the lulling sound of the surf or the carny atmosphere of a festive beach town. The waves are dependent on the water—during a good Northeast blow they pound the shores and threaten beach houses built decades ago. During the balmy days of midsummer the ocean can be as gentle as a farm pond, with barely audible waves lapping timidly at the shore.

One thing all the beaches share in common: They're washed by the frigid waters of the Gulf of Maine. Bouts of swimming tend to be very brief and often accompanied by shrieks and whoops. The beach season is brief and intense, running from July 4th to Labor Day. Before and after, beach towns tend to be rather sleepy.

On foggy or rainy days, plan to search out the south coast's rich history. More than 3 centuries ago, the early European newcomers first settled here, only to be driven out by hostile Native Americans, who had been pushed to the brink by treaty-breaking British settlers and prodded by the mischievous French. Settlers later reestablished themselves, and by the early 19th century the southern Maine coast was one of the most prosperous regions in the nation. Shipbuilders constructed brigantines and sloops, and ship captains plied the Eastern seaboard, the Caribbean, and far beyond. Merchants and traders constructed vast warehouses along the rivers to store their goods. Many handsome and historic homes near the coast today attest to the region's former prosperity.

A second wave came in the mid- to late 19th century, when wealthy city dwellers from Boston and New York sought respite from the summer heat and congestion by fleeing to Maine's coast. They built shingled estates (which they coyly called "cottages") with views of the Atlantic. After the turn of the century, aided by trolleys and buses, the wealthy rusticators were followed by the emerging middle class, who built bungalows near the shore and congregated at ocean-side boarding houses to splash in the waves.

THE YORKS

"The Yorks" are comprised of three towns that share a name but little else. In fact, it's rare to find three such diverse New England archetypes in such a compact area. York Village is rich with Early American history and architecture. York Harbor is redolent of America's late Victorian era, when wealthy urbanites flocked to the ocean's edge. And York Beach has a turn-of-the-century beach-town feel, with loud amusements, taffy shops, a modest zoo, and small gabled summer homes set in crowded enclaves near the beach.

ESSENTIALS

GETTING THERE   The Yorks are accessible from Exit 1 of the Maine Turnpike. Route 1A, which departs from Route 1 just south of the turnpike exit, connects all three York towns and loops north back to Route 1.

VISITOR INFORMATION   Travelers entering the state on I-95 can stock up on travel information for the region and beyond at the **Kittery Information Center** (☎ **207/439-1319**), located about a mile south of outlet row between I-95 and Route 1 (watch for signs). Open until 9pm in summer, it's amply stocked with brochures, and the helpful staff can answer many questions.

The **York Chamber of Commerce,** P.O. Box 417, York, ME 03909 (☎ **207/363-4422**), operates an attractive, helpful information center at 599 Route 1, a short distance from the turnpike exit. A trackless trolley (a bus fitted out to look like an old-fashioned trolley) regularly links all three York towns and provides a convenient way to explore without having to scare up parking spots at every stop. Hop the trolley at one of the well-marked stops for a 1-hour narrated tour ($3), or disembark along the way and explore by foot.

Southern Maine Coast

5

26

117

Turner

Winthrop

North
Waterford

5

South Paris

4

11

Norway

118

202

495

201

Mechanic
Falls

117

Lovell

302

Auburn

Lewiston

196

Lisbon
Falls

Richmond

95

Bridgton

*Long
Lake*

11

Casco

Bath

26

136

Naples

Saco R.

5

117

Gray

Brunswick

11

Hiram

N. Windham

*Sebago
Lake*

Yarmouth

Freeport

South Freeport

209

Cornish

35

302

Harpswell Center

South Harpswell

Bailey Island

5

25

202

Westbrook

Portland

*Casco
Bay*

Limerick

4

South Portland

Hollis
Center

95

Cape
Elizabeth

11

Shapleigh

5

TNPK.

Old Orchard
Beach

*Saco
Bay*

Alfred

111

Saco

Biddeford

109

Sanford

MAINE

1

202

4

109

Kennebunk

North
Berwick

Kennebunkport

Atlantic

Rochester

Berwick

95

Ocean

Somersworth

Wells

Ogunquit

Dover

Cape Neddick

**New
Hampshire**

Maine

York Beach

York Village

Durham

York Harbor

Kittery

108

Portsmouth

0   16 km
10 mi.

N

1A

Exeter

1-0607

BEACHES

York Beach actually consists of two beaches—**Long Sands Beach** and **Short Sands Beach**—separated by a rocky headland and a small island capped with scenic Nubble Light. Both offer plenty of room for sunning and Frisbees when the tide is out. When the tide is in, they're both a bit cramped. Short Sands fronts the town of York Beach with its candlepin bowling and video arcades. It's the better bet for families who have kids with short attention spans. Long Sands runs along Route 1A, across from a profusion of motels, summer homes, and convenience stores. Parking at both beaches is metered (50¢ per hr.).

DISCOVERING LOCAL HISTORY IN YORK VILLAGE

Old York Historical Society. South Side Rd., York. ☎ **207/363-4974.** $6 adults, $2.50 children 6–16 (admission to all buildings; individual buildings are $2). Tues–Sat 10am–4pm, Sun 1–5pm. Closed Nov–Apr.

John Hancock is famous for his oversized signature on the Declaration of Independence, his tenure as governor of Massachusetts, and the insurance company named after him. What's not so well known is his earlier checkered past as a businessman. Hancock was the proprietor of Hancock Wharf, a failed enterprise that's only one of the intriguing sites open to the public in York Village, a fine destination for those curious about Early American history.

First settled in 1624, York Village has several early homes open to the public. Tickets are available at **Jefferds Tavern,** across from the handsome old burying ground, where changing exhibits document facets of early life. Next door is the School House, furnished as it might have been in the last century. A 10-minute walk along lightly traveled Lindsay Road will bring you to Hancock Wharf, which is next door to the George Marshall Store. Also nearby is the Elizabeth Perkins House with its well-preserved colonial-revival interiors. The most recent acquisition is an old bank building, which now houses the society's library and offices. The library is open to historical-society members only.

The two don't-miss buildings in the society's collection are the intriguing **Old Gaol,** built in 1719 with its now musty dungeons for criminals and debtors. The jail is the oldest surviving public building in the United States. Just down the knoll from the jail is the **Emerson-Wilcox House,** built in the mid-1700s. Added on to periodically over the years, it's a virtual catalog of architectural styles and early decorative arts.

WHERE TO STAY

For basic accommodations, try York Beach, which has a proliferation of motels and guest cottages facing Long Sands Beach. Even with this abundance, however, it's best to reserve ahead during prime season. And don't expect any real bargains during midsummer, even among the most basic of motels. If the inns reviewed below are booked, try these: the **Anchorage Motor Inn** (☎ 207/363-5112), the **Sea Latch Motor Inn** (☎ **800/441-2993** or 207/363-4400), or the **Sunrise Motel** (☎ **800/242-0752** or 207/363-4542).

Dockside Guest Quarters. Harris Island (P.O. Box 205), York, ME 03909. ☎ **207/363-2868.** Fax 207/363-1977. 21 rms, 2 with shared bath. TV. Mid-June to early Sept $60–$159 double. Ask about off-season discounts. MC, V. Closed weekdays Nov–May. Drive south on Rte. 103 from Rte. 1A; after bridge, turn left and follow the signs.

David and Harriet Lusty established this quiet retreat in 1954, and recent additions (mostly new cottages) haven't dulled any of the friendly, maritime flavor of the place. Situated on an island connected to the mainland by a small bridge, the inn occupies nicely landscaped grounds shady with maples and white pines. Five of the rooms are in the main house, built in 1885, but the bulk of the accommodations are in small, town-house-style cottages constructed between 1968 and 1974. These are simply furnished, bright, and airy, and all have private decks that overlook the entrance to York Harbor. (Several rooms also offer woodstoves.)

Dining/Entertainment: The inn operates a popular restaurant on the property, serving mounds of fresh seafood and New England classics. It's moderately priced.

Facilities: Canoes, rowboats, 13-foot Boston whaler (no additional charge for boats), badminton, croquet, ocean swimming.

Nevada Motel. Rte. 1A (P.O. Box 885), York Beach, ME 03910. ☎ **207/363-4504.** 21 rms. A/C TV TEL. Mid-June to Labor Day $78 double; off-season $56 double. AE, MC, V. Closed Oct 15–May 15.

This unassuming, classic 1953 beachfront motel is a low, white, two-story affair with turquoise trim offering simple, comfortable rooms, most of which are on the small side. But the sound of surf reaches the rooms through louvered windows (Long Sands Beach is just across Route 1A), and there's a spacious deck on the second floor that affords wonderful views across the road to the ocean beyond. The Nevada is popular with a mix of guests, from families to couples, most of whom simply spend their day on the beach.

Stage Neck Inn. Stage Neck (P.O. Box 70), York Harbor, ME 03911. ☎ **800/222-3238** or 207/363-3850. 60 rms. A/C TV TEL. June through Labor Day $160–$220 double; early fall $130–$195 double; winter $105–$140 double; spring $130–$160 double. AE, DISC, MC, V. Head north on 1A from Rte. 1; make 2nd right after York Harbor post office.

A hotel in one form or another has been housing guests on this windswept bluff between the harbor and the open ocean since about 1870. The most current incarnation was constructed in 1972, and it defines modern elegance for the region. The hotel, while indisputably up-to-date, successfully creates a sense of old-fashioned intimacy and avoids the overbearing grandeur to which many modern resorts aspire (often with poor results). Almost every room has a view of the water, and guests enjoy low-key recreational pursuits. York Harbor Beach is but a few steps away. No smoking.

Dining/Entertainment: The dining room is very good, offering dinner entrees ranging from blackened Maine crab cakes to grilled pork medaillons with apple-Dijon-garlic glaze. Entrees run $13 to $22.

Facilities: Indoor and outdoor pools, ocean swimming, Jacuzzi, tennis courts, fitness room, sauna.

WHERE TO DINE

Cape Neddick Inn. 1233 Rte. 1, Cape Neddick. ☎ **207/363-2899.** Reservations recommended. Full dinners $18–$27; light entrees served à la carte $10–$14. AE, MC, V. Summer daily 6–9pm; closed 1 or 2 days weekly during off-season (call ahead). REGIONAL/CONTINENTAL.

This fine inn offers some of the consistently best dining in southern Maine. Located in an elegant structure (largely rebuilt after a recent fire) on a relatively undeveloped stretch of Route 1, the Cape Neddick Inn has an open, handsome dining area that mixes traditional and modern. The old comes in the cozy golden glow of the room. The modern is the artwork, which changes frequently and showcases some of the region's better painters and sculptors.

The highly creative menu also changes frequently to make the most of seasonal products. Depending on the season, the menu might include local venison with a wild-mushroom and roasted-shallot Madeira sauce; or a horseradish and ginger–encrusted salmon with a cider-jalepeño glaze.. Save room for dessert, which tends to be extravagant.

✪ **Chauncey Creek Lobster Pier.** Chauncey Creek Rd., Kittery Point. ☎ **207/439-1030** or 207/439-9024. Reservations not accepted. Lobsters priced to market; other meals $1.50–$8.50. No credit cards. Daily 11am–8pm (until 7pm during shoulder seasons). Closed Mon after Labor Day. Closed Columbus Day through Mother's Day. Take Rte. 103 from York toward Kittery Point; watch for signs. LOBSTER POUND.

It's not on the wild, open ocean, but Chauncey's remains one of the most scenic lobster pounds in the state, not the least because the Spinney Family, which has been selling lobsters here since the 1950s, takes such obvious pride in their place. You reach the pound by walking down a wooden ramp to the water's edge, where a broad deck and plenty of brightly painted picnic tables await. (If it's too crowded, order your meal to go and head to Gerrish Island State Park, just down the road.)

Lobster, served hot and fresh, is the specialty, of course, but they also serve up steamed mussels (in wine and garlic) and clams. This is an à la carte place—buy a bag of potato chips and sodas while waiting for your lobsters to cook. There's a BYOB policy, and you can bring in any other food you want, provided they don't sell it here. Afterwards, wash up at the outdoor sink (labeled "finger bowl") on the deck.

Goldenrod Restaurant. Railroad Rd. and Ocean Ave., York Beach. ☎ **207/363-2621.** Breakfast $2.10–$5.25; lunch and dinner main courses $1.75–$7.50. MC, V. Memorial Day to Labor Day daily 8am–10:30pm (until 9pm in June); Labor Day to Columbus Day Wed–Sun 8am–3pm. Closed Columbus Day to Memorial Day. AMERICAN.

This beach-town classic is the place for local color with breakfast or lunch. The Goldenrod has been a summer institution in York Beach since it first opened in 1896. It's easy to find: Look for visitors on the sidewalk gawking at the plate-glass windows, mesmerized by the ancient taffy machines hypnotically churning out taffy in volumes (63 tons a year) enough to make thousands of dentists very wealthy.

The restaurant, behind the taffy and fudge operation, is low on frills and long on atmosphere, and offers great value. Diners sit on stout oak furniture around a stone fireplace, or at the marble soda fountain. There are dark beams overhead and the sort of linoleum floor you don't see much anymore. Breakfast offerings are the standards: omelets, waffles, griddle cakes, and bakery items. Lunch is equally predictable, but also very well presented. As for dinner, you'd probably be better served heading to some place more creative.

OGUNQUIT

Ogunquit is a bustling beachside town that's attracted vacationers and artists for more than a century. Its fame as an artist's colony dates to 1890, when Charles H. Woodbury arrived and pronounced the place an "artist's paradise." He was followed by artists such as Walt Kuhn, Elihu Vedder, Yasuo Kuniyoshi, and Rudolph Dirks, who was best known for creating the "Katzenjammer Kids" comic strip.

Ogunquit is a hugely popular destination among gay travelers, as it has been for decades. There's a lively beach and bar scene in summer. In the winter, gay life is decidedly more mellow. Try **The Club,** 13 Main St. (☎ **207/646-6655**), during the summer rush.

The town bristles with restaurants and inns and often can feel overrun with tourists during the peak summer season, especially on weekends. The cure? Head for the expansive beach, which by and large has been protected from development, and is large enough to allow most of the teeming masses to disperse.

ESSENTIALS

GETTING THERE   Ogunquit is located on Route 1 between York and Wells. It's accessible from either Exit 1 or Exit 2 of the Maine Turnpike.

VISITOR INFORMATION   The **Ogunquit Welcome Center,** P.O. Box 2289, Ogunquit, ME 03907 (☎ **207/646-5533** or 207/646-2939), is located on Route 1 south of the village center. It's open daily Memorial Day through Columbus Day, and weekdays during the off-season. On the Web, head to **www.ogunquit.org**.

GETTING AROUND   The village of Ogunquit is centered around an awkward four-way intersection that seems fiendishly designed to cause massive traffic foul-ups in summer. Parking in and around the village is also tight and relatively expensive (expect to pay $5 or $6 per day). As a result, Ogunquit is best reconnoitered on foot, by bike, or on the trackless trolley.

EXPLORING THE TOWN

The village center is good for an hour's browsing among the boutiques or sipping a cappuccino at one of the several coffee emporia.

From the village you can walk a mile to scenic Perkins Cove along **Marginal Way,** a mile-long ocean-side pathway once used for herding cattle to pasture. Earlier in this century, the land was bought by a local developer who deeded the right-of-way to the town. The pathway, which is wide and well maintained, departs across from the Seacastles Resort on Shore Road. It passes tide pools, pocket beaches, and rocky, fissured bluffs, all of which are worth exploring. The scenery can be spectacular (especially after a storm), but Marginal Way can also be spectacularly crowded during fair-weather weekends. To elude the crowds, I recommend heading out in the very early morning.

Perkins Cove, accessible either from Marginal Way or by driving south on Shore Road and veering left at the Y intersection, is a small, well-protected harbor that seems custom-designed for a photo opportunity. As such, it attracts visitors by the busload, carload, and boatload, and is often alarmingly congested. A handful of galleries, restaurants, and T-shirt shops catering to the tourist trade occupy a cluster of quaint buildings between the harbor and the sea. An intriguing pedestrian drawbridge is operated by whomever happens to be handy, allowing sailboats to come and go. Perkins Cove is also home to several tour-boat operators, who offer trips of various durations throughout the day and at twilight. But if tourist traps give you hives, steer clear of Perkins Cove.

Not far from the cove is **The Ogunquit Museum of American Art,** 183 Shore Rd. (☎ **207/646-4909**), one of the best small art museums in the country. Set back from the road in a grassy glen overlooking the rocky shore, the museum's spectacular view initially overwhelms the artwork as visitors walk through the door. But stick around a few minutes—the changing exhibits in this architecturally engaging museum of cement block, slate, and glass will get your attention soon enough, since the curators have a track record of staging superb shows and attracting national attention. (Be sure to note the bold, underappreciated work of Henry Strater, the Ogunquit artist who built the museum in 1953.) A new 1,400-square-foot wing opened in 1996, adding welcome new exhibition space. The museum is open July 1 to September 30 from 10:30am to 5pm Monday through Saturday, and 2 to 5pm on Sunday. Admission is $3 for adults, $2 for seniors and students, and free for children under 12.

BEACHES

Ogunquit's main beach is 3 miles long, and three paid parking lots are located along its length. The most popular access point (with the most expensive parking) is at the foot of Beach Street, which connects to Ogunquit Village. The beach ends at a sandy spit, where the Ogunquit River flows into the sea, and offers changing rooms and a handful of informal restaurants. It's also the most crowded part of the beach. Less crowded, less expensive options are at **Footbridge Beach** (turn on Ocean Avenue off Route 1 north of the village center) and **Moody Beach** (turn on Eldridge Avenue in Wells).

WHERE TO STAY

The Aspinquid. Beach St. (P.O. Box 2408), Ogunquit, ME 03907. ☎ **207/646-7072.** Fax 207/646-1187. 62 rms. A/C MINIBAR TV TEL. June through Labor Day $110–$205 double; shoulder seasons $60–$115 double. AE, MC, V. Closed mid-Oct to mid-Mar.

Built on the site of the old Aspinquid Hotel in 1971, the new Aspinquid is a complex of modern, shingled buildings located an easy stroll across the bridge from Ogunquit's beach. Rooms range from basic motel units to two-room apartments, and all are equipped with most modern amenities. The hotel is home to a purebred Maine coon cat named Socrates. "If he is an unwanted visitor," notes a letter to the guests, "just shoo him out of your room."

Facilities: Swimming pool, spa, sauna, tennis courts.

Marginal Way House. Wharf Lane (P.O. Box 697), Ogunquit, ME 03907. ☎ **207/646-8801,** or 207/363-6566 in winter. 30 rms, some with showers only. TV. Peak season $76–$165 double; shoulder seasons $42–$138 double. MC, V. Closed late Oct to mid-Apr.

If you travel for vistas, this is your place. Even if your room lacks a sweeping ocean view (and that's unlikely), you've got the run of the lawn and the guest-house porch, both of which overlook Ogunquit River to the beach and sea beyond. This attractive compound centers around a four-story, mid-19th-century guest house, which is surrounded by four more or less modern outbuildings. The whole affair is situated on a large, grassy lot on a quiet cul-de-sac. Indeed, it's hard to believe that you're smack in the middle of Ogunquit, with both the beach and the village just a few minutes' walk away. All rooms have refrigerators ("for the caviar and champagne," the manager says), and all but two have air-conditioning for those few days when the sea breeze fails. For longer stays, one- and two-bedroom efficiencies are available.

WHERE TO DINE

✪ **Arrows.** Berwick Rd. ☎ **207/361-1100.** Reservations strongly recommended. Main courses $25.95–$29.95. MC, V. May and Columbus Day to Thanksgiving Fri–Sun 6–9:30pm; June and Sept to Columbus Day Wed–Sun 6–9:30pm; July–Aug Tues–Sun 6–9:30pm. Closed Thanksgiving to Apr. Turn uphill at the Key Bank in the village; the restaurant is 1.9 miles on your right. REGIONAL/NEW AMERICAN.

Ask well-heeled Mainers to name the five best restaurants in the state, and it's likely that Arrows will appear on most lists. Since owner-chefs Mark Gaier and Clark Frasier opened Arrows in 1988, they've managed to put Ogunquit on the national culinary map. And they've done so by not only creating an elegant and intimate atmosphere in a pleasant country setting, but by serving up some of the freshest, most innovative cooking in New England.

The food transcends traditional New England, and is deftly prepared with exotic twists and turns. Frasier lived and traveled widely in Asia, and his Far Eastern experiences often influence the menu, which changes nightly. Typically creative entrees might include grilled yellowfin tuna served with a mélange of golden chanterelles, warmed frisee, walnuts, and a wild-mushroom broth; or smoked duck breast with baby bok choy, garlic, jasmine rice fritters, and Sichuan marinated eggplant. The wine list is superb.

Barnacle Billy's & Barnacle Billy's Etc. Perkins Cove. ☎ **207/646-5575.** Web site: www.barnbilly.com. Reservations not accepted. Lunch $3.65–$11.95; dinner $10.95–$18.95. AE, MC, V. Daily 11am–9:30pm. Closed Nov to mid-Apr. SEAFOOD.

This pair of side-by-side restaurants under the same ownership are a bit like brothers, one of whom became a fisherman, the other an executive. The original Barnacle Billy's, a local landmark since 1961, is a place your order, take a number, and wait on the deck style restaurant with the usual nautical decor and pine furniture inside. Its younger and fancier sibling next door has valet parking, sit-down service, and shows somewhat better breeding.

In both places, you're largely paying for the same thing: the unobstructed view of Perkins Cove. At the original Barnacle Billy's, that means the food is at the high end of the price range for what you get. It's best to stick to simple fare, like chowder or boiled lobster. The prices are steeper but the value better next door, where the service seems less weary and more care is taken with the food. Entrees include a variety of broiled, fried, and grilled seafood, along with a selection of poultry and meat.

✪ **Hurricane.** Oarweed Dr., Perkins Cove. ☎ **207/646-6348** or 800/649-6348 (in ME and NH only). Reservations strongly recommended. Lunch items $6.95–$13.95; main dinner courses $14.95–$24.95. AE, DC, DISC, MC, V. Daily 11:30am–4pm; Sun–Thurs 5:30–9:30pm, Fri–Sat 5:30–10:30pm. NEW AMERICAN.

Tucked away amid the T-shirt kitsch of Perkins Cove is one of southern Maine's classiest dining experiences. The plain shingled exterior of the building, set along a curving, narrow lane, doesn't begin to hint at what you'll find on the inside. The narrow dining room is divided into two smallish halves, but soaring windows overlooking the Gulf of Maine make the rooms feel much larger than they actually are. The menu offers pleasant surprises, with creative concoctions like an appetizer of deviled Maine lobster cakes served with a tangy fresh salsa. Main courses include a lobster cioppino, and a baked salmon and brie baklava with a key lime béarnaise. Added bonus: Hurricane makes the best martinis in town.

THE KENNEBUNKS

"The Kennebunks" consist of the villages of Kennebunk and Kennebunkport, both situated on the shores of diminutive rivers. The region was first settled in the mid-1600s and flourished following the American Revolution, when ship captains, shipbuilders, and successful merchants constructed the imposing, solid homes for which the area is noted.

The two villages have decidedly different characters; a visit to these siblings provides contrasting looks at a coastal and an inland town. Kennebunk, an inland town just off the turnpike, doesn't draw as many tourists, but it is a dignified, small commercial center of white clapboard and brick that's worth checking out. **Tom's of Maine,** a natural-toothpaste maker, is headquartered here and has an outlet in a re-habbed industrial building (at the corner of Main and Water streets) that's open during regular business hours.

While summer is the busy season along the coast, winter has its charm: The grand architecture is better seen through leafless trees. When the snow flies, guests find solace curling up in front of a fire at one of the inviting inns.

ESSENTIALS

GETTING THERE Kennebunk is located off Exit 3 of the Maine Turnpike. Kennebunkport is 3.5 miles southeast of Kennebunk on Port Road (Route 35).

VISITOR INFORMATION   The **Kennebunk–Kennebunkport Chamber of Commerce,** P.O. Box 740, Kennebunk, ME 04043 (☎ **207/967-0857**), can answer your questions year-round by phone or at their offices on Route 35 (Port Road) just west of the intersection with Route 9. The **Kennebunkport Information Center** (☎ **207/967-8600**) is off Dock Square (next to Ben & Jerry's) and is open throughout the summer and fall.

EXPLORING KENNEBUNKPORT

Kennebunkport has national name recognition thanks to former President George Bush, whose family has summered here for most of this century. It also has the tweedy, upper-crust feel that you might expect of a town where the former president feels right at home. This historic village, whose streets were laid out during days of travel by foot and horse, is subject to epic traffic jams around the town center, called **Dock Square.** Your best strategy is to avoid driving near the square, park some distance away, then approach the square by foot.

Ocean Drive from Dock Square to Walkers Point and beyond is lined with opulent summer homes overlooking surf and rocky shore. This stretch is best appreciated by bike or on foot. You'll likely recognize the former president's home at Walkers Point when you arrive. If it's not familiar from the 4 years it spent in the spotlight, look for the swarming crowds with telephoto lenses.

Several local beaches are suitable for an afternoon's relaxation. To the south of the Kennebunk River is **Kennebunk Beach** and **Gooch's Beach;** to the north is **Goose Rocks Beach.** These beaches tend to be less crowded and noisy than the beaches in York and Ogunquit to the south, or Old Orchard Beach to the north. Parking at the beaches requires a permit, which can usually be obtained at the town offices or from your hotel.

✪ **The Seashore Trolley Museum.** Log Cabin Rd., Kennebunkport. ☎ **207/967-2800.** E-mail: carshop@biddeford.com. Web site: www.gwi.net/trolley/. $8 adults, $4.50 children 6–16, $6 seniors. Early to mid-May Mon–Fri 11am–1pm, Sat–Sun 11am–4pm; mid-May to June daily 11am–4pm; July to mid-Oct daily 10am–5:30pm; mid-Oct to mid-Nov Sat–Sun 11am–4pm (weather permitting). Closed mid-Nov to May. Head north from Kennebunkport on North St.; look for signs.

A short drive north of Kennebunkport on Log Cabin Road is one of the quirkiest and most engaging museums in the state. The Seashore Trolley Museum, a place with an excess of character and an intriguing history, is well worth a visit. This scrap yard masquerading as a museum ("world's oldest and largest museum of its type") was founded in 1939 to preserve a disappearing way of life, and today the collection contains more than 200 trolleys from around the world, including specimens from Glasgow, Moscow, San Francisco, and Rome. (Of course, there's also a streetcar named Desire from New Orleans.) About 40 of the cars still operate, and the admission charge includes unlimited rides on a 2-mile track. The other cars, some of which still contain turn-of-the-century advertising, are on display outdoors and in vast storage sheds.

A good museum inspires awe and educates its visitors on the sly. This one does so deftly, and not until visitors are driving away are they likely to realize how much they learned.

WHERE TO STAY

✪ **Captain Lord.** Pleasant St. and Green St. (P.O. Box 800), Kennebunkport, ME 04046. ☎ **207/967-3141.** E-mail: captain@biddeford.com. Web site: www.captainlord.com. Fax 207/967-3172. 16 rms (10 with shower only). A/C TEL. $149–$349 double. Rates include full breakfast. 2-night minimum on weekends and holidays. DISC, MC, V.

It's simple: This is the best building in Kennebunkport, in the best location, and furnished with the best antiques. The Captain Lord is one of the most architecturally distinguished inns anywhere, housed in a pale yellow Federal-style home that peers down a shady lawn toward the river. When you enter the downstairs reception area, you'll know immediately that you've transcended the realm of "wanna-B&Bs." This is the genuine article, with grandfather clocks and Chippendale highboys—and that's just the front hallway. Off the hall is a comfortable common area with piped-in classical music and a broad brick fireplace. Head up the elliptical staircase to the guest rooms, which are furnished with splendid antiques; 14 feature gas-burning fireplaces. If you're really looking to spoil yourself, book the new first-floor Captain's Suite with king-sized canopy bed, stereo, TV and VCR, whirlpool, exercise equipment, and shower with a multijet hydro-massage spa. No smoking.

The only complaint I've heard about this place is that it's too nice, too perfect, too friendly. That evidently puts some people on edge. But why not risk it?

✪ **The Colony Hotel.** Ocean Ave. (about a mile from Dock Sq.; P.O. Box 511), Kennebunkport, ME 04046. ☎ **800/552-2363** or 207/967-3331. Fax 207/967-8738. E-mail: info-me@thecolonyhotel.com. Web site: www.thecolonyhotel.com/me. 121 rms in 4 buildings. TEL. July–Aug $209–$314 double. Off-season rates available. Rates include breakfast and dinner. 2-night minimum on weekends and holidays. AE, MC, V. Closed mid-Oct to mid-May.

The Colony is one of the handful of ocean-side resorts that has preserved intact the classic New England vacation experience. This gleaming white Georgian Revival (built in 1914) lords over the ocean and the mouth of the Kennebunk River. The three-story main inn has 105 rooms, most of which have recently been updated. The rooms are bright and cheery, simply furnished with summer cottage antiques. Rooms in two of the three outbuildings carry over the rustic elegance of the main hotel; the exception is the East House, a 1950s-era motor hotel at the back edge of the property with 20 charmless motel-style rooms. During the day, activities include swimming in a heated saltwater pool (or at a small pebble beach across the street), golfing on the putting green overlooking the ocean, or renting bikes and exploring Ocean Avenue. No smoking.

Dining/Entertainment: The massive, pine-paneled dining room seats up to 400, and guests are assigned one table for the duration of their stay. Dinners begin with a relish tray, but quickly progress to a more contemporary era with regional entrees such as rainbow tortellini with lobster marinara sauce, or maple-cured ham with apricot-orange sauce. On Sundays, there's a jazz brunch. There's also a cocktail lounge and free refreshments in the lobby.

Services: Room service, social director, safe-deposit boxes, free refreshments in lobby.

Facilities: Bike rental, putting green, game room, library, heated saltwater pool, poolside sundeck, beach, conference rooms, gift shop.

Kennebunkport Inn. Dock Sq. (P.O. Box 111), Kennebunkport, ME 04046. ☎ **800/248-2621** (out of state) or 207/967-2621. Fax 207/967-3705. 34 rms (21 with shower only). A/C TV TEL. Summer $89.50–$237 double; Sept–Oct $79.50–$237 double; off-season $69.50–$209 double. Breakfast included Nov–Apr; MAP rates available summer and fall. 3-night minimum summer and holiday weekends. AE, MC, V.

Visible behind a scrim of maple trees a few steps from bustling Dock Square, the Kennebunkport Inn's exterior is busy with an amalgam of dormers, gables, porticos, awnings, and modern additions. Despite this architectural frenzy, the stately 1899 inn manages the mean feat of both blending in with *and* standing out from its surroundings. Inside, it's impeccably maintained. The rooms are nicely furnished, many with turn-of-the-century antiques and all with hair dryers. (Some equally well appointed rooms are located in the adjoining River House, built in the 1930s.) Smoking is allowed only in the bar and some guest rooms.

Dining/Entertainment: There's a handsome, clubby lounge and a well-respected dining room on the first floor, which is open summer and fall.

Facilities: Outdoor pool, sundeck.

✪ **White Barn Inn.** Beach St. ($^1/_4$ mile east of the junction of Rtes. 9 and 35; P.O. Box 560), Kennebunkport, ME 04046. ☎ **207/967-2321.** Fax 207/967-1100. 24 rms. A/C TEL. $150–$230 double; up to $375 suite. Rates include continental breakfast. 2-night minimum on weekends; 3 nights on holidays. AE, MC, V.

The White Barn Inn pampers its guests like no other lodging in Maine. Upon checking in, guests are shown to one of the inn's parlors and offered sherry or brandy while valets in dark uniforms gather luggage and park the cars. A tour of the inn follows, then guests are left to their own devices. They can avail themselves of the inn's free bikes (including a small fleet of tandems) to head to the beach, or walk across the street and wander the quiet, shady pathways of Saint Anthony's Franciscan monastery. The rooms are individually decorated in a refined country style that's comforting without being obtrusive. The inn has a heavily European atmosphere (no surprise: nearly half the staff is here on special visas from Europe), and the emphasis is on service. I'm not aware of any other inn of this size that offers as many unexpected niceties, like robes, fresh flowers in the rooms, and bottled water. Nearly half the rooms have wood-burning fireplaces. No smoking.

Dining/Entertainment: See "Where to Dine," below.

Services: Concierge, limited room service, dry cleaning, laundry service, newspaper delivery, in-room massage, twice-daily maid service, turndown service, valet parking, safe.

Facilities: Outdoor heated pool, bicycles, nearby ocean beach (a 5-min. walk away), conference rooms, sundeck.

WHERE TO DINE

Federal Jack's Restaurant and Brew Pub. Lower Village (south bank of Kennebunk River), Kennebunkport. ☎ **207/967-4322.** Web site: www.shipyard.com. Reservations not accepted. Lunch items $5.25–$12.95; main dinner courses $6.25–$21.95. MC, V. Daily 11:30am–4pm; Sun–Thurs 5–9pm, Fri–Sat 5–10pm. PUB FARE.

This light, airy, and modern restaurant is in a retail complex of recent vintage that sits a bit uneasily amid the scrappy boatyards lining the south bank of the Kennebunk River. From the second floor perch (look for a seat on the spacious deck in warm weather), you can gaze across the river toward the shops of Dock Square, which is within easy walking distance across a (nonworking) drawbridge. The menu features basic entrees like hamburgers, BBQ pork ribs, and pizza, and everything is well prepared. Watch for specials like the tasty crab and artichoke bisque. Don't leave without sampling the Shipyard ales, lagers, and porters brewed downstairs, which are among the best in New England.

✪ **White Barn Inn.** Beach St., Kennebunkport. ☎ **207/967-2321.** Reservations recommended. Fixed-price dinner $59. AE, MC, V. Daily 6–9pm (open later during peak season). Closed Jan. REGIONAL/NEW AMERICAN.

People don't come to the White Barn Inn just for special occasions, like anniversaries or birthdays. They come for *really* special occasions, like anniversaries or birthdays that end in "0" or "5." It's that kind of place (and one that charges that kind of price), but worth saving up for if you're bound and determined to make your stay in Maine unforgettable.

The setting is magical. The restaurant (attached to an equally magical inn) is housed in an ancient, rustic barn with a soaring interior. (The furnace runs nearly full time in winter to keep the space comfortable.) There's a copper-topped bar off to one side, rich leather seating in the waiting area, a pianist setting the mood, and an eclectic collection of country antiques displayed in the hay loft above. On the tables are floor-length tablecloths, and the chairs feature imported Italian upholstery that recalls early Flemish tapestries.

The menu changes frequently, but depending on the season you might start with a lobster spring roll with daikon, carrots, snow peas, and cilantro, then graduate to a crab-glazed poached filet of halibut on sweet-pea purée, or pan-seared veal and venison on bacon-roasted butternut squash. Anticipate a meal to remember. The White Barn won't disappoint.

Windows on the Water. 12 Chase Hill Rd. (above Lower Village), Kennebunkport. ☎ **800/ 773-3313** or 207/967-3313. Web site: www.biddeford.com/wow/. Reservations recommended. Lunch items $7.50–$15.50; main dinner courses $15.50–$30.50. AE, DC, DISC, MC, V. Daily 11:45am–2:30pm; Sun–Thurs 5:30–9pm, Fri 5:30–9:30pm, Sat 5:30–10pm. NEW ENGLAND/ INTERNATIONAL.

First off, the name's a bit of a misnomer. It's more like Windows on the Kennebunkport Brewing Co., although some glimpses of the river might be had, especially from the second-floor dining room. But the compromised views aren't much of a loss, since the interiors of this modern restaurant are tastefully if conservatively done, with pink tablecloths, oak chairs, and oak accenting.

The food here is quite good. The menu is based on classic New England cuisine, but with cooking techniques and spicing borrowed from around the world. There's seafood fettuccine Milanese, lobster ravioli, and grilled salmon fillet served on couscous and topped with wild mushrooms. The menu changes seasonally; a full dinner menu is available at lunch, along with lighter entrees such as lobster croissants and chicken Caesar salad.

3 Portland

Portland is Maine's largest city, and easily one of the more attractive, livable small cities on the East Coast. Actually, Portland has more the feel of a very large town than a small city. Strike up a conversation with a resident, and she's likely to give you an earful about how easy it is to live here. You can buy superb coffee, see great movies, and get delicious pad Thai to go (Portland has four Thai restaurants). Yet it's still small enough to walk from one end of town to the other, and postal workers and bank clerks know your name soon after you move here. Despite its outward appearance of being an actual metropolis, Portland has a population of just 65,000 (about half that of Peoria, Ill.).

ESSENTIALS

GETTING THERE   Portland is located off the Maine Turnpike (I-95). Coming from the south, downtown is most easily reached by taking Exit 6A off the turnpike, then following I-295 into town. Get off at the Franklin Street exit and follow this eastward until you arrive at the waterfront at the Casco Bay Lines terminal. Turn right on Commercial Street and you'll be at the lower edge of the Old Port. Continue on a few blocks to the visitor's center (see below).

The **Portland International Jetport** is served by regularly scheduled flights on several airlines, including **Business Express** (☎ 800/345-3400), **Continental** (☎ 800/525-0280), **Delta** (☎ 800/221-1212), **USAirways** (☎ 800/428-4322),

United (☎ 800/241-6522), **Pine State** (☎ 207/879-6111), and **Downeast Express** (☎ 800/983-3247). The small and easily navigated airport is located just across the Fore River from downtown. Metro buses ($1) connect the airport to downtown; cab fare runs about $10.

VISITOR INFORMATION   The **Convention and Visitor's Bureau of Greater Portland,** 305 Commercial St., Portland, ME 04101 (☎ **207/772-4994**), stocks a large supply of brochures and is happy to dispense information about local attractions, lodging, and dining. The center is open in summer weekdays 8am to 6pm and week-ends 10am to 5pm; hours are shorter during the off-season. Ask for the free *Greater Portland Visitor Guide* with map. *Casco Bay Weekly* is a free alternative paper distrib-uted Thursdays at many downtown stores and restaurants. The paper features listings of performers at area clubs and other upcoming events.

ORIENTATION   The city of Portland is divided into two areas: on-peninsula and off-peninsula. (There are also the islands, but more on that below.) Most travelers are destined for the compact peninsula, which is home to downtown Portland, and is where most of the city's cultural life and much of its commercial action takes place.

Viewed from the water, Portland's peninsula is shaped like a swaybacked horse, with the Old Port in the low spot near the waterfront, and the peninsula's two main residential neighborhoods (Munjoy Hill and the West End) on the gentle rises over-looking downtown. These two neighborhoods are connected by Congress Street, Portland's main artery of commerce. The western stretch of Congress Street (roughly between Monument Square and State Street) is Portland's emerging arts district, home to a handsome art museum, three theaters, the campus of the Maine College of Art (located in an old department store), an L.L. Bean outlet, and a growing num-ber of restaurants and boutiques.

PARKING   Parking is notoriously tight in the Old Port area, and the city's park-ing enforcement is notoriously efficient. Several parking garages are convenient to the Old Port, with parking fees less than $1 per hour.

SEEING THE SIGHTS IN TOWN

Any visit to Portland should start with a stroll around the historic **Old Port.** Bounded by Commercial, Congress, Union, and Pearl streets, this several square block area near the waterfront contains the city's best commercial architecture, a plethora of fine res-taurants, a mess of boutiques, and one of the thickest concentrations of bars you'll find anywhere. (The Old Port tends to transform as night lengthens, with the crowds growing younger and rowdier.) The narrow streets and intricate brick facades reflect the mid-Victorian era; most of the area was rebuilt following a devastating fire in 1866. Leafy, quaint **Exchange Street** is the heart of the Old Port, with other attrac-tive streets running off and around it.

Portland Museum of Art. 7 Congress Sq. (corner of Congress and High sts.). ☎ **207/775-6148.** E-mail: portlandmuseum@maine.com. Web site:www.portlandmuseum.org. Admis-sion $6 adults, $5 students and seniors, $1 children 6–12. Free Fri 5–9pm. Mon–Wed and Sat 10am–5pm, Thurs–Fri 10am–9pm, Sun noon–5pm. Closed Mon from mid-Oct to June.

This bold, modern museum was designed by I. M. Pei Associates in 1983, and dis-plays selections from its own fine collections and a parade of touring exhibits. The museum is particularly strong in American artists who had a connection to Maine, including Winslow Homer, Andrew Wyeth, and Edward Hopper, and has fine displays of Early American furniture and crafts. The museum shares the Joan Whitney Payson Collection with Colby College (the college gets it one semester every other year). The collection features wonderful European works by Renoir, Degas, and Picasso. Tours are offered at 2 and 6pm on Thursday and Friday.

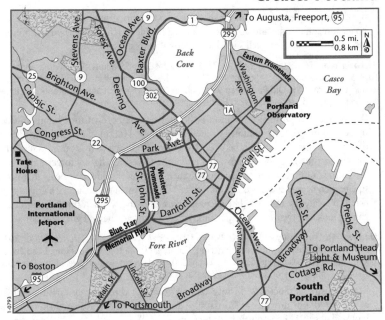

Children's Museum of Maine. 142 Free St. (next to the Portland Museum of Art). ☎ **207/828-1234.** Admission $5 per child or adult (under 1 year old free). MC, V. Mon–Sat 10am–5pm, Sun noon–5pm. Closed Mon–Tues from fall to spring.

Make a deal with your kids: they behave during a trip to the art museum, and they'll be rewarded with a couple of hours in their own museum.

The centerpiece exhibit of the Children's Museum is the camera obscura, a room-sized "camera" located on the top floor of this regal downtown building next to the art museum. Children gather around a white table in a dark room, where they see magically projected images that include cars driving on city streets and boats plying the harbor. The camera obscura never fails to enthrall, and it provides a memorable lesson in the workings of a lens—whether in a camera or an eye.

There's plenty more to do here, from running a supermarket checkout counter to sliding down the firehouse pole to piloting the mock space shuttle from a high cockpit. Budget time also for lunch at the cafe, where you can order up a peanut butter and jelly sandwich, a tall glass of milk, and an oatmeal cookie.

✪ **Portland Head Light & Museum.** Fort Williams Park, 1000 Shore Rd., Cape Elizabeth. ☎ **207/799-2661.** Web site: www.portlandheadlight.com. Grounds free; museum admission $2 adults, $1 children 6–18. Park grounds open daily year-round sunrise to sunset (until 8:30pm in summer); museum open daily June–Oct 10am–4pm; open weekends only in spring and late fall. From Portland, follow State St. across the Fore River to the T intersection at Broadway; turn left. At 2nd light turn right on Cottage Rd., which soon becomes Shore Rd.; follow this about 2 miles until you arrive at the park, on your left.

Just a 10-minute drive from downtown Portland, this 1794 lighthouse is one of the most picturesque in the nation. The light marks the entrance to Portland Harbor, and was occupied continuously from its construction until 1989, when it was automated and the graceful keeper's house (1891) converted to a small, town-owned museum focusing on the history of navigation. The lighthouse itself is still active and thus closed to the public, but visitors can stop by the museum, browse for lighthouse-themed gifts at the gift shop, wander the park grounds, and watch the sailboats and ships come and go. The park has a pebble beach, grassy lawns with ocean vistas, and picnic areas well suited for informal barbecues.

Victoria Mansion. 109 Danforth St. ☎ **207/772-4841.** $5 adults, $2 children under 18. Tues–Sat 10am–4pm, Sun 1–5pm. Closed Nov–Apr, except for holiday tours from end of Nov to mid-Dec. From the Old Port, head west on Fore St. to Danforth St. near Stonecoast Brewing; bear right and proceed 3 blocks to the mansion.

Widely regarded as one of the most elaborate Victorian brownstone homes in existence, this mansion (also known as the Morse-Libby House) is a remarkable display of high Victorian style. Built between 1859 and 1863 for a Maine businessman who made a fortune in New Orleans hotel trade, the towering, slightly foreboding home is a prime example of the Italianate style then in vogue. Inside, it appears that not a square inch of wall space was left unmolested by craftsmen or artists (11 painters were hired to create the murals). The decor is ponderous and somber, but it offers an engaging look at a bygone era. A gift shop offers Victorian-themed gifts and books.

Wadsworth-Longfellow House & Maine Historical Society. 489 Congress St. ☎ **207/ 879-0427.** Web site: www.mainehistory.com. Gallery and Longfellow house tour $4 adults, $1 children under 12. Gallery only $2 adults, $1 child. Longfellow House and gallery June–Oct Tues–Sun 10am–4pm; gallery only June–Oct Wed–Sat noon–4pm.

Maine Historical Society's "history campus" includes three widely varied buildings in the middle of downtown Portland. The austere brick Wadsworth-Longfellow House dates to 1785 and was built by Gen. Peleg Wadsworth, father of noted poet Henry Wadsworth Longfellow. It's furnished in an authentic Early American style, with many samples from the Longfellow family furniture still on display. Adjacent to the home is the Maine History Gallery, located in a slightly garish postmodern building. Changing exhibits explore the rich texture of Maine history. Just behind the Longfellow house is the library of the Maine Historical Society, a popular destination among genealogists. Don't miss the small, peaceful garden hidden in the back next to the library.

EXPLORING ON THE WATER

Casco Bay Lines. Commercial and Franklin sts. ☎ **207/774-7871.** Fares vary depending on the run, but are generally $4.50–$13.75 round-trip. Frequent departures 6am–midnight.

Six of the Casco Bay islands have year-round populations and are served by scheduled ferries from downtown Portland. (Most of these are part of the city of Portland; the exception is Long Island, which broke away in a secession bid a few years ago.) The ferries offer an inexpensive way to view the bustling harbor and get a taste of Maine's islands. Trips range from a 20-minute excursion to Peaks Island (the closest thing to an island suburb with 1,200 year-round residents), to the 5^{1}/$_{2}$-hour cruise to Bailey Island and back. All of the islands are well suited for walking; Peaks Island has a rocky back shore that's easily accessible via the island's paved perimeter road (bring a picnic lunch). Cliff Island is the most remote of the bunch, and has a sedate turn-of-the-century island retreat character.

Eagle Island Tours. Departing from Long Wharf (at Commercial St.) ☎ **207/774-6498.** $15 adults, $9 children under 9 (plus state park fee of $1.50 adults, 50¢ children). One departure daily at 10am.

Eagle Island was the summer home of famed Arctic explorer and Portland native Robert E. Peary, who claimed in 1909 to be the first person to reach the North Pole. (His accomplishments have been the subject of exhaustive debates among Arctic scholars, some of whom insist he inflated his claims.) In 1904, Peary built this simple

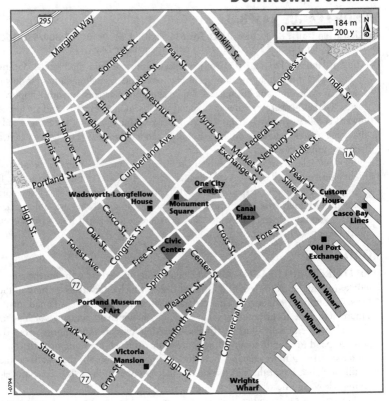

home on a remote, 17-acre island at the edge of Casco Bay; in 1912, he added flourishes in the form of two low stone towers. After his death in 1920, his family kept up the home, then later donated it to the state, which has since managed it as a state park. The home is open to the public, maintained much the way it was when Peary lived here. Island footpaths through the forest allow exploration to the open, seagull-clotted cliffs at the southern tip. Eagle Tours offers one trip daily from Portland. The 4-hour excursion includes a 1½-hour stopover on the island.

SHOPPING

Aficionados of antique and junk stores love Portland.

Good browsing can be had on **Congress Street.** Check out the stretches between State and High streets in the arts district, and from India Street to Washington Avenue on Munjoy Hill. About a dozen shops of varying quality will be found in these two areas.

More serious antique hounds will want to take in an **auction** or two. Almost any day of the week you'll be able to find an auction within a hour's drive of Portland. The best source of information is the *Maine Sunday Telegram.* Look under the classifieds for listings of auctions scheduled for the following week.

For new items, the **Old Port,** with its dozens of boutiques and storefront shops, is well worth browsing. It's especially strong in chic, contemporary one-of-a-kind clothing that's a world apart from stuff you'll find at a mall. Artisan and crafts shops are also well represented.

MINOR-LEAGUE BASEBALL

Portland Sea Dogs. Hadlock Field, P.O. Box 636, Portland, ME 04104. ☎ **800/936-3647** or 207/874-9300. Tickets $4–$6. Season runs Apr through Labor Day.

The Portland Sea Dogs are the Double-A team affiliated with the Florida Marlins, and they play throughout the summer at Hadlock Field, a small stadium near downtown that still retains an old-time feel despite aluminum benches and other improvements. Games here are a great way to spend an afternoon or evening, and are geared toward families, with lots of entertainment between innings and a selection of food that's a couple of notches above basic hot dogs and hamburgers. (Try the tasty french fries and grilled sausages.)

Getting tickets can sometimes be a problem—the more popular weekend and night games often sell out weeks in advance. Pick a date, and call for reservations. If a game's sold out, don't despair. Loose tickets are often for sale out front just before the games by folks who bought too many; they're almost always available at face value. If you buy general admission seats, get there at least a half-hour early so you don't end up way down the left field line.

ROAD TRIPS

OLD ORCHARD BEACH   About 12 miles south of Portland is the unrepentantly honky-tonkish beach town of Old Orchard Beach, which offers treats for most of the senses (taste buds excluded). This venerable Victorian-era resort is famed for its amusement park, its pier, and its long, sandy beach, which attracts sun worshippers from all over, especially Québec. (English-speaking folks are the minority here.) Be sure to spend time and money riding some of the stomach-churning rides (if you'd prefer something more relaxing, head for the antique carousel), then walk on the 7-mile-long beach past the mid-rise condos that sprouted in the 1980s like a model-train-scale Miami Beach.

The beach is broad and open at low tide; at high tide, space to plunk your towel down is at a premium. In the evenings, teens and young adults dominate the town's culture, spilling out of the video arcades and cruising the main strip. For dinner, do as the locals do and buy hot dogs and pizza and cotton candy; save your change for the arcades.

Old Orchard is just off Route 1 south of Portland. The quickest route is to leave the turnpike at Exit 5, then follow I-195 and the signs to the beach. Be aware that parking is tight, and the traffic can be horrendous during the peak summer months.

SEBAGO LAKE   Maine's second-largest lake is also its most popular. Ringed with summer homes of varying vintages, many dating from the early part of this century, Sebago Lake attracts thousands of vacationers to its cool, deep waters.

You can tour part of the lake and the ancient canal system between Sebago and Long lakes on the *Songo Queen* (☎ 207/693-6861), a faux steamship berthed in the town of Naples. Or just lie in the sun along the sandy beach at bustling **Sebago Lake State Park** (☎ 207/693-6613) on the lake's north shore (the park is off Route 302; look for signs between Raymond and South Casco). The park has shady picnic areas, a campground, a snack bar, and lifeguards on the beach (entrance fee charged). It can be alarmingly crowded on summer weekends, so you're better off heading here midweek. Bring food for barbecuing. A day-use fee is charged.

✪ SABBATHDAY LAKE SHAKER COMMUNITY   Route 26 from Portland to Norway is a speedy highway that takes you through hilly farmland and past new housing developments. At one point the road pinches through a cluster of stately historic buildings that stand proudly beneath towering shade trees. That's the

Sabbathday Lake Shaker Community (☎ **207/926-4597**), the last active Shaker community in the nation. The dozen or so Shakers living here today still embrace the traditional Shaker beliefs and maintain a communal, pastoral way of life. The bulk of the community's income comes from the sale of herbs, which have been grown here since 1799.

This community is open to the public daily in summer except on Sundays (when visitors are invited to attend Sunday services). Docents offer tours of the grounds and several of the buildings, including the graceful 1794 meetinghouse. Exhibits in the buildings showcase the famed furniture lovingly crafted by the Shakers, and include antiques made by Shakers at other U.S. communes. You'll learn a lot about the Shaker ideology with its emphasis on simplicity, industry, and celibacy. After your tour, browse the gift shop for Shaker herbs and teas.

Tours last either 1 hour ($5 adults, $2 children 6 to 12) or 1 hour and 45 minutes ($6.50 adults). Open Monday to Saturday, Memorial Day to Columbus Day from 10am to 4:30pm. The last tour is at 3:30pm.

The Shaker village is located about 45 minutes from Portland. Head north on Route 26 (Washington Avenue in Portland). The village is 8 miles from Exit 11 (Gray) of the Maine Turnpike.

WHERE TO STAY

Two sizable downtown hotels stand out against the skyline. The **Holiday Inn by the Bay,** 88 Spring St. (☎ **207/775-2311**), offers great views of the harbor from about half the rooms, along with the usual chain-hotel creature comforts. The **Radisson Eastland,** 157 High St. (☎ **207/775-5411**), is located in Portland's most venerable old hotel, and features two restaurants, a pleasantly dated rooftop lounge, and a spacious lobby imbued with an old-world elegance.

Budget travelers should seek out less expensive accommodations near the Maine Mall in South Portland and off the Maine Turnpike near Westbrook—two areas that are patently charmless, but offer reasonable access to the attractions of downtown, about 10 minutes away. Try **Days Inn** (☎ **207/772-3450**) or **Coastline Inn** (☎ **207/772-3838**) near the mall, or the **Super 8 Motel** (☎ **207/854-1881**) or **Susse Chalet** (☎ **207/774-6101**) off turnpike Exit 8 near the Westbrook town line.

The Danforth. 163 Danforth St., Portland, ME 04102. ☎ **800/991-6557** or 207/879-8755. Fax 207/879-8754. 10 rms (4 with shower only). A/C TV TEL. $105–$185 double; $235 suite. Rates include breakfast. Off-season discounts. AE, MC, V.

Located in an exceptionally handsome brick home constructed in 1821, The Danforth has been something of a work in progress since it first opened in 1994, when it had just two guest rooms. But it's getting close to its ultimate goal of becoming one of Portland's two most elegant small inns. (The Pomegranate is the other.) The inn is located at the edge of the Spring Street Historic District, and is within a 10-minute walk of downtown attractions.

The first floor benefited from a full restoration between 1996 and 1997, with an expanded breakfast room and attractive sitting room with fireplace. The guest rooms are handsomely decorated, many in rich and vibrant tones, although the furnishings tend to be a bit spare still (that's set to change). But the inn's extra touches are exceptional throughout, from the working fireplaces in most guest rooms to the richly paneled basement billiards room to the direct-line phones in the rooms (equipped with data ports for cyber travelers). Especially appealing is Room 1 with a sitting room and private second-floor deck, and Room 2 with high ceilings and superb morning light; be aware that Rooms 5 and 6 are smaller, housed in the old servant's wing. No smoking.

Services/Facilities: Access to an in-town health club, newspaper delivery, in-room massage, billiards room, bicycle rental.

Inn at Park Spring. 135 Spring St., Portland, ME 04101. ☎ **800/437-8511** or 207/774-1059. 7 rms (2 with shared bath; some with shower only). Summer $95–$115 double; off-season from $65 double. Rates include continental breakfast. AE, MC, V.

This small in-town B&B is housed in a comfortable, historic brick home dating back to 1835, and is the best-located inn for exploring the town on foot. The Portland Museum of Art is just two blocks away, the Old Port about 10 minutes, and great restaurants are all within easy walking distance. Guests can linger or watch television in the front parlor, or chat at the table in the kitchen. The rooms are all corner rooms, and most are bright and sunny. Especially nice is "Spring," with its great morning light and wonderful views of the historic row houses on Park Street, and "Gables," one of the shared-bath rooms on the third floor, which has a clean, contemporary design and abundant afternoon sun. Reservations are usually essential here, as the owner lives separately and comes to meet the guests.

✪ Pomegranate Inn. 49 Neal St., Portland, ME 04102. ☎ **800/356-0408** or 207/772-1006. Fax 207/773-4426. 8 rms (4 with shower only). A/C TV TEL. Summer and fall $125–$165 double; winter and spring $95–$125 double. Rates include full breakfast. 2-night minimum on summer weekends; 3 nights on long holiday weekends. AE, DISC, MC, V. Free on-street parking. From the Old Port, take Middle St. (which turns into Spring St.) to Neal St. in the West End (about 1 mile); turn right and proceed to inn.

This is Portland's most stunning B&B, and one of the best in northern New England. Housed in a handsome, dove gray 1884 Italianate home in the architecturally distinctive Western Prom neighborhood, the interiors are wondrously decorated with whimsy and elegance—a combination that can be fatally cloying but is executed here with impeccably good taste. Look for the bold and exuberant wall paintings by Heidi Gerquest, a local artist, and the wonderfully eclectic antique furniture collected and arranged by owner Isabel Smiles. If you have the chance, peek in some of the unoccupied rooms—they're all different with painted floors and faux-marble woodwork. Four of the rooms have gas fireplaces; the best of the lot is in the carriage house, which has its own private terrace, kitchenette, and fireplace.

The sit-down breakfasts in the cheery dining room are invariably creative and tasty. The inn is also well situated for exploring the West End, and downtown is about a 15-minute walk away. No smoking.

Portland Regency Hotel. 20 Milk St., Portland, ME 04101. ☎ **800/727-3436** or 207/774-4200. Fax 207/775-2150. Web site: www.theregency.com. 95 rms. A/C MINIBAR TV TEL. Summer $149–$229 double; off-season $119–$199 double. AE, CB, DC, DISC, MC, V.

Centrally located on a cobblestone courtyard in the middle of the trendy Old Port, the Regency boasts the city's premier hotel location. But it's got more than location going for it—it's also one of the most handsome and well-managed hotels in the state. Housed in a historic brick armory, the hotel offers a number of modern guest rooms nicely appointed and furnished with all the standard amenities. The one complaint I've heard is about the noise: The guest-room walls are a bit thin, and on weekends the revelry on the Old Port streets can penetrate even the dense brick exterior walls.

Dining/Entertainment: The hotel is home to the recently remodeled Market Street Grille, a well-regarded dining room with an emphasis on seafood. There's also The Armory, a popular, low-key tavern.

Services: Limited room service, valet parking, dry cleaning (Monday to Friday), baby-sitting (with prior notice), courtesy car to airport, safe-deposit boxes.

Facilities: Jacuzzi, sauna, fitness club with aerobics classes, conference rooms.

West End Inn. 146 Pine St., Portland, ME 04102. ☎ **800/338-1377** or 207/772-1377. 6 rms (1 with detached bath, 2 with shower only). A/C TV. $89–$169 double. Rates include full breakfast. AE, MC, V. Parking on street.

This brick, mansard-roofed 1871 duplex sits in one of Portland's more historic residential neighborhoods. The inn is well situated for walks in the West End and the Western Prom, two lovely turn-of-the-century neighborhoods with some of Portland's best architecture.

John Leonard and Teri Dizon have done a superb job making this urban town house into a welcoming retreat. The downstairs parlor features gold-leaf detailing on the ceiling, leather furniture, and Asian antiques. The guest rooms on two upstairs floors have canopy beds and are nicely decorated with bold wallpaper and antiques. Look for nice touches like bottles of Poland Spring Water in the rooms, and towels that match the decor in the bathrooms. No smoking.

WHERE TO DINE
EXPENSIVE

✪ **Street & Co.** 33 Wharf St. ☎ **207/775-0887.** Reservations strongly recommended. Main courses $11.95–$17.95. AE, MC, V. Sun–Thurs 5:30–9:30pm, Fri–Sat 5:30–10pm. MEDITERRANEAN/SEAFOOD.

This is one of the best seafood restaurants in the state, if not all of New England. A pioneer establishment on now trendy Wharf Street, Street & Co. specializes in seafood cooked just right. There's no smoke and mirrors—you pass the open kitchen as you're seated, where you can watch the talented chefs perform their magic in virtually no space. This intimate spot is a bit like something you might imagine stumbling onto while touring Provence: Low beams, dim lighting, and drying herbs hanging overhead nicely set the mood. Diners are seated at copper-topped tables, designed such that the waiters can deliver steaming skillets right from the stove. Try the lobster diavalo—a tangy mélange of lobster, mussels, and clams in a delectable red sauce. If you're partial to calamari, be sure to order it here. They know how to cook it so it's perfectly tender, a knack that's becoming lost elsewhere. Street & Co. fills up early, so reservations are strongly recommended. One-third of the tables are reserved for walk-ins each night, though, so it can't hurt to try if you're in the neighborhood.

✪ **West Side Restaurant.** 58 Pine St. ☎ **207/773-8223.** Reservations recommended. Main courses $13.95–$18.95. AE, MC, V. Tues–Fri 11:30am–2pm, Sun 9am–2pm; Tues–Thurs and Sun 5–9pm, Fri–Sat 5–10pm. NEW AMERICAN.

This intimate neighborhood bistro is quiet, elegant, and hugely popular with clued-in Portlanders. The West Side is off the beaten path, but it's well worth hunting down. In the winter a woodstove makes the place toasty; in summer there's dining on a second-floor deck.

It's hard to read all the way through the enticing menu without tackling a waiter and demanding to order immediately. The offerings change frequently but often feature a good selection of game dishes: There's the Maine venison medaillons with a wild-mushroom, tarragon, and red-wine sauce; duck breast with cranberries; and a tangy cassoulet with duck, lamb sausage, and pork. Other fine choices include delicate preparations of quail, sweetbreads, veal, salmon, and rabbit.

MODERATE

Café Uffa! 190 State St. ☎ **207/775-3380.** Reservations not accepted. Main courses $7.95–$11.95. MC, V. Wed–Sat 5:30–10pm, Sun 9am–2pm. MULTIETHNIC.

If you're looking to stretch your dollar without compromising on quality, this is the place. Uffa consistently manages to impress Portland's notoriously picky eaters with creative international fare. The specialty is fish grilled to perfect tenderness over a wood-stoked fire, but there's plenty else to choose from. The chefs share a predilection for perfectionism, and even simple side dishes like black beans are cooked with unexpected flair. Desserts are uniformly wonderful. With its mismatched chairs, last week's flea-market decor, and high ceilings, Uffa attracts a young crowd with its aggressively informal styling. Sunday brunches are also superb, but be prepared to wait. There's often a line to get in.

Katahdin. 106 High St. ☎ **207/774-1740.** Reservations not accepted. Main courses $9.95–$14.95. DISC, MC, V. Mon–Thurs 5–9:30pm, Fri–Sat 5–10:30pm. AMERICAN/REGIONAL.

Katahdin is a noisy place that prides itself on its funky interior and eclectic food. Artists on slim budgets stop here to order the nightly blue plate special, which typically features something basic like meat loaf. Wealthy business folks one table over dine on more delicate fare, like the restaurant's famed crab cakes. Other recommended specialties include lobster spring-roll appetizers, and a superb main course of grilled sea scallops with a spicy lime vinaigrette. Sometimes the kitchen nods, but for the most part it's good food at good prices. There's a long bar in the dining room where you can enjoy Portland's best martini while waiting for a table.

Uptown Billy's. 1 Forest Ave. ☎ **207/780-0141.** Reservations not accepted. Main courses $6.95–$20.95 (mostly $8–$10). AE, DC, MC, V. Mon–Sat 11:30am–2:30pm; Mon–Thurs 5–9pm, Fri–Sat 5–10pm, Sun 3–8pm. BARBECUE.

You needn't be embarrassed by the BBQ sauce on your chin at Billy's. This is the place to go for a plate of pork ribs and a mess o' beans.

Billy's started out in an authentic dive across the river in South Portland. Since moving uptown to a slightly larger venue, it's become "bistro-ized," adding more refined dishes like salmon and grilled portobello mushrooms. But it's still best known for the slow-cooked pork spare ribs, which require at least a dozen napkins per rack. The meals come with cornbread, buttermilk biscuits, and a choice of side dishes like macaroni and cheese, potatoes, or a zippy coleslaw. On weekends there's live entertainment, which is typically jazz, blues, or rockabilly.

Zephyr Grill. 653 Congress St. ☎ **207/828-4033.** Reservations recommended. Main courses $10.95–$16.95. AE, CB, DISC, MC, V. Wed–Sun 5–10pm. UPSCALE GRILL.

The name suggests the elegance of a fine meal on a dining railcar circa 1939, and this relatively new spot, which opened in 1996, doesn't disappoint. Situated in one of Portland's less elegant commercial neighborhoods, the Zephyr Grill sets an inviting mood with rich colors (squash-colored walls and teal wainscoting), soft lighting, and pinpoint spotlights over the tables that carve out alluring islands of light. The menu is extremely appealing, with starters like grilled eggplant with goat cheese, sun-dried tomatoes, and roasted peppers, and Thai-style spring rolls with shrimp. Main courses might include crispy duck breast with seared cabbage, bok choy, and peppers, or local scallops with a Thai coconut curry over basmati rice. About half the seats are kept open for walk-ins, so take a chance and stop by even if you don't have reservations. There's a good selection of wines.

INEXPENSIVE

Seng's 2. 921 Congress St. ☎ **207/879-2577.** Reservations not accepted. Main courses $5–$9.95. No credit cards. Daily 11am–10pm. THAI.

Portland's best Thai food is found in a small, somewhat dingy spot in a cheerless part of town near the bus station. Don't come here expecting atmosphere—unless you're a connoisseur of buzzing fluorescent lights. Come here expecting a big pile of delicious food at great prices. The spicy pad Thai has developed a cult following among knowledgeable Portlanders. Five dollars will buy you a plateful that's nearly big enough for two. The curries are delicious, as are the hot basil leaves with chicken, beef, or tofu. Everything is available to go.

Silly's. 40 Washington Ave. ☎ **207/772-0360.** Reservations not accepted. Lunch and dinner items $1.25–$5.95; pizza $5.95–$16.90. No credit cards. Mon–Sat 10am–10pm. ECLECTIC & TAKEOUT.

Silly's is a favorite cheap joint among young Portlanders. Situated on an aggressively charmless urban street (it's across from an industrial bakery), the interior is informal, bright, and spunky, with a superb selection of mismatched 1950s-era dinettes, funky-retro accessories, and Tracy Chapman playing in the background. The menu is creative and the selections tasty. Many of the meals are served in hubcap-sized pita bread (the shish kebab roll-up is especially delicious), the pizza is superb, and there's beer on tap. Don't overlook the french fries, or the huge old-fashioned milkshakes and malts. They offer free delivery for orders over $6, so you can have a picnic delivered to your in-town hotel room.

PORTLAND AFTER DARK

Portland is lively in the evenings, especially on summer weekends when the testosterone level in the Old Port seems to rocket into the stratosphere with young men and women prowling the dozens of bars and spilling out onto the streets. Among the bars favored by locals are **Three-Dollar Dewey's,** at the corner of Commercial and Union streets (try the great french fries); **Gritty McDuff's Brew Pub,** on Fore Street near the foot of Exchange Street; and **Brian Ború,** slightly out of the Old Port on Center Street. All three bars are informal and pubby, with guests sharing long tables with new companions.

Beyond the active Old Port bar scene, a number of clubs offer a good mix of live entertainment throughout the year. There's been considerable upheaval and turmoil among clubs and club owners in the past couple of years; check the free alternative paper, *Casco Bay Weekly,* for performers and show times.

4 The Western Lakes & Mountains

Maine's Western Mountains are a treasury of sparkling destinations if your idea of getting away involves heading into the outdoors and away from the crowds. This rugged, brawny region, which stretches northeast from the White Mountains to the Carrabassett Valley, isn't as commercialized as the Maine coast, and the villages aren't as quaint as you'll find in Vermont's Green Mountains. But it has azure lakes, ragged forests of spruce, fir, and lichens, and rolling hills and mountains that take on a distinct blue hue during the summer hiking season.

Cultural amenities are few here, but natural attractions are legion. Hikers have the famed Appalachian Trail, which crosses into Maine in the Mahoosuc Mountains (near where Route 26 enters into New Hampshire), and follows rivers and ridgelines northeast to Bigelow Mountain and beyond. Canoeists and fishermen head to the noted Rangeley Lakes area, a chain of deepwater ponds and lakes that has attracted sportsmen to rustic lodges along their shores for more than a century. And in the winter, skiers can choose among several downhill ski areas, including the two largest ski areas in the state, Sunday River and Sugarloaf.

BETHEL

Until the mid-1980s, Bethel was a sleepy, 19th-century resort town with a friendly, family-oriented ski area that seemed destined for certain extinction—until a guy named Les Otten came along. This brash, young entrepreneur bought Sunday River Ski Area and proceeded to make it into one of New England's most vibrant and successful ski destinations. (Successful enough that Otten subsequently snapped up most of the major ski areas in New England, including Killington, Attitash, Sugarbush, Sugarloaf, Mt. Snow, and Waterville Valley.)

With the rise of Sunday River, the white clapboard town of Bethel (located about 7 miles from the ski area) has been dragged into the modern era, although it hasn't yet taken on the artificial, packaged flavor of some other New England ski towns. The village (pop. 2,500) is still dominated by respected prep school Gould Academy, the village common, and the Bethel Inn, a turn-of-the-century resort that's managed to stay ahead of the tide by adding condos, but hasn't forfeited its pleasant, timeworn character.

ESSENTIALS

GETTING THERE   Bethel is located at the intersection of Routes 26 and 2. It's accessible from the Maine Turnpike by heading west on Route 26 from Exit 11. From New Hampshire, drive east on Route 2 from Gorham.

VISITOR INFORMATION   The **Bethel Area Chamber of Commerce,** 30 Cross St., Bethel, ME 04217 (☎ **207/824-2282,** or 800/442-5826 for reservations assistance), has offices in the Bethel Train Station at the back of the movie theater. It's open year-round Monday through Saturday from 9am to 5pm and on Sundays "by chance."

EXPLORING THE TOWN

Bethel's stately historic homes ring the **Bethel Common,** a long, rectangular greensward created in 1807 atop a low, gentle ridge. (It was originally laid out as a street broad enough for the training of the local militia.) The town's **historic district** encompasses some 27 homes, which represent a wide range of architectural styles popular in the 19th century. The oldest home in the district is the **1813 Moses Mason House,** which is now a fine, small museum housing the collections and offices of the **Bethel Historical Society** (☎ 207/824-2908).

GETTING OUTSIDE

Hiking

The **Appalachian Trail** crosses the Mahoosuc Mountains northwest of Bethel. Many of those who've hiked the entire 2,000-mile trail say this stretch is the most demanding on knees and psyches. The trail doesn't forgive; it generally foregoes switchbacks in favor of sheer ascents and descents. It's also hard to find water along the trail during dry weather. Still, it's worth the knee-pounding effort for the views and the unrivaled sense of remoteness.

One stretch of the Appalachian Trail crosses **Old Speck Mountain,** Maine's third highest peak, in Grafton Notch State Park off Route 26. There are no views since the old fire tower closed a few years ago, but an easy to moderate hike from Route 26 to an 800-foot cliff called **"The Eyebrow"** provides a good vantage point for the Bear River Valley and the rugged terrain of Grafton Notch. Look for the well-signed parking lot where Route 26 intersects the Appalachian Trail in Grafton Notch State Park. Park your car, then head south on the AT; in 0.1 mile you'll intersect the Eyebrow Trail and its moderate ascent to the fine vistas.

The Appalachian Mountain Club's *Maine Mountain Guide* is highly recommended for detailed information about other area hikes.

Alpine Skiing

The *Sunday River Express* (☎ 888/724-5754) is the East's only **ski train,** serving Sunday River from Portland and offering a relaxed way to get to the slopes and back. Launched in 1993 by Sunday River and sold to another concern in 1996, the train pulls out of an industrial lot on Portland's outskirts early in the morning, then follows rivers and historic train routes on its 2^1/$_4$ -hour run to Bethel Station. Skiers are then transferred to a fleet of buses for the final 7-mile shuttle to the slopes, and are usually on the slopes by 9:30 or 10am. A winter weekend trip to sample Portland's restaurants and attractions could easily be packaged with a 1- or 2-day excursion to Sunday River, combining the best of urban Maine with some of the best skiing in New England. The train typically runs on weekends and school holidays. The train costs $19 round-trip, or $59 with lift ticket.

✪ **Sunday River Ski Resort.** P.O. Box 450, Bethel, ME 04217. ☎ **207/824-3000** or 800/ 543-2754 for lodging. Web site: www.sundayriver.com. Vertical drop: 2,340 ft. 15 chairlifts (3 high-speed), 1 surface lift. Skiable acreage: 639. Lift tickets $46 adults on weekends, $43 weekdays; $29 children 6–12 on weekends, $28 weekdays.

Sunday River has grown by leaps and bounds in recent years, and today competes in the same league as major New England winter resorts like Mount Snow and Killington. Unlike ski areas that have developed around a single tall peak, Sunday River has expanded along an undulating ridge about 3 miles wide encompassing some seven peaks. As a result, you'll never get bored making the same run time and again.

The descents offer something for virtually everyone, from steep bump runs to glade skiing to wide, wonderful intermediate trails. A decade ago, Sunday River was regarded as an intermediate's mountain. That changed dramatically with the expansion to the adjacent peaks and the addition of steep new runs. It's now got the reputation of a mountain with great bumps and sheer descents. Sunday River is also blessed with plenty of water for snowmaking, and makes tons of the stuff using a snowmaking system it developed.

My chief complaint with Sunday River is that the superb skiing conditions are offset by an uninspiring base area. Everything seems a bit raw and unfinished at the bottom of the mountain. The lodges and condos are architecturally dull, dull, dull, and the less than delicate landscaping is of the sort created by graceless bulldozers. And spread as widely as it is, there's no real sense of place, as there is at more established resorts like Sugarloaf or Waterville Valley. Each year, though, it seems to be improving bit by bit.

Ski Mt. Abram. P.O. Box 120, Locke Mills, ME 04255. ☎ **207/875-5003.** Vertical drop: 1,030 ft. 2 chairlifts, 3 T-bars. Skiable acreage: 135. Lift tickets $29 weekends for adults, $18– $24 for children and teens; $19 midweek for adults, $15–$17 for children and teens.

Mount Abram is a welcoming intermediate mountain that's perfect for families still on the learning curve. It has a friendly, informal atmosphere that's in sharp contrast with nearby Sunday River. You don't have to expend much energy on logistics here, planning when to meet up or at what base lodge. You don't have to expend nearly as much cash, either.

WHERE TO STAY

Bethel Inn. On the Common, Bethel, ME 04217. ☎ **800/654-0125** or 207/824-2175. 57 rms (some with showers only) plus 40 2-bedroom condos. TV TEL. Summer $198–$360 double; winter $138–$260 double. Rates include breakfast and dinner; lodging only (no meals) available in Apr and Nov. Ask about package rates. AE, DC, DISC, MC, V.

The Bethel Inn is a classic, old-fashioned resort built on the Common in 1913. You can tell which buildings are part of the inn by their distinctive color—the pale Bethel Inn yellow. The main inn, on 200 acres, has a quiet, settled air throughout, which seems appropriate since it was built to house patients of Dr. John Gehring, who put Bethel on the map treating nervous disorders through a regimen of healthy country living. (Bethel was once known as "the resting place of Harvard" for all the faculty treated here.) The quaint, homey rooms aren't terribly spacious, but they are welcoming and pleasingly furnished with country antiques. The deluxe rooms have separate sitting rooms; modern condominium lodging is also available, but these sorely lack the charm of the inn. While the cost is high, don't be scared off; the inn offers a number of packages that bring down the daily rate if you stay a few days.

Dining/Entertainment: The inn's dining room serves passable meals in a classically elegant dining room, with specialties like a lobster-filled ravioli, venison medaillons, and broiled duck breast. It's not great food; the more basic the preparation, the more likely you'll be satisfied.

Facilities: Fitness center with an outdoor heated pool (open year-round), golf course, tennis, cross-country skiing, shuttle to ski areas. There's also lake swimming at the inn's Lake House, picturesquely located amid pines on a small lake a short drive away.

Holidae House. Main St., Bethel, ME 04217. ☎ **800/882-3306** or 207/824-3400. 7 rms (4 with shower only). TV TEL. Winter $89–$150 double; summer $70–$98 double. 2-night minimum on weekends Jan–Mar. Rates include continental breakfast. AE, MC, V.

Innkeeper Tom McGinniss has done an exemplary job making over this century-old village home on Bethel's Main Street. The exterior is unusually handsome, painted in rich but muted colors, and the inside is superbly decorated in a style that nicely straddles high Victorian and low whimsical. Every room is furnished with antiques and Oriental carpets; some have delightful hand-painted ceiling murals and whirlpool tubs. (Number 5 was my favorite, decorated with classically inspired elegance.) Among the accommodations are a studio apartment that sleeps four, and a three-bedroom apartment that sleeps eight. The inn is a 5-minute walk from the Bethel Common, and a 10-minute drive to skiing at Sunday River.

L'Auberge Country Inn. Bethel Common (P.O. Box 21), Bethel, ME 04217. ☎ **800/760-2774** or 207/824-2774. E-mail: lauberge@nix.com. 7 rms (1 with hall bath). $60–$120 double. 2-night minimum on winter weekends. Rates include continental breakfast. AE, DISC, MC, V. Closed mid-Apr to mid-May and mid-Oct to Thanksgiving.

L'Auberge was originally built as a barn in the 1890s, but other than a few exposed beams, its lineage isn't immediately evident. Located on a spacious and shady lot down a small lane just off the Bethel Common, the inn has a settled, European air inside. You enter through a high-ceilinged living room with a Steinway, ticking antique hall clock, fireplace, and decanter of sherry. Kit the golden retriever may be present to give you a low-key greeting. The rooms are furnished in a comfortable country style, some with stenciling and brass beds.

Dining/Entertainment: The inn is well known locally for its dining room, which serves French-influenced fare. Guests choose from three small dining rooms; the best is an intimate space painted "gregarious red" that gives off a gentle, candlelit glow in the evening. (The dining room is open to the public; reservations recommended. Entree prices range from $14 to $24.)

WHERE TO DINE

Moose's Tale. Rte. 2 (at Sunday River Rd.). ☎ **207/824-4253.** Reservations not accepted. Main courses $5.95–$15.95 (mostly $6–$8). AE, MC, V. Daily 11:30am–12:30am. PUB FARE.

Sunday River Brewing Co. opened this modern brew pub a few years ago on prime real estate at the corner of Route 2 and the Sunday River access road. This is a good choice if your primary objective is to consume robust ales and porters. The brews are awfully good (although some claim they're way too hoppy); the food (burgers, nachos, chicken wings) doesn't strive for any culinary heights. The design of the restaurant is a bit idiosyncratic; you have to elbow your way in through the bar. The best tables are by the stone fireplace in the main dining room, and in a side room near the pool tables. Come early if you're looking for a quiet evening; it gets real loud in the evening when bands take the stage.

Mother's. Upper Main St. ☎ **207/824-2589.** Reservations accepted for parties of 6 or more. Lunch $4.75–$8.95; dinner $6.50–$19. MC, V. Daily 11:30am–9:30pm. AMERICAN.

Appropriate to its name, Mother's is a homey, informal place housed in a pale green Victorian home adorned with gingerbread trim. Inside, diners are ushered to small, darkly paneled rooms, each of which has four or five tables and walls hung with portraits of dour Victorians. (In summer, there's also dining on the front deck.) The meals are basic and well prepared, and the service is always friendly. For lunch there's hamburgers and crab-cake sandwiches; for dinner, try the sea scallops with artichokes, or the pork ribs grilled with a lemon barbecue sauce.

RANGELEY LAKES

Mounted moose heads on the walls, log cabins tucked in the spruce forest, and cool August mornings that require not one sweater but two come to mind when speaking of the Rangeley Lakes region. Although Rangeley Lake and its eponymous town are at the heart of the region, it extends much further, consisting of a series of lakes that feed into and flow out of the main lake. Upstream is Maine's fourth largest lake, Flagstaff, a beautiful, wind-raked body of water created in 1949 when Central Maine Power dammed the Dead River. (Below the dam it's no longer dead; in fact it's now noted for its white-water rafting—see section 8, "The North Woods," below). From Rangeley Lake, the waters flow into the Cupsuptic Pond, which in turn flow to Mooselook-meguntic Lake, through the Upper and Lower Richardson Lakes, down remote Swift River and to Lake Umbagog, which feeds the headwaters of the Androscoggin River.

The town of Rangeley (pop. 1,063) is the regional center for outdoor activities. It offers a handful of motels and restaurants, a few fishing guides, and a smattering of shops, but little else. Easy to visit attractions in the Rangeley area are few, and most regular visitors and residents seem determined to keep it that way. The wise visitor rents a cabin or takes a room at a lodge, then explores the area with the slow pace that seems custom-made for the region. Rangeley is Maine's highest town at 1,546 feet, and it usually remains quite cool throughout the summer.

ESSENTIALS

GETTING THERE   Rangeley is 122 miles north of Portland, and 39 miles northwest of Farmington on Route 4. The most scenic approach is on Route 17 from Rumford. Along the way, you'll pass one of the most stunning overlooks in New England, with a sweeping panorama of Mooselookmeguntic Lake and Bemis Mountain.

From New Hampshire, drive 111 miles north on Route 16 from North Conway through Gorham, Berlin, and Errol. Route 16 from Errol to Rangeley is especially remote and scenic.

VISITOR INFORMATION   The **Rangeley Lakes Region Chamber of Commerce,** P.O. Box 317, Rangeley, ME 04970 (☎ **800/685-2537** or 207/864-5364),

Weird Science

My vote for the quirkiest destination in Maine is **Orgonon,** former home of the controversial Viennese psychiatrist Wilhelm Reich (1897–1957). A tour of his hilltop estate includes a compelling story about a driven man, a glimpse at some provocative theories about the nature of matter and sexuality, and a close-up look at an architecturally distinctive stone house. Even if the history of psychiatry or architecture holds little allure for you, stop by anyway. You'll find something to intrigue you, even if it's just the wonderful lake vistas.

A brief overview: Wilhelm Reich was an associate of Sigmund Freud during the early days of psychoanalysis. Like Freud, he believed that underlying sexual tension governed much of our behavior. But Reich took Freud's work a few steps further. Building on the hypothesis that pent-up sexual energy—a sort of psychological blockage—resulted in many neuroses, Reich developed techniques to release that energy. His persistent belief in Freud's libido theory (even after Freud had largely abandoned it) forced a break with Freud; the clouds of World War II forced his departure from Austria.

After some time in Scandinavia spent actively involved in the European sexual-politics movement, Reich settled in Rangeley, where he refined his theories and developed the science of "orgonomy." In his research, Reich concluded that living matter was animated by a sort of life force called "orgone." This floated freely in the atmosphere and was blue, which Reich believed explained the hue of the sky. Reich maintained that orgone imbalances within people were at the root of many behavioral problems, and to cure those imbalances he invented orgone energy boxes, which were said to gather and concentrate ambient orgone. These boxes were just big enough to sit in, and featured 6-inch walls of metal and asbestos, which Reich believed was the right combination of material to capture orgone.

Reich also invented a rather large and fearsome-looking device called a cloudbuster, which to the uninitiated looks a bit like an anti-aircraft weapon (it's on display at Orgonon). This was said to draw energy from the atmosphere, thereby changing the energy balance and affecting weather patterns. During the period Reich felt most persecuted because of his ideas, he even threatened to use these machines to cause storms and flood the United States. He did not have the opportunity. Reich was sentenced to federal prison for contempt on matters related to the interstate transport of his orgone boxes, and that is where he died in 1957. While many have dismissed Reich's theories as pure quackery, he still has adherents, including those who maintain the museum in his memory.

Orgonon, built in 1948 of native fieldstone, has a spectacular view of Dodge Pond and is built in a distinctive American Modern style, which stands apart from the local rustic lodge motif. Visitors on the 1-hour guided tour of the estate can view the orgone boxes and the orgone gun, along with other intriguing inventions and stark, dramatic canvases painted by Reich, who took up the brush at age 55.

Orgonon (☎ **207/864-3443**) is located 3.5 miles west of Rangeley just off Route 4 on Dodge Pond Road. Admission is $3 adults, free for children 12 and under; it's open July and August Tuesday through Sunday from 1 to 5pm, and in September on Sunday only.

maintains an information booth in town at a small park near the lake that's open year-round Monday through Saturday from 9am to 5pm.

CANOEING

The Rangeley Lakes area is a canoeist's paradise. Azure waters, dense forests, and rugged hills are all part of the allure. Rangeley Lake has a mix of wild forest and old-time camps lining the lakeshore. The southeast coves of Mooselookmeguntic Lake suffered an unfortunate period of haphazard development during the 1980s, but much of the shore, especially along the Phillips Preserve and the west shore, are still very attractive. Upper Richardson Lake's shoreline is largely owned by the state, and is the most remote and wild of the chain.

Primitive campsites along the shores of both Upper and Lower Richardson Lakes are managed by the **South Arm Campground** (☎ 207/364-5155), located at the tip of Lower Richardson Lake and accessible via dirt road from the town of Andover.

HIKING

The **Appalachian Trail** crosses Route 4 about 10 miles south of Rangeley. A strenuous but rewarding hike is along the AT northward to the summit of **Saddleback Mountain,** a 10-mile round-trip that ascends though thick forest and past remote ponds to open, arcticlike terrain with fine views of the surrounding mountains and lakes. Saddleback actually consists of two peaks over 4,000 feet (hence the name). As on the lakes, be prepared for sudden shifts in weather, and for the high winds that often rake the open ridgeline.

An easier 1-mile hike may be found at **Bald Mountain** near the village of Oquossuc, on the northeast shore of Mooselookmeguntic Lake. (Look for the trailhead 1 mile south of Haines Landing on Bald Mountain Road.) The views have grown over in recent years, but you can still catch glimpses of the clear blue waters from above.

ALPINE SKIING

Saddleback Ski Area. P.O. Box 490, Rangeley, ME 04970. ☎ **207/864-5671.** Vertical drop: 1,830 ft. 2 double chairs, 3 T-bars. Lift tickets $34 adults on weekends, $22 juniors and students on weekends; all tickets $20 midweek.

With only two chairlifts, Saddleback falls under the category of "small mountain." But there's the surprise: Saddleback has an unexpectedly big-mountain feel. It offers a vertical drop of just 1,830 feet, but what makes Saddleback so appealing is its rugged alpine setting (the Appalachian Trail runs across the high, mile-long ridge above the resort) and the old-fashioned trails. Saddleback offered glade skiing and narrow, winding trails well before the bigger ski areas sought to re-create these old-fashioned slopes. The 2.5-mile Lazy River Trail is one of the more scenic beginners descents in New England.

WHERE TO STAY & DINE

The Rangeley area has a scattering of bed-and-breakfasts, but many travelers destined here spend a week or more at a sporting camp or rented waterfront cottage. Among the best known of the sporting camps is **Grant's Kennebago Camps** (☎ 800/633-4815 or 207/864-3608), situated down a long and dusty logging road on Kennebago Lake—the biggest "fly-fishing only" lake east of the Mississippi. Rates are $100 per person per day, including all meals. **Mooselookmeguntic House** (☎ 207/864-2962) offers a cluster of cabins on or near the shores of Mooselookmeguntic, along with access to a handsome beach and marina.

For weekly rental of a private cabin, a good place to start is the local chamber of commerce's free *Accommodations and Services* pamphlet (☎ **800/685-2537** or 207/864-5364). The chamber can book cabins for the week for you. You might also try **Vacation Realty Rental Properties,** P.O. Box 430, 86 Main St., Rangeley, ME 04970 (☎ **207/864-3300**).

Kawahnee Lodge. Rte. 142 (P.O. Box 119), Weld, ME 04285. ☎ **207/585-2000** or 207/778-4306. E-mail: strunk@saturn.caps.maine.edu. 9 rms (5 with private bath) plus 12 cabins. $60–$95 double; $95–$160 cabin. Closed Oct 15–May 15. MC, V.

The rustic Kawahnee Lodge is located about 30 miles southeast of Rangeley, but it's worth the drive if you're looking for that ineffable lakeside Maine experience. Originally built in 1929 to house parents visiting their children at neighboring Camp Kawahnee, the lodge is full of creaks and shadows, as befits a spot built by a teacher of industrial arts. There are columns of yellow birch, handsome caned chairs original to the lodge, a cobblestone fireplace with a moose head above, and breathtaking views across the lake to Mount Blue (a state park offering great hiking).

The lodge rooms are Spartan but attractive, and noises tend to carry. Five of the rooms have private baths; the other four share one bath. The one-, two-, and three-bedroom cabins are usually booked by the week (rates range from $415 to $600), but some are available on a nightly basis, especially during the shoulder seasons.

Dining/Entertainment: The rustic dining room is open nightly though Labor Day and serves moderately priced fare including sirloin steak, roast duck, seafood, and a selection of vegetarian dishes, including Szechuan vegetable stir-fry.

Facilities: Lake beach, motorboat and canoe rentals.

Mallory's Bed and Breakfast Inn. 1 Hyatt Rd. (P.O. Box 9), Rangeley, ME 04970. ☎ **800/722-0397** or 207/864-2121. Fax 207/864-2066. 5 rms (sharing 3 baths). $56–$72 double. Rates include continental breakfast. Children 2–10 sharing parent's room are charged $10 extra. AE, MC, V.

This very handsome and historic shingled home is set amid white birches on 660 feet of waterfront. The five rooms share three baths, but you'll soon forget this minor inconvenience as you fill your time strolling around the property, lolling in the Adirondack chairs on the front porch, and sunning on the floating dock. There are paddle boats, canoes, sailboats, and bikes available to guests free of charge; motorboats are available for rent. The guest rooms are bright, spare, and comfortable, and are welcoming for a few days' getaway.

Rangeley Inn. P.O. Box 398, Rangeley, ME 04907. ☎ **800/666-3687** or 207/864-3341. Fax 207/864-3634. 51 rms (several with shower only). TV (motel only). $69–$114 double. AE, DISC, MC, V.

The architecturally eclectic Rangeley Inn dominates Rangeley's miniature downtown. Parts of this old-fashioned, blue-shingled hotel date back to 1877, but the main wing was built in 1907, with additions in the 1920s and the 1940s. A 15-unit motel annex was built more recently behind the inn on Haley Pond, but those looking for creaky floors and a richer sense of local heritage should request a room in the main, three-floor inn. The rooms at the inn and motel are each unique—some in the motel have woodstoves, kitchenettes, or whirlpools; in the inn you'll find a handful of rooms with claw-foot tubs perfect for an evening's soaking. David and Rebecca Schinas bought the inn in 1996 after a long run by the Carpenter family, and they've made some small improvements without compromising the historic feel of the place.

Dining/Entertainment: The gracious, old-worldish dining room serves hearty, filling meals, most of which are traditional New England but often prepared with some flair.

CARRABASSETT VALLEY

The Carrabassett Valley can be summed up in six words: big peaks, wild woods, deep lakes.

The crowning jewel of the region is Sugarloaf Mountain, Maine's second highest peak at 4,237 feet. Distinct from nearby peaks because of its pyramidal shape, the mountain has been developed for skiing, and offers the highest vertical drop in Maine, the best selection of activities daytime and night, and a wide range of accommodations within easy commuting distance.

Outside of the villages and ski area, it's all rugged hills, tumbling streams, and spectacular natural surroundings. The muscular mountains of the Bigelow Range provide terrain for some of the state's best hiking. And Flagstaff Lake is the place for flat-water canoeing amid majestic surroundings.

ESSENTIALS

GETTING THERE   Kingfield and Sugarloaf are on Route 27. Skiers debate over the best route from the turnpike. Some exit at Auburn and take Route 4 north to Route 27; others exit in Augusta and take Route 27 straight through. It's a toss-up time-wise, but exiting at Augusta is marginally more scenic.

VISITOR INFORMATION   The **Sugarloaf Area Chamber of Commerce** (☎ 207/235-2100) offers information from its offices 9.5 miles north of Kingfield on Route 27. The office is open year-round Monday to Saturday 10am to 4pm (until 5pm in winter). The chamber will book lodgings in and around Sugarloaf; call ☎ 800/843-2732. (For accommodations on the mountain, contact Sugarloaf directly at ☎ 800/843-5623.)

ALPINE SKIING

✪ **Sugarloaf/USA.** R.R. #1, P.O. Box 5000, Carrabassett Valley, ME 04947. ☎ 207/237-2000, or 800/843-5623 for lodging. Web site: http://www.sugarloaf.com. Vertical drop: 2,820 ft. 13 chairlifts, including 1 gondola and 1 high-speed quad; 1 surface lift. Skiable acreage: 1,400 (snowmaking on 475 acres). Lift tickets $46 for adults on weekends, $43 weekdays.

Sugarloaf is Maine's big mountain, with the highest vertical drop in New England (after Killington, in Vermont). And thanks to quirks of geography, it actually feels bigger than it is. From the high, open snowfields (which account for much of Sugarloaf's huge skiable acreage) or the upper advanced runs like Bubblecuffer or White Nitro, skiers develop a bit of vertigo looking down at the valley floor.

Sugarloaf attracts plenty of experts to its hard-core runs, but it's also a superb intermediate mountain, with great cruising runs. A gentle bunny slope extends down through the village; the "green" slopes on the mountain itself are a bit more challenging.

The main drawback is the winds. Sugarloaf seems to get buffeted regularly, with the higher lifts often closed due to gusting.

Sugarloaf has more of a destination feel to it than many resorts, since it's nearly 3 hours from Portland (5 hr. from Boston) and gets relatively little day-tripper traffic. Most people who ski Sugarloaf stay at the base complex, a well-run, convivial cluster of hotel rooms, condos, minisuites, and the like offering 7,500 beds. The accommodations, the mountain, the restaurants, and other area attractions are well connected by chairlifts and shuttle buses, making for a relaxed visit here even during a fierce blizzard.

CROSS-COUNTRY SKIING

The **Sugarloaf Ski Touring Center** (☎ 207/237-6830) offers 57 miles of groomed trails that weave through the village at the base of the mountain and into the low hills covered with young, scrappy woodlands south of the Carrabassett River. The trails are impeccably groomed for striding and skating, and wonderful views open here and there to Sugarloaf Mountain and the Bigelow Range. The base lodge is simple and attractive, all knotty pine with a cathedral ceiling, and features a cafeteria, a towering stone fireplace, and a well-equipped ski shop. Trail fees are $10 daily for adults; $7 to $8 for juniors, seniors, and children. The center is located on Route 27 about 1 mile south of the Sugarloaf access road. A shuttle bus serves the area in winter.

HIKING

The 12-mile **Bigelow Range** has some of the most dramatic, high-ridge hiking in the state, a close second to Mount Katahdin. The Bigelow Range consists of a handful of lofty peaks, with Avery Peak (the east peak, named after Myron Avery, one of the Appalachian Trail's founders) offering perhaps the best views. On exceptionally clear days, hikers can see Mount Washington to the southwest and Mount Katahdin to the northeast.

A strenuous but rewarding hike for fit hikers is the 10.3-mile loop that begins at the **Fire Warden's Trail.** (The trailhead is at the washed-out bridge on Stratton Brook Pond Road, a rugged dirt road that leaves eastward from Route 27 about 2.3 miles north of the Sugarloaf access road.) Follow the Fire Warden's Trail up the steep ridge to the junction with the Appalachian Trail. Head south on the AT, which tops the West Peak and South Horn, two open summits with stellar views. One-quarter mile past Horns Pond, turn south on Horns Pond Trail and descend back to the Fire Warden's Trail to return to your car. Hikers pass two lean-tos along this route (free; first come, first served), making this suitable for an overnight hike. Allow about 8 hours for the loop; a map and hiking guide are strongly recommended.

Detailed directions for these hikes and many others in the area can be found in the AMC's *Maine Mountain Guide.*

OTHER OUTDOOR PURSUITS

In summer, Sugarloaf/USA's 18-hole **golf course** (☎ 207/237-2000) attracts duffers by the cartload. It's invariably ranked the number-one golf destination in the state by experienced golfers, who are lured here by the Robert Trent Jones, Jr., course design and dramatic mountain backdrop. Sugarloaf hosts a well-respected golf school during the season.

WHERE TO STAY & DINE

For convenience, nothing beats staying right on the mountain in winter. Skiers can pop right out the door and onto the lifts. Sugarloaf is nicely designed to allow skiers access to the village; a long, gentle slope extends from the base of the mountain through the clusters of condos and hotels, allowing skiers to glide home after a long day. A low chairlift takes you up to the base first thing in the morning.

Many of the condos are booked through **Sugarloaf/USA Inn** (☎ 800/843-5623 or 207/237-2000), which handles the reservations for more than 300 condos and minisuites. The units are spread throughout the base area, and are of varying vintage and opulence. All guests have access to the Sugarloaf Sports and Fitness Center.

Another option at the base village is the **Sugarloaf Mountain Hotel** (☎ 800/ 527-9879), a towering structure right at the lifts with more than 100 guest rooms.

The chamber of commerce will also book lodgings in and around Sugarloaf; call ☎ 800/843-2732.

The Herbert. Main St. (P.O. Box 67), Kingfield, ME 04947. ☎ **800/843-4372** or 207/ 265-2000. 40 rms. $89–$150 double. Discounts available midweek. AE, DC, DISC, MC, V.

The Herbert, located about 15 miles from the slopes at Sugarloaf/USA, has the feel of a classic North Woods hostelry—sort of Dodge City by way of Alaska. Built in downtown Kingfield in 1918, the three-story hotel featured all of the finest accoutrements when it was built—fumed oak paneling and incandescent lights in the lobby (look for the original brass fixtures), a classy dining room, and comfortable rooms. The Herbert's 1982 renovation cost $1 million, and was nicely done—right down to the two stuffed moose heads, the baby grand piano, and the fireplace in the lobby. The rooms are furnished in a fairly simple and basic style, although some feature whirlpool bathtubs (there's also a family whirlpool for rent at $10 per half-hour in the basement). Room furnishings tend toward flea-market antiques, with some newer additions.

Dining/Entertainment: The open but intimate dining room off the lobby of The Herbert recalls the days when hotels served the best meals in town. The chef offers some nice interpretations of regional classics, like shiitake mushrooms with venison medaillons, and haddock baked with feta cheese and served with a lemon-garlic dressing. The meals are good, not excellent, but the service is friendly and the experience altogether enjoyable.

5 The Mid-Coast

Veteran Maine travelers contend that this part of the coast is fast losing its native charm—it's becoming too commercial, too developed, too much like the rest of the United States. The grousers do have a point, especially regarding Route 1's roadside— but get off the main roads and you'll find pockets where you can catch glimpses of another Maine. Back-road travelers will stumble upon quiet inland villages, dramatic coastal scenery, and a rich sense of history, especially maritime history.

FREEPORT & ENVIRONS

If Freeport were a mall (and that's not a far-fetched analogy), L.L. Bean would be the anchor store. It's the business that launched Freeport, elevating its status from just another town off the interstate to one of the two outlet capitals of Maine (the other is Kittery). Freeport still has the form of a classic coastal village (the main Y intersection in town was designed such that 100-foot masts could be hauled to the water's edge without making any sharp turns), but it's a village that's been largely taken over by the national fashion industry. Most of the old homes and stores have been converted to upscale shops and now sell name-brand clothing and housewares. Banana Republic occupies an exceedingly handsome brick Federal-style home; even the McDonald's is in a tasteful, understated Victorian farmhouse—you really have to look for the golden arches.

While a number of more modern structures have been built to accommodate the outlet boom (there are now more than 100 stores in town), strict planning guidelines have managed to preserve much of the local charm, at least in the village section. Huge parking lots off Main Street are hidden from view, making this one of the more aesthetically pleasing places to shop anywhere in the United States. But even with these vast lots, parking can be scarce during the peak season, especially on rainy summer days when every cottage-bound tourist between York and Camden decides that a trip to Freeport is a winning idea. Bring a lot of patience and expect teeming crowds if you come at a busy time.

ESSENTIALS

GETTING THERE   Freeport is on Route 1, but is most commonly reached via I-95 from either Exit 19 or 20.

VISITOR INFORMATION   The **Freeport Merchants Association,** P.O. Box 452, Freeport, ME 04032 (☎ **800/865-1994** or 207/865-1212), publishes a map and directory of businesses, restaurants, and accommodations. The free map is available widely around town at stores and restaurants, or you can contact the association to have them send you one.

The best source of information for the region in general is found at the **Maine State Information Center** (☎ **207/846-0833**) just off I-95 in Yarmouth. This state-run center, which is usually open until 7pm during the summer, is stocked with hundreds of brochures and free newspapers, and is staffed with a helpful crew that can provide information on the entire state, but is particularly well informed about the mid-coast region.

SHOPPING

At last count, Freeport had more than 100 retail shops between Exit 19 at the far lower end of Main Street, and Mallett Road, which connects to Exit 20. Shops have recently begun to spread south of Exit 19 toward Yarmouth. If you don't want to miss a single shopping opportunity, get off at Exit 17 and head north on Route 1.

The bargains can vary from extraordinary to nonexistent, so plan on racking up some mileage if you're a bottom feeder looking for outrageous deals. A more relaxed strategy is to just pick three or four shops and focus your efforts there.

Among national chains with a presence in Freeport are The Gap, Anne Klein, Levi's, Boston Traders, Patagonia, Nike, J. Crew, Timberland, Maidenform, and many others.

But the granddaddy of 'em all, of course, is **L.L. Bean,** Main and Bow streets (☎ **800/341-4341**). Monster outdoor retailer L.L. Bean traces its roots to the day Leon Leonwood Bean decided that what the world really needed was a good weatherproof hunting shoe. He joined a watertight gumshoe bottom with a laced leather upper. Hunters liked it. The store grew. An empire was born.

Today L.L. Bean sells millions of dollars' worth of clothing and outdoor goods to customers nationwide through its well-respected catalogs, and it continues to draw hundreds of thousands through its door. This modern, multilevel store is the size of a regional mall, but tastefully done, with its own indoor trout pond and lots of natural wood.

L.L. Bean is open 365 days a year, 24 hours a day (no locks or latches on the front doors), and it's a popular spot even in the dead of night, especially around summer and holidays. Selections include Bean's own trademark clothing, along with home furnishings, books, shoes, and plenty of outdoor gear for camping, fishing, and hunting.

In addition to the main store, L.L. Bean stocks an outlet shop with a relatively small but rapidly changing inventory at discount prices. It's located in a back lot between Main Street and Depot Street—ask at the front desk of the main store for walking directions.

Other noteworthy stores include **Cuddledown of Maine,** 231 U.S. Rte. 1, between exits 17 and 19 (☎ **207/865-1713**). Down pillows are made right in this shop, which carries a variety of European goose-down comforters in all sizes and thicknesses.

Benefiting the Freeport Historical Society, the **Harrington House Museum Store,** 45 Main St. (☎ **207/865-0477**), sells an array of unique Maine items, including antique reproduction furniture, jewelry, and packaged gourmet foods.

A Maine shoemaker since 1830, **J. L. Coombs** today carries a wide assortment of imported and domestic footwear at its two Freeport shops, including a good selection of those favored by teens and college kids, like Dr. Marten, Ecco, and Mephisto.

There's also outerwear by Pendleton and Jackaroos. Look for locations at 15 Bow St. and 278 Rte. 1, between Exits 17 and 19 (☎ **207/865-4333**).

The Mangy Moose, 112 Main St. (☎ **207/865-6414**), is a cute souvenir shop with a twist: Virtually everything in the place is moose related. There are moose hackey sacks, moose wineglasses, moose trivets, moose cookie cutters, and, of course, moose T-shirts. And much more. The merchandise is a notch above that you'll find in other tourist-oriented shops.

Maxwell's Pottery Outlet, 47 Main St. (☎ **207/865-1144**), offers a good selection of practical and fancy pottery, candlestick holders, and other household items. Prices are reasonable.

WHERE TO STAY

Harraseeket Inn. 162 Main St., Freeport, ME 04032. ☎ **800/342-6423** or 207/865-9377. 84 rms. A/C TV TEL. Summer and fall $155–$235 double; spring and early summer $140–$235 double; winter $105–$235 double. $10 midweek discount. Rates include breakfast buffet. 2-night minimum on holidays. AE, DC, DISC, MC, V. Take Exit 20 off I-95 to Main St.

The Harraseeket Inn is a large, thoroughly modern hotel two blocks north of L.L. Bean. It's to the inn's credit that you could easily drive down Main Street and not notice it. A late-19th-century home is the soul of the hotel, but most of the rooms are in later additions built in 1989 and 1997. Guests can relax in the common room with the baby grand player piano, or in the Broad Arrow Pub. The guest rooms are on the large side and tastefully done, all with quarter-canopy beds and a nice mix of contemporary and antique furniture. All have hair dryers and coffeemakers; about a quarter have gas- or wood-burning fireplaces, and 23 have whirlpools. (The new wing was still under construction at press time, so I can't vouch for its quality. If past experience is any guide, the guest rooms won't disappoint.)

Dining/Entertainment: There are two restaurants on the premises. The well-regarded Maine Dining Room is on the pricey end of the scale, offering New American dining with a heavy emphasis on local ingredients; entree prices are $13 to $26. The Broad Arrow Tavern, which is slated to be moved to the new addition and equipped with a wood-fired oven and grill, has a more informal setting with a less ambitious menu, with dinner entrees ranging from $9.95 to $14.95.

Services: Concierge, limited room service, dry cleaning/laundry, safe-deposit boxes.

Facilities: Indoor pool, business center, conference rooms.

WHERE TO DINE

Even hard-core shoppers need sustenance to sustain their consumerism. For a quick and simple meal, you might head down Mechanic Street (near the Mangy Moose at 112 Main St.) to the **Corsican Restaurant,** 9 Mechanic St. (☎ **207/865-9421**), for a 10-inch pizza, calzone, or king-sized sandwich. Nearby is the tiny **Chowder Express and Sandwich Shop,** 2 Mechanic St. (☎ **207/865-3404**), where you can pick up a New England chowder, sandwich, bagel, or muffin. A favorite spot among locals for quick, reasonably priced lunch close to L.L. Bean is the **Falcon Restaurant,** 8 Bow St. (☎ **207/865-4031**).

Harraseeket Lunch & Lobster. Main St., S. Freeport. ☎ **207/865-4888.** Reservations not accepted. Lobsters, market price (typically $6–$9). No credit cards. Open daily 11am–7:25pm for lunch and dinner. Closed mid-Oct to Apr. From I-95, take Exit 17 and head north on Rte. 1. Turn right at the huge Indian statue; continue to stop sign in S. Freeport; turn right to waterfront. From Freeport, take South St. (off Bow St.) to Main St. in S. Freeport; turn left to water. LOBSTER POUND.

Located at a boatyard on the Harraseeket River about a 10-minute drive from Freeport's main shopping district, this lobster pound is an especially popular destination on sunny days—although with a heated dining room, it's a worthy destination anytime. Order a crustacean according to how hungry you are (from a pound on up), then take in the river view from the deck while waiting for your number to be called. Be prepared for big crowds; a good alternative is to come in late afternoon between the lunch and dinner hordes.

Jameson Tavern. 115 Main St. ☎ **207/865-4196.** Reservations encouraged during peak season. Tap Room main courses $5.25–$9.95; Dining Room lunch $5.75–$10.95, dinner $10.95–$19.95. AE, DC, DISC, MC, V. Tap Room daily 11:30am–11pm; Dining Room daily 11:30am–2pm and 5–10pm. AMERICAN.

Located in a handsome, historic farmhouse literally in the shadow of the L.L. Bean store (it's just north of the store), the Jameson Tavern touts itself as the birthplace of Maine. (In 1820 the papers were signed here legally separating Maine from Massachusetts.) Today, it's a dual restaurant under the same ownership. As you enter the door you can head left to the historic Tap Room, a compact, often-crowded spot filled with the smell of fresh-popped popcorn. (You're better off outside on the brick patio if the weather's good.) Meals here include fare like crab-cake burgers, lobster croissant, and a variety of delectable build-your-own burgers. The other part of the house is the Dining Room, which is rather more formal in a country-colonial sort of way. Meals here are more sedate and gussied up, with dinners like crabmeat-stuffed and baked haddock, apple-mustard chicken, and filet mignon. While not overly creative, the meals in both the Dining Room and Tap Room are well prepared and presented.

BRUNSWICK & BATH

Brunswick and Bath are two exceptionally handsome and historic towns that share a strong commercial past. Today, both are vibrant with commercial activity. Many travelers heading up Route 1 pass through both towns eager to reach the areas with higher billing on the marquee. That's a shame, for both are well worth the detour.

ESSENTIALS

GETTING THERE   Brunswick and Bath are both situated on Route 1. Brunswick is accessible via Exits 22 and 23 off I-95.

VISITOR INFORMATION   The **Bath–Brunswick Region Chamber of Commerce,** 59 Pleasant St., Brunswick, ME 04011 (☎ **207/725-8797** or 207/443-9751), offers information and lodging assistance from its offices near downtown Brunswick. The chamber also staffs an information center on Route 1 just west of Bath.

EXPLORING BRUNSWICK

Brunswick was once home to several mills along the Androscoggin River; these have since been converted to offices and the like, but Brunswick's broad Maine Street still bustles with activity. A number of galleries, shops, and bookstores invite leisurely browsing.

Brunswick is also home to **Bowdoin College,** one of the nation's most respected small colleges. The school was founded in 1794, offered its first classes 8 years later, and has since amassed an illustrious roster of prominent alumni, including Nathaniel Hawthorne, Henry Wadsworth Longfellow, President Franklin Pierce, and arctic explorer Robert E. Peary. Civil War hero Joshua Chamberlain served as president of the college after the war.

A walking tour of the campus is pleasant enough, but be sure to allow time to visit two fine collections.

The **Bowdoin Museum of Art** (☎ 207/725-3275) is housed in a stern, neoclassical building designed by the prominent architectural firm of McKim, Mead & White. While the collections are small, they include a number of exceptionally fine paintings from Europe and America, along with early furniture and artifacts from classical antiquity. The artists include Andrew and N. C. Wyeth, Marsden Hartley, Winslow Homer, and John Singer Sargent. Admission is free and the museum is open Tuesday through Saturday from 10am to 5pm, and on Sunday from 2 to 5pm.

A few seconds' stroll from the art museum is the **Peary-MacMillan Arctic Museum** (☎ 207/725-3416). While Admiral Robert E. Peary (Bowdoin class of 1887) is better known for his accomplishments (he claimed to be the first man to reach the North Pole at age 53 in 1909), Donald MacMillan (class of 1898) also racked up an impressive string of achievements in Arctic research and exploration. You can learn about both men and the wherefores of Arctic exploration in this manageable museum on the Bowdoin campus. The front room includes wildlife from the Arctic, including some impressive stuffed polar bears. A second room outlines Peary's historic 1909 expedition, complete with extensive excerpts from his journal. The last room includes varied displays of Inuit arts and crafts, some historic, some modern. This compact museum can be visited in about 20 minutes or so. Admission is free, and it's open the same hours as the art museum, described above.

MARITIME HISTORY IN BATH

Eight miles to the east of Brunswick is Bath, nicely situated on the broad Kennebec River. It's Maine's premier center of shipbuilding. The first ship ever built in the United States was constructed downstream at the Popham Bay colony in the early 17th century; in the years since, shipbuilders have constructed more than 5,000 vessels in the area.

Bath shipbuilding reached its heyday in the late 19th century, but it continues to this day. Bath Iron Works remains one of the nation's preeminent boatyards, constructing and repairing ships for the U.S. Navy. The scaled-down military has left Bath shipbuilders in a somewhat tenuous state, but it's still common to see the steely gray ships in the dry dock (the best view is from the bridge over the Kennebec), and the towering red-and-white crane moving parts around the yard.

You don't have to be a ship aficionado to enjoy the **Maine Maritime Museum and Shipyard,** 243 Washington St. (☎ 207/443-1316). But those who do have a passion for boats love it here and are hard to drag away. This contemporary museum on the shores of the Kennebec River (it's just south of Bath Iron Works) features a wide array of displays and exhibits related to the boatbuilder's art. The location is appropriate—it's sited at the former shipyard of Percy and Small, which built some 42 schooners in the late 19th and early 20th centuries. Indeed, the largest wooden ship ever built in America—the 329-foot *Wyoming*—was constructed on this lot in 1909. If you snoop around in the reeds, you can even find the ways used in launching the ship.

The centerpiece of the museum is the striking brick Maritime History Building. Here, you'll find changing exhibits of maritime art and artifacts. (There's also a gift shop with a good selection of books.) The 10-acre property houses plenty of additional displays, including an intriguing exhibit on lobstering and a complete boatbuilding shop. Here, you can watch handsome wooden boats take shape in this active program. Kids enjoy the play area (they can search for pirates from the crow's nest of the play boat). Be sure to wander down to the docks on the river to see what's tied up, or to inquire about cruises on the river (extra charge).

Admission is $7.75 for adults, $5 for children 6 to 17, $22 for a family. Open daily from 9:30am to 5pm.

Exploring the Harpswell Peninsula

Extending southwest from Brunswick and Bath is the picturesque Harpswell Peninsula. It's actually three peninsulas, like the tines of a pitchfork, if you include the islands of Orrs and Bailey, which are linked to the mainland by bridges. While close to some of Maine's larger towns (Portland is only 45 minutes away), the Harpswell Peninsula has a remote, historic feel with sudden vistas across meadows to the blue waters of northern Casco Bay.

Toward the southern tips of the peninsulas, the character changes as clusters of colorful Victorian-era summer cottages displace the farmhouses found further inland. Some of these cottages are for rent by the week, but many book up years in advance. Inquire with local real-estate agents if you're interested.

There's no set itinerary for exploring the area. Just drive south until you can't go any farther, then backtrack for a bit and strike south again. Among the "attractions" worth looking for are the wonderful ocean and island views from **South Harpswell** at the tip of the westernmost peninsula (park and wander around for a bit), and the clever **Cobwork Bridge** connecting Bailey and Orrs islands. The humpbacked bridge was built in 1928 of granite blocks stacked in such a way that the strong tides could come and go and not drag the bridge out with it. No cement was used in its construction.

This is a good area for a bowl of chowder or a boiled lobster. One of the best places for chowder off the beaten track is at the down-home **Dolphin Marina** (☎ 207/833-6000) at Basin Point in South Harpswell. (Drive 12.2 miles south of Brunswick on Route 123, turn right at Ash Point Road near the West Harpswell School, then take your next right on Basin Point Road and continue to the end.) Find the boatyard, then wander inside, where you'll discover a tiny counter with seating for six and a handful of pine tables and booths with stunning views of Casco Bay. The fish chowder and lobster stew are reasonably priced and absolutely delicious, and the blueberry muffins are warm and have a crispy crown. The servers appear easily flummoxed, so bring some patience.

For lobster, several sprawling establishments specialize in delivering crustaceans fresh from the sea. On the Bailey Island side there's **Cook's Lobster House** (☎ 207/833-2818), which seats 280 diners and has been serving up a choice of shore dinners, most involving lobster, since 1955. The restaurant has two decks for outdoor dining. Near Harpswell is the **Estes Lobster House** (☎ 207/833-6340), which serves lobster (including an artery-clogging triple lobster plate) amid relaxed, festive surroundings.

Where to Stay

Driftwood Inn & Cottages. Washington Ave., Bailey Island, ME 04003. ☎ **207/833-5461,** or 508/947-1066 off-season. 18 double rms, 9 single rms, 6 cottages (most rms share hallways baths). $45–$50 single; $65–$70 double. Weekly rate $335 per person including breakfast and dinner. Cottages $450–$550 per week. No credit cards. Closed mid-Oct to mid-May.

The ocean-side Driftwood Inn dates back to 1910 and is a coastal New England classic. It isn't for those seeking luxury, but it's an ideal location to if your primary goal is to keep company with the sea. A rustic summer retreat on 3 acres at the end of a dead-end road, the inn is a compound of four weathered, shingled buildings and a handful of housekeeping cottages on a rocky, ocean-side property. The Spartan rooms of time-aged pine have a simple turn-of-the-century flavor that hasn't been gentrified in the least. Most rooms share baths down the hall, but some have private sinks and toilets.

Your primary company will be the constant sound of surf surging in and ebbing out of the fissured rocks. The inn has an old saltwater pool and porches with wicker furniture to while away the afternoons, and roadway walks in the area are pleasant. But I'd advise bringing plenty of books and board games.

The dining room (open late June through Labor Day) serves basic fare in a wonderfully austere setting overlooking the sea; meals are extra, although a weekly American plan is available.

WHERE TO DINE

✪ **Robinhood Free Meetinghouse.** Robinhood Rd., Robinhood. ☎ **207/371-2188.** Reservations recommended. Main courses $16–$21. DISC, MC, V. Summer daily 5:30–9pm; Sun 10am–2pm. Limited hours in winter; call first. FUSION.

This is a bit of a drive from the Harpswell peninsula (it's a couple of peninsulas to the east), but it's worth it. Chef Michael Gagne's menu is huge, featuring more than 30 entrees, and it's wildly eclectic—from Thai grilled vegetables to Wiener schnitzel to salmon en papillote. Remarkably, Gagne rarely serves a mediocre meal. As with the meals, extraordinary attention is paid to detail throughout this historic meetinghouse on a quiet side road. Eating here is not inexpensive, but it tends to be magical and offers tremendous value for the price.

BOOTHBAY HARBOR

Although Boothbay Harbor is 11 miles from Route 1, this small, scenic town exerts an outsized allure on passing tourists, and has become one of the prime destinations of travelers in search of classic coastal Maine. As a result, it's a popular stop for bus tours, and the village has been infiltrated by kitschy shops (T-shirts, stained-glass unicorns) and mediocre restaurants that specialize in fried foods. The harbor is hemmed in somewhat by boxy, bland motels, but there's still an affable charm that manages to rise above the clutter, especially on foggy days when the horns bleat mournfully at the harbor's mouth. And visitors should also find some measure of satisfaction that a nickel will still buy 24 minutes at the town parking meters.

ESSENTIALS

GETTING THERE   Boothbay Harbor is 11 miles south of Route 1 on Route 27. Coming from the west, look for signs shortly after crossing the Sheepscott River at Wiscasset.

VISITOR INFORMATION   There are three visitor information centers in and around town, reflecting the importance to tourism in the region. At the intersection of Route 1 and Route 27 is a new center that's open May through October and is a good place to stock up on brochures. A mile before you reach the village is the seasonal **Boothbay Information Center** on your right (open June to October). If you zoom past it or it's closed, don't fret. The year-round **Boothbay Harbor Region Chamber of Commerce,** P.O. Box 356, Boothbay Harbor, ME 04538 (☎ **207/ 633-2353**), is at the intersection of Routes 27 and 96.

SEEING THE SIGHTS

Boothbay Harbor is ideal for exploring by foot. Pedestrians naturally gravitate to the long, narrow footbridge across the harbor, first built in 1901, but it's more of a destination than a link—other than a few restaurants and motels, there's really not much on the other side. The winding, small streets in town also offer plenty of boutiques and shops that cater to the tourist trade and offer decent browsing.

The most enjoyable way to see the Boothbay region is on a boat tour. Nearly two dozen tour boats berth at the harbor or nearby, offering a range of trips from an hour's tour to a full-day excursion to Monhegan Island. You can even observe **puffins** at their rocky colonies far offshore.

Balmy Day Cruises (☎ 207/633-2284) runs trips to Monhegan Island in the 65-foot *Balmy Days II*, allowing passengers about 4 hours to explore the island before returning (see the "Monhegan Island" section, below). The company also offers harbor tours and 2-hour dinner cruises with onboard dinners of chicken, lobster roll, and lobster. The Monhegan run is $29 ($18 for children), harbor tours are $8.50, and dinner cruises are $22.

Cap'n Fish's Scenic Nature Cruises (☎ 800/636-3244 or 207/633-3244) offers sightseeing trips of 1¼ to 4 hours duration, including puffin and whale watches. The four boats in the fleet each carry between 130 and 150 passengers. The vessels are truly piloted by folks named Capt. Fish—John and Bob Fish, who both hail from a Boothbay family that's long messed around in boats. Prices range from $10 to $25 ($5 to $15 for children).

A short excursion to **Ocean Point** is well worthwhile. Follow Route 96 southward from west of Boothbay Harbor, and you'll pass through East Boothbay before striking toward the point. The narrow road runs through piney forests before arriving at the rocky finger; it's one of the few Maine points with a road around its perimeter, allowing wonderful ocean views. Bunches of colorful Victorian-era summer cottages bloom along the roadside like wildflowers.

WHERE TO STAY

Five Gables Inn. Murray Hill Rd. (P.O. Box 335), E. Boothbay, ME 04544. ☎ **800/451-5048** or 207/633-4551. Web site: www.maineguide.com/boothbay/5gables. 16 rms (12 with shower only). TEL. $90–$160 double. Rates include breakfast buffet. MC, V. Closed Nov to early May. Drive through E. Boothbay on Rte. 96; turn right after crest of hill on Murray Hill Rd. No children under 8.

The 125-year-old Five Gables Inn was painstakingly restored a decade ago, and now sits proudly amid a small colony of summer homes on a quiet road above a peaceful cove. It's nicely isolated from the confusion and hubbub of Boothbay Harbor; the activity of choice here is to sit on the deck and enjoy the glimpses of the water through the trees. It's a good base for biking—you can pedal down to Ocean Point or into town. It's also handy to the Lobsterman's Wharf for good, informal dining. The rooms are pleasantly appointed, and the common room is nicely furnished in an upscale country style. No smoking.

Lawnmeer Inn & Restaurant. Rte. 27, Southport, ME 04576. ☎ **800/633-7645** or 207/633-2544. 32 rms. TV. Summer $88–$168 double; spring and fall from $58 double. MC, V. Closed mid-Oct to mid-May.

The Lawnmeer, a short hop from Boothbay on the northern shore of Southport Island, offers easy access to town and a restful environment. This was originally built as a guest home at the turn of the century, and the main inn has been updated with only a slight loss of charm. More than half of the guest rooms are located in a motel-like annex, which makes up for its lack of character with private balconies offering views of the placid waterway that separates Southport Island from the mainland.

Dining/Entertainment: The locally popular dining room, serving breakfast and dinner, is comfortable and homey, with broad windows overlooking the water. The menu offers contemporary American fare.

Newagen Seaside Inn. Rte. 27 (on the south tip of Southport Island; P.O. Box 68), Cape Newagen, ME 04552. ☎ **800/654-5242** or 207/633-5242. 26 rms (2 with shower only). $100–$175 double. Rates include breakfast. MC, V. Closed late Sept to early June. Take Rte. 27 from Boothbay Harbor and continue on until the inn sign.

This 1940s-era resort has seen more glamorous days, but it's still a superb small, low-key resort offering stunning ocean views and walks in a fragrant spruce forest.

The inn is housed in a low, wide, white-shingled building that's furnished simply with country pine furniture. There's a classically austere dining room, narrow cruise-ship-like hallways with pine wainscoting, and a lobby with a fireplace. The rooms are plain and the inn is a bit threadbare in spots, but never mind that. Guests flock here for the 85-acre ocean-side grounds filled with decks, gazebos, and walkways that border on the magical. It's hard to convey the magnificence of the ocean views, which may be the best of any inn in Maine. No smoking.

Dining/Entertainment: The handsome, simple dining room with ocean views offers a menu with traditional New England fare and some more creative additions.

Facilities: Freshwater and saltwater pools, badminton, shuffleboard, horseshoes, tennis, sundeck, free rowboats.

Spruce Point Inn. Atlantic Ave. (P.O. Box 237), Boothbay Harbor, ME 04538. ☎ **800/553-0289** or 207/633-4152. E-mail: thepoint@sprucepointinn.com. Web site: sprucepointinn.com. 65 rms. TV TEL. July–Aug $264–$396 double; shoulder seasons $190–$296 double. Rates include breakfast and dinner. Ask about packages. 2-night minimum on weekends; 3 nights on holidays. AE, MC, V. Closed mid-Oct to Memorial Day. Turn right on Union St. in Boothbay Harbor; proceed 2 miles to the inn.

The Spruce Point Inn was originally built as a hunting and fishing lodge in the 1890s, and evolved into a summer resort in 1912. After years of quiet neglect, it benefited in the late 1980s from a long-overdue makeover that retained much of the rustic charm—at least in the main lodge. Guests typically fill their time puttering around the inn's 15-acre oceanfront grounds, or idling in the wicker chairs on the porch overlooking the rocky shore.

The eight guest rooms in the venerable, gabled main building are simply furnished and clean, but rather austere and motel-like. Better are the rooms in the outbuildings flanking the lodge. These have a woodsy, country pine feel, and most have private porches with ocean views. If your preference is for modern accommodations, the inn has those as well. The newer "Ocean Houses," built in 1988 in the woods at the back of the property, are contemporary, condominium-like town houses with plenty of amenities (including kitchenettes) but little in the way of native charm. And at press time 16 brand-new deluxe motel-style rooms with ocean views, gas fireplaces, and whirlpools were under construction, replacing two older cottages.

Dining/Entertainment: See "Where to Dine," below.

Services: Concierge, laundry/dry cleaning, in-room massage, baby-sitting, safe, free shuttle bus to Boothbay.

Facilities: Croquet, shuffleboard, two outdoor clay tennis courts, Astroturf putting green, ocean-side saltwater pool, heated freshwater pool, whirlpool, sundeck, conference rooms, self-service Laundromat, game rooms.

Topside. McKown Hill, Boothbay Harbor, ME 04538. ☎ **207/633-5404.** 28 rms (1 with shower only). July 1 through Labor Day $70–$100 double; June and Sept–Oct $75–$95. MC, V. Closed mid-Oct to June.

The looming old gray house on the hilltop above the motel-style building may bring to mind the Bates Motel, especially when a full moon is overhead. But get over that, because Topside offers spectacular ocean views at a good price on its quiet hilltop compound in downtown Boothbay. The inn itself features six comfortable rooms, furnished with a mix of antiques and contemporary furniture. (Some may find the building a bit overly carpeted and wallpapered.) At the edge of the inn's cambered lawn are two outbuildings housing basic motel units, which are simply and basically furnished. Guests return here year after year not for the styling, but for the spectacular ocean views.

WHERE TO DINE

Boothbay Region Lobstermen's Co-op. Atlantic Ave., Boothbay Harbor. ☎ **207/ 633-4900.** Reservations not accepted. Sandwiches $1.25–$8.75; dinners $6.50–$9.95. No credit cards. Daily 11:30am–8:30pm. Closed late Oct to Apr. By foot, cross footbridge and turn right; follow road for ⅓ mile to co-op. SEAFOOD.

WE ARE NOT RESPONSIBLE IF THE SEAGULLS STEAL YOUR FOOD, reads the sign at the ordering window of this casual, harborside lobster joint. And that sets the tone pretty well. Situated across the harbor from downtown Boothbay, the lobstermen's co-op offers no-frills lobster and seafood. You order at a pair of windows, then pick up your meal and carry your tray to either the picnic tables on the dock or inside a garagelike two-story prefab building. Lobsters are priced to market (figure on $8 to $10), with extras like corn on the cob reasonably priced at under a buck. A bank of soda machines provides liquid refreshment for 75¢ a can. This is a fine place for a lobster on sunny day, but it's uninteresting at best in rain or fog.

Lobsterman's Wharf. Rte. 96, E. Boothbay. ☎ **207/633-3443.** Reservations for parties of 6 or more only. Lunch from $4.50; dinner $13.25–$22.95 (mostly $14–$16). AE, MC, V. Open Apr–Oct. SEAFOOD.

Slightly off the beaten path in East Boothbay, the Lobsterman's Wharf has the comfortable, pubby feel of a neighborhood bar, complete with pool table. And that's appropriate, since that's what it is. But it's that rarest of pubs—a place that's popular with the locals, but also one that commands the respect of finicky diners and makes travelers feel at home. If the weather's cooperative, sit at picnic table on the dock, admiring views of a spruce-topped peninsula across the Damariscotta River; you can also grab a table inside amid the festive nautical decor. Entrees include a tasty mixed-seafood grill, a barbecued shrimp and ribs platter, grilled swordfish with béarnaise sauce, and succulent fresh lobster offered four different ways.

✪ Spruce Point Inn. Atlantic Ave., Boothbay Harbor. ☎ **207/633-4152.** Reservations recommended. Main courses $14.75–$24.25. AE, MC, V. Daily 7:30am–9:30am and 6–9pm. Closed mid-Oct to Memorial Day. Turn right on Union St. in Boothbay Harbor; proceed 2 miles to the inn. CONTEMPORARY NEW ENGLAND.

This classic resort dining room is certain to surprise you with its creativity. And what else would you expect from an inn that once won a statewide cooking contest with a recipe for "lobster succotash"? Diners are seated in an elegant, formal dining room—the tables are arrayed with an almost military precision, the maitre d' wears a tux, and men are requested to wear jackets at dinner. Guests enjoy wonderful sunset views across the mouth of Boothbay Harbor as they peruse the menu, which offers an inviting mix of seafood and meat dishes. The lobster spring rolls are terrific for starters. Next, you might opt for the two-texture duck (served with a shiitake and ginger gravy), or shrimp amaretto. If you're not feeling overly adventurous, you can take refuge in the more basic choices, like pork tenderloin, grilled chicken breast, or filet mignon.

MONHEGAN ISLAND

Brawny and remote, Monhegan is Maine's premier island destination. Visited by Europeans as early as 1497 (although some historians insist earlier Norsemen carved primitive runes on neighboring Manana Island), the island was first settled by fishermen attracted to the sea's bounty in the offshore waters.

Starting in the 1870s and continuing to the present day, noted artists discovered the island and came to stay for a spell. These included Rockwell Kent (the artist most closely associated with the island), George Bellows, Edward Hopper, and Robert

Henri. The artists gathered in the kitchen of the lighthouse to chat and drink coffee; it's said that the wife of the lighthouse keeper accumulated a tremendously valuable collection of paintings. Today, Jamie Wyeth, scion of the Wyeth clan, claims the island as his part-time home.

It's not hard to figure why artists have been attracted to the place: There's a mystical quality to it, from the thin light to the startling contrasts of the dark cliffs and the foamy white surf. There's also a remarkable sense of tranquillity to this place, which can only help focus your inner vision.

If you have the time, I'd strongly recommend an overnight on the island at one of the several hostelries. Day trips are popular and affordable, but the island's true character doesn't start to emerge until the last day boat sails away and the quiet, rustic appeal of the island starts to percolate back to the surface.

ESSENTIALS

GETTING THERE   Access to Monhegan Island is via boat from New Harbor, Boothbay Harbor, or Port Clyde.

The hour-and-10-minute trip from Port Clyde is the favored route among longtime island visitors. The trip from this rugged fishing village is very picturesque as it passes the Marshall Point Lighthouse and a series of spruce-clad islands before setting out on the open sea. Two boats now make the run to Monhegan from Port Clyde. The *Laura B.* is a doughty work boat (building supplies and boxes of food are loaded on first; passengers fill in the available niches on the deck and in the small cabin). A new boat—the faster, passenger-oriented *Elizabeth Ann*—now also makes the run, offering a large heated cabin and more seating. You can't bring your car, so pack light and wear sturdy shoes. The fare is $25 round-trip for adults; $12 for children 1 to 12 years old. Reservations are advised; call the **Monhegan Boat Line** at ☎ 207/372-8848. Parking is available near the dock for an additional $4 per day.

VISITOR INFORMATION   Monhegan Island has no formal visitors center, but it's small and friendly enough that you can make inquiries of just about anyone you cross on the island pathways. The clerks at the boat dock in Port Clyde are also quite helpful. Be sure to pick up the inexpensive map of the island's hiking trail at the boat ticket office or at the various shops around the island.

A NOTE ON SMOKING   Because a forest fire could destroy this breezy island in short order, smoking is prohibited outside of the village.

EXPLORING THE ISLAND

Walking is the chief activity on the island, and it's genuinely surprising how much distance you can cover on these 700 acres (about $1\frac{1}{2}$ miles long and half a mile wide). The village clusters tightly around the harbor; the rest of the island is mostly wildland, laced with some 17 miles of trails. Much of the island is ringed along its shoreline with high, open bluffs atop fissured cliffs. Pack a picnic lunch and hike the perimeter trail, and plan to spend much of the day just sitting and reading or enjoying the surf rolling in against the cliffs. During one lazy afternoon on a bluff near the island's southern tip, I spotted a half-dozen whale spouts over the course of a half hour, but never did agree with my friend whether it was one whale or several.

The inland trails are appealing in a far different way. Deep, dark **Cathedral Woods** is mossy and fragrant; sunlight only dimly filters through the evergreens to the forest floor. Look for the small "fairy houses" in the woods; these fanciful structures of twigs, bark, and other forest-floor detritus are crafted by island kids and visitors. You're welcome to build your own, provided you don't use live moss.

Bird-watching is an exceedingly popular activity in the spring and fall. Monhegan Island is on the Atlantic flyway, and a wide variety of birds stop at the island along their migration routes. Bring your binoculars.

The sole attraction on the island is the **Monhegan Museum,** located next to the 1824 lighthouse on a high point above the village. The museum, open from July through September, has an engaging collection of historic artifacts and provides some context for this rugged island's history. (Plans are also in the works for a small and select art museum to open in 1998 near the lighthouse; it's slated to feature works of Rockwell Kent and others.) But the real draw is the spectacular view from the grassy slope in front of the lighthouse. The vista sweeps across a marsh (which seems to attract deer at twilight), past one of the island's most historic hotels, past melancholy Manana Island and across the sea beyond. Get here early if you want a good seat for the **sunset;** it seems most visitors to the island congregate here after dinner to watch the sinking of the sun. (Another popular place is the island's southern tip, where the wreckage of the *D. T. Sheridan,* a coal barge, washed up in 1948.)

One other popular activity is to visit the studios of Monhegan artists, who still gather here in great number. Artists often open their workspaces to visitors during limited hours, and are happy to have people stop by and look at their work, talk with them a bit, and perhaps buy something to bring home. Some of the artwork is predictable seascapes and sunsets, but much of it rises above the banal. Look for the bulletin board along the main pathway in the village for walking directions to the studios and a listing of the days they're open.

WHERE TO STAY & DINE

Monhegan House. Monhegan Island, ME 04852. ☎ **800/599-7983** or 207/594-7983. 32 rms (all with shared bath). $80 double. AE, DISC, MC, V. Closed Columbus Day to Memorial Day.

The handsome Monhegan House has been accommodating guests since 1870, and it has a comfortable, worn patina. The downstairs lobby, with its fireplace, is a welcome spot to sit and take the fog-induced chill out of your bones (even in August it can be cool here). The front deck is a nice place to lounge and keep a close eye on the comings and goings of the village. The accommodations are austere but comfortable; there are no closets, and everyone uses dormitory-style bathrooms down the hall.

The restaurant offers three meals a day, with a selection of filling but simple meat and fish dishes, along with vegetarian entrees. Main courses range in price from about $9 to $16.

Trailing Yew. Monhegan Island, ME 04852. ☎ **207/596-0440.** 37 rms in 4 buildings (1 rm with private bath). $116 double. Rates include breakfast, dinner, taxes, and tips. No credit cards. Closed mid-Oct to mid-May.

At the end of long summer afternoons, guests congregate near the flagpole in front of the main building of this rustic hillside compound. They sit in Adirondack chairs or chat with newfound friends. But mostly they're waiting for the ringing of the bell, which signals them in for dinner, summer camp style. Inside, guests sit around long tables, introduce themselves to their neighbors, then pour an iced tea and wait for the delicious, family-style dinner. (You're given a choice, including vegetarian options, but my advice is to go for the fresh fish.)

The Trailing Yew, which has been taking in guests since 1929, is a friendly, informal place, popular with hikers and bird-watchers (meals are a great time to swap tales of sightings) who tend to make fast friends here. Guest rooms are eclectic and simply furnished in a pleasantly dated summer-home style; only one of the four guest buildings has electricity (although all bathrooms have electricity); guests in rooms without electricity are provided a kerosene lamp and instruction in its use (bring a flashlight just in case).

6   Penobscot Bay

Traveling eastward along the Maine coast, you'll notice around Rockland that you're suddenly heading almost due north. The culprit is Penobscot Bay, a sizable bite out of the Maine coast that forces a northerly detour to cross the head of the bay where the Penobscot River flows in at Bucksport.

You'll find some of Maine's best coastal scenery in this area—spectacular offshore islands, high hills rising above the blue bay, and weathered rocks pounded by the surf. Although the mouth of Penobscot Bay is occupied by two large islands, its waters can still churn with vigor when the seas are running.

The west shore of Penobscot Bay gets a heavy stream of tourist traffic, especially along Route 1 and through the scenic villages of Rockport and Camden. These are good destinations to get a taste of the Maine coast, especially for those in a hurry to get to Acadia National Park. Services for travelers are easy to find, although during the peak season a small miracle will be required to find a weekend guest room without a reservation.

In contrast, the bay's eastern shore, formed by the Blue Hill Peninsula, Cape Rosier, and Deer Isle, is much more remote, laced with shady back roads and dotted with small inns. By and large it's overlooked by most tourists, especially those who get nervous when they find themselves on narrow roads that suddenly dead-end or inexplicably start to loop back on themselves. If you're the sort who enjoys getting a little lost when exploring, the east side of the bay is a superb destination.

ROCKLAND & ENVIRONS

Few visitors refer to Rockland as "quaint." Located on the southwest edge of Penobscot Bay, Rockland has long been proud of its brick and blue-collar waterfront town reputation. Built around the fishing industry, Rockland historically dabbled in tourism on the side. But with the decline of the fisheries and the rise of the tourist economy in Maine, the balance is gradually shifting—Rockland is slowly being colonized by restaurateurs and other small-business folks who are painting it with an unaccustomed gloss.

There's a small park on the waterfront from which the fleet of windjammers comes and goes (see below), but more appealing than Rockland's waterfront is its commercial downtown—it's basically one long street lined with sophisticated historic brick architecture. If it's picturesque harbor towns you're seeking, head to Camden, Rockport, Port Clyde, or Stonington. But Rockland makes a great base for exploring this beautiful coastal region, especially if you have a low tolerance for primness and tourist hordes.

ESSENTIALS

GETTING THERE   Route 1 passes directly through Rockland. During the peak summer season, you can avoid the coastal congestion of Route 1 by taking the Maine Turnpike to Augusta, then heading to Rockland via Route 17.

Rockland's tiny airport is served by **Colgan Air** (☎ **800/272-5488** or 207/596-7604), with daily flights from Boston and Bar Harbor.

VISITOR INFORMATION   The **Rockland/Thomaston Area Chamber of Commerce,** P.O. Box 508, Rockland, ME 04841 (☎ **800/562-2529** or 207/596-0376; E-mail: **rtacc@midcoast.com**), staffs an information desk at Harbor Park. It's open daily from 9am to 5pm in summer, weekdays only the rest of the year.

Penobscot Bay

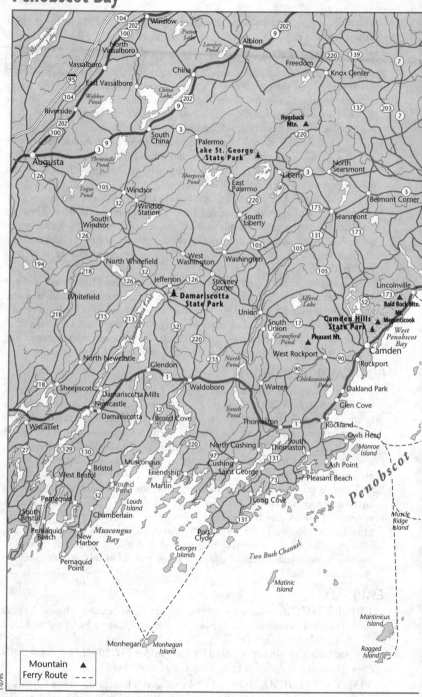

Mountain ▲
Ferry Route - - - -

634

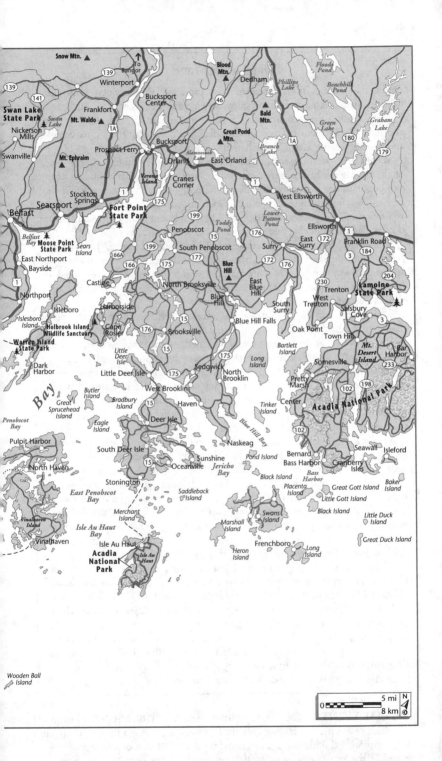

Windjammer Tours

During the long transition from sail to steam, captains of the fancy new steamships belittled the old-fashioned sailing ships as "windjammers." The term stuck, and through a curious metamorphosis the name evolved into a term of adventure and romance. Maine is the capital of windjammer cruising in the United States, and two of the most active Maine harbors are Rockland and Camden.

Windjammer vacations combine adventure with limited creature comforts—sort of like lodging at a backcountry cabin on the water. Guests typically bunk in small two-person cabins, which usually offer cold running water and a porthole to let in fresh air, but not much else. (You'll conclude this isn't like a stay at an inn when you see one ship's brochure boasting "standing headroom in all 15 passenger cabins," and another crowing that all cabins "are at least six feet by eight feet.")

Cruises last from 3 days to a week, during which these handsome, creaky vessels poke around the tidal inlets and small coves that ring beautiful Penobscot Bay. It's a superb way to explore Maine's coast the way it's historically been explored—from the outside looking in. The price runs around $100 per day per person, with modest discounts early and late in the season.

Cruises vary from ship to ship, and from week to week, depending on the inclinations of the captains and the vagaries of the mercurial Maine weather. The "standard" cruise often features a stop at one or more of the myriad spruce-studded Maine islands (perhaps with a clambake on shore), hearty breakfasts enjoyed sitting at a table below decks (or perched cross-legged on the sunny deck), and a palpable sense of maritime history as these handsome ships scud through frothy waters. A windjammer vacation demands you use all your senses, to smell the tang of the salt air, to hear the rhythmic creaking of the masts in the evening, and to feel the frigid ocean waters as you leap in for a bracing dip.

At least a dozen windjammers offer cruises in the Penobscot Bay region during the summer (many migrate south to the Caribbean for the winter). The ships vary widely in size and vintage, and guest accommodations range from cramped and rustic to reasonably spacious and well appointed. Ideally, you'll have a chance to look at a couple of ships to find one that suits you before signing up. If that's not practical, call ahead to the **Maine Windjammer Association** (☎ 800/807-9463) and request a packet of brochures, which allow some comparison shopping. If you're angling for a last-minute cruise, stop by the Chamber of Commerce office at the Rockland waterfront (see above) and ask if any berths are available.

All the commercial windjammers are Coast Guard–inspected and each has unique charms. Among the ships worthy of note are the 40-passenger *Victory Chimes* (☎ **800/745-5651** or 207/594-0755), the largest schooner at 132 feet. The smallest in the fleet is the seven-passenger *Summertime* (☎ **800/562-8290**), a 53-foot schooner based in Rockland. The 26-passenger *J&E Riggin* is captained by a native Maine couple, who provide a lively running commentary on Maine history and lore. And the 31-passenger *Angelique* (☎ **800/282-9989** or 207/236-8873), based in Camden, may be the most handsome ship in the fleet with its dark sails and sleek lines, and features two below-deck hot-water showers.

SPECIAL EVENTS   The **Maine Lobster Festival** (☎ **800/562-2529** or 207/596-0376) takes place at Harbor Park the first weekend in August (plus the preceding Thursday and Friday). Entertainers and vendors of all sorts of Maine products—especially the local crustaceans—fill the waterfront parking lot and attract thousands of festival-goers who enjoy this pleasant event with a sort of buttery bonhomie. The event includes the Maine Sea Goddess Coronation Pageant.

TWO FINE MUSEUMS

Farnsworth Museum. 352 Main St. ☎ **207/596-6457.** Admission $5 adults, $4 seniors, $3 children 8–18. MC, V. Summer Mon–Sat 9am–5pm, Sun noon–5pm. Opening time 1 hr. later in winter. Closed Mon Columbus Day to Memorial Day.

Rockland, for all its rough edges, has long and historic ties to the arts. Noted sculptor Louise Nevelson grew up in Rockland, and in 1935 philanthropist Lucy Farnsworth bequeathed a fortune large enough to establish Rockland's Farnsworth Museum, which has since become one of the most respected small art museums in New England.

Located in the middle of downtown Rockland, the Farnsworth has a compact but superb collection of paintings and sculptures by renowned American artists with some connection to Maine. This includes not only Louise Nevelson and three generations of Wyeths (N. C., Andrew, and Jamie), but Rockwell Kent, Childe Hassam, and Maurice Prendergast. The display space is modern and well designed, and the shows professionally prepared.

The museum is poised for even greater growth. Plans are underway for a new Farnsworth Center for the Wyeth Family in Maine, which will house Andrew and Betsy Wyeth's personal collection of Maine-related art. The center is slated to open in 1998 in the former Pratt Memorial Methodist Church. And in late 1996 a benefactor bought and donated to the museum a sizable abandoned storefront next door. At press time, it was uncertain how the new space will be integrated into the museum.

The Farnsworth also owns two other buildings open to the public. The Farnsworth Homestead, located behind the museum, offers a glimpse into the life of prosperous coastal Victorians. And a 25-minute drive away in the village of Cushing is the Olson House, perhaps Maine's most famous home, immortalized in Andrew Wyeth's noted painting, *Christina's World*. Ask at the museum for directions and information.

Owls Head Transportation Museum. Rte. 73 (3 miles south of Rockland), Owls Head. ☎ **207/594-4418.** Web site: www.midcoast.com/~ohtm. Admission $6 adults, $5 seniors, $4 children 5–12; families $16. Apr–Oct daily 10am–5pm; Nov–Mar Mon–Fri 10am–4pm, Sat–Sun 10am–3pm.

You don't have to be a car or plane nut to enjoy a day at the Owl's Head Transportation Museum, which has an extraordinary collection of cars, motorcycles, bicycles, and planes, nicely displayed in a tidy, hangarlike building at the edge of the Knox County Airport. Look for the beautiful early Harley Davidson, and the sleek Rolls-Royce Phantom dating from 1929. The museum is also a popular destination for hobbyists and tinkerers, who drive and fly their classic vehicles here for frequent weekend rallies in the summer. Call ahead to ask about special events.

WHERE TO STAY

Capt. Lindsey House Inn. 5 Lindsey St., Rockland, ME 04841. ☎ **800/523-2145** or 207/596-7950. Fax 207/236-0585. E-mail: kebarnes@midcoast.com. Web site: http://www.midcoast.com/~kebarnes. 9 rms (7 with shower only). A/C TV TEL. Peak season $95–$160 double; Columbus Day to Memorial Day $65–$110 double. Rates include continental breakfast and afternoon tea. DISC, MC, V.

The very handsome Capt. Lindsey House is a magnificently well-appointed three-story downtown hotel. The solid brick building, located just a couple minutes' walk from the Farnsworth Museum, originally was erected as a hotel in 1835, but went through several subsequent incarnations, including a stint as the headquarters of the Rockland Water Co. (The inn's front desk is where locals once paid their water bills.)

The upstairs rooms are also superbly decorated in a contemporary country style, generally with bold, modern colors and patterns applied to traditional design. Even the smaller rooms (like no. 4) are well done (this one in a sort of steamship nouveau style); the rooms on the third floor all feature yellow pine floors and antique Orientals. All rooms have nice details, like handmade bedspreads, hair dryers, down comforters, and bathrobes.

East Wind Inn. P.O. Box 149, Tenant's Harbor, ME 04860. ☎ **800/241-8439** or 207/372-6366. Fax 207/372-6320. 26 units, 14 with shared bath. Summer $82–$120 double, $150–$260 suite or apt; off-season $55–$99 double. Rates include full breakfast. Drive south on Rte. 131 from Thomaston to Tenant's Harbor; turn left at the post office. AE, DISC, MC, V.

The East Wind Inn manages to attract the corduroyed old-money crowd, even though more than half the guest rooms share baths. How did old money get that way? Evidently through frugality and thrift, and the East Wind's shared bath rates are among the better bargains in the region. The inn itself, formerly a sail loft, is perfectly situated next to the harbor with water views from all rooms and the long porch. It's a classic seaside inn, with busy wallpaper, simple colonial reproduction furniture, and tidy rooms. (The 10 guest rooms across the way at a former sea captain's house have most of the private baths.) The atmosphere is relaxed almost to the point of ennui and the service is very good.

Dining/Entertainment: Meals are served in an Edwardian-era dining room. The menu includes hearty Yankee fare, usually with an ample selection of fresh-caught seafood.

WHERE TO DINE

✪ **Cafe Miranda.** 15 Oak St. ☎ **207/594-2034.** Reservations strongly recommended. Main courses $9.50–$14.50. DISC, MC, V. Tues–Sun 5:30–9:30pm. ECLECTIC/GLOBAL.

Hidden away on a side street, this tiny, contemporary restaurant features a huge menu with big flavors. The fare draws liberally from cuisines from around the world, and given its wide-ranging nature, it comes as something of a surprise that the kitchen can consistently maintain quality. The char-grilled pork and shrimp cakes (served with a ginger, lime, and coconut sauce) are superb. Other creative entrees include barbecued pork ribs with a smoked jalapeño sauce, and Indian almond chicken. While the prices aren't cheap compared to the basic diner fare available in town, Cafe Miranda offers one of the best values for the buck of any restaurant in Maine.

CAMDEN

Camden is quintessential coastal Maine. Set at the foot of the wooded Camden Hills on a picturesque harbor that no Hollywood movie set could improve, this affluent village has attracted the gentry of the Eastern seaboard for more than 100 years. The quirky mansions of the moneyed set still dominate the shady side streets (many have been converted into bed-and-breakfasts), and Camden is possessed of a grace and sophistication that eludes many other coastal towns.

Camden's charms haven't gone unnoticed. The village and the surrounding communities have become a haven for retired U.S. Foreign Service and CIA personnel, and has attracted its share of summering corporate bigwigs, including former Apple Computer CEO John Sculley. (The area seems to be the destination of choice for retired computer executives: the family of Thomas Watson, the former CEO of IBM, has a summer compound just offshore at North Haven.) More recently, the town received an economic injection from the phenomenal growth of MBNA, a national finance company, which has restored historic buildings and contributed significantly to Camden's current prosperity. It also explains the high number of clean-cut young men in white shirts and ties you may see in and around town.

The best way to enjoy Camden is to park your car as soon as you can—which may mean driving a block or two off Route 1. The village is of a perfect scale to reconnoiter on foot, which allows a leisurely browse of the boutiques and galleries. Don't miss the hidden town park (look behind the library), which was designed by the landscape firm of Frederick Law Olmsted, the nation's most lauded landscape architect.

ESSENTIALS

GETTING THERE   Camden is located on Route 1. Coming from the south, travelers can shave a few minutes off their trip by turning left on Route 90, 6 miles past Waldoboro, bypassing Rockland. The most traffic-free route from southern Maine is to Augusta via the Maine Turnpike, then via Route 17 to Route 90 to Route 1.

VISITOR INFORMATION   The **Rockport-Camden-Lincolnville Chamber of Commerce,** P.O. Box 919, Camden, ME 04843 (☎ **800/223-5459** or 207/236-4404; E-mail: **rclchmbr@midcoast.com**), dispenses helpful information from its center at the Public Landing in Camden. The chamber is open year-round weekdays from 9am to 5pm and Saturdays from 10am to 5pm. In summer, it's also open Sundays from noon to 4pm. For information on the Web, head to **www.midcoast.com/~rclchmbr**.

EXPLORING CAMDEN

Camden Hills State Park (☎ **207/236-3109**) is nicely situated about a mile north of the village center on Route 1. This 6,500-acre park features an ocean-side picnic area, camping at 112 sites, a winding toll road up 800-foot Mount Battie (with spectacular views from the summit), and a variety of well-marked hiking trails. There's a day-use fee to enter the park.

One easy **hike** I'd recommend strongly is an ascent to the ledges of **Mount Megunticook,** preferably early in the morning before the crowds have amassed and when the mist still lingers in the valleys. Leave from near the campground and follow the well-maintained trail to these open ledges, which requires only about 30 to 45 minutes' exertion. Spectacular, improbable views of the harbor await, as well as glimpses inland to the gentle valleys. Depending on your stamina and desires, you can continue on the park's trail network to Mount Battie, or into the less trammeled woodlands on the east side of the Camden Hills.

For a view from the water back to the hills, **Maine Sports Outfitters** (☎ **800/722-0826** or 207/236-8797) offers **sea-kayaking tours** of Camden's scenic harbor. The standard tour lasts 2 hours and costs $30, and takes paddlers out to Curtis Island at the outer edge of the harbor. This is an easy, delightful way to get a taste of the area's maritime culture. Longer trips in the area and instruction are also available. The outfitter's main shop, located on Route 1 in Rockport, has a good selection of outdoor gear and is worth a stop for outdoor enthusiasts gearing up for local adventures or heading on to Acadia.

What to do in the evening? Besides quaffing a pint at the Sea Dog Brewing Co. (see below), you might take in a foreign or art film at the **Bayview Street Cinema,** 10 Bayview St., on the second floor (☎ **207/236-8722**), a short stroll from Camden's main intersection. The theater boasts a superb sound system, and there's an excellent lineup of frequently changing films throughout the year.

WHERE TO STAY

Camden vies with Kennebunkport and Manchester, Vt., for the title of bed-and-breakfast capital of New England. They're everywhere. Route 1 north of the village center—locally called High Street—is a virtual bed-and-breakfast alley, with many handsome homes converted to lodging. Others are tucked on side streets. (*One note:*

High Street is thick with cars and RVs during the summer months, and you may find the steady hum of traffic diminishes the small-town charm of the establishments that flank this otherwise stately, shady road.)

Despite the preponderance of B&Bs, the total number of guest rooms is fairly limited, and during peak season lodging is tight. It's best to reserve well in advance. You might also try **Camden Accommodations and Reservations** (☎ **800/236-1920**), which offers assistance with everything from booking rooms at resorts to finding cottages for seasonal rental.

If the inns and B&Bs listed below are booked up or too pricey, a handful of motels and hotels may be able to accommodate you. On Route 1 north of town, there's the **Lighthouse Motel** (☎ **207/236-2758**) and the **Mount Battie Motel** (☎ **800/ 224-3870**). A bit closer to the village center are the **Cedar Crest Motel,** 115 Elm St. (☎ **207/236-4839**), and the **Towne Motel,** 68 Elm St. (☎ **207/236-3377**). And right in town, just across the footbridge, is the modern **Camden Riverhouse Hotel,** 11 Tannery Lane (☎ **800/755-7483** or 207/236-0500).

The Belmont. 6 Belmont St., Camden, ME 04843. ☎ **800/238-8053** or 207/236-8053. E-mail: foodeez@midcoast.com. 6 rms (2 with shower only). $260–$360 double. Rates include 2 nights accommodation, 1 dinner, 2 breakfasts. 2-night minimum. MC, V. Closed Nov–Apr. Coming from the south on Rte. 1: Turn right at first stop sign in Camden; continue straight for 1 block; inn is on your left. From the north: After passing through town on Rte. 1, turn left at blinking yellow light; continue straight for 1 block; inn is on your left.

The Belmont is in a handsome, shingle-style 1890s home set in a quiet residential neighborhood of unpretentious homes. Step inside, though, and you're instantly transported to world of elegance and repose. The Belmont has a strong sense of understated style throughout. All the guest rooms are nicely furnished with eclectic antiques and have polished wood floors; the simplicity lets this house of clean, uncluttered lines speak for itself. Downstairs there's an elegant common room with a fireplace alcove and two built-in benches; adjacent is a cozy bar. Smoking is restricted to the bar and parlor.

Dining/Entertainment: The dining room (open to the public) seats about 50, with diners choosing from a plum-carpeted main room, or a sunporch with wood floors and contemporary sculpture. The meals are among Camden's finest, with the menu changing weekly. A typical meal around foliage time might include late summer squash stew in a coconut-and-curry broth, or veal loin with wild mushrooms. The dining room is open Thursday to Tuesday in season from 6 to 9pm. Entrees are $16 to $28, and reservations are encouraged.

Inn at Sunrise Point. Rte. 1 (P.O. Box 1344), Camden, ME 04843. ☎ **800/435-6278** or 207/236-7716. Fax 207/236-7716. 7 rms (4 in cottages). TV TEL. $160–$325 double. Rates include full breakfast. AE, MC, V. Closed Nov–Apr.

This peaceful, private sanctuary 4 miles north of Camden Harbor seems a world away from the bustling town. The service is crisp and helpful, and the setting can't be beat. Situated on the edge of Penobscot Bay down a long, tree-lined gravel road, the Inn at Sunrise Point consists of a cluster of contemporary but classic shingled buildings set amid a nicely landscaped yard full of birches. The predominant sounds here are of birds and waves lapping at the cobblestone shore. A granite bench and Adirondack chairs are arrayed on the front lawn to allow guests to enjoy the bay view; breakfasts are served in a sunny conservatory. The guest rooms are spacious and comfortable and full of amenities, including VCRs (for those rainy days) and individual heat controls. The cottages are at the deluxe end of the scale, and all feature double Jacuzzis, fireplaces, wet bars, and private decks. No smoking.

✪ **Maine Stay.** 22 High St., Camden, ME 04843. ☎ **207/236-9636.** E-mail: mainstay@midcoast.com. Web site: www.distinctiveinns.com/mnsty. 8 rms (6 with private bath; 5 with shower only). $80–$135 double. Rates include breakfast. Discounts available off-season. AE, MC, V. No children under 10.

The Maine Stay is Camden's premier B&B. Located in a home dating to 1802 but expanded in Greek Revival style in 1840, the Maine Stay is a classic slate-roofed New England homestead set in a shady yard within walking distance of both downtown and Camden Hills State Park. The eight guest rooms on three floors all have ceiling fans and are distinctively furnished with antiques and special decorative touches. My favorite: the new downstairs Carriage House Room, which is away from the buzz of traffic on Route 1 and boasts its own stone patio.

The three downstairs common rooms are perfect for unwinding, and the country kitchen is open to guests at all times. Breakfast is served in a country pine dining room, or, when the weather permits, on a deck overlooking the landscaped backyard. Hikers can set out on trails right from the yard into the Camden Hills. No smoking.

✪ **Norumbega.** 61 High St., Camden, ME 04843. ☎ **207/236-4646.** Fax 207/236-0824. E-mail: norumbeg@acadia.net. Web site: www.acadia.net/norumbega. 12 rms (4 with shower only). TV TEL. July to mid-Oct $195–$450 double; mid-May to June and late Oct $165–$375 double; Nov to mid-May $135–$295 double. Rates include full breakfast and evening refreshments. AE, DISC, MC, V.

You'll have no problem finding Norumbega. Just head north of the village and look for cars pulled over so their occupants can take photos of this Victorian-era stone castle overlooking the bay. One of the priciest inns in the state, Norumbega is the natural habitat of high-powered businessmen of a certain age. And it's no wonder they're attracted here. The 1886 structure is both wonderfully eccentric and finely built, full of wondrous curves and angles throughout. There's extravagant carved oak woodwork in the lobby, and a stunning oak and mahogany inlaid floor. The downstairs billiards room is the place to pretend you're a 19th-century railroad baron. (Or an information-age baron—the home was owned for a time by Hodding Carter III.) The guest rooms have been meticulously restored and furnished with antiques. Five of the rooms have fireplaces, and the three "garden-level rooms" (they're off the downstairs billiards room) have private decks. The inn is big enough to ensure privacy, but also intimate enough to get to know the other guests—mingling often occurs at breakfast, at the optional evening social hour, and in the afternoon, when the inn puts out its famous fresh-baked cookies.

The Spouter Inn. Rte. 1 (P.O. Box 270), Linconville Beach, ME 04849. ☎ **207/789-5171.** E-mail: terrapin@tidewater.com. 7 rms (2 with shower only). A/C. Summer and early fall $85–$185 double; off-season $75–$135 double. Rates include full breakfast. 2-night minimum stay July–Aug. AE, DISC, MC, V. No children under 7.

The Spouter Inn is situated about 5 miles north of Camden in Lincolnville Beach, just far enough from the congestion to imbue your stay with a slower pace. This elegantly restored 1832 farmhouse is also within walking distance of everything there is to do in Lincolnville (which is blessedly little). You can loll around on the beach across the road, enjoy a lobster at a nearby restaurant, or rent a bike from the inn ($15 per day) and grab the ferry to the gracious island of Islesboro for an afternoon adventure.

The rooms are furnished in a light country style. All have at least glimpses of the water; some have full-blown views and decks. Among the best rooms are the two suites, both of which feature Jacuzzis, decks, and plenty of space. The 1995 addition, with three new guest rooms, blends well inside and out with the rest of the inn, and all units have great bay views and wood-burning fireplaces. No smoking.

Whitehall Inn. 52 High St., Camden, ME 04843. ☎ **800/789-6565** or 207/236-3391. Web site: www.whitehallinn.com. 50 rms, including 10 rms across the street in 2 cottages (6 rms with shared bath). TV TEL. July to late Oct $130–$145 double; late May to June $90–$110 double. Rates include breakfast. AE, MC, V. Closed Nov to mid-May.

The Whitehall is a venerable Camden establishment, the sort of place where you half expect to find Cary Grant in a blue blazer tickling the ivories on the 1904 Steinway in the lobby. Set at the edge of town on Route 1 in a structure that dates to 1834, this three-story inn has a striking architectural integrity with its columns, gables, and long roofline. This is the place you think of when you try to picture the time-worn New England summer inn.

Inside, the antique furnishings—including the handsome Seth Thomas clock, Oriental carpets, and cane-seated rockers on the front porch—are impeccably well cared for. Guest rooms are simple but appealing, and feature rotary dial phones that will provoke nostalgia in older visitors and mild befuddlement among younger guests. The Whitehall also occupies a minor footnote in the annals of American literature— a young local poet recited her poems here for guests in 1912, stunning the audience with her eloquence. Her name? Edna St. Vincent Millay.

Dining/Entertainment: The Whitehall's dining room boasts a slightly faded glory and service that occasionally limps along. But it remains a good destination for reliable American fare like veal with sweet vermouth, sage, and prosciutto; or baked haddock stuffed with Maine shrimp. Entrees are $14.75 to $17.50. And, of course, there's always boiled Maine lobster.

WHERE TO DINE

Frogwater Cafe. 31 Elm St. ☎ **207/236-8998.** Main courses $8–$15. MC, V. Tues–Sun 5–9:30pm (slightly later on weekends). BISTRO.

The Frogwater is cozy and comfortable if a little generic, with blond wood, pine wainscoting, laminate tables, and blue-gray industrial carpeting. The meals are well above average, however, and range from down-home (twice-cooked spaghetti cake or double hamburgers) to borderline elegant (oven-roasted lamb chops). The meats are smoked by the chef; the wild-mushroom ravioli is especially delectable.

Sea Dog Brewing Co. 43 Mechanic St. (at Knox Mill, 1 block west of Elm St.). ☎ **207/ 236-6863.** Reservations not accepted. Main courses $6.95–$10.95. AE, DISC, MC, V. Daily 11:30am–3pm and 5–9pm. PUB FARE.

The Sea Dog Brewing Co. is one of a handful of brew pubs that have found instant success in Maine, and it makes a decent destination for quick and reliable pub food like nachos or hamburgers. It won't set your taste buds to dancing, but it will satisfy basic cravings.

Located in the ground floor of an old woolen mill that's been renovated by MBNA, a national credit-card company, the restaurant has a pleasing pub atmosphere that, save for the waterfall outside the windows, could be anywhere—maybe the Midwest, maybe a mall. While not original, the place is comfortable, with its booths, wooden chairs and tables, a handsome bar, and views through tall windows of the old millrace. And the beers are uniformly excellent, although some suffer from a regrettable cuteness in naming (for example, Old Gollywobbler Brown Ale).

BELFAST TO BUCKSPORT

This region was once famed for its fine shipbuilding. In the mid-19th century, Belfast and Searsport produced more than their share of ships and the captains to pilot them on trading ventures around the globe. In the last century, the now quiet village of Searsport had 17 active shipyards that turned out some 200 ships. In 1856 alone, 24 ships of more than 1,000 tons each were launched from Belfast.

You can learn about that salty heritage at the **Penobscot Marine Museum** (☎ 207/548-2529), one of the best small museums in New England. Housed in a cluster of eight historic buildings atop a gentle rise in tiny downtown Searsport, the museum does a deft job of educating visitors about the vitality of the local shipbuilding industry, the essential role of international trade to daily life in the 19th century, and the hazards of life at sea. The exhibits are uniformly well organized, and wandering from building to building induces a keen sense of wonderment at the vast enterprise that was Maine's maritime trade.

The museum is just off Route 1 at Church Street. It's open from Memorial Day through mid-October, Monday to Saturday from 10am to 5pm and Sunday from noon to 5pm. Admission is $5 for adults, $4 for seniors, $2 for children 7 to 15.

Another appealing detour is aboard the scenic **Belfast and Moosehead Lake Railroad** (☎ 800/392-5500 or 207/948-5500), which departs from both downtown Belfast and the inland town of Unity. The railroad was chartered in 1867 and financed primarily by the town; in fact, until 1991, the B&ML railroad remained the only railroad in the nation owned by a municipality. The rail line was purchased by entrepreneurs, who have spruced it up considerably. In 1995, the company acquired 11 vintage rail cars from Sweden, including a 1913 steam locomotive, and opened the new station in Unity, near the end of the 33-mile-long line.

The 1½-hour tour offers a wonderful glimpse of inland Maine and its thick forests and rich farmland. (The train also edges along Passagassawakeag River, a name which provokes considerable amusement among all but the most melancholy of children.) The train features a dining car, where beer and wine may be purchased, and entertainment in the form of a holdup by some unsavory desperadoes known as the Waldo Station Gang. An optional tour of northern Penobscot Bay on a handsome riverboat can also be packaged with the train excursions.

The trains run twice daily from mid-May to the end of October. Fare is $14 for adults, $7 for the first child (ages 3–16), and $3.50 for each additional child.

WHERE TO DINE

When you first pull into the dirt parking lot at **Young's Lobster Pound** (☎ 207/338-1160), you'll gaze upon an unlovely red corrugated industrial building on the East Belfast waterfront and think: "There must be some mistake." This doesn't look like a restaurant at all. But head inside the hangar-sized door, and you'll find a counter where cordial folks will take your order amid the long, green lobster tanks loudly gushing water. After placing your order, scope out the operation then stake out a seat. You can eat upstairs, where picnic tables are arrayed in an open, barnlike area, or out on the deck, with views across the river to Belfast. This is a place to get good and messy without embarrassment. While you can order from a variety of dishes, the smart money sticks to the shore dinners and steers away from the stews, which are a bit bland and thin.

It's open April through November daily until 8pm (7pm in the slower seasons). From Belfast, take Route 1 east across the river; take the next right on Mitchell Avenue after Perry's Nut House; follow the road to water. No credit cards are accepted.

CASTINE & ENVIRONS

If I had to choose the most graceful village in Maine, I would without hesitation choose Castine.

It's not so much the stunningly handsome mid-19th-century homes that fill the side streets, virtually all of which are meticulously maintained. Nor is it the location on a quiet peninsula, 16 miles south of tourist-jammed Route 1. No, what lends Castine most of its charm are the splendid, towering elm trees, which still overarch many of the village streets. Before Dutch elm disease, much of America once looked like this, and it's easy to slip into a profound nostalgia for this most graceful of trees, even if you're too young to remember the elms of America. Through perseverance and a measure of luck, Castine has managed to keep its elms alive, and it's worth the drive here for this alone.

For American history buffs, Castine offers more than trees. This outpost served as a strategic town in various battles between the British, Dutch, French, and feisty colonials in the centuries after it was settled in 1613. It was occupied by all of them at some point, and historical personages like Miles Standish and Paul Revere passed through during one epoch or another. (Paul Revere, in one of his less heroic feats, was involved in the horrendous loss of 44 American ships during the Revolution, a setback that came after a failed colonial attack on British-held Castine.) The town has a dignified, aristocratic bearing, and it somehow seems appropriate that Tory-dominated Castine welcomed the British with open arms during the Revolution.

ESSENTIALS

GETTING THERE   Castine is located 16 miles south of Route 1. Turn south on Route 175 in Orland (east of Bucksport) and follow this to Route 166, which winds its way to Castine. Route 166A offers an alternate route along Penobscot Bay.

VISITOR INFORMATION   Castine lacks a formal information center, but the clerk at the **Town Office** (☎ **207/326-4502**) is often helpful with travel questions.

EXPLORING THE TOWN

An excellent brief history of Castine by Elizabeth J. Duff is published in brochure form by the Castine Merchant's Association. The brochure, which includes a walking tour of Castine, is entitled *Welcome to Castine* and is available widely at shops in town and at the state information centers.

Castine is also home to the Maine Maritime Academy, which trains sailors for the rigors of life at sea with the merchant marine. The campus is on the western edge of the village, and its hulking gray training ship is often docked in Castine, threatening to overwhelm the village with its sheer size. Tours of the ship are offered in summer.

One of the town's more intriguing attractions is the small **Wilson Museum,** on Perkins Street (during the day, call ☎ **207/326-8753,** or, from 5 to 9pm, call the curator at ☎ **207/326-8545**), an attractive and quirky anthropological museum that contains the collections of John Howard Wilson, an archaeologist and collector of prehistoric artifacts from around the globe. Don't miss the display of summer and winter hearses, or the Early American kitchen. The museum is open from the end of May through September, Tuesday through Sunday from 2 to 5pm, and admission is free.

WHERE TO STAY

Castine Inn. Main St. (P.O. Box 41), Castine, ME 04421. ☎ **207/326-4365.** Fax 207/326-4570. 20 rms (some with shower only). $85–$135 double. Rates include full breakfast. MC, V. Closed mid-Dec to May. No children under 5.

The Castine Inn is a Maine Coast rarity—a hotel that was originally built as a hotel (not as a residence), in this case in 1898. This handsome cream-colored village inn, designed in an eclectic Georgian-Federal revival style, has a fine front porch and attractive gardens. Inside, the lobby takes its cue from the 1940s, with wingback chairs and love seats, and a fireplace in the parlor. The guest rooms on the two upper floors are attractively if unevenly furnished in Early American style—some aren't much of an improvement over standard motel rooms, but others are graciously appointed with antiques. Likewise, some rooms feature glimpses of the harbor, while others don't, so ask to see your room before you sign in. No smoking.

Dining/Entertainment: The elegant dining room, with its heavy wooden chairs and rustic wraparound mural, serves the best fare in town. The chef emphasizes regional dishes like rabbit, scallops, and salmon, and adds a deft global spin with often exotic ingredients. Entrees range from $15 to $26. There's also an intimate, dark lounge decked out in rich green hues, reminiscent of an Irish pub.

Pentagöet Inn. Main St. (P.O. Box 4), Castine, ME 04421. ☎ **800/845-1701** or 207/ 326-8616. 16 rms (7 with showers only). $95–$125 double. Rates include full breakfast. MC, V. Closed last week of Oct to mid-May. No children under 12.

Here's the big activity at the Pentagöet: Sit on the wraparound front porch on cane-seated rockers and watch Castine go by. That's not overly appealing to those looking for a fast-paced vacation, but it's the perfect salve for someone seeking respite from urban chaos. This quirky yellow and green 1894 structure with its prominent turret is tastefully furnished downstairs with hardwood floors, oval braided rugs, and a woodstove. It's comfortable without being overly elegant, professional without being chilly, personal without being too intimate. The rooms on the upper two floors of the main house are furnished eclectically, with a mix of antiques and old collectibles. The five guest rooms in the adjacent Perkins Street building—a more austere Federal-era house—are furnished simply and feature painted floors. There's no air-conditioning, but all rooms have ceiling or window fans. No smoking.

DEER ISLE

Deer Isle is well off the beaten path, but worth the long detour off Route 1 if your tastes run to pastoral countryside with a nautical edge. Loopy, winding roads cross through forest and farmland, and travelers are rewarded with sudden glimpses of the azure ocean and mint green coves. An occasional settlement crops up now and again.

Deer Isle doesn't cater exclusively to tourists. It's still occupied by fifth-generation fishermen, farmers, longtime rusticators, and artists who prize their seclusion. The village of Deer Isle has a handful of inns and galleries, but its primary focus is to serve locals and summer residents, not transients. The village of Stonington, on the southern tip, is a rough-hewn sea town that's still dominated by fishermen and the occasional quarry worker.

ESSENTIALS

GETTING THERE Deer Isle is accessible via several winding country roads from Route 1. Coming from the west, head south on Route 175 off Route 1 in Orland, then connect to Route 15 to Deer Isle. From the east, head south on Route 172 to Blue Hill, where you can pick up Route 15. Deer Isle is connected to the mainland via a high, narrow, and graceful suspension bridge, built in 1938, which can be somewhat harrowing to cross in high winds.

VISITOR INFORMATION The **Deer Isle–Stonington Chamber of Commerce** staffs a seasonal information booth just beyond the bridge on Little Deer Isle. The booth is open daily in summer from 10am to 4pm, depending on volunteer availability.

Sea Kayaking & Camping Along "Merchant's Row"

Peer southward from Stonington and you'll see dozens of spruce-studded islands between here and the dark, foreboding ridges of Isle au Haut. These islands, ringed with salmon pink granite, are collectively called Merchant's Row, and they're invariably ranked by experienced coastal boaters as among the most beautiful in the state. Thanks to these exceptional islands, Stonington is among Maine's most popular destinations for sea kayaking. Many of the islands are open to day visitors and overnight camping, and one of the Nature Conservancy islands even hosts a flock of sheep.

Experienced kayakers should contact the **Maine Island Trail Association** (☎ 207/761-8225) for more information about paddling here; several of the islands are open only to association members. Aspiring kayakers who lack seafaring experience should sign up for a guided trip. No outfitter is currently based in Stonington (they've come and gone in the past), but several Maine-based outfitters lead multiday camping trips to Merchant's Row and Isle au Haut. Contact **Maine Sports Outfitters** (☎ 207/236-8797) or **The Phoenix Centre** (☎ 207/374-2113).

EXPLORING DEER ISLE

Deer Isle, with its network of narrow roads to nowhere, is ideal for perfunctory rambling. It's a pleasure to explore by car, and is also inviting to travel by bike, although hasty and careening fishermen in pickups can sometimes be a bit unnerving. Especially tranquil is the narrow road between Deer Isle and Sunshine to the east. Plan to stop and explore the rocky coves and inlets along the way. To get here, head toward Stonington on Route 15 and just south of the village of Deer Isle, turn east toward Stinson Neck and continue along this scenic byway for about 10 miles over bridges and causeways.

Along this road, be sure to visit the **Haystack Mountain School of Crafts** (☎ 207/348-2306). The campus of this respected summer crafts school is visually stunning. Designed in the early 1960s by Edward Larrabee Barnes, the campus is set on a steep hillside overlooking the cerulean waters of Jericho Bay. Barnes cleverly managed to play up the views while respecting the delicate landscape by building a series of small buildings on pilings that seem to float above the earth. The classrooms and studios are linked by boardwalks, many of which are connected to a wide central staircase, ending at the "Flag Deck," a sort of common area just above the shoreline. The buildings and classrooms are closed to the public, but visitors are welcome to walk to the Flag Deck and stop by the college store, which sells art supplies and craft books. There's also one public tour weekly, which offers glimpses of the studios. Call for information.

Stonington, at the very southern tip of Deer Isle, consists of one commercial street that wraps along the harbor's edge. While a handful of bed-and-breakfasts and galleries have established themselves here, it's still a rough-and-tumble waterfront town with strong links to the sea, and you're likely to observe lots of activity in the harbor as lobstermen and urchin divers come and go. If you hear industrial sounds emanating from just offshore, that's probably the stone quarry on Crotch Island, which has been supplying architectural granite to builders nationwide for more than a century. You can learn more about the stone industry at the new **Deer Isle Granite Museum** on Main Street; it was slated to open in June 1997.

A DAY TRIP TO ISLE AU HAUT

Rocky and remote Isle au Haut offers the most unique hiking and camping experience in northern New England. This 6-by-3-mile island, located 6 miles south of Stonington, was originally named Ille Haut—or High Island—in 1604 by French explorer Samuel de Champlain. The name and its pronunciation evolved—today, it's generally pronounced "aisle-a-ho"—but the island itself has remained steadfastly unchanged over the centuries.

About half of the island is owned by the National Park Service and maintained as an outpost of Acadia National Park (see section 7 of this chapter). A 60-passenger "mailboat" make stops in the morning and late afternoon at Duck Harbor, allowing for a solid day of hiking while still returning to Stonington by nightfall. At Duck Harbor the NPS also maintains a cluster of five Adirondack-style lean-tos, which are available for overnight camping. Advance reservations are essential. Contact **Acadia National Park,** Bar Harbor, ME 04609, or call ☎ **207/288-3338.**

A network of superb hiking trails radiates out from Duck Harbor. Be sure to ascend the island's highest point, 543-foot Duck Harbor Mountain, for exceptional views of the Camden Hills to the west and Mount Desert Island to the east. Nor should you miss the Cliff or Western Head trails, which track along high, rocky bluffs and coastal outcroppings capped with damp, tangled fog forests of spruce. The trails periodically descend down to cobblestone coves, which issue forth with a deep rumble with every incoming wave. A hand-pump near Duck Harbor provides drinking water, but be sure to bring food and refreshments for hiking.

The other half of the island is privately owned, some by fishermen who can trace their island ancestry back 3 centuries, and some by summer rusticators, whose forebears discovered the bucolic splendor of Isle au Haut in the 1880s. The summer population of the island is about 300, with about 50 die-hards remaining year-round. The mailboat also stops at the small harborside village, which has a few old homes, a handsome church, and tiny schoolhouse, post office, and store. Day-trippers will be better served ferrying straight to Duck Harbor.

The **mailboat** (☎ **207/367-5193**) to Isle au Haut leaves from Stonington. In summer, the *Miss Lizzie* departs for the village of Isle au Haut daily at 7 and 11am; the *Mink* departs for Duck Harbor daily at 10am. The round-trip boat fare is $18 for adults to either the village or Duck Harbor. Children under 12 are charged half-price. Reservations are not accepted, but surprisingly few passengers are turned away, even in midsummer.

WHERE TO STAY

Goose Cove Lodge. Goose Cove Rd (P.O. Box 40), Sunset, ME 04683. ☎ **207/348-2508.** Fax 207/348-2624. E-mail: goosecove@hypernet.com. 23 rms (some with shower only). High season $179–$260 double including breakfast and dinner; low season $90–$170 double including full breakfast. 1-week minimum stay July–Aug (Sat–Sat). MC, V. Closed mid-Oct to mid-May.

Goose Cove Lodge, a rustic compound adjacent to a nature preserve on a remote coastal point, is a superb destination for families. Exploring the grounds offers an adventure every day. You can stroll out at low tide to salty Barred Island, or take a guided nature hike on the five trails. You can mess around in boats in the cove (the inn has both kayaks and canoes), or borrow one of the inn's bikes for an excursion. When fog or rain puts a damper on things, curl up with a book in front of a fireplace. (Twenty of the rooms offer fireplaces or Franklin stoves.) And parents take note: Every evening from 5:30 to 8 there's a supervised children's program, which includes dinner (in a separate dining room) and a playtime overseen by counselors, offering some quiet time for you during dinner.

The rooms are divided among cottages, most of which have ocean views, and two annex buildings. The nicest rooms are in the annex off the main lodge, but all are furnished adequately if simply.

Dining/Entertainment: Each evening begins with a cocktail hour at 5:30 in the lodge, followed by a single seating at 6:30 for dinner. The maple-floored dining room wraps in a semicircle around the living room, and guests dine while enjoying great views of the cove and distant islands while swapping information on the day's adventures (guests are often seated family style with other guests). There's always a vegetarian option at dinner, along with one or two other entrees, like pecan-crusted chicken with a pesto broth. Fridays feature a lobster bake on the beach (weather permitting). The dining room is also open to the public as space permits, with reservations essential (fixed price $30; Sunday $25).

Inn on the Harbor. Main St. (P.O. Box 69), Stonington, ME 04681. ☎ **800/942-2420** or 207/367-2420. Fax 207/367-2420. 13 rms (2 with shower only), suite. $100–$125 double. Rates include continental breakfast. AE, CB, DC, DISC, MC, V. Closed Jan to early Apr. No children under 12.

This quirky waterfront inn benefited from a major overhaul between 1995 and 1997. In its former incarnation as The Captain's Quarters, the inn had the indisputably best location in town—perched over the tidal harbor smack in the middle of town. (The location was made all the more desirable since the harbor was cleaned up a few years ago.) The old inn was funky, with small rooms and 1970s-era furnishings. Under new management, the rooms have been enlarged (with the loss of several rooms) and nicely appointed with antiques and sisal carpets. Yet, with its warrens spread about a handful of buildings, and the spacious wooden deck overlooking the harbor, the place still retains an unconventional charm. This is a great location for resting up before or after a kayak expedition, or for making a day trip out to Isle au Haut. A few details: Smoking is permitted only on the outside deck. All rooms except the suite, located across town, feature in-room phones. Because of the decks over the water, the inn is recommended primarily for children 12 and over.

Pilgrim's Inn. Deer Isle, ME 04627. ☎ **207/348-6615.** 13 rms, 2 cottages (10 rms with private bath, 5 with shower only). $150–$175 double, $135–$205 cottage. Rates include breakfast and dinner. $10 surcharge July–Aug. MC, V. Closed mid-Oct to mid-May.

Set between an open bay and a millpond, the Pilgrim's Inn is a historic, handsomely renovated inn in a lovely setting. It's the best choice for high-end lodging on Deer Isle. This four-story, gambrel-roofed structure will especially appeal to those intrigued by Early American history. (Two nearby cottages are also available.) The inn was built in 1793 by Ignatius Haskell, a prosperous sawmill owner. His granddaughter opened the home to boarders, and it's been housing summer guests ever since. The interior is tastefully decorated in a style that's informed by Early Americana, but not beholden to historical authenticity. The guest rooms are well appointed with antiques and painted in muted colonial colors; especially intriguing are the rooms on the top floor with impressive diagonal beams. Activities here include strolling around the village, using the inn's bikes to explore (free), and setting off on scenic drives. No smoking.

Dining/Entertainment: Dinners start with cocktails and hors d'oeuvres in the common room at 6pm, followed by one seating at 7pm in the adjacent barn dining room. Only one entree is served, but it's not likely to disappoint. You might feast on tenderloin of beef with lobster risotto, or a bouillabaisse made of locally caught seafood. Dinner is open to the public by reservation at a fixed price of $29.50. Credit cards are not accepted at the restaurant.

WHERE TO DINE

For fine dining, head to the Pilgrim's Inn (see above). For more basic fare, see below.

Fisherman's Friend. School St. (up the hill from the harbor past the Opera House), Stonington. ☎ **207/367-2442.** Reservations recommended peak season and weekends. Sandwiches $1–$5.95; main dinner courses $6.95–$14.50. No credit cards. Daily 11am–9pm. Closed Dec–Feb. SEAFOOD.

One of the paradoxical attractions of Stonington is that it lacks a single restaurant catering to tourists. The eating houses are for locals, and tourists are welcome only as long as they mind their manners. This seems especially true with Fisherman's Friend, located slightly inland and above the Stonington waterfront. This lively, boisterous restaurant is usually as crowded as it is unpretentious. Simple tables fill a large room, and long-experienced waitresses hustle about to keep up with demand.

But the food! There's fish, and then some. The menu typically includes a wide range of fresh fish, prepared in a variety of styles. (The locals seem to like it fried.) If you find yourself beset with a fierce craving for the local crustacean, do yourself a favor and bypass the tired boiled lobster with bib. Instead, head straight for the lobster stew, which is brimming with meaty lobster chunks and is flavored perfectly. It's not a light meal, but travelers often find themselves lingering another day in Stonington for yet another hearty bowl of stew. Bring your own wine, beer, or cocktails.

BLUE HILL

Blue Hill (pop. 1,900) is fairly easy to find—just look for gently domed, eponymous Blue Hill Mountain, which lords over the northern end of Blue Hill Bay. Set between the mountain and the bay is the quiet historic town of Blue Hill, which clusters along the bay shore and a burbling stream.

There's not much going on in town. And that seems to be exactly what attracts summer visitors back time and again—and may explain why two excellent bookstores are located here. Many old-money families still maintain retreats set along the water or in the rolling inland hills, but Blue Hill offers several excellent choices for lodging if you're not so blessed. It's a good destination for an escape, and will especially appeal to those deft at crafting their own entertainment.

When in the area, be sure to tune in to the local community radio station, WERU at 89.9 FM. It started some years back in the chicken coop owned by Noel Paul Stuckey (of Peter, Paul & Mary fame). The idea was to spread around good music and provocative ideas. It's become slicker and more professional in recent years, but still maintains a pleasantly homespun flavor.

ESSENTIALS

GETTING THERE   Blue Hill is located southeast of Ellsworth on Route 172. From the west, head south on Route 15, 5 miles east of Bucksport.

VISITOR INFORMATION   Blue Hill does not maintain a visitor information booth. Look for the *Blue Hill, Maine* brochure and map at state information centers, or write the **Blue Hill Chamber of Commerce,** P.O. Box 520, Blue Hill, ME 04614. The staff at area inns and restaurants are usually able to answer any questions you might have.

SPECIAL EVENTS   The **Blue Hill Fair** is a traditional country fair with livestock competitions, displays of vegetables, and carnival rides. The fair takes place at the fairgrounds northwest of the village on Route 172 on Labor Day weekend.

EXPLORING THE AREA

A good way to start your exploration is to ascend the open summit of **Blue Hill Mountain,** from which you'll have superb views of the azure bay and the rocky balds on nearby Mount Desert Island. To reach the trailhead from the village, drive north on Route 172, then turn west (left) on Mountain Road at the Blue Hill Fairgrounds. Drive 0.8 mile and look for the well-marked trail. An ascent of the "mountain" (elevation 940 ft.) is about a mile, and requires about 45 minutes. Bring a picnic lunch and enjoy the vistas.

Blue Hill has traditionally attracted more than its fair share of artists—especially potters. On Union Street, stop by **Rowantrees Pottery** (☎ 207/374-5535), which has been a Blue Hill institution for more than half a century. The shop was founded by Adelaide Pearson, who said she was inspired to pursue pottery as a career after a conversation with Mahatma Gandhi in India. Rowantrees pottery is richly hued, and the potters who've succeeded Pearson continue to use glazes made from local resources.

Another inventive shop, the family-run **Rackliffe Pottery** on Ellsworth Road (☎ 207/374-2297), uses native clay and lead-free glazes, and the bowls, vases, and plates produced here have a lustrous, silky feel to them. Visitors are welcome to watch the potters at work. Both shops are open year-round.

Even if you've never been given to swooning over historic homes, you owe yourself a visit to the intriguing **Parson Fisher House** (contact Blue Hill Tea & Tobacco at ☎ 207/374-2161 for information), located on Routes 176 and 15, half a mile west of the village. Fisher, Blue Hill's first permanent minister, was something of a Renaissance man when he settled here in 1796. Educated at Harvard, Fisher not only delivered sermons in six different languages, including Aramaic, but was a writer, painter, and minor inventor whose energy was evidently boundless. On a tour of his home, which he built in 1814, you can see a clock with wooden works he made, and samples of the books he not only wrote but published and bound himself.

Parson Fisher House is open from July through mid-September daily except Sunday from 2 to 5pm. Admission is $2 for adults; children under 12 are admitted free.

WHERE TO STAY

Blue Hill Inn. Union St. (P.O. Box 403), Blue Hill, ME 04614. ☎ **207/374-2844.** Fax 207/374-2829. 12 rms (3 with shower only). $140–$210 double. Rates include breakfast and dinner. MC, V. Closed mid-May to Nov and Jan–Mar. No children under 13.

The Blue Hill Inn has been hosting travelers since 1840, so by now the place has got hospitality down pat. Situated on one of Blue Hill's busy streets and within walking distance of most everything, this Federal-style inn features a colonial American motif throughout, with the authenticity enhanced by creaky floors, door jambs slightly out of true, and quirky touches like a heavy iron safe employed as an end table. Innkeepers Mary and Don Hartley have furnished all the rooms pleasantly with antiques and down comforters; four rooms feature wood-burning fireplaces. New in 1997 was a contemporary suite built in an annex, which features cathedral ceiling, fireplace, kitchen, and deck. No smoking.

Dining/Entertainment: The one part of the inn that doesn't feel old (and is the least interesting) is the dining room, in a boxy, shedlike addition to the old house. But the superb French-style cooking of chef Andre Strong makes up for the slightly disappointing atmosphere. The meals are made chiefly with local organic ingredients and might be described as creative continental cuisine. You might start with chanterelle mushroom flan with diced tomatoes, then follow with lobster with a vanilla beurre blanc or a roast duck with green-peppercorn sauce. The fixed-price dinner ($30 for five courses, $22 for three courses) is served Wednesday through Sunday and is open to the public; reservations required.

John Peters Inn. Rte. 176 East (P.O. Box 916), Blue Hill, ME 04614. ☎ **207/374-2116.** 14 rms. $105–$165 double. Rates include full breakfast. MC, V. Closed Nov–Apr.

The long and narrow dirt driveway of the John Peters Inn sends a signal that you're entering into another world. You ascend a gentle hill between a row of stately maples; to the right are glimpses of the bay, to the left is the handsome 1810 home that, with its later architectural embellishments, could be a modest antebellum plantation home. Toto, I don't think we're in Kansas anymore.

Inside, it's strictly New England, decorated with antiques that have an uncommon elegance. Innkeepers Barbara and Rick Seeger have an eye for detail. There's nothing grand here—it's all simple Early American style, done with exceptionally good taste. The guest rooms, nine of which boast fireplaces and four of which have private phones, all feature love seats or sofas, and are hard to tear yourself out of. But do try. The inn sits on 25 lovely shorefront acres, and has been lightly landscaped— to do more would be to gild the lily. There's also an unheated outdoor pool that will appeal mostly to those of stout constitution.

Breakfast in the simply decorated dining room is a sublime treat, with offerings like freshly squeezed orange juice, poached eggs with asparagus, lobster omelets, and a variety of waffles. No smoking.

WHERE TO DINE

The **Left Bank Bakery and Cafe** (☎ 207/374-2201) is Maine's preeminent counterculture outpost. Located on Route 172 north of town, the Left Bank serves up good food and good music, although service has historically been spotty. (New owners have done a good job of speeding things up.) Tasty fresh-baked products are piled high at the counter in the older front section of the restaurant; a renovated side section down a few steps is open and airy, and hosts regular evening performances by notables like Maria Muldaur, Jonathan Edwards, Tom Rush, and Mose Alison. Call ahead (or check the handy Web site at **www.downeast.net/com/leftbank**) to find out who's playing in the coming weeks.

✪ **Firepond.** Main St. ☎ **207/374-9970.** Reservations recommended. Main courses $15.95– $21.95. AE, MC, V. Daily 5–9:30pm. Closed Tues in fall; Jan to mid-May. REGIONAL GOURMET.

Firepond, located right in the village, is a drop-dead gorgeous restaurant that happens to serve exceptionally fine food. Ideally sited along a small stream in a former blacksmith's shop, Firepond has old pine floors and is lavishly decorated with dry and live flowers. The decor flirts with a Martha Stewart run amok look, but it pulls back in the nick of time and carries off its elegance unusually well. The best seats are downstairs in the covered porch overhanging the stream, but it's hard to go wrong anywhere here for setting a romantic mood. If you're not sure this is the place for you, try this: Stop by the handsome bar with its wrought-iron stools for a drink and an appetizer. The odds are you'll decide that staying for dinner is a good idea.

The meals are adventurous without being overly exotic. Traditional regional fare updated for the 1990s dominates, with grilled chicken served with a vegetable salsa and amarillo sauce, veal with sun-dried tomatoes, and lobster served on fresh pasta with a cream sauce of boursin and Romano cheese. Whatever you choose, expect it to be prepared with a deft touch.

Jonathan's. Main St. ☎ **207/374-5226.** Reservations recommended in summer and on week-ends year-round. Main courses $16.95–$21.95. MC, V. Daily 5–9:30pm. Closed Mon–Tues in Nov–May. ECLECTIC.

Don't order the boiled lobster at Jonathan's. There's nothing wrong with it, of course, but you're better off sampling the more innovative cuisine served up here, saving the boiled crustacean for a picnic table. The menu changes frequently, but among the fine dishes often served here are churrasco (a Cuban-style marinated flank steak with Caribbean condiments); a mixed grill of quail, rabbit, and venison sausage; and a simple poached salmon with dill sauce. Appetizers run along the lines of warm salad of smoked mussels and chèvre, or Indonesian shrimp satay.

Located in the middle of Blue Hill, Jonathan's attracts a younger local crowd as well as the old-money summer denizens. The background music is jazz or light rock, the service brisk and professional, and the wine list is extensive and creative. Guests choose between the barnlike back room, with a comfortable knotty pine feel, or the less elegantly decorated front room facing Main Street, done up in green tablecloths, captain's chairs, and booths of white pine.

7 Mount Desert Island & Acadia National Park

Mount Desert Island is home to spectacular Acadia National Park, and for many visi-tors the two places are one and the same. It's true, Acadia dominates the economy and defines the spirit of Maine's largest island. And it does feature the most dramatic coastal real estate on the Eastern seaboard.

Yet the national park holdings are only part of the appeal of this popular island, which is connected to the mainland via a short, two-lane causeway. Beyond the parklands are scenic harborside villages and remote backcountry roads, quaint B&Bs and exceptionally fine restaurants, oversized 19th-century summer "cottages" and the unrepentant tourist trap of Bar Harbor. Those who arrive on the island expecting untamed wilderness invariably leave disappointed. Those who understand that Acadia National Park is but one chapter (albeit a very large one) in the intriguing story of Mount Desert Island will enjoy their visit more thoroughly.

Mount Desert (pronounced "de-*sert*") is divided into two lobes separated by Somes Sound, the only legitimate fjord in the continental United States (a fjord is a valley carved by a glacier that is subsequently filled with rising ocean water). Those with a poetic imagination see Mount Desert shaped as a lobster, with one large claw and one small. Most of the parkland is on the meatier east claw, although large swaths of na-tional park exist on the leaner west claw as well. The eastern side is more developed, with Bar Harbor the center of commerce and entertainment. The western side has a more quiet, settled air, and teems with more wildlife than tourists. The island isn't huge—it's only about 15 miles from the causeway to the island's southernmost tip at Bass Harbor Head—so visitors can take their time adventuring. The best plan is to explore mostly by foot, bicycle, or kayak.

ACADIA NATIONAL PARK

It's not hard to fathom why Acadia is consistently one of the biggest draws in the U.S. national park system. The park's landscape is a rich tapestry of rugged cliffs, restless ocean, and deep, silent woods.

Acadia's landscape, like so much of the rest of northern New England, was carved by glaciers some 18,000 years ago. A mile-high ice sheet shaped the land by scour-ing valleys into their distinctive U shapes, rounding many of the once jagged peaks, and depositing huge boulders about the landscape, such as the famous 10-foot-high

"Bubble Rock," which appears to be perched precariously on the side of South Bubble Mountain.

The park's more recent roots can be traced back to the 1840s, when noted Hudson River School painter Thomas Cole packed his sketchbooks and easels for a trip to this remote island, then home to a few fishermen and boatbuilders. His stunning renditions of the surging surf pounding against coastal granite were later displayed in New York and helped trigger an early tourism boom as urbanites flocked to the island to escape the heat and to "rusticate." By 1872, national magazines were touting Eden (Bar Harbor's name until 1919) as a desirable summer resort. It attracted the attention of wealthy industrialists, and soon became summer home to Carnegies, Rockefellers, Astors, and Vanderbilts, who built massive summer "cottages" with literally dozens of rooms (one cottage even boasted 28 bathrooms).

By early in this century, the huge popularity and growing development of the island began to concern its most ardent supporters. Boston textile heir and conservationist George Dorr and Harvard president Charles Eliot, aided by the largesse of John D. Rockefeller, Jr., started acquiring large tracts for the public's enjoyment. These parcels were eventually donated to the federal government, and in 1919 the public land was designated Lafayette National Park, the first national park east of the Mississippi. Renamed Acadia in 1929, the park has grown to encompass nearly half the island.

Rockefeller purchased and donated about 11,000 acres—or one-third of the park. He's also responsible for one of the park's most extraordinary features. Around 1905 a dispute erupted over whether to allow noisy new motorcars onto the island. Resident islanders wanted these new conveniences to boost their mobility; John D. Rockefeller, Jr., whose fortune ironically grew from the oil industry, strenuously objected, preferring the tranquillity of the car-free island. Rockefeller went down to defeat on this issue, and the island was opened to cars in 1913. In response, the multimillionaire set about building an elaborate 57-mile system of carriage roads, featuring a dozen gracefully handcrafted stone bridges. These roads, which are today open only to equestrians, bicyclists, and pedestrians, are concentrated most densely around Jordan Pond, but also ascend to some of the most scenic open peaks and wind through sylvan valleys.

JUST THE FACTS

GETTING THERE   Acadia National Park is reached from the town of Ellsworth via Route 3. If you're coming from southern Maine, you can avoid the coastal congestion along Route 1 by taking the turnpike to Bangor, picking up I-395 to Route 1A, then continuing south on Route 1A to Ellsworth. While this looks longer on the map, it's by far the quickest route in summer.

Daily flights from Boston to the airport in Trenton, just across the causeway from Mount Desert Island, are offered by **Colgan Air** (☎ **800/272-5488** or 207/667-7171).

ENTRY POINTS & FEES   A 4-day park pass, which includes unlimited trips on Park Loop Road, costs $10 per car (no extra charge per passenger). A daily pass is $5.

The main point of entry to Park Loop Road, the park's most scenic byway, is at the visitor center at **Hulls Cove.** Mount Desert Island consists of an interwoven network of park and town roads, allowing visitors to enter the park at numerous points. A glance at a park map (available at the visitor center) will make these access points self-evident. The entry fee is collected at a toll booth on Park Loop Road, one-half mile north of Sand Beach.

VISITOR CENTERS   Acadia staffs two visitor centers. The **Thompson Island Information Center** (☎ **207/288-3411**) on Route 3 is the first you'll pass as you enter Mount Desert Island. This center is maintained by the local chambers of commerce, but park personnel are often on hand to answer inquiries. It's open May through mid-October, and is a good stop for general lodging and restaurant information.

If you're primarily interested in information about the park itself, continue on Route 3 to the National Park Service's **Hulls Cove Visitor Center,** about 7.5 miles beyond Thompson Island. This attractive stone-walled center includes professionally prepared park service displays, such as a large relief map of the island, natural-history exhibits, and a short introductory film. You can also request free brochures about hiking trails and the carriage roads, or purchase postcards and more detailed guidebooks. The center is open mid-April through October.

Information is also available year-round, by phone or in person, from the park's **headquarters** (☎ **207/288-3338**) on Route 233 between Bar Harbor and Somesville. Your questions might also be answered on the park's Web page at **www.nps.gov/acad/anp.html**.

PARK ACCOMMODATIONS   Unlike many of the other "crown jewel" national parks, Acadia doesn't have its own rustic park lodge. In fact, the park itself offers no overnight accommodations at all, other than two campgrounds (see below). But visitors don't have to go far to find a room, especially in Bar Harbor. It's teeming with motels and inns. The rest of the island also has a good selection of places to spend the night. See "Where to Stay," below.

SEASONS Visit Acadia in September if you can finagle it. Between Labor Day and the foliage season of early October, the days are often warm and clear, the nights have a crisp northerly tang, and you can avoid the hassles of congestion, crowds, and pesky insects. Not that the park is empty in September. Bus tours seem to proliferate this month, which results in crowds of tourists at the most popular sites. Not to worry: If you walk just a few feet away (literally, in some cases) you can find solitude and an agreeable peacefulness. Hikers and bikers have the trails and carriage roads to themselves.

Summer, of course, is peak season at Acadia. Some of the roads in and around the park can resemble New York's Central Park at rush hour if you arrive at the wrong time. That's no surprise. The weather is perfect for just about any outdoor activity in July and August. Most days are warm (in the 70s or 80s), with afternoons frequently cooler owing to ocean breezes. While sun seems to be the norm, come prepared for rain and fog, which are both frequent visitors to the Maine coast. And once or twice each summer a heat wave will settle into the area, producing temperatures in the 90s, dense haze, and stifling humidity, but this rarely lasts more than 2 or 3 days. Soon enough, a brisk north wind will blow in from the Arctic, churning up the waters and forcing visitors into sweaters at night. Sometime around the last 2 weeks of August, a cold wind will blow through at night and you'll smell the approach of autumn, with winter not far behind it.

AVOIDING THE CROWDS Late summer and early fall are the best times to miss out on the mobs yet still enjoy the weather. If you do come during midsummer, try to venture out in the early mornings and early evenings to see the most popular spots, like the Thunder Hole or the summit of Cadillac Mountain. Setting off into the woods is also a good strategy. About four out of five visitors restrict their tours to the loop road and a handful of other major attractions, leaving the Acadia backcountry open for more adventurous spirits.

The best guarantee of solitude is to head to the more remote outposts managed by Acadia, especially Isle au Haut and Schoodic Peninsula.

REGULATIONS Guns may not be used in the park; if you have a gun, it must be "cased, broken down, or otherwise packaged against use." Fires and camping are allowed only at designated areas. Pets must be on leashes at all times. Seat belts must be worn in the national park (this is a federal law). Don't remove anything from the park, either man-made or natural; this includes cobblestones from the shore.

RANGER PROGRAMS Frequent ranger programs are offered throughout the year. These include talks at campground amphitheaters and tours at various locations around the island. Examples are the Otter Point nature hike, Mr. Rockefeller's bridges walk, Frenchman Bay cruise (rangers provide commentary on commercial trips; make reservations with boat owners), and a discussion of changes in Acadia's landscape. Ask for a schedule of events at the visitor center or either of the two campgrounds.

Seeing the Highlights

Three or 4 days is a good amount of time to spend exploring the park. If you're passing through just briefly, try to work-in at least three of the four following activities.

DRIVE THE PARK LOOP ROAD This almost goes without saying, since it's the park's premier attraction. This 20-mile road runs along the island's eastern shore, then loops inland along Jordan Pond and Eagle Lake. The road runs alternately high along the shoulders of brawny coastal mountains, then dips down along the boulder-strewn coastlines. The dark granite is broken by the spires of spruce and fir, and the earthy tones contrast sharply with the frothy white surf and the steely, azure sea.

The two-lane road is one-way along the coastal stretches; the right-hand lane serves as a parking area, so it's easy to make frequent stops to admire the vistas.

Ideally, visitors will take at least two trips on the loop road. The first is for the sheer exhilaration and to get a feel for the lay of the land. On the second trip around, plan to stop more frequently, leaving your car behind while you explore the trails and coastline.

Attractions along the coastal loop include scenic **Sand Beach,** which is the only sand beach on the island and offers good swimming during infrequent hot spells and brutally cold swimming the rest of the time; **Thunder Hole,** a shallow ocean-side cavern into which the surf surges, compresses, and bursts out with explosive force and a concussive sound (young kids seem to be endlessly mesmerized by this); and **Cadillac Mountain,** at 1,530 feet, the highest point on the island and the place first touched by the sun in the United States during certain times of year. The mountain-top is accessible by car, but the lot at the summit is often full to overflowing. You're better off hiking to the top, or scaling a more remote peak.

HIKE A MOUNTAIN   This quintessential Acadia experience shouldn't be missed. The park is studded with low "mountains" (they'd be called hills elsewhere) that offer superb views over the island and the open ocean. The trails weren't simply hacked out of the hillside; they were crafted by experienced stonemasons and others with high aesthetic intent. The routes aren't the most direct, or the easiest to build. But they're often the most scenic, taking advantage of fractures in the rocks, picturesque ledges, and sudden vistas. See "Hiking," below, for suggested climbs.

BIKE A CARRIAGE ROAD   The 57 miles of carriage road built by John D. Rockefeller, Jr., are among the park's most extraordinary hidden treasures. (See the introduction above for a brief history.) While built for horse and carriage, these grass-and-gravel roads are ideal for cruising by mountain bike. Park near Jordan Pond and plumb the tree-shrouded lanes that lace the area, and take time to admire the stone-work on the uncommonly fine bridges. Afterwards, stop for tea and popovers at the Jordan Pond House, which has been a popular island destination for over a century, although it's unlikely as much Lycra was in evidence 100 years ago. For bike rentals, see "Mountain Biking," below.

EAT A LOBSTER   While you can't feast on boiled lobster served ocean-side within Acadia National Park, several lobster pounds offer the opportunity right outside the park's borders. It's the perfect way to end a day spent in the park.

The best places are those right on the water, and where there are no pretensions or frills. The ingredients for a proper feed at a local lobster pound are a pot of boiling water, a tank of lobsters, some well-worn picnic tables, a good view, and a six-pack of Maine beer. Among the best destinations for lobster are **Beal's Lobster Pier** (☎ 207/244-7178) in Southwest Harbor, which is one of the oldest pounds in the area. **Abel's Lobster Pound** (☎ 207/276-5827), on Route 198, 5 miles north of Northeast Harbor, overlooks the deep blue waters of Somes Sound; eat at picnic tables under the pines or indoors at the restaurant. It's quite a bit pricier than other lobster restaurants at first glance, but they don't charge for the extras like many other lobster joints.

On the mainland just north of the causeway is the wonderful **Oak Point Lobster Pound** (☎ 207/667-6998). This is off the beaten path (although still very popular and often crowded), where you can enjoy your lobster with a sensational view of the island's rocky hills. To get here, turn west off Route 3 onto Route 230 before crossing to Mount Desert, then continue 4 miles to the restaurant.

Sports & Outdoor Pursuits

CANOEING   Mount Desert's several ponds offer scenic if limited canoeing, and most have public boat access. Canoe rentals are available at the north end of Long Pond in Somesville from **National Park Canoe Rentals** (☎ 207/244-5854). Long Pond is the largest of the island ponds, and offers good exploring. Pack a picnic and spend a few hours reconnoitering the pond's 3-mile length. Much of the west shore and the southern tip lies within Acadia National Park.

CARRIAGE RIDES   Carriage rides are offered by **Wildwood Stables** (☎ 207/276-3622), a national park concessionaire located a half-mile south of Jordan Pond House. The 1-hour Day Mountain trip departs three times daily, yields wonderful views, and costs $12 for adults, $7 for children 6 to 12, and $4 for children 2 to 5. Longer tours are also available; reservations are encouraged.

HIKING   Acadia National Park has 120 miles of hiking trails in addition to 57 miles of carriage roads. The Hulls Cove Visitor Center offers a one-page chart of area hikes; combined with the park map, this is all you'll need since the trails are well maintained and well marked. It's not hard to cobble together loop hikes to make your trips more varied. Coordinate your hiking with the weather; if it's damp or foggy, you'll stay drier and warmer strolling the carriage roads. If it's clear and dry, head for the highest peaks with the best views.

Among the most extraordinary trails is the **Dorr Ladder Trail,** which departs from Route 3 near The Tarn, just south of the Sieur de Monts entrance to the Loop Road. This trail begins with a series of Homeric stone steps ascending along the base of a vast slab of granite, then passes through crevasses (not for the wide of girth) and up ladders affixed to the unyielding granite. The views east and south are superb.

An easy lowland hike is around **Jordan Pond,** with the northward leg along the pond's east shore on a hiking trail, and the return via carriage road. It's mostly level, with the total loop measuring just over 3 miles. At the north end of Jordan Pond, consider heading up the prominent, oddly symmetrical mounds called **The Bubbles.** These detours shouldn't take much more than 20 minutes each; look for signs off the Jordan Pond Shore Trail.

On the western side of the island, an ascent of **Acadia Mountain** and return takes about an hour and a half, but hikers should schedule in some time for lingering while they enjoy the view of Somes Sound and the smaller islands off Mount Desert's southern shores. This 2.5-mile loop hike begins off Route 102 at a trailhead 3 miles south of Somesville. Head eastward through rolling mixed forest, then begin an ascent over ledgy terrain. Be sure to visit both the east and west peaks (the east peak has the better views), and look for hidden balds in the summit forest opening up unexpected vistas.

✪ **MOUNTAIN BIKING**   Acadia's carriage roads (see introduction, above) offer some of the most scenic, relaxing mountain biking anywhere in the United States. The 57 miles of grassy lanes and gravel road were maintained by John D. Rockefeller, Jr., until his death in 1960. Afterwards, they became somewhat shaggy and overgrown until a major restoration effort brought them back beginning in 1990. The roads today are superbly restored and maintained.

Where the carriage roads cross private land (generally between Seal Harbor and Northeast Harbor), they're closed to mountain bikes. Please respect these restrictions.

A map of the carriage roads is available at the park's visitor center. More detailed guidebooks are sold at area bookstores.

Mountain-bike rentals are easily found along Cottage Street in Bar Harbor. Some bike shops include locks and helmets as basic equipment; ask what's included before you rent. Also ask about closing times, since you'll be able to get a couple extra hours in with a later-closing shop. Try **Bar Harbor Bicycle Shop** (☎ 207/288-3886) at 141 Cottage St.; **Acadia Outfitters** (☎ 207/288-8118) at 106 Cottage St.; or **Acadia Bike & Canoe** (☎ 207/288-9605) at 48 Cottage St.

SEA KAYAKING   Experienced sea kayakers flock to Acadia to test their paddling skills along the surf at the base of rocky cliffs, to venture out to the offshore islands, and to probe the still, silent waters of Somes Sound. Novice sea kayakers also come to Acadia to try their hand for the first time with guided tours, which are offered by several outfitters. While many new paddlers have found their inaugural experiences gratifying, others have complained that the large numbers of paddlers taken out on quick tours during peak season make the experience a little too much like a cattle call to truly enjoy. The following outfitters each offer half- and full-day tours: **Acadia Outfitters** (☎ 207/288-8118) at 106 Cottage St.; **Coastal Kayaking Tours** (☎ 207/288-9605) at 48 Cottage St., and **National Park Sea Kayak Tours** (☎ 207/288-0342) at 137 Cottage St.

CAMPING

The National Park Service maintains two campgrounds within Acadia National Park. Both are extremely popular; during July and August, expect both to fill by early to mid-morning.

The more popular of the two is **Blackwoods** (☎ 207/288-3274), located on the island's eastern side. Access is from Route 3, 5 miles south of Bar Harbor. Bikers and pedestrians have easy access to the loop road from the campground via a short trail. The campground has no public showers, but an enterprising business offers clean showers for a modest fee at an operation just outside the campground entrance. Camping fees are $16 and limited reservations are accepted through a **reservation service** (☎ 800/365-2267).

Seawall (☎ 207/244-3600) is on the quieter, western half of the island near the fishing village of Bass Harbor. This is a good base for road biking, and several short coastal hikes are within easy striking distance. Many of the sites are walk-ins, which require carrying your gear a couple hundred yards or so to the site. The campground is open late May through September on a first-come, first-served basis. In general, if you get here by 9 or 10am, you'll be pretty much assured of a campsite, especially if you're a tent camper. No showers. The fee is $13 for those arriving by car, $8 for those coming by foot or bike.

Private campgrounds handle the overflow. The region from Ellsworth south boasts some 14 private campgrounds, which offer varying amenities. Contact the **Thompson Island Information Center** (☎ 207/288-3411) for details.

WHERE TO DINE

Jordan Pond House. Park Loop Rd., Acadia National Park (near Seal Harbor). ☎ 207/276-3316. Reservations recommended for lunch, tea, and dinner. Lunch $5.50–$14; afternoon tea $5.50–$6.50; dinner $8–$16. AE, DISC, MC, V. Daily 11:30am–8pm (until 9pm July–Aug). Afternoon tea served 2:30–5:30pm. Closed late Oct to mid-May. AMERICAN.

The secret to the Jordan Pond House is location, location, location. The restaurant traces its roots back to 1847, when an early farm was established on this picturesque property at the southern tip of a pond looking toward The Bubbles, a pair of sizable glacially sculpted mounds. The spot first caught on during the local mania for teahouses in the late 19th century. But tragedy struck in 1979 when the original structure and its birch bark dining room was leveled by fire. A more modern, two-level dining room was built in its place—it's got less charm, but it still has the location. If the weather's agreeable, ask for a seat on the lawn with its unrivaled views.

Afternoon tea is a hallowed Jordan Pond House tradition. Ladies Who Lunch sit next to Lycra-clad mountain bikers, and everyone feasts on the huge, tasty popovers and strawberry jam served with a choice of teas or fresh lemonade. Dinners are reasonably priced and include classic resort entrees like prime rib, steamed lobster, and baked haddock.

BAR HARBOR

Bar Harbor has its recent historical roots in the grand resort era of the late 19th century. Sprawling hotels and boardinghouses once cluttered the shores and hillsides, as the newly affluent middle class flocked here in summer by steamboat and rail from Boston, New York, Philadelphia, and Washington, D.C. When the resort was at its peak near the turn of the last century, Bar Harbor had rooms enough to accommodate some 5,000 visitors. Along with the hotels and guest houses, hundreds of cottages were built by the wealthiest rusticators who came here season after season.

The tourist business continued to grow through the early part of the 1900s, then all but collapsed as the Great Depression and the growing popularity of automobile travel doomed the era of the extended vacation. Bar Harbor was dealt a further blow in 1947 when a fire fueled by an unusually dry summer and fierce northwest winds leveled many of the most opulent cottages and much of the rest of the town. (To this day, no one knows how the fire started.) The fire destroyed 5 hotels, 67 cottages, and 170 homes. In all, some 17,000 acres of the island were burned. Downtown Bar Harbor was spared, and many of the grand homes in town along the oceanfront were missed by the conflagration.

After a period of quiet slumber, Bar Harbor has been rejuvenated and rediscovered in recent years as tourists have poured into this area and entrepreneurs have followed them, opening dozens of restaurants, shops, and boutiques. The less charitable regard Bar Harbor as just another tacky tourist mecca—Pigeon Forge, Tennessee, with moose horns and spruce. And it does share some of those traits—the downtown hosts a proliferation of T-shirt vendors, ice-cream shops, and souvenir palaces. Crowds spill off the sidewalk and into the street in midsummer, and the traffic and congestion can be truly appalling.

But Bar Harbor's vibrant history, quirky architecture, and beautiful location along Frenchman Bay allow it to rise above its station as mild diversion for tourists. Most of the island's inns, motels, and B&Bs are located here, as are dozens of fine restaurants, making it a desirable base of operations. Bar Harbor is also the best destination for the usual supplies and services; there's a decent grocery story and Laundromat, and you can stock up on other necessities of life.

ESSENTIALS

GETTING THERE   Bar Harbor is located on Route 3 about 10 miles southeast of the causeway.

VISITOR INFORMATION   The **Bar Harbor Chamber of Commerce,** P.O. Box 158, Bar Harbor, ME 04609 (☎ **207/288-5103;** Web site: **www.acadia.net/bhcc**), stockpiles a huge amount of information about local attractions at its offices at 93 Cottage St. Write, call, or E-mail (**bhcc@acadia.net**) in advance for a full guide to area lodging.

EXPLORING BAR HARBOR

Wandering the small commercial area on foot is a good way to get a taste of the town. Don't overlook the residential side streets, which are leafy and quiet, lined with homes that range from Victorian quaint to sturdy but unremarkable.

The best views in town are from the foot of Main Street at grassy **Agamont Park,** overlooking the town pier and Frenchman Bay. From here, set off past the Bar Harbor Inn on the Shore Path, a winding, wide trail that follows the shoreline for a short distance along a public right of way. The pathway passes in front of many of the elegant summer homes (some converted to inns), offering a superb vantage point to view the area's architecture.

Bar Harbor also makes a terrific base for offshore **whale watching.** Several tour operators offer excursions in search of humpbacks, finbacks, and others. The largest of the fleet is the sizable *Friendship V* (☎ **800/942-5374** or 207/288-2386), which operates out of the Bluenose Ferry Terminal, 1 mile north of Bar Harbor. The tours are on a fast, twin-hulled excursion boat that can hold 350 passengers on three decks and in two spacious heated cabins. The 2- to 3-hour whale-watch tour costs $30 for adults, $19 for children 6 to 14. **Frenchman Bay Boat Cruises** (☎ **800/508-1499** or 207/288-3322) leads passengers in search of whales aboard the 105-foot, two-deck *Whale Watcher.* Tours range from 1 to $3^{1}/_{2}$ hours, with tour prices from $10 to $28. Discounts are offered for seniors and children.

Bar Harbor in the evening tends to be rather low-key, although you can often find some live music or a watering hole to while away a few hours. One of the great evening attractions is the **Criterion Theatre** (☎ **207/288-3441**), a movie house built in 1932 in a classic art deco style and which has so far avoided the horrors of multiplexification. (It has benefited, however, from recent reupholstering and a new surround-sound system.) The 900-seat theater, located on Cottage Street, shows first-run movies in summer and is worth the price of admission for the beautiful interiors; the movie is secondary. It costs extra to sit in the private loges up above—go ahead and splurge.

WHERE TO STAY

Acadia Hotel. 20 Mt. Desert St., Bar Harbor, ME 04609. ☎ **207/288-5721.** 10 rms. TV. Peak season $59–$95 double; off-season $45–$65 double. Rates include continental breakfast. AE, DISC, MC, V.

The Acadia Hotel is perfectly situated overlooking the Village Green, and easily accessible to all in-town activities. This handsome, simple home dating from the late 19th century has a wraparound porch (where in summer you can enjoy the continental breakfast) and attractive guest rooms newly decorated in a pleasant floral motif. The rooms vary widely in size and amenities; some have whirlpools, some have air-conditioning, one has a kitchenette. Ask for the specifics when you book.

✪ **Balance Rock Inn.** 21 Albert Meadow (off Main St. at Butterfield's grocery store), Bar Harbor, ME 04609. ☎ **800/753-0494** or 207/288-2610. 21 rms. A/C MINIBAR TV TEL. Peak season $195–$435 double; off-season $135–$265 double. Rates include breakfast. AE, DISC, MC, V. Closed Nov–Apr.

It's quite simple: If you can afford it, stay here. Everyone seems to speak in whispers, even the staff—not because it's a snooty place, but because one and all seem in awe of this oceanfront mansion, built in 1903. It's an architecturally elaborate affair of gray shingles with cream, maroon, and forest-green trim. The common rooms are expansive yet comfortable, with pilasters and coffered ceilings, arched doorways and leaded windows. There's even a baby grand piano. The favored spot among serious loungers is the front covered patio with its green wicker furniture and a recessed bar

Bar Harbor

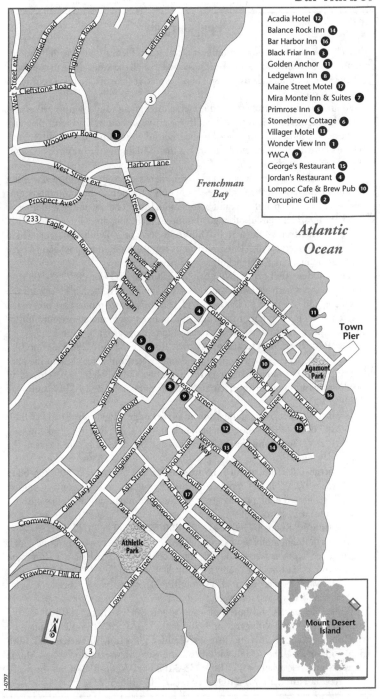

Acadia Hotel **12**
Balance Rock Inn **14**
Bar Harbor Inn **16**
Black Friar Inn **3**
Golden Anchor **11**
Ledgelawn Inn **8**
Maine Street Motel **17**
Mira Monte Inn & Suites **7**
Primrose Inn **5**
Stonethrow Cottage **6**
Villager Motel **13**
Wonder View Inn **1**
YWCA **9**
George's Restaurant **15**
Jordan's Restaurant **4**
Lompoc Cafe & Brew Pub **10**
Porcupine Grill **2**

Frenchman Bay

Atlantic Ocean

Town Pier

Mount Desert Island

Pillow Talk

Bar Harbor is the bedroom community for Mount Desert Island, with hundreds of hotel, motel, and inn rooms. Be forewarned that all share one thing in common: They're filled during the busy days of midsummer. It's essential to book your room as early as possible.

A number of modern hotels and motels cluster along Route 3 just northeast of the village center; this is your best bet if you arrive without reservations. Be aware that even the most basic of rooms can be frightfully expensive in July and August. There's virtually no motel available for less than $50 during the summer; bed-and-breakfasts start at about $85.

In the full listings on the adjacent pages, there's space enough to review just a handful of the best choices. These represent only a fraction of the accommodations available. Don't despair if you can't book a room in any of these fine establishments.

There are still dozens of other good options, including those listed below.

The Acadia Inn, 98 Eden St. (☎ **800/638-3636** or 207/288-3500), opened in 1996. This modern, stylish three-story hotel features an outdoor pool and Jacuzzi. Peak season rates are $129 including continental breakfast.

The Golden Anchor, 55 West St. (☎ **800/328-5033** or 207/288-5033), is smack on the waterfront, with some rooms looking across the harbor toward the town pier and others out to Bar Island. (The less expensive rooms have no view at all.) There's a pool and hot tub right at the harbor's edge, and an oceanfront dining room that serves basic fare. Peak season rates range from $110 to $165.

The Park Entrance Oceanfront Motel, Route 3 (☎ **800/288-9703** or 207/ 288-9703), is nicely situated on 10 handsome waterfront acres close to the park visitor center. The inn has an attractive private pier and cobblestone beach, and an outdoor swimming pool and Jacuzzi. Summer rates are $129 to $149; suites are $169 to $299.

Great views greet guests at the **Atlantic Eyrie Lodge,** Highbrook Road (☎ **800/ 422-2843** or 207/288-9786), perched on a hillside above Route 3. Peak rates are $125 to $180. Some units have kitchenettes and balconies; all share access to the ocean-view pool.

The ocean-side **Holiday Inn SunSpree Resort,** 123 Eden St. (☎ **800/234-6835** or 207/288-9723), has 217 rooms, a children's program, and numerous amenities, including a heated pool, putting green, marina, and restaurant and lounge. Room rates run from $149 to $189.

The Colony, Route 3, Hulls Cove (☎ **800/524-1159** or 207/288-3383), consists of a handful of motel rooms and a battery of 55 cottages arrayed around a long green. The Colony is across Route 3 from a cobblestone beach, and a 10-minute drive into Bar Harbor. The rooms are furnished in a simple 1970s style that won't win any awards for decor, but all are comfortable; many have kitchenettes. Summer rates are $50 to $90 for two.

Reputable motels and hotels offering rooms for less than $100 include the conveniently located **Villager Motel,** 207 Main St. (☎ **207/288-3211**), a family-run motel with 63 rooms; the 79-room **Wonder View Inn,** 50 Eden St. (☎ **800/ 341-1553** or 207/288-3358), with its sweeping bay views; the downtown **Maine Street Motel,** 315 Main St. (☎ **800/333-3188** or 207/288-3188); and the B&B-style **Acadia Hotel,** 20 Mount Desert St. (☎ **207/288-5721**).

off to the side. The sound of the sea drifts up gently. And then there's the view, which is among the best in Maine: You look across a wonderful pool, and down a long verdant lawn framed by hardwoods to the rich, blue waters of Frenchman Bay. The service is impeccable, and the rooms wonderfully appointed, many with whirlpool baths or fireplaces. The inn also features a fitness center in an air-conditioned carriage house on the property.

The Bar Harbor Inn. Newport Dr. (P.O. Box 7), Bar Harbor, ME 04609. ☎ **800/248-3351** or 207/288-3351. 153 rms. A/C TV TEL. Peak season $139–$265 double; spring and late fall $75–$179 double. Rates include continental breakfast. Packages available in shoulder seasons. AE, DISC, MC, V. Closed Dec to mid-Mar.

The Bar Harbor Inn, located just off Agamont Park, manages to nicely mix the traditional and the contemporary. Situated on shady waterfront grounds just a minute's stroll from downtown boutiques (it's also at the start of the Shore Path), the inn offers both convenience and gracious charm. The main shingled inn, which dates back to the turn of the century, has a settled, old-money feel, with its semicircular dining room with ocean views, and the button-down elegance of the lobby.

The guest rooms, located in the main inn and two additional structures, are decidedly more contemporary. Guest rooms in the Oceanfront and Main Inn both offer spectacular views of the bay, and many have private balconies; the less expensive Newport building (constructed in 1994) lacks views but is comfortable and very up-to-date.

Dining/Entertainment: The Reading Room restaurant serves up well-regarded meals along with one of the best ocean views in town.

Services/Facilities: Heated outdoor pool, hot tub, morning newspaper, conference space, limited room service, afternoon coffee and cookies.

Ledgelawn Inn. 66 Mt. Desert St., Bar Harbor, ME 04609. ☎ **800/274-5334** or 207/288-4596. Fax 207/288-9968. 33 rms (9 with shower only). A/C TV TEL. July–Aug $125–$275 double. Rates include full breakfast. Discounts available off-season. AE, DISC, MC, V. Closed Nov–Apr.

The Ledgelawn features a handsome sunporch lounge with a full bar, and when you first set foot inside you half expect to find Bogart flirting with Bacall in a corner. This hulking cream and maroon 1904 "cottage" sits on a village lot amid towering oaks and maples, and has a mid-century elegance to it, although updated with modern amenities; on the property you'll find a pool and hot tub for soaking. Inside, the recently renovated common area around the fireplace has a plush, quiet, upholstered feel. The breakfast room is unexpectedly formal; it feels like a setting for a fancy wedding reception. The guest rooms all vary somewhat as to size and mood, but all are comfortably if not stylishly furnished with antiques and reproductions. Some rooms feature fireplaces that burn Duraflame-style logs.

Mira Monte Inn. 69 Mt. Desert St., Bar Harbor, ME 04609. ☎ **800/553-5109** or 207/288-4263. Fax 207/288-3115. 12 rms, 3 suites (some with shower only). A/C TV TEL. $120–$150 double; $180 suite. Rates include breakfast. AE, DISC, MC, V. Closed Nov–Apr.

This handsome grayish green Italianate mansion, built in 1864, is blessed with a profusion of balconies and fireplaces—most guest rooms have one or the other; some have both. The common rooms are furnished in a pleasant country Victorian style, and there's a piano for evening entertainment. The 2-acre grounds are handsomely landscaped and include a cutting garden to keep the house in flowers. There's a nice brick terrace away from the street, which makes a fine place to enjoy breakfast on warm summer mornings. As for decor, the guest rooms tend to be a bit schizophrenic.

Some are dim and almost sepulchral in that heavy Victorian style; others have the bright and airy feel of a country farmhouse. Ask to look first to find a room that fits your tastes. Unless you're traveling with a family, I'd avoid the suites in a separate outbuilding; they're not all that charming, and guests have the vague feeling of staying in someone's borrowed apartment.

Mount Desert YWCA. 36 Mt. Desert St., Bar Harbor ME 04609. ☎ **207/288-5008.** 35 rms (all with shared bath). $25 single; $85 per week single; $140 per week double. No credit cards.

If you're a woman traveling alone, the best deal in Bar Harbor is the $25 bed at the YWCA, which is clean and centrally located. It's available only to women, and rooms can be rented by the night or week. If you choose to stay a week or more you'll be assessed a $10 membership fee and a $25 security deposit (refundable). The Y is open year-round, but during summer it fills up rather fast; it's advisable to make reservations early.

WHERE TO DINE

George's. 7 Stephens Lane. ☎ **207/288-4505.** Reservations recommended. Main courses $23; fixed-price dinner $32. AE, DISC, MC, V. Daily 5:30–10pm; shorter hours after Labor Day. Closed Nov to early May. CONTEMPORARY MEDITERRANEAN.

George's takes some sleuthing to find, but it's worth the effort, because this is one of Bar Harbor's classics, offering fine dining in informal surroundings for nearly 2 decades. (By the way, it's located in the small clapboard cottage behind Main Street's First National Bank.) George's captures the joyous feel of summer nicely in its setting, with four smallish dining rooms (with plenty of open windows) and additional seating on the terrace outside, which is the best place to watch the gentle dusk settle over town. The service is upbeat, and the meals are wonderfully prepared. All entrees sell for one price ($23), and include salad, vegetable, and potato or rice. You won't go wrong with the basic choices, like steamed lobster or roast chicken, but you're even better off opting for the more adventurous fare like tangerine scallops or the house specialty—lamb in its many incarnations, including charcoal-grilled lamb tenderloin and rolled lamb stuffed with wild mushrooms.

Lompoc Cafe and Brewpub. 32 Rodick St. ☎ **207/288-9392.** Reservations not accepted. Sandwiches $3.75–$5.75; dinner $10.95–$14.95. DISC, MC, V. Daily 11:30am–1am. Closed Dec–Apr. AMERICAN/ECLECTIC.

The Lompoc Cafe has a well-worn, neighborhood bar feel to it, and it's little wonder that waiters and waitresses from around Bar Harbor congregate here after hours. The cafe consists of three sections—there's the original bar in the pine-floored dining room, a trim and tidy garden just outside (try your hand at bocce), and a small and open barnlike structure at the garden's edge to handle the overflow. The on-site brewery produces five unique beers, including a locally popular blueberry ale (intriguing concept, but ask for a sample before you order a full glass), and the smooth Coal Porter, available in sizes up to the 20-ounce "fatty." Whisky drinkers will be busy here: the Lompoc claims the largest selection of single-malts north of Boston. Bar menus are usually predictably tiresome, but this one has some pleasant surprises, with an around the world in 80 minutes–style selection. Select from tasty entrees like Indonesian chicken, Mediterranean scallops, shrimp étouffée, and Vermont pork tenderloin. About half the menu is vegetarian. Live music is offered some evenings, when there's a $2 cover.

Porcupine Grill. 123 Cottage St. ☎ **207/288-3884.** Reservations recommended. Main courses $17.50–$21.95. AE, DC, MC, V. Daily 5:30–9:30pm. Closed spring and winter. NEW AMERICAN.

The Porcupine Grill is a pleasant surprise. Housed in a nondescript home on the slightly frayed commercial end of Cottage Street, the grill's interior is beautifully arrayed around a magnificent oak bar, which has the regal presence of an altar. Guests sit upstairs and down amid a smattering of antiques and enjoy the fresh flowers placed about as they peruse a wonderful menu, which is updated frequently to reflect the seasonal changes in the local bounty. You might begin with the delicate salmon cakes, served with a fresh ginger, chili, and coconut sauce, then move on to filet mignon served with portobello mushrooms and wild-boar bacon, or grilled sea scallops with a peppercorn and sun-dried tomato beurre blanc. The signature Porcupine stew is outstanding—a savory mélange of lobster, scallops, fish, and mussels served in a tomato-caper broth. Desserts are equally superb.

ELSEWHERE ON THE ISLAND

Acadia National Park is the main island attraction, of course, and Bar Harbor has hidden charm and plenty of character. But there's plenty else to explore outside of these areas. Quiet fishing villages, deep woodlands, and unexpected ocean views are among the jewels that turn up when one peers beyond the usual places.

ESSENTIALS

GETTING AROUND   The east half of the island is best navigated on Route 3, which forms the better part of a loop from Bar Harbor through Seal Harbor and past Northeast Harbor before returning up the eastern shore of Somes Sound. Routes 102 and 102A provide access to the island's western half.

VISITOR INFORMATION   The best source of information on the island is at the **Thompson Island Information Center** (☎ 207/288-3411) on Route 3, just south of the causeway connecting Mount Desert Island with the mainland. Another reliable source of local information is **Mount Desert Chamber of Commerce,** P.O. Box 675, Northeast Harbor, ME 04662 (☎ 207/276-5040).

EXPLORING THE REST OF THE ISLAND

On the tip of the eastern lobe of Mount Desert Island is the staid, prosperous community of **Northeast Harbor,** long one of the favored retreats among the Eastern seaboard's upper crust. Those without personal invitations to come as house guests will have to be satisfied with glimpses of the shingled palaces set in the fragrant spruce forests and along the rocky shore. But the village itself is worth investigating. Situated on a scenic, narrow harbor, with the once-grand Asticou Inn at its head, Northeast Harbor is possessed of a refined sense of elegance that's best appreciated by finding a vantage point, then sitting and admiring.

One of the best, least publicized places for enjoying views of the harbor is from the understatedly spectacular ✪ **Asticou Terraces** (☎ 207/276-5130). Finding the parking lot can be tricky: Head one-half mile south on Route 3 from the junction with Route 198, and look for the small gravel lot on the water side of the road with a sign reading ASTICOU TERRACES. Park here, cross the road on foot, and set off up a magnificent path made of local rock that ascends the sheer hillside with expanding views of the harbor and the town. This pathway, with its precise stonework and the occasional bench and gazebo, is one of the nation's hidden marvels of landscape architecture. Created by Boston landscape architect Joseph Curtis, who summered here for many years prior to his death in 1928, the pathway seems to blend in almost preternaturally with its spruce-and-fir surroundings. Curtis donated the property to the public for quiet enjoyment.

Continue on the trail at the top of the hillside and you'll soon arrive at Curtis's cabin (open to the public daily in summer), behind which lies the formal **Thuya Gardens,** which are as manicured as the terraces are natural. These wonderfully maintained gardens, designed by noted landscape architect Charles K. Savage, attract flower enthusiasts, students of landscape architecture, and local folks looking for a quiet place to rest. It's well worth the trip. A donation of $2 is requested of visitors to the garden; the terraces are free.

From the harbor visitors can depart on a seaward trip to the beguilingly remote **Cranberry Islands.** You have a couple of options: Either travel with a national park guide to Baker Island, the most distant of this small cluster of low islands, and explore the natural terrain, or hop one of the ferries to either Great or Little Cranberry Island and explore on your own. On Little Cranberry there's a small historical museum run by the National Park Service that's worth seeing. Both islands feature a sense of being well away from it all, but neither offers much in the way of shelter or tourist amenities, so travelers should head out prepared for the possibility of shifting weather.

WHERE TO STAY

Asticou Inn. Rte. 3, Northeast Harbor, ME 04662. ☎ **800/258-3373** or 207/276-3344. 44 rms. TEL. $197–$232 double. Rates include breakfast. DISC, MC, V. Closed mid-Oct to Apr.

The once grand Asticou Inn, which dates back to 1883, occupies a prime location at the head of Northeast Harbor. Its weathered gray shingles and layered eaves gives it a slightly stern demeanor, but yellow window shades leaven its appearance with a mild eccentricity. The Asticou is, unfortunately, more elegant on the exterior than on the interior. The furnishings, including the plastic porch furniture, seem to have come from some best-forgotten interregnum between the dapper golden era and the present day. Nonetheless, a wonderful old-world gentility seems to seep from the creaking floorboards and through the thin walls. The rooms are simply furnished in a pleasing summer-home style, as if a more opulent decor was somehow too ostentatious.

Dining/Entertainment: Jackets are requested for men in the evening; the dinner dance and elaborate buffet on Thursday nights in summer are hallowed island traditions and well worth checking out.

✪ **Claremont.** P.O. Box 137, Southwest Harbor, ME 04679. ☎ **800/244-5036** or 207/ 244-5036. Fax 207/244-3512. 30 rms (2 with tub only), 12 cottages. TEL. July through Labor Day $120–$145 double, including breakfast; $195 double, including breakfast and dinner. Off-season from $80 double. No credit cards. Closed mid-Oct to mid-June.

The early prints of the Claremont, built in 1884, show an austere four-story wooden building with a single severe gable overlooking Somes Sound from a low, grassy rise. And the place hasn't changed all that much since then. The Claremont offers nothing fancy or elaborate—just simple, classic New England grace. It's wildly appropriate that the state's most high-profile and combative croquet tournament takes place here annually in early August; all those folks in their whites seem right at home. The common areas and dining rooms are pleasantly appointed in an affable country style. There's a library with rockers, a fireplace, and jigsaw puzzles waiting to be assembled. Two other fireplaces in the lobby take the chill out of the morning air.

Most of the guest rooms are bright and airy, furnished with antiques and some old furniture that doesn't quite qualify as "antique." The bathrooms are modern. Guests taking dinner at the inn are given preference in reserving "seaside" rooms overlooking the water; it's worth it. There's also a series of cottages, available for a

3-day minimum. Some are set rustically in the piney woods; others offer pleasing views of the sound.

Dining/Entertainment: The dining room is open nightly and is open to outside guests. Meals are mainly reprises of American classics like grilled salmon, steamed lobster, and rib-eye steak served with a mushroom demiglaze.

Facilities: One clay tennis court, rowboats, bicycles (free to guests), croquet court.

Inn at Southwest. 371 Main St. (P.O. Box 593), Southwest Harbor, ME 04679. ☎ **207/ 244-3835.** E-mail: innatsw@acadia.net. Web site: www.acadia.net/iaswh. 9 rms (5 with shower only; 2 with hall bath). Summer and early fall $90–$135 double; off-season $60–$95 double. Rates include full breakfast. MC, V. Closed Nov–Apr.

Jill Lewis and her golden retriever, Bronco, acquired the architecturally quirky Inn at Southwest in 1995, and both have done a fine job making this mansard-roofed Victorian a hospitable place. There's a decidedly turn-of-the-century air to this elegant home, but it's restrained on the frills. The guest rooms are named after Maine light-houses, and are furnished with both contemporary and antique furniture. All rooms have ceiling fans and down comforters. Among the most pleasant rooms is Blue Hill Bay on the third floor, with its large bath, sturdy oak bed and bureau, and glimpses of the scenic harbor. Breakfasts offer ample reason to rise and shine, featuring specialties like vanilla Belgian waffles with raspberry sauce, and crab potato bake.

Le Domaine. Rte. 1 (P.O. Box 496), Hancock, ME 04640. ☎ **800/554-8498** or 207/ 422-3395. Fax 207/422-2316. 7 rms (2 with shower only). $200 double. Rates include break-fast and dinner. AE, DISC, MC, V.

Although it's a half-hour drive from Mount Desert, Le Domaine has firmly established its reputation as one of the most elegant and delightful destinations in Maine. Set on Route 1 about 10 minutes east of Ellsworth, this inn has the continental flair of an impeccable auberge. While the highway in front can be a bit noisy, the garden and woodland walks out back offer plenty of serenity. The rooms are comfortable and tastefully appointed without being pretentious.

Dining/Entertainment: The real draw here is the exquisite dining room, which serves up the most elegant French cuisine in the state. Chef Nicole Purslow carries on the tradition begun by her mother, who emigrated here from France and opened the restaurant in 1946, by offering superb French country cooking in the handsome candlelit dining room with pine-wood floors and sizable fireplace. The sauces make the entrees sing—witness the Atlantic salmon with a sorrel-and-shallot sauce, or rabbit served with a surprisingly delightful prune sauce. The restaurant also boasts a 5,000-bottle wine cellar, with all selections from France. Dinner is served May through October Wednesday through Monday (daily in August) between 6 and 9pm. Entrees are $20.75 to $25.

✪ **Lindenwood Inn.** 118 Clark Point Rd. (P.O. Box 1328), Southwest Harbor, ME 04679. ☎ **207/244-5335.** 23 rms (some with shower only). July–Aug $85–$195 double; Sept to mid-Oct $75–$185 double; mid-Oct to June $65–$175 double. Rates include full breakfast. AE, MC, V.

The Lindenwood offers a refreshing change from the fusty, overly draped inns that tend to proliferate along the coast. Housed in a handsome 1902 Queen Anne–style home at the harbor's edge, the inn features rooms that are modern and uncluttered, the colors simple and bold. The adornments are relatively few (those that do exist are mostly from the innkeeper's collection of African and Pacific art and artifacts), but clean lines and bright natural light more than create a relaxing mood—you'll even begin to view the cobblestone doorstops as works of art. Especially appealing are the spacious suites, which feature great harbor views.

If you're on a tighter budget, ask for a room in the annex, housed in an 1883 home just a minute's walk down the block. The rooms are somewhat less expansive and more simply decorated, but still offer nice touches (like bright halogen reading lamps) and make a superb base from which to explore the area. Eight of the rooms feature fireplaces; most also have telephones, but ask when you book, if this is important to you. No smoking.

Dining/Entertainment: The Lindenwood features an excellent, intimate restaurant on the ground floor, with an emphasis on creatively prepared organic and local foods. Prices range from $17 to $20.

Facilities: Jacuzzi, outdoor pool, boat dock.

WHERE TO DINE

The Burning Tree. Rte. 3, Otter Creek. ☎ **207/288-9331.** Reservations recommended. Main courses $13.75–$19.50. MC, V. Wed–Mon 5–9pm (open daily in Aug). Closed Columbus Day to mid-June. REGIONAL/ORGANIC.

Located on busy Route 3 between Bar Harbor and Northeast Harbor, The Burning Tree is an easy restaurant to speed right by. But that would be a mistake. This low-key restaurant, with its bright, open, and sometimes noisy dining room, serves up the freshest food in the area. Much of the produce and herbs come from its own gardens, with the rest of the ingredients supplied locally wherever possible. Seafood is the specialty here, and it's consistently prepared with equal parts imagination and skill. The menu changes often to reflect local availability. Typical appetizers include chili-orange noodle-and-scallop salad, and smoked salmon served with a corn-and-caper relish. Entrees might include Cajun crab and lobster au gratin, grilled swordfish with a watercress-lime sauce, or monkfish baked with clams, artichokes, and olives and served with a saffron orzo. Desserts are equally enticing, especially the ginger-orange cheesecake.

✪ **Redfield's.** Main St., Northeast Harbor. ☎ **207/276-5283.** Reservations strongly recommended in summer. Main courses $17.95–$19.95. AE, MC, V. June–Oct Mon–Sat 6–9pm; Nov–May Fri–Sat 6–9pm. CONTEMPORARY.

One of the great surprises of Redfield's is that a restaurant with such a superb sense of service and such a fine mastery over the kitchen can thrive in such a small village. Then again, quietly wealthy Northeast Harbor isn't your typical small village. Located in a storefront in the tiny downtown, this restaurant is decorated with a subtle and restrained elegance. A couple of large sprays of flowers set the tone.

Patrons can enjoy a libation at the wonderful marble bar (it was taken from an old soda fountain), then settle in and peruse the short but tempting menu, which draws its inspiration from cuisines around the world. Choices change with some frequency, but might include appetizers of smoked mussels with a sauce of corn, tomato, and serrano chili; or eggplant and roasted red peppers baked with cheddar on a corn tortilla. The delectable entrees are prepared with style and care, and include a salmon fillet with ginger-tamari sauce, and venison tenderloin with dried cranberries and blueberries.

✪ **Restaurant XYZ.** Shore Rd., Manset. ☎ **207/244-5221.** Reservations recommended weekends. Main courses $11–$15. MC, V. Summer daily 5:30–9:30pm; limited hours (usually weekends only) during shoulder seasons. MEXICAN.

Every so often you come upon a restaurant that's so unexpectedly good that it catches you thoroughly off-guard. Restaurant XYZ is just such a place. It doesn't promise much at first: It's on the ground floor beneath a run-of-the-mill motel overlooking the harbor, and the interior is adorned with kitschy imports from Mexico that might best be described as "stuff."

But the food! Drawing on the traditions of central Mexico and the Yucatán, the fare here is spicy, earthy, and tangy. Don't look for thin sauces and melted cheese. Expect a remarkably savory mole (especially good with chicken), and a chipotle salsa that positively sings. Start with one of the standout margaritas (made with fresh lime juice), and then head straight to the main courses. (The appetizers don't offer especially good value.) Among the more notable entrees are the pork dishes, including *tatemado* (a pork loin baked with guajillo and ancho chilies), and Yucatecan-style pork rubbed with achiote paste and marinated with citrus before baking. By passing on appetizers, you've saved room for dessert—the offerings are limited, but equally delicious. The flan is especially good. Aficionados of authentic Mexican cooking will be delightfully surprised to find such excellent dining deep in the home turf of boiled lobster and fried clams.

8 The North Woods

There's the perception of Maine's North Woods, and then there's the reality.

The perception is that this region is the last outpost of big wilderness in the East, with thousands of acres of unbroken forest, miles of free-running streams, and more azure lakes than you can shake a canoe paddle at. A look at a road map seems to confirm this, with only a few roads shown here and there amid terrain pocked with lakes. Indeed, Maine accounts for about half of New England, and northern forestlands with no formal local government—called the "unorganized townships"—comprises about half of Maine. So about one-quarter of New England is undeveloped forestland in northern Maine.

But undeveloped does not mean untouched. The reality is that this forestland is a vast plantation, largely owned and managed by a handful of international paper and timber companies. An extensive network of small timber roads (about 25,000 miles at last count) feed off major arteries and open the region to extensive clear-cutting. This is most visible from the air. In the early 1980s, *New Yorker* writer John McPhee noted that much of northern Maine "now looks like an old and badly tanned pelt. The hair is coming out in tufts." That's even more the case today following the acceleration of timber harvesting, thanks to technological advances and demands for faster cutting to pay down debts incurred during the leveraged buyout mania of the late 1980s.

While the North Woods are not a vast, howling wilderness, the region still has famously remote enclaves where moose and loons predominate, and where the turf hasn't changed all that much since Thoreau paddled through in the mid-19th century and found it all "moosey and mossy." If you don't arrive expecting utter wilderness, you're less likely to be disappointed.

THE MOOSEHEAD LAKE REGION

Thirty-two miles long and 5 miles across at its widest point, Moosehead Lake is Maine's largest lake, and it's a great destination for hikers, boaters, and canoeists. The lake was historically the center of the region's logging activity; paradoxically, that preserved the lake and kept it largely unspoiled by development. Timber companies still own much of the lakeside property (although the state has acquired a significant amount in recent years), and the 350-mile shoreline is mostly unbroken second- or third-growth forest. The second-home building frenzy of the 1980s had some noticeable impact on the southern reaches of the lake, but the woody shoreline has absorbed most of the boom rather gracefully.

The first thing to know about the lake is that it's not meant to be seen by car. There are some great views from a handful of roads—especially from Routes 6 or 15 as you near Rockwood, and from the high elevations on the way to Lily Bay—but for the most part the roads are a distance from the shores, and offer rather uninteresting driving. To see the lake at its best, you should plan to get out on the water by steamship or canoe, or fly above it on a charter floatplane (see below).

Greenville is the de facto capital of Moosehead Lake, scenically situated at the southern tip. Most services are located here, and you can stock up on groceries and camping supplies. The descent into Greenville on Routes 6 or 15 is becoming a bit cluttered with commercial strip development, but the town is still holding on to its remote, woodsy flavor.

ESSENTIALS

GETTING THERE   Greenville is 158 miles from Portland. Take the turnpike to the Newport exit (Exit 39) and head north on Routes 7 or 11 to Route 23 in Dexter, following that northward to Routes 6 or 15 near Sangerville. Follow this to Greenville.

VISITOR INFORMATION   The **Moosehead Lake Chamber of Commerce,** P.O. Box 581, Greenville, ME 04441 (☎ **207/695-2702**), maintains an information booth that's open Monday to Saturday year-round from 10am to 4pm, just south of the village on Routes 6 or 15. Information is also available on the Internet: E-mail is **moose@moosehead.net**, and the Web address is **www.moosehead.net/ moose/chamber.html**.

HIKING

The famed **100-Mile Wilderness** of the Appalachian Trail begins at Monson, south of Greenville, and runs northeast to Abol Bridge near Baxter State Park. This is a spectacularly remote part of the state, and offers some of the best deep-woods hiking in Maine. This trip is primarily for independent and experienced backpackers— there are no points along the route to resupply—although day trips in and out are a possibility.

One especially beautiful stretch of the trail passes by **Gulf Hagas,** sometimes called "Maine's Grand Canyon" (a description that's a bit grandiose, to my mind). The Pleasant River has carved a canyon as deep as 400 feet through the bedrock slate; the hiking trail runs along its lip, with side trails extending down to the river, where you can swim in the eddies and cascades. The gulf is accessible as a day hike if you enter the forest via logging roads. Drive north from Milo on Route 11 and follow signs to the Katahdin Iron Works (an intriguing historic site worth exploring), pay your fee at the timber company gate, and ask directions to the gulf. Also nearby is **The Hermitage,** a Nature Conservancy stand of 120-foot white pines that have been spared the woodsman's axe.

Another inviting hike is **Mount Kineo,** a sheer, broad cliff that rises from the shores of Moosehead. This hike is only accessible by water; near the town of Rockwood look for signs advertising shuttles across the lake to Kineo (folks offering this service seem to change from year to year, so ask around). Once across, you can explore the grounds of the famed old Kineo Mountain House (alas, the grand, 500-guest-room hotel was demolished in 1938), then cut across the golf course and follow the shoreline to the trail that leads to the 1,800-foot summit. The views from the cliffs are dazzling; one hiker I know says he has no problems on any mountain except Kineo, which gives him an inexplicable case of vertigo. Be sure to continue on the trail to the old fire tower, which you can ascend for a hawk's-eye view of the region.

WHITE-WATER RAFTING

Big waves and boiling drops await rafters on the hairy run through Kennebec Gorge at the headwaters of the **Kennebec River,** located southwest of Greenville. Dozens of rafters line up along the churning river below the dam, then await the siren that signals the release. Hop in, and you're off, heading off through huge, roiling waves and down precipitous drops with names like Whitewasher and Magic Falls. Most of the excitement is over in the first hour; after that, it's a lazy trip the rest of the way down the river, interrupted only by lunch and the occasional water fight with other rafts. Also nearby is the challenging Dead River, which offers about a half-dozen release dates, mostly during the early summer.

A number of commercial white-water outfits offer trips throughout the summer at a cost of about $75 to $115 per person. **Northern Outdoors,** P.O. Box 100, The Forks, ME 04985 (☎ **800/765-7238;** Web site: **www.northernoutdoors.com**) is the oldest of the bunch, and offers rock climbing, mountain biking, and fishing expeditions as well, plus snowmobiling in winter. Other reputable rafting companies to check with include **Wilderness Expeditions,** P.O. Box 41, Rockwood, ME 04478 (☎ **800/825-9453**), and the **New England Outdoor Center,** P.O. Box 669, Millinocket, ME 04462 (☎ **800/766-7238**).

MOOSEHEAD BY STEAMSHIP & FLOATPLANE

During the lake's golden days of tourism in the late 19th century, visitors could come to the lake by train from New York or Washington, then connect with steamship to the resorts and boarding houses around the lake. A vestige of that era is found at the **Moosehead Marine Museum** (☎ **207/695-2716**) in Greenville. A handful of displays in the small building suggest the grandeur of life at Kineo Mountain House, a sprawling Victorian lake resort that once defined elegance. But the real showpiece of the museum is the **SS *Katahdin,*** a 115-foot steamship that's been cruising Moosehead's waters since 1914. The two-deck ship (it's now run by diesel rather than steam) offers a variety of sightseeing tours, including a twice-a-week excursion up the lake to the site of the former Kineo Mountain House. Fares vary depending on the length of the trip.

Moosehead from the air is a memorable sight. Stop by **Folsom's Air Service** (☎ **207/695-2821**) on the shores of the lake in Greenville just north of the village center on Lily Bay Road. Folsom's has been serving the North Woods since 1946, and has a fleet of five floatplanes, including a vintage canary yellow DeHavilland Beaver. A 15-minute tour of the southern reaches of the lake costs $20 per person; longer flights over the region run up to $60. A nice adventure is the canoe-and-fly package. For $85 per person, Folsom's will drop you and a canoe off at Penobscot Farm; paddle up to Lobster Lake, where you'll get picked up and returned to Greenville later that day.

SNOWMOBILING

You'll need more than just good luck finding a room in Greenville some weekends in winter. The town has become a snowmobilers' mecca of sorts, with hundreds of sledders descending on the town during good winter weather before striking out into the remote woods. The **Moosehead Trail,** which runs around the perimeter of the lake, offers lodging and meals at various stops along the way. For snowmobile rentals, contact **The Birches Resort** (☎ **800/825-9453**), **Kokadjo Trading Post and Camp** (☎ **207/695-3993**), which is located about 15 miles north of Greenville, or the **Greenwood Motel** (☎ **207/695-3321**).

WHERE TO STAY & DINE

Chesuncook Lake House. P.O. Box 656, Greenville, ME 04441. ☎ **207/745-5330.** 4 rms (all share 2 baths), 3 cottages. $170 double. Rates include all meals. No credit cards. Closed Nov–Apr.

The Chesuncook Lake House is a perfect destination for those who like a bit of comfort with their adventure. This 1864 farmhouse, located on the shores of remote Chesuncook Lake, is accessible via seaplane or 18-mile boat shuttle from Chesuncook Dam. (It can also be reached by canoe.) It's run with tremendous rustic charm by Bert and Maggie McBurnie, who've been hosting guests here since 1957. (Bert grew up in Chesuncook Village when it was an active logging center; Maggie is from Paris, France.) The rooms are furnished simply and eclectically; there's running water in the shared bathrooms, and gas lamps provide the light in the evening. All meals are included in the rates, and Maggie's superb cooking makes good use of produce from her sizable garden. During the day, guests can explore the remnants of Chesuncook Village (Thoreau passed through here in the mid-19th century), canoe over to 3,000-acre Gero Island, or just pass the time on the porch enjoying the views of Mount Katahdin 35 miles to the east. If you stay 3 days or longer, the boat shuttle is free; otherwise there's a charge for it. No smoking.

Greenville Inn. Norris St., Greenville, ME 04441. ☎ **888/695-6000** or 207/695-2206. E-mail: gvlinn@moosehead.net. 5 rms, 1 suite, 6 cottages. Summer $115–$195 double; off-season $85–$165 double. Rates include continental breakfast buffet. DISC, MC, V. No children under 8.

This handsome 1895 lumber baron's home sits regally off a hilly side street in a residential neighborhood a short walk from Greenville's commercial district. The interiors are manly and sumptuous, with wonderful cherry and mahogany woodworking and a lovely stained-glass window of a pine tree over the stairwell. There's a handsome small bar, where you can order up a cocktail or Maine beer, then sit in front of the fire or retreat to the front porch to watch the late afternoon sun slip over Squaw Mountain and the lake. The rooms vary in size (the new master suite with lake views is the best and most expensive), but all are richly appointed. Four new cottages were built on the property in 1995, adding to the two already there. The trim cottages are furnished in a light summer-cottage style, and have views of the lake. No smoking.

Dining/Entertainment: The dinners served in the elegant dining room are delicious. The menu offers continental fare with a regional twist, with entrees like roast duckling with an orange-apricot glaze, or haddock with red onion and dill. The popovers are delectable and roughly the size of a football. The restaurant is open for dinner daily late May through October; entrees range from $17 to $28, with the great majority under $20.

✪ **Little Lyford Pond Camps.** P.O. Box 1269, Greenville, ME 04441. ☎ **207/695-2821** (radio phone via Folsom's). Fax 207/534-7428. E-mail: katecf@moosehead.net. Web site www.moosehead.net/lyford/lyford.html. 8 log cabins (each with private outhouse). $170 double. Rates include breakfast, lunch, and dinner. 2-night minimum on weekends and holidays. No credit cards. Closed spring and late fall/early winter. Accessible by logging road in summer, by snowmobile or ski-plane in winter. No credit cards.

Kate and Bud Fackelman left Massachusetts for this remote lodge more than a decade ago, and they've made this backwoods logging camp one of the most welcoming and comfortable spots in the North Woods. Guests stay in small log cabins originally built to house loggers in the 1870s. Each has a small woodstove, propane lantern, cold running water, a private outhouse, and plenty of rustic charm.

Guests gather in the more spacious main lodge for meals, to browse the inn's books, and to play board games in the evening. During the day, activities aren't hard to find, from fishing or canoeing at the two ponds down a short trail, or hiking the Appalachian Trail to Gulf Hagas, just 2 miles away. There's a wood-fired sauna and a solar shower for keeping clean. In winter, the cross-country skiing on the lodging's private network is superb.

BAXTER STATE PARK & ENVIRONS

Baxter State Park is Maine's crown jewel. This 201,000-acre state park in the remote north-central part of the state is unlike more elaborate state parks you might be accustomed to elsewhere—don't look for fancy bath houses or groomed picnic areas. When you enter Baxter State Park, you enter near wilderness.

The park was single-handedly created by former Maine governor and philanthropist Percival Baxter, who used his inheritance and investment profits to buy the property and donate it to the state starting in 1930. Baxter stipulated that it remain "forever wild," and caretakers have done a good job fulfilling his wishes.

You won't find paved roads, RVs, or hookups at the eight drive-in campgrounds. (Size restrictions keep RVs out.) You will find rugged backcountry and beautiful lakes. You'll also find Mount Katahdin, that lone and melancholy granite giant rising above the sparkling lakes and severe boreal forest of northern Maine.

To the north and west of Baxter State Park are several million acres of forestland owned by timber companies and managed for timber production. Twenty-one of the largest timber companies collectively own much of the land and manage recreational access through a consortium called North Maine Woods, Inc. If you drive on a logging road far enough, expect to run into a North Maine Woods checkpoint, where you'll be asked to pay a fee for day use or overnight camping on their lands.

One bit of advice: Don't attempt to tour the timberlands by car. Industrial forestland is boring at its best, and downright depressing at its cutover worst. A better strategy is to select a pond or river for camping or fishing, and spend a couple of days getting to know a small area. Buffer strips have been left around all ponds, streams, and rivers, and it can often feel like you're getting away from it all as you paddle along, even if the forest sometimes has a Hollywood facade feel to it. Be aware that, outside of Baxter State Park, no matter how deep you get into these woods, you may well hear machinery and chain saws in the distance.

ESSENTIALS

GETTING THERE   Baxter State Park is 86 miles north of Bangor. Take I-95 to Medway (Exit 56), and head west 11 miles on Routes 11 or 157 to the mill town of Millinocket, the last major place for supplies. Head northwest through town and follow signs to Baxter State Park. The less used entrance is near the park's northeast corner. Take I-95 to the exit for Route 11, drive north through Patten then head west on Route 159 to the park. The speed limit within the park is 20 miles per hour. Motorcycles and ATVs are not allowed within park boundaries.

VISITOR INFORMATION   Baxter State Park offers maps and information from its **headquarters** at 64 Balsam Dr., Millinocket, ME 04462 (☎ **207/723-5140**).

For information on canoeing and camping outside of Baxter State Park, contact **North Maine Woods, Inc.,** P.O. Box 421, Ashland, ME 04732 (☎ **207/ 435-6213**).

Help finding cottages and outfitters is available through the **Katahdin Area Chamber of Commerce,** 1029 Central St., Millinocket, ME 04462 (☎ **207/723-4443;** E-mail: **kachambr@agate.net**).

FEES   Baxter State Park visitors with out-of-state license plates are charged a day-use fee of $8 per car. (It's free to Maine residents.) The day-use fee is charged only once per stay for those camping overnight. Camping reservations are by mail or in person only.

The private timberlands managed by North Maine Woods levy a day-use fee of $3.50 per person for Maine residents, $7 per person for nonresidents. Camping fees are additional (see below.)

HIKING

With 180 miles of maintained backcountry trails and 46 peaks (including 18 over 3,000 ft.), Baxter State Park is the destination of choice for serious hikers in Maine.

The most serious peak is 5,267-foot **Mount Katahdin**—the northern terminus of the Appalachian Trail. An ascent up this rugged, glacially scoured mountain is a trip you'll not soon forget. Never mind that it's not even a mile high (although a tall cairn on the summit claims to make it so). The raw drama and grandeur of the rocky, windswept summit is equal to anything you'll find in the White Mountains of New Hampshire.

Allow at least 8 hours for the round-trip, and be prepared to abandon your plans for another day if the weather takes a turn for the worse while you're en route. The most popular route leaves and returns from Roaring Brook Campground. In fact, it's popular enough that it's often closed to day hikers—when the parking lot fills, hikers are shunted to other trails. You ascend first to dramatic Chimney Pond, which is set like a jewel in a glacial cirque, then continue to Katahdin's summit via one of two trails. (The Saddle Trail is the most forgiving; the Cathedral Trail most dramatic.) From here, the descent begins along the aptly named "Knife's Edge," a narrow, rocky spine between Baxter Peak and Pamola Peak. This is not for acrophobes or the squeamish: In places, the trail narrows to 2 or 3 feet with a drop of hundreds of feet on either side. It's also not a place to be if high winds or thunderstorms threaten. From here, the trail follows a gentle ridge back down to Roaring Brook.

Katahdin draws the largest crowds, but the park maintains numerous other trails where you'll find more solitude and wildlife. A pleasant day hike is to the summit of **South Turner Mountain,** which offers wonderful views of Mount Katahdin and blueberries for the picking in late summer. The trail also departs from Roaring Brook Campground and requires about 3 to 4 hours for a round-trip. To the north, there are several decent hikes out of the South Branch Pond Campground. You can purchase a trail map at park headquarters, or consult *50 Hikes in Northern Maine.*

CAMPING

Baxter State Park has eight campgrounds accessible by car, and two backcountry camping areas, but don't count on finding anything open if you show up without reservations. Park headquarters starts taking reservations in January, and dozens of die-hard campers spend a cold night outside headquarters on January 1 to secure the best spots. Many of the most desirable sites sell out well before the snow melts from Katahdin. The park is stubbornly old-fashioned about its reservations, which must be made either in person or by mail, with full payment in advance. No phone reservations are accepted. Don't even mention E-mail. Camping at Baxter State Park costs $6 per person ($12 minimum per tent site), with cabins and bunkhouses available for $7 to $17 per person per night.

North Maine Woods, Inc. (see above) maintains dozens of primitive campsites on private forestland throughout its 2-million-acre holdings. While you may have to drive through massive clear-cuts to reach the campsites, many are located on secluded coves or picturesque points. A map showing logging road access and campsite locations is $3 plus $1 postage from North Maine Woods headquarters (see "Visitor

Information," above). Camping fees are $4 per person in addition to the day-use fee outlined above.

WHITE-WATER RAFTING

A unique way to view Mount Katahdin is by rafting the West Branch of the Penobscot River. Flowing along the park's southern border, this wild river offers some of the most technically challenging white water in the East. Along the upper stretches it passes through a harrowing gorge that appears to be designed by cubists dabbling in massive blocks of granite. The river widens after this, interspersing sleepy flat water (with views of Katahdin) with several challenging falls and runs through turbulent rapids. At least a dozen rafting companies offer trips on the Penobscot, with prices around $75 to $100 per person, including a lunch along the way. Try **Unicorn Rafting,** P.O. Box T, Brunswick, ME 04011 (☎ **800/864-2676**), or **Magic Falls Rafting Co.,** P.O. Box 2820, Winslow, ME 04901 (☎ **800/207-7238** or 207/ 663-2220; Web site: **www.magicfalls.com**).

CANOEING

The state's premiere canoe trip is down the ✪ **Allagash River,** which starts just west of Baxter State Park and runs northward for nearly 100 miles to finish at the town of Allagash. The Allagash Wilderness Waterway was the first state-designated wild and scenic river in the country, and has been protected since 1970. The river runs through heavily harvested timberlands, but a 500-foot buffer strip of trees protects the forest views along the entire route.

The trip begins along a chain of lakes involving light portaging. At Churchill Dam, there's a nice stretch of Class I–II white water for about 9 miles, then it's back to lakes and a mix of flat water and mild rapids. Toward the end, there's a longish portage (about 150 yards) around picturesque Allagash Falls before finishing up above the village of Allagash. (Schedule in enough time for a swim at the base of the falls.)

Most paddlers spend between 7 and 10 days making the trip from Chamberlain Lake to Allagash. Eighty campsites are maintained along the route; most have outhouses, fire rings, and picnic tables. The camping fee is $4 per night per person for Maine residents, $5 for nonresidents.

Several outfitters offer Allagash River packages, including canoes, camping equipment, and transportation. **Allagash Wilderness Outfitters,** Box 620, Star Route 76, Greenville, ME 04441 (radio ☎ **207/695-2821**) rents a complete outfit (including canoe, life vests, sleeping bags, tent, saw, axe, shovel, cooking gear, first-aid kit, etc.) for $23 per person per day. **Allagash Canoe Trips** (☎ **207/695-3668;** E-mail: **alcanoe@moosehead.net**) in Greenville offers 7-day guided descents of the river, including all equipment and meals, for $625 adults, $475 children under 18.

SNOWMOBILING

Northern Maine is laced with a magnificent network of snowmobile trails. If the conditions are right, you can even cross over into Canada and take your sled to Québec. Although a handful of maps and guides outline the network, the trails are still largely a matter of local knowledge. Don't be afraid to ask around. A good place to start is **Shin Pond Village**, R.R. #1, Box 280, Patten, ME 04765 (☎ **207/528-2900**). Six cottages and five guest rooms are available (starting at $42 double for guest rooms and $62 for the cottages), and snowmobile rentals are $100 to $140 per day. Shin Pond is located within one-quarter mile of two ITS trails (the chief snowmobile routes).

Index

ACCOMMODATIONS INDEX

WHEREVER YOU TRAVEL, *H*ELP IS NEVER FAR AWAY.

From planning your trip to providing travel assistance along the way, American Express® Travel Service Offices are always there to help.

New England

CONNECTICUT
American Express Travel Service
Stamford
203/359-4244

NEW HAMPSHIRE
Griffin Travel Service (R)
Manchester
603/668-3730

MAINE
American Express Travel Service
Portland
207/772-8450

RHODE ISLAND
American Express Travel Service
Cranston
401/943-4545

MASSACHUSETTS
American Express Travel Service
Boston
617/439-4400

VERMONT
Milne Travel (R)
Brattleboro
802/254-8844

American Express Travel Service
Cambridge
617/868-2600

American-International Travel (R)
Burlington
802/864-9827

Travel

http://www.americanexpress.com/travel

American Express Travel Service Offices are located throughout New England. For the office nearest you, call 1-800-AXP-3429.